HANDBOOK OF NORTH AMERICAN BIRDS

*Sponsored by American Ornithologists' Union and*

*New York State Museum and Science Service*

# HANDBOOK OF

# NORTH AMERICAN BIRDS

VOLUME 3

*Waterfowl (concluded)*

EIDERS
WOOD DUCKS
DIVING DUCKS
MERGANSERS
STIFFTAILS

EDITED BY RALPH S. PALMER

*New Haven and London, Yale University Press, 1976*

Library of Congress catalog card number: 62–8259
International standard book number: 0–300–01903–3

Designed by John O. C. McCrillis
and set in Caledonia, By Eastern Typesetting Company,
Hartford, Connecticut
Printed in the United States of America by
Vail Ballou Press, Inc. Binghamton, New York

Published in Great Britain, Europe, and Africa by Yale
University Press, Ltd., London.
Distributed in Latin America by Kaiman & Polon, Inc., New
York City; in Australasia and Southeast Asia by John Wiley &
Sons Australasia Pty. Ltd., Sydney; in Japan by John
Weatherhill, Inc., Tokyo.

# CONTENTS

## COLOR PLATES

## Steller's Eider

*Polysticta stelleri* (Pallas)

Siberian or Little Eider of Russian authors. Very much smaller than any other eider. Feather margin at top base of bill truncated and not extending farther forward than on sides (among eiders, this is diagnostic of all ages, including downy young); the bill more typically ducklike than in other eiders, although it appears quite squarish at distal end in dorsal view and lateral portions of distal half of upper mandible are rather soft and fleshy; speculum dark, vivid to muted bluish depending on Plumage and sex, with prominent white bar at its forward and another at its trailing edge. The drake's trachea is uniform in diam. until it gradually enlarges in its distal quarter; the small asymmetrical bony bulla (illus. in 2 views in Schiøler 1926) at the other end differs decidedly in several respects from those of all other eiders; see text and illus. of Humphrey (1958b); the bronchi are not enlarged and are of equal size.

Length ♂ ♀ 16½–19½ in., wingspread to 30, usual wt. of ♂ about 2 lb., ♀ about 1¾. No subspecies.

DESCRIPTION Two Plumages/cycle, definitive by the 3rd cycle in the ♂ and by the 2nd in the ♀. Differs from all other eiders in various details of feather replacement; for example, the Juv. tail feathers are lost quite early and "quite simultaneously," and Basic I Plumage definitely includes all feathering except the wing (Portenko 1952); all scapulars are renewed twice/cycle (in all other eiders the longest ones are renewed once/cycle).

▶ ♂ Def. Alt. Plumage (all feathering except wing, tail, and apparently the abdomen), LATE FALL through WINTER and until some time in SUMMER. **Bill** medium or darker grayed bluish, nail paler; **iris** rather dark brownish or brownish red. **Head** and upper neck white except: face anterior to eye washed pale green, or this is concentrated as a darker muted greenish area between eye and bill; an occipital patch of darkish grayed green, the feathers elongated as a short crest; blackish spot on rear side of head at lateral terminus of occipital patch; oval blackish area around (and more extensive behind) eye; chin and throat dull blackish; posterior lower half of neck black with strong ultramarine-violet gloss and connected narrowly to black of throat. **Upperparts** black with strong gloss like hindneck; scapulars curved, the innermost ones short, pointed, outer webs white, inner webs blackish; middle ones long, lanceolate, white on inner webs, iridescent cobalt-ultramarine on outer; outermost ones shorter, broad, with variable longitudinal pattern of blackish gray and white. **Underparts** usually a narrow white collar immediately below the dark one; upper breast cinnamon, becoming progressively deeper colored posteriorly, blending with darker lower breast and abdomen (both may be retained Basic feathering); sides of breast, sides and flanks

1

much paler, varying from tawny to nearly white, blending gradually with color of midunderparts except posterior portion of flanks which contrast sharply with blackish brown (apparently retained Basic) abdominal feathers; a small black spot on either side of breast near bend of folded wing. Much individual variation in depth of color of underparts. Legs and **feet** grayish or quite dark bluish gray, webs nearly black, claws yellowish gray. Tail and wing are retained Basic feathering; part of the venter apparently is retained Basic, but possibly is acquired at a time offset from other periods of molting.

▶ ♂ Def. Basic Plumage (entire feathering), the head–body worn from about MID-SUMMER into EARLY FALL and, at the latter time, the Basic wing and tail grow and are retained and worn with the succeeding Alt. (and apparently the Basic abdomen also is retained). **Bill** muted brownish gray. Head and neck brownish olive, darkest on crown and chin; a faintly paler eye ring. **Upperparts** dark brownish olive anteriorly, shading to dull blackish on most of back and upper tail coverts; a faint ultramarine-violet iridescence, particularly posteriorly; scapulars broader, less pointed than in Alt., blackish brown, some of the longest with slight cobalt-ultramarine sheen on outer web. **Underparts** upper breast barred sepia or blackish and cinnamon; lower breast rich cinnamon to tawny, sometimes vaguely barred blackish, becoming progressively deeper posteriorly to blackish brown on abdomen and under tail coverts; sides of lower breast, sides and flanks deep blackish brown. **Tail** cuneate, dull blackish above, brownish olive below, occasionally (Stejneger 1885) with white mark at tip of outer web of outermost pair of feathers. **Wing** primaries nearly black shading to fuscous on inner web above, medium gray with brownish tinge below; innermost secondary straight, white on outer web, blackish on inner; next 6 or so secondaries curved down over primaries in closed wing, deep iridescent cobalt-ultramarine on outer portion of outer web, remainder white; remaining secondaries sepia with broad white tip, all except outermost with cobalt-ultramarine sheen on outer web, forming white-edged speculum in closed wing; greater primary coverts like primaries; alula blackish with contrasting white edges; small feathers under alula (middle primary coverts) blackish mixed with white; a few blackish feathers among the marginal coverts; remainder of upper and under wing coverts and the axillars white.

NOTES   At Izembek Bay, Alaska, on Sept. 14, 1968, many drakes were just beginning to regain flight, while many ♀ ♀ were just beginning their flightless period (R. D. Jones, Jr.). The duration of the flightless period is unknown.

Stejneger (1885) described a considerable amount of white in the primaries and primary coverts of one wing of a drake.

▶ ♀ Def. Alt. Plumage (all feathering except wing, tail, and apparently the abdomen), worn from FALL (some time in Oct.) through WINTER into late SPRING. **Bill** muted bluish gray, **iris** dark brownish. **Head** crown dark sepia with black and pinkish cinnamon bars, mostly concealed; sides of head barred black and rich tawny, with whitish area encircling eye, washed with buffy brown; chin and throat cinnamon to tawny, washed with blackish on chin; a broad collar around neck of black or blackish brown feathers with whitish or pale cinnamon subterminal bars. **Upperparts** blackish, barred with pinkish cinnamon, deepening to tawny chestnut on rump, bars often obsolete on upper tail coverts; scapulars brownish black, paling, especially with wear, to buffy brown or tawny at tip. **Underparts** breast blackish, the feathers with broad, deep tawny bars and edges; extent of barring posteriorly varies individually, may be correlated with age; color deepens toward rear, with the apparently retained Basic feathering of lower breast, abdomen, and under tail coverts rich blackish chestnut to almost black (some individuals have conspicuous pinkish buff bars on middle of abdomen, but significance of this type of marking is unknown); flanks like breast but darker, and barring less clearly defined. Legs and **feet** bluish gray to olive. Wing, tail, and part of venter (apparently) are retained Basic feathering.

▶ ♀ Def. Basic Plumage (entire feathering), head–body worn from some time in SPRING or later until well into FALL, when the late-acquired Basic wing and tail grow (these, and apparently the Basic abdomen, are long retained and worn with the succeeding Alt.). Differs from Def. Alt. as follows: **head** paler, cinnamon rather than rich tawny; more distinctly barred (except chin and throat); eye ring poorly defined or absent. New **dorsal feathers** much like old; center of **abdomen** and under tail coverts

♂ Def. Alt.     ♀ Def. Alt.

cinnamon (Portenko 1952). **Tail** blackish above, deep smoky gray brown below. **Wing** primaries blackish brown above, grayish brown below; secondaries as in ♂, except inner web of outermost sepia rather than blackish; curved inner secondaries with inner web and inner part of outer web sepia, frosted silvery gray; cobalt-ultramarine iridescence of outer webs of secondaries duller than in ♂, giving way to dark sepia with little or no iridescence on speculum of outer secondaries; greater coverts tipped white, forming anterior margin of speculum; remainder of upper side of wing sepia, the smallest coverts more or less faintly edged with pale cinnamon or buff; under primary coverts silvery gray; marginal and lesser under wing coverts, axillars, and under greater secondary wing coverts white.

AT HATCHING  Small and very dark; in size much like Black Scoter duckling; often with 4 indistinct spots on dorsum, which the scoter lacks; cheeks are marked with light rosy buff, while the scoter has a pale grayish cheek patch.

The 2 pairs of dorsal spots, particularly the anterior, tend to be obsolete in darker individuals and are difficult or impossible to detect in older downies. J. C. Phillips (1926) stated "there are no white dorsal patches," but the anterior one shows clearly on his col. pl. 80. Cheeks and sides are slightly paler than back; a whitish eye ring, narrowly interrupted immediately above and below center of eye, connects posteriorly to

3

a short pale cinnamon stripe behind eye; a pale cinnamon spot on lores (shown too high on pl. 80 in Phillips, correctly on a pl. in Millais 1913b). Underparts smoke gray, with vaguely defined darker band across upper breast; chin and upper throat washed pale cinnamon. Wings blackish fuscous like back, above; pale smoke gray below. Soft-part colors in life not recorded, but shown as dark in Phillips' col. pl.

The body down of the Juv. Plumage appears earlier than the Juv. body feathers, giving larger downy young a different appearance; dorsally the incoming body down is mostly hidden by the long natal down but short, pale precursors of Juv. body down are pushed out by the tips of the growing downs, giving an appearance superficially like the 2 generations of natal down of loons and some other birds; these short, pale downs are briefly quite conspicuous against the much darker and longer natal down. Ventrally the incoming Juv. body down is less hidden by the short natal down and is conspicuously paler smoke gray in color.

▶ ♂ Juv. Plumage (entire feathering), worn in its entirety briefly, in FALL, but apparently a considerable amount is retained into winter by some individuals; the wing is retained into following summer. **Bill** dark olive greenish. **Head** crown streaked sepia and cinnamon, the former predominating; neck and sides of head pale buffy brown, with sepia tips giving mottled appearance, palest on cheeks, vaguely defined spot around eye and on lores paler, almost white, with sepia tips; chin and throat pale buffy brown with little or no mottling. **Upperparts** blackish sepia, each feather with terminal bar of buffy brown (palest on upper back, then deepening to chestnut on lower back, then slightly paler on rump and upper tail coverts), these bars giving a scaled appearance; scapulars broad, not elongated, color as adjacent back. **Underparts** breast and sides barred, individual feathers having deep tawny terminal bar, blackish subterminal bar, remainder of feather white (those on upper breast with an additional sepia bar); flanks and abdomen similar, but feathers deep smoke gray rather than white for basal half; general appearance of underparts barred black and tawny, darkest on abdomen; under tail coverts sepia, tipped in some individuals with deep tawny. Legs and **feet** medium gray. **Tail** shorter, less cuneate than in older birds, each feather notched where natal down precursor broke off; brownish black above, dark brownish olive below. **Wing** primaries as in Def. Basic but shorter; inner secondaries shaped as in Def. Basic, but shorter and less sharply downcurved; inner webs dark sepia, outer blackish with varying degree of deep bluish iridescent wash; outer secondaries narrowly tipped with white, dark smoke gray on inner web, outer web blackish with varying degree of deep bluish iridescent wash; greater coverts dark sepia with white tips forming a white bar (anterior border of speculum); remaining upper coverts dark sepia or blackish with buffy brown terminal bar; alula blackish; marginal coverts and anterior lesser under wing coverts blackish margined with pale smoke gray; under primary coverts like primaries; remainder of wing lining and axillars white.

▶ ♀ Juv. Plumage (entire feathering), acquired as in ♂, worn in entirety briefly, then timing of loss of various portions variable, and wing retained nearly a year. Similar to ♂ except: dark sepia markings of head somewhat less pronounced; terminal bars paler and more vivid on back, scapulars, rump, upper tail coverts, and wing coverts; underparts paler, less reddish brown; marginal coverts and anterior lesser under wing coverts with whiter margins. Contrary to Kortright (1942), the blue wash ("speculum")

4

on the secondaries is present in many Juv. ♀♀, but av. more muted than in Juv. ♂♂.

▶ ♂ **Basic I Plumage** (all feathering except wing), acquired beginning some time in 1st FALL or later and worn until some time in WINTER or even spring. As Juv. except: **head** and neck darker, more regularly barred; chin and throat blackish, feathers white for basal half; **upperparts** incoming Basic I feathers on upper back and scapulars recognizable by bright pinkish cinnamon terminal and subterminal bars; new upper tail coverts blackish, unbarred; **underparts** upper breast brighter cinnamon than Juv., with less prominent blackish subterminal bars; flank feathers more barred (Juv. feathers have terminal bar only); new **tail** as in ♀ Def. Basic.

NOTE Portenko (1952) pointed out that Basic I includes entire new underparts and that all Juv. tail feathers are renewed (in one bird as early as Sept. 24) during the Prebasic molt. He had 3 specimens; they showed considerable individual variation in coloring, especially of scapulars, sides, and underparts—for example, abdomen and under tail coverts "pure cinnamon" in 1 and "with mixture of deep yellow bars" in the others.

▶ ♂ **Alt. I Plumage** (all feathering except wing, tail, and apparently abdomen; some individuals evidently acquire less body feathering, however), may begin to appear as early as FEB. or as late as May (individual variation); it is retained until some time in SUMMER, i.e., not as long as later Alts. **Bill** very dark, at least sometimes. The following is based on a single specimen that was not fully into Alt. I. **Head** chiefly dark brownish olive faintly barred blackish or sepia; feathers of posterior half of head whitish at base, those of nuchal region extensively white at base; a few pure white feathers scattered here and there; slightly elongated nuchal crest present, with markings of Def. Alt. vaguely suggested; chin and throat dull blackish, the feathers basally white; a poorly defined dark sepia collar around neck, merging with sepia of dorsum. **Upperparts** among the mixture of Juv. and Basic I dorsal feathers (which have mostly lost their pale tips through wear) appear a few blackish feathers with faint purplish sheen. **Underparts** narrow white collar immediately posterior to dark sepia collar, the feathers with sepia subterminal bars; breast similar in ground color to Def. Alt., but feathers barred with sepia or blackish; 2 or 3 new flank feathers pale yellowish buff, white for basal half. **Legs** and **feet** dark. Remainder of feathering consists of Juv. (wing, etc.) and Basic I (tail, some body feathering). Specimens described and figured in Millais (1913b), on pls. 38 and 39 of Schiøler (1926), and in text by Portenko (1952), definitely indicate that individuals renew more feathers than in the one just described.

▶ ♀ **Basic I Plumage** (all feathering except wing) acquired in 1st FALL and worn until some time in WINTER. Described in Witherby (1939) and by Portenko (1952); author has seen a single example. In general, quite like Basic I of ♂: predominantly variants of cinnamon; head and part of neck reddish brown, vaguely barred dark; dark spots on mantle; forward underparts yellowish, then breast rusty tawny, both with scattered dark markings, then abdomen and under tail coverts unmarked cinnamon, not blackening rearward (Portenko).

▶ ♀ **Alt. I Plumage** (all feathering except wing, tail, apparently abdomen, and possibly some other feathering), acquired some time in WINTER and worn until some time in SPRING or early summer. As Def. Alt., but paler overall.

▶ ♂ **Basic II Plumage** (entire feathering), head–body acquired late in 2nd SUMMER and worn until early in 2nd FALL, when the Basic II tail and wing grow; these, and apparently the abdomen, are long retained, i.e., worn with Alt. II. As Def. Basic except: **dorsum** with less sheen; **wing** alula feathers lack white edges; small feathers under alula (middle primary coverts) browner, with little or no admixture of white; bend of wing and under wing coverts with much less white, more dull brownish olive or sepia. So far as body feathering goes, a fall Plumage, often not evident until Aug. and after Sept. it is lost. See Portenko (1952) for various additional details.

▶ ♂ Alt. II Plumage (all feathering except wing, tail, and apparently abdomen), acquired in 2nd FALL (about Oct.) and worn through winter into 3rd SUMMER (July or later). As Def. Alt. but upperparts have less sheen; birds at this stage are most easily recognized by characters (see above) of retained Basic II wing.

▶ ♀ Basic II Plumage (all feathering), all except tail and wing acquired some time in SPRING or early summer (before age 1 year), then retained until late summer or FALL and, after a flightless period, the Basic II wing and tail grow and are worn with the incoming Alt. II. The "final eclipse" (Portenko), i.e., definitive. Well developed blue speculum.

▶ ♀ Alt. II Plumage (inclusive feathering as in ♀ Def. Alt.), acquired in late summer or EARLY FALL (at age 13–14 mo.) and retained through WINTER into following SPRING. Definitive; "scarcely subject to change" in subsequent Alts. (Portenko 1952). Birds at this stage may prove to be recognizable if there are distinguishable characters in retained Basic II wing.

**Measurements**   17 ♂ (from Alaska, Siberia, n. Scandinavia, and Japan): BILL from nostril 24–27.5 mm., av. 26.4; WING 204–223, av. 212.2; TAIL 83–92, av. 87.4; TARSUS 37–40, av. 38.4;   14 ♀ (Alaska, Siberia): BILL from nostril 25.5–29.3 mm., av. 27.5; WING 205–226.5, av. 211.5; TAIL 71.5–93.3, av. 82; TARSUS 34.7–41.5, av. 39.5 (ETS).

Another series, perhaps overlapping above sample, bill meas. from feathers, wing flattened, 12 ♂ (11 Alaska, 1 Siberia): BILL 36–41 mm., av. 39; WING 210–228, av. 218; TAIL 82–90, av. 87.7; TARSUS 37–40, av. 38.7;   11 ♀ (9 Alaska, 1 Bering Strait, 1 Siberia): BILL 40–44 mm., av. 41.6; WING 212–223, av. 215.6; TAIL 78–90, av. 85; TARSUS 38–40, av. 39.7 (ETS).

Siberian birds, WING (how meas. not stated): 31 ♂ 207–229 mm., av. 221; 40 ♀ 203–233, av. 216 (Rutilevskii 1957).

June–early July specimens from ne. Yakutia, bill from feathers and evidently wing flattened: 19 ♂ BILL 36–43 mm., av. 39.7; WING 212–238, av. 223;   14 ♀ BILL 37–48 mm., av. 43.8; WING 208–235, av. 227.2 (S. Uspenskii et al. 1962).

For another series, WING meas. over the curve, see Witherby (1939).

**Weight**   ♂ 719–954 gm., ♀ 780–945 (compilation, various sources). In ne. Yakutia in June–early July: 19 ♂ 670–900 gm., av. 793.7; 14 ♀ 750–1,000 gm., av. 852.8 (S. Uspenskii et al. 1962). Series that included both breeders and older prebreeders, from New Siberian Is.: 29 ♂ 628–822 gm., av. 759; 28 ♀ 651–999, av. 836 (Rutilevskii 1957). For Kamchatka, Averin (cited in Dementiev and Gladkov 1952) gave for ♂ ♂ in May 850 gm., in Oct. 500–800, in Nov. 1,000; a ♀ in July and another in Sept. each 720.

At Izembek Bay, Alaska, in late Jan.: 4 ♂ 1 lb. 12 oz. to 2 lb. 1 oz., av. 1 lb. 13 oz. (about 820 gm.); 2 ♀ 1 lb. 12 oz. and 1 lb. 14 oz. (R. D. Jones, Jr.).

**Hybrids** none known.

**Geographical variation** none (Portenko 1939; present author). KCP (early draft), expanded by RSP.

FIELD IDENTIFICATION    Approximately the size of the Lesser Scaup, but more elongated. Smallest, trimmest, and the most agile of the eiders. Straight thin bill. Swimming birds often have their tails angled upward more or less. Drakes resting on the water appear patchy—mostly white with some black—and truncated, the rear end being black. Unless extended, the black neck is inconspicuous. If a drake rears up on the water, the variably tawny venter is exposed and, if the wings are flapped, a large white area is prominent. (The drake Oldsquaw is dark breasted; the drake Smew has a prominent black patch from bill to around eye and much of the body is white or almost white, back to the tail.) Drake Steller's in Basic (Aug.–early Sept. mainly) are quite ♀-like (dark brownish), not largely black as are the other eiders when in Basic.

The ♀ in Alt. (fall–spring) is quite evenly dark brownish with decidedly reddish cast (generally being darker overall than most ♀ ♀ of other eiders), with head shaped like that of a shoal-water duck, and more or less bluish bill. The head and neck, at least from fall into spring in mature birds, generally appears very markedly paler than the body; a light eye ring is conspicuous. The duck has a quite Mallard-like wing pattern, without the large white area present in drake Steller's; the blue speculum and at least its trailing white edge show even when the wing is folded, the white at anterior edge of the speculum often being more or less concealed. The 2 white stripes in the wing are fairly wide and show well when the duck is flying.

Some of the predefinitive stages, described earlier, are quite ♀-like, with feathering some variant of reddish brown.

When the birds are not closely packed in a raft, they tend to be in scattered groups of about 15–40 individuals. As noted in winter, such flocks usually fly 30–50 meters above the sea, while other eiders typically fly lower (Belopolskii 1934). The large white wing patch of the drakes shows well at a considerable distance. The birds fly swiftly and buoyantly, their wings producing a louder whistling noise than the wings of Goldeneyes (*Bucephala* spp.); in a fog, the whistling is heard long before the birds are seen, if they are seen at all. When a huge assembly of Steller's flies up, steeply, there is a roar of wings at times audible a mile away (McKinney 1965c).

For excellent photographs of Steller's swimming, commencing to dive, and flying, and for size comparison with Common Eider, see Grastveit (1971). RSP

VOICE    Near Hooper Bay, Alaska, in the nesting season, the calls of both sexes of breeders when disturbed by man resembled the growling or barking of a young dog; a drake, on station on a pond, uttered an occasional barking sound, like the playful yelping of a little dog (Brandt 1943). In ne. Siberia in summer, growls from parties of flying birds (Percy, in Bannerman 1958).

When displaying birds were studied at a distance at Izembek Bay, Alaska, McKinney (1965c) was "never able to detect any male call," but he noted that captive drakes in hostile situations give calls that are similar in tone to those of the duck. According to Blair (in Bannerman 1958), it is when the drake is displaying that he most frequently utters his peculiar call, a murmuring croon, harder but not as loud as the cooing of the Common Eider.

The duck has a display named Rippling call (see beyond), with harsh, guttural, rapid stuttering that rises in pitch.

A constant chattering from flocks.

There is further information on voice below under both "Reproduction" and "Habits."

The striking wing noise, which may serve to keep a flock or members of a pair in contact in foggy weather, was mentioned in the previous section. RSP

HABITAT **Nesting areas** generally are away from the sea, at some distance inland. Steller's commonly nest in areas of tundra where there are numerous ponds with elevated margins or dry areas interspersed. It nests in areas of *Carex* or grassy hummocks, in some places on moss–lichen tundra (shared with Spectacled Eider) or even barren rocky tundra (shared with King Eider). Occasionally on ridges near the sea.

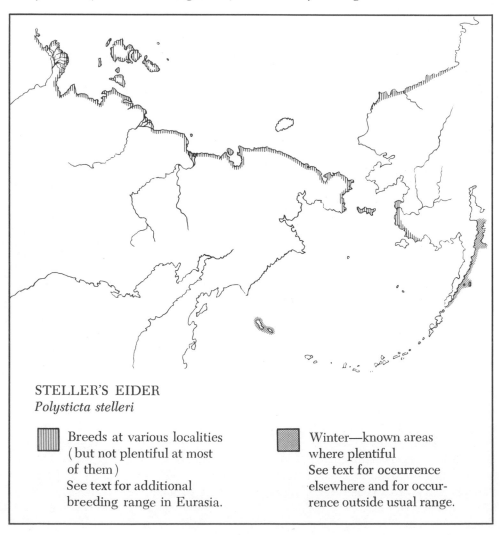

STELLER'S EIDER
*Polysticta stelleri*

▥ Breeds at various localities (but not plentiful at most of them)
See text for additional breeding range in Eurasia.

▨ Winter—known areas where plentiful
See text for occurrence elsewhere and for occurrence outside usual range.

When **on the sea,** a littoral bird. Prefers very shallow waters, such as the intertidal zone along rocky shores of marine bays, or around reefs, or in lagoons and inlets; *Ulva*, *Zostera*, or *Fucus* grow here; small mollusks and swimming crustaceans are plentiful. Groups of these little eiders commonly rest on beaches, sandbars, and flats exposed by the falling tide.

Lateral portions of the bill are fleshy in both Steller's Eider and the extinct Labrador Duck, which is the main basis for several authors having referred to these waterfowl as ecological counterparts. RSP

DISTRIBUTION   The majority of the birds are in arctic Siberia in summer and in waters adjacent to the Alaska Pen. in winter.

**Breeds** in N. AM. along the Bering Sea coast of Alaska between the Kuskokwim and Yukon deltas (plentiful at Igiak Bay, for example) and probably elsewhere, possibly on Nunivak I. and smaller is. thereabouts nearer the mainland, and occasionally nests on St. Lawrence I.; also along the arctic coast of Alaska at various places including vicinity of Wainwright, Barrow (common, at least formerly), and suitable localities eastward perhaps nearly to the Alaska–Yukon boundary. Possibly also in coastal Yukon Terr.

E. PALEARCTIC   Bering Sea coast of Chuckchee Pen. locally from Providence Bay northward; then w. along the arctic coast and on some nearby is. to the Lena Delta and Anabar tundra, a few beyond in Khatanga Gulf (one banded when adult at Izembek Bay, Alaska, has been recovered there in summer). Generally prevalent as a nester in New Siberian Is.: Little and Big Lyhakov (plentiful on the latter), Stolbov, Belkovskii, Kotelny, Faddevski, New Siberia, and s. part of Zemlya Bunge; does not nest farther n. at the DeLong Is. (Rutilevskii 1957).

W. PALEARCTIC   These birds may be termed the Barents Sea unit. Maximum numbers of Steller's, among the counts reported recently by Kokhanov (1974), include: at Murmansk [evidently includes Varanger Fjord]—presently not over 2,000 in winter; Vost Listy to Kochkovki—about 1,050 on March 27, 1968, about 1,180, on March 4, 1971, and at Dumbov Bay about 500 (87% ♂) in March 1971; in e. Murman from Daln Zelents to Ryndy—180 in May 1966 and 520 (33% ♂) in March 1971; entrance to White Sea—up to 130 in Oct.–Nov. 1971; Tersk Shore of White Sea—300 (mostly ♂) on 15 km. of coast at end of July 1971, on another section of Tersk shore about 130 molting drakes on July 18, 1972, also up to 90 along still another stretch of coast.

According to S. M. Uspenskii (1972), Steller's nests sporadically along the Barents and Kara sea coasts; nests have been found at Varanger Fjord, Matochkin Shar on s. Novaya Zemlya, on w. Yamal Pen., and w. Taimyr. Thus the number of records is very few. The nest at Varanger Fjord was found e. of Vadsø in 1924.

S. Johnsen (1938) postulated that, when the sea ice remains packed along the Asiatic coast e. of the Taimyr Pen. in summer–fall, but milder weather and open water prevail to the west, some of these eiders would move toward ice-free waters, i.e., shift from the e. to w. Palearctic.

**Summer**   Prebreeders are widely distributed, a very few sometimes remaining even on winter range. There are scattered flocks at both e. Asian and N. Am. Bering Sea localities and the rest are beyond, on shallow seas, in areas not remote from nesting localities. In n. Norway, prebreeders generally are in Varanger Fjord in some numbers in summer and a few are scattered westward, occasionally as far as the Lofoten Is.

9

**Winter** Widely scattered along Bering Sea coasts as far up as there is any open shallow water. In N. Am., however, most numerous s. of Bering Sea—around Kodiak and is. to the west (Shumagins and others) and in bays along the s. edge of the Alaska Pen. There are some in the easternmost Aleutians and a few s. in Pacific waters down to Prince William Sd. On approach of spring, some 200,000 assemble at 3 large lagoons at outer end of the Alaska Pen.: Nelson Lagoon, Izembek Bay, and Bechevin Bay.

Apparently this eider now is a very scarce winterer approximately from Umanak westward in the Aleutian chain; O. Murie (1959) stated that it may have occurred there long ago when reportedly it was much more plentiful.

In e. Asia, countless numbers are said to have wintered formerly in the Commander Is. Steller's is abundant there at the present time, at its preferred stations, the shallow waters along the w. side of Bering I. (Marakov 1966). Along the outer coast of Kamchatka there are scattered small flocks, giving an impression that the species is plentiful even though the total number of birds is small. They winter in the n. Kurils: Schumschu, Paramushir, and Onekotan. Upper limit of wintering may be any ice-free stretches of water along the Anadyr coast, where Belopolskii (1934) saw them at 2 localities in March.

In the w. Palearctic in winter there have been none in some former seasons to hundreds in some recent ones around northernmost Fennoscandia, notably in Varanger Fjord. Numbers there are highest in spring, the largest tallies (Grastveit 1971) being 1,000 in mid-march of 1969 and 1,100 in mid-March of 1970. A Steller's Eider was taken in Feb. in the White Sea. (Also see below.)

**Straggler** to widespread localities. In N. Am. to B.C. (Queen Charlotte Is.), Mackenzie (C. Bathurst), s. Baffin I. (Cumberland Sd.), Que. (N. Shore of Gulf of St. Lawrence—2 records), and Me. (Scarborough). In Md. a flock of 8 on Jan. 4, 1967; of these, 3 were shot and the hunter had no idea what they were; one of those shot had been banded Sept. 7, 1962, at Izembek Bay, Alaska.

Greenland: 3 singles captured, on the west coast in Disko Fjord, June 15, 1878, at Godthaab, Nov. 24, 1954, and near the ne. coast at Sabine I., June 14, 1922.

In the e. Palearctic: Wrangel I. (occasional) and Herald I.; in Okhotsk Sea to Sakhalin I. (where supposedly it occurred in some numbers in the previous century); and southward beyond the Kurils to n. Japan (Hokkaido—2 records).

In the w. Palearctic, and omitting information given above: recorded down the Atlantic coast of Norway to Andenes, and numerous records in and around the Baltic (including Gulf of Finland and the Kattegat) and to the south. There are at least 29 records, almost all in the previous century, for "Middle Europe" (which includes the s. Baltic); details in Bauer and Glutz von Blotzheim (1969). Recorded from France. To June, 1971, there were 8 acceptable records for the Brit. Isles.

Bones of Steller's Eider have been identified from **archaeological sites** in Alaska at Kodiak I., Little Kiska I., St. Lawrence I., and C. Prince of Wales; see Brodkorb (1964a) for full references. RSP

MIGRATION The schedule of this little eider is greatly weather influenced. The following pattern probably fits the majority of the birds. In spring the scattered flocks come together at staging areas, then migrate rather late. After their travels northward, mature drakes and prebreeders (both sexes) return early to these same staging areas to molt or, in tardy seasons, molt in assemblies on the sea near breeding areas and return to the staging areas much later. In the "normal" (former) situation, the long journey back is a molt migration and the rather short distance scattering of flocks afterward (and much later) is the only true fall migration; in the latter situation, molt migration is short (although distance varies) from breeding areas to wherever they molt, while the much later fall migration consists of both the return flight to staging areas and the scattering from there to wintering places. Breeding ♀ ♀ normally make a long return flight to staging areas prior to the flightless stage of molting.

Young Steller's Eiders probably begin migrating soon after they attain flight.

It is now known that at least the bulk of the birds that gather in spring at lagoons at w. end of the Alaska Pen. migrate to arctic Siberia; see R. D. Jones, Jr. (1965) for details, including 16 banding recoveries in Siberia w. to the delta of the Lena plus 1 from Pt. Barrow, Alaska. As of early 1971, among 31 recoveries of birds banded when flightless at Izembek Lagoon, 11 were from arctic Yakutia. The following were from even more distant places: banded Sept. 10, 1962 and recovered in Sept. 1965 at Little Lyhakov I. (about lat. 142° E); banded Sept. 7, 1962 and recovered in July 1964 at Syndassko in Khatanga Gulf (about lat. 110° E). There were no recoveries in N. Am. distant from place of banding except 1 from Pt. Barrow and 1 from Md., which is mentioned earlier. (Data from R. D. Jones, Jr.)

According to Bent (1925), Steller's Eider migrates in spring westward along the Aleutians to the Commander Is., then up the Bering Sea Coast of Siberia, and travels this route in reverse in fall, but as O. Murie (1959) indicated, there is no supporting evidence for this theory. Asiatic winterers go up the w. rim of Bering Sea, but Am. winterers evidently keep fairly close to the Alaskan side. There are not many records for the Pribilofs.

**Spring**   In N. Am. the scattered wintering flocks s. of the Alaska Pen. cross over and assemble in lagoons near its w. end. About half of them are in Nelson Lagoon, the remainder being divided between Izembek Lagoon and Bechevin Bay. These areas then are ice-free, but waters to the north still are frozen. The birds begin moving out in the latter half of April and all have departed by about May 20. The breeders move on; yearlings (prebreeders) tend to linger, then travel leisurely, numerous flocks only going as far as the shallow waters along the s. and w. coasts of St. Lawrence I. To the north, there are mass flights through Bering Strait, generally from late May to about mid-June. The species has been noted on the Am. side of Bering Strait, at Wales, as early as May 12 and in arctic Alaska at Barrow on June 5. The majority of Alaskan winterers go westward from Bering Strait, along the arctic coast of Siberia. One year, they appeared en masse (and flocks contained more drakes than ducks) in ne. Yakutia at Krumski Bay as early as May 5, when the first thawed pools were on the ice; migration began to slacken by the middle of June, but continued to the end of the month (S. Uspenskii et al. 1962). In the New Siberian Archipelago they generally arrive around mid-June; in 1939 first seen June 14 and mass arrival June 21; in 1949 first on June 17 and in mass June 19–23 (Rutilevskii 1957). They go to any open water, such as thawed pools inland. A great many prebreeders reach the nesting areas, often in unisexual groups or flocks, but they soon depart.

On e. Asiatic winter range, flocks combine in April and pass along the Kamchatkan coast during May. They are gone from the Kurils by mid-April, from Kamchatka and the Commander Is. by late May, and Gulf of Anadyr by about June 10. It is not known whether they are bound for Siberian or Alaskan destinations.

The w. Palearctic birds have their staging area in Varanger Fjord, where they reach peak numbers in mid-March.

**Summer**   There is insufficient information to unravel what happens to the various categories—breeding drakes, breeding ♀ ♀, prebreeders of both sexes, and young of the year—during favorable and variably severe adverse seasons. From known fragments, the following is suggested.

In arctic Siberia the first birds to leave on **molt migration** are any early-arriving prebreeders, to a considerable extent evidently in unisexual flocks. Next go the drakes whose mates are incubating. In the New Siberian Archipelago, according to Rutilevskii (1957), their departure is inconspicuous and begins by early July; the shores still are icebound; the drakes form in small groups that later combine into flocks of 40–60 birds and fly eastward. The flight is on a broad front if they find much open water; that is, the more open water the less concentrated the flight. Birds bound from Siberia to Alaska near midnight on July 24, 1969, and tracked on a broad front by radar at C. Prince of Wales, were suspected of being Steller's Eiders (Flock 1972). Sometimes there are mixed flocks, containing Oldsquaws and King Eiders along with Steller's. It is believed that a few drakes remain behind and molt near nesting areas. The postnesting ♀ ♀ leave much later, and their young later still, and go eastward. The birds fly to Bering Strait and (those that are to winter in Alaska) thence to the lagoons at outer end of the Alaska Pen., where they arrive in Aug. In 1957–62 inclusive, "most, if not all" (birds of both sexes) arrived in Aug. (R. D. Jones, Jr., 1965) and soon the drakes became flightless. At this time some rafts consist almost entirely of drakes, and others of ducks.

In other years, as in 1963 and 1964, the birds arrived at the lagoons almost 3 months later, having molted beforehand elsewhere. In 1964 they arrived between sunset on Nov. 6 and midmorning on Nov. 9. When the lagoons freeze, they leave and scatter.

Off the sw. coast of Stolbov I. (New Siberian Archipelago) in mid-Aug. of 1956 there was a raft of not less than 3,000 Steller's Eiders. "Apparently ice conditions that year induced bachelor birds [postbreeding drakes] to remain in the Laptev Sea for molting" (Rutilevskii 1963, transl.). The latest date that any were seen thereabouts was Aug. 23.

**Late fall**   Evidently, in both e. Asia and Alaska, flocks are not stationed at most areas where they occur through winter until late Oct. or some time in Nov. They are said to occur in the Commander Is. from early Sept. onward (which may indicate that this also is a staging area), but do not arrive in the Kurils until late Nov.

NOTES   On the s. side of St. Lawrence I. on June 25, 1913, there were a number of large, very dense, flocks consisting mostly of drakes (W. S. Brooks 1915). Considering the date, these probably were ♂ ♂ that had left their incubating mates and had come there prior to molting.

There are reports of small flocks, generally containing both sexes (presumably of prebreeders), molting in late July and early Aug. on the arctic coasts of Siberia and Alaska.

In the case of so adverse a season as to inhibit nesting entirely, there is no information as to whether the birds return immediately or else molt beforehand. The latter is probable, as in the very cold summer of 1964, when they arrived late at outer end of the Alaska Pen. RSP

BANDING STATUS   According to the Bird Banding Laboratory, in Alaska a total of 861 were banded through the year 1964 and there were 2 recoveries through 1961. R. D. Jones, Jr. (1965) reported that at Izembek Bay, Alaska, a total of 833 were banded when flightless in 1961 and 1962, and he listed (and mapped) 17 returns through June, 1963. As of early 1971, a total of 986 had been banded at Izembek Bay and there were 31 recoveries, some of which have been mentioned earlier. RSP

REPRODUCTION   Age when first breeds unknown, evidently at least 2 years, i.e., not as yearlings. At least most breeders are paired long before they arrive at nesting areas. Displays were studied in April at Izembek Bay, Alaska, by McKinney (1965c) and the same names were used for them as for their presumed homologies in the Common Eider. The birds are highly social and, compared with the Common Eider, their displays are much more rapid and there is a greater amount of aerial activity. For photos of some displays, see Johnsgard (1964a); for some diagrams, see McKinney's paper.

In **pair-formation** activity, 3–7 drakes crowd around a duck, displaying, chasing one another, apparently having a constant urge to make SHORT FLIGHTS, and there is occasional fighting. The flights usually are for only a few hundred yds. at most, often on a curving course. There is traffic between groups, new drakes flying to join a group, while members that take flight may drop out, i.e., not return to the group. In pursuit flights of a group of drakes and a duck one ♂ usually was seen to keep close to the ♀ when others dropped out; in such cases presumably the duck and attending drake already had formed a pair bond. After alighting, the drake would make aggressive rushes at other drakes. Drake displays at this time were Shake, Head-toss, and Head-turn. The known repertoire of the sexes is as follows.

**Displays of the duck**   INCITING threatening (pointing) movements toward another bird alternate with upward movements of the head that resemble Head-toss of drake. A rapid action. A loud *coooay* during upward motion of the head. RIPPLING CALL constant chatter from flocks, harsh and gutteral, rapid stuttering *a-a-a-a-r*, rising in pitch to give rippling effect. PRONE with head forward along water surface, as in Common Eider. BATHE as by drake. PREEN-DORSALLY as drake.

**Displays of the drake**   REARING done rapidly by swimming bird; head and body suddenly moved backward so that the bird is up-ended, conspicuously showing the tawny venter; the bill points skyward; then the bird returns to normal swimming posture. HEAD-TOSS bill tossed upward and backward very rapidly; performed afloat and ashore. SHAKE a rearing up and then settling again on the water, as in a comfort movement; the head is flicked forward, then back quickly before the breast is again in the water. HEAD-TURN bill moved mechanically from side to side a variable number of times, rapidly. In most striking form, performed with head held high as drake swims away from the duck. Preen-dorsally bird nibbles at forward mantle. BILL-DIP head moved forward so that bill touches, or almost touches, the water. BATHE stereotyped head dipping, as in normal bathing; a continuous series of dipping actions, up to 17 noted. HEAD-ROLL cheek rubbed on shoulder. HEAD-SHAKE laterally, very rapidly.

13

ERECT head high, tail cocked in varying degree; a flight-intention posture of both sexes; frequently assumed by drakes in social phase of display; also often assumed, by drakes especially, after postcopulatory Rearing. SHORT FLIGHT from Erect position, drake rises steeply, with rapid wingbeats, flies a very short distance (perhaps 6 ft.), and alights with a splash. Very similar to display flight of the Bufflehead.

The first 4 drake displays listed are closely associated with overt hostility between drakes and are given in different order and in various combinations, as 4 + 1, or 4 + 1 + 4, or 3 + 4 + 1 + 4, etc.

Rearing normally occurs in the following sequence: Erect + Shake + Head-turn (as ♂ STEAMS toward ♀) + Rearing + Head-turn (as ♂ Steams away from ♀) (Johnsgard 1964a).

**Copulation** These are McKinney's (1965) observations in April at Izembek Bay. The pair avoids interference by moving, or drifting, away from the group and the display pattern that follows is similar to that of the Common Eider. The duck is inactive in PRONE posture; The drake swims around her, continually displaying; his commonest repertoire includes PREEN, Bill-dip, and Bathe, the following being less frequent: Head-shake, Head-roll, and Head-turn. The order in which they occur is not random; that is, they are linked in combinations such as Preen + Bathe, Preen + Bill-dip, etc. Then the drake performs a single Shake, rushes rapidly across the water, and mounts. On dismounting, the drake Rears, then assumes Erect posture, and sometimes gives Head-turns. The duck may make Inciting movements and usually bathes briefly. Not long afterward, the drake makes one or more Short flights away from the duck, or the pair takes wing and rejoins the group, the social bond evidently being maintained until pairs disperse after terminating spring migration.

So far as known, **nests** are distributed without a tendency toward grouping; this is the most solitary of the eiders as a nester. The nest site often is in a slight depression, as between hummocks, hence difficult to find; others are on slightly elevated spots; often within 2–3 meters of a pond. At Hooper Bay, Alaska, 5 nests were made of grass lined with a thick wall of down; dimensions were: outside diam. 23–50 cm., inside diam. 14–15 cm., and depth of cup 9–10 cm. (Brandt 1943). The **nest down** is very dark, sooty brown, and the center spots are so slightly lighter as to be scarcely noticeable. Occasionally there is a small white spray included. Intermingled breast feathers are light brownish (nearly white) for their basal half and shade to medium gray-brown or even blackish brown at the tip and are practically indistinguishable from those of the Oldsquaw. They are figured on pl. 90 in Witherby (1939). Usually there is much vegetation intermingled with the down.

As noted earlier, copulation has been observed in April at an assembly area in Alaska. Blair (1936) saw it in late June in E. Finmark.

In a late season at Hooper Bay, Alaska, **fresh eggs** were found on June 19 and it is likely that, in a "normal" season, clutches are begun there early in the month. On main breeding range in arctic Siberia and Alaska, clutches apparently are initiated from about mid-June to early July, with variation beyond this span depending on whether spring comes early or late. Unlike other eiders, Steller's lays large clutches, usually 7–8 eggs. Five clutches at Hooper Bay: 1 (of 7 eggs), 3 (8), and 1 (9) (Brandt 1943).

One **egg** each from 18 clutches from Alaska **size** length $59.41 \pm 2.16$ mm., breadth

14

40.94 ± 1.34, radii of curvature of ends 15.73 ± 1.40 and 11.55 ± 1.04; **shape** approximately subelliptical, elongation 1.44 ± 0.072, bicone −0.030, asymmetry +0.148 (FWP). Omitting recorded variation, the published av. of some other series are as follows: 75 av. 61.4 × 42 mm. (Bent 1925); 30 av. 62.9 × 40.78 (J. C. Phillips 1926); and, converting Brandt's (1943) inches to mm., 40 from Hooper Bay, Alaska, av. 58.7 × 40.9. **Color** of fresh eggs is some variant of pale olive buff, but they are much darker when stained. They resemble in color the eggs of the Oldsquaw and Common Eider.

In the New Siberian Is., July 16, 1948, the total wt. of a 7-egg clutch was 363 gm., this being 46.7% of the wt. of the sitter (Rutilevski 1957).

The incubating duck is a close sitter. The drake stays nearby on a pond until sometime probably quite early in incubation, then joins with other drakes and soon they depart. **Incubation period** unknown.

Females with **broods** are seen on tundra ponds, brackish inlets, and occasionally on salt water. Brandt (1943) felt that gulls and other predators took a heavy toll of ducklings on ponds, reducing to 3–4 the number of young in a brood by the time those remaining were half-grown. Almost nothing, however, is yet known about the preflight period. Most ♀♀ probably go away to molt, leaving their still flightless young on ponds, deltas, and coastal inlets. Many young are flying by the end of Aug. RSP

HABITS Steller's, quite unlike the large eiders, is an agile bird when ashore; it walks well, with a slight waddle, and runs with ease. It is one of the most highly social waterfowl, except when nesting, the birds packing into compact assemblies or dense rafts. Often they are, at most, only inches apart and so appear like a solid carpet on the sea. When they feed, however, they scatter in bunches and long irregular lines. Flightless molting birds form in large and notably dense rafts, preponderantly of birds of one sex, after the manner of the King Eider. The birds tend to dive in unison. At one moment perhaps a thousand are on the surface, a few seconds later none are in sight; they not only dive but also reappear simultaneously, as if getting food by some concerted action (R. D. Jones, Jr.). A raft of feeding birds throws up a shower of spray that is visible for a great distance (McKinney 1965c).

When starting to dive, the wings are out from the body as shown in an excellent photo in Grastveit (1971). Food is swallowed under water; at least they are not seen to emerge with it in their bills. The items they ingest are mostly small. Much feeding is done in shallows, on a falling tide; the birds swim and wade in pools and runoff channels and move about on exposed tidal flats. They up-end in shallow water, dabble at the surface, and even pick up stranded items. In fall at Izembek Bay they feed on gastropods and pelecypods that inhabit the eelgrass leaves; these items are very small and many are required for nourishment, but they are extremely abundant (R. D. Jones, Jr.). They rest and sleep in close formation, in the lee or on a calm sea, or in scattered bunches on weed-covered rocks and on sandbars in the intertidal zone, at times also above tideline on shore.

When taking wing, Steller's rises easily and steeply, then flies swiftly, generally at a fair height above the sea. They fly in a wavy frontal (transverse) line. They are said to fly as swiftly as Oldsquaws, with which they associate occasionally. They also are said not

15

to prefer the company of other eiders, the King excepted, which may merely reflect the fact that the King and Steller's have in common certain preferences of time and place. In mid-Aug. near Stolbov I. (in New Siberian group), there was a raft of not less than 3,000 molting Steller's and, nearby, another of about 10,000 King Eiders; the rafts came together at times, but "remained independent" (Rutilevskii 1963).

In banding operations at Izembek Bay, when a small flock is held captive in a channel, the ducks are very talkative. They utter a quiet *ta ta ta ta ta* but, when driven into a trap, the volume of sound rises. When dipped from the trap, the duck's call is a loud squawk. The drakes submit to handling in silence; the ducks invariably are noisy, invariably struggle, and scratch with their sharp nails. In captivity, the ducks are much easier to keep alive than the drakes. (Data from R. D. Jones, Jr.)

On the Alaska Pen., where these little eiders are known as "Scotchies," they are not particularly sought after in the hunting season, being passed up when more desirable birds such as Brant are obtainable. In certain Asiatic localities, the flesh of wintering birds has the odor of iodine, which may indicate that they have been eating sea lettuce (*Ulva*) (Gizenko 1955).

The total number of Steller's Eiders in winter may be of the order of 400,000 birds, possibly fewer. An estimate of "around 500,000" by S. Uspenskii (1972) seems rather high. Surely the bad seasons that have such disastrous effect on breeding of Brant and King Eider are equally detrimental to Steller's. Both weather and predation may seriously diminish the number of ducklings before they are able to maintain themselves. But this is largely guessing, since there is very little information of any sort on various aspects of the biology of this little eider. RSP

FOOD  Examination of 66 stomachs of birds taken in summer in extreme e. Siberia and w. Alaska showed 87% animal food, crustaceans mainly, also mollusks, insects, worms, and fishes, and 13% vegetable matter, principally pondweeds and eelgrass. Unexpectedly, the food of "juveniles" contained only 60% animal matter, the vegetable rising to 40% (Cottam 1939).

**Animal**  Crustaceans (amphipods—15 genera, isopods, barnacles, and crabs) 45.2%, mollusks (*Mytilus, Siliqua, Nucula, Mya, Natica, Littorina*, Olividae, etc.) 19.3% insects (Chironomid larvae, Trichoptera larvae, and miscellaneous— *Limnophila, Scatella, Spilogna, Chrysops*, Dytiscidae, Carabidae) 13%, annelid worms 3.3%, sand dollars (Exocycloida) 2.8%, fishes 2.3%, foraminiferans 1.1% (Cottam 1939).

In Alaskan islands, fed mainly on amphipods (*Allorchestes, Pontoporeia*) and mollusks (*Neverita, Cardium, Melanella*) (Preble and McAtee 1923, Bretherton 1896). Marine worms (Gephyrea) (Murdoch 1885) and sea fleas (Orchestiidae) (W. Palmer 1889) also mentioned. In April, near end of Alaska Pen. at Nelson Lagoon, a flock fed for several days on an accumulation of dead shrimp in shallow water at the edge of the beach (McKinney 1965c).

In n. Norway, crustaceans (*Gammarus, Amphitöe*) and mollusks (*Littorina, Lacuna, Trophon, Margarita, Amnyx, Podocerus, Buccinum, Pleustes*) (Collet 1894). At sea, food almost entirely animal, chiefly mollusks. Siivonen (1941) reported much the same

16

food: mollusks (11 genera), Crustacea (3 Families), echinoderms (2 genera), also numerous very small gizzard stones.

In U.S.S.R. in summer on tundra lakes the animal food (87.1%) consists mainly of amphipod crustaceans (45.2%), insects (including larvae of caddis flies and chironomids) 13%, mollusks (mainly barchiopods) 19.3%, and small quantities of polychaetes and fishes (Dementiev and Gladkov 1952). The stomach of a drake taken near Markov on the Anadyr R. on June 7 contained a great number of stone fly (Perlidae) larvae, aquatic beetles, a water boatman (*Corixa*), and much gravel (Portenko 1939).

In ne. Yakutia, in the early days after the birds arrived (June 5–10), they fed on sprouts, panicles, and spikelets of grasses, shoots of *Equisetum*, fruiting spikes on *Carex*, as well as Tipulidae larvae, Neuroptera, and moss. Later (June 11–July 7), a large proportion of their food was chironomid larvae. And the stomach of a ♀ taken Aug. 4 in the Indigirka delta contained only vegetative parts of plants and seeds of *Ranunculus*. These data are from S. Uspenskii et al. (1962).

On the n. Anabar tundra, ♀ ♀ taken June 13–20 had stomachs full of chironomid larvae and aquatic plants; the wt. of wet contents of alimentary tracts full of these larvae was 12.5 gm., the stomach alone 10 gm. (S. Uspenskii 1965c).

**Vegetable** Pondweeds (*Zostera, Potamogeton*) 3.4%, crowberry (*Empetrum*) 1.1%, algae 1%, miscellaneous (*Carex, Hippuris, Rubus, Potentilla, Rosa, Arctostaphylos, Cornus, Sparganium, Equisetum, etc.*) 7.6% (Cottam 1939). Seen feeding on a marine "grass" [*Zostera?*] in Alaska (Conover 1926). In April at Izembek Bay at end of Alaska Pen., the large flocks fed mainly around extensive beds of *Zostera* (McKinney 1955c). AWS

## Common Eider

*Somateria mollissima*

Also called Eider or Eider Duck. Large, heavy-bodied marine duck, some populations consisting of the largest of any species of eider. Elongated wedge-shaped facial profile. Side of upper mandible has a naked extension (frontal process or lobe) back into the forehead. Feathering near lower side base of upper mandible extends forward nearly to or even past level of rear of nostril, but feathering on top midline of bill ends far short of this (reverse of King Eider). In the ♀ , apparently in all Plumages but especially Alt., the feathers of upperparts and sides have more broadly rounded ends in the Common than in the King Eider (in which they are more tapering, i.e, approaching pointed). The difference is accentuated by the shape of the black area within the feather, the distal end of this area being more toward transverse than the outline of the feather in *S. mollissima* and more toward pointed (especially scapulars) than the feather outline in *spectabilis*. The drake Common in Def. Alt. Plumage is unique among the Anatids in having the combination of white back and breast plus black belly and sides.

The drake's trachea has uniform diam., the asymmetrical bony bulla at proximal end is similar to but slightly larger than that of the King Eider; see Humphrey (1958b) for figs. of various bullae and text comparison of trachael apparatus of the eiders. Although 1 bronchus is noticeably larger than the other in the King Eider, in the Common it is very markedly larger; see fig. 50 in Schiøler (1926) and pl. 248a in Heinroth and Heinroth (1928).

With the very considerable geographical variation in size included: length ♂ about 21–28 in., ♀ 20–26, wingspread ♂ 32–43, ♀ 30–42, usual wt. of ♂ varies from about 3½ to 5¾ lb., ♀ 3–5½. Seven subspecies recognized here, 5 in our area.

DESCRIPTION    Two Plumages/cycle in both sexes. Definitive condition generally is attained in 3rd cycle in ♀ and 4th in ♂ , but perhaps sometimes earlier in both sexes. Major previous work on the species: Schiøler (1908 and especially 1926), Millais (1913b and especially 1913c), A. C. Meinertzhagen as revised in Witherby (1939), all on *S. m. mollissima;* and Portenko (1952), on *S. m. v-nigra.* Beginning with the earliest of these papers, it has been a practice to give estimated age of individuals described, the stated ages not being for birds of known age. Many such estimates, no doubt, are fairly accurate; there is now some evidence, however, that timing of attainment of the definitive condition is variable. As in other *Somateria* (and various other ducks), the molts in the first cycle may be "on schedule," protracted, interrupted, or delayed and, commonly, may not include all of the body; for example, some Juv. feathering frequently is retained for a time. "Offset" or delayed molting of some earlier-acquired feathering and individual variation in timing are common even in later cycles.

Both Schiøler and Millais were unclear as to the number of feather generations in the first cycle. For example, many waterfowl—not just the Common Eider—illustrated in Schiøler's major opus (1925, 1926) and labeled "Juv." have acquired some or all of the succeeding Basic I.

There has been some confusion from describing age-class by calendar year; in the

18

present text a bird aged 12 mo., although well into its 2nd calendar year, is designated as a yearling and not as a 2-year-old.

There is variation in coloring and markings of feathering acquired at certain pre-definitive molts: some birds "advance" toward what one would anticipate as first oc-curring in the comparable Plumage of the succeeding cycle; others have "retarded" characteristics; occasionally there is a mixture. Such matters raise particularly difficult problems with ♀♀, because of resemblance of their Plumages to one another.

*S. m. dresseri*, the subspecies of the Maritimes and e. U.S., is described below; also see col. pl. facing p. 376. This extends geographical coverage of detailed Plumage studies of the species.

▶ ♂ Def. Alt. Plumage (all feathering except the long scapulars, tail, and all of wing), acquired by prolonged molting that begins some time in AUG. or EARLY SEPT. and is completed by some birds in Oct. but in others even as late as early Dec., then retained through WINTER into the following EARLY SUMMER. Molting often begins (on head and upper breast) even while the abdomen, rump, and even the scapular area still are ac-quiring some of the preceding (Basic) generation and, in turn, the venter and rump may not be fully in Alt. until Nov. or later. Occasionally, some Basic feathering on the venter is retained into winter.

**Bill** in winter a vivid orange-yellow, but in spring turns greenish yellow or greenish olive. **Iris** dark brownish. **Head** crown to below eye and narrow band along lower mar-gin of frontal lobes black with some ultramarine-violet iridescence; posterior margin of the black crown area divided by a cream or straw yellow streak extending to point above eye (feathers of this streak white except at tips); nape, anterior sides of neck, upper cheeks, and a line extending a varying distance along lower edge of black band below frontal lobes, pale yellow-lime (greenish), washed with straw yellow; rest of head and throat white; in new feathering the white and green feathers of the face may be tipped with black which, exceptionally, may persist through winter. Sometimes, on underside of head, there is a V (with point forward); if present, it varies from rather obscure and finely drawn to heavy and black. **Upperparts** from posterior neck to sides of rump (and including visible areas of scapulars) white, often with straw yellow tinge; center of rump black, extending in a median line to center of back and becoming grayer. **Underparts** upper breast white, heavily suffused with color varying from cream to pinkish buff; this color fades with wear, and pigments are partly evanescent, fading rather quickly after death. In addition, some breast feathers when new have narrow black margins that wear off. Remainder of underparts black except **1** if any Basic still is retained on the venter, it is faded and brownish and contrasts with black Alt. feathering of sides that has a faint bluish bloom when new, and **2** on sides of rump a more or less oval white or creamy area, continuous anteriorly with white of back, and the feathers (which come in late) are much longer than the surrounding ones. Legs and **feet** quite vivid to muted yellow, webs olive (greenish), claws pale brownish. Tail, wing, and the 2 long scapulars are retained Basic, described below.

NOTES   In the drake Common Eider the cheek feathers are long and soft, not mod-ified, stiff, and relatively erect (plushlike) as in the drake King and Spectacled Eider and Labrador Duck.

The upper scapulars are molted twice/cycle, being white in Alt. and dark in Basic. At

19

least 2 long white scapulars underneath, the ones with "scooped" ends, are acquired late, often in Nov. or Dec., during terminal stage of molting of body. Thus the long scapulars are acquired by an offset (much delayed) fragment of molting into Basic. Hence they are worn first with Alt., then Basic head–body.

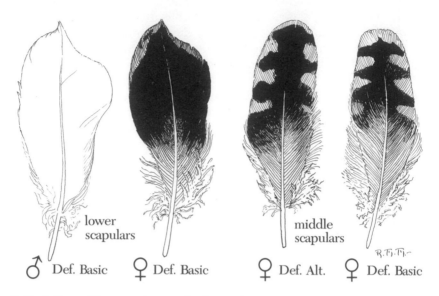

♂ Def. Basic    lower scapulars ♀ Def. Basic    middle scapulars ♀ Def. Alt.    ♀ Def. Basic

▶ ♂ Def. Basic Plumage (entire feathering), MIDSUMMER into FALL, except entire wing, tail, and late-acquired longest scapulars are long retained. Order of molting: head, breast and upper back, and shorter scapulars (all usually in late June–July), then more of breast, the sides, and posterior underparts (about Aug.) then tail, and the new feathering may be worn 2–4 weeks before the wing is molted (usually in Aug.); later stages overlap onset of Prealt. Molt (and see note above regarding long scapulars). Drakes appear to be largely in Basic for an estimated 2 mo.

**Head** crown and nape brownish olive, the feathers with blackish tips creating obscure barring; feathers (except tips) paler along streak through eye, creating a poorly defined transocular line; lores, cheeks, and sides of neck sooty sepia, loreal feathers often tipped white; often a small tuft of white feathers immediately behind ear opening; chin and throat similar to crown but paler. **Upperparts** anterior mantle and upper scapulars sooty or brownish olive, the scapulars with varying amount of white along shaft and on outer web; the 2 long scapulars are broad, with "scooped" outer margin so that they curve upward and show as a rounded or somewhat triangular projection above the contour of the back; the projections (homologous with the "sails" of the King Eider) are erectile and thus prominent at times in live drakes, but not at other times and not conspicuous in prepared skins; posterior mantle feathers variable, some resembling anterior ones, some pure white, some white with broad sooty margins giving scaled effect; midback usually white; lower back and upper tail coverts sooty black, the feathers on former with narrow white edges that soon wear away; area on side of rump a mixture of white and more or less brownish feathers, or white feathers that are

20

brownish laterally, this area connected anteriorly to white of midback. **Underparts** upper breast feathers variable, usually with more or less white at base or centrally, with black subterminal and sepia terminal band; amount of white increases down breast, sometimes absent on upper breast; lower breast, abdomen, and under tail coverts blackish, becoming brownish with wear and fading; sides and flanks dark brownish olive (feathers much shorter and distally broader than in Alt.). **Tail** feather vanes angle to a point; the feathers are dull blackish above, usually with narrow white tips when fresh, and are dark smoke gray below. **Wing** primaries brownish black (several innermost ones sometimes tipped white); all short secondaries black (at least some distal ones generally tipped white), and all these remiges paler on inner web; elongated innermost secondaries falcate, curving down over closed wing, and white; greater primary coverts and alula dull blackish brown, usually tipped white in new feathering; lesser primary coverts also nearly black with prominent white tips; greater coverts (except innermost) black, often with white tips increasing in width from outer to inner; innermost greater covert white with black tip on outer web; remainder of upper surface of wing white; underside of remiges and under primary coverts light gray, remainder of wing lining and axillars white.

NOTE    In sea ducks there is little information on length of interval between approximately simultaneous loss of flight feathers and sufficient growth of new ones to sustain flight (but see below under ♀ Def. Basic).

▶    ♀ Def. Alt. Plumage (all feathering except longest scapulars, tail, and all of wing), acquired beginning in LATE SUMMER or FALL and retained until EARLY SPRING. (Since the Basic venter and rump quite often are long retained, one may get the impression that the Alt. generation is not as inclusive as is actually the case.) Occasionally a few feathers (particularly upper scapulars) appear as early as late June; most molting is in Aug.–Sept., then may continue gradually or else there is a pause and it is completed much later.

**Bill** dusky greenish to olive green, the unguis pale brownish to pale plumbeous gray with brownish tinge, the basal areas of bill sometimes yellowish but less vivid than in ♂. **Iris** dark brownish. **Head** and neck tawny, darkest on crown, finely streaked black (streaks variable—usually heaviest on crown, nearly absent on chin–throat; the crown is well defined). Cheeks and side of head tend to be lighter than rest of head (usually the reverse is true of Def. Basic.). **Upperparts** variably (usually heavily) barred black and rusty, the black bars broadest on upper scapulars. **Underparts** breast, flanks, and under tail coverts tawny, barred (often heavily) with black (broadest on flanks); abdomen highly variable, in some individuals virtually unmarked blackish brown, but most have an indication of barring, more or less obscure, broadest anteriorly. (Authors who have studied other subspecies have suggested the possibility that older ♀ ♀ have paler and/or less heavily marked underparts.) Legs and **feet** colored approximately as in ♂. Tail, wing, and long scapulars are retained Basic feathering, described below.

NOTE    An idea which has some currency, that the ♀ molts later and more rapidly than the ♂, calls for explanation. In many N. Hemisphere waterfowl (eiders included) in which the ♀ has a spring molt (of head–body) into Basic, that much of the molting must be subtracted from the total that occurs postnesting when comparing with the ♂. The postbreeding drake molts head–body twice (into Basic and back into Alt.), but the

21

postnesting ♀ has merely to molt wing–tail and a few other feathers to complete her molt into Basic and then has only 1 head–body molt (back into Alt.). The postnesting ♀ thus may require less time, but does less molting.

▶  ♀ Def. Basic Plumage (entire feathering), head and almost all of body acquired in SPRING (commonly in April) and retained until very late summer or some time in FALL; the tail and wing are acquired in early fall or later and retained nearly a year; the 2 longest scapulars apparently are acquired late, in fall (contemporaneous with molting back into Alt.), and also are retained nearly a year; they are broad, "scooped" at the end, with rather abrupt tips, and are dark sepia with tawny margins.

In general, **head–body** more muted, much less rusty-colored than Def. Alt., but individuals vary from deep rusty to palish (toward tan); there is more pronounced streaking on head–neck which apparently is reduced in older individuals; border of crown poorly defined or not evident, i.e., head–neck appears quite uniformly darkish in many individuals; light tips of back and breast feathers narrower; feathers of upper back barred rather than tipped tawny; the longest scapulars have less "scooped" ends than in the ♂; comparatively heavy dark barring on sides and flanks; abdomen often very dark.

**Tail** blackish fuscous above, narrowly tipped pale buffy brown (the tips may wear off), its undersurface deep smoke gray, the feathers with pale shafts. **Wing** primaries blackish fuscous, paler on inner web; outer secondaries fuscous, broadly tipped with white on outer web (forms white stripe at trailing edge of wing which becomes frayed or even worn off); inner secondaries fuscous, heavily washed on outer webs with tawny-chestnut; innermost secondaries (variably lengthened and downcurved) have dark tawny terminal and vague blackish subterminal bands; greater primary coverts fuscous with vaguely defined tawny-cinnamon edges and tips; greater secondary coverts fuscous with narrow tawny-cinnamon outer margin and distinct white tip to outer web (and blackish subterminally), forming white line or band at anterior border of speculum; median coverts barred black or dark fuscous and tawny; lesser coverts and alula nearly black with tawny edges; underside of remiges and under primary coverts smoke gray, darkening along outer webs of primaries; under median coverts whitish; axillars white, longest ones shading to sepia along midline; remaining feathers of underwing dark fuscous with tawny-buff edges.

NOTES  The above description may cover "typical" individuals; the wing may lack 1 or both white bars or have 1 or both reduced.

It is generally assumed that older ♀ ♀ tend to be paler overall, but undoubtedly there are exceptions.

Females are subject to extreme wear and fading; the description given applies to relatively new feathering.

In a ♀ *dresseri* that lived in captivity from duckling stage to age 2½ years, all flight feathers and upper coverts of the wing dropped within a "few days" and "the new ones" started to grow very rapidly. Judging from this captive bird, the flightless condition lasts about three weeks in the wild state (R. A. Johnson 1942). In very lean postnesting ♀ ♀ it would seem likely that the period is longer. For both sexes, it is estimated tentatively to be 4 weeks.

AT HATCHING  See vol. 2, col. pl. facing p. 370; for monochrome photo of 7 young still in the nest, see Gross (1938). As observed while still in the nest, downy *dresseri* seem to be quite consistently dark dorsally, but some ducklings are lighter ventrally than others. For some days, the young have much the same appearance; then the lighter parts begin to lighten and take on a browner cast; then the down shows increasing wear and fading until finally it disappears.

▶ ♂ Juv. Plumage (entire feathering), fully developed by some time in LATE SUMMER OR FALL (depends on hatching date), probably at age about 10–11 weeks; then the Juv. tail may remain until any time from early Oct. to as late as the following spring; all of the wing is retained into the following summer.

**Bill** more or less bluish gray, grading to greenish yellow nail; **iris** dark brownish. **Head** crown black or blackish brown, more or less streaked with rich buffy brown anteriorly; sides of head sepia, streaked buffy brown, these streaks somewhat broader and paler in the superciliary region, forming a vaguely defined stripe; light streaks of face become obsolete posteriorly so that the neck is fairly uniform sepia or grayish sepia; chin and throat pale to buffy brown, palest on chin, vaguely streaked posteriorly with sepia. **Upperparts** back (including scapulars) blackish sepia, the feathers edged tawny, longest scapulars broadened, with fairly abruptly pointed tips and no light edgings; rump and upper tail coverts edged tawny or tawny-chestnut. **Underparts** blackish sepia, the feathers tipped tawny (tipping broad anteriorly and on sides, flanks, and under tail coverts; narrow on abdomen); breast feathers with distinct barring in sequence (from tip to base) brown-black-white-black-white. Legs and **feet** variants of grayed olive, webs blackish. **Tail** blackish sepia, the feathers with notched ends. **Wing** blackish sepia, all upper coverts narrower than in later (Basic) wings; small coverts with faintly lighter and more rufous edges than the larger ones; innermost secondaries short, slightly downcurved, and with rounded ends; underside of primaries and their coverts deep smoke gray; under greater coverts and axillars white; remainder of undersurface of wing grayed sepia in specimens examined.

NOTES In *S. m. mollissima* and without having known-age material, Millais (1913c) concluded that the young were in full Juv. feathering and capable of flight at age 60 days and Schiøler (1926) estimated age at first flight as approximately 2½ mo. (Also see end of section on "Reproduction.")

According to Schiøler, the Juv. head–body feathering is long retained in those northernmost birds (as within *borealis*) which are hatched late, but is molted soon, except for belly, in southerly birds (nominate *mollissima* at southerly breeding stations). He may have been correct—molting may be delayed until after migration in northerly birds—or he may have confused Juv. with Basic I. The timing varies much in *dresseri*, as also do hatching dates.

The Juv. tail feathers are succeeded by pointed blackish ones (Basic I). At least in southerly nominate *mollissima* (hatched in the Baltic and southward), a great many grow the new tail in Sept.; that is, they acquire it approximately in their 3rd month posthatching. In the nominate subspecies as a whole, and including all young regardless of hatching date, the new tail may be acquired in fall, or some time in winter, or occasionally may be retained until the following spring or even later.

All tawny feather edgings of the Juv. Plumage fade quickly to buff.

▶ ♀ Juv. Plumage (entire feathering), much of it lost soon after it is fully grown, but at least all of wing retained into the following summer. Similar to ♂ Juv. except: breast

23

feathers less distinctly barred, with less (or no) white; light edgin. on wing coverts broader, paler, more contrasted. As in the ♂, the notched Juv. tail feathers generally are lost in year of hatching, but occasionally later.

NOTE    Material examined does not show certain differences between ♂ and ♀ Juv. that have been claimed, namely, that ♂ has darker upperparts and wider eye stripe than ♀ (*dresseri*), or that ♂ has sides of head darker and wing lining paler than ♀ (nominate *mollissima*).

▶    ♂ Basic I Plumage (at fullest development includes all feathering except tail and all of wing, but many individuals apparently acquire a lesser amount, i.e., retain more or less of the Juv. mantle, rump, and venter). In general, this is a LATE FALL–EARLY WINTER Plumage, with much more clear-cut pattern than Juv. There is a molt of body down in Sept. (Beetz 1916).

In "advanced" birds there are some Basic I short scapulars by late Aug. Molting may proceed rapidly, teminating some time in fall; usually it is more prolonged, being completed well along in Dec.; in "tardy" individuals it goes slowly, or there may be a pause, so that some fresh Basic I feathering may be found in midwinter. Apparently head–neck commonly acquire less than all of Basic I, rather than all as in the King Eider. Most obvious elements of Basic I: barred flank feathers, longer and broader than those of Juv. Plumage; scapulars barred near tip rather than plain sepia with pale tip as in Juv.; entire venter and much of sides often quite finely patterned, the feathers variably brownish with black margins, or on belly and abdomen variably brownish with distal whitish spot; and on upper breast the feathers show more white than in Juv. The time when Basic I tail feathers grow varies; see above under ♂ and ♀ Juv. Since renewal of the tail generally concludes the molting into Basic I, it may be assumed that a bird with a new tail also has about all the other Basic I feathering it ever will acquire. Molting into Basic I is sometimes concluded as early as Oct.

NOTE    Basic I is the "first stage" of molting out of Juv., as described by Millais (1913c) for nominate *mollissima*.

▶    ♂ Alt. I Plumage (excepting the Basic I long scapulars, all, or a lesser amount, of head–body; usually includes at least head and foreparts of body, the shorter scapulars, and scattered feathers elsewhere; tends to succeed Basic I portions and there still may be some retained Juv. feathers, as on rump, part of venter, and always all of wing). The tail worn with Alt. I typically is Basic I, but occasionally some Juv. feathers still are retained. In general, Alt. I is worn from some time in 1st WINTER into the following SUMMER (to age slightly over 1 year). Some drakes, by April or May, have essentially all of head–body in Alt. I: white, black, and browns; see col. pl. facing p. 376.

The impression gained from examining a rather limited series of 1st fall–winter–spring drakes is that individuals are molting into Alt. I at any time during this span. It begins to show on "advanced" birds before the end of Oct.; more commonly it begins to appear in winter (probably following more gradual attainment of the antecedent Basic I and/or a pause thereafter). "Tardy" birds first show it as late as in spring, in which case the antecedent molting probably also was "tardy" or prolonged, then a pause, then Alt. I comes in late and rapidly. There is support for these generalizations from reinterpretation of various literature plus observations of live individuals.

The drake's Alt. I is highly variable, especially on head–neck. Frequent pattern: **head** most of feathers white at base; crown and nape feathers barred black and buffy brown near tip, so that crown appears blackish overlaid with buff, latter prevailing on forehead; cheeks and superciliary area blackish olive, the feathers more or less barred at tip with buffy brown to buff; face gradually paling to buff toward point of feathering that projects along side of bill; transocular line variably paler than cheeks and superciliary; an area above and anterior to eye blackish; chin and throat white or whitish, spotted or washed pale brownish olive. More "highly developed" individuals approach more closely the Def. Alt. head pattern: again, most feathers white at base; crown feathers barred black and buffy brown at tip; line from eye to bill white tinged pale green; area between this line and crown black, mixed or tipped with buff; sides of face blackish sepia much mixed with white, latter increasing posteriorly; sides of occipital region white washed pale green; chin, throat, and neck white. **Upperparts** new upper scapulars white or same mixed with brownish olive or darker, apparently always appear, as do blackish sepia upper tail coverts. Extent of molting of remainder of upperparts variable; upper back varies from a few new white feathers to extensively white; lower back and rump grow a varying number of new blackish sepia feathers. **Underparts** most new feathers of upper breast white, but number varies from a scattering to a complete replacement of this area; some feathers, especially toward sides of breast, have blackish edges giving scalloped appearance; some side and flank feathers apparently always renewed, and under tail coverts usually, all of these feathers being blackish sepia except for light patch on flanks (more or less buffy or white); new blackish sepia feathers appear mixed in among worn Juv. feathers of lower breast and abdomen in some individuals, but few except in "advanced" birds. As previously indicated, the Juv. wing and the Basic I long scapulars and tail are worn with Alt. I.

At least as early as midwinter, the drake's bill becomes muted greenish yellow or more vivid and the feet greenish olive.

NOTES Alt. I is the "second stage" of molting out of Juv., as described by Millais (1913c) for *S. m. mollissima*. He stated that, when drakes are acquiring the white chin and throat of Alt. I, the molting "nearly always leaves a broad V-shaped line of brown feathers" on the chin, which is retained through summer and is an "interesting parallel to the V-shaped mark" that is found in some adult drakes.

▶ ♀ Basic I Plumage (probably all of body sometimes, but in material examined consists of head down to include foreparts of body, also at least the scapulars, the sides, flanks, upper tail coverts, and tail; the remainder is retained Juv. feathering). Typically a very LATE FALL or EARLY WINTER Plumage. There is a molting of body down in fall. Most ♀ ♀ in Basic I are quite buffy brownish overall, many feathers with clear-cut contrasty pattern.

Differs from Juv. thus: head tawny buff to buff streaked blackish, the streaks obsolete in interramal area, and coalesced on crown to give effect of black with fine light streaks; eye stripe buffy, more or less streaked blackish; breast feathers distinctly barred; upper tail coverts barred (not merely edged) tawny-buff or tawny; other new feathers (anterior dorsum, at least upper scapulars, the sides and flanks) with broader tawny-buff edges, in striking contrast to faded worn edges of any retained Juv. feathers.

25

NOTES  Too few birds were examined to ascertain the full extent of variation in timing of this Plumage.

Some individuals are very dark overall, sepia, with reduced cinnamon feather markings and dark breast more mottled than barred.

In winter, some ♀ ♀ evidently acquire a Basic I venter that is more or less gray, the feathers narrowly but densely barred blackish. Often this is retained and worn for some time with the succeeding Alt. I.

Perhaps because there is more or less continuous molting of ♀ ♀ in their first year, when studying nominate *mollissima*, Millais and Schiøler did not distinguish between Juv. and Basic I as separate feather generations. That is, they did not recognize Basic I of the ♀ in the sequence: Juv. (to 1st fall), Basic I (late fall or early winter), Alt. I. (midwinter or earlier into spring), Basic II (late spring until well into summer).

▶  ♀ Alt. I Plumage (almost all of head–body, but sometimes a lesser amount may be acquired). Typically acquired in JAN. and retained into SPRING. More richly colored than the preceding Basic I.

Head, neck, and breast generally warm browns (rather than buffs) and any markings are fine and very dark; the crown appears brownish (not blackish) and not markedly different from sides of head; feathers of scapular area (upper scapulars) rich browns barred blackish; rump same; sides and flanks rich browns barred black. If the venter has much narrow transverse dark barring, this may be late-acquired feathering of the previous (Basic I) generation.

▶  ♂ Basic II Plumage (entire feathering), almost all of head–body acquired in SUMMER (beginning at age just over 1 year) and retained into LATE SUMMER or EARLY FALL, the long scapulars, tail, and wing later and retained nearly a year.

Based on material examined, like Def. Basic except: **breast** feathers with less white; middle and lower **back** with less white, more black or dark olive gray; short scapulars with more dark olive gray, less white; bend of **wing** and most lesser coverts blackish olive rather than white; under wing coverts with more smoke gray, less white; innermost secondaries not as curved and are blackish distally. The body down is molted in June–July. The new breast feathers appear in July, then more new feathering through summer (sometimes with interruption), then the old (Juv.) wing and tail are dropped and there is a flightless period, then the Basic II long scapulars, tail, and wing grow (about Sept.) at onset of molting of most of head–body into Alt. II.

The light area in the Basic II wing typically is somewhat mottled darkish; lesser coverts dark brown (leading edge of wing is dark), but median coverts are gray-buff edged brown; innermost secondaries curled down at ends, which are at least edged black.

▶  ♂ Alt. II Plumage (all of head–body, except sometimes some Basic II on venter, rump, and the long scapulars always, are retained in addition to Basic II tail and wing), generally acquired beginning in EARLY FALL (about Aug. at age 14–15 mo.) and ending in DEC. or up to weeks earlier. Then it is retained until the following SUMMER. The earliest Plumage in which lower breast to vent is all black (except in very "advanced" birds in Alt. I).

As Def. Alt. except; **head** white crown stripe obsolete, the feathers being extensively tipped with black or brown; variable amount of black tipping on white facial feathers (it wears off); green of cheeks and nape usually paler, perhaps less extensive; **upperparts** a few black or dark brownish tips to white mantle feathers; center of back may be brown or mixed brown and white; white area on side of rump less extensive, generally mottled darkish, and separated from midback by a fuscous or darker area; **underparts** color of breast somewhat paler. The long scapulars and the tail are retained Basic II, as also is the wing, its presence being the most obvious indicator that the accompanying Alt. is II.

NOTES   In an addendum to Millais (1913b) there is mention of a captive-reared drake that, at age 48 days, "is showing a considerable number of white feathers on the back." The bird was nominate *mollissima*.

Another, hatched in captivity in July at a small waterfowl aviary near Uppsala, Sweden, was stated by its owner and another experienced observer (Lindorm Liljefors) to be in "fully adult" feathering in Dec. of the following year. This was considered remarkable. There is no evidence that the wing had been examined carefully. This drake had been disposed of prior to a visit to this aviary by R. S. Palmer in May, 1969.

▶   ♀ Basic II Plumage (entire feathering), head–body generally acquired quite rapidly in SPRING (before age 1 year) while the faded and worn Juv. wing still is present; in summer (about late July or in Aug.) the Basic I tail and Juv. wing are dropped; then, in EARLY FALL, within the flightless period when the "offset" Basic II tail and wing are growing, the head–body begin molting out of Basic II into Alt. II. The body down is molted in June–July. It is probable that the long scapulars are renewed late, i.e., in fall.

As Def. Basic except: **head**–neck av. toward buffy brown with blackish streaks somewhat more distinct; **wing** white tips to outer secondaries and greater coverts, which form parallel borders to the speculum, very narrow or even (especially on ends of secondaries) obsolete; innermost secondaries somewhat less curved and with paler edging.

NOTES   Because various feather edgings wear off, under field conditions in summer some individuals appear to be almost black.

▶   ♀ Alt. II Plumage (all feathering except long scapulars, tail, and wing), acquired beginning in FALL (at age around 15 mo.) and retained into the following SPRING. General coloring rich browns, such as deep rusty. As Def. Alt. so far as known; the accompanying tail, wing, and long scapulars are predefinitive, being Basic II.

▶   ♂ Basic III Plumage (entire feathering), acquired by prolonged, probably interrupted, molting in summer–fall (at age about 25–28 mo.). Head–body begin showing some Basic some time in JUNE; generally most or all of it is acquired and worn for a considerable time before the wing is molted (flight feathers simultaneously, then a flightless period), also the tail; then, in FALL, while Basic III wing and tail are growing, the early-acquired portions begin to be succeeded by Alt. III. The Basic III long scapulars evidently grow in fall.

In birds believed to be of this Plumage, **wing** differs from Def. Basic as follows: marginal coverts along bend mostly grayish olive rather than white; small coverts lying under alula feathers mostly grayish olive (are much mixed with white in definitive wing); lesser under wing coverts and axillars with varying amount of pale grayish olive or smoke gray; counting outward, the 1st secondary to be other than all white (usually the outermost that shows distinct curvature) usually grayish olive on inner web, black

27

on outer, white centrally, whereas this feather in definitive wing usually has pure white inner web, black edge along outer web only; tips of curved inner secondaries sometimes marked with gray or blackish.

▶  ♂ Alt. III Plumage (all feathering except the long scapulars, tail, and wing), acquired through FALL (see above under Basic III) at age about 27–29 mo. and retained through WINTER into the following SUMMER.

Like Def. Alt. except: **head** dark tips sometimes present in white crown stripe; **upperparts** white area between midback and lateral rump patches sometimes less clearly defined, mixed with grayish olive to blackish fuscous; the Basic III wing (for its characters, see above) and tail, also the modified long scapulars, are worn with this Plumage.

NOTE  At this stage (Alt. III with Basic III wing) and later, it is quite probable that there is individual variation in whether there is any dark coloring on ends of innermost secondaries and in the wing coverts.

**Estimating age from characteristics of feathering**  Treatment here is tentative and subject to revision when there is adequate information from known-age individuals. These assumptions, for southerly colonies of *S. m. dresseri*, are made: hatching date June 15, preflight period 70 days and, when molting, flightless period of 4 weeks. If it can be demonstrated that some individuals attain their "final" (definitive) condition when younger or older than is usual, allowance for this will have to be made.

▶  ♂ To age 70 days—some natal down still present until about age 40 days, thereafter the Juv. Plumage with notched tail feathers.

▶  ♂ Age 2½ mo. (Sept. 1) to 13 mo. (July 15)—Juv. wing has all coverts narrow, dark, and varying with individual from unicolor to margined somewhat paler and browner; the several innermost secondaries graduated in length, with rounded ends, and the longest is shorter than the middle secondaries; notched tail feathers are diagnostic if still present, but are succeeded by pointed ones at any time beyond about 3 mo. posthatching.

▶  ♂ Age 14 mo. (Sept. 15) to 25 mo. (July 15)—Basic II wing has some white in upper surface, mainly middle coverts over the secondaries, but also some white in lesser coverts; innermost secondaries downcurved, pointed, their basal halves varying (with individual) from white to smoke gray, grading to blackish distally.

▶  ♂ Age 26 mo. (Aug. 15) to 37 mo. (July 15)—in the Basic III wing the smaller secondary coverts are white except for some darkish ones at bend of wing at leading edge and occasionally a few elsewhere; the 2 longest alula feathers are black and the small primary coverts underlying them are mostly or entirely black; the elongated, downcurved, pointed, white innermost secondaries often are dark at their tips; primaries and 10 adjoining secondaries black (no white ends).

▶  ♂ Age 38 mo. (Aug. 15) and, except during wing molt, thereafter—the wing (Basic IV and later Basics) has the elongated, downcurved, innermost secondaries and all middle and lesser coverts white; the small primary coverts same with dark intermixed; the short alula feathers generally white and the longest one with light end and/or margins; greater primary coverts often tipped white (inner ones may be almost entirely white); generally some white on ends of black secondaries (if present, it decreases in amount inwardly); generally some white on tips of the black greater secondary coverts, increasing in amount from outer inward.

▶  ♀ Preflight stage as ♂.

28

▶  ♀ Age 2½ mo. (Sept. 1) to 13½ mo. (Aug. 1)—the Juv. wing is plain, as in the ♂, the smaller coverts being narrow, darkish, and unicolor or margined warm brownish; the wing lacks white bars, but the greater secondary coverts may grade to palish ends. Innermost secondaries short and rounded. Notched Juv. tail feathers, as long as they are present, are diagnostic.

▶  ♀ Age 14½ mo. (Sept. 1) to 26 mo. (Aug. 15)—in the Basic II wing the middle and lesser coverts are broad, rounded, and with sharply defined and much paler margins; the innermost secondaries have broadly wedge-shaped (not rounded) ends and sometimes the longest may exceed the length of the middle secondaries. It is sometimes indicated that this stage is characterized by a white bar (anterior border of speculum). However, there is great individual variation, from no bar at all to a conspicuous one, or even another consisting of ends of about 10 outer secondaries (trailing edge of wing), and width of both bars is variable.

There is some evidence that these young ♀ ♀ (some are nesting at age about 23 mo., in May) have darker, richer head–body coloring than older age-classes and this may prove to be a more constant criterion of age than wing characters.

▶  ♀ Age about 27 mo. (Sept. 15) and, except when in wing molt, thereafter—the wing (Basic III and later Basics) perhaps generally, but not invariably, has a white bar at trailing edge of about 10 outer secondaries and another comprised of ends of the greater secondary coverts (along anterior border of speculum). The longest of the curved innermost secondaries may fall short of the middle secondaries in length, or vary to the extent that several are much elongated; these feathers typically are narrower than in Basic II and slightly more pointed; there is much individual variation in their pattern. The head–body feathering at about 34½ mo. (age when all ♀ ♀ presumably nest) may av. paler than a year earlier; that is, pale breeders may generally be at least nearly 3 years old.

**Aberrant individuals** (in the species). A drake-feathered ♀ was taken July 9, 1900, in Spitzbergen (Roth et al. 1902). An "old" ♀, "partly assuming" drake feathering, killed on the Norwegian coast, had the long secondaries unusually curled, much black in flanks, and white in scapulars (Millais 1913b). Another ♀, even more drakelike, was taken in Denmark on Jan. 19, 1908 (see pl. 65 in Schiøler 1926). Another, resembling a 2nd-year ♂, was taken June 12, 1939, on Wrangel I.; the ovary was finely granular and, on left side at oviduct, there were "elongated thickenings resembling undeveloped testes" (Portenko 1952). The same author also described a ♀-feathered drake, molting into 2nd winter [Alt. II] Plumage, taken Nov. 30, 1937, at Providence Bay (Bering Sea: sw. Chuckchee Pen.).

All records found to date of pale to all-white individuals seen or captured are for Atlantic–arctic (none for Pacific–Bering) area.

**Hybrids** in the wild of S. mollissima with S. spectabilis, also observations of these at Icelandic cider farms, are discussed under King Eider. See Gray (1958) for additional references, plus references to alleged wild crosses of S. mollissima with Anas acuta, A. platyrhynchos (2 or 3), and ♂ Melanitta fusca paired with ♀ Common Eider (and 3 eggs, but further result of mating unknown). Mention of drake Steller's mated to ♀ Commons in Iceland (Gudmundsson 1932) evidently was a case of mistaking hybrid King × Common drakes for Steller's.

**Measurements** of S. m. dresseri 12 ♂ (2 Labrador, 2 New Bruns., 7 Mass., 1

29

R.I.): BILL 56–60, av. 57.8 mm.; WING 287–300, av. 292.5; TAIL 92–97, av. 94; TARSUS 51–55, av.52.7;   12 ♀ (4 N.S., 1 New Bruns., 6 Mass., 1 R.I.): BILL 49–53, av. 50.8 mm.; WING 274–298, av. 283; TAIL 82–98, av. 89; TARSUS 49–53, av. 50.7 (ETS).

In this series wing meas. across chord; 16 ♂ (from Nfld., N.S., Me., Mass., R.I., and N.Y.): BILL 49.1–60, av. 52.9 mm.; WING 275–295, av. 287.2; TAIL 83.4–95.5, av. 88.7; TARSUS 49–54.4, av. 50.9;   21 ♀ (from Labrador, Me., Mass., R.I., and N.J.): BILL 42.2–56, av. 50.9 mm.; WING 265–288, av. 276.8; TAIL 70.3–92.3, av. 82.9; TARSUS 44.6–52, av. 48.7 (H. Friedmann).

**Weight** of mature *dresseri* in Me., 1972–75:  119 ♂ 1.70–2.45 kg., 143 ♀ from about 850 gm. (incubating) to 2,560 (prelaying). Minimum wt. of breeding ♂ ♂ coincides with molting in late summer–early fall; maximum is attained in Feb. and wt. decreases through March and April. (No drakes have been weighed during the nesting season, but apparently wt. is decreasing.)

By Oct., postnesting ♀ ♀ weigh an av. of 1,830 gm. Av. wt. (98 records) increases only slightly thereafter through March. Then they attain maximum wt. just before egg-laying (their wt. includes hypertrophied reproductive organs, gastrointestinal tract, pectoral muscles, and fat deposits). Three ♀ ♀ collected during laying had significantly reduced gizzards, livers, and intestines, indicating that these organs may serve as a protein reserve for the rapid laying of large eggs. During laying, ♀ ♀ attempt to feed, but size of food items (primarily *Mytilus*) and quantity are much reduced. At termination of laying (onset of incubation), ♀ ♀ av. slightly less than 2,000 gm. Thirty ♀ ♀ weighed on final day of incubation av. 1,300 gm.—an av. loss of 35% of post egg-laying wt. or about 45–50% of prelaying maximum wt. The ♀ ♀ that hatch clutches early in the season weigh significantly more than those that hatch clutches in the later part of the season.

Birds in 1st fall (Juv. tail, large bursa): ♂ 12 in Oct. 1.45–1.90 kg., mean 1.74; and 8 in Nov. 1.50–2.04 kg., mean 1.84;   ♀ 14 in Oct. 1.22–1.98 kg., mean 1.69; and 10 in Nov. 1.46–1.99, mean 1.75.

Ducklings while still in the nest: 74 ♂ 60–91 gm., mean 76.6, and 101 ♀ 62–89 gm., mean 76.4.

All the above wt. data are from Me. and supplied by C. E. Korschgen.

**Geographical variation in the species**   The V or chevron mark on the throat of drakes apparently is an ancient condition. It is characteristic of the King Eider, almost always present in the Bering–Pacific population of the Common Eider, and rare in the Spectacled Eider. It is "lost" in most Atlantic–arctic Common Eiders, but occurs in a few birds, at least in nominate *mollissima* even in Alt. I (Millais 1913b, Schiøler 1926); Norton (1897) was the first of several authors to describe this mark in *dresseri*.

Size variation shows no obvious geographical pattern, the smallest birds being the Faeroe population, the largest being those of Hudson Bay and the Bering–Pacific area. Taking middle-sized eiders as the norm in physical proportions, the smallest birds (*faeroeensis*) appear stoutish and foreshortened, less typically "eiderlike," and the largest ones appear to be somewhat elongated. Salomonsen (1972) compared wing meas. of drakes from Spitzbergen, s. Greenland, England, Norway, Faeroes, and the Baltic; there was little variation, except wings are much shorter in the Faeroes and slightly longer in the Baltic; a parallel condition exists in the Black Guillemot (*Cepphus grylle*).

30

These color characteristics vary in drakes: black V on throat (discussed above); amount of green on side of head, most extensive in Am. populations; and color of bill. Most authors attribute bright yellowish or orange bills only to Pacific and some n. birds

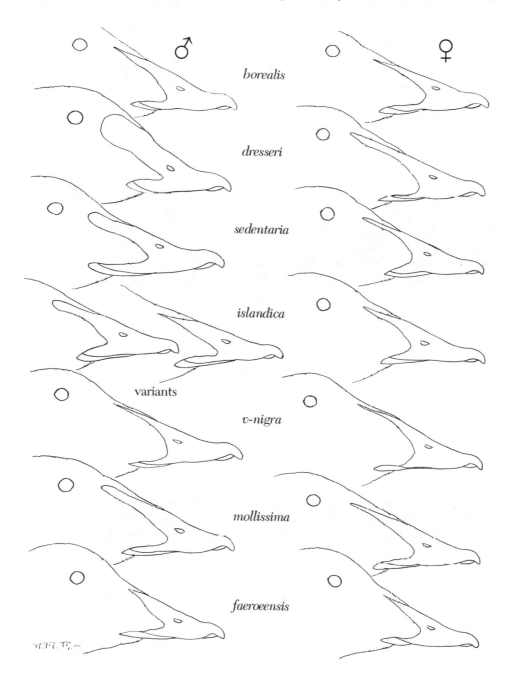

♂ borealis ♀

dresseri

sedentaria

islandica

variants

v-nigra

mollissima

faeroeensis

(*v-nigra* and *borealis*). Johansen (1956) divided Atlantic populations into western (yellow billed) and eastern (greenish-yellow billed). Delacour (1959) attributed an orange-yellow bill to the more southerly w. Atlantic birds (*dresseri*). Forbush (1925) stated "bill in spring orange-yellow, varying at other times from gray to green," which matches many observations of live *dresseri* in the wild. Schiøler (1926) included within a yellow-brown-billed race the *islandica* birds from s. and e. Greenland and from Iceland and Spitzbergen. Salomonsen (1950) lumped all Greenland breeders with the yellow-billed *borealis* of nw. Greenland (the Gitz-Johansen plate in his volume is at variance, perhaps indicating artistic license). Delacour (1959) called all Greenland plus Spitzbergen eiders *borealis*, but lumped Icelandic birds with European *S. m. mollissima* (which they resemble in bill color and more or less in roundness of tips of narrow frontal lobes). Hans Johansen (1956) considered the eiders of Iceland, s. Greenland, n. Norway, and Spitzbergen to be intermediate between *borealis* and nominate *mollissima*, suggesting an origin by secondary intergradation between w. and e. Atlantic populations when sharing a refugium during the most recent glaciation, and advocating the use of the name *islandica* Brehm for all these birds—the treatment followed in the present volume. Within this assemblage there are regional differences which (contra Schiøler 1926) are below the subspecies level.

Occasionally someone reports one more subspecies in which it has been observed that some portion of the modified long scapulars of drakes is raised above the contour of the back. All Common Eiders have these feathers, which are more developed in the drake. Commonly, during the span from late fall into the nesting season, many drakes show such "bumps" or "sails." In conflict situations, drakes change from smoothly contoured to raised scapular and then back to smooth again later. The same drakes that display "bumps" in spring lack them later on when they have left their incubating mates and are showing no aggression while in unisexual groups; they still have these modified feathers, but look as if they have lost them. [It is not the pointed tips of the long scapulars, but a rounded portion of a vane, that forms the erectile "bumps" homologous with the permanently erect triangular "sails" of the ♂ King Eider and contoured seasonally erectile "bumps" of the ♀ King. Fuertes (in Eaton 1910) was in error in depicting pointed "sails" on the ♂ Common Eider.]

Color of Alt. Plumage of mature ♀ ♀ varies, on the average, as follows: *borealis* is the most reddish and with comparatively few dark markings (many are redder than is typical of the ♀ King Eider); *dresseri* is dark and richly colored; *v-nigra* is dark but less richly colored; nominate *mollissima* is more toward buffy brown; regional units of *islandica* vary between *borealis* and the nominate subspecies; *sedentaria* is very conspicuously the palest—"washed out"; and *faeroeensis* is much the darkest.

Whether there is geographical variation in clutch size can be debated; see data below under "Reproduction."

Although geographical variation in downies has been the subject of some discussion, notably by Schiøler (1908, 1926), it still awaits adequate treatment. The subspecies differ more or less in overall coloring (with some individual variation) and in bill configuration. All have a pale stripe above the eye; cheeks are at least darkish. Faeroe downies are very dark; *dresseri* and *borealis* are relatively dark, with *v-nigra*, *islandica*, and nominate *mollissima* somewhat lighter and the last 2 notably variable; *sedentaria* is markedly pale (the only Am. subspecies distinguishable on color alone) and slightly larger. The frontal processes on the forehead are rounded and more conspicuous (less hidden in the natal down) in *dresseri* and *sedentaria*.

Geographical variation in shape of bill and frontal processes, in adults of both sexes, is shown earlier in a diagram. It is of interest that *v-nigra* differs from all others in that the feathered area projecting forward along sides of upper mandible is broad and generally rounded, and that the skull is relatively longer, so that the eye is more distant from base of bill; the frontal processes also are nearer the midline of the skull (less laterally placed) than in any other population.

See Schiøler (1926) for geographical variation in meas. of certain skeletal elements of this species. KCP (early draft), expanded by RSP

SUBSPECIES  **In our area** *borealis* (Brehm)—northern, in Atlantic area; both sexes with frontal lobes narrower and more pointed than in *dresseri;* ♂ with less green on side of head; bill seasonally orange-yellow or orange (as in *dresseri*). Schiøler (1926) regarded the birds (both sexes) from nw. Greenland as having the most highly colored feathering of all Common Eiders; the ♀ in Alt. Plumage tends toward rich reddish brown overall, with cheeks nearly unmarked, yet ♀ ♀ in Basic Plumages tend to be pale and grayish, quite different from the dark *dresseri*. Sex for sex, size av. smaller than *dresseri*. Nine ♂ (1 Greenland, 3 Labrador, 2 Que., 2 New Bruns., 1 Me.): BILL 48–57, av. 52.3 mm.; WING 283–298, av. 288; TAIL 85–96, av. 90.2; TARSUS 46–54, av. 50.6;  12 ♀ (1 Greenland, 7 Labrador, 2 Strait of Belle Isle, 1 Que., 1 New Bruns.): BILL 46–54, av. 48.7 mm.; WING 273–297, av. 281.6; TAIL 86–92, av. 88.4; TARSUS 47–52, av. 50.3 (ETS).

Another series, wing meas. across chord; 15 ♂ (from Greenland, Ellesmere I., and n. Labrador): BILL from anterior end of median feathering 45–53, av. 50.7 mm., and from posterior end of frontal maxillary process 64–77.2, av. 68.9; WING 278–293, av. 285.7; TAIL 82.5–93, av. 86.9; MIDDLE TOE without claw 63–70, av. 65.9;  22 ♀ (from nw. Greenland, Ellesmere I., Baffin I., and n. Labrador): BILL meas. as in ♂ 42–51, av. 43.7 mm. and 56.1–65, av. 62; WING 265–286, av. 276.5; TAIL 78–98.2, av. 84.1; MIDDLE TOE without claw 56.2–65.3, av. 61.5 (H. Friedmann).

For large series from sw. Baffin I., the WING meas. across chord, see Macpherson and McLaren (1959); they also gave wt. of a few drakes.

**Intergradation**  Some *borealis* birds occur with *dresseri* from fall to spring (time of pair formation). Intergrades are known: drakes (Townsend, in Beetz 1916, text and accompanying pl. 15) and ♀ ♀ (H. L. Mendall). Although mixed pairs quite likely are formed away from nesting areas, it is also possible that some ♂ *dresseri* that go northward early on molt migration into the Labrador coastal breeding range of the later-nesting *borealis* still are sexually active and may pair briefly with ♀ ♀ of the latter. For these or other reasons, there is a zone of occurrence in the nesting season of both subspecies plus intergrading individuals (Labrador coast: Cartwright to Makkovik).

In w., and especially sw. Greenland, and perhaps the southerly e. coast, there are eiders that are larger than *borealis* and have fairly wide frontal lobes (toward those of *dresseri* in shape); these birds, which nest there, are assigned to *islandica* in the present text. In addition, a drake *dresseri* was taken near Godthaab in April. Furthermore, both typical and atypical *v-nigra* have been taken, not breeding; details, including meas., in Schiøler (1926). Perhaps a few *v-nigra* in the Canadian arctic join flocks of *borealis* (or even of King Eiders) which fly to molting and wintering localities in sw. Greenland. Schiøler stated that they occur there every winter. Presumably any such *v-nigra* individuals then would form mixed pairs with Greenland birds and the resulting progeny would show some *v-nigra* characteristics. This assessment is contrary to that of J. C. Phillips (1926), who regarded the birds in question as "merely individual variants and not true Pacific Eiders."

*dresseri* Sharpe—full descr. and meas. given above; southerly w. Atlantic range.

**Intergrades** with *borealis* along the Cartwright to Makkovik section of the Labrador coast.

*sedentaria* Snyder—James and most of Hudson Bay; definitely recorded away from there only once. Females and young (including downies) pale, toward gray-buff; in both sexes the frontal lobes are variable in shape, but usually shorter and considerably narrower than in *dresseri*. The birds are about as *v-nigra* in size, i.e., largest Common Eiders. Twelve ♂ (from Hudson Bay) WING 300–332, av. 312 mm.; 10 ♀ (Hudson and James Bays) WING 290–316, av. 302. WING (chord) 8 ♂ 284–303, av. 290.6 mm.; and 4 ♀ 274–289, av. 281.5 (Snyder 1941a).

Ten ♀ July 21–Aug. 6, from near Port Harrison (e. coast of Hudson Bay): BILL 48–54, av. 50.9 mm.: length of bare frontal processes 18–22, av. 20.25; width of processes 6–7.5, av. 6.6; WING (across chord) 273–296, av. 285.5 (Manning 1949).

**Weight** of paired breeders prior to nesting, June 4, 1960, at the Belcher Is.: 5 ♂ 2,450–2,725, av. 2,500 gm., 3 ♀ 2,575–3,025, av. 2,866 gm.; also, June 21, an incubating ♀ 2,275 gm.; and July 7 two ♀ 1,575 and 1,825 gm. (Freeman 1970). From w. side of Hudson Bay at McConnell R. (lat. 60° 50′ N), 3 ♀ : 2,640 gm. (June 10, moderately fat), 2,679 gm. (June 21, little fat, 3 ruptured follicles), and 1,780 gm. (July 8, no fat); and 2 ♂ : 2,560 gm. (June 10, moderately fat) and 2,134 gm. (June 21, no fat) (C. D. MacInnes).

See Snyder (1941a) for various information, including comparative meas. of both sexes of *sedentaria*, *dresseri*, and *borealis*, also nominate *mollissima;* see Todd (1963) for general account of eiders in Hudson Bay; the useful literature was listed recently by Freeman (1970).

**Intergradation** Snyder (1941a) and especially Todd (1963) went to considerable length to try to establish that *sedentaria* is reproductively isolated from *borealis*. In the collection of the Coop. Wildlife Research Unit, Univ. of Me., are 3 eiders—2 postnesting ♀ ♀ and a ♂ in Def. Alt.—taken in late June far down the w. coast of Hudson Bay at McConnell R.; they have all the characters of *sedentaria* except size, in which respect they match small examples of *borealis*. The highly migratory *borealis* probably is on a different spring–summer schedule than the local Hudson Bay birds, the differences controlled by climatic conditions in their respective areas. Perhaps there is no geographical summer "boundary" between the subspecies in nw. coastal Hudson Bay, but far up the e. side of the bay they are separated by a nearly complete absence of nesting habitat from C. Smith n. to C. Wolstenholme.

*islandica* Brehm—occurs as breeder in the *Handbook* area in southern Greenland (limits uncertain). It is the breeding bird of Iceland, Spitzbergen, some other is., and

n. Norway; see discussion earlier under variation. Drake's bill more muted in color than that of *borealis*, and green on face less extensive, seldom extending onto cheeks. Much variation in ♀ ♀ in Def. Basic, from various browns to much gray, as observed in the great colonies in nw. Iceland (R. S. Palmer). See Schiøler (1926) for meas.

**Intergradation**    (See comments earlier under *borealis*.) Along the w. side of Greenland, climatic fluctuations have caused extensive changes in nesting distribution (Vibe 1967); whether this has resulted in a mixing of different populations in any season is a moot point. The situation is complicated.

*v-nigra* Bonaparte—both sides of the n. Pacific, the Aleutians, Bering Sea, beyond on arctic coasts and is. of E. Siberia, and clockwise around Alaska and beyond to Coronation Gulf in n. Canada. Both sexes have narrow frontal lobes lying close to midline of head and feathered area along sides of bill board and terminally rounded; head longer, with eye farther from nostril, than in other populations; feet paler. In drakes, green on sides of head is maximal for the species (about as in *dresseri*); bill at least seasonally vivid orange-yellow or orange. Black V on chin of ♂, but there are a few southerly birds in Tauisk Gulf (within Okhotsk Sea) that lack this mark but otherwise are typical *v-nigra* and same holds for occasional drakes from the Chuckchee Pen. The total known number of such variant individuals is small; see discussion by Portenko (1972).

Twelve ♂ (1 E. Siberia, 11 Alaska); BILL 53–59, av. 54.3 mm., WING 302–328, av. 313.3; TAIL 91–100, av. 95.4, TARSUS 52–57, av. 54;   11 ♀ (1 Siberia, 11 Alaska): BILL 43–53, av. 50 mm., WING 290–305, av. 301; TAIL (of 10) 90–102, av. 94; TARSUS 50–54, av. 52 (ETS).

Drakes (from n. coast of Alaska and w. Canadian arctic): BILL (of 25) 44.4–54, mean 49.44 ± .55 mm.; WING (of 22) 280–315, mean 303.2 ± 1.9;   20 ♀ (n. Alaska and w. Canadian arctic): BILL 42–51.4, mean 47 ± .45 mm.; WING 283–307, mean 292.9 ± 1.4 (Manning et al. 1956).

This series includes wing meas. across chord: 20 ♂ (from Alaska, nw. Canada, and Copper I. in Commander group): BILL from anterior end of median feathering 48–56.2, av. 52.7 mm., and from posterior end of frontal process 66.4–78, av. 71.6; WING 290–315, av. 303.4; TARSUS 50.4–55.2, av. 52.7; MIDDLE TOE without claw 64.3–71, av. 66.1;   ♀ (13 from Alaska): BILL meas. as in ♂ 44.2–52.5, av. 48.9 mm., and 58.2–72, av. 65.2; WING 270–295, av. 288.5; TAIL 81–95.2, av. 87.3; TARSUS 48.5–54, av. 51.3; MIDDLE TOE without claw 61–67.5, av. 64.5 (H. Friedmann).

From New Siberian Is., methods of meas. and sample size not stated: WING ♂ 277–325, av. 311 mm., ♀ 279–300, av. 284; and **weight**, dates not given (wt. fluctuates greatly in summer): 4 ♂ 1,987–2,740 gm., 12 ♀ 1,629–2,726 (Rutilevskii 1957).

For many additional data, including various meas. of the BILL and the WING meas. by tape over the curve, see Portenko (1972).

**Intergradation**    Although this subspecies has a discrete Bering–Pacific winter range, there is limited contact with *borealis* (which see), presumably beginning in summer, and intermediates are known.

**Extralimital**    *mollissima* (Linnaeus)—breeds: Brit. Isles, w. Europe from the Netherlands to s. Scandinavia, Baltic coasts and is., the White Sea and vicinity, and Barents Sea localities to s. Novaya Zemlya and Franz Josef Land. For lengthy treatment see especially Schiøler (1908, 1926), Millais (1913b, 1913c), Witherby (1939), and Dementiev and Gladkov (1952). There is a problem of where to draw the line between breeding *islandica* of n. Norway and nominate *mollissima* to the eastward; Varanger Fjord may be the approximate boundary.

From Danish and s. Swedish waters, slightly more than half of 300 museum skins were of drakes and 18 of these have a more or less distinct V on their throats. However, these specimens, when in the flesh, were selected from a very large number of individuals. In the winter of 1908–09, only 11 out of 20,000 drakes examined in the market had such a mark, i.e., one per thousand (Schiøler 1926).

**Intergradation** with *islandica* is a possibility.

*faeroeenis* Brehm—Faeroes; smallest range of any subspecies; not migratory in the usual sense, having only very local movements (which is true of some other eiders also); small birds with small bills, ♀ ♀ notably dark in all seasons—some have the brown feather edgings and white feather ends in wing so much reduced that the birds appear more like scoters than eiders; see Schiøler (1926) for further details.

**Intergradation** none; there is no evidence that these birds ever leave the Faeroes or that other Common Eiders go there. KCP (early draft), expanded by RSP

FIELD IDENTIFICATION In all 4 species of eider, after early stages, the pattern of drakes is sharply defined and very contrasty. In the Common: most of head and down to include breast and mantle white or very light and the white extends far out on wing and to side of rump; most of remainder of body feathering is black. That is, a bulky, white-backed, light-breasted sea duck (the King is dark backed, the Spectacled white backed but dark breasted, and the little Steller's is patchy and tricolored). Both sexes and all ages appear long headed, ♀ ♀ especially so, because of sloping facial profile (but the King is quite round headed and relatively stubby billed). The ♀ Common in all seasons is, overall, in the tan to very dark brownish range, bleaching toward buff (especially in summer), and with various feathers (most conspicuously on sides and flanks) barred. The drake in Basic Plumage (midsummer into fall) appears almost sooty, with some white in wing and light area on side of rump through most of the molting. At times, especially when flightless, Common Eiders swim very low in the water, generally with heads drawn back on forepart of their flat-appearing bodies. Scoters swim in this fashion also, but dorsal body profile generally appears rounded upward.

The 3 large eiders have strong steady flight. The King has relatively longer wing and less "heavy" flight than the larger Common; but this difference may be evident only when direct comparison can be made, and then black vs. white mantle of drakes is more useful in species recognition. The large eiders commonly fly in long strings, at right angle to line of flight, or curved, or swept back, less often in wedges (with one side generally much longer than the other), sometimes in rather open groups. An approaching or receding string has a kind of rippling or undulating movement within it which seems to be unique with eiders. The wing motion is comparatively slow and, at times, flapping is interrupted by periods of short glides.

The drake Common in certain displays has the bill angled up so that the chin is visible. The black V, characteristic of the chin of Pacific birds and infrequent elsewhere, has been seen in the w. Atlantic under particularly favorable conditions of observation.

The voice of drakes of the various large eiders, especially when heard from invisible birds in foggy weather, has a ghostly quality and is not easily forgotten. The Common tends to utter a 2-syllabled *a-ooo*, while the King has a wavering call, the several syllables run together. The ♀♀ croak. (Also compare with accounts of the other eiders.) RSP

VOICE  When alarmed, the drake has a series (length indefinite) of rather hoarse, grating, *kor-korr-korr* notes, but is best known for the muffled cooing which accompanies certain displays. This commonly is 2 syllabled, as *a-ooo*, or longer. It is heard in

all seasons, though only rarely from midsummer into fall. The duck, when nest-site hunting, has a mixture of croaking and groaning sounds; from some time in incubation onward to include her association with crèches of young, her notes vary with circumstances from rather subdued and spaced out to rapid, harsh, grating croaks. In certain display situations, the croak is modified to rapid *gogogog*, length indefinite. The peeping of ducklings has variations to fit such situations as brooding, complaint, cohesion, contentment, and desertion.

All of the above calls as they relate to "Reproduction" are mentioned in context under that heading. RSP

HABITAT  (Of the species.) A shoal-water marine duck. Varied **nesting habitat.** For example, islets and shores of ponds and lagoons close to, and with outlet to, the sea—as at various Aleutian localities, St. Lawrence I., outer N. Shore of Gulf of St. Lawrence and s. Labrador, Bear I. (perhaps exclusively at such places here), and at scattered Eurasian localities. There are comparable conditions at some places in Iceland, where the birds nest on sheltered lower terrain near the sea and drink and bathe in streams of meltwater that flow from higher ground. Many Common Eiders also nest on islands and islets in fjords, estuaries, and the open sea, but preferably not remote from sheltered shallow coves and bays where the ducklings can feed. Smaller is., under 75–100 acres (30–40 ha.) are preferred, with sloping or well-drained terrain; the vegetative cover varies from grassy (or even grazed by sheep) to shrubby to dense coniferous or mixed forest, or any combination of these. That is, this eider is not restricted to open situations, since a great many nest within stands of conifers, as at the largest colonies on is. in the inner St. Lawrence, on others in the Gulf of Me., and at some localities near the White Sea. The nesting ♀ ♀ may get some rainwater, or else may drink saline water if no fresh is available.

This eider also colonizes headlands, slopes, and shores of bays of larger is. and the mainland. Scattered pairs occasionally nest a considerable distance inland, as in Iceland and Spitzbergen. In the Faeroes, to the "top of Hestø, which certainly is between 1,000 and 1,200 ft. high" (Müller, in Schiøler 1926). In the Aleutians, some nest on cliff ledges, where they are safe from introduced foxes.

In **spring** at various boreal localities, the birds seek the first open marine water along shore near nesting places or, if there is any fresh water ashore, respond to the thaw there. (The King Eider does likewise earlier, responding to the inland thaw while the sea still is frozen.) Yet just why the timing of nesting at Common Eider colonies at more southerly places where the sea does not freeze differs in the same year on adjacent is. is not yet understood.

In **various seasons** enters estuaries and river mouths; migrants occasionally stop on rivers and lakes. Daily schedule on the sea is attuned more or less to the tide—feeding on falling tide, especially at ebb, and resting on rising tide—but it moves shoreward at evening and seaward in morning where persecuted. Migrates preferably over water along coasts but, in a few places, the distance is shortened by crossing land, usually at night. Birds of all ages rest at times on rocks, sandbars, and drifting or stranded ice. Evidently they drink at puddles of meltwater on ice. RSP

DISTRIBUTION   (See map.) Panarctic-boreal; also nests well to the south, down to about lat. 43° N in e. N. Am. The Common is not as highly migratory as the King Eider, which is reflected in their respective distributions. In the Eurasian arctic, for example, Common Eiders from the west (Barents Sea and vicinity) seldom occur eastward beyond the e. side of Vaigach I. and few of those coming from the east (Chuckchee Sea) go w. beyond the Yana Delta. Thus the 2 "ends" of distribution are far apart. (The King closes the gap by regularly reaching the midpoint, the Taimyr Pen.) In the Am. arctic a corresponding gap is much narrower (midpoint is about at long. 100° W); a few Common Eiders must cross it in at least one direction, since some Pacific–Bering birds have reached w. Greenland.

There has been great reduction, even local extinction, of breeding stock in widely scattered areas of the breeding range of the Common Eider. Yet this bird responds rapidly to adequate protection and not only has recovered lost areas but also, in recent decades, has extended its breeding range in w. Europe, Brit. Isles, w. Atlantic, and elsewhere.

Although both Common and King Eider occur occasionally well beyond usual range, the former is less likely to be found far inland.

*borealis*—fairly large breeding range. Some records of summer occurrence at high-arctic localities are not necessarily evidence of breeding at these places.

**Breeds** in Canada from somewhere in the Hamilton Inlet region, Labrador, counterclockwise around Ungava, but evidently not down into ne. coastal Hudson Bay; also is. across the mouth of Hudson Bay (Mansel, Coats, Southampton) and probably not

38

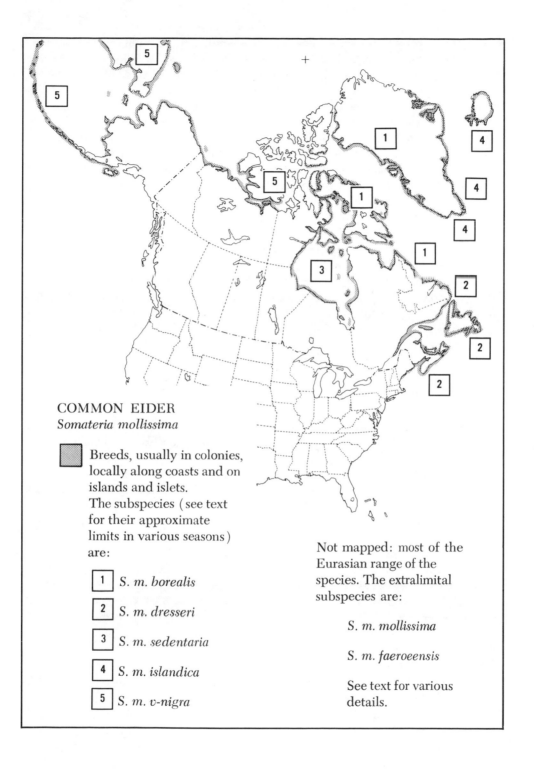

**COMMON EIDER**
*Somateria mollissima*

Breeds, usually in colonies, locally along coasts and on islands and islets.
The subspecies ( see text for their approximate limits in various seasons) are:

| 1 | *S. m. borealis* |
| 2 | *S. m. dresseri* |
| 3 | *S. m. sedentaria* |
| 4 | *S. m. islandica* |
| 5 | *S. m. v-nigra* |

Not mapped: most of the Eurasian range of the species. The extralimital subspecies are:

*S. m. mollissima*

*S. m. faeroeensis*

See text for various details.

down into the bay (Ottawa Is., Sleeper Is.); w. of Southampton, from somewhere in the Chesterfield Inlet region at least to Boothia Gulf localities; recorded (most westerly record, not nesting) at Cresswell Bay on e. side of Somerset I., about long. 92° W, but has nested n. to s. Cornwallis I. and s. Ellesmere I. In nw. Greenland, nests at least from C. York (lat. 76° N) northward into Hall Land (above 81° N), opposite extreme ne. Ellesmere I.; perhaps this also is the main subspecies that nests farther s. in w. Greenland, where there have been very extensive weather-induced changes in summer distribution (see discussion beyond under *islandica*). In **winter** there are large numbers of eiders along the sw. coast of Greenland, from vicinity of Holsteinborg southward (presumably they all are *borealis* and any local-nesting *islandica* go elsewhere); evidently a few on open water around se. and s. Baffin I. and perhaps along the Labrador coast; evidently occurs in some numbers somewhere in the Gulf of St. Lawrence (not in the estuary); abundant around e. and se. Nfld.; some on coasts of Maritimes; regular, in some numbers, in extreme easternmost Gulf of Me.; straggler beyond to s. New Eng. and to N.Y. (♀ taken at Montauk, Dec. 15, 1945).

*dresseri*—**breeds** from somewhere along the Labrador coast southward to include Nfld. (very few, in extreme n. part of Hare Bay and off the ne. coast at the Wadham Is.), St. Lawrence estuary and Gulf, in the maritimes, and in Me., where reduced to one known breeding station in 1907 (for history, see Gross 1944) but has doubled in numbers repeatedly (about 20,000 nesting pairs in 1970—H. L. Mendall) and by 1969 nested w. of Casco Bay off the York Co., Me., coast. Some of the northerly birds, in summer, have a molt migration to well within southerly breeding range of S. *m. borealis* (example: molting drake taken at Hopedale, Labrador, July 6, 1944—Gross 1937).

In **winter** from Nfld. (rarely?) and abundantly southward, with major concentrations in Gulf of Me. (w. Me. to Mass., including s. of C. Cod, but a claim of a half million off Monomoy, Mass., in late 1951 is difficult to accept), in some winters in some numbers to e. Long I., N.Y. There are scattered occurrences down the Atlantic coast to Va., N.C., and Fla., for which there are several records, the southernmost (Petrovic and King 1972) being a long-dead bird found in the Dry Tortugas on April 3, 1967.

In Greenland a drake was taken near Godthaab in April, 1907, and was illus. in color on pl. 54 in Schiøler (1926).

*sedentaria*—**breeds** on coasts and is. of Hudson Bay, on the w. side n. to include the mouth of Chesterfield Inlet; on the e. side on some of the innumerable is. n. to the C. Smith area; the Belcher Is. in se. Hudson Bay are major nesting areas and they also nest to the north on the Ottawa and Sleeper Is.; to the south they nest on various is. in James Bay. In **winter** in numbers on open water w. of the Belcher Is. and evidently elsewhere, in unknown numbers, on open waters of Hudson–James Bays. One record as a **straggler:** 3 eiders seen (young ♂ collected) at Navy I., Ont., on the Niagara R. a short distance above Niagara Falls, Nov. 21, 1936.

Except for land-fast ice along shore, ice forms earliest in the n. sections of Hudson Bay and advances southward as the cold intensifies. Evidently the last area to freeze (except for persisting open leads) is w. and s. of the Belcher Is. The shore lead in the bay is widest and most persistent along the w. and nw. coasts, due to offshore winds. There always is open water in Hudson Bay—enough to maintain eiders—see Lardner (in

Beals and Shenstone 1968) and Danielson (1971) for details. Most of James Bay freezes, but there is a curved area of open water across its mouth, which varies in width after the manner of a shore lead. The eiders thus are isolated much of the year; in winter they are confined to limited areas of harsh but relatively constant environment and they have become relatively sedentary and morphologically distinct.

*islandica*—the most westerly **nesting areas** probably are somewhere in sw. Greenland. Vibe's (1967) important analysis of climatic fluctuations vs. changes in eider nesting distribution are in outline as follows. 1 Drift-ice stagnation stage (about 1810–60)—the ice did not advance far up Davis Strait, the w. Greenland climate was relatively cold, dry, and stable, and nesting eiders were concentrated southerly. 2 Drift-ice pulsation stage (about 1860–1910)—the ice advanced far n., either early or late in summer; the climate southerly became unstable and wet and the eiders were concentrated farther northward in cent. w. Greenland. 3 Drift–ice melting stage (about 1910–60),—the ice decreased in Davis Strait and eiders again became distributed far down the coast; conditions improved even in nw. and in e. Greenland. 4 A new drift-ice pulsation stage is beginning.

This subspecies also **nests** at a few localities in e. Greenland, in Iceland (long protected, very abundant locally except comparatively few on the s. coast), Jan Mayen, Spitzbergen, Bear I., and all along the coast of Norway. [The Common Eiders of Franz Josef Land have not been identified to subspecies and perhaps represent a northerly outpost of nominate *mollissima.*]

Assuming that subspecies are essentially separate in the seasons of pair formation, the eiders **wintering** along w. Greenland approximately from Holsteinborg southward are *borealis* and the *islandica* birds of sw. Greenland go elsewhere. Probably all the birds from southerly e. Greenland go to Iceland; Jan Mayen—no basis even for speculation; Spitzbergen—to nearest open water of suitable depth; Bear I.—apparently nearby, within the winter limits of sea ice; Norway—a shift down the coast (known from banding recoveries).

A bird banded in Spitzbergen in July was found dead in Oct. of the same year in Iceland (G. Timmermann 1949). In general, however, the various units assigned to *islandica* consist of birds that evidently are quite local in their travels.

*v-nigra*—**breeds** in N. Am. in Alaska at Glacier Bay, Cook Inlet region, Kodiak and nearby is., s. side of Alaska Pen., in the Aleutians (except where locally extirpated), n. side of Alaska Pen., and to the north on is. and sections of the Bering Sea coast, and clockwise beyond around the perimeter of Alaska on is. and coast; and in Canada on is. coast e. into Coronation Gulf, and on several arctic is. (sw. Banks, w. side of Victoria and se. at least to Cambridge Bay area, and on nearby Jenny Lind I.). Easternmost record in Canada: Coronation Gulf, about long. 150° W (but some have reached w. Greenland).

In e. Asia breeds on Medny (Copper) I. in the Commander group, where it is said (Marakov 1966) to be present all year and not to visit neighboring is. An apparently disjunct subpopulation breeds in ne. Okhotsk Sea from Tauisk Gulf e. into Penzhinskaya Gulf. Plentiful locally on ne. coast of Kamchatka and the Koryak coast. Nests locally around the perimeter of the Chuckchee Pen., on the arctic side greatly declining in numbers w. of Chaun Bay and Aion I. (Portenko 1972). Yet it nests far beyond, at

41

localities as far as the Yana R. estuary (about long. 137° E). Plentiful on Wrangel I. In the New Siberian Archipelago said only to visit Great and Little Lyakhov and Stolbov, but nests in some numbers to the north (New Siberia w. to Kotelny inclusive). Western-most records are for 3 ♀ ♀, banded on St. Lawrence I. in the summer of 1940; 2 were killed in nesting seasons of 1943 and 1946 at Tiksi Bay (about long. 130° E) and the other killed Aug. 22, 1952 (12 years after banding) in Khatanga Bay (long. 110° E). According to Rutilevskii (1957), this eider reaches the De Long Is. (n. of the main New Siberian group) but does not produce young there.

In **winter** on the Am. side, depending on ice conditions, from n. Bering Sea southward (and in some years perhaps a few as far n. as there is any open water in Beaufort Sea near Alaska), and around is. (including the Aleutian chain) and along the Pacific (Gulf of Alaska) coast, but in dwindling numbers in waters of the Alexander Archipelago; very few beyond in B.C.; recorded in Wash.

Apparently a few birds migrate southward (up rivers) from Beaufort Sea inland, which might account for occurrences inland southward even into conterminous U.S., (N.D., Minn., Kans., Iowa).

On the Siberian side, winters on perimeter of Bering Sea, also in Commander Is. (only resident birds?). It is quite possible that arctic-nesting birds from both Asia and N. Am. winter primarily in Am. waters, with distribution centered in Aleutian–Alaska Pen. area.

In w. Greenland, best known from Godthaab Dist., because of active collecting in that area (but probably has occurred elsewhere); records are for Jan.–April and July.

**Extralimital subspecies** Nominate *mollissima*—**breeds** on arctic coasts and is., apparently from somewhere in Varanger Fjord area eastward locally on the Murman coast, also in w. and s. White Sea, Kanin–Pechora coast, se. side of Kolguev I. (not many), w. and n. side of Vaigach I., along w. side of Novaya Zemlya and around to the ne. coast (the s. island has largest colonies at present in w. U.S.S.R.), and those that go n. to Franz Josef Land may be of this subspecies. The Common Eider rarely goes e. beyond Vaigach I. into the Kara Sea where, according to Belopolskii (1957), the inshore benthic fauna on which the eiders feed is much reduced as compared with Barents Sea (yet the King and Steller's Eider penetrate even farther eastward). In **winter** some eiders occur along the edge of the shore ice on w. side of Novaya Zemlya. Others pass the season along the w. Murman coast and westward into Norway. The White Sea is an important wintering area since parts of it (Gulf of Onega, areas along the Tersk coast) do not freeze. For local numbers and distribution in various seasons, see Bianki et al. (1967b). At present the total number of Common Eiders in the Barents Sea–White Sea area is a small fraction of the total population of *S. m. mollissima*.

According to Schiøler (1926), "it is certain" that birds from the White Sea sometimes occur in winter in Swedish and Danish waters. There the matter rested until, in late April–early May, 1969, flocks of eiders were seen (and one flock was followed for some distance) going from Trondheim Fjord in Norway eastward to Sweden and presumably beyond to the White Sea, and there was movement in the opposite direction in early Sept. (Folkestad and Moksnes 1970). Possibly these birds winter somewhere in the North Sea. A few eiders occur on Finnish lakes, at least in spring.

**Also nests** in the Baltic (the center of abundance) and its outlet and to the Netherlands (where, by the late 1960s, there was one of the largest colonies in w. Europe), and a few places in the Brit. Isles, and a record for France (several nests on an islet in the Loire estuary in 1932). For summer and winter distribution in Britain, see J. H. Taverner (1967) and his earlier papers which he cited. **Winter range** includes parts of the Baltic (Danish waters mainly), along the North Sea coast, and parts of the e. Atlantic (as around Brit. Isles) down to include n. France.

For a recent cursory summary of numerical changes of nominate *mollissima* in various countries, see Kumari (1966).

Has **straggled** to the Kara Sea (as previously noted), to s. shore of Bay of Biscay, to Portugal, and w. Mediterranean (various records as far as w. coast of Italy), Adriatic (Dalmatian coast), Aegean, and nw. coast of Black Sea (both sexes in small numbers in spring–summer since 1964). There are a few inland records; in Europe, for example, in Switzerland and Yugoslavia, and some of the stragglers just listed obviously had made overland flights. One taken near Zurich, Switzerland, in 1951 had been banded 4 mo. earlier in Sweden.

*faeroeensis*—known only from the Faeroes, where locally plentiful.

The species has been reported as **fossil** from the Pleistocene of Ireland, Scotland, Norway, and Denmark (various localities); and from **archaeological sites** in Denmark (various localities) and Alaska (6 is. and 2 mainland localities); see Brodkorb (1964a) for full references. The Danish records are from Winge (1903); he listed localities under these headings: Ice Age, Old Stone Age, New Stone Age, Iron Age, and Middle Ages to Present. Bones from middens of Stone Age and Iron Age reveal that the birds were of the same size as presently occurring nominate *millissima* (Schiøler 1926). RSP

MIGRATION    (Of the species.) Such a complicated subject can be treated only briefly here, to show some facets of the general pattern. There are few helpful banding data, except for w. Greenland and the Baltic.

Movements are weather influenced, even drastically in cold climates where timing of spring thaw and fall freeze-up are highly variable. In addition, in various places there is a supplanting effect: birds of an area are absent seasonally and their place is taken by others from elsewhere. There are long-distance migrants (some Bering–Pacific birds), many that travel shorter distances (as Baltic birds), and still others that are essentially sedentary (as at Copper I. in the Commanders and in the Faeroes).

One might generalize that Common Eiders on molt migration go toward their wintering areas, though there are striking exceptions. When the wintering area of a unit is close to its nesting area, then molt migration is local (but see, for example, *dresseri* below) and generally to some intermediate place. The time of molt migration of post breeding drakes seems to vary in relation to peaks of nesting dates, beginning somewhat sooner in highly migratory cold-climate breeders. And for age categories that have a molt migration (all birds after their first winter), true fall migration varies from essentially no travel (in sedentary birds) to extensive travel, mostly in Oct.–Nov.

It has been said that spring migration of the Common Eider is rapid and fall migration leisurely. Yet for many of them spring migration requires considerable time. And, since movement from summer to winter quarters is a complex matter (includes molt migration) and can extend from some time in June until into early winter, this gives a superficial appearance that "fall migration" is leisurely.

As with other eiders, there is much, often complete sex and/or age segregation in flocks. Many postbreeding drakes go in flocks by themselves on molt migration. Some later flocks are entirely or preponderantly of ♀ ♀, and some still later contain only young of the year (both sexes included). There is a tendency for these last not to travel as far as older birds but there are exceptions. In spring, flocks of older prebreeding drakes (2-year-olds) form the vanguard of migrants and so these unisexual flocks occur along migration corridors and near breeding areas. Soon afterward come flocks consisting of mated breeders. About the time the latter arrive in numbers, the flocks of prebreeding drakes move away. They are the earliest to begin molt migration. Some of them, however, may obtain mates. Sometime after nesting ♀ ♀ begin incubating, their mates (now postbreeding drakes) depart. In the case of some highly migratory units, apparently older ♂ prebreeders plus postbreeding drakes either travel together or else their schedules overlap greatly. At some northerly localities, heavy flights of drakes in the first half of July evidently contain birds of both categories. During spring migration, yearlings tend to accompany later-migrating breeders; some of the young birds go only part of the distance to breeding areas, then either stop to molt or else alter their direction and go to a molting area. Especially where seasonal movements are rather short, the pattern outlined here is obscured by intermingling of birds of more than one category, or from different breeding units, on overlapping schedules.

PACIFIC–BERING birds begin moving not later than some time in March; their passage (all categories included) through Bering Sea extends from about mid-April into early June. They arrive at St. Lawrence I. in numbers about mid-May. Beyond Bering Strait, at least older ♂ prebreeders plus paired breeders are traveling in May and arrive in "normal" seasons at or near distant breeding places in the w. Canadian subarctic and arctic in the last third of May and first third of June (but some, in some years, much earlier; perhaps all, in very tardy seasons, beginning some time in June). Some yearlings go to breeding places, but many stop en route (or turn back?); for example, large numbers molt at St. Lawrence I.

At least 2 species of eider—Common and King—are known, from birds forced down on land by adverse weather, to cross over the Seward Pen., and all 4 eider species have thus been found also to migrate over the arctic coastal plain s. of Pt. Barrow. From radar observations (Flock 1973), it is now known that the birds fly very high overland, unseen, well beyond the range of human vision. Also, eiders apparently go from the Barrow region on a direct course over the sea, the Common Eider to sw. Banks and to Victoria I.

It would not be surprising to discover that there is also spring migration overland on the Asiatic side, from Anadyr Gulf northward across the Chuckchee Pen.

Older prebreeding plus postbreeding drakes begin leaving nesting areas, on **molt migration,** in very late June–early July; great numbers go down through Bering Strait in July and very early Aug. (the Strait usually is ice-free by the first week in July). For the next 2 weeks, postbreeding (and other?) ♀ ♀ are preponderant in migrating flocks; young of the year and a few ♀ ♀ travel still later. The return flight is close to the Alaskan arctic coast and there are radar observations (Flock 1973) of migration (the birds could be eiders) up to 40 mi. inland. At Pt. Barrow, throughout the 5-day period Aug. 25–29, 1969, as observed on radar, waterfowl passed at a rate of 2,740 birds/hr., more than ever reported in visual counts. It is probable that 3–4 times as many waterfowl migrate over the Pt. Barrow area than actually can be seen at the duck camp, Birnik. There is a heavy return flight also along the e. Siberian arctic coast.

Although large numbers of Common Eiders molt along the s. shore of St. Lawrence I., it is far from certain that this is the only major molting area in or near Bering Sea. The number of birds is very great and there may be other suitable shoal-water areas in n. Bering Sea (which generally is not frozen July–Sept. inclusive) or perhaps the eiders continue on toward or to widely scattered wintering areas. If the latter, then molt migration and fall migration are one and the same.

A considerable number of Pacific–Bering birds may have only rather local seasonal travels—for example, those that nest in Shelikov Gulf, the Commanders (definitely), Aleutians, Kodiak I. area, etc.

W. ATLANTIC birds have a complicated pattern, a result of birds of different breeding areas having different routes or schedules and, to an unknown extent, different wintering areas. For the n. Gulf of St. Lawrence, Beetz (1916) still is a useful source, now supplemented by banding recoveries and studies done to the southwest in the St. Lawrence estuary beginning in the 1960s. The following is tentative, however, since much remains unknown.

At s. limits of nesting in the Gulf of Me., there are flocks of drakes (presumably older prebreeders) through spring. Most paired breeders are in the vicinity of nesting is. in that area not later than some time in April, generally accompanied by yearling pre-breeders (some drakes, at least, recognizable as yearlings). Postbreeding drakes remain until about the middle of June and many remain thereafter all through the flightless period. On molt migration, some older prebreeding and postbreeding drakes apparently go n. via the Bay of Fundy, cross overland late in the day or at night, and probably molt in the Gulf of St. Lawrence. There is a major molting area around Prince Edward I. (Boyer 1966). The **molt migration** is rapid and northward, i.e., in opposite direction from the much later fall migration. A great many (or all?) young of the year remain and molt, by themselves, in the e. Gulf of Me. In fall migration, the main route of Common Eiders is out around the Maritimes, but some cross overland. In Oct. the latter fly high when southbound over Kings Co., N.S. (Tufts 1962), en route to the Gulf of Me. From whatever route by which they arrive they shift sw., many to waters around C. Cod, Mass., and in some winters reach e. Long I., N.Y., in numbers.

Drakes from colonies in the lower St. Lawrence (not the Gulf beyond) evidently move out into the Gulf and molt there. The postnesting ♀ ♀ and their young move, at first leisurely, into the Gulf (where the former presumably molt) and all age-classes and both sexes are believed to travel out around the Maritimes. They go around N.S. and, by Nov., banded postbreeding ♀ ♀ are in the Gulf of Me.; during Dec. and Jan. the birds are scattered from Me. to C. Cod, having taken a 1,400-mi. route via water to reach winter quarters that, if they had crossed directly southward overland, are scarcely 400 mi. distant (Reed 1972). The inner St. Lawrence birds are believed to travel the same circuitous water route when northbound in spring.

Drakes from the N. Shore of the Gulf of St. Lawrence, plus at least older prebreeders fly e. on molt migration, in the period June 15–July 15, through the Strait of Belle Isle and then go n. to places along the Labrador coast—some definitely as far as Hopedale, perhaps some even farther. A considerable number of ♂ *dresseri*, therefore, molt within the Labrador nesting range of later-nesting *borealis*.

In fall these *dresseri* reverse their course and, in Sept.–Oct., go well w. along the N. Shore of the Gulf of St. Lawrence, past Anticosti I., and turn southward. Then presumably they circumnavigate the Maritimes to reach the Gulf of Me. and there spread to wintering localities where there are vast beds of blue mussel.

It is of interest that *dresseri* more or less vacates the Gulf of St. Lawrence, which becomes part of the winter range of *borealis*, and that many *dresseri* have a molt migration in the direction opposite from their later fall migration.

Where the drake *borealis* from colonies along the n. ⅔ of the Labrador coast molt remains a mystery. In fall, *borealis* of both sexes and all ages go down toward the n. tip of Nfld. From there a vast number go to winter range all along the outer Nfld. coast and clockwise around to Fortune Bay on the s. side. A much smaller number goes through the Strait of Belle Isle and the birds turn s. before reaching Anticosti I. These must include the birds that, from some time in Nov. to early spring, occupy the ne. corner of the Gulf of Me. (which then is largely vacated by *dresseri*). They must arrive via Cabot Strait and the outer perimeter of N.S. The return in spring of *borealis* breeders to nesting places in Labrador is rather late, about May 15–June 15.

The schematic arrangement of winter distribution appears to be as follows: Long I., N.Y., to somewhere in Me.—almost exclusively *dresseri*, the young in their 1st winter being at least mostly from within the Gulf of Me. (and with some hatched in Me. even scattered ne. into N.S. waters); extreme ne. Gulf of Me.—*borealis*, over 1½ years old; outer coast of Maritimes—mature *borealis* and some (mostly young) *dresseri;* Gulf of St. Lawrence—primarily *borealis,* also some *borealis–dresseri* intermediates; along e. and se. Nfld.—*borealis,* mostly 1½ years old and older.

E. CANADIAN ARCTIC  The majority of eiders (*borealis*) are believed to have a molt migration back to within the general area of the winter range of this subspecies in sw. Greenland waters, with the young going there also. A few may remain through winter in areas of "permanent" open water within the e. Canadian arctic. Whether there is any movement between Greenland and Ungava is a question and whether the birds that molt in Ungava Bay all are local breeders is another question.

GREENLAND  The eiders of nw. Greenland (*borealis*) evidently are in widely scattered flocks when molting and they later shift southward; their later-arriving young are concentrated in the n. part of the w. Greenland winter range. Any *islandica* birds of sw. Greenland presumably vacate this area seasonally, perhaps going to Icelandic waters. Salomonsen (1972) suggested that beforehand in summer prebreeding ♂ ♂ go n. in w. Greenland waters to molt, leaving the food resources near nesting places to ♀ ♀ and young. In e. Greenland there is no known migration of Common Eiders along the coast in any season; Schiøler (1926) was the first to suggest that the birds summering there spend the winter in Icelandic waters. One or two banding recoveries partially support this suggestion.

HUDSON AND JAMES BAYS   The *sedentaria* birds remain on unfrozen waters; a major wintering area is w. of the Belcher Is. in se. Hudson Bay.

ELSEWHERE   Icelandic eiders molt and also spend the winter on surrounding waters, so far as known. Jan Mayen—no information. Spitzbergen—at least one molting area (of drakes) is known, near the extreme sw. coast; in fall the eiders disappear (Common Eiders have been seen in this season to the southward toward Bear I., also some to the sw. at sea toward Norway); one banded in Spitzbergen has been recovered in Iceland; in winter, evidently they are near the shore ice. Bear I.—apparently present thereabouts all year. Norway—some shifting along the coast; some southerly birds cross the Skagerrak and winter in Danish waters. Faeroes—very local movements.

For nominate *mollissima* there are many data, treated here in brief outline, going from n. to s. On the Murman coast (which is warmed by the Gulf Stream), even in Jan., with the lengthening days, flocks begin shifting eastward. Some nest in w. Murman. Others, in March, gather in e. Murman localities and, later, some of these go into the White Sea, others to Novaya Zemlya, and a few to Franz Josef Land (arrival beginning in April, but bulk in last third of May). Winter range also includes open water along the ice edge off sw. Novaya Zemlya and unfrozen portions of the White Sea. Within the White Sea, the birds arrive at nesting places (as in Kandalaksh Bay) as soon as there is much open water locally; flocks of 1st-winter ♀ ♀ (or with some ♂ ♂ of same age) tend to keep by themselves and come near the nesting areas later than breeders (Bianki et al. 1967a). As to **molt migration,** drakes from w. Murman localities go eastward, about June 12–July 12, clockwise, into the entrance of the White Sea and then molt on the e. side (Tersk coast), where they are joined by others from within the White Sea (as from Kandalaksh Bay). (The w. Murman birds thus go in the opposite direction from their fall migration, which is back toward Norway, just as some *dresseri* of the W. Atlantic go in the opposite direction to molt.) There is also a major molting area along sw. Novaya Zemlya and off Vaigach and Kolguev is.; molting drakes, at least, are scattered elsewhere. According to Bianki et al. (1967a), ♀ ♀ tend to remain and molt on waters near the various nesting places.

In the Baltic, the birds go to breeding places mostly in March, some in April. On molt migration, many of the birds from northerly localities gather and molt off Gotland and on coasts of Latvia and Estonia. But the majority of Baltic birds, from the end of June into Aug., go sw. to Danish water, cross over s. Denmark, and molt on the Waddensea of Slesvig (North Sea coast). Fall migration from the Baltic coast of Sweden to the North Sea occurs in Oct.–Nov. For lengthy coverage of molt migration of Baltic birds, see Salomonsen (1968) and especially Joensen (1973) for data by age-class and sex.

Dutch birds shift southward and there is banding evidence that some individuals cross over to England.

In Scotland–England the local nesters do not travel far, in general only up to 100 km., and some are truly sedentary. In those that have migratory movements, 1st-winter birds (the sexes together) tend to keep to themselves and go shorter distances than older birds (just as most 1st-winter *borealis* from Labrador only go to the Gulf of St. Lawrence). Evidently all age-classes are more or less together in spring. In the first half of April the breeders return to nesting places; beginning in summer, they go some distance (in direction of wintering places) to molting areas; several were listed by Milne (1965). The shift later to winter quarters is a short movement.

It is of special interest that, at a nesting place in Scotland, there are both sedentary and migratory eiders. They tend not to mingle, but instead to nest in contiguous areas, and they differ genetically. This difference is maintained by the units being separated in seasons when pair formation occurs (Milne and Robertson 1965). RSP

BANDING STATUS   In N. Am., 307 were banded through 1964 and there were 6 recoveries through 1961; main places of banding were Que., N.B., Me., and Alaska (data from Bird Banding Laboratory). There have been local programs subsequently, but few data are at hand. In the St. Lawrence estuary the number of adult ♀ ♀ banded 1963–70 inclusive was 903; through 1970 there were 106 recaptures at nesting places and 39 recoveries elsewhere in fall (Reed 1972). In Me. in 1970, 159 nesting ♀ ♀ were banded and there were 37 recoveries of ♀ ♀ banded in previous years; also, 133 preflight young and molting birds of older age-classes were banded that year (H. Mendall). The total for Que., N.S., N.B., Me. (all summer bandings, mostly adult ♀ ♀), and Mass. (winter bandings) was 2,676 through Aug. 1971 and there were 428 recoveries (H. Mendall).

In w. Greenland, 2,247 were banded 1946–65 inclusive, with 494 recoveries, all in Greenland, in that period (Salomonsen 1966). The program has continued. For locations of 515 recoveries and discussion of banding data, see Salomonsen (1967a).

Elsewhere there have been various banding programs, in the n. Atlantic and Baltic especially, with some findings scattered in the literature. A fine example of use of many banding data, with list of recoveries included, is that of Paludan (1962) on eiders in Danish waters. The number banded in the Brit. Isles through 1969 was 7,904 and there were 646 recoveries; within this area, in ne. Scotland 1960–72, some 5,000 were banded, some wing-tagged. RSP

REPRODUCTION   This is a composite account, drawn from information from various parts of the range of the species; not all major papers have been consulted. The most useful data utilized are on nominate *mollissima*, *borealis*, *islandica*, and *dresseri*, with relatively little on the others. Older compilations still are useful: Bent (1925), J. C. Phillips (1926), Witherby (1939), Dementiev and Gladkov (1952), and others.

It must be emphasized that most studies to date have been local and of rather short duration, hence are not entirely comparable. For example, the general picture of spring–summer activities may vary depending on whether a unit is expanding in size, near-stable, or declining, whether highly migratory or quite sedentary, and whether the season when a study was made was early, average, or late. An important variable is energy reserves of the ♀ ♀—whether the birds are in good physical condition when they begin the span ashore during which they get no or almost no nourishment. Still another relates to disturbance before, during, and after nesting; this varies all the way from year-round protection plus seasonal reduction of various predators (as at eider farms), to situations in the wild where there is frequent disturbance and heavy predation (including by man) to the extent of disrupting nesting and killing the birds. Even

48

though existing studies reflect these and many other variables, in different combinations, they also show similarity in general pattern of breeding biology in all units which have been studied.

It is generally believed, based as yet on rather few known-age banded individuals, that not all ♀ Common Eiders **first breed** at 2 years of age—i.e., some not until a year older—and ♂♂ generally not until their third year (at age about 34 mo.).

Some Common Eiders do not travel very far, and thus expend little energy, when returning to nesting areas, as in the Aleutians, Hudson Bay, Faeroes, parts of Britain, and w. Europe. To reach the more distant colder parts of their range they must travel far and, where both Common and King Eider nest in the same region, the former generally begins arriving about 1–2 weeks after the latter. Older ♂ prebreeders (unisexual flocks, of drakes) come first, then pairs that had formed much earlier and the remaining prebreeders (see "Migration"). The sex ratio is more balanced after early-arriving flocks of drakes move away (or some find mates) and have been succeeded, near breeding areas, by paired breeders. These have formed pairs earlier, from fall on. Thus a great many breeders are paired during spring migration, hence arrive paired at their destinations. The sequence of events outlined here is not as evident where eiders of both sexes and all age-classes have short travels in spring, or the same with additional migratory flocks passing through their area.

The time of year when **display first is manifest** apparently varies, depending on such factors as temperature and, again, on whether the birds are sedentary or decidedly migratory. Inclement weather has an inhibiting effect. In highly migratory units, the considerable sexual segregation that begins at the time of wing molt of the drakes may continue long afterward, but probably not in relatively sedentary birds. In southerly birds on both sides of the Atlantic, display occurs in fall, apparently first in a social context, as in groups or sizable assemblies containing both sexes, and without the activities of a drake being directed toward a particular duck. In both nominate *mollissima* and *dresseri* there is much tossing upward of the head, cooing, neck stretching, and ritualized Wing-flapping by drakes in autumn, on a calm sea on sunny days. It may seem rather surprising that, in that season, some ♀♀ assume the Prone position and apparent copulation is quite frequent. Many birds (*dresseri* and nominate *mollissima* at least) already are in pairs in fall and it seems probable that in instances in which Common Eider mates are not very distant from each other at any time (do not make long flights), they occasionally may rejoin for another nesting season (renewed pair bond). In the species in general, pairing is apparently frequent in fall, infrequent in midwinter, then frequent in late winter and spring; the early-paired birds continue displaying to maintain the pair bond. On warm days in spring, flocks on the sea near nesting localities are very active and noisy—much commotion and a far-carrying chattering as of many people all talking at once. There is considerable display even by yearling drakes (in Alt. I. Plumage) and some of these form pair bonds of unknown duration with ♀♀ of unknown age(s).

**Display** and **pair formation**　The actual genesis of display, as previously noted, evidently occurs within a group, the drake not directing it toward a particular duck. (Potential breeders of both sexes obviously must be together by some time in fall or later, even though they may have been separated beginning some time in the preceding summer.) Most observations do not begin until a late phase in which assemblies break into small gatherings, typically consisting of a single duck and several (up to 10) drakes, and the pair bond is formed in this situation.

Although there is some display ashore and on ice, in this later phase it occurs most actively on water (displaying groups swim and dive rather than fly), in 3 main situations that culminate in production of a fertile clutch: **1** in groups, **2** during aggressive encounters between pairs, and **3** before and after copulation. The same postures may be given in all 3 situations, but frequency varies. Some displays are continued long after pair formation, to maintain the bond, and even after the time the drake leaves his incubating mate. In the following list the terminology is that of McKinney (1961), most of it being a literal translation from the Dutch of the pioneer study by Hoogerheide (1950); displays of both sexes are included. In addition, the last entry in this list is here first described.

COOING MOVEMENT 1 by ♂; breast swells and head is thrown back to touch mantle as cooing note *a-ooo* is given.

COOING MOVEMENT 2 by ♂; the preceding display may be given singly or be followed immediately by 2, in which head is brought forward with a slight jerk so that crown points forward and upward to accompaniment of call *a-ooo*.

COOING MOVEMENT 3 by ♂; and infrequently by ♀; first the bird adopts a head-high posture with neck vertical, then head–neck are brought forward until bill touches water, a conspicuous bulge appears in the neck, and call *woo-hooo* is given. Females do not coo, but with this movement they give a loud, throaty cawing version of the drake's call.

DOUBLE COOING MOVEMENT by ♂; probably equivalent to or linkage of Cooing movement 2 + 1.

TRIPLE COOING MOVEMENT by ♂; probably represents linkage of Cooing movement 2 + 1 + 2.

NECK-STRETCHING by ♂; crown is moved suddenly upward and slightly forward, bill points slightly down, and neck is fully stretched (more than in Cooing movement 2). There is normally no call.

HEAD-TURN frequent and pronounced in unpaired ♂♂ and as a precopulatory display; bill is moved rather slowly from side to side several times.

ROO-CALLING rather quiet calls given by ♂♂.

PREEN by ♂; brief and quite stereotyped nibbling with tip of bill in middle of back or shoulder region.

BATHING a series of dipping movements in which the head is submerged and water is thrown over back, much more frequently by the ♂; and SPLASH BATHING, much more vigorously by the ♂ who vanishes from sight within a shower of spray.

WING-FLAP by ♂, less frequently by ♀; bird rears up and remains poised with wings open for a moment before giving 2 rapid flaps. (This ritualized movement differs from the normal comfort activity of flapping the wings, during which the pause is absent and 3, 4, or more flaps may be given in series. The former produces a loud noise; the latter is comparatively noiseless.)

Wing-flap

SHAKE by ♂, less often by ♀; on water, bird rises, pushing breast forward slightly, and rotates head with a rapid flick before subsiding again.

HEAD-ROLL by ♂; cheeks are rolled over the back, first to one side and then to the other.

CHIN-LIFTING by ♀ only; bill is tossed up rapidly a number of times; closely linked with threatening movements, the whole performance constituting INCITING. Chin-lifting is directed toward the duck's mate and alternates with the same used as threatening toward another bird, a common Anatid behavioral pattern.

51

GOG-GOG calling by ♀; a series of throaty calls *gogogogog* (length indefinite).

ELEVATED   A further posture of the drake was described by Hoogerheide, in which head and tail were held erect as in Bubble display of the Ruddy Duck (*Oxyura jamaicensis*).

TREADING WATER by individuals of both sexes; seen in late May–early June in members of pairs and, among unpaired birds, at least in drakes. It differs from puddling for food principally in that the bird does not rear up. The feet paddle quite rapidly, the body trembles or "shivers," and there is no evident forward progression on the water. It occurs at the season when the birds ingest little or no food, is inconspicuous except at very close range, and (like puddling) is done silently (R. S. Palmer).

**Behavior when in groups**   Intensity of pursuit of the ♀ varies. At times, the group cruises along slowly, drakes giving displays and chasing one another, the duck threatening some of the drakes. Fights in which drakes beat each other with their wings occur occasionally. In other groups, ♂♂ actively pursue the ♀; she is forced to dive and an underwater chase ensues. In most cases, ♂♂ do not behave aggressively toward the ♀, but occasionally in a displaying group a ♂ dashes across the water at the

♀. This somewhat ritualized surface chase is the nearest equivalent to Short flights of some other waterfowl; the ♂ seldom catches up with the ♀; the 2 birds usually appear to be in the process of becoming paired.

The commonest activities of the ♂♂ in displaying groups are chasing other ♂♂ and performing Cooing movements. Head-turn and Shake also are common displays. Drakes compete for position nearest the duck. The most aggressive ♂♂ perform more double Cooing-movements while the least aggressive ones perform Cooing-movement 3 more often. There is considerable interchange of birds; for example, an unpaired drake may swim away and join another group; the ♀ may take flight and not return.

**Encounters between mated pairs**   There is no defense of a definite area, but there are frequent conflicts when pairs happen to come close together on water or on land.

Drakes chase and perform the same displays they do in groups, while ♀ ♀ Chin-lift and threaten. Drakes stationed on land near their incubating mates, with their off-duty mates, also when sunning on rocks, ice, or beaches, typically keep spaced a short distance out of reach of neighboring birds. (The relations of the sexes as observed during incubation are discussed later.)

**Copulation** This is very frequent and, in spring, has been observed more than 2 months before the first eggs are laid. The ♀ assumes a PRONE posture on the water, neck stretched forward, and the drake swims around her for a variable length of time, performing his displays. The frequency of these varies. Thus, the displays of drakes in full definitive feathering which precede a successful copulation include many Preens, Bathes, Neck-stretches, Shakes, and Head-rolls; the Wing-flap and Head-turn are less frequent; Cooing movements are rare. The Preen tends to be more common at the start of the sequence, while Head-turn and Cooing movements occur mainly just before mounting. When precopulatory behavior is influenced by the presence of other birds nearby, more Cooing movements are included. As the drake dismounts, he assumes a rather upright posture and bends forward to perform Cooing movements, then, while Head-turning, he swims away from the duck. At times the ♀ performs these post-copulatory displays as well, but more often she begins to bathe at once. Especially after unsuccessful copulation attempts, the ♀ may chase or threaten the ♂.

Younger drakes, not yet in definitive feathering, have fewer Preens and Neck-stretches plus more Cooing movements and Head-turns than do older ones. In the latter, however, when activity is at low intensity, the whole sequence is slower and the Preen is relatively more frequent than is "normal."

Less detailed descriptions of displays by many observers and from scattered parts of the range of the species add essentially nothing to what is given above. Most observations are for the spring season, after most breeders already are paired.

In general, the Common Eider is **seasonally monogamous**—at least for a single clutch—but there are exceptions. In a situation in which ♀ ♀ of *S. m. dresseri* greatly exceeded "adult" ♂ ♂ in number, Gross (1938) reported an instance in which a ♂ copulated with 3 ♀ ♀ in the course of 30 min. A trio of 1 ♂ and 2 ♀ nominate *mollissima* was observed by F. McKinney at the Farne Is. and the ♂ was seen to copulate with both ♀ ♀. In 1973 at Aethey, in Isafjord in nw. Iceland, there was at least one trio: 2 ♂ kept close company with the same ♀ while she was incubating and wherever she went when flushed from her nest. Also in nw. Iceland, trios consisting of ♂ King plus ♂ Common mated to a ♀ Common may be as frequent as ♀ Common mated only to a ♂ King Eider; the writer has photographed 2 of these mixed-species trios. Drake Common Eiders, in the period immediately after they become "detatched" from their incubating mates, display toward and consort with ♀ ♀ other than their mates of the season, and probably including late-season nesters, failed breeders, and prebreeders, depending on circumstances.

Generally a **colonial nester**, in highest density plus largest numbers under more or less controlled conditions at eider farms. There also are areas of high density in large colonies that are strictly wild. It has been stated that *v-nigra* is not colonial in Alaska, but density varies from colonial (as 100 nests/acre on small is. in southerly lagoons of St. Lawrence I., Fay 1961) to widely dispersed nests; Rutilevskii (1957) stated that the nests are widely scattered in New Siberian Is., but in the U.S.S.R. most are colonial. In *faeroeensis* scattered nests are common, but most nesters are in colonies.

In spring, on **arrival near breeding places**, the assemblies of mated birds (plus any accompanying prebreeders) spend under ideal conditions a considerable period undisturbed on sheltered waters. Numbers increase; that is, they do not all arrive together. The drakes continue displaying (pair-bond maintenance). The ♀ ♀ feed and now attain their maximum wt. The eiders are shy at this time and at the slightest disturbance they close ranks and either swim away from shore or take wing. Nominate *mollissima*: the ♀ ♀ become heavy, from fat, also enlarged reproductive organs, so that some have difficulty in taking flight (V. S. Uspenskii 1946); unlike in other seasons, the ♀ ♀ now feed at twice the rate of ♂ ♂ (Gorman and Milne 1971). It follows that if migrant eiders are delayed by an adverse season they arrive late, in poor condition, and have little opportunity to rest and gain wt. before going ashore. This adversely affects reproduction: smaller clutches are laid, the eggs produce less viable ducklings, nests may be abandoned by weakened ♀ ♀, or there even may be no nesting.

The change from a marine life to nesting ashore is a considerable adjustment for the Common Eider. In a sense, it is gradual under "normal" circumstances; the birds come ashore to "prospect" for a nest site, then to begin nest construction, and then egg-laying, but return to the sea. Many pairs begin coming ashore in the morning or on a rising tide, and the ♀ ♀, closely followed by their mates, return to the vicinity (or actually to) their former nest sites. The birds come ashore in a "wave"—Tinbergen (1958) called it an invasion—and, presumably, later comers find the transition to life ashore easier because the others already are there. When they first come ashore, the heavy ♀ ♀ have a gait quite different from later on. In S. *m. dresseri* it is almost certain that some ♀ ♀ are too heavy to fly at the time of their first visits ashore; later after they have finished laying, they weigh much less (C. E. Korschgen).

**Site selection** (including reoccupation) proceeds in the following way at colonies of *borealis* near C. Dorset on Baffin I. (Cooch 1965). Scouting forays and visits to the lakes on the islands are made on the incoming tide; at first the pairs fly low over the ground, the ♀ slightly in the lead. The drake usually is silent but the duck keeps up an incessant moaning or croaking. Desirable areas are circled many times. At the end of a flight the pair alights on water nearest to the selected nesting area. The duck leaves the water, the drake follows, and they walk to the chosen place. Gudmundsson (1932) described similar behavior in Iceland—the birds visit the colony (eider farm) on the incoming tide; they do not alight at the nesting area, the trip to and from the sea or a pond being accomplished on foot. The duck may make nest-building movements at spots over a considerable area, but tends to settle finally on or near her previous site.

Yet where eiders nest comparatively far from any temporary pools or other water, the duck (with or without the drake) does fly inland and alight; then she stands nearly motionless, scanning the surroundings for possible predators, and then walks the remaining distance to the chosen spot or, later, the nest and eggs; then she settles down quickly. In early June in Me., at a colony of *dresseri* where numbers were increasing, small groups of eiders were seen to fly over incubating ♀ ♀ on the peripheral zone of an island and to alight on unoccupied grassy turf in the interior. This occurred most often at dawn. Some of these birds behaved as though mated, i.e., had formed at least temporary pair bonds; some of the drakes were in dark feathering with white upper breast (yearlings); the ages of both attached and unattached ♀ ♀ were, of course, unknown. On alighting, the birds scattered and behaved as though on a search mission. Presumably the ♀ ♀ were seeking an area to which they formed some degree of attachment and would return there the following year to nest (R. S. Palmer).

There are many factors that influence site selection and **nesting density**; for nominate *mollissima*, Gerasimova and Baranova (1960) listed these: topography, dispersal of plant cover, shelter from wind, time of disappearance of snow cover, characteristics of the vegetation, type of littoral zone and composition of its fauna. The chosen site varies greatly, from fully sheltered (as within a cavity or under driftwood) to fully exposed (as on a sand spit, tundra desert, or rubble). In the subspecies *dresseri*, some birds nest under tangles of fallen dead and also thick stands of live spruces (Gross 1938, Guignion 1968); on some is. in Penobscot Bay, Me., they nest in cow parsnip (*Heracleum maximum*), which grows early; they also show a preference for sites where cover types meet—an "edge effect" (Choate 1966). *S. m. mollissima* goes into forests at some White Sea localities (Gerasimova and Baranova). In his study of *borealis* on the permafrost tundra near C. Dorset, Cooch (1965) found 90% of nests sheltered by rocks or under an overhang of rocks; favored sites were along ridges facing s. or sw., these being well drained and snow-free early. Of 5,700 sites he examined, 40% were within 100 ft. of an area of water while at least 10% were more than 900 ft. from water. In nominate *mollissima* in the w. Soviet arctic (Barents Sea), nest sites were divided arbitrarily into 4 classes, and each illustrated, by Belopolskii (1957) and also Gerasimova and Baranova (1960): **1** covered—beneath tussocks, overhanging rocks, or other shelter, thus concealed from predators and shielded from wind and more or less from rain; **2** half covered—between loose rocks and other objects, but open above and occasionally at the sides, having good protection from predators and sufficient from wind; **3** half open—next to a rock, ledge, shrub, or other object, hence limited protection from predators and wind; and **4** open—on level tundra, or peat, rubble, ledge, or sand, totally unshielded.

The Common Eider has a strong preference for nesting close to a prominence or local landmark—a rock, mound, some driftwood, even an occupied human dwelling. In early May, 1969, at Utholmen, a low island on the w. side of Gotland in the Baltic that is cropped by sheep outside the eider-nesting season, there were 18 incubating eiders within a patch of rotted timbers where a building once had stood; some ♀ ♀ were nearly in contact with one another. In the Belcher Is. in se. Hudson Bay, the birds tend to avoid the areas of barren rock and to be concentrated where soil and vegetation have accumulated in the cracks; 10 nests/25 sq. yds. is not unusual (Freeman 1970). More or less sheltered sites predominate at Kandalaksh Bay (White Sea) and on the Murman coast, but exposed ones at Novaya Zemlya. A breeding unit often appears to consist of fairly to conspicuously evident groupings of nests, plus others more randomly scattered and presumably less favorably located. In a new or "young" colony, probably grouping is more evident, the distribution being nearer even overall when there are additional birds in later years if the colony thrives. There are interesting diagrams showing distribution patterns of nominate *mollissima*, on various is. in the Kandalaksh Reserve in w. White Sea, in Gerasimova and Baranova (1960). Nests are spaced with remarkable evenness, to some extent with the aid of man, over sizable areas on some Icelandic eider farms; see photos in Pettingill (1959a) and D. Munro (1961).

Man-made shelters over eider nests are in use in Iceland, the Faeroes, Fennoscandia, the U.S.S.R., and experimentally in Me. in the U.S. There are various kinds, such as A-frame and lean-to; if flat stones are available, they are used as roofs of stone cubicles. In the absence of adequate natural cover, they protect against aerial predators and the weather. Their relative effectiveness may be roughly comparable to a natural situation in the St. Lawrence estuary, where Milne and Reed (1974) reported hatching success as 15% on open habitat, 30% where considerable vegetation exists, and 36% on wooded islands, i.e., sheltered.

**Reuse of the same site,** or else nesting nearby, has been demonstrated on a large scale with banded birds in the Gulf of Finland, by Grenquist (1965). Cooch found that, of 23 ♀ *borealis* banded at nests in 1955, 18 nested the next year within 50 ft., and 2 more within 100 ft., of their former sites; those that did not actually use old sites but shifted to new ones all nested on the same ridges or beside the same ponds. Late-lingering snowdrifts covered some sites in 1956 that had been used the previous year and this presumably caused some minor shifts. Other evidence of reuse of sites includes: **1** mated pairs often were seen inspecting old nests that still contained last year's down; **2** nests normally are reoccupied if the down is not removed, or the ♀ nests very close to the former site if the down has been removed (Cooch 1965); and **3** in Iceland, Gudmundsson observed "gray" ♀ ♀ driving "brown" ♀ ♀ (he assumed the latter were younger) away from old sites which the latter had occupied. Cooch saw this also in *borealis*. In the Baltic, a one-eyed ♀ nested 14 years in succession under the same juniper (Nordberg 1950). It may be concluded that ♀ ♀ return to the same locality with more constancy than to the identical site.

If the ♀ reoccupies her nest of the previous year, or if a former nest is taken over by any ♀, any weathered, old nest-down still present is useful for covering the eggs before the ♀ begins adding new down. This may be of importance in shielding the eggs from avian predators and, in cold climates or seasons, keeping the first-laid eggs from chilling.

Empty sites, but especially those containing uncovered or partly covered eggs, are a powerful magnet to other ♀ ♀ ready to lay; joint layings (quite commonly to 10, occasionally to 19 eggs) are known and there is competition between (or among) the "owners" for possession of the accumulated eggs. Sometimes 2 nests are very close, the sitters even touching each other. Eiders also lay in nests of other birds—scoters, mergansers, gulls; eiders will use old gull nests and gulls, eider nests; eiders sometimes take possession of gull nests complete with eggs (V. S. Uspenskii 1946). On is. off the Me. coast one finds both eider and Herring Gull eggs in Herring Gull nests, also in eider nests. Eiders have occupied the nests of Barnacle Geese in Spitzbergen.

It should be noted that at least in colder climates there is a difference between a nest used only once and one used repeatedly. At first, if the nest is on turf, the rim of the cavity tends to be flush with the ground. In successive years the rim becomes larger and higher, a mixture of nest down, feathers, plant materials, and anything else (mollusk shells, pebbles, and so on) that the ♀ pulls to the rim from around its perimeter. Thus the ♀ clears a zone around the nest and extending out as far as she can reach while sitting. In nominate *mollissima* in Novaya Zemlya (and as observed by the author in Iceland), an elevated rim gradually develops. The activities of the sitter tend to deepen the cavity and part of the material from within works out toward the rim. After 2 or 3 seasons, the ring of accumulated organic matter begins to decay and form humus. This change, aided by warmth of the sitting bird, accelerates growth of plants at the edge of the rime and this, in turn, provides some shelter from wind and concealment from predators (Belopolskii 1957). The same author stated that the situation is different on the Murman coast, where the nesting eiders are spread out thinly and there are many vacant sites. Most sites are not used for several consecutive seasons. Usually, a bird nests very close to her site of the previous year. An abundance of flea (*Ceratophyllus*) larvae in old sites has been suggested as one of the probable reasons for change, but there must be others.

Especially in warmer parts of the breeding range, where some units are relatively sedentary and the nesting season is longer, a site may be utilized more than once in a season. This results in some apparently anomalous situations, such as a new egg in a nest containing abundant nest down (when a clutch had been removed), or even a clutch with a surplus of nest down because the 2nd ♀ added hers to that already present. In brief, while replacement clutches at new sites have essentially no nest down, the situation is not the same when ♀ ♀ lay their first, or even replacement, clutches in nests lined earlier by other ♀ ♀.

In *borealis*, Cooch found that the final **preparation of the site** normally is not accomplished on the first visit to it and an egg normally is not laid on the first trip unless late in the season or a new nest is constructed. Scouting forays usually precede the laying of the first egg by 2 or 3 days. On the first visit to the site, the old material in the depression is churned up by the ♀'s bill and this permits air to circulate and dry out the site. During preparation for the first egg, and during formation of a new nest, the duck squats on the ground, pushing downward with her breast and scraping backward with her feet; by rotating in this posture, a circular hollow is formed. As observed in nominate *mollissima* in the Farne Is. (Tinbergen 1958), drakes that accompany their mates to the nest site perform typical building movements—squatting on the ground, picking up pieces of grass in the bill and placing them to one side of the body. The drake does not, however, take part in preparation or construction of the actual nest site.

The **eggs** usually **are laid** at rate of 1/day, as determined in at least 4 subspecies. In *borealis*, Cooch (1965) found that laying virtually ceases during inclement weather. As with nest initiation, the duck visits the nest to lay on a rising tide or at high tide. The drake accompanies his mate during laying and remains only a few ft. away from the nest. Immediately after laying, some ♀ ♀ begin a prolonged bout of "nest-building," with sideways movements of the head being performed continuously for many minutes.

All through the laying span, various couples join in little communal groups and "doze", on a slope or on the shore of a pond or the sea. At least at some Icelandic eider farms, a continuation of this activity consists of groups of spaced-out drakes, on higher ground overlooking incubating ♀ ♀ and away from any water, and ♀ ♀ join them if disturbed from their eggs. In nominate *mollissima* and in *dresseri*, and at least into the laying span, copulation still occurs. So does some displaying.

The **nest down** is medium gray-brown, paling to lighter tips and center (illus.: Broley 1950); intermingled feathers typically are rather light brownish with wide and much darker transverse barring (illus.: Witherby 1939, Broley 1950). The duck stands in the nest and inserts her bill in among the feathers of her venter; when the bill is withdrawn, there is down adhering to it; then this is shaken or rubbed off into the nest. This activity continues intermittently for at least several days. Usually it begins after the 3rd egg is laid; that is, the stimulus from seeing the early eggs results in a loosening of the down, which then is preened out (not plucked) and added to the nest. The usual accumulation of down weighs about 18–25 gm. and, in the absence of the ♀, forms a quite bulky covering that surrounds the eggs. In joint layings, the 2nd ♀ may add her down, as well as eggs, and it has been stated by Gerasimova and Baranova (1960) that prebreeding (nonlaying) ♀ ♀ will "adopt" nests and add down. The actions of the ♀, as when settling on the nest or rotating the eggs, result in various extraneous matter becoming worked into the down.

Only at the very end of the incubation period does the ♀ begin to grow any new down on her venter (V. S. Uspenskii 1946). Therefore if, after early loss of her clutch, the ♀ renests at a new site, there is little or no down (but often a considerable number of small feathers).

After the first egg is laid, the duck more or less covers it if loose material is available at the site (there may be none unvegetated turf), the pair returns to water, and the ♀ bathes. Few ♀ ♀ sit on a single egg. There is much individual variation in the time spent on the nest during laying; in general, duration of the visit increases each day until finally the ♀ spends nearly all of her time on the nest. In *borealis* this stage may be reached before the clutch is completed, by most ♀ ♀ after the 3rd egg is laid (Cooch 1965).

In *borealis*, during the first week of **incubating** the ♀ makes short visits to the nearest pond to bathe and drink; apparently she eats little, probably nothing; thereafter she incubates continuously unless frightened from the nest. Perhaps some water is gotten from plants, or during storms when it collects in a depression in the back feathers (Cooch). In Iceland when it rains, according to eider farmers, the incubating eiders drink rainwater that collects in a shallow depression between their wings. (Gudmundsson 1932). In nominate *mollissima* the digestive tract shrinks, with "complete disappearance" of endoparasites from the intestine (M. Belopolskaia, cited in S. Uspenskii 1972). In *dresseri* in Me., there is evidence that ♀ ♀ eat small items of food while egg-laying; the extent of shrinkage of the digestive tract is remarkable, however, and it contains neither food nor live parasites by the end of 5 days' incubation (C. E. Korschgen). If ♀ Common Eiders are in good condition at the start of incubation, evidently they are fully capable of going longer than the entire period without ingesting food. Minus food, probably they can maintain themselves best if they can get fresh (rather than salt) water during any off-duty periods. Tinbergen (1958) observed nominate *mollissima* that became so weak that they abandoned their nests, even clutches of pipped eggs. He wrote that they had to stop and rest at intervals when on their walk to the sea. Even healthy birds, however, have "rest stops" when on their way to water, as though a drive to incubate temporarily was ascendant over a desire to drink. Again *borealis*: by the 2nd week, when incubating continuously, there is a change in behavior when ♀ ♀ are disturbed; instead of fleeing and remaining absent for a time, they would not fly far and would return and alight very close to their nests while uttering harsh grating croaks of a sort not heard at other times (Cooch). They defecated a liquid when getting off their nests.

**Defecation at the nest** If the duck is frightened she does not cover her clutch, but on taking wing defecates a green, oily liquid on or close to her nest; it has a very bad odor and is repulsive to canines, yet it does not prevent the taking of eggs by foxes. It dries to a powder and falls off. The excrement of the ♀ at other times than during incubation is firm, cylindrical, gritty, and about 25–40 mm. long, as described for *dresseri* by Beetz (1916). Nest fouling does not deter avian predators such as gulls and ravens.

Common Eider **eggs** are large and moderately variable in both size and **shape**— typically subelliptical; they av. larger, but proportionately are less elongated, than those of the King Eider. Since the former is mostly colonial, many large series of eggs have been measured and only a portion of the extant data are referred to below. Egg **color** usually is a grayed "olive," with yellowish or greenish cast, rarely a quite vivid green or clear bluish; generally they are unmarked, but some have obscurely defined slightly darker blotches or mottling. The shell is quite smooth, with little luster, but some have a slight sheen when fresh.

**Egg measurements** Schönwetter's (1961) compilation included 5 series, 1 each for 5 subspecies, with combined total of 769 eggs; in the different series, av. length varies from 75.8 to 78.9 mm. and breadth from 50.2 to 51.9 mm. Part of his data are included below.

*borealis*—76 eggs "in various collections" length av. 75.4 mm. (73.2–83) and breadth 50.4 (46–53) (Bent 1925). A sample of 103 eggs taken in 1934 near Hopedale, Labrador, av. 77.07 × 50.87 (Gross 1937).

*dresseri*—1 egg each from 20 clutches (1 Me., 1 New Bruns., 3 N.S., 12 Que., 3 s. Labrador) **size** length av. 76.71 ± 3.06 mm., breadth 51.64 ± 1.43, radii of curvature of ends 20.21 ± 1.16 and 13.75 ± 1.09; **shape** elongation 1.49 ± 0.055, bicone −0.027, and asymmetry +0.186 (FWP). For 59 eggs "in various collections," Bent (1925) gave length av. 76 mm. (65–83.5) and breadth 50.7 (41.5–54.8).

*sedentaria*—from Robertson Bay in Belcher Is., 1960, mean and standard error: 71 eggs length 75–89 mm., mean 80.8, SE 1.174, breadth 50–55, mean 52.9, SE 0.597 (Freeman 1970).

*islandica*—188 eggs from Iceland length av. 76.2 mm. (69.5–86.2) and breadth 52 (47–54) (Gudmundsson 1932). From Spitzbergen and Bear I., 167 eggs length av. 77 mm. (67.5–89) and breadth 49.94 (46.5–51.5), meas. by le Roi (Hartert 1920b).

*v-nigra*—1 egg each from scattered localities (mostly in Alaska) **size** length av. 76.24 ± 2.62 mm., breadth 50.38 ± 1.31, radii of curvature of ends 19.16 ± 1.19 and 12.01 ± 1.28; **shape** elongation 1.51 ± 0.041, bicone −0.057, and asymmetry +0.216 (FWP). Eighty-five eggs in U.S. National Museum and Bent collections length av. 75.9 (74.5–86.5) and breadth 50.4 (47–52) (Bent 1925).

S. m. *mollissima*—for meas. and wt. of large series from 4 different localities in w. U.S.S.R., see Gerasimova and Baranova (1960); the largest eggs were from the Kandalaksh Reserve (White Sea), the smallest from Novaya Zemlya. The statistics for 730 eggs from the Estonian portion of Gulf of Finland are length av. 77.24 mm. (67.8–94.9) and breadth 51.50 (47.5–60.5) (Onno, in Kumari 1966); the averages are nearly identical with those for a composite sample of 400 from w. U.S.S.R., Spitzbergen, n. Europe, and Greenland (includes nominate *mollissima*, *islandica*, and perhaps *borealis*) given by Schönwetter, namely 77 × 51.5 mm.

There is some evidence, from nominate *mollissima*, that egg size varies in different colonies in the same geographical area in the same year, also at the same colony in different years, also between early and late clutches in the same year at the same colony. It would seem, then, that existing data from various parts of the range of the species are too inexact to permit any conclusion as to whether there is appreciable geographical variation in egg size.

*faeroeensis*—14 eggs meas. by Jourdain (in Hartert 1920b): av. 78.85 × 51.89 mm. (max. 85.7 × 54, min. 72.7 × 52.5 and 77.8 × 49.5). Hartert commented that these eggs, from the smallest Common Eiders, were in no way smaller than those of larger Common Eiders. In a clutch of 4, length varied 71–75 mm. and breadth was 49, the av. being 73.3 × 49 (Schiøler 1926).

**Egg weight** In *dresseri* a fresh egg weighs about 120 ± 10 gm. and this will serve as a rough figure for other Common Eiders. See Gross (1938) for meas. and wt. of individual eggs in 10 clutches. He stated that the loss of wt. during incubation is about 14% of fresh wt. In *v-nigra*, Rutilevskii (1957) gave some figures for percentage of wt. of sitter that her clutch comprised, unfortunately without indication of how long the ♀ ♀ (and eggs) had been losing wt. during incubation. Part of his data: ♀ 1,837 gm., her 6 eggs 518 gm. (28%); ♀ 1,629, her 5 eggs 414.5 (25.4%); ♀ 2,095, her 4 eggs 397.5 (19%); and ♀ 1,960, her 3 eggs 258 (13.2%). Examples of *dresseri* in Me., with days of incubation: ♀ 1.53 kg. (4 days) and 6 eggs 724 gm. (47.32%); ♀ 1.75 kg. (5–8 days) and 6 eggs 736 gm. (42.06%); ♀ 1.76 kg. (10 days) and 5 eggs 612 gm. (34.77%); and ♀ 1.60 kg. (15 days) and 4 eggs 452 gm. (28.25%) (C. E. Korschgen).

**Clutch size** in *borealis* near C. Dorset on Baffin I., in 1,598 clutches (5,496 eggs): 48 (of 1 egg), 211 (of 2), 520 (3), 669 (4), 118 (5), 24 (6), and 8 (7), the av. for the combined samples from the different areas being 3.44 eggs/clutch (Cooch 1965). See his paper for tabulation of data for *islandica* (Iceland), *borealis* (Payne Bay within Ungava Bay, his own data from C. Dorset), and *dresseri* (3 areas in St. Lawrence estuary and Gulf). Near Hopedale, Labrador, in 1934, av. size of "nearly 100" clutches was 4, smallest was 2 and largest 7 (Gross 1937). In the Upernarvik Dist. of w. Greenland in 1965, most common clutch size was 4 eggs, the av. for 1,815 clutches being 3.4 (Joensen and Preuss 1972).

Cooch found that, in *borealis*, clutches begun earlier at is. in the C. Dorset area were larger than those begun later; even a day's delay in inception of laying made a difference, as it does also in Blue/Snow Geese, small Canada Geese, Brant, and some other waterfowl. Av. clutch size differed from one island to another in the same year; the snow cover remained later on one than another, possibly older ♀♀ lay larger clutches, etc. (Cooch). The many variables hinder any attempt to establish geographical variation in clutch size, using extant data.

*dresseri*—commonly lays 3–5 eggs. Various studies were cited by Paynter (1951); from these plus his own data he concluded that there was a trend of increase in clutch size from Penobscot Bay, Me. (3.25 ± .10) to the N. Shore of the Gulf of St. Lawrence (4.04 ± .03), but the matter needs further study. One of his conclusions was that there was no difference between mean clutch size of nests that produce young and those that do not, but in a later study of 1,030 nests (data for 2 seasons combined) in Penobscot Bay, Choate (1967) reported that clutches of 4 or more eggs were more successful in producing ducklings than smaller ones. The latter found that av. clutch size varied among is. in the same year and on the same island in successive years (1964 and 1965), the variation between is. in the same year being somewhat greater than from one year to the next. He cited Hildén (1964a), who pointed out (from study of nominate *mollissima*) that differences in the number of ♀♀ nesting for the first time could be a reason for yearly fluctuations in clutch size at a locality. In full clutches of 2–8 eggs at islets in the St. Lawrence estuary in 1966, mean clutch size was 4.33 eggs in 315 nests (Guignion 1968).

*sedentaria*—in 1960 at Robertson Bay, Belcher Is., 61 clutches on June 21: 2 (of 1 egg), 6 (of 2), 5 (3), 8 (4), 22 (5), 17 (6), and 1 (7), av. 4.59 eggs/clutch (Freeman 1970).

*v-nigra*—on the nw. Canadian arctic mainland and nearby islets, generally 5 eggs/clutch, rarely more, in total of over 1,000 eggs taken (MacFarlane 1891). On Amchitka I. in the Aleutians, in 1956, 3 eggs (in 13 nests) and 4 (in 20) were the commonest clutch sizes in 65 nests (Kenyon 1961). In New Siberian Is., 3–6 eggs, av. 4.4 in 18 clutches (Rutilevskii 1957).

*islandica*—in Spitzbergen, on one island most clutches in over 200 nests were of 3 eggs, none had more than 4, and many others had been emptied by gulls; on another island, where gulls were killed by the human inhabitants, over 100 nests had an av. clutch size of 7 and some had 9 eggs (Wrigley 1964). [One suspects that, on the first island, early eggs may have been gathered for human consumption.] For an important discussion of clutch size vs. predation in Spitzbergen, see Ahlén and Andersson (1970); they reported that evidently the av. clutch is 4.5–5 eggs in undisturbed colonies and that other authors have reported even higher averages; in 19 ♀♀ taken, the av. number of eggs they had laid was 6.2 "until they were collected."

At Bear I., an islet in a lake had almost 200 nests and clutch size almost invariably was

5 (Bertram and Lack 1933). For Iceland, Hantzsch (1905) made the general statement that most first clutches are of 5–7 eggs, with 3–4 in replacement sets. Usual clutch size there is 5–6 (G. Timmermann 1949). But Gudmundsson (1932) gave normal clutch size as 6–7, with less than 5 rare and over 10 presumably the product of more than 1 female. At eider farms, according to regulations, any excess over 4 can be and often are taken for food by the landowners.

For low-arctic w. Greenland, Salomonsen (1972) gave an av. of 3.79 eggs for 2,059 "undisturbed" clutches in 1954.

*S. m. mollissima*—in European U.S.S.R. clutch size varies in different years at the same locality. At Seven Is. Reserve (Murman coast) 1940–58 inclusive, the low figure was 3.28 eggs/clutch (904 clutches) in 1958, ranging to a high of 4.28 (1,500 nests) in 1941 (Gerasimova and Baranova 1960). The figures in Belopolskii (1957) show a decrease northward in av. number of eggs/clutch from 5.15 in the White Sea to 3.52 in Novaya Zemlya. In the Baltic, in Estonia, the variation 1958–65 inclusive was from 4.56 ± 0.10 (80 clutches) in 1961 to 5.00 ± 0.19 (25 clutches) in 1965; 4–6 eggs were commonest by far (Onno, in Kumari 1966). For many detailed data for 10 years, from Finnish localities in the Baltic, see Grenquist (1965); he discussed some of the factors influencing clutch size.

As pointed out earlier, Common Eider nests may contain some eggs that are incubated much longer than others; that is, a ♀ may appropriate a partly incubated clutch, add to it, and incubate the accumulated eggs.

The following may serve as a rough indication as to when **full first clutches** may be expected.

*borealis*—C. Dorset region of Baffin I., laying started June 19, 1955, and continued 29 days; and it started June 23, 1956, and continued 25 days (Cooch 1965). Near Hopedale, Labrador, on July 6, 1934, the vast majority of eggs were fresh or not long incubated (Gross 1937). In high-arctic Greenland, nesting is about a month later than to the Southward in low-arctic (Salomonsen 1972), which probably would mean full clutches at high latitudes around the third week in July.

*dresseri*—in Penobscot Bay, Me., there may be as much as 2 weeks' difference between inception of laying at different islands; at the earliest places, clutches are completed throughout a span of perhaps 20 days beginning about April 18; cold weather and late snow may retard laying at all stations. At least at some stations there are 2 peaks of laying, the 2nd about 2 weeks after the first. See Choate (1966) for further details. Generally speaking, most ♀ ♀ have full first clutches by some time in the 3rd week of May. At Kent I., New Bruns., laying begins some time in the first half of May, with peak in June. In the inner St. Lawrence the entire span is about May 10–June 25.

*sedentaria*—in 1960 at the Belcher Is., Freeman (1970) calculated that laying started around the end of the first week in June and was mostly finished by the first week in July. However, since he assumed a 28-day incubation period (actually it is 24–25), laying must have occurred somewhat later. At Chesterfield Inlet there were young a few days old on July 20, indicating laying by mid-June (Savile 1951). At Gasket Shoal I. in James Bay, first eggs pipping July 9 (Manning and Coates 1952).

*v-nigra*—one might expect that clutches would be completed fairly early in warmer parts of the Aleutians. There is very little information, however. At Amchitka, laying begins about June 8–10 and continues into late June (Kenyon 1961). Beyond, in Bering Sea, Chuckchee Sea, E. Siberian Sea, and Beaufort Sea, the seasons evidently vary greatly. At northerly stations in a "normal" season, full clutches may be expected beginning in the middle third of June, but in tardy seasons considerably later. At Kotelny I. (New Siberian group), the earliest date for a large clutch is 6 eggs on June 26, 1948, with most clutches completed by July 5, and span of laying being about June 21–July 18 (Rutilevskii 1957).

*islandica*—in Iceland, clutches are completed from about May 20 until well into June, depending on locality and season. At those farms where there are thousands of pairs of eiders, the birds arrive and come ashore over a considerable period of time, hence clutches are initiated over a span of time. Spitzbergen—early June in sw. part, later elsewhere. Bear I.—2nd week in June or later. In low-arctic w. Greenland—about the last week in June.

*S. m. mollissima*—in parts of Britain, the Netherlands, and Denmark, many clutches completed in latter third of April. In the Baltic, at the beginning of May at some stations, a week later at others, and seasonal variation. In Kandalaksh Day (White Sea) and w. Murman coast (Barents Sea) by about mid-May; in e. Murman about May 15–June 10, depending on year; on warmer parts of sw. Novaya Zemlya, about June 10–15 when ice conditions permit (Gerasimova and Baranova 1960); at Franz Josef Land, about June 15–25 unless the season is late (Belopolskii 1957).

*faeroeensis*—clutches completed from end of May to mid-June (Salomonsen, in A. S. Jensen et al. 1934).

The duck's **routine during incubation** is variable, as the following reports indicate.

In *borealis* near C. Dorset, Baffin I., as previously noted, the ♀'s absences become briefer and then cease, so that incubation is constant after the first week.

In *dresseri* in New Bruns., the ♀ leaves for long periods, to 3½ hrs., when hatching is very close (Gross 1938). [The possibility of reaction to human interference must be kept in mind.]

In *islandica* in Iceland, where the birds are adjusted to man and predators are more or less controlled, the ♀ leaves the nest at least once each 24 hrs. to drink fresh water and bathe. As observed at a farm in Dyrafjord during the time when drakes still were ashore: between nests and ponds there was a steady procession of birds, on foot and on the wing. Mostly they were in pairs (mates), walking, "stopping frequently to crouch and rest, as if the exercise were too strenuous. At the ponds the birds first drank and later bathed, but they did not feed" (Pettingill 1959a). There is nothing for them to eat in these meltwater ponds. On the nesting turf at this locality in 1972, there were a few score of little patches of weathered ground-up mollusk shells; presumably the eiders had defecated these earlier when the first came ashore. The eiders were not seen to defecate while afloat on these ponds, nor was there any evidence of fecal matter in suspension in the water or on the mud on the bottom (Palmer 1973). Icelandic eider farmers state (correctly) that the birds do not eat while ashore.

In Spitzbergen in early July, 18 incubating ♀♀ were watched continuously for 48 hrs. and not one left the nest (Ahlén and Andersson 1970).

Nominate *mollissima*. At Inner Farne (Northumberland, England), the ♀ left the nest usually every 2nd or 3rd day, "but only went to drink" (Tinbergen 1958). At Forvie

(Aberdeenshire, Scotland), apparently they stay on the nest for many days, if not the whole incubation period (Milne 1963). The latter was of the opinion that there was little or no feeding for at least 20 days after incubation was begun; toward the very end, there were remains of *Mytilus* and *Littorina* in the fecal liquid. The pattern appears to be similar in *dresseri* (C. E. Korschgen).

In Finland (Baltic Sea), usual absence is 1–2 hrs./day, but when incubation is advanced it is more of the order of ½ hr. (G. Bergman 1939). At Finnish localities, 1960–64 inclusive, 482 ♀ ♀ weighed during the "end-phase" of incubation av. 1,592 ± 139 gm. (Grenquist 1965), which is about 1 kg. less than when they first come ashore.

In Onezh Bay in the White Sea, the ♀ has an off-duty period of, at first, up to several hrs. in each 24, but duration of absence diminishes as incubation advances. The duck goes to water (where at first she is joined by the drake) to drink and bathe, at maximum low tide. Flint (1954), who used an automatic recorder to determine this schedule, and not on any one ♀ for the full incubation period, also reported that there is shrinkage of the digestive tract as a result of partial starvation. The alimentary tracts of nesting ♀ ♀ (collected) showed that, even on the 25th day of incubation, shells of *Littorina* occur; he stated that these, after ingestion, are retained only a brief time, measured at most in hours.

And at Kandalaksh Bay in the White Sea, early in incubation, the ♀ leaves the nest 2–3 times/day for a total of 1½-2½ hrs. and goes away quite a distance on the water; in the middle of incubation she leaves for 1½ hours; on the last day she does not leave (Gerasimova and Baranova 1960). These authors discussed the activities of the ♀ at considerable length and cited variations in routine, including conflicting reports on whether the off-duty ♀ ingests any food.

When nesting in captivity, the ♀ "never or rarely takes food," even if a constant supply is provided close by (St. Quintin, in Millais 1913b).

In wild colonies, if the duck is flushed from her eggs, she tries to get back to them fairly soon. Yet in the Gulf of Bothnia, Hildén (1964a) considered the Common Eider to be the waterfowl species most likely to desert; sometimes nests were deserted when the ♀ was flushed only once.

At an Icelandic eider farm in Dyrafjord, during the time when drakes still were ashore, as noted in 1972, often there was considerable commotion when a duck (followed by her mate) went to drink and bathe. As she walked among the other nesters, she made Chin-lifting and threatening movements. Various drakes and ducks responded by leaving their nests and gathering around her like a coterie of followers. Some would drop out and return to their mates; others continued on with her to water. The duck enters a pond, drinks, Wing-flaps, and immediately bathes. Her mate remains close by, but the others swim away, some soon Splash-bathe, and eventually they return singly to their sitting mates.

The **drake's routine** also is variable. In *dresseri*, Gross (1938) claimed that the ♂ never approaches the nest, but may linger on the sea and, usually at high tide, come to the shore to rest and preen. This may be explained either in terms of incomplete observations or, more likely, frequent interference by the observer, since the drake, except where persecuted and therefore shy, accompanies his mate during site hunting and the laying of each egg. In colonies undisturbed by man, at least some drakes tend to continue for a while to keep station close to their mates when the latter return to the nests to incubate; if there is even occasional disturbance by man, the drakes tend to stay on the shore or the sea as long as they remain in the vicinity. But at eider farms in Iceland, where such predators as gulls and ravens are discouraged by use of guns and lethal drugs and the eiders are adjusted to man's presence, drakes keep station ashore beside their mates for approximately the first 10 days of incubation.

The variations in pattern appear to be responses to different levels of predation and disturbance, with temperature also an influence. In wild colonies, with gulls constantly coursing overhead, the ♀ ♀ evidently tend to sit close and long, especially in cold weather. In absence of human interference, the drakes may come ashore for a time. There are degrees of response, the limit being at some eider farms where there is reduced predation, a conditioning to man's presence by at least scores of generations of eiders, and conveniently located fresh water. In this optimal situation, both sexes drink daily during their respective "starvation" periods ashore and the drake keeps close company with his mate until very shortly before he departs on molt migration.

It is well known that some ♀ ♀ , on being flushed from their eggs, have a distraction display ("feign injury"); they also splash along on the water if disturbed when with a young brood. At an eider farm, in the period when both sexes were ashore, some individuals (both sexes) retreat if approached, others remain at the nest even when approached closely (and some ♀ ♀ can be lifted from their eggs), and still others are aggressive. The drake points his bill toward the observer, with head lowered, puffs up his feathers (including his cheeks), spreads his tail, and opens his wings slightly. If further disturbed, or even sometimes without this preliminary display, the drake sometimes rears up and Wing-flaps before retreating. It is more common, however, for the drake to retreat and for the duck to get off her eggs, rear up, and Wing-flap. The double flap produces a startling sound, more muffled in the duck than in the drake.

It is often overlooked that the drakes eat nothing for a span of nearly 2 weeks when they are ashore (as at eider farms) and little, if anything, when they spend the corresponding period nearby on the sea. In this span, in nominate *mollissima*, drakes lose 200–300 gm. of wt.

In nominate *mollissima* in w. U.S.S.R., time and again "young" ♀ ♀ were trapped on unattended clutches, while starting to add their own nest down and to incubate the eggs already present (V. S. Uspenskii 1946). From this it may be inferred that 1 prebreeders, although incapable of producing eggs, have a drive to incubate; 2 that the deposition of nest down can antedate the ability to produce eggs; and 3 it may be to the disadvantage of the rightful owner to be absent from the nest when there are prebreeding ♀ ♀ in the vicinity.

The incubating eider turns her eggs 20–24 times/24 hrs. (Gerasimova and Baranova 1960).

There is a distinction between loss of an incomplete clutch, with the ♀ laying the remainder elsewhere ("continuation laying"), and a true **replacement clutch,** laid after a full clutch is lost. The elapsed time, or so-called renesting interval, before a new clutch is begun is variable. In *borealis*, if both down and eggs were removed, the ♀ prepared a new site, usually within a few ft. of the original one, and in 12 renestings clutch size av. 2.33 eggs (Cooch 1965).

**Incubation period**   24–25 days, i.e., shorter than the 28-day figure usually given. In nominate *mollissima* in U.S.S.R., it is 25–29 days (Flint 1955), 25–28 days (Gerasimova and Baranova 1960), and in the Baltic in Estonia in 6 nests the variation was 24–28 days, av. 26 (Onno, in Kumari 1966). The period is said to be a little shorter in harsher climates, because ♀ ♀ sit closer there (Gerasimova and Baranova 1960). In *dresseri* in Me., the av. period for 11 clutches was 26 days and there was some evidence from 18 other clutches that often it may be shorter (Choate 1966). In the same subspecies in the St. Lawrence estuary, it was 23 days at 1 nest, 24 at 8, 25 (11), 26 (19), 27 (9), 28 (7), and even as long as 30 days (Guignion 1968). The "normal duration" in an incubator under conditions suitable for hatching domestic duck eggs is 24–25 days; details in Rolnik (1943). In marked eggs of *borealis,* invariably the first one laid was the first to hatch; a 7-egg clutch hatched in a span of 24 hrs., 2- and 3-egg clutches within 4 hrs. (Cooch 1965).

If the nest becomes damp, with lower surface of eggs cooler than surface in contact with the sitter, incubation is slowed or, if a great difference (say 15°), the embryo is killed (Gerasimova and Baranova 1960). The same authors discussed growth of the embryo. Unhatched eggs left in nests are eaten quickly by gulls, crows, ravens, jaegers, and so on. After such predation, it is difficult to distinguish between deserted and destroyed nests.

**Nesting success**   In sw. Spitzbergen the eiders nesting in Arctic Tern (*Sterna paradisaea*) colonies were most successful, to 93%, dropping to 63% in scattered nesters away from terns. Also, eiders in dense parts of eider colonies were more efficient in defending against predators, notably the Glaucous Gull (*Larus hyperboreus*), with 83% success, and only 40% in scattered nesters. The number of nests that survive, also the number of eggs in them (clutch size) varied depending on level of predation. From a total of about 3,300 pairs of eiders and total annual production of approximately 20,500 eggs, only about 5,500 eggs (27%) hatched. Almost all the difference, about 15,000 eggs, was consumed by predators. (From Ahlén and Andersson 1970.)

On an island in Penobscot Bay, Me., the eiders suffered very little nest predation from gulls, presumably because terns also were present, but eider nest desertion was higher than usual because of harassment by the terns. Eiders can have good hatching success even in colonies shared with gulls, provided nesting cover is good and there is no human disturbance. (Data from H. L. Mendall.)

When the eggs are pipped and **hatching** is imminent, the duck becomes restless and utters croaking calls, as described for *dresseri* by Gross (1938). In nominate *mollissima* in the Orkneys, D. J. Robertson (1929) reported that additional ♀ ♀ gather around a nest containing hatching eggs or newly hatched young, and they "escort" mother and brood to water. In many cases, presumably the "aunts" are failed breeders that still have a drive to brood or to associate with ducklings. (Many prebreeding ♀ ♀ depart early to molt, before many clutches hatch.) In the Farnes, Tinbergen (1958) observed as many as 3 or 4 "aunts" gathering about the mother at the nest. If a duckling came near an "aunt," the latter would back away, or occasionally peck at the downy bird; the mother would make aggressive movements and keep the "aunts" a "couple of feet" away. A family (duck and brood) may depart by itself or with "aunts," or several families may combine and have not only mothers but also an escort of "aunts." The mothers lead, croaking. The young follow, even among boulders, or may tumble down cliffs 10 meters high (V. S. Uspenskii 1946).

In Spitzbergen, on the trek to water, if a gull approaches, the ♀ stops, utters a repeated croaking, and assumes a defense posture: wings out, tail spread, head pointed toward the attacker and moved up and down repeatedly. The young rush under her and often she settles down on them. The "aunts" adopt the same posture. For further details of defense against the Glaucous Gull by eiders with young, both ashore and afloat, see Ahlén and Andersson (1970).

Ducklings on their 2nd day, following the ♀, do not hesitate to launch into surf; they go up the slope of a wave, precisely gauge when the crest will break, and dive just beforehand and reappear after the crest has moved on (V. S. Uspenskii 1946). The usual pattern is for ♀ ♀ with broods or aggregations of ducklings to seek sheltered shallow waters—coves, inlets, quiet bays, where the ducklings can obtain food readily, especially at low tide.

The development of young and **vocalization by the young**, plus some reactions of the ♀, are summarized here from Driver's (1960) study of *borealis*.

Beginning before hatching, the duckling pushes its bill through the shell membrane into the air space in the large end of the egg. Beginning then, it has 1 a "brooding note"—monosyllabic, showing contentment when brooded, and 2 a "complaint"—an insistent disyllable, 2nd syllable higher and rising, uttered when the duckling is uncomfortable.

After hatching: 1a "cohesion call"—4 or 5 ascending notes, at frequent intervals, in maintenance of contact with brood mates; 1b same with upward nod is used as a greeting; 2 contentment notes—as cohesion call but faster, high pitched, and more monotonic. When the young are feeding in the water, these are the 2 most common acoustic signals.

3 A distress call—monosyllabic, insistent pipping, as in other Anatidae, when danger threatens; it alerts the others, including the ♀ parent. (The latter has an "alarm whirr"—descending, throaty, whirring, and the young respond by banding together close to her and they remain thus as long as she continues to call.) If danger is very imminent, the duckling "crash dives," going under in about $1/5$ sec. This dive, in modified form, is used in food getting; it evolves into a "juvenile feeding dive" (a smooth forward plunge) and, at age about 3½ weeks, is succeeded by the "adult feeding dive," a kick forward and down from a head-under position (the young bird is heavy anteriorly at this age). When the primary feathers have grown, the bird "flies" when submerged, the wings being out from the body but not spread. There is also 4 a "question or investigatory note"—a thin ascending monosyllable about 1 sec., uttered when in a puzzling situation, such as at sight of a stranger on the horizon.

**Travel** In *borealis*, Cooch (1965) reported that the ♀ often takes the brood to a freshwater pond on their natal island and they stay there for 2–3 days (they are absorbing yolk and do not have to forage very actively) and then go via the outlet or overland to the sea. Others go directly to the sea. Within a week after hatching, gatherings of many young and relatively few ♀ ♀ traveled from the nesting islands to tidal pools along the mainland coast. They remained there for nearly a month, then moved out to the vicinity of reefs and islands. By this time, the preflight young may have gone up to 50 mi.

67

from where they hatched (Cooch, letter). It follows that eiders can nest some distance from areas best suited for the growing young.

At Aethey, in Isafjord, nw. Iceland, the writer was told that many young first are led to ponds on the island and that, later, the trek to the sea is made rapidly in the boreal night when the sun is low.

In a sense, the young are quite independent of mature birds beginning early in the downy stage. For example, they eat different food from that of their mothers and "aunts," i.e., at first small (including various soft) items—amphipods, small *Littorina*, and so on, and eventually mussels (*Mytilus*) when they have the strength to utilize them.

**Growth** There are 2 published graphs of wt. vs. age, both apparently compiled and not specific information from particular known-age individuals. That of Belopolskii (1957) shows a rather even wt. increase to "adult" wt. at 80 days; in that of Pethon (1967) there is a pronounced curve, to about 1,700 gm. in approximately 10 weeks, then it levels off. In captivity, the young reach "adult size" in 80–90 days (Gerasimova 1954, cited in Belopolskii 1957).

**Crèches** or flotillas (aggregates of ducklings), with and without adults in attendance, have been discussed by various authors; the subject may be outlined as follows:

1 Broods when still ashore, ready to go to water, may combine. Thus there is a potential for more crèches to form in a dense colony on open terrain at peak of hatching. Crèches also form on the sea, where one or more ducklings may leave one group to join another, different groups may combine, or a group may disperse among other groups. The opportunities for such interchange must vary depending on number of young in an area. Size of crèches is negatively affected by predation, also adverse weather when the ducklings are small, and positively by any increments from later-hatching broods.

2 Ashore, failed-breeding and even incubating ♀♀ within visual range evidently respond to behavioral (including vocal) changes in a ♀ at the time her brood hatches. In response, they join the ♀ and brood—become "aunts"—and "escort" the duck and brood to water. Incubating ♀♀ then return to their nests. Apparently there is a limit to the number of accepted "aunts," about 3 or 4. On the sea, visual response to the behavior of a mother who is defending her charges from a predatory gull results in ♀♀ swimming or even flying to join in the defense.

3 Among ducklings, a social drive is strong, with aggression evidently lacking. But among (or between) ♀♀ there appears to be conflict for dominance when broods combine. Rather commonly, a ♀ may switch from one brood to another as long as she remains in their vicinity.

4 Not all young are in crèches. Broods, attended and unattended, are common. In Icelandic waters the young broods tend to remain separated at first (F. Gudmundsson). In the Gulf of Bothnia, single broods tend to remain as such; crèches tend to be less stable in size (Hildén 1964a). In the St. Lawrence estuary, groups are small and the parental bond appears to be long maintained—to 7–8 weeks after hatching—and a ♀ with a brood or crèche has less time to devote to feeding if there are no "aunts" to share guard duties (Bédard and Munro *Fourth An. Que. Waterfowl Seminar* 1972).

5 In the U.S.S.R., clutches have been taken (the wild mothers then renest) and hatched in an incubator; then the young were released at age 2–3 days to join wild

groups, i.e. to increase the total number of young (L. Belopolskii, in Kumari 1968). But in Scotland, attempts to introduce ducklings into groups of eiders and young failed unless an adult ♀ also was released with the brood (Milne 1963).

**6** Most crèches of preflight young contain 20–30 or fewer individuals, but some contain up to 50 and a few at least 150 birds. The size of crèches may not relate closely to number of young in an area.

**7** The length of time that a ♀ accompanies ducklings after nesting successfully must be highly variable. If she finishes her "starvation period" in good condition, renewal of molting is not imminent, and food is available, then presumably she may remain longer. If she nests late, is in a weakened condition by time of hatching, and/or renewal of molting is imminent, presumably she leaves sooner. In ne. Scotland, based on marked ♀ nominate *mollissima*, Gorman and Milne (1972) determined that adult ♀ ♀ with crèches usually were individuals that recently had hatched young and that there was a constant turnover of these ♀ ♀; an individual remained with the young, on the average, only 4 days. Then the ♀ ♀ joined other groups of adults. In *dresseri* in Me., evidently a ♀ may leave her brood at any time after they reach water. Both ♀ and young can remain in the same locality (there is food for both) and ♀ ♀ begin feeding at or even shortly before they lead their broods to water.

**8** That it is usual for "aunts" to be ♀ prebreeders (H. F. Lewis, in Terres 1961) is unlikely, although some may fill this role early in the season before they move away to molt.

**9** Early in the hatching season, drakes that still are present may swim near broods or crèches and even display to some extent to the attending ♀ ♀, but they are not known to participate in defense of the young against gulls.

**10** As summer advances, unattended groups of preflight young, often composed of birds of assorted sizes, become increasingly common. They swim in very close formation, appearing to be in contact, forming a dark patch on the water. On a falling tide they move to sheltered shallows to feed, then out again on a rising tide. In the life of the individual this is the earliest segregation (by age class) and it continues long after flight is attained, into winter in many instances.

A drive for social contact, very often ascendant over maintenance of family grouping, is widespread among sea ducks, mergansers, and some other waterfowl. Observations of marked young eiders in ne. Scotland suggest that the crèche system has more survival value for breeding ♀ ♀ than for their offspring; the former go to a safe location and replenish the body reserves consumed during incubation (Milne 1969). The pattern of molt migration in waterfowl in general relates to adequate food plus the safety of the birds, whether breeders or prebreeders.

In the Common Eider there are very high **losses of young** in most years, near-disaster in some years, and occasional years of high survival; there is compensation in that those that do survive have a comparatively long av. life span. This pattern, which is characteristic of various waterfowl that nest in boreal climates, applies in some measure to Common Eiders that nest in milder climates.

**Age at first flight** seems not to have been determined from marked wild birds; the range of guesses and close estimates varies from 6 to 12½ weeks. Captive-reared young "are full feathered on the 40th day, but traces of down remain on head and neck.

Primaries still undeveloped" (Lord William Percy, in an addendum in Millais 1913b). In *borealis*, Driver (1960) inferred that the primaries are fully developed at "age about 8 weeks" and Cooch (1965) estimated 60 days for attaining flight. In *v-nigra*, Rutilevskii (1957) stated that the young can fly well in 40–45 days, which is too short a period. In nominate *mollissima*, estimates include 75 days (Britain), 70–75 (e. Murman coast), and 60–65 (Novaya Zemlya), yet proof is lacking that the period is shorter in higher latitudes. Pending accurate determination, a tentative figure—and no doubt there is considerable individual variation—is 60–65 days in the wild. Perhaps some additional time is needed after first flying before the young can begin extensive migratory travel. RSP

SURVIVAL   Mean annual adult survival rate, based on published Swedish and Dutch and unpublished British recoveries, was estimated at 0.61 by Boyd (in Le Cren and Holdgate 1962). In a study of eiders in Danish waters, the mean annual mortality (including hunting kill) among "adults" was found to be about 20% (Paludan 1962). In Denmark in winters from 1950–51 to 1959–60 inclusive, the hunting kill rose (unevenly) from an estimated 22,800 to 109,100, being very much greater than the kill in Sweden and Finland combined. Yet the eiders thrived and well over a half million (mostly Baltic) birds reportedly entered or traversed Danish waters (Paludan). Since the Baltic birds have continued to thrive in the face of hunting kill plus "natural" mortality, the survival rate of 1st-year birds must be greater there than appears to be the case elsewhere.

In the St. Lawrence estuary, preliminary estimates, from band-recovery data, suggest an av. annual mortality of 20% for ♀♀ of breeding age (Reed 1972). In a later study there, from an estimated 73,500 eggs, about 6,000 ducklings were thought to have survived to flight age (Milne and Reed 1974).

The rate of survival of eiders through their 1st year apparently fluctuates quite widely around a low av. figure. This may be especially true in higher latitudes; in a "good" year the birds recoup from several "bad" ones. The highest losses evidently occur in the downy stage, especially in the first week posthatching. In Iceland, where there is considerable local predator control and no hunting kill, 5%–10% survival of 1st-year birds is considered a good year (F. Gudmundsson). In Scotland the figure is less than 5% in most years, but much higher in occasional favorable years (Milne 1969). In Me., where *dresseri* has been increasing very markedly, aerial censuses in spring in 2 years gave an av. figure of about 8% identified as "subadult" individuals (H. L. Mendall).

The pattern of losses from natural mortality (not hunting kill) was stated in general terms by Gordon et al. (1964) as follows: more "young" die than "adults," adult ♀♀ more often than ♂♂ (losses of ♀♀ of breeding age are heavy in the postnesting period), and deaths of "immatures" (meaning beyond the duckling stage) are high in Feb.–May prior to age 1 year. RSP

HABITS (Of the species.)   A trend toward symposia devoted to a single waterfowl species is exemplified by the conference on Common Eider held in Estonia in May, 1966, with full proceedings edited by Kumari (1968). Another (without formal publication) was held at Laval University in Que. on April 18, 1972. There is much literature on the species, in various languages; only a few topics of general interest can be touched upon here.

**Flocking**  In migratory movements, flocks contain from a few birds up to about 400, commonly 25–100, but in spring as the birds approach their nesting areas the larger gatherings break into small bunches. Solitary pairs are common. Flocks are said to be smaller in fall than spring. On the water, gatherings of various sizes seem to combine,

then divide, quite readily. At times they form in large rafts, which break up without evident pattern or unit size; this is influenced by rhythm of the tides, location of food, changes in weather, and probably other factors. The going and coming, joining and separating, has some of the same characteristics as the unstable dimensions of the crèches of ducklings. Beyond this, however, there is a pattern of age and sex segregation (see "Migration"), although it is not always clearly evident.

Outside the nesting season, the largest assemblies—up to many thousands of individuals—occur at molting areas on the sea. The birds may be in bunches, large flocks, and strings, the total extending for some miles over the water. No aggressive or sexual behavior is evident. Very large numbers of the birds may close ranks, forming a dense raft, when resting or shifting with the tide. Molting birds prefer the security of the sea but come ashore where not disturbed. They also tend to keep to themselves, only occasionally mingling with other molting waterfowl such as King Eiders or scoters.

**Preflight movements,** when there are any, consist of lateral Head-shaking. In nominate *mollissima*, flight speed (av. of 345 spring records) was 70 ± .03 km./hr (Ryden and Kallander 1964).

**Behavior ashore**  Generally speaking, eiders are wary ashore, evidently feeling less secure than when at sea. A common pattern is for a few birds to alight or swim near the water's edge, then walk ashore. They are very uneasy at this time and generally engage in a vigorous bout of preening; then they settle down, spaced just out of each other's reach, and appear to sleep. Their presence attracts others, which may walk ashore or, if the sea is rough, alight ashore, so that a sizable assembly of birds—the individuals quite evenly spaced out—is formed. Their behavior is much the same when they rest on ice.

**Diving** A frightened eider submerges very rapidly, with a splash. In the usual feeding dive the bird goes forward and downward quite smoothly, using the feet plus a stroke of half-folded wings. Both the half-folded wings and the feet are used during descent and more or less in horizontal underwater propulsion, but only the feet when maintaining station or seeking food on the bottom. Then, on ceasing all propulsion, the bird rises buoyantly to the surface. Various observations were summarized by Humphrey (1958c) and underwater "flying" was described graphically by Tinbergen (1958).

Near the end of the Alaska Pen., at Izembek Lagoon, up to several hundred eiders have been seen to dive simultaneously; it appeared that they were obtaining food by some concerted action (R. D. Jones, Jr.). At Tjörnin (the lake) in Reykjavik, where the writer has spent many hours watching the self-tamed eiders, it is commonplace to observe all downies in a brood up-ending or attempting to dive simultaneously.

Depth and duration of diving have been much discussed, as summarized by Pethon (1967). Most feeding dives are to a depth of 2 meters or less, but the birds are capable of going down 16 meters. There is an unverified report of their going much deeper. Duration of submergence varies greatly in any depth; it lasts about as follows: 10 sec. (to 1 meter), 10–30 sec. (1–3 meters), and 30–40 sec. (16 meters). Longest are escape dives, to 106 sec., by nearly fledged young birds (Pethon).

**Feeding** Eiders get their food below the water's surface and it is said (Belopolskii 1957) that they will not eat blue mussels (*Mytilus edulis*) exposed by the falling tide. They feed as readily by head dipping and up-ending in very shallow water as they do by diving in deeper water. The writer has watched hundreds of drakes (*dresseri*, also nominate *mollissima*) at all stages of tide, at the time when their mates were ashore incubating; the drakes spent their time sunning and cruising about, and at ebb tide there was some dipping and up-ending in the shallows, but these birds were not seen to bring anything to the surface and whether they were feeding is very questionable.

In winter in Scotland one method of feeding consists of an eider, fairly upright in very shallow water over a mussel bed, "pushing mussel shells around with its feet like a hen scratching for insects"; then it explores the hole with its beak, seeking food; at ebb tide the mussel beds appear cratered; see Player (1971) for details and an excellent photo of the "craters." They do the same in the Aleutians, i. e., churn holes in the mud with their feet; at these places small clams and worms would be available (R. D. Jones, Jr.). At least in early summer eiders of either sex, afloat on shallow water, rear up and paddle vigorously with their feet; when done by a ♀ with downies this appears to be a signal for the latter to dive (or partially dive) and feed. The adult does not feed (also see Treading water, listed earlier under displays).

There seem to be conflicting ideas as to whether length of daylight (with feeding periods in early morning and toward dusk) or rhythm of the tides (feeding on a falling tide and at ebb tide) governs the schedule. Possibly it differs between localities where the amplitude of the tides is small and where it is large, but it is tide dependent to a considerable extent. The birds feed in daylight, since they must see the food they bring to the surface in order to disentangle it from extraneous matter, such as attached seaweed, before swallowing it. In this process, as when vigorously shaking a mussel, often the food is dropped; then the bird dives quickly to retrieve it. Picozzi (1958) observed that, on surfacing with a crab, the eider holds it by a leg and shakes until the crab falls into the water; then the bird swallows the leg, dives to retrieve the crab, and repeats this until all legs are eaten; then it eats the body.

**Ice years**    This is a topic deserving much more study. In the literature on the Palearctic it has been suggested that when inshore waters remain frozen or freeze the eiders are forced out to waters so deep they cannot dive for food, and so they starve.

Some Icelandic data are more explicit and rather different. In the winter of 1917–18 the polar pack-ice reached the n. and e. coasts of Iceland; in a single night in Jan. it filled the fjords and bays. Then the temperature dropped and the surface of the sea was solid thereafter into May. Various alcids and the eiders, caught along the coast in this freeze, later were found starving, dying, and dead on the ice in large numbers (Gudmundsson 1932). There was much ice again in n. and e. Iceland (but not the nw. fjords) in the winters of 1965–68, but there was open water among the floes. The nesting eiders decreased in numbers for a time; the harvest of eiderdown in that part of Iceland declined by half. One probable relationship is that an ice year is very destructive to the invertebrate life of the littoral zone, i.e., to foods of the eider.

A listing of adverse seasons in the arctic, primarily in the Am. sector, is given under King Eider, starting on p. 131.

**Eiderdown** is unique. No synthetic product as yet manufactured, nor chopped goose or chicken feathers, is any match for the genuine article in insulating quality combined with lightness. The human use of bird down and feathers, especially of domestic geese, is a very ancient practice, notably in China. The taking of down from the nests of eiders is an ancient and widespread practice among Eskimos; small amounts were, and in some places still are, taken to line mittens and sleeping bags. Some data on harvesting eiderdown follow.

U.S.S.R.    The down has been collected since time immemorial. Documents of the 17th century record "bird down" sold to Dutch merchants (Dementiev and Gladkov 1952). Until some time before about 1917, the U.S.S.R. was the main source of this product for world trade. The amount of cleaned down may have exceeded 10 tons annually, but was reduced to 2 tons in the 1940s and continued to decline (S. Uskenskii, in Kumari 1966). (If the 10-ton figure is valid, it represents well over a half million nests, over twice the recent annual harvest of Iceland! There is now some inclination to question the claims of very great numbers of eiders having nested formerly in w. U.S.S.R.) In the Barents Sea–White Sea area, the decline in eider numbers continued through the 1950s and, in the 1960s, the largest remaining colonies (total of about 25,000 nests?) were on the w. side of s. Novaya Zemlya. The harvesting of down continues. Much effort has been expended in trying to increase the number of nesting eiders in the Barents Sea–White Sea colonies. The eider has had legal protection in the U.S.S.R. since 1931, but only on reserves is any protection effectively carried on.

NORWAY    The down has been gathered for more than 1,000 years and eiders have

73

been protected for a long time. (Undoubtedly it also was collected elsewhere in Scandinavia in the past.) In Spitzbergen, eggs and down have been collected (Lovenskiøld 1964) and the same undoubtedly applies to other is. in the ne. Atlantic area.

FAEROES    From ancient times, the down has been taken at the large colony on the islet Kirkebøholmm off Stromø. In the 1960s it still was collected on the island of Sunnbiarholmúr, where stone shelters are built to protect the incubating ♀ ♀.

BRITAIN    In A.D. 677–84, St. Cuthbert was on the Inner Farne, a small island on the North Sea coast of Northumberland. He is said to have tamed all the eiders (a vernacular name for the Common Eider is St. Cuthbert's Duck) and to have used their down and eggs. A thousand years later, John Ray (1678) wrote that, at the Farnes, eider eggs were taken, and the down to stuff beds and quilts.

ICELAND    The down has been gathered for over a thousand years. An interest in the welfare of the eiders is indicated in a document, still preserved, dating from the 12th century. The birds have had legal protection for over 150 years, are regarded as private property, and hardly ever are shot. In the early 1960s there were about 200 eider farms, including about 100 of major economic importance to their owners. The largest had briefly as a peak number several decades earlier, about 12,000 nests. The colonies in the early 1960s had a combined total of about 250,000 nesting pairs and each nest yields an av. of 18–20 gm of cleaned down. The Jan., 1973, price per kg. paid to farmers for cleaned down of best grade was 5,700 Icelandic kronur (about $64.00 U.S.).

The amount of down collected in Iceland and sold has fluctuated. Gudmundsson (1940) published data for the years 1898–1938 inclusive and his graph may be summarized as follows: high (av. over 3,500 kg. of cleaned down) 1898–1901, sharp drop to low in 1902–06 (av. about 3,200 kg.), gradual increase to a peak (over 4,000 kg.) in 1912–16, sharp drop to a low (about 3,300 kg.) in 1919–21, gradual rise to a peak (4,000 kg.) in 1927–29, and gradual decline to a low (av. about 2,900 kg.) 1935–38. The yearly av. for the 4 decades was about 3,582 kg.

The first 2 lows, 1902 and 1918, follow the winters when polar pack ice extended to the Icelandic coast. The downward trend that began after the 1928 high continued to about 1950; then, in 1950–1963, there was slight annual variation; after 1963, production evidently has continued to decline down to the present (1973). In 1965–68, as discussed earlier under "ice years," the down harvest declined by half in n. and e. Iceland. Known figures include 2,897 kg. of down in 1940 and 1,588 in 1963. According to Finnur Gudmundsson, to whom the author is indebted for many of the data given here, annual figures for 1940–63 have not been compiled and published and probably would be less reliable than earlier figures, cited above. There are no figures after 1963.

The interrelations of eiders with the local environment and also the changing social and economic patterns in Iceland are many. The decrease in nesting eiders since 1928 has varied with locality. The great colonies in the nw. part of the country, which are tended with diligence, have decreased much less than various others elsewhere. The mink (*Mustela vison*), escaped from fur farms and now present throughout Iceland, is a predator of some importance when the birds are nesting. Large gulls (*Larus*) and Ravens (*Corvus corax*) prey on eggs and the gulls get a great many small ducklings on the sea. Where flat stones are available, cubicles are built over the eider nests and, at a colony in Önundarfjord, A-frame shelters are provided, as protection against egg-eating Ravens. At many colonies there is active predator control by scattering eggs containing a powerful drug, by shooting of gulls and Ravens, and by hunting mink with dogs. Where eider nesting density is very high and predators are dealt with efficiently, as at Mýrar, egg losses are inconsequential. Where the eiders are more scattered and Ravens are abundant, as at Aethey, the Ravens took an estimated 12,000+ eggs in 1973 and 223 Ravens, numerous gulls, and several mink had been killed by July 7 of that year. The sporadic firing of guns at predators at these eider farms perhaps surprisingly does not adversely affect the incubating eiders.

Most Icelandic farmers are of the opinion that avian predators are solely responsible for the decline in numbers of nesting eiders, but this viewpoint is not correct. In the quarter century before 1960, the number of Icelanders engaged in agriculture decreased by 40%, partly from a desire to flee the rigors of farm life, partly from centralization of the fishing industry in a few major ports, and partly from growth of industries and commerce. Some eider colonies are no longer tended properly due to ignorance or to scarcity of labor, and some farms with colonies have been abandoned. The netting of lumpfish (*Cyclopterus lumpus*) has become very profitable (the roe is sold as caviar); it is done in the littoral zone and large numbers of eiders are caught and perish in the nets. There has also been heavy eider mortality from oil pollution on marine waters; it was especially serious during World War II. In addition, beginning about 1960, the general cooling trend of climate, which has had deleterious effects on the nesting of waterfowl in the N. Am. arctic, has affected Iceland considerably, but whether it is detrimental to the eiders there is speculative.

In the colonies, the nest down is collected several times in a season, the schedule sometimes depending on when help is available to gather it. The first collected, early in incubation, is the cleanest, since it is newly deposited and the sitters have not had time to work extraneous materials from the nest rim and nearby into it. That portion of the down which is left in the nest when the first is collected is mixed with a small quantity of dry grass and fluffed up, to give it bulk. The final, often the third, collection is made after the nests have been vacated and, hopefully, before the down is soaked and matted by rain.

A flea (*Ceratophyllus garei*) is abundant in eider nests; it is so bothersome to some people that they cannot engage in gathering the raw down and processing it.

Long ago, the down was cleaned by first drying it in any way possible, then spreading a certain quantity of it on a frame about 1 meter square and strung with evenly spaced taut string (codline), then beating it with a wooden paddle—a very time-consuming process. It is now done by machine.

1   The down is dried in a double-walled cylindrical chamber, a water jacket about 1 m. tall and of same diam. The down is warmed, but not overheated, by the temperature of the water in the surrounding jacket, and warm dry air is forced, by a electric fan, up through the loaded chamber. Thus the down is dried at a carefully controlled temperature. Or, opportunity permitting, it can be more or less dried by spreading it out in the sun.

2   The dried down is put in a motor-driven horizontal cylinder whose sides are movable rods with vanes; the cylinder also is surrounded by rods, parallel to the vanes, and the vanes hit against these outer stationary rods when the cylinder is rotated

rapidly. In this spinning (centrifugal force) operation, which is timed carefully (it is not so prolonged as to damage the cohesiveness and elasticity of the down), the debris is forced out between the rods. Even in down collected early from grassy turf, there is a surprising amount of this. The cleaned down is wonderfully cohesive and at the same time fluffy, but still there are small feathers intermingled.

3   About 1 full working day is required for a person to pick the feathers from 1 kg. of cleaned down. There is a machine, not yet in general use in Iceland, which separates the feathers from the down.

The large farms have their own machine for drying and cleaning the down, but the smaller ones send the uncleaned product to cooperatives for processing. The cooperatives establish the price paid for the cleaned down. About 50–60 nests are required to produce 1 kg. of cleaned down. There have been 2 or 3 grades of down sold, and priced accordingly, the best evidently being taken early from nests on grassy turf; of poorer grade is down from nests on rubble, seaweed, and under scrub growth (containing fragments more difficult to remove), also down wetted by much rain, and so on. At some farms there is not much variation in nest sites and all the down can be mixed and sold as best grade. About 1 kg. of down is required to make a bed coverlet which can be folded compactly for storage and which expands greatly when unfolded. These coverlets are very warm and, in the writer's experience in mild weather, usually end up by sliding off the bed onto the floor! Most of the Icelandic down is marketed in West Germany. It loses its cohesiveness and elasticity in about 30 years.

There are brief accounts of Icelandic eider farming by Pettingill (1959a) and D. Munro (1961).

GREENLAND   A native practice consists of killing the eiders, plucking their feathers, then using the skins (with the down still attatched) to make garments; 15–25 skins sewn together make an undergarment called a "tingmiaq" and a new one is needed annually. The Greenlanders also collect nest down, which they sell. The gathering is done along the cent. w. coast (mainly Disko I., Upernavik, and Umanaq Dist.) and the quantity decreased from about 3,000–5,000 lb. a century earlier to about 600–700 lb. (Salomonsen 1950). For many data on fluctuations in the amount of down gathered in Greenland, see Vibe (1967). For legal restriction on collecting the down, see Salomonsen (in Fuller and Kevan 1970). According to Joensen and Preuss (1972), the down still is collected in many eider colonies. Approximately 10 kg. of raw down yields 1 kg. of cleaned down. All the down from w. Greenland is sent to Upernavik for cleaning, the production now being about 100 kg. of cleaned down/year.

CANADA   Much is known about the marketing of skins of our native swans in former times (see account of Trumpeter Swan), but the history of down collecting at eider colonies is obscure. The Eskimos have gathered small amounts for their personal use from time immemorial. The various Canadian attempts to encourage down collecting on a sizable scale seem finally to have resulted in enough practical experience and technology to maintain a viable industry. Some historical data follow.

On s. Baffin I. there are little rows of stone cubicles with open fronts; some historians have considered these to be possible evidence that the Vikings were there a thousand years ago and that they developed an eiderdown harvest (D. Munro 1961). In the 19th century, Moravian missionaries collected eiderdown (for their own use, also to sell?)

along the Labrador coast. In an 1893 diary, A. P. Low stated that 600 lbs. of eiderdown were exported annually from Ft. Chimo in n. Ungava, but possibly part of it was ptarmigan (*Lagopus*) feathers (Manning 1949); a decade earlier, L. M. Turner (in Bent 1932) had estimated that the feathers of over 25,000 ptarmigan were shipped from Chimo to England in a single year. At Pangnirtung on Baffin I., the Eskimos were taught crude down-cleaning methods by whalers as early as 1890 and, at C. Dorset, several cleaning frames still were in use in 1955–56; a few Eskimos were collecting a small amount annually for lining sleeping bags and mittens (Cooch 1965).

In 1925, when Director of the Canadian Wildlife Service, Harrison Lewis, first reported experimental efforts to start an eiderdown industry along the N. Shore of the Gulf of St. Lawrence. Early attempts were unsuccessful. Nearer the city of Quebec, the Provancher Society encouraged the preservation of nesting eiders and establishment of an eiderdown industry (Potvin 1954). The latter seems to have gained momentum in the late 1950s and, by the early 1960s, the down was being collected from various localities in the St. Lawrence estuary. By 1965, some down was being received from N.B., also from an Eskimo cooperative at Frobisher Bay on Baffin I.; the total was about 500 lbs. of cleaned down that year. That is, several hundred lbs. of cleaned down were being produced annually; most of it was sold in Europe. Somewhere along the way there were difficulties in marketing and so efforts were made to use the product in down-filled garments in Canada. Because these were costly in comparison to substitutes, the eiderdown venture continued but did not thrive.

From 1939 through 1943, a total of 3,792 lb. of uncleaned down was collected in s. Baffin at C. Dorset, Lake Harbour, and Frobisher Bay. It was believed that a great many eider nests were destroyed in the process of gathering the down. The experiment was terminated for lack of facilities to clean the down plus failure to give close supervision to the Eskimos (Cooch 1965).

There have been continuing attempts to promote the collecting of eiderdown without disturbing the nesting eiders unduly. As of the early 1970s, the collecting of down by persons having the required permit which is issued by the Canadian Wildlife Service was carried on locally in N.B., N.S., the St. Lawrence estuary and Gulf, Nfld., and counterclockwise around the Ungava Pen. down to Port Harrison in e. Hudson Bay. To the north beyond Ungava, it was being collected on s. Baffin in the C. Dorset and Frobisher Bay areas. There are no permits outstanding for w. Hudson Bay or farther westward in Canada. No figures are available on the amount of cleaned down resulting from current operations, but apparently it is a few thousand lbs. at most. The genuine product is more or less of a luxury item in N. Am., being much more expensive, for example, than the down of domestic geese imported from the People's Republic of China.

In se. Hudson Bay, at the Belcher Is., the Eskimos use 20–25 eider skins to make a "mitvin" (eider parka), as in Greenland. An inner parka is worn with the down-side inward, then an outer one with it outward; for excellent photos of both, see Bruemmer (1971). A caribou parka is decidedly preferable, being lighter and more durable; in the 1880s or about then, however, according to Flaherty (1918), a thaw and then a sudden freeze covered the Belchers with ice and all the caribou perished.

**Wildness and tameness** The wildest birds probably are at colonies where avian predators are a constant hazard to the eggs, there is more or less molestation by man, and the birds are disturbed in other seasons and are hunted. Drakes rarely, if ever, visit their mates ashore after the clutch is completed; ducks soil their nests when they depart in fright. Drakes on the water do little cooing, even when joined by their mates, and their mates while ashore usually are silent. In Penobscot Bay, Me., Choate (1966) did not find the birds any tamer during the 2nd year of his study, yet he reported that the percentage of ♀ ♀ that soiled their nests when flushed was 64% in 1964 and 55% in 1965. See Choate (1967) for further information.

Near C. Dorset, Baffin I., in areas of high nesting density, if a person walks with a slow stealth and stooped over, the ♀ ♀ will flush but go only a few meters and soon are back on their eggs. They are shier where nests are scattered. In a 2-year study there, personnel agreed that the nesting ♀ ♀ seemed to be tamer the 2nd year. Some ♀ ♀ trapped and noted as wild in 1955 were handled easily in 1956. In another study of down collecting there (Houston, cited in Cooch), in 1957, increased tameness was reported. (Summarized from Cooch 1965.)

At St. Lawrence I. in n. Bering Sea, the eiders seemed to be attracted to the vicinity of some human habitations and nested close by (Fay and Cade 1959). In Norway they have occupied crannies in old masonry and niches in human habitations.

On Utholmen, a small island near Gotland, in the Baltic, there were several hundred eider nests in early May, 1969. There is considerable control of gulls and, when the eiders are away, the island is grazed by sheep. During early incubation a few drakes were ashore. A person could walk about and, although the ♀ ♀ usually vacated their nests before being approached closer than about 15–20 m., they made little (usually no) attempt to cover their eggs and few defecated (soiled their nests) on takeoff.

At eider farms in Iceland, when the drakes are ashore, there is variation in the tameness of the nesting eiders and their mates roughly comparable to the individual differences within a barnyard flock of domestic fowl. A person, moving without undue haste, can go among the nesting eiders; often both ducks and drakes are reluctant to move aside. Some ♀ ♀ can be lifted from their eggs; some are quite aggressive when this is attempted. There is a steady but not loud noise of drakes cooing and displaying, and ♀ ♀ croaking. Since most ♀ ♀ are not frightened, they seldom soil the nest down by defecating on it. At fringes of a colony, where nests are more scattered, most of the birds are shier.

In the Farnes, St. Cuthbert was said to have moved about among tame eiders and to have handled them freely. In the early 1800s, at a place in Norway, the eiders often nested in kitchens of inhabited houses, where they could be stroked, lifted from their eggs, and replaced (Boie 1822). Again at the Farnes, Tinbergen (1958) wrote that the ducks ashore became "tame" and that good "neighbourly relations" prevailed between naturalists and the birds. In a harbor, where the eiders had lost all fear of man, they gathered about fishermen's boats and swallowed fish offal thrown overboard. At a place in the Faeroes, eiders were seen feeding on limpets (*Patella*) thrown to them by some children (Potts 1961). Some of the self-tamed birds at the lake in the city of Reykjavik, Iceland, will take bread from the hand.

**A gull–eider relationship** Various *Larus* gulls are known to take food brought up by diving eiders. The most detailed report is that of Ingolfsson (1969), on the Glaucous

Gull (*L. hyperboreus*), as observed Aug.–Jan. inclusive in sw. Iceland. The pattern is as follows. A gull rests on the water, near or among eiders, and seemingly pays no attention until an eider brings food to the surface. Then the gull flies straight at the eider, which dives frantically and usually lets go of the food; the gull dives from the air and, if quick enough, retrieves the food. The pattern goes beyond this, however, since a raft of eiders or part of a raft is defended by the gull against other adult Glaucous Gulls but not against immatures of its own kind or against the Great Black-backed Gull (*L. marinus*). Adult Blackbacks also defend eider rafts, against other adults, and so does the Herring Gull (*L. argentatus*). The defense of rafts is a territorial phenomenon.

At Stonington, Me., in Jan.–Feb., a raft of about 150 Common Eiders, which fed regularly on small crabs, nearly always was accompanied by a Herring Gull. The gull never was seen to take food directly from an eider, but if part or all of a crab was dropped, usually the gull was quicker at retrieving it. If the gull got an entire crab, the bird flew to a ledge and there broke the crab into bits (Hundley 1970).

At Little Green I., Knox Co., Me., June 1–9, 1967, there were many nesting eiders, Herring Gulls, and some Great Blackbacks. Flocks and small groups of drake eiders often shifted about, along the shore, on the changing tide. A Herring Gull would fly out and settle close to the eiders. As the latter moved on by, the gull would depart and return to his station among the nesting gulls ashore. There were several gulls, scattered along the shore, that in turn "visited" the eiders as they moved by. These groups of eiders did no feeding and they paid no heed to their escorts.

**Hunting with bolas** The Chuckchee Eskimos (down to the present) and those of Alaska (until very recently?) used bolas for catching eiders. A number of thongs, 4–10 in number and about 60–70 cm. long, were tied or plaited together and on the free end of each a weight—an ivory ball, walrus tooth, or fragment of walrus tusk—about the size of an egg or prune, was attached. The weights were held in one hand, the joined opposite ends of the cords in the other, and the bola hurled upward into a flock of eiders approaching in dense fog. In a whirling action the weights spread out radially. Eiders struck on head or wing were brought down alive, usually only 1, sometimes 2 or 3, in a successful throw. Portenko (1972) illustrated a modern Chuckchee bola in which the plaited handle contained Oldsquaw (*Clangula*) primaries. A great number of bola weights have been found in Alaska, especially in excavations on St. Lawrence I. Rudenko (1947) illustrated many bola weights and pointed out that the bola appeared relatively late in Eskimo culture.

**Disease** is too large a subject to be covered in other than cursory fashion here. Some factors conducive to heavy parasite infection and spread of disease include: high nesting density of eiders, or the same in association with nesting gulls and other birds; bathing and drinking during the season ashore at rainwater pools, where gulls also bathe—see Ganning and Wulff (1969) for the biological dynamics of such pools on a Baltic island; large numbers of ducklings, more or less attended by mature birds, feeding at remnant pools of seawater at low tide; the crowding of eiders on patches of unfrozen seawater in winter and spring; and the sharing by northerly migrants of pools of meltwater on ice floes.

Certain combinations of circumstances probably set the stage for increased levels of eider mortality. For example, unseasonably warm weather at posthatching raises the temperature of tide pools which, in turn, favors the proliferation of various endoparasites prior to their being ingested by the birds. Beginning a few weeks later, the young eiders molt almost constantly until well into the following spring; when this energy drain occurs in a hard winter, it must reduce the resistance of the birds to infection. Female eiders, having starved through the incubation period, presumably are more vulnerable to parasites and disease for a period thereafter.

Known endoparasites of the eider include at least 35 species of worms (Gerasimova and Baranova 1960). On the reserve islands in Kandalaksh Bay (White Sea), over a period of years, 1,621 dead young eiders were found; 98.1% were under 10 days of age and most were victims of the highly pathogenic flukes *Paramonostromum* and *Spelotrema*—details in Kulachkova (1960). There is considerable evidence that very young eiders soon are heavily parasitized, which is a factor contributing to or causing mortality.

Various endoparasites have life stages in common food items of the eider, in small mollusks such as the tiny seaweed snail (*Hydrobius*) and periwinkle (*Littorina*), for example, and in crustaceans. The acanthocephalid *Polymorphus botulus* has crustaceans—amphipods (*Gammarus*) and sand crab (*Carcinus maenas*)—as intermediate hosts. This Holarctic worm has been found in at least 4 subspecies of Common Eider, also in the King Eider. Epizootics caused by *Polymorphus* have been recurrent and well known from the 1930s on in the Baltic and there has been recorded mortality in the Netherlands, Britain, and e. U.S. (Me. and Mass. in fall of 1956—G. M. Clark et al. 1958). Fatalities have not been limited to downies; among mature birds in the Baltic and Britain, for example, there has been a loss especially of ♀ ♀. For summaries, see Garden et al. (1964) and Grenquist (1965, 1970). For recent Swedish data and an important list of relevant literature, see Persson et al. (1974).

Several recent outbreaks of fowl cholera (the causal agent is a bacillus, *Pasturella multocida*) in *S. m. dresseri* have been well documented: 1963—summer, local, in e. part of Penobscot Bay, Me., in eiders and gulls (*Larus*) (Gershman et al. 1964); 1966—summer, very severe epidemic in St. Lawrence estuary (Reed and Cousineau 1967); 1970—peak about June 12–15, Muscongus Bay to w. Penobscot Bay; many ♀ ♀ died on their nests and in nesting cover, but most were found on island beaches; other victims included the Herring Gull, Double-crested Cormorant (assumed but not confirmed), and Harbor Seal (H. L. Mendall). RSP

FOOD  Almost entirely animal. The bulk consists of mollusks and crustaceans, other items generally occurring in minor quantity at most localities. Some of the vegetable matter taken probably is ingested accidentally, as when foraging among filamentous algae, but evidently there are exceptions.

In s. Norway the eiders usually feed twice/day and maximum recorded crop content weighed 185 gm.; the diet consisted of the most abundant species (amphipods, isopods, *Mytilus edulis*), while some other common and accessible species (*Asterias rubens*, *Nereis* sp., and *Carcinus maenas*) rarely were found. Small downies ate small crustaceans and mollusks in about equal quantity and probably these are more readily digestible by young birds. The older age-classes showed a significant changeover from mainly *Mytilus edulis* in spring and early summer to mainly small crustaceans in Aug.–Oct., then a return to *Mytilus*. Since there was no corresponding change in composition of available food, there must be some other explanation for the switch in diet. It was noted that the young birds were on such a diet during the period preceding Juv. feather development, and older age-classes when growing new feathers during late summer. (Summarized from Pethon 1967.)

Molting drakes in Spitzbergen lived mainly on sea slugs (holothurians) (Løvenskiold 1964).

Eiders disgorge large coarse shell fragments, just as raptorial birds and gulls disgorge pellets (V. S. Uspenskii 1946). In the Am. arctic in spring–summer, such fragments plus fecal droppings are scattered on ice where the birds rest after feeding. V. S. Uspenskii, whose observations were made at the Seven Islands Reserve (w. Murman coast of Barents Sea), stated that when eiders come ashore to nest they feed readily on last year's fruit of crowberry (*Empetrum nigrum*), green vegetation, and that on occasion they break open the eggs of gulls and even eggs of their own species. All this seems possible, especially after a hard winter.

The following summarizes much of the Nearctic but little of the Palearctic data; it is listed by general region rather than by subspecies of eider.

PACIFIC–BERING    Sixty-one stomachs from the Alaskan coast contained 95.3% animal and 4.7% vegetable matter. Mollusks were *Mytilus, Modiolaria, Siliqua, Tellina, Astarte, Littorina, Thais*, etc., for a total of 45.97%; crustaceans included *Telmessus, Lopholithodes, Oregonia, Hapalogaster, Pagurus, Gammarus*, etc. 30.65%; echinoderms *Echinarachnius, Strongylocentrotus, Lepasterias*, etc. 14.4%; fishes Heterostomata and Cottidae 1.5%; marine worms, hydroids, foraminiferans, sea spiders, brine fly larvae (*Ephydra*), etc. 2.7%. Vegetable matter included algae (mainly *Ptiloa*) 3.53%; *Zostera, Carex, Elymus villosissimus*, and *Loiseleuria procumbens* were found. This is summarized from Preble and McAtee (1923) and Cottam (1939).

This eider (and others) eats the green sea urchin (*Strongylocentrotus drobachiensis*) and, as a result, their bones become pigmented purplish (R. D. Jones, Jr., 1963b), just as do those of the sea otter.

HUDSON BAY    Mollusks (*Acmaea, Tonicella, Margarita* (*Margarites*), *Crenella*) *Hyas* and other crustaceans, Ophiuroida, Teleostei, and algae (Halkett 1905). Those shot at the Belcher Is. in the summer of 1960 had eaten *Mytilus edulis* and *Macoma baltica* (Freeman 1970).

E. CANADIAN ARCTIC    In. s. Baffin I., at the C. Dorset colonies, the ducklings at first are surface feeders, on fresh and brackish ponds, but soon go to salt water and become proficient at diving. After they leave the ponds, fish lice (*Argulus* sp.) appeared to make up a large part of their food; graduated later to *Mytilus*. (From Cooch 1965.)

W. ATLANTIC    The 96 stomachs collected from Labrador to R.I. contained 66.7% mollusks (*Mytilus edulis*—by far the most important, *Modiolus, Cyprina, Saxicava, Astarte, Macoma, Venus, Urosalpinax, Crepidula, Natica, Littorina*, etc.); crustaceans (*Hyas, Cancer, Neopanope, Pagurus*, etc.) 6.9%; echinoderms (*Strongylocentrotus, Ophiopholis*, etc.) 5.3%; and insects (caddis fly larvae (Trichoptera), diving beetles (Dytiscidae), etc.) 2.2% (Cottam 1939).

On the N. Shore of the Gulf of St. Lawrence, young birds were reported by Beetz (1916) to eat only prawns and much herbage.

In the St. Lawrence estuary the 407 birds collected were mostly "adult" ♀♀ and ducklings. *Littorina* was found in 96% of the ducklings and 67% of "adults"; *Mytilus*, a

81

staple food elsewhere, in only 30% of "adults" and 9% of ducklings. Additional items were mainly gammarids, *Nereis*, and herring eggs. It was estimated that the eiders could consume 33,000 metric tons of food from mid-June to early Oct. in the intertidal zone, and that they could deplete the supply of *Littorina* during the rearing period. (From Canton and Bédard 1972 *Fourth Que. Waterfowl Seminar.*)

None of the stomachs from Kent I., New Bruns., examined by Gross (1938) contained fish or plant material. G. H. Mackay (1890b, 1894) found, in Mass., specimens of horse mussels (*Modiolus*), slipper shell (*Crepidula fornicata*), sea urchins, and spawn of sculpins. A bird from Long I., N.Y., had fed mainly on sand crabs (*Cancer irroratus*) (Whitfield 1894). Birds from off Monomoy I., Chatham, Mass., contained blue crabs (*Callinectes sapidus*) and the mollusks *Brachydontes demissus* and *Nassarius obsoletus* (Burnett and Synder 1954).

GREENLAND   Birds from w. Greenland had generally eaten shrimps (H. C. Hart 1880). Five birds in ne. Greenland: bivalves (*Mya, Saxicava, Mytilus, Crenella*); univalves (*Buccinum, Tritonofusus, Natica,* and *Bulla*) totalling 45%; gastropods 20%; crustaceans (*Atylus, Corophium*) 7.2%; vegetable matter 1.4%; and miscellaneous 0.4% (Cottam 1936). One adult, sculpins (mostly *Myoxocephalus*) 74% and bivalve (*Astarte*) 23%; and a downy young eider had eaten young fishes (Cottidae 92% and plant material (mainly *Fucus*) 8% (Cottam and Hanson 1938). Recorded also from Greenland: mollusks (*Macoma, Portlandia, Cylichna, Modiolaria, Luniata, Sipho*), the crustacean *Gammarus*, fish spawn, and the capelin *Mallotus villosus* (Degerbøl and Möhl-Hansen 1935, Salomonsen 1950).

N. ATLANTIC   In Iceland, principally *Mytilus* (B. Roberts 1934). For Spitzbergen, there is a long and interesting list of foods; also, pellets of grass and seaweeds, small quantities of body down, and pebbles; see summary by Løvenskiold (1964).

BRITAIN   Mollusks were the principal food in 42 stomachs (W. Evans 1909). Twenty-four birds had eaten 95.5% animal and 4.5% vegetable matter: mollusks (20 genera) 51.5%, crustaceans 24.5%, annelids 6.5%, fishes 5%, echinoderms 4.5%, and insects 3.5% (Collinge 1924–27). In Scotland: *Littorina, Mytilus,* and *Balanus* (Florence 1912).

For Britain there also are many brief published items, not included here. Dunthorn (1971), for example, gave interesting data on the quantity of blue mussels eaten at a locality in Scotland.

W. EUROPE   In Denmark, examination of 296 specimens showed mollusks 68% (bivalves 51% and gastropods 17%), crustaceans 15.5%, fishes 5.5%, echinoderms 10.5%, and annelids 0.5%; in order of importance: blue mussel (*Mytilus edulis*), shore crab (*Carcinus maenas*), starfish (*Asterias rubens*), periwinkles (*Littorina* spp.), and the mollusks *Nassa, Cardium, Mya,* and *Buccinum* (Madsen 1954).

The very important study done in Oslofjord, se. Norway, by Pethon (1967) was referred to at the beginning of this section; it dealt with foods re age of birds and season, feeding habits, and nutritive value of foods; and it listed many papers omitted here.

BARENTS AND WHITE SEAS   V. S. Uspenskii (1946) did pioneer work and there have been various important studies more recently. The reader is referred to Belopolskii (1957) and, especially for comparison of information from various localities, to Gerasimova and Baranova (1960). AWS

## Spectacled Eider

*Somateria fischeri* (Brandt)

Fairly large marine duck, but considerably smaller than Common and King eiders. In downy and all later stages: **1** an area of down or feathers ("spectacle") encircling the eye is different in texture and/or color from surrounding areas; **2** the down or feathers of loreal area continue out onto the bill, the margin extending in low angle forward up side of culmen so that, on top, it terminates over or (usually) beyond the nostrils. After early age, eye color sexually dimorphic: iris pale bluish in the drake, brown in the duck. In the Common, King, and Spectacled eiders the tracheal apparatus of drakes is similar but with progressively smaller bulla (that of the Spectacled figured by Humphrey 1958b), its left chamber in the Spectacled expanded laterally.

Length 20–23 in. (both sexes included), wingspread of ♂ to 36 in., ♀ to about 33, usual wt. of ♂ about 3¾ lb., ♀ 3 lb. No subspecies.

DESCRIPTION  Two Plumages/cycle, the drake being definitive in the 3rd cycle, the ♀ from Basic II or Alt. II onward. Present findings align well with Portenko (1952), who had less material available and described fewer Plumages. Treatment still is somewhat tentative, especially because of lack of winter–early spring specimens. It is probable (by analogy with other large eiders) that in both sexes all the head–body (except longest scapulars) are renewed during each molt by at least most individuals, i.e., lesser amounts listed below reflect a shortage of information.

▶   ♂ Def. Alt. Plumage (all feathering except tail, wing, longest scapulars, and possibly rear of dorsum and posterior venter), acquired in FALL (beginning in Aug.) and retained through winter into SUMMER. **Bill** reddish orange (most vivid near base) with pale nail; **iris** nearly white, darkening to bluish toward outer edge. **Head** circular area (in which eye is somewhat anterior of center) silvery white, surrounded by a line of stiffened velvety black feathers; this line almost obsolete along lower margin, broadest along anterior and posterior margins, and the latter continued downward as a short line behind cheeks; a band at base of bill (angling along culmen) white or cream, blending posteriorly with an area of stiffened feathers anterior to "spectacles"; these latter feathers are pale yellowish green or a grayed green when bird faces observer, but much darker in lateral or postero-lateral view; cheeks similar in color or less yellowish green, but feathers longer and less stiff; crown and nape like cheeks but somewhat paler, the feathers lengthened to form a rounded but shaggy nuchal crest; chin, throat, and neck posterior to nape white. **Upperparts** anterior back and scapulars white to cream, the latter coloring possibly adventitious to some extent; tips of uppermost scapulars dissected and hairlike (the modified longest scapulars are retained Basic; see below); white of interscapular area continues as V-shaped area (point foremost), more or less continuous with an oval white patch at either side of rump. Lower back and upper tail coverts blackish gray with an ashy bloom, the feathers (especially anteriorly) tipped with white. (It is not clear whether much of this blackish gray area may represent retained Basic feathering; extent of feather replacement in this area at Prealt. molt may vary individually and with age.) **Underparts** upper breast and flanks blackish gray with ashy bloom (slightly browner on flanks). (Remainder of underparts appear to be retained Basic feathering.) Legs and **feet** "dull olive brown, except scales on front of tarsus and toes, which are dingy yellowish" (E. W. Nelson 1887). Longest scapulars, tail, and wing are retained Basic feathering.

▶ ♂ Def. Basic Plumage (entire feathering), the head–body portion worn from about EARLY JULY to LATE AUG. then, after a flightless period, the Basic wing, tail, and long scapulars grow and are retained nearly a year. **Head** and neck brownish olive, variegated with buff and smoke gray; "spectacles" distinguished by texture of feathers and by more uniform, less variegated, gray color. **Upperparts** anterior back and upper scapulars dark brownish olive to blackish gray; the 2–3 longest are off-white, broadened, scooped at outer web, then abruptly pointed at tip; posterior back, rump, and upper tail coverts blackish gray with brownish tinge. **Underparts** upper breast, sides, and flanks rich buffy brown to deep tawny, more or less barred with black or blackish brown; remainder of underparts blackish gray. Tail rounded, 14 feathers, dull brownish black above with smoke gray tips, dark smoke gray below. **Wing** primaries, outer secondaries, primary and greater coverts, and alula dull brownish black, the secondaries and greater coverts with narrow white tips when unworn; middle primary coverts mixed white and smoke gray; remainder of upper surface of wing white; innermost secondaries ("tertials") pointed, curved down over primaries in closed wing; undersurface of primaries, outer secondaries, and major under wing coverts light gray; smaller under coverts, axillars, and marginal coverts white, the last sometimes with a few brownish gray feathers mixed in.

♀ Def. Basic  ♂ Def. Alt.

▶ ♀ Def. Alt. Plumage (full extent of feathering not established due to lack of specimens, but excludes tail, wing, long scapulars, and sometimes possibly some additional body feathering), acquired in FALL and retained through winter into SPRING. **Bill** muted bluish with paler nail, **iris** medium or darker brownish. **Head** mostly buff to buffy brown base, more or less streaked sepia on crown, cheeks, and sides of neck; "spectacle" paler buff with very fine sepia streaks; forehead and lores usually predominantly sepia; chin, throat, and foreneck buff, immaculate or lightly streaked darker; hindneck darker. **Upperparts** back, shorter (upper) scapulars, rump, and upper tail coverts rich tawny (fading with wear to buff) heavily barred with blackish sepia. **Under-**

84

parts breast, sides, flanks, and under tail coverts tawny (fading with wear to buff), barred rather narrowly with black or blackish sepia (bars broader on flanks); abdomen deep smoke gray, sepia, or blackish sepia, varying in different individuals from (usually) uniformly colored through faintly barred to rather distinctly barred. Legs and **feet** brownish yellow, the joints and webs dusky. Tail, wing, and longest scapulars are retained Basic, described below.

▶ ♀ Def. Basic Plumage (entire feathering), the head–body (except longest scapulars) acquired in SPRING and retained into FALL, when the tail, wing, and longest scapulars are renewed concurrently with molt of remainder of feathering back into Alt. The flightless period begins in late Aug. or early Sept., its duration unknown. The late-acquired parts of Basic are retained nearly a year. **Bill** varies, bluish gray to slaty, the nail olive to greenish gray. **Head,** neck, and **body** quite like Def. Alt. except streaking on head usually much heavier; the 2 longest scapulars are broadened, rather abruptly pointed at tip, and sepia with rich tawny margins. Portenko (1952) stated that Basic is "dull dark color" in general appearance, compared with "dark rufescent" of Alt. **Tail** sepia, the feathers edged with rich tawny above, outer web of outermost rectrix often barred with tawny; deep smoke gray below. **Wing** remiges, larger coverts, and alula sepia to blackish sepia, paling to smoke gray on tips of secondaries and inner margins of primaries; greater coverts indistinctly margined with cinnamon or tawny, becoming richer colored distally; innermost secondaries ("tertials") usually distinctly margined with rich tawny or buffy brown, sometimes indistinctly variegated with this color near tip; these feathers are somewhat pointed, more or less curved down over primaries in closed wing as in ♂ ; smaller wing coverts black or blackish sepia, margined or barred with tawny or cinnamon; lesser under wing coverts grayish cinnamon, the feathers with sepia centers or shaft-stripes; rest of undersurface and the axillars pale smoke gray.

NOTE A ♀ taken June 23, 1922, at Wales, Alaska, was so bleached as to appear pale creamy brownish, especially on the venter.

AT HATCHING See vol. 2, col. pl. facing p. 370. Identifiable to species by unique "spectacle" which is darker than surrounding areas, the reverse of its color relationship later in life when in Alt. Plumage. For additional details, see C. Nelson (1964). On comparing that source with paragraph and photo in Johnsgard (1964b) and with skins of downies (1 ♂, 1 sex?) from Igiak Bay, Alaska, it appears that there may be slight individual variation in overall coloring.

▶ ♂ Juv. Plumage (entire feathering), acquired rapidly in SUMMER. In captives of unknown sex, Juv. feathering appeared in the scapular region "after 17 days" and flight feathers of wing broke through their sheaths "after 21 days" (Johnsgard 1964b); another bird was "almost completely feathered" at age 4 weeks (C. Nelson 1964); the full Juv. Plumage is worn briefly, but at least all of the wing is retained through winter and into the following summer.

**Bill** of an unsexed month-old bird still "light grayish blue" (C. Nelson 1974), but E. W. Nelson (1887) stated that, in 1st fall, it is "dark olive brown" in both sexes; in live birds approaching flight age it varies from grayish brown to slaty (C. Dau). Iris dark brown. **Head,** forehead and face anterior to "spectacle" smoke gray to brownish olive, paling slightly in area over nostrils; crown, occiput, and sides of head posterior to "spectacle" sepia finely streaked with pale cinnamon; "spectacle" pale grayish cinnamon with faint sepia streaks, these sometimes virtually absent (the area was "light golden buff " in a month-old unsexed bird—C. Nelson 1964); lower cheeks, chin, throat and neck grayish cinnamon to smoke gray, the hindneck obscurely streaked sepia. **Upperparts** blackish sepia, edged with tawny buff on anterior back, scapulars, and upper tail coverts, and with deep tawny on lower back and rump; most anterior feathers of back, shortest scapulars, rump, and upper tail coverts mostly barred as well as edged with the lighter color; 2 longest scapulars broadened, but narrower, more symmetrical, and more gradually tapered than in later Basics. **Underparts** cinnamon to deep tawny, most vivid but palest on breast, darkest on lower abdomen; the feathers of upper breast with a central sepia spot that broadens, on lower breast, to a subterminal bar; lower breast and abdomen closely barred with sepia; flanks and under tail coverts broadly barred with sepia. Legs and **feet** "dull yellowish, shaded with olive-brown" (E. W. Nelson 1887). **Tail** colored as in ♀ Def. Basic, but feathers narrower, notched at tip where natal down precursor broke off. **Wing** similar to ♀ Def. Basic except: secondaries tipped and margined with rich tawny; tawny margins of greater coverts more distinct; all coverts narrower; innermost secondaries narrower, more pointed, with paler, narrower, edgings.

▶   ♀ **Juv. Plumage** (entire feathering), timing as ♂ Juv. As ♂ except: crown av. darker; streaking of "spectacle" more distinct; rump feathers edged but not barred with deep tawny; barring of lower breast and upper abdomen usually less regular; light margins on wing coverts paler, less contrasting.

▶   ♂ **Basic I Plumage** (definitely includes head, neck, upper back, upper scapulars, upper tail coverts, upper breast, the sides, flanks, and at least 2 central tail feathers; probably includes all of head–body–tail, but specimen evidence lacking), acquired beginning some time in FALL and probably retained only into EARLY WINTER (but only fall specimens examined). Just when the drake's iris becomes pale bluish is unknown. **Head** anterior to "spectacle" grayish buffy brown; crown feathers basally white and remainder black obscurely barred with buffy brown at tip; nape and sides of head similar, but with more white; "spectacle" feathers dark gray tipped white—"frosted"; sides of neck medium gray; chin not molted in specimen examined, but Portenko (1952) stated coloring is "dull white with a mixture of gray feathers"; throat white. **Upperparts** anterior back dark gray with brownish tinge; upper scapulars white and dark gray in varying proportions; upper tail coverts blackish gray. **Underparts** upper breast, sides, and flanks blackish gray. Any new **tail** feathers (accompanying retained faded Juv. ones) are blackish gray and with rounded ends.

▶   ♂ **Alt. I Plumage** (consists at least of head, neck, smaller scapulars, and variable number of back feathers; probably includes all of head–body except longest scapulars), present by spring, but probably acquired beginning before MIDWINTER; retained into SUMMER (at age approximately 1 year). **Iris** pale bluish. **Head** feathers anterior to "spectacle" white at base with more or less of a subterminal area of dark gray or blackish brown, and a pale tip—head thus appearing "frosted" gray or brownish; crown, nape, and sides of head behind "spectacle" mixed blackish brown, white, and pale yellowish green in varying proportions, all feathers tipped blackish brown; "spectacle" feathers blackish gray at base, more or less silvery white at tip, giving an off-white appearance;

the black posterior margin of the "spectacle" of Def. Alt. vaguely indicated; a dark area below and behind "spectacle" formed of mixed black, white, and grayish green feathers, this patch outlined in white; below this dark patch, on lower cheeks, a patch of dark smoke gray; chin and throat white. **Upperparts** varying amount of new white feathers on upper back and smaller scapulars. **Underparts** apparently no new feathers, although by analogy with the ♀ and with other eiders they would be expected at least on upper breast and flanks; that is, the discrepancy is probably due to inadequacy of material examined. The wing is retained Juv.; the tail, longest scapulars, and also some body feathering are retained Basic I.

▶ ♀ Basic I Plumage (amount of new feathering at least as extensive as in ♂ Basic I; probably includes all of head–body–tail), present in FALL birds and probably not retained very long. The new feathering is like the Juv. except: head darker, more richly colored; area anterior to "spectacle" much darker, sepia mottled with buffy brown; "spectacle" cinnamon buff, nearly immaculate or with faint streaks or spots of sepia; upper breast, upper back, sides, flanks, uppermost scapulars, and upper tail coverts rich tawny barred with black or blackish sepia.

▶ ♀ Alt. I Plumage (variable amount of feathering in head, neck, upper breast, upper back and upper scapulars, sides, flanks, and upper tail coverts of individuals examined, but may include all of head–body except longest scapulars in some individuals), acquired in WINTER, being present in early spring specimens; it is retained until some time in SPRING. The incoming feathers are similar to those replaced except: head ground color paler, more buffy, thus contrasting more with streaks; "spectacle" finely but densely streaked sepia or blackish sepia; cheeks and sides of neck lightly but definitely streaked; even the throat may be faintly streaked or spotted. As in the drake, the wing is retained Juv., the tail and some body feathering are retained Basic I.

▶ ♂ Basic II Plumage (entire feathering), the head–body (except longest scapulars) acquired in LATE JULY or from then into Aug., the tail, wing, and evidently the longest scapulars in Aug. or EARLY SEPT. (while remainder of Basic is being succeeded by Alt. II). As Def. Basic except: head much paler, the base of bill to forehead creamy white, darkening along crown to smoke gray and brownish olive; underparts breast duller buffy brown; lower breast sometimes with a vaguely defined area of blackish sepia and cinnamon barring (such barring possibly is individual variation in drakes of various ages); wing middle primary coverts, marginal wing coverts, and smaller under wing-coverts with much more brownish gray (less white) than in succeeding Basics.

▶ ♂ Alt. II Plumage (inclusive feathering as in Def. Alt.), worn beginning in 2nd FALL through winter into 3rd SUMMER. As Def. Alt. except: blackish gray area of back extends farther forward, to interscapular area; the oval white patches at sides of rump usually isolated (not connected to white of back). Drakes in this feathering have retained Basic II wing (its characteristics are given above), tail, and longest scapulars.

▶ ♀ Basic II Plumage (entire feathering) head–body acquired in spring (before age 1 year), all of the wing then being retained Juv. feathering, the tail (and long scapulars?) retained Basic I. In late summer or early fall there begins a period of molting from Basic II to Alt. II head–body and, after a flightless period, the "offset" acquisition of Basic II wing, tail, and long scapulars (these then being retained and worn with Alt. II head–body). In Basic II the bill is gray tinged yellowish or bluish; the venter appears mottled dark on light (not darker and more uniform as in nesters); and the retained Juv. wing, especially the innermost secondaries, is very worn and bleached.

▶ ♀ Alt. II Plumage—presumably definitive.

**Measurements** Some of the same specimens are included in both of the 2 following series.

Fourteen ♂ (8 Alaska, 6 Siberia): BILL from nostril 25–27 mm., av. 26.2 (Alaska) and 25.5–27.5, av. 26.3 (Siberia); WING 249–265, av. 256 (Alaska) and 252–260, av. 257 (Siberia); TAIL 76.5–83.5, av. 80 (Alaska) and 77–85, av. 80 (Siberia); TARSUS 47.5–60, av. 52.9 (Alaska) and 45–49, av. 46.8 (Siberia); 10 ♀ (Alaska): BILL from nostril 25–27.5 mm., av. 26.4; WING 244–269, av. 252; TAIL 73–93, av. 80; TARSUS 45–47.5, av. 46.1 (KCP).

Twelve ♂ (11 Alaska, 1 Siberia): BILL from feathers 23–27 mm., av. 24; WING 253–272, av. 264; TAIL 75–86, av. 80; TARSUS 46–50, av. 47.8; 12 ♀ (Alaska): BILL from feathers 24–28 mm., av. 26.3; WING (of 10) 250–263, av. 256.5; TAIL (of 10) 71–83, av. 76; TARSUS 45–49, av. 46.2 (ETS).

Drakes from Siberia, WING meas. over the curve: 3 Juv. av. 252 mm. and 8 Basic av. 267 (Portenko 1952).

Summer specimens from ne. Yakutia (methods of meas. not stated); 7 ♂ : BILL 24–28 mm., av. 25.5; WING 265–280, av. 272.5; 5 ♀ : BILL 23–27 mm., av. 24.6; WING 233–280, av. 263.4 (S. Uspenskii et al. 1962).

For series with WING meas. across chord, see J. C. Phillips (1926); other series, WING meas. over the curve, see Witherby (1939).

**Weight** ♂ 1,500–1,850 gm., ♀ 1,183–1,850 (compilation, various sources). Three ♂ June 5–18 weighed 1,400–1,850 gm. and 2 on Aug. 5 weighed only 1,200 and 1,300 (S. Uspenskii et al. 1962).

Four young at hatching weighed 44.8–49 gm., the mean wt. being 46.2 gm (Smart 1965a); also see Johnsgard (1964b).

**Hybrids** none known.

No **geographical variation** has been reported; measured series (see above) show some differences, notably in tarsal length of drakes.

The following **individual variation** is of interest. A Bailey (1948) reported an "adult male with a black V on the throat, similar to that of the Pacific race of Common Eider." This specimen, Colo. Mus. Nat. Hist. no. 8,633, has been examined. The V-mark actually is gray rather than black. Another, in the same collection, no. 20,873, has fainter indication of a similar mark. Both (from Wainwright, Alaska) are in Alt. II rather than Def. Alt. ("adult male"). A drake in Def. Alt, having a faint throat chevron, was taken in the Yukon Delta in spring, 1973 (C. Dau). A young drake, U.S. Nat. Mus. no. 75,888 (St. Michael, Alaska, Sept. 9, 1877) is like no other specimen examined. It appears to be in an early stage of Prebasic II molt, with most of the very worn Juv. abdomen feathers and rectrices still present. The incoming wings are unique; there are no completely white feathers except 1 or 2 median coverts, all major wing feathers including the curved innermost secondaries ("tertials") being blackish sepia in color. The longest scapular feathers are shaped like those of Def. Basic, but are not white. They are brownish gray washed with white, with a very narrow white margin. KCP (early draft), expanded by RSP

FIELD IDENTIFICATION Smaller than the King and the Common Eider, with evenly sloping "forehead." Older drakes, fall–winter and into summer, have much white in upperparts (as in Common Eider) and remainder of body very dark, though not black (in Common and King Eiders the breast is pale or white). If close enough for details to be seen, the rather bizarre white "spectacle" contrasts with the surrounding greenish feathers. Contour of hindpart of head not smooth (it is in the King Eider), but somewhat irregular, like an uneven haircut. The drake's dark Basic Plumages are worn when, evidently, the birds are away from land. In Basic I (late 1st fall), upperparts and head (including "spectacle") are mostly various grays. In later Basics (midsummer into fall), the blackish body has white in the scapular area and on upper back, but most of head (including "spectacles") is largely various grays.

The ♀ Plumages and Juv. Plumages of both sexes are somewhat like corresponding Plumages of the Common Eider, but the "spectacles" generally are more or less paler than, i.e., contrast with, the darker feathering around them, especially anteriorly.

During the nesting–rearing season, in flying ♀ ♀ seen in good light, breeders have darker, more uniform wing coloration and darker belly. Yearling prebreeders have the belly mottled and, to a varying degree, lighter—a useful character to distinguish them when they are standing or walking. They still retain the Juv. wing, now much worn and faded, the pale innermost secondaries being a useful character when the birds are afloat or ashore. In flight, the general overall paleness of the dorsal surface of the Juv. wing is the most useful distinguishing feature of ♀ ♀ of this age-class. (Data from C. Dau.) RSP

VOICE In the Yukon Delta, no calling was heard from either sex during spring migration (C. Dau).

Captive drakes uttered a faint *hoo-hoo* during Head-forward + Rearing Display similar to but weaker than that of the Common Eider during Cooing movement 3 (Johnsgard 1964a), but neither this display nor call was heard during several seasons' study at nesting areas (C. Dau). A drake, circling with his mate over a pond after the nearby nest had been discovered, was heard "quacking in protest" (Brandt 1943). Females, when Inciting, utter calls much like the corresponding calls of ♀ Common and King Eiders (Johnsgard) and there is a call (heard but not described) uttered by a ♀ "while conducting her brood out of danger" (E. W. Nelson 1887).

During the latter half of incubation, flushed ♀ ♀ may remain 2–7 meters from the nest and they vary in behavior and in variety of calls. Most common—a short guttural croak at about 2-sec. intervals; less common—a rapid clucking like barnyard fowl, the 2nd syllable loudest. The first of these calls later is used in alarm, to send the ducklings scurrying for cover; the second is used to call the brood and they always respond to it. (Data from C. Dau.)

The young at first have a slurred whistle, later gradually altering to a clucking like that of the ♀ parent. It is used in greeting, accompanied by considerable nodding (like ♀ Inciting). A whistling purr was heard, but only once, from an older preflight bird. (Data from C. Dau.) RSP

HABITAT Nests mainly on coastal floodplain, from very near the sea to well inland in some places, where there are innumerable ponds and lakes and/or deltas and tidal inlets, i.e., areas that are about half water and half land. In Bering Sea coastal Alaska, at s. base of the Askinuk Range, preferred habitat extends into submontane valleys. In Siberia, in the Indigirka delta, penetrates inland farther than any other eider—to 50–100 km. (Bëme et al. 1965).Chosen areas generally consist of sedgy or grassy hummocks and slight ridges, also drier areas of sedge/moss and moss/lichen ground cover; some sheltered areas relatively remote from the sea have more or less upright woody growth. Nests are on islands and islets in tundra ponds and lakes, as well as ashore.

Evidently a bird of marine habitat when not breeding, including prebreeders in all seasons and excepting any that stay at or near nesting areas. RSP

DISTRIBUTION (See map.) In Alaska there are not many known **nesting localities,** from the vicinity of Baird Inlet (lat. 61° N) on the Bering Sea coast clockwise

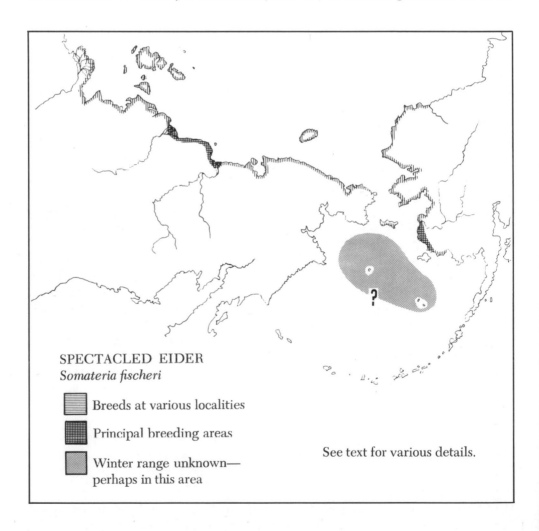

SPECTACLED EIDER
*Somateria fischeri*

Breeds at various localities

Principal breeding areas

Winter range unknown—
perhaps in this area

See text for various details.

around to the Colville delta area on the Beaufort Sea coast. The principal area in N. Am. is the Yukon Delta coastal plain. Occasionally nests on St. Lawrence I.; the summering birds there are mostly prebreeders.

Perhaps not now plentiful anywhere in Siberia. On the Chuckchee Pen. it nests only along the n. coast, in rather small numbers, and not every year at some known localities (Portenko 1972). To the north, there are 2 known occurrences (not nesting) at Wrangel I. Continuing westward, it nests at various mainland localities and on some adjacent is. (Aion, for example). In 1906 it was reported to be the commonest nesting eider in the Kolyma delta and in 1935 the commonest in the Indigirka delta. Vorobiev (1963) regarded it as still plentiful on coastal tundra between the Kolyma and the Indigirka. Still farther westward, there are few certain records; it has nested in the Yana delta, also somewhere in the Lena delta (long. 125°–129° E.) At the present time the largest numbers probably occur in the deltas of the Indigirka and Kolyma and on intervening coastal lowland.

There are a few known occurrences, both sexes included and sometimes with King Eiders, in the New Siberian Archipelago, but no proof of nesting there.

According to Belopolskii (in Dementiev and Gladkov 1952), apparently it visits along the [Bering Sea] coast" of the Chuckchee Pen., since it is known to the Eskimos of Kresta Gulf.

**Winter range** unknown. W. Cooke (1906) stated that it is "probable" that the Aleutians are the "principal winter home" and various later N. Am. authors have described the purported winter range by listing certain few presumed delimiting occurrences at that season, all of which possibly are stragglers. There is no satisfactory evidence of wintering along the Asiatic or N. Am. coasts, nor near the Commanders, nor more than occasional individuals at this season anywhere. Conover (1926) and subsequently various Russian authors have stated or implied that the main winter quarters are in Bering Sea, in or near pack ice or on more extensive open water. Such an area, for example, was mapped as principal winter range in Dementiev and Gladkov (1952). Down to the present, however, attempts to find any numbers of them anywhere during winter have been unsuccessful.

Less given to **straggling** than Steller's Eider. The following records are for localities remote from known "normal" range: drake seen at Banks I. in w. Canadian arctic, June 20, 1952 (Manning et al. 1956); drake seen of s. Vancouver I., Sept. 22, 1962 (Godfrey 1966); one shot at Bitterwater L. in San Benito Co., Cal., in Feb., 1893 (Moffitt 1940). This eider has been reported in Alaska outside the breeding season, at Wales, the Pribilofs, Izembek Lagoon, and on the Kenai Pen. In w. Eurasia there are records for s. Novaya Zemlya, Pechenga (Murmansk region), and a drake shot at Vardö, Norway, on Dec. 12, 1933.

Bones have been identified from an **archaeological site** on St. Lawrence I. (Friedmann 1934) and a single humerus from a prehistoric Eskimo midden on Kodiak I. (Friedmann 1935). RSP

MIGRATION Most of the explicit data pertain to spring passage in n. Bering Sea and beyond and the early return flight of postbreeding drakes. Flocks and smaller groups are more or less strung out, on routes used contemporaneously by other eiders. The northerly birds are funneled through Bering Strait; others are s. and nest in Alaska on the ne. periphery of Bering Sea, as discussed in the last paragraph of this section.

SPRING movement, in general, is later than that of the King and Common Eider but earlier than Steller's. Total span of time during which the Spectacled Eider passes through Bering Strait extends from about the beginning of May until late June, with main flight late in May, but there is much variation depending on season. Early flights have a preponderance of ♂ ♂, probably older prebreeders. Most breeders already are paired. Prebreeders of both sexes are included in spring migration. The majority, at least of breeders, turn westward and continue along the arctic Siberian coast to nesting areas. They arrive in ne. Yakutia at the very end of May or in early June (Vorobiev 1963), in one year arriving in Kromsk Bay en masse on June 5 (S. Uspenskii et al. 1962). A pair was seen on New Siberia I. on June 10 in 1902. On the Am. side they were seen far n. of Bering Strait in 1958 at the end of April, which is exceptionally early (M. T. Myres). In the Wainwright–Atanik area that year, the birds turned inland, going up river valleys, then crossed over and went down other (northward-flowing) rivers, such as the Meade and Inaru which drain into Dease Inlet not far e. of Barrow. Although total numbers seen were not large, this was the most numerous migrating eider on these rivers May 30–June 4 (M. T. Myres). Although the easternmost known nesting place is in w. part of the Colville delta, this eider has been taken much farther eastward—about 35 mi. w. of the Alaska–Canada boundary—as early as June 12. None of the Russian literature at hand suggests any overland migration across the Chuckchee Pen. But, if the birds do occur in Kresta Gulf, that location would be a logical point of departure for taking a short cut overland to the arctic coast.

**Molt migration** When the ducks are about half way through incubation, the drakes leave their mates and assemble nearby in groups. These combine into flocks which presumably move toward the still unknown winter range to molt, although occasional individuals and small groups may linger elsewhere. One year, in the Indigirka delta region at Kromsk Bay, groups of drakes were eastbound beginning June 19 and the movement was practically concluded by the 25th (Priklonskii et al. 1962). At Uelen, close to C. Dezhnev (E. Cape), on July 11, 1921, A. Bailey (1948) saw a "wonderful flight" of all 4 eider species, there being thousands and the majority were males, "no doubt returning from the breeding grounds."

A considerable number of yearling prebreeders have been seen at nesting areas (♀ ♀) or on waters thereabout (some ♂ ♂). It seems probable that the majority, at least of ♂ ♂, terminate their spring travels by going to as yet unknown molting areas somewhere at sea. Quite a few, however, molt near St. Lawrence I. in n. Bering Sea. V. M. Zenzinov "found females at sea July 18–Aug. 8 in flocks of hundreds," in waters off the Indigirka Dist. (Mikhel 1935). Since nesting ♀ ♀ are ashore at this time, and since molting prebreeders of both sexes would appear dark at a distance, the flocks most probably were molting prebreeders.

It is now known that some drakes of this species molt near Stuart I. in Norton Sd., Alaska (C. Dau).

FALL Whether postbreeding drakes have a true fall migration (after molting) will remain unknown at least until their winter range is discovered. The northerly birds vanish soon after entering Bering Sea. Successfully breeding ♀♀, soon after their young can fly, leave at the same time as the young and go to sea, in the latter part of August. Just when postbreeding ♀♀, and prebreeders of any age, return to wherever they spend the winter is conjectural. There is some evidence that movement down into Bering Sea of other than postbreeding drakes may occur at least throughout Sept., but this is the month when most postbreeding ♀♀ are believed to be flightless. No hint exists of an overland flight anywhere in fall. In arctic Alaska the birds must travel above range of human vision or at sea; at least there seem to be no reports of flights touching the coast anywhere. Nor is this eider found on the Chuckchee arctic coast in any numbers (Portenko 1972).

**Bering Sea breeders and young** (Data from C. Dau.) **Spring** time of coming ashore may be variable, depending on season. On the av., it may be as much as 3 weeks earlier in the Yukon Delta than on the Alaskan arctic coast. The nesting schedule and, apparently, the various subsequent activities are correspondingly advanced.

In the Yukon Delta, at a place about 18 mi. se. of Hooper Bay in 1972, a single bird was seen on May 10, and 3 small groups of paired birds on May 22. The major influx occurred May 23–26, when groups of up to 25 appeared. Most of them came from a northwesterly direction. In several seasons' study at Yukon Delta localities, it appeared that migrants generally arrive about the 3rd week in May, since many clutches are initiated at the very end of the month.

**Summer** Yearling ♀♀, in early to mid-June, come to the areas where older ♀♀ are nesting and become common. They remain into the rearing period; some even join parents with broods, but in other cases they are driven away. Evidently they go to sea by some time in Aug. A few yearling ♂♂ are seen in spring, occasionally associating with mated pairs. They have been seen on nearby sheltered waters until well into July; the whereabouts of any other yearling drakes at this time is unknown.

Mature drakes remain for a time in the area where their mates are nesting; they are increasingly less attentive as incubation proceeds and by midincubation the pair bond is terminated. They then gather in moderate-sized flocks on larger waters nearby and soon vanish. RSP

BANDING STATUS   In N. Am. the total number banded through 1964 was 120 and there was a single recovery through the year 1961; all banding was done in Alaska (data from Bird Banding Laboratory). In 1970–72 inclusive, C. Dau banded about 60, mostly preflight young, in the Yukon Delta region. RSP

REPRODUCTION   Age when **first breeds** unknown, presumably 2 years.

Most breeders already are paired during spring migration, hence **pair formation** occurs earlier, at sea. A few pairs are formed during the week or two before nesting begins (P Mickelson). Yearling prebreeders, mostly ♀♀, occur at nesting areas. Known displays have been observed only at or near the most southerly nesting localities, or among captives; there are no data on an initial, social, phase of display, which probably occurs at sea. Johnsgard (1964b) stated that the greenish feathers on rear sides of head are "not raised during display." Brandt (1943) mentioned them twice, once rather offhand, as used in display, and again very specifically in another context: mates swam close together on a pond, alarmed by the presence of the observer, and the drake "occasionally" would "partly elevate" his "crest" and "raise his white scapulars above his back." (Raising the scapulars occurs also in the drake Common and ♀ King Eiders; they are so constructed as to be permanently raised in the drake King.) The following behavioral information is based on Johnsgard (1964a, 1965), supplemented by some more recent information.

**Displays of the duck**   INCITING resembles that of the other large eiders and is quite distinct from that of the small Steller's; a croaking call is uttered. HEAD-ROLL rolling or rubbing movements of the cheeks on the anterior dorsum. (Also see below.)

**Displays of the drake**   SHAKE breast raised rapidly out of water, the head (with bill pointed downward) vigorously shaken, then head drawn back as bird settles down on water; much as in Steller's Eider. WING-FLAP no distinct pause beforehand, no orientation toward a ♀. REARING rapid jerk upward and backward of head–neck, the dark breast raised and prominent; done very rapidly; homologous to Rearing of Steller's Eider. HEAD-FORWARD+REARING neck first stretched vertically, then head swung forward and quickly retracted, producing a rearing of the body; closely corresponds to Reaching in the King Eider and Cooing movement 3 in Common Eider; a weak *hoo-hoo* accompanying it was heard from captives. BILL-TOSS corresponds to and is "certainly homologous to" Cooing movement 1 of Common Eider. NECK-JERK equivalent to Cooing movement 2 of Common Eider; the Bill-toss has only been seen linked to Neck-jerk, but independent Neck-jerk has been observed. Head-roll, as described above for the ♀, occurs in both sexes through spring and so long as the drakes remain, also in mature ♀ ♀ thereafter, in yearling ♀ ♀, and in the young beginning soon after they leave the nest (C. Dau). HEAD-TURN laterally, infrequent and inconspicuous.

According to C. Dau, in paired birds the Shake sometimes is performed at the same time by both individuals and they also Splash-bathe together.

**Copulation**   A drake performed the Shake only once, immediately before mounting; after treading, the drake released the duck's nape, performed as single Head-forward+Rearing and then 4 Head-turning movements; the ♀ Bathed. According to M. T. Myres, in a presumably incomplete copulation, the ♂ performed several Rearing like actions, the last time Rearing far back and Wing-flapping, then swam around the PRONE ♀ and mounted. Johnsgard (1964a) listed all of the following, in the order in which they occur in the drake's precopulatory repertoire: PREEN-BEHIND-THE-WING, PREEN-DORSALLY, PUSHING, Bathing, Head-roll, BILL-DIP, and Wing-flap. In 3 instances the ♂ performed an UPWARD-STRETCH. Postcopulatory displays: Head-forward+Rearing, then Head-turning. The ♀ usually bathed. Copulation has been observed in the Yukon Delta Region about a week before onset of nesting (P. Mickelson).

By June 1 at Onumtuk (about 24 mi. se. of Hooper Bay), Alaska, ♀ ♀ commonly were "**prospecting**" for nest sites (C. Dau); sometimes they are alone, sometimes accompanied by the drake (P. Mickelson). Selection occurs during the spring thaw and runoff when the water is high in ponds; a chosen site thus may be nearer water than later, after some ponds have subsided or dried up. Usually there is a single pair at a pond, or several at a large one having an irregular shoreline. Nests are near shore, or on peninsulas, or on islets. According to Johnsgard (1964b), where this eider is relatively plentiful, there is a tendency toward grouping of nests; 2 were as close as 12 ft. apart, 3 were around a pond less than an acre in area, and 2 each at 2 other small ponds. In a more recent study of this eider, distance from water varied from 10 in. to 240 ft. (usually about 6½ ft.), mean distance between nests was 889 ft., and there was no evident grouping (C. Dau).

**Nests** usually are in grass or sedge habitat at Onumtuk, commonly on a slightly raised site, a hummock or low ridge. They are very exposed, having no concealment until the new vegetation grows. An old site, still containing nest down of the previous year, now matted and quite wet, often is used (or reused). Whether a site is new or reused, the duck adds a substantial layer of vegetation, plucked or pulled, to the cavity; it becomes compressed and later is intermingled more or less with nest down as the ♀ arranges and covers her eggs (C. Dau).

**Laying season** On the Bering Sea coast of Alaska at Igiak Bay, Brandt (1943) generalized from 1924 data that June 10 "appears to be the opportune time" to seek full first clutches, but seasons vary; in 1963, most laying began there at least 2 weeks earlier (Johnsgard 1964b). On Onumtuk, 24 mi. se. of Hooper Bay, in 1969–72 inclusive, laying began in the last third of May and ended in the fourth week in June; in 1972, all eggs were laid May 31–June 28, with peak of clutch initiation at the very end of May (P. Mickelson). For Alaska, Bent (1925) gave dates for 12 clutches as June 8–July 4 (6 of them June 15–26); he included localities both s. and n. of Bering Strait. He reported a clutch of 9 on June 15 beyond Bering Strait at Point Hope. From various Russian papers it appears that, on the average, full clutches may be expected in arctic Siberia beginning in the third week in June. Near the Chuckocha R. in n. Yakutia, a clutch of 6 eggs found on July 12 hatched before July 15 (Vorobiev 1963).

An egg is laid daily, usually in early afternoon (C. Dau), often with a day skipped after the 4th or 5th egg (P. Mickelson).

**Clutch size** Brandt (1943) noted 5–6 eggs/clutch plus one clutch of 7 in 7 clutches in 1924 at Igiak bay and Johnsgard found 3–6, av. 4.25, in 11 clutches there in 1963. At the Onumtuk study area in 1969–72, clutches contained 1–8 eggs; the av. ranged from 4.06 (37 clutches) in 1969 to 4.90 (33 nests) in 1972; the 4-year av. for 169 nests found (not all had full clutches) was 4.44 and the av. number incubated was 4.69 eggs; 5 other studies in Alaska have yielded almost identical figures (P. Mickelson). Russian authors usually state 5–6 eggs/clutch, but as high as 9, presumably from Bent as mentioned above.

The **nest down** is added usually beginning with the laying of the 2nd or 3rd egg, sometimes quite rapidly, or sometimes gradually into early incubation. It is dark, fuscous or sepia or variants, with inconspicuous lighter centers; some intermingled small feathers are mottled, others barred fuscous at their ends.

One **egg** each from 20 clutches (mostly from Alaska) **size** length 66.78 ± 2.90 mm., **breadth** 44.22 ± 1.76, radii of curvature of ends 17.31 ± 1.42 and 10.19 ± 1.88 [this last figure is high because of 2 eggs of unusual shape], **shape** between subelliptical and long oval, elongation 1.50 ± 0.066, bicone −0.064, asymmetry +0.262 (FWP); **color** olive buff or light brownish buff, shell with considerable gloss, but soiled eggs are dark and without luster. For other published series, see Bent (1925), Brandt (1943), Dementiev and Gladkov (1952), Schönwetter (1961), and Johnsgard (1964b).

At the Onumtuk study area, se. of Hooper Bay, Alaska, in 1969–72 inclusive; 640

eggs: length 67.9 ± 3.0 (spread 44.6–77.3) and breadth 45.3 ± 1.53 mm. (spread 31.1–48.6) (P. Mickelson).

**Egg weight** in 1973 in the Yukon Delta: in 3 clutches in which av. wt. of eggs was about 80 gm, mean length was 70.5 mm. (69.3–72.5) and breadth 46.7 (46.5–47.0); in 25 clutches in which eggs av. about 70–80 gm., mean length was 68.3 (65.3–71.0) and breadth 45.5 (43.3–47.0); and in 13 clutches in which eggs weighed an av. of about 60 up to 70 gm., mean length was 67.3 mm. (65.0–70.8) and breadth 44.8 (41.1–46.2); thus it can be seen that av. dimensions and wt. of eggs varies from clutch to clutch, i.e. from different ♀ ♀ (C. Dau).

**Mixed clutches** Spectacled Eider eggs have been found in nests of the Cackling Canada Goose and vice versa, also a clutch of 4 eggs of this eider plus 3 of the Greater Scaup (C. Dau).

**Renesting** is not known, but one or two very late nests without eggs have been found (C. Dau).

**Behavior during incubation** The duck is a close sitter, possibly beginning sometimes before the last egg is laid; at least one individual has been touched and photographed while on her eggs. An off-duty ♀, observed carefully, was seen to feed by up-ending to obtain aquatic vegetation; she also ate midges (Chironomidae) which literally covered the surface of a pond (C. Dau). Late during incubation, if a ♀ is flushed from her nest, commonly she performs a "broken wing" distraction display, sometimes with tail erected and spread (C. Dau). At nesting ponds, frequently a pair would swim close to another pair sitting by the water's edge with no sign of conflict; also, at various times, drakes were seen accompanied by 2 or even 3 ♀ ♀, perhaps failed breeders (Johnsgard). Approximately half way through incubation, the pair bond is terminated and soon afterwards the drakes disappear.

The **incubation period** is 24 days (Johnstone 1970), the details not given. In 3 nests in the Yukon Delta in 1972, the period from laying of the last egg to hatching of all was 24 days (C. Dau, P. Mickelson).

**Nesting success** is fairly high, varying from 50% to 84% in adequate samples in 4 successive years in the Yukon Delta and the combined av. for 120 broods hatched was 4.13 young/brood (P. Mickelson). A hatching peak, in the Yukon Delta, occurs in the last few days of June or very beginning of July.

**Rearing period** The duck is known to be very attentive to her young brood and has been seen on ponds on the Bering Sea coast of Alaska with older young as late as the 2nd week in Sept. Sometimes broods join together, but such crèches as have been observed are small and they are not common. On a pond on June 22, 1972, there were 20 young plus 13 ♀ eiders of which at least 4 were yearlings (C. Dau). Typically, the young are accompanied by an adult ♀ —presumably their parent—until the former can fly, and they are reared within 1 to 2 mi. of where they hatched and always on fresh or slightly brackish water (C. Dau). When the family moves between ponds, it is led by the ♀ and goes very rapidly (Dau).

At the Onumtuk study area se. of Hooper Bay, within approximately 1 week after the young were on the wing the families left the inland area and moved out to coastal flats, before the adult ♀ ♀ became flightless. Age at **first flight** of a marked young bird in the wild was 53 days or less (C. Dau); development is rapid, as suggested earlier (see "Description" of ♂ Juv.). RSP

96

HABITS  The Spectacled Eider evidently spends much of its life on waters well away from shores. Sometimes it flies in fairly compact flocks, usually of less than 50 birds; at other times, as during spring migration, singles, pairs, bunches, and strings are seen, frequently in loose association with other waterfowl, especially the King Eider. At least in spring, the Spectacled has been observed resting on sea ice.

**Diving**  The wings are held out from the body as this eider commences its feeding dive and W. Percy (in J. C. Phillips 1926) observed that it can remain submerged a long time, a useful attribute of a bottom feeder.

**Feeding** (The following 4 paragraphs are data from C. Dau.)  The liquid defecated when a ♀ is flushed from her eggs contains some evidence of vegetable matter (C. Dau); in other instances it was clear (P. Mickelson).

During the nesting season, Spectacled Eiders feed to some extent at tundra ponds, by surface-dipping (head partly submerged), dipping (head well below the surface), and up-ending (as in puddle ducks). Diving is rare at this season, but has been observed even in downies. Early in life, the young commonly acquire a heavy parasite load (cestodes) which weakens them. Yearling ♀ ♀ and to a lesser extent young of the year have been seen feeding ashore, the yearlings on short sedges (*Carex*), both yearlings and young by "rooting" in waterlogged marshy places. Shore-feeding was verified by collecting a number of birds and examining their digestive tracts.

In August, adult ♀ ♀ with broods rest and feed on upland tundra, on berries then ripening. They feed for short periods, not over 30 min., and very selectively. Based on field observations and on stomachs examined, crowberry (*Empetrum nigrum*) was favored over the also abundant *Rubus* (probably cloudberry, *R. chamaemorus*). They are agile birds ashore.

In late Aug.–early Sept. the eiders move from inland environment to sheltered coastal waters, in preparation for going to sea. This may be a critical period in the lives of the young birds, since now they must adapt to very different foods and must obtain them by diving.

**Climatic factors**  Although the environment of the Spectacled Eider is subject to rapid and at times violent weather changes, the mean monthly air temperature in Bering Sea is mild in fall and even in winter—not far from freezing, a few degrees below the mean for arctic nesting areas in June. But spring is another matter. In northward flight into and beyond the Chuckchee Sea, the eiders pass through a tremendous temperature gradient. In some years there are hardly any open leads in sea ice, nor yet any thaw ashore; there are adverse winds at times, or driving sleet, freezing rains, and fog as dense as any on earth. Examples could be cited, at least from 1882 onward, of these factors in various combinations resulting in conditions unfavorable for travel or feeding by various eiders; see "Habits" of the King Eider for details. Later on, time of nesting is weather influenced, being favored by an early thaw and resultant runoff of surface water at nesting areas, or hampered by tardy seasons such as occur at least every few years.

**Predation**  Although the Spectacled Eider is a close sitter and solicitous parent, jaegers, gulls, and foxes (both red and arctic) get some eggs and surely get some ducklings. The Alaskan native practice of driving and killing any molting birds (though probably not this eider) and preflight young apparently ceased long ago. No nest in the vicinity of native settlements, however, is safe from man or roving dogs. There is some

97

shooting of migrants and it is known among Alaskan Eskimos (and no doubt in Siberia) that this eider is better eating than the King Eider, the duck better than the drake, and preflight young are a delicacy. It is certain that the Spectacled Eider became greatly reduced in numbers in the St. Michael area of Alaska in the previous century, allegedly from overexploitation by native residents. Especially because summer travel is practically impossible on marshy coastal tundra, there may be still-unknown nesting areas in Alaska, but the total number of birds must be small. In the Indigirka delta in Siberia, where the Spectacled Eider nested in comparative abundance, the eggs were gathered and local residents stated that the numbers of this eider were diminishing (Dementiev and Gladkov 1952). The decline in numbers appears to be general. It is probable that the total number of Spectacled eiders of breeding age does not exceed a few tens of thousands of pairs as of 1970; S. Uspenskii (1972) estimated a total of 500,000 individuals (all age-classes combined) in the species.

**Uses of skins**    The Chuckchees use the skins of the heads of drakes as ornaments on clothing (Vorobiev 1963); Alaskan natives use (or have used) them decoratively, on headgear, also (along with skins from heads of the King and other eiders) they have sewn them into handsome mats. There is a beautiful vest made entirely of the skins of the heads of drake Spectacled Eiders in the natural history museum of Washington State University. RSP

FOOD    When on marine waters, evidently mollusks mainly; elsewhere, insects, a few crustaceans, and various plant materials (including berries). Stomachs of 16 "adults" taken in summer contained 77% animal and 23% vegetable matter. Plants are much more important than with the other eiders, being the principal food when the birds are ashore; see the preceding section for various details. Diet of "juveniles" contained 54% animal and 46% vegetable matter (Cottam 1939).

**Animal**    Mollusks (*Siliqua* mainly, *Mytilus*, *Modiolaria*, *Natica*) 42.3% insects (larvae of caddis flies—Trichoptera, and midges—Chironomidae) 31.5%, crustaceans (mainly isopods—*Mesidotea entomon*) 2.6%, miscellaneous (foraminiferans, bryozoans, and sea urchins, sand dollars, starfishes, bones of sculpin) 1% (Cottam 1939). Contents of 2 stomachs from the Pribilof Is. showed 90% amphipods among which *Bathymedon obtusifrons* was identified; also the mollusks *Rochefortia* and *Lora* (Preble and McAtee 1923).

Small mussels and seaweed came out of the bill of a drake when shot on Dec. 12 in n. Norway (S. Johnsen 1938).

On tundra lakes in U.S.S.R. in summer, main food is aquatic insects (51.1%) of which caddis fly larvae form 42.4%, chironomids 8.3%, gastropods 9.4%, and crustaceans 2.6%. There is a considerable amount of vegetable food (37%), of which the leaves and rhizomes of *Potamogeton pectinatus* constitute 10.2%; also the succulent parts of grasses, sedges, aquatic plants, and berries of *Empetrum nigrum*. (From Dementiev and Gladkov 1952.)

In ne. Yakutia, the stomachs of birds taken June 5–8 contained stems and leaves of grasses, seeds of *Ranunculus*, remains of marine gastropods, remains of larvae of Rhagonidae and Carabidae; in mid-June, along with plant remnants, large quantities of chironomid larvae; and stomachs of adults and young taken Aug. 5 on a branch of the

Kolyma contained larval cases of Trichoptera, also leaves of grasses and *Carex*, and seeds of *Carex* and *Ranunculus* (S. Uspenskii et al. 1962).

On the sea the food is 95.8% animal, mainly mollusks (Dementiev and Gladkov 1952).

**Vegetable**  In addition to items mentioned in the section on "Habits" and also in the above paragraphs: pondweeds (*Potamogeton pectinatus, Zannichellia palustris*) 7%, crowberry 1.5%, mares tail (*Hippuris vulgaris*) 1.4%, grasses and sedges 2.2%, and miscellaneous (*Ranunculus, Rubus, Potentilla, Cornus*, algae, mosses) 10.6% (Cottam 1939). AWS

### King Eider

*Somateria spectabilis* (Linnaeus)

Large, heavy-bodied marine duck; one of the large eiders. Feathering extends from center of forehead narrowly far forward, approximately to level of nostrils; it does not reach the nostril on side base of upper mandible (reverse of Common Eider). Both sexes have rather small bills and—exaggerated seasonally in the drake—roundish heads (not wedge-shaped facial profile). Females and young ♂♂ in certain stages av. more toward reddish tan or rufescent in general coloring than is characteristic of most populations of Common Eider. Mantle and upper scapular feathers of ♀ have somewhat tapering ends (not as broad as in Common Eider) and the terminal border of the black portion, which comprises most of the feather, is V-shaped or at least angled back

Common Eider                                                        King Eider

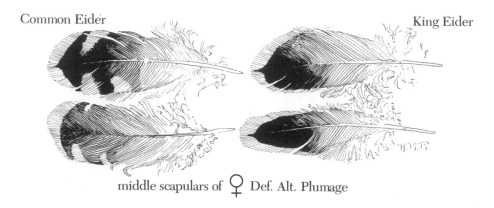

middle scapulars of ♀ Def. Alt. Plumage

from the shaft (rather than curved or nearly transverse as in Common Eider). In drakes, the frontal lobes (also called frontal processes or bulges, frontal or lateral protruberances) at top base of bill become progressively larger until perhaps 3rd year and especially in mature birds vary with season from being essentially flat to greatly swollen; most of back and all of secondaries black. Drake's trachea has uniform diam., the asymmetrical bony bulla at proximal end very similar to but slightly smaller than that of Common Eider; the bulla is best illus. in Schiøler (1926), both trachea and bulla in Humphrey (1958b) whose accompanying text gives comparison with other eiders.

Length ♂ to at least 25 in., ♀ to 24; wingspread ♂ to 40, ♀ to about 36; usual wt. of ♂ about 4 lb., ♀ about 3½. No subspecies.

DESCRIPTION Two Plumages/cycle in both sexes; sequence as in Common Eider; attainment of definitive feathering probably by 3rd cycle in ♀, 4th in ♂, but perhaps some individual variation. As in the Common Eider, there is individual variation in timing (especially duration) of molts, amount of new feathering acquired during certain molts, details of coloring, etc. As in the other eiders, the tail, all of the wing, and the modified long (lower) scapulars are molted only once/cycle, i.e., are Basic. Of the various studies (some not entirely independent of earlier ones but based on different material), these are especially important: Schiøler's (1926) text, based on examination of over 450 specimens, and excellent col. and monochrome pls.; Meinertzhagen's

100

concise treatment (in Witherby 1924, revised in Witherby 1939); Portenko (1952); and Parkes (in Todd 1963), which is based on much of the same information used here. Millais (1913b) is still useful, especially the photos of skins. Various Plumages are shown in a rather general way on pl. 19 in Thomson (1964).

♀ Def. Basic  ♂ Def. Alt.

T.Pengel

▶  ♂ Def. Alt. Plumage (head–body, except long scapulars), may be acquired beginning in SEPT., but OCT.–DEC. seems to be principal period; worn through winter into the following summer. Frontal lobes are most highly developed and colored vivid yellow or even toward orange in spring, and the **bill** scarlet with white nail. **Iris** black (not yellow as sometimes stated or illustrated). **Head** nape, crown, and forehead pearl gray, palest anteriorly; nape feathers elongated (posteriormost sometimes tipped dark gray), forming rounded puffy crest; a white line margining this gray area from anterior corner of eye to sides of nape; frontal lobes outlined in black; cheeks pale green and iridescent, extending back (somewhat darker) along white margin of sides of crest; the cheek feathers are stiff and plushlike; throat white, with V-shaped mark (its point forward), varying in darkness to (usually) black and its degree of development not correlated with age. **Upperparts** neck to interscapular region white; upper scapulars dull blackish and unmodified in shape (for lower scapulars, see below); remaining upperparts black. **Underparts** upper breast pinkish or yellowish buff (any black tips on new feathers soon wear off), paling to white toward neck; flank feathers nearly black or black; a white patch on each side of rump; venter black (or when abraded Basic is retained, it contrasts with the large new black Alt. flank feathers). Legs and **feet** vivid yellow in late spring, the webs dusky, nails black.

Retained Basic, worn with the above-described Alt., includes: 1 the 2 longest scapulars on each side, which are stiff, black, the upper one most prominent, and both modified in shape to form the triangular "sail" on each side of back; 2 tail; and 3 all of wing.

▶  ♂ Def. Basic Plumage (entire feathering); these feathers begin showing on head–neck and then body in JULY and these areas generally are renewed almost completely by sometime in AUG.; then wing and tail are molted and their new feathers begin to grow; from about OCT.-DEC. the drake loses the Basic head-body and acquires Alt.,

101

but the modified Basic scapulars are "offset" in timing so as to grow contemporaneously with the incoming Alt.

The lobes at base of **bill** shrink in late June; their most reduced stage lasts more than 3 mo. and during this time they are fleshy yellow with dark brownish spots on some portions (Portenko 1952); near Pt. Barrow, Alaska, by late July, the bulges are "shrunken and dull in color and the head and neck are mottled brown" [incoming Basic] (D. Q. Thompson and Person 1963). **Head** crown and nape dark brownish olive obscurely barred black; vaguely defined paler line formed of buff or grayish buff feathers with blackish terminal shaft streaks extends from base of bill diagonally to eye, then posteriorly, disappearing along sides of nape; cheeks like crown but slightly paler; throat buffy white, a few sepia feathers primarily where the black V of Alt. Plumage occurs. **Upperparts** neck sepia; anterior mantle sepia, the feathers with a white subterminal spot which increases in size on more posterior ones; mixed with these are

Def. Basic    Basic 1    Def. Basic

R.T.T.

King Eider—modified scapulars

some white feathers with black tips and pale sepia bases; general effect mottled white and dark sepia; **scapulars** blackish brown to black, the 2 longest "offset" ones (worn with Alt.) are broad, with scooped and twisted outer web; remainder of back blackish brown, somewhat mixed with white in interscapular area; on side of rump a patch of white feathers with dark sepia margins. **Underparts** upper breast feathers variable, mostly barred black and buffy brown, interrupted with white along shaft; amount of white on feathers increases posteriorly (down breast); intermixed are white feathers with black terminal band or slight terminal barring; remaining underparts dull blackish, or toward brownish on flanks. Legs and feet probably less colored than in winterspring. **Tail** blackish brown above, somewhat lighter below. **Wing** primaries, their coverts, and alula blackish brown; secondaries and greater coverts black, some of the latter sometimes tipped white; inner secondaries falcate, curving downward over closed wing to light rump patch; a white patch formed by median and lesser coverts; feathers of bend of wing mixed white sepia; underside of remiges and primary coverts dark smoke gray, remaining under wing coverts and axillars white.

NOTE    Drakes generally are flightless by mid-Aug.; it has been surmised that they regain flight quite rapidly, but the time required is unknown.

▶    ♀ Def. Alt. Plumage (head–body, except long scapulars), acquired from late SUMMER and early FALL into very late fall, even WINTER (peak of molt usually well along in fall); sometimes the molt is very protracted or even incomplete so that some very worn

102

Basic is retained on venter and rump. So great is individual variation in timing that a bird taken Jan. 24 may be scarcely farther advanced than various mid-Oct. specimens and with most of head–body still are in very worn and faded Basic.

**Bill** pale greenish gray to yellowish green; the frontal processes are somewhat swollen in spring–early summer. **Iris** dark brownish (not yellowish as has been stated). **Head** and neck rich tawny-rufescent, darkest on crown, finely streaked black; chin and throat nearly immaculate or finely spotted black posteriorly. **Upperparts** feathers black tipped deep reddish brown, some of the upper scapulars with an additional tawny bar, some other feathers notched laterally with tawny; the 2 longest scapulars, which are modified in shape, are late-acquired Basic (described below). **Underparts** upper breast barred black and rusty, the bars becoming obsolete posteriorly so that abdomen varies, from tawny to sepia with obscure barring, to almost solid blackish sepia; flank feathers blackish with tawny ends and sometimes an additional poorly defined lighter bar; under tail coverts buffy brown barred black. Legs and **feet** greenish gray to yellowish, webs dusky to nearly black.

Retained Basic, worn with the above Alt., includes 1 modified longer scapulars or "sails", 2 tail, and 3 all of wing; sometimes, in addition, more or less of venter and rump.

▶ ♀ Def. Basic Plumage (entire feathering), the head–body except long scapulars acquired during SPRING (head often last, mid-May to early June), tail and wing in late SUMMER or early FALL, and the modified long scapulars in SUMMER or later. The succeeding long scapulars are retained through winter, spring, into summer or later; the Basic tail and wing are retained at least into late summer.

Differs from Alt. as follows: **head** and neck buffier, with heavier black streaks; throat mostly finely spotted or streaked instead of nearly immaculate; **upperparts** the feathers, including on rump and flanks, barred and tipped tawny; **underparts** feathers of upper breast paler with black bars averaging narrower, venter often more nearly unicolor (darkish), but much individual variation in color and pattern.

In addition: **longest scapulars** modified in shape, but not as exaggerated as in the ♂, and dark brownish; **tail** feathers blackish fuscous above, deep smoke gray below; **wing** primaries, their coverts and alula blackish fuscous, paler on inner web; outer secondaries fuscous, 5–8 of this group tipped with white on outer web to form band at trailing edge of wing; inner secondaries fuscous, outlined (especially outer web) with black and edged with tawny; innermost secondaries elongated and downcurved (less than in ♂); greater coverts fuscous with narrow deep tawny outer margin, all but 5–6 outermost with white tip to outer web (white band within wing at forward edge of speculum); remaining feathers of upper surface of wing blackish fuscous with tawny tip; underside of remiges and the primary coverts smoke gray; under median coverts whitish; axillars white; rest of underwing feathers dark fuscous with buffy brown edgings.

NOTES Nesting ♀♀ vary in general coloration, from a palish or pale reddish tan to much darker—either individual variation in Basic feathering or, perhaps, younger ♀♀ tend to be darker.

Much more than the Alt., the Basic feathering of head—body becomes abraded and bleached, toward buff: under certain conditions some ♀♀ become somewhat darker from loss of light ends and edges of various feathers.

There is some seasonal enlargement of the frontal processes of at least some ♀♀. A

103

pale ♀ in ne. Greenland had a "well developed prominence on the forehead" (Manniche 1910); also see photo of an incubating ♀ in Ytreberg (1960).

It is now known, from observations of P. Lamothe at Bathurst I. in arctic Canada and from observations of a single ♀ in nw. Iceland, that the modified long scapulars are seasonally erectile in the ♀; they appear as small rounded "sails", smaller than the permanently erected triangular ones of the drake. That is, they appear somewhat like the seasonally erectile rounded "sails" of the drake Common and Spectacled Eiders.

On Bathurst I., when an incubating ♀ was caught and handled, the modified long scapulars were loose and fell out (P. Lamothe). That is, they were dropped weeks after this duck had molted into the rest of Basic head–body.

AT HATCHING   See vol. 2, col. pl. facing p. 370; differs from other eiders in configuration of frontal and loreal feathering; see opening paragraph under this species. Upperparts paler than in the Common Eider; sides of head patterned and with cinnamon-buff cast. In young hatched in captivity, this cast had "almost completely disappeared" by end of 1st week (Johnstone 1961).

There is much fading as the ducklings grow; facial pattern becomes indistinct or absent. Discrepancies in published illus. may be accounted for partly by different ages of ducklings examined; also, Manning et al. (1956) stated that Banks I. downies varied thus: 1 usually a close similarity among members of a brood, but considerable variation among broods in relative amount of black and brown in dorsum and 2 none showed face and neck similar to the Southampton I. specimen illus. by Sutton (1932). Plate 32 in Sutton shows soft-part colors and head–pattern, the dark band across upper cheek being too pale. Among extant illus., the col. fig. on pl. 34 in Kortright (1943) is generally satisfactory in the 1st printing; Schiøler (1926: pl. 61) has a good fig. of an older, much faded duckling showing beginnings of Juv. Plumage. There is a strong facial pattern in 3-day-old downies shown in photo in Johnstone (1961); and same photo printed again, plus one of an older downy having blurred facial pattern, in Wildfowl Trust 13th *Report* (1962).

▶ ♂ Juv. Plumage (entire feathering), in entirety retained a few weeks at most (head-body generally molting out of Juv. in SEPT.), at least all of wing retained into following SUMMER. **Bill** variants of bluish gray, grading to somewhat yellowish on frontal lobes; iris very dark. **Head** crown and nape pale buffy brown, each feather with broad black shaft-streak; sides of head smoke gray with blackish olive streaks; a poorly defined transocular streak formed by paling of ground color (but streaking equally heavy); chin and throat smoke gray with only vague streaking, especially posteriorly, or slightly darker color. **Upperparts** blackish sepia, the feathers edged tawny or (scapulars) pale tawny, edgings bleaching rather quickly; edgings of mid- and lower back (area concealed when wings folded) obsolete or absent; longest scapulars broadened, pointed, but not scooped as in older birds, edged with tawny only on terminal third of inner web. **Underparts** breast feathers distinctly barred, with sequence (from tip to base) cinnamon-buff, black (or blackish sepia), white, and smoke gray; cinnamon-buff tips of some feathers have additional, interrupted, dark bar across; abdomen variable, but gives appearance of dense barring of brownish olive and buff or smoke gray; pale bars become obsolete posteriorly in some individuals, so lower abdomen appears almost solid brownish olive to blackish sepia; flanks strongly barred blackish sepia and cinnamon. **Legs** and **feet** "dull brown, darkest on webs and at joints" (Sutton 1932) or

104

pale yellowish with dusky lobes and webs (Schiøler 1926: pl. 62). **Tail** blackish sepia tipped with cinnamon. **Wing** brownish black, coverts edged with deep tawny-chestnut; some inner greater coverts with buff edges; innermost secondaries slightly elongated and downcurved, edged cinnamon; underside of wing as in ♀ Def. Basic.

NOTE   In 3 reared in captivity, the Juv. feathering began to show at 14 days and at age 1 mo. the birds "were virtually fully feathered"; the Juv. feathering was "lighter brown" than Common Eider and the sexes were similar [but see below]; at age 3 mo. the ♂'s bill was developing a pinkish hue and tail feathers were prominent (Johnstone 1961). There are photos of these captives, at 4 different ages, in Wildfowl Trust 13th *Report* (1962).

▶   ♀ Juv. Plumage (entire feathering), timing probably as ♀, at least the entire wing retained into following SUMMER. Based on museum skins examined, as ♂ except: **breast** feathers less distinctly barred, with less (often no) white; light edgings of **wing coverts** more contrasting; edgings usually present and conspicuous on **back** (where absent or obscure in ♂); in some individuals an indication of white speculum borders (tips of secondaries, greater coverts, or both).

▶   ♂ Basic I Plumage (perhaps all feathering except all of wing, but a lesser amount sometimes acquired: head–neck, foreback, varying amount of scapulars, upper tail coverts, breast, flanks, and tail), acquired beginning in SEPT. or OCT., but mostly Oct–Nov., and succeeded by Alt. I in WINTER.

**Bill** and developing frontal lobes become yellowish or somewhat orange as early as Dec., or (Schiøler 1926) even as early as Nov. 10 in Greenland. **Head** crown and nape rich buffy brown, each feather with black bar at or near tip; a narrow paler buff trans-ocular line; cheeks somewhat paler than crown, densely spotted rather than barred blackish; chin and anterior throat pale buffy gray; posteriorly, feathers tipped blackish gray giving "dirty" appearance, these feathers extending around neck behind nape. **Upperparts** new brownish black feathers may appear at this time in scapular area, also upper tail-coverts. The long Basic I scapulars are modified in shape, being quite like those of the ♂ Common Eider in Def. Basic but narrower. **Underparts** breast, sides, and under tail coverts buffy tan, the feathers with somewhat crescentic subterminal blackish bar, hence a broken pattern; lower breast to vent more evenly dark, the tan terminal portions of the feathers being greatly reduced and soon frayed.

▶   ♂ Alt. I Plumage (very variable in amount of inclusive feathering), acquired from about MIDWINTER on, often largely in spring; retained until some time in SUMMER. So variable in amount of feathering, pattern, coloring, etc., that no single description is adequate. Extremes range from individuals molting head only (into feathering resembling the antecedent Basic I) to those molting practically all of head–body into a Plumage strongly reminiscent of Def. Alt. An example of the former type has crown and nape appearing gray vaguely barred darker (feathers have gray terminal and blackish subterminal bar); cheeks similar but browner, a few blackish feathers intermixed; chin and throat grayish buff, darkest anteriorly, with V vaguely indicated in brownish olive or blackish; posterior throat pure white, the posteriormost feathers with blackish tips; a semicollar of mixed black and white feathers. A more "advanced," but by no means extreme individual, is shown as left-center fig. on pl. 62 in Schiøler (1926). The bird has much of crown and nape gray, the throat and breast and "collar" are almost pure white, the V on chin is blacker, and there has been substantial feather replacement on scapulars, sides, flanks, and lower rump, i.e., much black feathering. Even more "advanced" individuals may have entire crown gray, cheeks white or greenish. Highly characteristic is a "white-collared" stage (photos: Millais 1913b). Lower breast to vent, including sides, white, the feathers with black terminal band (av. narrower than in Basic I), but amount of black highly variable, or same with retained Basic I abdomen to tail.

NOTES   The short (black) scapulars are new Alt. I, but the 2 longest, which are modified in shape, are retained Basic I feathers.

A drake in "fullest" Alt. I also has all of Juv. wing, sometimes some retained Juv. feathering on abdomen, always the Basic I tail, and the above-mentioned 2 longest Basic I scapulars.

A drake reared in captivity, at age 8 mo., showed highly "advanced" Alt. I; face mostly white, crown–nape darkish, neck and forepart of body white, much black feathering (much of back, the rump, sides, and flanks), and the Basic I "sails" on the back are highly developed; see photo in Wildfowl Trust 13th *Report* (1962).

In the Aleutians at Unalaska, May 18–30, 1877, large flocks about the outer harbors "were just assuming the breeding dress" (E. W. Nelson 1887)—young drakes were molting into Alt. I.

▶   ♀ Basic I Plumage (variable amount of feathering—much of head–body), generally acquired about SEPT. and retained into DEC., but timing variable; acquired earlier than in ♂ and usually includes more feathering—head–neck, back and scapulars, upper breast, sides and flanks, under tail coverts, and at least central rectrices—but not in all individuals. Quite like Juv., but more clear-cut markings; also: **head** more tawny, **scapulars** with rich tawny edges (contrasting with bleached Juv. feathers), **flank** feathers darker and have almost no contrast at edges at first but show more when fully grown. It is probable that the long scapulars come in late and are worn with the next (Alt. I) Plumage; they are modified in shape.

▶   ♀ Alt. I Plumage (as in ♂, amount of new feathering acquired is highly variable), acquired gradually during LATE WINTER, the new feathering retained only until LATE SPRING (heavy molting in March and April specimens examined). Includes head–neck, also (at fullest development) much of dorsum including visible scapulars, upper breast, sides and flanks; molting on breast extends farther caudally than in Prebasic I, the new feathers somewhat less contrastingly barred and duller. In general, pattern and coloring of new feathering foreshadows Def. Alt.  Worn with it are at least all of Juv. wing and often posterior venter, Basic I tail (but some Juv. feathers may remain), and apparently Basic I long scapulars.

▶   ♂ Basic II Plumage (entire feathering), most of head–body acquired by EARLY JULY, the tail and wing later (and after a flightless period), the long scapulars perhaps still later, in LATE SUMMER–EARLY FALL (when head–body are molting back into Alt.). All of the Basic wing, tail, and the modified long scapulars are retained into the following SUMMER or later; the Basic abdomen also tends to be retained and worn for at least some time with Alt. II.

**Head** crown and nape very dark sepia, feathers tipped with black giving vaguely barred appearance; conspicuous buffy whitish line with black streaks beginning at or just before eye; cheeks dark buffy brown, streaked anteriorly and barred posteriorly with black; an unmarked dark sepia area lying along posterior side of frontal lobe; chin and throat pale smoke gray, finely spotted sepia posteriorly. **Upperparts** blackish brown, the shorter scapulars with faintly brownish edgings. **Underparts** upper breast feathers barred black and white, with buffy brown to tawny tips; amount of white and distinctness of barring diminish posteriorly, blending with blackish brown of lower breast and abdomen; flank feathers blackish sepia with browner tips. **Tail** as in Def. Basic. **Wing** as Def. Basic except white patch on coverts greatly reduced, confined to median coverts, and occasionally absent, and falcate inner secondaries av. less well developed. The head of this Plumage is well shown in upper left fig. on pl. 64 in Schiøler (1926), who also showed a ♂, mostly still in this Plumage, just beginning the succeeding molt—pl. 62, right cent. fig.

▶ ♂ Alt. II Plumage (extent of feathering as in Def. Alt.), worn from 2nd FALL through winter into 3rd SUMMER. Like Def. Alt. except: **face** in new feathering often heavily marked with black; much of this usually wears off but, exceptionally, black-faced birds may retain this until next molt. The retained Basic II wing has diagnostic features described earlier.

▶ ♀ Basic II Plumage (entire feathering), acquired beginning in 2nd SUMMER, substantially earlier than later Basics; head–body molt by end of June but flight feathers not dropped until AUG. or SEPT.; then new wing and tail grow, also the "offset" long scapulars, while rest of head–body molt back into Alt. Like Def. Basic except: **head** slightly duller with slightly paler, more blurred, streaking; white margins of **speculum** of wing much reduced, sometimes virtually absent, or may wear off. Abdomen may av. darker than in older birds.

▶ ♀ Alt. II Plumage (all of head–body except longest scapulars), acquired earlier than subsequent Alts., in FALL, and retained until late WINTER or SPRING. Like Def. Alt. except: **dorsal feathers,** including visible scapulars sometimes, somewhat grayer on edges. The wing is retained Basic II.

▶ ♂ Basic III Plumage (entire feathering), acquired beginning in 3rd SUMMER, in stages (like Def. Basic), and most of head–body retained a few weeks at very most. Analogy with Common Eider suggests that individuals with somewhat less white on wing (particularly at bend) may be of this age-class; otherwise presumably as Def. Basic.

▶ ♂ Alt. III Plumage—definitive. Norton (1900) gave a very detailed description of the drake's "perfected" feathering.

▶ ♀ Basic III on—definitive as far as known.

**Aberrant individuals** Schiøler (1926: pl. 65) figured a ♂ in Alt. having the normally black areas (except on head) variants of grayed brownish, lighter on upperparts. Portenko (1952) described a drake, believed to be in 3rd calendar year, taken June 21; it had a brownish ashy cap, broad black stripe from bill through eye to auriculars, and lower portions of head whitish ochraceous with scattered cinnamon-colored plumelets and V-mark; instead of a white patch on side of rump, the feathers were dark brown with broad yellowish brown borders. Otto Helms had an all-white drake, taken Oct. 10, 1897, in Arsuk Fjord, Greenland. Several ♀ ♀ have been seen or captured in which overall coloring was very pale, even white.

Krabbe (1926, 1929) described and illustrated 2 King Eiders he regarded as ♂

107

hybrids with Common Eider; Schiøler (1926) believed that they were, instead, ♀ Kings "with abnormal genitalia" that had molted into a more or less drake pattern. Counting these as of the latter sort, Schiøler had 6 ♀ in ♂ feathering, from Greenland (see his pls. 61 and 65 for color illus. of 3 of these). Portenko (1952) also reported ♀ ♀ in ♂ feathering.

**Hybrids** with *S. mollissima* have been reported at various times for over a century. The following, which does not include all of the published evidence, consists of mention of mixed pairs seen and of hybrids seen or collected, all these being Alt.-Plumaged drakes, undoubtedly the easiest birds of mixed parentage to recognize.

For Krabbe's presumed hybrids, see above under aberrant birds.

In Spitzbergen on June 28, 1921, a ♂ King and ♀ Common were seen sitting beside an empty nest, which probably had been robbed (van Oordt 1921). In Spitzbergen in 1931 a similarly mixed pair was seen and the 4 eggs were fertile (Dalgety 1933).

Portenko (1952) described 2 hybrids in detail: one, "no younger than" 3rd calendar year taken July 2, 1901, at Edge I. (in Spitzbergen); another, not dated, from Novaya Zemlya. The former more closely approximates *spectabilis*.

In the great nw. Iceland colonies of Common Eider, regular occurrence of a few drake Kings mated to Commons has been known since about the 18th century. Iceland is outside the "normal" breeding range of the King Eider. The species occurs, in some numbers, in Icelandic waters in winter–spring and mixed-species pairs presumably form during that time and the *mollissima* ducks lead their *spectabilis* mates to nesting colonies of the former. It is believed that hybrid offspring rarely are produced. A drake hybrid was captured, about 1929, not far from Reykjavik; 2 hybrids are in the natural history museum in that city. See Gudmundsson (1932) and Pettingill (1959b) for some further details; the latter included a color photo of a Common Eider on her nest with drake King on station close by. In 1960, in the colony where that photo was taken, 2 ♂ Kings were mated to Commons; also, there was a ♂ *spectabilis* × *mollissima* mated to a ♀ *mollissima* and the clutch of this ♀ "proved to be infertile." See Pettingill (1962) for further details and photo of this pair. There were at least 5 drake Kings mated to Commons in colonies of the latter in nw. Iceland in 1970 (F. Gudmundsson). R. S. Palmer spent the last days of May, 1972, at the locality which Pettingill had visited earlier, the eider farm of Gisli Vagnsson at Mýrar, on Dyrafjord. There was a drake King mated to an incubating Common (4 eggs) in among other nesting Commons. Away from other nesters there was a drake King and also a drake Common, both mated to the same ♀ Common (incubating a single egg); both ♂ ♂ kept station amicably near the incubating ♀ and accompanied her when she went to a pond to drink and bathe. There was a hybrid drake mated to a ♀ Common (incubating 4 eggs), surrounded by incubating Commons and their mates.

In 1973 Palmer first visited Aethey, an island in Isafjord, then returned to Gisli's farm at Mýrar. At Aethey there have been at least 3 drake Kings annually since Helge Thorarinsson began residence in 1961, also usually 1 or 2 on the nearby island of Vigur. In 1973 at Aethey, there were 3 drake Kings mated to incubating Commons, including a trio bond (♂ King and ♂ Common sharing a ♀ Common). More Kings were seen on June 2: 7 more mature drakes, a yearling drake, and a mature ♀. A total of 5 drake Kings, associated with nesting ♀ Commons, was found there subsequently. At Mýrar a total of 12 drake Kings appeared one year, about 1940; there were 3, mated to Commons and including a trio bond, in 1973. A yearling drake (not mated) also was present for a time. No drake hybrids were seen at either colony in 1973, but F. Gudmundsson saw one, mated to a Common, at another colony (Arncs) in nw. Iceland, where there also was a King–Common pair. For 1972 photos of the eider farm at Mýrar and a hybrid drake beside his incubating Common Eider mate, see R. S. Palmer (1973). It is quite commonplace to find trios at the colonies in nw. Iceland.

The reciprocal mating (♂ *mollissima* × ♀ *spectabilis*) has not been reported. Gudmundsson (in Pettingill 1959b) suggested that, if it did occur in Icelandic waters, for example, the drake Common would follow the ♀ King to the latter's nesting place, i.e., the pair would not remain in Iceland.

**Measurements**   12 ♂ (8 Alaska, 2 N. W. T., 2 Greenland): BILL (from angle with forehead on top midline) 26–34 mm., av. 30.7; WING 271–292, av. 280; TAIL 79–89, av. 83; TARSUS 46–50, av. 47.7;   11 ♀ (4 Alaska, 4 N. W. T., 1 Me., 1 Conn., 1 N. C.): BILL (from end of feathering on top midline) 31–36 mm., av. 33.7; WING 251–282, av. 270.3; TAIL (of 10) 73–87, av. 81; TARSUS 45–48, av. 46.3 (ETS).

For meas., also with WING flattened, of 3 series of "adults" from localities from Banks I. to Baffin I. and Hudson Bay, see Manning et al. (1956).

For series with WING meas. over the curve, see Witherby (1939).

Portenko (1952) stated that the Juv. WING of drakes meas. under 27 cm. and in Basics it is over 28 cm. His recent data (Portenko 1972) on WING (meas. over curve) are:  ♂ 27 Juv. 24.9–27.5 cm., av. 26.1 and 107 Basic 26.3–29.5, av. 28; ♀ 25 Juv. 24.4–27.1 cm., av. 25.6 and 57 Basic 26–29.1, av. 27.3.

Schiøler (1926) gave various meas. of series from several Atlantic areas, also of a few Alaskan specimens. His flattened WING meas. of w. Greenland series show the expected age differences:  ♂ 50 first-year birds (Juv.) 242–270 mm., av. 256.5; 26 2-year-olds (Basic II wing) 252–280, av. 268.5; 75 "adult" (presumably Basic III and older) 261–293, av. 278; ♀ 30 first-year (Juv. wing) 230–275 mm., av. 248.9; 50 "breeders" 248–281, av. 265.

The meas. of additional series from Canada–Greenland agree with those of Schiøler (Hørring 1937) and for some further Greenland data see P. Johnsen (1953).

From New Siberian Is., WING (method of meas. not stated) 18 ♂ 263–296 mm., av. 282; 26 ♀ 260–286, av. 279 (Rutilevskii 1957).

**Weight**   Drakes of breeding age usually have much subcutaneous fat in winter–early spring, but are lean by late June (probably from getting less adequate food, plus onset of Prebasic head–body molt) and they do not gain much wt. until at least well along in fall (after peak of molt into Alt. head–body). In drake prebreeders the leanness begins earlier, even in late May (with earlier onset of Prebasic molt), and ends earlier. Age for age, the cycle is roughly similar in ♀♀, but summer wt. loss is greater, especially in successful breeders. First-winter birds of either sex seldom have much subcutaneous fat (they are in almost continuous molt, Prebasic I and Prealt. I). The wt. cycle in both sexes and any age is subject to various influences—weather, scarcity or abundance of food, etc. These statements, based to a considerable extent on Portenko (1952), align with available N. Am. data.

"Adult" spring migrants at Hooper Bay, Alaska, May 4–15, 1924:  16 ♂ weighed 3 lb.

6 oz. (1.53 kg.) to 4 lb. 7 oz. (2.01 kg.), av. 4 lb. 1 oz. (1.83 kg.); 8 ♀ 3 lb. 5 oz. (1.5 kg.) to 4 lb. 2 oz. (1.87 kg.), av. 3 lb. 13 oz. (1.75 kg.) (Brandt 1943).

At the duck camp (Birnik) near Pt. Barrow, Alaska, 8 ♂ (3 May 16, 1949, and 4 May 26, 1951) weighed 1,593–2,085 gm., av. 1,813; and 5 ♀ (3 May 26, and 2 June 4, 1951) weighed 1,433–1,772 gm., av. 1,653 (R. Rausch and E. Schiller).

In Alaska 18 ♂ taken Feb. 8–March 21 inclusive (12 in the period March 10–12): 2 lb. 2 oz. to 4 lb. 9 oz., av. 4 lb. (1.8 kg.) (R. D. Jones, Jr.).

In the very tardy spring of 1958, when many starved migrants were found dead on the coastal plain in the Barrow area, these wts. of adult birds were recorded at Birnik: May 10–11, 45 ♂ mean wt. 1,765 gm. and 35 ♀ 1,610 gm.; southwestward at Wainwright on May 26, 36 ♂ mean wt. 1,908 gm. and 15 ♀ 1,830; and at Birnik on June 10–11, 27 ♂ mean wt. 1,912 and 25 ♀ 1,836 (M. T. Myres). A ♂ found dead with empty stomach weighed only 1,020 gm. (Myres). Far eastward, at Banks I., an "apparently starving adult" ♂ captured July 11, 1952, "weighed 1.0 kg. when dead next day" (Manning et al. 1956). Four starved dead drakes found in May, 1964, at Anderson R. delta weighed 840, 900, 1,021, and 1,137 gm. (Barry 1968).

At Birnik in 1953, "adults" during the period of westward passage on molt migration showed some wt. increase through Aug. Weights with standard error: ♂ 22 (Aug. 4–8) 1,629 ± 83, 10 (Aug. 11–14) 1,740 ± 116, 7 (Aug. 14–17) 1,645 ± 44, and 2 (Aug. 14–22) 1,813; ♀ 1 (Aug. 4–8) 1,275, 12 (Aug. 11–14) 1,562 ± 129, 44 (Aug. 14–17) 1,561 ± 120, and 84 (Aug. 14–22) 1,574 ± 117; mean wt. of all ♂ 1,668 gm. and all ♀ 1,567 (D. Q. Thompson and Person 1963).

From New Siberian Is., and without information such as dates, whether breeders, etc.: 18 ♂ 1,391–1,900 gm., av. 1,580, and 26 ♀ 1,247–2,368, av. 1,463 (Rutilevskii 1957).

**Geographical variation** evidently none in the species. KCP (early draft), expanded by RSP

FIELD IDENTIFICATION The drake in Def. Alt. Plumage (fall through winter into summer) is mostly black, with anterior third (forepart of body plus head–neck) almost entirely white; in Common and Spectacled drakes, practically all of the dorsum is white. The difference is evident in swimming drakes at long distance. In flight, the drake King is black-backed (black intervenes between white of anterior body and white area on wing); in Common and Spectacled, white of dorsum continues out to include white in the wing. Again, the distinction is apparent at a distance.

In Def. Basic (late summer into fall), drakes of the 3 large eider species appear very dark at a distance; the King, however, tends to have a grayish cast, the Common and Spectacled blackish. At say 100 meters distance, with the unaided eye, the stubby bill and steep forehead of the King can be seen, while the others have a "smoother" facial profile. Generally, in any assembly of molting drakes (even yearlings) there are among the birds in full Basic head–body some individuals on a sufficiently different schedule to be showing diagnostic amounts of Alt. Plumage.

The ♀ King in all seasons has stubby bill and more rounded head than the other 2 large eiders. A ♀ King in among Commons may show decidedly more color (rufescent) than most ♀ Commons.

Probably the greatest difficulties are with separating first fall–winter Kings from Commons; the differences in facial profile are present but not as well developed as in older birds and differences in feathering are not very obvious. "All data from the Murman coast and Kandalaksh Bay in the White Sea would indicate that the King Eider is a much more regular inhabitant of these areas than previously supposed. Evidently this is explained mainly by the difficulty in distinguishing ♀♀ and young of the King and Common Eider. Especially hindering determination of species composition of flocks is the fact that young Kings often stay in mixed flocks of young and adult Common Eiders (even sometimes with adult ♂♂ only). In such cases, if the birds are seen at a distance, even an experienced observer may take the whole flock to be Common Eiders" (Kokhanov 1967).

When in hand, downies are readily identifiable by configuration of frontal and loreal feathering, as described earlier. RSP

VOICE   At least the ♀♀, and possibly both sexes, call during migratory flight—a murmuring growl, becoming louder as a flock approaches and, when they swing by, "each bird" is uttering a "low, grating croak comparable to that of a big frog" (Dufresne, in Gabrielson and Lincoln 1959). The chorus from a slightly disturbed flock on the water that Drury (1961) heard in summer at Bylot I. was "a soft murmuring sound rising in intensity."

The drake's call, during Pushing and Reaching displays, is rather hollow and dovelike, a speeded-up and wavering *hooooo*, giving a tremolo effect quite different from the separate-syllabled cooing of the Common Eider. Descriptions, and the call itself, vary. Examples: triple, strongly reminiscent of the call of the Blackcock (*Lyrurus tetrix*) (Höhn 1957); dovelike moan *gug gug gugguggug grooooooooo* (Drury 1961); triple call-note *croo croo croooo* (H. C. Hanson et al. 1956); a sort of drumming *urrr-urrr-urrr*, last syllable loudest (W. S. Brooks 1915). Yet usually it diminishes in loudness, at least as heard in summer.

A drake, accompanying his mate who was nest-site hunting, uttered a ♀-like *kwack* in threat toward the observer (P. Lamothe).

The ♀'s voice consists of variants of croaking and grunting. At Victoria I. in June, ducks responded to displaying drakes by occasionally uttering a low *kuck* or *kwack* (Parmelee et al. 1967). In ne. Greenland in summer, when flying very low over land, ♀♀ "sometimes uttered a slight growling or grunting sound." A nesting ♀ flew to a pond and there circled the observer, her utterance being "angry grunting." Then, on the water, she approached the observer while uttering a "peculiar growling and hissing" and now and again "cackled" like a domestic hen. The duck, if disturbed when with brood, has a "grunting" call. (Summarized from Manniche 1910.) RSP

HABITAT   Circumboreal breeder, from high-arctic (beyond lat. 82° N in Greenland) down into the subarctic, generally near fresh water. On arctic coasts of continents the distance penetrated inland varies, evidently being greatest where there are scattered ponds and lakes. Nesting habitat also includes islets and islands in ponds and lakes, hummocky marshes, even (as in Spitzbergen) hummocks surrounded by fresh water. The King nests in the interior of various major peninsulas in both N. Am. and Eurasia, except scarce in interior Taimyr. Also in suitable habitat apparently at any distance from the sea on various large arctic is.; examples in the Nearctic include Banks, Victoria, Southampton, and ice-free portions of Baffin; and in the Palearctic include Novaya Zemlya (both is.), Vaigach, and the New Siberian group.

Local nesting habitat often is a ridge or slope (these are free of snow early), but also more or less flat terrain that may be vegetated (sedges, grasses, etc.) or else rocky, gravelly, or sandy—arctic desert. In some areas where there are polygonal frostcracks they nest in these.

This eider nests on some marine islets and islands within the general breeding range of the Common Eider, also beyond at one locality in ne. Greenland. Along arctic coastal Alaska, apparently a favored nesting environment is gravelly coastal is. and spits where there is stranded flotsam.

On the Foxe Pen., sw. Baffin I., King and Common Eiders "observed a meticulous segregation" during the nesting season, "not only locally but to such lengths that one or the other may be utterly excluded over extensive coastal areas. At the same time, overlapping of local breeding ranges takes place in some localities" (Soper 1946). Later attempts to verify this segregation have been, at best, inconclusive.

Many prebreeders (drakes) remain on salt water, but many (mostly ♀ ♀) also go to fresh waters in nesting areas. Ducks with broods have a decided tendency to leave inland areas and go to sea and molting birds of both sexes are on marine waters so far as known. That is, they tend to leave fresh waters, which may freeze early.

In much of the year the King is a marine bird, probably resting on drifting ice much more than on land. Some remain about as far n. as there is both open water and adequate obtainable food, as in parts of Bering Sea, off w. Greenland, and in Barents Sea. Flocks and even solitary individuals tend to occur much farther away from land than Common Eiders. RSP

DISTRIBUTION   (See map) The King Eider and the Oldsquaw are the most northerly-nesting ducks. Both also are northerly winterers. The King, in migrations, is the eider most likely to occur as a straggler in continental interiors. For comparison of summer distribution of King and Common Eiders, see under the latter species.

**Breeders**   In the Nearctic area the great majority nest in the Canadian arctic, evidently in largest numbers approximately from Boothia Pen. w. to include Banks, Victoria, and other is. thereabouts. But many also nest elsewhere, from Greenland to arctic Alaska. The King has nested above lat. 82° N on both Ellesmere I. and in Greenland, but apparently is not numerous anywhere above lat. 78°; it has nested farther s. in the Nearctic than anywhere in the Palearctic area: into Bering Sea (St. Lawrence I., also St. Matthew I., and R. D. Jones, Jr. collected a preflight ♀ on Sept. 27, 1957, at a pond near Izembek Lagoon at outer end of the Alaska Pen.); in Hudson Bay (on the w. coast, also the s. coast at C. Henrietta Maria in Ont., and perhaps regularly in the n. Belcher Is. and other small is. n. of this group, and Todd (1963) gave records for well down in James Bay). There are surprisingly few nesting records for n. Ungava. In w. Greenland it nests rarely s. into the Egedesminde Dist.

In the Palearctic region: the King has not been found nesting in Iceland (except there are some drakes mated to Common Eiders); it nests in parts of Spitzbergen, but evidently not on Bear I., reportedly not at Franz Josef Land, nor Severnaya Zemlya, although it has occurred at some of these places at various times.

In the summer of 1812, the climax of a period of cold years, William Bullock toured Orkney and Shetland. On Papa Westray, one of the northernmost Orkneys (lat. 59° 20′ N), at the end of June, he found the nest of a "King Duck" with 6 yellowish white eggs

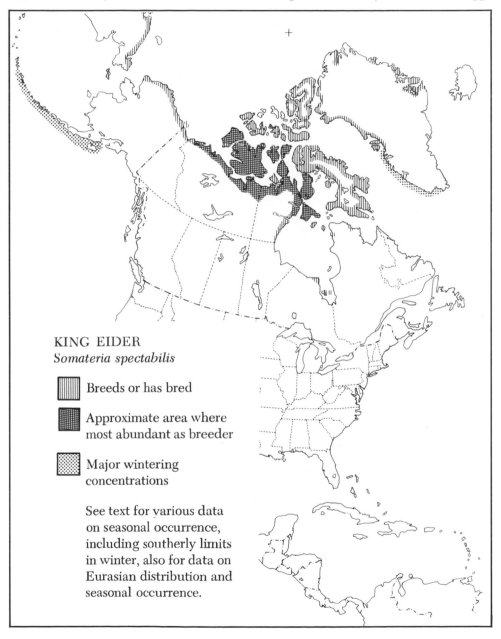

KING EIDER
*Somateria spectabilis*

Breeds or has bred

Approximate area where
most abundant as breeder

Major wintering
concentrations

See text for various data
on seasonal occurrence,
including southerly limits
in winter, also for data on
Eurasian distribution and
seasonal occurrence.

rather smaller than those of the Common Eider. This report, as recorded in the appendix to *Suppl. to the Ornithol. Dict.* (London, 1813) by G. Montagu, seems acceptable. Less satisfactory and not firsthand is a report that this species bred in the Orkneys for 2 consecutive years in the 1870s (Buckley and Harvie-Brown *Vert. Fauna of the Orkney Is.* Edinburgh 1891).

In Eurasia, most nesting occurs on arctic is. and mainland peninsulas, from e. part of the Kola Pen., on Novaya Zemlya, and on Vaigach I. eastward to include the Chuckchee Pen. (where it nests commonly on the n. coast). Few, if any, nest on Wrangel I.; recently S. Uspenskii (1972) stated none nest there. The following are outlying records, going from w. to e. In addition to old reports for Norway, there is a recent one far down the coast: in 1957 a pair (with 5 eggs) in a Common Eider colony on Tuatra I. in Trondheim Fjord, about lat. 63° N (Ytreberg 1960). In the White Sea, 2 broods in late Aug., 1937, and this eider is believed to nest occasionally near ponds in from the Tersk (nw.) coast (Kokhanov 1967). S. Uspenskii (1972) stated that it occurs in summer and breeds sporadically in the White Sea area, chiefly at the Solovetski Is., also on the e. side of the Kola Pen. On the Asiatic side, in Bering Sea, it has nested down the Chuckchee coast to Providence Bay and w. to the n. shore of Kresta Gulf (within Anadyr Gulf).

**Summer** In addition to some places mentioned above, it also has occurred elsewhere n. of known nesting range—for example, to lat. 83° N in Greenland and to Bennett I. n. of the main New Siberian group. Adults and younger birds sometimes are found s. of regular breeding range in summer; examples: molting birds in the White Sea; 2 out of 6 occurrences in the Faeroes; 2 ♀ in July, 1971, in Nova Scotia; a report (*Am. Birds* **26** 732. 1972) of 2 flightless birds seen on May 20, 1972, at Mullet Key in n. peninsular Fla.

Many prebreeders occur away from regular breeding areas, some in Anadyr Gulf, large numbers in w. Bering Sea and around St. Lawrence I., large numbers in w. Greenland waters, and some from n. Fennoscandia eastward to the Barents Sea coast. Beginning in July, older drakes move toward winter range or intermediate places.

**Winter** In the Pacific, on the Siberian side, occurs in small numbers in Anadyr Gulf where there is open water, occasionally in the Commander Is., has occurred down the e. coast of Kamchatka and beyond into the n. Kurils, also in Shelikov Gulf (n. Okhotsk Sea), and southernmost record is inland from the Sea of Japan and not far n. of Vladivostock near L. Talmi in South Primor.

Main Pacific–Bering range (probably includes many birds from the Asiatic side) consists of Aleutian waters from around Adak I. (long. 177° E) eastward, primarily the deep-water bays along the s. side of the Alaska Pen. and around the many is. s. of the inner Aleutians and Alaska Pen. There are few records for the outer Aleutians. In the n. Gulf of Alaska, numbers decline rapidly to the east.

If there is open water, some remain through winter in Bering Sea, off the n. side of the Alaska Pen., for example, around Amak I. nw. of Cold Bay. There is a possibility that some winter farther northward, even perhaps in the Chuckchee Sea—if, for example, the lead off Point Lay, Alaska, remains open.

On the Am. side of the Pacific, there are records down the coast to include several for Cal. In interior N. Am.: at various places, s. into conterminous U.S. to include Kans. and W. Va.

In the Canadian high-arctic, n. of Baillie Hamilton I., at lat. about 76° N, there is an open lead because of strong currents; the area supports pinnipeds and polar bears. King Eiders have been seen there in April (C. J. Jonkel), but whether they could pass the long dark winter there is doubtful.

In the w. Atlantic area, large numbers winter on open water along the sw. coast of Greenland. There is no information as to whether they also occur farther northward in the North Water, which is inhabited all year by various marine mammals; for description of this area, see Dunbar (1969) and Aber and Vowinkel (1972). The King may winter off the outer coast of Labrador; a great many occur farther southward. It winters around Nfld. (it is even occasional at sea on the Grand Bank), including within the Gulf of St. Lawrence; a very sizable number winter in Atlantic waters of s. Nfld. and e. N.S. It occurs fairly regularly in the e. Gulf of Me. and there are scattered records down the Atlantic coast to the Carolinas, Ga., and 2 for Fla. (see earlier for a Fla. summer record). High figures: in a very cold winter, late Feb. 1971, 41 Kings at Longpoint, N.J., and 21 at the Chesapeake Bay bridge tunnel.

In the w. Palearctic, occurs in winter in Icelandic waters (small numbers?), in Norwegian waters and around to include the Barents Sea coast of Kola Pen., and evidently many winter in e. Barents Sea. Known to have wintered on the Finmark coast as long ago as 1698; in some winters in thousands, in others in smaller numbers; in Feb., 1907, huge flocks (containing both sexes) all along the Norwegian coast from Vardø down to Harstad (Schiøler 1926). Unusually plentiful on the Norwegian Atlantic coast in winter of 1972–73. Winters in some numbers where open water in n. White Sea and also some other open areas in that sea; details in Kokhanov (1967). Frequently reaches the Baltic, at least the fall–winter records being birds that probably crossed overland from the White Sea.

Recorded s. to the Brit. Isles (various records, most frequent in Shetland), Channel coast of France, cent. Europe (Czechoslovakia, Hungary), and n. Italy (4 specimen records). A record for Voronezh in interior w. U.S.S.R.

Known from **archaeological sites** at 5 island and 2 mainland localities in Alaska; references in Brodkorb (1964a). RSP

MIGRATION  For most breeders, the general pattern consists of a long flight to breeding places and, as early as possible, a molt migration back toward winter range, and much later a movement over any remaining distance to wintering areas where there is permanent open water and available food. In the molt migration, older prebreeding and then postbreeding drakes go first, beginning in late June and in early July; then come various other categories, in overlapping periods of time, as the season advances. The latest are mostly young of the year. In spring, many yearling prebreeders (♂ ♂ preponderantly) do not go all the way to breeding areas, but instead halt at some intermediate place and molt or else alter their direction and go to molting areas; some, however, go the whole distance, then remain at breeding areas for a time before departing to molt. Spring and fall travel are greatly weather influenced.

SPRING  The King is the first eider to migrate and has the farthest to go. In N. Am., some come from the west, around Alaska, the others from easterly areas (Nfld. to Greenland, etc.). From the 2 sides they either meet or have a zone of overlap in the Canadian arctic at about long. 100–110° W; there are 7 recoveries of Greenland-banded birds at long. 90–100° W and one from farther westward at long 107° W (on s. Victoria I.), as mapped by Salomonsen (1967a, 1968), who placed an arbitrary dividing line between westerly and easterly birds diagonally nw. through Dease Strait and Victoria and Banks I.

In the **Pacific–Bering** area, great numbers of King Eiders that winter from w. Gulf of Alaska westward to include the inner Aleutians come together in large rafts on lagoons and estuaries on the n. side of the distal end of the Alaska Pen. These are figures for 1964: March 31—50,000 in Ugashik Bay, April 5—large rafts between Moffett Lagoon and Nelson Lagoon, April 8—100,000 in Nelson Lagoon, April 10—20,000 in Kululak Bay, May 1—22,000 in Port Moller, May 4—10,000 at Cinder R. Lagoon, and May 22—10,000 at Port Heiden (R. D. Jones, Jr.).

On the Bering Sea coast of Alaska at Hooper Bay, Brandt (1943) saw vast numbers of migrants. They had been going past for 2 weeks prior to May 9 in the tardy spring of 1924; the peak occurred May 11–15 (estimated 75,000 on the 15th) and a great many were paired. It seems likely that the birds had begun their migration not later than early April. (It is of interest that, in a casual search of the literature, the writer has not found useful information on the size of any flights on the Asiatic side of Bering Sea. Even with few observers, if there are heavy flights, one would expect them to have been mentioned.)

In n. Bering Sea at St. Lawrence I., aside from the Oldsquaw, King Eiders are the earliest and most numerous migrants seen along the w. coast; they become abundant about April 25 and pass on northward, intermittently, for about a month; judging from their directions of flight, they are bound both for Siberian and N. Am. destinations (Fay 1961).

Still farther n., at Bering Strait, A. Bailey (1948) wrote that King Eiders appeared off Wales in small numbers by mid-March and were seen there throughout April. Northerly movement depended on weather. Thus, in early May, if the wind blew from the south, thousands and thousands of this species and other eiders massed over open leads. Migration was at its height on calm days. Great strings of eiders, often several hundred yds. long, advanced, the birds more or less abreast, the line of them having a "rhythmic undulating movement." The birds flew low, from just above the ice to higher up but well within shotgun range. They moved on northward, from one lead to another.

Those bound for N. Am. destinations pass off and along the nw. (Chuckchee Sea) and n. (Beaufort Sea) coasts of Alaska. Although most of their routes are over marine waters (frozen or open), at least in 1958 there was a line of travel e. of Bering Strait across the Seward Pen. from the Imuruk Basin northward (M. T. Myres). In various (or all?) years there is movement overland some distance s. of Barrow, the birds cutting across eastward toward Dease Inlet, a route mentioned long ago by Murdoch (1885). At this season they fly very high, unseen; the majority do not follow the Alaskan–w. Canadian arctic coast but instead go over Beaufort Sea directly toward is. in the Canadian arctic.

Spring came very late in 1958 and dead starved King Eiders were scattered inland s. of Barrow. (A distinction between sea and land routes may be rather trivial since, when both marine ice and the coastal plain are covered with snow, they are different but not greatly so.) Evidently a rather small portion of the birds goes to mainland destinations.

The others may be expected in waters near their distant arctic island breeding places beginning in the latter half of May, with more coming until sometime in June. Time of first sightings varies greatly, depending on season; in different years at Banks I. on April 10, May 13, and June 2 (Manning et al. 1956). As soon as there is thawed water at ponds or on the perimeter or surface of lakes, small parties and pairs go there. Then, as the thaw progresses, the eiders copulate and this seems to be a prelude to very low reconnaissance flights over the tundra to select (or sometimes reoccupy?) nest sites as soon as they are acceptably dry.

The travels of **easterly birds** (Greenland–e. N. Am.) from winter quarters to breeding areas are less well known. Numbers of Kings diminish on at least southerly winter range beginning in March. Movement is very widespread in April, the limits of travel in some areas possibly being dependent on whereabouts of open water. A large number go from the Atlantic into the Gulf of St. Lawrence via Cabot Strait, passing off C. Ray (sw. Nfld.). Along the N. Shore of the Gulf of St. Lawrence, the King departs eastward late in spring, the last ones leaving May 15–June 15 (Beetz 1916). (Probably many of the late ones are yearlings.) Major lines of travel into the Canadian arctic probably are via Hudson Strait and across s. Baffin I. Some winterers off sw. Greenland may travel via Baffin Bay and Lancaster Sd. (around the top of Baffin I.). At C. Dorset, sw. Baffin I., 2 ♀ were shot as early as March 2, 1929, and migration extended until June 21 (Soper 1946). In another year at C. Dorset, there were thousands of King Eiders— almost all drakes—on April 25 and migration continued until well into June (Macpherson and McLaren 1959). Apparently breeders are widely distributed not distant from southerly breeding places by some time in May and reach northerly ones in "average" seasons in the first half of June. Especially to the north, the birds fly over still frozen sea and the first thawed water is at shallow ponds inland on islands.

Those bound for nw. Greenland move far up the coast in April; they have been seen in large numbers on open water at lat. 81° N. in mid-May. In "normal" years they arrive near their northernmost breeding places in the 2nd week in June.

**Yearlings**, at least some of them, migrate comparatively late in spring. A great many halt before going anywhere near as far as breeders and evidently they then gather early at molting places. In sw. Bering Sea, off the Nushagak Pen. (within Bristol Bay), on May 26, 1960, there was a flock of young Kings several hundred yds. in width and extending for 8 mi., which was estimated to contain at least 100,000 birds (Jim King, Henry Hansen). In n. Bering Sea, in late June and July, there are large flocks of molting yearlings around St. Lawrence I. (Fay and Cade 1959). On the Siberian side, large numbers occur around the Chuckchee Pen., from Bering Sea waters (Anadyr Gulf) around into Chuckchee Sea waters (arctic coast), as mentioned in Dementiev and Gladkov (1952). On the other hand, some yearlings evidently are scattered, at least for some time, even within remote breeding areas. For example, on July 18–20, 1949, there were groups of ♀ ♀ on a creek in the Perry R. area (n. Mackenzie–Keewatin boundary) and 2 collected proved to be yearlings (H. C. Hanson et al. 1956). In May –June of 1958, very few "subadult" King Eiders were seen during migration in the Barrow, Alaska, area (M. T. Myres), as one would expect. There are some yearling prebreeders of both sexes in the Canadian high-arctic, as at Bathurst I. In w. Greenland waters, the yearlings do not move very far n. from winter quarters before they stop at places where they will molt. Both sexes become flightless up to several weeks earlier than breeders of either sex.

As to **e. Eurasia** in spring, a great many King Eiders that come via Bering Strait turn westward to Siberian localities. Evidently the major nesting areas are westward beyond Chuckcheeland; the birds that travel farthest reach the e. side of the Taimyr Pen. (earliest date there is June 8). The New Siberian Archipelago is reached early in some years; May 3 at Kotelny I. is an early date. In adverse seasons the early migrants fly in very cold weather, over the still frozen E. Siberian Sea. According to Rutilevskii (1957), older ♂ prebreeders plus breeders of both sexes, westbound, travel out over the sea (not near the mainland) to Khatanga Gulf, and return via the same route. They fly along any open leads n. of main New Siberian Is. in the last third of May and in early June (but earlier in early seasons). The return eastward (molt migration) of older ♂ prebreeders occurs while some breeders and yearlings still are westbound, in the latter part of June and later. (From the Chuckchee Pen. westward there must also be a flight nearer the coast or else overland, since the King nests at places along the coast w. to the Yana delta.) Some yearling prebreeders go to breeding areas. For example, on the n. Anabar tundra in early July, there were flocks of 10–20 ♀ ♀ on lakes and those collected proved to be yearlings weighing 1,300–1,400 gm. (S. M. Uspenskii 1965c).

In the **w. Eurasian** sector there is, except very rarely, open water the year round along the Finmark and Murman coasts and to the east toward Kolguev I. Older birds, at least, move through Finmark and Murman waters in Feb.—March and continue in April; their eastward movements vary more as they reach areas where the ice is more regular and persistent. Migration on the Murman coast ends in late June, but some birds (mostly young) remain and molt at various places, such as around Ainov I. Many King Eiders go to Novaya Zemlya. Others move eastward, to areas even as far as the w. side of the Taimyr Pen. (The King Eider occurs, but is scarce, in interior Taimyr.) Many prebreeders assemble near Kolguev I. and molt there. For various additional information, including movements in the White Sea, the reader is referred to Kokhanov (1967).

SUMMER The most spectacular movement, namely the **molt migration,** first of older ♂ prebreeders and then ♂ postbreeders, begins in late June and very early July. Postbreeding drakes from the nw. Canadian is. and mainland begin taking leave of their incubating mates in the last third of June and they are gone from fresh water localities in about a week. They occur briefly in small groups on salt water and these, in turn, combine, probably along their routes of travel. They go westward along the Canadian–Alaskan edge of Beaufort Sea. Long ago, Murdoch (1885) wrote that from the 2nd week in July to mid-Sept. flocks of drakes came from the east and passed via the duck camp (Birnik) or eider pass at Pt. Barrow. As the season advances, there come postnesting ♀ ♀ and, later, more of these and young of the year; some prebreeders of various ages are included at some time also.

The passage of eiders at the duck camp was observed July 14–Sept. 1, 1953, by D. Q. Thompson and Person (1963). They estimated that, in an entire season, at least a million eiders (mostly Kings, also some Commons) pass by. Of 497 flocks (both species), 73% contained less than 100 birds each (modal group was 26–50) and less than 7% contained over 300 birds. The largest flock was of 1,100. In the period Aug. 8–17, the King Eider sex ratio shifted from a preponderance of drakes to a preponderance of ♀ ♀ . That is, postincubating ♀ ♀ leave their preflight young and join the molt migration. The young of the year, after they attain flight, and those older birds (mostly ♀ ♀) that remained longest in breeding range make up the late flocks. Murdoch (1885) stated that in 1882 at the duck camp young of the year first were seen Aug. 30. He added: "small flocks and single birds are to be seen till the sea closes, at the end of Oct. . . ." It was a mild season. He reported that many were seen as late as Dec. 2, when there still were patches of open water. (Generally there is an open lead not far from Barrow all winter.)

Just where both Siberian and w. N. Am. King Eiders of breeding age occur when they are flightless still is not entirely clear. There were flocks totaling thousands of birds (in Basic feathering) in the Chuckchee Sea and down through Bering Sea in Aug.–Sept., 1881 (E. W. Nelson 1887). Probably most of them were flightless. In Alaska at Atanik (not far sw. of Barrow), at the end of July in former times, King Eiders were driven into inshore ice (if it stayed close in) and were killed in puddles on the ice, according to P. Sovalik (M. T. Myres). T. Brower (in D. Q. Thompson and Person 1963) mentioned that there is an assembly place in the vicinity of Pt. Lay, some 200 mi. sw. of Barrow and 300 mi. n. of Bering Strait. (There is also a report of permanent open water off Pt. Lay and that northbound King Eiders stop there in spring.) It seems probable that a considerable number of King Eiders, perhaps yearlings and postbreeding ♀ ♀, molt on shallow water that extends far out from the Alaskan coast from the vicinity of Pt. Lay southward in the Chuckchee Sea. Young in their first fall also may spend some time n. of Bering Strait.

As to older prebreeding plus postbreeding drakes, their return flight past Barrow has been mentioned already and, on the Siberian side, various recent Russian authors confirm earlier evidence that great numbers fly eastward toward Bering Strait. They are said not to remain and molt along the arctic coast of Chuckcheeland (Portenko 1952). Early in July, W. Percy (in J. C. Phillips 1926) saw huge flocks of drakes, some already in head–body molt, fly s. through Bering Strait. Thus there is evidence that large numbers of drakes arrive early at Bering Strait, before they become flightless. They probably molt on shallow waters in n. Bering Sea. The lack of evidence of any huge gatherings of molting prebreeders on the Am. side (even though, collectively, the flocks at St. Lawrence I. might be considered such) prompted Salomonsen (1968) to suggest that such may occur on the Soviet side, but it seems more likely that many are in widely scattered flocks.

In the w. Soviet arctic it has been reported that postbreeders pass the flightless stage of molting at these localities, listed from e. to w.: near Yamal Pen., around Vaigach I., w. side of s. Novaya Zemlya, and around Kolguev I. (where prebreeders are congregated all year). At Novaya Zemlya on July 16 vast flocks of postbreeding drakes had congregated on the sea of s. Belusha Bay; on July 21 and 25, there were flocks of flightless drakes near islets along the coast; on Aug. 16 there were drakes still in full Basic and still flightless along the s. shore of Admiralty Pen. (Portenko 1952). A few molt in the White Sea.

Movements in much of the e. N. Am.–w. Greenland area are fairly well known from field observations reinforced by data from recoveries of birds that had been banded when flightless in cent. w. Greenland waters. In w.-cent. Ellesmere I. at Fosheim Pen., the drakes leave their mates in early July but remain in the fjords there until early Aug. (Parmelee and MacDonald 1960); this is the time when postbreeding drakes are

## North American Wood Duck

### *Aix sponsa*

Heads in all Plumages are shown, numbered (♂ 1-5 and ♀ 6-10), for each sex in the sequence in which they are acquired.

1 and  6  Juvenal. Has streaky venter.

2 and  7  Basic I. Short "mane" at nape; earliest white-bellied Plumage.

3 and  8  Alt. I.

3 and  9  Def. Basic.

5 and 10  Def. Alt. In the head, there may be no clear-cut difference between Alt. I and Def. Alt.; the Alt. I individuals illustrated both still retained the Juv. wing.

(For a day-old downy in color, see vol. 2 plate facing p. 370.)

RSP

molting into Basic head–body, prior to becoming flightless. In Lancaster Sd. at the n. end of Bylot I., in 1957, King Eiders appeared on June 26 and numbers increased daily until, on July 6, there was a raft of 2,400 individuals (mostly ♂ ♂) in an inlet w. of C. Hay; and on July 15, a census of "molting" King Eiders along a 15-mi. strip of coast from C. Hay westward yielded an estimate of 10,400 individuals (Tuck and Lemieux 1959). Whether they were flightless there or moved on to Greenland waters beforehand is a matter of conjecture.

The majority of postbreeding drakes from all except the westerly part of the Canadian arctic fly to waters extending along the cent. w. Greenland coast from s. of to well n. of Disko I. They come via water routes n. (Lancaster Sd.) and s. (Hudson Strait) around Baffin I., but most of them cross over the midportion of Baffin and thus take the shortest route to their molting area. Their flight across Baffin I. was described graphically by Wynne-Edwards (1952). Other postbreeding drakes come down from nw. Greenland to the same area. Also, there are large numbers of prebreeders that, earlier, had migrated from molting places directly to this molting area. Here, in early Aug., the number of molting King Eiders is some 100,000 individuals (Salomonsen 1968), but for the entire season the number occurring must be much larger. They are close-packed when flightless and the flocks may be driven ashore.

**Failed breeders** On high-arctic Bathurst I. in 1971, almost all ♀ ♀ lost their eggs during laying or very early in incubation to arctic foxes. Then the ♀ ♀ formed in groups of 2–11 birds and remained close to and at inland ponds from early July to Aug. (peak numbers in mid-July). They often rested on the tundra and, at least in the first half of July, their loosened nest down and ventral feathers commonly were preened out or were blown out by the wind, the presence of these indicating where the birds had rested. In the first week in Aug. there were small groups of these ♀ ♀ on salt water around the island. Few drakes (mates of these ♀ ♀) remained inland after July 10–13 and they vanished, rather than remaining nearby on any open salt water. The later departure of the ducks would result in flocks consisting only of the latter. (Data from Philip Taylor.) The pattern was the same in the very tardy summer of 1972 (P. Lamothe).

**Post incubating** ♀ ♀ (after they leave their preflight young) plus the young when they can fly presumably begin traveling in that sequence. Most older birds evidently go to some molting area, but it seems likely that the young of the year may tend, later on, to go more or less directly to wintering localities. Opposite the w. Greenland molting area, on the e. side of Davis Strait along the Eglinton Fjord–Clyde Inlet coast of Baffin I., Dalgety (1936) saw large flocks of ♀ ♀, July 14–20, 1934. It had been an adverse season, which had prevented nesting, and the ♀ ♀ were flocking early. Salomonsen (1968) stated that they "probably intended" to pass the flightless period there. They would be molting by themselves, i.e., in unisexual flocks.

In late Aug., 1969, at high-arctic Bathurst I., some failed-breeding ♀ ♀ and young of the year (about 75 birds altogether) were observed flightless there at Bracebridge Inlet (P. Lamothe).

At False R. estuary in Ungava Bay, Aug. 21, 1958, there was an assembly of about 2,000 Common and King Eider young and "molting adults" (Driver 1958).

There must be additional molting areas.

FALL–WINTER   Dates of departure of the last birds from waters within breeding range vary greatly. There are records of scattered very late lingerers on open water in high latitudes, but the usual pattern of birds older than young of the year is to move out early (prior to becoming flightless), but not to go all the way to winter quarters. Arrival at wintering areas is late, in Nov. and into Dec. almost everywhere. In n. Bering Sea at St. Lawrence I., the Kings return with the ice, in Dec. (Fay 1961). Cahn (1947) stated that King Eiders do not arrive at Dutch Harbor (Unalaska I. in the **Aleutians**) until Dec. On Dec. 2, 1955, near the outer end of the Alaska Pen., large amorphous flocks were seen coming in from Bering Sea and crossing overland to Morzhovoi Bay (Jim King). It is evident that birds in their first winter (both sexes) go to the main Aleutian–Alaska Pen. wintering area since, in the following spring, they are included in the later flights northward.

For **e. Canadian–w. Greenland** birds, postmolting travel (fall migration) occurs fairly late in the year. From the molting area along coastal cent. w. Greenland, the birds move down to the s. third of the w. coast. They pass the winter here in large numbers, being less littoral than the wintering Common Eiders. The King occurs around Nfld. approximately from late Nov. into April, and (in very small numbers) on the U.S. Atlantic coast mostly from Dec. through March. In fall they come down the Labrador coast and through the Strait of Belle Isle and then go along the w. coast of Nfld. (rather than the N. Shore of Gulf of St. Lawrence); in some winters there are many near Anticosti I. (Beetz 1916). Apparently others do not come through the Strait, but instead go to outer Nfld. waters. A bird banded at Sukkertoppen, w. Greenland (lat. 65° N) in Jan., 1948, was taken in 1963 (15 years later!) at Kegashka on the N. Shore of the Gulf of St. Lawrence (Salomonsen 1965).

Almost nothing seems to be known about movements of King Eiders that go to **ne. Greenland**. There seems to be no eider migration down the e. Greenland coast and so the birds are presumed to go out to sea. A bird banded as a preflight young on Aug. 1, 1933, in Jameson Land was recovered on Dec. 12 of that year in ne. Iceland. Presumably on this evidence plus winter occurrence of some King Eiders along the n. and e. coasts of Iceland, Salomonsen (1967a) mapped that area as the winter range of the ne. Greenland birds.

In **Spitzbergen** the King Eiders are thought to join the spring and fall movements of the Common Eider, which evidently does not travel very far. It also has been suggested that the Spitzbergen Kings spend the winter off the Norwegian coast. At least in one year in late summer, flocks of drake Kings molted in extreme sw. Spitzbergen, from Hornsund to Sorkapp I. (Lovenskiøld 1964).

For **e. Eurasian** birds, as indicated earlier, winter range is s. of Bering Strait, probably on the Am. side primarily.

In **w. Eurasia,** King Eiders begin arriving on the Murman coast in Oct. and, in due course, some go westward into Norwegian waters. Some occur during winter in other places, such as on open water in the White Sea; for numbers and places of occurrence, see Kokhanov (1967). Except in severe winters, however, most of them evidently remain in Barents Sea.

NOTES   **Sex segregation**   Postbreeding drakes and postnesting ♀♀ begin their molt migration at different times, so there are many migrating unisexual flocks. Later, at known places where postbreeders occur when flightless, dense flocks on the water often consist almost entirely of ♂ ♂ and some others (later) almost entirely of ♀ ♀. Occurrence of unisexual flocks of failed-breeding ♀ ♀ in July was mentioned earlier. In winter and spring there must be no separation of the sexes of potential breeders, since pair formation occurs then and most birds are paired when they migrate in spring. There are, however, observations of ♂ flocks on dates from March into June. These are older prebreeders that resemble breeders except in detail. Examples: extreme nw. U.S.S.R. at C. Bashenka (Rybach Pen. on w. Murman coast)—March 25, flock of about 2,500 with 98% ♂ ♂ (Skalinov 1960); e. Canadian arctic (s. Foxe Pen., Baffin I.)—April 25, thousands, almost all ♂ ♂, but in a few days ♀ ♀ had increased in numbers (Macpherson and McLaren 1959); w. Canadian arctic (Banks I.)—June 2, three flocks of ♂ ♂ totaling over 200 individuals (Manning et al. 1956); cent. Canadian arctic (Adelaide Pen.)—June 11, a flock of 26 ♂ ♂ (Macpherson and Manning 1959). (Later dates for ♂ flocks are omitted here, since they might pertain to postbreeding drakes.)

**Possible intercontinental exchange** Siberian and w. N. Am. birds certainly are together during passage through Bering Strait. Aside from this, there seems to be no definite evidence that birds from the 2 continents mingle at any time. Yet it is a reasonable supposition that most of the birds that come down through Bering Strait go to the main known wintering area, which is on the Am. side.

**Inland occurrence** The King is the eider that lingers n. of continental landmasses until arctic waters freeze. If forced to move, scattered birds may take a fairly direct southward course, which would account for occurrences in the interior of continents. RSP

BANDING STATUS In N. Am., 15 King Eiders were banded in 1964 and there have been no recoveries (data from Bird Banding Laboratory). Two incubating ♀ ♀ were banded on s. Victoria I. in July, 1960; one of them was captured in June of the following year at a location probably within 5 mi. of the 1960 nest (Parmelee et al. 1967). There have been a few recent bandings in N. Am.; for example, 4 were banded on Bathurst I. in 1971.

The number banded in Greenland, 1946–65 inclusive, was 3,868, and there have been 607 recoveries, mostly in w. Greenland (Salomonsen 1966). As a result, the best-documented travels of the King Eider are along w. Greenland; also, the taking of Greenland-banded birds in the Canadian arctic demonstrates that birds from a large segment of Canadian breeding range migrate to w. Greenland winter range. For tabulation of banding recoveries in Greenland by district and month, and full discussion of all banding results, see Salomonsen (1967a).

The number banded in U.S.S.R. through 1954 was 162, then none in 1955–59 inclusive; the author has seen no more recent information. There may have been some banding elsewhere in the Palearctic, but no data are at hand. RSP

REPRODUCTION Emphasis in this section is on Nearctic data, although various literature for the Palearctic has been consulted also. There is no information, from banded known-age individuals, on age when King Eiders **first breed**. It is well established, from smallness of gonads of specimens collected, that neither sex breeds at age

1 year. Schiøler (1926) presumed that some 2-year-old ♀ ♀ breed and that drakes generally begin when a year older. He surmised that, when nesting is late at more northerly localities, the resulting late broods require an additional year to attain breeding age. According to Portenko (1952), in season the gonads enlarge slightly in yearlings and are progressively larger each succeeding year up to breeding age; from rather scant specimen evidence, he concluded that a few two-year-olds (birds in their third calendar year) breed and that all (of both sexes) are capable of breeding when a year older.

Although the earliest flocks of spring migrants may consist entirely of drakes (older prebreeders), by the time the flight is heavy the sex ratio has altered (a great many birds are paired breeders). In general, therefore, much pair formation occurs in the span from fall to early spring. Various displays have been seen along migration routes and, to some extent, in or near nesting areas. Although this may indicate that some pairing occurs after departure from winter range, more likely most of this activity is related to pair bond maintenance plus some display and perhaps temporary pairing by prebreeders.

Practically all information on **display activities** pertains not to the pairing season but to later on, plus some data from captives. The picture derived from these sources surely is incomplete, especially as to what may transpire on the water in winter, and nothing definite is known regarding any possibly relevant aerial activity. It is known that a number of drakes—up to about 10—gather around a ♀, as in the Common Eider; the best observations of this are from summer range and possibly are of older prebreeding or even postbreeding drakes displaying toward either unmated mature or else prebreeding ♀ ♀. The known displays of this species have their homologues in both Spectacled and Common Eiders; see tabulation of them, also photographs of displaying captive King Eiders, in Johnsgard (1964a). Display movements of the King are faster in tempo than those of the Common Eider.

**Displays of the duck** INCITING as in Common Eider; a threatening action—neck forward, or same with bill flipped up (Chin-lifting) and sometimes opened. The throat appears somewhat inflated, as if there were a bubble in it (Drury 1961). The series of notes uttered has a hollow, wooden quality. The duck, at least in summer, often Incites actively whether or not there is any drake response. The ♀ apparently also has at least rudiments of several of the drake's displays.

**Displays of the drake** Among the following, numbers 1, 3, 6, and 7, as observed among captives, may be the major pair formation displays.

1 HEAD-TURNING head rotated horizontally, so that each side is presented alternately to the ♀ (Höhn 1957); commonly linked to other displays. A drake in early summer, on station close to his incubating mate, was approached rather closely; the drake turned his head at an angle and it could be seen that the short feathers on the side of the head were erected in such a fashion as to open a deep V-shaped furrow forward of the white line that extends down across the rear of the cheeks. Then the drake retreated in alarm (R. S. Palmer). 2 UPWARD-STRETCH the drake rears up, revealing his ventral surface, and rotates his head (wags it "ponderously"—Drury 1961) or shakes it, then settles down on water. Drakes standing on ice had a rapid shaking of the whole body while moving the head up to vertical position (Höhn 1957). 3 WING-FLAP begins as the preceding; when the body is almost vertical and the bill angled steeply upward (reveals

black marking on chin), the wings are held outstretched momentarily, then flapped twice, then folded as the bird settles down on water. Typically, the drake faces the duck when doing this. 4 CHIN-LIFTING as in ♀ ; rather rapid; a flashing of the chin pattern. 5 NECK-STRETCHING as in alert posture, sometimes with more or less horizontal rotating of the head. 6 REACHING the neck is upstretched, then the head swung down forward so that the tip of the bill is close to (or into?) water, then the head is retracted quite rapidly. During the forward motion, breast and throat appear inflated and, while the head is being drawn back, the drake utters a rolling, somewhat dovelike, call that diminishes in volume. The head, while being retracted, pats the breast repeatedly, about 2 pats/sec. (Drury 1961). As described by Höhn (1957), the display starts with a forward rocking movement of the long axis of the body; that is, as the breast is lowered, the tail is raised to vertical (which makes conspicuous the white area at its side base); the head goes down simultaneously and then is brought forward, then retracted until the bill is on the puffed-out breast, and then a gulping forward motion of the head is executed. This display is homologous to Cooing movement 3 of the Common Eider (Johnsgard 1964a) and usually is followed by Head-turning. 7 PUSHING the neck is retracted, then the head is moved forward and upward in deliberate fashion as though pushing against some object, while the bill is pointed nearly vertically downward. The breast appears to be greatly inflated and a wavering *hoooo* is uttered as the head goes forward (M. T. Myres). Between short series of (usually 3–4) Pushing movements, the bird returns to a resting position. This display frequently is followed by Head-turning. It occurs as long as the pair bond is maintained, i.e., into the nesting period. Drury (1961) described a very vigorous, rapid, version. The bill was held down, then thrust forward with such violence that the tail bobbed out of the water and the triangular "sails" trembled; then the head was drawn back to the breast and the tail went back down. Then, while patting his breast with his bill, the drake uttered a prolonged dovelike moan. W. S. Brooks (1915) observed 3 ♂ ♂ in June, on a beach, performing

Pushing

Wing-flap

Reaching

this display while squatting around a ♀. He described the ♂ call as *urrr-urrr-urrr* with last syllable loudest, a sort of drumming call as when one expels air forcibly through the mouth with the tongue lightly pressed against the palate. **8** PREEN-DORSALLY behind the wing, etc., by individuals in a group. **9** HEAD-ROLL cheeks and crown rubbed on anterior dorsum. **10** BATHING very animated; head dipped under water, then pulled vigorously back so that water splashes over the dorsum.

NOTES    If one observes both Common Eider and King, the most striking contrast is in the "heightened" characteristics of the latter—rapid voice and displays, "sails" (modified scapulars) permanently erect in the drake, more elaborate pattern and coloring. The drake's cooing is so accelerated that it sounds as though the bird were trying to call while in haste and shivering, with a wavering effect, not separate syllables.

It has been discovered recently, from observations in Iceland and from those of P. Lamothe at Bathurst I. in the Canadian arctic, that the modified scapulars of the ♀ are erectile: her "sails" are up under certain conditions, at least in late spring–early summer. That is, they are erectile in the same way they are in the drake Common and Spectacled Eider. An observation in Iceland confirms this.

The precise function of the "sails" is not yet apparent. They vibrate during the drake's Upward-stretch, are above the pivotal point in Reaching, and are prominent in the Pushing display. S. Johnsen (1938) suggested that these feathers "may have an acoustic function, beginning to vibrate and give forth a sound when the birds throw themselves down in the water from some height, an action generally performed at great speed." Yet it seems more likely that their effect is visual and their function is seasonal, since they are erect only seasonally in the ♀ King and in the ♂ Common and Spectacled.

**Copulation**    Johnsgard (1964a) made the following observations of captives. The duck gradually assumes the PRONE position while the drake is performing various displays in no set sequence. These include Bathing, Upward-stretch, Head-roll, Wing-flap, Reaching, Bill-dip, Pushing (in series), and Preen-dorsally. A common sequence is Bathing followed by Upward-stretch and Wing-flap or Head-roll. Just prior to mounting, the drake was seen either to Wing-flap or Upward-stretch. The drake retains hold of the duck's nape for a few sec. after copulation presumably is terminated, then does a single Reaching display and swims away while performing lateral Head-turns. The duck swims away. Essentially the same behavior has been photographed in wild birds by P. Lamothe.

King Eiders of reproductive age presumably are monogamous ordinarily for the period required to produce a fertile clutch and begin its incubation, i.e., **seasonal** and single-clutch **monogamy.** The possibility that drakes while still paired or afterward may consort with other ♀ ♀ (including prebreeders) already has been mentioned; such activity is now confirmed from observations on Bathurst I. **Aberrant bond** In the great eider colonies in nw. Iceland, in the absence of ♀ Kings, not only are there some ♂ Kings mated to ♀ Commons, but also trio bonds (♂ King and ♂ Common sharing the same ♀ Common); this occurs regularly (see earlier section on hybrids).

After the thaw has begun ashore, small groups and single pairs of King Eiders fly very low over the tundra, the ♀ leading her mate and uttering a moaning or growling sound, while inspecting the terrain. It is very easy for man to discover nest sites of the

126

previous year once they are free of snow, because last year's weathered and faded nest down is in the cavity or scattered about, waving in the wind. If the duck has nested previously, in all likelihood she returns to the same area. Having chosen a site, if there is fresh water within convenient walking distance, the duck (and drake for a while) probably walk there from the water, but they fly to within walking distance of sites located on waterless tundra. The drake accompanies the duck to the site during laying. At Victoria I. a pair was flushed from an empty fresh scrape at 2:30 P.M. and the scrape contained a fresh egg at 4 P.M. the same day (Parmelee et al. 1967). The drake in an undisturbed situation accompanies the duck at least for some time after laying, keeping station close to her as she sits on her nest. Drake Kings keep station thus at least well into incubation in those instances in which they are mated to Common Eiders in nw. Iceland. In truly wild conditions, after the period of accompanying the ♀, drakes may have their stations on the nearest water for a while prior to departing to molt.

Typically a **solitary nester,** the King Eider is said to be intolerant of other eiders if they nest in too close proximity. There are practically no records of King Eider nests less than several meters apart, except perhaps for reported **semicolonial** nesting on islets (mentioned below) and with actual spacing of nests not on record. The drake of a pair of Kings that nested within a large protected colony of Commons in Norway was so quarrelsome that it became necessary to shoot it (Boie 1822). In Iceland in former times there was a belief that the drake King was an old Common Eider that had acquired modified feathering and was overbearing or domineering, the king of the eiders. In mid-May in Iceland a flock of about 30 Commons on the water near shore also contained a drake King; during 3 hours of observation, this drake was seen to spend his time in aggressive actions toward both ♀ and ♂ Commons, occasionally taking time out to dive for food (Hantzsch 1905). In late May at an Icelandic eider farm, the more aggressive of 2 drake Kings in the colony (both were mated to incubating Commons) attacked several drake Commons in succession at distances as far from his mate's nest as 10–15 ft. (Pettingill 1959b). At the same locality in 1972, while their (Common) mates

127

were incubating, 2 drake Kings were quick to attack if approached closely by drake Commons, but a fight sometimes was settled in favor of the latter. That is, the Kings acted speedily, but were not always dominant. A mated hybrid King × Common drake did not seem to be especially quarrelsome, even toward very close neighbors.

In the Perry R. region (n. Mackenzie–Keewatin boundary), where the King Eider is the most numerous breeding duck, nests were scattered widely on the flat coastal tundra which extends up to 20 mi. inland, but some also nested semicolonially on is. in tundra lakes (H. C. Hanson et al. 1956)—14 nests on an islet 30–40 yds. long (P. Scott 1951)—and some nested on coastal is. (Gavin 1947). On sw. Baffin I. at Foxe Pen., they nest inland and also on the Wildbird Is. (Macpherson and McLaren 1959) which are sizable, i.e., not islets. On Victoria I. there are areas 60 mi. inland where the King apparently nests as commonly as near the coast. On se. Baffin I., breeding places include is. in Gabriel Strait and in Frobisher Bay (Soper 1946). On Southampton, many are distributed over the tundra, often far from water (Sutton 1932); also in the immediate vicinity of water—swampy coastal areas preferred—the nests situated just above high water on is. within the area of tidal flats (Bray 1943). In Greenland, in from the coast near fresh water or on islets in fresh water, and P. Johnsen (1953) recorded nesting on marine islets within Jorgen Brønlunds Fjord. In U.S.S.R., nests generally are scattered, but on some small river islands, where the birds are secure from the arctic fox (*Alopex*), they are close together and the terrain frequently is shared with nesting geese and gulls (Dementiev and Gladkov 1952).

**Nest sites** are varied. Preferred locations are snow-free early, dry, and away from but not distant from water. Many are on sloping terrain. Some sites, such as sedge hummocks, are well vegetated; at some there is prostrate or low woody growth, grass, or moss–lichen ground cover; some are on stretches of sand, gravel, or rubble. Many are close to a rock or some very slight prominence, but others are on seemingly featureless terrain. Where there are shallow and often polygonal surface cracks, caused by frost, these commonly are utilized.

There is a slight cavity, either natural (commonly) or made by the duck. Here the eggs are deposited, the rate of laying at Bathurst I. in 1971 being approximately 1/day. In arctic desert, nothing is available, hence nothing added, to the cavity during laying of as many as 6 eggs (P. Johnsen 1953); on Victoria I. the first eggs of a clutch are scantily covered with vegetable material until some nest down has accumulated (Parmelee et al. 1967) and the same occurs on Bathurst I. (R. S. Palmer) and in Greenland (Schiøler 1926). That is, the duck covers the egg(s) even before any nest down is added and a nest at this stage is very well concealed. **Nest down** Beginning usually before the termination of laying, the down is added over a period of time. It is quite different from that of the Common Eider, being much darker—a sooty brownish with faint light centers and a few scattered whitish sprays. Any included feathers generally are small, pale grayish basally, grading to medium gray-brown distally; see pl. 90A in Witherby (1939).

Complete **first clutches** usually contain 4–6 eggs, with any number over 7 (to at least 16 have been recorded) assumed to be the product of more than one duck. A sampling of published data: Victoria I. and Jenny Lind I.—27 clutches consisted of 3 eggs (in 1 nest), 4 (in 7)), 5 (9), and 6 (10) (Parmelee et al. 1967); Prince of Wales I.—26 nests contained clutches of 1–8, the mean being 4.1 (Manning and Macpherson 1961); King William I.—clutches of 3–5 (Fraser 1957); Adelaide Pen.—6 clutches of 2–6, av. 4.4

(Macpherson and Manning 1959); Perry R. region—14 nests av. 4.9 eggs and, in addition, 2 clutches of 8 and 1 of 9 (H. C. Hanson et al. 1956); Greenland—4–6 recorded, 5 being commonest (Salomonsen 1950); Novaya Zemlya—normal clutch size 4–7, most frequently 5 (Dementiev and Gladkov 1952); New Siberian Is.—clutches of 1–7, usually 5–6 but frequently 7 (Rutilevskii 1957).

The **eggs** are smaller and generally paler than those of the Common Eider; **shape** somewhat more slender than in Common Eider; **color** some variant of (greenish) olive buff, often stained during incubation; shell smooth, with slight gloss when eggs are fresh. Combined **measurements** of two clutches of 6 each from Victoria and Jenny Lind is.: length 61.7–67 mm., av. 64.36, and breadth 39.9–44.2, av. 43.16 (Parmelee et al. 1967). Meas. of 152 eggs "in various collections": length 61.3–79.5 mm., av. 67.6, and breadth 41.5–52, av. 44.7 (Bent 1925). Both these extremes and averages are very close to combined series of 200 eggs from Europe, Asia, and N. Am. given by Schönwetter (1961).

**Weight of fresh eggs** about 73–75 gm., less than ¾ as much as most Common Eider eggs.

There is little point in giving scattered records of dates when first clutches are begun (or presumably completed), since the seasons vary greatly and there are no adequate data for several seasons at any locality. Generally speaking, unless the weather turns severe, the earliest eggs are laid within a week after the birds go inland. The King nests earlier than the Common Eider. In the Nearctic area, **clutches are completed** in "normal" seasons beginning about June 15 in warmer parts of the nesting range and not until well into July at some high-arctic localities. In N. Ellesmere I. a clutch as early as June 25 is indicated by a brood of 5 hatched July 18 (Savile and Oliver 1964); this locality is warmer than others farther s. and w. On the Eurasian mainland, many clutches normally are completed in the last third of June, but later on is. to the north. In the New Siberian Is., ducklings have been found as early as July 19 (Rutilevskii 1957).

**Replacement clutches** no information. At least in high latitudes, as at Bathurst I., if part of the clutch is lost during laying, the duck completes laying that clutch somewhere else. The activities of failed breeders were discussed earlier (see "Migration").

Even on monotonous and barren arctic desert, **the incubating duck** is inconspicuous. If one walks facing the sun and scanning the ground, her whereabouts is revealed by the light reflected from her feathers. Some individuals can be touched, or even lifted off the eggs. Some, when thus handled and banded early in incubation, have abandoned their nests. Others depart hastily if approached, not covering the clutch, and defecating a malodorous watery discharge which soils both eggs and nest down. The arctic fox is said not to eat smelly eggs (Schiøler 1926), which is doubtful; but the soiling certainly does not deter avian predators such as jaegers and gulls.

At least for a time, and probably at quite regular intervals throughout incubation, the duck covers her eggs and goes to water to drink, bathe, and preen. During incubation, ♀♀ do not eat very much and probably can go without food; afterward, while the young are growing, ♀♀ gain wt.; drakes, on arrival in spring and throughout their stay in summer, feed only sporadically (Rutilevskii 1957). At high-arctic Bathurst I. in 1971, at least during laying and early incubation, mated birds of both sexes were observed in pairs, evidently feeding at a lake; only drakes were shot and all 3 contained masses of chironomid larvae.

**Incubation period** of eggs under a bantam hen 23 days (Johnstone 1961) and on Victoria I. the last (marked) egg in a 5-egg clutch hatched in not less than 22 nor more than 24 days (Parmelee et al. 1967). The period, therefore, may be slightly shorter than in *S. mollissima*. All 6 eggs in a clutch hatched within a span of 24 hrs. (Parmelee et al. 1967).

Duck and brood go to the nearest water and during the **preflight period** there is probably considerable moving about so that broods soon are mostly on large ponds and lakes (also see Savile and Oliver 1964 and Parmelee et al. 1967). A great many that are not remote from coasts move downstream, or perhaps overland from pond to pond, to the sea (compare with Common Eider). Beginning at any time posthatching, broods combine, forming crèches (assemblies) of a few to well over 100 individuals, often of various ages. Some time postnesting, the parent ♀ leaves any young with which she may have been associated and soon begins her molt migration. There still are ♀ ♀, one to several, that accompany crèches of growing preflight birds for a while; some of these may be failed breeders, or perhaps also prebreeders. In such circumstances, the number of ♀ ♀ associated with crèches increases for a while, then diminishes as the ♀ ♀ depart. Many crèches, however, are unattended even when the ducklings are quite small; a great many are unaccompanied by mature ♀ ♀ during the latter part of the preflight period; and many young migrate by themselves.

On n. Ellesmere I., a half-grown brood often swam in the shallow margins of ponds, with their heads below the surface, apparently feeding on an abundant shrimp *Lepidurus arcticus* (Savile and Oliver 1964).

Not only do King Eiders sometimes starve en route to breeding areas, but also there are seasons when adverse weather lasts into summer—if one can call it summer—and the birds either fail to nest or to produce young. Recorded instances include: ne. Greenland in 1907 (Manniche 1910) and in 1933 (Bertram et al. 1934) and part of e. Baffin I. in 1934 (Dalgety 1936). The summer of 1961 was a failure, at least in the e. Canadian arctic; the disastrous summer of 1972 is discussed later in this account, along with seasons when migrants starved. Losses of eggs and of laying and incubating ♀ ♀ to foxes during times of peak fox abundance is severe and fairly regular, but more local than very adverse seasons; sometimes only those Kings that nest on fox-free islets have any chance of succeeding.

There is very little information on **growth** of young King Eiders, other than that captive-reared birds are well feathered when a month old (see earlier under Juv. Plumage). Allowing 7 days for laying, 23 for incubation, and 50 (a guess) for age when young first can fly well, the total is 80 days; this matches the 80–85 day estimate by Rutilevskii (1957), but does not include the period prior to laying and may include too short a preflight period for the young. RSP

SURVIVAL   No statistical information.

HABITS   Among eiders, the King is a cold-weather bird. Little is known about the Spectacled and Steller's, however, so comparison of King and Common is about all that can be made with any confidence. There is good evidence that the King generally dives in deeper water, hence may remain submerged longer, than the Common. The two readily join forces at times, when their needs or travel schedules coincide; at other times, as when nesting and molting, they tend to stay apart. The King has been found, usually away from breeding range, with both Spectacled and Steller's, while singles and small groups occasionally associate with Oldsquaws.

In **flight** the King seems more maneuverable and more buoyant than the Common; like the latter, it flies swiftly, with rapid wingbeats, and flocks seem intent on maintaining course; the best description probably is that of Hersey (in Bent 1925). There is a somewhat growling or croaking noise, at least from flocks containing ♀ ♀. Often they travel in long lines that are more or less at right angles to line of flight, or somewhat diagonal or swept back, or wedges—the 2 sides of the wedge generally being very unequal in length—and the entire line of birds has the same undulating motion as that of the Common Eider. Sometimes they travel in what might be described as small clouds, the flocks maintaining no particular shape very long. The birds frequently glide during flight, and often they make a long glide when approaching to alight; their descent to water varies from gradual to swift, when they touch down hard, with a great splash.

They **dive** smoothly, with little apparent effort, or at times give a vigorous rapid kick and go down hurriedly amidst flying spray. The bend of each wing is out from the body, but tips of flight feathers are on or close to the rump, and the feet stroke alternately during the dive. Descriptions of feeding activity differ. For example, duration of dives in 7 meters of water av. 45 sec., with pauses of 3–10 min., and they also were seen dabbling, "perhaps for plankton," according to Macpherson and McLaren (1959). On the other hand, Schiøler (1926) described them as making several dives, between each showing only part of the head above water and, after a series, surfacing completely. The King has been taken in a net at a depth of 55 ft. and surely can go deeper still.

The King has nasal glands of same size as the Common, although the former is a considerably smaller bird; compare figs. 48 and 52 in Schiøler (1926).

There are various sightings of groups of a few birds sleeping, or at least **resting,** on shore in spring and early summer; flocks rest on ice, or at pools of water on ice, in various seasons.

**Adverse seasons**   From ne. Pacific waters and s. Bering Sea, King Eiders on spring migration pass through a tremendous temperature gradient as they move up through Bering Sea into Chuckchee Sea and beyond in Beaufort Sea on the N. Am. side and East Siberian Sea on the Asiatic side. Seasons vary. The birds move on, generally when the wind is in their favor or on calm days, over the ice, from one stretch of open water to the next, if any exist. If they do find an open lead, they may stop for a time. But if spring breakup comes late, the early migrants especially are weakened and forced down by freezing sleet, adverse winds, and ice-fog. In the N. Am. sector, known years when starved dead King Eiders have been found on land and/or sea ice are as follows:

1882 FIRST HALF OF MAY   Barrow region; details in Murdoch (1885).

1919 SPRING   Colville R. delta (information supplied by P. Sovalik to M. T. Myres).

1927 SPRING   Flaxman I. (Sovalik, to Myres).

1936 SPRING   Se. Victoria I., Common (and King?) Eiders (H. P. Alexander, to Myres).

1941 SPRING   Wainwright area (D. Bodfish, to Myres).

1949 SPRING    Banks I., 16 plucked drake Kings found below a Peregrine eyrie probably were downed migrants (Porsild 1951).

1953 SPRING    From Barrow area at least to the Colville delta (Myres); at Banks I., Höhn was given a starving drake King on June 10 and another on July 11; Eskimos said they frequently saw drake Kings too weak to fly and attributed this to starvation (Höhn 1957).

1958 BEGINNING BY MAY 1    Wainwright to Barrow region plus a number of localities beyond eastward to Canning R., large numbers found dying and dead ashore or on sea ice (on both at some localities) (M. T. Myres).

1960 LATE APRIL–EARLY MAY    Banks I., sudden cold weather froze the open leads and Eskimos found several dead drake Kings on the ice (Barry 1968).

1964 MAY ON    Very severe season in the w. Am. arctic; heavy mortality in the Barrow area (long. 157° W) and various points eastward into Franklin Bay (long. 125° W), also northward at Mould Bay on Prince Patrick I. (long. 118° W); an estimated 100,000 eiders, mostly Kings, died, this being at least 10% of the av. annual number of King Eiders using the Beaufort Sea route. See Barry (1968) for many additional details.

Some years of **nonbreeding**, usually without adult mortality, are listed here by geographical area:

(ICELAND lies outside the breeding range of the King Eider, but note "ice years" under "Habits" of Common Eider.)

GREENLAND    No nesting in the ne. part in 1907 and 1939. Also, the data on effects of climatic change on the Common Eider in Greenland (in Vibe 1967) are suggestive, but not explicit, for the King Eider.

NEARCTIC AREA    In 1972, "summer" was the most tardy ever recorded—at least from Greenland westward to include ne. Asia—and only some King Eiders nesting at lower fringes of breeding range produced any young.

In 1974 no young waterfowl were produced in the Canadian high-arctic and southward to include at least n. Baffin, most of Victoria, and Banks I.

PALEARCTIC    In May of 1902 and 1903, starving King Eiders were found in the New Siberian Archipelago (references in Pleske 1928). The year 1933 was one of nonbreeding on the Taimyr Pen., while 1949, 1961, and 1968, were bad years for all eider species in the area from n. Europe eastward to cent. Siberia (S. M. Uspenskii 1972). Farther eastward, at Wrangel I., Lesser Snow Geese had 4 or 5 consecutive bad years beginning with 1969; presumably the adverse weather was more widespread and affected eiders also.

To return to the 1958 Alaskan episode, as investigated in the Barrow region by M. T. Myres (personal communication), dead starved drake King Eiders picked up on the tundra had shrunken frontal lobes, empty gizzards, and lacked subcutaneous fat; breast muscles were reduced noticeably in size; and some had visceral contents heavily stained with bile. Weights of starved drakes have been given earlier (see "Description").

The instances of starvation during spring, as they were reported, have emphasized drakes (which are easier to find), but ♀ ♀ also have perished in large numbers. Since the earliest migrants are flocks consisting of older prebreeding drakes, i.e., birds not mated for the coming nesting season, their loss would not affect the number of pairs breeding that year. But paired breeders come soon afterward.

In late June–early July, 1960, T. W. Barry made an aerial survey of waterfowl nesting areas on Banks I. The King Eiders had a "fairly successful" year, with an estimated 100,000 individuals present (the estimate, by other observers, had been 150,000 in 1952 and in 1953). In 1961, when Barry surveyed the island's best eider-production area on July 25, and made further observations on the island to Aug. 9, he found a total of 6 live eiders. He did find remains of 125 "young and female" King Eiders along 2½ mi. of lake shoreline. All were flightless; they died presumably from an epidemic or from having been caught in a sudden freeze. Barry estimated the loss of King Eiders on Banks I. that season at about 50,000 birds (the drakes apparently had escaped loss) and he concluded that there were few ♀ ♀ to return to the island in 1961. [Apparently he assumed that ♀ ♀ found dead were postnesters that had become flightless near nesting places instead of leaving beforehand as drakes do. It is known that some prebreeding ♀ ♀ go to breeding range and their loss would reduce somewhat their particular cohort of ♀ ♀.] The very high lemming (*Dicrostonyx*) population on Banks I. "crashed" in the winter of 1960–61, but arctic foxes survived this reduction in their food supply and preyed heavily on eider nests in 1961. Survey flights showed that the eiders were "still absent" in 1962.

It is of interest that practically all information relates to cataclysmic events; the effect, for example, of less than complete starvation is less well known.

Adverse weather can result in heavy mortality during spring travel, later can reduce or prevent successful nesting, and still later can result in losses of whatever birds occur at or near breeding places. Both sexes normally fatten in a period ending by the time the ♀ begins laying and both probably are capable of surviving on little (or nothing) for a considerable period thereafter. Yet nobody knows how any adaptation to reduced feeding fits in with any actual shortage of food in spring and summer. The 1972 thaw came as late as ever recorded, at least in the N. Am. and E. Siberian arctic (includes Wrangel I.). No young Greater Snow Geese were produced nor, except at southernmost stations, any Lesser Snow/Blues, Ross' Geese, and Brant. Some King Eiders attempted belatedly to nest even in the high-arctic; young were produced only on the southern perimeter of their breeding range—that is, well south in the subarctic. The weather influence extends into fall, since late-hatched young may be caught by an early freeze. To these adversities must be added predation (by gulls and jaegers, as well as foxes), which is very heavy in some localities and seasons, and debilitation from endoparasites plus effects of disease. Since these factors, which themselves are variable, mostly tend to have a differential effect on the sexes and age-classes, the population structure must be changing constantly and quite drastically.

Since yearling prebreeders (both sexes) tend not to travel to harsh climates, but instead stop and molt somewhere along migration routes, the hazards they face are different and probably much less severe than those encountered by breeders.

The **native kill** of King Eiders has been considerable in the past in Alaska, Greenland, and certainly elsewhere. In the w. Palearctic, the annual take of flightless molters around Kolguev I. was about 12,000–14,000 (Dementiev and Gladkov 1952). At the present time, the native kill is greatly diminished in most places, but the King Eider can become very important any time other foods are scarce or not as readily obtainable. On. w. Victoria I. in 2 weeks in June, 9 Eskimo families killed an estimated 6,468 Kings, not including escaped cripples (T. G. Smith 1973). The Eskimos bite off the swollen frontal lobes of spring drakes and regard them as a special delicacy, as noted in Greenland (Schiøler 1962) and in 1958 near Barrow, Alaska (M. T. Myres). The skin of the head of drakes is decorative and used by native peoples in various ways.

Barry (1968) estimated the number of migrant eiders (mostly Kings) using the Beaufort Sea route at 1,108,000 with annual native kill of 1% or less, which is negligible compared with other mortality. For a guess, the recent total average annual Holarctic population of the King Eider may be of the order of 2½ million individuals.

In the Nearctic, in addition to **legal protection** most of the year in Canada and the U.S., taking eggs is forbidden in Greenland, as are taking the birds when inland, flightless Kings anywhere, or taking this eider in ne. Greenland. RSP

FOOD Stomachs of 85 "adults" showed approximately 95% animal matter (mollusks mainly, also crustaceans, echinoderms, and insects) and 5% vegetable matter (Cottam 1939). Stomachs of downy young contained fragments of crustaceans and plants (Manniche 1910).

**Animal** Mollusks (*Mytilus, Modiolaria, Saxicava, Siliqua, Tellina, Tachyrhynchus, Littorina,* etc.) 45.8%, crustaceans (*Dermaturus, Cancer, Pagurus*) 18.6%, echinoderms (*Echinarachnius parma, Strongylocentrotus*) 17.2% insects (caddis fly and mayfly larvae, beetles, water bugs) 5.2%, sea anemone (*Aulactinia capitata*) 2.4%, miscellaneous (bryozoans, marine worms, sea squirt, fishes, hydroids, etc.) 5.4% (Cottam 1939).

In S.C. a bird had fed entirely on mussels (*Modiolus plicatulus*) (Chamberlain 1937). A ♀ taken on the Seneca R., N.Y., had eaten 72 amphipods (*Gammarus fasciatus*), a johnny darter (*Boleosoma nigrum*), leopard frogs (*Rana pipiens*), aquatic insects (*Gyrinus, Corixa*), and mollusks (*Planorbis, Asellus, Physa, Limnea*) (Embody 1910). One taken at Buckeye L., Ohio, in early Dec. contained 3 small gizzard shad (*Dorosoma cepedianum*), a few grains of corn, and gravel (Trautman 1940). Eiders from Long I., N.Y., contained crabs (*Cancer irroratus*) and shells of mollusks (*Mytilus, Luniata*) (Whitfield 1894). In Me., birds had fed on crustaceans (*Gammarus locusta, Cancer irroratus*) and young holothurians (*Pentacta frondosa*) (Norton 1900, 1909). Bryozoans (*Crisia, Menipea, Myriozoum, Cellepora*) were reported from the Pribilof Is. (Osburn 1921). The following data from R. D. Jones, Jr., not tabulated, are for 14 drakes (4 taken in Feb., 10 in March) from Cold Bay, Alaska: the food was 100% animal—limpets, cockles, mussels, scallops, crabs, snails, and other invertebrates; there also were varying amounts of grit. In the Barrow region of Alaska in spring of 1958, some of the birds found dead had fed on gastropod mollusks, over a considerable range of size, and on crabs (M. T. Myres). In May at Foxe Pen. on Baffin I., clam and whelk shells littered the ice upon which King Eiders roosted and a drake was shot in the act of swallowing a soft-shelled clam (*Mya truncata*) 75 mm. long (Macpherson and McLaren 1959). In subarctic Canada at Perry R. in summer, the birds had eaten some hydromedusae, ground beetles, and spiders (H. C. Hanson et al., 1956).

134

In 3 drakes taken inland in early July, 1971, at high-arctic Bathurst I., even the lower ends of the large intestines were distended with the remains of thousands of midge larvae; when samples of this material were dropped in water, it was seen that a considerable number of chironomid larvae still were intact after having passed through the digestive tract (R. S. Palmer). Based on field observations, the summer food of both sexes at Bathurst is mainly insects but also includes some plant material (P. Lamothe).

Food at sea in Greenland consists principally of mollusks (*Mytilus*, *Modiolaria*, *Leda*, *Saxicava*, *Pecten*, *Trophon*, *Turritella*, *Volutomitra*), also young sea urchins (*Strongylocentrotus*), plus ophiurids, actinians, and occasionally crutaceans and fish spawn (Salomonsen 1950, Winge 1898); marine worms and a whelk (*Buccinum*) (Bird and Bird 1941); bivalves (*Portlandia arctica*, *Saxicava arctica*) (P. Johnsen 1953). In ne. Greenland, 6 young birds while still living on lakes: *Branchinecta* primarily, also gastropods, Ophiuridae, and unidentified vegetable matter (P. Johnsen 1953).

In April, 1972, n. of Vardø, Norway, Kings were feeding on eggs of capelin (*Mallotus villosus*); their digestive tracts contained these fish eggs and mud from the ocean bottom (Gjøsaeter et al. 1972).

There is seasonal variation in food in n. U.S.S.R. While on tundra pools in spring–summer, food consists mainly of the larvae of aquatic insects and amphipod crustaceans. Stomachs from Taimyr and from the New Siberian Archipelago in May–June were filled with the abundant larvae of midges. When the birds return to sea there is a radical change in diet. In Novaya Zemlya: mainly mollusks (*Mytilus* and *Saxicava*) with some crabs, in July at Bezymyannya Bay almost exclusively the crustacean *Idothea entomon*, and Aug. 14 at Great Karmankul Bay, drakes 15–20 km. from shore were feeding on pteropod mollusks (*Clio borealis* and *Lomacina limacina*) which were swarming in the water. (Summarized from Dementiev and Gladkov 1952.)

The following 3 paragraphs, based on observations in ne. Yakutia, are summarized from S. Uspenskii et al. (1962).

There are definite changes in foods taken by the King Eider through spring and first half of summer, the period of observation. When the birds first arrive, their stomachs, as a rule, contain remnants of marine mollusks (the gastropods Naticidae, *Buccinacea*, *Sipha*, and *Volutopsius*, and the bivalves *Taxodonta*, *Loldia*, *Loldinella*, and *Saxicava*). The mollusks must have been taken where the sea had normal, or slightly less than normal, salinity, a silt bottom, and depth not less than 5 meters. They could have been taken most readily in Bering Sea; hence King Eiders apparently migrate rapidly from Bering Sea to nesting areas without feeding along the way. [Beyond Bering Sea, at least in some years they are flying continuously over ice.]

On arrival, at thawed pools and lake margins, this eider feeds on trichopterous larvae (in volume up to 90% of stomach contents) and eats fruit of *Ranunculus*, *Sparganium*, and *Carex*, plus small amounts of vegetative parts of *Carex* and grasses. From the beginning of thawing of freshwater ponds, the major elements are caddis fly (Trichoptera) larvae—stomachs contained 200–300 larval cases—and chironomid larvae. At this time vegetable food is eaten in small amounts. Later, they switch almost entirely to feeding on chironomid larvae. The total wt. of these in a stomach was 11 gm., plus 20 gm. in the esophagus. The total number of larvae in this instance, assuming a larva weighs 2 mg., is over 10,000.

During the whole period of observation, the Ob lemming (*Lemmus obensis*) had a definite place in the diet; in 10% of full stomachs examined, one would find lemming remains of as many as 4 or 5 individuals. Judging by the size of the bones, the eiders had eaten only young lemmings. These authors commented that Sdobnikov and other authors also had reported finding rodents in digestive tracts of the King Eider.

S. Uspenskii later (1972) stated that lemmings found in King Eiders weighed 20 gm. each. The Ob lemming is not a small species and one would expect the young to much exceed 20 gm. before they were moving about. Then too, the King Eider cannot swallow very large objects. A search for other references to King Eider vs. lemmings has turned up only Sdobnikov's (1959b) paper on waterfowl of w. Taimyr. It translates: "In most cases the stomachs of killed King Eiders were empty. In 2 stomachs were found, in 1, skull bones of a lemming, in the other, fragments of a reindeer bone, small pieces of reindeer hoof, small bones of lemmings, fish bones, and cases of some worms or larvae. All these finds were made at breeding time [end of June]. Therefore it can be supposed that by swallowing the bones of lemmings and other animals, the Kings replenish within themselves a deficiency of the calcium necessary for eggshell formation."

**Vegetable**   Eelgrass (*Zostera marina*) and trace of wigeon grass (*Ruppia maritima*) 2.4%, algae (*Ptilota*) 2.2%, and miscellaneous plants 0.9% (Cottam 1939).

On Canadian high-arctic Bathurst I., when the Kings first arrive (over frozen sea) they feed on plant materials; after the emergence of chironomid larvae in the ponds, there is a shift and aquatic invertebrates comprise at least 70% of the diet (P. Lamothe). Plants were reported to be major food items at fresh water in ne. Greenland (Manniche 1910), but P. Johnsen (1953) reported otherwise for preflight birds (see above). On Spitzbergen, stems of grasses and unidentifiable leaves of phanerogams (Koenig 1911). Five birds from the Perry R. region of mainland Canada had eaten twigs, buds, leaves, and catkins of *Salix*, stems of moss, florets of *Calamagrostis* and *Poa*, bracts of *Eriophorum*, seeds of *Ranunculus*, and bulblets of *Polygonum viviparum* (H. C. Hanson et al. 1956).

Algae formed about 10% of material ingested at the Pribilofs (Preble and McAtee 1923). AWS RSP

## Canvasback

*Aythya valisineria* (Wilson)

Medium-sized diving duck, although averaging somewhat larger than any other species of *Aythya*. The sloping crown–bill profile, evident even in newly hatched downies, gives the head an elongated appearance and is diagnostic among waterfowl breeding in N. Am. (but perhaps excepting the Common Pochard, *A. ferina*, which has straggled to our area). Bill long (for a diving duck), straight, tapering and flattened distally (in lateral view), with inconspicuous nail, sides parallel (in dorsal view), and totally dark-colored (after early life) in both sexes. Bill shape, including the evenly curved feather margin at side base, and meas., differentiates *valisineria* from the most similar-appearing members of the pochard group (*A. ferina* and *americana*) occurring in N. Am.; see fig. on p. 157. Crown feathers short. Eye color sexually dimorphic after early life (♂ brownish orange to scarlet, ♀ very dark).

Drake in Def. Alt. Plumage (most of year): head and all of neck mostly reddish brown, with blackish face; forepart of body blackish, mantle and most of underparts very light (back and flanks white or nearly so, finely vermiculated blackish), posterior feathering very dark, and these various areas sharply delineated; the accompanying Basic wing has proximal half nearly all white. The ♀ has the flanks and much of back generally much lighter than forepart of back and the breast (instead of nearer alike as in Common Pochard, Redhead, and scaups). In the Canvasback, in the ♂ Basic wing, both the secondaries and their coverts are about equally light-colored, and in ♂ and ♀ Juv. and ♀ Basic, they are about equally medium dark; that is, they do not contrast in this species. In the Redhead ♂ and ♀, both Juv. and Basic wing, the coverts are conspicuously darker than the secondaries, i.e., they contrast. In corresponding sex and Plumage, the Common Pochard is somewhat intermediate, being nearer the Canvasback.

The drake's trachea tapers gradually toward its distal end, with a distinct enlargement 1 in. long about 3 in. from the distal end, and the bulla at the inner end is "very similar" to that of *A. americana* and *A. ferina* (J. C. Phillips 1925). Although first described in 1824 and redescribed several times, apparently no illus. of the bulla of *valisineria* has been published.

Length ♂ 19½–23 in., ♀ 19–22½, wingspread ♂ to 35½, ♀ to 33½, usual wt. of ♂ nearly 3 lb., ♀ 2½. No subspecies. The Canvasback of the Nearctic region and the slightly smaller Common Pochard of the Palearctic are different species, but are much alike in appearance and total biology.

DESCRIPTION   Two Plumages/cycles in both sexes; 2nd cycle earliest definitive; The ♀ molts into Basic head–body in spring. In the 1st cycle, the amount of feathering in Plumages after the Juv. is not fully known (inadequate available specimen material); in later cycles, after almost all of a Plumage is acquired, the molt quite often is slowed or interrupted so that traces of a preceding Plumage may remain for weeks or months, a common situation in diving ducks. Ferrous staining on head and dorsum is common.

▶   ♂ Def. Alt. Plumage (all feathering except the tail and, in the wing, includes only the innermost secondaries and their coverts), worn from LATE SUMMER or FALL (Aug.–Nov.) through winter and spring into SUMMER (June–July). **Bill** blackish, **iris** reddish (to scarlet); most of **head** and neck reddish brown, but blending on front of face and the crown to very dark (toward blackish brown); small white chin spot; **upperparts** upper back black; mantle and scapulars pale grayish (fades to white), quite densely covered with fine blackish brown vermiculations; lower back dusky brownish, speckled and vermiculated pale gray; rump and upper tail coverts blackish brown; **underparts** breast black; sides and belly white, latter especially becoming pale gray faintly vermiculated blackish brown posteriorly; under tail coverts black, faintly speckled smoke gray; legs and **feet** bluish gray, webs dusky. Retained Basic feathering includes the tail, and the wing except: elongated innermost secondaries ("tertials") which appear solidly white (though there is some dark) and their outer webs (except on the innermost feather) are narrowly margined black; and their overlying coverts also are predominantly white.

In s. Man., some drakes are well into Alt. by early Sept. and most have acquired it fully by mid-Oct. or early Nov. (Hochbaum 1944).

NOTE   In captivity, drakes in their first 3 years had complete molt out of Alt. into Basic; older ones had an incomplete molt (retained some Alt. feathers), and an 8-year-old individual retained his Alt. Plumage until the next Prealt. molt, i.e., then molted from Alt. to Alt. head–body without intervening Basic feathering, although the Basic wings were shed with "usual flightless period" according to Hochbaum (1944). Seldom "vigorous enough to molt normally in captivity" (J. C. Phillips 1925).

▶   ♂ Def. Basic Plumage (total feathering; worn a few weeks at most, except the tail and most of the wing are retained and worn with the next-incoming Alt. Plumage), acquired in SUMMER (beginning June to early Aug., depending on the individual) and head–body feathering succeeded by Alt. in LATE SUMMER or FALL (beginning in Aug. or Sept., depending on the individual). General appearance: pearly gray bird with brownish head and neck. **Iris** becomes flecked with yellow and brown (Hochbaum 1944). **Head** and neck grayed brownish or dusky, sometimes mottled lighter, and some individuals have a light eye ring (as in some ♀♀ in Alt.); **upperparts** scapulars and upper back more broadly and conspicuously marked dark than in Alt. Plumage; rump and upper tail coverts brownish black, the feathers mostly pale tipped; **underparts** upper breast brownish black or same mixed with brown and gray feathers; sides and flanks more broadly and conspicuously vermiculated dark than in Alt. Plumage; lower breast and belly more or less mottled with pale grayish or brownish; under tail coverts nearly black with whitish tips. **Tail** feathers blackish brown, faintly speckled buffy at tips. **Wing** secondary coverts white, most of them finely and densely vermiculated dark; primary coverts blackish brown with white vermiculations or flecking (especially toward tips); primaries blackish brown, becoming medium smoke gray near shafts, the outer webs of inner primaries faintly flecked white; outer secondaries white, lightly vermiculated pale grayish brown and this increases and becomes darker on inner secondaries, the innermost ones being darkest and more or less coarsely vermiculated grayish brown or grayish; wing lining pale grayish, axillars white.

Some drakes already show some Basic feathers while their mates still are laying (Hochbaum 1944). There may be some degree of correlation of timing of the drake's molt and his mate's nesting schedule—i.e., early molters being mated to early nesters (but also see beyond under ♀ Def. Basic). Among captives, nonbreeding drakes go into molt late, according to Hochbaum (1944), who believed that timing of molt in "unmated" wild drakes was similarly late, although it probably is not.

Captives require 2½–4 weeks for "renewal" of the wing (Hochbaum 1944); drakes in the wild probably are flightless for at least 3 weeks. Observations in Man. of flightless wild drakes: earliest was June 30, they were uncommon until after mid-July, and peak numbers occurred between late July and late Aug. (Hochbaum 1944). As in at least most ducks that have been studied, the Canvasback acquires most or all new Basic head–body feathering before the flight feathers of wing and the tail feathers of the preceding Basic generation are dropped; and the Basic head–body, in turn, is beginning to be replaced by Alt. before the wing again has grown sufficiently to permit flight. Therefore, as stated by Hochbaum (1944), one may see flightless drakes in full Basic and others with only a few Basic feathers remaining. The former condition is normal for birds early in flightlessness, the latter for birds toward end of that period when molt back into Alt. head–body is well advanced.

▶  ♀ Def. Alt. Plumage (all feathering except tail and, in the wing, only a few innermost feathers), acquired beginning in early FALL (later than in ♂ ) and worn until LATE WINTER–SPRING.

Quite clear-cut pattern, the dark forepart of body terminating in a well-defined edge. A comparatively gray ♀ Plumage. **Bill** nearly black, **iris** dark brownish; **head** forehead, crown, nape, and much of lower neck brownish olive; elsewhere, palest (whitish) behind eye and on chin and upper throat; the remainder gray-brown (reddish brown is ferrous staining), except for a white eye ring (not always distinct) and sometimes a poorly defined darkish stripe across lower cheek; **upperparts** mantle and scapulars appear rather light gray, the white feathers being finely and heavily vermiculated dark; lower back and rump toward sooty, many feathers with some fine white vermiculations; upper tail coverts dusky; **underparts** breast browner than anterior dorsum and the feathers pale ended (the ends wear off); sides and flanks palish gray (white, finely vermiculated blackish); belly white, but darkening on rear of abdomen and in vent area (these feathers, too, are vermiculated); under tail coverts whitish. Legs and **feet** grayish blue, webs dusky.

Tail is retained Basic feathering, also the wing except several innermost secondaries ("tertials") which are elongated, tapering (with tips rounded), and medium gray or darker with white flecking near their ends, and with narrow blackish outer margins; the 2 longest (innermost) feathers are very dark with tips slightly vermiculated whitish; and the retained overlying coverts are gray, heavily marked with white distally.

The last Alt. feathers to grow are the innermost feathers of wing (often still growing in late Nov.–early Dec.) and scattered feathers on the rump; traces of the preceding Basic Plumage often remain on the rump into winter.

NOTE   Def. Alt. ♀ Canvasback and Common Pochard are very similar, but the latter has a darker occiput.

▶  ♀ Def. Basic Plumage (total feathering), the head and body acquired during SPRING and retained until well along in SUMMER or into EARLY FALL; the Basic tail and wing are acquired beginning in late summer (late Aug.) or early fall, while the remainder of the Basic is molting back into Alt.

A blended, brownish Plumage. **Head** forehead and crown dark brownish olive, grading to buffy brown laterally and on nape, hindneck, and lower sides of neck; side of face, chin, and foreneck smoke gray faintly mottled buffy brown; indistinct white eye ring, or only the lower lid white; **upperparts** feathers of upper back medium brownish olive, the more posterior ones with narrow buffy margins; most of mantle and the scapulars darker than in Alt., and further darkening on lower back and upper tail coverts, and various feathers have coarse white vermiculations; **underparts** much of breast some variant of tawny, richest laterally, and with lower margin not well defined; feathers of sides and flanks buffy brown with pale ends; belly pale smoke gray, becoming darker on rear of abdomen and vent area; under tail coverts smoke gray with broad whitish margins. **Tail** grayish fuscous.

**Wing** primaries blackish brown with large portions of inner and outer webs of 6 outer feathers smoke gray; outer webs of most of the exposed secondaries light grayish with broad grayish fuscous subterminal band and white ends; innermost secondaries rounded (not tapering) and dark without blackish outer border; upper wing coverts mostly variants of grayish fuscous, the longest ones more or less flecked whitish near their ends; wing lining pale grayish, axillars white.

Females may become flightless as early as July 20 in s. Man., but wing molt usually does not begin until Aug., and a still flightless ♀ was seen as late as Oct. 9 (Hochbaum 1944). Duration of flightlessness is 3 or 4 weeks (Hochbaum).

NOTE   Definitive-feathered ♀ ♀ occasionally have some white feathers on back of head; compare with Redhead.

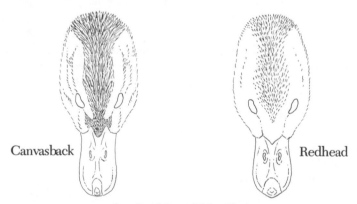

Canvasback                    Redhead

heads of day-old ducklings

AT HATCHING   See vol. 2, col. pl. facing p. 466. Contrasty pattern; darker upperparts than Redhead; dark forehead. See text fig. comparison of dorsal views of heads. The sloping head–bill lateral profile is not a good field character until the ducklings are 4–5 weeks old (Hochbaum 1944).

As early as age 30 days (before there is an eye-color difference), the ducklings can be sexed by difference in incoming Plumage (see below under ♂ and ♀ Juv.). For details of fading, color difference in the 2 down generations, growth (wt., meas.) and loss of down from known-age captives, see Dzubin's (1959) illus. and text. Captive ducklings lose most of the down by age 7 weeks (it may wear off sooner in the wild).

▶ ♂ Juv. Plumage (entire feathering). Probably perfected at age about 70–80 days, worn in entirety briefly, then largely replaced by succeeding feather generations, but most of wing retained through winter into following summer.

**Bill** mostly dark. **Iris** probably olive-yellow when entire feathering is Juv. (color change comes later). Feathering superficially like ♀ Def. Basic, but notable differences include: presence of quite distinct white eye ring; **heads** of some drakes are distinctive dark cinnamon, others tend toward buffy browns. (The dark flecking that appears on cheeks of some ♂♂ by age 56 days belongs to the succeeding feather generation, i.e., Basic I.) **Upperparts** mantle and scapulars medium grayish fuscous to medium buffy fuscous with faint smoke gray vermiculations. **Underparts** side of breast medium brownish olive, the feathers with pale buffy margins; upper breast grayish fuscous, the feathers margined pale buffy; sides and flanks medium smoke gray with feather tips paler; lower breast and belly pale silvery smoke gray, becoming darker posteriorly and in vent region. Legs and **feet** probably quite dark (data lacking). Tail fuscous, the feathers blunt and with abraded ends. **Wing** paler than ♀ Basic; recognizable as Juv. and as ♂ (as early as 30th day—Dzubin 1959) by upper secondary coverts which are medium gray to medium dusky brown, faintly or moderately speckled white or buffy (♂ Basic wing has upper secondary coverts finely but abundantly vermiculated dark on white), and the greater coverts over the exposed secondaries often have indistinct whitish terminal margins (which wear off).

The sequence in which tracts begin to show Juv. feathering is very similar in the several *Aythya* that have been reported on, including the Redhead in N. Am. In the Canvasback, the scapulars begin to appear as early as the 14th day and, beginning as early as age 30 days, their diagnostic sex difference is evident—♂ dark or smoke gray, vermiculated pale gray; ♀ brownish olive, usually unmarked. Drakes also tend to have darker head color, especially after the 45th day. These data are from Dzubin (1959); see his paper for many additional details.

▶ ♀ Juv. Plumage (entire feathering), timing as ♂, i.e., worn rather briefly, except most of wing long retained.

As ♂ except: **head** generally not as dark; **mantle,** including scapulars, and upper wing coverts variants of brownish olive, usually plain (indistinct paler vermiculations sometimes present); in the **wing** the innermost secondaries are narrow, tapering, medium gray, sometimes plain and sometimes with whitish vermiculations to heavy dotting distally; their overlying greater coverts are comparatively narrow, squarish ended, indistinctly edged whitish (it may wear off) and lightly to heavily dotted whitish; overlying middle coverts frosted grayish.

NOTE   The interval between breaking of primary sheaths and sufficient growth of the Juv. wing for the young to fly in captive birds in Alaska was 19 days (Schneider 1965), in known-age wild-trapped young in Man. 20 days (Dzubin 1959).

▶ ♂ Basic I Plumage (probably all of head–body, tail, and innermost feathers of wing, but less extensive in material examined). A transitory stage in 1st fall, but sometimes retained longer, tail evidently retained into following summer.

A dark Plumage. **Bill** blackish, **iris** variants of grayed orange. **Head** and neck dusky brown to blackish brown, the feathers shorter than in next-incoming Alt. I. **Upperparts** quite dark, light to medium brownish olive faintly speckled buffy, various feath-

141

ers with narrow pale buffy margins. **Underparts** variants of dusky brownish or mottled brown and gray, upper sides and flanks lighter grayish. **Tail** medium gray. Innermost feathers of wing evidently much as in ♂ Def. Basic.

▶    ♂ Alt. I Plumage (head–body and innermost feathers of wing) ordinarily acquired in 1st FALL, Oct.–Nov. and worn into following SUMMER (to age 1 year). **Iris** color at about 10–12 weeks posthatching approaches scarlet (Hochbaum 1944). Incoming Alt. I feathers are like Def. Alt., except there tend to be coarser vermiculations on **mantle,** sides, and flanks. From late Oct. on, the new innermost secondaries and their coverts appear and resemble those of Def. Alt. The tail is retained Juv. or Basic I (the latter generally present by early Dec.); most of the wing is retained Juv. feathering.

▶    ♀ Basic I Plumage (inclusive feathering not fully known; probably all of head–body, the tail, and innermost feathers of wing, but inadequate specimen data). Transitory, usually within the span SEPT.–OCT. Generally similar to ♀ Def. Basic; in material examined, however, the venter somewhat darker and less evenly colored. The Basic I tail may come in late, when the bird is molting out of much Basic I and into the next Plumage; most of the wing is retained Juv.

▶    ♀ Alt. I Plumage (all feathering except tail and, in the wing, only a few innermost feathers), generally acquired in very LATE FALL (commonly in Nov.) and retained until LATE WINTER or early spring. Apparently as succeeding Alts.; the tail is retained Basic I and most of the wing is retained Juv.

▶    ♀ Basic II Plumage (entire feathering), head–body and a few innermost feathers of wing acquired in EARLY SPRING (before age 1 year), most of the wing and the tail not until late summer or EARLY FALL (in which season the head–body molt into Alt.). Thus most of the Juv. wing is worn with the Basic II head–body until the late summer flightless period, after which the Basic II wing and tail grow.

**Color phases**    none; note early sex differences under ♂ Juv. above.

**Measurements**    12 ♂ (from Alta. to Que. and s. into Texas, mostly Oct.–Dec.): BILL 59–65 mm., av. 62.7; WING 229–248, av. 235; TAIL 56–60, av. 57.1; TARSUS 44–47, av. 45.3;    12 ♀ (B.C. and Alta. s. into Cal. and N.C., varous seasons): BILL 57–63 mm., av. 59.1; WING 221–234, av. 229; TAIL 56–59, av. 57.9; TARSUS 43–47, av. 44.2 (ETS).

Spring birds, WING meas. across chord: 5 ♂ av. 241 mm. and 5 ♀ 227 (Dzubin 1959). For another series, also with chord of wing, see J. C. Phillips (1925). Certain meas. of wild ducklings, at intervals from their first day to attainment of flight, also were given by Dzubin (1959).

**Weight** (mean and range) of Canvasbacks at Seneca L. in N.Y.: "adult" birds Jan. 9–March 31, 191 ♂ 1,252 ± 9 gm. (850–1,600) and 54 ♀ 1,154 ± 14 (900–1,530); "immature" 57 ♂ (Jan. 9–March 29) 1,250 ± 11 gm. (1,020–1,510) and 26 ♀ (Jan. 13–March 24) 1,149 ± 29 (950–1,390) (Ryan 1972).

At Delta, Man., mean wt. with standard error in parentheses: 18 young (mostly ♀) in Sept. 1,076 gm. (12.2), 18 "adult" ♂ in May 1,238.4 (12.4), 9 "adult" ♀ in May 1,216 (25.9), and 5 ♀ attending broods in June 1,115 (Dzubin 1959). See his paper for wt. and growth analysis of ducklings; individual wts. in a brood of 10 on day of hatching were 43–48 gm.

The Canvasback was the heaviest duck weighed in Ill. in fall by Bellrose and Hawkins (1947); 4 ♂ "adult" 2.98 lb. (mean), one 1st fall ♀ 2.20, 2 "adult" ♀ 2.58 (mean) and 5 1st fall ♀ 2.35 (mean).

Sixty-two fall drakes av. 2.8 lb. (1.17 kg.), max. 3.5 (1.59 kg.), and 79 fall ♀ av. 2.6 lb. (1.18 kg.), max. 3.4 (1.54 kg.) (A. L. Nelson and Martin 1953).

Flightless molting "adults" at Ohtig L. in ne. Alaska: 48 ♂ max. 3 lb., min. 1 lb. 12 oz., mean 2 lb. 7 oz. (1,105 gm.); 20 ♀ max. 2 lb. 12 oz., min. 1 lb. 15 oz., mean 2 lb. 5.6 oz. (1,065 gm.) (Yocom 1970a). They may not have had food for several days.

There are some additional data on wt. in A. Leopold (1921) and J. C. Phillips (1925).

**Hybrids** in the wild with Lesser Scaup (*Aythya affinis*) and Mallard (*Anas platyrhynchos*) are known (J. C. Phillips 1925). Also see under Redhead for a cross with a captive ♀ Canvasback and for mixed pairs of these 2 species in the wild. In captivity, with 3 *Aythya* and 2 *Anas* species; this includes a fertile cross with the Redhead (C. L. Sibley 1938) and probably fertile with the Common Pochard (Phillips). Most wildfowlers, if they shot *Aythya* hybrids, would be unlikely to recognize them as such.

Captive-reared Redhead × Canvasback hybrids resemble the Common Pochard.

**Geographical variation** none reported. RSP

FIELD IDENTIFICATION   The Canvasback is the largest of our inland ducks, being slightly larger than the Mallard. Afield, however, size is a relative characteristic usable only when various species are together.

The long tapering bill plus sloping forehead give the head a thin wedge-shaped outline, decidedly thinner than the Common Pochard (which is only a straggler to our area). Drakes, especially, tend to occur on wide shallow waters, where common associates are scaups and the Redhead. Females and young, in small bunches, also visit much smaller waters such as are preferred at times by the Ringneck.

The Canvasback and Ruddy probably are our fastest-flying ducks; wingbeat is rapid and flight direct. The Canvasback's very light wings with dusky tips add to the impression of an essentially white bird. The pattern of the ♀ is less contrasty, although her profile is the same. They fly in bunches on local flights, at other times in compact wedge- or U-shaped flocks and usually closer to the water surface and in smaller flocks than the Mallard. They prefer to fly around projecting points of land when in low altitude flight, rather than cross over them.

The back of the drake usually appears much nearer white than the grayish back of Lesser and Greater Scaups, especially in autumn, and the scaups are much more chunky birds. (In winter, the backs of scaups, especially the ♂ ♂, are lighter than in summer–fall and, at a distance, then appear almost as light as the Canvasback.) Scaups in bright reflected light may appear to have white backs. (Also compare with Ringnecked Duck.) When Canvasbacks and scaups are together, however, a difference in back color is apparent. Moreover, the former appears to ride higher on the water. The Redhead is dark backed and round headed, hence quite readily distinguished.

From some time in summer into fall, various *Aythya* (adults in Basic, young in Juv. Plumage) tend to look much alike at a distance, having somber, blended, coloring. Still, the Canvasback's head profile is diagnostic, except perhaps from the Common Pochard, which has a profile intermediate in shape between Canvasback and Redhead. FCB

VOICE  The drake generally is silent except during certain displays, as discussed under "Reproduction." Then he has a trisyllabic call that ends with a cooing syllable (frequently uttered), an in-breathing sound, and a monosyllabic cough (seldom). The ♀, when Inciting or Neck-stretching, has a low guttural purring, much like that of the ♀ Redhead and Common Pochard; a drawn-out whine, in flight when pursued by drake(s); and a repeated *Kuck,* commonly heard in late spring–summer when she is with her brood; all are mentioned below in context with associated activities.

The approximate frequency range of hearing of a drake was 190–5,200 cycles/sec.; that is, the "lower limit was about half an octave below middle C and the upper limit was a few notes above the highest note on the piano" (E. P. Edwards 1943). RSP

HABITAT  Nests in shallow-water marshes bordered by emergent vegetation. Prefers hardstem bulrush (*Scirpus acutus*) as nesting cover, but uses other plants also, especially cattail (*Typha latifolia*) and flooded cane (*Phragmites communis*). At farmland "potholes" it often nests in stands of whitetop grass (*Scholochloa festucacea*) flooded by spring runoff. Sometimes it nests at potholes as small as 20–30 yds. in diam.; under these conditions, the drake "waits" and the pair loafs and feeds on open water of a larger slough or lake nearby. In larger marshes, some nest in dense island stands of bulrush far from shore. Young are reared in the same environment as used for nesting, but broods do much feeding and traveling in open water. In small-marsh regions, broods regularly walk overland from one pothole to another (C. D. Evans 1951).

**Midsummer–early fall**  Birds of the year and many adult ♀ ♀ congregate on larger marshes where they are especially attracted to submerged beds of sago pondweed (*Potamogeton pectinatus*). Drakes on molting waters, such as boreal lakes, also congregate over beds of pondweeds. Apparently, in the annual cycle of this bird, the pondweed family (Najadaceae) is more important than the wild celery (*Vallisneria spiralis*) after which the species is named (Cottam 1939).

**Autumn** migrants stop to feed and rest on lakes, rivers, and large marshes, small groups of ♀ ♀ and young on smaller water areas at times.

**Winter**  Some Canvasbacks pass the season on deep lakes, such as Cayuga and Seneca in cent. N.Y., but most move to or near coasts, to brackish or alkaline waters where wild celery and pondweeds thrive. Namely: estuaries, upper reaches of the tide, shallow bays (mouth of Susquehanna R.; Chesapeake Bay), harbors, and the freshwater lakes of the Mississippi delta region. All these are preferred to the open sea.

**Spring**  Return to breeding areas is by way of most of the same stopover places used in autumn, but at this season Canvasbacks also visit flooded farmland and small marshes where they seldom are seen during fall passage. HAH

DISTRIBUTION  (See map.) R. E. Stewart et al. (1958) is a prime source of information on overall range and on seasonal density distribution. Data published subsequently add more range in Alaska where, since some time in the 1950s, this species has increased greatly. Canvasbacks reached "peak numbers" there in 1959 and 1960, "after the onset of the current drought on the prairies"; an "influx of displaced prairie birds" into Alaska during drought is "nothing new" (Hansen and McKnight 1964). Ir-

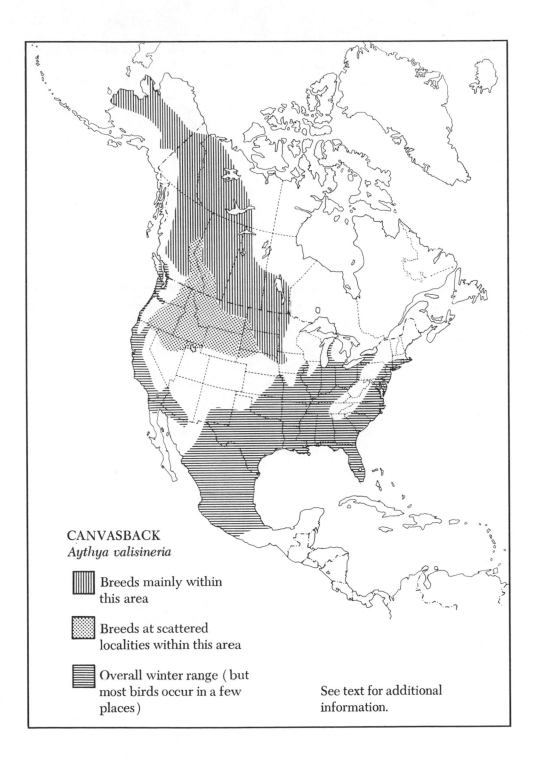

CANVASBACK
*Aythya valisineria*

||||| Breeds mainly within
this area

::::: Breeds at scattered
localities within this area

≡≡≡ Overall winter range (but
most birds occur in a few
places)

See text for additional
information.

respective of this, the continuing decline in the total Canvasback population surely has resulted in at least local changes elsewhere in distribution.

**Summer**   Highest nesting densities occur in areas of se. Man., n. Alta. and n. Yukon Terr.; medium to medium-high densities occur in a large area of prairie astride the conterminous U.S.–Canadian boundary and breeders occur in medium density on the Ft. Yukon area (Alaska) and the Old Crow flats (Yukon Terr.) In conterminous U.S., and excepting the area astride the international boundary, the places where the Canvasback breeds are few and widely scattered, from the prairies and some peripheral areas nearly to the Pacific coast.

Some examples of peripheral breeding: in Iowa (Bennett 1937), Tule L. in Cal. (Jewett 1947), and Overton in s. Nev. (G. T. Austin 1970).

Occurrence in breeding season extends beyond the perimeter of known breeding range. In conterminous U.S., for example, occasional birds remain to the south and east. In Alaska, in the interior, a small flock on June 19 on the John R. within the Brooks Range (J. M. Campbell 1969b) in 1959 and 1960, recorded from the lower Kuskokwim R. up the Bering Sea coast to Kotzebue Sd. (H. A. Hansen 1960, Hansen and McKnight 1964). In the case of various northerly marginal occurrences, it is not clear whether the birds are molting drakes, or failed breeders, or possibly birds that did not attempt to breed (nonbreeders).

The whereabouts of many birds after their molt migration is mentioned below under "Migration."

**Winter**   There is some overlap of breeding and winter range. The birds occur where there is suitable sheltered open water and food. Because of diagonal as well as other migration routes, Canvasbacks occur at very widely scattered localities. In decreasing order of number of birds present (at least prior to 1958), largest wintering concentrations occurred in: Chesapeake Bay area, San Francisco Bay area, Detroit area, s.-cent. Mexico (central plateau), delta lakes of s. La., and e. Great Lake–upper Mississippi area.

**Examples of changed status**   Now occurs only occasionally along the St. Lawrence in se. Ont. and close by in s. Que., where it was regular formerly. Now occurs in the Cook Inlet region of Alaska as a migrant in spring and fall (Hemming 1966). As of 1970 or earlier, wintered at Adak I. in the cent. Aleutians and recorded eastward toward or to the Alaska Pen.

For an earlier summary of range, which included some examples of local changes in status, see J. C. Phillips (1925).

**Straggler** in continental N. Am. to New Bruns. (2 localities), N.S. (3 localities), interior Sonora in nw. Mexico, and interior Guatemala. In the Atlantic area: Bermuda, Cuba, and (subject to doubt) Jamaica. Bering–Pacific area: in Alaska, St. George I. (Pribilof group) and see summer data given above; Clipperton I. (10° N, 109° W) sw. of Mexico; Hawaii—Maui in 1948, 1949, 1960, and 1965, and Molokai in 1964; taken twice in winter in Japan.

NOTE   Authors continue to mention the reports by Reichenow, dating from 1899 and 1901, of occurrence of the Canvasback in the Marshall Is. in e. Micronesia. Reichenow even reported that duck skins from the Marshalls included this species. The matter was discussed by J. C. Phillips (1916). Evidently no corroborating evidence

146

has turned up and, in his later monograph, Phillips (1925) mentioned the reports very briefly, and followed by an exclamation point.

Recorded as **fossil** from the Pleistocene of Fla. and from **archaeological sites** in Alaska (at Dutch Harbor), Wash., Cal., Iowa, and Ill.; all these were listed by Brodkorb (1964a). Also the Pleistocene of New Mex. (Howard 1971). RSP

MIGRATION Canvasbacks typically fly in rather small flocks, a mixture of ♀ ♀ plus young of both sexes, or somewhat larger ones consisting of about a dozen or even scores of drakes. The flocks meet to form large assemblies at various places.

"Principal migration routes" were diagrammed by R. E. Stewart et al. (1958) and, for the U.S. e. of the Rockies, Bellrose (1968) described and illustrated "migration corridors" (a concept: wider than "routes") and gave approximate numbers of Canvasbacks that used these in fall in the mid-1960s. These papers should be consulted for many details. The corridor used by most birds is broad; from the Canadian prairies it goes diagonally down to s.-cent. Minn., then veers e. across L. Michigan to the Detroit and extreme s. Ont. area; from there it swings more se. toward Chesapeake Bay. From se. Minn. there is also a heavy, though lesser, flight to se. Iowa and then directly toward s. La. Flocks also travel n. of the main corridor, to L. Ontario and cent. N.Y.; then many of them fly se. or southward to coastal areas. A fraction of the birds that reach Chesapeake Bay continue on down to the coast of the Carolinas and some continue on to n. interior Fla. Canvasbacks use various other corridors e. of the Rockies, from the Canadian interior and n. U.S. to n. Fla., the Gulf Coast (mostly La. and Texas), and Mexico. Canvasbacks from interior Alaska, Yukon Terr., and nw. Canadian prairies go via the continental interior mostly e. of the Rockies; then most of them veer diagonally sw. over various lines of travel (over Mont., Idaho, Wash., Ore., and part of Nev.) and converge on the coast of cent. Cal.; some, from northerly areas, go more eastward down the interior into Mexico; and a few continue from the cent. Cal. coastal area southward (where some other minor routes join it) in that state and over a route inland from the coast down into s. Mexico. There also are routes from e.-cent. Alaska via interior B.C. southward and then out to the Pacific coast to conterminous U.S.

It is known from band recoveries that there is some interchange or overlap; for example, some of the Canvasbacks banded on winter range in La. have been captured subsequently on the Atlantic coast, also some on the Pacific coast. (Birds destined for all 3 of these regions may occur at the same place, in season, on the Canadian prairies.)

Fifty adult Canvasbacks, when flightless during wing molt, were banded at Takslesluk L. (confluent with Baird Inlet), not distant from Bering Sea coastal Alaska, in 1964. From those banded Aug. 8, there have been 7 widely scattered recoveries in subsequent hunting seasons: Cal.—♂ and 2 ♀, e. Texas Gulf Coast—♂, Minn.—♀, Mich.—♂, and Md.—♂ (J. G. King).

Spring passage presumably is approximately the reverse of fall passage, although stopover places or number of birds occurring at a particular one may vary. Some individuals, as already mentioned, may have changed routes.

**Spring** Canvasbacks probably begin leaving s.-cent. Mexico at least as early as mid-Feb. A great many leave the U.S. Gulf of Mexico coastal area during that month and nearly all have left Fla. before the first of March. In the Chesapeake Bay area, migration begins in late Feb., is heavy from early March to early April, and ends in early May. Usually they are gone from the Long I., N.Y., region by early April. They begin arriving in the upper Mississippi drainage and thereabouts beginning some time in March and peak numbers evidently pass through in the first half of April. They are first seen, in an av. year, on the s. Canadian prairies about the beginning of April and the bulk arrive in the second half of that month. As with several other waterfowl, departure from Cal. is comparatively late—in March and April—and a great many of these birds go to Alaska and Yukon Terr. where the nesting season also is comparatively late. There seem to be few northerly arrival dates on record, but migration is known to continue well into May in n. Canada and, at least in tardy seasons, probably continues into June in both Yukon Terr. and interior Alaska.

**Summer**   About the time the ♀ begins to incubate her clutch (a date that varies with season, locality, and individual), her mate takes leave and soon goes on **molt migration.** This is not an abrupt termination of the pair bond; that is, the drake may commute for a few days between his "waiting place" and some other water area, meanwhile forming a social bond with a few other drakes, and then the group departs. They molt on lakes of all sizes and depths, all having areas of abundant submerged and floating aquatic vegetation, notably *Potamogeton* spp.; some are in parklands and some are within the conifer belt and are bordered with spruce. The drakes, in hundreds and even tens of thousands, in large, loosely structured flocks, are scattered over the water well out from shore. Other molting waterfowl, such as scaups, Redheads, and shoalwater species, may occur at the same locality, but each tends to keep more or less separate, in its own preferred niche. The distance drakes travel to molt is probably quite often considerable, even several hundred miles. Molting lakes mentioned in the literature include: Alaska—Butterfly L. and Old Albert L. (H. A. Hansen 1960), several large lakes in the Yukon flats area (Yocom 1964); Man.—L. Manitoba, Swan L., Dauphin L., and Kawinaw L. (the 2nd is w. of L. Winnipegosis, the 3rd s. of it, and the 4th e. of it) and Long I. Bay of L. Winnipegosis; Sask.—Belanger L. w. of Le Pas (in Man.); most of these were mentioned in Hochbaum (1944); Cartwright and Law (1952) stated that they could name a half dozen lakes in Sask. and Alta., used almost exclusively by Canvasbacks, Lesser Scaups, or both; also some waters in Athabaska delta; in se. Idaho—lakes in Camas Refuge (Oring 1964).

R. D. Bergman (1973) described several molting lakes in sw. Man., including the available waterfowl food; at Swan L. there was an early (low) peak of numbers in July of molting Canvasbacks (95% drakes), and a later (high) premigration peak from mid-Aug. through Sept. (90–95% drakes); they ate various species of *Potamogeton*.

Long after the drakes have departed to molt, the ♀ ♀ leave their preflight young (even as early as several weeks before the latter can fly) and gather in small groups; then most of the ♀ ♀ become flightless on the rearing areas rather than joining the drakes. The ♀ ♀ are again able to fly about the time the young are on the wing—that is, several weeks after mature drakes are again flying. The ♀ ♀ and the young (of both sexes) then combine in small flocks. Thus there are flying flocks of mature ♂ ♂ (from late summer on), and mixtures of mature ♀ ♀ and young (early Sept. on), forming a postmolting separation of the sexes in mature birds.

**Fall** The pattern, somewhat oversimplified, appears to be as follows. Although the mature drakes are capable of migrating first, apparently they tend to linger until forced to move by weather and they tend to go the shortest distance, to more northerly wintering places. The ♀ ♀ after they regain flight and the young when they attain flight begin migrating earlier and travel farther, waves of migrant ♀ ♀ and young "leapfrogging" over the mature drakes and going to more southerly centers of winter distribution. (The young of the year are molting into Alt. I head–body during fall and as a consequence closely resemble fully mature birds after early Nov.; age-classes are not distinguishable in the field when winter censusing is done.) The pattern, as outlined here, is masked considerably by overlapping times of travel and of destinations of different groups, also seasonal differences, variation in time spent at stopover places, and so on. At any rate, association of individuals is based on a social (not sexual) drive in fall–winter and flocks that are preponderantly (or entirely) of mature drakes occur at northerly localities, while elsewhere there are flocks preponderantly of ♀ ♀ and young birds. This is the situation until there is a mixing of birds in late winter or in spring.

A breakdown into age and/or sex categories seldom is given in available sources, hence the following dates are general and inclusive. Many Canvasbacks begin entering conterminous U.S. as early as late Sept., but the majority begin arriving about mid-Oct. or even as much as 2 weeks later in exceptional seasons. Usually the last birds have left the Canadian prairies by about mid-Nov. Ordinarily they begin arriving at Chesapeake Bay about mid-Oct., with a peak lasting about 4 weeks and beginning around mid-Nov. They seldom are seen in waters around Long I.( N.Y.) before Nov. and they increase there in numbers into Dec. They arrive in n. Fla. beginning in late Nov. or early Dec. and by that time also in La. and Texas. Movement in Pacific coastal states is largely in Nov.–Dec. Probably few or none arrive in Mexico before Nov. and southerly travel may continue into the last third of Dec.

There is more of a tendency in fall than in spring for Canvasbacks to mingle on the water with other species.

**Winter** There is considerable movement during this season. For example, in N.Y. in Jan.–Feb., groups (not all the birds present) may disappear for a while and then reappear at the same locality. Some of the Canvasbacks on Canandaigua L. fly overland a few miles to Seneca L. and, as determined by live-trapping, even may return on the same day (S. Browne). RSP

BANDING STATUS Over 70,000 were banded between 1925 and 1972 and the number of recoveries through 1973 was over 8,800. Largest numbers were banded in N.Y., Md., the Canadian prairies, Mich., Del., Cal., Va., and Alaska. Banding data have been utilized by several authors, notably by R. E. Stewart et al. (1958). RSP

REPRODUCTION Both sexes (all individuals?) first breed when approaching age 1 year. Although there is some pairing behavior among the older age-classes while the birds still are at wintering localities, most of this activity occurs beginning after some time in March and reaches a peak (in most years) in early April. In the first (social) phase, groups of several (to 10) drakes swim about rapidly, in close proximity to a compact group of several ♀♀, or near a lone ♀. A drake may leave such a gathering and move on to another one. The initial stage was described well by A. A. Allen (in Bent 1923). After various displays, a ♀ and the drake of her choice leave the group. Because there is a coming together of various flocks at these stopover places, the sex ratio that was vastly unbalanced locally and earlier becomes nearer even. As spring advances, more and more pairs move away from the remaining unpaired birds. Pair bond form **seasonal** (single-clutch) **monogamy.**

**Displays of the duck** INCITING consists of an alternating of threatening movements and NECK-STRETCHING (head elevated high) with bill pointed toward the preferred drake. Neck-stretching occurs without any accompanying threat; when one or more drakes perform it, the ♀ does likewise, at the same time uttering a soft *krrr-krrr*. HEAD-THROW as ♂; was done occasionally by a captive, but not seen in wild ♀♀.

**Displays of the drake** KINKED-NECK (Courtship-call of Hochbaum 1944). The neck is drawn back and head lowered, with bill parallel to the water's surface. There is a bulge in the upper throat ("lump under the chin"—J. C. Phillips 1925) and the eye blazes in brilliant scarlet (the dark pupil is contracted). At the time the "lump" appears, the bird utters part or all of the cooing call described under the next display.

HEAD-THROW without preliminaries, the head is snapped abruptly backward so that the crown touches the back, then is thrown quickly forward. On the backward motion the notes uttered are *ick-ick* and on the forward throw a *cooo*. The *ick-ick* is feeble; the *cooo* (it comes after a momentary pause and sounds like *cu-oo* when heard closeup), a sort of asthmatic groan, is far carrying; when many drakes are displaying at a distance, it sounds soft and dovelike.

NECK-STRETCH head elevated as high as possible for a min. or more, the bill aimed forward and angled upward, as the drake swims in the presence of the ♀. Sometimes the head is turned stiffly from side to side, or the bill bobbed. Other drakes frequently join in, whereupon the drake utters a sort of in-breathed cough *hfff*.

COUGHING bird swims in "normal" posture, the wings and tail flicked slightly, and the above-described cough uttered.

SNEAK the neck is stretched forward and bill rests on water, in a posture resembling an escaping wounded bird (or a ♀ preliminary to treading), and the drake attempts to approach the ♀ or else merely Sneaks about her in a seemingly aimless fashion.

TURNING-THE-BACK-OF-THE-HEAD as drake swims past or ahead of the ♀ in response to her Inciting.

PREEN-BEHIND-THE-WING may occur but has not been reported.

**Displaying** drakes strive to keep station close to an unmated ♀; she often dives to avoid them or takes flight, the drakes following closely. While being pursued, she utters a coarse whine, which a person may imitate by pronouncing *whaa-aaa-aaa* with an indrawn breath. Displays and aggression continue immediately when the birds return to water. The ♀ threatens ♂♂ aggressively but, if their attention lags, she Incites by tugging at the flank or scapular feathers of a drake, then quickly assumes the Neckstretch with accompanying call. She also has a low *kuck* note in indefinite series. Eventually, a drake is able to remain constantly at a ♀'s side. Then they Neck-stretch mutually, betweentimes showing threat toward other drakes, and the latter gradually break away from the newly formed pair. The time required for pairing is unknown;

150

some groups of still unpaired birds interrupt their displaying to migrate together to the next stopping place.

Pairs en route to nesting areas feed and travel together. **Copulation,** however, which occurs frequently in the latter half of April, is accomplished at some distance from the group. The drake's precopulatory activity consists of ritualized Preening (of dorsum), alternating with Bill-dipping, and the ♀ assumes a flattened posture. After treading, the drake utters a single call (same as in Kinked-neck display), then swims away from the ♀, and bends his neck abruptly so as to touch his breast with tip of bill (Bill-down posture).

Once arrived on **breeding range,** pairs leave the group, more or less isolating themselves from others of their kind. There is, however, no clear-cut defense of any part of the area they utilize during the breeding season. When approached closely by other pairs or by unmated drakes, the ♂ challenges with Head-throw. Mates continue to Neck-stretch mutually and, in flight, the drake frequently attempts to grasp the tail of his mate in his bill.

**Utilized area** consists of the nesting place plus one or several ponds, or small lakes, or open stretches of water, where the drake "waits" while his mate is absent laying eggs and where they also join (as long as the drake remains) to feed and loaf in her off-nest periods during incubation. The terrain utilized by a color-marked pair in Minnedosa, Man., pothole country was about 1,330 acres; this same area was overlapped in occupancy by 8 to 15 other pairs (Dzubin 1955). Density of pairs in 1952 av. about 1 pair/10 sq. mi. in pothole country in S.D., the same in the Newdale–Erickson pothole district of Man. and in the Caron pothole country of Sask., 4.6 pairs/sq. mi. near Redvers, Sask., and 8 pairs/sq. mi. near Rosneath, Man. (Fish and Wildlife Service 1952).

As indicated above; **nests** usually are widely dispersed; but several ♀ ♀ may use sites near one another in a single stand of bulrush. The bulky nest is built above shallow water (usually less than 3 ft. deep); it is constructed by the ♀, using the previous year's growth of plant materials gathered at the site. Sometimes the nest is on a muskrat house, seldom on dry ground. In size and shape it resembles that of the Redhead; also, somewhat, the egg nests and brood nests of the Coot (*Fulica americana*). It may be distinguished from the former by the **nest down,** which differs from that of the Redhead, being pearly gray with inconspicuous white tips; intermingled breast feathers have the proximal third of the shaft light, the dark portion of the vane ends in a fairly straight transverse line, and the light distal portion of the vane generally encompasses nearly half of the total area of the feather (Broley 1950). The duck builds up her nest to raise the eggs above water level in periods of flood.

**Laying** begins before the nest is completed and the duck does not begin to deposit nest down until after several eggs are laid. Usually they are laid at a rate of 1/day and usually in the morning.

One **egg** each from 20 clutches (from localities from conterminous U.S. into Alaska) **size** length av. $62.84 \pm 2.04$ mm., breadth $43.75 \pm 2.00$, radii of curvature of ends $16.76 \pm 0.97$ and $13.20 \pm 1.90$; **shape** elliptical, elongation $1.42 \pm 0.048$, bicone $-0.019$, asymmetry $+0.117$ (FWP). The av. of 103 eggs at Delta, Man., was $62.8 \times 44.5$ mm., the extremes being $66.7 \times 44.5$ and $59.9 \times 44.8$ (Hochbaum 1944). The meas. of 88 eggs given by Bent (1923) are very similar. **Color** Canvasback eggs are a grayed olive or greenish drab and less blunt and slightly larger than those of the Redhead. The latter often lays in the nest of the former, but the reciprocal seldom occurs.

Near Cumberland House, Sask., av. size of a large series of **clutches** was 7.2 ± 0.9 eggs (G. H. Townsend 1966). At Delta, Man., the av. for 38 complete clutches, exclusive of Redhead intrusions, was 10 eggs. Twenty-two of these nests also contained Redhead eggs, an av. of 6.4/nest (Hochbaum 1944). In Ore., the av. number of Canvasback eggs was 9.9 in 7 unparasitized nests and 7.7 in 47 parasitized. In Man., Weller (1959) found 1 unparasitized nest (8 eggs) and 38 parasitized (av. 6.6 Canvasback eggs); as he pointed out, in ducks, "additions of parasitic eggs to the clutch will have a depressing effect on ovulation" of the host. See his paper for many details; also see under Redhead.

**Egg dates**    These are rough estimates of the time when full clutches may be expected: around May 10 in conterminous U.S., May 20–25 at midlatitudes of the Canadian prairie provinces, and June 5 or later in Alaska–n. Yukon. Bent (1923) gave "egg dates" as follows: Man., Sask., and Alta., 17 records May 26–June 27 (includes 9 for June 1–11); Minn. and N.D., 12 for May 9–June 25 (6 for May 31–June 11); and Colo. and Utah, 4 for May 23–June 20.

The duck is on the nest almost constantly the last day or two before the clutch is completed. All eggs, however, often hatch within a span of 12 hrs. and seldom are more than 24 hrs. required. Eggs artificially incubated most frequently have an **incubation period** of 24 days; but varies from 23 to 29 (Hochbaum 1944). The drake "waits" on open water not far away during laying, then departs at onset of incubation or within a few days thereafter. The duck becomes more broody as time passes and, in later stages of incubation, sits very tightly on approach of a human intruder. Distraction display is rare.

**Hatching**    After an egg is pipped, the duckling emerges from the shell in 18–48 hrs.; a longer hatching time seldom produces vigorous young (Hochbaum 1944). The shells are submerged in water nearby or are crushed in the nest. The ducklings start preening and oiling as soon as they are hatched and swim when dry. They are brooded in the nest for several hours, longer in bad weather and the duck may return there to brood her young after their first excursion.    **Hatching success**    At least some eggs hatched in 66% of 22 nests studied by Kalmbach (1937) and 58% of 24 nests studied by Sowls (1948). The Crow (*Corvus brachyrhynchos*) is a serious predator during nesting. The Canvasback, however, has a higher nesting success than the land-nesting Mallard and other shoal-water ducks, which are more vulnerable to mammalian predators. Renesting has not been studied in this species.

The **ducklings** are led from the nest by the ♀, the young following in response to her low-pitched and not harsh *kuk-kuk-kuk* (length indefinite) calls; see Collias and Collias (1956) for details. The young forage for their own food beginning immediately after they leave the nest. The traveling brood maintains a tight grouping when very young, but their formation becomes loose and more strung out as they grow older. In the presence of a human intruder, the duck sometimes gives a distraction display which is less intense than in the Pintail and other shoal-water ducks. The brood ranges widely from its birthplace after the first day, often feeding out on open water far from shore, and periods of greatest activity are early morning and during twilight. The duck leaves her preflight young at some time up to several weeks before they can fly and joins a group of adults (it also may include Redheads and other species) to molt; the young often join other parentless broods to form large bands.

From about 44 gm. at hatching, wt. increases (it may be graphed as a sigmoid curve) to nearly 1,000 gm., i.e., to wt. of spring adults, by the time the birds first take wing. For many details of growth and a synopsis of feather development, see Dzubin (1959), both text and illus. According to various authors (table in Weller 1957), the age at which flight is attained varies from 54 to 84 days; most Canvasbacks, however, probably **first fly** when 60–70 days old. Then several weeks pass before they are as proficient on the wing as adults.

In s. Man., the first downy young hatch in late May or early June; these birds are flying by late July or early Aug. The majority, however, begin flying during the last half of Aug. and first week in Sept.; some late-hatched birds do not fly until early Oct.

For additional information, see Hochbaum (1944 and 1960). HAH

SURVIVAL   Based on band-recovery data: **1** the annual mortality rate in year of hatching was 77% and the annual rate for "adults" varied from 35% to 50%; **2** the rate is higher for ♀♀ than ♂♂; **3** hunting was estimated to account each year for more than half of the deaths of all birds of flying age; **4** relatively large numbers of ♀♀ and young of the year are shot early in the season and relatively large numbers of ♂♂ of older age-classes late in the season; **5** both hunting-season length and daily bag limit affect the size of the kill (A. D. Geis 1959).

Based on the above source, the estimated mean annual adult survival rate for cent. Canada is 0.59 (Boyd, in Le Cren and Holdgate 1962).

DeGraff et al. (1961) analyzed records of 9,361 Canvasbacks banded in cent. N.Y. in the years 1955 to 1958. The data indicated a more rapid decline in numbers of ♀♀, "which seems attributable to factors other than hunting." The higher the av. age of fall–winter birds, the greater the preponderance of ♂♂ —which is especially accentuated when there are repeated failures to produce a crop of young.

Differences among patterns of vulnerability to shooting of first-fall birds and of older ♂♂ and ♀♀ were discussed at length by Olson (1965). RSP

HABITS   The Canvasback is gregarious, except for the span beginning when pairs disperse to nest and ending (for drakes first) when the pair bond terminates and the drakes form in groups that go to a molting place. Largest gatherings of Canvasbacks include the many loosely organized groups scattered over the water at molting lakes, the assemblies that form at migration stopover places (31,000 on L. Christina, Minn., April 12, 1942—J. D. Smith 1946), and those at various wintering places. The summer pattern of movement and the resulting separation of mature drakes from the majority of the other Canvasbacks is discussed earlier under "Migration."

This duck associates on the water with other ducks, notably the Redhead and Lesser Scaup, but seldom occurs with other species during flight. During the period of spring migration, some Canvasbacks mingle on the water with feeding bands of Tundra Swans and take gleanings from the swans' activities. Canvasbacks feed mostly during

153

early morning and evening, with regular flights from resting places on open bays and lakes to shallow-water feeding areas. Generally they rest well away from shore, but they seek protected shorelines during heavy winds. They dive for food, propelled only by the feet, generally in shallow water (3–12 ft. deep), remaining submerged 10–20 sec. In water that is only inches deep, the bird "puddles" with its feet, then tips to feed. It is a surface feeder also, when aquatic insects are hatching, and it snaps flying insects from the air.

The Canvasback is capable of 72 mph when chased (M. Cooke 1937), but normal air speed is 30–55 mph, giving ground speeds of 60–70 mph or even more when traveling with a tail wind.

Canvasbacks become very tame when not molested; some ♀♀ rear their broods in village ponds or beside heavily traveled roads, and they nest in farmyard sloughs. The young in their first autumn are unwary and easily shot. Although Canvasbacks become increasingly wild as the season advances, they never are as wary as the American Black Duck (J. C. Phillips 1925).

The Canvasback population has fluctuated, trending downward in numbers, for many decades; see J. C. Phillips (1925) for earlier history. As to very recent times, there was a steady decline in the 1950s and later. As of early 1964, the av. number counted in winter (post-hunting-season census) in 14 annual counts (included Mexico) was 358,420 (H. A. Hansen 1964), and declining; the number found in Mexico in early 1964 was 12,894. In Jan. 1966, the total figure (excepting Mexico) was 272,000; in Jan. 1970, it was just over 228,000 (Mexico included). Their number reportedly was about 240,000 in Jan., 1973. This fine waterfowl is endangered by steady reduction of breeding range, resulting from drainage, by periods of drought, and by excessive mortality from hunting. The heaviest kill is along migration corridors in the interior. The young of the year and adult ♀ ♀ are especially vulnerable to gunning on prairie marshes in Sept. and early Oct. There was no legal hunting of this species in the U.S. in 1960–63 and 1972–73.

The raccoon (*Procyon lotor*) in recent years has expanded its range northward into the e. half of the nesting range of the Canvasback. This mammal enters the water and swims readily to raid duck nests.

It is an unusual circumstance in waterfowl that a closely related species, the Redhead, by its habit of nest parasitism, can be detrimental to the breeding success of the Canvasback. HAH

FOOD Examination of 427 stomachs showed that vegetable matter formed 80.6% of the food, pondweeds being of the most importance. The remaining principal items were wild celery, water plantains, grasses and sedges. The animal matter (19.4%) was about equally divided between mollusks and insects. The food of "juveniles" comprised 64.4% aquatic plants and 35.6% insects (Cottam 1939).

**Vegetable** Seeds and tubers of pondweeds (*Potamogeton*), wigeon grass (*Ruppia*), naiad (*Najas*), horned pondweed (*Zannichellia*), and eelgrass (*Zostera*) 29.9%; wild celery (*Vallisneria spiralis*) 8.8%; water plantains, principally *Sagittaria* 7.8%; grasses, principally wild rice (*Zizania*) 7.5%; sedges (*Scirpus*) 6.3%; waterlilies (*Castalia, Brasenia, Nymphaea*) 4%; bur reeds (*Sparganium*) 2.5%; water milfoils (*Myriophyllum, Hippuris*) 2%; muskgrass (Characeae) and other algae 1.5%; miscellaneous plants (*Polygonum, Ceratophyllum, Galium, Vitis, Chenopodium, Lemna, Bidens*) 10.2%.

Frogbit (*Limnobium*), blue flag (*Iris versicolor*), water starwort (*Callitriche*), and bladderwort (*Utricularia*) mentioned by Yorke (1899). Pondweeds form principal food in Mich. (Pirnie 1935) and Wis. (Kumlien and Hollister 1903). Eelgrass (Gabrielson and Jewett 1940) and wapato (*Sagittaria*) (D. W. Huntington 1903) important on Pacific coast. Acorns utilized in La. (Lowery 1931).

The 91 birds from upper Chesapeake Bay had eaten principally the vegetation and rootstalks of wild celery and eelgrass, and the vegetation, rootstalks, and seeds of pondweeds, and wigeon grass (R. E. Stewart 1962). The food in 28 specimens from Ill. consisted of 65% plant and 35% animal matter. The chief plant foods were *Potamogeton* spp. 33.61%, *Sagittaria latifolia* 18.13%, and *Ceratophyllum demersum* 10.91% (H. G. Anderson 1959). Ten birds in Mo. consumed 95.4% plant and 4.6% animal matter. Only 2 genera of plants were of importance, *Potamogeton* spp. 44.6% and *Scirpus* spp. 43.3% (Korschgen 1955). The 38 gizzards from Reelfoot L., Tenn., contained 74.2% plant and 25.8% animal matter. Principal plant foods were *Potamogeton* spp. 37.76%, *Polygonum* spp. 5.92%, and *Cephalanthus occidentalis* 5% (Rawls 1958).

Sixteen captive young birds were fed over a period of 72 days a ration consisting of

155

*Vallisneria spiralis* 63.7%, *Elodea canadensis* 15.1%, and invertebrates (mainly mollusks) 13.3%. The av. daily consumption was 0.78 lb. wet wt., or 0.05 lb. dry wt. (Longcore and Cornwell 1964).

**Animal**  Mollusks (*Macoma, Mactra, Gemma, Astarte, Neritina, Planorbis, Mitrella, Anachis, Nassarius, Acteocina, Bittium, Lymnea, Turbonilla, Fluminicola*) 8.8%; insects: principally caddis fly (Trichoptera) larvae and cases, and midge (Chironomidae) larvae; also nymphs of mayflies (Ephemerida), dragonflies and damselflies (Odonata), water boatmen (Corixidae), back swimmers (*Notonecta*), and water striders (*Gerris*) 8.1%; small fishes 2%; miscellaneous items, crustaceans, and annelid worms 0.5% (Cottam 1939).

Recorded from the upper Chesapeake are 9 species of mollusks, Decapoda (*Callinectes sapidus*), Xanthidae, and Polychaeta. In Ill., Arthropoda (mainly chironomid larvae) 25.28% and Mollusca 7.35%; in Mo., Pentatomidae 3.5%, Carabidae 0.9%, and Gastropoda 0.2%; and at Reelfoot L., Insecta 15.92%, Gastropoda 5.13%, and Pelecypoda 4.74%.

Gizzard shad (*Dorosoma cepedianum*) captured extensively at Buckeye L., Ohio (Trautman 1940). One bird had eaten 9 shad averaging 3.5 in. long. Principal food along the Cal. coast comprises shellfishes (*Mya arenaria, Odostomia*, and *Cerithidea californica*) (J. Grinnell et al. 1918). Decayed salmon mentioned (Dawson and Bowles 1909). A stomach from the Pribilof Is. contained only larvae and cases of caddis flies (Preble and McAtee 1923). AWS

Important papers that postdate the preparation of the above summary are the following:

Quay and Crichter (1965) reported on winter food of 62 birds from Currituck Sd., N.C. In both frequency of occurrence and in volume, *Potamogeton* spp. ranked first; others which were high in frequency were *Ruppia, Najas, Scirpus, Myrica*, and *Polygonum*. There was only a trace of animal matter.

Bartonek and Hickey (1969) described in great detail the food of 175 birds, taken from late spring to early fall in sw. Man., with separate tabulation for "juvenile," "adult female," and "adult male" individuals. During summer, ♀♀ and young had similarly high percentages of aquatic invertebrates (largely the immature stages of insects), while the mature drakes remained high in plant materials. By fall, the young had shifted to an adult diet, mainly plant matter—*Potamogeton* spp. and other Najadaceae being dominant. This paper, which discusses the food of Canvasbacks generally, also tabulates certain findings of other authors, and cites the relevant literature (including items omitted from the present summary).

For amount of grit ingested, see Bartonek (1969). RSP

## Common Pochard

*Aythya ferina* (Linnaeus)

Pochard of British list; other English language names include White-backed Pochard and Red-headed Diver or Pochard. Intermediate morphologically between Canvasback (*A. valisineria*) and Redhead (*A. americana*). The bill is closer to that of the latter in shape (but straighter distally, with smaller and narrower nail); the drake is nearer the former in eye color and color of Alt. Plumage (there is sexual dimorphism in both eye color and color of feathering). Sex for sex, the bill is approximately similar in length in *ferina*, *americana*, and also the very different Ringneck (*A. collaris*), all being decidedly shorter than in *valisineria*. Beginning not long after the Juv. stage, the midsection of the bill of *ferina* becomes paler in both sexes and the distal end very dark; both sexes of *americana* also have a lighter subterminal area (not sharply defined as in *collaris*), while the bill is unicolor (quite dark) in both sexes of *valisineria*. Individuals in predefinitive stages can be identified by bill characters.

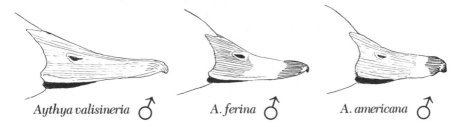

*Aythya valisineria* ♂        *A. ferina* ♂        *A. americana* ♂

The drake's tracheal apparatus was illus. by Heinroth and Heinroth (1928), but see Schiøler (1926) for details of the bulla.

Length ♂ to at least 18 in., ♀ to about 17, wt. of ♂ 1¾–2½ lb., ♀ about 1¼–2¼. No subspecies. Not conspecific with the Canvasback which, in total biology, is the nearest counterpart in the Nearctic of the Common Pochard in the Palearctic.

DESCRIPTION    Two Plumages/cycle in both sexes; in the definitive cycle they acquire Alt. head–body in fall and the ♀, as in other *Aythya*, molts out of this portion of her feathering in late winter–spring, i.e., into Basic head–body well before the nesting season. The following is abbreviated treatment. For some further details see Schiøler's (1926) text and color illus., Heinroth and Heinroth (1928), Veselovsky (1953) for growth data, and Witherby (1939) for downies and later stages. Predefinitive stages, especially of the ♀, have not yet been studied in detail.

▶    ♂ Def. Alt. Plumage (head–body plus innermost feathers of wing), acquired from late SUMMER into or through FALL and retained into following SUMMER. **Bill** black at tip and base, more or less grayed bluish in between (palest subterminally); **iris** brownish orange, becoming scarlet in winter; **head** and upper neck brownish red, a white spot on chin, lower neck black; **upperparts** ends of the bird black or nearly so, the midsection finely vermiculated medium blackish brown on pale gray (may appear almost white); **underparts** breast and under tail coverts black, belly white to pale buffy or silver gray, most of this area more or less vermiculated darker, and becoming darker posteriorly; sides and flanks rather pale, finely vermiculated medium blackish brown on pale gray; legs and **feet** a variant of light bluish gray, webs and joints nearly black. In the **wing**, several innermost secondaries are grayish to dark brownish gray, flecked white, with narrow black border on outer web (except it is lacking from the innermost feather); the longer coverts overlying the secondaries are similarly grayish and flecked; remainder of wing and the tail are retained Basic feathering.

▶ ♂ Def. Basic Plumage (entire feathering), head–body acquired beginning in early JULY, the wing and tail beginning in Aug. or early SEPT. (after a flightless period); then head–body and innermost feathers of wing molt back into Alt., but the Basic tail and almost all of the wing are retained into the following SUMMER. **Head** crown dark brownish, the remainder and much of neck very muted reddish brown (toward chocolate); **upperparts** feathers of anterior back dark gray with pale, quite yellowish brown margins; remainder of mantle including scapulars dark gray with coarse grayish vermiculations; rump blackish; **underparts** breast feathers dark grayish with very pale, somewhat yellowish, margins; sides and flanks a mixture of vermiculated gray feathers and dark gray ones having buffy brown edges; **tail** brownish gray. **Wing** primaries dark (toward fuscous), most of them paling (to a grayish) on at least the basal half of inner webs and outer ones often have white dots; secondaries pale grayish, tipped and more or less coarsely vermiculated white (spread wing shows gray area that includes most of the secondaries and basal half of most primaries, with narrow white line at trailing edge formed by ends of the secondaries); most upper coverts medium brownish gray with variable amount of white vermiculation (usually much); wing lining white except for some gray along leading edge.

▶ ♀ Def. Alt. Plumage (head–body and innermost feathers of wing), acquired in FALL and retained until LATE WINTER–SPRING. **Bill** mostly variants of bluish slate (tip darkest) with pale subterminal band; **iris** muted yellow or slightly orange. **Head** crown feathers blackish brown tipped cinnamon, nape near cinnamon, chin and throat white or same spotted dusky, feathers of remainder of head–neck dusky with cinnamon brown tips and (when fresh) narrowly edged white; **upperparts** upper back cinnamon-brown; rump and upper tail coverts blackish brown; remainder of upperparts a deep, somewhat brownish, gray coarsely vermiculated pale grayish; **underparts** feathers of upper breast dark, becoming cinnamon toward their tips and broadly edged white; lower breast and belly feathers nearly white (slightly grayed); the body down on venter brownish gray (not black) feathers of sides and flanks vermiculated white; feathers of rear of abdomen darker, also the under tail coverts which have narrow white tips (they wear off); legs and **feet** grayed yellowish, webs and joints medium gray or darker. In the **wing**, the several innermost secondaries are dark grayish brown with some whitish vermiculations on outer web, their longer overlying coverts also are gray-brown and speckled white distally; remainder of wing and the tail are retained Basic feathering.

NOTE    Sage (1957) reported 2 ♀ that had white areas on side of head behind the eye, in about the same position as the white on head of the ♀ Bufflehead. (See also under Redhead for comments on white feathers in head.)

▶ ♀ Def. Basic Plumage (entire feathering), head–body acquired in LATE WINTER–EARLY SPRING, but tail and most of wing not until early FALL (when the rest of this

Plumage is being succeeded by Alt.). Major differences from Alt. are: **upperparts** darker, browner, and much less vermiculated, the scapulars very dark brown (but the dorsum bleaches to a yellowish brown); **underparts** feathers of sides and flanks rich brown with buffy brownish tips; the down on the venter is nearly black; **tail** brownish gray; the **wing** is patterned much as in the drake, but is overall more brownish, the several innermost secondaries are plain (without light markings) and there are no (or occasionally a few) vermiculations on their longer overlying coverts.

AT HATCHING  See color illus. in Schiøler (1926) or description in Witherby (1939) general coloring of upperparts muted dark brownish with olive tinge, underparts lightly greenish yellow.

▶  ♂ Juv. Plumage (entire feathering). Perfected about the time flight is attained, in late SUMMER (varies depending on hatching date); by then, the head–body feathering is beginning to be succeeded by Basic I; the Juv. tail is succeeded by the Basic I tail at any time from FALL into WINTER; the Basic I tail and most of the Juv. wing are retained into the following summer. A rather ♀ -like Plumage; **dorsum** nearly plain (vermiculated feathers may be incoming Basic I); **underparts** various grays, mottled (by light feather tips); **tail** feathers with notched ends; **wing** much like ♀ Def. Basic and differs from ♂ Basic in having vermiculations (if present) on secondaries only toward tip, the innermost several dark brownish with some white dotting, and most upper coverts dark brownish gray with creamy dots (rather than paler with white dotting). See Veselovsky (1953) for development of the Juv. feathering.

▶  ♀ Juv. Plumage (entire feathering), timing probably as ♂ , i.e., begins to be succeeded by Basic I not long after flight is attained. Body as ♂ Juv. except: **upperparts** mantle, including scapulars, and flanks without vermiculations, the mantle and scapular feathers tipped buffy brown; **wing** as ♀ Def. Basic except no dotting on secondaries or upper coverts.

▶  ♂ Basic I Plumage (apparently includes all feathering, excepting all but a few innermost feathers of wing). In FALL this succeeds the corresponding Juv. feathers, the tail being renewed last, sometimes not until during the next head–body molt. This Plumage is worn briefly, sandwiched in between Juv. and Alt. I. It is a "dull" though clear-cut Plumage, very like ♂ Def. Basic, but the feathers are narrower and less broadly rounded terminally. Most of the Juv. wing is retained.

▶  ♂ Alt. I Plumage (apparently all feathering, excepting the tail and all but innermost feathers of wing). Most of the molting into Alt. I occurs in very late FALL or early WINTER, the belly molting late and sometimes concurrent with replacement of Juv. by Basic I tail. Many drakes are well into Alt. I as early as Nov.—i.e., they then appear "adult"—but others are later. This feathering is retained through winter into the following SUMMER. Coloring as Def. Alt. The eye becomes reddish some time in 1st fall. This is the last drake Plumage with which any Juv. Plumage (minimum is most of wing) is worn.

▶  ♀ Basic I Plumage (apparently all feathering, excepting most of wing). Usually acquired in early FALL, but more gradually or later by some individuals. The notched Juv. tail feathers are replaced by rounded Basic ones at end of this molt; sometimes the innermost secondaries and their longer coverts are renewed (but perhaps not invariably). Color and pattern essentially as ♀ Def. Basic, but various feathers are narrower. Most of the Juv. wing is retained.

159

▶ ♀ Alt. I Plumage (apparently all feathering, excepting the tail and almost all of the wing). Succeeds Basic I during late FALL or into WINTER. This Plumage is retained into late WINTER or early SPRING, when the ♀ molts into Basic II head–body—this being the last feathering with which the Juv. wing (except innermost feathers) is worn.

**Measurements** 12 ♂ (7 Britain, 4 Europe, 1 China): BILL 47–52 mm., av. 48.3; WING 206–216, av. 213.4; TAIL 51–59, av. 54.2; TARSUS 37–40, av. 39; 10 ♀ (4 Britain, 3 Europe, 1 Egypt, 1 India, 1 Afghanistan) BILL 43–49, av. 46.2 mm.; WING 202–219, av. 207.3; TAIL 52–57, av. 54.5; TARSUS 37–41, av. 37.6 (ETS).

For series with WING meas. over the curve, see Witherby (1939).

**Weight** J. C. Phillips (1925) gave range for "adults" as ♂ 2 lb. 2 oz. to 2 lb. 6 oz. (.96–1.07 kg.), occasionally to 2 lb. 8 oz. (1.13 kg.); ♀ 1 lb. 5 oz. to 2 lb. 4 oz. (.59–1.02 kg.). For seasonal changes in wt., see Isakov (in Dementiev and Gladkov 1952).

**Hybrids** Has crossed in the wild with 3 *Aythya* (*fuligula*, *marila*, and *nyroca*) and allegedly (J. C. Phillips 1925) also with *Bucephala clangula*, *Anas acuta*, and *Anas crecca*. Displays of wild *ferina* × *fuligula* hybrids were intermediate between those of the parent stocks (Bezzel 1960). In captivity reportedly has crossed with these genera: *Tadorna*, *Aix*, *Anas*, *Aythya*, and *Netta* (references in Gray 1958). The tracheal bullae of crosses of *ferina* with *A. fuligula* and with *A. nyroca* were illus. by Beer (1968).

Both ♂ and ♀ crosses between the Redhead and Canvasback resemble the Common Pochard "very closely" (Weller 1957). Common Pochard–Tufted Duck (*A. ferina* × *fuligula*) hybrids are of several "types," including a "Lesser Scaup type" (Perrins 1961, Gillham et al. 1966, Harrison and Harrison 1970).

**Geographical variation** none reported. RSP

FIELD IDENTIFICATION  In N. Am., where there are 2 other "white-backed pochards" (Canvasback and Redhead), the Common Pochard more closely resembles the former in coloring and the latter in configuration. A fair approximation of a drake Common Pochard would be a drake Canvasback with dark mud on the end of its bill. In both ♂ and ♀ Common Pochard, the bill is dark basally, light in midsection, and dark distally. Identifying young birds, also adults in late summer, may be very difficult, if in fact possible. RSP

HABITAT  For **breeding,** prefers shallow inland waters—lakes, ponds, slow-moving streams—margined with floating and emergent vegetation. Similar waters in **other seasons,** also sheltered brackish and salt waters—Caspian Sea, Black Sea, marine estuaries, and sheltered bays. RSP

DISTRIBUTION  For details of summer and winter range, see especially Bannerman (1958), Dementiev and Gladkov (1960), and Vauric (1965); breeding range was mapped by Voous (1963); probably the best map of breeding range in U.S.S.R. is that of Flint et al. (1968).

**Breeds** mainly in temperate latitudes of Europe and eastward only to w.-cent. Siberia, but locally in additional areas. Has spread westward in Europe (including Scandinavia) and in the Brit. Isles, the changes during 1850–1950 being mapped in Bezzel (1969). It has continued to increase its breeding range in Europe. For history of spread in Britain and Ireland also see Bannerman (1958). For Iceland, G. Timmermann (1949) recorded 2 stragglers, but Gudmundsson (in Bannerman 1958) reported that, by 1956, a few pairs were breeding in the Mývatn district. **Straggler** in the Atlantic to the Faeroes, Azores, and Canary Is. In n. Pacific area: possibly breeds in Kamchatka; a record of occurrence at Bering I. (Commander group), May 13, 1911.

For records of **fossil** occurrence in the Palearctic Pleistocene, see Brodkorb (1964a).

**In our area** Alaskan records: taken on St. Paul I. (Pribilofs) on May 4, 1912, and ♀ seen there June 6–7, 1973; in the Aleutians, on Adak I., ♂ and ♀ seen in late May 1970, late May through June 1971, a ♂ in mid-June 1972, and pair remained through mid-June 1973; on Amchitka I., a ♀ through June 13 in 1973. (For a good photo of a drake on Adak, see *Am. Birds* **25** 894. 1971). RSP

MIGRATION  **Spring** travel begins not later than early March and ends not earlier than some time in May. That drakes have a **molt migration,** while their mates are incubating, is well known; see Bezzel (1969) for various details. In the U.S.S.R., according to Isakov (in Dementiev and Gladkov 1952), part of the drakes molt, singly and in small groups, in breeding areas; the others depart and molt, in assemblies, at traditional molting lakes that are mostly in the steppe or wooded steppe zone; they also molt at deltas, bottomland forest reservoirs, and at Matsal Bay in the Gulf of Finland. There is movement in **fall** beginning in Sept. and lasting at least through Nov. In w. Europe and Britain, as known from banding (Boyd 1959b, Bezzel 1969), many of these birds go from interior Europe westward to winter on the eastern fringes of the Atlantic. The separation of sexes and of age-classes during the summer molting is reflected during fall movements, also in winter when numerous flocks at more northerly places are composed preponderantly of drakes. RSP

REPRODUCTION  Both sexes (all individuals?) **first breed** at age 1 year. For voice and displays, see full discussion by Bezzel (1968, 1969). A rather late nester. The **nests** are built on floating vegetation, or other vegetation above shallow water, or close to shore, and typically are sheltered by an overstory of herbaceous or woody growth. The **eggs** are very similar to those of the Tufted Duck, but the **nest down** is different— brown with light centers in the Common Pochard, very dark (sooty) with inconspicuous light centers in the Tufted Duck. The "normal" **clutch** is about 7–10 eggs, but many individuals are **parasitic,** laying in the nests of other individuals of their own species, or in "dump" nests (to 89 eggs at 1 site), also in the nests of other birds. Mixed clutches with 6 other species of ducks, also the Coot (*Fulica atra*), were listed by Bezzel (1969). Although the **incubation period** has been given as 23 days, this is too short; it is 24–25 (and to 28) (Bezzel 1969). For development of captive young, see Veselovsky (1953); they reportedly **attain flight** as early as age 55 days, but 60–65 may be more typical. RSP

HABITS and FOOD  Very gregarious; unwary, but becomes quite shy if persecuted. Feeds in shallows generally. On short flights, travels in compact groups; on long flights, as on migration, in wavy lines and wedges. A listing of foods includes the same genera of plants, also of aquatic invertebrates or larval stages, preferred by the Canvasback; see Olney (1969) and Bezzel (1969) for many data.

For monographic treatment of this species, see Bezzel (1969). RSP

161

## Redhead

*Aythya americana* (Eyton)

Medium-sized diving duck, in the broad-billed pochard group. Bill has "typical" shape for a duck, with slight uptilt distally; it is even in width, has large and decidedly hooked nail, and the feather margin at side base of upper mandible is slightly curved but essentially at right angles with long axis of bill; see fig. on p. 157. Beginning at age about 4 mo., the drake's bill develops a pattern of bluish basal ⅔, then white subterminal band, and sharply delineated black end; the ♀'s usually is quite evenly dark, but sometimes reflects the drake's pattern (lightest subterminally, darkest terminally). In Alt. Plumage, the drake's crown feathers are elongated, giving the head a somewhat enlarged and rounded profile. Drake's iris after early life varies with age and season from orange-yellow to muted yellowish; the ♀'s averages more toward yellowish brown or brownish. Drake in Def. Alt. Plumage (most of year): head and upper neck brownish red, remainder of neck and forepart of body black, most of dorsum and sides grayish and finely vermiculated black, rump and undertail area very dark, the various areas clearly delineated; ♀ Def. Alt. (fall–winter): head, neck, dorsum, breast, and sides much the same in color, variants of grayed brownish, with mantle slightly vermiculated. See below for other Plumages.

The drake's tracheal apparatus resembles that of *A. ferina* (which has been illustrated several times), i.e., the trachea is nearly uniform in diam., but tapers slightly at proximal end, and the bony bulla is flattened and smaller than in the Canvasback (J. C. Phillips 1925). The trachea and bulla were illus. by Johnsgard (1961c).

Sexes differ in coloring, including eye color after early age, and in av. meas. and wt. Length ♂ to 20½ in., ♀ to 19½, wingspread ♂ to 32, ♀ to 30½, usual wt. of ♂ about 2¼ lb., ♀ 2 lb. No subspecies.

"Considering both color and structural characters, it would be difficult to say which species, the Canvasback or the Redhead, actually represents [the Common Pochard] *ferina* on the American continent" (Hollister 1919). Although the Common Pochard and Redhead were regarded as conspecific long ago, morphologically the difference is greater between these species than between Common Pochard and Canvasback.

DESCRIPTION  Two Plumages/cycle in both sexes; beginning with the 2nd cycle, the ♀ (as in many ducks) acquires much Basic (all of head–body) in spring. In the first year of life, the ♂ progresses through Juv. and Basic I into Alt. I approximately in the span Aug.–Dec. inclusive; the ♀, additionally, goes from Alt. I into Basic II head–body well before attaining age 1 year. Certain of the younger stages still are not fully known. The most detailed information is from penned birds, but data on any *Aythya* kept in captivity must be treated with caution. Treatment here includes considerable reinterpretation of Weller (1957 and 1970).

▶ ♂ Def. Alt. Plumage (all feathering, excepting the tail and all but innermost feathers of wing), illus. in color in right-center fig. on plate in Weller (1957), acquired during FALL (usually by late Oct.) and retained through winter and spring into SUMMER. **Bill** upper mandible light turquoise-cobalt, grading quite abruptly to white subterminally, then a sharply defined black end. **Iris** orange-yellow (varies from vivid to rather muted). **Head** and upper neck brownish red, in new feathering with considerable magenta or even some violet iridescence; lower neck black. Forward portion of mantle and the breast black (continuous with lower neck), this typically ending abruptly, transversely, and farther toward belly than breast coloring of earlier Plumages (but in some examples the breast feathers have progressively longer whitish tips toward the belly, i.e., the lower breast appears nearly white, although the light feather ends may wear off later). Most of **mantle** light gray finely vermiculated black, rump blackish.

R.M.Mengel-

Sides and flanks as mantle; **belly** white, usually grading to darkish posteriorly (vermiculated feathering); under-tail area nearly black. Legs and **feet** dark bluish gray, the webs and joints much darker.

In the wing the elongated innermost secondaries ("tertials") taper to a rounded tip, are near sooty in color, and almost always are finely flecked white distally (but this may wear off toward spring as the feathers become frayed and pointed); their overlying longer coverts usually are more extensively and densely flecked white; remainder of wing and the tail are retained Basic feathering (described below).

▶   ♂ Def. Basic Plumage (entire feathering), most of it worn rather briefly (largest amount usually in latter half of AUG.) but almost all of wing and the tail retained and worn with the succeeding Alt. The head–body feathering is acquired over a period of weeks beginning in LATE JUNE or in JULY and then succeeded by Alt. through FALL; this span includes a flightless period and the new Basic wing is at least partly grown when the head–body begin to molt back into Alt. A quite blended brownish Plumage. The head appears ♀-like because the feathers are short. The **bill** loses the bluish color

163

for a period in summer and becomes very dark, like the ♀ in spring; **iris** muted orange-yellow (Weller 1957). **Head** and upper neck buffy to somewhat reddish brown; anterior portion of mantle, the breast, and sides mixed brownish and blackish and with margins of these areas not clearly defined; **upperparts** largely brownish, somewhat mottled lighter; some scapulars may have some dark coarse vermiculations on lighter background; from lower breast back to include part of **abdomen** the feathers are almost entirely white except many have darker ends, giving a somewhat patterned effect; under tail coverts blackish brown with light edging. **Tail** some variant of fuscous, the middle feathers somewhat tapering and pointed.

**Winter** primaries and their upper coverts dark grayish brown, the former darkest on outer webs and ends; beginning distally, most of the secondaries are silvery gray, darkening subterminally, and with white end (at least on outer vane); some (usually 3) more proximal ones have narrow black outer margins and reduced white on ends; the several innermost are not appreciably elongated, not tapering (they are quite broadly rounded), and their ends are plain (sooty); most of the upper wing coverts, which are broadly rounded, are medium or darkish gray (depending on the individual) and have fine white flecking in their exposed portions; there is no white tipping on greater coverts; wing lining mostly white but some light gray along leading edge.

In the final phase of the Prebasic molt the drake becomes flightless, usually well along in summer. All remiges are cast in less than a week; their successors, which grow faster than those of the Juv. generation, are fully hardened in 5–6 weeks; the drake probably is flightless for 3 weeks or longer.

▶ ♀ Def. Alt. Plumage (all feathering, excepting the tail and all but a few innermost feathers of wing), usually acquired beginning about mid-Aug. and often not fully grown until Oct., then worn through winter into SPRING. In new feathering, quite grayish and with fairly clear-cut pattern.

**Bill** dark slaty with pale subterminal band, iris brownish yellow or brownish. **Head** and neck medium fuscous, grading to white at side base of bill and on chin, the eye ring also light (to whitish) and a poorly defined palish line or stripe extends back from eye. **Upperparts** medium fuscous, various mantle feathers margined (the margin wears off) and faintly vermiculated light grayish brown; rump brownish olive. **Underparts** upper breast brownish fuscous and toward the belly the breast feathers have progressively wider white ends so that the surface grades ventrally to all-white (but, unlike the white belly feathers, the basal portions of all breast feathers are quite dark); feathers of sides and flanks quite brownish fuscous with pale buffy edgings and some often are vermiculated whitish; belly white, this grading on abdomen to light grayish fuscous and the feathers quite often with whitish margins and some faint vermiculations; longest under tail coverts almost entirely white. Legs and **feet** more toward slaty than in ♂. In the wing the elongated, tapering, innermost secondaries are plain (not flecked nor vermiculated) and their overlying coverts are plain or with no more than faint light flecking; remainder of wing and the tail are retained Basic feathering.

NOTES Females usually have some white feathers on the head, especially on rear of crown and on upper nape (illus. in Weller 1957), the number of these seemingly increasing with age but the most conspicuous increase occurs during 2nd fall–winter. Nearly all wild ♀♀ have a few white feathers, captive ♀♀ rarely. The location of such feathers is an indication that they occur as a result of damage to feather follicles when the drake pinches the head of the ♀ during copulation (Weller). A ♀ in Feb. had a white throat, ventral upper neck, patches on forehead and lores, and also white feathers distributed sparsely on cheeks, nape, and sides and back of neck.

A ♀ and ♂, both in Def. Alt. Plumage, were live-trapped on Feb. 21 at Seneca Lake, N.Y., and examined by the writer; the irises of the ♀ were somewhat more vivid orange-yellow than those of the drake.

▶ ♀ Def. Basic Plumage (entire feathering), the head–body and some innermost feathers of wing acquired in SPRING (March–April) and lost during LATE SUMMER– FALL (Aug. or later); the tail and most of the wing are acquired in late summer or early fall and these portions are retained and worn with the next-incoming Alt. A brownish Plumage, especially head and sides. Color illus: left center fig. (new feathering) and lower left fig. (worn and faded feathering) on pl. in Weller (1957).

The **bill** becomes very dark with obscure paler subterminal area during summer. **Head,** neck, much of breast, the sides, flanks, and scapulars muted buffy brownish to (in some individuals) deep tawny, the chin and foreneck white. **Upperparts** much of mantle somewhat darker brownish, many feathers with narrow lighter edging (which wears off); belly and **abdomen** mostly white, plain to mottled brownish, under tail coverts white with brownish olive patches. **Tail** brownish fuscous. In the Basic **wing** the innermost secondaries, which have broad ends and are not elongated, are plain dark fuscous; the next 3 have narrow black outer edges and no white on tips; the remainder (outer ones) are pearly gray, darkening somewhat subterminally, then ends of both vanes are white; the various upper coverts are broadly rounded and a grayed fuscous, with variable amount of faint light vermiculations or flecking toward their ends; axillars white; wing lining white except for some grayish along leading edge.

NOTE Females escorting broods often are in full body molt in Aug., but flightless ♀♀ never were seen with broods (Weller)—that is, the former take leave of the latter before the wing quills are dropped.

AT HATCHING See vol. 2, col. pl. facing p. 466, also this volume, p. 140. Much like Canvasback, but has light forehead and usually has slightly darker upperparts. Some downy Redheads may be darker than Canvasbacks (Hochbaum 1944). The nail on the bill of the Redhead always is much wider than that of the Canvasback; posterior margin of nostril of downy Canvasback is about ⅓ the distance from lores to bill tip and in the Redhead it is about ¼ the distance (Hochbaum). Downy Ringnecks (*A. collaris*) also differ in having light-colored forehead which contrasts with darker crown and nape.

▶ ♂ Juv. Plumage (entire feathering), much of it succeeded by Basic I over a considerable span of time, the tail still later; the wing (except for a few innermost feathers) is retained into the following late summer. The timing of attainment of full Juv. Plumage, and consequently of subsequent events, varies depending on date of hatching; in conterminous U.S. and on the Canadian prairies, early-hatched young are flying in the last week in Aug., the great majority probably by about mid-Sept., and the latest-hatched not until about mid-Oct.

At 8–10 weeks posthatching the **bill** tip darkens and an indistinct subterminal light band appears; the **iris** then is a muted straw yellow. **Head** and neck some variant of buffy brown (tan), paling on chin and throat; **upperparts** feathers brownish gray, indistinctly edged lighter brownish; at 5–6 weeks the ♂'s mantle has some white vermiculations (but this is very rare in the ♀) (Weller); **underparts** breast, sides, and rear of abdomen to tail more or less buffy brown; belly whitish, mottled and streaked brownish; legs and **feet** a somewhat greenish gray, webs darker.

The Juv. **wing** differs from the later (Def. Basic) wing thus: upper coverts narrower, with more squarish ends, with faint white flecking on some, and some greater coverts have white ends; innermost secondaries narrow, tapering, rounded at ends (but soon become frayed) and unicolor (darkish).

NOTE    It is believed rather commonly that late-hatched waterfowl attain flight at a younger age than early-hatched. This subject was studied in the Redhead by Smart (1965b); eggs were hatched in an incubator (June 15–25 and July 17–20) and the ducklings were pen-reared and examined twice weekly. In the early-hatched group the primaries required 7–10 more days to emerge and this temporal difference remained constant throughout feather growth and maturation. In the late-hatched group the primaries not only matured sooner but also when somewhat shorter. As graphed, the peak of ages at which the captive-reared birds became capable of flight was about 63 days in early-hatched and about 54 in late-hatched. The av. age at which all primaries were clear and hard was 78 days (early-hatched) and 70 days (late-hatched). C. W. Dane (1965) also observed a difference in rate of maturation in Redheads, but no difference in Blue-winged Teal.

▶    ♀ Juv. Plumage (entire feathering), perhaps not fully developed before it begins to be succeeded by Basic I; most of the Juv. wing long retained. At age 8–10 weeks the **bill** of the duck is not as conspicuously patterned as that of the drake at that age and the **iris** is muted greenish yellow with brownish center (Weller). **Feathering** as ♂ Juv., except head and breast not as brown nor as dark; mantle at 5–6 weeks lacks any white vermiculations; wing has no light flecking on upper coverts. Greater secondary coverts usually have partial or complete terminal white bar.

▶    ♂ Basic I Plumage (definitely includes head–neck, much body feathering, and tail; probably includes all feathering excepting all but innermost feathers of wing). Most of this Plumage is acquired through LATE SUMMER and FALL (by the majority, but later in late-hatched individuals), sandwiched in between overlapping molts: Juv. to Basic I and Basic I to Alt. I. The first noticeable Basic I feathers, on lores and cheeks, are brownish red or toward chestnut, short (compared with Alt.), have relatively little sheen, and on hatchery-reared birds are visible on some drakes at age 8 weeks and on all by 9 weeks (Weller). Thus they appear even before all the Juv. primaries are "hard." The drake's eye color becomes more vivid than in Juv. at 12–16 weeks of age. More Basic I is acquired (and, in overlapping molt, it is being succeeded by Alt. I) until into DEC. The reddish brown Basic I **head–neck** grows and is quickly lost. The **mantle** is predominantly grayish brown; breast quite rich brownish and with lower border poorly defined; **belly** whitish, quite finely, and evenly marked somewhat darker (not as coarse, irregular, and conspicuous as Juv.), and the concealed portions of these feathers are very light. **Tail** variably fuscous.

This feather generation (Plumage) perhaps cannot be seen in its entirety on any individual, since it is part of a continuum of molting. That is, head–neck molt out of Basic I into Alt. I (while most of the body is in Basic I). As already noted, the first of the Basic I feathers are visible by age 9 weeks; the last of the Basic I tail feathers may not be acquired until age about 28 weeks, by which time the drake has Alt. I head–body.

▶ ♂ Alt. I Plumage (probably all feathering, excepting the tail and all but innermost feathers of wing), begins to appear on head–neck in FALL, probably in the majority of individuals in Aug., thus quickly succeeding that part of Basic I. It is fully acquired from some time in JAN. to as late as some time in MARCH (at age about 6½–8 mo.) and retained through spring into SUMMER (to age just over 1 year). **Bill** has dark tip and noticeable subterminal light band; proximal ⅔ lightens during winter, toward pale cobalt (Weller 1957). **Feathering** approximately as Def. Alt. but somewhat less vividly colored; not as much iridescence on head; less contrast between background and vermiculations on flanks and scapulars (appear dull); dark of breast sometimes does not terminate in a clear-cut transverse demarcation. The belly is white, the concealed portions of the more anterior feathers tend to be gray vermiculated white. This is the earliest Plumage in which vent to tail nearly black, except longest under tail coverts, which are pale and faintly vermiculated dark (as in later Alt. Plumages). Innermost feathers of wing as in Def. Alt., the remainder being retained Juv. The Basic I tail is retained.

NOTE  A few drakes still are molting into Alt. I to some extent as late as April and possibly a few may retain some earlier (Basic I) feathering even until the molt into the next Basic beginning in summer.

▶ ♀ Basic I Plumage (evidently includes all feathering except, in the wing only the innermost feathers). Begins to appear early, even before the Juv. Plumage is fully developed, usually in AUG. (but timing varies depending on hatching date) and the last of this feather generation (part of venter, also the tail) may not grow until DEC. or JAN. (and by this time at least much of the Basic I already has been replaced by overlapping molt into Alt. I). Coloring of **head–neck** differs from either Juv. or Alt. I, being nearer the former but difficult to describe more precisely. Less white on scapulars than in later Basics and few or no white feathers on back of head (Weller 1957). **Under tail coverts** usually speckled buffy brown on white background. **Tail** brownish fuscous. The innermost secondaries and their longer coverts have broader, more rounded ends than their Juv. precursors and are colored as corresponding feathers of later Basics.

▶ ♀ Alt. I Plumage (most, probably all, of head–body plus innermost feathers of wing). As stated above, succeeds Basic I during overlapping molt which usually begins by EARLY WINTER. This Plumage is retained longer than its predecessor, being lost in SPRING (before age 1 year). Coloring, etc., essentially as Def. Alt.

▶ ♀ Basic II Plumage (entire feathering). Acquired (as are all later Basics) by an interrupted molt—the head–body and innermost feathers of wing during EARLY SPRING, the tail and all of the wing after a flightless period and not until late summer or EARLY FALL, at which time the head–body begin molting back into Alt. This is a brown Plumage, quite different from the preceding, grayer Alt. and apparently identical with succeeding Basics. The last head–body feathering with which any Juv. (most of the wing) is worn.

**Measurements**  Tarsus reaches full size in 6th or 7th week posthatching and culmen nearly full length by 10th week, as determined from hatchery-reared birds (Weller 1957).

167

Twelve ♂ (from widespread localities, fall, winter, spring): BILL 44–49 mm., av. 47.5; WING 231–240, av. 235.7; TAIL 54–62, av. 57.6; TARSUS 38–45, av. 42.2; 10 ♀ (from widespread localities, fall, winter, spring): BILL 44–48 mm., av. 46.1; WING 221–235, av. 226; TAIL (of 7) 53–62, av. 57; TARSUS 39–42 mm., av. 41 (ETS).

WING meas. across chord: ♂ 230–242 mm., ♀ 210–230 (J. C. Phillips 1925). For some variation in length of Juv. WING, see above under ♂ Juv. Plumage.

BILL of ♀ : 46 from Utah av. 44.9 mm. and 49 from Man. av. 45.1 (Weller 1957).

**Weight** of known-age embryos, also of young from hatching through 1st fall, and older birds April–Oct. inclusive, were given by Weller (1957). Adults are relatively heavy prior to fall migration and then, by Oct., may av. 7–8 oz. lighter. Presumably the wt. lost in fall is regained in winter or spring, since spring migrants av. heavier than fall migrants. (The ♀'s gain in spring is due to a considerable extent to enlargement of re-productive organs.) Then there is a decrease, much greater in the ♀ than ♂ , during the laying–incubating span of the ♀ , both sexes averaging least wt. at terminus of this de-cline. (Summarized from Weller.)

Part of Weller's wt. data: in spring migration 1,157 ♂ av. 2 lb. 7 oz. (1.1 kg.) and 485 ♀ av. 2 lb. 3 oz. (.99 kg.); "pre-molt" (summer): 32 ♂ av. 2 lb. 1 oz. (.94 kg.) and 71 ♀ av. 2 lb. (.9 kg.); in fall migration: 40 ♂ av. 2 lb. 3 oz. (.99 kg.) and 52 ♀ av. 2 lb. (.9 kg.); heaviest bird was a drake at 3 lb. 1½ oz. (.1.4 kg.).

Wt. of flightless molting birds in ne. Alaska in Aug.: 6 ♂ 2 lb. 4 oz. to 2 lb. 8 oz., the mean being 2 lb. 6.7 oz. (1,097 gm.); and 7 ♀ 1 lb. 12 oz. to 2 lb. 4 oz., the mean being 2 lb. (907 gm.) (Yocom 1970a). These birds had been confined up to several days, possi-bly without food.

For wts. of adequate series of birds, in Jan.–Feb. at Seneca L. in N.Y., tabulated by sex and by age-class, see Ryan (1972). There was a decrease in wt. during the 2-month span; also, comparing the years 1960 and 1971, the loss was greater in the latter year, probably because of colder weather and possibly because of less suitable available food.

Seventeen newly hatched ducklings weighed 33–41.3 gm., the mean and standard error being 37.6 ± 0.40 and S.D. 1.67 (Smart 1965a).

**Hybrids** Has crossed in the wild with the Ringneck (*Aythya collaris*), as described and illus. by Weller (1957). Allegedly there have been natural crosses also with the Pintail (*Anas acuta*), both scaups (*Aythya marila, A. affinis*), Wood Duck (*Aix sponsa*), and Hooded Merganser (*Mergus cucullatus*). The long list of crosses in captivity in-cludes various *Aythya* and *Anas*, also *Aix* (both species) and *Netta* (2 species). See Gray (1958) for references. Crosses of Redhead with various other *Aythya* probably are fertile.

A wild ♂ Redhead crossed with a captive ♀ Canvasback (*Aythya valisineria*); both ♂ and ♀ hybrids were "intermediate in morphological and plumage characters," resem-bling the Common Pochard (*Aythya ferina*) "very closely" (Weller 1957). Three in-stances of Redhead–Canvasback associations in the wild, 2 of 1 species displaying to the other and 1 of a mixed pair, were reported by Timken (1967) and Weller (1967).

**Geographical variation** none reported. Birds from different wintering areas may meet at the same stopover place in spring when pair formation is occurring. Most of the individuals that make major shifts in routes traveled are drakes. RSP

FIELD IDENTIFICATION   Fairly sizable duck, smaller than the Canvasback, about the size of the Greater Scaup. The round head, and abrupt forehead, add up to a profile very different from the elongated one of the Canvasback. Like most diving ducks, the Redhead uses both the feet and wings in propelling itself on the water during takeoff. More often than our other common diving ducks (excepting the Ringneck), Redheads are found on ponds, shallow lakes, and bays where they feed on underwater vegetation.

Although not quite as fast in flight as the Canvasback and Ruddy, the Redhead is faster than most ducks. It wheels and turns in flight more than the Canvasback. Usually it occurs in smaller flocks and gatherings than the scaups and Canvasback but, mainly at a few of its wintering localities, rafts contain up to tens of thousands. In a general area, such as a bay, where the birds feed, they move from place to place in compact irregularly shaped masses, usually higher above the water than our other diving ducks.

The drake, except in late summer, has a reddish chestnut head and a sooty gray back, the latter being darker than that of scaups and of the Canvasback. In flight, the sooty gray wings with light grayish speculum contrast with the dark ends of the body. When Redheads pass overhead, the black breast contrasts with the white belly (as in other *Aythya* species). The drake is more uniformly colored, rather brownish, and with trim head profile, in late summer–early fall. The duck, in fall–winter, appears almost uniform sepia, except for white belly and whitish chin and throat. Female Redheads, scaups, and Ringnecks, also our rarer *Aythya*, resemble one another in a general way in both pattern and subdued coloring, but differ in profile, size, etc. And at close range scaup ♀ ♀ usually have a white facial front, the Ringneck a very definite white eye ring. The ♀ Redhead is quite brownish beginning in spring and this bleaches (as in other *Aythya*) to yellowish brown by the time she is tending small downies. The latter are quite yellow; the young later appear somewhat mottled at the time they first fly.

Also see earlier under hybrids and compare with the Common Pochard. FCB

VOICE   When displaying, the drake utters a *meow* "exactly like that of a cat," decidedly more catlike than the call of the Common Pochard (J. C. Phillips 1925). It carries 150 yds. on a quiet day. It is uttered during Kinked-neck and Head-throw displays, also during trio flying and postcopulatory displaying. Phillips reported that a captive drake, while making jerky movements with its bill, several times made a short coughing sound barely audible at 25 yds. This may be the rather feeble *pheep pheep* of drakes, heard March 11, 1920, near Mt. Vernon, Va., by F. Harper. It is uttered during mutual Neck-stretch display.

The ♀ utters an *err* sound when Inciting. There is also a coarse *kurr-kurr-kurr*, or *kurr-r-r*, much like ♀ Common Pochard or Greater Scaup but more guttural and rolling than the latter's call; it is uttered in any season, but is most prevalent during nest-site hunting and the laying span. Also see below under trio flying. Wetmore (1920) described what may be a variant or modification of this call, a *quek que-e-ek* terminating in a rather peculiar rattling. RSP

HABITAT   For **breeding**, the Redhead prefers extensive marshy areas—shallow water openings in cattail marshes, lakes, or "potholes" bordered by emergents such as

169

hardstem bulrush (*Scirpus acutus*) and other sedges, cattail (*Typha latifolia, angustifolia*, and their hybrids), and cane (*Phragmites maximus*). (In comparison, the Canvasback favors scattered small water areas, or has low nesting density in large marshes.) Hardstem bulrush is preferred throughout much of breeding range, as revealed, for example, by studies in Cal., Utah, Mont., Iowa, and Man. Use of other emergents depends on their area and spatial relationship to open water, where the drake has his "activity center" and, later, the young are reared. In w. U.S., greatest nesting concentrations are found where suitable areas are not numerous and generally there is a quite abrupt transition from wetland to fairly dry or even very arid terrain. For nesting density (nests/sq. mi.), see fig. in Weller (1964) or beyond under "Reproduction."

Stopping places during **migration** usually are lakes and shallow, slow-moving rivers where submerged aquatic plants are abundant, the rooted basal portions being available in spring and the mature plants in fall.

**Winter** habitat is primarily saline waters that are rich in plant foods—coastal lagoons and bays—and certain fresh waters inland. In the late 1960s, some 420,000 Redheads (probably there had been over a million before the 1950s) wintered in se. Texas in the lower Laguna Madre; for a description of this hypersaline lagoon, which has an av. depth of only about 18 in., see McMahan and Fritz (1967). Unlike the Canvasback, which is more of a freshwater bird, flocks of Redheads show no hesitation in alighting and resting on the open sea.

Weller (1964) suggested that the Redhead species may have evolved at alkaline lakes in what is presently the conterminous U.S. The Redhead is social, almost colonial, as a nester and is a smaller and more southerly bird than the Canvasback. The 2 species now overlap on a major portion of their respective breeding ranges and probably they compete for nesting habitat. They compete in a very direct way, via nest parasitism, when Redheads lay in Canvasback nests. MWW

DISTRIBUTION (See map.) The Redhead is, among Nearctic waterfowl, a comparatively southerly nester in the w. continental interior; it is a coastal winterer, although some remain on open waters inland. Discussion here is brief; the reader is referred especially to Weller (1964) for many further details.

Although overall geographical limits of **breeding** (except northward) evidently have not changed a great deal since published records began, there has been a serious reduction in wetlands as a result of periodic drought and drainage. The occupation by the Redhead of breeding range in nw. Canada and in Alaska beginning in the late 1950s is believed to indicate a northward shift of birds displaced elsewhere by periodic drying up of breeding habitat. As to e. Canada and e. conterminous U.S., breeding at scattered localities is not a new phenomenon, but the number of birds occurring at some places and the number of known localities has increased. Attempts to establish this species by release outside the breeding range of pen-reared birds has resulted in local breeding at 3 widely separated localities in N.Y.; possibly those found breeding at L. St. Francis in Que. are derived from one of these introductions. (For a history of the releases, of 50 young birds in 1952 and 1,972 young plus 1,911 adults between 1957 and 1963, and numerous recoveries of these banded birds, and earlier publications on them, see Benson and Browne 1969.)

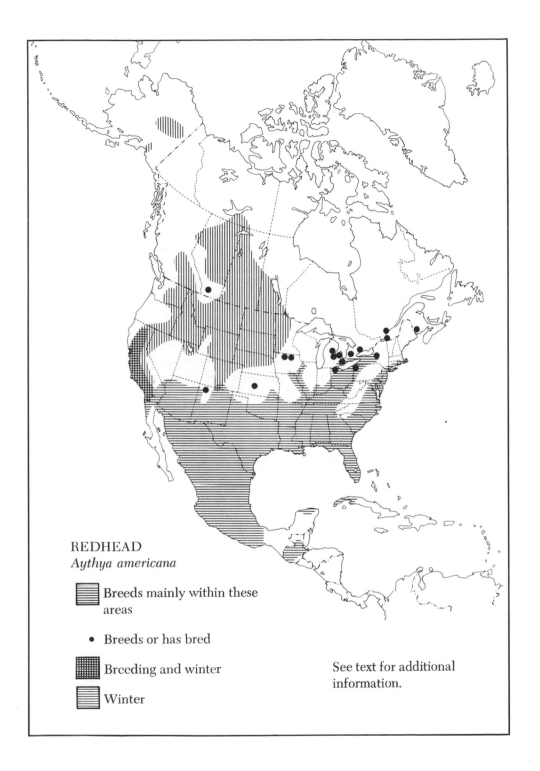

REDHEAD
*Aythya americana*

Breeds mainly within these areas

• Breeds or has bred

Breeding and winter

Winter

See text for additional information.

In the summer of 1973 there were perhaps 200 Redheads at Laguna de Zapotlan (19° 41′ N, 103° 30′ W), approximately 100 mi. s. of Guadalajara, Jalisco, Mexico; 5 broods of preflight young were seen (S. O. Williams III 1975).

**Summer**   After separating from their nesting mates, many drakes go northward, even hundreds of miles. Large summer aggregations, especially on lakes within the forest zone, that consist predominantly of molting drakes plus a few ♀♀. Known localities are mentioned beyond under "Migration" (also see under Lesser Scaup). In brief, total summer distribution is more extensive than nesting distribution.

**Winter**   In 1951–56, 78% of the Redhead population occurred at this season in sheltered waters along the coast of w. Texas and Tamaulipas (Mexico). About 9% wintered in Chesapeake Bay–N.C. waters, 5% in Fla., 2% scattered along the Pacific coast of Mexico and Guatemala, and other occupied areas each had less than 1% (Weller 1964). Northerly limits of wintering are the Puget Sd. region on the Pacific coast, Lakes Michigan, Erie, and the Finger Lakes in N.Y. in the interior, and occasionally n. New England and Bay of Fundy on the Atlantic Coast. Southern limits are in the Caribbean area and down the Pacific coast of Mexico or in Guatemala.

**Stragglers**   A drake was taken on Great Lyhakov I. (New Siberian Archipelago) on June 5, 1961, and another presumed Redhead was seen there the previous year (S.M. Uspenskii and Filin 1965). In the Pribilofs, one reportedly was taken on St. Paul in 1844. A pair, thought to be of this species, was seen on Amutka (about long. 171° W) in the Aleutians and an Aleut stated that similar-appearing birds (*Aythya americana?* *A. ferina?*) nested and wintered in the area. This species was recorded from Kodiak I. in 1896, long before the recent records in the Alaskan interior. In n. Alaska there are records for a pair and a single drake at Umiat.

Far out in the Pacific, on the island of Hawaii, a ♀ was taken in 1960 and another Redhead was seen in 1961 (Berger 1972).

In Greenland a drake was taken in Godthaabfjord on June 10, 1953. There is no acceptable record for Nfld. There are at least 5 fall–winter records for N.S. Rare in Bermuda. In the W. Indies, recorded from the Bahamas (Andros I., New Providence), Cuba, and Jamaica (Nov. 11–March 5) (J. Bond 1961a). On Hispaniola, 100 birds were recorded in 1953 in the Dominican Republic (Weller 1964). Saunders (in Paynter 1955) reported 200 on the Yucatan Pen. This species is rare in interior Mexico, but occurs down the Pacific coast and, as mentioned above, in Guatemala.

Recorded as **fossil** in the Pleistocene of Ore., Cal., Texas, and Fla.; for localities and references, see Brodkorb (1964a). RSP

MIGRATION   Redheads migrate between the interior (breeding range) and coasts (winter range), although some spend the winter on inland lakes. In general, this species nests later and goes farther s. to winter range than the Canvasback. The 3 major wintering areas are: Gulf Coast (se. Texas and Tamaulipas), U.S. e. coast (mainly Chesapeake Bay area and s. to include Fla.), and w. coast (Puget Sd. s. into Guatemala). Stated oversimply: most birds from the prairies and vicinity, including e. Great Basin, go s. to the Gulf Coast, except that a progressively greater percentage northeasterly of birds from across the prairies go diagonally se. to the e. coast, to Chesapeake Bay (shortest route to salt water); birds from s. interior B.C., the westerly Great Basin, and other more westerly breeding areas go mostly to the w. coast. Redheads banded in ne. Cal. (most were banded as preflight young) have been recovered in Canada, conterminous U.S. from coast to coast (to N.Y., Va., and Fla.) and s. to the Gulf Coast (Texas, Mexico) and w. coast of Mexico (Reinecker 1968). Unlike the Canvasback, whose largest movement is to and from Chesapeake Bay, about ⁴/₅ of the Redheads go s. over mostly dry terrain to sheltered saline waters along the Gulf Coast.

Birds banded along a particular migration route or "corridor" (of Bellrose 1968) tend to return to the same wintering area via the same corridor in successive years, but a small percentage of birds of both sexes may shift to another corridor. Drakes travel farther, and shift about more, than ♀ ♀.

Apparently there are no great differences between corridors traveled in spring and those described by Bellrose for fall. The one used by the most birds extends from the Canadian prairies to the Texas–Mexico Gulf Coast and is called the "eastern plains corridor"; the one of next importance e. of the Rockies, is the "Chesapeake Bay corridor." For the latter, timing of movement in fall from the prairies to and on down the coast, based on recoveries of winter-banded individuals, was shown in a table in Benson and DeGraff (1968). Redheads tend to travel in flocks by themselves, but share various stopover places with Canvasbacks, scaups, etc.

There seems to be no information on routes or corridors to and from Yukon Terr. and Alaska; the birds evidently travel through the interior nw. of the prairies.

The subject of Redhead migration was covered in detail by Weller (1964), whose paper is the main source of information given here.

**Spring** The lower part of the Texan (there is also a Mexican) portion of Laguna Madre is the main winter range of the Redhead. The bulk of the birds are present by Nov. 15 and remain until about Feb. 13 (McMahan and Fritz 1967). Movement from this area, therefore, must begin in Feb. Up through the U.S. interior, Redheads begin arriving in Kans. in the first week in March and in the n. tier of states and adjoining s. Canada in late March or early April; in the latter area, migration continues into early May. On the Atlantic coast, in the Chesapeake Bay area, where there are both winter residents and transients from farther s., migration extends from early March through April (mainly mid-March to about April 20). In Cal., migration occurs through March and April. In w. Mont., Redheads usually begin arriving in March. On the n. Canadian prairies, migration probably continues well into May.

**Summer** Drakes take leave of their nesting mates during laying or early in incubation; some evidently go to the nearest suitable lake or reservoir but others, probably in groups, travel northward on molt migration. Some may go hundreds of miles to lakes where they spend the flightless stage of molting. Some ♀ ♀ also make such flights; perhaps the earliest of these are parasitic individuals (that lay but do not incubate) and, later, failed breeders. At least at local molting waters (not distant from nesting areas, as in the Klamath Basin, for example) the drakes and early-arriving ♀ ♀ are joined later (after having grown new flight feathers) by many successful nesting ♀ ♀ and their broods. The overall result of these movements is a partial segregation of adults from young (although the latter have a tendency to wander northward in late summer) and, among the former, a great preponderance of drakes over ducks at various molting places. As of about 1970, few molting lakes actually were a matter of published record;

best known, and probably a southerly one, is L. Winnipegosis, which also is used by Canvasbacks and Lesser Scaups. To the west, they molt on Swan L. Other lakes include Kazan and Witchikan, both in n. Sask., and part of L. Claire, w. of the Athabaska delta in n. Alta.

At Long I. Bay in L. Winnipegosis, there is an early (low) peak in numbers of Redhead drakes from late July to Mid-Aug. (molting), then a later (high) peak from early Sept. to late Oct. (premigration); *Chara* is an abundant food at this locality (R. D. Bergman 1973).

The shift n. to molt may bring some westerly birds into more easterly lines of subsequent travel, and vice versa. Little is known about the movement in the period beginning when adults at molting places again can fly; in Aug. and Sept., however, there is considerable movement, some of it northward, of young birds after they first become capable of flight.

**Fall** migration within the breeding range begins in Sept. and reaches a peak in Oct. At Laguna Madre, some Redheads arrive as early as Oct., but the big flights are in Nov. or Dec. Movement of birds from the interior to the e. coast is indicted by arrival dates for the Chesapeake Bay area: about Oct. 10 to past mid-Dec., greatest numbers usually present Nov. 10–Dec. 10; this is both a stopover and wintering area. Some fall seasons a great many Redheads still are on L. Erie at a time when tens of thousands or even more have arrived in Fla. They arrive in Fla. in numbers in the latter half of Nov. in some years (at least 100,000 on the Gulf Coast side, Nov. 17, 1970) and regularly in Dec. Movement toward the U.S. w. coast begins as early as some time in Sept; along the coast, there is migration from early Oct. to at least late Dec.

A few birds (mostly adults?) go ne. down the St. Lawrence R. and some are killed in upper N.Y., s. Que., and thereabouts (under "Distribution," note release of penreared stock) and presumably such a movement is at least partly the basis for sightings and captures on the ne. Atlantic coast in fall.

Segregation of sexes and ages, beginning with summer–early fall movements, is reflected later on; there are, for example, wintering flocks comprised almost entirely of mature drakes. Perhaps a balanced sex ratio is not approached until flocks have left wintering areas and mingle at stopover places after spring migration begins.

**Winter** Recoveries of adults banded in the Carolinas during the fall season show a northerly movement into Chesapeake Bay prior to Jan. 31. According to Weller (1964), this implies either shifting from s. to n. on wintering areas or that the birds start shifting n. soon after they reach the terminus of their southward travel. A shift in winter (Jan.– Feb.) of some birds from Md. n. into N.Y. is indicated by band-recovery data (Benson and DeGraff 1968). Movement in Feb. in Texas (mentioned earlier under "spring") may be some sort of shift prior to actual migration.

The various divers, notably the Canvasback, Redhead, and the scaups, shift about during winter months, probably in relation to food supply. At least to some extent, such movements result in mingling of the sexes in a more balanced ratio when they engage in pair formation activities. RSP

BANDING STATUS The total number of Redheads banded through 1964 was 108,449 and the total number of recoveries through 1966 was 12,660. Main places of banding: N.Y., Man., Utah, and Md. (Data from Bird Banding Laboratory.)

The banding data have been used extensively, notably by Hickey (1952), Rienecker (1968), Weller and Ward (1959), Weller (1964), and Benson and DeGraff (1968). RSP

REPRODUCTION Most individuals **attain sexual maturity** by age 1 year. The first flocks to arrive in the general area where nesting will occur are small, of paired birds, and usually they arrive at night. Later flocks contain some unpaired drakes. There have been several studies of sex ratio, showing an excess of ♂ ♂ during northward migration, evidently with somewhat diminishing excess as the season advances. Displays leading to pair formation begin on wintering areas and are especially prevalent at stopover places en route northward. The formation of a firm bond probably requires days in the wild, but occurred in 8 min. when a wing-clipped ♀ was introduced among free-flying wild drakes (Weller 1959). **Pair bond** form is **seasonal,** probably single-clutch monogamy. The following data on displays are almost entirely from Weller (1967).

**Displays of the duck** INCITING The bill is lowered, angled downward, then quickly raised as the bill is pointed back toward side; this may be done repeatedly. An *err* call is uttered during the lifting movement. Threat is done as by drakes, but ♀ ♀ seem to hold their heads higher; they give a low gutteral call with bill open. Drakes may peck the ♀'s head or scapulars and ♀ ♀ often threaten, chase, and peck at undesirable drakes.

MUTUAL NECK-STRETCH After encounters with displaying drakes, ♀ ♀ may rejoin their mates and both members of the pair Neck-stretch (fully upward) while facing or with bodies at right angles, breasts often in contact. The drake's throat and upper neck appear swollen; he utters a quiet *pheep-pheep*. After a few seconds the 2 birds swim away together.

**Displays of the drake** KINKED-NECK the neck drawn back slightly, head quite high and its feathers erected, pupil contracted, the bill opened slightly, and throat appears swollen. While in this posture the drake gives a peculiar wheezy catlike *whee-ough* or *meow* call. This display has a role in pair formation, is seen regularly when 2 pairs meet in breeding areas (threat?), and is a response to disturbance.

AERIAL COURTSHIP NOTE in trio flight (2 ♂, 1 ♀), the hindmost drake, probably the ♀'s mate, may hold his wings arched downward and call *meow* as he loses altitude, then quickly resume station. Presumably this is an aerial version of the preceding display.

HEAD-THROW done when 2 or more drakes are displaying to a single ♀; with a rapid motion, the head is laid back until crown touches lower back and the tip of the upper mandible almost touches the water above the nearly submerged rump; then the head is brought forward still more rapidly while the same *meow* as in Kinked-neck display is uttered. Intent to begin this display is indicated when a drake stops swimming, with head held high. In the Head-throw the head is slightly off-center, skewed toward the ♀.

TURNING-THE-BACK-OF-THE-HEAD is an occasional ♂ response to Inciting by a ♀; not highly ritualized in this species. Drakes while swimming in front of ♀ ♀ move the bill from side to side, apparently displaying their head feathering.

THREAT AND CHASE head-low posture, the crown feathers depressed as the drake swims toward an intruding ♂ or aggressive ♀; the bill often is slightly open and wheezing notes may be uttered. In attack, the paired ♂ pecks at rival drakes.

PREEN-BEHIND-THE-WING done occasionally.

UNDERWATER CHASE and AERIAL CHASE if the ♀ attempts to evade intensively displaying drakes by diving, the drake(s) make a sudden splash dive and the ♀'s mate tries to maintain station near her under water, or scurries to her when she emerges. If the ♀ takes wing pursued by drakes, some of the latter may drop out and others may join the flight (maximum of 14 seen). Usually the group returns to the point of departure, where displays continue until the bond seems to deter additional displaying.

AERIAL TAIL-PULL Drakes of pairs (or occasionally in trio flying) attempt to pull the ♀'s tail; sometimes a drake is successful and grips it momentarily. This occurs mostly during prelaying and laying, but has been seen later, also rarely in winter.

**Copulation** The drake or both birds BILL-DIP (pseudodrink) and both PREEN-DORSALLY. Mounting is brief, followed by stereotyped BILL-DOWN position by drake or both birds. They swim a short distance, then resume "normal" stance and preen and bathe. The *meow* call may be included in postcopulatory behavior.

Head-flick and Swimming-shake are "comfort movements" that occur between and also after various displays; whether they have signal functions is unknown.

The sequence of events is as follows. The interest of one sex in the other is first manifest in late Dec. or early Jan., on wintering areas. At first, only a few birds show any overt behavior, but the percentage increases throughout the wintering period; data suggest (Weller 1965) that the duration of ♂–♀ association is longer in March–April than in Jan.–Feb. In the early stage there is a tendency for ♀♀ to "follow" drakes, an indication of sexual interest at least by the former. This leads to group activity (a ♀ and a number of ♂♂) and a drake often defends a following ♀; at times, the ♂ follows the ♀. Other ♀♀ are distributed on the water, often in twos and threes, without reference to the whereabouts of drakes.

Late during the period when the birds are on wintering areas, and afterward during migration and after arrival on breeding areas, drakes normally follow ♀♀. Display groups, usually of 4–7 unpaired drakes, form and then direct their attentions toward a ♀ already accompanied by a drake. Even within a large assembly of Redheads, such groups are conspicuous because of their close formation, alert postures, and synchronized movements. The paired ♂ tries to keep station close to the ♀ (he swims close to her flank) and both birds (but especially the ♀) are aggressive toward other drakes. Common activities during this phase include: Kinked-neck, Head-throw, Inciting, mutual Neck-stretch, some Aerial chasing, and much aggressive behavior.

During migration (April into May) and after arrival at breeding areas (May into June), additional elements of display include: Aerial chases (during migration), Aerial courtship notes (of trio flying), and Aerial tail-pull (occasional in winter and during migration, common after arrival). Copulation has been observed both at migration stopover places and after arrival.

Many Redheads are paired during migration and perhaps almost all that are going to breed are paired on arrival in general vicinity of nesting areas. There still are some extra drakes, however, and these display toward already paired ♀♀. This phase, which may last several weeks at more southerly breeding areas, is at its peak when large numbers of Redheads are on large expanses of water and migrants still are passing through. The social drive then wanes and pairs move away, to smaller waters, and the

♀ ♀ begin prospecting for nest sites. At this time the Aerial tail-pull, Aerial courtship note, and the harsh *kurr-r-r* uttered by ♀ ♀ as they fly over the marsh are conspicuous; pair members engage mainly in mutual display.

**Spacing** There is no territory in the classic sense, but rather a seeming avoidance of other pairs. Aggressive displays now are by the drake only, when his mate is approached very closely by another drake or a pair. The drake may use a single water area or several small ones as "activity centers" where he loafs, feeds, is joined by his mate, and the pair copulates; the ♀ nests at another small water area. In w. Mont., observations of recognizable (marked) individuals gave an av. distance of 180 yds. from "breeding pair" potholes to "nesting" potholes (Lokemoen 1966).

**Nests** usually are well dispersed, but concentrations occur where good cover is well interspersed with water. Nest densities/acre of cover have been reported as follows: Man. .04 (Weller 1959); Iowa .09 (J. B. Low 1945); Utah .11 (C. S. Williams and Marshall 1938b), .41 (Weller 1959), and 1.00 (Wingfield and Low 1955). Nests usually are constructed over shallow water (6–14 in. deep), not many yds. from shore, but occasionally are on dry ground (especially in w. conterminous U.S.) or over water as much as 4 ft. deep. The ♀ builds, using dried vegetation of the previous year at the site, and often pulls vegetation over the nest for concealment. Averages for nests in Man. and Utah: height of nest above water or ground 150 mm. (94 nests), depth of bowl 77 mm. (93 nests), inside diam. 195 mm. (69), and maximum outside diam. of nest 342 mm. (in 69).

Nesting, in the usual sense, is irregular because of the ♀'s parasitic tendencies. Some ♀ ♀ are "**normal**" and lay in the nests that they construct. Most are **semiparasitic**, laying an av. of about 10 eggs in the nests of other waterbirds and then nesting normally. Some appear to be **completely parasitic**, never constructing a nest nor incubating a clutch. For further details, see Weller (1959).

In the Flathead R. valley of w. Mont., the period from establishment of the first nest (May 10) to hatching of last clutch (July 19) in 1960 was 71 days; in 1961 it started April 28 and lasted 78 days (Lokemoen 1966). By June 10, initial nest establishment generally was completed.

Parasitic and "normal" ♀ ♀ start **laying** at the same time. Dates vary with weather conditions (J. B. Low 1945). Earliest recorded date, or same with span of laying: Utah, April 25 (Wingfield 1951) and April 30–June 25 (Weller 1959); w. Mont., see above; Iowa, May 1 (J. B. Low 1945); and Man., May 5–June 24 (Weller 1959). About 71% of nests in Iowa were started by June 1 (Low); the last ones in Man. probably are started by mid-July.

Because of parasitism, true **clutch size** is difficult to determine. Some reported sizes: Iowa, av. 8.9 eggs in 21 nests (Bennett 1938) and 9.8 in 115 nests (J. B. Low 1945); Utah, 12.5 in 212 nests (C. S. Williams and Marshall 1938b) and 13.5 in 151 nests (Wingfield 1951); Cal., 13.8 in 27 nests (A. W. Miller and Collins 1954). True size of most clutches probably is 9 eggs. A number of ♀ ♀ parasitize a single nest, which then may not (or cannot) be incubated. Joint layings have included 30 eggs, 39, 50, 74, and 87; a "dump" nest contained 74 eggs of Redhead plus 1 of the Black Tern (Weller 1959). The Redhead is a known parasite on the Canvasback, Mallard, Cinnamon Teal, Pintail, Gadwall, Baldpate, Ruddy Duck, and even the American Bittern, both during first nestings and renestings in the case of some of the duck species. In turn, Redhead nests occasionally are parasitized by other species—Mallard, Blue-winged Teal, and Ruddy Duck (Lokemoen 1966).

One egg each from 20 clutches (3 Cal., 2 Utah, 3 Sask., 7 N.D., 3 S.D., 2 Mich.) **size** length av. 59.83 ± 3.78 mm., breadth 43 ± 2.63, radii of curvature of ends 15.73 ± 1.64 and 13.20 ± 1.24; **shape** elliptical to slightly subelliptical, elongation 1.38 ± 0.063, bicone −0.067, asymmetry +0.082 (FWP). For additional meas., of 79 eggs, see Bent (1923); for 237 from Iowa, see J. B. Low (1945); and 50 from Man., see Weller (1959); there is little variation from the meas. just given. The eggs are smooth and without markings, with a sort of waxy texture; **color** creamy white, about 5% are buffy brownish or, less commonly, greenish. There is a ratio of 1 "runt" egg to about 2,000–3,000 normal ones. Evidently no wts. of fresh eggs are on record, but 30 during 1st week of incubation av. 64.1 gm.

Rate of laying av. slightly less than 1/day, because of occasional days skipped. They are laid at any time of day, but usually in the morning. As to replacement clutches, the few ♀ ♀ that nest late either may have failed earlier in the season or perhaps are late-maturing yearlings nesting for the first time. Lokemoen (1966) believed that a few ♀ ♀ do renest.

The drive to incubate is relatively weak in the Redhead. The duck begins **incubating** within 48 hrs. or less after she ceases laying. The **nest down** varies depending on the individual from white to medium gray (it is darker in the Canvasback) and about half of all birds (not nests) examined had mixtures of white and gray (Weller 1957). Feathers included in the down in nests are relatively large and the darkened portion of the shaft matches the adjacent portion of the vane, i.e., there is a gradation from white to some shade of gray in both (Broley 1950). The down and feathers accumulate beginning late during laying and continuing into incubation.

Low recorded an av. attentive period of 17.5 hrs. of incubation/day for 4 ♀ ♀. Incubation behavior is essentially as reported for the Mallard by McKinney (1953). The drake "waits" for the ♀ on water not far from the nest during laying and early incubation, usually departing by the end of the 1st week of incubation, but sometimes even by the time incubation begins (J. B. Low 1945, Oring 1964). The **incubation period** usually is 24 days, but varies from 23 to 29 (Hochbaum 1944).

**Hatching** occurs over a span of 5–10 hrs. The shells of the first eggs to hatch may be carried away or submerged in water at the edge of the nest; the remainder may be partially eaten by the duck or be crushed by her weight (Weller 1959). At hatching 53.8% of 636 ducklings were ♂ (Sowls 1955).

Distraction displays during incubation are rare; the duck usually sneaks away. Injury feigning on the water is done occasionally by the ♀ when the brood is very young, but rarely is it performed very effectively.

**Reproductive success** is low in the Redhead, as a result mainly of desertion caused by interference by parasitic individuals, also flooding of nests, drying of potholes, and predation (mostly mammalian). The percentage of nests in which at least some eggs hatch has been reported as follows: 56.2% in Iowa (J. B. Low 1945), 31.4% in Utah (Wingfield 1951), 15.2% in Mont. (Lokemoen 1966), and 45% in Cal. (A. W. Miller and Collins 1954). The percentage of eggs ("normal" plus parasitic) that hatched in Redhead nests varied, in 6 studies, from 21.8% to 70%, averaging 32% in a combined total of 10,802 eggs, as summarized in Weller (1959). In w. Mont., 68% of 202 eggs in 21 successful nests hatched, as also did 8 of 57 Redhead eggs laid in the nests of other species of ducks (Lokemoen 1966). No difference is apparent in fertility of "normal" and parasitic eggs. The entire subject of parasitism by the Redhead, including possible effects on other host species, is complicated; see lengthy treatment by Weller (1959).

**Hatching to independence** The length of time the ducklings remain in the nest depends on time of hatching and on weather; they are led away by the ♀ in 18–30 hrs. Prior to departure they may feed while at the nest or in water at its edge, in company of the duck. The young spend time oiling, preening, and feeding when their down is dry. Imprinting occurs during the first 24 hrs. (Collias and Collias 1956). In w. Mont., ♀♀ lead their broods from small potholes ("nesting potholes") to larger ones ("brood potholes," which are deeper, have more aquatic food, and are less likely to dry up) and eventually to a reservoir, where they remain until fall migration (Lokemoen 1966). From a wt. at hatching of about 37–40 gm., increments may be plotted as a sigmoid curve to 700 gm. at time of first flight at 8½–9 weeks (Weller 1957). (Most individuals **attain flight** at 60–65 days and the reported variation is 56–84 days.) The duck usually takes leave of her brood when the young are 3–5 weeks old. The latter may maintain brood ties, but often combine with other broods, especially at 6–8 weeks of age. MWW

SURVIVAL An analysis of recovery data for individuals banded mostly in Utah suggests that the first-year mortality is about 70% and the mean annual mortality rate for adults about 55% (Hickey 1952). A total of 6,915 Redheads were banded in ne. Cal. from 1948 through 1963; analysis of recoveries indicated a first-year mortality of 78% during years in which there was a hunting season and 75.8% during years without a season (the av. hunter cannot identify the species), and av. annual adult mortality of 41% (Rienecker 1968). Also see Benson and DeGraff (1968) for analysis of recoveries of 10,388 Redheads banded in winters of 1955 to 1960 in N.Y. Prior to restrictive regulations, annual mortality rates for adult Redheads were about 55%; for the period of very restrictive regulations, annual mortality-rate estimates ranged from 14 to 21% (A. D. Geis and Crissey 1969).

In summarizing various data on hatching success of eggs in Redhead nests, Weller (1959) stated "it may be concluded that the average nesting female hatches 3.4 ducklings each year." Allowing 30% mortality of young prior to fall migration, the figure is reduced to an av. of 2.3. If foster parents rear 1 young for each parasitic Redhead ♀ and an av. of 2.3 are produced by the 60% of Redheads that nest, the statistically av. number of young produced per ♀ in the entire population would be only 2.3. In his mortality studies, Hickey (1952) concluded that each ♀ would have to have 3.6 young surviving to Sept. 1 if the population were to remain stable. This would require an egg success of at least 40%; the lower figure (32%) given above "may easily be a result of the presence of the investigators during these studies" (Weller). For further discussion of this subject, see Lokemoen (1966). At any rate, reproductive success is low, mostly because of parasitic behavior. The population is characterized by rapid changes not fluctuating synchronously with those of other waterfowl (Hochbaum 1946). DSF

HABITS The Redhead is highly **gregarious.** This trait persists or is reflected to some extent even in the nesting season, when assemblies of pairs break up and yet tend to be concentrated locally when nesting. The drakes molt in large assemblies; Redheads migrate in compact flocks; on winter range, the birds "raft up" at times, typically with few or no individuals of other species within the raft. In winter in Fla. waters, rafts contain 5,000–20,000 birds; a total of some 80,000–90,000 Redheads frequently have been observed in the vicinity of Cedar Key, where generally they stay 5–15 mi. offshore and seldom come within a mile of shoreline (Chamberlain, Jr., 1960). A raft in se. Texas contained an estimated 76,000 Redheads (Jennings and Singleton 1953). At lower Laguna Madre (se. Texas), on windy days and nights, the birds seek protection from the weather by rafting up on water so shallow that they scarcely can float (McMahan and Fritz 1967).

In nesting areas the Redhead **associates,** or at least shares the same habitat, with the Canvasback, Lesser Scaup, and American Coot; in winter, also with Greater Scaup, Baldpate and, to some extent, the Pintail. When on breeding range, Redheads seem to have no well-defined feeding periods but, according to J. C. Phillips (1925), migrants rest during midday and **feed** most actively in morning and evening. They dive and swim submerged, propelled by the feet, a common method of feeding. They usually seek food in water less than 6 ft. deep and rarely remain submerged more than 15 sec. Up-ending in shallow water and taking food from the surface, in the manner of dabbling ducks, are done commonly.

**Flight speed** (ground speed) 42 mph (M. Cooke 1937); 31, 50, 51, and 55 mph (Cottam et al. 1942).

**Numbers** All authors agree that the Redhead population has declined as much or more than almost any other duck in N. Am., due to decrease in suitable habitat (A. C. Martin et al. 1951) and overshooting (Forbush 1912, Hochbaum 1946). The Redhead is easy to kill; it comes to decoys readily, being both innately curious and gregarious. Forbush (1912) and J. C. Phillips (1925) cited hunting club records that indicated a serious decline in Redhead numbers by the early 1900s. Known numbers were low in the 1930s (but Laguna Madre winterers had not been discovered), then gradually increased under protection until the 1950s when, for a while, they appeared to be relatively stable. For the species as a whole, winter inventories for the various years in the span 1948–62 inclusive were listed by Weller (1964); the highest figure was 1,407,064 for Jan. 1956, the lowest was 310,967 for Jan. 1960, and the last listed was 475,556. The Jan. 1966 total, which did not include the comparatively small number wintering in Mexico, was 688,100 (Hansen and Hudgins 1966). Because Redheads concentrate in winter in only a few areas, aerial surveys provide a very useful index of trends in numbers.

Probably, at the main wintering area in se. Texas and extending into Mexico (lower Laguna Madre), over a million Redheads wintered in some past years (before the 1950s); the figure was about 700,000 for Dec. 1951; it was down to an estimated 420,000 in the winter of 1966–67 (McMahan and Fritz 1967). MWW

FOOD Analyses of 364 stomachs from 26 states and 5 Canadian provinces, mostly collected in the fall, showed 90% vegetable and 10% animal matter. The latter was mainly aquatic insects, grasshoppers, and nymphs of damselflies (Cottam 1939).

Bartonek and Hickey (1969) gave a detailed analysis of food of 99 birds, late spring into fall, in Man.; the data were tabulated for "juveniles" and "adults" by sex. In the young birds, plant and animal matter were ingested in about the same frequency. The summer adults ate mainly animal matter (aquatic larvae of insects). Eleven adults, when flightless in molt in late Aug., had eaten winter buds of *Potamogeton* almost exclusively. In fall, plant foods, *Chara* being very important.

**Vegetable**  Pondweeds: true pondweeds (*Potamogeton*), seeds and other parts of wigeon grass (*Ruppia*), naiads (*Najas*) 32.3%; muskgrass (Characeae) and other algae 23.2%; sedges (Cyperaceae), principally *Scirpus* 7.8%; seeds of grasses (Gramineae), *Zizania, Fluminea, Panicum, Echinochola* 6.3%; wild celery (*Vallisneria spiralis*) 2.7%; duckweeds (*Lemna*) 1.3%; waterlilies (Nymphaceae), *Castalia, Brasenia, Nymphaea* 1.3%; coontail (*Ceratophyllum demersum*) 1.3%; smartweeds (*Polygonum*) 1%; miscellaneous 12.7% (Cottam 1939).

Frogbit (*Limnobium*), iris (*Iris*), water milfoil (*Myriophyllum*), water starwort (*Callitriche*), bladderwort (*Utricularia*), mare's tail (*Hippuris*) also mentioned (Yorke 1899, Gabrielson and Jewett 1940). Principal food in Mich.: seeds and tubers of pondweeds (Pirnie 1935).

The gullets and gizzards of 99 birds from the upper Chesapeake region contained the vegetation and rootstalks of *Potamogeton pectinatus, P. perfoliatus, Zostera marina, Ruppia maritima, Elodea canadensis,* and the seeds of *Najas* sp. and *Potamogeton perfoliatus* (R. E. Stewart 1962).

Fourteen birds in Ill. had consumed 78% plant and 22% animal matter. The plant material consisted mainly of the seeds of *Potamogeton nodosus* 33.45%, *Ceratophyllum demersum* 14.31%, and *Echinochloa crusgalli* 8.32% (H. G. Anderson 1959). The 21 gizzards from Mo. contained chiefly the seeds of *Polygonum* spp. 40.7%, *Potamogeton* spp. 21.2%, and *Scirpus* 8% (Korschgen 1955).

Quay and Crichter (1965) reported on winter foods of 44 birds from Currituck Sd., N.C.; most important in quantity and frequency were *Potamogeton, Ruppia, Najas,* and *Scirpus*.

McMahan (1970) reported that shoalgrass (*Diplanthera wrightii*), a submergent spermatophyte, formed 80% by volume of the diet in winter at Laguna Madre.

**Animal**  For seasonal changes from plant to animal, see Bartonek and Hickey, cited above.

Insects: grasshoppers, midge larvae, caddis fly larvae, and miscellaneous insects 5.9%; mollusks, chiefly gastropods 3.9%; miscellaneous, mainly amphipods, arachnids, polychaetes (*Nereis*) 6%. A specimen from Ala. had consumed 400 snails (A. H. Howell 1924). Consumption in quantity of fish, e.g., gizzard shad in Ohio, is exceptional (Trautman 1940). The upper Chesapeake birds had eaten Pelecypoda (*Macoma balthica, Mya arenaria, Gemma gemma*) and Isopoda (*Erichsonella filiformis*). The animal food (22%) of the Ill. birds consisted almost entirely of chironomid larvae.

**Grit**  Bartonek (1969) reported that older birds have more grit in their digestive tracts than do young ones. AWS

The above summary by AWS does not include certain earlier papers on Redhead foods that have been cited by Bartonek and Hickey (1969). The references these authors cited, plus others given above, are believed to include all the important ones up to 1970. RSP

Baer's Pochard

*Aythya baeri* (Radde)

Also known as Eastern White-eyed Pochard (to distinguish it from *A. nyroca*, the White-eyed Pochard or Ferruginous Duck.) Smallish diving duck, a member of that group known as white-eyed pochards and which contains several species all superficially rather similar. The skull of *baeri* is relatively massive, larger than in other members of the genus (Dementiev and Gladkov 1952). The drake in Alt. Plumage has very dark and mostly greenish head and dark brown mantle (reverse of *A. nyroca*). The drake's trachea is swollen toward the middle; at its proximal end there is a partly bony, partly membranous bulla (Finn 1900), which is said to be very similar to that of *A. australis*, which in turn is said to be "almost identical in shape" to that of *A. collaris* (Johnsgard 1965). The sexes differ mainly in Alt. Plumage (see below), in eye color (♀ dark; ♂ nearly white, beginning probably in 1st fall or winter), and size (♂ larger). Probably, like other *Aythya*, in the definitive cycle the ♂ has a Prebasic molt beginning in summer and the ♀ a Prebasic head–body molt in spring. Length ♂ 18½–19½ in., ♀ about 16½, wt. ♂ about 1 lb. 15 oz., ♀ about 1 lb. 9 oz. No subspecies.

At least as early as Hartert (1920a) and as recently as Dementiev and Gladkov (1960), *baeri* sometimes has been treated as conspecific with *A. nyroca*, but currently they are regarded as two full species. Their respective characteristics were given by Delacour (1959).

DESCRIPTION    Two Plumages/cycle in both sexes.
▶    ♂ Def. Alt. Plumage (head, body, and probably innermost feathers of wing). **Bill** slaty, darker near tip and at base; **iris** pale straw color; **head** and neck nearly black with muted greenish sheen, except dark rufous at side of head adjoining the bill and there is a small white chin spot; **mantle** dark brown with obscure cinnamon vermiculations; **breast** rich rufous chestnut; sides and flanks sepia to fuscous, the feathers with light tips; **belly** white; under-tail area mostly white but blackish brown laterally; legs and **feet** lead gray, darker at webs and joints.
▶    ♂ Def. Basic Plumage (entire feathering). Quite like ♀ Alt. (see below), but **breast** more vividly colored; **under tail coverts** white, the lateral feathers brown banded with narrow crescentic bars of white, giving a pencilled effect; **tail** blackish brown; **wing** mostly dark brown, primaries margined internally with light smoke gray; whitish patch (speculum) on secondaries with dark line along trailing edge.
▶    ♀ Def. Alt. Plumage (probably all feathering except tail and almost all of wing). **Bill** mostly muted slaty; **iris** medium or darker brownish; feathering colored much as drake's Alt. but more muted—**head** and neck have only a hint of greenish gloss on crown and nape and there is a wash of rich reddish brown on lores and sides and some individuals have pale-edged feathers at side base of bill; a white spot on chin; **mantle** dark brown; **underparts** breast muted brown suffused with rufous; belly white, becoming rather dusky brownish in vent region; under tail coverts white with area of brown at sides.

182

▶ ♀ Def. Basic Plumage—little information; by homology with other *Aythya*, probably differs, but not strikingly, from Alt. Tail and wing much as in ♂ Def. Basic.

AT HATCHING very similar to *A. marila*, but crown slightly darker, area behind vent lighter.

▶ Predefinitive Plumages—almost no useful information. Dementiev and Gladkov (1952) stated that the iris is dark in both sexes at the Juv. stage, upperparts uniform brownish, most of breast brownish, some white with brown spots on lower breast, abdomen rusty, and under tail coverts white.

**Measurements** of definitive-feathered birds from Manchuria, 9 ♂: BILL 44–46 mm., av. 45; WING 206–215, av. 212; TAIL 54–64, av. 59.3; TARSUS 36–37, av. 36.4; 7 ♀: BILL 40–45 mm., av. 43; WING 196–209, av. 201; TAIL 57–60, av. 58.5; TARSUS 34–36, av. 34.6 (ETS).

For meas. of WING across chord, see E. C. S. Baker (1929). RSP

DISTRIBUTION For map, see Dementiev and Gladkov (1952). **Breeds** primarily in the Amur Basin in Manchuria, also in adjoining areas to the north and west. Migratory. **Winters** locally from Korea and e. China s. and w. to e. India. Older Japanese records for *A. nyroca* probably refer to *A. baeri*, although the former has been taken at least once (Kuroda 1961c). Presumably has **straggled** to w. Siberia (dead bird purchased in market at Tomsk) and taken once in Kamchatka.

**In our area** 2 were taken, about 1841, in "Oregon" (when the concept of Oregon Territory encompassed more area than the present State); the specimen still extant is no. 12,773 in the National Mus. of Nat. Hist. coll.; details in Friedmann (1949), who pointed out that the captures were in such a remote area and at so early a time as to preclude the birds having been escaped captives and that Baer's Pochard was reported to have strayed as far from its natural range as England.

The first time the writer examined the extant specimen, which is in poor condition, he had some doubts as to its identity. It lacks a white facial "front" and it has white under tail coverts, characters typical of *baeri*, but the under tail coverts of ♀ *Aythya marila* are not invariably all dark and the face evidently lacks white sometimes. Yet it seems unlikely that the specimen is a hybrid. Having reexamined it, the writer is satisfied that it is *baeri*.

A belief that Baer's Pochard strayed far distant from its usual range, to England, was discredited by the discovery (see E. H. Gillham et al. 1966) that some Tufted Duck (*A. fuligula*) × Ferruginous Duck (*A. nyroca*) hybrids resemble Baer's Pochard. RSP

OTHER TOPICS Baer's Pochard has been reported as "nowhere abundant" (Tougarinov 1941) and "rare" (Dementiev and Gladkov 1960). The most useful accounts in English of this species are by J. C. Phillips (1925) and the 1967 translation of Dementiev and Gladkov (1952). Older information on displays was summarized in Phillips and there are some recent data in Johnsgard (1965). In threat toward another drake and in HEAD-THROW display, the drake contracts the pupil of the eye until it is almost lost to view (Millais 1902b), as is known to occur also in some other *Aythya*; an effect is created of almost a white flash (of the iris) when the head is in rapid motion.

This duck is reported to feed extensively in spring on frogs in ponds and meadows; wintering birds in India are considered inedible because of their fishy flavor (Dementiev and Gladkov 1952).

Baer's Pochard was reared for the first time in captivity in 1962 at Breezand, Holland (Delacour 1964). SDR

### Ring-necked Duck

*Aythya collaris* (Donovan)

Small diving duck, one of the smaller *Aythya*. Superficially scauplike but actually more pochardlike. Bill has "normal" duck shape and after early age has a transverse white band distally in both sexes. No actual speculum, the area being predominantly a light grayish, hence not contrasting with rest of wing. Alt. Plumage: ♂'s crown feathers elongated so that, in lateral profile, the head is highest toward rear of crown (but with smooth contour except for slight indentation at rear); in the ♀ the elongated feathers form a mere "bump" toward rear of crown. Drake's iris near orange, ♀'s yellowish to yellowish brown. Sexes differ most in Def. Alt. Plumage: ♂ almost black (strong ultramarine-violet sheen on head) with inconspicuous chestnut collar (unique in *Aythya*), the belly and sides very light; ♀ brownish gray, with well-defined white eye ring (unique in *Aythya*), head color pales toward bill and chin (to white), belly white. See below for other Plumages. In general, the drake's tracheal apparatus resembles that of Common Pochard, Southern Pochard, and Greater Scaup (J. C. Phillips 1925), the bulla being well developed, with strong bony keel and membranous windows; for an illus. of the entire trachea and bulla, see Bonaparte (1824).

Length ♂ 16–18 in., ♀ 14–18, wingspread ♂ to 29½, ♀ to 28, usual wt. ♂ 1³/₅ lb., ♀ about 1½. No subspecies. The similarities of and differences between the Ringneck and Tufted Duck (*A. fuligula*) were pointed out by Hollister (1919) and A. Brooks (1920); it may be an oversimplification to regard these species as counterparts on different continents, since the Lesser Scaup (Nearctic) may be more nearly the counterpart of the Tufted (Palearctic). The Ringneck is a pochard, not a scaup.

DESCRIPTION Two Plumages in definitive cycle in both sexes, the ♀ with the usual pattern of molting into Basic head–body in late winter or early spring. Mendall (1958) is the main source of recorded information, here modified and supplemented by various additional specimen data.

▶ ♂ Def. Alt. Plumage (all feathering except tail and most of wing), acquired in LATE SUMMER–FALL (within the span Aug. into Oct. or later) and retained through winter into the following SUMMER (June–July). **Bill** mostly grayish or greenish blue, the upper mandible having base, sides, and sometimes nostril narrowly edged white, distally there is a broad white band, and the end beyond is dark grayish (bill color usually does not attain full vividness until Dec. or Jan.); **iris** some variant of orange. **Head** and upper neck black with mainly ultramarine-violet sheen; white spot not always present on chin; narrow, usually inconspicuous, chestnut collar around lower neck; **upperparts** glossy black (but fade toward brownish); lower back has slight metallic sheen. **Underparts** breast black, sharply and transversely delimited from white belly and the white extends upward in a triangle toward dorsum forward of the folded wing; the belly grades into light or medium gray posteriorly because of dark vermiculations; sides and flanks light gray (white, finely vermiculated dark), the upper edge white and this increases in amount on flanks (feathers tipped white). **Legs** and **feet** usually dark grayish or slaty with bluish cast, webs and joints darker. **Tail** is retained Basic feathering. **Wing** is retained Basic except: innermost secondaries elongated and somewhat curved, black or nearly so with greenish sheen when new; and coverts overlying these, which are broadly rounded, similar in color and sheen, and (sometimes) with light flecking on smaller ones.

Most drakes have acquired much of this Plumage by late Sept.–early Oct.

▶   ♂ Def. Basic Plumage (entire feathering), the head–body acquired in SUMMER (usually beginning by early July); and later (after a flightless period estimated as 3–4 weeks) the wing and tail (beginning in Aug.), and soon the early-acquired Basic is molting back into Alt. **Bill** color darkens (no stripe around base). Most obvious retained ♂ character is orange-yellow iris. A muted Plumage. **Head**–neck smoky gray or slightly brownish; the crown feathers short; **upperparts** blackish brown; **underparts** breast feathers blackish with white edging; belly white or same blotched gray (usually the feathers are gray with wide white terminal band); abdomen and under-tail area dark grayish; sides paler; the feathers a dusky olive or smoky, broadly margined paler and browner, and with a few fine pale dots. **Tail** blackish brown. **Wing** primaries and their coverts grayed fuscous; darker on outer webs and ends; most (about 8 or 9 distal)

secondaries pearly gray; darkening near ends and the very tips white, 2 nearer secondaries evenly colored gray except have more extensive white ends; innermost ones are
dark brownish olive, not elongated or curved, and have broad ends; the coverts over
the secondaries have rounded ends, are dark olive brownish (or even blackish) with
some sheen (greenish), the smaller proximal coverts plain (compare with Alt.); wing
lining mostly various grays (little white); axillars white.

There is considerable variation in the time the Basic head–body are acquired, some
drakes having much of it by early July when others still are mostly in Alt. In Me.–N.B.;
av. time of peak number of flightless drakes is Aug. 10–20 (extremes are July 25–Sept.
15); a July 9 date for B.C. (J. Munro 1945) is exceptionally early.

NOTES   Molting adult Ringnecks are very shy, hence specimens of drakes in Basic
head–body are rare. The above description of head–body is largely from a flightless
drake taken Aug. 16 in N.B. by Mendall.

At a game farm in early fall, the writer saw what at first glance looked like rather
dullish Canvasbacks. Various *Aythya* in Basic are quite nondescript. It is of interest
that the first impression of these Ringnecks in Basic was that they were pochards, not
scaups.

▶  ♀ Def. Alt. Plumage (head–body plus innermost feathers of wing), acquired in late
SUMMER–FALL (within the span Aug.–Nov.) and retained until LATE WINTER or EARLY
SPRING. A grayish or gray-brown Plumage, the head capped very dark. **Bill** mostly
gray-blue, a white transverse band (somewhat narrower than in ♂) distally, and dark
tip; **iris** yellow. **Head** a conspicuous white eye ring; crown and upper sides of head
nearly black, separated by a narrow whitish line (extends back from eye) from grayish
cheeks, the head feathering lightens to a narrow white facial front which extends back
to include underside of head; nape dark like crown, remainder of neck gray-brown;
**upperparts** mostly some variant of grayed fuscous, many feathers broadly tipped
lighter and browner; **underparts** breast a medium warm brownish, the feathers narrowly tipped buffy or white (this wears off); belly white (area not sharply delineated);
sides and flanks warm brownish, the feathers with broad paler margins; rear of abdomen plain dark or sometimes speckled white; under-tail area also dark, but longer
feathers have progressively more white vermiculations. Legs and **feet** dark gray with
bluish cast. In the **wing** the elongated innermost secondaries are dark gray-brown,
their ends narrower than in Basic; seldom any white on exposed edge of more than 1 or
2 of them; their longest overlying coverts similarly dark, sometimes with light tipping
and/or flecking. Remainder of wing and the tail are retained Basic feathering.

NOTE   Females often have some white feathers in head and upper neck (compare
with ♀ Redhead).

▶  ♀ Def. Basic Plumage (entire feathering), the head–body acquired in WINTER–
EARLY SPRING (within the span late Jan. through March), the tail and wing (after flightless period) not until FALL—usually beginning in Sept.—at which time head–body and
then innermost feathers of wing begin molting back into Alt.

A brownish, blended Plumage. The **bill** shows little or even no white. **Head** pattern
blended, gray-brown or quite brownish, except sides coarsely marked gray-brown on
white, and coloring pales around base of bill and on chin to whitish; **upperparts**, also
part of **underparts** (breast, sides, flanks) rich brownish, but rapidly bleaches to yel-

187

lowish brown; belly feathers are darkish with white ends; under-tail area tends to be patchy (feather ends are light); **tail** very dark brownish. **Wing** pattern essentially as ♂; innermost secondaries shorter than in ♀ Def. Alt., with broader ends, and are more brownish; overlying coverts colored similarly; wing lining variable, from little white and much gray to nearly all white; axillars white.

NOTE    In some individuals the head coloring does not gradually lighten toward bill, but instead there is an abrupt change (white patch around base of bill and extending back on chin), giving a scauplike appearance. This may develop in early summer, as a result of feather wear. There is general fading also and, most evident on underparts, much wear; by late May the white (or very light) ends of belly feathers wear off irregularly, exposing the more basal darker portions so that the belly appears mottled or even totally darkish long before it is molted.

AT HATCHING    See vol. 2, col. pl. facing p. 466; pochard-type pattern; clear-cut and more contrasty than Redhead or Canvasback, not somber and blended as in scaups. Nail on bill comparatively narrow (in Redhead it is nearly as wide as bill), feather outline at top base of bill ends bluntly (it projects out in a point in Redhead). Yellow forehead contrasts sharply with dark crown. After the first few days, the down shows progressive fading. Downies can be sexed by cloacal examination and, at least in dead ones, by determining whether there is a bulla at inner end of trachea (present in ♂ only).

▶    ♂ Juv. Plumage (entire feathering), begins to appear at age 13–15 days and is perfected at age about 8 weeks; soon afterward, part of it is molted but most of wing is retained nearly a year. A blended, brownish Plumage, without white on venter. **Bill** blackish with indistinct bluish band distally, **iris** golden brownish (it gradually differentiates from ♀, becoming more yellowish, and still later toward orange). **Head** crown dark brownish olive; cheeks near buffy brown (any darker mottling may be incoming Basic I); loreal area pale smoke gray to dull tawny; chin, throat, and neck smoke gray, the back of the last being darker. **Upperparts** mostly somewhat grayed brownish olive, the feathers narrow. **Underparts** feathers of breast, anterior belly, sides, and flanks pale silvery smoke gray to pale buffy brown; abdomen medium dusky brown; under tail coverts same, the feathers with narrow silvery gray margins. **Tail** brownish olive, ends of the feathers notched (where the down broke off). Legs and **feet** light greenish gray, webs and joints darker. **Wing** has muted coloring compared with the later Basic wing; innermost secondaries tapering (and soon much frayed by wear), upper coverts narrow (ends approach squarish, not broadly rounded), without sheen. According to Bent (1923), the gray feathers of the speculum area are dusky subterminally and only narrowly, if at all, tipped white.

▶    ♀ Juv. Plumage (entire feathering), timing as ♂. As ♂ except: iris remains brownish, or with hint of yellow; crown, neck, upper breast, and flanks not as dark. By age 5 weeks the lighter coloring of the ♀ can be detected in many individuals (they then have acquired sufficient Juv. Plumage) and, by 7–8 weeks, the difference is unmistakable (Juv. Plumage well developed).

▶    ♂ Basic I Plumage (head–body, tail, and innermost feathers of wing). This Plumage begins to appear (first on head–neck) not long after the Juv. Plumage is fully grown; thus it is acquired in EARLY FALL and retained until LATE FALL or EARLY WINTER. Because part of it (as head–neck) are succeeded by Alt. I by the time other

188

parts (mantle, tail) develop, previous describers of 1st-fall drakes have (when they did mention elements of Basic I) included this Plumage as part of Juv. and/or "1st nuptial" (Alt. I).

The drake has dull brownish **head**–neck, without chestnut neck ring; **upperparts** also dark brownish, some feathers with paler margins; **underparts** breast feathers brownish with sharply demarcated white terminal zone; the light triangle in front of folded wing is not well defined and is buffy brown like the sides and flanks; much of the belly is white or mottled or blotched darkish (the feathers are medium gray with terminal white zone, or vary to largely medium gray or darker); the lower belly grades into gray-brown of abdomen and under-tail area. By the time (very late fall or into winter) the notched Juv. tail feathers are succeeded by the wide but distally pointed blackish Basic I **tail**, at least the head–neck already are in Alt. I, as also scattered (black) feathers on dorsum, some vermiculated feathers on sides and flanks, and scattered white ones on forward sides and anterior belly. Innermost feathers of wing essentially as ♂ Def. Basic.

Birds usually are in transition from Basic I to Alt. I as migrants and on winter range, i.e., last half of Nov. through first half of Jan.

▶  ♂ Alt. I Plumage (head–body and a few innermost feathers of wing), usually acquired during LATE FALL, but sometimes into winter, and retained into the following SUMMER. Essentially as Def. Alt., but some differences as follows: **head**–neck sometimes with less sheen; usually a sizable white area on chin; chestnut collar sometimes indistinct or even lacking; **underparts** the triangle in front of bend of folded wing usually somewhat vermiculated black (most of these feathers typically are unmarked white in later Alts.); flank feathers not as large and seldom with clear white margin on exposed web.

Many drakes are in fully developed Alt. I by Nov., but others acquire it more gradually, or even later, retaining portions of Juv. and Basic I longer and not being fully into Alt. until late winter. Regardless of variation in timing, retained and worn with the completed Alt. I are at least most of the Juv. wing plus the Basic I tail. By early winter, most drakes have fully "adult" coloring of iris, bill, legs, and feet.

▶  ♀ Basic I Plumage (all feathering except most of wing), acquired in FALL and retained into EARLY WINTER, the dating somewhat later in "tardy" individuals. **Bill** has pale subterminal band; **iris** yellowish or yellowish brown. **Head** crown blackish brown, the feathers tipped lighter brownish; cheeks mostly quite dark brownish but grade to off-white at side base of bill and on throat and foreneck; **upperparts** blackish brown, some feathers with lighter brownish margins; **underparts** breast feathers dark gray and terminally buffy brown (upper breast) or white (lower breast); belly white but becomes mottled darker with wear (the feathers are 2-zoned, the white ends being sharply delineated); sides and flanks brownish and not vermiculated and the broad feathers (not narrow as in Juv.) have yellow-brown terminal zones; rear of abdomen quite dark; under-tail area medium fuscous speckled brownish olive and white, the longest feathers with broad white margins; **tail** feathers broad distally and nearly black; innermost feathers of wing as ♀ Def. Basic. The Basic I tail is present as early as Oct. or is acquired at any time into Jan., possibly even later; that is, it is acquired last, commonly when some other feathering already has molted into the succeeding Alt. I.

▶  ♀ Alt. I Plumage (all feathering, excepting tail and all but innermost feathers of

189

wing), usually acquired beginning well along in FALL, sometimes later; retained until late WINTER or early SPRING. Not many specimens seen but, from material examined, this Plumage differs from all others in the species. **Head**, from eye upward, nearly black; cheeks medium gray; the facial front is white at sides and under bill, but tends to be darker (brownish) at top base of bill than typical of ♀ Def. Alt. The white area is well defined. There is much individual variation in the head; some have most of it (except cap and facial front) mottled or quite densely marked black; some have fine black dotting on cheeks only; some have white throat and foreneck; the eye ring is white; a more or less obvious white line extending back from eye is usual. **Upperparts** feathers of anterior mantle rich dark brownish; those of back darker but margined same color as forebody; long scapulars blackish with slight greenish sheen; lower back black. **Underparts** breast rich buffy brown (the feathers much darker basally), belly white (concealed portions of the feathers medium gray); feathers on sides and flanks dark brownish with broad edging that is buffy tan and whitish, finely dotted dark; vent to tail plain dark (not dark and light as in Basic I). Innermost feathers of **wing** as ♀ Def. Alt.; the remainder of the wing, with its narrow coverts and muted "speculum" area, is retained Juv., the tail retained Basic I.

▶ ♀ Basic II Plumage (entire feathering), the head–body acquired in EARLY SPRING (before age 1 year), the wing and tail much later (after flightless period and after nesting). Head–body evidently as succeeding Basics; there is no evidence of a spring molt of the tail (Basic I tail probably retained); at least almost all of the Juv. wing is retained until the flightless period, when the Basic II wing is acquired.

**Measurements**   12 ♂ (from various parts of range, mostly fall and spring): BILL 44–49 mm., av. 47; WING 194–205, av. 201; TAIL 55–65, av. 59; TARSUS 34–36, av. 35.2;   11 ♀ (from scattered localities, mostly fall and spring): BILL 44–48 mm., av. 45.5; WING 188–200, av. 192; TAIL 56–59, av. 58; TARSUS 33–36, av. 34.5 (ETS).

In various external, skeletal, and gonadal meas., birds in their first spring after hatching ("yearlings") av. smaller than older age-classes taken the same season. Part of the data (includes flattened wing) are as follows:

"Adult" ♂ BILL (of 78) 47.5 ± 1.43 mm., WING (of 94) 203 ± 4.08, TAIL (of 43) 56.80 ± 2.78; ♀ BILL (of 53) 45.68 ± 1.47 mm., WING (of 72) 194 ± 3.57 mm., TAIL (of 32) 54.91 ± 2.61.

"Yearling" ♂ BILL (of 53) 47.19 ± 1.93 mm., WING (of 60) 202 ± 4.26, TAIL (of 29) 54.30 ± 3.18; ♀ BILL (of 48) 45.18 ± 1.34 mm., WING (of 51) 191 ± 3.69, TAIL (of 24) 54.60 ± 2.82 B. W. Anderson and Warner 1969a).

The same authors tabulated meas. from earlier sources, the WING probably measured in various ways.

For size of the bursa of Fabricius, in spring birds approaching age 1 year and in older age-classes at that season, see B. W. Anderson et al. (1969).

**Weight**   See Mendall (1958) for his own and also summary of previously published data. Part of his data: "adults" in fall 7 ♂ 1 lb. 8 oz. (.68 kg.) to 2 lb. 1 oz. (.94), av. 1 lb. 11 oz. (.76); and 6 ♀ 1 lb. 2 oz. (.51 kg.) to 1 lb. 15 oz. (.88), av. 1 lb. 8 oz. (.68); "adults" in spring 22 ♂ 1 lb. 9 oz. (.70 kg.) to 1 lb. 15 oz. (.88), av. 1 lb. 10 oz. (.74); and 10 ♀ 1 lb. 5 oz. (.59 kg.) to 1 lb. 9 oz. (.70), av. 1 lb. 7 oz. (.65).

Another series, age-classes not distinguished, reported in tenths of lb. by A. L. Nelson and Martin (1953): 285 ♂ av. 1.6 lb. (.73 kg.), max. 2.4 (1.09); and 151 ♀ av. 1.5 lb. (.68 kg.), max. 2.6 (1.18). These maxima are the heaviest recorded weights.

**Hybrids** several wild crosses with the Redhead (*Aythya americana*) have been recorded; see Weller (1957) for descriptions and photos of a ♂ and ♀. A presumed Ringneck × Lesser Scaup (*A. affinis*) hybrid was observed, but not collected, in the wild in Me.; it was in company with a ♀ Ringneck (Mendall 1958). A presumed Lesser Scaup × Ringneck hybrid ♀, taken Oct. 24, 1967, near Vermillion, S.D., was described and illus. by B. W. Anderson and Timken (1969). In captivity, the Ringneck reportedly has crossed with at least 4 *Aythya* species, also *Netta rufina* and *Anas crecca*.

**Geographical variation** none reported in the species. RSP

FIELD IDENTIFICATION    Smallish duck, body size about as Lesser Scaup or Hooded Merganser. When at rest, rides high on water like the scaups and Tufted Duck. From fall to spring (♀) or to summer (♂), the head appears somewhat angular or semicrested, that of the drake especially, because of elongated feathers on crown. Most often confused with scaups and Redhead (which are comparatively common), but most similar to the Tufted Duck (which is rare in our area) in general appearance.

The drake Ringneck, from fall into following summer, is best described as appearing blackest of the *Aythya* group, the sides being mostly gray (not all white as in the Tufted Duck)—hence the name "Blackjack" on the Mississippi. On the water, the white bordering the black breast extends upward toward the dorsum in a conspicuous crescent or tall narrow triangle (not a small white triangle as in Tufted Duck). The white transverse band distally on the bill shows well at a distance; "Ring-billed Duck" is appropriate, the chestnut ring on the neck being a poor diagnostic feature afield. The drake is much more nondescript, with less evident pattern to bill, in late summer–early fall (see Def. Basic Plumage).

From fall to spring, the ♀ on the water appears darker than our other *Aythya* (excepting the Tufted Duck), with more angular head, and distinct white eye ring; the head pales to white at base of bill and on throat, rather than having a clear-cut white facial front as in scaups and Tufted Duck. The white transverse stripe on bill is quite prominent and is diagnostic. Most of these characteristics are modified or obscured from spring to fall, when bird is in Def. Basic Plumage. The voice of the ♀ is softer, lower pitched, and notably less discordant than that of scaups and Redhead.

Some of the predefinitive stages (described earlier) are quite nondescript; see Plumage descriptions and also compare with other *Aythya*.

In flight, the gray wing stripe and very black appearance distinguish the drake. The ♀ in flight differs from the scaups in also having the wing stripe gray, but often cannot easily be distinguished from ♀ Redhead. HLM

VOICE    The drake usually is silent except during displays and when joined by his mate when off-duty from the nest; his call then is a low-pitched, hissing whistle audible for a relatively short distance. Like the "sound produced by a person blowing through a tube" (Audubon 1843). The duck has a scauplike call typical of *Aythya* but less discordant or harsh; it is a purring growl, generally low pitched when she is curious, also dur-

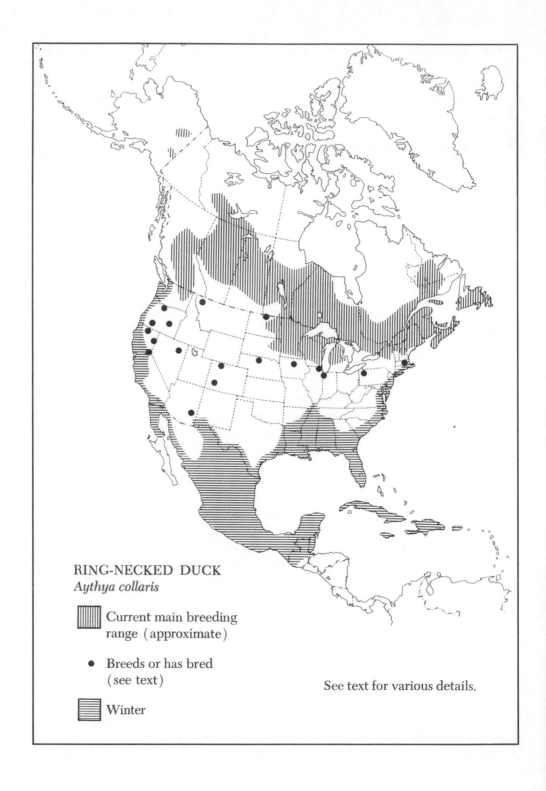

RING-NECKED DUCK
*Aythya collaris*

Current main breeding
range (approximate)

● Breeds or has bred
(see text)

Winter

See text for various details.

ing displays and when mildly disturbed, but shorter and higher pitched when she is badly frightened. (See "Reproduction" for calls in context with displays.) The duck with brood, under normal conditions, utters a low, husky *cut-cut-cut* call. HLM

HABITAT   Essentially a duck of freshwater marshes, frequenting shallower water and denser vegetation than our other diving ducks.

**Summer–early fall**   Might be described as a forest-dwelling Pochard. Sedge marshes and bogs are most favored habitat throughout much of range. In the wetlands classification of Shaw and Fredine (1956), important types are: shallow fresh marshes, bogs, and swamps. Small potholes, sloughs, and beaver flowages sometimes are utilized for nesting, if near larger lakes or rivers. When the Ringneck began expanding its nesting range northeastward, at first it preferred sedge meadows and bogs, but by the early 1970s it was making increasing use of older beaver flowages with grass and sedge borders and sedge hummocks for nesting. Molting assemblies, as observed in N.B. and se. Ont., occupied large, open areas of water having an abundance of submerged vegetation and a fringe of emergent "escape cover." In N.S. they have molted on ponds as well as on lakes. Females that have nested successfully usually molt in their breeding areas.

During **migrations** and on **winter range** (especially the more southerly portion) often occurs on estuaries and other tidal waters, but generally in fresh or brackish portions of these. Seldom found on strictly saline waters. HLM

DISTRIBUTION (See map.)   W. Cooke (1906) described the **breeding** range as consisting of 2 areas separated by the Rocky Mts.—a large one extending from the Great Lakes nw. to L. Athabaska and a smaller one extending from s. B.C. (Cariboo Dist.) locally down to the Klamath Basin in Ore. J. C. Phillips (1925) summarized the older records; his map showed less breeding range w. of the Rockies, an increase of midcontinent range eastward (in Great Lakes area), and "sporadic" nesting at 6 localities from s. New Eng. to N. Shore of Gulf of St. Lawrence. The Ringneck has a long history in the northeast; see R. S. Palmer (1949) for Me.–N.B. The map in Mendall 1958) showed much more breeding range eastward, particularly from Ont. to Nfld. inclusive; the changes are real, not merely better reporting. The map in Godfrey (1966) showed some further changes.

The easterly increase came about from birds breeding at widely scattered areas, then in the areas in between, rather than gradually adding increments in an easterly direction (Mendall 1958). For an historical summary, see Baillie (1969). The Ringneck seems to have gone through a stage of having 3 foci: w. of the Rockies, in midcontinent, and a rather sprawling easterly one. These now have more or less coalesced, but with some separateness between 1st and 2nd where the Rockies intervene. Westerly changes appear to be recent, but perhaps are partly a matter of better reporting. Southerly in midcontinent, there has been some loss as a result of drought and agriculture; the map is not up-to-date with these changes. To the north there has been an increase in breeding range and, beyond, summer occurrences of molting (or perhaps breeding) birds to localities around James Bay, se. Hudson Bay, and n. of Great Slave Lake—this last on probable route to interior e. Alaska. In Ungava, upper limits of known breeding now are approximately to cent. Que. and then northeastward nearly to Hopedale, Labrador.

Another focus may be developing in Alaska. The species was recorded in some numbers in the e. interior beginning in 1957—perhaps at first molting birds—and it bred at Tetlin in 1960 and on Yukon flats in 1964 (Kessel and Springer 1966). It now probably breeds regularly in small numbers.

South of main breeding range the Ringneck has nested at widely scattered localities, the following list probably being incomplete: Ore.—Klamath Co. (1888 and 1954), Clackmas Co. (1963 and 1964), Harney Co. (1964), and probably continuing at same places; Cal.—Lassen Co. (continuing), Siskiyou Co. (continuing), and L. Tahoe (1926); Nev.—Ruby Lakes Refuge (1950); Colo.—Mineral Co. (1949) and North Park (1952 and 1955); Ariz.—White Mts. (for a long time, locally, and continuing at least into 1960s); N.D.—scattered nesting for a very long time, probably most birds in Turtle Mts. region (Duebbert 1966b); n.-cent. Nebr. (mapped by Mendall 1958); n. Iowa—Clear Lake (turn of century) and a few in n.-cent. Iowa from the late 1940s to the present; Ill.—in ne. part (early 1950s, probably an extension from Ind.); Ind.—nw. part as mapped by Mendall (1958); nw. Pa.—Pymatuning (1936); N.Y.—Adirondack region (a locality in 1946 plus others later, and continuing); Mass—Concord (1947 and 1951); Me.–N.B. border—Calais region (absent after about 1876, but by late 1930s this area again part of easterly breeding range).

**Winter**  Has occurred in Alaska, for example at Petersburg, Feb. 27, 1940. Has occurred in sw. B.C., easterly Great Lakes, and n. New Eng. and nearby Maritimes, but winters widely in ice-free fresh and brackish waters southward into Cent. Am. Aside from the area mapped, there are occasional occurrences in the interior, as in Nev. and n. Texas. Has occurred in winter in Bermuda, and from the Bahamas down through the Caribbean region to Margarita I. and Trinidad.

**Straggler**  Beyond Guatemala in cent. Am. there are few records, the southernmost being several for Panama. One for mainland Venezuela.

Hawaiian Is.—reported from Maui in 1948 and 1949 and Oahu in 1966 (Berger 1972).

In England, the type specimen, obtained in Leadenhall Market, is said to have been taken in Lincolnshire in Jan., 1801. There was no other British record until 1955. From then through the 1960s there were scattered occurrences in the Brit. Isles and Europe. Bruun (1971) listed these totals: Britain and Ireland 9, France 1, Switzerland 4, Belgium 1, Netherlands 3, Denmark 1, and n. Norway 1. Probably there is some duplication of individuals in this list. Most records were for winter–early spring, and for drakes, except a ♀ in France, Switzerland, and Denmark. At least in the Brit. Isles, at present the probability that some occurrences are of escapees is considerable.

In N. Am. the Ringneck is reported as **fossil** from the Pleistocene of Ore., New Mex., Texas, and 6 Fla. localities; and from **archaeological sites** in Ill. (4), Ohio, and Fla. (2); references in Brodkorb (1964a). RSP

MIGRATION  Duvall (in Aldrich 1949) provided some information, mostly on midcontinent birds, Mendall (1958) treated the ne. Ringnecks, and Bellrose (1968) gave some figures for numbers using various migration "corridors" in fall from the

Rockies eastward. There is no single source for those nesting w. of the Rockies or for flights from anywhere continuing into Mexico and beyond.

Evidently those nesting w. of the Rockies (mostly in s. B.C.) go to the Pacific coast and have that as their main route to and from winter quarters. In fall the midcontinent birds tend to fan out, the more westerly (and northerly) ones going toward the w. Gulf of Mexico (and some continuing into Cent. Am.) and the others going to inland localities in the lower Mississippi drainage, many to the Gulf Coast eastward from the Mississippi delta, others to Fla. (a great many) and S.C., and comparatively few go diagonally se. from the Great Lakes region to the Chesapeake Bay area and then down the Atlantic coast. The birds that nest from Ont. to Nfld. for the most part tend to go by several direct routes to the U.S. Atlantic coast, then some continue on as far as into Fla. Comparing figs. 5 and 6, also text, in Mendall (1958), the easterly birds have important differences between fall and spring lines of travel. For example, in fall there is a route across the Gulf of Me. from N.S. to s. New Eng., but in spring they go around via the mainland of Me. and N.B. Another difference: instead of coming up the Atlantic coast, part of the birds that winter in Fla. go inland to Ind. and then veer ne. and travel via L. Erie. The migratory pattern of easterly Ringnecks is of special interest because its development must have been concurrent with the great increase in Ringnecks in the northeast that began roughly in the early 1930s. See Mendall (1958) for routes and other information.

From Chesapeake Bay southward into Fla. there is a mingling in winter of Ringnecks from the midcontinent and northeasterly summering areas. For example, birds in S.C. have been recovered at points from the Maritimes w. into Sask.

**Spring** Northward movement must begin in Mexico by early Feb.; in conterminous U.S. the main time of passage is March and, in northerly states, to past mid-April.

The schedule of the better-known ne. birds is as follows. They begin to leave s. and cent. Fla. about Feb. 20 and most are gone by March 1; peak of movement in e. S.C. is about March 10, and in Chesapeake Bay 10 days later. There are early arrivals on breeding areas in e. and cent. Me. about March 30 and in the St. John Estuary, N.B., April 15. Arrival dates in Me. and N.B. are variable and correlated with ice clearing, but peak numbers show considerable annual regularity. The early arrivals in Me. consist of mated pairs plus groups engaged in pair formation activity and having an excess of drakes. These are followed by unpaired birds, with large excess of drakes. Late arrivals are, again, mated pairs and display groups but with more nearly balanced sex ratio. The ultimate ratio, after migration, is approximately 3 ♂ : 2♀. (Summarized from Mendall 1958.)

**Summer** Drakes leave their incubating mates, form in small groups, and soon depart on **molt migration**. Some, however, remain and molt locally; perhaps others travel northward. The whereabouts of assemblies of molting drakes is largely a mystery; Mendall (1958), for example, found only 1 locality—Musquash I. lagoon in the St. John R. estuary, N.B., used by 200–300 birds. Erskine (1972b) reported that, in 1960–70, he found molting assemblies at a lake and at 3 ponds on C. Breton I., N.S.; earliest dates June 23 and 27; highest counts June 28–Aug. 14 (130 at 1 locality on July 30); latest dates Sept. 6 (25 ♂) and 8 (21 ♂). The birds were very shy. Some failed-breeding ♀♀ join the drakes. There is some evidence, from the midcontinent Ringnecks, that their molt migration is more or less northward within the forest zone. Beginning well along in summer, when they have attained flight, young Ringnecks are given to extensive wandering; limited band-recovery data on Me. and Que. birds indicate that these have a nw. and w. trend of movement.

**Fall** The picture of movement is complicated from the time (in summer) when drakes depart on molt migration to largely unknown destinations. Dating from then, they are in unisexual ♂ flocks, sometimes joined by a few ♀ ♀. There is some evidence of sex segregation even among the young in their 1st fall.

Movement this season begins at variable dates, from about Sept. 20 onward, but usually and mainly in Oct.–Nov. in conterminous U.S. Again, the pattern is best known for the ne. birds. Some years there is little movement out of general breeding range until late Oct. or Nov., but in other autumns heavy withdrawals in late Sept. There seems to be little apparent correlation with weather conditions. Often, but not always, they arrive at wintering areas in S.C. and Fla. in large numbers in the first half of Nov. At least the earlier arrivals in coastal S.C. are almost all drakes. Birds of the midcontinent breeding stock begin arriving in the Mississippi delta and along the Gulf Coast from some time in Oct. until well into Nov.

**Winter** It is not a simple matter to divide the shifting about into late fall migration, winter movement, and beginning of spring migration. For example, birds banded in La. in winter and recovered that same season showed an "explosive" pattern of travel (Duvall, in Aldrich 1949, text and map). Ringnecks arrive at some wintering areas as in Gulf Coast states and s. Cal. and, some time in late Jan. or early Feb., a considerable number of them shift to somewhere else. (Compare with winter activities of other *Aythya*.) HLM

BANDING STATUS The total number banded through 1964 was 50,904 and the total number of recoveries and returns through 1966 was 5,914; main places of banding were La., S.C., Fla., and Minn. (data from Bird Banding Laboratory). RSP

REPRODUCTION **First breeds** at age approximately 1 year (known from banded individuals), is single-brooded, and **seasonally monogamous.** A small percentage of the birds, believed to be older (2 and more years), are paired before arrival in breeding areas. According to Erskine (1964), large numbers of apparently nonbreeding Ringnecks were noted in 3 consecutive summers of study on C. Breton I., N.S., a possible explanation being that not all yearlings breed.

Displays begin at places where the Ringneck winters, with some pair formation evidently accomplished in late winter; there is much pair formation activity at spring stopover places, but some pairs are not formed until the birds are within breeding range. There is the usual *Aythya* pattern: first a grouping of birds (mostly drakes), with displays of the various drakes not oriented toward a ♀; later there is more directed action and pairs are formed. Relatively little aerial activity has been observed. After pair formation, and at least as long as any flocking occurs, the bond is maintained by relatively passive display.

**Displays of the duck** INCITING is pochardlike, an alternating of threatening movements and NECK-STRETCHING, in both with bill toward the drake; a low *krrr* is uttered. PREEN-BEHIND-THE-WING is performed occasionally. There may be other still undescribed ♀ displays, such as Head-throw.

**Displays of the drake**　KINKED-NECK much as in the Canvasback, but with less bending of the neck; a soft "breathing" call, weaker than that of the Canvasback, is uttered.

HEAD-THROW much as in the Redhead; the head is moved back almost to the rump and slightly off center plane (toward ♀), then brought forward comparatively slowly (for an *Aythya*). The Kinked-neck call is uttered. NECK-STRETCH vertically, with in-breathing call. LATERAL THREAT when a ♂ approaches another ♂ and near the latter's mate, the drakes swim side by side, 1–3 ft. apart and in the same direction; their heads are high (neck stretched), the feathers flattened on the side of the head facing the rival, but the cheek facing away is puffed out (Ripley 1963, with illus.). This was observed in captives and obviously relates to pair bond maintenance. NODDING drake swims rapidly, near ♀, nodding with his crest feathers conspicuous and appearing triangular in outline; the in-breathing call may be uttered. COUGHING frequent and conspicuous, the wings flicked noticeably and "cough" uttered. SNEAK apparently as in Canvasback. TURNING-THE-BACK-OF-THE-HEAD with crown feathers depressed, in response to In-citing by the ♀. PREEN-BEHIND-THE-WING seldom observed.

**Copulation**　The drake BILL-DIPS and PREENS-DORSALLY and the ♀ Bill-dips; after treading, the drake utters the Kinked-neck call and swims away while assuming BILL-DOWN posture (tip touches breast), or perhaps both birds do this.

The pattern of activities leading up to and subsequent to **pair formation** is essentially as in other pochards. That is, after flocks arrive in the general breeding area, the mated birds leave the group, the ♀ seeks a place to nest (it may be one used in a previous year), and the drake has at least one station on open water. Pairs seem to occupy terrain on a "mutual respect" basis, vigorous defense seldom being observed. Pairs regularly share feeding and resting areas. Such defense as has been noted is confined largely to the period immediately preceding selection of a nest site and the drake defends his mate rather than a specific area.

The **pair bond** is maintained longer and is stronger than in some other waterfowl. Among early-nesting Ringnecks in Me. and N.B., most drakes remain with their mates until just prior to the time the clutch hatches. Even in late nesters (July), drakes usually are present for at least part of the incubation period. There also is circumstantial evidence that some ♀♀ that lose their nests and do not renest, i.e., become failed breeders, accompany their mates to a molting area. Furthermore, Ringnecks often behave as though paired in fall, but it is unknown as to whether this represents continued maintenance of a bond by individuals that were mated earlier. A color-marked pair in Me. was known to have remained together, in summer habitat, in excess of 60 days and during 2 nestings, both of which were unsuccessful (Marquardt 1955).

Except where otherwise indicated, the remainder of this section is based on data from Me. and N.B. (in Mendall 1958).

**Nest-site** selection is by the ♀ accompanied by her mate. The interval between selection and laying varies from 1 to 10 or more days, being influenced by prevailing weather. Such nest building as is done accompanies, rather than precedes, laying. There is no evidence that the ♀ makes "scrapes." The first eggs are laid when the future **nest** has a minimum of material and shape. There is no bowl until the 3rd or 4th egg is present. The **nest down** is added gradually after the 5th egg is laid; it is dark (sooty) with fairly conspicuous white centers, and intermingled feathers typically are darkest up against the terminal white band (not a lightening toward the band as in Lesser Scaup); see Broley (1950) for illus. There is no evidence that nests are begun and abandoned, except under conditions in which the ♀ was disturbed. No nest parasitism has been observed. Of 518 nest sites classified, more than ⁴/₅ were either on floating islands or among hummocks and brushy clumps in open marsh. Solid islands were utilized only sparingly. The species differs from some other diving ducks in seldom nesting in emergent vegetation over water. Practically all nests were on a dry to semidry foundation but in proximity to open water. Seventy percent of all nests were within 15 yds. of permanent open water. Cover types were determined for 411 nests: a sedge–sweetgale–leatherleaf type comprised 69% (285) of all nests.

**Laying**   The earliest recorded laying is approximately May 1 in Me. and N.B. coastal belt, but usually does not start before the 2nd week in the month. There is much annual variation in early dates, but laying "peaks" are more constant. The peak av. May 23 in the region studied (primarily ne. and cent. Me. and sw. N.B.) for a 13-year period (1943–55). The latest recorded laying was in 3rd week in July. **Clutch size** 423 complete first clutches contained 6–14, av. 9.04 eggs, as follows: 6 eggs (10 clutches), 7 (52), 8 (92), 9 (116), 10 (92), 11 (36), 12 (22), 13 (2), and 14 (1). In **replacement clutches** (48 records) the range was 5 to 9 with av. 6.96 as follows:  5 eggs (6 clutches), 6 (7), 7 (20), 8 (13), and 9 (2).

Near Cumberland House, Sask., earliest nesting was May 6, mean date for laying (2 years' data) was the end of the month, and the av. clutch in 46 nests was $8.4 \pm 0.4$ eggs (G. H. Townsend 1966).

One **egg** each from 20 clutches (from localities from Ariz. to n. Canada, none from the northeast) **size** length $55.36 \pm 2.70$ mm., breadth $39.52 \pm 1.57$, radii of curvature of ends $15.03 \pm 0.90$ and $12.67 \pm 0.97$; **shape** elliptical to slightly subelliptical, elongation $1.39 \pm 0.052$, bicone $-0.015$, and asymmetry $+0.084$ (FWP). In Me. the size varies considerably, but the av. is in accord with $57.5 \times 39.8$ mm. given for the species by Bent (1923). There is much variation in **color,** but nearly always it is constant in a given clutch. The majority are of 2 "phases," olive-gray or olive-brown, with the former predominating. Others are light buffy brown; a small minority are creamy buff. They are laid at a rate of 1/day with deposition at any time during daylight hours, most known instances being between 7:00 and 11:00 a.m.

**Incubation** by the ♀ usually starts with laying of the last egg of the clutch, the period being 25–29 days with majority hatching at end of 26th or 27th day. There is some tendency for longer periods at beginning of the nesting season, believed to be correlated with degree of attentiveness of the ♀ , to a lesser extent with weather conditions. The drake's waiting area often is quite close to the nest when the local habitat is such that there is suitable open water nearby. During the early stage of incubation, under these conditions, the ♀ is off the nest frequently. The drake often appears to warn her of approaching danger by taking wing and circling the nest.

**Nesting success** (nests in which 1 or more eggs hatched) was 70% of 473 first nests and 61% of 49 renestings. The av. hatch from 329 first nests was 8.5 ducklings and from

198

28 renestings was 6.8. The majority of egg losses in successful nests was from infertility, dead embryos, and eggs accidentally rolled out of nests. Nest losses (171) were due to: predation 79.5%, flooding 15.8%, and desertion 4.7%. Three predators—in order of importance: mink, Crow (plus Raven), and raccoon—caused 71% of all identified predation losses. Greatest losses were during laying and 1st and 4th weeks of incubation. Nest losses varied with sites, floating islands being safest with only 17% loss.

**Renesting**   The Ringneck is quite a persistent renester, particularly when the first or even succeeding attempt is broken up in May or early June; it is estimated that over 50% of initial nest losses are compensated for by renesting.

In Lassen Co., Cal., E. G. Hunt and Anderson (1966) captured and color-marked 10 ♀ and 8 renested, the eggs having been taken to "simulate nest destruction." The interval between nestings varied 5–27 days (assuming no abortive attempts occurred and were undiscovered). In the 8 nests, first clutches were of 7–9 eggs, av. 7.9, and in the renestings 2nd clutches were of 6–9, av. 7.8. One ♀ renested twice, laying 7–8–7 eggs. Distance between 1st and later nests av. 591 yds.

**Preflight young**   Pipping precedes hatching by 24–48 hrs. and generally the last chick emerges within 6 hrs. of the first. Unless disturbed, the young are brooded in the nest a minimum of 12 and sometimes as long as 24 hrs., then are led to nearest water. The family may return to the nest for brooding if adjacent rearing habitat lacks dry spots. The ducklings are brooded extensively for the first 4 or 5 days, with only a few hrs./day on water for feeding and traveling. Exceptions occur if the birds are disturbed frequently or if physical conditions of the habitat are unfavorable. At such times they may travel several mi. in a few hrs. The brood is under the close care of the ♀ and her distraction display is highly developed, rivaling that of the Blue-winged Teal. Aquatic insects and other animal organisms are obtained by the ducklings on the surface of the water for the first few days. Initial dives for food ordinarily occur at age about 5 days and increase thereafter. Little vegetable food is utilized until age 3–4 weeks, then progressively more of it. At 4–5 weeks, the dives by the young are nearly as frequent and prolonged as in adults. Throughout the rearing period, the ♀ and brood seek safety in emergent vegetation more extensively than many other diving ducks. The young develop rapidly and sexual differences in feathering begin to be apparent at 4–5 weeks. At 6 weeks they are almost fully feathered and **initial flights** begin at or shortly after 7 weeks (usually between ages 49 and 55 days).

If the ♀ is nearing the flightless stage before the young are half adult size, the latter usually remain with her during that stage of molting; that is, under such conditions, the family group may remain intact after the ♀ has regained flight and the young are on the wing.

The total span of the rearing season was about 4 mo. on Me. and N.B. study areas; June 6 was the earliest recorded hatching, while flightless young still attended by the ♀ were observed in early Oct. HLM

SURVIVAL   Data from Me. and N.B., from Mendall (1958). The heaviest mortality occurs immediately after hatching and again at about age 3 weeks when the first independent wanderings of the young are noted. Brood sizes (using the age classification of Gollop and Marshall 1954): class I 7.0 young (488 records), II 6.0 (361 records), III 5.2

199

(141 records). Other N.B. data, not duplicated in the foregoing, from B. Wright (1954): Class I 6.6 young (123 records), II 6.4 (82 records), and III 6.0 (35 records). Chief causes of losses are exposure, accidents, and predation; the mink and snapping turtle are the most important known predators—also the easiest to identify so interpretation of the data must be qualified.

"Adult" losses during the breeding season are primarily from accidents and predation; spring muskrat trapping is a prime cause of the former. There is little evidence of mortality from diseases or parasites in the northeast. There is a differential mortality rate between the sexes, with ♀♀ more susceptible to loss. HLM

HABITS   (This section is based on Mendall 1958, including sources he cited.)

A gregarious species; even during nesting, there are many interludes of flocking and sharing of local space. As with various other waterfowl, where habitat is favorable, high breeding densities are maintained.

The Ringneck has many characteristics considered more typical of a surface feeder than a diving duck. Examples: it often swims with tail clear of the water; it rides high in the water; it can spring at a steep angle upward from water or nest; the Ringneck often soars and "towers" at a great height in typical Mallard or Black Duck fashion, the young usually are taken to thick vegetation for safety, rather than to open water as is usual with most divers; it often feeds on surface vegetation and occasionally (in Me.) is observed to up-end to feed, as well as to wallow in mud with Black Ducks seeking snails and other animal life. In the northeast it associates with the Black Duck and teals more than with diving ducks.

The Ringneck usually feeds where water is 2–5 ft. deep (Me. and N.B. data), while optimum depth at Seney Refuge in n. Mich. was only 2–3 ft. Occasionally it may feed in water 40 ft. deep according to Kortright (1942). Timed dives in Me. were 8–25 sec. with 10–15 sec. most common. Daily feeding routine is quite regular, the morning flights to feeding places only moderately early, near sunrise in Me. and in S.C.; they feed again in early to mid-afternoon, and there is evening feeding from shortly before sunset to dark. There are exceptions to this schedule; during the display period and early stages of nesting, and if bird is extensively hunted in a restricted area, feeding is intermittent all day. There is little evidence of feeding at night, but it has been observed in Me. during bright moonlight. The usual diet is rather restricted, with a few plant groups providing the bulk of food; nevertheless, it is quick to adapt to a changing environment, feeding in flooded grain fields at Calais, Me., and in newly flooded smartweed beds at Mt. Holly, S.C.

Curiosity is a well-developed trait, also trustfulness when not molested. The Ringneck is relatively "tame" at start of hunting, but becomes gun-shy and wary very quickly.

Flight is easy, sustained, very agile, and fast. The Ringneck is among the fastest flying of all N. Am. ducks, with several authors commenting on its speed.

A restlessness and wandering trait is well developed in the Ringneck; "pioneering," as discussed by Hochbaum (1955), is a characteristic which may in part be responsible for the recent expansion of breeding range.

The Ringneck has increased as a breeder, from Ont. eastward, from virtually

200

nothing prior to 1925 to a status of common to abundant in various areas. By the late 1950s, it was second in abundance to the Black Duck (among game species) in Me. and much of the Maritime Provinces. Judging from available sources, the number of birds breeding w. of the Rockies was declining. The midcontinent population was showing some slight changes, with marked annual fluctuations, and subsequently has expanded its distribution—as into Alaska. During the 1960s the ne. Ringneck subpopulation was known to be increasing. The midcontinent and ne. birds have overlapping winter ranges and evidently some exchange of individuals; generally speaking, however, the ne. breeding subpopulation may be considered as restricted outside the breeding season to the Atlantic coastal area and nearby inland. Maximum nesting densities on 13 study areas in Me. and N.B. varied from 1 pair per half acre to 1 in 112 acres. Adult sex ratios show considerable excess of drakes, varying from about 60: 40 on breeding areas to as high as 75: 25 at some wintering areas; there are, however, large gaps in information, plus differentials in migration of the sexes (see "Migration"), so the discrepancy may be more apparent than real. A sex differential in mortality has been mentioned earlier. Limited secondary sex ratios, from incubator hatches in Me., indicate a near 1:1 ratio. HLM

**FOOD** Seeds, bulbs, and succulent parts of waterlilies, pondweeds, sedges, grasses, and smartweeds; also aquatic insects and mollusks. Examination of 742 stomachs, mainly fall and winter in the south, showed 81.5% vegetable, and 18.5% animal matter (Cottam 1939).

**Vegetable** Seeds of waterlilies (*Brasenia, Nymphaea, Castalia*) 14.6%; seeds, rootstalks, tubers, and succulent parts of pondweeds (*Potamogeton, Najas, Ruppia, Haldule, Zannichellia*) 13.4%; seeds of sedges (*Eleocharis, Scirpus, Carex, Cladium, Cyperus, Rynchospora, Fimbristylis*) 8.3%; seeds of grasses (*Zizania, Zizaniopsis, Echinochloa, Panicum, Setaria*, etc.) 8.1%; smartweeds (*Polygonum*) 6.4%; muskgrasses (Characeae) and other algae 4.8%; delta duck potato (*Sagittaria platyphylla*) 3.8%; coontail (*Ceratophyllum demersum*) 3.6%; bur reeds (*Sparganium*) 1.3%; miscellaneous plants 17.0% (Cottam 1939).

In Me. and N.B., little difference in the amounts of vegetable food (av. 88%) and animal food (av. 12%) consumed in spring, summer, and fall. During these seasons the principal plants consumed are respectively: Cyperaceae, 39.9, 16.3, and 39.9%; Najadaceae, 17.9, 32.4, and 21.6%; Sparganiaceae, 13.3,——, and 8.6% (Mendall 1958). Bushy pondweeds (*Najas minor* and *N. flexilis*) formed principal food on lower Hudson R. (Foley and Taber 1951). The principal food items in the gullets and gizzards of 34 birds from the upper Chesapeake region were: vegetation and rootstalks of pondweeds (*Potamogeton* spp.) and naiad (*Najas* spp.); acorns (*Quercus palustris*); seeds of smartweed (*Polygonum punctatum*), rice cut-grass (*Leersia oryzoides*), spike rush (*Eleocharis quadrangulata*), and bur reed (*Sparganium americanum*) (R. E. Stewart 1962). Seeds of *Brasenia, Castalia, Polygonum, Ceratophyllum*, and *Eleocharis* form the important foods in Fla. (A. H. Howell 1932).

Analysis of the gizzard contents of 120 fall specimens from Ill. showed 66% plant and 34% animal matter. Seeds: *Ceratophyllum demersum* 17.41%; *Zea mays* 13.92%; *Potamogeton* spp. 13.86%; *Polygonum* spp. 6.19%; *Cyperus* spp. 3.94%; and miscellaneous 10.51% (H. G. Anderson 1959). The 59 gizzards from Mo. contained only 1.6% animal matter. The chief plant foods were the seeds of *Polygonum*, *Scirpus*, *Potamogeton*, and *Quercus* (Korschgen 1955). The 295 gizzards from Reelfoot Lake contained 82% plant and 18% animal matter. The principal plant foods were the seeds of *Potamogeton* spp., *Ceratophyllum demersum*, and *Nuphar advena* (Rawls 1958).

**Animal** Nymphs of damselflies and dragonflies (Odonata), larvae and cases of caddis flies (Trichoptera), larvae of midges (Chironomidae), water boatmen (Corixidae), diving beetles (Dytiscidae), etc.; mollusks, grastropods (*Goniobasis*, *Neritina*, *Mitrella*, *Planorbis*, *Amnicola*, etc.), and pelecypods; miscellaneous: fish, water mites, crabs, water fleas, amphipods, annelid worms, etc. (Cottam 1939). The Chesapeake birds had consumed Gastropoda (*Oxytrema virginica*), nymphs of Libelluloidae, and larvae of Trichoptera and Chironomidae; in Illinois, Mollusca 25% and Arthropoda 8.2%; and at Reelfoot Lake, Gastropoda 11.61%, Pelecypoda 3.33%, and Insecta 2.25%.

Stomachs of "juveniles" taken in Canada, mainly in July, contained 63% vegetable matter, largely *Zizania* and *Sparganium*; and 37% animal matter comprising insects of the orders Anisoptera, Trichoptera, Zygoptera, Hemiptera, and Coleoptera. Sixteen stomachs of downy young from Me. and N.B.: vegetable matter, Cyperaceae (principally *Scirpus torreyi* and *S. subterminalis*) 19.7%; horsetail (*Equisetum* sp.) 11%; bur reed (*Sparganium* sp.) 8.9%; pondweeds (*Potamogeton*) 6.5%; and miscellaneous 5.3%. Animal matter, caddis flies (Trichoptera) 23%; beetles (Chrysomelidae, Haliplidae, Curculionidae, Elateridae) 13.5%; bugs (Gerridae, Corixidae) 5.5%; nymphs of dragonflies (Anisoptera) and damselflies (Zygoptera), 4.9%; miscellaneous 1.8% (Mendall 1958). AWS

### Tufted Duck

*Aythya fuligula* (Linnaeus)

Small diving duck, a member of the scaup group but, in N. Am., most likely to be confused with the Ring-necked Duck *A. collaris* (which is a pochard). The Tufted's "tuft" actually is a tassel, pendant from the occiput, in fullest development (Def. Alt. Plumage) to about 2½ in. long in the ♀. Bill small and not much broadened; in dorsal view the feathering projects the same distance forward on top of bill as on sides. Speculum area white (not gray as in the Ringneck). Sexually dimorphic in color (beginning with downies) and pattern; after early life, there is appreciable sex difference in eye color.

all birds in Def. Alt. Plumage

The bill of the Tufted has very little white, close to the tip (it is a broad band, farther back, in the Ringneck); the head is very round in lateral profile, with or without "tuft" at rear (in the Ringneck in Alt. Plumage the crown is heightened, there is a slight indentation at the occiput, and no pendant feathering); in the drake Tufted the white of underparts extends to include the sides and also projects upward somewhat at forward end of folded wing (in the Ringneck the gray ventral surface pales on upper sides to white and this projects upward strikingly, beyond folded wing toward dorsum).

Differences among Plumages of the Tufted, rather than differences from other *Aythya* species, are emphasized below. In specimen identification, bill size and shape are diagnostic of the species.

Beginning with Latham and Romsey (1798), the tracheal apparatus of the drake has been described and/or illus. repeatedly. The "bony box-like portion of it [the bulla] 'is elevated' and not otherwise to be distinguished from that of the Scaup [*A. marila*] except by its smaller size" (J. C. Phillips 1925). The best illus. are 2 views of the bulla in Schiøler (1926).

Length ♂ to about 17 in., ♀ to about 16; wingspread of ♂ to about 27 in., ♀ to 25; usual wt. of ♂ 1½–1¾ lb., ♀ 1¼–1½. No subspecies.

DESCRIPTION   The usual *Aythya* pattern—2 Plumages in definitive cycle in both sexes, with the ♀ molting from Alt. back into Basic head–body in spring. Both sexes, usually before the end of the calendar year of hatching, have 3 feather generations—Juv., which is succeeded early by Basic I, then this by Alt. I. The ♀

203

Tufted varies considerably in color and pattern, also there is variation in timing (including duration) of molting. The Juv. Plumage and its development are well known, but the succeeding predefinitive stages commonly are misunderstood. The following treatment is terse, but considerable variation is mentioned.

▶ ♂ Def. Alt. Plumage (all feathering excepting the tail and all but a few innermost feathers of the wing), acquired in LATE SUMMER–FALL or sometimes from then into early winter and retained until following SUMMER. **Bill** slaty blue, often lightening somewhat distally, then a subterminal narrow white line and black tip; **iris** orange-yellow to a vivid yellow; **head** (including pendant tuft) and neck black, the head–neck with violet-magenta sheen; some have white on chin and/or white feathers in forepart of face; **upperparts** black, generally with extensive fine pale dotting, and greenish sheen; underparts breast black, the very tips of the feathers white (they wear off); **underparts** belly, sides, and flanks white, occasionally with dusky dotting especially on flanks; abdomen white, grading posteriorly to dusky; vent to tail black, or occasionally with white area included; legs and **feet** slaty blue with dark joints and webs; in the **wing** the next to innermost secondary has white outer and dusky inner web, the innermost is black with some greenish sheen (and both are longer and narrower distally than in Basic); the longest coverts overlying them also are black with sheen; remainder of wing and the tail are retained Basic feathering.

▶ ♂ Def. Basic Plumage (entire feathering), then head–body acquired in SUMMER and retained a few weeks at most; then, while this is being succeeded by incoming Alt. (which also includes innermost feathers of wing) the new Basic tail and wing grow. **Head** and neck brownish black, often with scattered whitish showing on chin and/or throat and foreneck (these feathers are light except terminally); no "tuft"; **dorsum** very dark, with fine white dotting and slight greenish sheen; **underparts** breast blackish brown, the feathers edged white distally; sides and flanks browner, sometimes with intermingled white feathers (the brown feathers vermiculated pale, the white ones darkish); abdomen much the same except white predominates; vent to tail mostly dark; **tail** black (it fades toward brownish), the feathers with broadly rounded ends.

**Wing** primaries very dark, their inner webs paler and this extends to outer web of inner primaries; secondaries white with black ends (a black stripe at trailing edge of wing), the innermost secondaries evenly dark, not as long as in Alt., and with broadly rounded ends; upper coverts sooty black, with some greenish sheen when feathers are new, and the smaller ones generally have very fine buffy yellow dots; wing lining mostly white, but some dark near leading edge; axillars white, usually dotted dusky distally.

▶ ♀ Def. Alt. Plumage (all feathering, excepting the tail and all but a few innermost feathers of wing), acquired in LATE SUMMER–FALL or sometimes into early winter, and retained into LATE WINTER–SPRING. **Bill** slaty gray (darkish to palish), quite often with a very small amount of white adjoining the very end, which is black. **Iris** vivid to slightly brownish yellow. **Head** and neck vary as follows: generally a sepia brown with some black-tipped feathers intermingled, the crown and pendant "tuft" (which varies from short but obvious to 1½ in. long) nearer black; in some, however, the head–neck–tuft are much more ♂-like, i.e., are almost entirely black with pronounced violet or violet-magenta sheen on head–neck; quite commonly there is some white at sides and top of base of bill (area sharply defined), but rarely as extensive as the white facial front in Def. Alt. ♀ Lesser and Greater scaups; more commonly, there is a white spot or patch on chin. **Upperparts** mostly a blackish brown with some greenish gloss, various feathers margined cinnamon, and some are finely dotted white; in more ♂-like individuals the dorsum varies to black with very marked greenish sheen; lower back to tail very dark; **underparts** upper breast generally concolor with lower neck, but farther down the feathers commonly are edged cinnamon broadly, and on lower breast they are edged whitish; sides and flanks a more brownish sepia, the feathers with lighter (even to yellowish brown) margins; belly white (sometimes dark feathers intermixed, though usually this is a stage of molting from Basic to Alt., i.e., in fall); the underlying down is a gray-brown (not sooty); vent to tail (a) darkish, with or without some fine white markings, or (b) white. **Wing** innermost secondaries elongated, tapering at ends, and nearly black or with some white on outer web of next to innermost one, and the overlying coverts nearly black. The tail and remainder of wing are retained Basic feathering.

▶ ♀ Def. Basic Plumage (entire feathering), the head–body acquired in LATE WINTER–SPRING, the tail and wing not until LATE SUMMER or EARLY FALL (concurrently with molting of head–body and innermost feathers of wing back into Alt.). A muted Plumage. The feathers have broadly rounded ends and fairly wide lighter (brownish) margins most obvious on dorsum and sides. No "tuft." **Head** varies with individual from all dark to same with feathers close to side of bill white grading into dark of cheeks (not an abrupt change); the light area varies from conspicuous to much reduced to barely indicated, depending on the individual. Pronounced variation in this Plumage also involves overall coloring, from quite brownish to sepia (and after wear and bleaching some individuals are quite yellowish brown), and ventral pattern—the belly white in some, or same intermixed with same color as breast and sides, or all of underparts dark (the feathers uniformly colored or with some indication of broad barring) or with a mere indication of white on belly. The nest down is nearly black (sooty) with somewhat lighter centers.

**Wing** about as ♂, but browner; there is less dark on ends of secondaries (narrower dark stripe along trailing edge of wing); innermost secondaries shorter than in Alt., with broadly rounded ends, and evenly dark, as also the overlying coverts.

NOTE The blotching on the venter of some ♀♀ in late summer is a result of abrasion of light feather ends, exposing their darker basal portions.

AT HATCHING According to Veselovsky (1953): ♂—cheeks completely dark; ♀—cheeks more or less yellowish with dark zones and spots. In both sexes, iris gray, bill dark brownish with fleshy red nail. Rather complicated but blended pattern and somber coloring. Much of head and dorsum some variant of brownish olive, paling on underparts to a yellowish; also see text in Witherby (1939) and col. pl. in Heinroth and Heinroth (1928). Legs and feet bluish gray, joints and webs very dark.

▶ ♂ Juv. Plumage (entire feathering), well developed by age 7 weeks, but some further growth of wing quills and other feathers. The eye of the ♂ is a more vivid yellow than that of the ♀ by age 35 days (Kear 1970). Apparently by age 8–9 weeks the drake starts molting into Basic I, but most of the Juv. wing is retained into following summer. The **bill** becomes bluish gray. **Head** and neck dark brownish (darker than in ♀); no "tuft." Some white may be present near side base of bill and on chin from about 5th week of age (E. H. Gillham 1957). **Upperparts** dark, the feathers narrow and with cinnamon margins; scapulars and feathers of lower back finely dotted white. **Underparts** breast feathers patterned predominantly darkish but with somewhat streaky effect, and this grades into belly which is predominantly white but still more or less streaky (not plain); sides and under-tail area also patterned.

The transition from downy to the Juv.-feathered stage was described by Veselovsky (1953) and again by Kear (1970), both indicating some differences between the sexes.

▶ ♀ Juv. Plumage (entire feathering), timing as ♂ (Kear 1970); **bill** dark brownish, **iris** brownish yellow (by age 35 days obviously not as vivid as ♂ of same age), **head**–neck lighter brownish than ♂ Juv.; remainder of feathering essentially as ♂, including streaky venter.

▶ ♂ Basic I Plumage (all feathering, excepting all but a few innermost feathers of wing) begins, when or soon after the young bird first can fly, to succeed the Juv. feathering; much of it is retained until some time in FALL (to age about 14 weeks posthatching), the tail grows last (see below).

**Head**–neck dark brownish; sometimes there is a slight indentation at occiput, but no pendant "tuft." **Upperparts** very dark, unmarked or with a few whitish vermiculations. **Underparts** upper breast concolor with neck, then farther down the feathers have increasing amount of white (barred white and dark area), then the belly white (earliest white-bellied Plumage); feathers on sides light with dusky brownish areas or vermiculations; posteriorly on abdomen there is a transition to white streaked dusky, then predominantly dusky on rear sides of body and vent to tail; **tail** feathers dark gray-brown with rounded ends (the Basic I tail feathers succeed the notched Juv. ones at any time from late fall to midwinter, rarely later). Innermost feathers of **wing** as ♂ Def. Basic, the remainder being retained Juv.

NOTE This feather generation (Plumage) generally has not been recognized as such, but instead regarded as Juv. or as a stage in molting, supposedly from Juv. to Alt. I (of 1st winter). Veselovsky (1953) was correct in reporting 3 different feather generations on the flanks (the 2nd is Basic I), but he did not fully diagnose this Plumage. For ventral views of good examples of Basic I, see figs. 2 and 3 on col. pl. facing p. 48 in Millais (1913a). Since the molt out of Basic I (and into Alt. I) begins with the head–neck, there are specimens largely in Basic I but having the rudiments of a "tuft" from incoming Alt. I; see upper left fig. on pl. 14 in Schiøler (1926).

▶ ♂ Alt. I Plumage (all feathering, excepting the tail and all but a few innermost feathers of wing), acquired in LATE FALL–EARLY WINTER (begins to appear at 14–16 weeks posthatching) and retained into following SUMMER. Earliest Plumage having black **head**–neck, a "tuft" at occiput, and white upper sides. **Upperparts** essentially as ♂ Def. Alt.; **underparts** breast very dark brown to black (individual variation), the lower part sometimes alternating light and dark rather than a clear transition from blackish breast to white of belly and sides; abdomen, going posteriorly, there is increasingly more dusky coloring (largely barring) to vent area; then vent to tail very dark in some individuals and white in others. The Basic I tail is retained. **Wing** innermost secondaries and their longer overlying coverts as ♂ Def. Alt.; the remainder is still-retained Juv. feathering.

206

NOTE    Occasional individuals are "tardy" or have an interrupted molt; that is, they are not fully into Alt. I until some time in winter or even not until spring.

▶    ♀ Basic I Plumage (all feathering excepting all but innermost feathers of wing), timing as ♂ Basic I, i.e., much of it succeeds the Juv. early and rapidly. **Head**, neck, upper breast, and sides brownish, at least the head–neck averaging lighter than in ♂ Basic I, and generally a roundish or oval white patch (varies from vaguely to clearly defined) at side base of bill. No "tuft." **Underparts** belly and much of abdomen white and, posteriorly, becomes streaked or somewhat barred dusky; vent to tail generally mixed whitish and dusky (predominantly latter). **Tail** dusky. **Wing** innermost secondaries plain dark and broad distally, their overlying coverts dark (remainder of wing is retained Juv.)

NOTES    The "♀ Juv." on pl. 13 in Schiøler (1926) actually is in white-bellied Basic I Plumage.

Although a plain white belly is typical of this Plumage, some ♀ ♀ have varying numbers of dusky feathers throughout the venter, forming a more or less blotchy pattern.

▶    ♀ Alt. I Plumage (all feathering excepting the tail and all but innermost feathers of wing), generally acquired in NOV.—DEC., i.e., beginning 14–16 weeks posthatching; retained only until LATE WINTER–SPRING. This Plumage is very like ♀ Def. Alt., with similar individual variation to considerable ♂-like coloring. A roundish or oval white patch at side base of bill, foreshadowed by the same in Basic I, is common and is sharply defined. This is the earliest ♀ Plumage having a pendant occipital "tuft" and it varies in individuals from nearly absent to well over an inch long. Tail is retained Basic I, innermost feathers of wing as ♀ Def. Alt. (the remainder is retained Juv.).

▶    ♀ Basic II Plumage (entire feathering), head–body acquired in LATE WINTER or SPRING, or sometimes from then into early summer, the tail and almost all of the wing not until late SUMMER or FALL (at which time the other Basic II feathering is being succeeded by Alt. II). Basic II is like succeeding Basics and shows much wear and fading by the time the ♀ is tending her brood. This is the last Plumage with which any Juv. feathering (most of the wing) is worn.

**Measurements** of specimens from widely scattered localities 11 ♂: BILL 39–42 mm., av. 40.9; WING 198–212, av. 204; TAIL 51–56, av. 53.4; TARSUS 34–36, av. 35; 10 ♀: BILL 37–43 mm., av. 40.2; WING 186–208, av. 199; TAIL (of 9) 51–59, av. 52.5; TARSUS 34–36, av. 35 (ETS).

For series with WING meas. over the curve, see Witherby (1939).

The Juv. WING is shorter than the Basic wing; these are averages of series, from Schiøler (1926): ♂ 197.9 vs. 202, ♀ 190 vs. 194.8.

For comparative meas. of the bills of the parent species of *Aythya* alongside those of Greater Scaup × Tufted and Common Pochard × Tufted crosses, see Sage (1963a).

**Weight** ♂ about 500–900 gm. (usually about 700), ♀ 400–850 (usually about 600). For data by sex and season for U.S.S.R. localities see Isakov (in Dementiev and Gladkov 1952); for the same fall–spring in s. France see Hoffmann and Muzzucchi (in Bauer and Glutz von Blotzheim 1969).

On day of hatching, 100 weighed 30–43 gm., the mean being 35.3 gm. (Kear 1970).

**Hybrids**    The Tufted has crossed both in the wild and in captivity with Common Pochard (*Aythya ferina*), Ferruginous White-eye (*A. nyroca*), and Greater Scaup (*A.*

*marila*); the hybrids are fertile. It also has crossed in captivity with *Aix* (1 species), *Anas* (6), *Aythya* (3 additional species), *Bucephala* (2), and *Netta* (2) (Gray 1958). Even in the wild, ♂ Tufteds have been seen copulating with ♀ Mallards (Clegg 1971). This list of hybrids now is incomplete.

The literature on hybrids that include Tufted Duck parentage is quite extensive; the reader is referred especially to E. H. Gillham et al. (1966), both text and illus., for crosses within the genus *Aythya*. Among first-generation hybrids they described the following: Common Pochard × Tufted = "Lesser Scaup type," "Pochard type," and "Tufted Duck type"; Greater Scaup × Tufted = "Scaup type"; and Tufted × Ferruginous White-eye = "Baer's Pochard type." The study was based almost entirely on ♂ hybrids. There can be little doubt that different Plumages and stages of molting, plus ♀ hybrids, plus various possible backcrosses, would add up to a bewildering spectrum of variation. For ♀ hybrids of Common Pochard (*A. ferina*) × Tufted Duck, see Harrison and Harrison (1970); they are scauplike.

There were sightings in 1965 and 1967, thought to be of a different individual each year, of "Scaup type" (Greater Scaup × Tufted) hybrid near Reykjavik, Iceland. Bengtson (1968) reported seeing 16 Tufted Duck–Greater Scaup mixed pairs at Mývatn, Iceland; in 14 the drake was a Tufted Duck and 2 of these were accompanied by both a ♀ Greater Scaup and a ♀ Tufted.

**Geographical variation** none reported. RSP

FIELD IDENTIFICATION   All scaups, but especially the Tufted Duck have seemingly foreshortened bodies. The drake's pattern most of the year is sharply defined and very contrasty: white sides and ventral midsection and black elsewhere except part of spread wing. The white does extend up the forward sides, but not as prominently as in ♂ Ringneck (which is a pochard, not a scaup). The head is very round (less so when feathers are sleeked down) and, at close enough range for the appended "tuft" to be visible, one may also note a near-absence of white in the bill.

The head of the ♀, from fall to late winter, varies from having no white facial front (commonly) to having an appreciable one (rarely as large as typical say of Lesser Scaup). The very front of the face is light in the ♀ Ringneck, but this grades into dark and, at a range where it is visible, a white subterminal band shows on the bill. Females of Lesser and Greater Scaup in fall to late winter typically have much white adjoining unicolor bill, and most of the mantle is much lighter than the ends of the body.

Various diving ducks, especially the scaup group, rest high on the water but have less buoyancy (tail nearly flush with surface) between dives when feeding. The undertail area, which can be seen in the high position, is dark in some ♀ Tufteds and light in others; it is typically quite light in ♀ Ringneck and dark in Lesser and Greater Scaup. These are differences from late fall to late winter.

When active, the Tufted is a very lively bird. Except when breeding, it occurs in flocks, sometimes in large assemblies. Stragglers commonly associate with other *Aythya* species. Although "dumpy" in appearance when idle, the Tufted is very trim in flight. Then the secondaries show much white, with black rear border (the Ringneck has grayish speculum area).

See the preceding section for other Plumages and for additional variation in the ♀.
RSP

VOICE   Generally silent except during displays. The ♂ has a hoarse *whee-oo* uttered during Head-throw and Kinked-neck displays, also a rapid, whistled, 3-syllabled call that is rather drawn-out at end, uttered during Coughing display; the ♀ utters a soft *karr* when Inciting and has been heard uttering a *quack* or *gack*. For further information see Veselovsky (1953) and Johnsgard (1965).

In preflight young the sexes were becoming distinguishable by voice at age 37 days and, by the 44th day, all ♀ ♀ were uttering the "adult" *karr* call, while drakes were squeaky (Kear 1970). RSP

HABITAT   Essentially as Lesser Scaup but some breed at larger (including marine) waters. RSP

DISTRIBUTION   The relevant literature on this bird is most interesting, but can only be touched on here. The Palearctic breeding range was mapped in considerable detail in the revised (1963) edition of Voous; both breeding and winter ranges (which overlap) were described by Vaurie (1965). This species has been extending its breeding range both w. and n. in Europe and thereabouts for over a hundred years; there are various relevant papers, especially Arnhem (1959). Atkinson-Willes (1969) mapped winter distribution and density in the Brit. Isles; Moreau (1967) discussed occurrence in Africa; and Brodkorb (1964a) listed records from the Pleistocene and from archeological sites in Europe.

**Outside our area**   Off the European mainland, and omitting history of occurrence and spread in the Brit. Isles, the following are of interest. A pair was seen on Bear I. in June–July 1932 and a single bird in W. Spitzbergen on June 13, 1968. The first breeding record for the Faeroes was in 1966. The species was first noted in Iceland in 1895, it bred in some numbers at Mývatn in the years 1904–08, and it continued to increase and to extend its range in Iceland; widespread and locally common breeder by 1950 (Gudmundsson 1951); now widespread in lowland areas and possibly still increasing in numbers. It is know from band recoveries that Icelandic birds migrate to the Brit. Isles, also to localities from s. Norway to Portugal, but most of them winter in Ireland.

In the N. Pacific area this species breeds in Kamchatka, also on the mainland northward e. to about long. 165° E, and has occurred in summer in the Commander Is.; authors usually state "probably breeds" there. Apparently it has not been recorded on the Chuckchee Pen., but Schaaning (cited in Portenko 1972) reported 4 downy young taken June 27, 1915, on Wrangel I.!

In the cent. n. Pacific there are 1959 and 1963 records for Sand I. in Midway Atoll and 1963, 1964, and 1965 occurrences at Green I. in Kure Atoll; the dates range from Oct. 30 to Jan. 7 and most of the birds were sick, emaciated, or found dead (Clapp and Woodward 1968).

**In our area**   It must be kept in mind that the Tufted Duck is a favorite of aviculturalists and that some birds have escaped into the wild. For example, see Gochfeld (1968), also Bull (1964), who reported the escape of 2 individuals. Yet it is obvious that the species also has occurred naturally. Recent reports of sightings (as of 1972 there was no breeding record) are so scattered that surely some have been missed in preparing the following summary.

ATLANTIC   There are a few fall records for sw. Greenland, beginning in 189, also one for May 1948 (Salomonsen 1967a).

Mass.—Marshfield, early 1954 (tame); Newburyport, early 1954, 2 seen (shy); Falmouth and Carver, early 1963, pair; C. Cod (Falmouth and thereabouts), regular, 1 or 2 birds in winter–spring since1963; Conn.—at least 2 records for 1971; N.Y.—greater N.Y. area, singles in late 1955, early 1962, and early 1966 (all possibly escapees) and other records subsequently including 4 throughout winter of 1971–72 (earlier records summarized by Post 1968), and se. L. Ontario, one in spring of 1971 at Nine Mile Point; N.J.—Bayhead area, drake in late Feb. 1972.

BERING–PACIFIC   Alaska—undoubtedly, J. C. Phillips (1925) was correct that the birds Turner (1886) reported as having occurred at St. Michael and on Amchitka and in winter on Attu were Tufted Ducks instead of Ringnecks.

In the Pribilofs, May 9, 1911 (specimen); seen there on several occasions in spring and fall, specimens June 7 and Oct. 7 in 1961, and a pair seen June 3–4, 1962 (Sladen 1966). In the Aleutians, at Attu—2 ♂ and 2 ♀ seen in May, 1945; on Amchitka—both sexes now regular in small numbers, sometimes in pairs and presumably mated; at Adak—various records beginning in the late 1960s, mostly fall–winter, but also both sexes present into summer beginning in 1970, with maximum of 6 birds at any one time (spring 1971).

B.C.—at Vancouver, young ♂ seen Nov. 4, 1961; at Victoria, a drake in late March 1970; and a drake at Saltspring I. on Feb. 9, 1972. Wash.—Seattle, one in Dec. 1967, Jan. 1969, and Jan.–March 1970. Ore.—♂ photographed at Portland and present Feb. 14–March 26, 1960. Cal.—Alameda Co., ♂ shot some time between Dec. 23, 1948, and Jan. 8, 1949; Arcata, drake in spring and fall 1968; Palo Alto area, drake early Feb.–early March 1971; the area around San Francisco produced various records in winter of 1971–72 (for good photo see *Am. Birds* **26** 650. 1972).

INTERIOR   Wyo.—7 mi. w. of Laramie, ♂ seen April 10, 1966. RSP

OTHER TOPICS   This species, which occurs farther n. in Eurasia in winter than the Common Pochard, is not an early spring **migrant** and is a decidedly **late nester**, these being *Aythya* characteristics. In both sexes, the majority **first breed** at age 1 year. For displays, see Bezzel (1968) and papers he cited. There is a tendency toward **colonial nesting**, although isolated nests are common. Preferred places are islands and islets in lakes, ponds, and rivers, also marine is. (as in the Baltic), and mainland shores. The site typically is concealed (more so as vegetation grows), close to water, or above very shallow water, or sometimes on matted floating vegetation. Commonly they are among reeds or under bushes, but some are fully exposed on stranded flotsam or on rocky ground or turf. Most nests are on a firm substrate. The Tufted commonly nests in gull and tern colonies; see discussion by G. Bergman (1957). Material is obtained at the site, also nearby if a nest in shallows must be built up to escape rising waters. Old sites are used again, by the same or other individuals. During and after laying the very dark **nest down**, with intermingled small feathers (usually darkish, with white ends), is added, seldom in large quantity.

Probably "normal" **clutch size** is 7–10 eggs; at Mývatn, Iceland, the mean of means for a very large number of clutches in the years 1961–70 inclusive was 10.06 ± 0.06

210

(Bengtson 1971c). Especially in semicolonial situations, however, there are ♀♀ that lay in the nests of others; up to 14 eggs are common, over twice that number occur occasionally, and there are "dump" sites where many eggs are deposited and never incubated. The eggs are large for the size of the ♀, averaging about 58 × 41 mm.; when fresh they are palish olive (greenish), with little sheen. **Incubation period** usually 24 or 25 days, but see Mednis (1968) for variation from 23 to 29 days. There are detailed observations by E. H. Gillham (1958, also papers he cited) on rearing period, etc., from observations in St. James's Park, London, which are more or less applicable to other localities. He found that the ♀ usually leaves the young by the time they are 6 weeks old (before they can fly), but her time of departure to molt varies from a few days after hatching on. Some ♀♀ remain through the wing molt (flightless period estimated to last 30–32 days), hence are associated with broods much longer. There does not seem to be a strong drive for broods to gather into bands, but the extent of combining may vary with circumstances. Growth of captive young has been described by Veselovsky (1953) and in greater detail by Kear (1970). Veselovsky gave **age at first flight** as 59 days; E. H. Gillham (1958) calculated it at 7–8 weeks; and the graph in Kear (1970) shows a reversal (to a decline) in wt. at 7–8 weeks, this being about the time the young become able to lift themselves off the ground, although their flight feathers are not yet fully grown. For further data on reproduction, see Frederickson (1968) for details of the parasitic habit, and Havlin (1966), Mednis (1968), and Mihelsons et al. (1968) for all other facets of reproductive biology. Mihelsons et al. found that banded ♀♀ had the highest reproductive success in their 2nd nesting season; in older birds it was lower.

During laying or (usually) incubation, drakes depart and form small groups, some of which molt on open water nearby, but many have a **molt migration.** Evidently they seldom go more than perhaps 150 mi. (although this extends summer distribution that much n. of breeding places), and probably most go to the nearest suitable molting area—a shallow lake, quiet stretch of river, or the sea (Baltic, Okhotsk Sea). Apparently there are seldom as many as 2,000 individuals at a locality, smaller gatherings than are common in some other *Aythya*, and commonly they are more or less intermingled with other molting waterfowl. Peak numbers of molting drakes may be expected at the end of July and early in Aug.

**Fall migration** begins in Sept. and is protracted, into Dec.; unusually cold weather causes additional movement at least into midwinter. The considerable segregation of sexes in molting adults (some ♀♀ join the ♂♂) results in great variation in sex ratio subsequently at different times and localities. There also appears to be a tendency for ♀♀ and young to migrate farther than mature drakes, as in various other *Aythya*. Movements from late winter on must result in at least a temporarily more balanced sex ratio to facilitate mate selection.

There are many interesting accounts of the habits of this bird, including the useful earlier ones by Millais (1913a) and J. C. Phillips (1925). This duck is in some respects intermediate between shoal-water ducks and sea ducks. Its **food** is quite largely animal—mollusks (especially various snails), insects, fish eggs and small fishes, tadpoles, etc., and parts of aquatic plants. The subject of food has been covered by Madsen (1954) and both food and feeding habits by Olney (1963b). A bird taken in the Pribilofs had eaten grass, "cress," small seeds, and a few larvae (Evermann 1913). AWS RSP

## Lesser Scaup

*Aythya affinis* (Eyton)

Rather small diving duck, the smaller of the 2 species of scaup commonly called "bluebill" or "broadbill" in N. Am.; smaller (usually) than Greater Scaup; bill has smaller nail (width under 7 mm.—usually appears to be about half as wide as nail of Greater Scaup); bill widens distally and laterally (shape toward spatulate); it is unicolor (as in Greater Scaup) or without clear-cut pattern (it is patterned in the Ringneck); head profile in life not roundish as Greater Scaup but instead (because of somewhat elongated crown feathers, especially in ♂) rather "bumpy," highest toward rear of crown (it is highest toward forecrown in the Ringneck); primaries grayish or buffy brownish (in most Greater Scaups the white area of secondaries continues outward beyond onto the primaries); the dark area along trailing edge of speculum is even in width (does not

Lesser Scaup        Greater Scaup

taper distally as in Greater Scaup). Sexually dimorphic in feathering, especially Alt. Plumage, and to a considerable degree in eye color, the ♂ orange-yellow after early age, the ♀ changing from darkish (as a yearling) to olive-yellow or yellow (at 3 years). The drake in Def. Alt. Plumage has predominantly violet iridescence on head (it is green in the Greater Scaup). General pattern as Greater Scaup, but Alt.-Plumaged drake usually has more dark on sides (amount is variable in both species), ♀ has narrower white facial "front" when it is present (but numerous individuals lack it).

Based on definitive-feathered individuals: ♂ nostril to tip of bill less than 29.5 mm., width of nail on bill 7 mm. or less, flattened wing 212 mm. or less; and ♀ 29 mm. or less, 6.5 or less, and 205 or less. All these are less than those for Greater Scaup (which see), but further sampling perhaps may reveal some overlap.

The drake's tracheal apparatus seems not to have been described, unless that of "scaup" in A. Wilson (1829) was of this species and not *A. marila*.

212

The sexes differ in av. meas. and wt. Length ♂ 16½–18½ in., ♀ 15–17¾, wing-spread ♂ 27–31, ♀ 27–30½, usual wt. of ♂ slightly under 2 lb., the ♀ about 1¾. No subspecies.

DESCRIPTION   Two Plumages/cycle in both sexes. In both of our scaups the tail is molted only once/cycle (as is most of the wing). The ♀ Lesser in most Plumages, and perhaps the ♂ in predefinitive Plumages, have much more individual variation in coloring than generally reported.

▶   ♂ Def. Alt. Plumage (all feathering except tail and most of wing), acquired in FALL (mainly Sept. into Oct., but some individuals are molting into WINTER) and retained into following SUMMER (white on flanks generally still conspicuous in July). **Bill** pale bluish with very dark nail; **iris** orange-yellow or vivid yellow. **Head** and neck black with violet iridescence; some drakes have a small white chin spot; **upperparts** upper back and rump black; mantle and scapulars white with coarse blackish brown vermiculations (the effect lighter than typical of ♂ Alt. I); **underparts** breast black, this ending transversely, and dark feathers near the lower edge usually with narrow white margins (they wear off); belly white, becoming grayish and somewhat vermiculated blackish brown near vent; sides and flanks white and vary from heavily vermiculated dark (usually) to only slightly vermiculated or even almost unmarked; under-tail area black; legs and **feet** usually a dusky or grayed greenish, the webs much darker. Tail is retained Basic feathering, as is the wing except innermost feathers. The elongated innermost secondaries (which are acquired late during molting) tend to be longer and more tapering than in Basic and are dark, finely flecked or vermiculated light; any new coverts over these are similarly flecked.

▶   ♂ Def. Basic Plumage (entire feathering), head–body acquired in summer, generally beginning in LATE JUNE, with heavy molting in July–Aug.; in FALL (beginning some time in Sept., before the Basic is completed by full growth of flight feathers of wing), the head–body begin losing Basic and acquiring Alt. (but in some the body–molt is later); most of the Basic wing and the tail are worn into the following SUMMER.

The **bill** becomes darker when Basic is worn, except for lighter subterminal band (Pirnie 1928). **Head** and neck dingy brownish to blackish, except chin, and often some feathering elsewhere around base of bill, whitish; lower neck not as dark as upper neck; **upperparts** general shade of mantle, including scapulars, dark (rather brownish, heavily marked with blackish); **underparts** upper breast buffy brown, not terminating sharply at lower margin; sides and flanks have much brownish, belly usually white or whitish, mottled darker. **Tail** blackish brown. **Wing** primaries a variant of buffy brown with tips and outer vanes of the 3 outermost feathers blackish brown; almost all secondaries white with very narrow black exposed border and broad blackish ends the latter quite commonly more or less flecked white; innermost secondaries have broadly rounded ends and are unmarked blackish; greater coverts nearly black with or without white flecking (often without on distal ones); middle and lesser coverts heavily flecked or vermiculated light on blackish background; underside of wing and axillars as in Greater Scaup.

The Prebasic molt on head–body begins early, before the drake leaves his incubating mate to go to a large water area (where he becomes flightless later during this molt), according to Hochbaum (1944). The same author also stated that, in captivity, birds 1–3 years old have a complete Prebasic molt but that it is incomplete in some older birds—that is, they retain some Alt. feathers through the Basic stage and until the next (Pre-alternate) molt. Various *Aythya* frequently do not molt in normal fashion in captivity, however.

The duration of the flightless period has been estimated as between 2 and 3 weeks (McKnight and Buss 1962), probably being at least 3 weeks.

▶ ♀ Def. Alt. Plumage (all feathering except, in wing, only a few innermost feathers, and the tail), acquired in FALL (or beginning earlier in prebreeders and nonbreeders) and, in some individuals, molting continues into early WINTER. This feathering is succeeded by Basic in SPRING.

**Bill** muted bluish (shade varies) with dark nail; **iris** usually yellow. **Head** individuals vary from (a) area of face around bill white and sharply defined, remainder of head down to foreneck and breast dark (variant of chestnut or sepia); to (b) entire head rather light (variant of buffy brown); any individual may have some white feathers or small patches on head–neck, especially nape (from injury to skin; compare with ♀ Redhead). **Upperparts** apparently vary correspondingly: (a) birds having most of the head dark have much of mantle dark flecked whitish or variably off-white with dark wavy lines or vermiculations, seldom clearly indicated (may be somewhat clearer on scapulars), total effect—upper midsection of body somewhat lighter than the ends (reflects pattern of drake); and (b) if head is light and plain, then most of remainder of body is light and plain or nearly so (some variant of buffy brown); throughout range (a–b) of variation, sides and flanks rich dark brownish, a broad darker terminal zone of the feathers vermiculated white. **Underparts** belly white (the individual feathers are all-white), abdomen somewhat grayish brown, under-tail area very dark and generally somewhat vermiculated white. The ventral down is lighter (grayish) than the nest down acquired in spring. Legs and feet some variant of bluish gray, webs dusky. **Tail** apparently retained Basic feathering. Wing retained Basic except: any new innermost elongated secondaries are plain, dark, seldom having sparse light flecking near tips, and any new overlying greater coverts are finely flecked white distally and near (but not to) edges.

▶ ♀ Def. Basic Plumage (entire feathering), head–body usually acquired beginning in EARLY SPRING (much molting in March), but some individuals have this portion of the molt prolonged into April or even May; this feathering is retained into EARLY FALL, when the Prebasic molt is concluded by growth of new Basic wing and tail, and concurrently or beginning not long after, the head–body begin molting back into Alt.

**Bill** becomes dark grayish. Possibly the iris darkens. **Head** usually has facial "front" mixed brownish and white, hence not clearly defined, but some lack it, and many individuals with or without it have a poorly defined whitish auricular patch; remainder plus upper neck a dark brownish (individuals vary) more or less mottled lighter; lower neck usually medium fuscous; **upperparts** foreback near medium fuscous, mantle darkish brown, finely and variably vermiculated white, rump dark; **underparts** upper breast some variant of buffy brown (quite dark), some feathers much darker and with white ends (and some individuals also have feathers with faint white vermiculations), lower breast and most of belly white (the concealed portions of the feathers are gray), posteriorly becoming pale and grayish brown; feathers on sides and flanks brownish (lighter than in Alt. Plumage) with quite light ends (to white flanks), which frequently become much abraded; under-tail area dark brownish (varies with individual). **Tail** dark brownish olive.

**Wing** general pattern as ♂; the dark coloring largely fuscous; innermost secondaries have rounded ends and generally are plain dark (sometimes slightly flecked white terminally); greater coverts vary with individual from plain dark to same flecked white; middle and lesser coverts flecked light (densest near terminal margins); white margin at trailing edge of wing [compare with ♂]; underwing as Greater Scaup—lining white, except primary under-coverts medium gray and some light-margined dark feathers adjoining leading edge; axillars white.

NOTE    A few ♀ ♀ have ♂-like characters; for example, head–neck (except for white facial "front") as dark as ♂ Alt. I.

AT HATCHING    See vol. 2, col. pl. facing p. 466. See under Greater Scaup for comparison of Lesser with that species and with the Ring-necked Duck.

▶    ♂ Juv. Plumage (entire feathering), worn rather briefly after it is fully grown at estimated 50–55 days posthatching, generally in late AUG. or in SEPT.; tail and most of wing long retained. The Juv. is acquired by the pushing out of the natal covering which is retained briefly on tips of the Juv. feathers. Differences from ♀ Def. Basic include: **iris** darker; facial "mask" less clearly defined; **scapulars** plain; belly appears white, the individual feathers being white laterally with internal tapering gray area; posterior **abdomen** brownish and rather streaky; **tail** feathers have notched ends; **wing** elongated innermost secondaries narrower, nearly pointed (and soon much frayed), upper coverts (especially greater) narrower, a few over innermost secondaries may have some flecking (but most are plain). The ♂ Juv. usually is darker in general appearance than ♀ Juv., hence white facial mask is more conspicuous.

▶    ♀ Juv. Plumage (entire feathering), timing as ♂. Some individuals lack a white facial mask; no flecking on any greater coverts (invariably?); otherwise as ♂ except as mentioned above. **Iris** very dark brownish.

At Tetlin, Alaska, tagged known-age ducklings were confined to a pond where, in absence of parent birds (no maternal care), 6 of 88 individuals survived to attain flight at 53–61 days. Details, including wt. increase, growth of tarsus and culmen, and development of the Juv. Plumage (with increase in length of certain particular feathers), were reported by Schneider (1965). Judging from his and other data he cited, Lesser Scaups in the wild probably first fly at age 7–7½ weeks. By that time the Juv. Plumage is almost fully developed and possibly the first traces of Basic I have begun to appear.

▶    ♂ Basic I Plumage (all feathering except, in the wing, only a few innermost feathers), during FALL soon succeeds the Juv. Plumage and, in turn, soon afterward is succeeded by Alt. I. The innermost Basic I wing feathers come in late, the tail still later. The iris evidently changes from darkish to yellow during the Basic I stage or soon after.

A rather plain darkish Plumage. **Head** and neck much darker than Juv., toward sooty; **mantle**, including scapulars, brownish and more or less (usually quite sparsely) finely vermiculated white; **underparts** belly white (concealed portions of feathers grayish), upper sides and flanks a rather dingy brownish, under-tail area evenly darkish. **Tail** feathers dark and with rounded ends. **Wing** innermost secondaries fairly broad and typically plain dark, as are their longer overlying coverts; remainder of wing is retained Juv.

NOTE    The Basic I head is acquired and lost rapidly. Most specimens that show much Basic I on the body already have the head–neck molted into Alt. I. Birds in transition from Basic I to Alt. I are common through Nov. and Dec., many being shot on winter range.

▶    ♂ Alt. I Plumage (all feathering except tail and, in wing, only a few innermost feathers), generally acquired in LATE FALL, but in some later or else molting is protracted into WINTER. Much as ♂ Def. Alt. except: head–neck have little sheen, mantle usually more coarsely vermiculated (heavy wavy black lines), light feather ends on flanks often more heavily vermiculated or barred dark. Considerable Basic I ventral feathering often is long retained, while the Basic I tail sometimes is not acquired until after much Alt. I has grown. Wing—innermost feathers as Def. Alt., remainder is retained Juv.

NOTE    The comment elsewhere on variation in molting of young ♂ Greater Scaups applies here also.

▶    ♀ Basic I Plumage (inclusive feathering as ♂ Basic I), timing as ♂. This is a FALL Plumage, commonly found from late Sept. into Oct.

A brownish, blended Plumage. Typically there is a large roundish white patch, well delineated, at side base of bill. This character may be unique to ♀ Basic I, except it occurs occasionally also in ♂ Basic I.

**Iris** brownish olive or brownish. **Head**, neck, forepart of body, sides and flanks all nearly the same somewhat buffy brownish shade; **back** darker, some feathers with slightly lighter buffy yellow margins; **belly** white (the feathers are terminally white, otherwise gray); abdomen mixed medium gray and white; feathers of under-tail area dusky with white ends. It is common for ♀ ♀ to retain all Juv. tail feathers (i.e., not acquire Basic I tail) until much of the bird has molted out of Basic I and into Alt. I.

▶    ♀ Alt. I Plumage (all feathering except most of wing and the tail). Earliest good example was dated Oct. 19; usually this Plumage is worn from some time in NOV. to some time in MARCH.

A darkish, rather evenly colored Plumage. The earliest in which the white facial "front" assumes definitive shape and is sharply delineated on cheeks and chin. **Iris** variably brown. **Head** various dark browns (darkest adjoining white on front of cheeks), the neck paler browns; **dorsum** muted (darkish) browns, some of the feathers on back commonly well vermiculated white; **underparts** breast feathers darkish with buffy brownish to whitish ends; belly feathers totally white; abdomen at first may be rather streaky (from any long-retained Juv.) or somewhat barred (from retained Basic I), but finally becomes evenly smoky gray; feathers of under-tail area heavily vermiculated black on white, the longest ones mostly white. The tail sometimes is still-retained Juv. (notched feathers), but Basic I is the usual condition by the time the head–body is in Alt. I.

▶    ♀ Basic II Plumage (entire feathering), the head–body and a few innermost feathers of wing are acquired in SPRING (before age 1 year), the tail and most of wing not until LATE SUMMER or FALL, when the ♀ is molting from Basic back into Alt. head–body while also acquiring the Basic II tail and most of wing. This Plumage is as later Basics, differing only in that it is the last one with which, for a time, most of the Juv. wing still is worn. **Iris** brownish to brownish-yellow.

NOTES    The size of the Bursa of Fabricius has been used commonly to distinguish birds of the year from older age-classes of ducks in fall and early winter, but it is unreliable later on. B. W. Anderson et al. (1969) were able to distinguish 1st-year from older Lesser Scaups in spring; they were, however, dissecting dead birds rather than examining live ones.

Females by age 3 years have definitive eye coloring, i.e., olive yellowish or yellow, occasionally brownish yellow.

**Measurements**    12 ♂ (in various seasons and from widespread localities): BILL 40–43 mm., av. 41.5; WING 194–208, av. 202.4; TAIL 48–57, av. 52.7; TARSUS 34–37, av. 35.7;    12 ♀ (also various seasons and localities) BILL 40–43 mm., av. 41; WING 191–202, av. 195.6; TAIL 51–56, av. 53; TARSUS 32–38, av. 35.4 (ETS).

The wing is flattened in this series also. In Minn., in late March–early April: "adult" ♂ BILL (of 290 birds) 38.2–45.2 mm., mean 41.37; WING (of 381) 191–220, mean 208; TAIL (of 131) 46.9–61.8, mean 52.32;    ♀ BILL (of 140 birds) 36.2–43.6 mm., mean 40.35; WING (of 184) 192–213, mean 203; TAIL (of 70) 48–57.6, mean 52.30; "yearlings" [in spring before age 1 year] ♂ BILL (of 94) 37.6–44.4 mm., mean 41.50; WING (of 115) 193–217, mean 206; TAIL (of 46) 47.2–63, mean 51.18;    and ♀ BILL (of 92) 38–44.4 mm., mean 40.60; WING (of 105) 190–210, mean 199; and TAIL (of 56) 40.2–57, mean 50.20 (B. W. Anderson and Warner 1969a). These authors also gave other, including certain skeletal, meas.; birds in their first spring av. smaller in all meas.—skeletal, body, gonadal—than birds from older cohorts at that time of year. As expected, the Juv. WING is shorter than the Basic.

J. C. Phillips (1925) gave the meas. of WING (across chord) as ♂ 190–201 mm. and ♀ 185–198.

**Weight** of 112 ♂ was 1 lb. 6 oz. (.62 kg.) to 2 lb. 5 oz. (1.05), av. 1 lb. 14 oz. (.85); and 118 ♀ 1 lb. 3 oz. (.54 kg.) to 2 lb. 2 oz. (.96), av. 1 lb. 12 oz. (.79) (Saunders et al. 1950). The wts. are similar in A. L. Nelson and Martin (1953).

Averages in Ill. in fall: ♂ 9 "adult" 1.85 lb. (.84 kg.) and 26 "Juv." 1.78 lb. (.80); ♀ 6 "adult" 1.72 lb. (.78 kg.) and 27 "Juv." 1.73 (.78) (Bellrose and Hawkins 1947).

At Seneca L. in cent. N.Y., in early Jan. to late March: "adults" 147 ♂ 600–1,040 gm., mean 838 ± 6, and 21 ♀ 570–970, mean 801 ± 29; and "immature" [= 1st winter] 92 ♂ 670–970, mean 813 ± 5, and 35 ♀ 600–940, mean 761 ± 10 (Ryan 1972).

Birds flightless when molting, in Aug. in ne. Alaska: 113 ♂ 510–794 gm., mean 625 (1 lb. 6½ oz.) and 14 ♀ 454–680, mean 527 (1 lb. 2½ oz.) (Yocom 1970a). They may have had no food for up to 4–5 days.

For wt. of untended captive known-age young up to flight age, in Alaska, see Schneider (1965).

**Hybrids**    J. C. Phillips (1925) stated that "wild hybrids" with the Redhead (*Aythya americana*) and Canvasback (*A. valisineria*) had been recorded by Poll (1911), but more details of this would have been desirable. There have been a number of apparent wild hybrids of Lesser Scaup × Ringneck (*A. collaris*); for photo of a ♀ and summary of records, see B. W. Anderson and Timken (1969). In captivity, the Lesser Scaup is reported to have crossed with *Anas* (1 species), *Aix* (1 species), and *Aythya* (6 species, including those mentioned above). The characteristics of both ♂ and ♀ captive-reared *A. affinis* × *A. ferina* hybrids were described by Sage (1963b). J. C. Phillips commented that crosses of Lesser with Greater Scaup (*A. marila*), if they occurred, would be "difficult, if not impossible, to distinguish unless in full male plumage."

Tufted Duck (*Aythya fuligula*) × Common Pochard (*A. ferina*) ♂ crosses resemble the Lesser Scaup; see Perrins (1961, photo and text). For additional discussion and photos of "Lesser Scaup type" hybrids, see E. H. Gillham et al. (1966).

**Geographical variation**  A group of 1,142 Lesser Scaups, victims of pollution on the Mississippi R. in Minn. in spring of 1963, apparently were birds that had converged there during migration from salt water and from freshwater habitats. The birds with large salt glands (presumably from salt water) had, on the average, smaller sternums and longer appendages than those with smaller salt glands (presumably from fresh water), "perhaps suggesting geographical variation among populations of Lesser Scaup" (B. W. Anderson and Warner 1969b). RSP

FIELD IDENTIFICATION  Medium-sized to smallish diving duck. Most abundant diving duck inland in N. Am.—on large rivers and lakes, also on various coastal bays, including rim of Gulf of Mexico and some places farther southward. Often in tremendous "rafts," covering up to hundreds of acres of water.

In flight, a white patch, in both sexes, usually is limited to the secondaries (in the Greater Scaup it extends onto the primaries and in the Ringneck it is gray). Both scaups, but especially the Lesser, fly in compact but irregular formations that dart about like squadrons of pursuit planes. They are prone to dart into flocks on the water, rather than scale down to them in the manner of Canvasbacks and Redheads. Canvasbacks fly in quite distinct formations, in direct, powerful, purposeful flight, giving the impression of a squadron of bombers.

On the water, Canvasbacks ride higher than scaups (both species) and their sides and backs appear nearer white. In fall, the backs of mature drake scaups of both species often are not as light as later on, a result of prolonged molting.

In other than ♂ Alt. Plumage the 2 scaups are not easily separable. The young ♂ of each species in fall is more or less like the ♀ at same season and seldom has much Alt. head–body feathering (dark ends, light midsection) before late winter. Season for season, the ♀ has the same characters as ♀ Greater Scaup, and at least as much individual variation (as in presence, absence, or size of light area on cheeks from spring into late summer). Various *Aythya* in Basic Plumage are not obviously different from one another; compare their descriptions for details.

In hand, as when netted for banding, the 2 scaups are separable in all seasons by width of nail on bill (see opening paragraphs under both species), extent of white in wing, and perhaps by av. difference in general size.

Yearling Lesser Scaups are separable from older cohorts under certain conditions; see below under "Reproduction." RSP

VOICE  Very similar to Greater Scaup. The drake generally is silent, except during displays. According to F. Bellrose, however, both sexes have a short purring *br-r-r-p* uttered singly or in series of 2 or 3, in flight and at rest. In autumn, more vociferous than our other common diving ducks but less so than, for example, various puddle ducks.

Calls of the drake: a single *whew* in Coughing display; a fast *whee-ooo* in Kinked-neck, Head-throw, and probably in postcopulatory display. The ♀, when Inciting, has a harsh call, rendered as *kerr-urr* or *hurr,* and so on. A soft purring note (J. Munro 1941) is uttered during distraction display. RSP

HABITAT **Summer** Nests, often semicolonially near grass-margined ponds and lakes, sometimes where there is a floating shoreline, also on islands in such waters; in river deltas and on flats that are seasonally flooded with silt-laden waters; on stretches of marshy terrain near waterways; in the aspen–grassland–alkaline lake region of B.C., largest nesting concentrations are in marshes of *Scirpus acutus* bordering lakes where amphipods are abundant; similar habitat in Peace R. region e. of the Rockies. Undergoes wing molt on lakes where invertebrates and submerged and floating aquatic plants are abundant, mostly within limits of general breeding range.

**During migrations** Via inland lakes and rivers, again, where invertebrates and aquatic plants are available; also sheltered coastal waters.

**Winter** Sheltered bays, estuarine waters, flooded coastal marshes, and unfrozen fresh waters near coasts and well inland. More sheltered habitat than preferred by the Greater Scaup.

Contrary to some authors, the Ringneck, rather than the Lesser Scaup, is the nearest N. Am. ecological counterpart of the Tufted Duck of the Palearctic. RSP

DISTRIBUTION (See map.) This species is a small, primarily inland-wintering derivative of the same ancestral stock as the Greater Scaup.

**Breeding** Widely distributed, but rather local within sizable segments of the overall area. Main concentrations are away from the prairies, to the west and north.

In Alaska the Lesser is the nesting Scaup of the upper Yukon–Porcupine drainage (most common nesting duck on Yukon flats) and locally westward at least to the confluence of the Tanana and Yukon. There are scattered nesting records elsewhere in the interior—n. into the Brooks Range and s. into McKinley Park; one near the Gulf of Alaska in the Glacier Bay area is an outpost of the extension of breeding range across extreme n. B.C. Although the Lesser Scaup is the bird of the far interior and the Greater nests mainly in a broad zone of the Bering Sea perimeter, the 2 species share some nesting localities in Alaska (Minto L. area nw. of Fairbanks, for example) and in Canada. The Lesser is the most abundant nesting duck in parts of the Athabaska delta and in similar habitat elsewhere in nw. Canada.

The map shows a vacant strip between sw. breeding and nw. wintering ranges; the species has nested within this strip, also beyond (within general winter range) in Cal. The species has nested beyond se. limits of main breeding range. At the present time it appears to be extending and enlarging its breeding range eastward in Canada. Breeds (in some numbers) at Tule–Klamath in extreme n. Cal. and (in smaller numbers) at Mountain Meadows, Lassen Co., ne. Cal. There are records (some old) for n. Idaho,

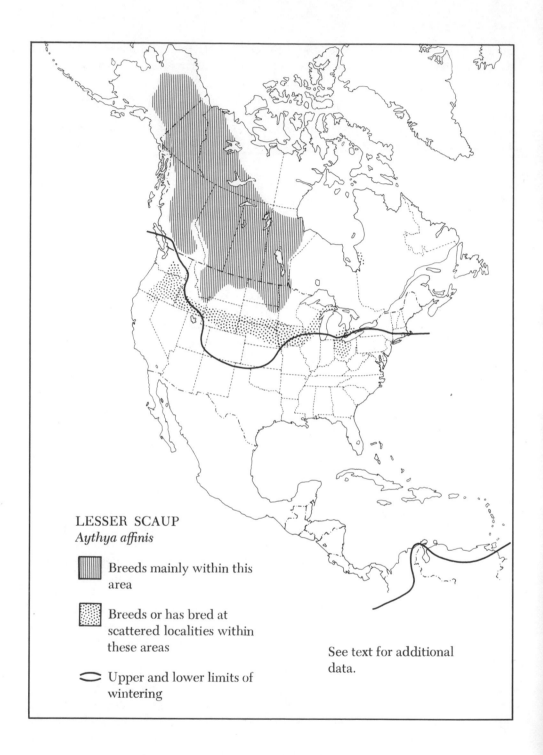

LESSER SCAUP
*Aythya affinis*

▥ Breeds mainly within this area

▦ Breeds or has bred at scattered localities within these areas

◠ Upper and lower limits of wintering

See text for additional data.

ne. Colo., Nebr., s. Wis., ne. Iowa, and Ohio. In e. Canada: several localities in Ont., one on Ont.–Que. border, and on e. side of James Bay; details in Godfrey (1966).

**Summer** There are various records, into or even through this season, of nonbreeding Lesser Scaups remaining far s. of breeding range.

At least in Alaska, a few birds may move to places beyond general breeding range prior to wing molt; about 20 at Umiat, June 23, 1971.

**Migrations** May occur almost anywhere on the continent s. and se. of breeding range.

**Winter** Primarily s. of range of Greater Scaup, but considerable overlap. Large numbers are along and close to coasts—on Pacific side from s. B.C. down to bays of Cal. and coastal lagoons of w. Mexico (more than half of Pacific winterers are in these lagoons); in the interior, abundant on some natural waters and impoundments in sw. U.S.; others are scattered on open water in the main Mississippi drainage; a few thousand far n. near Detroit, Mich.; others along n. edge of Gulf of Mexico w. into Texas, with over a million in the Mississippi delta region; on the Atlantic coast, outnumbers the Greater Scaup on the lower Hudson R., but occurs mainly from the Potomac R. southward (in Fla. the most abundant wintering duck, on coastal sounds, interior lakes, and rivers). Apparently local and not in sizable numbers in Cent. Am.

Bermuda—a few in winter. May occur almost anywhere in and around the Caribbean. There are records from the Bahamas around the Caribbean (few from Lesser Antilles) to S. Am., also for various is. off the Venezuelan coast as listed by Meyer de Schauensee (1966).

Southern limits of recorded occurrence include, on the S. Am. mainland: Colombia (E. Andes and Cauca valley), w. Ecuador (1 record), and n. Venezuela.

**Straggler** to sw. Greenland (3 records). A Nfld. specimen record (Nov. 12, 1889), recently reconfirmed. Formerly scarce in N.S., but now regular from mid-Sept. to Dec.

Hawaiian Is.: on Oahu—recorded in 1946 and most years from 1960 on and now may be regular in winter in small numbers; Lanai—1914; Maui—1965 and 1970 (Berger 1972).

**Erroneous record** for Kamchatka (Dementiev and Gladkov 1960).

Reports of occurrence in Britain and Europe are suspect, because the cross *Aythya fuligula* × *A. ferina* resembles the Lesser Scaup.

Recorded as **fossil** of Pleistocene age from Ore., Cal., Texas (2 localities), Kans., and Fla. (10 localities); and from **archaeological sites** in Alaska (Kodiak I.), Cal., Texas, Iowa, Ill. (3 sites), Ohio, and Fla. (4 sites); details in Brodkorb (1964a). RSP

MIGRATION No general coverage of this topic has been published. Aldrich (1949) gave an analysis based on 1,683 banding recoveries; there are important data on birds banded in and also recovered in Fla. in Hyde (1958); Bellrose (1968) gave estimates of numbers that migrate via certain "corridors" in conterminous U.S. e. of the Rockies. Very large gaps in published information concern the whereabouts in winter of birds from northerly localities, also the movements of birds that migrate and/or winter in waters of the arid sw. U.S. From available information, the following generalizations appear to be valid.

Near Columbus, Ohio, the daily schedule of feeding and resting autumn migrants is regulated by light intensity. Resting birds became more active as light diminished in evening. There was more activity on dark than on bright days. Strong winds induced compact rafting, the birds facing the wind. It was theorized that, as a weather front arrived, there was a buildup in flock organization in response to decreased light, strong winds, and possibly other weather factors; when clearing follows, mutual stimulation in an organized flock facilitates movement from the area. Summarized from Miskimen (1955).

Aldrich (1949) found no difference in migration patterns of birds of different ages or sexes.

Apparently spring routes are largely, but perhaps not entirely, the reverse of fall routes.

East of the Rockies in conterminous U.S., the greatest numbers of birds travel up and down the interior; that is, between the Canadian prairies and Gulf of Mexico.

As with various nesters on the n. prairies, the majority of easterly birds tend to go se. and s. to winter quarters, westerly birds tend to go toward the Pacific coast and, especially in the s. half of Alta., birds from the same locality may go to the Pacific coast, or down the w. interior and to anywhere in Mexico, or to n. Gulf of Mexico, or Fla., or to the mid-Atlantic coast (Long I. Sd. to Chesapeake Bay and then some may shift s. to Fla.).

The birds from interior Alaska and nw. Canada migrate in the interior rather than via the nearest coast (of se. Alaska and upper ⅔ of B.C.); the Greater Scaup appears to be the bird of that coastal area. Lesser Scaups banded in interior Alaska (Minto lakes, Yukon flats, Tetlin lakes) have been recovered at places from n. Alta. to s. Mexico and from the Pacific coast to the Atlantic coast; greater numbers from these banding localities apparently winter along the Gulf of Mexico coast of Texas and La.

Many northerly breeders, of interior Alaska and nw. Canada, evidently go se. via the Great Lakes region to the Atlantic coast (Long I. to Chesapeake Bay).

Thirty-one adult Lesser Scaups were banded when flightless during wing molt at Takslesluk L. (confluent with Baird Inlet), not distant from Bering Sea coastal Alaska. Two ♀ ♀ banded Aug. 8, 1964, have been recovered in subsequent hunting seasons, in n. Mich. in 1964, and in N.C. in 1967 (J. G. King).

The large wintering concentrations in Fla. come, in part, via the Mississippi valley down to coastal La. and then turn eastward; a goodly number go e. to places as far as L. Erie and then down the interior to Fla.; still others reach the Atlantic coast (Chesapeake Bay region) and then move southward.

Apparently there are regional differences in schedules, as yet not analyzed, both in spring and fall, indicating some tendency of Lesser Scaups to behave as subpopulations; this probably would be minimized by any shifting of individuals from one wintering segment to another.

**Spring** In s. conterminous U.S., movement begins by very early March and coastal birds go inland mostly from around mid-March to late April. Often many thousands still are on waters near the Gulf of Mexico coast and in Fla. until past mid-April. In late March and through April the birds spend time at stopover places, where there is much pair formation activity. Local breeders begin arriving on deeper ponds on the Canadian prairies as soon as these open, in very late April and early May; from then on, even into early June, they scatter to smaller waters and nest nearby. There is continuing migration on the prairies, at least through May, as flocks pass through en route to more northerly nesting areas. They usually arrive May 9–19 in interior Alaska (sometimes a few days later than the Greater Scaup), with peak numbers appearing May 15–21. Probably, in an av. season, all breeders have reached open waters even at northerly nesting areas by some time in early June.

**Summer**  Those yearlings that do not breed are the first birds to congregate on molting lakes, beginning soon after mid-June. They are joined later by drakes, which have left their incubating mates. There is a tendency for this molt migration, at least of mature drakes from the prairies and parklands, to be in a northerly direction, to waters in forested areas. The actual whereabouts of most molting Lesser Scaups has not been reported. J. Munro (1941) mentioned several molting lakes with up to several hundred birds ("adults" and "yearlings") in s. B.C. Lakes in the w. part of the Saskatchewan R. marshes in Man. are utilized heavily for molting by Lesser Scaups and Canvasbacks. At McCallum L. in n. Sask., there were an estimated 25,000 Lesser Scaups per mi. of shoreline (Cartwright and Law 1952). Ohtig L., within the Yukon flats area in Alaska, is a known molting place. Also waters in the Minto Lakes region nw. of Fairbanks and lakes in the Tetlin area in e. interior Alaska. A few flightless molting birds have been captured far w. of known breeding range in Alaska, at Takslesluk L. (lat. 61°4′ N, long. 162° 52′ W.), mentioned earlier.

Many ♀ ♀ that are successful in hatching a first clutch evidently remain with their young until very late in or even through the preflight stage of the latter, but late nesters and renesters (a large percentage) leave earlier and go to molting lakes. Late gatherings of flightless birds are largely ♀ ♀.

Various lakes where bands of preflight young occur also are molting lakes.

**Fall**  Migration is rather late, just ahead of freeze-up. As in various other waterfowl, since the drakes are through the flightless period ahead of the ♀ ♀ and before many young are flying, there are migrant (also wintering) flocks comprised almost entirely of drakes. The birds start moving in Sept., linger at stopover places, and those bound for the e. U.S. and Gulf coasts generally are not present there in numbers until some time in Nov. Arrivals continue well into Dec.

**Winter**  In Alaska there have been recent fall and winter sightings from near Cordova and at Kodiak.

In southerly areas there is a shifting of birds through Dec., probably into Jan. There is also local movement elsewhere, as from more exposed tidewater earlier in the season to sheltered inlets and flooded marshes as the days grow longer.

In Fla., numbers in the Merrit I. and Indian R. areas sometimes build to a peak of over 300,000, then there is a sharp decline in early Jan., possibly a mass movement to n. Gulf of Mexico coast (Chamberlain, Jr., 1960). This shift may be back along the route by which the birds arrived in Fla. RSP

BANDING STATUS  The total number banded through 1964 was 190,989 and the total number of recoveries and returns through 1961 was 10,531; main places of banding were La., Alta., Alaska, Mich., and Fla. (Data from Bird Banding Laboratory.) RSP

REPRODUCTION From histological examination, McKnight and Buss (1962) found evidence of ovulation in 12 of 16 yearling ♀ and concluded that most, but not all, ♀ of this age are physiologically capable of breeding. In s. B.C., J. Munro (1941) noted that, when flocks first arrive, yearling drakes are distinguishable by darker appearance—an admixture of gray in the nearly white areas (as on flanks) that is more pronounced in early July (when the young drakes are more advanced in molting into Basic), at which time older ones still are in full Alt. (with white flanks, etc.). Thus it can be determined that early molters are yearling drakes, which may be classed as pre-breeders until another year. In July yearling ♀ ♀ that did not nest had head–neck faded to pale buff or cinnamon, "whereas these regions of the adult were rich brown in contrast." The summer (Basic) Plumage of ♀ ♀ is subject to rapid fading; presumably the ♀ ♀ that remain out on open water become much paler than those that are more sheltered from sunlight while incubating. Munro mentioned various lakes where there were gatherings, including yearlings of both sexes, at a time when breeding ♀ ♀ would have eggs or small young. In the Yellowknife area, Mackenzie Dist., Trauger (1970) found that less than 5% of marked yearling ♀ ♀ attempted to nest and only 3 were observed with broods. Thus it may be concluded that some Lesser Scaups, ♀ ♀ at least, first breed as yearlings, others not until older.

**Pair formation** occurs decidedly late in this species (Weller 1965), permanent bonds for the nesting season being formed perhaps most commonly in March. Thus it is a spring activity, when the birds are about to begin migrating or are at stopover places en route to nesting areas. As in various other *Aythya*, presumably there is much pair bond maintenance display as long as the pairs are in flocks—up to the time the ♀ ♀ scatter to nest. Stated otherwise, by J. Munro (1941), "courtship" continues through April and May.

The birds are paired (except for an excess of ♂ ♂) when they arrive near nesting areas. Then their schedule is "adjusted," i.e., there is a waiting period of variable length, from the time the birds (still in flocks) are in the vicinity until sites are suitable for occupancy. In the Sask. R. delta, there is a decrease in clutch size of 1 egg for every 10.3 days' delay in nesting (G. H. Townsend 1966). Many are nesting at southerly localities before all transients have arrived there or moved on.

At Kindersley, Sask., many pairs remained on a study area through late June without attempting to nest (Dzubin, in D. Munro 1969). In Man., nonbreeding was associated with deteriorating habitat and nonflooding of nesting cover (Rogers 1964). That is, nesting may be inhibited by unfavorable environmental factors such as declining water levels.

**Displays of the duck** INCITING as in Greater Scaup, but the call is even weaker. Preen-behind-the-wing is frequent during pair formation, later mutually by mates (from Johnsgard 1965).

**Displays of the drake** differ from those of the Greater Scaup mainly in speed (are more rapid) and in accompanying calls (which are weaker). COUGH as in Greater Scaup; a whistled *whew* uttered. KINKED-NECK as in Greater Scaup; a faint *whee-oo* uttered. (Possibly it is in this display that a lump appears to travel upward and disappear before reaching the throat—Brooks in J. C. Phillips 1925.). HEAD-THROW after an introductory Head-shake, done extremely fast (fastest known in pochard tribe), only a blur to the human eye. The bill is angled up, generally less than 45°, and the head is kept in median plane. Kinked-neck call uttered. SNEAKING as in Greater Scaup. TURNING-THE-BACK-OF-THE-HEAD as Greater Scaup, i.e., a low profile with head feathers depressed. PREEN-BEHIND-THE-WING is frequent; later it is a mutual display. (From Johnsgard 1965.)

**Copulation**  The drake BILL-DIPS, PREENS-DORSALLY, and Preens-behind-the-wing and the duck may or may not do likewise before she assumes a PRONE position. After treading, the ♂, usually also the ♀, swims with BILL-DOWN and the ♂ probably utters the Kinked-neck call. (From Johnsgard 1965.)

Although nothing seems to have been reported about any aerial activity associated with pair formation or bond maintenance, it is evident from Wetmore's (1920) observations that displays include an underwater component.

There is a strong tendency for breeding ♀ ♀ to return to the same pond and nesting area in succeeding years, with a lesser percentage of yearling ♀ ♀ returning to natal ponds (Trauger 1970). There also is a tendency for nests to be concentrated within an area, rather than scattered randomly. The **nest site** usually is dry and sheltered under fairly heavy cover of nettles, grasses, low brush, even stranded driftwood. Many are very close to the water's edge and the ♀ can slip from the eggs, submerge, and swim away. Islands in lakes are used commonly, mainly the perimeters of larger ones, and higher densities are reached there than is typical of mainland areas. Some nest in tussocks in more or less flooded marshes and, at times, the eggs in the bottom of nests are wet. A few nests are in exposed situations where grass is low, also on muskrat houses. They have been found nesting on floating bogs among cattail and sedge (Harper, in J. C. Phillips 1925).

**Nest**  The duck makes a slight hollow, in among the standing or sheltering vegetation, and some dry plant materials may accumulate in it. After several eggs are laid, the **nest down** is added gradually until some time during incubation. As in the Greater Scaup, it is very dark with inconspicuous light centers. Unlike the Greater Scaup, the dark portion of intermingled feathers grade gradually to a wide white terminal band (Broley 1950, text and illus.).

**Egg dates**  A late nester. At Tule–Klamath in extreme n. Cal., back-dating from reported hatching dates, evidently clutches were begun in 1952 from the 1st week in May onward (A. W. Miller and Collins 1954), but apparently later in 1957 (or else early clutches were destroyed), when 1st hatching was about June 22 (Rienecker and Anderson 1960). In s. B.C., laying evidently begins by early June, but J. Munro (1941) stated that the majority of "nests" (with clutches) were found in July and Aug. In se. Alta., the mean date of initiation of the first 50% of successful clutches in a 5-year span varied from May 27, in 1957, to June 7 in 1953 (Keith 1961). At Miquelon L. in se. Alta., in 1964–65, the earliest clutch was begun May 17–18, with largest number begun about June 10–21, and others until into early July (Vermeer 1968). In the Sask. R. delta (s. of Cumberland House, Sask.), the mean date of clutch initiation in 1963–64 was during the 1st week in June (G. H. Townsend 1966). In interior Alaska, nesting begins in mid-June (McKnight and Buss 1962). Most recent data: a few ♀ ♀ begin laying there in late May, but usually it begins in the 1st week of June (B. Kessel).

The duck lays at a rate of an egg a day, or with a day skipped during clutch deposition.

225

**Clutch size** usually 9–11 eggs. At Sask. R. delta 84 clutches av. 9.0 ± 0.3 eggs (G. H. Townsend 1966). At Miquelon L., 59 clutches av. 10.5 eggs (Vermeer 1968). In se. Alta., in 131 clutches, those before June 16 av. 10.6 ± 0.06; those of June 16–30 av. 10.2 ± 0.2; and after June 30 the figure was 8.5 ± 0.7; that is, **replacement clutches** av. smaller (Keith 1961). A "dump nest" of 26 eggs was mentioned in J. C. Phillips (1925).

At Mountain Meadows in ne. Cal., clutches were taken to "simulate nest destruction." Five color-marked ♀♀ renested and one did so twice. Though all 1st clutches were taken before incubation began, the length of subsequent renesting interval varied considerably—from 5 to 27 days (although some ♀♀ may have made undiscovered abortive attempts). Five first clutches contained 9–12 eggs, av. 10.6; 5 second clutches from the same ♀♀ were of 8–11, av. 8.8; the ♀ that renested twice had clutches of 9–7–7. The distance between 1st and subsequent nests of the same ♀ av. 464 yds. (Summarized from E. G. Hunt and Anderson 1966.)

One **egg** each from 20 clutches (from localities in conterminous U.S. and in Canada) **size** length av. 57.39 ± 1.66 mm., breadth av. 39.93 ± 1.26, radii of curvature of ends 15.49 ± 1.38 and 12.84 ± 1.10; **shape** between elliptical and long subelliptical, elongation 1.43 ± 0.049, bicone −0.021, and asymmetry +0.096 (FWP). The figures in Bent (1923) for 88 eggs are very similar: length 50–61.5 mm., av. 57.1, and breadth 35.5–42.5, av. 39.7. **Color** toward greenish, a variant of olive buff; shell smooth, without much gloss. As in diving ducks in general, the ♀ voids an odorous liquid on the eggs and nest if flushed from them.

Evidently, in the case of first clutches, the drake may leave the ♀ at any time from beginning of incubation on. If they leave at the beginning of incubation, the drakes are scattered in small groups for a period prior to their departure to a molting area. There is less intervening time for those that leave later.

**Incubation period** 21–22 days. According to Vermeer (1968), in 18 clutches it varied 21–27 days. Wild-taken eggs (under a hen?) 22–23 days (Wolfe, in J. C. Phillips 1925).

**Nesting success** In the Yellowknife area, 1967–69, 33%–41% of ♀♀ hatched some eggs (Trauger 1970). South of Cumberland House, Sask., lumping island and mainland nests, success in 33 nests in 1963 was 73 ± 16% and in 50 nests in 1964 was 64 ± 14% (G. H. Townsend 1966). In 115 nests in se. Alta., there was 27% success (Keith 1961). At Miquelon L., eggs hatched in 60 of 67 nests, or 89.5% (Vermeer 1968). At prairie potholes in sw. Man., success was very low, partly due to increased predation, in years of low water (Rogers 1964). It probably is safe to generalize that the birds are more successful away from the prairies, in areas where water levels are more stable.

**Hatching success** As in waterfowl generally, the number of eggs that hatch in nests in which at least some hatch is high. For example, in se. Alta., 83.3% of the eggs in 18 clutches hatched (Keith 1961). In se. Alta. in 1964, 59 clutches contained 619 eggs and 91% hatched (Vermeer 1968).

**Hatching dates** for various areas can be calculated by adding 30 days (for laying plus incubation) to dates of clutch initiation given above. Apparently, except for Cal., most clutches hatch some time in July. In interior Alaska the peak of hatching occurs during the 2nd or 3rd week of July and a few clutches hatch as late as early Aug. (B. Kessel).

**Nest parasitism**   Even though most nests are rather well concealed, hence not a conspicuous stimulus to laying ♀♀, some ♀♀ do lay in the nests of others. Vermeer (1968) mentioned a double clutch in a nest; its neighboring clutch never had more than 2 eggs. A Lesser Scaup laid in a Gadwall nest. It also is recorded as laying in the nests of the Baldpate, Shoveler, Redhead, and White-winged Scoter; the Ruddy Duck, in turn, has laid in the nest of the Lesser Scaup (J. C. Phillips 1925).

**Ducklings**   The duck and brood are soon on water, where there is frequent combining of families, often under joint care of several ♀♀. The following are from J. Munro's (1941) observations in s. B.C. He saw young switch from one ♀ to another, also untended young. One band of 64 young of various ages was accompanied by 7 ♀♀. Another of 34 and one of 35 were with 3 ♀♀ each; the young swam in grouped (coordinated) formation. A band of 55 downies had a ♀ leading and 2 following; the young swam in a long line or, at times, in a compact group. According to Hochbaum (1944), amalgamations result from "battles" between brood ♀♀ when they meet. Some families, however, remain by themselves.

At first, the ♀ or ♀♀ lead the brood away. As the season wears on, ♀♀ show less interest in broods or aggregations and may take wing if approached; the young run over the water or dive (Munro). Apparently ♀♀ stay longer with early hatched-young. Young hatched at molting lakes are more or less mingled in the molting assemblies. Young at other waters after attaining flight may join the groups at molting lakes. **Age at first flight** closely estimated as 47–54 days. In interior Alaska, some young can fly by mid-Aug. and most during the last week of Aug. and 1st week of Sept. (B. Kessel). For a graph of weight vs. age in weeks of pen-reared and (as estimated) of wild ducklings, see L. G. Sugden and Harris (1972). RSP

SURVIVAL   Recoveries through 1968 from 1,772 banded birds showed a 73.9% mortality rate for "juveniles" and 41.7% for "adults" (Trauger 1970). RSP

HABITS   The Lesser Scaup population greatly exceeds the N. Am. population of the Greater Scaup. It is one of our most numerous ducks, definitely the most numerous diver inland. Compared with the Greater, it is more widespread, prefers milder climate for nesting, and more sheltered and milder (southerly) environment in winter.

Both scaups tend to be rather shy when present in large numbers, especially if persecuted; the rafts remain well out on open water. Yet where not molested, small groups of Lesser Scaups become conditioned to feeding on grains thrown into shallow water or, in a few places, actually take food from the hand. This seems to be a natural consequence of their curiosity. For example, small flocks will visit any other ducks, or decoys of any sort, swinging in low and rapidly, in a dense bunch. If they decide to alight, they come right on in with a splash, then may move apart in a group by themselves.

At least away from tidewater the Lesser Scaup feeds most actively in early morning, then rests well out from shore in a compact flock or even a raft containing scores, hundreds, or thousands of individuals. When resting, the birds tend to be spaced quite evenly. Sometimes, as when migrating through the arid southwest, the birds fill reservoirs and arroyos from shore to shore, and overflowing ashore. On tidewater it is probable that their feeding schedule varies to some extent with the tide; at least they feed nearer shore at high tide. They are known to feed at night.

Lesser Scaups feed in shallow water and by up-ending where it is somewhat deeper; usually they dive, preferably in water 1 to 3 meters deep. Kilham (1954) watched 6 birds in winter, on a falling tide, feeding where they were not quite afloat, perhaps having remained to feed there after the water had become too shallow for diving. Sometimes, between dives or when resting, a bird rolls on its side, preening, and the white belly flashes briefly before the bird rights itself.

Lesser Scaups are very animated when feeding. A bird springs or "leaps" forward and upward, then goes down with wings closed and tail partly spread. Cleaves (1947) observed their activities as he took underwater photos at Silver Springs, Fla. In swimming on the surface the feet stroke alternately; in diving, they are spread laterally and stroke in unison. Sometimes 2 birds dived close together at the same time and fed so close that their bodies collided gently; they came to the surface "as if by mutual understanding." The birds appeared to swallow food (grains) as fast as they picked it from the bottom. After feeding, a bird would right itself, relax, and shoot up almost vertically from its own buoyancy. Occasionally there were 1 or 2 kicks, the feet stroked simultaneously. Sleeping birds (as viewed from underneath) allowed the feet to hang limp, kicking at intervals with 1 foot only to maintain station. As seen above the surface, they had their heads on their backs and bills tucked in the feathers. This probably is "pseudo-sleeping" behavior, as described by D. W. Anderson (1970).

Near Delta, Man., in May, Ring-billed Gulls (*Larus delawarensis*) have been observed pirating food from foraging Lesser Scaups (Siegfried 1972).

In a comfort movement, when a bird reared up ("stood on its tail") and beat its wings, it was observed underwater that the feet were stroking alternately (treading water) and so fast that the human eye could not follow the movement.

It is very probable that Lesser Scaups can pass at least an entire season without coming ashore. Yet at times they rest on flats, mudbars, or even ice.

Although the 2 scaups consort at times and in various seasons, each species seems to have a strong drive to keep with its own kind. Many large rafts of Lesser Scaups contain practically no other ducks. This tendency to homogeneous grouping is strong in various *Aythya*, as at a molting lake where one section will be preempted by Lesser Scaups, another by Canvasbacks, and so on. If disturbed, the different kinds intermingle, but sort out again when left to themselves.

Not much is known with any real certainty about the past status of the Lesser Scaup. Forbush (1912) thought there had been a great reduction in numbers between 1878 and 1900. J. C. Phillips (1925) was puzzled about this and suggested a decrease of 40–60% had occurred in New Eng. and Fla. in the preceding 30 or 40 years, then some increase. At any rate, in the late 1960s, the total number of wintering Lesser Scaups was perhaps on the order of 4,000,000 birds. Beyond the yearling age-class there appears to be a decidedly unbalanced sex ratio—a surplus of drakes—for reasons not yet understood. As mentioned earlier, the majority of them nest in fairly stable boreal habitat, which is reflected in a fairly stable production of young from year to year.

As a table bird the Lesser Scaup has been cursed, dismissed as not worth mentioning, and praised. J. C. Phillips (1925) considered it "one of the poorest for the table." He went on to remark that Lesser Scaups were "very rank" in Fla. and got worse the longer they stayed there! Yet, in summing up, he noted that some authorities have rated the bird highly and so concluded "it is never safe to generalize." RSP

FOOD   On the basis of 1,051 stomachs, about 60% consists of the seeds and other parts of aquatic plants, largely pondweeds, grasses, and sedges; and 40% of animal matter, mainly mollusks and aquatic insects. Food of "juveniles," however, is only about 10% plant material, the 90% of animal matter consisting almost entirely of insects (Cottam 1939).

**Vegetable**   Pondweeds (*Potamogeton, Ruppia, Najas, Zannichellia*, and *Zostera*) 18.4%; grasses (*Zizania* and miscellaneous) 9.6%; sedges (*Scirpus* mainly) 6.3%; wild celery (*Vallisneria spiralis*) 5.2%; muskgrass (Characeae) and other algae 2.6%; waterlilies (Nymphaeaceae) 2.1%; coontail (*Ceratophyllum*) 1.5%; water milfoils (*Myriophyllum*) and mare's tail (*Hippuris*) 1.4%; smartweeds (*Polygonum*) 1.3%; arrowheads (*Sagittaria*) 1.0%; miscellaneous 10.2% (Cottam 1939). The 922 stomachs used by Kubichek (1933) were collected over a wide area. The food was 59.96% vegetable: Naiadaceae 23.79%, Graminae 10.43%, algae 5.0%, and miscellaneous 20.74%.

In Mass., seeds of bur reed (*Sparganium*), bayberry (*Myrica*), and saw grass (*Cladium effusum*) (J. C. Phillips 1911). The food in Conn. coastal waters consisted of 38.3% plant and 61.7% animal matter. The plant matter was almost entirely sea lettuce (*Ulva lactuca*) (Cronan 1957). The food of 42 birds on the upper St. Lawrence was 21% plant and 79% animal. Wild celery formed 9.4% (Kutz et al. 1948). In contrast, on the lower Hudson R. the food in 17 stomachs was 86.6% plant and 13.4% animal. Of the identifiable plants, pondweeds (*Najas minor* and *N. flexilis*) amounted to 35.7% (Foley and Taber 1951). The 63 specimens from the upper Chesapeake region had consumed the vegetation and rootstalks of *Ruppia maritima, Potamogeton perfoliatus*, and *Zostera marina*, the seeds of *Potamogeton* spp., *Scirpus olneyi, Sparganium americanum*, and *Rosa paustris* (R. E. Stewart 1962).

Based on 220 gizzards from Illinois birds, the food was only 9.65% plant, and 90.35% animal. The principal plants were *Potamogeton* spp. and *Ceratophyllum demersum* (H. G. Anderson 1959). The ratio of plant to animal matter was just the reverse for the 44 gizzards analyzed from Mo. The principal plant foods were *Chara* 17.3%, *Scirpus* spp. 15.0%, and *Polygonum* spp. 13.6% (Korschgen 1955). The food of 122 birds from Reelfoot Lake, Tenn., was about equally divided between plant and animal. The principal plant foods were the seeds of *Platanus occidentalis* 10.37%, *Ceratophyllum demersum* 8.40%, *Potamogeton* spp. 7.21%, and algae 5.29% (Rawls 1958). In Puerto Rico, seeds of panic grass (*Panicum*) (Wetmore 1916). Twenty-one immature birds were fed a mixed diet of *Vallisneria spiralis, Elodea canadensis*, and Mollusca. The av. daily intake was 0.49 lb. wet wt., or 0.03 lb. dry wt. (Longcore and Cornwell 1964).

**Animal**   Gastropods (*Amnicola, Carinifex, Planorbis, Nassarius, Lymnaea, Bythinella, Bittium, Turbonilla*, etc.) 25.0%; insects: caddis flies (Trichoptera), dragonflies and damselflies (Odonata), water boatmen (Corixidae), midges (Chironomidae), and beetles (Coleoptera), 12.0%; crustaceans 1.4%; miscellaneous 2.1% (Cottam 1939).

229

A stomach from Me. contained snails predominantly (Mendall and Gashwiler 1940). Mass. birds had eaten snails (*Lunatia heros*) and ants (J. C. Phillips 1911). A stomach from Md. contained 75 snails (*Amnicola, Goniobasis,* and *Planorbis*) (Judd 1902). The animal food on the upper St. Lawrence was almost entirely gastropods (Kutz et al. 1948) and in the coastal waters of Conn. largely Pelecypoda, mainly *Mulinia lateralis* (Cronan 1957). Birds in upper Chesapeake Bay had consumed Gastropoda (*Oxytrema, Amnicola, Gillia, Planorbis, Sayella, Acteocina, Laevicardium,* and *Odostomia*): Pelecypoda (*Mulinia, Gemma brachidontes, Macoma,* and *Mya*); Isopoda (*Chiridotea coeca*); Pisces (Centrachidae) and Libelluloidea nymphs (R. E. Stewart 1962). Eight Fla. specimens contained mollusks, chiefly *Rissoina cancellata* (F. C. Baker 1890). A stomach from Puerto Rico contained mainly the usual aquatic insects (Wetmore 1916).

In Ill.: Gastropoda (*Gyraulus, Viviparus, Campeloma, Lioplax,* and *Amnicola, Fluminicola, Somatogyrus, Pleurocera,* and *Neritina*) 43.35%; Pelecypoda (*Pisidium, Musculium,* and *Sphaerium*) 42.74%; and Insecta 4.14% (H. G. Anderson 1959). In Mo., Odonata 9.2%, and Mollusca and Hydrophilidae 2.1% (Korschgen 1955). Reelfoot Lake specimens had consumed Insecta 23.85%, Gastropoda 18.40%, Pelecypoda 3.16%, and Pisces 3.07%. (Rawls 1958). The food of 32 birds from the La. coast consisted almost entirely (99.8%) of dwarf surf clams (*Mulinia lateralis*) (Harmon 1962). Seven birds from Ore. had fed almost exclusively on mollusks (*Fluminicola, Planorbis,* and *Lymnaea*) (Gabrielson and Jewett 1940). In fall at Great Salt Lake, Utah, the birds feed on brine shrimp (*Artemia fertilis*) and larvae of alkali flies (*Ephydra* spp.) (Wetmore 1917a).

Since the above survey was prepared, a number of studies of food of the Lesser Scaup have appeared. These reveal that this species feeds predominantly on animal material. Amphipods appear to be the main food on breeding range and bulk large at inland places where the birds occur as migrants. These studies, which contain much detail are summarized very briefly here.

The percentage of animal vs. vegetable foods, in the earlier studies, was tabulated by Rogers and Korschgen (1966). They also gave data on the food found in 164 birds, as follows: 39 from a breeding area in Man.—91.1% animal (crustaceans, insects, annelids, etc.), plus miscellaneous plants; 88 from a fall concentration area in Ill.—93.5% animal (gastropods, pelecypods, insects, etc.), plus miscellaneous plants (*Potamogeton,* others); and 37 birds from 2 wintering areas in La.—63.7% animal (fish fragments, Crustacea, Gastropoda), and various plants.

In sw. Man., 47 "juveniles" and 24 "adults," late spring and early fall—more animal than plant matter; aquatic invertebrates, especially amphipods, also gastropods, midge larvae, caddis fly larvae and cases, water boatmen, and leeches (Bartonek and Hickey 1969).

In Sask. R. delta, May–Oct. inclusive, by month, combined to form 66% animal and 34% vegetable. Invertebrates, aquatic seeds; there were changes in proportion of animal to plant between months; an apparent correlation with changing abundance of food items; these subjects treated in detail by Dirschl (1969).

North of Great Slave L., N.W.T., 25 "adults" (in June) and 38 "juvenile" (late July to early Aug. and in Sept.) having food in their esophagi were collected. The food was animal, less than 1% being vegetable. The main food, both in frequency of occurrence

230

and in quantity, of the "adults" was Amphipoda, Gastropoda, and Pelecypoda. The "juveniles" collected in late July to early Aug. had fed mainly on free-swimming organisms—Dipterous (midge) larvae, Conochostraca (clam shrimps), and Gerridae (water striders); those collected in Sept. had fed primarily on bottom-associated fauna—Amphipoda, Anisoptera (dragonfly) nymphs, Corixidae (beetles: water boatmen) (Bartonek and Murdy 1970).

In s. Alta. the young are essentially carnivorous during the preflight period. Food: amphipods 52%, dipterous larvae 16%, and gastropods 16%. Chironomids were the most important Diptera. Older young ate relatively more amphipods, a change attributed to movement of the birds from small to larger ponds. Although newly hatched young did considerable surface feeding, this was not reflected in their diet and apparently was inefficient compared with diving. They preferred to feed in deeper water than that used by the several species of dabbling ducks present. Summarized from L. G. Sugden (1973).

There is a buildup of grit in gizzards, older birds contain more of it than "juveniles" (Bartonek 1969). AWS RSP

## Greater Scaup

*Aythya marila*

Medium-sized diving duck, the larger of the 2 species of scaup commonly called "bluebill" or "broadbill" in N. Am. Differs from the Lesser Scaup in being larger (there is a slight overlap in size); bill av. longer and has decidedly larger nail; in proportion to its size, however, the bill of the Greater widens less distally and laterally (appears less spatulate); head profile in life smoothly contoured and nearly round; white of secondaries ("speculum") usually continues distally as white or light area on 6 inner primaries (but there is individual variation in its extent). Bill unicolor (like Lesser Scaup), not patterned (as in Ringneck and Tufted Duck). Iris yellow in both sexes, possibly from 1st fall on (the sexes differ in Lesser Scaup, more so in early age).

Definitive-feathered individuals, i.e., those with Basic wing: ♂ —nostril to tip of bill 30.5 mm. or more, width of nail on bill rarely less than 7.5 mm., and flattened wing rarely less than 220 mm., and ♀ —29.5+, 7+, amd 212+. These figures exceed those for Lesser Scaup (which see), but further sampling perhaps may reveal some overlap.

After early life drake has "belted" pattern—both ends of the bird very dark, midsection light (to white on sides and underparts). Alt.-Plumaged drake has predominantly green iridescence on head, rather than variants of violet (as in Lesser Scaup). The ♀ in Alt. has a clear-cut white facial front (larger than typical of Lesser Scaup, much larger than the poorly defined one of the ♀ Ringneck) and the "belted" pattern is evident even though the midsection does not contrast greatly with darker ends of the bird. Both sexes are more uniformly colored in Basic feathering and the facial front of the ♀ often is reduced to lateral patches (may be poorly defined). See below for individual variation and for predefinitive Plumages of both sexes.

The drake's trachea is slightly enlarged and flattened in distal ⅔, then tapers to considerably smaller at inner end where the left-sided bony bulla is large, flattened, and very like that of the Ringneck (*A. collaris*), Common Pochard (*A. ferina*), etc. Most useful illus.: p. 214 in Schiøler (1926).

The sexes differ in coloring of feathers (but not of eyes) and somewhat in pattern. Length ♂ 17–20 in., ♀ 16–19; wingspread of ♂ to 32½, ♀ to 31; usual wt. of ♂ under

2½ lb., ♀ about 2 lb. There are 2 subspecies, slightly differentiated, and both in our area—1 widespread, the other as a straggler to Greenland.

DESCRIPTION  *A. marila mariloides.* Two Plumages/cycle in both sexes (no evidence of 3 in the definitive cycle of the ♀, although such a possibility was suggested in Schiøler 1926. Some ♀♀ are quite ♂-like in appearance, i.e., have black head with greenish sheen and other "drake" characters. The tail in both sexes (like most of the wing) is molted once/cycle. There are 3 Plumages in calendar year of hatching, in both sexes, with molt from Juv. into much Basic I occurring early. Molting and its variation in the definitive cycle were described by Billard and Humphrey (1972) who, however, consistently transposed the terms Basic and Alt. when referring to ♀♀.

▶   ♂ Def. Alt. Plumage (all feathering except tail and most of wing), acquired in FALL (late Aug. through Sept., occasionally later) and retained into following SUMMER (usually molted beginning in latter part of June). **Bill** somewhat muted turquoise-cobalt with blackish nail; **iris** vivid yellow. Head, neck, forepart of body (upper back and all of breast) black, the head with predominantly greenish iridescence, occasionally a white chin spot, and more rarely a paler (brownish or even partly whitish) neck ring; **upperparts** mantle white to very pale grayish, coarsely vermiculated black; rump black; **underparts** the black of breast ends in an even transverse line; belly white, this extending up to include sides and flanks or else they become clouded with very fine dark vermiculations, and posteriorly the abdomen appears grayish, being more or less vermiculated dark; under-tail area black. Legs and **feet** as bill but coloring more muted, webs blackish.

**Wing** elongated innermost secondaries tapering, blackish, with sparse to considerable light flecking distally but not extending to margins (plain border zone), their longer overlying coverts similar except flecking extends to margins; remainder of wing, also the tail, are retained Basic feathering.

NOTE  For important data on individual variation in ♂ Alt. Plumage, see L. Bishop (1895a). In new Alt., some ♂♂ have the breast feathers edged white.

▶   ♂ Def. Basic Plumage (entire feathering), the head–body–innermost feathers of wing acquired in SUMMER, usually beginning in latter part of June or very early July, and the tail and remainder of wing acquired in FALL when the remainder of the bird is molting back into Alt. In general, quite like ♀ Def. Alt. except no white facial front (although occasional white feathers) and **upperparts** are more coarsely vermiculated. **Head** and neck variants of blackish brown, lighter on cheeks and chin, often with scattered white feathers (especially around base of bill), and nape darkest with intermingled gray feathers having coarse black vermiculations; dark breast feathers have white edging; white of **underparts** generally more or less mottled brownish, the under-tail area mixed dark (not black) and white. **Tail** dark grayish.

**Wing**, typically, 4 outer primaries blackish brown, the 6 others having progressively more whitish on basal ⅔ and on both webs (as an extension of speculum) but L. Bishop (1895a) showed that drakes vary individually from white on all primaries to white on none; innermost secondaries have broad ends and are unmarked blackish; the next 2 are greenish black with narrow black outer margins; the others are white with black ends (broadest on proximal and grading to narrowest on distal one); upper wing coverts

233

dark, most of the greater ones plain, the middle and lesser ones lightly to heavily ver-miculated whitish; wing lining white except primary coverts medium gray and some light-margined dark feathers adjoin leading edge of wing; axillars white.

▶ ♀ Def. Alt. Plumage (all feathering, excepting the tail and all but innermost feath-ers of wing), acquired in FALL (Sept.–Oct., sometimes even to mid-Nov.) and suc-ceeded by Basic head–body in LATE WINTER or EARLY SPRING.

**Bill** rather slaty bluish; **iris** yellow. **Head** and neck vary with individual from buffy brownish to very dark brown to essentially black with greenish sheen, except a clear-cut and typically wide white facial front (always present?) which extends all around base of bill and often there are scattered white feathers elsewhere on head and neck; **upperparts** variable, but generally a brownish fuscous, with (especially on scapulars) more or less coarse white vermiculations on distal ends of feathers; rump dark; **under-parts** breast, sides, and flanks usually a warm brownish, the lower feathers of breast often white edged, those of sides and flanks with paler brown borders; also, on sides and flanks, some brown feathers are vermiculated white distally and there may be in-termingled some white feathers that are vermiculated dark; belly white (the underly-ing body down is ashy brown); grading on abdomen toward dusky and then sooty or same mottled lighter; under-tail area white, generally with considerable dark vermicu-lations. Legs and **feet** lead-colored, the webs darkest. **Wing** innermost secondaries usually unmarked dark, rarely slightly speckled white near tips, the overlying coverts plain dark; remainder of wing and the tail are retained Basic Plumage.

NOTE Occasional ♂-like individuals, although they possess the white facial front of the ♀, not only have ♂-like color of head, but also ♂ pattern on dorsum, sides, and under-tail area. For a color illus. of this variant in nominate *marila*, see pl. 19 in Schiøler (1926).

▶ ♀ Def. Basic Plumage (entire feathering), the head–body acquired beginning in FEB. (exceptionally, earlier) with heavy molting in spring (late Feb. to mid-March) and retained until EARLY FALL; the tail comes in late, and most of the wing not until (in fall) the head–body are molting back into Alt. This is a more blended, generally somewhat darker (toward brownish olive) Plumage, but it bleaches toward yellowish brown dur-ing summer. **Head** white facial front tends to be poorly defined or ragged at its poster-ior margin; sometimes it is reduced, there being only a whitish area on each side and very little white on chin; quite commonly there is a light (to white) auricular patch, often well developed in the Greater (but seldom the Lesser) Scaup in the last third of May (and probably due in part to feather wear); **upperparts** feathers toward sooty brownish, margined paler brownish (but they bleach and their ends become frayed); sometimes there are some intermingled buffy brown feathers vermiculated dark; **under-parts** breast, sides, and flanks generally a rather warm dark brownish, various feathers (especially on sides) with broad paler margins; white of belly (the feathers are at least subterminally gray and have white ends) and forepart of abdomen generally not sharply delineated, and sometimes darkish feathers are scattered throughout; the ven-tral down is very dark with conspicuous light centers; under-tail area toward sepia, plain or with whitish flecks or vermiculations; **tail** dark brownish olive.

**Wing** primaries medium blackish brown, inner portion of both webs of 6 innermost feathers off-white; most secondaries white with dark brownish ends (form a stripe at trailing edge); innermost secondaries blackish brown (unmarked) and comparatively broad near ends (but are very tapering in worn condition), the greater coverts over them also plain (always?) and dark; the dark middle coverts do not always have white flecking (it is near the edges if present); when it is present, it is a diagnostic difference from ♀ Juv. wing (which has plain coverts). Wing lining as ♂ Def. Basic.

NOTE   The venter, in worn condition, often is very patchy (dark and light).

AT HATCHING   **Bill** blackish, often yellowish at tip, the lower mandible yellow; **iris** dark. **Head** forehead buffy brown becoming brownish olive with buffy streaks on crown and nape; superciliary area, lores, cheeks, chin, throat, and sides of neck pale buffy brown to buffy yellow; small, indistinct brownish olive streak in front of eye; **upperparts** brownish olive to dark brownish olive, with more or less buffy brown on upper back and small pale buffy brown scapular marking; **underparts** very pale yellowish buffy, becoming darker at sides and under tail; **tail** brownish olive; **wing** brownish olive dorsally without ulnar markings.

Age for age, downy Lesser Scaups (*A. affinis*) are smaller than Greater (*A. marila*), with smaller nail on bill; they also differ somewhat in head pattern and a pale ulnar spot is present. Young Ringnecks (*A. collaris*) differ from both in having very dark crown contrasting greatly with light forehead.

▶   ♂ Juv. Plumage (all feathering; in entirety retained briefly, most of wing retained nearly a year), acquired by late SUMMER (Aug.–Sept.), depending on date of hatching. Feathers of belly come in first, then scapular area, tail, side of head, and then front of face, rear of crown, and midportion of back; bird appears full-sized before the last down disappears from neck; flight feathers of wing are last to develop (many young do not attain flight until very late Aug. or early Sept.—in Alaska usually early Sept.).

**Bill** slaty; **iris** brown to yellowish brown. Differs from ♀ Def. Basic thus: **head** narrow off-white facial front, even more poorly defined at its rear margin; remainder of head and the neck paler brownish or with palish area on side of head; **upperparts** between sepia and buffy brown, various feathers with paler margins and a few sometimes with whitish vermiculations; **underparts** upper breast medium brownish, terminating unevenly; lower breast and belly white, becoming somewhat streaked darkish posteriorly; upper sides and flanks quite pale brownish, the feathers narrow and with slightly paler margins; under tail coverts grayish brown (not patterned). **Tail** paler and browner, the feather ends blunt or notched. Legs and **feet** slaty. **Wing** differs from ♂ Def. Basic thus: innermost elongated secondaries narrow, rounded at very ends (but soon become frayed and pointed), plain darkish or, in some individuals faintly speckled white; greater and middle upper coverts narrower, their ends not smoothly rounded, the former generally plain, the latter vermiculated or slightly flecked white except for plain border on each feather.

▶   ♀ Juv. Plumage (all feathering; in entirety retained briefly, most of wing retained nearly a year), timing as ♂. Similar to ♂ Juv. except: **upperparts** generally plain; **wing** greater coverts over narrow elongated innermost secondaries are plain (not flecked); middle coverts usually plain, occasionally lightly flecked near edges.

NOTE   The Juv. Plumage and its variation, in both sexes, needs study. Some specimens are dark headed and others vary to having a well-indicated white facial front and/or a pale area on side of head. Whether there are diagnostic differences between

♂ and ♀ Juv. Plumage remains unknown. The matter has been complicated by authors confusing Basic I with Juv. Plumage. The iris evidently becomes yellow quite early in life in both sexes, but details are unknown.

▶ ♂ Basic I Plumage (probably all feathering except, in wing, only a few innermost feathers), generally begins to be evident in SEPT. and quite rapidly succeeds various portions of Juv. Plumage; by the time most of it has appeared, the head and sides are beginning to lose it and to acquire Alt. I (black head, white sides). The Basic I tail comes in last, in late FALL or even WINTER—after much of the remainder of Basic I has been succeeded by Alt. I—and is much faded and frayed by early summer.

A rather plain dusky Plumage. **Head**, neck, and **dorsum** almost uniformly fuscous, or with scant fine white dotting or vermiculation on some mantle feathers; much of breast fuscous, the feathers when new margined a pale warm brownish; on lower **breast** they are basally white, subterminally fuscous, and broadly white terminally; belly white and, posteriorly on abdomen, the feathers become increasingly darker with progressively less white on ends, so that the effect is somewhat of barring (white and dark) and such a pattern extends to include under-tail area; sides and flanks gray-brown, the long flank feathers sometimes with some white vermiculations. **Tail** feathers grayish brown. **Wing** innermost secondaries very dark, plain, and broader distally than their Juv. precursors; their longest overlying coverts also plain dark; remainder of wing is retained Juv. feathering.

▶ ♂ Alt. I Plumage (inclusive feathering as Basic I, except no new tail), usually begins to succeed Basic I in late SEPT. or Oct., and molting commonly continues into Nov., in some individuals into WINTER. Even after much of it has appeared, the last of Basic I (the tail) grows; the Basic I belly and abdomen often are retained into winter. The Alt. I feathering is worn into the following SUMMER, usually past mid-June.

In general, Alt. I is like ♂ Def. Alt., but differs in various details. The black **head** seldom has much greenish sheen; **upperparts** on dorsum the black and white pattern is more irregular, rump not as dark; **underparts** dark of breast tends to terminate somewhat farther forward and often in an uneven fashion (not an abrupt transverse boundary); feathers on sides and flanks often white, sparingly vermiculated fuscous; belly white, posteriorly (on abdomen) more or less evenly gray-brown; vent to tail same or somewhat darker, even with a few black feathers, but not all black as in Def. Alt. **Wing** innermost feathers as in Def. Alt., remainder is retained Juv. feathering, the **tail** retained Basic. I.

NOTE Apparently individuals vary from molting continuously from Juv. into Basic I and then into Alt. I during fall to having an interruption or delay (often after much Basic I is acquired); that is, different drakes are acquiring much Alt. I at any time from early Oct. at least through Jan.

▶ ♀ Basic I Plumage (probably all feathering except most of wing); as in ♂, much of it rapidly succeeds the Juv., often in SEPT. This Plumage is much like ♀ Def. Basic. However, the white facial front commonly is reduced to a more or less oval patch on each side of head, with or without a small amount of white on chin; auricular area generally palish; sparse speckling on the dark dorsum; breast, sides, and flanks plain brownish; white of belly grades into dusky on abdomen and the under-tail area is very dark and the feathers have light ends. **Wing** inner feathers as ♀ Def. Basic and remainder is retained Juv. feathering.

236

▶ ♀ Alt. I Plumage (probably all feathering except, in wing, only a few innermost feathers), commonly succeeds at least much of Basic I in OCT.–NOV., but as late as Jan. in some tardy individuals. Then it is succeeded by most of the next Plumage (Basic II) beginning in early SPRING. Alt. I is like later ♀ Alts., i.e., white **facial front** (variable in size), **dorsum** has some black and white vermiculations (scapulars mainly), white area of **belly** sharply defined; under-tail area all very dark, etc. **Wing** innermost feathers as ♀ Def. Alt., remainder is retained Juv. feathering.

NOTE As in young drakes (see above), ♀ ♀ show considerable variation in timing of Basic I and Alt. I. Also as in drakes, the Basic I tail comes in late and is retained and worn with Alt. I, and the Basic I belly and abdomen commonly is retained at least until well after the remainder of head–body are in Alt. I. The ♀ Alt. I Plumage shows the same extensive individual variation as ♀ Def. Alt.

▶ ♀ Basic II Plumage—as succeeding Def. Basics. The head–body acquires this feathering beginning in early SPRING (before age 1 year); the molt commonly is quite prolonged or somewhat delayed (in most individuals at least from early March through May) and the terminal phase, molting from Juv. into Basic wing, occurs not long before molting of head–body back into Alt.—somewhat earlier than in older age-classes (breeders).

**Measurements** 12 ♂ (from scattered localities, Alaska to Conn., mostly winter): BILL 44–49 mm., av. 46; WING 218–231, av. 223; TAIL 53–61, av. 56.8; TARSUS 38–42, av. 39.8; 11 ♀ (Alaska to Conn., mostly winter): BILL 42–45 mm., av. 43.8; WING 208–225, av. 215.6; TAIL 52–59, av. 55.6; TARSUS 38–41, av. 38.8 (ETS).

For series meas. across chord of WING, see J. C. Phillips (1925).

**Weight** ♂ adult 2 lb. 4 oz. to 2 lb. 10 oz. (1.0–1.1 kg.), exceptionally 2 lb. 12 oz. (1.2 kg.), and in Dec. in N.C. the av. was 2 lb. 5½oz.; ♀ adult 2 lb. to 2 lb. 5 oz. (0.9–1.0 kg.), the av. in Dec. in N.C. was 2 lb. 2 oz. (J. C. Phillips 1925).

In Alaska, in the Brooks Range at Anaktuvik Pass, May 24–June 4–17 ♂ 844–1,046 gm., av. 932; and May 27–June 10, 9 ♀ 856–1,117, av. 957 (Irving 1960). At Minto Lakes, Alaska, June 4—4 ♂ 840–983 gm., av. 920; and 5 ♀ 990–1,088, av. 1,008 (B. Kessel).

Molting birds at Minto Lakes, 3 ♂ July 31–Aug. 1 weighed 819–896 gm., av. 863; and 12 ♀ July 29–Aug. 2 weighed 714–810 gm., av. 765 (B. Kessel); after confinement up to several days at Ohtig L. (e. of Ft. Yukon) on Aug. 10, 3 ♂ 680.4–907.2 gm. and 2 ♀ 681–907 (Yocom 1970a); and 12 ♀ at Selawik, Aug 1–18, av. 1 lb. 12 oz. (about 795 gm.) (B. Kessel). (It is of interest that, in the nominate race at Mývatn, Iceland, the mean wt. of ♀ ♀ in the breeding season showed marked variation in different years, evidently depending on fluctuations in amount of available food—see Bengston 1972c).

In fall hunting season, age-classes and localities not stated: 60 ♂ av. 2.2 lb. (998 gm.), max. 2.9 (1,317 gm.), and 43 ♀ av. 2 lb. (908 gm.), max. 2.9 (1,317) (A. L. Nelson and Martin 1953).

Wintering birds at Seneca L. in cent. N.Y., early Jan. to late March: ♂ 44 "adult" 850–1,350 gm., mean 1,054 ± 13, and 40 "immature" [= 1st winter] 830–1,150, mean 990 ± 8; ♀ 23 "adult" 740–1,260 gm., mean 976 ± 36, and 29 "immature" 830–1,170, mean 987 ± 27 (Ryan 1972).

Four ducklings on day of hatching weighed 42.5–45 gm., the mean being 43.9 (Smart 1965a).

**Hybrids**   J. C. Phillips (1925, citing Poll) listed 4 species with which *Aythya marila* had crossed, including the Redhead (*A. americana*) of N. Am., and stated that he knew of no instances of *marila* hybridizing in confinement. He must have intended "except in confinement," since there seems to be no certain evidence of natural crosses of *marila* with any other species in N. Am.

The worldwide list (in Gray 1958) of species with which *Aythya marila* has crossed included 1 *Anas*, 6 *Aythya*, 1 *Bucephala*, and 1 *Oxyura*; of these, presumed natural hybrids were listed only with *Aythya nyroca* and *Bucephala clangula* (both in the Palearctic).

The cross (captive, also wild-shot) *A. marila* × *A. fuligula* is a "scaup type" hybrid; 3 such drakes were described and illus. by E. H. Gillham et al. (1966). Evidently the head is not smoothly contoured, but instead has a "bump" on top in these drakes.

Presumed wild *marila* × *fuligula* crosses were seen near Reykjavik, Iceland, in 1965 and 1967. In 7 years' observations at Mývatn, Iceland, 16 mixed pairs were seen; in 14 the ♂ was *fuligula* and 2 of these ♂ ♂ were accompanied by both a ♀ *marila* and a ♀ *fuligula*; since the latter species forms pairs and nests earlier than *marila*, and there is a greater excess of *fuligula* ♂ ♂, presumably these ♂ ♂ can find unmated ♀ *marila* more easily than *marila* ♂ ♂ can find *fuligula* ♀ ♀ (Bengtson 1968).

Very few wild ♀ *Aythya* hybrids have been recognized and reported.

**Geographical variation** in the species is slight and apparently is evident only in Alt.-Plumaged drakes; individual variation is greater than has been generally noted. Drakes in Def. Alt. have coarser dark barring on upperparts, especially on the scapulars, in N. Am. than in Palearctic. Hartert (1920a) gave smaller wing meas. for drakes of far eastern Asia, so that they have been referred to generally (without further investigation) as smaller birds than those from anywhere else. (Apparently he was referring to the birds that winter on the Asian Pacific border.) In Eurasia and westward to include Iceland and Greenland, drakes have finer dorsal markings. N. Am. drakes usually have near-white to white on fewer primaries (usually the 6 inner ones) than those of Eurasia. L. Bishop (1895a), who examined drakes taken on winter range in the e. U.S. (Conn.), found great individual variation in wing pattern (and other characters); the amount of white or light ranged from none on any primary to at least some on all primaries. The latter apparently also is the usual condition in drakes from Iceland and eastward across Eurasia. RSP

SUBSPECIES   Authors formerly listed 3, but several recent ones have listed none. Hellmayr and Conover (1948) and Parkes (1958) have shown that, on the basis of coloring of Alt.-Plumaged drakes, the species can be divided into coarsely barred (Nearctic) and finely barred (Palearctic) populations. The birds differ little, if at all, in size (J. C. Phillips 1925). Females and predefinitive-feathered drakes probably are not supspecifically identifiable. Treatment below accords with Delacour (1959, text, not map).

*mariloides* (Vigors)—includes "*nearctica*" of authors; full descr. and meas. are given above; Alt.-Plumaged drakes have coarsely barred upperparts and usually have near-white or white on only 6 inner primaries; N. Am., including the Aleutians.

*marila* (Linnaeus)—Alt.-Plumaged drakes have finely barred upperparts and usually white on more (generally all) primaries; breeds from Iceland eastward across Siberia.

Stragglers to Greenland are assigned to this subspecies, since evidently some Icelandic birds go there; most Greenland specimens are ♀♀ or ♂♂ in predefinitive feathering, but the several Alt.-Plumaged drakes are nominate *marila* (Salomonsen 1967a).

Thirteen ♂ (Iceland, Britain, w. U.S.S.R., and 1 winter from Japan): BILL 40–46 mm., av. 44.5; WING 215–228, av. 221.8; TAIL 56–64, av. 59.2; TARSUS 38–41, av. 39.5; 6 ♀ (1 Iceland, 1 Netherlands, 2w. U.S.S.R., and 2 in winter from Japan): BILL 40–44 mm., av. 42.3: WING 212–216, av. 214; TAIL 47–60, av. 57.7; TARSUS 37–40, av. 38 (ETS).

For meas. over curve of WING, also full descr. of this subspecies, see Witherby (1939); for additional meas. (WING flattened) and 2 especially fine color plates, see Schiøler (1926). RSP

FIELD IDENTIFICATION   In N. Am. The Greater and Lesser Scaup are so nearly similar in appearance that they are difficult, in fact often impossible, to distinguish at any distance. The single most useful character is the white wing stripe, which, typically, in the Greater Scaup extends outward beyond the secondaries well onto the primaries (it ends at the primaries in the Lesser). Although sometimes impossible to see when the wingbeat is fast, the stripe shows well when the birds have their wings set for alighting. It shows best when resting birds stretch their wings (comfort movements).

The drakes of the 2 species most of the year are very dark ended and very light around the middle; the middle appears white in strong light. The Greater has a very rounded (not angular) head profile and the upper sides of the body often are nearly white. There is some, but much less, difference in head shapes of ♀♀. In both our scaups the ♀♀ have unicolor (rather dark) bills and typically have well-defined white facial fronts, from fall through winter and at least into spring. This distinguishes them as scaups. From late spring into early fall, many ♀♀ of both scaups have a poorly defined pale auricular patch and a similar patch is found in some young ♂♂ in fall. This patch, however, is most evident in mature ♀ Greater Scaups, from the last third of May on (few ♀ Lessers show it then).

Most of our *Aythya* species during summer and early fall molting (when wearing much Basic Plumage) are very similar-appearing, foreshortened or "dumpy," nondescript ducks. This includes the scaups, Ringneck, Tufted Duck, and Redhead; the Canvasback has a more obviously distinctive bill–head profile (attenuated sloping "forehead"). Unless disturbed, the various species when molting tend to keep more or less apart, even when on the same lake; an occasional early or tardy molter may have enough Alt. Plumage for this to be an aid in identification.

Away from breeding areas, the Greater Scaup tends to "raft up" on open waters. Under such circumstances it is a wary bird, but small flocks become rather tame. The Lesser prefers more sheltered, also fresh, waters.

Compare "Field Identification" of the various other *Aythya* species. FCB

VOICE   Little useful information. Perhaps usually silent except during certain displays, and then not noisy. The ♂ in Coughing display has a rather weak rapid whistle; in Kinked-neck, Head-throw, and postcopulatory displays, a soft rapid *wa-hoo*. J. C.

239

Phillips (1925) stated that "almost all sportsmen" are familiar with the ♀'s loud, hoarse note, which would seem to imply that it is uttered commonly. It has been variously rendered *kaup kaup* or *karr karr karr* and so on. It is guttural and rasping, especially when the ♀ is disturbed with her brood. A rasping *arr*, varying from loud to rather quiet, is uttered by the ♀ when Inciting. She is said also to have a rather weak crooning note.

Clearly the full repertoire of calls and contexts in which they are given remain undescribed. RSP

HABITAT   In N. Am. Breeds from within the forest zone (on open flats, windswept is. in lakes) n. through a mixture of open terrain with many areas of water and patches of trees and beyond to richly vegetated low tundra. This environment begins with the discontinuous permafrost zone and extends onto the continuous one; after spring runoff, local water levels are fairly stable. Occurs in equivalent habitat away from permafrost in sw. Alaska, the treeless Aleutians, and various places in Canada eastward to e. Nfld.

Molts (passes flightless period) in assemblies on inland lakes, to a limited extent also on the sea.

In migration occurs both on larger inland waters (especially lakes) and on brackish and inshore marine waters.

In winter mainly on salt and brackish coastal bays, estuaries, and other broad expanses of marine and nearby unfrozen fresh waters. Generally in less sheltered places than preferred by Lesser Scaup. RSP

DISTRIBUTION  (See map.)  *Aythya marila* is boreal–subarctic when nesting and a more or less marine species in winter.

*A. marila mariloides*—since the last glaciation this scaup has spread as a nester from the Bering Sea region eastward across Canada, along the general route of migrants traveling (in both directions) between Alaska and the Atlantic coast. In the process, there has developed an overlap of general breeding ranges of Greater and Lesser Scaup, plus some outlying breeding places of the Greater far to the east, as in n. Ungava. It is difficult, however, to escape an impression that the vast majority of Greater Scaups in N. Am. still nest in Alaska.

**Breeding**   Has been found nesting in Alaska in all major duck-producing areas where ground studies have been made; most abundant in westerly areas, as from Kotzebue Sd. to Bristol Bay; common in the interior; common in the Aleutians, especially on Amchitka and Unalaska; widely distributed on the North Slope; evidently in fewest numbers in e. areas (Yukon flats, Tetlin Lakes) and s.-cent. areas (Nelchina, Anchorage), except locally plentiful in the Copper R. delta.

Perhaps locally common in some areas in nw. Canada, but information is rather scant. Has nested in extreme nw. B.C. In June, 1971, a pair was found some 300 mi. beyond known breeding range at a place about 100 mi. ne. of Bathurst Inlet at lat. 67°24′ N, long. 140°42′ W. Southern limits in w. Canada are hard to define, in part because of confusion with Lesser Scaup. J. Munro (1938) published 2 photos of a nesting ♀ labeled Lesser Scaup, taken in 1931 at Ministik L., Alta. (lat. 53°21′ N, long.

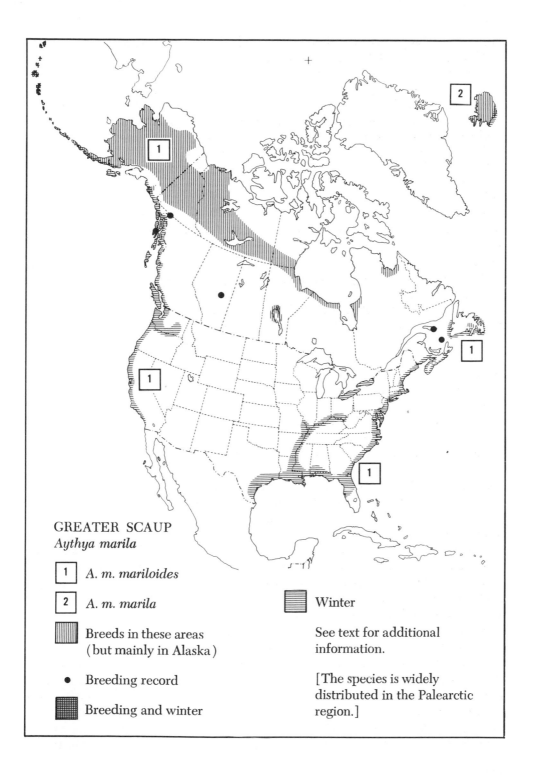

GREATER SCAUP
*Aythya marila*

1   *A. m. mariloides*

2   *A. m. marila*

▥   Breeds in these areas
    (but mainly in Alaska)

●   Breeding record

▦   Breeding and winter

▤   Winter

See text for additional
information.

[The species is widely
distributed in the Palearctic
region.]

113°01′ W.); it appears to be a Greater Scaup. The Greater is a common nester in the n. L. Winnipeg area—details in Vermeer et al. (1972).

The Greater Scaup's nesting distribution extends along the s. border of Hudson Bay, then across to the e. side of James and Hudson Bays; it definitely nests in the Chimo region of n. Ungava, possibly also near the Labrador coast. It nests commonly in an area of perhaps 40 sq. mi. located inland from the se. shore of Nfld.; it has nested on Anticosti and in the Magdalens, both in the Gulf of St. Lawrence.

Alleged nesting in N.D. is very doubtful and the Mich. record (both are in the 1957 A.O.U. *Check-list*) was given originally as Lesser Scaup. There are other supposed breeding occurrences in the w. conterminous U.S., none recent. A few birds linger s. of known breeding range.

**Summer**    The places to find assemblies of molting drakes are the larger lakes within the general breeding range. Examples: Takslesluk and Dall Lakes and probably Baird Inlet in the Yukon–Kuskokwim delta region, Beaverhouse L. on the Minto flats, the Minto Lakes (a few birds), definitely at various lakes on the Seward Pen. and probably such places as Shismaref Inlet and Lopp and Arctic lagoons, also probably the larger lakes on the North Slope.

Along the arctic (Beaufort Sea) Alaskan coast, from the Colville delta e. to Demarcation Pt., molting flocks of 100–200 Greater Scaups occur in the bays and about is., reefs, and spits; they total perhaps 2,000 (being greatly outnumbered by molting Old-squaws) and evidently equal in numbers only to a small fraction of ♂ breeders on the North Slope.

Interestingly, no molting Greater Scaups are known to occur in the Aleutians, in lagoons, bays, or on the sea.

**Migrations**    The Greater Scaup may occur almost anywhere, from molting and breeding areas southward on the continent and along coasts, but is very scarce from the Canadian prairies southward in the interior. Has occurred in Bermuda.

**Winter** range includes Aleutian localities and the Copper R. delta in Alaska, and the Am. rim of the Pacific, especially from s. B.C. down to s. Cal. In the interior, Lakes Erie and Ontario (in long spells of freezing weather the birds move to the lower Niagara R.), possibly also s. L. Michigan. In N. Am. Atlantic waters, occurs at various localities around Nfld. (except n. part), also around the Maritimes, then plentiful in Mass. and coastal N.Y. (probably over 100,000 in some years), s. to cent. Fla. (along both coasts) and s. Fla. (a few); on the upper Gulf of Mexico coast (probably few in most winters); and to a very limited extent inland up the main Mississippi drainage (most birds there are Lesser Scaups). May occur, irregularly and in small numbers, on open water almost anywhere in the continental interior—for example, records for Utah and Colo.

Southern limits in N. Am.: on the Pacific side to nw. Mexico (n. Baja Cal. and Sinaloa); on the Atlantic side to s. Fla., the Bahamas, and w. Cuba.

NOTES    Between Alaska and Siberia the species has occurred on St. Lawrence I. (May, June, and Oct. records) and has been taken in the Pribilofs. As to the Asiatic side, under the subspecific name *mariloides*, Portenko (1972) stated (here translated): "On Chuckchee Pen. they occur as strays during migration, also vagrant nonnesting pairs or molting drakes, but rarely, and mostly in w. localities. No nests, eggs, or young have been found, but nuptial behavior has been observed. Has not been recorded for

Wrangel I." The nesting localities nearest to N. Am. are in from the s. rim of the Okhotsk Sea and the far eastern birds winter principally from Sakhalin I. down through Japan.

Reported in the Hawaiian Is. (some published reports probably are inaccurate) as follows: Kauai—1961; Oahu—1946, 1967, and 1969; Hawaii—1902 (Berger 1972). To the south, this species is reported (Gallagher 1960) as seen on Christmas I.

*A. m. marila*—in the N. Atlantic area this bird is widespread and plentiful as a nester in Iceland; a few hundred remain through the winter in the sw. sector; their main wintering area is Ireland, but Britain and the Netherlands are important also. Presumably it is birds from Iceland that straggle to Greenland, where there are a few records for 1860–1940 at localities from ne. and e. Greenland, also from s. Greenland and up the w. coast to Sukkertoppen (Salomonsen 1967a).

The nominate race winters in e. Atlantic waters and on various inland seas (unfrozen portions of the Baltic, also the Mediterranean, Black, and Caspian) and has occurred widely elsewhere (it is *mariloides* that breeds in far e. Asia and winters on the Asian Pacific coast).

In the Nearctic the species is recorded as **fossil**, of Pleistocene age, from Ore., Nev., and Fla., and from 2 **archaeological sites** in Alaska; in the Palearctic as **fossil** in Ireland (2 localities), Denmark (several localities), Italy (2 localities), and from an **archaeological site** in England. References to all these were listed by Brodkorb (1964a); for Fla., also see Ligon (1965).

Serebrovsky (1941) described *A. m. asphaltica* from 2 fossil (Pleistocene) crania from the Binagada deposits in Azerbaijan. RSP

MIGRATION In N. Am.    Not much useful published information exists. The following is tentative.

The birds from n. and much of interior Alaska and probably nw. Canada go se. in fall (over the general Canadian breeding range of the species), more or less toward s. Hudson Bay. Those continuing on a more northerly course go to e. L. Erie, L. Ontario, and the upper (inner) St. Lawrence; later they cross over to Atlantic coastal waters and are plentiful in winter in New Eng. (mainly Mass.). Others travel farther s. (from n. Man.), via the n. edge of Lakes Superior and Huron, also to Lakes Erie and Ontario, and thence to Long I., N.Y., and probably some places farther to the south. Still others come down through w. Man. (L. Winnipegosis) to lakes in Minn. and Wis. and then cross eastward to Chesapeake Bay and waters thereabouts. There is considerable shifting of birds down along the coast, to points as far as the upper half of Atlantic coastal Fla.; some probably cross to the west into the Gulf of Mexico. Which birds shift southward, and how far they go, evidently varies greatly depending on severity of season.

A very few Greater Scaups probably travel to and from s. destinations (n. Gulf of Mexico) within the continental interior, in company of Lesser Scaups and other divers.

The N. Am. Pacific migrants occur in winter at localities extending from the Aleutians and Copper R. delta in Alaska down to s. Cal., apparently with center of abundance in coastal conterminous U.S. waters. In fall the birds are numerous on lakes in B.C., presumably stopping there when coming via an interior route from breeding areas to the Pacific coast. On salt water, some remain at northerly places and others shift southward. In spring the birds migrate somewhat earlier than Lesser Scaups. There is a sizable movement along the B.C. coast. Yet it seems probable that, when or before they reach the n. B.C. coast, many go inland, and later westward, and so arrive at various Alaskan localities by a partially inland route.

**Dates**   The following are very general statements. SPRING Atlantic winterers are moving at coastal localities by early March and continuing until late April; in the latter month the majority of them go inland. They stop at various waters and begin arriving at nw. localities within the forest zone by about the end of the first week of May.

Pacific winterers are moving in March, on the s. B.C. coast beginning in that month, and most have moved on by late April. On breeding range they are intermingled more or less with Atlantic winterers.

In Alaska, migrants are abundant in the Copper R. delta from late April to mid-May (there are wintering birds in the area; others probably have come via marine routes). In the interior at Fairbanks they generally arrive May 9–14, either a few days earlier than or in close association with Lesser Scaups; the main passage lasts about 2 weeks. In 1955 they arrived at Selawik on May 17. Generally they arrive at Yukon Delta nesting areas about May 18 in "normal" seasons and to May 28 in "tardy" ones. Most migratory flocks have disappeared by June, the latest in some years by about June 7.

SUMMER–FALL   At first the birds are assembled on larger lakes (in Alaska principally from the cent. interior westward; most abundant duck in the Yukon–Kuskokwim delta region) and drakes are the first to regain flight after wing molt. There is some movement beginning early in Sept. (when drakes first regain flight), but on the larger, deeper, lakes (which do not freeze early) both scaup species still are present until early Oct. The birds stop at various inland lakes, often for a considerable time. They arrive on both Pacific and Atlantic coasts mainly from about mid-Oct. to mid-Nov.; then there is movement southward, sometimes until late Dec., on salt water.

NOTES   Although drakes complete the wing molt first, they are not necessarily the earliest birds to travel any distance in fall; they tend to slow down once they reach salt water, which results in a preponderance of ♂♂ at northerly wintering localities through fall or even into winter.

Some of the birds that winter on N. Am. Atlantic and Pacific waters are together when nesting and/or molting in w. Alaska; this association (the company an individual keeps) explains why some individuals are known (from banding) to have wintered on opposite coasts in different years.

At Takslesluk L. (confluent with Baird Inlet), not distant from Bering Sea coastal Alaska, 2,291 Greater Scaups were banded when flightless during wing molt in 1963–65 inclusive. There have been 50 recoveries, all of drakes. Thirteen were taken in the same area in subsequent molting seasons. Other recoveries are widely scattered in N. Am.: coastal Gulf of Alaska; s. B.C. to cent. Cal. (many); in the interior, especially Great Lakes region but also e. to the inner St. Lawrence (s. Ont., s. Que.); Atlantic coastal waters, Conn. to N.C. inclusive; and one banded Aug. 8, 1964, was recovered in coastal La. on Nov. 28 of the same year. (J. G. King).

Greater Scaup banded at Minto lakes (cent. interior Alaska) have been recovered primarily in conterminous U.S. in the Great Lakes region and in Atlantic coastal areas from New Eng. to Chesapeake Bay. BK RSP

244

BANDING STATUS   The total number banded in N. Am. through 1964 was 24,269 and the total number of recoveries through 1961 was 1,169; main places of banding: N.Y., Alaska, N.J., and Ore. (data from Bird Banding Laboratory). RSP

REPRODUCTION   The rather scant N. Am. data are summarized, supplemented by some information (mainly on displays) of nominate *marila*. Contrary to former belief, it is now known that various *Aythya* **first breed** as yearlings. For the Greater Scaup in N. Am. there are a few data on banded ♀ ♀ that demonstrate this and there is good evidence from examination of gonads of shot drakes that they also can breed as yearlings. Some yearling drakes having enlarged testes and paired to nesting ♀ ♀ of older cohorts have been collected.

In early winter the birds begin showing incipient sexual behavior, such as ducks following drakes and a number of the latter grouping about a ♀, but active pair formation occurs principally in Feb., March, and April. Thus many that are long-distance travelers either are paired before they migrate or become paired en route. Much of the display seen at stopover places presumably is for purposes of bond maintenance and synchronization of reproductive cycles of mates; other birds, perhaps mainly those approaching age 1 year, are actively engaged in pair formation until well along in spring. Display continues, although details are not fully known, up to the time when flocks break up and ♀ ♀ begin nesting.

**Displays of the duck**   INCITING the duck neck-stretches (vertically), occasionally makes lateral movements of bill, utters an *arrr* call, and sometimes Bill-dips. PREEN-BEHIND-THE-WING is directed toward a ♂ under various circumstances, later in mutual display.

**Displays of the drake**   Not all of the probable repertoire is known—for example, nothing on aerial and underwater activity. The following is based mainly on Johnsgard (1965), presumably from observations of captive *A. m. marila*.

COUGH drake utters a very rapid soft whistle *week week whew* (or a variant) and flicks wings and tail. A frequent display. HEAD-THROW in a display group (a number of ♂ ♂ near a ♀), a drake approaches a ♀, stops swimming, and gives one or more head shakes; the neck is held vertical and is distended with air, bill at an upward angle of 50°–60°, then there is a quick throw-back of the head (in median plane) and a soft rapid *wa-hoo* (accent on 1st syllable) is uttered. The ♀ responds by Inciting. KINKED-NECK as observed on the B.C. coast in Feb.–March: between periods of diving to feed, ♂ ♂ suddenly commence to bow, thrusting the head forward with neck arched until tip of bill touches water, then raising the head until the bill points upward vertically or slightly past the vertical, and the same call uttered as in the preceding display (J. Munro 1941). BILL DIP a less vigorous action than the preceding; the bill is dropped gently to the surface and then raised slightly above the horizontal, as though drinking (Munro). SNEAKING (of Johnsgard 1965); compare with Threat and Chase as described under Redhead. Head low, crown feathers depressed, as drake swims toward another ♂ or sometimes a ♀; done silently or perhaps with an inaudible call. TURNING-THE-BACK-OF-THE-HEAD with crown flattened, the ♂ swims ahead of the ♀; also occurs as mutual display of mates. PREEN-BEHIND-THE-WING directed toward ♀ ♀. NOD-SWIM apparently lacking (Johnsgard).

**Copulation**   The drake's precopulatory displays are Bill-dip, PREEN-DORSALLY, and Preen-behind-the-wing; the ♀ performs these and assumes a PRONE posture; after treading, the ♂ gives Kinked-neck call and swims with BILL-DOWN (neck erect, bill almost vertically downward), the ♀ swims briefly in same posture and then bathes.

Generally, when the flocks disintegrate, the ♀ ♀ go to fairly flat, low, open areas where there is dead herbage of the previous year, usually close to ponds and watercourses. Some nests are distant from water, up to perhaps a thousand meters. They also nest on islands and islets in lakes, as in Greak Slave Lake (P. A. Taverner 1926, Weller et al. 1969). The **nest site** often is a slightly elevated spot with an unobstructed view and the ♀ can walk the short distance to water rapidly if disturbed. A few nests are near or sheltered by low woody growth.

At Minto Lakes in Alaska, both scaups prefer open habitat adjacent to water, often nesting on floating vegetation supported primarily by buckbean (*Menyanthes trifoliata*). Preferred cover, however, is grass–sedge, largely *Glyceria*, along shores of lakes, ponds, and channels (R. Kirkpatrick). At Selawik, where the Greater is the only nesting scaup, many of the early nesters used sites at the exact high-water mark, about a week after water levels began to recede. Most such sites were grassy (P. E. K. Shepherd).

Very exceptional **concentrations** have been reported occasionally. There were about 50 nests, "some not over 2 ft. apart, others 10 ft. at most," along the edge of weeds on only a portion of an island about 4 acres in size near the end of the Alaska Pen. (Littlejohn 1899). The ultimate in recorded nesting density was described by Millais (1913a), as observed in nominate *marila* in the Mývatn dist. of Iceland. On 3 or 4 acres of open farmland there "must have been over 100 nests," sometimes 2 or 3 touching one another, in other cases 2 with a Mallard or Wigeon nest in between.

The ♀ makes or uses (and sometimes reuses) a slight cavity. During laying and into incubation, nest down and broken plant materials are accumulated, forming a lining and a covering for the eggs and often a substantial rim.

The **nest down** is very dark, quite like that of the Oldsquaw. At Hooper Bay, Alaska, it varied in different nests from black to blackish to darker browns, with inconspicuous slightly paler centers (Brandt 1943). Included feathers either were whitish or mottled gray and white. In 3 nests there was no down, but instead only small gray feathers; the ♀ ♀ collected from 2 of these nests were found to be thin and without subcutaneous fat. These gray feathers were not found in nests lined with down. According to Broley (1950), the dark portions of included feathers from the venter are evenly colored and the tip is narrowly white (not a gradation to a wide white terminal band as in the Lesser Scaup).

**A late nester**   Judging from fragments of information, full clutches may be expected in normal seasons in much of the breeding range in Alaska in the 2nd week of June—perhaps considerably earlier in the Aleutians and definitely so at some localities well within interior Alaska and in Canada. At Minto Lakes, Alaska, some ♀ ♀ began laying in late May in 1953 and 1954. As to late eggs, these are dates for the e. side of James Bay in Canada: July 8—nearly full-sized yolk in oviduct; July 14—egg in oviduct plus an empty follicle; July 17— ♀ with yolk in oviduct plus 3 emply follicles (Manning and Macpherson 1952). A ♀ from Selawik, Alaska, had a soft-shelled egg in oviduct July 29 (B. Kessel). Also see below for late hatching dates.

**Egg size** 180 eggs "in various collections" length 54.5–68.5 mm., av. 62.4, and breadth 40.7–48, av. 43.7 (Bent 1923); **shape** between long elliptical and long subelliptical (wider in proportion to length than in the Lesser Scaup); shell quite smooth but not glossy, **color** toward greenish, a variant of olive buff (very similar to Lesser Scaup).

Av. of 9 clutches (84 eggs) at Minto Lakes in 1954 was 62.8 × 43.7 mm. and wt. (stage of incubation not recorded) av. 62.5 gm. (B. Kessel).

**Clutch size** commonly 7–9 eggs. At Minto Lakes in 1954—14 complete clutches ranged 7–13, av. 9.8; Selawik in 1955—av. of 16 nests was 7.3 eggs (no indication of stage of clutch completion); Copper R. delta in 1959—18 nests av. 6.9 eggs (completed clutches?). At the West Mirage Is. in Great Slave Lake. N.W.T., 34 warm clutches contained 5–12 eggs, the mean and SD being 8.5 ± 1.55 (Weller et al. 1969). In addition, there were joint layings—16 eggs in each of 2 nests and 22 in another. A Red-breasted Merganser clutch of 4 also had 2 Greater Scaup eggs; a Greater Scaup clutch of 8 had an added Lesser Scaup egg; another consisted of 10 Greater Scaup and there were 1 Greater and 3 Lesser Scaup eggs outside the nest, indicating that some fighting had occurred between ♀♀. At Hooper Bay, Alaska, Brandt (1943) found 10 eggs of Greater Scaup plus 1 of Oldsquaw. Some 25 mi. se. of Hooper Bay, Alaska, in 1972, a nest contained 4 eggs of Spectacled Eider plus 3 of Greater Scaup; the eider incubated and all but 1 scaup egg hatched on July 3 (C. Dau). In Iceland a Greater Scaup and an Oldsquaw were found sitting on the same nest (Shepard, in S. F. Baird, et al. 1884b).

At Mývatn, Iceland, Bengtson (1971c) examined a very large number of clutches each year 1961–70 inclusive; clutch size varied from a low of 9.01 ± 0.16 for 117 clutches in 1970 to a high of 9.83 ± 0.10 for 192 clutches in 1961.

There seem to be no N. Am. data on **incubation period**. It is 24–25 days in *A. m. marila* in Finland (Hildén 1964b).

Some **hatching dates** in Alaska: Minto Lakes, in 1951—first broods July 7, peak of hatch about July 28, and some newly hatched ducklings as late as Aug. 2 or 3; in 1953—first hatch July 8, the peak in 2nd week in July, and a few broods (renestings?) Aug. 4–11; 1954—first hatch July 5, with peak at end of 2nd week in July; at Umiat in 1949—day-old young on July 26; Selawik in 1955—estimated first hatch date was July 16, the peak July 21–22, and 2 late broods Aug. 7.

The **young** are led to nearby water, where families may join company. The few reports of untended gatherings of preflight young would indicate that the ♀♀ leave them, probably not until they are quite large and well feathered, to join assemblies of molting drakes. By analogy with better-known *Aythya*, it is probable that young *marila* attain flight in 9–10 weeks. In interior Alaska a few young can fly by mid-Aug., but most attain flight in the last week of Aug. and 1st week in Sept. RSP BK

SURVIVAL No N. Am. data. In *A. m. marila*, calculating from published recoveries of birds banded in Iceland, plus Russian data (Isakov, in Dementiev and Gladkov 1952), the estimated mean annual adult survival rate is 0.48 ± .06 years (Boyd, in Le Cren and Holdgate 1962). RSP

HABITS In N. Am. A saltwater bird much of the year, capable of feeding in deeper, rougher water than the closely related pochards and white-eyes. The Greater

Oldsquaw

*Clangula hyemalis*

The 3 Plumages of the definitive cycle of both sexes are shown.

1 ♂ Def. Alt. (with retained Basic wing, tail, and possibly abdomen). Winter. Note long white scapulars and white upper sides. Head feathering is longest in Alt.

2 ♂ in late spring after acquiring part of Def. Basic. The scapulars are bicolored and intermediate in length. Sides still are in white Alt. The Basic head feathering is short.

3 ♂ well along in summer; at least part of Def. Basic body feathering now is succeeded by corresponding portions of Def. Suppl. In the dorsum (including scapulars) the new feathers are short, broad, rounded, and muted in coloring. Upper sides have molted from white (Alt.) to dark (late-incoming Basic). The drake is flightless, having molted the wing, and soon will molt the tail.

4-6 The duck has the same sequence as the drake, but timing is later. Compare scapulars: 4—Alt., 5—Basic, and 6—Suppl. As in the drake, the white (Alt.) of upper sides is succeeded late by dark (Basic) feathering. The duck in fig 6 is flightless and soon will molt the tail. The difference in amount of white on foreneck in figs. 5 and 6 is individual variation.

(A day-old downy Oldsquaw is shown in color in vol. 2 on plate facing p. 466.)

R.T.T. Trengel—

Scaup is highly gregarious in late fall and winter, the large rafts of birds generally occurring on wide expanses of water and being difficult to approach. Yet this scaup comes to decoys readily. J. Munro (1941) wrote of small groups that became so tame that they would come on signal to be fed. The birds move with the tide, or at other times keep station at a particular place, and rest on the sea. Except for nesting ♀ ♀, not much time is spent ashore; drakes rest at times along shorelines and on spits in the general vicinity of incubating ♀ ♀. Both sexes swim rather low, but appear more buoyant when asleep or resting. They dive very actively, wings closed, legs out laterally, and preferably in about 1 to 4 meters of water. The flocks tend to keep by themselves at times, but at other times are found mingled in with other divers, shoal-water ducks, and Coots (*Fulica americana*). They take wing with relative ease and tend to gain altitude immediately; they fly in compact flocks and their mobility is great in contrast to the actions of the less agile species of divers (J. Munro 1941).

The following are from Cronan's (1957) studies of wintering Greater Scaups in coastal Conn. The birds fed at any daylight hour (no night studies were made). They normally do not feed on mudflats, but take submerged mussels at all levels of tide. They fed regardless of rain, snow, and sleet, even when there were 3-ft. waves, and in breaking surf. They fed readily among various other ducks. Herring Gulls often robbed them of food, but this interfered rather little with their feeding. They fed mostly in less than 5 (but up to 23) ft. of water, where the blue mussel (which is a shoal-water mollusk) was abundant. They were easily driven away by human activity. Their av. time of submergence in feeding dives was 20.4 sec., range 9–33, and pause between dives was slightly less than duration of submergence.

In a raft, the birds at one end might be feeding, the others resting. Occasionally, feeding and resting birds were interspersed. On a current, the raft would be strung out in a line and the birds fed as they drifted by a feeding area; after having drifted a certain distance beyond, they would fly up-current and drift by again. In "drift feeding" there were periods of hours in which there was a constant procession of birds flying up-current. Yet at other times they fed by maintaining station in the same current, with no apparent difficulty. RSP

FOOD  *A. marila mariloides*. Nearly equally divided between vegetable 46.5% and animal 53.5% from the examination of 752 stomachs. The chief vegetable foods are pondweeds, muskgrass, water milfoils, sedges, wild rice, and wild celery; and animal: mollusks, insects, and crustaceans. Three "juveniles" from Alaska had consumed 58% vegetable matter and 42% animal matter, chiefly water fleas (Cladocera) and larvae of caddis flies (Trichoptera) (Cottam 1939). Some other studies show a preponderance of animal food.

**Vegetable**  Pondweeds (*Potamogeton, Ruppia, Zostera, Phyllospadix, Zannichellia*) 18.9%; muskgrass (*Chara*) 5.4%; water milfoils (*Hippuris, Myriphyllum*) 4.9%; sedges (*Scirpus, Carex, Eleocharis*) 3.3%; seeds of wild rice (*Zizania*) and other grasses (*Panicum, Paspalum, Echinochloa, Setaria, Leersia, Poa*) 2.9%; wild celery (*Vallisneria*) 1.5%; miscellaneous plant material 9.6% (Cottam 1939).

The 16 stomachs from the upper St. Lawrence contained 79.8% plant material consisting of *Vallisneria spiralis* 39.3%, *Scirpus americanus* 11.2%, and unidentified

249

24.9% (Kutz et al. 1948). On the lower Hudson the food was entirely vegetable, consisting of 37.9% *Najas minor* and 62.1% unidentified (Foley and Taber 1951). The 44 Long I. (N.Y.) specimens had eaten only 18.75% of plant material of which the identified portion (3.78%) was *Ulva lactuca* (Foley and Taber 1952). This was also the chief plant eaten in Conn. waters (Cronan 1957). Forty-four upper Chesapeake Bay birds had consumed eelgrass, wild celery, pondweeds and their seeds, and wigeon grass and its seeds (R. E. Stewart 1962). The 644 stomachs used by Kubichek (1933) were collected widely in N. Am. The food was 67.14% vegetable consisting mainly of *Potamogeton, Ruppia, Najas, Zannichellia,* and *Zostera.* Also in Mich. muskgrass (*Chara*), and seeds of bur reed (*Sparganium*) (Pirnie 1935). In 79 stomachs from Okanagan and Swan Lakes, B.C., *Chara* was the chief food, others being miscellaneous vegetable matter and mollusks; details in J. Munro (1941).

**Animal** Bivalve mollusks, especially the blue mussel (*Mytilus edulis*), oyster (*Ostrea lurida*), *Macoma, Protothaca, Mulinia, Gemma, Nucula, Arca, Modiolus,* etc. 23.20%; snails (*Nassarius, Lymnaea, Campeloma, Amnicola, Mitrella,* etc.), 15.92%; insects (Trichoptera, Chironomidae, Odonata, Dytiscidae, Corixidae, etc.), 7.2%; crustaceans (Amphipoda, *Hemigrapsus, Balanus*), 6.8%; miscellaneous, fishes, sea urchins, water mites, polychaete worms, etc., 0.4% (Cottam 1939).

A wintering bird from the Fox Is., Me. was filled with *Macoma balthica* (Norton 1909). Two specimens from Wenham Lake, Mass., contained *Gemma gemma* (J. C. Phillips 1911). The 81.25% animal matter consumed by Long I. birds contained 52.41% of bivalves of which the blue mussel formed 33.17%; undetermined mollusks 10.69%; and crustaceans 4.77% (Foley and Taber 1952). The blue mussel was also the chief food in Conn. waters along with *Mulinaria lateralis,* and undetermined Pelecypoda (Cronan 1957). In R. I. the food was also principally mollusks but mainly young sea clams (*Mactra solidissima*) (Lynch 1939). In upper Chesapeake Bay the animal food consisted of Pelecypoda (*Macoma, Laevicardium, Mulinia, Brachidontes,* etc.), and Gastropoda (*Bittium, Mitrella, Nassarius, Anachis, Aceteocina, Ilyanassa,* and *Oxystrema*) (R. E. Stewart 1962). Mollusks formed 84.7% of the stomach contents of birds from Oyster Bay, Wash., 41.6% consisting of oysters (*Ostrea lurida*) (Kubichek 1933). At Biloxi Bay, Miss., the birds fed on dead gulf menhaden (*Brevoortia patronus*) and where shrimp heads had been dumped (Christmas 1960).

In B.C., at coastal streams and lakes, foods in order of importance were vegetable matter, mollusks, salmon eggs, and salmon flesh; on salt water, gastropods, sea lettuce (*Ulva*), crustaceans, and eggs of Pacific herring (*Clupea pallasii*). The ducks visit salmon-spawning streams and, after a peiod of spawning, drifting eggs are easily obtainable from the stream bottom, i.e., need not be extracted from reeds. In March–April, unattached herring eggs settle to the bottom and are a chief food. (Summarized from J. Munro 1941.)

*A. m. marila* In Ireland, almost exclusively minute univalves (*Littorina littorea, L. retusa, Lacuna quadrifasciata, Rissoa ulvae, Cerithium reticulatum*); also the bivalve *Nucula margaritacea,* and minute crustaceans (*Idothea*) (W. Thompson 1851). In England mussels (*Mytilus edulis*), snails, and other mollusks, crabs, and starfish. Lives almost entirely on the snail, *Littorina littorea,* in the Baltic (Naumann 1905b). Stomachs of birds taken in Switzerland contained mollusks (*Valvata antiqua, Bythinia*

250

*tentaculata, Pisidium amnicum, Limnaea auricularia, L. stagnatilis*), larvae of diving beetles (Dytiscidae), dragonflies (Anisoptera), and skimmers (Libellulidae) (Fatio 1904). Principally fresh water mollusks (*Limnaea, Pisidium,* and *Succinea*) in Iceland (Slater 1901).

The food in Denmark in winter was 97% animal consisting of: Pelecypoda (*Mytilus, Cardium*) 67%; Gastropoda (*Littorina, Nassa, Hydrobia, Rissoa*) 23%; Crustacea (*Idothea*) 2.0%; Pisces (*Gobius*) 3.5%; and Annelida 1.5% (Madsen 1954).

The food in Russia is about equally divided between plant and animal. In the Pechora region 10 stomachs contained dragonfly larvae, mollusks, fish, and green parts of plants, especially *Potamogeton.* At the Rybinsk Reservoir in October 31.5% of the food was mollusks, the most common being *Valvata* 16%, then *Unio* and *Anodonta;* larvae of aquatic insects 24% of which *Phryganea grandis* formed 14%, and *Tendipes plumosus* 8%. Important were the rhizomes of *Potamogeton lucens* 33%, torn off in length of 3 to 5 cm.; and 10.5% of seeds.

Mainly mollusks (*Sphaerum, Vivipara, Bythinia*), some *Notonecta,* and a small amount of plants consumed in Oct.–Nov. in the Kiev and Chernigov areas in the Ukraine. In the Lenkoran area on the Caspian in winter the food is composed entirely of *Cardium edule,* the av. being 45 to a stomach with a maximum of 65. Birds wintering farther n. on the rocky shores of Azerbaijan consume *Mytilaster lineatus.* On the White Sea, almost entirely mollusks, especially *Littorina, Mytilus, Nassa,* and *Cerithium,* and on the bays *Dreissensia;* and occasionally crustaceans, worms, and seeds of *Zostera marina* (Dementiev and Gladkov 1952, citing Niethammer). AWS

251

### North American Wood Duck

*Aix sponsa* (Linnaeus)

Wood Duck of A.O.U. list (but there are other waterfowl called Wood Duck on other continents); Carolina Duck of some older literature. Smallish duck; extension of bill projects in a point into each side of forehead, head crested in Alt. Plumages, strikingly so in Def. Alt. of both sexes; eye very large and sexually dimorphic in color; belly white or predominantly so (beyond Juv. stage); legs and feet more or less yellow. Because of rich and varied pattern of drake's Alt. Plumage, generally considered our most beautiful waterfowl. The ♀ is differently colored and patterned.

The trachea of the ♂ was figured by Eyton (1838); the bulla is left-sided, very thin walled, and nearly 2 cm. in longest diam. (J. C. Phillips 1925). For a recent illus. see Johnsgard (1961c).

Length 17–20 in. (♂ av. larger within this span), wingspread to 29½, wt. usually about 1½ lb. (♂ av. heavier than ♀). No subspecies.

DESCRIPTION    Two Plumages/cycle in both sexes (see col. pl. facing p. 120) although all previous authors have stated or implied only 1 in the ♀. Basic I, the earliest white-bellied Plumage, evidently has been misconstrued to be an early stage in the development of Alt. I ("first winter"). In the ♀ the various Plumages after the Juv. are not strikingly different; furthermore, the differences are masked partly by individual variation and the molts are gradual enough not to cause any abrupt change in appearance in birds observed over a span of time in captivity. After the first cycle, the ♀ goes into Basic head–body gradually, usually (but by no means invariably) beginning prior to or during the time she is incubating her first clutch of the season. In substance, the timing of molts of ♂ and ♀ roughly coincide.

▶    ♂ Def. Alt. Plumage (all feathering except, in wing, includes only the innermost, modified, secondaries and their longest coverts), acquired in LATE SUMMER–EARLY FALL (usually beginning in July or early Aug. in n. U.S.) and retained through WINTER into SUMMER. It is acquired up to several weeks earlier, and also lost correspondingly earlier, in s. U.S. and at least part of Cal.; elsewhere, sometimes it is not fully acquired until Dec.

**Bill** upper mandible yellow at very base, then scarlet (most vivid in fall) with black patch between nostrils, then the scarlet grades distally to white and nail is black; lower mandible black or, in some, with intervening flesh-colored areas. **Iris** scarlet (nearer ruby in fall), eyelids scarlet. Feathers on sides of **head** short and velvety; long crest on crown and upper nape of black, iridescent greens, blues, and violets; white line extends from lateral projection of top base of bill back over eye and through crest, another from behind eye through base of crest; white of chin–throat has broad extension up middle of very dark cheek and another up side of head where it joins the neck. **Upperparts** mostly black with various metallic sheens; scapulars long, broad, with squarish ends. **Underparts** breast purplish chestnut (becomes brownish red in worn condition) with triangular white spots; on side forward of folded wing a broad transverse (vertical in the swimming bird) white bar with black one behind it; feathers of

252

sides yellow (often vivid) with fine irregular black lines, the uppermost feathers terminating in alternating black and white crescents; feathers on side of rump reddish violet, some shaped lanceolate and with orange-tawny shaft stripes; belly white, shading to dusky under tail. Legs and **feet** mostly vivid orange-yellow (paling to yellow by spring), webs dusky. **Tail** feathers black with bronzy sheen. In the **wing** the 11th secondary (1st "tertial") is very broad and truncated, its outer web velvety black, the end white; next feather short, no white tip (further details in DeW. Miller 1925); longest coverts over these are medium violet in color; remainder of wing is retained Basic feathering.

▶ ♂ Def. Basic Plumage (entire feathering), worn briefly in SUMMER, the wing (except innermost secondaries and their longer coverts) retained through winter into following summer. In n. U.S. most drakes are in Basic head–body–tail by very early July, but in s. U. S. and at least part of Cal. they reach this condition up to several weeks earlier.

Head without crest or even a mane. Obvious ♂ characters are: extensions of white up side of head, reddish iris, and colorful bill; otherwise remotely ♀-like. Crown dark, sides of **head** gray, except usually a dark area just in front of eye, this sometimes with an extension around under eye, also typically a poorly defined darkish stripe back from eye; at least in specimens examined, no white line around base of bill (it is present in Basic I); **scapulars** comparatively short and rather rounded. **Tail** black with some sheen. **Wing** inner webs of primaries mostly deep bluish and outer webs grayish (silvery) distally, their coverts dark; 10 distal secondaries largely cobalt, becoming black subterminally, and the white tip is narrow on both webs of each of these feathers; innermost secondaries plain, dark, and essentially unmodified in shape; at least greater, middle, and a few lesser secondary coverts largely ultramarine-violet, terminally margined black; smaller coverts medium gray; and all coverts have broadly rounded ends. In the underwing the smaller coverts are white with black marks, in some individuals the black predominates; the greater under coverts are light to medium gray, some with broad distal white bars and all with white ends; the white axillars have transverse black markings (narrow to wide depending on the individual).

The molt into Def. Basic head–body–tail, which requires up to a month, sometimes extends out to include at least many upper wing coverts well in advance of onset of flightless period. (The best color illust. of ♂ Def. Basic is by Fuertes, in F. M. Chapman 1934.) Then comes the flightless period (probably of about 22–24 days), during which Alt. begins succeeding Basic on head and body.

▶ ♀ Def. Alt. Plumage (extent of feathering as in ♂ Def. Alt.), usually acquired beginning in EARLY FALL in n. U.S. and retained through WINTER into SPRING or (by some individuals ) early summer. It is both acquired and lost much earlier in s. U.S. and at least part of Cal. **Bill** has rather indistinct pattern of various grays, muted fleshy or rose, white, and black. **Iris** dark brownish, the eyelids yellow. **Head** crown and nape with large crest, colored dark gray and with bronzy and purplish sheens; conspicuous white area (generally large, but varies in size with individual) around eye, tapering rearward, and sharply defined; seldom any black in front of the white; chin–throat white, without the 2 upward projections (which ♂ has) on side of head, the white sharply defined, and it does extend upward as a conspicuous line or narrow stripe around base of bill. **Upperparts** various olive greens or grays with sheens ranging from bronze to violet. Scapulars comparatively long and square ended. **Underparts** most of breast has comparatively broad tan streaks on dark (gray-browns or grays); the feathers on lower breast have wide white ends, then a broad transverse dark bar (not a double-spotted effect); belly white; most under tail coverts white, the others increasingly marked black (finely), the longest ones darkest; feathers along sides are various medium browns or grays, the light area within each (lengthwise astride shaft) comparatively broad, usually paler than the breast marks, and so arranged as to form interrupted stripes. Legs and **feet** more or less yellowish, webs nearly black. **Tail** feathers as dark or darker than dorsum, with greenish bronze sheen. In the **wing** the innermost secondaries ("tertials") are rather pale, toward olive, with bronzy sheen, and their ends are broadly rounded; the longest coverts over them are pale greenish; remainder of wing is retained Basic feathering.

NOTE  Occasionally, as a result of gonadal atrophy or other malfunction, a ♀'s feathering has many characteristics of ♂ Def. Alt. (See also below under ♀ Alt. I)

▶ ♀ Def. Basic Plumage (entire feathering; worn rather briefly, except most of wing long retained), becomes noticeable on head and breast sometime in SPRING and remainder of head–body–tail then acquired over a period of weeks. Thus it is a SUMMER or LATE SUMMER Plumage in n. U.S., but is acquired and also lost at least several weeks earlier in s. U.S. and at least part of Cal. Everywhere, if a bird renests after loss of earlier clutch(es), the molt out of Basic evidently is slowed or interrupted. As to the early molting, even as early as mid-May in s.-cent. U.S., ♀♀ often show some molting on head–body and sometimes drop 1 or more secondaries and a few proximal upper wing coverts in nest cavities while incubating. In n. U.S., still-flightless ♀♀ occur throughout Sept., occasional ones even in Oct. There are no Cuban data on timing of this molt.

**Head** crown darker but not well defined from cheeks; a small mane at most (not a crest) on upper nape; white area around eye much reduced in size (at least in the few specimens seen) and with ragged margins (or this may indicate molting); often much black adjoins the white (or encroaches on it) in the area anterior to the eye and this commonly extends as a black border to the white around under the eye; white of chin–throat not always sharply defined and rarely streaked darkish; **upperparts** have little or no sheen and the rounded scapulars have broader black distal margins than in Alt.; **underparts** upper breast predominantly brownish (rather than toward grayish), the light streaking very pale; feathers on lower breast have subterminal dark zone on each vane rounded, giving an effect of concealed coarse spotting; pattern along upper sides quite blended, the darker coloring predominantly brownish; tail more brownish than greenish and with little sheen.

The new Basic **wing** grows mostly during a flightless period estimated at 22–24 days; its pattern is much as in ♂, but with less extensive and less vivid colors; the white on tips of 10 distal secondaries is much wider on outer than on inner web (as also in ♀ Juv.); innermost secondaries olive and with rounded ends, their longest coverts rather pale; the other greater secondary coverts have both webs iridescent cobalt-ultramarine, their black margins even in width; such coloring usually extends to include a total of 3 or more rows of coverts; longest underwing coverts light grayish, without barring, and with white ends; axillars white with (in specimens examined) a few narrow black crossbars. By the time the new Basic wing is growing, much of the remainder of the bird is losing Basic and acquiring Alt. (of fall–spring).

A ♀ taken March 15 in Fla. already had Def. Basic head–body. On the other hand, some northerly ♀ ♀ apparently have acquired very little Basic up to the time they begin incubating their first clutch.

AT HATCHING    See vol. 2, col. pl. facing p. 370. The dark stripe back from the eye varies in width in different individuals; also it is not always sharply defined and, in some, it bifurcates. The buffy yellow of sides of head and underparts fades to near-white in a few days at most. The tail is broad and long; the toes have needle-sharp nails. There may be geographical variation in coloring (paler westerly?). Internally, the tracheal bulla is present (as in other Anatids having one) in the ♂ from some time prior to hatching.

▶    ♂ Juv. Plumage (entire feathering), perfected about the time flight is attained (at age 9 weeks) and, except for most of the wing, soon is succeeded by Basic I (which begins to appear while flight feathers of Juv. wing still are growing). In the U.S., the Juv. is a SPRING to LATE SUMMER Plumage; add 9 weeks to date of hatching. **Bill** upper mandible mostly dark but with yellowish edges; iris dark. **Head** may be recognized as ♂ (but also see note below under ♀ Alt. I) by white of chin–throat having an extension up cheek (which first appears at age about 6 weeks) and another up side of head where it joins the neck (both are present thereafter throughout life); and as Juv., rather than Basic I, by very dark broad stripe extending back from eye (it reflects the downy pattern). Crown dark, most of cheeks gray, some white or near-white at or around eye but no white line at side base of bill; **upperparts** more or less fuscous; all scapulars comparatively narrow, tapering, and with rounded ends. **Underparts** the light brownish streaking on breast (on darker base) tends to be broader than in ♀ Juv.; the upper belly sometimes is nearly unmarked, but typically most or all of underparts are quite heavily spotted dark (the spots in rows, i.e., streaked effect) with gradual transition from this to pattern on sides, where the feathers are gray-brown except paler (light tan) along shafts. **Legs** and **feet** dusky and yellowish, webs dusky. **Tail** colored as dorsum, the feathers with protruding shafts.

The Juv. **wing** is much like the Basic wing (previously described); some differences include: innermost secondaries ("tertials") pale bronze and with tapering ends; their longest coverts are muted greenish, comparatively narrow, and short; greater and middle coverts over the other secondaries have reduced amount of purplish, without much sheen; any "frosting" usually is limited to outer vanes of 6 distal primaries; the greater coverts have more white barring, so that the white ends of the feathers appear not to contrast as much with the gray portions. As in Basic, the 10 distal secondaries are black subterminally and have white ends, with amount of white approximately the same on both webs of each feather; the black borders on the larger upper wing coverts also are even in width.

According to Grice and Rogers (1966), the Juv. Plumage develops about as follows, the figures in parentheses being known age in days: down pattern becoming indistinct, first Juv. tail feathers appear (20); first scapulars visible (25); wing coverts emerging from sheaths, first feathers on breast and belly visible (30); first upper tail coverts visible, tips of secondaries still sheathed (35); primaries breaking from sheaths, pin feathers visible on crown (40); white mark up cheek visible, underparts feathered (45); body feathering appears complete except on back (55); many individuals able to fly, drake's eye begins to change from dark to red (60); all except most "retarded" individuals able to fly, Juv. Plumage practically complete (70). In the table from which this is condensed, the next Plumage (Basic I) was not recognized as a separate feather generation following Juv. and preceding Alt. I.

For an especially good photo of ♂ Juv., see 1960 *Condor* **62** 411.

▶ ♀ Juv. Plumage (entire feathering), timing of development as in ♂ (Grice and Rogers 1966), then succeeded (except for most of wing) by Basic I. The Juv. thus is a SUMMER or LATE SUMMER Plumage, depending on date of hatching, but it is instead a spring Plumage in early-hatched birds in Fla.

**Bill** upper mandible various grays, edges whitish; iris dark brownish. **Head** may be recognized as ♀ by lack of upward extensions on cheeks and side rear of the white of chin–throat; and as Juv. by the blackish stripe back from eye. Crown dark; light areas around eye small and not sharply defined; light stripe above eye; no white line bordering side base of bill; cheeks mostly grayed brownish; white of chin–throat typically not sharply defined; **upperparts** some variant of fuscous, usually without sheen, the longest scapulars tapering and with rounded ends; **underparts** breast has longitudinal tan streaks on medium fuscous background; lower breast to under tail coverts whitish and usually all heavily spotted dusky. Legs and **feet** darkish with hint of yellow, webs dark. **Tail** as dorsum, the ends of the feather shafts protruding (where the precursor down broke off). **Wing** much as ♂ Juv.; longest coverts over innermost secondaries greenish yellow; greater coverts and adjoining ones (total of 3 rows) over most of the secondaries have at least some iridescence (on deep bluish) on outer webs and the black border on these feathers is uneven in width; on the 10 outer secondaries the white is much more extensive on the end of the outer web than on the inner.

▶ ♂ Basic I Plumage (all feathering except, in wing, perhaps only the innermost secondaries and their longest coverts), begins to succeed the Juv. head–body–tail at least as soon as the latter is fully grown (but even before the Juv. flight feathers of wing attain full length) and soon is succeeded by incoming Alt. I. Since most of Basic I is acquired by the time the drake is slightly over 3 mo. old, this generally a FALL Plumage in most of range, but timing varies depending on date of hatching. This Plumage was first mentioned by Finn (1904).

256

Diagnostic features: small amount of white adjoining eye may be bordered anteriorly and ventrally with black; no broad blackish stripe back from eye (it was present in Juv.); white line adjoins side base of bill (lacking in Juv.); at most a mane (no prominent crest) at nape; belly and most of under tail coverts typically immaculate white (as in Alt. I), but sometimes with scattered small dark spots; tail feathers (which are nearly grown by the time the drake is 4 mo. old) are fairly broad, lack notched ends, and at least 4 central ones have some sheen.

The **upper mandible** begins to develop high coloring (reds, plus black and white) during the time this Plumage grows; **iris** scarlet-orange. **Head** crown and nape dark, with slight sheen; most of side of head (excluding white areas) and most of neck medium brownish gray; **upperparts** dark with slight greenish sheen; scapulars rather short and rounded; **underparts** breast narrowly streaked pale tan on brownish gray; sides much the same; lower belly to well behind vent white, sometimes spotted dark. **Tail** feathers have some greenish sheen. Legs and **toes** largely yellow, webs dusky. **Wing** innermost secondaries, not modified in shape, are bronzy at least on outer web, none with white end, and their longest overlying coverts are rather short; remainder of wing is retained Juv. feathering.

NOTE   The white up sides of cheeks sometimes is reduced, being entirely lacking on both sides in some drakes and on one side in a museum specimen examined. This raises a question as to whether drakes seen without such projections are assumed to be ♀♀. The opposite situation also occurs; a few Juv. ♀♀ have white "fingers" on their cheeks and thus appear to be drakes.

▶   ♂ Alt. I Plumage (all feathering, excepting all but innermost feathers of wing), begins appearing when the drake is about 100 days old and its full growth usually requires several weeks. Thus the drake, at least in much of the breeding range of the species, generally goes into Alt. I through FALL or from then into EARLY WINTER (depending on his date of hatching) and retains this Plumage through his first winter and into EARLY SUMMER, to age approximately 1 year. (Drakes of older age-classes are in full Alt. at least a month earlier than 1st-fall birds.)

As Def. Alt., including soft-part colors, except: white line over eye sometimes incomplete; crest usually not as large; longest scapulars not as broad distally, but have quite squarish ends; often little coloring on sides of rump; modified inner secondaries sometimes shorter and narrower, but with proportionately same amount of white on end of one of them. This is the earliest Plumage in which the sides and flanks are largely yellow with fine black lines and heavy crescents; it is the last Plumage with which the Juv. wing is worn. A winter-taken drake in Alt. I head–body has mostly full-length Basic I tail feathers, the others being half-grown Alt. I feathers.

According to Heinroth (1910), in the molt into the first "adult" (Alt.) Plumage, the only wing feathers that are not shed are primaries and secondaries.

▶   ♀ Basic I Plumage (probably entire feathering, except much of Juv. wing retained), acquired at same age as in ♂. That is, this Plumage generally succeeds the Juv. through EARLY FALL (but timing varies considerably depending on date of hatching); timing of its replacement by Alt. I apparently is approximately as in ♂ in some individuals, but perhaps is considerably later in some others.

Diagnostic features: **head** crown rather slaty (less toward brownish than Juv.); a

257

small mane at nape; sides of head mostly gray, in some with a grayish stripe back from eye (not a wide blackish one as in Juv.); white area around eye typically a narrow zone or, in some, nearly lacking; at least a trace of white line adjoining side base of bill (lacking in Juv.); margins of white on chin–throat vary with individual from poorly to well defined. **Upperparts** have a slight bronzy sheen; **underparts** breast narrowly streaked whitish tan on brownish; pattern on sides rather blended; lower breast to beyond vent white, or with only scattered dusky spotting (i.e., earliest white-bellied ♀ Plumage). Most of wing is retained Juv. feathering.

A ♀ in Basic I was taken as early as July 6 in Cal., indicating early nesting; another was taken as late as Oct. 21 in Fla. (a migrant from farther north?). Two ♀ ♀ in Basic I, taken April 10 in Cuba, presumably were hatched in early Feb.

▶ ♀ Alt. I Plumage (full extent of feathering probably as in ♂ Alt. I), begins to replace Basic I at about age 3½ mo. and then requires considerable time for full development. That is, in most of the species' breeding range, it is acquired during FALL into WINTER (but timing varies depending on date of hatching) and is retained into following SPRING, rarely later.

Diagnostic features: more contrasty pattern than Basic I; **head** with moderate crest (earliest crested Plumage); crown dark gray with greenish cast, sometimes with brownish feathers intermingled; side of head gray; conspicuous white line at side, base, and top of bill; the white area around eye is comparatively large and sharply defined, hence conspicuous; usually there is some blackish in the loreal region; **upperparts** have some sheen that is more purplish (less bronzy) than in Basic I; **underparts** light markings on breast and along sides are variable in width, but usually narrower than in succeeding Alts.; upper belly to beyond vent unmarked white; some longer under tail coverts are dark, at least on outer webs (i.e., much darker than the brownish of earlier Plumages); **wing** innermost secondaries ("tertials") pale, bronzy, with ends rounded, their longest overlying coverts violet-magenta.

NOTES Some ♀ ♀ in Basic and even in Def. Alt. have more or less of an indication of the white "fingers" (typical of the ♂) on cheeks and side rear of head; in some it consists chiefly of feather tips, which soon wear off, but in others it includes more of the individual feathers and so is retained until they are molted. A number of individuals that were banded as ♂ ♂ were, when recaptured subsequently, lacking the white "fingers," i.e., were ♀ ♀ (L. H. Fredrickson). In captivity, old ♀ ♀ are known to assume the ♂ pattern and coloring; see, for example, Finn (1916).

Delacour (1959) reported a blond mutation in both sexes in captives.

▶ ♀ Basic II Plumage (entire feathering), head–body and tail are acquired in SPRING (but earlier in southerly localities), before age 1 year and are similar to succeeding Basics; the Basic wing is acquired much later, evidently depending on length of time devoted to nesting attempts; in the meantime, most of the worn and faded Juv. wing is retained.

**Measurements** of specimens from conterminous U.S. plus a ♀ from Ont., taken fall–spring 12 ♂: BILL 32–36 mm., av. 34.7; WING 218–240, av. 228; TAIL (of 10) 100–118, av. 115; TARSUS 34–39, av. 36;   12 ♀ BILL 31–35 mm., av. 33.5; WING 211–231, av. 221; TAIL 91–106, av. 98; TARSUS 33–36, av. 34.5 (ETS).

For WING meas. across chord, J. C. Phillips (1925) gave erroneous meas. for the drake, and for the ♀ 230 mm.

**Weight** in fall 248 ♂ av. 1.5 lb. (681 gm.), max. 2 lb. (907 gm.); 163 ♀ av. 1.4 lb. (635 gm.), max. 2 lb. (A. L. Nelson and Martin 1953).

Live-trapped birds taken in Sept. in Ill.: 13 ♂ "adult" av. 1.54 lb. (700 gm.), 46 ♂ "juvenile" av. 1.46 lb. (653 gm.), and 32 ♀ av. 1.42 lb. (645 gm.) (Bellrose and Hawkins 1947).

Free-flying zoo birds: ♂, fat in fall, to 890 gm., in June 200 gm. lighter; fat ♀ 630–650 gm., but lean birds as little as 350 gm. (Heinroth 1910). The ♀'s wt. declines during incubating and into brood rearing; some double-brooded ♀ ♀ recover before laying their 2nd clutch of the season, and then again decline.

**Hybrids** none reported in the wild. In N. Am. there are several known instances of wild drakes forming pair bonds with ♀ Mallards.

An aviculturalist in Germany, at the suggestion of O. Heinroth, placed together in a pen a ♂ Wood Duck and a ♀ Mandarin (*Aix galericulata*), and in another pen the reciprocal of these. Although allegedly there was frequent copulation, the ♀ ♀ laid infertile eggs. Next, the same individuals were mated with their own kind and both ♀ ♀ laid fertile eggs. This suggests that producing hybrids is not as simple as the similarity of the ♀ ♀ of these 2 species might lead one to expect (Heinroth 1910). Earlier, however, Finn (1904) had written: "Of late years, if I recollect aright, a hybrid was bred . . . which did not live to attain maturity." Recently Johnsgard (1968b) described and illustrated several apparent ("putative") hybrid drakes.

In the late 1960s at a private waterfowl collection in Scottsdale, Ariz., a ♂ Mandarin and ♀ Wood Duck were put in a holding pen in a secluded place. Since they showed no signs of mating, another drake Mandarin was added later, whereupon the ♀ "had to make up her mind." She paired with one of the drakes and produced 8 eggs, of which 2 hatched; 1 duckling was lost; the survivor (♂) was dark, but had "sails" like the Mandarin. The following year the same duck and drake produced another clutch; 2 eggs hatched and the young were dark. (Data from Mrs. H. E. Carnes.)

In captivity the Wood Duck also allegedly has crossed with various *Anas* species, several *Aythya*, and even 3 additional genera; see listing in Gray (1958) and discussion by Johnsgard (1968b). (Gray's listing of *Bucephala* × *Aix* was an error.)

In Seattle, Wash., a captive ♀ Hooded Merganser (*Mergus cucullatus*) "mated with a drake Wood Duck, laid, and the eggs were fertile but the young died in the shell just before hatching. Mr. Pilling reports that the young looked like young Wood Duck, but unfortunately none was preserved" (Ripley 1956).

No fertile hybrids with the Wood Duck are known.

Beer (1968) figured the tracheal bullae of crosses with *Anas flavirostris*, *A. sibilatrix*, and *Netta rufina*.

**Geographical variation** evidently none in morphological characters, or possibly some in coloration of small downies (see "At hatching" above). RSP

**FIELD IDENTIFICATION** Wood Ducks commonly are seen in pairs, small groups, and as singles; there are, however, aggregations of hundreds and even thousands at so-called "roosts" (water areas), the largest numbers being present in autumn and winter.

The Wood Duck is truly a woodland dweller, perching on stumps, snags, and limbs of trees. No other N. Am. waterfowl, not even the Hooded Merganser, flies as readily among or through crowns of trees or is as much at home under a closed woodland canopy. Usually it is found in or near shade, not regularly well out on open water unless the light is of rather low intensity or they are attracted by an abundance of food. In flight it shows (except in Juv. Plumage) a white belly and long squarish-tipped tail. The bill usually is angled downward. (Other white-bellied ducks with which it might be confused have small or pointed tails and fly with bill pointed forward. Compare with Hooded Merganser.) It rides high on the water, tail angled up (more so in alarm), the drake showing his striking pattern, the duck her white eye patch. A plaintive *oo-eek oo-eek* . . . is diagnostic and the basis of such vernaculars as "squeaker" and "squealer." This, the usual call heard, is uttered only by the ♀. The thin lisping or reedy call of the drake, a most unducklike sound, may be heard especially at dawn, twilight, and after dark, as groups of Wood Ducks enter and leave their "roosts," also at any time of day when they are on the water feeding or resting, and during displays. RSP

VOICE   A considerable vocabulary. Seldom very vocal in flight, except on takeoff and when about to alight. The following are nonsexual calls, as reported by Heinroth (1910), J. C. Phillips (1925), and Lorenz (1941); for the others, see "Reproduction."

In general, thin, squeaky, unducklike. The drake's conversational call is a drawn-out *ji-ihb*, accent on 2nd syllable, or very low squeaky *jeeb* kept up for a long time, audible only at close range, and resembling the lisping of the Pine Siskin (*Spinus pinus*). A more clipped variant is a warning call. The ♀'s flight call *oo-eek oo-eek* . . . (written *u-ih* by Heinroth) has variants; a clipped *huick* in warning. Her going-away call, uttered especially when nest hunting (and the accompanying drake utters his), is a soft rapid *tetetetetet*. For a general call note she has a raucous *ku-ack*, seldom heard. In young ♀♀, even after attaining flight, the *oo-eek* is so fine and acute as to be confused with the *ji-ihb* of older drakes.

Very small ducklings have a double *peep* conversation call and in alarm, as when deserted, a *piep* in couplets but so close as to sound like 2 syllables. (According to Lorenz, the distress whistle is double or multiple in geese and perching ducks, rather than 1 syllabled as in typical shoal-water ducks.) RSP

HABITAT   Shallow quiet inland waters in or near deciduous or mixed woodland.

For **nesting** requires natural cavities in trees, nests of Pileated (and formerly also Ivory-billed) Woodpeckers, or suitable nest boxes. Preferred nest location is about 5–40 ft. above water or ground, and over water or else ashore but within about 200 yds. of water. Readily nests near human habitations.

For brood rearing and **summer** molting, ideally a combination of spreading brushy overstory (concealment from above), much floating and emergent vegetation (habitat of invertebrates sought for food), small open-water passages (for moving about), and scattered fallen dead limbs, trees, or stumps, muskrat houses, etc. (for perching).

At **other times** sheltered waters where food is available, such as open to wooded swamps, flooded lowland forest, ponds, and some fairly large areas of open water in marshes (in these various places, in season, many assemble to spend the night).

Occurs on upper fresh- and brackish-water reaches of tidal streams and estuaries;

260

seldom on salt water, although it has crossed broad expanses of it, as to Nfld., Sable I. (N.S.), Bermuda, and Caribbean localities.

For further information on habitat and a listing of relevant literature, see McGilvrey (1968). RSP

DISTRIBUTION  (See map.) Although very abundant in Audubon's time, the Wood Duck was so reduced in numbers in N. Am. (and Cuba?) early in the present century that there was general speculation that it might soon become extinct. As a result of protection, it has reoccupied remaining areas of suitable breeding habitat within its former range; in addition, it has extended its main breeding range northward and locally westward, also in various directions in w. N. Am., and presumably southward in Texas (where its early range is difficult to determine). Range increase northward may be a result of overflights by yearlings over nesting areas already in use.

In 1968, at Arrowhead Nat. Wildlife Refuge in e.-cent. N.D., captive-reared young were released and nest boxes were installed; by these artificial means, the breeding range was extended to this locality in 1969 (Doty and Kruse 1972).

The reader is referred to J. C. Philips (1925) for detailed summation of older distributional data. A map of "principal breeding and wintering range" in continental N. Am., based on records through 1938, was published in Jahn (1966); breeding range in N. Am., as of the late 1960s, was mapped in McGilvrey (1968).

Present treatment is brief and by locality rather than season, for the most part, although the latter usually is self-evident except for some older records for localities away from breeding range. Factors affecting distribution include: latitude, elevation, season, sex, age, availability of nesting cavities, and breeding density. Breeding distribution and the breeding-season distribution of drakes are different, the latter being more extensive because drakes leave their incubating mates and go elsewhere to molt. (Also see "Migration.")

**Mainly peripheral records**  E. Canada (Data mainly from M. Smith, in Jahn 1966, and Godfrey 1966.) James Bay area (Ont.–Que.)—records (not breeding), include Charlton I.; Cringan (1971) has documented the rapid increase of this species in Ont. Que.—northernmost records are sightings in Aug. of 1963 and 1965 near Ft. Chimo (lat. 58° 21′ N); has occurred on N. shore of Gulf of St. Lawrence and on Anticosti I.; Gaspé Pen.—occurs, plus an influx of drakes. Nfld.—several drakes captured and several sightings; old report of eggs from Hamilton Inlet, Labrador, is very questionable (Todd 1963). Miquelon—banded drake taken Oct. 31, 1963. Prince Edward I.—has bred (Godfrey); a few drakes banded each summer 1960–64, but no young or ♀ ♀ seen in 7 years of field work (M. Smith). N.S.—C. Breton I., breeding record; Sable I., recorded in May, July, Sept., and Nov. (McLaren and Bell 1972); on the mainland, captive-reared birds have been released near Truro "each year"; the species breeds regularly in cent. and s. parts of the province; birds banded in New Eng. have been secured in the province in Oct. of the same year. New Bruns.—has bred at least for decades in St. John R. valley, but in much of the province the records are for drakes only; birds banded in New Eng. have been taken in N.B. in fall.

**W. Canada**  There are summer–fall records away from breeding areas, across the s. half of the prairie provinces. For Cumberland House (now in Sask.) there are satisfac-

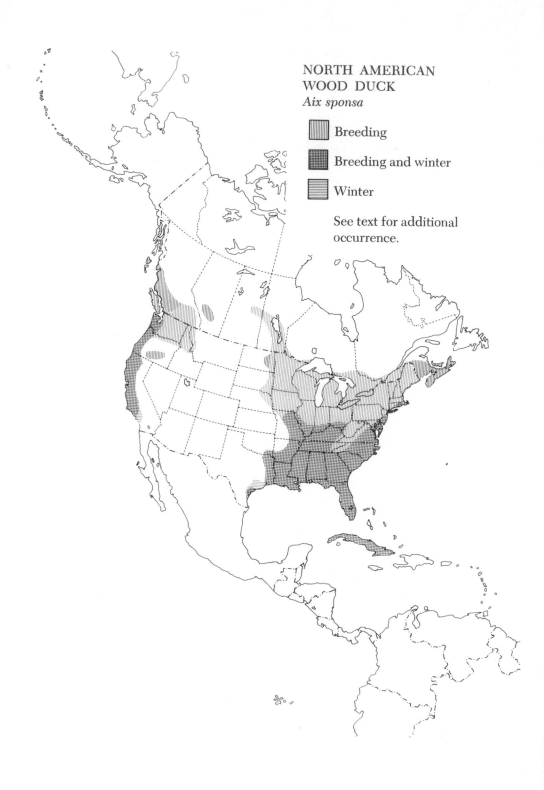

NORTH AMERICAN
WOOD DUCK
*Aix sponsa*

⬛ Breeding

⬛ Breeding and winter

⬛ Winter

See text for additional
occurrence.

tory old records (1820, 1827), possible breeding (in 1890, single egg in hollow tree), and according to F. Bard, some 30 mi. s., along the Carrot R., the species has been sighted regularly in recent years.

**Conterminous U.S.**   In various seasons in the area in w. interior left blank on the map, there are up to several records of occurrence at hand for all states except Wyo.

There are 2 recent breeding records for s. Texas.

At least in milder winters, the species occurs well n. of main winter range—to s. B.C., se. Minn., s. Ont., Mass., and N.S.

**Mexico**   Although the Wood Duck may occur as an occasional straggler, evidence of regular wintering (implied or stated in various books) is not proven; apparently acceptable records (some are sightings) consist of these: Sinaloa 1, Distrito Federal 1, and another n. of there (Hidalgo?), and Tamaulipas 1.

**Atlantic**   Bermuda—recorded in fall and winter (not regular); Bahamas—reported from New Providence; Cuba—resident, more common in w. part; Hispaniola—doubtful (old) record; Jamaica—old records.

**Abroad**   Although the closely related Mandarin apparently now is established in a feral state locally in se. England and in Scotland, there still is uncertainty as to whether the Wood Duck is self-supporting in the se. part and in E. Anglia in England.

Surely the very few free-flying birds seen or shot in Europe were escapees from captivity.

In. N. Am. recorded as **fossil** from the Pleistocene of Ont., Kans., and 3 localities in Fla.; known from **archaeological sites** in Ill. (2 localities), Ohio, and Fla. (2); see Brodkorb (1964a) for references. To this list add Pleistocene of New Mex. (H. Howard 1971) and an additional Fla. locality (Ligon 1965). RSP

**MIGRATION**   Southerly ♀ ♀ are essentially resident, with dispersal movements; northerly Wood Ducks (both sexes) in the main breeding range of the species mostly migrate to below 35° N lat. into range of the southerly ones. Generally speaking, after New Eng. birds reach Md. in fall migration, their further travel is confined largely to a strip some 100–125 mi. wide adjoining the Atlantic coast; a few, however, reach destinations as far w. as La. Birds from the n. interior tend to fan out, reaching destinations from Texas to Ga. Pacific birds—from B.C., Mont., Wash., and Ore.—concentrate in n. Cal. above lat. 38° N., and those Cal. breeders that nest at higher elevations move lower seasonally.

It seems quite possible that a drake may be migratory one year and not the next, if he mates one winter with a northerly breeder, the next with a southern bird, as he supposedly accompanies the duck to her breeding place. Or that he may mate one winter with a duck from Wis., the next with one from the Maritimes, so that he begins successive breeding seasons at n. localities far apart. At a locality in Mo., of 30 drakes (mostly paired) captured in spring, none had been banded or tagged locally; of 30 ♀ ♀ captured, 17 had been banded or tagged there previously (L. H. Fredrickson).

What follows is based mostly on banding evidence, the main sources being P. A. Stewart (1957, 1958b) and Naylor (1960).

**Summer–early fall**   Drakes, commonly late in the period when their mates are incubating, depart and, as singles or having combined in small groups, go to a secluded place where they remain at least through the flightless stage of molt. Distance to a molting place may be short; a good many, however, go a considerable distance on molt migration, even several hundred miles. When they again are able to fly, they join groups or assemblies at favored feeding places. Small ducklings (except those hatched at a local gathering place), move locally with the duck to a place offering a suitable combination of water and concealing cover; several broods may amalgamate as a result of these travels. When the ducklings are about 5 weeks old (and before they can fly), the duck leaves them, either going to some place not far away to molt or, if not yet ready to begin the flightless period, joins with other ♀ ♀ that have left their broods. The young, after attaining flight, and the ducks, after regaining it, also move to favored feeding places, moving as much as 8 mi. (data from banded birds). Early-hatched young in Mass. begin this movement as early as about mid-July. The assemblies thus formed sometimes are large and contain both sexes and young and older birds, but perhaps there is some segregation of young from older birds at this time.

Later—mainly in Aug., prior to southward migration—there is radial dispersal (except not over salt water) from these gathering places; most individuals go less than 20 mi., but some go several hundred. Drakes disperse much farther than ♀ ♀. This dispersal is a characteristic of all local breeding units; it occurs much earlier in La. than, for example, in Ohio. In late summer in Cal., the birds apparently leave the Central Valley and go to foothill streams of the Sierra Nevada and Coast ranges (R. E. Jones and Leopold 1967).

**Late fall**  Radial dispersal, just discussed, may be regarded as an Aug. phenomenon, with concentrations in Sept., and fall migration in Oct. and continuing into Nov. The birds travel in small groups for the most part.

**Winter**  There is some shifting about, depending on food supply and whether or not the birds are disturbed, and apparently a continuous southward drift.

**Spring**  The birds travel in small groups of about 6–12 individuals and also as lone pairs. Older birds (mostly paired) that are local breeders arrive first, then transients and yearling ♀ ♀ with their mates. There is movement regularly as early as 3rd week in Feb., with peak in southerly areas in March. In Cal. they return to nesting places in March. They arrive in southern New Eng. by mid-March and the peak occurs before mid-April. They arrive at n. limits of breeding range beginning about mid-April in normal seasons and migration elsewhere in the main range is largely over by then. Western birds at corresponding latitudes are somewhat earlier than eastern ones. RSP

BANDING STATUS  The total number banded through 1964 was 153,882 and total number of recoveries and returns through 1966 was 15,683; banding has been done throughout main range of the species, but with smallest numbers banded in southern U.S. (Data from Bird Banding Laboratory.) Data from banded birds have been used by several authors, for example by Kaczynski and Geis (1961), Grice and Rogers (1966), and P. A. Stewart (1959). RSP

REPRODUCTION  Enough information is given here to indicate the general pattern, without including all known details and variants. Display data are mostly from observations of semicaptive birds; the bulk of the other information is derived from observations at places where nest boxes were provided.

In captive-reared birds, low-intensity display by drakes first becomes evident about the time they have acquired enough of Alt. I Plumage to appear adultlike (in Sept. in Mo.). Intensity of display increases during fall, but wanes with the approach of cold weather. The display of these young drakes resembles that of mature ones, but the former lack the orientation and posture exaggeration seen in mature birds and they are less successful in forming pairs, even during the following spring. Yet some pair formation does occur in 1st fall; its frequency and the durability of such bonds are unknown (L. H. Frederickson).

Both sexes can **first breed** as yearlings, as known from aviary and from wild stock. Many ♀ ♀ in their first spring after hatching fail to nest successfully (although some lay eggs); perhaps especially in late-hatched individuals all the drives essential to successful reproduction have not matured by the following breeding season. **Pair formation** activity begins about midwinter (but has been seen in Oct. in Va.), at least in birds that are to migrate, and probably first among birds old enough to have bred previously. Pointing movements (bill aimed and back-and-forth pumping of head), as when swimming about in search of food, are frequent and are intermingled with the various displays. Principal descriptions of the latter are by Heinroth (1910), Lorenz (1941), and Johnsgard (1965).

**Displays of the duck** COQUETTE CALL (of Heinroth) a *houi* note, dropping in pitch, uttered as the bird suddenly points her bill near-vertically downward; functionally similar to Nod-swim of Mallard (Lorenz). The ♀ ♀ frequently give this call at a roost at night, commonly in late fall (Nov.), either as incipient or actual early display. FLIGHT CALL a prolonged loud *u-ih*, believed by Lorenz to be homologous to Decrescendo call of ♀ *Anas*. INCITING rapid, direct, pointing movements, made while calling softly, and alternating with "caressing" movements toward preferred drake. BILL-FLICK similar to drake's; rapid, upward to vertical, used in greeting and threat.

**Displays of the drake** Drakes chase and beat one another with their wings, doing no serious damage. INTRODUCTORY SHAKE rare, not functionally introductory. DRINKING ritualized movement; separate display, also always precedes the next following. PREEN-BEHIND-THE-WING rather frequent and striking; primaries and secondaries spread momentarily in full view of ♀. BURP a lisping, squeaky, siskinlike call, uttered while vertically stretching neck and raising crest. CHIN-LIFTING the white area oriented toward ♀; separate display, or linked to next. TURNING-THE-BACK-OF-THE-HEAD toward ♀ as she swims on parallel course and slightly ahead; drake's tail is tilted away from ♀, which may emphasize the vividly colored elongated feathers on side of rump (the ♀ may Incite as ♂ thus displays). DISPLAY-SHAKE ("whistle shake" of Lorenz) elaborate, highly ritualized general shake of body accompanied by whistling note; analogous to Grunt-whistle of Mallard. DOWN-UP (not homologous to Mallard's) single rapid upward flick of bill, flashing the white chin; used in greeting or sexual display toward ♀ ♀ and as threat toward ♂ ♂. WING-AND-TAIL-FLASH sudden upward jerk of closed wing and tail, bill angled steeply down, crest prominent; observed both in Wood Duck and Mandarin (Johnsgard).

The feathers on the cheeks of the drake are surprisingly long; they can be erected somewhat, giving a puffy appearance and, as noted by Wall (1963), rendering the white mark thereon more conspicuous. This occurs during the Burp display, probably also in some others.

Although J. Munro (1950) mentioned seeing a pair in "display flight," some sort of 3-bird flight (mated pair plus drake) is not uncommon, in habitat where it is nearly impossible to observe it from start to finish.

In rather poetic phrases, Audubon (1835) stated that the drake, while raising his crest momentarily, bows before the ♀ [Down-up display] and utters a "guttural sound." The duck swims beside him, now and again touching his feathers with her bill, and shows hostility toward any other ♀ that approaches. Then they are paired. They "repeat every now and then their caresses" and fly away to seek a nesting cavity. Johnsgard (1965) stated that the ♀ often nibbles the white chin region of her mate; he also (Johnsgard 1968a) mentioned "mutual" nibbling. Finn (1904) cited a French work on aviculture by M. G. Rogerson, in which it was reported that the drake calls the ♀ to take some morsel he has secured, but if she does not hasten, he swallows it. According to Heinroth (1910), here translated: "When the ♂ finds a large piece of food, he takes it up and holds it in his bill tip in a charming way with his head held high toward the ♀. She takes the food and eats it." To date, there are no published observations of similar behavior in wild Wood Ducks. Evidently 1 either sex may touch the other, 2 the ♂ has been seen to "feed" the ♀, and 3 all observations of physical contact, including Audubon's, probably relate to birds already paired. The actual sequence of events (which may vary) through to pair formation apparently are not known. Pair bond form is at least **temporary monogamy,** or possibly should be described in terms of number of his mate's clutches the ♂ fertilizes—perhaps not all that are laid by some ♀ ♀ in some seasons.

Many yearling ♀ ♀ return to the area in which they were reared and others nest not far (within a few mi.) away. This tends to restrict occupation of additional **nesting areas.** Once they nest, they tend to return to the very same locality, often the same nest, in succeeding years (Hester 1965, Grice and Rogers 1966, other authors). Older ♀ ♀ (with their mates) arrive earlier than yearlings (with theirs). At first, and in early morning, the ♀ accompanied by her mate may perch in the vicinity, as though looking it over. Within a few days, however, she begins entering tree cavities or nest boxes; she may enter several and make a nest scrape in the bottom of each one. The drake perches nearby, or at times may cling at the cavity entrance and peer in (noted both in semicaptive and wild birds) or, when opportunity occurs, enter (semicaptives observed by Heinroth). Sometimes, by himself and for reasons unknown, the drake visits cavity entrances in the general vicinity. Both sexes have been seen to cling, quite woodpeckerlike, and brace themselves with their tails, at nest entrances; for photo of ♂ at entrance, see Heinroth (1910), and of ♀, see Dixon (1924). The **cavity** which the ♀ selects for laying may be at any height, preferably not far from water (often over it), and the drake's waiting place is not necessarily nearby. Quite often a prospecting duck descends a chimney and, in some localities, chimneys are screened because the ducks are such a problem (P. A. Stewart 1971a). Some nest in barns and abandoned camps. An ideal site has an elliptical entrance, 4 in. (10 cm.) wide and 3 in. (7.5 cm.) high; the cavity should be at least deep enough so that the eggs and sitting bird are beyond arm's reach by a raccoon; about 24 in. (60 cm.) is satisfactory, but the floors of some occupied

266

cavities are 6–8 ft. below the entrance. The interior should have a diam. of about 11 in. (27.5 cm.), or a nest box be 10 in. (25 cm.) square inside, and the bottom should have a layer of dried particles and fragments of rotted wood or sawdust and shavings in a nest box. Nests of Flickers and Pileated Woodpeckers become usable if the wood has rotted so as to enlarge both entrance and cavity. Many authors mention use of Pileated nests, notably Cringan (1971) for Ont. In Md. the Starling (*Sturnus vulgaris*) is a serious competitor for nest boxes, but a horizontal structure with semicircular entrance hole 11 in. (28 cm.) in diam. is acceptable to the ducks but not to Starlings (McGilvrey and Uhler 1971).

Among nest sites not already mentioned (see J. C. Phillips 1925 for references) are these: in Cuba, hollow palms and other trees, especially fallen ones, and crevices in rocks; also Audubon's report of a nest with 10 eggs in a fissure in a rock on the Kentucky River. One used a twig and leaf nest (with nest down added) supported by small branches 32 ft. above water in an oak, at Montezuma Refuge in cent. N.Y. (M. S. Hall 1969).

The reports by Boardman and by Anderson of **joint layings** of Wood Duck and Hooded Merganser also were cited by Phillips. In the St. John valley of New Bruns., there was little competition between Wood Ducks and Common Goldeneyes for natural cavities; they appeared to use different forest areas (Prince 1968). Bolen and Cain (1968) found a joint laying of 4 Wood and 8 Red-billed Whistling Duck eggs; all hatched and all young left the nest cavity. Bellrose (1943) found 2 ♀ Wood Ducks incubating in the same cavity; it was big enough to allow both birds to sit comfortably. This has occurred also in Mo. (L. H. Fredrickson).

Wood Ducks do not defend an area, at least not one including the nest site (nothing seems to be known about relations among drakes in the period when they have waiting places). The drake, however, defends his mate if another ♂ or a pair approaches her; he makes threatening rushes toward the approaching bird(s) and/or takes station between his mate and the other Wood Ducks. When 2 nest-seeking ♀ ♀ entered the same cavity, they did not fight; however, the first drake to arrive and perch near the site chased another drake who came too close to him (Heinroth 1910). As a consequence of lack of territoriality, very high nesting densities can be created by providing numerous nest boxes, even in open marshes (rather than wooded swamps which are "typical" natural areas). That is, within certain limits terrain is unimportant if nest cavities are available. An abundance of the latter also concentrates predation (Grice and Rogers 1966, Strange et al. 1971, and other authors).

In the Sacramento Valley, Cal., nest boxes were provided for a local breeding unit, which was studied 1957–65 inclusive. Along with an increase in ♀ ♀ of breeding age there was interference and disruption of some of them by others so that, in the latter years of the study, the breeding population became essentially self-limiting; see R. E. Jones and Leopold (1967) for details. In Mass., many yearling ♀ ♀ and also some older ones failed to nest when the local population was high; they were unable to compete successfully with older ♀ ♀ (Grice and Rogers 1966).

**Copulation** The ♀ assumes a PRONE position with bill along water and tail angled slightly upward. The drake swims around her, usually with Drinking, Chin-lifting, and pecking at her head and dorsum. He mounts and, after treading, quickly swims a few feet away and at the same time Turns-the-back-of-the-head, then generally points his bill toward the ♀ as she bathes. (The extent to which the copulatory pattern is ingrained and stereotyped is indicated by Heinroth's observations of semicaptive homosexual pairs, both ♂–♂; and ♀–♀; displays and postures in "mock copulation" were the same as in heterosexual unions.)

**Laying period** The duck pays a brief visit to the nest and lays, early in the morning; her mate perches a short distance away, uttering his reedy call, and follows the ♀ when she departs. The first few eggs usually are buried in the detritus at the bottom of the cavity (except in joint laying). The nest down and a few feathers accumulate generally beginning about the time the 4th to 8th egg is laid and continuing into incubation, and the eggs no longer are buried. (The semicaptives studied by Heinroth seldom deposited any nest down before 11 eggs were laid.) This down, which drops out or is preened out (not plucked), is pale grayish white with white centers and any included breast feathers are wide and white webbed; see illus. in Broley (1950). (Hooded Merganser feathers are narrow and off-white; some Goldeneye feathers are white, others gray.) Unless frightened from the cavity, the ♀ covers her eggs with down before departing.

**Clutch size** usually 9–14 eggs, the frequent large sets (to over 40 eggs) being the result of joint laying by 2 or more ♀ ♀. The following data are from nest-box studies: Mass.—including joint layings, in 918 successful nests the av. was 13.3 eggs; it was 12.2 in 509 unsuccessful nests; clutches in nests over land were smaller than those over water, the latter more frequently being joint layings (McLaughlin and Grice 1952); for later information in detail on about 2,000 clutches, see Grice and Rogers (1966); Iowa—omitting joint layings, the av. proved to be "about" 11.8, with early clutches averaging 13.9 and late ones 11.0 (F. Leopold 1951); Miss.—in nest boxes in 1966–69 inclusive, 7,279 eggs were laid, 2,145 (29%) hatched, 2,061 ducklings departed, and 1,292 eggs (18%) were destroyed by predators; the percentage of eggs that hatched, depending on year and locality, varied from 91 down to 5 (in 1969); birds—mainly the Yellow-shafted Flicker (*Colaptes auratus*)—pecked and thus destroyed 814 eggs; see Strange et. al. (1971) for further details; Cal.—commonest sizes in 125 successful nests were 10–14 (av. 11.8) eggs, but when smaller clutches and joint layings were included the overall av. was 13.3 (Naylor 1960).

In Mass., assuming that more than 15 eggs indicated joint laying, clutches of 9 and 19 eggs were of equal frequency and 57% of successful nests contained more than 15 eggs; joint layings actually may increase the number of ducklings produced because many contributing ♀ ♀ also ultimately hatch a clutch at another site (Grice and Rogers 1966, Heusmann 1972). The same authors believed that, if a previously used nest was taken over by a yearling ♀ who laid in it, the original owner (older bird) drove the younger one away and added her own eggs to those already laid. In Ore., joint laying was common even when there were available unused nest boxes; the net effect was production of more ducklings early in the season (when chances of survival are better) than would have resulted from single layings (T. E. Morse and Wight 1969); these data, however, may be subject to some other interpretation.

Grice and Rogers (1966) thought it possible that some yearlings may pass through a parasitic stage of laying eggs in nests of other ♀ ♀ before eventually establishing nests of their own. More recent data indicate that "dump nesting" is done by ♀ ♀ of all age-classes (yearling on) and that the same individuals additionally in a given season may produce a clutch and incubate it. In Mo., some yearling ♀ ♀ "dump" only a few eggs (5 or 6), may or may not develop an incubation patch, and the ovary regresses (L. H. Fredrickson).

The times when complete **first clutches** may be expected are as follows or may be calculated from these observations: Cuba—probably midwinter (downies have been found in late Sept: a very late brood of the same year or a very early one of the next?); Fla.—April (probably also much earlier; report of young March 19); Ga.—clutch April 5, broods April 15–May 9, including 3 half-grown young on May 1, and small young on

July 19 (Burleigh 1958); Cal.—April and May; N.C.—some ♀♀ are "prospecting" for nest-sites in Jan. and laying begins in Feb.; they start laying in Feb. in Mo. (L. H. Fredrickson). Ark.—report of young as early April 4; Iowa—late March through April; Ohio—many clutches complete by about April 10 in central part and 10 days later in n. part; Md.—April; N.J.—small young on April 25; N.Y.—April 10–30; New Eng.—late April into June; New Bruns.—laying begins April 15–20, with peak number of full first clutches May 1–5 (H. Prince).

One **egg** each from 20 clutches (localities from Ont. and Mass. to Texas and Fla.) **size** length av. 50.70 ± 3.04 mm., breadth 39.03 ± 1.99, **shape** usually between elliptical and subelliptical, radii of curvature of ends 15.98 ± 0.97 and 13.20 ± 1.00, elongation 1.30 ± 0.051, bicone −0.027, asymmetry +0.093 (FWP). For another series, of 99 eggs, see Bent (1923), and for 51 from Cal. that av. smaller, see R. H. Robinson (1958). Weight of 16 fresh ones from Cal. was 40.5–47.2 gm., av. 42 (Dixon 1924).

Female yearlings (prebreeders) begin nesting later than older age-classes; the data from Mass. yield 2 overlapping curves of dates of "nest-initiation," the first with peak April 13 (older birds) and the second maintaining a high level April 27–May 18; see Grice and Rogers (1966).

**Replacement clutches**    F. Leopold (1951) stated that the span from nest selection to completion of incubation is about 50 days. Depending on how early this is interrupted, and probably for various other reasons, the interval before renesting varies greatly; see discussion in Grice and Rogers (1966). In regard to semicaptives, Heinroth (1910) reported that, if the first clutch is taken [soon after completion?], the replacement clutch seldom contains a different number of eggs, but the third clutch contains fewer eggs and of smaller size. Smaller late clutches, as in F. Leopold (1951, and in Jahn 1966), presumably include repeat attempts. Whether or not the original drake is the partner in late renestings has not been determined (Grice and Rogers 1966). There are more infertile eggs in late clutches. (See below for 2 broods/season.)

The duck turns her eggs, as determined from a marked clutch (P. A. Stewart 1971b). The usual **incubation routine** of the ♀ includes absences of about 40 min. to 1 hr., twice daily—very early in the morning and at evening—to join her mate (as long as he remains) at his station and to feed, drink, and rest. The schedule is variable; see Breckenridge (1956) and P. A. Stewart (1962). When the duck returns, the drake follows her and both are silent; although he may perch momentarily, he generally does not stop but instead flies back to his waiting place. In early nestings this situation typically prevails until near the end of incubation; in late nestings the drake may leave the area even as early as immediately after the clutch is completed (F. Leopold 1951). That is, **termination of the pair bond** is progressively more imminent as the season advances. Drakes that depart early in the season still have most of their Prebasic body molt while away from their mates; those that leave late generally are in heavy body molt and are due to become flightless soon.

The **incubation period** is a function of incubation temperature, within limits. It was reported over a century ago, by Sclater (1859), to be 30 days; this was based on zoo birds and is close to 31 days given by Heinroth (1910) for semicaptives. Other older published figures range down to 27 days. H. C. Hanson (1954) published illus. showing the extent of development of artificially incubated embryos at intervals through 27 days. The period, as "precisely determined" at 5 nests, ranged from 31 to 35 days (R. E. Jones and Leopold 1967), longer than given by Dixon (1924), F. Leopold (1951), and Breckenridge (1956). In 3 clutches, Breckenridge found the period to range from 25 to 31 days and he believed that the longer periods were the result of cooling of the eggs in the absence of the sitter. According to F. Leopold (in Jahn 1966), at the time the last 2 or 3 eggs are being laid, the duck may return late in evening and spend the night in the nest box (he stated that this "does not start development" of the embryos, as all eggs later hatch on the same day); also, incubation begins immediately after the last egg is laid, infrequently not until a day later.

A ♀ incubated 21 eggs for 62 days and another incubated 12 eggs for 59 days (F. Leopold, in Jahn 1966). In England, the ♀ of a captive pair deserted her infertile eggs; the "drake," when flightless in molt, walked up the ramp to the nest entrance, incubated at various times, and covered the eggs with nest down before departing (Rollin 1957). (But some "drakes" are ♀♀; see earlier under "Description.")

Although **fertility** sometimes is reported as low in eggs from captive stock, it is high in the wild. In Ill., of 467 wild-taken eggs, 40 (8.6%) were infertile (H. C. Hanson 1951); a study one year in Mass. showed a minimum of 92% of eggs in successful nests were fertile (McLaughlin and Grice 1952).

**Hatching** was reported by Heinroth (1910) to require 2 days (other authors usually estimate about 30 hrs.) from time the shell is pushed out at one spot, i.e., pipped; on the 2nd day the duckling calls from within the egg. According to Gottlieb (1963), the duck begins to vocalize when the eggs are pipped, and her rate of calling increases as the time draws near for the young to emerge from the shell. P. A. Stewart (1968) reported that the duckling rotates inside the shell, cutting around the large end, and this activity plus emergence required only 8 min. in one instance and 9½ in another. According to F. Leopold (in Jahn 1966), the newly hatched ducklings are "nearly helpless" for a few hrs.; Weatherbee and Weatherbee (1961) put one in water and it tried to swim but sank and drowned. As they become dry, the sheath on the down disintegrates and then the ducklings are fluffy and very active in half a day. They weigh 20–24 gm. (Heinroth 1910); 4 av. 23.53 gm. (Weatherbee and Weatherbee 1961). Usually they leave the nest cavity in the morning of the day after hatching.

A drake (probably the parent) was seen at one nest containing ducklings and he drove away a curious Blue Jay (F. Leopold 1951). A drake has been seen with a family a few times.

The duck, at the cavity entrance, on a nearby limb, or near the base of the nest site, signals with a repeated soft cooing *kuk* note; the **ducklings** at once jump toward the cavity entrance, bracing with their tails, clinging with their claws, while uttering a staccato double *peep* call, then launch into space and fall to ground or water. All depart within a few min. They may actually bounce when they land; in a bad landing they are stunned, usually only momentarily; and, in watching hundreds of jumps from nest boxes, F. Leopold (in Jahn 1966) saw only one duckling killed. Excellent photos of ducklings launching into space have been published, for example, by Bellrose (1955) and P. A. Stewart (1961). The duck leads the brood away while they are small. Duck and brood

271

may remain for some time in the general vicinity if there is at least some water and concealing shelter, or (Hardister et al. 1965) they may go directly overland for some distance to favorable rearing habitat.

At least after the ducklings are about 2 weeks old (and probably earlier), the ♀ often leaves her brood and feeds elsewhere in morning and evening. It appears to be the rule that the ♀ tends her brood longer, commonly to age 5 weeks (at which time the young cannot yet fly) if it is early-hatched (see McGilvrey 1969), but may depart up to at least 10–12 days sooner after hatching if late-hatched. That is, the ♀ seeks solitude as the time to become flightless draws near, and the interval is progressively shorter the later the brood hatches. Early broods thus have a better chance of survival. Broods may combine, in which case only one duck is in attendance, or none in older assemblies.

Young Wood Ducks are very independent by nature. It is possible that, from age about 10 days on, some may leave the brood on their own, i.e., they are not abandoned by the ♀.

For considerable information on **growth** and on general habits of the young during their preflight stage, see Dreis (1954), Grice and Rogers (1966), and McGilvrey (1969); for a few photos of older downies and succeeding Juv. Plumage in known-age young, see H. C. Hanson (1951b).

The young **attain flight** in 8–9 weeks in the wild. Well-nourished captives flew at age about 60 days but, when fed reduced levels of protein, required 12.9 days longer (N. F. Johnson 1971). If the brood or an assembly of broods that have amalgamated is not broken up (by predation, for example), possibly they sometimes remain together until time of radial dispersal (see "Migration"). There are, however, observations to indicate that commonly they scatter widely at age 5–6 weeks.

After an early and successful nesting the Wood Duck, at least in part of its breeding range, may produce a **second brood,** as reported in N.C. in 4 instances, Mo. 5, Md. 2, and Mass. 1; the renesting interval varied from 28 days to 12 weeks; see Rogers and Hansen (1967) for details. Later information, into 1974, brings the total in se. Mo. to 24 known instances which include: a ♀ hatched 2 broods/year for 3 consecutive years, another did so in 3 out of 4 years, and another did so for 2 consecutive years; second clutches varied from larger to smaller, averaging about the same size as first ones; of over 50 ♀ ♀ weighed at intervals, all showed good recovery between clutches; one ♀ weighed less at 9 days on her second than at 30 days on her first clutch (J. L. Hansen, L. H. Fredrickson). There are 27 records of 2 broods/season in ne. Ark. (B. W. Brown 1973). RSP

SURVIVAL   Of 2,548 banded Wood Ducks that were shot, 69.3% were killed within 1st year after banding. After 1st year, mean annual mortality rate was 35.7%; this rate for all years, exclusive of the last, was 38.3% (P. A. Stewart 1959).

The first-year mortality of Wood Ducks banded before they attained flight was considered to be about 80% (Bellrose et al. 1964).

New Eng. data (3 states), based on band recovery, gave a mean annual mortality rate of 62.8% for "adults" and 76.7% for "juveniles." Thus, more than 95% of the birds banded in any one year disappeared from the population by the end of their third year of life. The av. life expectancy after banding was 1.4 years for "adults" and 1.2 years for "juveniles" (Grice and Rogers 1966). The same authors presented a "life equation" for a hypothetical stable local population in Mass., with "production" balancing "mortality."

At Patuxent, Md., data were compiled on an estimated 223 broods in 1964–67 inclusive; mortality from hatching to age 6 weeks av. 47%; that is, the av. number of young/brood declined from 9.8 (at hatching) to 5.2 (at 4–6 weeks); of this mortality, 90% occurred in the first 2 weeks (McGilvrey 1969).

For important data on chance of survival of early-hatched vs. late-hatched young, see Grice and Rogers (1966) and McGilvrey (1969). RSP

HABITS    Much has been written about this particularly attractive waterfowl. Especially noteworthy are Heinroth's (1910) study of free-flying park birds, J. C. Phillips' (1925) summarizing account of the bird in its natural setting and in captivity, the detailed study in Mass. by Grice and Rogers (1966), and the symposium edited by Jahn (1960). A spate of journal papers appeared in the 1950s and 1960s. The following touches only on portions of all known information.

**General characteristics**    The Wood Duck is unwary, almost tame where not molested. It associates, temporarily and not closely, with various other waterfowl, notably with the Black Duck; see A. A. Saunders (1926) for interesting observations. Because it also takes wing when near the wary Black Duck and the latter is flushed, it must gain some protection from associations of this sort. It keeps fairly close company with gallinules in parts of its range. Forward "pointing" movements of the head, when swimming or walking (like head movements of domestic fowl and pigeon), are done more rapidly as flight-intention movements. All the feathers are held down smooth, making the body appear more slender, the tail is elevated, and sometimes there is some lateral head-shaking. On taking wing, the ♀ utters her *oo-eek* call and the ♂ occasionally his squeaky lisp; both calls are surprisingly far-carrying sounds. There is a subdued whistling of wings in flight. Under experimental conditions, in horizontal flight with no wind, speeds were 27.8–34.8 mph (av. 31.2), with 7–7.5 wingbeats/sec. and 6.5 ft. of forward movement per beat at av. speed (P. A. Stewart 1958a). In early Aug. in Wis., flocks flew at a speed of 39–55 mph, averaging about 47 (Lokemoen 1967). There seems to be no special flight organization; instead, a loose group, the birds changing relative position, with a straggler or two behind. This is indicative of the usual unit, even in the breeding season, of large numbers of small groups of Wood Ducks. There are rather ragged assemblies when groups come together.

The Wood Duck is a surface feeder generally, but often immerses head and neck; it does not up-end much. Preflight young dive readily when pursued and can swim submerged (P. A. Stewart 1958a). The Wood Duck has been seen diving and catching fish. While either afloat or ashore, it is adept at catching insects that fly close by. It is agile ashore, walking about under trees or even among shrubbery, seeking acorns, beechnuts, and other foods. The large size of acorns and cypress "balls" and the hard shells of hickory nuts that it eats are rather surprising. It feeds also in fields, at times after the harvest, where corn, wheat, and other cereals are grown, and in Ohio particularly in farmers' hog lots (P. A. Stewart).

**Daily routine** of groups includes a morning flight to feed. When the sun is high the

273

groups splash-bathe, then rest ashore or on the water. Later, there is another feeding flight; still later, the evening flight to "roost"—on water in a marsh, swamp, or pond. All these movements appear to be more pronounced when the birds are present in sizable numbers. (See "Migration" for seasonal movements.) The Wood Duck flies skillfully in restricted quarters, as among branches, in very poor light, a trait even more marked in its eastern Asian relative the Mandarin. As Heinroth (1910) pointed out, the Wood Duck does not need to fly over trees when going from one pond to another, and it flies into tree cover if pursued by the Peregrine.

**History**    The Wood Duck was plentiful in Audubon's day and even later, until the early 1880s, in the e. (main) part of its range; it was common and widespread in Cal. from the San Joaquin Valley n. at the time of early settlement. But destruction of habitat, chiefly by cutting of mature forest and by drainage and overshooting in all seasons reduced this bird to near-extinction over much of its range by the year 1905. In the e. U.S. it fared better in the south than north. In 1913 the Wood Duck received federal protection (a "permanent" closed season in the U.S.) and the Migratory Bird Treaty Act of Aug., 1916, provided special protection in the U.S. and Canada for this species and the Common Eider. In the U.S., federal protection was continued to 1941 and the bird was not legal game in New Eng. until 1942; after that, it was protected some years in Mass., N.J., and W. Va., and in Mass. the season was closed from 1943 to 1951. For further details, see Reeves (in Jahn 1966).

There was a long period of rather gradual increase and reoccupation of parts of its range, during which many Wood Ducks were shot accidentally by gunners. Certainly by the early 1930s there was an increasingly upward trend in numbers, aided by better protection, some releases of pen-reared stock—for example, several hundred annually 1925–1939, reared in Conn. and released at various places (Ripley 1951)—and the posting of nest boxes came into practice. Although the Wood Duck has been reared in captivity at least since the 1840s (see Lee and Nelson, in Jahn 1966, for historical summary), far more important to the welfare of the bird has been the construction and posting of many thousands of nest boxes. The extent to which these have been utilized in some localities was summarized by Van Deusen (in Jahn 1966). There is a continuing effort to design housing that satisfies the requirements of the duck and, at the same time, is as "predator proof" as possible; see McGilvrey (1968) and papers cited therein, also McGilvrey and Uhler (1971).

**Hunting kill**    In the U.S. e. of the Rockies the 1960 pre-shooting-season population estimate was nearly 2,000,000 Wood Ducks, with subsequent kill estimated at 266,000 (Kaczynski and Geis 1961). For B.C., Wash., w. Mont., n. Idaho, Ore., and Cal., the 1958 preseason estimate was about 84,000, including an estimated 15,860 breeding pairs (Naylor 1960); the subsequent kill was estimated at over 22,400. The kill in conterminous U.S. was estimated at 374,700 in 1964 and 559,900 in 1965 (H. A. Hansen and Hudgins 1966). More figures are hardly necessary. There was a decline in numbers in at least a considerable portion of the main range to a low level in the early 1950s, and subsequent increase; by the late 1960s there was speculation that numbers again were decreasing, or at least that the previous high would not be regained.

**Roosts**    As in early times, the birds gather in scores and hundreds at favored places. In early winter, 1940, there was a "roost" of at least 5,000 Wood Ducks in Camden Co.,

Ga. (Hebard 1941); nearly 2 decades later, 2 quite sizable concentrations were noted in Cal. (Naylor 1960). The largest gathering on record was 5,400 birds in 3 foci within slightly less than a sq. mi. at Green I., Jackson Co., Iowa, in 1960 (see Hein and Haugen 1966 for details); and an estimated 10,000 at Rimini Swamp near the upper end of L. Marion, Sumter Co., S.C., which was abandoned in early Dec. after a 4-ft. rise in water level occurred (McGilvrey 1966a). There are relatively brief early-season gatherings of premolting drakes, but "roosts" are occupied principally by young of the year, beginning well along in summer, then joined by adults after their wing molt; largest numbers are present in fall prior to (and during?) migration. The birds are best seen in the low light of sunset and sunrise, as they fly to and from these places. Quite likely, if their activities are not overly affected by hunting or other disturbance, many go from one "roost" to another, so that peak numbers occur progressively farther south at such places as the season advances.

**Predation** Besides man's checks on the Wood Duck population through cutting nest trees, manipulating the water level, catching them unintentionally in muskrat traps, and shooting, there are other hazards. Many ♀ ♀ are lost when they enter chimneys while nest-hunting. The raccoon preys heavily on eggs and sitting birds; the fox squirrel gets numerous eggs, as do the bull snake and rat snake, the latter being the most serious predator in the south. Snapping turtles catch many ducklings at some localities and the bullfrog and alligator are known predators. On shallow ponds, if the young are disturbed and dive, they may become entangled in filamentous algae and drown.

Regardless of existing hazards, protection most of the year plus the posting of nest boxes has resulted in a great increase in Wood Ducks. By and large, man-made housing is more weatherproof, more favorably located, and more predator-proof than many of the inadequate number of natural cavities. (The boxes also attract Starlings, Tree Swallows, Carolina Wrens, Flickers, American Kestrels, Crested Flycatchers, flying squirrels, mice [mostly *Peromyscus*], honeybees, etc.). Satisfactory internal dimensions were mentioned earlier (see "Reproduction"); the boxes should be cleaned out and then provided with a layer of dry sawdust or chips before the ducks begin "prospecting." For further information, see Bellrose (1955), Webster and Uhler (1964), and various papers in Jahn (1966). RSP

FOOD Seeds and other parts of aquatic plants, seeds of trees (especially acorns) and shrubs; also aquatic and land insects, and crustaceans. Examination of 399 stomachs of specimens from 24 states, taken Aug. to Dec. and Feb. to March inclusive, showed 90.2% vegetable and 9.8% animal matter (Mabbott 1920). The Wood Duck consumes larger amounts of acorns than our other species of waterfowl.

Young consume a large number of insects: mayflies (Ephemerida) and larvae, caddis flies (Trichoptera) and larvae, and grasshoppers (Locustidae). Frogs occasionally. They are fond of duckweeds (*Lemna*) (Judd 1901, Gigstead 1938). In Me., young 4 days of age had eaten insects only; at age of a week, vegetation was taken in increasing quantity (Coulter 1957). For the shift of young birds from animal to plant foods, in Tenn., see Hocutt and Dimmick (1971).

**Vegetable** Duckweeds (*Lemna, Spirodela*) 10.4%; cones and galls of cypress

(*Taxodium*) 9.2%; sedges: seeds of bulrush (*Scirpus*), beak rush (*Rynchospora*), saw grass (*Cladium*), nut rush (*Scleria*), chufas, (*Cyperus*), *Carex, Fimbristylis*, and spike rush (*Eleocharis*) 9.1%; grasses: seeds of wild rice (*Zizania*), meadow grass (*Panicularia*), panic grasses (*Panicum*), wild millet (*Echinochloa*), cut-grasses (*Zizaniopsis, Homalocenchrus*), love grass (*Eragrostis*) 8.2%; numerous true pondweeds (*Potamogeton*), bushy pondweed (*Najas*), wigeon grass (*Ruppia*) 6.5%; seeds of Fagaceae: beechnuts (*Fagus*), acorns (*Quercus rubra, palustris, nigra, macrocarpa, lobata, marylandica*) 6.3%; seeds of waterlillies (*Nymphaea, Castalia, Brasenia*), stems and leaves of *Caboma* 6%; seeds of Urticaceae: water elm (*Planera*), hackberries (*Celtis*), elm (*Ulmus*) 4.8%; Polygonaceae: dock (*Rumex*), smartweeds (*Polygonum*) 4.7%; coontail (*Ceratophyllum*) 2.9%; Araceae, Compositae, and miscellaneous families 22.2% (Mabbott 1920). Seventy-five individuals had eaten 11.6% wild rice (McAtee 1911).

Seeds of arrow arum (*Peltandra*) are eaten extensively in Mass. (J. C. Phillips 1925) and in S.C. (Mabbot 1920); *Scirpus* and bulbs of *Sagittaria* in Me. (Norton 1909, Mendall and Gashwiler 1940). In Me. in spring the chief foods were Cyperaceae (mainly *Carex*) and Sparganiaceae (mainly *Sparganium*), while in fall *Zizania aquatica Potamogeton* spp., *Sparganium spp.*, *Scirpus subterminalis*, and *Quercus* spp. (Coulter 1955, 1957). Chief fall foods on the lower Hudson R. were *Solanum dulcamera* 47.3% by volume, *Zea mays* 16.4%, and *Quercus vetulina* 10% (Foley and Taber 1951). Ten stomachs from the upper St. Lawrence region contained principally acorns (*Quercus borealis*) 25.4%, seeds of rice cut-grass (*Leersia oryzoides*) 23.1%, and wild celery (*Vallisneria americana*) 14.9% (Kutz et al. 1948). The gullets and gizzards of 77 specimens from the upper Chesapeake region showed chiefly beechnuts, acorns, seeds of smartweed (*Polygonum arifolium, P. punctatum*), hornbeam (*Carpinus caroliniana*), black gum (*Nyssa sylvatica*), and aquatic plants (*Peltandra, Sparganium, Potamogeton, Elodea*) (R. E. Stewart 1962).

In s. Wis. the acorns of *Quercus macrocarpa* are a favored food (Kumlien and Hollister 1903). Twenty-two fall specimens from Horicon Marsh, Wis., contained *Quercus* spp. 65% by volume, *Sparganium eurycarpum* 15%, *Leersia oryzoides* 6%, and *Ceratophyllum demersum* 4% (Stollberg 1950). The food in 26 gizzards from Illinois specimens in fall was quite different: *Zea mays* 48.4% *Quercus* spp. 15%, and *Echinochloa crusgalli* 12% (H. G. Anderson 1959). Utilized especially during the flightless peroid: *Cephalanthus, Forestiera, Nelumbo lutea, Scirpus fluviatilis, Polygonum muhlenbergii* (Hawkins and Bellrose 1940). Thirty-eight gizzards from Mo. contained *Quercus* spp. 42.4%, *Fagopyrum sagittatum* 28.2%, and *Zea mays* 7.9% (Korschgen 1955). The 36 Reelfoot Lake specimens showed a high utilization of seeds of *Taxodium distichum* 50%, along with *Quercus* spp. 32.8%, *Zea mays* 2.8%, and surprisingly *Carya* sp. 2.6% (Rawls 1958). Seeds of swamp privet (*Forestiera acuminata*) are utilized extensively in the middle south (McAtee 1915), and of water chinquapin (*Nelumbo lutea*) in La. (Beyer et al. 1907). In the 1961 hunting season at L. Marion, S.C., 6 plants made up 98% of the total volume of food in 108 stomachs; 5 were tree fruits—water oak (*Quercus nigra*) and willow oak (*Q. phellos*) [not pin oak as originally reported], bald cypress (*Taxodium distichum*), sweet gum (*Liquidambar styraciflua*), and water hickory (*Carya aquatica*); the sixth was corn (*Zea mays*); the small amounts of

9 others included green hawthorn (*Crataegus viridis*) and American hornbeam (*Carpinus caroliniana*) (McGilvrey 1966a).

Foods in Cal.: waterweed (*Anacharis*), water buttercup (*Ranunculus aquatilis*), and acorns of valley oak (*Quercus lobata*) (Dixon 1924). Two stomachs from Ore. contained seed of *Myriophyllum*, seeds and vegetative parts of *Hippuris vulgaris*, seeds of *Polygonum hydropiper*, *Triglochin maritima*, and *Symphoricarpos* (Gabrielson and Jewett 1940).

**Animal** Dragonflies (Anisoptera), damselflies (Zygoptera), especially nymphs, 2.5%, bugs (Heteroptera, Homoptera) 1.6% beetles (Coleoptera) 1%, Orthoptera, Diptera, Hymenoptera, Arachnida, and miscellaneous animal foods (mollusks, amphibians, crustaceans, fishes) 4.7% (Mabbot 1920). One stomach was filled with a small Coleopteran, *Donacia* (Nuttall 1834). The spring food in Me. contained 9% animal matter consisting entirely of the insects Ephemeridae, Coleoptera, Diptera, Membracidae, Orthoptera, Plecoptera, Gyrinidae, Gerridae, and Lepidoptera (Coulter 1955). Seen to catch and swallow fish in Jan. in N.Y. (Scheider 1957). One had eaten a mouse (A. L. Nelson 1944). AWS

277

## Muscovy Duck

*Cairina moschata* (Linnaeus)

A very large duck with short stout legs and fairly long tail. In **wild stock** both sexes are largely very dark or black with more or less purplish or greenish gloss, underparts brownish, and upper and under wing coverts and axillars white in definitive feathering. In the drake the feathers of forehead to upper neck are elongated (combined crest and mane); the skin is bare, from around the eye to the bill, and blackish with purplish or pinkish caruncles (enlarged seasonally); bill dusky with pink end (except dark nail) and pink transverse stripe. The drake weighs up to 5.5 lb. (2.5 kg.). The duck is much smaller (weighs about half as much), has reduced crest and mane, no bare facial area, and bill dusky except pinkish near tip. Although Delacour (1959) stated that *Cairina* has "no eclipse plumage" (meaning 1 Plumage/cycle), this remains to be demonstrated. The Juv. wing has no white. In downies the eye stripe begins at back of the eye (as in *Aix*). **In domestication,** after 2 or 3 generations (Delacour 1959) Muscovies become heavier, with larger caruncles; domestic strains include birds that are more or less streaked whitish, or are all white, or some variant of buffy brown, or even bluish.

The drake's tracheal apparatus has been described repeatedly, from 1779 on; see J. C. Phillips (1923a) for a description.

No subspecies.

**Measurements** of specimens from widespread localities, 9 ♂: BILL 60.9–76.2 mm., av. 67.9; WING across chord 345–408, av. 385; TAIL 164–184, av. 176; TARSUS 62.1–69.1, av. 64.7;　and 4 ♀: BILL 47.2–54.3 mm., av. 51.4; WING across chord 294–318, av. 307; TAIL 139–156, av. 148; TARSUS 48.3–54.2, av. 51.9 (H. Friedmann). RSP

DISTRIBUTION　**Natural range** includes Mexico from Sinaloa, Nuevo Leon, and Tamaulipas southward, also Cent. Am., Trinidad, and S. Am. down into Peru, Paraguay, and e. Argentina. Kept in **domestication** within its natural range and beyond, including conterminous U.S., Britain, Europe, and probably elsewhere.

**In our area** occurs in Texas as a **feral** bird in Live Oak and San Patricio cos. (Bolen 1971b) and perhaps locally elsewhere in the Gulf of Mexico coastal region.

**Introduced** in Fla., but whether presently established in the wild is unknown. In 1966, 4 birds from Paraguay were received in Aug., and 97 from Venezuela in Nov.; most of this stock was liberated at various Fla. localities. Some evidence was obtained that ♀ ♀ first bred when about 2 years old. It also was discovered that some of the birds developed white spotting and were rather tame, i.e., showed evidence of being progeny of domesticated stock. Plans were being made to import more Muscovies. These data are from a report by E. D. Crider to the Fla. Game and Fresh Water Fish Comm. dated Sept. 15, 1967. Serious reservations, for stated reasons, regarding release of this waterfowl into the natural range of our native species have been expressed by Weller (1969) and Bolen (1971b). The birds released in Fla. in 1966, however, are said to have been exterminated by raccoons or other predators. RSP

OTHER TOPICS　This duck is a hole nester, i.e., a forest species. It is aggressive toward other waterfowl. It hybridizes with the Mallard, producing infertile crosses. On

278

arrival of Columbus in the W. Indies, his men found domesticated "ducks as large as geese" among the Indians, according to J. C. Phillips. The species was listed as "common in domestication" on Hispaniola by Wetmore and Swales (1931), but there seems to be no evidence that it has occurred naturally in the Caribbean area n. of Trinidad. It was found in domestication in S. Am. in the early 1500s and is known to have been imported to Europe by 1550 and to England by 1670. The vernacular name "Muscovy" is a corruption of a name applied to certain Nicaraguan Indians. In addition to these historical data, there is much else of importance in J. C. Phillips (1923a) and sources he cited; for some further information, see Delacour (1959). RSP

### White-winged Scoter

*Melanitta fusca*

Includes Velvet or European White-winged Scoter or authors. Large, stocky, short-necked diving duck; dark (to black) except for white patch in wing, some white on head (location and amount depend on sex and Plumage) and venter (in some Plumages).

*M. fusca deglandi*

Bill has sides convex (as viewed from directly above); nail broad, flattened, and scarcely hooked; feather margin on side base extends forward, then is angled upward, and across the top it is more or less truncated; drakes have a "hump" or even a knobby protuberance (its size varies geographically) on top basal half of bill, but it is less developed in younger drakes and not evident when they first fly; the large nostrils are within the swollen area and, the larger the hump, the more nearly circular they become. The bill of ♀ ♀ in lateral profile is rather wedge-shaped and with distal half angled upward slightly. The iris becomes white in the drake, being dark brown in young of both sexes and in ♀ ♀ of all ages. Tail feathers comparatively broad, only narrowing near their ends to a point (Basic Plumage). Tenth (outer) primary longer than the 8th and its inner vane not narrowed.

Tracheal apparatus of the drake: in N. Am. birds the windpipe has distal half enlarged in diam. and then, near the midpoint, there is a smallish, more or less bony swelling, and no enlarged bulla at the inner end; in w. Palearctic birds, part of the distal ⅔ is enlarged, then there is a spherical bony enlargement. The 2 variants just described were figured together by deW. Miller (1926), but the latter one is best shown in Schiøler (1926), and the tracheal apparatus of the Asiatic population (*stejnegeri*) apparently has not been described or figured.

Length ♂ to about 23 in., ♀ to 22, wingspread ♂ to about 39, ♀ to 37, wt. of ♂ 2½–4 lb., ♀ 2–3. Three subspecies, 1 in N. Am., another (w. Palearctic) has straggled to Greenland, and the third (e. Palearctic) reaches the Commander Is.

DESCRIPTION *M. f. deglandi.* Two Plumages/cycle in both sexes. In the first cycle, molting often is fairly protracted, thus Plumages often overlap in time on the individual. In succeeding cycles, both sexes have a fairly long molt into most of Basic in spring (the duck beginning first), the wing portion of the molt being offset into late summer. Because 1 there is individual variation in duration of molting in healthy birds, 2 some birds in collections were in poor health when captured, from oiling, and 3 some specimens, expecially of young birds, appear to have been wrongly sexed, it is difficult or impossible to assign some specimens to particular Plumages with certainty.

▶ ♂ Def. Alt. Plumage (all feathering except wing and tail), typically acquired from some time in JULY or AUG. well into SEPT., but individuals commonly continue acquiring some new feathers into WINTER; it is retained into SPRING.

In general, black and white with some bluish gloss (mostly on head–neck). **Bill** proximal portion (including hump) black and this continues narrowly along sides of maxilla (but did not completely outline it in any bird examined) to the nail, and some black along top midline; forward sides of bill scarlet or ruby, the nail orange, and top of distal half of bill white (with or without narrow black lateral border). **Iris** white with dusky outer margin. **Head** and neck black with ultramarine gloss and with smallish tear-shaped or crescent-shaped white area, somewhat variable in size, that surrounds the eye and extends back from it; often some head feathers are white with dark ends and the dark may wear off; the neck feathers are somewhat furrowed (not smooth). **Body** black, except feathers of sides and flanks brownish (longest feathers, on flanks, taper to a point). Legs and **feet** in the rose to magenta range (outer side of tarsus), darkening to black on rear of tarsus, webs, and joints. Wing and tail are retained Basic feathering.

▶ ♂ Def. Basic Plumage (entire feathering), the head–body and part or all of tail acquired in SPRING, sometimes more gradually (or molt perhaps interrupted) into early SUMMER; the wing is acquired in LATE SUMMER or FALL, in the span during which the spring-acquired Basic begins to be succeeded by Alt.; the Basic wing is retained nearly a year.

This is a sooty Plumage, without gloss, with white area at eye, and venter whitish or same mottled dark. On **upperparts** and sides many of the feathers have paler margins, giving a scalloped or somewhat barred effect; feathers on sides, and especially flanks, are broad, rounded (not pointed), sooty brownish, color not appreciably different from lower sides and breast. **Belly** sometimes white, but usually the feathers have sooty ends, giving an irregularly and densely spotted effect. Tail blackish.

**Wing** mostly black with large white patch at trailing edge. The innermost secondaries are elongated, downcurved, pointed, and generally all-dark, and their overlying coverts are equally dark; the next 4 secondaries are white, the next 2 outward are white tipped black, the next has more black on tip and basal half also black, and the ends of greater coverts overlying the white area are broadly tipped white. In the wing lining some coverts have much white, especially the longer ones over bases of the primaries and this, plus pale sheen of undersurface of primaries, plus white area in secondaries, combine to give the appearance of a very light underwing.

▶ ♀ Def. Alt. Plumage (all feathering except wing and tail), generally acquired beginning in very LATE SUMMER or some time in FALL, although new feathers commonly continue to appear into very late fall; it is retained until SPRING.

A very dark Plumage, varying with individual from sooty to olive brownish; in fresh feathering, some bluish sheen on head–neck and mantle. **Bill** dark, except for light band adjoining nail; **iris** dark brownish. **Head** check feathers on at least some individuals are whitish basally and, after they become abraded, some white may show; upper **sides** and flanks generally somewhat browner than other feathering; **belly** varies with individual from all-dark (usually) to broken pattern (dark-ended light feathers) to nearly all-white (exceptional). Legs and **feet** have quite muted reddish cast, grading to dusky on rear of tarsus and the webs. Tail and wing are retained Basic feathering.

▶ ♀ Def. Basic Plumage (entire feathering), the head–body and sometimes part of tail acquired usually in MARCH–APRIL or this molt prolonged into early summer; the wing is acquired later, after nesting, and beginning then or some time later the spring-acquired portion of the Basic starts molting back into Alt. The Basic tail and wing are retained nearly a year.

Usually quite brownish, but some individual variation toward dark olive grayish. **Head** varies from all dark to same with a poorly defined light area on cheek near base of bill and another on rear of cheek; feathers on side of head white basally, hence more white shows after abrasion. Many feathers on **upperparts** have wide margins that vary from slightly paler to very distinctly paler (scalloped pattern). **Underparts** sides and flanks generally as dark as dorsum but somewhat browner, the feathers plain or margined (as on dorsum) and rounded in shape; belly varies with individual—some shade of brown, or a smoke gray, or rarely whitish, or dark-ended light feathers that give a mottled or even a quite barred effect. **Tail** as back. **Wing** mostly sooty brownish (some coverts often lighter margined); nearly as much white in secondaries as in the drake, but adjoining greater coverts only narrowly white-tipped.

NOTES   This Plumage sometimes bleaches to a buffy brownish.

Females have been found flightless Aug.–Oct., some even as late as Nov.

In both Alt. and Basic, individuals vary from toward black to somewhat brownish.

AT HATCHING   See vol. 2, col. pl. facing p. 466. Apparently there is some individual variation, as in absence or some indication of a whitish patch in scapular area and also on side of rump. M shaped feather margin at top base of bill distinguishes downy Whitewings from Surf and Black Scoters.

▶   ♂ ♀ Juv. Plumage (entire feathering), fully developed at estimated 70 days post-hatching, then is replaced during FALL by Basic I, except the Basic I tail sometimes does not succeed the Juv. until early winter, and the Juv. wing is retained nearly a year.

This is a rather dingy Plumage, darkest on **head**–neck and anterior mantle, and with 2 poorly defined whitish (or same speckled dark) areas on side of head; upper **breast** to vent light mottled darkish (not unmarked white). **Tail** feathers narrow and with notched ends. The dark **wing** has a white patch that is smaller than in the Basic wing, does not include tips of overlying greater coverts, and varies somewhat in size in different individuals (or a sex difference?).

NOTE   Dwight (1914) stated that birds still wholly in Juv. may be found from Oct. to April, but he included at least Basic I in the Juv. Plumage.

▶   ♂ Basic I Plumage (all feathering except wing), generally succeeds the corresponding portions of Juv. in OCT.–NOV., although the tail may come in considerably later. There is considerable variation in timing and rate of molting into Basic I. Generally it is retained only until EARLY WINTER.

**Head**–neck black, only the lower eyelid being light; **dorsum** blackish; **underparts** breast, sides, and flanks somewhat brownish, grading into unmarked whitish belly; **tail** feathers blackish with rounded ends.

NOTE   This Plumage appears first on head–neck, then back, breast, and sides, then remainder of underparts and the tail. Commonly the head–neck molt out of Basic I before or soon after the venter acquires Basic I.

▶   ♂ Alt. I. Plumage (all feathering except wing and tail) generally acquired beginning in very LATE FALL or EARLY WINTER and retained into SPRING.

A black Plumage with some sheen on head–neck and dorsum. There is only a trace of white crescent encircling the eye, or no sign of it, the feathers being dark-ended although white basally. About the time this Plumage begins to appear, the eye lightens, the hump enlarges on the bill, and the feet show considerable reddish color.

NOTE   The molting from Juv. through Basic I into Alt. I is, typically, a more or less continuous process that extends into winter. It may be interrupted or delayed, so that various stages described above occur later than usual. Good examples of Alt. I generally are dated Jan. or later.

▶   ♀ Basic I Plumage (all feathering except wing), timing as ♂. The dark brownish or somewhat sooty **head** has a quite well-defined white patch on the cheek and a less distinct one from below the eye nearly to the bill, or sometimes the forepart of the face is palish brown. The **dorsum** is dark, breast brownish, sides and flanks dark brownish (the rounded feathers usually have somewhat paler broad margins); breast and sides grade into white **belly** (or this may be partly or entirely marked with pale brownish).

▶   ♀ Alt. I Plumage (all feathering except wing and tail), timing apparently as ♂ Alt. I. Generally all dark, more or less sooty brownish; some have more or less white on belly that is very coarsely marked sooty brownish.

NOTE   The timing of the sequence Juv.–Basic I–Alt. I in the ♀ may be even more variable than in the ♂; some apparently do very little molting out of Juv. in fall, then go through the other stages quite rapidly in winter. This results in individuals that appear to have skipped portions of "normal" molting, or that have feathers that are intermediate in character rather than clearly typical of any Plumage.

▶   ♂ Basic II Plumage (entire feathering), molting resumes in SPRING (before age 1 year), into new head–body resembling Def. Basic; at first the Juv. wing is worn, i.e., is retained into summer (to age about 1 year), then it is molted and the Basic II wing grows. Many yearlings become flightless as early as the 2nd week in June. If not already present, the new tail grows with the new wing. Then Basic II head–body are succeeded by Alt. II beginning not earlier than well along in SUMMER, but the wing and tail are retained nearly a year.

▶   ♀ Basic II Plumage (inclusive feathering as ♂ Basic II), the head–body and sometimes tail acquired in SPRING, all or remainder of tail and the wing later (LATE SUMMER or FALL) when head–body are molting back into Alt. Feathering evidently as ♀ Def. Basic.

**Color phases** none. Millais (1913b) stated that *M. f. fusca* ♀ ♀ were of 2 "distinct types," gray and rich reddish brown, but these are extremes of individual variation. Variation from toward dark gray to a dark brownish occurs also in ♀ ♀ of at least the Am. population.

**Measurements** of 2 series of "adults" are given here; those in the second series were labeled "*dixoni*," but note that the first series also includes western drakes.

First series 12 ♂ (9 New Eng., 1 Wash., 1 Alta., 1 B.C.): BILL 39–44 mm., av. 41.2; WING 274–298, av. 284.3; TAIL 76–86, av. 81.2; TARSUS 49–54, av. 51;   12 ♀ (3 New Eng., 2 Ill., 1 Wis., 1 N.D., 1 B.C., 3 Alta., 1 Yukon Terr.): BILL 35–43 mm., av. 38.8; WING 256–280, av. 267.7; TAIL 73–82, av. 77.7; TARSUS 48–51, av. 49.3.

Second series 12 ♂ (11 B.C., 1 Cal.): BILL 36–47 mm., av. 41.2; WING 272–289, av. 279.2; TAIL 69–87, av. 81.4; TARSUS 46–52, av. 49.3;   12 ♀ (1 Cal., 1 Wash., 9 B.C., 1

Alaska): BILL 35–41 mm., av. 38.2; WING 258–274, av. 268; TAIL 75–88, av. 79; TARSUS 45–50, av. 48.2 (ETS).

Independently, Rand (1946) measured bills of many of the above birds; also see bill meas. in Irving (1960).

The Juv. WING undoubtedly is shorter than the Basic wing in *M. f. deglandi*, since Schiøler (1926) found these av. differences in flattened wing of *M. f. fusca*: ♂ 13 Juv. 260 mm. and 22 Basic 275, ♀ 9 Juv. 249 mm. and 18 Basic 261.

**Weight** of 13 ♂ av. 3.4 lb. (1.5 kg.), max. 4 (1.8 kg.); 19 ♀ av. 2.7 lb. (1.2 kg.), max. 3.5 (1.5 kg.) (A. L. Nelson and Martin 1953). Perhaps they were weighed wet when retrieved; the series in Kortright (1942) weighed less. Six ♂ taken in mid-June at Anaktuvuk Pass, Alaska, weighed 1,413–1,907 gm., av. 1,650; and 2 ♀ (June 17, Aug. 6) 1,548 and 1,700 gm. (Irving 1960). Three flightless ♀ in Aug. in Alaska weighed 794–1,247 gm., the mean being 964 gm. (Yocom 1970a). A drake taken in late Dec. at Clallam, Wash., weighed 1,994 gm. (4 lb. 7 oz.) (G. E. Hudson). Maxima were given as ♂ 4 lb. 9 oz. and ♀ 3 lb. 8 oz. by Forbush (1925).

**Hybrids** a presumed wild cross between the European Whitewing and the Common Goldeneye (*Bucephala clangula*) was described by Leverkühn (1890). In Iceland a drake Whitewing was found paired with a ♀ Common Eider (*Somateria mollissima*), with 3 eggs in the nest, but any further result of this was not known (Gudmundsson 1932). S. F. Baird et al. (1884b) described a drake from Alaska that was suspected of being a *fusca–perspicillata* cross; it was, however, a somewhat unusual example of the latter (Surf Scoter).

**Geographical variation in the species** All "white-winged" scoters have been treated as comprising a single species by Hartert (1920b), J. C. Phillips (1926), Delacour (1959), and others. The w. Palearctic ("European") birds, however, have some minor structural differences (see "Subspecies") that are qualitative, hence some authors have continued to treat this population as having evolved to the species level. It is, perhaps, best treated as a semispecies, with the other two subspecies included in another semispecies. The other two are larger in size and are much more nearly alike otherwise, except that bill characters of drakes of the Nearctic ("American") population are "exaggerated" in the e. Palearctic ("Asiatic") population. The two also differ (mainly in ♂ Alt. Plumage) in coloring of sides and flanks. W. S. Brooks (1915) split the Am. population into 2 subspecies on the basis of alleged differences in bills, but further investigation has revealed that there is considerable individual variation within a single subspecies. RSP

SUBSPECIES The first listed probably can be distinguished always from the others, since loreal feathering ends at least 5 mm. distant from rear edge of nostril. Between the latter 2, in both of which the loreal feathering approaches much closer to the nostril, ♀ ♀ and young apparently are not identifiable to subspecies.

*fusca* (Linnaeus)—European White-winged or Velvet Scoter. Sides of bill nearly straight and parallel; drake's bill has, at most, only a slight swelling on top near base (no hump), light areas of bill (except nail) are yellow, and the nostrils are elongated oval in shape; the bill of the ♀ is comparatively long; trachea of drake has distal third enlarged and, $2/3$ way from its distal end, there is a spherical structure (tracheal rings fused) having about twice the diam. of the enlarged distal portion; feathers on sides and flanks slightly differentiated (toward brown) in coloring, most evident in ♂ Alt. Plumage. For meas. see especially Schiøler (1926), the WING flattened, also Witherby (1939), WING meas. over curve. Has straggled to Greenland.

*deglandi* (Bonaparte)—American White-winged Scoter. Description and meas. given earlier. Sides of bill convex; drake has hump near top base of bill, the nostrils are short oval in outline, and lateral portions of bill are scarlet or orange; trachea of drake has distal half enlarged and, at midpoint, the tracheal rings are further enlarged and somewhat fused, forming a pronounced swelling (not spherical enlargement); feathering on sides and flanks tends to be differentiated in coloring (decidedly brown or chocolate in ♂ Alt. Plumage). Nearctic distribution; has straggled to e. Asia.

*stejnegeri* (Ridgway)—Asiatic White-winged Scoter or Hump-billed Turpan (Russian). As preceding except: hump on bill of ♂ so developed as to be a forward-projecting knob and the nostrils are circular; feathering on sides and flanks not (or little) differentiated in coloring, being blackish gray or black in ♂ Alt. Plumage. Tracheal apparatus undescribed. There seem to be almost no published meas.; said by Delacour (1959) to be the "same size" as the preceding. Eastern Palearctic in distribution; winter range includes the Commander Is. RSP

**FIELD IDENTIFICATION** The thickset dark scoters are very difficult, at times impossible, to identify to species at a distance. They tend to be strung out in lines when idling on the water and to be in scattered parties when diving for food. They fly in lines and bunches and frequently shift formation. Usually they are well away from shore, but in some places and seasons they tend to move shoreward to feed. They are not particularly shy. They prefer to remain a long time in one place; then they take wing heavily and fly low and swiftly over the water.

The White-winged, in all stages, has a white patch that extends inward from proximal part of trailing edge of the wing. It is not visible in the folded wing, but shows well when the birds flap, a rather frequent comfort movement. At closer range the drake's knobby bill and inverted white crescent at the eye can be seen; ♀ ♀ and certain young stages have two sizable, poorly defined white or pale areas on side of head. Compare with the other scoters. Generally speaking, scoters have a rather different profile—

285

more roundish overall, with shorter head–bill—than the dark stages of the Common Eider. RSP

VOICE    N. Am. data are few. Generally silent. Both sexes definitely call in flight as well as on water, usually a rather guttural, harsh, rattling call, between croaking and quacking. During display, both have a thin, somewhat whistled, call; the drake's is double noted and has been rendered *whur-er*. It is uttered decrescendo. An alarmed young drake made a low purring noise (Brooks, in J. C. Phillips 1926). The duck's alarm call, with variants used to warn or assemble her brood, ranges from rather nasally trilled grunting to harsh *kerr kerr* notes. A low cheeping from preflight young. (The Am. data are very incomplete; see, for example, Koskimies 1957 for calls of ♀ ♀ and young *M. f. fusca*.)

Although this species does not have the striking "wing music" of the Black Scoter (*M. nigra*), a distinct whistling can be heard at close range from groups making circular flights after their arrival at breeding localities. RSP

HABITAT    *M. f. deglandi*.    Breeds about ponds, lakes, oxbows, and sluggish streams, and on islands and islets in inland waters, also near rivers, and well inland from coasts (in nw. Canada and Alaska), in treeless or relatively open country, where there is dense and usually low ground cover (herbaceous, woody, or mixed). In other seasons (and most prebreeders all year), on marine and brackish waters along coasts where they like shallow water over shellfish beds, where the bottom is hard and usually sandy or gravelly. Occurs (regularly?) through winter on the Great Lakes (fresh water). RSP

DISTRIBUTION    (See map.) A boreal–subarctic nester. Compare with the section on "Migration," which points up some of the complexities of seasonal distribution of the sexes and age-classes in N. Am.

*M. f. fusca*—westward off continental Europe, has occurred in Sptizbergen, the Faeroes, Iceland, and in our area on w. coast of Greenland (records for Dec., Jan.–Feb., March, and May). See Bannermann (1958) and Vaurie (1965) for details of distribution elsewhere.

*M. f. deglandi*—**breeds** in N. Am. from w. Ont. westward throughout a large segment of Canada n. onto the barrens, and at various localities in interior Alaska w. to the vicinity of Kotzebue Sd., but concentrated in extreme nw. Canada and ne. Alaska; s. limits extend from Canada down into conterminous U.S. in ne. Wash. and upper half of N.D.

**Summer distribution** also includes much of marine winter range on Pacific and Atlantic coasts, plus interior areas where flocks travel on **molt migration,** plus molting areas (for example, se. Hudson Bay and Atlantic waters to include the outer coast of Labrador n. nearly to C. Chidley). The center of abundance of summering prebreeders is, on the Pacific side, in waters of se. Alaska, and on the Atlantic side in the Gulf of St. Lawrence and adjacent waters of Nfld. and s. Labrador.

Has occurred in summer westward into Siberia (coast of s. Primor, May 2, 1944), on

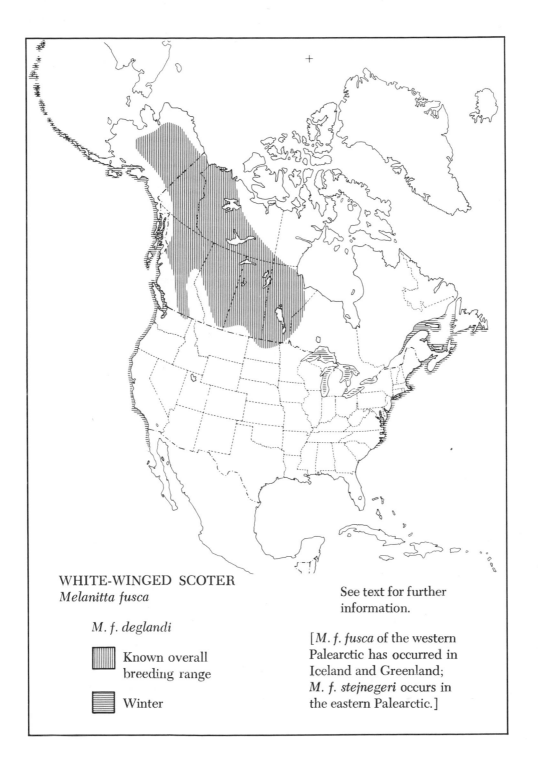

**WHITE-WINGED SCOTER**
*Melanitta fusca*

*M. f. deglandi*

Known overall
breeding range

Winter

See text for further
information.

[*M. f. fusca* of the western
Palearctic has occurred in
Iceland and Greenland;
*M. f. stejnegeri* occurs in
the eastern Palearctic.]

St. Lawrence I. (several records, including small flocks), the Pribilofs, and inner Aleutians (few records are w. of Umanak I.); northward in Canada at C. Bathurst (it nests not far away), w. Victoria I., mouth of Coppermine R., Foxe Pen. on Baffin I. (several records), Hudson Strait, Ungava Bay, and taken in w. Greenland at Nugssuak on July 1, 1944. To the south, on the Pacific coast into Cal. and on the Atlantic coast usually at least to Long I., N.Y.

**Winter** In Bering–Pacific waters: large numbers in the Aleutians (even sighted w. to Attu) and along the Alaska Pen., plentiful in se. Alaskan waters and in B.C., also in Wash., and in fair numbers down into Cal.

In the Commander Is. the birds (fairly common migrant; rare in winter) are *stejnegeri*, but there are 3 specimens (April, May, and Nov.) identified as *deglandi* (Hartert 1920b, Dementiev and Gladkov 1952, Johansen 1961).

In interior N. Am.: Great Lakes, where evidently only small numbers occur and possibly not regularly present.

Atlantic: Gulf of St. Lawrence and s. Nfld. southward to the Carolinas (evidently concentrated from w. Me. to Chesapeake Bay), occasionally to Fla. At the present time it is by far the most numerous wintering scoter in New Eng. waters.

**Southerly limits of recorded occurrence** in N. Am.: Mexico (Baja Cal.), Ariz. (2 localities), New Mex. (at least 4 reports), and inland and/or Gulf Coast records for Texas, La., Ala., and Fla. Formerly it was the commonest scoter in n. Gulf of Mexico, but is now the rarest.

In the Nearctic region, *M. fusca* (*M. deglandi* of earlier authors) is recorded as **fossil** from the Pleistocene of s. Cal. (2 localities) and from **archaeological sites** in Alaska (10 localities, mostly on is.); details in Brodkorb (1964a). To these add a Pleistocene locality in Ore. (Jehl 1967) and one in Md. (Wetmore 1973), and an archaeological site in Cal. (H. Howard 1933).

**Extralimital** *M. f. stejnegeri*—**breeds** nearest to N. Am. on the Kamchatkan Pen. and in Anadyrland, and thence westward to the upper (southern) reaches of the Yenesei. (This species is not recorded in any season from the Chuckchee Pen. and Wrangel I.) To the south it has an interesting and (as in *M. f. deglandi* in N. Am.) very discontinuous breeding distribution; it breeds around the n. part of L. Baikal (details in Gusev 1962) and about some widely scattered smaller lakes at high elevations in mountainous areas, for example in Kazakhstan (details in Dolgushin 1960). The various localities were listed by Vaurie (1965).

For Palearctic **fossil** localities, see under *M. fusca* in Brodkorb (1964a).

NOTE Contrary to some distribution maps, in n. Eurasia the breeding ranges of *M. f. fusca* and *M. f. stejnegeri* are not known to meet; in the intervening gap, either prebreeders or postbreeding molting *M. f. fusca* have been recorded occasionally. RSP

MIGRATION *M. f. deglandi*. Travels by day and night over water but prefers to travel by night over land; travels high (often passes unnoticed) on long overland flights and with few stops on deep-water lakes and on rivers where the birds rest but apparently do not feed. The 2 major wintering units are on opposite sides of N. Am. and the birds go from both sides to the interior to nest, the Pacific–Bering birds being more northerly as breeders.

W. Cooke (1913a) stated that Atlantic winterers go overland in spring from s. New Eng. and elsewhere toward Man. and that their return route to winter quarters is "due east to the coast of the most eastern part of Labrador," thence down through the Gulf of St. Lawrence and on southward. That is, different spring and fall routes. He also stated that the Pacific coastal wintering birds moved n. in spring to near the nw. corner of B.C. and disappeared, presumably flying overland toward the Mackenzie drainage, and reversed this route to return to salt water. He made no distinctions among age-classes or sexes, but J. C. Phillips (1926) raised the question of whether breeding drakes fly to some place to molt. Lincoln (1950a), although he distinguished age-classes, stated that Atlantic winterers go se. from breeding range (reverse of spring route) to winter quarters, with no elliptical route of breeding drakes and no mention of molt migration. The earlier concept seems nearer correct for breeding ♂♂, even though numerous questions remain unanswered.

From piecing together various fragments of information (time of occurrence at or absence from various places, known dates when flightless at some localities), the following generalizations seem valid:

**1** Two-year-olds and older birds make long flights to the interior (a few that go to breeding range may not breed), but at least most of the younger birds remain on salt water.

**2** The majority (but not all) of the breeding drakes leave their mates early in incubation and, usually some weeks later, make a long molt migration back to salt water.

**3** Yearlings (prebreeders) in spring move up both coasts (March into June), the terminal phase of this journey being, in essence, a molt migration. In fall they take the reverse route, southward, from some time in Sept. on (movement usually ends on winter range in late Nov. or early Dec.).

**4** For breeders in spring, although there is at first a shift northward, their long overland flight (both from the Atlantic and Pacific) comes late, not earlier than some time in May. True fall migration (which comes after molt migration and molting) also is not early, but occurs mostly in Oct.–Nov., and greatest winter abundance is more northerly than for prebreeders.

**5** Breeding ♀♀ first, and their broods averaging somewhat later, travel approximately the reverse of the spring route of the former (easterly winterers), reaching Atlantic waters probably at various points from the Gulf of St. Lawrence to the Gulf of Maine; then there is a general shift southward of younger birds in coastal waters so that their greatest winter abundance is more southerly than that of drakes of breeding age.

**6** Allowing for differences in geography, Joensen's (1973) summary by sex and age-class of movements of *M. f. fusca* in Danish and other n. European waters aligns fairly well with the above generalizations.

**Atlantic-wintering unit** occurs in winter from s. Nfld. to the Carolinas. There is movement up along the U.S. coast beginning in March (if not earlier), with much movement even in the Maritimes and beyond in April, and cessation of movement not until some time in June in outer Gulf of St. Lawrence and coastal Labrador. Through the summer, they are scattered from the marine waters of N.Y. to about lat. 60° N on the Labrador coast, the majority of both sexes occurring from the n. Maritimes northward and many ♂♂ apparently going farthest, to Labrador. A great many of these prebreeders become flightless (terminal phase of Prebasic molting) as early as the 2nd and 3rd weeks of June.

In mid-May, or even later, breeders (both sexes) go from Atlantic coastal points (possibly from as far s. as Chesapeake Bay, more certainly at least from Long I. Sd. to Gulf of St. Lawrence) westward overland toward Man. (southerly breeding range). A great many form in assemblies on the s. Mass.–Conn. coast and then fly inland. The Great Lakes are resting places for an unknown number of spring migrants. After the ducks are incubating, the drakes gather, at first in small groups, and some remain to molt on larger waters nearby, but the majority vanish from breeding range, on molt migration. Some are flightless in molt far to the east in se. Hudson Bay in the first 3 weeks in Aug., but it appears that the great majority continue on eastward across Ungava (none are known to breed or molt in the interior) to the s. third (or more?) of the outer coast of Labrador. Many are flightless in middle third of Aug., some 7–8 weeks later than the beginning of the flightless stage of some yearling prebreeders.

At various large lakes in Alta., from mid-June through July, drakes make circling flights for 2–2½ hrs. every evening, for a total of some 4,000 mi. at about 40 mph, and "finish where they began" (Rowan 1931). The distance traveled is the equivalent of flying from their breeding places to the Equator. Some important questions remain unanswered. First, whether Rowan was seeing the same drakes or different ones, i.e., whether circular flights in fact add up to as much mileage for the individual. Also, it is not clear whether these particular birds were Atlantic or Pacific winterers, whether their flying was equivalent to a molt migration (without the drakes going anywhere), or whether they make a subsequent flight to a molting place. At least for a time, the ♀ ♀ join in these flights.

There are small flights of White-winged Scoters to New Eng. waters in late July –early Aug.; if they are "old males" as J. C. Phillips (1926) stated, perhaps they flew se. from the interior instead of making the roundabout passage via Labrador. The ♀ ♀ and their young reach Atlantic waters at more southerly places than is typical of breeding drakes (more nearly the reverse of spring migration). [The birds that occur in great rafts, often far from shore on the Great Lakes, that Pirnie (1935) stated were present as early as Sept., may be molting birds rather than autumn migrants.] They reach salt water from some time in Sept. on and there follows a shift down along the coast. The majority of mature drakes moves s. along the coast in Oct.–Nov., few going beyond Long I., N.Y.

**Great Lakes wintering unit**   Size unknown; no useful information on movements. Since usually there are mature White-winged Scoters on s. Man. breeding range by May 10 (an earlier date than is usual for departure of winterers from the Atlantic), one wonders if these early arrivals wintered on the Great Lakes. The first White-winged Scoters arrived May 6 in 1965 at Miquelon L., Alta. (Vermeer 1969).

**Alaska to Cal. winterers** have, as in the Atlantic, a center of winter abundance of mature drakes more northerly than of yearlings of either sex. Also as in the Atlantic, there is movement northward beginning in March. Then the yearlings remain and molt on salt water, mostly from B.C. to around the Alaska Pen.; breeders, from localities both in B.C. and s. Alaska, fly overland toward ne. Alaska and the lower (northerly) part of the Mackenzie drainage, departing well along in May. Some stop to rest on interior waters. In general, the Pacific birds occupy the northerly sector of inland breeding range. In molt migration (mainly in July) the drakes fly in small parties and flocks back over the mountains to salt water, where they form large gatherings and become flightless. At Graham I. in the Queen Charlotte Is., in the latter part of Aug., the beach frequently was "littered with feathers" of molting drakes (Patch 1922). The ducks and their broods also fly sw., probably on a broader front, and mostly in Sept. The southward coastal movement extends from at least some time in Sept. through Nov.

**Aleutian and Kodiak winterers** Scant information. North of the Alaska Pen. at Nushagak Bay (within Bristol Bay) a mass flight inland was seen on May 26 (O. Murie 1959). It would seem probable that the Whitewings seen flying eastward up the Porcupine R. drainage at Old Crow, Yukon Terr., in last third of May (Irving 1960), were following a continuation of the route of the birds Murie saw and were near the end of their journey. RSP

BANDING STATUS   In N. Am. the total number banded was 1,823 through the year 1964 and there were 27 recoveries through 1961; main places of banding were Alaska, Alta., Sask., and B.C. (data from Bird Banding Laboratory). RSP

REPRODUCTION   *M. f. deglandi.* Minimum **breeding age** 2 years, but perhaps some do not breed until older. A few birds (in the 2-year age-class?) go to breeding range and remain in small flocks on larger waters until some time in summer; then they depart.

There is much chasing and **display** among groups on winter range, especially as the season wears on, and at least most breeders are paired prior to spring migration. Edson (in Bent 1925) observed the following performance at Bellingham Bay, Wash., on Dec. 24 and again on Feb. 11. About 10 birds were together, actively swimming and plunging in an area perhaps 10–12 ft. in diam.; he could not distinguish the sexes. In the center, 2 birds would assume a pose as if billing and caressing each other, 1 with head elevated, the other's head depressed, bills in contact. This lasted 2–3 sec. at a time. There was constant interruption by interloping birds that would approach one or both performers from behind, and which were driven away. On one date, he believed the same 2 birds still were engaged in this activity when he left after watching the group for half an hour. M. T. Myres has seen a drake with bill downward and head and neck appearing much swollen; he believes that this posture has some connection with pair formation.

Known displays are few and simple; these data are from Myres (1959a), from field observations in B.C. coastal waters. **Displays of the duck** CHIN-LIFTING (equivalent to Inciting), a thin whistle uttered, display directed toward a particular drake. Ritualized DRINKING. **Displays of the drake** NECK-ERECT-FORWARD (threat) while swimming rapidly. Ritualized DRINKING. WATER-TWITCH bill dipped in water with slight shake of head, then raised and swung around to one side. PREEN-BEHIND-THE-WING has several variants and preening is not limited to wing; bill color, white iris, white area adjoining eye, and white in wing are conspicuous against black body. UPWARD-STRETCH and WING-FLAP are frequent and apparently ritualized. The drake has a whistling note, uttered some time during display.

Pursuit-flights have been noted on breeding range—a ♀ and 2 pursuing ♂ ♂, each of the latter striving to become stationed just behind the duck. Bent (1925) stated that drakes give voice during this activity. The drake has been known to try to grasp the flying duck's tail in his bill, but cannot hold on as the duck maneuvers to avoid him.

Beginning in early June (on breeding range) mated pairs, also groups of pairs, fly in wide circles over nesting terrain or around nearby waters; afterward, each pair goes to each drake's particular water area, which is defended more vigorously against intruding drakes than against mated pairs. From observations at several Alta. lakes, Rowan (1931) ascribed such flying to drakes only and he stated it occurs from mid-June through July.

Pair bond form is **single clutch monogamy**, so far as known.

**Copulation** has been described by Myres (1959b). There is mutual Drinking and drakes perform Water-twitch and Preen-behind-the-wing (the 2 frequently linked). The duck assumes a PRONE position; after the drake mounts, he performs a double WING-FLICK; on dismounting, sometimes he holds the ♀'s nape very briefly so that the 2 birds rotate slightly on the water. Then the drake swims away slowly, with some wing movement; the duck behaves similarly, sometimes flapping her wings.

The interval between arrival of the birds and initiation of clutches is comparatively long; the birds arrive late and nest very late. In general, full **fresh clutches** should not be expected until the last third of June and in some areas perhaps not until July. At Miquelon L., Alta., in 20 nests (1964–65 data combined) the first egg was laid from June 7 to July 2; the av. interval between laying of eggs in a clutch was 1.6 days; and **clutch size** in 12 clutches was 6–16 eggs (Vermeer 1968). Clutch size was given as 9–14 eggs by Bent (1925).

The **nest site** is a shallow depression, preferably in a patch of brush or herbaceous growth, occasionally more in the open; close to water (commonly), some distance away (uncommonly), ½ mi. from water (rarely). Often on islets or islands, in which case sometimes a high nesting density; for example, 20 nests on less than ½ acre on a small willow-covered island in Chip L., Alta. (R. Smith). Various is. in Alta. lakes are shared with nesting gulls (*Larus*) and several duck species; see Vermeer (1968) for details. The nest depression sometimes contains some plant materials gathered at the site; the **nest down**, deposited from some time during laying until some stage in incubation, is a deep grayed or olive brownish with small white centers (illus.: Broley 1950).

The duck swims to shore and walks to the nest; the drake has a waiting area (on water not far away) where his mate joins him between layings and when off-duty from incubating, until he departs. He defends his water area, at least against other ♂ Whitewings, and rarely, if ever, goes ashore.

One **egg** each from 20 clutches (from widespread localities) **size** length 67.19 ± 1.99 mm., breadth 45.96 ± 1.12, radii of curvature of ends 18.19 ± 1.09 and 12.50 ± 1.40; **shape** nearly elliptical (very slightly subelliptical), elongation 1.46 ± 0.050, bicone −0.019, asymmetry +0.182 (FWP). The mean meas. of 100 eggs from Miquelon L., Alta., were length 67.33 mm. and breadth 46.33; see Vermeer (1968a) for additional details. The length av. less than in the above 2 series in the 71 eggs reported in Bent (1925). Eighty eggs in Schönwetter's (1961) list av. 65.6 × 45.8 mm. Egg **color** creamy buff, without gloss.

Incubation by the duck; soon after it begins, the drake joins with other drakes and, sooner or later, either molts on larger waters nearby or (more typically) makes a long flight to salt water and becomes flightless there. The only datum on **incubation period** of *M. f. deglandi* is 25 days for a clutch at Miquelon L., reported by Vermeer (1969). In 25 clutches of *M. f. fusca* it was 26–29 days, av. 27.5 (Koskimies and Routamo 1953).

At Miquelon L., of 10 clutches of known fate, 5 hatched (50 eggs—38 hatched, 10 did not, and 2 disappeared), 4 were destroyed by predators, and 1 was deserted (Vermeer 1969).

**Preflight ducklings** These data from Swarth (1926) are from observations at L. Como in nw. B.C. When a day or 2 old, the young dive "expertly, making long stays below the surface." Soon after hatching, broods merged into loose assemblies and sometimes 2 or 3 ♀ ♀ attended 16–20 young; one had 32 small ducklings. The latter are very self-reliant; sometimes 6–8 would forage unattended. In this "colony" individuals, young and old, gathered "together into larger or smaller groups as suited their convenience at the time." In Man., Hochbaum (1944) saw a duck with 84 young, all under 2 weeks of age. (There are many data on crèches, or brood amalgamations, of *M. f. fusca* in the Baltic.) At first the ducklings tend to stay close to the duck; later they are strung out in single file and, if alarmed, they dive and are widely scattered on resurfacing. Some ducks may stay with a brood or amalgamation and go through the flightless stage of molting, but probably it is the rule that they desert the ducklings, late-hatched young sooner than earlier ones. The postnesting ducks, most of which molt within or near breeding range, are very secretive when molting. As estimated from field observations, the young attain flight in 63–77 days (Hochbaum 1944), in the latter half of Sept. or even later.

NOTE Although, as is apparent from the above account, little is known about *M. f. deglandi*, there is practically monographic treatment of reproduction and survival of *M. f. fusca* in a series of papers by Finnish authors. Most of these were cited by Koskimies (1957); there is additional information, especially on survival of young, in Koskimies (1958) and Grenquist (1959). RSP

SURVIVAL No N. Am. data; the Finnish data on *M. f. fusca* may be found in sources mentioned in the preceding paragraph. RSP

HABITS *M. f. deglandi.* Except when in wing molt (summer into fall), decidedly unwary, especially young birds in their first calendar year. At times, one can sail or row downwind to within shooting range of them before they fly. In New Eng., where the "patch-wing coot" was hunted from dories, the birds sometimes returned repeatedly to within target range. According to some authorities, they come to decoys more readily than do other "coots" (scoters), but other authorities claim just the opposite. It is well known among wildfowlers that making a loud noise—firing a gun, banging on gunwales, "hollering" (shouting), etc.—when a flock is high overhead or off to one side out of range, will cause the flock to break formation and the birds "tumble" toward the water, even in the direction of waiting gunners. New Englanders say these birds are "hollered in." Even during high migration flights, in both spring and fall, a flock sometimes "tumbles" hundreds of ft., with a great rushing noise.

Except for ♀ ♀ when nesting, this scoter normally may never come ashore.

293

When there are large numbers of these scoters on saltwater bays, the birds generally are not all together but instead tend to spread out, the social unit apparently being about 10–15 individuals, which swim as well as often fly in single file. They patter along the surface in cumbersome takeoff into a light breeze, but fly fast once they are fully airborne. Sutton (in Todd 1963) once saw a huge flock of drakes fly through a ship's rigging during a storm. They use more shoreward lines of travel than many other seafowl.

On flights between feeding and resting areas they are strung out, low, just clearing the waves in heavy weather. They prefer to rest and feed in sheltered, rather shallow bays and on the leeward side of islands. When starting high-altitude (migratory) flights, the various flocks move about, as though seeking the appropriate heading and altitude, the lines, wedges, and bunches changing configuration as the birds get suitably organized and oriented; then they start overland toward distant destinations.

They are daytime feeders, although reliable observations have been made that they also are crepuscular and nocturnal; see, for example, Reif 's (1966) very interesting account of nocturnal feeding in Me. in Aug. They prefer shallow water, even less than a fathom deep, as at low tide in places where shellfish abound, and they make repeated short feeding dives with intervals at the surface about half as long as time under water. Sometimes they appear to synchronize their activities, taking regular turns at diving. Usually after less than a half hour they quit feeding and spend at least equal time dozing, resting, or preening. On deeper water, to about 5–8 fathoms, the spans of apparent idleness on the surface are somewhat longer.

A. Brooks (1945) termed their diving posture "peculiar"—the wings flipped outward at the "bend" as the bird plunges; while submerged, the wing tips are crossed over the upper tail coverts, the secondaries are spread and show the white patch well, and the alulae are so extended as to appear like a pair of small pointed wings. On surfacing, these winglets still are outstretched. When resting between consecutive dives, the wings remain outside the flank feathers, carpus submerged, and tail slightly submerged. In one pair of birds, watched over a period of 6 weeks, the ♂ dived with wings out and the ♀ invariably had them closed. Subsurface propulsion is by lateral strokes of the large feet.

While hidden on a wharf, J. Munro watched 2 drakes feeding in about 5 ft. of clear still water. A bird would grasp a mussel in its bill and, paddling vigorously with its feet, would assume a vertical head-down position in order to tear the mussel loose. Having torn it free, the drake would reverse position—neck upstretched, bill pointing straight up—and come straight to the surface (J. Munro and Clemens 1931).

Small food is swallowed under water; larger mussels, brought to the surface, are swallowed with some difficulty. The bird points its head up, stretches its neck, and gives a series of convulsive gulps (J. Munro and Clemens 1931). Kortright (1942) commented on the grinding power of the gizzard; oysters and other mollusks, swallowed shell and all, are "readily ground and chemically disintegrated." He mentioned 10 oysters (shells about 2 in. long) in the gullet of a bird and "remains of 46" in another. Gravel and pebbles are swallowed, but the sandy or gritty texture of this duck's droppings (as with other sea ducks) is caused by ground-up shells. Shedding the gizzard lining was noted by McAtee (1917), who reported it also in 23 other Anatids.

If scoters, including this species, feed in numbers at commercially valuable shellfish beds, they are capable of causing extensive depletion.

A few of these scoters have been taken in fishermen's nets in L. Michigan. Approximately 300 were taken in one haul on L. Ontario in May, 1938 (Snyder 1941b).

There are several dozen vernacular names for this scoter, most of them alluding in some way to the white wing patch. A large flight of these birds, referred to at the time as "black ducks," gave origin to the place name of Black Duck, Minn.

Judging from the fact that 2 dozen bones of this scoter were found in a midden in Cal. (H. Howard 1933), this bird has been utilized by man for a long time. The young birds, newly arrived from inland, are excellent eating; the older ones that have spent much time in marine environment are quite something else and the scoter stew of New Englanders is a fine solution to a rather difficult problem. According to Brewster (1924), whether the birds are fat or lean, if they are stuffed, wrapped in paper or birch bark, and then baked by being surrounded by hardwood coals in a hole in the ground, they are excellent eating.

There never was much hunting of this scoter inland; the birds stay far from shore, when and if they stop, and the more usual species of ducks in such places are more readily taken. On the Atlantic coast there was a reported decrease in White-winged Scoters during the decades of unrestricted wildfowling, but the birds now are plentiful. There is considerable evidence that this scoter, during the past 50 years, has been decidedly the most numerous scoter to migrate through Massachusetts Bay in fall, while the Surf Scoter showed a great decline until some time in the 1960s. Few gunners currently engage in such rigorous activity as hunting from dories and it is likely that, in various years, oil pollution on marine waters on both coasts has killed many more of these scoters than have wildfowlers. On the southerly portion of the Atlantic winter range, fowl cholera (a bacterial disease) killed many of these scoters in early 1970.

In the Kattegat in March, 1972, probably the majority of the birds in the largest Danish wintering concentration of *M. f. fusca* were destroyed by oil pollution (Joensen 1972).

For further information on this species, see especially Mackay (1891), Bent (1925), and J. C. Phillips (1926). RSP

FOOD   Chiefly mollusks and crustaceans, also aquatic plants, insects, and occasionally fishes.

*M. f. fusca* **Animal**   Chief food in the Orkneys razor clams (*Ensis*) and crabs (Millais 1913b). In Scotland, the mollusks *Mactra, Tellina, Solen, Mytilus, Cardium, Donax*, the species being dependent on the locality (MacGillivray 1852); also *Buccinum, Bythinia, Pectunculus, Valvata*, and small crabs (in Witherby 1939). In Denmark in winter, principally mollusks (*Cardium, Nassa, Mytilus*) 86%; crustaceans (*Carcinus maenas, Eupagurus bernhardus*) 6%; echinoderms (*Echinocardium cordatum, Strongylocentrotus droebachiensis*) 4%; polychaetes (*Arenicola marina, Pectinaria*) 2%; and fishes (*Gasterosteus aculeatus, Clupea harengus, Gobius*) 2% (Madsen 1954). Young fed on Diptera and other insects, and on *Cancer pulex* and other small crustaceans. In captivity, refused everything but flies (Gadamer 1855).

No information on food in summer in U.S.S.R. Stomachs of birds shot during the fall flight on Pechora R. contained gastropod mollusks and plant (*Potamogeton*) remains. In Oct. at Rybinsk Reservoir, 99.5% animal matter (mollusks 62.5%, larvae of aquatic insects 30%, and small fishes 7%). The winter food is entirely mollusks. On the Caspian Sea, chiefly *Cardium edulis*, and on North Sea and Baltic, this mollusk and others (in Dementiev and Gladkov 1952).

*M. f. deglandi*   Three-fourths mollusks; also crustaceans, insects, fishes, and aquatic plants. Examination of 819 stomachs of adults showed 94% animal and 6% vegetable matter. Stomach contents of 4 "juveniles" showed approximately the same percentages (Cottam 1939).

**Animal**   Mollusks (*Ostrea, Pecten, Venus, Mya, Thais, Protothaca, Mytilus, Macoma, Tellina, Siliqua, Cardium, Nassarius*, etc.) 75.3%; crustaceans (*Hemigrapsus, Cancer, Neopanope, Hexapanopeus, Pagurus*, etc.) 13.2%; insects (larvae of caddis flies, dragonflies, lacewings, and midges, grasshoppers, etc.) 2.5%; fishes (*Porichthys, Moxocephalus, Ammodytes*, Heterostomata) 1.7%; miscellaneous—sand dollars (*Echinarachnius*), sea urchins (*Strongylocentrotus*), starfishes, brittle stars, total 1.4% (Cottam 1939). Stomach contents of 2 birds taken in the Pribilofs in Feb. were about equally divided between amphipods and bivalves (principally *Saxicava arctica*) (Preble and McAtee 1923).

Gizzard shad (*Dorosoma cepedianum*) and snails (*Physa*) found in Ohio birds (Trautman 1940). On the Pacific coast, mollusks (*Olivella, Nassa, Mangilia, Alectrion*), crabs, and sand dollars (J. Grinnell et al. 1918, McKernan and Scheffer 1942); and herring eggs in small quantity (J. Munro and Clemens 1931).

In nw. Cal., at Humboldt Bay and on the ocean in winter–spring: animal matter occurred in all 106 digestive tracks examined; over 85% of them contained mollusks, principally crabs (*Protothaca staminea, Macoma irus*), olive shell (*Olivella pycna*), dog whelk (*Nassarius fossatus*), mussel (*Mytilus edulis*), and jackknife clam (*Solen secarius*). Crabs (*Cancer magister*) occurred in 15% of them. When on the ocean, the birds had eaten primarily the jackknife clam. None had eaten oysters. See Grosz and Yocom (1972) for details.

**Vegetable**   Pondweeds (*Zostera, Potamogeton, Ruppia, Vallisneria*) 2%; bur reed (*Sparganium*) 1.2%; miscellaneous (*Ceratophyllum, Rumex, Carex, Hordeum, Brasenia, Myriophyllum*) 2.7% (Cottam 1939). Of the 106 birds from Humboldt Bay and vicinity (see above), 52% had ingested sea lettuce (*Ulva*) and 9% contained miscellaneous vegetation. On a Wis. lake, buds of wild celery formed the exclusive diet for a time (McAtee 1911). Yorke (1899) mentioned Lemnaceae, Najadaceae, Selaginellaceae, Salviniaceae, Elatinaceae, Gentianaceae, Pontederiaceae, and Myracaceae. Vegetable food is important on nesting and rearing areas.

The digestive tracts of about half of the birds from Humboldt Bay and vicinity contained sand and rock, but it is assumed that shell material may be a substitute for grit (Grosz and Yocom 1972).

*M. f. stejnegeri*   Five drakes taken in June around Markov in Anadyrland had eaten larvae of caddis flies (Trichoptera) and stone flies (Perlidae) (Portenko 1939). AWS

**Surf Scoter**

*Melanitta perspicillata* (Linnaeus)

Stoutish, medium-sized diving duck with quite evenly sloping head–bill profile. Head feathering tapers to a point far forward on top of bill (to nearly over nostrils); on the sides it is truncated (terminates in a straight vertical line). Bill more or less swollen on sides near base. Inner vane of outer primary in both sexes has distal third narrowed (but much less so than in *M. nigra*). The outer primary is longest. No white in upper surface of wing. The dark iris of young birds later becomes whitish in both sexes.

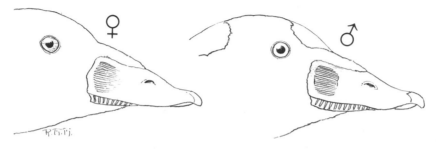

Feathering mostly black or dark, usually with white or whitish areas on head and, in some early stages, a pale belly. The drake's tracheal apparatus includes a large spherical bony bulb, larger and also nearer the inner end of the trachea than in *M. fusca deglandi*; at the inner end there is no left-sided bony bulla proper, only a slight dilatation; for useful illus. see deW. Miller (1926).

Length ♂ 20–21 in., ♀ 18–19, wingspread ♂ to 31½, ♀ to 29½, usual wt. of ♂ about 2¼ lb., ♀ about 2 lb. No subspecies.

DESCRIPTION  Two Plumages/cycle in both sexes. Sequence of molts and resultant Plumages as in the White-winged (*M. fusca*), i.e., overlapping molts in young birds, molting sometimes slowed, interrupted, or delayed, and older birds of both sexes have an extensive spring molt (in addition to molting from late summer on). As in other scoters, some feathering on venter and rump is molted last, or sometimes retained until the next period of molting, which gives an impression that the inclusive feathering is less in some Plumages than is actually the case. There is more individual variation in pattern and coloring than usually is reported.

▶ ♂ Def. Alt. Plumage (all feathering except wing and tail), acquired beginning usually in AUG. and continuing into FALL, even into winter (much variation in timing) and worn until the following SPRING.

Black, with white head markings and highly colored bill. **Bill** orange-yellow distally, then upper mandible has zone of scarlet that extends upward (surrounds nostril) to forward extension of feathering, then white area on side, a lateral swelling which is black, and narrow zone between this and feathering is scarlet-orange or scarlet. **Iris** nearly white. **Feathering** almost entirely black, with some cobalt-ultramarine gloss (which disappears); a white patch (size and shape vary) on forecrown and, beginning at rear of crown, another that tapers down onto nape (latter comprised of hairlike white

297

feathers—a kind of short mane—that conceals underlying short black feathers). Drakes in late Aug.–Sept. often have white on forecrown only, perhaps indicating that the white nape patch appears later or possibly is an additional (Supplemental) generation of feathers. An occasional individual, even in midwinter, has white only on the nape. Some individuals have a white line below the eye. One has white bar across lower foreneck and a longitudinal white streak on chin. Scapulars comparatively long and tapering. Feathers on sides and flanks long and rather lax, latter narrowly rounded at ends. Feathers on underparts lighter (toward brownish) basally; the belly has a ragged or blotched appearance after much wear. Legs and **feet** scarlet-orange, joints dusky, webs black. Tail and wing are retained Basic feathering.

NOTE  Quite often the badly abraded venter consists in part of not-yet-molted feathering of the previous (Basic) generation.

▶  ♂ Def. Basic Plumage (entire feathering), beginning with head to forepart of mantle, the head–body feathers and sometimes more or less of tail are acquired through SPRING; in some individuals the molting is slowed or interrupted (during migration) and may not be completed (especially on abdomen) until into SUMMER. The Basic wing grows (after a flightless period) during the period of molting (of head–body back into Alt.) in LATE SUMMER–FALL and is retained nearly a year.

**Bill** coloring muted. Most of **feathering** sooty, except white patch on nape only and the underparts vary toward dusky brownish. Scapulars comparatively short, as also feathers of upper sides and flanks. **Tail** black (but bleaches to grayed brownish), the feathers quite rounded at ends. **Wing** mostly black, inner vanes of various flight feathers toward brownish, innermost secondaries not elongated and are broad distally, upper coverts have broadly rounded tips, some grayish and white in wing lining; much fading and wear.

▶  ♀ Def. Alt. Plumage (all feathering except tail and wing), acquired in LATE SUMMER–FALL (by some, continuing into early winter) and worn until the following SPRING.

**Bill** very dark, sometimes with even darker (blackish) patch on side base of upper mandible. **Iris** nearly white. In general, **feathering** dark and plain, the cap darker than rest of head and neck, and 2 poorly defined light areas on side of head, one close to bill, the other behind the eye and adjoining the dark cap; a smallish nape patch (white and blackish feathers intermixed) varies with individual from well developed to entirely absent—see L. Bishop (1895b) for individual variation. Some individuals are lighter, some darker; some have feathers of sides and flanks tipped whitish, on other individuals blackish. Legs and **feet** orange-yellow, grading to dusky on joints, rear of tarsi, and webs. Tail and wing are retained Basic feathering.

▶  ♀ Def. Basic Plumage (entire feathering), all except wing and usually tail acquired through SPRING, but some apparently do not acquire all of it then and molting is slowed during migration. This feathering is retained into LATE SUMMER or FALL and then begins a period of molting out of most of the Basic and back into Alt.; in this period the "offset" Basic wing is acquired after a flightless period and this portion (and usually the tail) is retained nearly a year. Compared with Def. Alt.: light areas on **head** even less clear-cut; no white on nape; **scapulars** short and broad, as also feathers on upper sides and flanks; **tail** feathers quite broad at ends. **Tail** blackish brown. **Wing** dark sepia, upper coverts with broadly rounded ends, inner webs of flight feathers palish, some whitish in wing lining.

AT HATCHING feathering projects forward on top of bill, tapering to a point (while in M. fusca this is M-shaped and in M. nigra the feathering terminates in a transverse line). Bill dark slaty, iris dark. Apparently never a white spot at lower eyelid. Upperparts blackish brown or dark brownish olive, cheeks and throat grayish; dark band (like back) across upper breast; most of remainder of underparts silvery gray. Legs and feet dark.

▶ ♂ ♀ Juvenal Plumage (entire feathering), probably fully developed soon after flight attained; generally head–body is lost in FALL, the tail later (see below under Basic I and beyond), but the wing is retained nearly a year. Apparently the sexes are similar, except ♀ av. smaller.

Bill all dark, iris dark brownish. Head crown much darker than the rest, a sizable and rather well-defined whitish patch extends back from side base of bill and there is a less distinct one on upper rear of cheek (they become larger with wear and tend to merge); upperparts various dark browns or sepia; underparts feathers lighter than ♀ definitive stages, breast and upper sides colored much like mantle, the feathers edged brownish buff (fade toward whitish), feathers from belly to vent at least subterminally whitish and with darkish ends (mottled effect). Tail feathers have notched ends (the precursor down breaks off ends of the shafts). Wing quite like ♀ Basic (not black), but upper coverts have narrow (not broadly rounded) ends; some whitish in wing lining.

▶ ♂ Basic I Plumage (all feathering except wing); generally begins to appear on head –neck by OCT. and the remainder soon after, then the tail in LATE FALL or WINTER; a few birds acquire Basic I more gradually, or do not begin to acquire it until EARLY WINTER. Thus some birds are going out of Basic I into Alt. I in Nov., but others not until weeks afterward. Quite often more or less of the Juv. abdomen is retained and worn with Basic I.

Feathering blackish, without gloss; the head gets a small white nape patch (but none on forecrown). The new black tail feathers are somewhat pointed. The iris pales during the first winter or earlier and the bill and feet acquire some color.

▶ ♂ Alt. I Plumage (all feathering except tail and wing), in some individuals begins (first on head–neck) to succeed Basic I in LATE FALL; in others, the earlier molts are delayed or protracted, so that Alt. I does not begin to appear until EARLY WINTER. Possibly some birds may not acquire all of this Plumage. It is retained until SPRING and the Juv. wing plus Basic I tail are retained into summer.

A black Plumage. White nape patch now elongated, pointing down neck as in later Alts., rather than a shortish transverse area as in Basic I. No white frontal patch in specimens examined. Iris whitish, bill and feet vividly colored, though lateral swelling of bill continues to develop later on. If the Juv. abdomen is retained, it shows much wear. (Good examples of Alt. I apparently are scarce in museum collections.)

▶ ♀ Basic I and Alt. I Plumages (inclusive feathering as in ♂), timing variable as in ♂ so far as known; inadequate specimen data. In both Plumages the ♀ is darker than in Juv. and, on the head, this reduces contrast between cap and sides; the 2 white areas on side of head are smallish and poorly defined. In winter or spring the bill becomes somewhat swollen basally. The Juv. abdomen sometimes is retained throughout. As in the drake, the Juv. wing is worn with these Plumages, also with Basic II head–body, thus nearly a year.

▶ ♂ ♀ Basic II are essentially as Def. Basic; the last Plumage with which the Juv. wing is worn (the Basic II wing succeeds it about the time of molting out of Basic II head–body).

**Measurements** 12 ♂ (3 Alaska, 5 B.C., 1 P.E.I., 2 Mass., 1 Conn.): BILL 36–40, av. 37 mm.; WING (233)+241–252, av. 245; TAIL 79–84, av. 82; TARSUS 43–45, av. 44; 12 ♀ (1 B.C., 4 Cal., 1 Labrador, 1 Mass., 3 Conn., 1 N.Y., 1 N.C.): BILL 37–40, av. 38.8 mm.; WING 215–240, av. 228; TAIL 68–74, av. 72; TARSUS 40–44, av. 42 (ETS). See especially J. C. Phillips (1926), WING not flattened, and Witherby (1939) for other series, the latter with WING meas. over the curve.

**Weight** scant data; 12 ♂ av. 2.2 lb. (1 kg.), max. 2.5 (1.1 kg.); 10 ♀ av. 2.0 lb. (0.9 kg.), max. 2.5 (1.1 kg.) (A. L. Nelson and Martin 1953). Data in Kortright (1942) are very similar. J. C. Phillips (1926) gave greater maxima. In a small series from Wash., 2 ♂ in Dec. weighed 1,157 and 1,297 gm. (G. E. Hudson). Irving (1960) gave wt. of 5 drakes taken in summer in interior Alaska as 964–1,006 gm., av. 987.

**Hybrids** no reliable records (see under *M. fusca*).

**Geographical variation** apparently none. RSP

**FIELD IDENTIFICATION** A black or dark, thickset duck, generally in flocks that are strung out on the water, well away from shore. Quite commonly associates with other ducks, including other scoters and various eiders. The Surf Scoter has an evenly sloping (eiderlike) profile that can be seen at some distance and, when wing-flapping (a frequent comfort movement), it may be noted that there is no white in upper surface of wing. The drake, most of the year, is black with white patch on forehead and another on nape, or at least the latter (and ♀ ♀ may have the latter)—hence "skunk-head coot" and "bald coot" of gunners. Females and young typically have two white patches on sides of head, generally not well defined (are best defined in young birds), and they tend to merge if the feathering becomes abraded. Also in ♀ ♀ and young, the cap contrasts in some measure with patterned sides of head, but not as in Black Scoter, which has a sharply delineated dark cap that extends down to eyes and evenly palish cheeks and neck. RSP

**VOICE** (N. Am. data.) Said to be generally silent. Drakes in "mating season" (near breeding places) utter a low clear whistle (E. W. Nelson 1887); in display a liquid explosive little *puk-puk* (J. C. Phillips 1926) like sound of water dripping in a cavern (A. Brooks 1920); a liquid gurgling call during Breast-scooping display (described below). Apparently these are different descriptions of the same call. The duck has a guttural croaking *krrraak krrraak* (Phillips), a rasping or crowlike call during Chin-lifting (described beyond) when threatening strange drakes; a harsh *crahh* with open beak when defending small young (Nero 1963).

The drake's wings produce a whistling sound during Flying-away display (described beyond); also see Nero (1963). RSP

**HABITAT** On breeding range—quiet and slow-moving waters of the forest zone and semibarrens, with nest in a dry place some distance away in brushy or forested surroundings, less often in herbaceous growth. Relatively abundant, for example, at Old Crow flats in Yukon Terr. In the lake plateau area of interior Ungava, preferred habitat is bog ponds and other waters in low-lying areas within open forest (lichen–spruce woodland). Here, as elsewhere in the interior, there are perhaps 10 times as many Surf Scoters as Black Scoters.

Prebreeders all year and breeders away from breeding range are more typically birds of the ocean littoral than are the White-winged and Black Scoters and, in migration, less often seen in bays and on fresh water. Winter range, however, includes the Great Lakes. RSP

DISTRIBUTION (See map.) A Nearctic species. Limits of **breeding** range are not well known, in Ungava, for example. Since prebreeders spend the summer on marine coasts and breeding drakes go to marine waters to molt, total distribution in summer is very different from breeding distribution, as in other scoters. This scoter is recorded inland rather seldom; either it flies nonstop overland or else it rests well out from shore on large waters. On winter range along marine coasts, the northerly winterers are very much closer to breeding localities than are southerly winterers. This species is a fairly regular straggler eastward in the Atlantic area and there are a few records of westward occurrences toward ne. Asia.

A breeding record for Akpatok I. in Ungava Bay perhaps is best listed as "according to" Bent (1925). Audubon's report of a nest at Little Mecatina on the North Shore of Gulf of St. Lawrence has been questioned by Todd (1963) and others.

**Summer** (especially late summer). On the Atlantic side there are flocks of molting birds along the Labrador coast at least as far n. as Nain (and probably considerably farther). A few breeders may molt in Gulf of St. Lawrence, but summering birds in the Maritimes and southward probably are, for the most part, prebreeders. This scoter occurs in numbers in se. Hudson Bay in summer—at least molting postbreeding drakes, but perhaps not these exclusively. There are scattered small groups of molting drakes on interior waters in extreme w. Canada and, at least in Alaska, evidently a few prebreeders also molt inland. This scoter occurs in flocks off the arctic coast of nw. Mackenzie, Yukon Terr., and Alaska—perhaps postbreeding drakes only—and large numbers molt in Bering Sea waters of Alaska. At Stuart I. in Norton Sd., Aug. 23, 1878, there was an assembly of drakes "forming a continuous band around the outer end of the island" for about 10 mi., and ½ to ¾ mi. wide (E. W. Nelson 1887). They could fly; judging from the date, it seems probable that they very recently had regained flight after molting. Some distance southward (s. of Hooper Bay), at Angyoyaravak Bay, on Aug. 31, 1972, there were large flocks of molting birds (C. Dau). Apparently a few of these scoters molt around the inner Aleutians and near the s. side of the Alaska Pen., but the Surf Scoter is rare in the cent. Aleutians. The summer assemblies in se. Gulf of Alaska waters and along the B.C. coast perhaps contain more than one generation: i.e., both prebreeders and postbreeding drakes that have returned to salt water. There are other scattered summer occurrences to the south.

**Winter** Atlantic coast—occurrence extends from Nfld. and Gulf of St. Lawrence to the Carolinas, occasionally to Fla. The bulk of them are concentrated from s. New Eng. (s. of C. Cod) to Va. In the interior—apparently has wintered on several of the Great Lakes: Michigan, Erie, and Ontario. Pacific coast—s. side of Alaska Pen. s. to n. Gulf

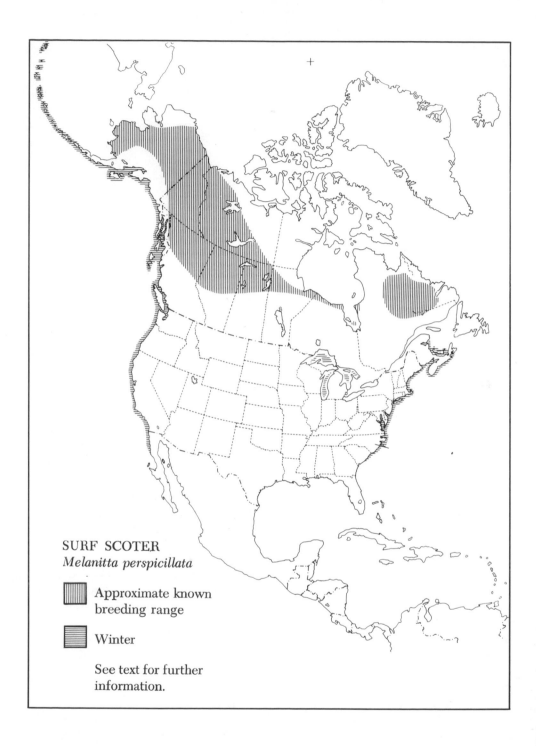

**SURF SCOTER**
*Melanitta perspicillata*

Approximate known
breeding range

Winter

See text for further
information.

of Cal. in Mexico, with concentrations from se. Alaska to Cal. Southern limits of recorded occurrence: Gulf of Cal. (and those in spring on Salton Sea, Cal., surely are migrants from there), Ariz., New Mex., coastal Texas, La., Ala., and inland and on both coasts of Fla.

**Straggler** A record for Repulse Bay in ne. Keewatin may fit in this category. Has occurred in Bermuda in late fall–winter. Also recorded in Greenland (6, mostly "adult" drakes), Faeroes, Norway, Sweden, Finland, Denmark, Holland, Belgium, France, Switzerland, and Britain (where many records, mostly Sept.–May; now recorded in most years). There are no known captive stocks in Europe and Britain. Bruun (1971) suggested that the Fennoscandian records were for individuals that had joined wintering European White-winged Scoters and later had accompanied them on northward migration.

Hawaii—reported from Oahu in 1959 (Berger 1972).

Chuckchee Pen.—on the e. end at Mechigamen Bay, a "Juvenal" ♂ was taken on Aug. 6, 1843, this being the evidence for the "only authenticated instance of nesting" (Portenko 1972). On the n. coast at C. Vankarem, a bird of this species was taken on Aug. 1, 1881.

Bering–nw. Pacific—there is a single record for the Pribilofs. The only evidence of occurrence at St. Lawrence I. is from an archaeological site. For the Commander Is., reports differ depending on author, but apparently add up to a number of May–June occurrences (only drakes specifically stated) plus Oct. (a drake) and Nov. 6 (drake).

The published **fossil** record seems surprising, if correct, in view of this being a Nearctic species; Pleistocene finds in England and Scotland, and in N. Am. in Ore. and 2 localities in Cal.; reported from **archaeological sites** in Alaska—St. Lawrence I., Kodiak I., Dutch Harbor, and Little Kiska. See Brodkorb (1964a) for references. RSP

MIGRATION By day and night, very high when overland; any stops inland apparently are brief and for resting, not feeding. Migrating flocks seem to be changing formation constantly, from clusters, or so many birds as to resemble a black cloud, to straggling lines and Vs, then bunching again.

J. C. Phillips (1926) summarized briefly the then-existing information; the most important fact learned since then is that breeding range—terminus of spring migration for breeders—extends in a great arc from interior Ungava, with more or less of a gap in n. Ont.–Man., through w. Canada and, with other gaps, to the Bering Sea coast of Alaska. It seems probable that the great majority of breeders go to nw. Canada and Alaska and comparatively few to Ungava. The general pattern of migration resembles that of the White-winged Scoter: a concentration of breeders in the n. interior and main winter range along the e. and w. coasts of the continent.

SPRING There is movement in southerly portions of winter range on both coasts beginning by late Feb., but most movement on salt water is in March and first 3 weeks in April. Breeders apparently move farther n. up both coasts than do Whitewings before heading inland and they go overland earlier (late April usually). Prebreeders move up along the coasts, their upward movement continuing after breeders have departed.

SUMMER **Prebreeders,** almost all of which spend this season on salt water, are in molting assemblies containing other scoters also. The **molt migration** for prebreeders consists of the terminal portion of n. movement in spring and drakes tend to go farther than ducks so that there is a great preponderance of the former at northerly molting places. Prebreeders of both sexes molt early, generally being flightless by early July. For breeders, the presence of great numbers of drakes that are flightless in late July or in Aug. (as at marine localities on Bering Sea coast of Alaska and in inlets and bays along the Labrador coast of Ungava) would indicate that these birds left their mates and returned to sea to molt. If, as seems probable, the large number of Aug. molters in Labrador waters exceeds the number of males of breeding pairs in Ungava, then it follows that many drakes from more distant breeding range also fly eastward to molt. (Compare with White-winged Scoter.)

FALL    Prebreeders on marine waters move southward; ♀ ♀ and their young fly from the interior to marine waters and continue on southward; and drakes of breeding age that returned to salt water in summer move southward (averaging not as far as younger birds). The earliest molters (prebreeders) begin migrating quite early in Sept. and not all are at their most southerly destinations until early Dec. The ♀ ♀ and young reach salt water beginning in Sept. and, thereafter, shift farther southward. Breeding drakes begin moving from marine molting areas fairly soon after they regain flight, i.e., they too start migrating in Sept., and most are at wintering places by late Nov. Thus, with greatly overlapping dates, there is intermingling of these various categories, especially during heavy migration from about Oct. 10 to past mid–Nov., along saltwater portions of their routes.

The preceding paragraphs, worked out from fragments of information, leave much in obscurity. Information is scant indeed on such matters as: migration routes in Alaskan area (Alaska–Yukon birds probably all are Pacific winterers); overland routes generally (L. Mistassini in interior Que. apparently is on an Atlantic to James Bay or Hudson Bay route); whether the Great Lakes are stopover or wintering places for any number of birds; whether midsummer birds in such areas as Hudson Bay and waters e. and w. of the Mackenzie delta include any yearlings or are all of older age-classes; whether summering birds at more southerly coastal localities are "old" birds (which has been claimed, but is doubtful); and so on. RSP

BANDING STATUS    The total number banded was 30 through 1964, in Ont. and Alaska; there were no recoveries through 1966 (data from Bird Banding Laboratory). RSP

REPRODUCTION    Little information exists, except some observations of displays. Eggs of this scoter were discovered a century ago, but the first downy young known to science were taken in 1920.

Minimum **breeding age** presumably 2 years. Pair bond typically is formed on winter range; in April there, as Mackay (1891) reported, the drake keeps close company with the duck and, if she is shot, he returns to his dead mate repeatedly.

Various displays have been described and named, but little is known of their time and frequency of occurrence, relation to pair formation, etc. Flying-away (described below) and much active swimming about with tail cocked are drake activities in groups apparently consisting solely of yearling prebreeders in early summer. In older age-classes there is much activity of groups on the water, also aerial pursuit of a duck by several drakes; both occur in winter and have also been noted after arrival of the birds within general breeding range. The useful literature is Alford and other authors cited in Bent (1925), a paper by Nero (1963), and Johnsgard's (1965) summary, which drew heavily on M. T. Myres (1959a).

**Displays of the duck** CHIN-LIFTING she raises her head about 30° above horizontal, often with open beak, and utters a harsh rasping or crowlike call; it is directed toward a particular drake. She also performs several ♂ displays.

**Displays of the drake** The most commonly observed activity on the water is several ♂ ♂ displaying in close presence of a ♀. THREAT head forward low (the ♀ holds it higher in threat postures). SENTINEL POSTURE drakes swim to and fro rapidly, neck erect, at intervals dipping the bill in water. This may be what A. Brooks (1920) referred to as behaving "like whirligig beetles." The ♂ may swim from one ♀ to another, bowing toward a ♀, or darting forward in a crouched aggressive attitude. If she dives, so do the drakes, and they may stay down for 40 sec.; the drakes emerge one by one, then the ♀ accompanied by one drake. The other drakes may peck at one another. All this is repeated over and over. Probably there is underwater pursuit of the ♀. BREAST-SCOOPING drakes face ♀ ♀ and have a bowing action, a sort of combining of head-erect and breast-preening movements; a drake may immerse his head and follow this action with stereotyped bathing activity. He utters a liquid gurgling call. FLYING-AWAY drake flies only a short distance, slowly, past a ♀; his wings beat slowly and produce a loud whistling noise; as he alights and glides to a halt, the neck is stretched upward and both wings briefly are held extended vertically. The duck then swims or flies to the drake. CHIN-LIFTING plus HEAD-TURNING and TAIL-RAISED drake swims toward ♀ while alternately touching his beak to his breast and raising his head and shaking it laterally. CHEST-LIFTING then immediately he rears up and swings about so as to face away from her. His nape patch, which is erected, is displayed toward her. At height of this action his head is held high and bill depressed close to neck; throughout, the tail is raised.

Aerial activity includes extra drakes in pursuit of a ♀.

**Copulation,** as observed in midwinter in B.C., with no evidence of durable pair bond, by Myres (1959b). The ♀ holds a PRONE posture for up to 2 min. (long for a scoter). The ♂'s precopulatory repertoire consisted of WATER-TWITCH dips bill while shaking head laterally, PREEN-BEHIND-THE-WING and, in 4 out of 8 observations, ritualized DRINKING. He FLICKED-THE-WINGS during treading and not invariably assumed a Chest-lifting posture as he dismounted. The ♀ usually flapped her wings afterward.

**Nest** generally some distance from water (few have been found) on ground under low branches of deciduous or coniferous tree or, sometimes, in herbaceous growth in a more open situation. The **nest-down** is very dark brownish with whitish centers and tips; any included breast feathers are small, light brown, then rather abruptly darkening at tip (illus.: Broley 1950). **Fresh clutches** probably in the middle third of June; known egg dates for N.W.T.—12 records June 19–July 8, with 6 of them in the span June 25–July 1 (Bent 1925). Bent gave clutch size as "evidently" 5–9, usually about 7, but MacFarlane (1891) stated 5–7 plus 1 of 8. **Egg size** in sample of 33 length 58–67.5 mm., av. 61.6, and breadth 40.5–45, av. 43; **shape** nearly elliptical, slightly pointed;

305

shell smooth and without gloss, **color** creamy or whitish buff (adapted from Bent). **In-cubation period** unknown.

These close estimates of **hatching dates** are for the L. Athabaska region: July 2 (brood of 7 with extra ♀ in attendance), July 6 (1 of 8), July 9 (1 of 4), all young apparently a day or less old (Nero 1963). In the same region, large downies July 28 (Harper, in J. C. Phillips 1926); in Ont. between Ft. Severn and Winisk, 6 one-third grown on Aug. 3 (Simkin 1963). There also are a few Alaskan data in Gabrielson and Lincoln (1959). Practically nothing is known of the rearing period, etc. Phillips believed that after ♀ ♀ and young had flown to salt water in fall broods were smaller than in most ducks, but note above that clutch size is small. It is likely that the ♀ ♀ leave their preflight young and go elsewhere to molt. RSP

HABITS   Surprisingly little new information in recent decades. Most useful sources are the general accounts in Millais (1913b), Bent (1925), and J. C. Phillips (1926), plus Mackay's (1891) observations in s. New Eng.

Flocks quite commonly are smaller, under 40 birds, than in the other scoters, but the total number in assemblies of migrants in early spring on salt water and of molting drakes in late summer is very great. E. W. Nelson's (1887) report of a flock of molting drakes, some 10 mi. long and ½–¾ mi. wide, previously mentioned under "Distribution," is the largest single gathering on record. Fifty thousand to a hundred thousand may occur within a fairly small geographical area, along either e. or w. coast of N. Am. in early spring prior to the departure of breeders overland. Numbers to 120,000 have been reported in Long I. (N.Y.) waters (Bull 1964). Except for an occasional gutteral croak, Mackay heard no vocal utterance from them.

In flight the Surf Scoter, like the Black, is more maneuverable than the stockier White-winged Scoter. There is a whistling of wings as the birds get under way, but it dies down as they settle into steady flight.

Diving habits now are known to vary considerably (Humphrey 1957b). Wings may be flexed somewhat and with alulae outstretched, or may be closed; if the latter, the bird may spring clear of the surface as it lunges forward in a high arc and then downward on a near-vertical course, propelled by the feet. The neck is outstretched. Whether the wings always are open during submergence is unknown. In observed instances, they were out from the body and with alulae extended, but reports indicate that sometimes there is no movement of wings and in other instances they are moved in measured beats, like underwater flying, in unison with strokes of the feet. Ascent is vertical or nearly so, the head bowed with bill on breast, the wings and alulae out somewhat, the legs bent upward slightly, toes trailing relaxed. Sometimes the body rotates on its long axis. For information on dives and pauses, see Alford (1920) and D. Dow (1964). Quite likely this scoter ordinarily prefers depths under 6 fathoms. For interesting details of commensal feeding of Horned Grebes with Surf Scoter, see Pearse (1950) and Paulson (1969).

There seem to be no useful estimates of probable total population of this scoter. Judging from various reports for fall on C. Cod (Mass.) waters, there was a drastic decline in numbers of this scoter after 1915, down to perhaps 10%–20% of former numbers, then apparently a small increase recently (Hill 1965). At winter feeding areas it regularly associates with other seafowl, especially other scoters, which complicates estimating their respective numbers. As a table bird, this scoter rates about as the others (it can be excellent) and, except for a few hardy hunters of "sea coots," it is little sought by man.

Known mortality factors include debilitation and death from internal parasites and from floating oil along both Atlantic and Pacific coasts. RSP

FOOD Largely mollusks, with crustaceans, insects, fishes, and echinoderms. Plants consumed are mainly pondweeds and sedges. Examination of stomachs of 168 "adults" showed 88% animal and 12% vegetable matter (Cottam 1939).

**Animal** Mollusks (*Mytilus* mainly, *Macoma, Mactra, Siliqua, Protothaca, Nucula, Littorina, Nassarius, Polinices, Olivella,* etc.) 60.8%; crustaceans (*Emerita, Hemigrapsus, Neopanope, Hexapanopeus, Cancer, Pagurus*) 10.3%; insects: larvae of caddis flies (Trichoptera), dragonflies and damselflies (Odonata), diving beetles (Dytiscidae), etc., 9.0%, fishes (*Ammodytes, Fundulus*) 3.4%; echinoderms (*Strongylocentrotus* mainly, *Echinarchinius*) 1.8%; miscellaneous: marine worms, clamworms (*Nereis*), sea anemones, hydroids, etc. 2%.

**Vegetable** Pondweeds (*Potamogeton, Zostera, Ruppia, Zannichellia*) 3.2%; miscellaneous (*Vallisneria, Brasenia, Cladium, Sparganium, Scirpus, Carex, Prunus,* algae) 8.9% (Cottam 1939).

Audubon (1838) found fishes in all stomachs examined in Labrador. Stomachs of birds from B.C. contained 45%–90% herring eggs when feeding on spawning grounds (J. Munro and Clemens 1931).

Seven young had consumed about 80% animal and 20% vegetable matter. Coleoptera 16.72%, Ephemeroptera 14%, Hemiptera 12.57%, Trichoptera 6.86%, Odonata 1.14%, and miscellaneous 9.71%; mollusks (mainly Mytilidae) 18.57%. Vegetable food principally seeds of *Empetrum nigrum, Carex, Potamogeton, Eleocharis, Scirpus,* and *Cladium.* One bird contained 758 seeds of crowberry (*Empetrum*). AWS

## Black Scoter

### Melanitta nigra

Common Scoter *Oidemia nigra* (Linnaeus) of 1957 A.O.U. list and of various authors; the Nearctic subspecies formerly was called American Scoter. A sizable stout-bodied diving duck (smallest of the scoters), in definitive stages most or all feathering dark (to black).

Head feathering ends in a nearly straight line up side base of bill, angling outward on top barely enough to be noticeable. Bill has straight, nearly parallel, sides (is slightly wider just beyond nostrils); it is swollen at top base (not laterally) in drakes beginning during their 1st fall or winter, being enlarged most (to a knob) in w. Palearctic birds; in the ♀ the top profile of the bill either is angled down or is horizontal to a low point just

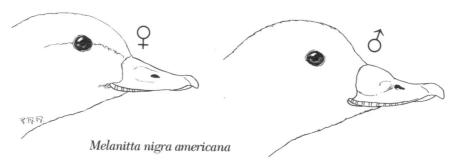

*Melanitta nigra americana*

beyond the nostrils, this being modified somewhat in that, near top base, it becomes rounded upward slightly. Iris dark in both sexes and all ages. For a scoter tail is comparatively long and graduated, i.e., each more lateral pair of feathers is considerably shorter than the next pair inward.

The outer primary is somewhat short (shorter than 8th in ♂ Basic); in ♂ ♀ Juv. and ♀ Basic wing, the outer primary is narrower than in corresponding stages of other scoters (to greatest extent in ♀ Basic); in ♂ Basic the inner web of this primary is greatly narrowed for half of total exposed length of the feather, as if much of it had been cut away. In the drake in Alt. Plumage, feathers on part of head–neck have distal barbs converging, the result being a crimped or somewhat striated effect as in neck furrowing of various geese.

It might be said that the trachea in both sexes somewhat resembles that of ♀ ♀ of other scoters, since it has no enlarged segment and the inner end is not even slightly enlarged. In both sexes of *nigra* the bronchi are quite bulbous. The 2 bulbous bronchi are spread out quite laterally in the ♂, but in the ♀ are more nearly parallel, being joined together farther from their bases (compare figs. 32 and 33 in Schiøler 1926). Among scoters, this species has much the shortest intestinal caecae, under 2.5 cm. in drakes (as in mergansers); see meas. for scoters in deW. Miller (1926).

Length ♂ to 21 in., ♀ to 19, wingspread ♂ to 36 and ♀ to 33, wt. of ♂ usually about $2^2/5$ lb., ♀ $1^4/5$. Two subspecies, both in our area (but 1 only as a straggler to Greenland).

308

DESCRIPTION  *M. nigra americana*. Two Plumages/cycle in both sexes; sequence and timing as in other scoters, with corresponding variation in molting.

▶  ♂ Def. Alt. Plumage (all feathering except tail and wing), acquired from LATE
SUMMER well into FALL (occasionally into Nov.) and retained until following SPRING
(March–April).

Black, with metallic gloss; part of head–neck feathering not smooth. **Bill** black, except upper mandible from forward of nostrils back to the feathers (and including bulge)
vivid orange-yellow, narrowly divided by black along top midline; **iris** dark brownish;
eyelids yellow. In unworn condition the black feathering has an ultramarine-violet
sheen on head and neck and it varies toward turquoise or emerald on forward mantle.
Feathering at base of bill soft, downy, without gloss, and on most of remainder of **head**
and neck (except chin and throat) it has the crimped or randomly striated condition
already mentioned. Feathers on sides and flanks long and, especially on latter, tend to
narrow to a point. Legs and **feet** dusky, webs and joints blackish. Tail and wing are
retained Basic feathering.

▶  ♂ Def. Basic Plumage (entire feathering). In SPRING the Basic grows first on head
and down foreparts of body, then scattered elsewhere on sides and dorsum, then on
rump, belly to tail, and tail. Sometimes there is a slowing or pause so that part of this
feathering (especially venter) grows in summer. Acquisition of the Basic wing is
"offset" into the next period of molting, beginning in LATE SUMMER, when it grows
(after a flightless period, often beginning in late July) and beginning some time thereafter the Basic head–body starts molting back into Alt. The Basic tail and wing are retained nearly a year.

The new **feathering** is black, at first with some gloss toward cobalt; feathering on
**head**–neck smooth; feathers on sides and flanks black terminally with sooty bases, their
ends rounded. **Tail** blackish, the feathers rounded at ends. **Wing** black with some gloss
at first, the innermost secondaries distally rounded; wing lining black, except under-
primary coverts have a pale sheen that matches that of inner webs of the primaries.

▶  ♀ Def. Alt. Plumage (inclusive feathering as ♂ Alt.), acquired apparently somewhat later than in ♂, in FALL, and retained until SPRING.

Quite sooty brownish overall, except for 2-toned head (dark cap sharply delineated
from much lighter remainder). **Bill** black, with hint of yellowish in basal part of upper
mandible and, at least in some, in profile appears very slightly swollen near top base;
**iris** dark brownish. **Head** cap sooty, remainder plus upper foreneck pale grayish
brown; **upperparts** dark brownish, varying with individual from plain to feathering
with palish tips (effect is indistinct barring), same variation on upper breast, also sides
and flanks but these feathers tend to be broadly margined paler (barred effect); **underparts** all dark or, in some, grade to whitish belly (may be unmarked or be faintly barred
or mottled). Lightest areas of legs and **feet** dusky with hint of yellow, the webs and
joints black.

▶  ♀ Def. Basic Plumage (entire feathering), head–body and more or less of tail acquired in SPRING, sometimes more gradually into early summer; the wing not acquired
until LATE SUMMER or FALL, after a flightless period (that generally begins in Aug.) and
when the Basic head–body is being succeeded by Alt. The Basic tail and wing are retained nearly a year.

Differences from Def. Alt.: head pattern well delineated but somewhat less contrasty (illus. of *M. n. nigra*: Sutton 1961); **dorsum** has distinct barring (lighter feather ends), feathers of **sides** and flanks broadly rounded and widely margined buffy brownish (broadly barred effect); **underparts** typically darkish with lighter feather ends, but in some plain darkish; none seen with light belly.

**Wing** plain darkish on upper surface, the coverts broad, rounded, and lighter toward ends (after fading and wear the covert area appears decidedly barred); wing lining mostly smoky or sooty, except under-primary coverts have pale sheen that matches that of inner webs of the primaries (2-toned effect on underwing).

AT HATCHING frontal feathering (top base of bill) ends in a transverse line; that is, neither indented nor with an outward projection. This distinguishes *M. nigra* downies from other scoters and from eiders except Steller's (whose bill is narrower and appears rather hooked in profile). Rather eiderlike pattern—upperparts various dark browns, without spotting; underparts nearly white with broad and not sharply defined darkish band across upper breast. Whether the sexual difference in the trachea (mentioned earlier) is evident in downies (which is probable) remains unknown.

▶    ♂ ♀ Juv. Plumage (entire feathering), no data on age when it is fully developed (about 60 days?). Sooty brown cap; remainder of **head** and the neck light smoky gray, somewhat mottled darker; **upperparts** rather smoky brown; scapulars short, narrow, rounded; **underparts** breast smoky brownish; sides and flanks also smoky brownish, the feathers soft, lax, narrow, and mostly with buffy brown ends; belly and abdomen whitish, mottled sooty. **Tail** feathers notched (not pointed). **Wing** outermost long primary slightly attenuated, the extent of this apparently varying somewhat among individuals in both sexes (no sex difference such as in Basic wing); darkest part of wing toward blackish gray, innermost secondaries not tapering at ends; middle and upper coverts narrow, ending in rather diagonal shape (not broadly rounded); wider webs of primaries have palish sheen on undersurface.

▶    ♂ Basic I and Alt. I Plumages (the former comprised of all feathering except wing, the latter all except tail and wing).

Basic I is quite blackish and generally has appeared on head and foreparts of body by early Oct. and more is acquired soon afterward. There is no sheen, at least in prepared skins. Feathers of lower breast to beyond vent are light with dark ends, giving a finely barred effect clear to base of tail. The tail usually grows in Nov., sometimes later, and the feathers taper to rounded tips. Molting varies, being sometimes slowed or late. Generally, molting (this time into Alt. I) starts again in late Oct. on head–neck and anterior body, and sweeps over the body. This Plumage is black with some sheen and some striated effect on head–neck. It is, in general, like ♂ Def. Alt. Not later than the time it begins to appear, the basal portion of the upper mandible begins to swell and turn yellow.

▶    ♀ Basic I and Alt. I (inclusive feathering of each as in ♂), timing apparently as in ♂ and with individuals varying similarly. In these Plumages the head–body correspond roughly to those of ♀ Def. Basic and Alt. In the ♀ in Alt. I the cap is dark and rest of head and the neck much lighter, a contrasty pattern; the feathers on venter are dark distally on and near the shaft, producing a fine and quite even pattern (lightest on belly); vent to tail black. The Juv. wing and Basic I tail are worn with Alt. I.

310

▶ ♂ Basic II Plumage (entire feathering), head–body acquired through SPRING, or sometimes into EARLY SUMMER; pattern and color as ♂ Def. Basic. In MIDSUMMER the Juv. wing and tail are molted and, after a flightless period, the "offset" Basic II wing (with greatly attenuated outer primaries) grows.

▶ ♀ Basic II Plumage (all feathering), timing apparently as ♂; color and pattern as ♀ Def. Basic. The much-abraded Juv. wing is worn until, beginning in midsummer or later, the Basic II wing grows.

**Measurements**  12 ♂ (2 Alaska, 4 B.C., 1 Wash., 1 N.B., 1 N.S., 2 Mass., 1 Conn.): BILL 40–47 mm, av. 43.3; WING 229–241, av. 234; TAIL 82–100, av. 91; TARSUS 45–49, av. 46.3;  11 ♀ (1 Kuril Is., 4 Alaska, 1 B.C., 3 Nebr., 1 Conn.): BILL 39–44 mm., av. 42.2; WING 206–230, av. 222; TAIL 69–82, av. 73; TARSUS 42–45, av. 43.6 (ETS).

For series with WING meas. across chord, see especially J. C. Phillips (1926).

**Weight**  Scant information. Eight ♂ av. 2.4 lb. (1.1 kg.), max. 2.8 (1.27 kg.): 4 ♀ av. 1.8 lb. (0.8 kg.), max. 2.4 (1.1 kg.) (A. L. Nelson and Martin 1953). A drake taken in Masoc Co., Wash., in mid-Dec., weighed 3 lb. 3 oz. (1.43 kg.) (G. E. Hudson).

**Hybrids** none known with certainty.

**Geographical variation** in the species—differences between E. Siberian–Nearctic and w. Palearctic populations apparently are constant. In the former, the end of the bill is more hooked in both sexes; drakes have smallish yellow hump on top base of bill, the yellow narrowly divided by black along top midline; in the latter the bill appears straighter (nail at end flatter) and av. longer in both sexes; drake has larger basal hump (truly a knob) on bill and the yellow portion is a broad stripe extending from top base nearly to the nail (it is widest at nostrils). Apparently there is no appreciable difference between the populations in overall size and wt. RSP

SUBSPECIES  *nigra* (Linnaeus)—w. Palearctic, wintering in the ne. Atlantic primarily, 12 ♂ (1 Sweden, 2 Denmark, 8 England, 1 Italy): BILL 47–50 mm., av. 48; WING 227–240, av. 235; TAIL 90–110, av. 95.4; TARSUS 43–48, av. 45.4;  12 ♀ (1 Scotland, 9 England, 2 Italy): BILL 43–48 mm., av. 45; WING 215–232, av. 224; TAIL 72–84, av. 76; TARSUS 41–47, av. 43.6 (ETS).

For additional meas., also with WING flattened, for ♂ and ♀ Juv. and Basic (the Juv. wing is shorter), see Schiøler (1926). For meas. of WING over the curve, see Witherby (1939). There are a few wt. data in Schiøler, but see also Dementiev and Gladkov (1952). For wt. of ♀♀ in nesting season at Mývatn, Iceland, see Bengtson (1972c).

*americana* (Swainson)—Nearctic and E. Siberian, wintering in the w. Atlantic and in the Pacific; descr. and meas. given at beginning of this account. RSP

FIELD IDENTIFICATION  In N. Am. Sometimes described as difficult to identify because of absence of any notable field marks. Older drakes: feathering entirely black, yellow patch on top of bill. Definitive-feathered ♀♀: rather uniform sooty upperparts, or the same faded, the head with very dark cap clearly delineated from paler sides, the bill usually all dark; young stages more ♀-like, but most drakes begin acquiring some black feathering late in 1st fall. On the wing, both sexes show conspicuous silvery undersurface of primaries and their coverts in contrast with very dark remainder of wing lining (same holds for other scoters, but is much less evident.)

311

Wings of drakes over a year old make a whistling sound. The duck's dark cap on light head shows in flight at a considerable distance.

Birds of both sexes in 1st fall, when in Basic I head–body feathering, are the "gray coots" of gunners. It is a long tradition among wildfowlers to regard birds at this stage as of a species distinct from the same species when in other feathering.

Various scoters tend to mingle where they occur in the same area, but this one is more likely to be found near exposed shorelines and out on open water at any hour, rather than seeking a lee shore or sheltered bay. The birds are strung out on the water, or in scattered bunches. No scoter rises gracefully from the water but, in comparison with the others, this one rises with decidedly less apparent effort and often at a greater angle with the horizon. They fly in strings and bunches and shift formation frequently. The sleigh-bell call is appropriately named, a far-carrying call of drakes, a pleasant, plaintive series of *cree* notes—hence "sleigh-bell duck"—but on the water at close range one also may hear the quite guttural chatter of ♀ ♀.

Compare with the other scoters, especially head pattern and wing. In poor light the Black Scoter possibly might be mistaken for the Harlequin, which is comparatively small headed, lively, and with patchy pattern. Young eiders have a humpy profile and long sloping foreheads. The Ruddy (in winter) has white cheeks, is a more compact bird, and probably does not occur where it might be confused with Black Scoter ♀ or young. RSP

VOICE   Silent at times, but most vocal of scoters in social and in pair formation activity. Humphrey (1957a) and Bengtson (1966b) are particularly useful sources of information.

Drakes in fall utter a shrill whistling *cree cree* . . . in ringing chorus, audible a half mile in calm air (Brewster 1924). This or a variant has been described as *tuk tuk* (accent on 2nd syllable). A. Brooks (1920) described the drake's common call as a prolonged plaintive whistle *cour-cour-cour-loo cour-lou*, the "most musical of duck cries, very different from the croaking notes of most diving ducks." Uttered by drakes in flight and on water, including during Tail-snap and Head-shake displays. A metallic *crek* note by drakes in groups in Erect display (a variant of *cree* or *tuk* syllables?). A rattling *tuka-tuka-tuka-tuk* during Bowing, Erect, Rush, and Short Flight displays.

The duck has a low growling call, uttered when excited, including toward a displaying mate. Gurgling, growling notes in alarm. Quite loud. A mated ♀ in circling flight in late June uttered a reedy *tooooo-it* and variants. A ♀ on being flushed from her nest uttered a *pe-e-e-e-e-ut*, the first portion higher and rapid, the last part a low croak. RSP

HABITAT   Breeds in n. part of the forest zone, also the semibarrens, and grassy or brushy tundra, usually quite close to water. At ponds, etc., at considerable elevations in some localities. Many prebreeders spend the summer on the sea; the vast majority of breeding drakes go there to molt, but others gather on large waters inland. As a migrant, occurs on lakes, estuaries, and coastal marine waters. In winter, prefers fairly shoal water over mussel beds along exposed coastlines, rather than vicinity of islets and ledges. Occasionally seeks sheltered waters in stormy weather. RSP

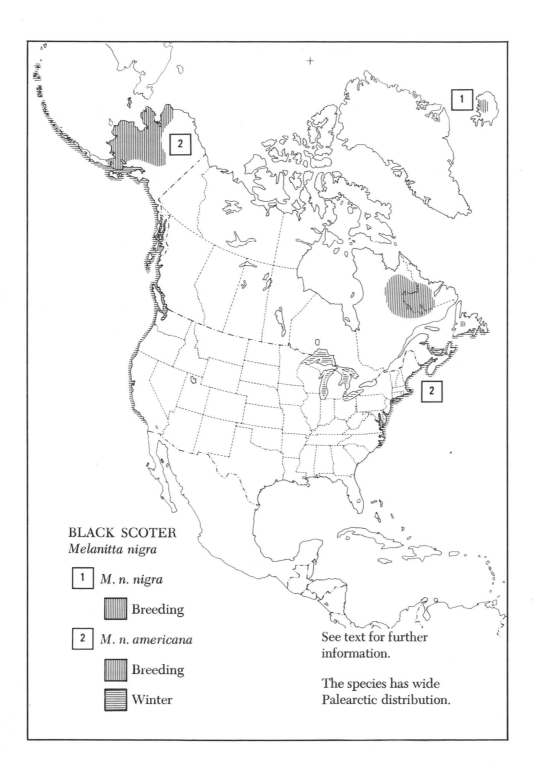

BLACK SCOTER
*Melanitta nigra*

1 | *M. n. nigra*

▥ Breeding

2 | *M. n. americana*

▥ Breeding

▤ Winter

See text for further
information.

The species has wide
Palearctic distribution.

DISTRIBUTION (See map.) This section should be read in conjunction with "Migration," since the latter indicates some of the unknowns regarding travels of this scoter, hence areas where it may occur in N. Am.

*M. nigra americana* in N. Am. **Breeds** in Alaska, in a few places around Bristol Bay (including Ugashik Lakes on Alaska Pen.), but mainly from Kuskokwim Bay n. to Norton Sd., then on Seward Pen. (including C. Prince of Wales and Shishmaref area), and in inner Norton Sd. (abundant in delta of the Kobuk); has nested farther n. at C. Lisburne. South of the Alaska Pen., has nested on Kodiak I. (1 record). In interior Alaska: McKinley Park, also ne. of Anchorage at L. Louise (one of most abundant nesters there).

Recently found breeding in interior Ungava, in the same habitat as the Surf Scoter but perhaps only a tenth as many birds.

Godfrey (1966) listed these scattered N. Am. localities: in s. Keewatin at Windy R.; in n. Que. within Ungava Bay at Leaf Bay; and in Nfld. (the Avalon Pen., also Missen Topsail, and near Grand Lake). Except for Grand Lake, these may not be regular breeding localities. Reported nesting at Gary I. in Mackenzie Bay, also Audubon's description of a nest on the N. Shore of Gulf of St. Lawrence, seem plausible even though they have been discounted by various authors. Both were mentioned by Bent (1925).

**Summer** distribution—very widespread; for both prebreeders and older birds, see beyond under "Migration." Upper limits are somewhere in Alaska (lower reaches of the Colville, possibly also the arctic coast), also Hudson Strait and Ungava Bay; southward in Pacific waters to include occurrence in Baja Cal., Mexico, and Atlantic waters at least to Long I., N.Y.

**Winter** In the Bering–Pacific area, from the Aleutians s. into Cal., the majority of the birds probably being in coastal waters of B.C. and se. Alaska; at Clam Lagoon on Adak I. (cent. Aleutians), however, it is the commonest sea duck from about mid-Oct. to June; in the interior, a few on the Great Lakes; in Atlantic waters from s. Nfld. to Ga. (now plentiful on the se. Atlantic coast), rarely to Fla.; on the Gulf Coast of Texas, once the rarest scoter but now the commonest, often flocking with scaups.

Has occurred in interior N. Am. s. into Colo., Kans., Mo., Tenn., La., and Miss.

**Straggler** There are 2 reports of mature drakes in Holland, in late Dec. 1954 and early Nov. 1967 (Bruun 1971).

This species is not recorded as fossil in N. Am., but has been reported from 6 **archaeological sites** in Alaska, on is. and mainland; details in Brodkorb (1964a).

In ne. Asia, *americana* nests from the Lena drainage eastward at least into Anadyrland, and se. to include the Kamchatkan Pen. and n. Kurils. The whereabouts of any summer assemblies of prebreeders and of postbreeding drakes is not reported. It is not recorded in any season on the Chuckchee Pen. Winter range extends s. to cent. Japan, rarely to coastal China.

*M. n. nigra* has occurred **in our area** only as a straggler to Greenland, twice in Nanortalik Dist. and once in Angmagssalik Dist.; details in Salomonsen (1967a).

**Elsewhere** breeds in Iceland (mainly at Mývatn, where it has decreased very greatly in recent years), Brit. Isles (very few localities), Orkneys, Bear I., Spitzbergen (2 records), and on the Eurasian continent from n. Scandinavia eastward in U.S.S.R. to the upper (southerly) Khatanga drainage. [Various authors have indicated continuous

314

breeding range of this species across Eurasia, but there appears to be a considerable gap between the Khatanga and Lena drainages whence only nonbreeding (prebreeding?) or molting individuals are known.] Has occurred in summer as far n. as Kolguev and Vaigach is. and s. Novaya Zemlya. The major molting area for prebreeders and postbreeding drakes of Icelandic origin apparently is off e. Scotland and for continental birds is along the North Sea coast of Denmark. Winters mainly in Baltic and North Sea areas, s. to include the Bay of Biscay (where birds banded in Iceland have been captured). Some also winter elsewhere and the species has straggled widely (data not summarized here).

In the Palearctic area this species is recorded as **fossil** from the Pleistocene of various localities in the Brit. Isles and Europe; see Brodkorb (1964a) for references. RSP

MIGRATION  This section combines speculation with known fact, to indicate a probable pattern.

*M. n. americana* in N. Am. In the Pacific–Bering area, the birds occur in **winter** along the coast, mostly from se. Alaska and B.C. southward through Cal. (some others are in s. Bering Sea and vicinity) and in **spring** at least the southerly winterers begin shifting upward along the coast by some time in April, probably much earlier. Then breeders, very late in April and in first third of May, depart on long, high-altitude and probably nonstop flights to waters within breeding areas. **Summer** After mid-May the breeding pairs begin to spread out and ♀ ♀ eventually occupy (or reoccupy) nest sites. The spring movement of prebreeders may terminate in a fairly long flight over the sea and the birds are in molting assemblies in Bering Sea (in Alaska mainly in coastal waters) around mid-May. They are molting from early June onward and remain through the summer. Ashore, about the time the ♀ ♀ begin incubating (middle third of June), most of their mates return to the sea, where they join the other molters. South of Hooper Bay at Angyoyaravak Bay, scoters of this species were molting in large flocks on Aug. 31, 1972 (C. Dau). Some mature drakes in small gatherings remain inland on larger expanses of water. Some ♀ ♀, probably failed breeders, go to sea also and, in the rearing period, many ♀ ♀ evidently leave their preflight young and also go to sea (or perhaps a few to large inland waters). The successfully breeding ♀ ♀ are the last to begin the wing molt. Most of the young of the year probably remain close to where they hatched until they attain flight; they then go to sea.

Referring back to spring, the **molt migration** of prebreeders consists of the terminal phase of their spring travel; for many breeders that return to the sea, the distance traveled is rather short.

In **fall**, periods overlap during which the different categories migrate. Prebreeders of both sexes (now over a year old and not distinguishable in appearance from older cohorts), which are the earliest to finish wing molting, probably are the first to travel; next, flocks consisting entirely or almost entirely of mature drakes; then mature ♀ ♀ and, finally, young of the year. Birds of the youngest cohort tend to travel farther than older ones, i.e., on winter range there is age segregation as well as, among birds of breeding age, more or less sex segregation until well along in the season.

In the e. Palearctic, although breeding and winter distribution are known in a general way, there is little useful information on migration—nothing, for example, on the

315

whereabouts of molting birds. Whether there is any movement between Siberia and Alaska is unknown.

In the w. Atlantic area the total number of individuals now is small in comparison with the other scoters, probably a few tens of thousands at most.

In **spring** the birds shift northward in coastal waters and then, from New Eng. waters mainly, most of the breeders disappear. Although these birds may vanish into the vastness of interior Ungava, it is possible that some of them really are Alaskan birds that make a very long flight across Canada to near the Bering Sea coast of Alaska. A probable route extends from s. Me. to s. James Bay (or inland just sw. of this bay) to nw. Man.– sw. Keewatin, then there seem to be no records between there and breeding areas in Alaska. **Summer** There are very few unquestionable easterly breeding records, which were listed earlier under "Distribution." The number now in Ungava is unknown but not large. Either a few prebreeders go inland and molt on James and se. Hudson Bay or else early June birds there are late-migrating breeders. In Atlantic waters, prebreeders are moving northward until at least late May and some spend the summer in the Gulf of St. Lawrence, around n. Nfld., and along Atlantic coastal Labrador. In the early 1880s this scoter was, according to Turner (1885), "abundant in Hudson Strait and eastern shore of Labrador where it is reported to breed sparingly." He had a specimen from the mouth of the Koksoak R., which enters Ungava Bay.

It is not beyond possibility that some postbreeding drakes in Alaska make a long flight back to e. Hudson Bay to molt, rather than molting on the edge of Bering Sea. **Fall** The early overland flights to the Me. coast (from the Hudson Bay–James Bay area?), beginning in Sept., consist mainly of drakes; young of the year—the "gray coots" of gunners—come later, in Oct., typically in flocks by themselves. There is southerly movement of yearlings from Labrador, the Gulf of St. Lawrence, and neighboring waters, and of other birds after they arrive on the coast from the interior. It is the youngest cohort, which arrives from the interior, that tends to travel farthest, to more southerly winter range. The southward shift from New Eng. of the various cohorts, on overlapping schedules, occurs from Oct. into Dec.

*M. n. nigra* (w. Palearctic)—the birds of Fennoscandia and w. U.S.S.R. winter in the s. Baltic and in Atlantic waters from North Sea localities to the Bay of Biscay. In spring some prebreeders may go directly to molting places along w. Denmark (and some to e. Scotland?), but a very large number evidently fly to s. Sweden and cross into the Baltic. The bulk of breeders do this and continue on, via the Gulf of Finland and Lakes Ladoga and Onega, to breeding places in the w. U.S.S.R. Somewhere along this route, the prebreeders turn back and cross Denmark from e. to w., beginning as early as mid-May. They molt, in dense assemblies on shoal water beyond the surf, along the sandy North Sea coast of Denmark. Later, mature drakes leave their mates and form in flocks. Seebohm (1880) reported seeing an estimated 10,000 in the arctic waters at mouth of the Pechora R. in mid-July. Beginning in July, the postbreeding drakes return and become flightless in molt in the same Danish waters as the prebreeders. On June 16, 1963, at Rømø, an aerial census showed about 50,000 (95% were ♂ ♂) not yet flightless; on July 29 there were 150,000 (90% were ♂ ♂) flightless (Joensen 1964). See the later paper by Joensen (1973) for many additional data, by sex and age-class.

See. G. Bergmann and Donner (1964) for many important data on spring migration in s. Finland, Salomonsen (1968) for general coverage of molt migration in the w.

Palearctic, and Jacobi and Jögi (1972) for details of the westward molt migration as studied in Estonia. RSP

BANDING STATUS    The total number banded in N. Am. through 1964 was 19 and there have been no recoveries; they were banded in Alaska and Alta. (data from Bird Banding Laboratory). Some results of Icelandic banding have been mentioned earlier. RSP

REPRODUCTION    For the species, the various papers on displays have been used and cited by these recent authors: Humphrey (1957a), McKinney (1959), and Bengtson (1966b). The data on other facets of reproduction, especially for N. Am., are scant. Minimum breeding age presumably is 2 years.

There is some display by migrants in fall at stopover places, as Brewster (1924) observed at L. Umbagog on the Me.–N.H. boundary. He described a "sort of revolving dance," all members of the flock following one another closely, in a great circle, swimming rapidly and energetically so as to keep most of the body above the surface, the wings not opened, and a continuous sound very like that of raindrops falling on a calm pond, doubtless caused by vigorous action of the feet. In another action (Erect position described below), a bird's body is upward, "like a bottle floating upright," momentarily; then the bird lowers its neck and settles on the water. He observed the Wing flap (also see below) less often.

Much **pair formation** activity must occur in winter, since at least many birds are paired long before they arrive on summer range. A social phase of display is indicated by the above data from Brewster. Furthermore, "the courting actions differ radically from those of other scoters, especially the courting flights when four to ten males may be seen wheeling about after one female" (A. Brooks 1945). There is a considerable problem in distinguishing comfort movements from displays, since it appears that some that may be classed as the latter are very slightly modified from the former. Displays are listed here in no particular order.

**Displays of the duck**    INCITING if ritualized, is difficult to recognize; possibly a slight chin lifting (tilting the bill slightly upward). Both sexes utter a whistled call at the same time, the birds in Erect position. At least the following drake patterns occur also in the duck: Preen-under-the-wing, Tail-snap, and Rush. Various comfort movements (lateral shaking of head, erect position, wing flapping, etc.) may have display functions. The duck has the same jerky bowing as the drake.

**Displays of the drake.**    HEAD-SHAKE laterally; ♂'s most frequent movement; commonly done just after calling; usually precedes Rush. RUSH (or Low Rush) head is lowered as drake starts to paddle forward and rushes over surface for 3–4 ft., churning up much spray; done in various situations including alongside ♀. SHAKE bird rears up briefly, the head high, and a shaking movement passes over the whole body, then a "striking forward twitch of the head, which seems peculiar to scoters" (McKinney 1959). ERECT (or Upward-stretch) same as preceding, but no shaking movement; wings are closed, bill pointed above horizontal. WING-FLAP several flaps, the body Erect; a comfort movement, frequent during bouts of displaying; whether it has a signal function is unknown. BOWING forward movements of head–neck, with plaintive whistling; the movements are rather jerky and the tail is angled about 45° above the

317

horizontal. This is similar to activities of both sexes when disturbed or curious (Humphrey 1957a). TAIL-SNAP tail snapped quickly to vertical or even angled forward over back, the neck stiffly upward (beak horizontal) and drake utters his plaintive whistling; occurs in group situations, also done by lone ♂ displaying to mate. Generally followed by Rush. Then the drake resumes bowing activity. SHORT FLIGHT common; drake flies 4–8 ft., just clearing surface of water at peak of flight; then a sudden braking action of feet, the head drawn back, and bird in Erect position as spray begins to fly; then the bird continues forward in Rush. Occurs when a group is displaying. STEAMING of ♂ toward ♀, as preceding but the bird seen to do this did not become airborne, the ♂ (2 others were nearby) briefly adopted a half-erect posture, head drawn back, breast forward ("chesty"). BREAST-PREEN the Rush is followed by very rapid head movements (resembling preening), difficult to observe because of flying spray; in one instance the bird nibbled in region of its shoulder or side of breast (McKinney). BREAST-PREEN as a separate display is common, as described and illus. in Bengtson (1966). PREEN-UNDER-THE-WING ritualized, illus. in Bengtson. WATER-FLICK bill and forepart of face submerged, then flicked upward; done by drake alongside or just ahead of duck. FORWARD STRETCH ♂ low on water, head somewhat forward (as though about to start Rush).

Some linkage of displays has been indicated above. According to Johnsgard (1965), the usual sequence of ♂ displays is as follows: Erect (with whistle), Tail-snap, Rush, Water-flick, Breast-preen, Forward-stretch, Erect, and Head-shake. From this sequence, Tail-snap plus Rush often are omitted.

Often the **nest site** is within a few meters of water, near a pond or lake, or on an island in one of these. A common site is a hummock, covered with dead grass of the previous year plus new growth, in a dried-out marshy area, or on moorland, or else a dry place among grasses, heaths, dwarf birches, or willows. Thus there is concealment and the duck is said to be shy. At Hooper Bay, Alaska, Brandt (1943) found them nesting on grassy hummocks (generally the largest one in the vicinity was selected), also dune ridges along the coast, embankments bordering estuaries, and on rolling upland tundra. The duck presumably forms the shallow cavity and adds some dry vegetation and then, beginning during laying, adds the **nest down** (dark brownish with fairly large white centers) and sometimes a few breast feathers (quite gray, some with broad white terminal band).

**Clutch size** 6–10 (usually 7–8) eggs, with occasional joint layings (to over a dozen). In *M. n. nigra* in 1961–70 inclusive at Mývatn, Iceland, variation in clutch size ranged from a low (in 27 clutches) of 7.56 ± 0.31 in 1970 to a high (in 10 clutches) of 9.00 ± 0.30 in 1964 (Bengtson 1971a). **Egg size** 58 eggs from N. Am. measure length 53–72.5 mm., av. 61.9, and breadth 33.6–46.2, av. 41.7 mm. (Bent 1925). For 35 Alaskan eggs (meas. in inches), see Brandt (1943). For eggs of nominate *nigra*, see Schönwetter (1961). They are nearly elliptical in **shape**, slightly pointed at one end, off-white or ivory **color**, and without gloss.

Although **full clutches** of nominate *nigra* may be expected occasionally as early as the end of May in Iceland, and commonly in early June in Iceland and Brit. Isles, the usual time for *americana* is about June 10–20. They are incubated by the duck, the drake remaining on nearby water only through laying or until very early in incubation. In nominate *nigra* the **incubation period** has been reported as 28 days or longer (to 33), also (Moody, in Witherby 1939) 27–28 days in confinement; there are no N. Am. data.

According to E. W. Nelson (1887), in Alaska, drakes may be found in the same places as ♀ ♀ through the season, but "these are pairs which bred late." He mentioned a fresh (replacement?) clutch on Aug. 3 and a brood of downies on Sept. 9. At Mývatn, Iceland, the ♀ ♀ nest ashore and on islands and at least some of the drakes molt on the lake; in N. Am., probably the vast majority of drakes molt on the sea.

Little is known about the posthatching period. E. W. Nelson reported that ♀ and **brood** stay on water near where the young hatched until the ducklings are half grown, then the family moves to the nearby coast and remains on salt water until the young are able to fly. More likely, the vast majority of young spend the preflight period on inland waters and, some time within this period, the ♀ leaves them and goes elsewhere to molt. Hantzsch's (1905) figure of 6–7 weeks for attainment of flight is only an estimate from field observations in Iceland; probably it is too short. RSP

SURVIVAL No N. Am. data. Based on a few recoveries of *M. n. nigra* banded in Iceland, Boyd (in Le Cren and Holdgate 1962) gave an estimated mean annual adult survival rate of 0.77 ± 0.04. RSP

HABITS In N. Am. The various published accounts actually contain rather little information. Most useful are the general summary in J. C. Phillips (1926) and Brewster's (1924) detailed observations inland in fall at L. Umbagog on the Me.–N.H. boundary.

This scoter is somewhat different from the others in certain respects. It is much more noisy, considerably more inclined to take wing, somewhat wary, and less inclined to associate with other waterfowl. The only species with which it is reported to occur with any regularity are the Surf Scoter and Greater Scaup. Fall flocks, especially of mature drakes, tend to keep to themselves.

The reader is referred to Brewster's detailed notes. Flocks, containing scores of birds, were seen to drop nearly vertically from a great height, seemingly with wings closed. They made a far-carrying rushing sound. They would arrive in the morning, stay well out on the lake and not feed and then, on the following evening, rise to a great height and continue their overland journey to the sea. Usually they resumed their overland journey about ½ hr. after sunset.

On marine waters in fall the birds fly in lines, sometimes just over the surface, or rise and fall, or form in bunches and then again space out in irregular lines. When actively feeding they tend to be in parties. They dive for mussels, preferably in 2–5 fathoms of water. If the tide is strong, the surfaced individuals drift away; then they fly back and again dive—drift feeding. According to A. Brooks (1945), this scoter does not open its wings or extend the alulae when submerged. It feeds in fairly smooth to even rough or choppy water. RSP

FOOD In N. Am., examination of the stomach contents of 124 "adults" gave 90% animal matter (mainly mollusks and crustaceans, with a few insects, fishes, and echinoderms) and 10% vegetable (principally pondweeds and algae) (Cottam 1939). Yorke (1899) mentioned, in addition, slugs, snails, frogs, tadpoles, and fish spawn. The next 3 paragraphs are Nearctic (*M. n. americana*) and the last 2 are Palearctic data.

NEARCTIC **Animal** Mollusks (*Mytilus* and *Siliqua* chiefly, *Protothaca*, *Venus*, *Tellina*, *Macoma*, *Littorina*, *Acmaea*, *Crepidula*, *Lacuna*, *Natica*, etc.) 65.2%; crustaceans: barnacles (*Balanus*, *Chthamalus*, *Lepas*), claw shrimp (*Limnadia*), crabs (*Neopanope*, *Hemigrapsus*, *Cancer*, *Pinnotheres*), crawfishes (*Cambarus*), shrimps (*Crago*), etc. 17.3%; insects: caddis fly larvae (Trichoptera), ants (Hymenoptera), etc. 3.2%; fishes 1.7%; echinoderms: sand dollars (*Echinarachnius*), sea urchins (*Strongylocentrotus*), starfishes (Asteroidea), brittle stars (Ophiuroidea), etc. 1.5%; miscellaneous (hydroids, marine worms, sea spiders) 0.8% (Cottam 1939).

Freshwater clams (*Unio*) preferred inland. Food of 13 Mass. birds consisted of 95% mussels and 5% starfishes and periwinkles (Forbush 1916). On Mass. coast G. H. Mackay (1891) found food to consist mainly of black mussel (*Modiolus modiolus*), small sea clams (*Spisula solidissima*) scallops (*Pecten concentricus*), and razor shells (*Siliqua costata*). In B.C., gastropods (*Margarites*, *Alectrion*, *Bittium*, *Cerithopsis*, *Acmaea*, *Littorina*, *Columbella*, *Merovia*, *Alnarria*, *Lacuna*) and the pelecypod *Mytilus* (J. Munro and Clemens 1931).

**Vegetable** Pondweeds (*Zostera*, *Potamogeton*, *Ruppia*) 4.7%, muskgrass (*Chara*) and other algae 2.1%, miscellaneous (*Scirpus*, *Carex*, *Cladium*, *Ranunculus*, *Hippuris*, *Empetrum*) 3.5% (Cottam 1939). For inland waters, duckweed (Lemnaceae), pondweeds (Najadaceae), flag (*Iris*), water milfoil (*Myriophyllum*), bladderwort (*Utricularia*), etc. (Yorke 1899). AWS

PALEARCTIC **Animal** In Europe, mollusks, *Mytilus edulis* up to 3.5 cm. in length (Millais 1913b), *Cardium edule*, *Solen vagina*, *Venus*, *Tapes*, *Tracia* (?), and larvae of Libellulidae (Madon 1935), shrimps and sandhoppers (*Talitrus saltator*) (Bolam 1912). At Mývatn, Iceland, ducklings less than half grown ate mainly adult insects and some seeds (chiefly *Potamogeton*); when older, chironomid larvae and some Cladocera. When over 2 weeks old they ate relatively more seeds of *Batrachium;* the few mature drakes examined had eaten fish eggs and some chironomids; mature ♀ ♀ ate mainly chironomid larvae, also some fish eggs, mollusks (*Lymnea*), and seeds (Bengtson 1971b). Food during nesting season in U.S.S.R. has not been studied but is known to consist of mollusks, insects, and rhizomes of aquatic plants. During migration along the Pechora R. they consume larvae of caddis flies and dragonflies, with some mollusks and fishes (*Phoxinus phoxinus*). In autumn at Rybinsk Reservoir, food is mainly mollusks (50%), larvae of caddis flies (16.3%) and of chironomids (20%). In winter on the sea, consumes mainly mollusks, chiefly species of *Mytilus* (in Dementiev and Gladkov 1952).

**Vegetable** In Europe, nodular roots of aquatic plants, probably *Polygonum amphibium* (Naumann 1905b). Have fed on horse beans and grain from wrecked cargo ships (A. Chapman 1887, Gätke 1895). AWS

**Labrador Duck**

*Camptorhynchus labradorius* (Gmelin)

EXTINCT   Ninety years after this species was made known to science the last alleged contact with it alive ended with the killing of one individual in 1878 near Elmira, N.Y., a most unlikely place. That this species was taken there is doubted by various authorities.

DESCRIPTION   Smallish diving duck whose closest affinities may be with the scoters (*Melanitta*), but are subject to debate. Sides of upper mandible flared and pendulous distally—"soft membranous expansions" (Audubon 1843)—and there are about 50 lamellae (combined total for 1 side each of both mandibles); white area in wing consisted of at least the secondaries and adjoining row of upper coverts, but in older drakes included practically all of upper surface of wing except alula, the primaries, and some adjoining coverts; "mature" drakes, at least most of year, had cheeks of plushlike feathers (as in the Spectacled and King eiders). The drake's trachea had an enlargement at either end plus 2 in between, the bony bulla at inner end being much the largest, round, and asymmetrical (A. Wilson 1829). Mature drake boldly pied (mostly black and white), ♀ and certain younger stages somber (mostly brownish slate with white wing patch). J. C. Phillips (1926) described known feathering and included a col. pl. by Fuertes of 3 stages (♂ "adult" and "immature" and ♀ "adult"); the unknowns include the downy young and apparently several Plumages. For some information on external appearance (including unfeathered areas), pterylosis, and on certain skeletal elements, see Humphrey and Butsch (1958).

   Length probably to 22½ in., ♂ larger than ♀. A drake, no. 29 in Hahn's (1963) list, measures BILL 44 mm., WING 222, TAIL 72, and TARSUS 40; no. 22 measures 42–219–74–37; ♀ no. 20 measures 42–211–71–37; and no. 31 measures 42–210–78–35 (ETS). J. C. Phillips (1926) gave the following, including chord of wing: ♂ BILL 44 mm., WING 215, TARSUS 40; ♀ BILL 40 mm., WING 208, TARSUS 38. RSP

DISTRIBUTION   Breeding range unknown. From available information on place of capture in any season (though mostly winter), localities include "Labrador" (a name in the past having inexact application to portions of the Ungava Pen., or even all of it), N.S., N.B., New Eng., N.Y. (minimum of 15 records for Long I.), and N.J. s. at least to the Delaware R. Beyond, Audubon allegedly saw it in Chesapeake Bay. Winter habitat included sandy bays and estuarine waters. Inland records: Laprairie, Montreal, Que., spring of 1862, and near Elmira, N.Y., Dec. 12, 1878. RSP

OTHER TOPICS   That the Labrador Duck ever really did occur in "Labrador" seems not to have been established until recently by Lysaght (1959, or see Todd 1963). Certain eggs, accredited to this species but lacking unassailable proof of specific identity, were described by Glegg (1951). Seven eggs "im Museum Tring und Dresden" measure 60–62 × 42–43.5 mm. (Schönwetter 1961). Even why the bird became extinct is a mystery. Known extant specimens, listed by Hahn (1963), total 54 skins and mounts plus very few separate skeletal items, notably a sternum with coracoids and furcula that were figured by Rowley (1877).

Bangs (in J. C. Phillips 1926) suggested that the peculiarities of this duck's bill indicated a specialized diet, but little pertinent information exists beyond Audubon's (1838) mention that it was caught on trotlines baited with blue mussel (*Mytilus edulis*), or that one had small shells in its digestive tract. [The lateral portions of the distal half of the upper mandible of Steller's Eider are rather soft and fleshy. The Blue Duck (*Hymenolaimus*) of mountain streams in New Zealand also has fleshy lateral flaps on the bill, which Kear and Burton (1971) suggested may function protectively when the bird is foraging under stones.] The Labrador Duck's "remarkably large" liver (A. Wilson and Bonaparte 1831) indicates it had ability to remain submerged a long time. We close this obituary with a surmise, not original here, that the Labrador Duck may have been a N. Atlantic ecological counterpart of Steller's Eider. RSP AWS

**Harlequin Duck**

*Histrionicus histrionicus* (Linnaeus)

Small stocky diving duck. Nail on upper mandible indistinct in outline and occupies entire breadth of bill. Margin of feathering on side base of bill convex (curves forward on bill) and, on top base, tapers to a point farther forward. There is a soft naked membrane at the base of the upper mandible, overlapping the edge and concealing the corner of the mouth and side base of lower mandible. Distance between loreal feathering and nostril as great or greater than length of nostril opening (it is less in the Oldsquaw). Patchy head pattern in both sexes. Alt.-Plumaged drake has very broken overall pattern of bluish, white, black, and rusty. The drake's speculum reflects in the cobalt to violet range; the duck's is muted and not very noticeable. The drake's trachea is large in diam. distally, then tapers gradually to a short constriction, then expands near the large round bony bulla that projects to the left side and lacks membranous windows; see Schiøler (1926) for detailed illus.

Length ♂ to about 17½ in., ♀ to 16½; wingspread ♂ to 26½, ♀ to 25; wt. of ♂ usually about 1½ lb., ♀ 1¼. No subspecies.

DESCRIPTION Two Plumages/cycle in both sexes. The drake's Juv. and Basics are somewhat ♀-like in pattern. There is individual variation in size of markings in both sexes. Timing and duration of molting vary considerably in both sexes. These factors, plus a complicated and bizarre color pattern, render it impossible to write descriptions that are comprehensive yet brief.

▶ ♂ Def. Alt. Plumage (all feathering, excepting the tail and all but innermost feathers of wing), acquired beginning in EARLY FALL and worn through winter into SUMMER. Best color illus. are of Greenland and Icelandic birds, in Schiøler (1926). **Bill** bluish gray with whitish nail; **iris** quite dark reddish brown; **head** and neck medium grayish blue except: chin, throat, and foreneck black; forepart of cheeks white and this continues, narrowing, upward in front of eye and along side of crown; lower eyelid white; small white oval auricular patch; white stripe on side of neck toward nape; black stripe from top base of bill back over crown onto nape bordered white narrowly (extension from cheek patch) on crown and then rusty and more broadly rusty posteriorly (much individual variation in amount of rusty); rather narrow white collar at base of neck (sometimes incomplete, especially in front), and most or all of these white markings except area on front of cheek have at least rear or lower margin bordered black. **Upperparts** upper back and mantle medium or darker bluish; scapulars white with narrow lead gray margins on outer webs; rump black. **Underparts** most of breast and forward sides bluish (as mantle), interrupted by a transverse (vertical in the swimming bird) black-bordered white stripe or crescent in front of folded wing; most of sides and the flanks rich brownish red or rusty; remainder of venter muted bluish gray, brownish, or rusty (individual variation); a small white spot in the black area of side of rump at base of tail; upper and under tail coverts black. Legs and **feet** variants of bluish gray with very dark webs. **Wing** innermost secondaries rather broad distally, their inner webs white with black border that does not continue around the end of the feathers; remainder of wing and the tail are retained Basic feathering (described below).

NOTE   A partial albino was mated to a "normal" ♀ (J. Grinnell 1910).

▶   ♂ Def. Basic Plumage (entire feathering); usually some Basic begins to show on head–neck in very LATE JUNE or EARLY JULY; most drakes are wearing Basic head–body from some time in July through Aug. and into SEPT.; drakes become flightless (duration of this unknown) in July and, usually by some time in Aug., the tail is being renewed and the new wing quills are growing; some drakes still are flightless until at least Sept. 10. The molt out of Basic head–body begins while the new tail and wing are growing and sometimes is not completed until late in FALL. In captive individuals, the time the "eclipse" [Def. Basic head–body] is worn is of "relatively short " duration (Derscheid 1941).

A very dark Plumage with blended pattern and greatly reduced number of markings, well illus. as "Ad. m. eclipse" in Witherby (1939). Sides of **head** and the breast and much of **upperparts** between sooty and lead color (somewhat bluish); most of remainder of head, neck, and body (including scapulars) sooty brownish. On the head the white loreal patch is larger than in Alt. (extends from bill back to and below the eye, in some also down to include the chin), many of the feathers with dusky tips; there is a small white auricular patch, but other white areas of head and foreparts that are present in Alt. are lacking. **Underparts** variable, in some solid dark, but in others the feathers are light with dark ends that produce a more or less evenly broken pattern. **Tail** nearly black with (at first) a gray bloom, the feathers pointed. **Wing** distal half sooty; smaller upper coverts on inner half bluish gray; several middle coverts usually with round or oval terminal white area; greater coverts toward sooty, several central ones with subterminal ultramarine band and white ends; innermost (longest) secondaries have white outer webs with complete blackish brown (not black) borders; speculum not conspicuous but reflects in the cobalt to violet range; wing lining mostly dark.

▶   ♀ Def. Alt. Plumage (all feathering except tail and all but innermost feathers of wing), acquired beginning in LATE FALL or later and retained into SPRING. More grayish or toward gray-blue (less brownish) than Basic and typically with belly mostly or all darkish. There are useful illus. on pl. 35 in Schiøler (1926). **Bill** bluish slaty, paling to whitish nail; **iris** medium brownish. On the **head** a large white loreal area (usually it extends from bill back to below eye and usually up onto side of forehead), except that part of the feathers are tipped dark so that the area contains a dusky stripe or area from near top of bill back to eye; a white postauricular spot; remainder of head and the neck various gray-browns. **Upperparts** gray-brown to bluish (individual variation), some feathers edged more or less paler (toward gray-buff); **underparts** variable, the sides and flanks more or less brownish (sometimes toward rusty), the remainder varying from quite evenly dark to more or less barred darkish on belly and abdomen, the basal portion of the feathers being light. Legs and **feet** grayed yellowish, the joints dark and webs blackish. In the **wing** the innermost secondaries are brownish with inner webs paler; remainder of wing and the tail are retained Basic feathering (described below).

▶   ♀ Def. Basic Plumage (entire feathering), acquired in stages, the head–body in spring, the tail and most of wing (after flightless period) in fall (usually beginning not earlier than late Sept.), by which time the head–body has begun molting back into Alt.

324

(The "adult female" on col. pl. in J. C. Phillips (1925) is in Basic, not Alt.) More brownish and blended than Alt. and typically with whitish belly. **Head** variable, in some all of forepart of face white except for a line from bill to eye, in others this white is reduced to a tiny spot on side of forehead and a patch below and in front of eye; there is a whitish auricular spot, variable in size; usually some white on chin; **upperparts** variably brownish, bleaching toward buffy brown; **underparts** breast as dorsum, also the sides; belly varies from unmarked whitish to same heavily mottled brownish and usually becoming darker well beyond vent. **Tail** dark brownish but fades considerably. **Wing** distal half blackish browns, upper coverts more brownish but darkening at ends and a few larger ones sometimes have very pale ends; and edging on innermost secondaries is brownish (not grayish); speculum toward ultramarine, but very muted; wing lining dark, a few coverts tipped white.

NOTES   As in waterfowl generally, failed-breeding ♀ ♀ evidently begin wing molt earlier than do successful ones.

In at least some successful breeders, the head–neck show some molting from Basic back into Alt. in Aug.; that is, the next molt begins while these ♀ ♀ still are attending preflight young.

AT HATCHING   Obvious differences from Oldsquaw downies: no dark band across upper breast; white extends farther up cheek (to edge of eye); a single white spot, in front of and above eye, in dark portion of head. There is some individual variation in number and size of light spots in dark dorsum, as noted in Nearctic and Icelandic downies. At first, the dark portions of small downies have a delicate, almost iridescent sheen, which disappears rapidly. Photos of Icelandic downies: still in nest—Wildfowl Trust 13th *Rept.* (1962); head pattern of 4 large downies—*Brit. Birds* 61 no. 5, pl. 30 (1968) and 63 no. 10, pl. 71 (1970), same photo again in Gudmundsson (1971).

▶   ♂ ♀ Juv. Plumage (entire feathering), appears first on scapulars and flanks, at age about 3 weeks, and present overall with only traces of down remaining on head by age 30 days (Derscheid 1941); "almost completely feathered when one month old" and "reach full size and are fully feathered in approximately six weeks" (Carr 1969), both authors referring to rapid development of captives. Apparently the entire Juv. feathering is retained for some time in wild birds. Not a white-bellied Plumage. **Bill** dark lead color; **iris** dark brown. Blended **head** pattern that includes poorly defined whitish patches above eye, below eye (variable in size), and auricular (small); remainder of head–neck more or less smoke gray, darkest on crown. **Upperparts** variably brownish olive, darkest on rump, and with medium buffy brown scapulars. **Underparts** breast more or less brownish, the feathers subterminally barred darker and margined paler (toward buff); belly and abdomen palish, the feathers having a quite dark subterminal area and pale ends; under tail coverts quite dark with pale tips. **Tail** dusky brownish, the feathers with notched ends. **Wing** differs from the later Basic in being entirely brownish, including coverts; it differs from ♀ Def. Basic in having the primaries and secondaries more muted brownish (not as dark), innermost secondaries shorter and narrower, and upper coverts smaller.

NOTES   A col. pl. in J. C. Phillips (1925) showed the ♂ and ♀ Juv. as having some evident differences, but the birds depicted are in Basic I; whether the sexes differ in Juv. is unknown.

325

▶   ♂ Basic I Plumage (apparently all feathering, excepting all but innermost feathers of wing), evidently begins to appear some weeks after the Juv. is fully developed. However, drakes with at least the head in Basic I are known from EARLY SEPT. on. A clear-cut rather than blended pattern. Earliest white-bellied Plumage. **Head** and neck grayish brown, paling on chin and throat; whitish malar patch that becomes more distinct after some gray-brown feather tips wear off; white loreal spot; larger white auricular spot (size of all these light areas is variable). **Upperparts**, including scapulars, grayish brown, the feathers with sharply delineated paler (somewhat brownish) margins; **underparts** breast dark like dorsum, sides and flanks brownish gray, sometimes darker, the feathers with broad pale margins; lower breast to vent white; under tail coverts evenly dark. Part or all of the Juv. **tail** generally is succeeded by dark, pointed Basic I feathers well along in fall or by early winter. In the **wing** the innermost secondaries are short.

▶   ♂ Alt. I Plumage (all feathering excepting the tail and all but innermost feathers of wing, but perhaps sometimes a lesser amount acquired), generally begins to appear by some time in OCT., is completed by EARLY WINTER, and retained until the following SUMMER.

The first conspicuous evidence of incoming Alt. I is white in the crescent area on forepart of face, then in the stripe area on forward sides. Apparently this Plumage differs from later Alts. thus: the darkest areas on head–neck are not clear black; less and paler rusty on crown; chin and throat not clear black; white collar often broken in front; in various white areas many feathers have narrow gray margins which may wear off; the scapulars (they come in gradually, some present beginning in Oct.) have less white; rump not as dark; on sides and flanks some feathers dull rusty with very fine dark vermiculations, others quite gray with rusty cast to tips. Apparently some individuals retain some Basic I, especially part of the venter, until at least into spring. Most of the Juv. wing is retained.

NOTES   Bengtson and Ulfstrand (1971) stated that yearling drakes, i.e., those in Alt. I, have "duller" Plumage than older drakes and so are distinguishable afield from the latter. The field work of these authors was done inland, however, and it is not clearly established that yearling drakes go inland.

The young ♂ ♂ that Bent (1925) saw in the Aleutians in June, judging from his description, already had begun molting into Basic II rather than being "especially backward" in completing the 1st cycle.

▶   ♀ Basic I Plumage (inclusive feathering as ♂ Basic I), timing as ♂—i.e., a first FALL Plumage. Apparently differs from Def. Basic in being more toward slaty brown overall, flanks somewhat grayer, and innermost secondaries shorter. Most of the Juv. wing is retained.

▶   ♀ Alt. I Plumage (inclusive feathering as ♂ Alt. I), acquired beginning in LATE FALL, sometimes later, and retained until SPRING. As later Alts., so far as known; most of the Juv. wing, with its narrow coverts, retained; also the Basic I tail.

▶   ♀ Basic II Plumage—although, when a year old, ♀ ♀ still retain most of the Juv. wing, they are indistinguishable afield from older ♀ ♀ at the same season.

NOTES   In both sexes, the feathering acquired in the 2nd cycle is similar to that of later cycles, although some individuals perhaps might have slight quantitative changes thereafter. According to Millais (1913a), the drake even after acquiring Alt. II is not as richly colored as later, but Derscheid (1941) stated that captive-reared individuals of known age were in "perfect plumage" when 20 mo. old.

Capt. Cartwright, in his Labrador journal, recorded that, at the St. Peter's Is. (ne. of outer end of Strait of Belle Isle) on July 29, 1770, he shot 7 "lords and ladies" which "were in full moult could not fly, but they were very fat" (C. W. Townsend 1911). Since he got both sexes, one suspects that the birds were yearling prebreeders in Basic II feathering.

**Measurements** 12 ♂ (6 Iceland, 1 Greenland, 3 Labrador, 2 Me.): BILL 25–29 mm., av. 27; WING 197–209, av. 205; TAIL (4 worn, 75–89) 94–102, av. of all, 93; TARSUS 36–39, av. 37.9; 10 ♀ (4 Iceland, 2 Labrador, 1 Nfld., 1 N.B., 2 Me.): BILL 25–27 mm., av. 25.8; WING 178–205, av. 192; TAIL (worn, 72) 73–89, av. of all 82.3; TARSUS 33–38, av. 36.2 (ETS). For another Atlantic series, WING meas. over the curve, see Witherby (1939); and for meas. by age ("young" and "adult") and sex, and with flattened WING, mainly of Icelandic and Greenland birds, see Schiøler (1926).

Among meas. given by Dickinson (1953) are these, for drakes: 32 Atlantic birds BILL 24.5–28, av. 26.3 flattened WING 189–208, av. 201.1, and 35 Pacific–Bering birds BILL 26–30 mm., av. 27.4, and WING 195–211, av. 202.8. Rand (1948b) gave BILL for 9 ♂ Atlantic birds (some are same ones measured by ETS) as 25–26.5 mm., av. 25.5, and 10 Pacific as 26–28.5, av. 27.1.

**Weight** of Alaskan birds: 9 "adult" ♂ taken June 2–Aug. 2 weighed 636–770 gm., av. 687, and 8 "adult" ♀ June–early Aug., 520–594, av. 557.7; and a "young" [yearling] ♂ on June 11 weighed 665 gm. (R. Rausch, P. Stettenheim).

In Iceland, 2 ♀ on rivers in early June weighed 485 and 496 gm. and a ♀ on a river on Sept. 20 accompanied by fledged young weighed 682 gm. (Gudmundsson 1971).

In N. Am. 5 ♂ av. 1.5 lb. (.68 kg.), max. 1.6 (.72 kg.) and 4 ♀ av. 1.2 lb. (.54 kg.), max. 1.3 (.59 kg.) (A. L. Nelson and Martin 1953).

Four ducklings, artificially incubated and newly hatched: 29.1–36.7 gm. (Smart 1965a).

**Hybrids** none reported.

**Geographical variation** Pacific–Bering birds apparently av. very slightly larger than Atlantic birds, although only bill length and its height at base generally are mentioned. In drakes everywhere, the amount of rusty coloring on head, size of white and black markings, and other details of feathering, are matters of Plumage (hence, to some extent, age) and individual variation. There seems to be no adequate justification for recognizing subspecies, as was done by W. S. Brooks (1915). Various persons have tried, but nobody seems to have improved on Stejneger (1885) who compared drakes from the Commander Is., Alaska, and "from the Atlantic shores, without finding any tangible difference." RSP

FIELD IDENTIFICATION   Very small and stocky; all dark at a distance; very buoyant on the water; tail often up-angled. None of our other ducks, not even mergansers, swim and fly in such compact little groups. Or they scatter somewhat on the sea and each bird follows its predecessor after an apparently measured interval in executing the same maneuver—altering course, diving, and so on. At various molting and wintering places, where many birds are present, they still tend to be in little groups or parties. Harlequins seldom mingle very long with other waterfowl. Much of the year they are not at all wary; in some places inland, as in Iceland (where they are protected), they are unbelievably tame.

Harlequins fly rapidly and with seeming purpose, very closely bunched, generally low over the sea or close to the surface of streams and rivers. They follow inland water-courses, no matter how crooked, rather than taking short cuts over dry terrain. They swim at times with jerky (pointing, not pumping) movements of the head; they stand in shallows and stand or sit on rocks and logs in streams or ashore or, in their contranuptial habitat, on ledges close to the surf.

At a distance on the sea, Harlequins appear small headed and thick necked (reverse of Oldsquaws). Drakes begin wearing their remarkable and variegated pattern well along in their first fall and wear it thereafter except for midsummer or later into fall (see the preceding section for the somber Basic Plumages). At close range and in direct sun-light, drakes are a vivid blue, broken by white stripes and patches, but Harlequins dwell where skies are cloudy and so they usually seem dark and quite colorless. The white on side of mantle shows up farthest on overcast days. The ♀ is mostly dark in all seasons, with white patches on the head (most white is in front of eye), white belly (fall to spring), and no light area in either surface of wing. Early Plumages of both sexes are quite ♀-like and, in general, differ thus from young Oldsquaws: more distinct auricu-lar patch, larger light area below eye, and light (white in Basic I, in fall) area on venter, most evident in flight, is smaller. RSP

VOICE   Quite noisy at times, but most calls are not far-carrying. Few utterances are even remotely ducklike. The following evidently includes variants of certain calls and/or different renderings of the same call.

Drake—there is no better comparison of any waterfowl voice than the likening of the usual call of ♂ Harlequins to the squeaking of fighting mice. In Me. in winter a "squeaking note like mice," hence the vernacular name "sea-mice" (Norton 1896). When Nodding, utters a high-pitched note, single or trilled, reminiscent of a "group of fighting mice" (Myres, in Johnsgard 1965). During forward action of Head-throw, a shrill whistling, descending in cadence, beginning with 2 long notes and ending in a trill (Bretherton 1896). A low piping whistle, reminiscent of a sandpiper (Alford 1920). In flights in groups in 2nd week in July in Iceland, a Harlequin occasionally would utter a "musical call-note which always reminded me of the distant trumpeting of a Whooper [*Cygnus cygnus*]" (Pool 1962). In spring in Iceland a low *giäk* or *gia* (Faber 1822). A hoarse *hu* or *hu-ek* when mate is nest-site hunting. A low hoarse *hu* or *heh heh* (Millais 1913a). A mated drake, inland in spring, uttered a loud clear *qua qua qua* (indefinite series) or occasionally a single note, particularly loud and clear; the same drake when with its mate, "carried on a low, chatty conversation," somewhat resembling calls of the Coot (*Fulica americana*) (Michael and Michael 1922). Drake while pursuing a flying ♀ *oy-oy-oy-oy* rapidly repeated, usually 7–8 times (Saunders, in Bent 1925). Alarm note of drake a soft *drüt* (Salomonsen 1950). A hissing of ♂♂ when fighting in winter (Turner, in J. C. Phillips 1926).

Duck—a croak, modified in various ways (Phillips); a harsh *ek ek ek ek* (Millais 1913a) uttered when nest-site hunting; a softer version of the drake's *gia* (Hantzsch 1905); low, croaking, somewhat ravenlike (Nicholson 1930); when both sexes present and drakes were Wing-flapping, the ducks uttered a very high-pitched staccato call, not a whistle, rather like the call of the Least Tern (*Sterna albifrons*) (Smith, in Johnsgard 1965). Hantzsch also mentioned a fine *du* and soft *da* as warning notes. RSP

HABITAT Of the species. As a breeder, the Harlequin is primarily boreal–subarctic, but also extends beyond northward into the low-arctic (Greenland, se. Baffin I., nw. Alaskan mainland, St. Lawrence I.) and to other relatively or entirely treeless areas (Iceland, n. Ungava, Alaska Pen., the Pribilofs, Aleutians, Commander Is., and elsewhere), and southward in montane environment in both w. N. Am. and e. Asia.

**Summer** requirements inland: shallow fast water, plentiful aquatic food, and sheltered nest sites. Nowhere dependent on when areas first become free of snow and ice, being a late nester. Especially in the N. Pacific–Bering area, it is likely that some Harlequins nest very close to the sea. In some mountainous areas in both N. Am. and e. Asia the Harlequin evidently nests along fast streams up through closed forest and then open forest, to valleys having patches of willow or alder, then perhaps not beyond on alpine terrain. There may be less food in the upper reaches of streams. Elsewhere, as in Greenland, it nests in tundra environment, far beyond the s. limits of the permafrost zone.

In Iceland, glacial rivers contain little food and so are used only as migration thoroughfares; the birds nest along other rivers, which contain abundant zooplankton, notably insect larvae; details in Gudmundsson (1971).

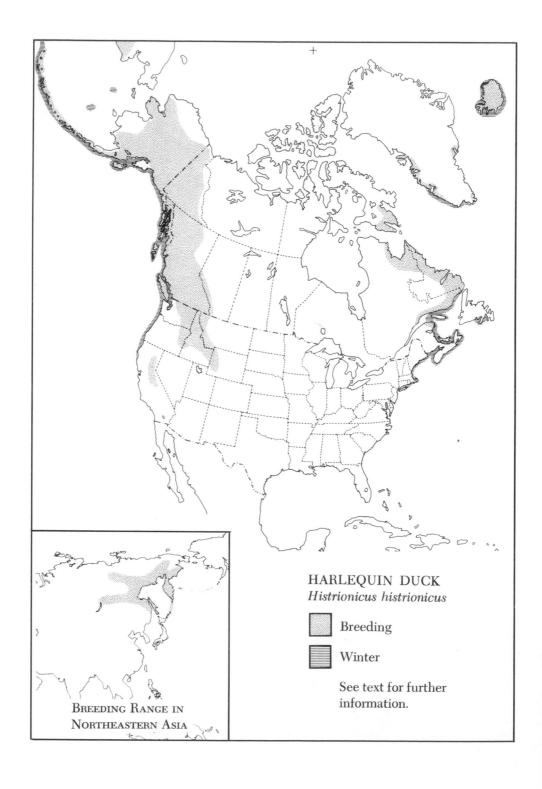

HARLEQUIN DUCK
*Histrionicus histrionicus*

Breeding

Winter

See text for further
information.

BREEDING RANGE IN
NORTHEASTERN ASIA

**Summer–fall** In early summer, prebreeders come into fjords, river mouths, even sheltered bays, and a few may go inland. But soon they move away, to relatively secure places on the sea where there is a rich bottom fauna on which they feed. Mature drakes later, and postbreeding ♀ ♀ not until fall, also go to sea, some probably joining prebreeders there. In parts of Alaska some mature birds remain in sheltered bays, some even on nearby lagoons and lakes.

In **winter** on marine waters along surf-pounded rocky coasts—not in sheltered bays and fjords, but instead where water is 1–2 fathoms deep, turbulent, and bottom fauna abounds. In w. N. Am. a few remain inland all year (Bent 1925) where warm springs or rapid current prevent freezing, but they do not remain inland in Iceland. RSP

**DISTRIBUTION** (See map.) Various published maps are useful: J. C. Phillips (1925) for general information, but shows breeding range extending too far n. in w. Greenland; Voous (1963) for total breeding range; Godfrey (1966) for breeding distribution in Canada; and Flint et al. (1968) for the same in e. Asia. Useful texts for the Palearctic include Tougarinov (1941), Dementiev and Gladkov (1952, 1960), and Vaurie (1965).

A similarity of breeding ranges of the Harlequin and Barrow's Goldeneye has been commented on by some authors. The Harlequin is a more northerly bird, however, and it also nests in e. Asia, a major segment of its range.

South of its main areas of breeding distribution, the Harlequin nests locally in montane environment—in N. Am. down into the conterminous U.S. and in e. Asia to the nw. Baikal district.

Whatever may have been its distribution in past geologic time, the Harlequin presently is in scattered, more or less disjunct, units. The Atlantic and the Pacific–Bering birds may be entirely separated, although a few individuals do straggle into the intervening area (interior N. Am.) and so might cross from one side to the other. Gudmundsson (1971) theorized that the Harlequins that have reached the Brit. Isles may have come from Iceland, Greenland, or even e. N. Am., but that the birds that have occurred in the White Sea, the Baltic, continental Europe, and Spitzbergen, probably came from ne. Siberia. (Compare with w. Palearctic distribution of Steller's Eider.)

Distribution is discussed below by geographical areas for convenience, since the birds occur in each geographical area where they nest all year round (have much overlap in seasonal distribution) and each is more or less separate.

ICELAND Widely scattered as a **breeder**, wherever there are small or large swift rivers having clear water and containing food, from near the coast to any elevation in the interior. There are concentrations only in a few places where aquatic food is very abundant. The total number of breeding pairs was estimated by Gudmundsson (1971) to hardly exceed 5,000; see his paper for map of breeding localities and concentrations. In **summer** prebreeders are on surrounding marine waters, a very few perhaps inland briefly before returning to the sea. In **winter** on marine waters all around Iceland, near rugged portions of the coast and seldom in sheltered places; probably in greatest numbers on the w. and sw. coast. Known wintering localities were mapped by Gudmundsson (1971).

E. ATLANTIC, EUROPE, AND VICINITY **Stragglers** Brit. Isles—less than a dozen

331

acceptable records. Spitzbergen—pair in July 1906. Faeroes—an old record. Fennoscandia—surprisingly few records, but these include the Baltic area; there are 2 or more records of occurrence eastward in the White Sea. Europe down to the n. Mediterranean—various records, some dating back many decades; easternmost are for Poland and Czechoslovakia and southernmost is for Italy.

GREENLAND  **Breeds** at a few places near the e. coast, notably Lindenow Fjord and in Angmagssalik Dist. They nest in fair numbers near the w. coast, from Julianehaab Dist. n. into the Holsteinborg Dist., perhaps occasionally in s. Upernavik Dist. In **summer** prebreeders are scattered along the w. coast, limits unknown. In **winter** in w. Greenland s. of the Holsteinborg Dist. **Straggler** to Scoresby Sd. in ne. Greenland.

E. N. AM.  **Breeding**  Baffin I.—a few in se. part. Ungava Pen.—around Ungava Bay and southeastward down through Labrador (center of abundance northerly) and apparently a few inland from the N. Shore of the outer Gulf of St. Lawrence; probably a very few far in the interior of Ungava (Indian House Lake); a few nest inland from the e. coast of Hudson Bay; details in Todd (1963). Gaspé Pen.—a record of preflight young. (Nfld.—aside from old and questionable hearsay reports of nesting, there are no inland records of this species.) In **summer** prebreeders are on marine waters, from the outer N. Shore of the Gulf of St. Lawrence northward (limits unknown). **Winter** n. limits unknown, perhaps outer Gulf of St. Lawrence; regular winterer in Nfld. at C. St. Mary's and probably elsewhere; winters around the Maritimes and into the Gulf of Me., apparently nowhere in more than appreciable numbers; a very few scattered, and not present annually, to Long I., N.Y., rarely to N.J.

**Straggler** in Hudson Bay to an island e. of the main Belcher group (♂ shot Sept. 2, 1927). Has occurred inland to L. Ontario, the Niagara R., L. Erie, and Ohio (more westerly stragglers inland in N. Am. are listed below). Southernmost localities: Mount Pleasant, S.C.; in Fla., reports of sightings plus a specimen from the ne. coast (♂, Matanzas Inlet, Feb. 21, 1967) (L. E. Williams, Jr., 1968) and reported seen Nov., 1971–March 1972 farther s. at Miami (*Am. Birds* **26** 594 1972.); Texas—pair seen at Rockport on Jan. 14, 1945 (C. Hagar 1945).

W. N. AM.  **Breeds** in conterminous U.S.; a few in mountainous terrain down into Cal., perhaps formerly into Colo. W. Canada—on the mainland through B.C. and across into the edge of Alta., n. to near the arctic coast of Yukon Terr.; also on various Pacific is., including Vancouver and the Queen Charlottes. Alaska—on the se. mainland and various is.; apparently absent from the Kenai Pen.; scattered breeder in the Alaskan interior (forested to alpine areas), n. to the cent. Brooks Range and to localities in approximately the same latitude westward, farthest nw. (Childs 1969) being the C. Lisburne area. Breeds in the s. side of the Alaska Pen. and evidently on many of the Aleutian Is., also on some is. in Bering Sea: St. Lawrence I., probably the Pribilofs. **Summering** prebreeders occur from B.C. northward in Pacific waters and beyond in Bering Sea (limits unknown). Flocks of molting postbreeding drakes occur n. at least to St. Lawrence I.

In **winter** about is. in Bering Sea, all along the Aleutians (a center of abundance), and down the N. Am. Pacific coast to n. Cal.; a few may winter inland on open waters in nw. conterminous U.S.

**Straggler** n. to Barter I. in Beaufort Sea near the Alaska–Canada boundary and rarely s. to s. Cal.; also down into interior N. Am.—w. Mackenzie (e. to Great Slave

L.), Alta., Sask., and Man. (stragglers in Ont. and Que. were mentioned earlier); also interior Cal., Idaho, N.D., Minn., Wis., Mich., Nebr., Iowa, Ill., Ind., Kans., and Mo.

HAWAII  Specimen from Laysan in 1906 (Bryan and Greenway 1944).

E. ASIA  On the Chuckchee Pen. the Harlequin "undoubtedly nests" at inland places and near the s. coast; singles and small numbers of molting birds are found on this coast in summer; it is abundant in Kresta Bay in spring; there are no records for the n. side of the peninsula nor for Wrangel I. (Portenko 1972).

Reports for the Commander Is. have been somewhat at variance. Stejneger (1885) stated that large numbers of Harlequins were present **all year**, that there were large assemblies throughout spring, "solid flocks" at Bering I. as late as the middle of June and, at Copper I. on July 1, flocks of "adult" ♂ ♂ "all in their most beautiful plumage." He stated that the Harlequin was not known to nest there, the flocks remaining through the summer being of birds "not propagating" for some reason or another. He suspected that the flocks observed July 1 and later, and comprised exclusively of adult drakes, were birds that had left their mates incubating in interior Kamchatka. Kartaschev (1961) reported the Harlequin to be the 5th most common bird (among 53 species), and by far the most numerous duck, in a census in June–Aug. 1960. Marakov (1966), who very likely was familiar with Stejneger's account, indicated that most of those present in summer are young birds (prebreeders) from elsewhere—the islands are "uniquely international" for the Harlequin—and scattered pairs nest along mt. streams. There is agreement among recent authors that this species **breeds** in the Commanders. In **winter** it is plentiful on the sea.

To the west, and stated oversimply, **breeders** are concentrated in the Okhotsk drainage basin and have "spilled over" various heights of land into the upper reaches of adjoining river systems; Harlequins also breed on the Pacific side of Kamchatka and for a distance northward. They nest on some is. in the Okhotsk Sea area, including s. Sakhalin; just how far down the Kuril chain (which forms the outer boundary of the Okhotsk Sea) they nest seems to be debatable. They are present in all seasons in the s. Kurils and nesting is suspected but not proven (Nechaev 1969).

In **summer** there are molters on marine waters in and n. beyond breeding limits; many molt all along the coasts of Anadyr Gulf (Dementiev and Gladkov 1952). A few (age-class?) molt in s. L. Baikal.

In **winter** occurs along coasts of s. Kamchatka, the Kurils, and around Sakhalin I., coasts around the Sea of Japan in decreasing numbers southward, and outer coasts of Japan from cent. Honshu northward.

**Straggler** inland in e. Asia beyond L. Baikal and s. beyond the larger Japanese is. to the Riukius.

Reported as **fossil** from the Pleistocene of Sweden (2 localities) and in N. Am. from Cal.; from **archaeological sites** in Alaska (3 island and 3 mainland); details in Brodkorb (1964a). RSP

MIGRATION  Emphasis on Nearctic data. Shortest seasonal shifts may be primarily in elevation, as where Harlequins go to sea from nearby mt. streams. Elsewhere the distance is longer, but Harlequins, by and large, are not long-distance travelers. Apparently, for some breeders (as in interior Iceland), the distance drakes fly from nesting areas to marine molting places may exceed any distance from the latter to wintering localities (or possibly the 2 coincide). That is, molt migration is longer than subsequent fall migration in some instances. Another point to be kept in mind is that, considering the distances some Harlequins have straggled, and that there are very few banding recoveries, there are almost no data on how far individual birds travel.

**Spring**  This is the general pattern. Flocks come together to form assemblies, sometimes of at least several hundred birds. These contain breeders (paired or mostly paired) and prebreeders (unpaired). The assemblies move toward coasts nearest to their nesting areas, into bays, fjords, and toward river and stream mouths. Then the breeders (and sometimes a few prebreeders?) go inland; then the prebreeders move away on the sea, to molting areas. The time of going inland varies; certainly it begins by very early April at southerly localities in w. N. Am., but may continue into early June in some colder parts of Alaska; flocks present on the Am. side of Bering Strait beginning on May 28 (A. Bailey 1943). The Harlequin arrives in Ungava Bay by May. 25 (Turner 1885).

In Iceland in April, the birds leave exposed coasts and go to bays, river mouths, etc. In late April and May they start ascending the now swollen rivers, gradually, flying and swimming. It is a kind of slow and hesitant upstream movement very different from a direct flight to nesting areas. The time of arrival at a particular place varies little from year to year, as compared with variation from place to place. (Based on Gudmundsson 1971.)

The above pattern must be modified in some mountainous areas in w. N. Am., also probably in various other places (some Greenland localities, parts of Ungava, part of breeding range in E. Siberia) in that pairs must make overland flights to some nesting localities.

**Molt migration**  As indicated earlier, the terminal portion of spring movement of most prebreeders on marine waters is to molting places. Presumably they arrive, depending on locality, from some time in May into June. If any prebreeders go inland, they leave early and go to sea. While ♀ ♀ are incubating, their mates gather in parties of a few to perhaps 2 score individuals and soon, usually in late June or early July in much of the species' breeding range, fly to marine waters to molt. Thus the drakes are at inland nesting areas not more than 4–5 weeks. Some failed-breeding ♀ ♀ may leave soon after. The ♀ ♀ that produce broods stay with them inland or sometimes families drift downstream and may not reach the sea until the young are well feathered. The postbreeding ♀ ♀ fly to molting places and are the last birds to become flightless. In some se. Alaskan localities, also probably in the Aleutians, where distance from nesting place to the sea is short and more or less navigable, ♀ ♀ arrive on the sea with preflight broods by early Aug., well ahead of the time when the adult ♀ ♀ begin their wing molt.

One cannot list molting areas because information is not specific and flocks are widely scattered. Interestingly, there may be more prebreeders on the sea than breeders ashore along the n. side of the outer Gulf of St. Lawrence. It is of interest also that considerable molt migration is in a northward direction; molters are numerous around the edge of Anadyr Gulf and midsummer is the time when Harlequins are recorded n. of breeding range elsewhere.

**Fall**  Postmolting travel presumably is not very extensive in Icelandic and Greenland waters, but there is a withdrawal from northerly areas (partial withdrawal in Iceland). Birds banded as preflight young on the River Laxá in the Mývatn region of Iceland have been recovered as follows: one banded Aug. 21, 1928 was shot 285 km. away on the sw. coast at Akranes on Nov. 14 of the same year; two others subsequently were taken on the n. coast (Gudmundsson 1971).

In e. N. Am., n. to include s. Baffin I., the total number of Harlequins cannot be very large; the number that travels s. to Nfld., the Maritimes, and farther southward probably is in the hundreds, certainly not now in thousands. There is movement from some time in Sept. to, in New Eng., some time in Dec. Timing is about the same on the Pacific coast of conterminous U.S. In the Aleutians, the birds begin to appear at wintering areas, in small flocks, around mid-Sept.

NOTES There are various published statements regarding sex segregation of Harlequins, most of which leave something to be desired. Parties of postbreeding drakes go to sea, hence are separated from their mates; the separation may continue for quite some time, because drakes complete their wing molt and again are flying at the time mature ♀ ♀ are flightless. Yet the sexes must come together sooner or later. On the coast at Comox, B.C., A. Brooks (in J. C. Phillips 1925) noted that drakes were in great preponderance at the end of March and no "young" birds had been seen for 2 months or more. There appears to be some sex segregation among yearling prebreeders on the sea, but statements are conflicting and precise information is lacking.

Considering the distances that a few Harlequins have traveled from their natural range, one wonders whether there also may be regular movement between e. Greenland and Iceland, or between w. Greenland and Labrador or places farther southward. In the Commanders and outer Aleutians it would seem possible that some winterers come from the Asian mainland. RSP

BANDING STATUS Nineteen Harlequins had been banded in Alaska through 1964 and there have been no recoveries (data from Bird Banding Laboratory). A few have been banded in Iceland and 3 of the recoveries are mentioned in the preceding section. A very small number has been banded in Greenland and one bird recovered there. RSP

REPRODUCTION Apparently, in both sexes earliest **breeding age** is 2 years. The only studies of reproductive behavior have been made in Iceland, where Harlequins are plentiful at a very few localities and are easy to observe; there is relatively little information from all other parts of the species' range. The following is a composite account, fragments of information from elsewhere being added to Icelandic data.

Since breeders are paired when they go inland in spring, at least most **pair formation** must occur earlier. Yet there is little information on activities during the winter season. In the flocks, usually of a few to perhaps 30 birds, there are periods of much activity: diving by both sexes, and jerky head movements; drakes swim in a tight circle or rotate on the water; they quarrel in the close presence of ♀ ♀, sometimes attacking one another vigorously, and there is much Wing-flapping and squeaky calling. At Comox, B.C., drakes chased ♀ ♀ all winter, usually on the wing; 5 to 9 drakes would flutter about after a single ♀, sometimes flying thus as high as 75 ft. above the water (A.

335

Brooks, in J. C. Phillips 1915). Such activities, presumably begun in the early (social) phase of display, are among those that are continued long after pair formation, i.e., are also used in bond maintenance.

When the birds go inland in spring, it is generally believed that the prebreeders (yearlings) remain on the sea and move away to summering areas. While the evidence is weak that any yearlings go inland, this is especially difficult to establish for ♀ ♀ because they are not distinguishable in appearance from older birds. Whether yearling drakes are distinguishable is conjectural.

Except for the information given above, the known repertoire of displays has been described almost entirely from or near nesting areas, i.e., after paired breeders are inland. Displays are relatively simple, Vocalizing is extensive, quite varied, and not yet adequately reported in context of displays, hence the extent of it is not indicated in the following paragraphs.

**Displays of the duck**  NODDING a variably modified pointing, the bill horizontal and moved in an elliptical path (Myres, in Johnsgard 1965); when a bird Nods while swimming against the current, the jerking and thrusting of the head give a false impression of having to strain to move forward. INCITING after the manner of goldeneyes; the ♀ lowers her chin, even to contact with water, and turns her head to one side and then the other (Bengtson 1966a). WING-FLAP as in the drake (see below), but much less frequent. BILL-SHAKE has been noticed only as a precopulatory display.

**Displays of the drake**  Michael and Michael (1922) observed a mated pair on a river, bobbing (Nodding) and turning, swirling around one another, touching bills, and uttering "chatty" sounds. Others have noted pairs or small groups, at least the drakes more or less ROTATING or pivoting and thereby rendering conspicuous all elements of their remarkable pattern. SHORT FLIGHT fluttering, as described above among winter activities. NODDING as described above for the duck; done in mild alarm, threat (which spaces pairs or individuals), and in display toward the ♀ (Myres, in Johnsgard 1965). If threat does not suffice, the head is lowered while pointed toward the opponent, or there may be actual attack, sometimes with open bill (Bengtson 1966a). Both sexes thus point, but drakes do most of the fighting. HEAD-THROW was described well by Betherton (1896): the head is thrown back against the dorsum, the bill opened wide and pointed vertically when the head is back and then, as the head is thrown forward and downward, the drake utters a high-pitched call that carries well; at this time the wings are opened slightly and drooped. BILL-SHAKE laterally, in water (Bengtson, in Johnsgard 1965; Bengtson 1966a). HEAD-SHAKE laterally, as in Black Scoter (Smith, in Johnsgard 1965). WING-FLAP a bird, swimming or standing, rears upward and flaps twice (rapidly); the sound is less than and not as sharp as, for example, that of the drake Common Eider. As noted where Harlequins are numerous in Iceland, loafing groups may be quiet for a while and then, for a short period, various individuals Wing-flap; it seems to be somewhat more prevalent when there is a mild degree of interaction of individuals, as when birds (either or both sexes) are arriving and/or departing. PEERING under water, as though seeking food; the drake thus dips when excited, then assumes a threat (Nodding) attitude and occasionally opens his bill while squeaking (Bengtson 1966a). PREEN-DORSALLY and PREEN-BEHIND-THE-WING have been observed (Bengtson 1966a).

336

**Copulation** has been described as seen April 3 on Vancouver I. (Pearse 1945), April 7 on the Merced R. in Cal. (Michael and Michael 1922), May 25 in the Coast Mts. of B.C. (R. Y. Edwards MS), June 7 in McKinley Park, Alaska (A. Murie 1963), and at various times in Iceland (Bengtson 1966a). The pair is apart from other Harlequins, on moving or quiet water. Mutual Nodding sometimes is prolonged, even to 30 min.; then both Bill-shake (in water) rapidly. The drake may mount immediately or, in other instances, he rushes toward the ♀ with his bill open, squeaking; sometimes, perhaps when the ♀ does not give the appropriate response immediately, there are numerous rushes over a considerable period. One drake reared upright (without Wing-flap) 5 times in less than 1 min. The drake seizes the nape of the PRONE ♀ and mounts; copulation is brief and without vocalizing. After the birds separate, the drake may more or less Rotate on the water, but no special postcopulatory display has been reported.

Harlequins not only return to the same stream in successive years, but to the same area on it; they often reoccupy the same loafing area. Twenty-two of 33 identifiable individuals in Iceland came back to within about a hundred meters of their nesting sites of the previous year (Bengtson 1972b). When they first arrive they are very restless; they fly to and fro, the ♀♀ uttering *ek-ek-ek-ek* and the drakes responding with a low hoarse *hu* or *hu-ek*. In Iceland in late May–early June, ♀♀ spent about 30% more time feeding than did ♂♂, with 3 peaks of activity: early morning, evening, and a lesser one in the low light around midnight (Bengtson 1972b). The drake follows the duck as she "prospects" for a nest site, on islets and stream banks, examining every cavity and sheltered spot; both birds are agile and noisy (Bengtson 1966a).

**Nest site**   Not a hole nester, but Harlequins often use sheltered cavities after the manner of the Red-breasted Merganser. Usually the site is within 2 meters of water, but occasionally up to 20 meters away; islets and islands in streams and rivers are preferred. In Iceland, only 7 of 98 nests were more than 5 meters from water (Bengtson 1972b). The site chosen usually has shelter overhead—a recess in a stream bank, for example, or among lava blocks (Iceland), or under shrubs, trees (sometimes semiprostrate), or stranded debris. Occasionally it is in an open area, but under shrubbery or other low vegetation, or even quite exposed on a stream bar. Contrary to Delacour (1959), there is no proof that the Harlequin ever nests in tree cavities. A nest on the slope of Mt. Hood, Ore., was concealed among roots and debris 3 ft. above ground on a large stump that had stranded on a gravel bar (Jewett 1931).

The Harlequin is a solitary nester although, at a few places such as near the source of the River Laxá in Iceland, where food is remarkably plentiful, many pairs nest in relatively close proximity. For details of **nesting density** there, see Bengtson (1972a). As many as 2 dozen birds may be seen at a loafing site. In June 1963, on some rivers that flow into the Okhotsk Sea in E. Siberia, Kistschinskii (1968) found an av. of 11 pairs per 10 km. of river, probably a fairly high density.

Like the scoters, the Harlequin nests late. The **nest** usually consists of some grass or other fine vegetation and, beginning during the span of laying, an ample lining of **nest down** is added. The individual downs are rather large, about 30–35 mm. in diam., and variably gray-brown with off-white centers; any intermingled feathers are small, darkish brown, and usually have a well-defined subterminal white band.

The time to expect **full clutches** is indicated by the following information. Iceland—

the majority of ♀ ♀ near the source of the River Laxá begin laying in the last week in May, with slight annual variations, and some 5–10 days later at a locality not far distant; the total laying span extends to mid-July (Bengtson 1972b). Greenland—eggs June 24 (Bent 1925). "Labrador"—eggs June 3 and 10 (Bent). Ore.—May 2, a dead ♀ contained a fully formed egg (Gashwiler 1961); May 31, on slope of Mt. Hood, 6 eggs slightly incubated (Jewett 1931); and a full clutch by about June 20 near Frazier L. is indicated by a ♀ having 2 downies on July 21 (Gabrielson and Jewett 1940). Wash.—May 7 near Port Angeles, clutch of 7 (D. E. Brown 1924); May 26, near Longmire, clutch of 7 (Flett, in Jewett et al. 1953). Mont.—eggs June 10 (Bent 1925). B.C.—May 24, near Penticton, 7 eggs apparently well incubated, and on June 1, 7 advanced in incubation (Tait 1949). Nw. Canada—eggs June 30 at Mackenzie Bay (Bent 1925). Alaska—4 records June 13–July 1 (Bent). Kolyma Highlands in E. Siberia—clutches must be completed by late June, since Kistschinskii (1968) stated that the young usually are hatched around the end of July.

The eggs are laid at intervals of 1 or 2 days (Bengtson 1972b) and **clutch size** usually is 3–7 eggs and "seldom exceeds" 9 (Bengtson 1966a). Eleven and 12 eggs in Icelandic nests perhaps were joint layings by 2 or more ♀ ♀ (Gudmundsson, in Blaedel 1961). Seventy-seven complete clutches in n. Iceland contained 3–9, mean 5.7 eggs, with decrease in size of clutches laid as the seasons advanced (Bengtson 1972b). A clutch contained 11 Harlequin eggs plus 2 of the Red-breasted Merganser (Gudmundsson, in Blaedel 1961; Gudmundsson 1971).

Harlequin eggs are slightly larger than Oldsquaw eggs. One **egg** each from 20 clutches (15 Iceland, 2 "Labrador," 1 N.W.T., 2 Alaska) **size** length 57.23 ± 2.07 mm., breadth 41.13 ± 1.17, radii of curvature of ends 16.76 ± 1.56 and 11.12 ± 1.64; **shape** approximately subelliptical, elongation 1.38 ± 0.060, bicone −0.024, asymmetry +0.190 (FWP). The shell, which is thin, quite fragile, and smooth, has almost no gloss; **color** creamy yellow when fresh, but the delicate creamy tint soon vanishes. In 400 eggs measured (Bent 1925, Witherby 1939, Derscheid 1941, Schönwetter 1961, and herein by FWP), length varied 52–62 mm., breadth 37–44.5 and averages were larger for the various other series than for the 20 eggs reported herein. Data on 105 Icelandic eggs: length 50.2–62.4 mm. (mean 57.5) and breadth 39.0–43.3 (mean 41.3) (Gudmundsson 1971).

**Incubation** is by the duck, who covers her eggs before departing (usually twice/day) and definitely is known to feed actively when off duty. She is a tight sitter from the beginning and sometimes can be touched; she hisses and even tries to bite the intruder (Bengtson 1966a). In Ore., a boy lifted a ♀ from her nest, released her, and soon she was back on her eggs (Jewett 1931).

Seventy-six Icelandic eggs were sent to Belgium, placed under bantam hens, and 59 hatched; the shortest incubation period was 29¼ days, 27 hatched in 30½–30¾ days, and the longest period was 33 days (Derscheid 1941). Under wild ♀ ♀ in Iceland, in 4 clutches in which all eggs hatched, the period from laying of last egg to hatching of last was between 27 and 29 days, the mean **incubation period** being 28 days (Bengtson 1972b).

Again, data from n.-cent. Iceland (Bengtson 1972b). Hatching begins in early July, with peak about July 20–25, and continues to about Aug. 14. **Hatching success** is high;

of 89 nests, 77 (87%) were successful; in 4 years, success ranged from 84% to 91%. Of 504 eggs, 408 hatched, 70 were destroyed in nests, and 26 disappeared from unsuccessful nests or did not hatch. The mean number that hatched in successful nests was 5.3 and, for the total number of nests, was 4.6 eggs.

Some **replacement clutches** are probably laid, since there are some very late broods (Bengtson 1972b).

The duck is quite secretive at first and leads her **brood** to a quiet stretch of water; if she encounters danger, she flattens herself on the surface, utters a "jarring sound," and the young hide along the banks under overhanging vegetation (Bengtson 1966). There is high mortality among downies for the first 10–14 days, then it declines (Bengtson 1966a, 1972b). The small ducklings, although good divers, take a considerable portion of their food from the water's surface and also snatch insects from vegetation along the shoreline, but feed in the same manner as adults by the time they are half grown (Bengtson 1972b). Then they are out on main streams and are quite conspicuous.

Two authors have stated that the small ducklings have a trait of stretching their bills toward the bill of a foster parent as though anticipating being fed by the latter, and from this it has been presumed that the parent feeds them in the wild. Such movements, however, are merely pointing or incipient Nodding. Moody (in Delacour 1959) had difficulty in getting his few aviary-hatched ducklings to start eating, but Derscheid (1941), who reared a large number of them, apparently did not consider feeding to be a matter worth mentioning.

Since drakes leave early to molt on the sea, obviously they normally do not associate with ♀ ♀ accompanied by broods. A recorded exception pertains to a drake in Iceland in early Aug.; it still was in Alt. head–body feathering but, perhaps through some accident, had lost the primaries of the right wing only (J. G. Harrison 1967). A photo of the group containing this drake appeared in *Brit. Birds* **61** (5): pl. 30, 1968, and again in Gudmundsson (1971).

Apparently, throughout the Harlequin's breeding range, it is commonplace for 2 or even several families to combine; i.e., there are aggregations or crèches, sometimes containing young of several sizes. There is no pronounced quarreling by the attending ♀ ♀; also, ♀ ♀ are not known to try to "rob" broods from other ♀ ♀; failed breeders sometimes join in attending broods or gatherings (Bengtson 1966a). Kistschinskii (1968) regarded combining of broods as the usual situation in the Kolyma Highlands.

Many ♀ ♀ remain inland, with broods or assemblies; others leave the young before they can fly, presumably to go elsewhere and become flightless. In interior Iceland, not until the young can fly, in Sept., do they and the ♀ ♀ go to sea, according to Gudmundsson (in Blaedel 1961), who also reported that ♀ ♀ with flying young occasionally still are inland as late as Sept. 20. Yet at places where Harlequins nest along streams near the sea families evidently do reach salt water even when some broods are not many days old. In Kamchatka, 5 broods still were flightless, inland, as late as Sept. 28 (Dementiev and Gladkov 1952).

Faber (1826) stated that the downy stage lasts 40 days, which has been construed as defining age at first flight. Derscheid (1941) thought that the preflight period was considerably shorter, since his captive-reared young were fully feathered and only wisps of down remained on them at age 30 days. They develop rapidly; it seems likely that they

**attain flight** in the wild at age 5 to 6 weeks (compare with the Oldsquaw), rather than the 60–70 days that Gudmundsson (1971) suggested.

The reader is referred to the various papers by Bengtson, also Bengtson and Ulfstrand (1971), for much additional information. Included are such topics as a discussion of mature ♀ ♀ that go to breeding areas but do not nest and the role of food supply in controlling reproductive success in the Harlequin. The paper by Gudmundsson (1971) also is a fundamental source of data. RSP

SURVIVAL    The only data are for Iceland, as follows. Field observations at Svartá suggest an annual adult survival rate for ♀ ♀ to be about 65%. Considering that the Harlequin does not face the hazards of long migrations and is not hunted, the annual survival rate may be as high as 80%–85% (Bengtson 1972b).

As to downies, after a high mortality in the first 1 or 2 weeks or less (if there is adverse weather), losses decline; the number that survived to flight age varied in different years, being 40%–75% of young hatched. There is a decrease in clutch size, number of young produced, and number of mature ♀ ♀ that lay (i.e., there are more nonbreeders) in years when summer food is scarce. Low productivity of young is reflected the 2nd year following in a reduced increment of breeders. The subject was discussed by Bengtson (1966a, 1972a, 1972b, 1972c) and by Bengtson and Ulfstrand (1971). RSP

HABITS    Some of the older comparisons of various Harlequin habits with those of other N. Hemisphere ducks now leave something to be desired; various differences seem less than formerly reported. But these apparently are certainties: the Harlequin is suited admirably to water in swift motion—rapids in rivers and streams, basins at the foot of waterfalls, close proximity to surf-pounded marine ledges, and the birds spend considerable time out of the water, seeming then to be almost indolent in contrast to their vigor when active afloat. But dangerous living has its price. A person in Me. who had handled 88 birds in the flesh was impressed by the number of mended broken bones he found, the breakage presumably having occurred during dives in turbulent water (R. S. Palmer 1949).

It is in a way odd that a bird of turbulent water should engage in social, stereotyped, SPLASH-BATHING. In summer on the River Laxá in Iceland, at a place where drakes and off-duty ♀ ♀ gathered to loaf, birds of both sexes would move off into the shallow swift water, and even while being drenched by flying spray they partly immersed themselves and shuffled their wings with great vigor, sending up more spray. There was no calling. Mated birds kept together, both duck and drake bathing. It is contagious in a group, a social activity during the nesting season. Soon a number of birds are bathing; a short while later this activity ceased.

Winter parties of Harlequins generally are small, probably 5–30 birds being usual, but there are considerable numbers at some favored localities—for example, several hundred sometimes near C. St. Mary's, Nfld. Through spring, parties of Harlequins are particularly noisy and active.

Generally speaking, they keep to themselves. On Icelandic rivers in summer, much squeaking by Harlequin drakes usually indicates that a drake Barrow's Goldeneye has approached. The territorial Barrow's drives any feeding or loafing Harlequins away.

340

Elsewhere, at times, perhaps only from preference for the same habitat, Harlequins associate with Oldsquaws, scoters, and various eiders. Norton (1896) saw some "pay a visit of inspection" to eiders and scoters, but they quickly rejoined their own flock. Toward the end of May at C. Prince of Wales, Alaska, a small flock was with a band of King Eiders, diving for snails (A. Bailey 1943). Harlequins respond to the alarm calls of the Black-backed Gull (*Larus marinus*) by quickly taking flight (Norton).

A Harlequin vigorously starts to dive by springing upward and forward, then plunging downward and, usually, flips its wings out somewhat from the body before submerging. On the sea the birds in a group dive in sequence, one by one; soon none are in sight and then, after about 15–30 sec. or longer per individual, they come to the surface, apparently with considerable awareness of their relative positions. The tail is flat on the surface (as with the Oldsquaw) between dives, but it is more or less cocked during various displays and at other times. A common pattern, at least in winter, is a series of vigorous rapid dives, interspersed with very short pauses afloat, and afterward a longer period of rest. When thus idling, they are as buoyant as bubbles and sometimes so bunched that some may be (or at least appear to be) in physical contact, and they are very deliberate about just when to vanish into an oncoming wave so as to emerge in relatively calm water after the crest has swept on by. Ashore, they stand or walk about quite gracefully—more like a Smew or a shoal-water duck than a sea duck—or rest on their bellies. They are at home on ice floes. After a time, either from a firm footing or the sea, the group suddenly takes wing and, tightly bunched, flies to some other place. Their takeoff is not heavy, but instead like that of the Oldsquaw, and they fly swiftly and generally quite low over the water.

Inland in summer, they prefer not to cross land, but instead follow every bend of a crooked watercourse, traveling close to the surface. In Iceland they fly under, not over, bridges, according to Bengtson (1966a); in the present writer's experience there they usually but not always fly under.

In summer in Iceland, if Harlequins are mildly disturbed, they make pointing movements, then sidle into the water and often ride the current downstream. In alarm, the neck is stretched upward fully. They prefer to escape by swimming or diving, rather than flying. According to Bengtson (1966a), when going upstream, they 1 dive repeatedly, especially when crossing a river; 2 they swim against the current, often hugging the shore, or in the lee of a rock, where the current is less swift; and 3, if the current is too strong, they skitter along the surface or become fully airborne.

The Harlequin is so far as known a day feeder, the days being short in winter and, in the opposite season, there is continuous daylight in northerly parts of the species' range. Five feeding methods were noted by Michael and Michael (1922) when watching a single pair in spring in the swift clear waters of the Merced R. in Cal.: 1 wading in shallows along shore, prying among stones; 2 swimming with bill below the surface, the mandibles in constant motion after the manner of a feeding Shoveler; 3 up-ending in shallow water, in Mallard fashion, to reach bottom; 4 diving and then walking on the river bottom while submerged, like a dipper (*Cinclus*) against the swift current, poking among the stones; and 5 diving in deep water—springing forward and downward with wings out from the body and using them during descent. A variant of #2 is swimming with eyes submerged, merganserlike, seeking food and/or feeding on small subsurface

341

animal life in suspension (compare with Peering display; see "Reproduction"). A Harlequin may start its dive in any position relative to direction of stream flow, but it faces into the current immediately. The bird has remarkable ability to maintain station, frequently coming up close to where it submerged, regardless of current or turbulence. On the surface a bird swims with head motionless relative to its body, but with pointing movements if at all disturbed. In Iceland, 3 feeding methods have been noted on rivers: 1 skimming the surface and dipping the head under water, 2 diving (commonest), and 3 up-ending; the mean duration of a dive in shallow fresh water is about 4 times as long as the pause between dives; that is, a dive/pause ratio of 4:1, a measure of the adaptability of this species to feeding in fast water (Bengtson 1972b). Submergence may be longer on deeper marine waters; see, for example, Cahn (1947).

Rich (1907) stated that, if a shot is fired, sometimes a flying flock will plunge into the sea; in an instance that he reported, they then swam a distance while submerged and dashed from the water "at full speed." They dive from the wing without having been shot at and also have a trait of dropping into the water and then immediately taking off again (Norton 1896).

The Harlequin's unwariness is almost proverbial. They have been known to swim to within a few yds. of fishermen on streams; a pair came repeatedly to an anchored "floating lunch counter" to obtain bread (Michael and Michael 1922); and, on salt water in Alaska, Turner (1886) noted that swimming birds sometimes would merely move aside or fly a few yds. so as to allow a canoe to pass among them. They are less confiding early in the nesting season and again when molting in late summer and fall, but even then they are less shy than other waterfowl under similar circumstances.

At sea, feeding Harlequins tear loose mussels and barnacles and gather various free-swimming invertebrates that swarm in and out of crannies in ledges and among seaweed in and below the intertidal zone. Thirty-nine tiny shells of a gastropod found in a bird taken in Long I. (N.Y.) waters "could only have been obtained in such numbers by a sort of sifting of the bottom mud" (Whitfield 1894). These items are large in comparison to the aquatic stages of blackflies and midges that are eaten in summer in Icelandic rivers and elsewhere inland. The common denominator seems to be abundance of animal organisms, in or near water in rapid motion, smallness of size being irrelevant if the items are numerous enough.

As noted at beginning of Description, the Harlequin has a small fleshy growth at corner of gape. The Brown Teal (*Anas aucklandica*) has a flap of hardened skin, similarly located, perhaps as a protection against sharp appendages of armored isopods which are eaten (Weller 1975).

In former times, when there was more gunning for various sea ducks, more Harlequins were bagged. Now, for the most part, they are an incidental and infrequent target. They do not come to decoys readily. However, their tight bunching on the water and in flight renders it possible to kill several at a single shot. Bretherton (1896) explained how, at Kodiak I., by getting ready when all birds of a flock were submerged, a practiced gunner could bag 6 or 7 by picking them off in sequence as they rose to the surface. On Sakhalin I., if a person stands still on shore, Harlequins swim within gunshot range; in this way a great many were shot, in part for food (Munsterhjelm 1922). At least formerly, Harlequins were shot for food in the Aleutians.

As with scoters, there are authors who have a high regard for the Harlequin as a table bird, but on a consensus basis it is not a much better culinary prospect than the Old-squaw. Millais (1913a) stated that the flesh of the young, before they go to sea, is eatable. The decorative skins of drakes were reported by E. W. Nelson (1887) to be given as playthings by the Yukon Indians to their children. In Me., certain haunts of this bird are named in reference to its voice—Squeaker Cove and Squeaker Guzzle (Norton 1896).

There is not much information on predation on Harlequins. In Iceland in the nesting season, predators of some importance include the Raven (*Corvus corax*), mink (*Mustela vison*, escaped from captivity and now widespread), Parasitic Jaeger (*Stercorarius parasiticus*), and arctic fox (*Alopex lagopus*) (Bengtson 1972b). In the Commander Is., according to Marakov (1966), the Harlequins come ashore to sleep on rocks and are stalked and taken by arctic foxes. He stated that the Gyrfalcon (*Falco rusticolus*) is especially successful in hunting Harlequins during storms. The Harlequins fly low over the water; the Gyr awaits his opportunity and, shielded by the high breakers, suddenly flies at its prey and seizes it before it can drop into the sea.

The taking of eggs of Harlequins in Iceland formerly was a regular and legal practice, the law requiring that 4 eggs be left in the nest; see full discussion by Bengtson (1966a). The taking of birds or eggs and their export now is banned; a few birds are caught accidentally in fishnets; eggs from which to rear birds for aviculturalists still were being taken in the Mývatn dist. until very recently.

Given seasonal protection, the Harlequin increased in Iceland (J. C. Phillips 1925). Phillips also stated that, in 20–40 years, there had been a "very marked reduction" in Harlequin numbers on winter range in the Maritimes and New Eng., but not on the N. Am. Pacific coast. A decrease on the Atlantic side seems to have continued, for reasons unknown. Oil pollution may be a contributing factor. On Long I., N.Y., there was a small (and temporary?) increase after 1950 (Bull 1964). No changes in the Pacific–Bering area have been reported. The Harlequin now has legal protection in all seasons in Iceland and Greenland.

Among the older accounts of the species, that of J. C. Phillips (1925) may be the best; there is much of interest in Schiøler (1926). For later information, with relevant literature listed, see the paper by Gudmundsson and those authored or coauthored by Bengtson that have been referred to earlier in the present account. RSP

FOOD Almost entirely animal, the vegetable items usually being taken accidentally.

ICELAND There are scattered data, from Faber (1822) down to the present. From the sea: crabs (*Cancer pulex*), mollusks (*Nerita*, Littorinidae), fish eggs, and aquatic plants (Faber, Hantzsch 1905). First-year birds examined had eaten principally crustaceans, but also some mollusks; one stomach contained polychaete jaws (Gudmundsson 1971). In summer inland: at n.-cent. localities, almost the entire food of adults is Diptera (*Simulium*) larvae and pupae, which constitute the bulk of benthic animal food present; since small ducklings take relatively more food from the surface than do adults, their diet is slightly more varied; see Bengtson (1972b) for full details. Because suitable food is scarce, except locally and for brief periods, Harlequins are widely scattered except at a few places (Bengtson 1971a, 1972b, Bengtson and Ulfstrand 1971).

343

Also see discussion of food by Gudmundsson (1971), who mentioned some published statements that evidently are erroneous.

GREENLAND AND E. N. AM.    On salt water in Greenland, mollusks and crustaceans; inland, snails, fish spawn, and larvae of gnats (Salomonsen 1950). Two birds taken in summer at Bonaventure I., Que.: 1 mollusks (*Margarites helicinus* mostly, also *Mytilus edulis* and *Littorina palliata*) 80%, barnacles 1%, amphipods (*Pontogeneia inermis, Calliopus laeviusculus, Gammarellus angulosus, Ischyrocerus anguipes*) 18%, hydroids and algae 1%; 2 almost entirely amphipods (U.S. Biol. Survey). Nine in winter from marine waters of Me.: marine worms (*Lepidonotus*), crustaceans (*Gammarus, Gammarellus*), sea spiders (Pyconogonidae), mollusks (*Chiton, Acmaea, Littorina, Purpura (Thais), Buccinum, Mytilus, Lucina, Saxicava*) (R. S. Palmer 1949). A bird from Long I., N.Y., had eaten mud crabs (*Panopeus depressa*), 39 of the gastropod *Astyris lunata*, and a few *Littorina* (Whitfield 1894). The blue mussel (*Mytilus edulis*) is considered the main food in New Eng. (Bent 1925).

E. PACIFIC AND BERING SEA Crustaceans (*Hemigrapsus, Pagurus, Dermaturus, Petrolisthes, Cancer, Oxyrhyncha, Pachycheles, Mesidotea*, etc.) 57.1%, mollusks (*Chiton, Lacuna, Littorina, Margarites, Acmaea, Mitrella, Odostomia, Buccinum, Natica, Bittium, Nassarius, Mytilus*, etc.) 24.7%, insects—nymphs of stone flies (Plecoptera), water boatmen (Corixidae), midges (Chironomidae), and miscellaneous 10.2%, echinoderms (*Strongylocentrotus*) 2.4%, fishes (Cottidae, *Salmo*) and fish eggs 2.4%, miscellaneous (nereid worms, ascidians, bryozoans, sea spiders, hydroids) 1.5% (Cottam 1939).

Inland in Cal. in summer: aquatic insects (J. Grinnell et al. 1918, Michael and Michael 1922, McLean 1925). In a bird from the B.C. coast: nearly 9,000 herring (*Clupea*) eggs and 20% sea lettuce (*Ulva lactuca*) (J. Munro and Clemens 1931). There were a few *Potamogeton* seeds in a bird taken in Alta. in summer. In Alaska, isopods and blue mussels (J. Grinnell 1909, Turner 1886). Over half of the food of birds taken in the Pribilofs consisted mainly of amphipods (*Anonyx, Gammarus, Hyale, Jassa, Metopa, Orchomenella*) (Preble and McAtee 1923). Three, taken April 21 at Amchitka, in the Aleutians, had eaten a combined total of *Littorina* 321, chitons 15, amphipods 7, and limpets 4 (Kenyon 1961).

A wild ♀ on the Merced R. in Cal. in summer ate the cooked potatoes, macaroni, raisins, and bread set out for it (Michael and Michael 1922).

E. ASIA    A bird taken at Bering I. in the Commander group had eaten a sculpin (*Cottus*), a small crab, and 2 periwinkles (*Littorina*) (Stejneger 1885). Birds killed on the upper Okhotsk Sea in late July and early Aug. had eaten gammarids, mollusks, and small fish 2–3 cm. long, and also had ingested gravel (Kistschinskii 1968). Inland, on the Anadyr R. at the beginning of June, larvae of caddisflies (Trichoptera) with up to 250 in a stomach, larvae of stone flies (Perlidae), and remains of small fishes (Dementiev and Gladkov 1952). In the Kolyma Highlands, adults fed mainly on fry of *Salvelinus malma* and *S. leucomaenis* and various insects (Kistschinskii 1968). AWS

**Oldsquaw**

*Clangula hyemalis* (Linnaeus)

Long-tailed Duck of various authors. Smallish diving duck. Small stout bill with distinct, narrower nail on upper mandible; the feathering angles slightly forward from side base of bill to top, where it is truncated; distance between feathering and nostril less than length of the large nostril opening; in the lower mandible the lamellae are fairly coarse, straight, and nearly at a right angle to the long axis (not finely spaced and each somewhat angled near its center to form herringbone pattern, as in the Harlequin). Upper surface of wing lacks a markedly obvious speculum, although outer webs

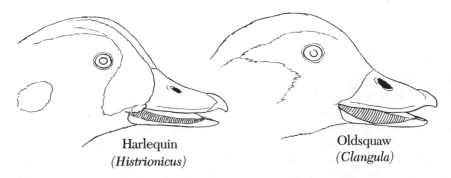

Harlequin
(*Histrionicus*)

Oldsquaw
(*Clangula*)

of most secondaries are toward rusty in the Basic wing. The 9th (next to outer) primary is slightly the longest, with outer web very narrow distally and then widening proximally to at least double that width in both Juv. and Basic ♂ and ♀ (corresponding widening is much less in the Harlequin). Alt. Plumages are sharply and contrastingly patterned, containing white to black; the others are variably darkish with more or less subdued browns in the mantle. The drake's tracheal apparatus was figured in detail by Schiøler (1926).

Length ♂ 19–22 in. (includes central tail feathers 7–10 in.), ♀ 15–17 (smaller, with shorter tail); wingspread ♂ to 31, ♀ to 29; usual wt. of mature ♂ about 1¾ lb., ♀ about 1½. No subspecies.

DESCRIPTION  See col. pl. facing p. 248. There are 3 Plumages/cycle in both sexes. In the definitive cycle the Alt. is acquired in a single fairly long period of molting; the succeeding Basic is acquired in 2 periods of molting (spring, late summer), the intervening pause being longest in the ♀; the third (Supplemental) Plumage, which replaces part of the Basic and is the least inclusive generation of feathers, also is acquired in 2 periods of molting—the first overlaps or coincides with the second period of molting into Basic and the second overlaps with early-incoming portions of Alt. Evidently because the hormonal milieu, which influences the nature of the feathering, varies within the long period from early spring to late fall, the earliest-incoming Basic (in spring) is intermediate in some respects (as in shape and length of scapulars) between the antecedent Alt. and succeeding Suppl.; again, during molting in fall, the last of the incoming Suppl. is intermediate in character toward the succeeding Alt.

345

The 3 Plumages occur also in the predefinitive cycle. The Suppl. then appears to include less feathering, or perhaps it often is not different enough to be identifiable as a separate feather generation unless one also were to determine the extent of molting from examining the flesh side of the skin of large series of specimens.

There are additional complications, as follows. 1 In the ♀ there is individual variation, from "brown" through intermediates to "gray" birds, from the Juv. Plumage on, but most pronounced in Def. Alt.; there is some variation in drakes also, terminating in Def. Alt. in which some lightest areas vary from white to pearly gray. 2 In most waterfowl having a Basic and Alt. Plumage, the feathering molted only once/cycle, i.e., Basic and retained nearly a year, consists of most or all of the wing and often the tail. In the Oldsquaw, beginning at the "post-pectoral line" (coincides with lower border of dark breast in the drake), the venter, but not sides and flanks, also are molted only once/cycle (Salomonsen 1942). That scheme is followed here, yet the writer suspects that the venter is molted twice, i.e., in spring (when the new ventral body down grows) as well as fall. Molting from white to white, especially if gradual, often is not readily apparent. 3 The length and shape of the innermost secondaries worn with the remainder of the Basic wing vary appreciably in shape, also they become pointed after wear. Most waterfowl that molt the body twice also renew some innermost feathers of the wing twice, but they are treated below as renewed only once in the Oldsquaw because the writer is uncertain as to whether they are renewed more often. At least sometimes the molting does extend out onto the upper covert area of the wing twice/cycle. 4 Many feather generations of waterfowl are noticeable first on head–neck, but in the Oldsquaw this portion tends to "lag" (in Alt. and Basic) or to appear so late as to be completely "offset" in time (Suppl.). 5 No schematic presentation can encompass all the variation in timing of events in the annual cycle of the Oldsquaw. For example, in the subarctic the birds are on a considerably earlier schedule, at least in some respects, than those that go to the high-arctic. The dating in the present account probably best fits birds of the subarctic and low-arctic. 6 Although there is much descriptive literature on the Oldsquaw, the significant publications, in chronological order, are Millais (1913a), Schiøler (1926), and Salomonsen (1942, 1949). The present writer has examined (in Copenhagen) some of the material used by Schiøler and Salomonsen, also series in several Am. museums. This has served to confirm many matters but, in the process, more additional problems were discovered than were solved. 7 Below, emphasis is on diagnostic features of Plumages plus their individual variation in coloring; variation in timing of molting is partly indicated, not being fully known.

▶ ♂ Def. Alt. Plumage (all feathering except tail, wing, and posterior underparts), usually acquired gradually, within the span SEPT. to NOV. or DEC., and retained until SPRING (usually April); the sides and flanks are retained until LATE SUMMER or LATER.

Very contrasty with much white; the "winter" or "display" feathering or "Prachtkleid" of authors. **Bill** bluish slaty with broad subterminal band that varies with time and individual from vivid pink to salmon, the ends of both mandibles (including large nail on upper) blackish. **Iris** varies from brownish yellow to quite brownish. **Head,** neck, most of anterior mantle, and upper breast white except: side of face palish gray or gray-brown, ring around eye white, area from rear of cheek down onto side of neck sooty brownish or same grading to warm brownish on neck; **upperparts** central portion of mantle dark brownish sepia (like breast) and this also includes lower back to tail; an area including the scapulars mostly pearly gray except: longest scapulars (to about 15 cm.) white, narrow, and tapering to a point, some shorter concealed ones blackish brown; **underparts** breast brownish sepia or sooty; sides pearly gray, the feathers with broad white upper margins, and the flank feathers elongated, tapering to a point, and mostly white. Legs and **feet** light bluish gray, webs slaty. The ventral **body down** is nearly white in winter. Retained Basic worn with the Alt. includes the long tail, the wing, and white of belly to tail.

In the molting into Alt. there is much change on the body before the antecedent Suppl. begins to disappear from the head–neck. Also, while the Alt. is incoming, the long central pair of Basic tail feathers still is growing. Early Alt. feathers to appear include some white or pale gray scapulars and the pearly feathers of upper sides and flanks. The molting of head–neck out of Suppl. into Alt. is late and quite prolonged. The molt into Alt. requires a minimum of several weeks on the individual.

NOTES   Key illus. include: Millais (1913a)—after p. 118, left-hand pl., fig. 8, and right-hand pl., figs. 6 and 7 (all in color, fig. 7 being a "gray" drake); Schiøler (1926)—pl. 32, upper right fig. (color) and pl. 34, center fig. (monochrome); present vol.—see p. 248 and facing pl. (color); Salomonsen (1942)—head only, pl. 3, fig. "a" (monochrome), and long scapular feather, pl. 4, left-hand fig. (color).

Drakes with all the light dorsal areas pearly gray are comparatively few.

In flocks, during April–May, one commonly sees drakes still in Alt. and others already having much Basic on head–body. On summer range, as in Bering Sea and arctic Alaska, drakes are seen throughout June in every stage of transition. A drake taken as late as July 8 at St. Lawrence Bay in Siberia still was in the transition "temple-mark" stage (described below), while another in Mass. had reached this stage as early as March 31.

▶   ♂ Def. Basic Plumage (entire feathering), acquired partly in SPRING and, after a long pause, the remainder is acquired beginning some time in SUMMER and extending into FALL. Most of the head–body is lost by fall, but the wing, tail, and venter from belly to tail are retained nearly a year.

The spring-acquired portion commonly appears in April and consists of head down to include the breast and much of the mantle. The light band on the bill begins to darken. **Head** down to anterior belly sooty brownish or even almost black, except: a large smoky or brownish gray area on side of face, plus some white extending from around or behind the eye posteriorly, and sometimes some tan or rusty feathering in foreneck; **upperparts** feathers of anterior dorsum have wedge-shaped very dark interiors and medium brownish margins; the exposed, tapering scapulars (to 11–14 cm. long) and some adjoining feathers similarly bicolored, but some underlying scapulars are entirely dark; remainder of dorsum dark (like breast). At this stage the drake has much dark feathering, with rich browns in the dorsum, and the pearly Alt. feathers of flanks and sides still are retained and are conspicuous.

NOTES   The resulting combination of portions of 3 feather generations is the "breeding" or "nuptial" feathering of various authors, including Salomonsen (1942).

The molting into this portion of Basic is quite prolonged, evidently during a period of changing hormonal influence. The resulting early-acquired feathers (such as the long

347

scapulars) tend toward Alt. in shape and even sometimes in coloring (pale margined); the later-incoming feathers of head–neck might be described as more typically Basic in characteristics.

The first signs of incoming Basic are rusty-edged feathers on the dorsum; the dark feathers of head–neck come in later and often gradually. As the dark increases on the neck and part of the head, it also appears as a line extending from behind up over the eye. This is the "temple-mark" stage of Salomonsen (1942) and it is not rare in collections.

Key illus.: Millais (1913a)—after p. 118, right-hand pl., 2 upper rt. figs. (color); Schiøler (1926)—pl. 32, right center (color), and pl. 34, left fig. (monochrome); Salomonsen (1942)—fig. 6 (monochrome); present vol.—see p. 248 and facing pl. (color); also in Salomonsen (1942)—"temple-mark" stage, fig. 2, also "b" on pl. 3; head in full Basic, fig. 4, also "c" on pl. 3; and long scapular feather, pl. 4, center (in color).

The head feathering is very short beginning in spring (Basic Plumage), giving a very different profile from the seemingly oversized light head of late fall–winter (Alt. Plumage).

Molting is renewed and is more or less continuous from LATE JUNE until well into FALL. An early event consists of acquiring some additional Basic and, more or less contemporaneously, having some of the spring-acquired Basic succeeded by a portion of the third generation of feathers (Supplemental Plumage) which also is acquired and lost in stages.

The **bill** has lost its pink color by summer. **Upperparts** the mantle molts from Basic to Suppl: the new feathers are short, roundish, with narrow and even buffy tan or gray-buff margins and dusky interiors; the longest scapulars are relatively short (to about 10 cm.) and wide for most of their length, with rounded (not pointed) ends; some underlying ones are plain dusky; **underparts** the sides and flanks now lose the conspicuous pale (Alt.) feathering and acquire broad, rounded feathers (Basic) that are fairly dark, a smoky gray; the remainder of the venter molts from white to white (Basic).

The **wing** is molted, usually in late July or early Aug. (duration of flightless period unknown).

NOTES The drake now is in the "semi-eclipse" of Millais (1913a) and "Schlichtkleid" of Salomonsen (1942).

A flightless drake, taken Aug. 9 at Herschel I., in Yukon Terr., had short sheathed primaries, rounded scapulars (Suppl.), dusky sides (Basic), and the ventral body down was smoky gray, somewhat paler than the flank feathers.

Key illus.: Schiøler (1926)—pl. 32, lower left (flightless but tail not yet molted) and lower rt. (new wing and short new tail) (both color); Lönnberg (1927)—in color; present volume—p. 248 and facing pl. (color); Salomonsen (1942)—long scapular feather, pl. 4, rt. fig. (color).

In the period from some time in SEPT. to about MID-OCT., the following events occur. While the new Basic wing is growing, the tail is dropped and a new Basic tail begins to grow. In addition, there is molting of head–neck, out of the dark Basic into white Suppl., with ill-defined darkish area on rear of cheek. The new **head** feathers are intermediate in length, i.e., not as long as the Alt. ones that will succeed them. By the time the head–neck are largely white, the new tail is well grown and, on the body, the molting of various areas out of Suppl. and Basic and back into Alt. is in progress—anterior **mantle** shows some white or pearly gray, same occurs in scapular area, and the **sides** and **flanks** have lost the dark Basic and again have pearly gray feathers with white upper margins (Alt.). The band on the bill again becomes pink.

**Tail** outer feathers white, with increasing amount of darkish gray in each of several successive pairs; the 3 innermost pairs: outer pair dark gray with white margins; next to inner are elongated (to 10–12 cm.), tapering and blackish; central pair greatly elongated (17–24 cm.), blackish, very narrow, tapering, somewhat upcurved, and each web is angled down about 45° from the horizontal. **Wing** all upper coverts very dark, toward sooty; secondaries variably brownish, often warm brown on outer web of exposed ones (this bleaches toward buffy brown); primaries blackish, paling on inner webs; lining and axillars some variant of fuscous.

NOTES    The total feathering that includes the essentially white-headed stage is the "fall" dress or "Herbstkleid" of Salomonsen (1942).

Key illus.: Schiøler (1926)—pl. 32, upper left fig. (color) and pl. 34, rt. fig. (monochrome); Salomonsen (1942)—fig. 9 and, head only, pl. 3, fig. "d" (both monochrome).

These events occur in the span from about MID-OCT. through DEC. There is molting of the **head–neck** from the intermediate-length white (Suppl.) feathers back to the Def. Alt. pattern of white, gray, sooty, and tan (the head now has its longest feathers); and various Alt. feathers complete their growth—scapulars, side and flank feathers.

▶    ♀ Def. Alt. Plumage (all feathering except tail, wing, and belly to tail), acquired beginning in FALL (Sept. or Oct., occasionally even later) and retained until SPRING (usually April, occasionally May). The Alt. sides and flanks evidently are retained much longer, as in the drake. This is the ♀ Plumage having the most white; head–neck has dark patches on white; hindneck always white; most of underparts white. Also the ♀ Plumage having the widest range of individual variation in general coloring, from rich rusty to gray birds.

**Bill** medium grayish or grayish blue, lighter subterminally with a trace of pinkish, and with dark tip. **Iris** yellowish brown. **Head** and neck mostly white, the crown and nape, also an area on rear of cheeks and another nearby on rear side of head, dusky to blackish, or the 2 patches on side of head more or less margined brownish. On **upperparts** great individual variation from rich reddish brown to somber dark grayish; most feathers have very dark centers and sharply defined lighter margins, reddish brown through a range of buffy browns to grays, depending on individual; rump usually very dark. **Underparts** upper breast and forward sides vary from browns to grays, more or less matching the dorsum; sides and flanks white. Legs and **feet** rather light gray-blue, webs much darker. Retained Basic feathering includes the tail, wing, and white of lower breast to tail. The ventral body down is whitish, much paler than in summer.

NOTE    "Brown" and "gray" extremes are shown well in color in the 2 bottom figs. on pl. 30 in Schiøler (1926), also see col. pl. facing p. 248 in the present volume for a "brown" individual. In winter-taken birds from L. Michigan there was a "complete spectrum" of individual variation from rich reddish brown through light browns and tans to gray; 240 ♀ were sorted as brown 17%, intermediate 50%, and gray 33% (Ellarson 1956).

▶ ♀ Def. Basic Plumage (entire feathering), at least head to lower breast plus mantle acquired in SPRING (usually April, but later in tardy birds) and retained into FALL (usually Aug.–Sept.), the remainder (rump, tail, wing, belly to tail) acquired usually in Sept.–Oct. and retained nearly a year. The tapering white (Alt.) feathers of sides and flanks are retained and worn with the early-acquired portion of Basic, i.e., are retained until at least well along in summer or early fall. Because overall coloring of Basic is muted, individual variation from "brown" to "gray" birds is not very conspicuous.

The spring-acquired feathering includes: **head–neck** very dark, more or less sooty brownish or even blackish, a large lighter area (usually a palish gray-brown) on side of face and some white within it at eye (mostly behind eye); white patch on foreneck variable in size and not always sharply defined; **upperparts** feathers are clearly patterned with dark brownish to gray-black interiors, tan to pale grayish margins; **underparts** breast varies from sooty brownish to dark gray, the feathers with pale tips that wear off. The very dark **nest down** is acquired at this stage of molting.

▶ ♀ Def. Suppl. Plumage (part of mantle, probably additional feathering). After a pause, and beginning some time well along in JUNE or in JULY, these events occur. There is molting on the **mantle** out of the spring-acquired Basic into Suppl. The new feathers have dusky interiors and buffy or gray margins; they are short and rounded. The white Alt. **sides** and **flanks** are succeeded by gray-brown Basic. Molting of the body elsewhere, including rump and belly to tail, continues and eventually extends out to the wing coverts. The flight feathers of the wing are dropped (duration of flightless period unknown). Little is known about molting of head–neck, in fall, into a Suppl. comparable to the white feathering of the drake; it is possible that such occurs, but without pronounced change in coloring. Some fall ♀ ♀ have head–neck white with very little dark on cheeks and top midline of head. The tail feathers are dropped late, after the flightless period begins.

The new **tail** is patterned as in the ♂, the central pair of feathers somewhat elongated, to perhaps 9 cm. The incoming Basic **wing** is dark overall, secondaries variably brownish; greater coverts have broad rounded ends, middle coverts variously margined from indistinct and toward buffy to distinct and broadly buffy brown; lining and axillars as ♂.

NOTES The late stage, showing the dark Basic sides and flanks, was illus. first by Lönnberg (1926); such specimens are scarce in museum collections. A flightless "gray" ♀, taken Aug. 8 on Southampton I., shows these characteristics: blended pattern on head–neck; area on side of head pale gray-brown; crown and continuing down hindneck and rear of cheeks medium gray-brown; a white eye ring; a white streak begins 3–4 mm. directly behind the eye and extends back to nape (becomes narrow); hindneck dark; side of neck pale grayish; throat and foreneck medium gray-brown; upperparts very dark, a mixture of grays to blackish (Suppl.); rump feathers black margined gray; underparts the gray-brown of foreneck continues down to include upper ⅔ of breast where the feathers become lighter terminally; sides and flanks have rounded gray-brown feathers which still are growing.

An instance of flying during the "flightless stage" was reported by Kartaschev (1962). At end of Aug., on a tundra lake on the Kola Pen., there was a flock of 6–7 Oldsquaws.

When alarmed, they flapped along the surface, headed into a weak wind, and took wing. Their wingbeats seemed faster than is normal. The birds were flushed several times and would not leave the lake and fly overland to the sea. Three "adult" ♀ were shot; they had long new wing coverts, but the primaries and secondaries had not begun to grow.

Key illus.: Schiøler (1926)—pl. 30, upper left fig. (brown bird with Basic scapulars), upper rt. (gray bird with Basic scapulars), and the bird shown with ducklings has some faded Basic plus new Suppl. in mantle (all these figs. in color); Lönnberg (1926)—Suppl. feathering in mantle, Basic gray-brown sides and flanks (color); present volume—see col. pl. facing p. 248.

The molting of the ♀ back into Def. Alt. head–neck and most of body is protracted and often not complete until Nov. or even some time in Dec. The **bill** again becomes somewhat pinkish subterminally. The blackish crown is sharply defined and there are 2 very dark, separate or joined, elongated brown-edged patches toward rear side of head. Some individuals do not have the head thus in full Alt. until late in Dec.

AT HATCHING   See vol. 2, col. pl. facing p. 466. Individual variation: the several white spots around the eye sometimes are joined to form a ring; sometimes there is a white spot in the auricular area. Downy Oldsquaws have a dark breast band which is lacking in Harlequins.

▶   ♂ ♀ Juv. Plumage (entire feathering), fully developed at 35–40 days posthatching. Birds with some down still adhering have a blended pattern—dorsum toward sooty brownish; upper breast and sides smoky, grading to white ventrally.

**Bill** medium grayish or gray-brown, darker at base and tip; **iris** muted brownish. **Head** dark crown and nape, off-white to white area around eye and this extends back to nape; often a nearly white area at side base of bill or the same extends back under eye; cheeks and throat smoky gray or even nearly as dark as crown (individual variation); front and sides of neck off-white to light gray. **Upperparts** scapular area shows the most individual variation (at least in ♀ ♀), from muted dark brownish to medium or lighter gray. **Underparts** upper breast smoky to rather sooty, grading to white or sometimes lower breast and upper belly are indistinctly mottled medium gray or lighter; sides and flanks rather smoky, sometimes more brownish, the feathers comparatively short; remainder of venter whitish. Legs and **feet** grayed buff in fall, webs toward blackish. The notched **tail** feathers are rather dusky with very narrow whitish edging (it wears off).

**Wing** darkish, blended (speculum area indistinctly brownish), upper coverts comparatively narrow, primaries rounded (not pointed). Innermost secondaries comparatively short and considerably rounded, with brownish to grayish edging and same range of individual variation in coloring occurs on middle coverts; lining and axillars dark.

NOTE   There seems to be no really adequate published illus. of the Juv. Plumage; the youngest bird in Schiøler (1926)—pl. 31, upper left fig., "♀ juv." apparently has lost some of the Juv. feathering. Yet the Juv. is retained evidently after it is perfected for a month or even considerably longer.

▶   ♂ ♀ Basic I Plumage (apparently all new feathering except wing) acquired during FALL (typically) but sometimes gradually into winter. Usually it is succeeded by much Alt. I by or before MIDWINTER.

This is a dark, almost blackish Plumage, darker than Juv. and more definitely patterned. The wide band on the bill becomes paler in the ♂ but remains bluish gray in the ♀. **Head**, neck, most of breast, and forward mantle sooty blackish except: side of face gray-brown with some white around eye, part of foreneck medium gray-brown; in the **upperparts** the scapular area is muted brownish; **underparts** dark of upper breast grades ventrally to much lighter, then belly to tail unmarked white; sides and flanks sooty gray. The Basic **tail** is acquired late, starting with the outer feathers (which are white). In early Feb. drakes have a single long central tail feather (Ellarson 1956). The Juv. wing is retained.

NOTES   The sexes may differ in Basic I, but the writer has not seen enough material to settle this point.

Key illus.: Schiøler (1926)—pl. 29, upper left fig., labeled "♀ juv." (color).

▶   ♂ Suppl. I Plumage (at least the scapular area, but inclusive feathering unknown), acquired well along in FALL or in EARLY WINTER and probably retained a very few weeks at most. By the time the drake is in transition from Basic I to Alt. I on the body, there are some short scapular feathers that are smoky gray with dark centers.

Key illus.: Schiøler (1926)—pl. 31, upper rt. fig., some Suppl. I plus incoming Alt. I (color).

▶   ♂ Alt. I Plumage (all feathering except tail, wing, and perhaps white of belly to tail). In the normal course of molting, this Plumage begins to appear within the span of OCT. to about MID-DEC. and is acquired quite rapidly, but it is later in "tardy" birds; it is retained until SPRING.

The band on the **bill** becomes pink by Dec. **Iris** yellowish brown. The feathering is much like Def. Alt. but, in material examined, these differences were noted: patch on rear of **cheek** and upper side of neck generally dark brownish (not nearly black); **upperparts** mixed black and white feathers on anterior mantle are common; scapulars pale grayish to white, the longest usually about 10–11 cm. (only 1–2 pale scapulars in Dec.–Jan., but their number increases to form a distinctive pale tract in March and April (Ellarson 1956) ); **underparts** white except a relatively narrow dark band across breast; sides and flanks more or less pale grayish. The Juv. wing still is retained, also the Basic I tail which has 2 long feathers by March.

Key illus.: Schiøler (1926)—pl. 31, left center fig. (color).

▶   ♀ Basic I Plumage—see above under ♂ ♀ Basic I.

▶   ♀ Suppl. I Plumage—probably exists, but no obvious examples examined. See Schiøler (1926)—pl. 29, top rt., the scapulars and anterior mantle apparently are Suppl. I and remainder of head–body mostly or all Alt. I.

▶   ♀ Alt. I Plumage (inclusive feathering as ♂ Alt. I), timing as ♂ so far as known.

Differs from subsequent ♀ Alt. Plumages as follows: **head** and neck have less clear-cut pattern; earliest ♀ Plumage in which the neck is white all around; **upperparts** anterior mantle and scapular area varies with individual from quite brownish to grayish, with intervening band of very dark feathers; the scapulars especially have very dark interiors and wide brown to very pale margins; **underparts** upper breast brownish to gray-brown (individual variation), paling to white on lower breast and this continues to tail; sides and flanks whitish. The tail is retained Basic I, the wing retained Juv.

NOTES  The above, for the most part, describes a brown individual; some are much more grayish.

Useful illus.: Schiøler (1926)—pl. 29, top rt. fig., Alt. I apparently with retained Suppl. I in anterior mantle and scapular area.

▶  ♂ Basic II Plumage (entire feathering), the earliest Basic to be acquired in 2 stages, in SPRING (at least head–neck, most of dorsum, and breast) and in SUMMER–EARLY FALL (remainder of feathering); part of the spring-acquired feathering is retained only into EARLY FALL, but the late-acquired portions (tail, wing, perhaps some body feathering) retained nearly a year.

The earliest ♂ Plumage having a clear-cut patch of brown-margined feathers on anterior **mantle** and long, attenuated, brown-edged scapulars; in the 2nd stage the still-retained white Alt. I **sides** and **flanks** are succeeded by smoky gray Basic II feathers. Also in the 2nd stage, the drake acquires the Basic II wing plus tail.

NOTES  Key illus.: Schiøler (1926)—pl. 31, lower left fig., stage 1, and lower rt. fig., stage 2 with dark flanks, also Suppl. II in dorsum (both figs. in color).

The bursa of Fabricius can be found in both sexes during the first winter and following spring, up to and including May (Ellarson 1956).

▶  ♂ Suppl. II Plumage (at least anterior mantle and the scapular area); these feathers, which are short, grow in LATE SUMMER when the drake is just over a year old and are retained briefly, into FALL. They have dusky interiors and wide muted brownish margins.

Key illus.: Schiøler (1926)—pl. 31, lower rt. fig. (color).

▶  ♂ Alt. II Plumage (inclusive feathering as later Alts.), LATE FALL to SPRING (when approaching age 2 years); presumably definitive.

▶  ♀ Basic II Plumage (entire feathering), acquired in 2 stages—the head–neck, mantle, and breast in SPRING (before age 1 year) and the remainder of underparts, the rump (?), sides and flanks, wing, and tail in LATE SUMMER–EARLY FALL (age just over 1 year); when the latter are being acquired, part of the stage-1 Basic is being succeeded by Suppl. II (described below), but most of the stage-2 Basic, except the dark sides and flanks, is retained nearly a year.

Some individuals in Basic II are among the darkest ♀ ♀ examined. Differs slightly from later Basics, as follows: **head** generally has smaller light (to white) area around eye; **upperparts** feather margins not as sharply defined and not as contrastingly lighter than their dark centers; **underparts** upper breast very dark, grading downward to white; **sides** and **flanks** variably dusky.

Key illus.: Schiøler (1926)—pl. 29, left center fig. (color).

▶  ♀ Suppl. II Plumage (at least anterior mantle and the scapular area), acquired well along in SUMMER or later, as mentioned above under ♀ Basic II, and retained only until the LATE FALL molting into Alt. on much of body plus head–neck. The very short darkish smoky gray **scapulars**, etc., have nearly black centers.

Key illus.: Schiøler (1926)—pl. 29, right center fig., Suppl. scapulars plus new Alt. on head, neck, breast, etc. (color).

▶  ♀ Alt. II Plumage (inclusive feathering as later Alts.), acquired in FALL–EARLY WINTER (at age over 1 year) and retained into SPRING (before age 2 years), except the sides and flanks retained into late summer. Presumably definitive.

**Measurements** of birds from localities in N. Am. 12 ♂: BILL 25–30 mm., av. 28; WING 225–237, av. 230; TARSUS 34–37, av. 35.2; TAIL 173–241, av. 208;  12 ♀: BILL 26–28 mm., av. 26.8; WING 201–220, av. 211; TARSUS 31–36, av. 34.7; TAIL 58–74, av. 68 (ETS).

The flattened WING of the drake, as given above, is 10–12 mm. longer than it is in the 3 N. Am. series measured, with wing also flattened, by Manning et al. (1956).

For Palearctic series, WING meas. over the curve, see especially Witherby (1939) and Dementiev and Gladkov (1952).

Judging from various meas. in Schiøler (1926), the flattened Juv. WING is considerably shorter than the Basic—probably 10–15 mm. shorter in the Juv. drake.

**Weight**  The mean in gm., plus sample size in parentheses, is given here for birds weighed wet after removal from fishnets in L. Michigan (Ellarson 1956). Drakes both of first-winter and older age-classes show an increase in Feb., then sharp decline to a low level in mid-March to mid-April, then rapid increase the next 4 weeks to above any previous level. Females show more than proportionately smaller fluctuations, with prebreeders under age 1 year having no recovery in May from the low level reached in March.

|        | ♂ "adult" |         | ♂ "juv." |        | ♀ "adult" |        | ♀ "juv." |        |
|--------|-----------|---------|----------|--------|-----------|--------|----------|--------|
| Nov.   | (11)      | 950     |          |        | (5)       | 822    |          |        |
| Dec.   | (60)      | 922.4   | (3)      | 975    | (37)      | 822.6  | (2)      | 855    |
| Jan.   | (4)       | 963     | (15)     | 954.3  | (2)       | 845    | (11)     | 851.8  |
| Feb.   | (108)     | 1,010.3 | (150)    | 977.3  | (190)     | 845.8  | (151)    | 829.8  |
| March  | (404)     | 913.9   | (264)    | 896    | (360)     | 797.2  | (247)    | 771.9  |
| April  | (64)      | 898.2   | (19)     | 898.6  | (36)      | 799.1  | (14)     | 773.2  |
| May    | (10)      | 1,034.5 | (4)      | 977.5  | (6)       | 856.7  | (7)      | 767.1  |

Summer wt. is considerably less than in midwinter; see Brandt (1943), Macpherson and McLaren (1959), Macpherson and Manning (1959), and Musacchia (1953) for N. Am. data. At Mývatn, Iceland, mean wt. of nesting ♀♀: 690 gm. (21 in 1968), 683 (16 in 1969), and 510 (18 in 1970), the last being a season of food scarcity (Bengtson 1972c).

**Hybrids**  None reported in the wild. In captivity, according to Delacour (1959), a drake mated with Chestnut Teal (*Anas castanea*) and 2 ducklings were hatched; they "looked much like" downy Oldsquaws and they soon disappeared.

**Geographical variation** none reported and probably there is none in morphological characters. RSP

FIELD IDENTIFICATION  Identifiable at a distance by actions—rolling careening flight, the birds showing their bellies, then their backs, as they fly swiftly. They travel in irregular masses, straggling lines, or bunches, just clear of the waves and then swinging upward 200 ft. or more. This behavior, which is unlike their direct and high migratory flight overland, is typical of wintering flocks as they move to and from feeding and resting areas. They are very active, restless, and noisy. Wingstroke, unlike that of eiders and scoters, is approximately from the level of the back steeply downward, and very rapid. Their flight is buoyant and unducklike. Often a flock alights with seeming impatience or great haste; the birds plunge headlong downward and splash breast first into the sea, sending up a shower of spray. When idling on the surface, their profile is very low, necks drawn in, tail nearly horizontal. Sizable flocks (to several hundred birds) usually break up into groups once they are on the water.

The far-carrying and at times quite musical baying of the drakes is unlike the voice of any other waterfowl; once recognized, it is unlikely to be forgotten. It has a friendly quality and is, perhaps, most memorable when heard during the quiet hours when the sun is nearest the horizon and observer is alone on the tundra. If Oldsquaws fly by at close range, there is a definite and rather even swish of wings; that is, a steady noise rather than a separate sound of each wingbeat. Porsild (1943) commented as follows on actions of small flocks on summer range in the Mackenzie delta: "The flight is so rapid that the birds can barely be followed by the eye. In downward swoop [from hills to river] the birds produce a buzz, not unlike that of a large calibre [artillery] shell passing overhead."

As to identification at close range, most Oldsquaws in winter appear to be patterned dark on white, in summer variably dark with much white in venter. (The Harlequin is mostly dark in all seasons.) There are many Plumages, a complex pattern of coloring, and variation in times of molting, described earlier. In both sexes the bill appears truncated, the wing dark (including undersurface) and without obvious pattern. Drakes in their 2nd year and older have very long central tail feathers, hence "Long-tailed Duck."

Oldsquaws and Harlequins in their first fall can be confused, although the latter are more evenly dark overall. Young Oldsquaws have lower breast to tail white, with upper breast and often the sides quite dark; in young Harlequins the lightest portion of the venter is ashy or dusky, not white, and this grades more gradually into adjoining darker coloring. The difference is evident even in swimming birds. RSP

VOICE   Very noisy, especially in late winter–spring, but quiet in latter part of breeding season and presumably also during the period of molting in late summer–fall.

Fifty years ago J. C. Phillips (1925) pointed out that much ink has been used in attempts to describe the drake's voice; more has been used since, usually without adding any new information. Individual calls vary, sounds of flocks vary with distance, number of birds, and so on, and all are difficult to communicate via written language. "Loquacious birds, like talkative people, are likely to be often misquoted" (Forbush 1925).

Commonest call, uttered by the drake in various seasons, consists of 4–5 syllables; the first 2–3 are low or slightly slurred downward, the next lower, and the last high with an *l*-like sound at its beginning—*ow owooolee* or *ow ow owoolik*. It is loud and it ends abruptly. Its quality, at close range, is somewhat like a nasal human voice. It is uttered when the bird is afloat or in flight, the bill somewhat open; not always accompanied (on water) by Head-throw display. Often heard on clear nights in nonbreeding seasons and in the breeding season at any hour.

The next 2 paragraphs, based mainly on Drury's (1961) summer data from Bylot I., appear to be the only attempt, at least in N. Am., to describe calls of birds in the wild in association with particular activities.

**Drake 1** Repeated *ahang-ahoo* with Head-tossing. **2** Series of *angh* notes, also with Head-tossing or, on last note, the head may be lowered, then tossed for *eeeoo*, or reverse may occur—bill lowered on former, raised on latter. **3** In flocks on water or in flight, *ah angnh* uttered repeatedly. **4** In small flying flocks containing both sexes, or 1–2 drakes in aerial pursuit of a duck, or occasionally a solitary flying drake, *ung ow geeooga* with more growling than baying character.

**Duck 1** Series of syllables *urk, ang, goo, gut, gooah,* about in that order, the various components uttered once or to several times, or some may be omitted, so that the entire call varies much in length and character; accompanied by Head-tossing. **2** Calls of ♀ ♀ in mixed flocks when the ♂ ♂ are giving their call described above under #3, a rather muffled *ah-angh.* **3** During nest-site hunting and continuing into laying or possibly incubating, flying single ♀ ♀ at ponds or pools—probably off-duty from laying or incubating—have series of *kuk* notes that may indicate mild alarm and/or appraise the drake of his mate's whereabouts. Rather similar calls are uttered by the ♀ if disturbed with brood. In general, duck's voice seems less varied, more repetitious, softer, and more toward barking than baying than the drake's.

Various groups of people have names for the Oldsquaw that imitate its voice. Eskimo renditions, from Alaska to Ungava and Greenland, consist of 2–5 syllables, variously accented, with somewhat melodious connotation, usually ending with an abrupt *il, ik,* or *luk* sound. N. Am. Indian names usually are shorter, 2–3 syllables, and some have been taken over by whites. For example, the Crees of nw. Canada say *ca-ca-wee* and essentially the same is used by persons of various ethnic origins around the Gulf of St. Lawrence (in French: le canard kakawi) and formerly by whites on the Me. coast. Because of its melodious, rather human, quality the drake's voice was incorporated in songs of the Canadian voyageurs and the bird was named "Organ Duck" by fur traders on the upper Yukon. The Russian book name "Moryanka" means "little sailor," but Russian vernaculars, such as "Avleika," are onomatopoeic after the voice of the drake. RSP

**HABITAT** The Oldsquaw and the King Eider are the 2 truly arctic ducks. The former apparently has greatest summer abundance more southerly; comparison is not a simple matter, however, since the 2 differ in certain requirements.

A tundra **breeder**, s. in some areas into semibarrens (open terrain plus scattered patches of trees), in some alpine areas on hills and mts. into the edge of the forest zone, also on treeless or nearly treeless is. in large lakes, and on is. of coasts s. beyond the upper limits of mainland forest, e.g., along the Labrador coast. Also on what might be described as semitundra in Iceland and parts of Fennoscandia. Nests are within short flight distance of a source of aquatic food—lakes, ponds, rivers, or the sea. Apparently absent as a nester from sizable areas of comparatively waterless terrain, also where snow persists very late. Some prebreeders pass the **summer** on lakes and rivers where surrounding terrain is unsuited to nesting. Huge numbers of postbreeders molt on the sea near some places (e.g., Wrangel I., Herschel I.) where very few Oldsquaws nest. Groups of molters come ashore to rest on sheltered beaches of islets and on sandy and gravelly bars, also to the water's edge in outer reaches of deltas.

Regular **winterer** in high latitudes where open water remains along coasts—n. Ber-

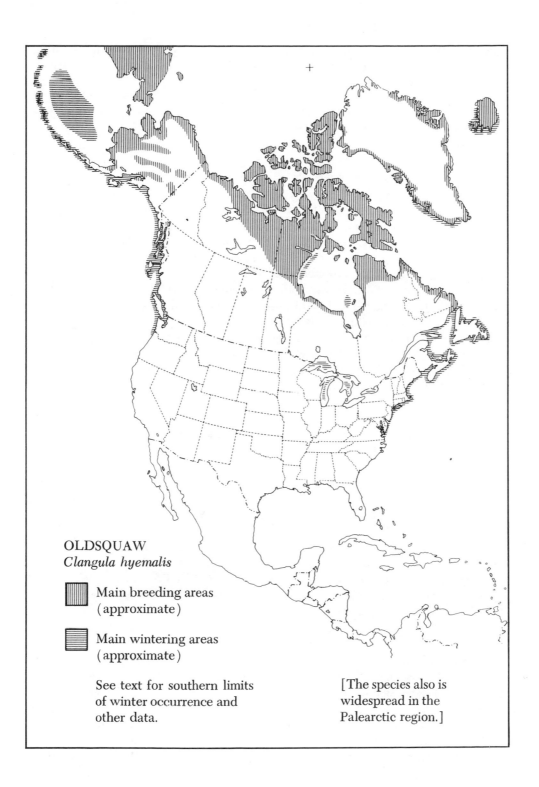

OLDSQUAW
*Clangula hyemalis*

Main breeding areas
(approximate)

Main wintering areas
(approximate)

See text for southern limits
of winter occurrence and
other data.

[The species also is
widespread in the
Palearctic region.]

ing Sea, s. third of w. Greenland, n. Fennoscandia, s. Novaya Zemlya—and southward into temperate marine and certain large inland waters. The flocks then are offshore, nearly pelagic, in habitat preference. RSP

DISTRIBUTION    (See map.) The Oldsquaw presumably survived the last glacial period in some high-latitude refugium.

A panarctic and subarctic breeder, in some places also farther southward as indicated above. In summer, molts at some n. areas where it is scarce or absent as a breeder. There are scattered southerly records for summer, probably for oiled or otherwise incapacitated individuals. Occurs in winter as far n. as there is open marine water, also on certain inland waters, s. through temperate-zone waters. Straggles s. beyond regular winter range. The following notes supplement the map.

N. AM. AND VICINITY    Has bred in extreme nw. B.C., apparently some distance from regular breeding range. Northernmost breeding records for this species are from Ellesmere I. and Greenland, to about lat. 83° N. In winter occurs in the Bering–Pacific area from Bering Sea down to Wash., in the interior on the Great Lakes (now perhaps excepting L. Erie), and in the Atlantic area in sw. Greenland and from Nfld. down to Long I. (N.Y.) and Chesapeake Bay. Extreme recorded limits in winter: Bering–Pacific area—n. to the Diomedes in Bering Strait (when any open water) and s. to southern Cal.; interior—s. to n. Texas and to Tenn.; mainland Atlantic coast—n. to Strait of Belle Isle and s. to S.C., very occasionally Fla. (and has occurred in Gulf of Mexico waters in Ala. and La.). Cold winters generally result in some southerly records in the continental interior.

A. P. Low (1906) stated that Oldsquaws remain on open water of Hudson Bay through the winter, with numbers killed at C. Fullerton (on the w. side of the bay) during that season. They remain through winter near the Belcher Is. and are captured for food (Freeman 1967).

For additional Nearctic data, see the 1957 A.O.U. *Check-list* and Godfrey (1966).

Reported as **fossil** from the Pleistocene of Ore. and Fla., and from **archaeological sites** in Alaska (1 mainland and 4 is.); references in Brodkorb (1964a).

PACIFIC OCEAN    Hawaii—reported from Midway Atoll in 1958 (Berger 1972).

ELSEWHERE    In Iceland, because of warming of the climate, it is being replaced as a breeder at Mývatn by the Tufted Duck (Gudmundsson 1951). Breeds s. to cent. Norway and there are 2 recent records for is. in the Gulf of Finland (brood hatched in 1963). There are records of former nesting in the Orkneys. Said to occur on Jan Mayen; breeds beyond at Bear I. and in Spitzbergen, but not reported from Franz Josef Land. Breeds on both is. of Novaya Zemlya, but perhaps not on is. n. of the Taimyr Pen. (Severnaya Zemlya, etc.); breeds in New Siberian Archipelago. As to Wrangel I., most authors from Tougarinov (1941) to S. Uspenskii et al. (1963) regarded breeding as not proven, but the species was mapped as breeding there by Flint et al. (1968) and Portenko (1972) stated that it nests there occasionally. In E. Siberia there may be (or has been) a disjunct breeding area near Gizhiga (upper end of Shelikov Gulf).

There are scattered summer occurrences in interior Eurasia, some northerly ones probably being for birds that had gone to such places to molt; some in E. Siberia have been reported, perhaps erroneously, as breeding. Apparently a few occur regularly inland in Europe.

The Oldsquaw is present in winter around Iceland and is very abundant in the Faeroes. The bulk of the e. Atlantic wintering birds occur in the North Sea area and in the Baltic (in the latter, limits depend on ice conditions); on top of the continent, Old-squaws winter on open water sw. of Novaya Zemlya and elsewhere in Barents Sea; in the w. Pacific area, marine waters from Bering Sea s. to include Japan.

S. limits of recorded occurrence in Eurasia: Azores, Madeira, Iberian Pen., the Mediterranean (Sardinia, s. Italy), Baluchistan, Sind, and Assam.

For some further details, see especially Dementiev and Gladkov (1952) and Vaurie (1965).

In the Palearctic, reported as **fossil** from the Pleistocene of Denmark and Azer-baijan; references in Brodkorb (1964a). RSP

MIGRATION  Northward movement in spring includes long flights from southerly places, the ultimate destinations ranging from the subarctic to high-arctic. The flocks break up, small groups of birds going to open water close to nesting areas and then, when islets and other terrain become suitable, the pairs disperse and ♀ ♀ begin nest-ing. (At least in the high-arctic, except for a very few places, first open water is inland at shallow ponds, not the sea.)  Summer movements vary in different localities and are

R. T. T. —

not yet well understood. Beginning with departure of drakes while their mates are in-cubating and continuing at least until late summer, movements result in considerable segregation, both by age and sex, which is reflected in the composition of flocks after-ward throughout winter and even into the following spring. In fall, when there also are long migratory flights, drakes—mature ones especially—tend not to travel as far as ♀ ♀. The following is more or less schematic and rather tentative, being based on frag-ments of information. There are few usable data from banding.

N. AM.  **Spring**  Atlantic area, Va. to Maritimes—the more southerly birds, at least, move early (mostly before mid-April); some perhaps go overland via the Great Lakes, but the main corridor is up along the Atlantic coast. There are short daytime movements, trending northward, beginning in early March. The birds avoid crossing land and eventually they assemble in thousands at what probably are traditional staging areas. During this shifting, and continuing after reaching these areas, flocks take flight, usually in the afternoon and not necessarily only once during the day, and mount in circles until they are nearly out of sight. Then they descend, on a zigzag course, with a loud far-carrying whirring sound. Finally, on an afternoon, usually in flocks of 100–200 birds, they tower high and begin their high-altitude long-distance northward flight overland. These flights occur mostly well along in May, when inland waters in Ungava and beyond still are frozen; almost surely the early birds do not stop until they at least reach Ungava Bay, or Hudson Strait, or any open water in similar latitudes westward. Drakes, apparently groups of unmated prebreeders, occur in these waters soon after mid-May and both sexes (paired mature birds) are present within a week or so. Small flocks and pairs move close to their ultimate destinations as soon as leads open nearby in the sea ice, or there are puddles on the ice, or tundra ponds start to thaw; in this fashion the terminal portion of their journey is adjusted more or less to seasonal variations in local climate.

Nfld.—the large wintering population moves out before late April. To the north, along the outer coast of Labrador, there seems to be no recorded evidence of a sizable flight of Oldsquaws in any season. Perhaps they pass that way unseen, flying high, or they may go w. to staging areas in the Gulf of St. Lawrence and later fly northward overland, or perhaps some even may go to Greenland.

Greenland—the Oldsquaw is a plentiful winterer on the unfrozen waters along the sw. coast. The birds move up both coasts (beyond the shore ice there is open water far n. off the w. Greenland coast) and the total span of migration extends from March well into June. In a normal season they are at upper limits of summer range, on thawed pools, margins of lakes, and inundated sea ice, long before any leads in the ice have opened; that is, they are present by the 2nd or 3rd week in June, in groups containing mated pairs.

There is at least some movement (demonstrated by band recoveries) from Iceland to Greenland and this species is present in Icelandic waters through winter; whether local birds or regularly also some from a distance (Greenland? Spitzbergen?) is unknown.

Interior N. Am.—large numbers of Oldsquaws pass the winter on at least the more westerly Great Lakes (Michigan, Superior) and a considerable number on L. Ontario; presumably they go overland to Hudson Bay, or the more westerly ones toward the cent. Canadian arctic. (Wintering on Hudson Bay was mentioned under "Distribution.") Scattered observations seem to indicate a long initial flight from the more westerly Great Lakes nw. toward L. Athabaska, then onward in small flocks in the last $^2/_3$ of May and continuing well into June in northerly areas. Earliest birds (middle third of May) are drakes (prebreeders?). In the s. Hudson Bay coastal area flocks begin arriving in the last third of May. As mentioned earlier, possibly some Atlantic winterers go overland to the Great Lakes, which would place them on an interior route through Canada.

N. Am. Bering–Pacific waters—southerly Pacific coastal flocks begin shifting northward, beginning in early March; in April–May many thousands of birds gather in the island channels along the se. Alaskan coast (includes many winterers there). That many of these birds fly overland toward the upper Yukon and Mackenzie drainages, seems more probable than that all of them go clockwise around Alaska. Wintering flocks are spread all along the Aleutians and, in n. Bering Sea, the birds number in the hundreds of thousands. At St. Lawrence I. in early April "they seem to be almost exclusively in unisexual flocks, but by the end of the month mixed flocks are seen" (Fay and Cade 1959). There is low-altitude migration, in stages as leads open in the ice, along the Bering Sea coast of Alaska (also elsewhere in Bering Sea) to Bering Strait; usually it reaches massive proportions in late April. Tremendous numbers go through the Strait (undoubtedly includes winterers from e. Asian, international, and Am. waters); then many go westerly along the n. Siberian coast, and a heavy flight goes ne., passing Pt. Barrow in peak numbers about mid-May. Timing everywhere varies depending on ice conditions. The Alaskan flight moves on eastward, part of it undoubtedly going to various is. of the w. Canadian arctic. Very large numbers, however, are spread throughout arctic Alaska in summer.

**Molt migration** Prebreeding yearlings of both sexes, many of which arrive comparatively late within the general breeding range, congregate at certain places on the sea and on lakes on arctic and subarctic is. and the mainland; loose assemblies of 200–500 birds are common. As in other ducks, prebreeders are the earliest to become flightless. Later there are failed breeders and, soon after, drakes of successfully-breeding pairs that leave their incubating mates. Some breeding ♀ ♀ molt on ponds and lakes close to where they nested; some are known to be flightless while accompanied by preflight young. There are also untended groups of ducklings, because many ♀ ♀ abandon them and fly elsewhere prior to becoming flightless. Since the time when a bird flies to a molting place varies depending on latitude, season, age, sex, and (if a breeder) whether successful in breeding, the span during which molt migration occurs is long.

Distances traveled to molting places must vary a good deal; probably it is longest for some prebreeders and for post breeding drakes. These are some observations of molting birds. There were "huge flocks" of molting drakes and "immature" Oldsquaws in the summer of 1968 in waters of the Thule Dist., far up the w. side of Greenland (Salomonsen 1972), a large proportion presumably having flown northward to molt. In Hudson Bay off Churchill—rafts of a thousand or more, mostly ♂ ♂, probably mates of ♀ ♀ then incubating (Taverner and Sutton 1934); sw. Baffin I.—flock of 45, containing both sexes, July 8, in a bay (Macpherson and McLaren 1959); Slidre Fjord in w.-cent. Ellesmere I.—drakes flocking in early July; flightless "adults" Aug. 20–26, but none seen in Sept.; mid-Aug. to Sept. 9, many flocks of up to 200 ("adults" and young of the year, both sexes) and in "certain places the water was covered with feathers" (Parmelee and MacDonald 1960); Demarcation Pt. (arctic coastal Alaska–Canada boundary)—after July 5, small flocks of ♂ ♂ constantly arriving from the east and congregating in Demarcation Bay to molt (W. Brooks 1915); Alaska (off the North Slope)—offshore is., reefs, and spits afford protection from winds and sea ice to tens of thousands of molting Oldsquaws (Bartonek et al. 1971); Alaska (Wales area)—wing molt in early Aug.; large bands of Oldsquaws on large tundra lagoons (A. Bailey 1943); Alaska (Wainwright area)—in Aug. big groups congregated on a long spit which extends into Wainwright Inlet, the majority unable to fly (A. Bailey 1948); Alaska (St. Lawrence I.)—prebreeders as numerous as breeders; in late June, flocks of up to 300 of the former on lakes and lagoons; in Aug., family groups and aggregations of molters on a coastal lagoon (Fay and Cade 1959). From E. Siberia, many thousands of Oldsquaws, mostly postbreeding ♂♂, have a northward molt migration to high-arctic Wrangel I. Although reports would seem to indicate that the largest assemblies of molting Oldsquaws are in U.S.S.R. waters, the numerous flocks or rafts of molters in N. Am. and vicinity would, in the aggregate, amount to very large numbers in the Thule Dist. of Greenland, in Ungava Bay, Hudson Strait, Fisher Strait (se. coast of Southampton I.), along the n. coast of Keewatin, Mackenzie Bay and vicinity, lakes and lagoons of St. Lawrence I., and tundra lakes and some coastal lagoons of the Bering Sea coast of Alaska.

**Late summer–fall** What happens after the older birds regain flight and the new generation first attains it is not clear. There is an urge to form flocks and, to an unknown extent, a tendency to be (or to remain?) segregated according to age-class and sex. There is a kind of buildup period during which flocks combine on certain preferred areas of the sea and towering flights, such as occur in spring, have been reported.

**Fall** Many Oldsquaws do not migrate until the land is frozen and ice is forming on the sea. In general, they are gone from land areas in n. portions of breeding range by early Sept. at the very latest. Various observations provide some hints regarding differences among age-classes or between sexes, such as: 1 older drakes are the earliest birds (in Sept.) to make major flights; 2 there appears to be some kind of dispersal movement in which some young birds may go in almost any direction and up to great distances; and 3 some wintering areas are occupied largely (or entirely?) by prebreeders and evidently also mature ♀♀ and other, more northerly, areas by drakes of breeding age. Apparently, even drakes in their first winter have a tendency to travel less distance than ♀♀. The high-altitude, long-distance, overland flights for long distances come late, generally after mid-Oct.

Arrival on wintering areas is about as follows. Sw. Greenland—prolonged, beginning at the very end of Sept. Nfld.—beginning early Nov. New Eng. coast and southward—begin arriving in Mass. in numbers about mid-Oct. with additions at least through Nov. According to Mackay (1892), the birds are flying high, in flocks of 75–100, when arriving from overland in New Eng. waters; on reaching a desired locality they circle several times before alighting, then remain together on the water for an hour or so, then break into groups of a dozen or more individuals. Southerly limits on Atlantic coast—they arrive from last third of Oct. until past mid-Dec. Great Lakes— aside from some flocks of drakes that arrive early, evidently they are not present before late Oct. and arrivals continue for some weeks thereafter. Oldsquaws are plentiful on L. Ontario in the latter half of Oct. Possibly part of the Great Lakes birds move on to the Atlantic seaboard. Time of passage in Alaska: 1 Pt. Barrow—latter half of Sept. and in early Oct.; 2 Bering Strait—latter half of Sept. and most of Oct.; 3 St. Lawrence I.—a conservative estimate of 50,000 in winter, moving as the wind packs the ice on one side of the island and forms openings on the other; they come in Dec., are in concentrations until mid- or late April and, by about mid-May, only local nesters remain inland; in June–Aug., prebreeders and breeders are about equally numerous on lagoons and on interior lakes; during Sept. the birds disperse from the island and are scarce or absent throughout Oct. and Nov. (Fay 1961); 4 Gulf of Alaska and southward—few data, movement probably from early Oct. on.

**Some banding data**   A total of 1,790 "adult" Oldsquaws, when flightless during wing molt, were banded at Takslesluk L. (confluent with Baird Inlet), not distant from Bering Sea coastal Alaska, in 1963–65 inclusive. There have been 31 recoveries. Some of these indicate that individuals of both sexes return in subsequent molting seasons to the same locality where banded. (Furthermore, a winter-banded ♀ returned to the same wintering area in Ont.—Allison 1974.) Recoveries elsewhere are scattered, in fairly high latitudes, over more than 140° of longitude. A drake banded Aug. 9, 1964, was taken far to the east, in Sept. 1967, in the Hope Pt. region, N.W.T. (mainland side of Dolphin and Union Strait). Of even greater interest are 13 recoveries from e. Asia. These include a ♀ recovered in Kolyushin Bay (n. side of Chuckchee Pen.). They are widely scattered, from n. Chuckcheeland westward, the most distant being a drake banded Aug. 7, 1965, and shot near Khatanga (about lat. 72° N, long. 102° E) in the middle third of June 1966. It had reached approximately the midpoint in longitude of subarctic U.S.S.R. Some of the recoveries were far inland, as in the Chersk region, also n. of Magadan, and in the cent. Kolyma drainage. For Kamchatka, there is a recovery on the se. coast (Petropavlovsk region) and another on the sw. (Okhotsk Sea) coast. Southernmost was a bird shot on extreme s. Sakhalin I. on May 2, 1965.

Except for a recovery in Kolyushin Bay (mentioned above) and for midwinter ♀ ♀ from Okhotsk Sea and Bristol Bay, all recoveries were of drakes. Also, except for nearby Bristol Bay, there were no recoveries s. of the banding site in N. Am. The evidence indicates that many Oldsquaws of the Yukon Delta winter in Bering Sea and Okhotsk Sea where they mingle with birds from across Siberia. Since pairing generally occurs at wintering areas, ♂ ♂ from the Yukon Delta disperse (by accompanying their mates in spring) and so occur across E. Siberia and also into Canada. Such wide dispersal may be common in the Alaskan Oldsquaws, which currently av. about 375,000 birds in fall. (Data from Jim King.)

Southerly N. Am. Pacific limits—Oldsquaws arrive beginning some time in Nov.

**Other banding data**   One banded in Godthaab Dist. of w. Greenland, July 18, 1959, was recovered in Iceland on Nov. 7, 1959 (Salomonsen 1961); another banded in Godthaab Dist., July 20, 1961, was shot at Pt. Verde, Placentia, Nfld., Nov. 20, 1961 (Salomonsen 1965); some Oldsquaw ducklings were banded at Sarqaq, near Disko I. in w. Greenland, in 1947; one was found as a "breeding bird" at Tuktoyaktuk (e. edge of Mackenzie delta) in June, 1950, and another wintering in Denmark (Baltic Sea) in Jan., 1951 (Freuchen and Salomonsen 1958); one banded at Mývatn, Iceland, July 15, 1928, was killed in Disko Bay, w. Greenland, May 27, 1929 (M. Cooke 1945); 9 others banded at Mývatn have been recovered in w. Greenland (Nanortalik Dist.—2 in Nov., 1 in Dec.; Julianehaab Dist.—1 Feb., 2 March, 1 May; Frederikshaab Dist.—1 in Nov.; and Christianshaab Dist.—1 in May) (Salomonsen 1971).

EURASIA   As in N. Am., there are lateral movements along the "top" of the landmass, also "cutting across corners," and movement part way down the "sides." Flights occur down and up far within the interior, over long-used routes, where the number of birds is rather small.

Westerly route—from Yamal Pen. (as demonstrated by banding recoveries) and in all probability even from w. side of Taimyr Pen., in fall the birds go westward toward the entrance of the White Sea; then some go out around Scandinavia to various wintering places, while a massive flight (it was a million birds) goes from the White Sea across the Karelian isthmus (via Lakes Onega and Ladoga) to the Gulf of Finland and on into the Baltic; their wintering localities are scattered from the Baltic to places around the North Sea, with heavier concentrations more southerly in colder winters. Fall movement begins in 2nd half of Sept., reaches a peak in Karelia and thereabouts usually in early Oct., and passage continues during Nov. At first, 80% are mature drakes, later come ♀♀ of various ages and younger drakes. For a discussion of fall and spring movement in n. Europe, and diagram of the routes, see Mathiasson (1970). Spring migration begins in March and, as ice conditions permit, the birds shift toward cent. Baltic–Gulf of Finland waters. Then, mostly in the last 3 weeks of May, they head overland toward the White Sea and on eastward beyond. Gulf of Finland: in low-altitude (200–300 meters) flight over water, speed av. 74 km./hr. (46 mph) and in high-altitude (500–2,000 meters) flight over land it is about 10% faster (G. Bergman and Donner 1964). Rather surprisingly, they fly slower than scoters (*Melanitta nigra*).

Easterly route—apparently begins on e. side of Taimyr Pen. Although there is migration all along the easterly arctic coast and down through Bering Strait, a great many Oldsquaws cross the Chuckchee Pen. to Bering Sea, or some may even cross farther w. from the Kolyma drainage southward. There are very large numbers, in flocks of up to hundreds and containing both sexes, in the Chuckchee Sea from Sept. at least through Oct.

Interior migration is mostly in Transuralia (e. of the Urals) in w. Siberia, mainly (although not exclusively) by birds in their first fall, and they go to various destinations. For details, see Pavlinin (1965), who stated that thousands pass through Transuralia in fall and that the number northbound in spring generally is smaller. Oldsquaws reach interior localities scattered from the Black Sea (in spring and fall) to the Caspian (in winter) and other waters including those in and near Kazakhstan, also far eastward at L. Baikal (winterer, perhaps also transient).

**Molt migration** An incomplete listing of Palearctic areas where Oldsquaws assemble to molt includes: around Kolguev I. (prebreeders, here outside breeding range), sw. coast of s. Novaya Zemlya, around Vaigach I., Belo I., lakes of n. Yamal Pen., n. interior lakes e. of the Urals (prebreeders), around New Siberian Is. (mostly prebreeders), Indigirka Delta (huge numbers), waters in Kolyma and Anadyr lowlands (mainly prebreeders in latter), Schmidt Cape (prebreeders mainly), and coastal lagoons and tundra lakes of Wrangel I. (many thousands, mostly postbreeding drakes). RSP

BANDING STATUS In U.S.–Canada the total number banded through 1964 was 1,503, with only a single recovery through 1961; main places of banding: Alaska, Dist. of Franklin, and Man. (data from Bird Banding Laboratory). The banding of 1,790 Oldsquaws in the summers of 1963–65 inclusive, w. of Bethel in Alaska, has been referred to earlier under "Migration."

In Greenland in 1946–64 inclusive, the total number banded was 228, with 24 recoveries in Greenland plus 4 abroad.

The second (1964) bulletin of the U.S.S.R. Bird-Ringing Bureau gave 685 as total number banded through 1959.

Numbers banded in other programs (Iceland, Scandinavia, perhaps elsewhere) presumably are small. RSP

REPRODUCTION   (N. Am. data unless otherwise indicated.) There is no satisfactory evidence that yearlings breed, although this has been claimed for ♀ ♀ presumed to have been still wearing much-worn Juv. wings (yearling prebreeders perhaps attend groups of ducklings hatched by older ♀ ♀). In drakes in their first fall–spring (Oct.–May inclusive), testicular volume does increase, but proportionately much less than in older age-classes; there is no evident follicle development in ♀ ♀ of corresponding age. In their 2nd year of life the birds are, to all outward appearances, "adult," and presumably they **attain breeding condition** when approaching 2 years of age. In "adult" drakes, testicular volume increases tremendously in May and, presumably, drakes have a relatively short period of active spermatogenesis in the arctic—late May to early July—as compared with a longer temperate-zone season in Mallards. No data were obtained by which the testis cycle of drakes from about age 18 mo. on could be distinguished from those of older age-classes; there may be no difference. (Summarized from Ellarson 1956.)

Sexual **displays** of the Oldsquaw consist first of group activity (by drakes, but soon oriented toward a duck) and then of single pairs (pair formation, bond maintenance, copulation). Drakes in groups begin calling, making Short Flights, and alighting with vigorous splashing. Soon they gather around a duck and direct their displays toward her. She may take wing and mount very high, closely followed by drakes; the group zigzags down to water. The duck, if hard pressed, dives and the drakes follow her under, back to the surface, and again over the water (E. W. Nelson 1887). In captivity also, the drake has been seen to pursue the ♀ under water (Washington 1972). In due course, pairs are formed and, thereafter, a drake attacks if another approaches his mate.

At least among birds already old enough to have bred, **pair formation** usually must occur prior to spring migration; migrant flocks contain mated pairs. All through the spring in the north country, drakes still in Alt. Plumage, as well as others that are acquiring part of Basic, are displaying very actively. Quite a few appear to be unmated, hence it would seem that pair formation, especially of birds beginning their first breeding cycle, may continue to occur in spring.

**Displays of the duck**   CHIN-LIFTING rapid, head kept down on "shoulders" (Myres 1959a), with various guttural calls (Drury 1961), presumably functionally equivalent to Inciting (Johnsgard 1965); ritualized BATHING (Drury).

**Displays of the drake**   Most frequent is AH-HAR-LIK CALL, with or without Bill-toss (Myres); also drake calls *ugh ugh ah-oo-ah*, 2nd syllable loudest, last 3 different in character and associated with REAR-END display, or *a-oo a-oo a-oo-gah* (accent on last *oo*); drake begins with neck vertical, then swings head down in forward arc as tail is erected to vertical and both feet kicked just out of water (Myres); sometimes the elevated tail is vibrated laterally; NECK-STRETCH tail up at 45° (Drury), may follow or be linked to TURNING-THE-BACK-OF-THE-HEAD (Myres); SHORT FLIGHT stiffly upward and abrupt return to water (Drury), tends to be a group activity; in a variant, usually late in the season, they fly along the surface in a group, their rear ends dragging in water, then they extend heads forward, low, and drop with a splash; ritualized PREEN-ING while partly "capsized," the white belly and side exposed toward the duck.

**Copulation** as observed in the wild: neither sex had any particular display before or after treading by the drake; the ♀ was PRONE from very briefly to 15 sec. in various instances (Myres 1959a). In the w. Canadian arctic at Victoria I., the birds copulated on the sea at the edge of the ice during the first 3 weeks of June (T. G. Smith 1973).

**Pursuit flights** of a pair plus an interloping ♂ (and with ♀ leading) occur as long as the pair bond is maintained, but seem most prevalent in the period from nest site prospecting into laying, i.e., are over nesting terrain. Pair bond form evidently is **single-clutch monogamy.**

There is some tendency toward a **grouping** of nests; that is, when groups disperse, apparently the pairs do not scatter widely. There are places where Oldsquaw nests are relatively plentiful; they are scarce or absent from what seem like equally suitable areas not far away. Especially on small islands and islets in tundra ponds and lakes, where the birds are free from terrestrial predators, nesting density sometimes is very high. At Mývatn, Iceland, there were 29 nests on an islet 60 yds. in circumference (Shepard, in S. F. Baird et al. 1884b). In Lopp Lagoon near Wales, Alaska, A. Bailey (1943) found at least a hundred nests on an island of unstated size. Referring to the same general locality later, he wrote of "colonies" as "more or less local" with "many birds in one place, and almost none in another" (A. Bailey 1948). Even so, widely scattered nests are very common and apparently are the basis for the idea that each pair has its own pond from which all other Oldsquaws are excluded.

The **nest site** is preferably not far from fresh water, sometimes at its very edge; generally dry. Often there is some concealment, under low or nearly prostrate woody growth (willow, birch, spruce), for example, or in a recess among rocks, or among sedges. Many sites are out in the open on turf, rocks, or sand, but even here the sitting bird seems to merge more or less into the surroundings.

Nesting in Arctic Tern colonies has been reported for localities in various parts of the Oldsquaw's total breeding range. They also nest near or among eiders (*Somateria mollissima*). In Iceland, according to Faber (1822), they laid eggs in nests of Greater Scaups (*Aythya marila*), drove the original owners away, and incubated the joint clutches. Also in Iceland, the Red-breasted Merganser (*Mergus serrator*) has been known to lay in nests of the Oldsquaw.

**Nest**  Considerable dry grass may be accumulated if available at the site, but often there are no plant materials. Before the nest down is added, the duck pulls over her eggs any plant material she has accumulated. Probably it is during early occupancy of the site that the duck is seen sometimes at the edge of a tundra pond plucking at vegetation; nothing is transported, however. Usually by the time the clutch is completed, sufficient nest down has accumulated to line the cavity and to cover the clutch before the duck departs. The sprays of **nest down** are small, nearly black with whitish centers, giving a mottled appearance in bulk. (That of Steller's Eider is evenly dark, the Pintail's much lighter.) An occasional breast feather is intermingled; these vary, some being white, others grayish (darkest distally).

**Clutch size** 5–7 eggs in "considerably over" 100 nests in nw. Dist. of Mackenzie (MacFarlane 1891). This is low for the species; Brandt (1943) stated 5–10, usually 6–8, for the Hooper Bay area of Alaska. Joint layings have resulted in up to 17 eggs in a nest. On the other hand, clutch size is reduced in adverse seasons. For variation in mean clutch size (low of 7.56 in 1970, high of 9.04 in 1968) during 9 consecutive years in the Mývatn area of Iceland, see Bengtson (1971a). Prolonged bad weather can result in delayed nesting, as at Churchill, Man., in 1972 (Alison 1973), or even nonnesting, as reported for several n. Greenland localities, Bear I., and elsewhere. (For a listing of seasons of partial or complete nesting failure in the arctic, see "Habits" of King Eider.)

One **egg** from each of 20 clutches (2 Alaska, 16 widespread in Canada, 2 Iceland): **size** length $54.80 \pm 2.95$ mm., breadth $38.10 \pm 1.59$, radii of curvature of ends $15.73 \pm 1.13$ and $10.57 \pm 1.21$; **shape** usually subelliptical but considerable variation, elongation $1.43 \pm 0.054$, bicone $-0.010$, asymmetry $+0.194$ (FWP). For other meas. that include eggs from much of the range of the species, see especially Bent (1925), Brandt (1943), Schönwetter (1961), and Witherby (1939); in the different series (total 503 eggs), averages of length vary within a range of 1.8 mm. and of width 1.2 mm. The shell is smooth, color some variant of pale grayish or brownish olive. Oldsquaw eggs av. smaller than Harlequin eggs. When not cleaned and polished they are indistinguishable from Pintail eggs, but after polishing they are identifiable by deeper color and high gloss (Brandt 1943).

If an Oldsquaw loses an incomplete clutch, evidently the remainder is laid at another site. Also, it is generally believed that if a completed clutch is lost, a **replacement clutch** is laid.

A rather **late nester.** Fresh clutches may be expected about as follows, but allowance must be made for earliness or tardiness of season: last third of May in warmer parts of Alaskan mainland and on various islands; about the beginning of June in nw. Alaska and much of Iceland; June 10—southerly breeding areas in Greenland; June 15–25— n. Canadian mainland including n. Ungava; June 25–30—much of arctic Alaska, Spitzbergen; early July—colder areas of the Canadian high-arctic, nw. Greenland, and is. n. of the Eurasian mainland.

The duck incubates and the drake remains nearby for a while on a tundra pond, river, or marine bay until some time during incubation, when he departs for a molting area. The ♀ is a close sitter, especially as the end of incubation nears, and occasionally a bird has been lifted from the eggs. In captivity, a ♀ regularly left the nest twice daily to bathe and feed (Washington 1972). **Incubation period** in the wild 24 days, based on data in Løvenskiold (1964); also "about" 26 days at Churchill, Man. (Alison 1973). A shipment of eggs was sent from Iceland to Britain and incubated under bantam hens; 30 hatched normally, 14 in 24 and 16 in 25 days (Derscheid 1938). Period stated to be 23 days (Johnstone 1970), but whether artificially incubated not stated.

There are no data on hatching success. The **ducklings,** some time after they are dry, are led to water and, contrary to some authors, swim well from the beginning and dive readily, to feed and to escape from predators. The duck, if alarmed, swims away from shore with her brood close to her. Using hip-length wading boots, the writer has gone into shallow tundra ponds after these broods; the duck soon flees, the brood scatters and, on close approach, the ducklings dive to the bottom and remain there for many seconds before bobbing to the surface. While they are on the bottom, a person can slide a foot over them gently to restrain them, then reach down and pick them up. Millais

367

(1913a), from observations in Iceland, stated that the duck dives and brings up food, which she places before her very young brood; few persons have studied Oldsquaws closely, but nobody else has claimed that such behavior occurs.

As to predation on the young, there is not much information, at least in the Nearctic area. Arctic foxes (*Alopex lagopus*) and roving dogs raid nests that they can reach; gulls (*Larus* spp.) get some eggs and ducklings; jaegers (*Stercorarius* spp.) are the most frequently mentioned predators, especially on young broods—see Millais (1913a) for a description of how they hunt ducklings; Ravens (*Corvus corax*) get eggs in some localities; native peoples are predators on eggs to some extent.

Oldsquaw families tend to vacate small waters soon. Presumably the duck leads her brood overland or downstream to larger inland waters or the sea. In n. Ungava, Turner (in Bent 1925) saw a duck lead 13 small ducklings at least a half mile to salt water. Some young stay on freshwater lakes until they can fly. Some broods are accompanied by a duck for a long time, even during the duck's flightless period; frequently, however, she departs long before they can fly and then amalgamations or crèches of ducklings, not necessarily of the same age, may be escorted or accompanied by none to several ♀♀. In the case of older preflight ducklings, especially on tidal waters, groups of 15–20, unattended, are quite common. Parmelee et al. (1967) reported a gathering of 138 unattended preflight young on Aug. 21 on Victoria I. Such groups are able to fend for themselves. On ponds in Chesterfield Inlet, Keewatin, in late July, broods joined forces and subdivided freely; it also became obvious that ducklings easily travel overland at least a quarter mile; by Aug. 24 some were on salt water where, by the 26th, they were forming flocks (Savile 1951).

According to Hantzsch (1905), the young are fully feathered and attain flight in "about" 5 weeks. Although accurate, this undoubtedly was an estimate. An egg from Iceland hatched July 22; the mantle and tail feathers appeared about Aug. 6; on Aug. 26 the bird would have flown if it had not been pinioned, according to Wormald (in J. C. Phillips 1925). Young in the wild at Churchill, Man., **attain flight** in 35 days (Alison 1973).

There are various observations of preflight young still on fresh water as late as the first week in Sept.; surely they would perish if the freeze-up came early. RSP

SURVIVAL   Based on published recoveries of Icelandic birds, an estimated mean annual adult survival rate of $0.72 \pm 0.04$ was calculated by Boyd (in Le Cren and Holdgate 1962). RSP

HABITS   Almost pelagic; frequently encountered a great distance from nearest land. Generally moves about in flocks of 50–200 or more and, after a flock alights, the birds tend to scatter in parties of about 7 to 15–20 individuals. Groups of this size seem to be the most closely knit social unit. Except under certain conditions in the breeding season, the Oldsquaw shows no inclination whatever to associate with other wildfowl. Even solitary individuals go their own way. The Oldsquaw is a very active bird. Sometimes flocks engage in a very animated social form of Splash-bathing, or the same with somersaulting. Flocks are noisy, even on clear nights. They are not wary of man. They prefer not to fly overland, but many do so, traveling very high when migrating.

Flocks tend to shift inshore to feed, then out again to rest, but their times of movement and daily routine in general vary greatly according to wind, tide, and depth of water. They have spectacular towering flights in both spring and fall, which were described by Mackay (1892). Although flightless birds during late summer and autumn molting rest on mudbars, low ledges, and elsewhere at the water's edge, winterers usually remain on the water constantly. They rest on ice occasionally, although recorded observations of this are scarce. On the island of Nantucket, Mass., they came occasionally to freshwater ponds in early spring (Mackay 1892), a habit also observed in the Palearctic region. Theinmann (1903), who kept some Oldsquaws through summer on a pond, stated that his birds never came ashore while healthy.

Intention to fly is shown by lateral HEAD-SHAKING. The birds rise with great ease, even in calm air, generally fly in a somewhat strung-out formation, and move noisily to some other locality. In spring, Speirs (1945) timed the flight of 12 groups; av. air speed was 50.5 mph and ground speed varied from 53.9 to 72.5 mph. This is somewhat faster than movement of migrant spring flocks in the Baltic, as determined by radar (see "Migration").

In preparation for diving, the Oldsquaw spreads and flattens its tail on (or even under) the water, opens its wings somewhat, and plunges forward and downward. Flying birds, if shot at, sometimes dive from the air (J. C. Phillips 1925). The diving bird reduces its specific volume by compressing its feathers (which reduces the amount of trapped air) and can proceed downward with minimum expenditure of energy. It has been stated that the wings are used for underwater propulsion. A dead Oldsquaw, kept submerged until it is saturated to the skin, sinks rather than floats (Ellarson 1956). Those caught in gill nets die without struggle (no damage to bird or net) in a particular posture with wings considerably out from the body (Ellarson). Diving to a depth of 10 fathoms probably is commonplace for this species. The deepest depth, believed to be reliably reported and based on birds taken on set hooks in L. Michigan, was 34 fathoms (Ellarson). For discussion of the physiology of deep diving and for various records of depths reached, see Schorger (1947). The Oldsquaw's unique anatomical specializations for such diving were discussed by Kuroda (1959). This species must have various feeding methods, judging from the variety of its known foods. At Izembek Bay, Alaska, members of a flock were seen to dive and also to reappear simultaneously, perhaps obtaining food by some concerted action (R. D. Jones, Jr.).

Because it is nearly pelagic, the Oldsquaw is safer from hunters than most ducks. On the Great Lakes, for example, the birds generally are so far out (7–10 mi. and beyond) that they cannot be seen from shore. On the other hand, in spring in the Finnish Archipelago in the Baltic, the writer has shot Oldsquaws over decoys at one of the outer islands. Formerly, when spring shooting was legal in N. Am., the Oldsquaw was hunted to some extent. Its numbers on this continent appear not to have diminished. In the recent past it has been considered an unimportant species, of so little consequence in sport hunting that it barely got passing mention in a 1965 federally sponsored volume, *Waterfowl Tomorrow*. Of 1,051 dead Oldsquaws taken from fishnets in L. Michigan and examined by fluoroscope in April, 1952, only 9 (1 first-winter and 8 older birds) were found with body-shot and none had ingested shot (Ellarson). The Oldsquaw, however, is taken both by netting and shooting in Eurasia and, apparently as a consequence of having some importance in man's economy there, it has received considerable study in recent years. The number of birds migrating via the Baltic has declined greatly over the past 50 years, the main cause evidently being oil from ship-wrecks and pumped from ships' bilges both in the Baltic and the North Sea. In the former, severe winters also have caused considerable losses.

On the Great Lakes, notably Michigan, the number of Oldsquaws taken in gill nets by fishermen may have approached 100,000 in the exceptional winters of 1949–50 and 1950–51; ordinarily, the catch is only 15%–20% as large (Ellarson). During April or May, 1917, about 15,000 drowned in nets off Rondeau in L. Erie and were found at a fertilizer plant on May 16 (data from a label on a specimen salvaged by W. E. Saunders). A fisherman at Saugatuck, Mich., reported having taken 27,000 during March, April, and part of May 1946 (Schorger 1947).

Off s. Mass., Mackay (1892) reported that, in the very severe winter of 1888 when there was much ice on the sea, Oldsquaws starved until they were "skin and bones" and many, particularly ♀♀ and birds in their first winter, died. From summary in Ellarson: 1880–81, L. Michigan—Oldsquaws froze in the ice off Milwaukee and boys peddled the emaciated corpses; 1897–98, a die-off at Sault Ste. Marie when the entire St. Mary's River froze over; 1903–04, L. Superior froze and dead Oldsquaws were picked up from the ice, also ashore nearby, and a few far inland. (Interestingly, 2 of the Great Lakes, Erie and Ontario, have not frozen over entirely in historic times, al-though sometimes they have frozen from shore at least as far out as the eye can see.)

Duben (1968) described mortality in the Tym R. valley on the e. side of Sakhalin I. caused by a severe storm on Nov. 22, 1965. Flocks of Oldsquaws were blown against trees, cables, snowdrifts, house roofs, and other objects.

Among waterfowl killed by fowl cholera (*Pasturella multocida*) in and near Chesapeake Bay in Feb.–March, 1970, the most numerous victims were Oldsquaws.

Around St. Lawrence I. in Bering Sea, the winds and currents keep opening and closing the leads in sea ice, so that vast numbers of wintering Oldsquaws keep shifting location (Fay and Cade 1959).

The Oldsquaw has a definite reputation as a table bird "several grades worse" than goldeneyes (J. C. Phillips 1925). Yet Ellarson ate the meat (but not the fat) and con-cluded that his experience was "not unpleasant." The writer once ate Oldsquaw in spring and found it quite satisfactory; the meal, however, had to be delayed so as to allow adequate time for cooking! The ventral body down of this bird has excellent in-sulating properties, but gathering it in summer is impractical because usually the nests are too widely scattered. Nor can it be obtained efficiently in winter; plucking dead Oldsquaws is very difficult and time-consuming.

Seven Oldsquaws, taken on L. Michigan on Feb. 1 when there was virtually no molt-ing in progress, were weighed, plucked (except for remiges, rectrices, scapulars, and head feathers), and the removed feathers were weighed: 2 ♂ "adult" 984.3 and 821.2 gm., the feathers 35.3 and 30.9 gm. (3.6% and 3.6% of total); a ♀ "adult" 813.4 gm., the feathers 34.4 (4.2%); 2 first-winter ♂ 869.2 and 869.1, feathers 30.5 and 31.6 (3.5% and 3.6%); 2 first-winter ♀ 811.8 and 822, the feathers 30.8 and 24 (3.8% and 2.9%) (Ellar-son).

On the Great Lakes the birds can survive the winter on a diet of an amphipod of the genus *Pontoporeia* (a tiny shrimplike bottom organism), taken at depths of 10–20 or more fathoms (Ellarson). Oldsquaws ingest sand and grit; there is considerable in alimentary tracts and the fecal matter has a gritty character (Ellarson). RSP

FOOD   Examination of the stomachs of 190 "adults" showed 88% animal matter consisting principally of crustaceans, along with mollusks, insects, and fishes. The 12% vegetable matter comprised mainly seeds of grasses and pondweeds. "Juveniles" had taken 77% animal matter, mainly crustaceans. The 23% of vegetable matter consisted largely of aquatic plants (Cottam 1939).

**Animal**   Crustaceans: amphipods (*Gammarus, Caprella*), mud crabs (*Neopanope, Hexapanopeus*), shrimps (*Crago*), crayfishes (*Cambarus*), mysids (*Thysanoessa*), fairy shrimp (*Lepidurus*), etc. 48.2%; mollusks (*Mytilus edulis, Lacuna, Littorina,* etc.) 15.7%; insects (Trichoptera, Chironomidae, *Corethra*) 10.8%; fishes (Pleuronectidae, Clupeidae, Cottidae, Cyprinidae) 9.7%; miscellaneous animal food 3.5% (Cottam 1939).

The animal food of downy young included 75.6% crustaceans (*Branchinecta, Daphnia,* etc.) and only 1.3% insects.

The nine-spined stickleback (*Pygosteus pungitius*) was rated an important summer food at Perry R., N.W.T. A second stomach contained pupa cases, apparently of caddis fly (H. C. Hanson et al. 1956). In Ungava waters, shrimps and small bivalves (Gross 1937); in interior Ungava, caddis fly larvae and cases (Polunin and Eklund 1953). In Mass., shellfish (*Venus, Siliqua, Astarte*), fishes, and crustaceans (Mackay 1892).

In N.Y., 52 small pike found in a stomach (Loring 1890). The reported finding of 140 shiners (*Notropis atherinoides*) averaging 2 in. long in a bird from the Chicago area (Hull 1914) seems incredible. In Ohio, earthworms and cutworms (Haynes 1900) and gizzard shad and crayfishes (Trautman 1940). Food in L. Michigan 99% animal: amphipods (*Pontoporeia affinis*) 77%; fishes and fish eggs (*Cottus, Perca, Notropis*) 18%; mollusks (Gastropoda and Pelecypoda) 3%; insects (Coleoptera, Trichoptera, Diptera) 1% (Ellarson 1956); chiefly *Pisidium* and *Pontoporeia* (Lagler and Wienert 1948).

Herring eggs taken in state of Wash. (Jewett et al. 1953). In the Pribilof Is., principally crustaceans (*Anonyx, Bathymedon, Caprella, Gammarus, Dermaturus,* etc.), *mollusks (Mytilus, Saxicava, Modiolaria, Littorina,* etc.) (Preble and McAtee 1923).

In Greenland, beetle (*Colymbetes dolobratus*) and larvae, Diptera (*Simulium, Sciara*), bud and capsule of *Polythricium* (Longstaff 1932); mollusks (*Modiolaria, Mya, Macoma, Margarita, Saxicava*) (Salomonsen 1950); shrimp (*Mysis relicta*) and other crustaceans, sculpins (Cottam and Hanson 1938); mainly insects and larvae in fresh water and mollusks and crustaceans in salt water (Manniche 1910).

At Mývatn, Iceland, Oldsquaws fed mostly in deeper water in the central part of the shallow lake; both sexes fed on chironomid larvae; fish eggs were relatively important in June–July and Cladocera in Aug.; newly hatched to half-grown birds fed almost exclusively on Cladocera; when larger, mainly Cladocera (Bengtson 1971b).

In Denmark mainly mollusks: bivalves (*Mytilus, Cardium, Spisula*) 51%; gastropods (*Littorina, Hydrobia*) 14%; crustaceans (*Gammarus, Idothea*) 27%; fishes (*Gobius, Gasterosteus*) 4.7%; echinoderms 1.5%; and annelids 1.8% (Madsen 1954).

Food reported from U.S.S.R. entirely animal. During the nesting season on the

371

tundra, consists of crustaceans and larvae of insects. In early spring on the Taimyr Pen., stomachs usually are filled with red larvae of midges. Food on Yamal Pen. consists of larvae of caddis flies, and crustaceans (Ostracoda, *Apus, Branchipus*). Stomachs in spring in Anadyr contained larvae of stone flies (Perlidae), sometimes as many as 100 in a stomach, larvae of caddis flies, also remains of small fishes, fish eggs, and elytra of beetles. Stated to feed on fish that died the previous autumn after spawning. During fall migration on the Pechora R. the food is chiefly insects and at Rybinsk Reservoir small fishes (73%), roach 52%, perch 21%, plus larvae of insects (*Tendipes plumosus, Glyptotendipes gripekoveni*) 20%. Of less importance: larvae of caddis flies, and mollusks (*Anodonta*). In e. Murmansk in winter, stomachs contained sandhoppers, and in Kamchatka the remains of mollusks (Dementiev and Gladkov 1952).

**Vegetable**  Seeds and vegetative parts of grasses 3.6%; seeds of pondweeds (*Potamogeton, Zostera, Ruppia, Zannichellia*) 1.5%; miscellaneous (*Vitis, Aronia, Lemna, Empetrum,* etc.) 7% (Cottam 1939).

"Juveniles" fed on *Hippuris, Empetrum, Potamogeton, Rubus, Carex, Ledum, Eleocharis, Ranunculus,* etc.

Tops of vernal grass (*Anthoxanthum odoratum*) eaten in Mass. (Mackay 1892). Yorke (1899) mentioned teal moss (*Limnobium*), blue flag (*Iris versicolor*), duckweed (*Lemna*), water plantain (Alismaceae), etc. Various parts of sedges and grasses, lupine (*Lupinus*), plume (Ceramiaceae), and filamentous algae (*Chaetomorpha*) consumed in the Pribilof Is. (Preble and McAtee 1923). Rootlets, moss, and especially algae in Spitzbergen (Le Roi, in Koenig 1911). AWS

# Common Goldeneye

*Bucephala clangula*

Moderate-sized diving duck; sexually dimorphic—mainly black and white (♂ Alt. Plumage) or dark grays or gray-browns and white with brownish head (other Plumages). Also shares with Barrow's Goldeneye such characters as: nostril nearer tip than base of bill; after early stages, iris, legs, and feet yellowish. Although the Alt.-Plumaged drake is readily identifiable by any of various characters (roundish white patch in front of eye, streaked scapulars, immaculate white area in the retained Basic wing), other stages in both sexes vary from less readily distinguishable to perhaps indistinguishable from corresponding stages of Barrow's; see full discussion by A. Brooks (1920). The nail on the bill of the Common generally is smaller, usually flush with the bill, and tends to become narrower (toward oval) proximally; dorsal profile of bill and frontal area of skull (not the feathering) align to form a continuously even slope (no bulge in frontal area); see diagrams on p. 400. The Common has more white secondaries in the Basic wing than does Barrow's (which usually has only 6).

In the midportion of the windpipe of the drake there is a very sizable bulbous enlargement, in which the bony rings are "irregular and confused in design"; preflight young show little or none of this specialization, but "complete development is reached by or before midwinter" (P. A. Taverner 1919). The bony bulla at inner end of the trachea is large (larger than in *B. islandica*) and asymmetrical. The tracheal apparatus has been described and/or illustrated many times, beginning in 1798. For a useful illus., see A. Brooks (1920); for a more detailed one, Schiøler (1926).

DESCRIPTION   Two Plumages/cycle in both sexes, the 2nd cycle being earliest definitive. In many of our ducks the ♀ acquires Basic head–body in spring, the ♂ beginning in summer or later; in the goldeneyes the timing is ♂-like in both sexes, i.e., no molting by the ♀ in spring prior to nesting.

▶   ♂ Def. Alt. Plumage (all feathering except tail and wing), acquired in FALL (often complete by mid-Oct.) and worn through winter into the following SUMMER. **Bill** nearly black, **iris** pale yellow. **Head** black with sheen (mostly greenish but some ultramarine-violet) and an oval (sometimes round) white area adjoining side base of bill which av. slightly larger in Alt. III than in Alt. II. **Upperparts** mantle and rump black, the long scapulars white with wide black border along both webs; neck and **underparts** white, the feathers on upper margins of sides and the flanks with broad black border at outer web and some feathers in vent area are brownish gray with white tips; legs and **feet** orange-yellow, the webs dusky. Tail and wing are retained Basic feathering.

NOTE   According to D. P. Olson (MS), who examined a fairly large series of birds in Me., most ♂♂ with no bursa of Fabricius or a short, blind, pit and (presumably in Alt. III or later Alts.) had the roof of the mouth entirely black and had larger (av. 18.3 × 26.7mm.) white face patches; of 10 ♂♂ with small bursas (presumably 18 mo. old and in Alt. II) 6 had areas of white or gray on the roof of the mouth but in 4 it was black, and all 10 tended to have smaller (av. 17.3 × 24.4 mm.) face patches. Since the actual ages of the birds were not known, these findings are tentative. The measurements given (averages with overlap in range) are too similar to be of much use, but the color differences may be helpful.

▶ ♂ Def. Basic Plumage (entire feathering), the head–body worn for an unknown period in LATE SUMMER–EARLY FALL, the tail and wing retained nearly a year. Generally speaking, drakes begin acquiring Basic head–body some time in late June or in July and lose it beginning in early autumn, in some individuals later, and they are flightless in Aug.

Distinguishable from ♀ Plumages because white patch in wing is not broken by any coloring on white coverts. **Head** paler than ♀ Def. Alt. There is little light color (no clear white) in **scapulars**. **Tail** rounded, rather dark grayish. **Wing** differs from Juv. in being nearly black, with some metallic sheen on inner coverts and innermost secondaries, and has large white area that includes: 7 or 8 middle secondaries (adjoining ones may be partly white), and a slightly larger number of greater and middle coverts (white does not extend to leading edge of wing); wing lining medium or darker grayish, the axillars also. The 2 outer primaries have narrow web, an "adult ♂" characteristic.

▶ ♀ Def. Alt. Plumage (all feathering except tail and wing), acquired in FALL and worn into following SUMMER. Distal third of **bill** (excluding nail) muted orange-yellow about Feb.–May, at other times more or less dark like base; perhaps rarely all of bill yellow (A. Brooks 1920); roof of mouth largely white or pink (as in all age-classes); **iris** pale yellow. **Head** sepia-brown. Nape toward slaty, the feathers tipped white. **Upperparts** including mantle and rump, also upper breast (but not foreneck) and most of sides, rather slaty; most of these feathers margined white, which wears off. Most of neck, also **underparts** from lower breast to vent, white; feathers from vent to tail medium gray with pale tips. Legs and **feet** yellow, the webs dusky. Tail and wing are retained Basic feathering.

NOTE  The ♀ remains in Alt., with pale ventral body down, through spring. That is, in *Bucephala*, the nest down is pale.

▶ ♀ Def. Basic Plumage (entire feathering), the head–body acquired beginning EARLY JULY to EARLY AUG. (early nesters begin molt early) and retained into FALL (probably Oct.); the late-acquired tail and wing are retained nearly a year, i.e., are also worn with the Alt. Plumage.

**Bill** all dark, or may be noticeably lighter distally. Differences from Def. Alt.: **head** more muted brownish; no white in neck (it matches mantle and most of breast; **sides** and flanks brownish rather than toward slaty. The ventral **body down** is not quite as pale as in spring. Legs and **feet** muted yellowish. **Tail** dark grayish brown. **Wing** differs from definitive ♂ in not having dark feathers as dark, also the white area usually is interrupted by 2 bars formed by medium to dark gray distal portions of greater and middle coverts; some middle coverts also have other grayed areas (individuals vary in amount); wing lining and axillars as in ♂.

AT HATCHING  See vol. 2, col. pl. facing p. 466. It has been claimed that a distinction exists between downy Barrow's (legs and feet greenish gray to dark greenish yellow) and Commons (legs and feet yellowish green, webs dusky), apparently based on Icelandic Barrow's and European Commons. In N. Am., both species have a hint of yellowish or orange-yellow in legs and feet (it is lacking in the Bufflehead); the iris is gray, bluish gray, brownish gray, and rarely brown in the Common and at least not bluish in Barrow's, so far as known. J. Munro (1939) stated that the 2 goldeneyes are indistinguishable except by the bill, which is shorter, narrows more steeply, with nail wider and rounder, in Barrow's. These differences are relative and not easy to use. Internally, the lemon-shaped bulge in the trachea of the ♂ Common does not develop until later on. Downy Buffleheads have a much smaller nail on the bill than either of the goldeneyes.

▶  ♂ Juv. Plumage (entire feathering), perfected by about age 7–8 weeks (when flight attained) and much of it (always excepting the wing) not retained very long afterwards. **Bill** dark, **iris** brownish. Compared with ♀ Def. Alt.: **head** more toward brownish olive; **upperparts** browner, with any pale feather edging narrower and grayish. **Underparts** upper breast light gray to smoke gray; sides and flanks near smoke gray, the feathers faintly and broadly margined lighter; lower breast and **belly** very light, altering toward smoke gray in region of vent; under tail coverts whitish with grayish markings. (The very light area on the venter is fairly well defined and the feathers have fairly distinct fine transverse wavy lines or small blotches, i.e., the Juv. belly is not plain white.) **Tail** feathers taper and have projecting shafts (where the down broke off); light **wing** patch generally larger in the covert area, but it is not always white (smaller coverts may be off-white); wing coverts narrower than in the later Basic wing, with less rounded ends, also a less orderly pattern of medium to dark grays on various light coverts.

Captive-reared *B. c. clangula* have their bodies covered with feathers at age 33 days (Blaauw 1909), but growth and development of the Juv. Plumage continues for 3–4 weeks thereafter.

▶  ♀ Juv. Plumage (entire feathering), timing as ♂. **Iris** brownish. Like ♂ Juv., but smaller light area in **wing** and the middle coverts within this area generally more grayed. Smaller av. size of ♀ (as in other stages) is somewhat useful in distinguishing the sexes.

▶  ♂ Basic I Plumage (evidently all feathering except tail and wing, but perhaps a lesser amount acquired sometimes), replaces much of the Juv. in 1st FALL and then much of it is, in turn, succeeded by Alt. I in 1st WINTER; both of these molts vary in timing. The **iris** changes from brownish to yellow, usually by Jan., exceptionally much later. **Head** dusky olive; dark parts of dorsum blackish brown; neck and most of **venter** white; sides and flanks medium slaty gray, the feathers with whitish tips; **tail** dark gray. Legs and **feet** become more or less orange-yellow, the webs dark brownish. The Juv. wing, and evidently sometimes some other Juv. feathering, is retained.

▶  ♂ Alt. I Plumage (includes head–body, but sometimes perhaps not all of latter is acquired), begins to appear very late in FALL (Nov.–early Dec. commonly), in some individuals in winter, and usually is retained into JULY. There is not only variation in timing, but also in coloring of incoming feathers. Some late Nov. birds have the head black with much sheen, sometimes purplish, and (for the first time) the white area begins to appear at side base of bill and av. less than 18 × 25 mm. in size (smaller than in older drakes); the neck is white; most new feathering resembles Def. Alt., but some

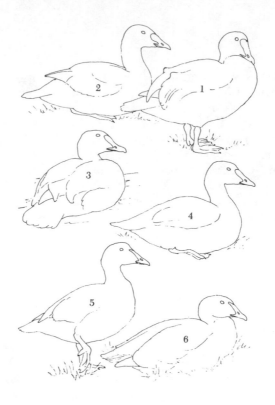

## Western Atlantic subspecies of Common Eider

### *Somateria mollissima dresseri*

1  ♂ Def. Alt. head-body with retained Basic wing, long scapulars, tail, and possibly abdomen. Winter. The Def. Basic inner secondaries are unmarked white and much downcurved. This drake's "sails" (modified long scapulars' are erected.

2  ♂ in much Alt. I (with retained Juv. wing, etc.). Age perhaps 10-11 months. The white breast is typical of Alt. I. There is much individual variation in Alt. I; head-neck often are very dark and forepart of mantle unmarked white.

3  ♂ Alt. II head-body with various retained Basic II feathering. A drake in 2nd winter. Typically, the more or less curved Basic II inner secondaries are black distally.

4  ♂ Def. Basic. Flightless during wing molt, in late summer or early fall. Variable, often darker overall than shown here and without white in dorsum.

5  ♀ Def. Alt. with retained Basic wing, long scapulars, tail, and possibly abdomen. Late fall-winter. Deep rich coloring is typical. Dark of crown sharply defined. Comparatively short black transverse markings on sides and flanks.

6  ♀ Def. Basic (entire feathering). Early summer (nesting). More muted than Alt.; crown less well defined; broader feathers on sides and flanks, hence longer black transverse barring. There is much fading; also, the white wears off ends of the secondaries and wing-coverts.

(For a day-old downy in color, see vol. 2, plate facing p. 370.)

R. T. Thengel-

differences: sides and flanks blackish brown or black and white (white areas usually mottled or speckled dark); usually much white in larger scapulars, their edging dark (seldom black) and narrower than in later Alts. The tail is retained Basic I, the wing retained Juv.

▶ ♀ Basic I and Alt. I Plumages, inclusive feathering of each and variation in timing probably as in ♂. The Basic I succeeds the Juv. in FALL, while the molt into Alt. I occurs in EARLY SPRING, later than in the ♂. Usually a yellowish cast to part of **bill** by late Dec.; the **iris** becomes somewhat yellowish in winter, usually yellow by April. The neck is off-white in Basic I (fall–winter) and becomes white in early spring (Alt. I). Basic I includes new tail, as in ♂. Legs and **feet** become yellow, webs dusky. At least the Juv. wing is retained throughout. Alt. I is retained until into June or even July.

**Measurements** of birds from Alaska, Canada, and n. conterminous U.S., mostly winter; 12 ♂: BILL 36–40 mm., av. 38.6; WING 223–239, av. 232; TAIL 89–94, av. 91; TARSUS 37–42, av. 40.9;    12 ♀: BILL 33–35 mm., av. 33.5; WING 199–220, av. 209; TAIL 77–86, av. 81.5; TARSUS 37–39, av. 38 (ETS).

Series from ne. N. Am.: 28 ♂ BILL 32–40 mm., av. 37, WING of 26 (across chord) 224–247, av. 237; TAIL (no. ?) 83–95, av. 89.4; TARSUS (of 28) 37–41, av. 39;    9 ♀ BILL 31–37 mm., av. 34; WING of 8 (across chord) 204–222, av. 216; TAIL 76–88, av. 80.5; TARSUS 32–37, av. 35 (D. P. Olson).

For another series, WING meas. across chord, see J. C. Phillips (1925).

**Weight** of 58 ♂ av. 2.2 lb. (1 kg.), max. 3.1 (1.4 kg.); 53 ♀ av. 1.8 lb. (0.8 kg.), max. 2.5 (1.1 kg.) (A. L. Nelson and Martin 1953).

Series from ne. N. Am.: first-fall birds 18 ♂ 31–40 oz., av. 36 (1.02 kg.) and 12 ♀ 20–31, av. 25 (0.7 kg.); "adults" 26 ♂ 33–45 oz., av. 39 (1.1 kg.) and 9 ♀ 25–31, av. 29 (.82 kg.) (D. P. Olson).

On day of hatching, 7 incubator-hatched young weighed 33.2–47.8 gm., the mean being 38.9 (Smart 1965a).

Wild **hybrids** are known of *B. clangula* with Common Pochard, Greater Scaup, Barrow's Goldeneye in N. Am. (2 ♂ collected, another seen) and in Iceland (♂ seen—Bengtson 1972d), White-winged Scoter, Smew (includes 5 reported by Millais 1913a), Hooded Merganser (at least 2 captured—Short 1969), and Common Merganser. A drake hybrid with Barrow's Goldeneye had iridescence on the head unlike that of either parent species and the trachea was intermediate in character (M. F. Jackson 1959). It is probable that hybrids between the 2 goldeneyes are more common than the few specimens indicate; ♀♀, for example, would be virtually indistinguishable even when in hand (Jackson).

In captivity, has crossed with at least 2 *Aythya* species. It is stated to have crossed with a Wood Duck (*Aix sponsa*), but this bird later was claimed to have been a hybrid *B. clangula* × *Anas querquedula*.

**Geographical variation** in the species is very slight in ♀♀. Drakes, especially, av. larger in the Nearctic region. Tougarinov (1941) stated that many Palearctic drakes are as large as most Nearctic ones, an av. size difference being insufficient to warrant recognition of subspecies. This view prevailed in Dementiev and Gladkov (1952), but the same authors later (Dementiev and Gladkov 1960) recognized subspecies, which is the current practice. In life and when handled in the flesh, adults of both sexes—at least in the w. Palearctic—have rounder (less triangular) heads and smaller bills than the Nearctic ones and there are other more subtle differences in appearance. RSP

SUBSPECIES *clangula* (Linnaeus)—Eurasia, straggling to our area; ♂ av. somewhat smaller than Am. birds. Winter–spring series from localities from Britain to Japan and Manchuria, 10♂: BILL 31–35 mm., av. 33.9; WING 215–234, av. 223.4; TAIL 83–89, av. 85.6; TARSUS 36–41, av. 39.7; 8 ♀: BILL 28–32 mm., av. 30.3; WING 193–210, av. 200; TAIL 72–86, av. 78.4; TARSUS 35–137, av. 35.7 (ETS). For additional meas. see: WING meas. across chord (J. C. Phillips 1925), Juv. and Basic WING of each sex, flattened (Schiøler 1926), WING meas. over curve (Witherby 1939), and flattened WING (Vaurie 1965).

   *americana* (Bonaparte)—N. Am., straggling elsewhere; ♂ av. larger; full description above. RSP

FIELD IDENTIFICATION   In N. Am. A medium-sized, stoutish duck; about 17–19 in. long, with short neck, large head, and stubby bill. Active and lively. "Whistling" flight.

   The drake most of the year has a very clear-cut pattern of black and much white. Blackish head is rather puffy and the apex of its somewhat triangular outline is above the center of the crown; this tricornered effect is visible at greater distance than the rounded white patch at side base of bill. On the water, all the white areas combined give an impression of an essentially white-bodied bird. (The Smew is largely white headed as well.) No dark extends down toward the waterline. In close view the head is seen to have a greenish sheen.

   The duck in all Plumages and young drakes (until late in first fall) have muted brown heads (no spot on side) and more or less brownish or grayed upperparts, upper breast, and sides. Mature ♀ ♀ from fall through winter into summer have a white collar; it is all or partly darkish in young birds. Drakes in their first fall have more contrast between brown of head and lighter color of breast than ♀ ♀ of any age, and their heads already have a slightly triangular ♂ profile. With practice, these differences can be recognized.

   The main problem is to distinguish between Common and Barrow's Goldeneyes. As Laing (1925) pointed out, mature drakes can be distinguished "almost as far" as they can be seen with binoculars—the Common being whiter, "more flashy," with no black down forward sides; Barrow's appears black backed, with this extending down forward to or nearly to the waterline. At closer range, drake Barrow's has a white crescent in front of eye and the white scapular streak is broken into spots. At a distance, distinguishing ♀ ♀ of the 2 goldeneyes is, "of course, impossible" (Laing).

   In various Plumages of the goldeneyes, a difference in head profile (more rounded in Barrow's) is evident. From late winter until into the nesting season, mature ♀ Commons have the distal portion of the bill yellow and in ♀ Barrow's it is all yellow, but in Iceland the ♀ Barrow's has a bicolored bill like that of the Common.

   Some Barrow's in early Juv. stage retain white down filaments on the cheeks; when viewed from a distance, such birds appear to have white cheek patches (J. Munro 1939). There are no comparable data on the Common, other than a brief statement on occurrence of filaments in Heinroth and Heinroth (1928). Very young ♀ ♀, and ♂ ♂ to

378

some extent, of the 2 goldeneyes are generally indistinguishable afield. In hand, the nail on bill of Barrow's is more or less raised (as it is sometimes in the Common); the "bump" of forehead bones of Barrow's is evident without dissection.

Common Goldeneyes fly swiftly, in compact small groups usually. The old drakes appear largely white-bodied and birds of both sexes and all ages have a large white area in inner half of wing that extends (interrupted in the ♀) from the trailing edge nearly to the leading edge. The wing music of the "Whistler" is loud from definitive-feathered drakes (whose outer primaries are the most narrowed) and audible from definitive-feathered ♀♀, but apparently not heard from young birds (Mayhoff 1918). In the U.S.S.R. a bookish name for this species is "gogol," but in some regions its true vernacular is "zvonok" (transl.: the bell), from the ringing sound from its wings. The sound is unique enough for the experienced wildfowler to identify flying goldeneyes in darkness. (It has been reported that the sound of the wings of Barrow's in Iceland is neither as loud nor as metallic as is characteristic of the Common Goldeneye elsewhere.)

Along N. Am. diving ducks, only the Bufflehead rises from the water more easily than the 2 goldeneyes.

The goldeneyes should not be confused with the mergansers, which are long-billed rakish birds, nor the little Bufflehead which has white area on head larger and behind the eye. Also compare with the Smew. RSP

VOICE   Both sexes are silent much of the time. The main source of the following information on display calls is Lind (1959), who studied zoo captives of the nominate race at close range. The display names are those used later in the present text, with Lind's added in parentheses.

**Drakes** appear to utter variants of a single type of call. When they are together and more or less aggressive, they have a faint short call, a subdued contraction of the prolonged *peent* that is uttered in Simple Head-throw (Snarl-throw I). The short form also may be uttered in Bowsprit (Oblique I) and Head-throw-bowsprit (Oblique II). Generally the full, downward-slurred *peent* (actually it is better rendered *yeeiiaaaah*), or same in doublets, does not carry far; according to Brewster (1911a), however, it can be heard a half mile on a calm day. It is harsh, not musical, and pitched from C#$_4$ to B$_3$ (A. A. Saunders). A call of "somewhat different timbre," similar to that uttered in last part of Slow-head-throw-kick (Kick-throw I) but fainter, always accompanies the stretching of the neck in Head-throw-kick (Crouched-up-down) and sometimes Head-throw-bowsprit (Oblique II). The same call is uttered in final stretching of the neck in Head-back (Mock-preening). Probably all "strongly ritualized drinking movements" are accompanied by the same type of call, but Display-drinking (Vertical Drinking) is silent (Lind). There is a grunting sound during Postcopulatory Steaming (M. T. Myres). (Some of these calls are mentioned again later in context with displays.)

The **duck** utters variants of a harsh croak, an upward-slurred *gwah*, often in series as when disturbed. During Head-forward, which is an Inciting activity, a faint *eeuu* (Lind 1959) and during Dip a purring or whining call (Brüggemann 1876); when prospecting for nest cavities, *cuk* notes in series (Harper, in J. C. Phillips 1925); also reportedly a special call to signal the ducklings to leave the nest cavity.

**Ducklings** have a whistled peeping, succeeded later by a low chirping (Phillips).

A **nonvocal sound** is the musical whistling of wings, pitch $G_4$ in the drake; apparently the birds can produce this sound or fly silently, at will (A. A. Saunders). Sometimes the drake at nearby water uses wing noise to communicate (alarm?) with his incubating mate. RSP

HABITAT   In N. Am. (but evidently the same elsewhere). In **nesting season** lakes, ponds, shallow stretches of rivers, and slower stretches of streams, all preferably with weedy margins. Nearby forest trees, sizable enough to include dead stubs with hollow tops or other nesting cavities, are essential unless nest boxes are provided. In N.B. and on C. Breton I. where this duck (which is not really a common breeder anywhere) is relatively plentiful, it nests in floodplain forests, which are few elsewhere in the Maritimes. Also in N.B., and perhaps in Me., it is about as plentiful at bog ponds and small lakes in the forest. At upper periphery of breeding range, a few Commons may nest away from stands of sizable trees, in abandoned buildings or possibly in cavities on slopes or among rocks. Prebreeders go to or near the same areas as breeders, but leave early to molt on other waters, mostly within overall breeding range. In **late summer** some birds molt on waters quite distant from stands of large trees—in N. Am., in Ungava Bay, for example. **Fall–spring** shallow coastal bays, estuaries (preferably brackish), and river mouths. Typically a bird of shallow bays, usually feeding by day in scattered parties and rafting at night well away from shore. Also occurs regularly in vicinity of marine is. and similar exposed situations. A very hardy species. Where lakes and rivers do not freeze and food is obtainable, sometimes in quite rapid stretches of rivers, for example, they remain inland through winter. RSP

DISTRIBUTION   (See map.) The Goldeneye probably originated in the Palearctic and spread to the Nearctic region. Although the species has a very large range in all seasons, the great majority in any season are concentrated in very much smaller areas. The species appears to be more nearly an obligate tree-cavity nester than Barrow's Goldeneye, which relates to some differences in breeding range.

*B. c. americana*—very large reported **nesting range,** but apparently nowhere a common nester, i.e., not known to reach local densities such as are known in B.C. for Barrow's Goldeneye and the Bufflehead. The vast majority are in 2 main nesting areas. **1** Interior Nfld., s. Que., parts of the Maritimes, and various areas in Me.; they are thinly scattered to the north and west into Minn. and beyond into Man. **2** From perhaps somewhere in nw. Man. westward and nw. through the Athabaska and Great Slave lakes regions toward the n. (lower) Mackenzie and also scattered in interior Alaska. Apparently they are most plentiful in the L. Athabaska and s. Great Slave L. region.

Since this bird may nest occasionally in terrestrial cavities, or go down chimneys or otherwise enter man-made structures, likely places to find it nesting away from trees include n. Ungava, parts of Keewatin, and scattered areas in Alaska.

Various reports, some quite old, of nesting in w. N. Am. from s. B.C. down into conterminous U.S. very likely are cases of mistaken identity; the ♀ Common and Barrow's are easily confused.

**Spring**   This duck may occur on open water almost anywhere between s. limits of wintering and n. limits of nesting.

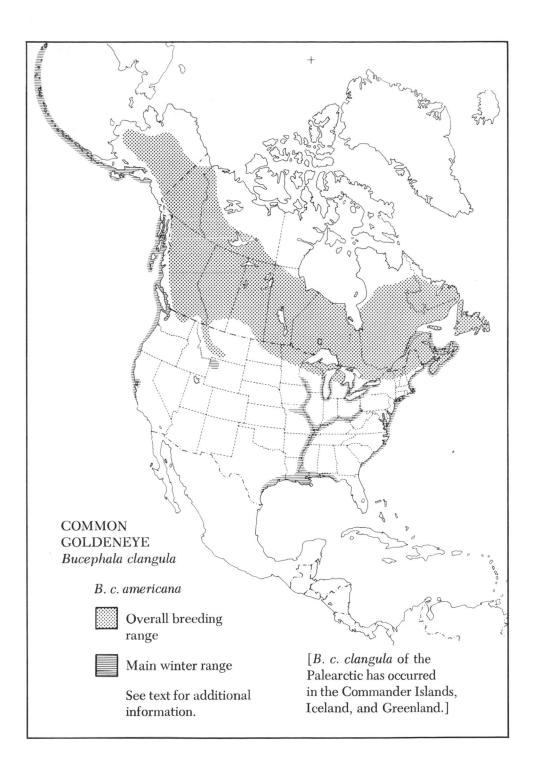

COMMON
GOLDENEYE
*Bucephala clangula*

*B. c. americana*

Overall breeding
range

Main winter range

See text for additional
information.

[*B. c. clangula* of the
Palearctic has occurred
in the Commander Islands,
Iceland, and Greenland.]

**Summer**    There is a molt migration, in general trending northward, and the birds apparently do not travel long distances. Thus there are molting flocks on various shallow waters within limits of nesting and at some places beyond. Examples of the latter: False R. estuary near Ungava Bay (Driver 1958); parts of James and se. Hudson Bay; the Mackenzie delta (Porsild 1943). A few molters occur on tundra lakes in Alaska.

**Fall**    As in spring, may occur almost anywhere within overall range, inland and on salt water.

**Winter 1a**    Easterly birds move toward or to Atlantic waters. They occur from se. and sw. Nfld., inner Gulf of St. Lawrence, coasts of the Maritimes, and down to Chesapeake Bay, a few beyond; they are concentrated in bays from n. New England down to include Chesapeake Bay. A few occur regularly in Bermuda. **1b** The following evidently pertains to some of the birds that nest in the continental interior. Some pass the season on the Great Lakes, especially Erie and Ontario, and move shoreward with the spring thaw. Occurs in the Mississippi drainage; formerly regular in the Mississippi delta region where now very scarce (winters are milder and they do not travel as far). In Fla. small numbers in winter, usually on the Gulf of Mexico side. **2** Westerly winterers occur in small flocks along the Aleutians (it is possible that some may be *B. c. clangula*), around Kodiak I., and in sheltered waters down the rim of the Pacific to some distance beyond San Francisco Bay; largest numbers are on coastal waters of se. Alaska and B.C.

Has occurred at a few localities in the w. interior, for example, at several places in s. Nev. A winter record for Imperial Co. in interior se. Cal.

**Straggler** to Greenland—drake shot on sw. coast in Godthaabsfjord on Jan. 16, 1906; Alaska—to various tundra localities including C. Prince of Wales, also the Pribilofs; Commander Is.—3 ♀ were taken in Oct.–Nov., 1911 (Hartert 1920b).

*B. c. clangula*—large total **nesting range,** but most of the birds are in parts of the forest zone from w. Siberia westward to include parts of Fennoscandia. A few scattered nesting records s. of usual limits. Nesting range extends eastward to include part of Koryakland, the Kamchatkan Pen., and n. half of Sakhalin I. There is no certain record in any season for the Chuckchee Pen.

In extreme w. U.S.S.R. and n. Fennoscandia, nesting range has been extended northward locally beyond occurrence of sizable trees by putting up nest boxes. Also 1 or more clutches in nest boxes in Scotland in 1971–72.

**Summer**    There are molting flocks within nesting range, also beyond on inner portions of the gulfs bordering the Kara Sea, to the west near the Kanin Pen., in the White Sea, and locally to or beyond Varanger Fjord.

In **migration**    Irregular in the Faeroes. Regular in very small numbers in spring and fall in the Commander Is.

**Winter**    For Iceland, G. Timmermann (1949) gave a few records; seen more frequently there since 1960; regular in sw. part (Gardarsson 1968); occurs on the island all year.

Winters in Brit. Isles; Faeroes (occasionally); parts of n. Europe (n. to Varanger Fjord), also on open water in the Baltic; small numbers reach the Aegean Sea; winters in n. part of the Black Sea and along s. rim of the Caspian. Some are scattered away from large waters, on any unfrozen water inland where they can get food, from the Iberian Pen. eastward across Eurasia to include parts of China; winters on Pacific waters from the n. Kurils southward to include Japan, Korea, and mainland coast beyond occasionally to the Formosan Strait. Occasional at this season in Commander Is.

**Straggler** A drake was taken in sw. Greenland in the Julianehaab Dist. in winter of 1930–31. Recorded from several places along the n. rim of Africa, at scattered Mediterranean localities, also in W. Pakistan, n. India, and Burma. A single record for Taiwan.

*B. clangula* is recorded as **fossil** from the Pleistocene of Sweden, Denmark (5 localities), Monaco, Italy, and Azerbaijan; and from **archaeological sites** in England, Denmark, and Alaska (2 on is., 1 on mainland); see Brodkorb (1964a) for references. RSP

MIGRATION N. Am. data unless otherwise indicated. An early traveler in spring and late fall. For many goldeneyes, spring travel is at first a movement up along coasts, then inland. On molt migration they go to shallow lakes or, if they are not remotely distant from the sea, toward the nearest coast and generally via waterways. For most saltwater winterers, fall migration is from inland to coasts and then southward. The flight to molting places is short in some areas, but probably up to at least 250 mi. in others; spring and fall migrations are, for some birds, much longer.

The Common Goldeneyes that occur in the continental interior molt on lakes and sluggish rivers and move s. to permanently open water—the Great Lakes, some other lakes, and rivers. "Brown heads" (young birds, also mature ♀ ♀) begin moving s. in fall earlier, and go farther, than mature drakes. Thus there is marked segregation by both sex and age in winter.

SPRING movement begins in s. part of winter range about the end of Feb., with peak in conterminous U.S. in late March–early April. Timing depends to some extent on advance of spring thaw, which occurs decidedly earlier on the Pacific coast than, for example, well within the continent. The birds move on before the ice breaks up or melts to any extent, stopping at very small areas of open water. Thus they arrive in late April or early May in n. wooded areas within the prairie provinces, after southerly warmer breeding places are occupied. The early flocks consist mostly of paired breeders, which tend to be scattered at night and to combine in feeding flocks during the day. Later flocks consist mostly of prebreeders. The breeders move on to nesting localities, leaving most of the prebreeders behind on rivers and lakes; thus the latter remain widely dispersed for a considerable time before they gather at molting places. Occupation of coldest parts of nesting range (nw. Canada, possibly cent. Ungava) must be delayed until there is some thaw in late May or early June.

SUMMER Evidently some birds from the interior of far w. Canada, on **molt migration**, go to Pacific waters, but mostly they occur at inland lakes. Near the easterly edge of summer range, in the Maritimes and Gulf of St. Lawrence region, there is considerable movement via watercourses to the nearest estuaries, river mouths, and coastal bays. There the drakes, which are very secretive, molt in scattered groups. The flight of yearling drakes evidently precedes, or their time of travel overlaps, that of mature (postbreeding) drakes. It is doubtful that any birds from well within the continent go as far as salt water to molt. In n. Ungava, rafts containing hundreds of birds occur in coastal waters as far n. as Ungava Bay, beyond the northerly limits of known nesting. Barrow's Goldeneyes mingle with them. Comparable northward movements are known in Eurasia. Nothing so far reported in N. Am., however, is as spectacular as the molting flocks of thousands in Kandalaksh Bay (an arm of the White Sea), or "massive gatherings" on waters of the forest steppe zone of w. Siberia, Transuralia, and the s. Urals, mentioned in Dementiev and Gladkov (1952). In the Pechora-Ilych Reserve area, after the ♀ ♀ are incubating, the drakes move upstream along the Pechora and Ilych Rivers; it is known that they travel via the Urals and molt on rivers in e. Poduralia (Teplov 1957).

FALL    Once the young are flying, and the ♀ ♀ that bred have regained flight after molting, apparently many of the former travel considerably and join flocks that have assembled at molting places earlier. At any rate, a very large percentage of Common Goldeneyes are concentrated, for a period prior to migration, in certain coastal areas and also on some interior waters. Without mentioning the composition of the flocks, Soper ( 1942b) reported seeing a total of "many thousands" of Common Goldeneyes in various-sized rafts at the w. end of L. Athabaska and on large rivers thereabout, from late Sept. to Oct. 16, 1932.

The inland birds tend to linger wherever open water remains, then are forced out by freeze-up. They migrate in scattered flocks, seldom in a concentrated flight. On arrival on salt water, the flocks combine at times into sizable rafts. Southward movement in the interior begins some time in Oct.; the movement reaches a peak in conterminous U.S. well along in Nov. and continues, at least for mature drakes, into late Dec. That is, ♀ ♀ and young of the year that are inland are forced to move by ice formation on shallow waters. The mature drakes, which went earlier to larger waters inland or to brackish or salt water along coasts, are not greatly weather influenced until weeks later and they do not go as far as the others. Some Common Goldeneyes probably travel rather short distances, but others certainly move 800–1,200 mi. between their boreal and austral destinations. RSP

BANDING STATUS   In N. Am. the total number banded through 1964 was 4,855 and the number of recoveries through 1961 was 174; main places of banding were: Alta., Minn., Mont., and Me. (data from Bird Banding Laboratory). There has been more banding subsequently. Example: 108 adult Common Goldeneyes, when flightless during molting, were banded at Takslesluk L. (confluent with Baird Inlet), not distant from Bering Sea coastal Alaska, in 1963–65 inclusive. The 3 recoveries, all of drakes, were singles each in the Chignik area on s. side of the Alaska Pen. in Jan. 1967, in the same area where originally banded, in July 1969, and in the Salton Sea area of s. Cal. on Jan. 17, 1967 (J. G. King).

There have been various programs in Eurasia. Johansen's (1959) statements on the travels of Common Goldeneyes in part of w. Siberia were based to a considerable extent on banding evidence. There are various published Russian and Finnish data—for example, Teplov (1957), Siren (1957b), and Rajala and Ormio (1970)—on return of ♀ ♀ to the same nest box in subsequent years. Boyd (1959b) mapped banding recoveries in Europe. Nilsson (1969) used banding data in discussing the migration of this species, including differences between sexes and age classes, in nw. Europe. Later (Nilsson 1971) he covered other topics, including estimated life expectancy. As of early 1970, 4 Swedish-banded Goldeneyes had been taken in Britain. Various other band-recovery data are scattered in the literature. RSP

REPRODUCTION  N. Am. data except where otherwise indicated. Although both sexes **first breed** when approaching age 2 years, yearlings engage in much (but less stereotyped) display. Some yearling ♀ ♀ "prospect" for nest sites. Sometimes a yearling ♂ and ♀ remain together and act generally as if paired (J. Munro 1939). Although Brewster (1900) was inclined to think that drakes are polygamous, pair bond form is single-clutch or **seasonal monogamy.**

**Displays** from Dec. on, leading to pair formation and maintenance of the bond, are more varied than the copulatory sequence described later on. The birds are in groups, not large assemblies, and the drake has up to 14 named displays, the duck at least 4. Size of the group (3–4 to perhaps 40 birds) is unimportant in determining what will occur. In both sexes, certain displays tend to be linked in a particular sequence (details in B. Dane and van der Kloot 1964) and there are differences in occurrence and frequency between what transpires in groups on winter range (where most observations have been made) and what happens after the birds have moved to nesting areas. The av. duration of various displays listed below are from Dane and van der Kloot; the descriptive material is from several sources, including observations by M. T. Myres. The relevant literature was listed by B. Dane et al. (1959), Lind (1959), and B. Dane and van der Kloot (1964), all including both Palearctic and Nearctic data. Lind's paper is especially useful in regard to vocalization during displays. The displays, at least for the drake, are given below roughly in the order they are added to the repertoire within the display season. The terminology is from Dane and van der Kloot, sometimes with that of Myres added in parentheses.

**Displays of the duck**  HEAD-UP (to 72 sec.) somewhat resembles alarm posture and may have affinities with head-turning (a)—see under Ticking display of drake; similar to Head-up of ♀ Bufflehead. Silent. Occurs more often and for longer periods as season progresses (B. Dane et al. 1959). HEAD-FORWARD (called Jiving by Myres) (0.85 sec.) most common response of ♀ ♀ to ♂ ♂, a lowering of head and neck forward (as in threat), often combined with sideways swinging of head and neck. The swinging is identical in appearance to Inciting of ♀ Mallard. This display occurs when the birds are in groups, particularly when the ♀ is following a leading ♂ who is performing Head-throw and Ticking. She may face right around, as she swims, and make passes at ♂ ♂ in her wake. The posture then may lead into a short rush with beak open. DIP (1.70 sec.) resembles 2nd part of Head-throw-kick of ♂, also Curtsy ("Knicks") of drake Red-breasted Merganser. Usually starts as Head-up, then brought forward and down, breast and neck thrust under water and beak points steeply upward. As head reaches water, rear of body is elevated and rounded by a paddling of the feet. Brüggemann (1876) recorded a purring or whining call. Posture seems to be directed at a particular drake. HEAD-FLICK (0.25 sec.) as ♂.

**Displays of the drake**  HEAD-THROW (1.40 sec.) first the head thrust straight forward, bill horizontal, then head lowered back onto rump (bill past the vertical, and tail is submerged. Usually, just after head touches rump, the bird gives a grating call described as like *peent* call of the Nighthawk (*Chordeiles minor*). It also has been called buzzing and insectlike, or creaking, or a high-pitched squeaky quack. Then, as the head is brought forward, it is very rapidly flicked first to one side and then other (double Head-flick).

The call note just mentioned is single. Heinroth (1911) and Lorenz (1941) stated that it could not be uttered without a stretching of the trachea during Head-throw; Daanje (1950), however, suggested that the call evolved after the display. This display is the most common one seen when groups are engaged in pair formation activities. Gunn (1939) described it aptly as a jackknife movement.

SLOW HEAD-THROW-KICK (2.20 sec.) starts as Head-throw erect posture, then head thrown back onto rump, then rear of body is humped up and feet drawn forward, and a downward pressure of feet at start of kick. Wings may show as projecting spurs above back. The neck may be submerged, but beak still points upward. Throat appears swollen; beak is open. Head then elevated upward and backward, finally beak closes, and bird assumes horizontal position; then a Head-flick. There may be a call when head placed on rump; there definitely is one as head and neck lifted in 2nd half of movement.

Common

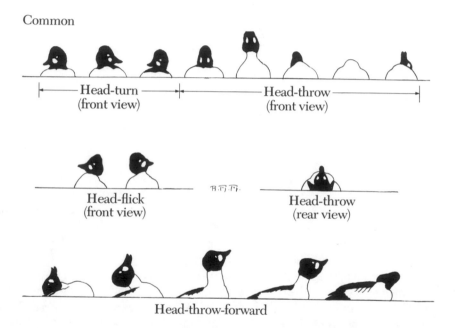

Head-throw-forward

Generally a double note, harsh, rasping, high pitched. Brewster (1911a) described this call as *paaap*, "not unlike" that of the American Woodcock (*Philohela minor*), and said it sometimes is doubled or trebled. Generally it is double, instead of the single note (*peent* or *paaap*) of the Head-throw. It is less synchronous with kick of feet than the homologous call in Barrow's Goldeneye. This display may be performed by a drake who is alone, has just alighted on water, or is approaching other birds from a distance. If one individual performs it, a nearby ♂ often does it also and almost at the same moment.

FAST-HEAD-THROW-KICK (1.25 sec.) head not elevated before being thrown back and does not reach rump. BOWSPRIT (Myres' Scoop) (1.95 sec.) head and neck lowered to water from normal position and a scooping movement made over water forward and upward as soft *rrrrrt* call uttered. Neck goes to about 45° angle and head held obliquely forward for about 1 sec. before neck withdrawn into shoulders and head flicked.

HEAD-THROW-BOWSPRIT (2.0 sec.) when the 2 displays are linked thus, duration of the former is either shorter or longer than single Head-throw; Bowsprit portion is briefer with shorter throw and longer with long throw. NODDING (Myres' Bowsprit-pumping) (individual nod 0.70 sec.) ♂ extends and withdraws his head, starting from position slightly above normal and thrusting it out very like Bowsprit; cheek and neck feathers

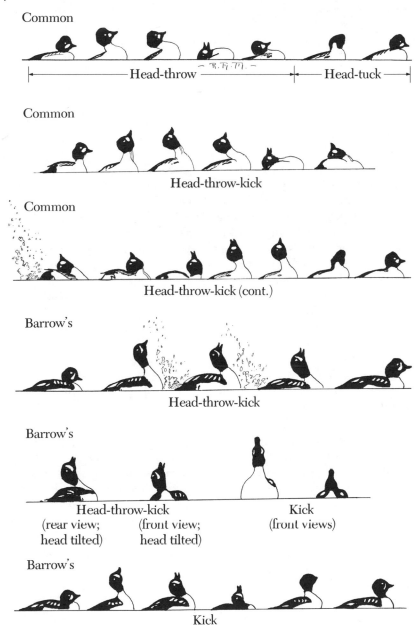

Common

|← Head-throw — R.Ti.Th. — →|← Head-tuck →|

Common

Head-throw-kick

Common

Head-throw-kick (cont.)

Barrow's

Head-throw-kick

Barrow's

Head-throw-kick          Kick
(rear view;   (front view;   (front views)
head tilted)   head tilted)

Barrow's

Kick

387

somewhat puffed. The beak tip follows an elliptical path, of lesser amplitude than in Barrow's Goldeneye. The visible effect of this elongating movement is that the beak appears longer and more finely pointed than in Barrow's and the flatter forehead augments this impression. Number of nods varies. MASTHEAD (4.80 sec.) drake lowers head to water level and holds position for as long as 3 sec.; head then quickly stretched out forward on water and, with neck extended, is jerked quickly up so that bill points vertically, causing a slight bend in the neck. Head feathers are sleeked. Then, quickly, the head is snapped down to water level and held there and, usually, the bird paddles vigorously. Then neck retracted for about 1.5 sec. before bird assumes normal stance. Movement is rapid, jerky, mechanical in character. Crest depressed during movement. Variation in total duration depends mostly on length of time the head is in the 2 down (on water) positions. J. C. Phillips (1925) and others have reported birds shooting backward for 1–2 ft. This goldeneye does move backward a little way in water, when lifting the head upward from threat (Head-forward) posture, which may be the origin of the other observations. Masthead is not recorded for Barrow's Goldeneye. TICKING (0.19 sec.) probably commonest action during goldeneye displays. Simple, frequently repeated movement of head from side to side (head turning) in horizontal plane; regularly interpolated in other displays. The faster the Ticking the smaller the arc described by the bill. Although various head-turning movements are stereotyped and it is convenient to lump them under Ticking, they probably are not homologous. (a) Occurs during intervals between successive movements of neck in Head-up-pumping; the neck elongated, beak opened, and a call uttered; the turning of the head is slow and jerky. (b) Occurs in intervals between Head-throws, especially when a ♂ is "leading" a ♀; neck not elongated; turning of the head frequent and even. During Postcopulatory steaming; neck upright and very elongated, beak open and call uttered; turning of the head frequent and even. It can be seen that each of these types is distinctive in combination of neck length and regularity of movement.

HEAD-FLICK (0.20 sec.) this movement (which is stereotyped finale to many other displays) consists of tilting the head usually once to right and once to left, bill down at 35° angle. Very brief; seldom detected. It occurs after Simple Head-throw, Wing-flick, Slow Head-throw-kick, Fast Head-throw-kick, Nodding, Postcopulatory Bathing, and Head-back-bowsprit in approximately that diminishing order of frequency. B. Dane et al. (1959) recorded it in isolation in precopulatory sequence, but it is not common then. HEAD-FORWARD (2.45 sec.) head extended and held close to water. Most frequently seen on waters near nesting areas where often associated with attack or fighting. HEAD-UP (2.60 sec.) head raised approximately 2 in. above normal and held in that position. HEAD-UP-PUMPING (Neck-withdrawing of Myres) (0.55 sec.) essentially the preceding repeated rapidly. As with Nodding and Ticking, may be performed as a single action or done in series, but usually a pause between the actions. The relative frequencies of Head-up and Ticking vary. Bernhardt (1940) noted that the ♂ exactly follows the ♀, turn by turn. HEAD-BACK (1.15 sec.) head snaked along back as in Fast Head-throw-kick, but stopped approximately half way to rump; possibly a call is uttered; finally the head snapped forward with a Head-flick. Seen only near nesting areas, where it is frequent. HEAD-BACK-BOWSPRIT (1.55 sec.) the Head-back, previously described, is followed by Bowsprit pose and latter held approximately 0.3 sec.

388

before head returned to normal with a Head-flick. Seen only near nesting areas, where frequent.

DISPLAY FLIGHT as in Bufflehead. Drake raises head as if in alarm, flies a short distance toward or away from flock; then he stalls and skids along water. During flight the head and neck held low, the head feathers elevated. Wingbeat short, fluttering; there seems to be less wing noise than might be expected. There also are short, irregular, flights of 3–4 birds, a ♀ invariably in the lead (Carter 1958).

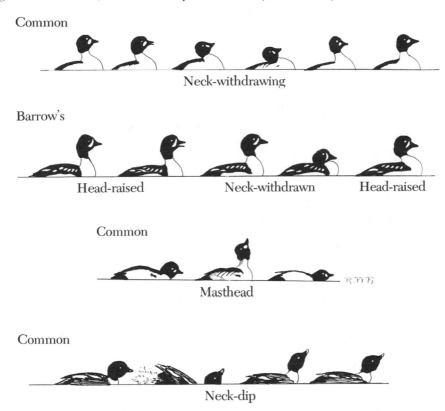

Common

Neck-withdrawing

Barrow's

Head-raised          Neck-withdrawn          Head-raised

Common

Masthead

Common

Neck-dip

**Fighting** is infrequent. Goldeneyes use diving as their main form of attack. The CROUCH (of Brewster 1911a) resembles the threat posture of Canvasback or Bufflehead. In Common Goldeneyes there is in addition a high-intensity Threat that is more effective in driving other individuals away. It resembles that of Barrow's Goldeneye—the head thrust forward as though on a stick, with bill above water or actually touching it, and body flattened. Brüggemann (1876) kept 2 pairs on a pond. Each drake defended a definite area of water. A drake would swim in Threat posture, then dive and swim submerged until near his rival, but even when below the surface neither bird invaded the other's territory and often they turned around suddenly under water when they reached an invisible boundary. When the 2 drakes met at a boundary, they both dived, but when they emerged they were farther apart than before. Actual battles did not occur.

Escape is by flying, swimming, or diving. In alarm posture the head is raised, crest expanded, and the bird may turn its head from side to side, as in Ticking, and utter grunting sounds.

**Displays of prebreeders** (young in 1st winter) include most of the known repertoire of mature drakes but prebreeders perform them with different relative frequencies. Young ♀ ♀ perform certain ♂ displays; their assumption of Bowsprit posture apparently caused great excitement among drakes (Brewster 1911); the latter then may perform Head-throw. Actions of young drakes are "odd", not stereotyped, sometimes so different from those of breeders that they are difficult to identify, but are of normal duration (B. Dane and van der Kloot 1964).

**Copulatory behavior** has been discussed by Lind (1959), Myres (1959b), and other authors. Myres compared it with that of the Bufflehead and scoters. Copulation may be initiated (especially on the sea) by the ♀ assuming a PRONE position, or by ♂ display (especially on waters near nesting places). The drake's Wing-and-leg stretch is the most certain indication that copulation is imminent, but Drinking also is more frequent at this time. Bill-shake, Wing-preen (fleeting movement of beak into dorsal feathers), and Precopulatory steaming are linked in that sequence and occur immediately before mounting. If a union is a failure, Postcopulatory steaming does not occur and the birds revert to earlier displays.

**The duck's copulatory actions**   PRONE stretched out, like a dead duck, largely submerged. May be held for 15 (exceptionally 30) min; occurs from Feb. on, but does not generally lead to copulation early in the season. As many as 3 ♀ ♀ have been seen Prone around a ♂ during the precopulatory sequence. DRINKING (2.10 sec.) as by ♂, but occurs rarely, sometimes during beginning of the precopulatory sequence. HEAD-LIFTING (1.05 sec.) rare; Prone ♀ sometimes lifts head and neck out of water to almost vertical position, then she returns to normal Prone. More rapid than Drinking. Ritualized BATHING (to about 12 sec.) as ♂.

**The drake's copulatory actions**   BILL-SHAKE (0.90 sec.). DISPLAY-DRINKING (2.0 sec.) chief difference from ordinary drinking is less in form than in frequency and duration. At other times than copulation it appears to be a mutual display, the ♂ (or ♀) often repeating it after the partner, up to a half dozen times. WING-AND-LEG-STRETCH (5.40 sec.) ♂ turns on side, exposing either white belly or dark back to ♀. Wing and leg which then are uppermost are stretched (exposes orange leg). If drake's back is toward ♀, his white wing patch is conspicuous in her view. Differs little from comfort movements, but repetition is clear indication it is a stereotyped display. HEAD-FLICK (0.25 sec.). HEAD-RUBBING (0.75 sec.) not common; head rubbed up and down on side of body, up to 6 times. CRESCENDO (7.25 sec.) variable number (3–10, av. 7) of rapidly repeated Bill-shakes. This is the first of a linked sequence of 3 actions, always occurring in the same order, prior to copulation. DISPLAY-DRINKING (0.50 sec.) drake raises head, turns it around over back, and points bill near the vertical downward. Head feathers raised. One wing is raised just off back and bill touches feathers behind the wing, then ♂ swings head back forward, bill horizontal.

**Copulation** (8.30 sec.) the ♂ overlies the Prone ♀ for some moments before he actually takes hold of feathers of her nape. By the time he does, she is nearly submerged. WING-FLICK (0.35 sec.) suddenly the ♂ lifts wings a little and snaps them briskly back into place. He spreads his tail, wagging it from side to side. He may remain mounted for as long as 45 sec., but usually 5–15 (at least on winter range). ROTATIONS (4.80 sec.) drake slides off ♀ sideways, but continues to hold onto her nape and starts to swim. His head feathers still puffed out and neck extended. He continues to swim with one foot braced against the ♀'s breast and these actions cause the pair to rotate once or twice on water before the drake releases ♀. POSTCOPULATORY STEAMING (13.60 sec.) drake immediately holds neck straight up, stiffly, his crest fully expanded, and he swims

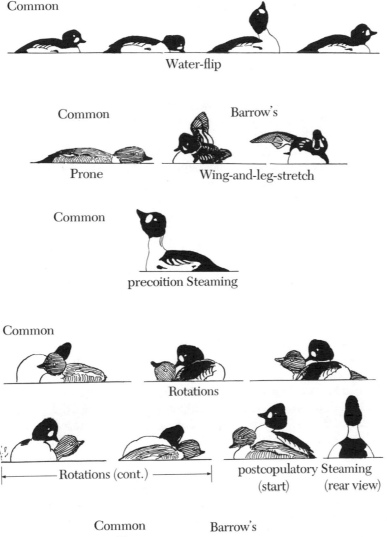

Common

Water-flip

Common                    Barrow's

Prone              Wing-and-leg-stretch

Common

precoition Steaming

Common

Rotations

Rotations (cont.)          postcopulatory Steaming
                              (start)      (rear view)

Common          Barrow's

postcopulatory Steaming

391

away. After swimming several yds., or perhaps immediately, he begins to turn head from side to side and "grunts"—Ticking (c). He may go some distance, fairly fast, or he may swing in broad arc and come back to the ♀. One went directly to another Prone ♀, performed the appropriate displays, and again copulated (B. Dane and van der Kloot 1964). POSTCOPULATORY BATHING (up to 10 sec.) after some sec., the drake subsides on water and begins exaggerated bathing actions, as does ♀ who remains crouched for some sec. after being released. The usual comfort actions occur: dipping, wing shimmering, upward stretch, wing flap, and tail wag.

The **nest site** of the Common Goldeneye typically is an open-top tree cavity, the tree or stub usually near or even in water; commonly on a forested shore bordering first open water in spring. In New Bruns., Carter (1958) noted that there always is water near the site when nesting starts but, after spring flooding subsides, some sites may be a considerable distance away. Both in N. Am. and in Eurasia, there are natural sites and nest boxes that are a considerable distance from water in any season. The entrance may be at any height, mostly 6–40 ft. up; occasionally the bottom of the cavity is so low that the eggs become flooded and are abandoned. For dimensions of 16 cavities in New Bruns., see Carter (1958).

In e. Alta. the majority of nests are in rotted-out Pileated Woodpecker (*Dryocopus pileatus*) cavities or, lacking these, hollow stumps and even chimneys. In the Fredericton, N.B., area, a few go down chimneys and thus are killed (Carter 1958). In the Lesser Slave L. area of Alta., the Common Goldneye is called "Chimney Duck," since all chimneys not screened are entered by them (A. J. Erskine).

In the bottomlands along the Mologa R. (upper Volga area in U.S.S.R.) there was extensive clearing of the forest in 1940. As a result, 32 of 53 clutches were not in the usual cavities; these included 5 between roots on the ground, 8 in hollow logs, 3 in semicavities of stumps and broken-off limbs, 2 in log piles, and 3 in haystacks (Dementiev and Gladkov 1952).

The birds use **nest boxes** readily, in Minn., for example, as readily as Wood Ducks (*Aix*). The boxes can be fastened to trees or placed on poles and there should be no dead limbs or other obstructions in front of the entrance. The duck appears to fly straight into the box, only checking her speed at the last possible instant. Boxes can be placed beside roads, on walls of houses, even in village yards. The Karelians and Lapps have provided structures, made from sections of hollow logs, since early times. In his *Tour of Lapland* (1732), Linnaeus mentioned them. Suitable dimensions for nest boxes are: inside meas. 9 × 9 × 24 in. deep (about 23 × 23 × 60 cm.), the entrance an ellipse 4½ in. wide and 3½ high (about 10.5 × 8 cm.), a few in. down from the top.

At Delta, Man., goldeneye eggs have been found in 11 nests incubated by Mallards in wooden nest boxes (Titman and Lowther 1971).

In the U.S.S.R. some cavities have been in use for 30 years in succession and a banded ♀ used the same one for several successive years (Teplov, cited in Dementiev and Gladkov 1952). In Sweden, R. S. Palmer has seen boxes that were used for at least 22 years. In Finland, a ♀ repeated for 5 successive years, but frequently a different site is used each year, although the bird usually moves less than 3 km. distance (Siren 1957b).

When cavities are scarce, **joint layings** by 2 or more ♀ ♀ occur, with over 30 eggs deposited (also see below on activities of 2-year-olds). In Bonaventure Co., Que., an elm had a hollow of some 20 in. diam. for about 20 ft. and a hole of about 5 in. diam. near top of the hollow section; when the tree was felled by wind, 28 dead ♀ Common Golden-eyes were found in the cavity (Mershon 1927). In the Lapland State Reserve in U.S.S.R. in 1951 a hollow pine in woods 600 meters from a lake shore was sawed down. A deep cavity was filled for 2–3 m. with the accumulations of years of goldeneye nest remains, including 2 abandoned clutches and the bones of 2 goldeneyes; on top, in 1957, were 14 eggs laid by 2 ♀ ♀ (Semenov-Tian-Shanskii 1960). Three goldeneyes to-gether in a nest were mentioned by Semenov-Tian-Shanskii and Bragin (1969). Gener-ally speaking, a suitable cavity does not extend more than 2–4 ft. below its entrance. Both goldeneye species have a clear preference for open-top, "chimney," or what might be called bucket-type tree cavities—very unlike the Bufflehead, which almost invariably uses a side entrance. When a cavity has both a top and a side entrance, a goldeneye uses the top one.

In N. Am., **mixed clutches** with Common Merganser, Hooded Merganser, Bufflehead, and Wood Duck are known, plus goldeneye and Hooder Merganser on top of eggs of Barred Owl. The published list of mixed usage is longest for Finland: Smew, Common Merganser, Mallard, Stock Dove, Jackdaw, squirrel (*Sciurus vulgaris*), Tawny Owl, and Starling (Grenquist 1962). Among the birds listed, the early nesters—Common Merganser, Stock Dove, and Jackdaw—are more detrimental to goldeneye nesting success (Grenquist). In mixed layings with Common Merganser, the goldeneye always abandons her eggs; if the goldeneye eggs hatch first, the duck-lings jump from the nest without any ♀ awaiting them (Grenquist).

The ♀ makes a rounded depression in rotted wood or chips at the bottom of the cav-ity and, beginning with laying of the first egg or soon after, adds some down. The **nest down** is wholly white and any intermingled feathers have white vane and dark shaft (Broley 1950); in the Palearctic, however, the down is said to be very pale grayish with lighter centers (in Witherby 1939). The down accumulates until there is sufficient for a nest and to cover the clutch. The ♀, unless so startled as to depart hurriedly, covers her eggs before leaving them. The eggs are laid, on the av., about every other day, but a day is not always skipped between layings. As time passes, eggs and down become soiled—more so if the ♀ is frightened repeatedly from the nest, as she then more often defecates when departing. Some of the body down generally clings to the cavity en-trance, thus revealing that a cavity is in use.

**Full clutches** may be expected in n. conterminous U.S. and the Maritimes of e. Canada about May 1–10, but N. Am. data for almost everywhere else are inadequate for making generalizations. South of Cumberland House, Sask., back-dating from mean date of hatching, in 2 years, many clutches were completed by May 23 (G. H. Townsend 1966). Probably clutches are not completed at upper limits of nesting range until some time in the first half of June, varying with earliness and tardiness of season. Two-year-olds lay considerably later than older birds.

Throughout laying and until some time in incubation, the **drake** remains nearby. Thus his continued presence in an area indicates the general location of a nest. On ap-proach of danger, the drake noisily (with whistling wings) rises from the water, a signal of danger to the duck; she leaves the cavity with agitated cackling and flies to water nearby (Dementiev and Gladkov 1952).

**Clutch size**—not all available data cited. In Ne Bruns., 9 clutches ranged 7—12 (av.

9) eggs (Carter 1958). For ne. U.S. and adjacent Canada the av. has been calculated at 8.8 (Gibbs 1962). In Finland, in clutches which were incubated to hatching, and in a rapidly increasing local population, av. 10.3 eggs (Grenquist 1963). In n. Finland, 53 clutches av. 8.11 ± (SE) 0.43 eggs, the sample not including any joint layings (Rajala and Ormio 1970). The U.S.S.R. data indicate some variation from year to year at Rybin Reservoir on the upper Volga (in Dementiev and Gladkov 1952). At Rybin, in 168 "clutches" in 1950–51, range was 5–24 eggs; 39 clutches contained 8–10 eggs (av. 9) and 53 had 12–14 (av. 13); this bimodal picture suggests 2 age-classes of layers, the older birds having larger clutches and laying earlier, two-year-olds having smaller sets later (in Dementiev and Gladkov); but the data are not very convincing. Sets of 12–14 were said not to be joint layings by more than 1 ♀. In the Pechora-Ilych Reserve, 137 clutches av. 6.8 eggs and about 93% of the clutches hatched (Teplov 1957).

One **egg** each from 20 clutches from Ungava to Alaska **size** length av. 60.47 ± 1.56 mm., breadth 43.68 ± 1.28, radii of curvature of ends 17.89 ± 1.18 and 13.58 ± 0.99; **shape** between long elliptical and subelliptical, elongation 1.38 ± 0.037, bicone 0.00, and asymmetry +0.138 (FWP). **Color** whitish green. Bent's (1925) measurements of 84 eggs are very close to those just given. In Eurasia, eggs av. nearly as long but about 1 mm. less in breath, judging from various published data.

**Replacement clutches** if any—no useful data.

There are various observations that ♀♀ are restless sitters, off and on more, and more easily disturbed from the eggs than most ducks. Semonov-Tian-Shanskii (1960), using a recording device, found that a ♀ stirred about so often that on a week-long record as shown on a graph it was not possible to distinguish the number of movements. According to Semenov-Tian-Shanskii and Bragin (1969), Common Goldeneyes abandon clutches more often than other ducks before and during incubation; possibly this is provoked sometimes by disordered laying in various nests. They also tend to abandon during prolonged periods of rain. **Nesting success** varies markedly from year to year.

Sometimes in the last 10 days of incubation a ♀ may even be removed from the cavity by hand and does not always flush when returned to the cavity (Dementiev and Gladkov). In New Bruns., Carter (1958) reported that well along in incubation one ♀ could be removed and returned to the nest.

During the time when mature ♀♀ are incubating, or even when they have preflight broods, young ♀♀ (prebreeders) "**prospect**" for nesting places. Apparently among yearlings this amounts only to "visiting." In Finland, 2-year-olds have been known to add to existing clutches, bringing the total to 20, 30, or even 40 eggs. Two such ♀♀ have been in a nest box together, with a third awaiting her turn outside on the cover (Grenquist 1963). This results in desertion of some sites. It has occurred where numbers were increasing rapidly, with many prebreeders and 2-year-olds present; compare with Barrow's Goldeneye. For some further details, also see Grenquist (1968).

**Incubation period** probably 30 days in the wild; it generally is given as 30 days, from Heinroth and Heinroth (1928), who very likely reported on eggs not under a goldeneye.

**Hatching dates** add 30 days to dates given earlier for completion of clutches. Usually hatching requires a few hrs., then the ducklings remain about a full day longer in the cavity. They have sharp curved nails and stiff tails (which may be used as a brace during climbing) and can get up out of a cavity even when it is deep, or up the side of a nest box made of rough boards. The ♀ may be outside, calling, but the climbing and jumping behaviors of the young are instinctive motor patterns and not dependent on maternal stimulation (Bjerke 1970). The ♀ is said to utter a special call and the ducklings immediately leave the nest.

**Hatching success** few N. Am. data. In New Bruns., Carter (1958) found not more than 1 egg per clutch that did not hatch, or 3.8% of 79 eggs. Gibbs (1962) reported on a Me. study in which (assuming 8.8 eggs/clutch) there was an av. loss of 3 young per successful nest by the time the ducklings were 2–3 days old. In Finland, Grenquist (1963) reported thus on 1,554 eggs: 50.6% hatched, 6.2% had incubation interrupted, 1.9% were infertile, and 40% were unincubated; also, 2 peaks of nesting success (80% and 75%) in the same year were followed by low hatching success (33% and 33%) 2 years later, apparently attributable to disturbance of older incubating birds by yearlings and 2-year-olds and site competition with Common Merganser and Stock Dove.

**Development of young** There are no detailed N. Am. data, such as exists for Barrow's Goldeneye. In U.S.S.R.: even the smallest ducklings dive well and can swim submerged; their contour feathers are well developed at 35 days, but feet still are dark; the ♀ is with the brood no more than 2–3 weeks, then the young combine in groups by themselves (Dementiev and Gladkov 1952). See Heinroth and Heinroth (1928) for a few details on growth, also several photographs, of known-age captive young of the Eurasian subspecies. In northern New. Eng., young broods break up naturally very early in the season (Brewster 1924). Finland: a ♀ leads her brood from open water to forest pools, leaving 1–2 young at a pool, and moves on to repeat this at other pools so that, by the time a duckling is old enough to fly, only 1 is left with her (Siren 1957a). In the U.S.S.R. at the Pechora-Ilych Reserve, the number of ducklings in 34 broods as observed in July of 10 years varied 4–8, av. 5 (Teplov 1957). In Me.: 15 broods (77 young) produced only 22 flying birds in 5 recognizable "broods" of which 1 brood was a combination of remnants of 4 others, another the combination of 2 (Gibbs 1962). In New Bruns., a quarter-grown Common Goldeneye was seen in a brood of Wood Ducks (*Aix*) of same age (Carter 1958). There is general agreement in available information that, so long as a ♀ remains with any of her brood, she stays in a very limited area. Then she flies to some other place and, in due course, begins the flightless stage of molting. As in Barrow's Goldeneye, however, there must be great variation in length of time ♀ ♀ tend any young.

**Age at first flight** in the wild probably is about 8 weeks. Two captive-reared young of the nominate race, in Holland, hatched June 26 and were able to fly on Aug. 25 (Blaauw 1909). The young sometimes are stated to attain flight in 57 days, which is based on "about" 57 days and before the wings are fully grown, for young of the nominate race in captivity, in Heinroth and Heinroth (1928). MTM MFJ RSP

SURVIVAL *B. c. clangula*—for Swedish birds, Nilsson (1971) calculated the annual adult mortality rate as about 37%, which is high, and expectation of adult life as about 6 years.

*B. c. americana* —there is no information on annual adult survival rate. At a locality in Me., there were heavy losses of young until they were 2–3 days old, then a high rate of survival thereafter to flight age (Gibbs 1962). In a 5-year study in N.B., an av. of 4.8 young/brood reached flying age (Carter 1958). RSP

HABITS There is considerable, rather widely scattered, information on the "Whistler"—especially on flocking, rafting at dusk, diving, generally restless nature, and on the hunting of this hardy bird. The summarizing accounts of Bent (1925) and J. C. Phillips (1925) are very useful; that of Millais (1913a) gives a fine picture of the activities of this goldeneye and of wildfowlers in pursuit of it. There has, however, been relatively little recent study of its habits.

Common Goldeneyes in their first fall are decidedly tame, in fact have been referred to as "stupid," but more experienced older birds are truly shy. Goldeneyes usually travel in small flocks of a few to perhaps a dozen individuals, but pairs and even singles are common. There is a good deal of interchanging of birds between flocks after they arrive on salt water and continuing well into winter. It is well known that, toward dusk, flocks combine in dense rafts, generally well away from shore; they scatter to feed in early morning; see Reed (1971) for various details. In spring, after the differentials in movement and in places of residence, by sex and age, that are so evident in fall and winter have been partly obliterated by subsequent flights, there are gatherings of all sizes. Many thousands may assemble at a stopover place, yet the prevalent social unit still seems to be a rather small group of individuals. The activities of the group are closely coordinated, all individuals taking flight together, even diving in unison, and so on. They tend to be restless, feeding in a most animated fashion at one spot for a while, then moving on.

In flight intention, Common Goldeneyes face into the wind, their heads erect, and there is some lateral head-shaking (Ticking). Then, if there is no breeze, they patter along the surface; if it is windy, they rise directly and easily, and mature birds (drakes especially) have the well-known far-carrying whistling sound. They keep low on short flights, as when shifting about to feed, but like sea ducks in general fly high on longer travels and when crossing over land. They are reported to fly at 9 wingbeats/sec. (Aymar 1935) and in Scandinavia have been timed at 72 km./hr. (Ryden and Kallander 1964). They have been seen to dive from the air. Toward dusk the groups move out to open water and join forces, or "raft up," for the night.

Goldeneyes feed very actively, usually by day but sometimes (Millais 1913a) on clear nights. They prefer depths of about 3–12 ft., the maximum reported being about 20. They swim with the neck angled forward, tail on (or even in) water, then dive with wings closed, tail spread, and feet out laterally (illus.: A. Brooks 1945). Generally a dive in 5–6 ft. of water is of about 20–25 sec. duration, which is more than twice the usual length of the intervening pause. They gather animal food from the bottom and also seek such items as insects and their larvae on subsurface vegetation and submerged logs and stumps; occasionally they catch small fishes. Millais (1913a) watched one from a bridge. It dived to the bottom in 8–10 ft. of water and at once began to turn over stones with its bill, to get insect larvae. Sometimes it found batches of small freshwater mussels and swallowed them. It had difficulty with a large stone and surfaced between attempts to move it. Millais stated that the Goldeneye goes down perpendicularly, or sometimes on a circular (spiral) course in quiet water, but at an angle upstream where there is a current. It reappears close to where it submerged. A group sometimes swims with heads at least partly immersed, in merganser fashion, preparatory to diving. Brewster (1911a) saw one feeding in shallows, with head submerged, on aquatic beetles.

On a river in New Bruns., Carter (1958) observed that they dive smoothly in a continuous motion and come up like a cork, in sitting posture, not headfirst. They faced into the current when diving and resurfaced 10 yds. downstream. This resulted in a gradual drifting and every few min. they flew back upstream to continue drift feeding.

There does not seem to be much information of a quantitative nature on factors affecting Goldeneye numbers. As with other seafowl, they have been victims of oil spills. If they are weakened by internal parasites or disease, presumably they are more likely to succumb in cold weather. Competition for nest holes results in a wastage of eggs. Bad weather seems to increase nest abandonment and is detrimental to small downies. In the Queen Charlottes the Bald Eagle (*Haliaeetus leucocephalus*) catches goldeneyes of both species (A. Brooks 1922). At Red Rock Lakes, Mont., in late fall–winter, both the Common and Barrow's are captured in flight by the Golden Eagle (*Aquila chrysaetos*), but on the water they can avoid the eagles and show no fear of them (W. M. Sharp 1951). A Herring Gull (*Larus argentatus*) attacked a presumably healthy Common Goldeneye (Trautman 1943). A Blackback (*Larus marinus*) captured and killed a ♀ (Cleghorn 1942). The Glaucous-winged Gull (*L. glaucescens*) has been seen robbing them of rotted salmon flesh (Pearse 1921).

This writer has hunted the "Whistler" without outstanding success. They are fast fliers and tough birds. There is no point in risking shots at long range, since a cripple is almost surely lost. Authors seem to rate this bird a better culinary prospect than most of the true sea ducks. On limited experience, the writer concurs, but some individuals—perhaps those recently arrived from freshwater localities—are better than others.

The Common Goldeneye probably is not hunted enough anywhere to have much effect on its numbers. In some localities in the European part of the U.S.S.R., the nest down and part of the clutch are taken from nest boxes (Dementiev and Gladkov 1952). The total number of Common Goldeneyes throughout the Holarctic range of the species is small when compared with most shoal-water ducks.

(Compare with Barrow's Goldeneye, since much that is known about that species well may apply to the Common also). RSP

FOOD (Emphasis on Nearctic data.) Largely crustaceans, insects, and mollusks, with a small amount of seeds and other parts of aquatic plants. Examination of the stomachs of 395 "adults" showed 74% animal matter and 26% plant matter. With "juveniles" the proportion of animal food is higher, 84%, and consists mainly of insects (Cottam 1939).

**Animal** Crustaceans, principally mud crabs (*Hemigrapsus*) on the Pacific coast, *Cancer, Pagurus, Cambarus, Astacus*; amphipods (*Gammarellus, Hyalella, Ischyrocerus, Pseudalibrotus*); shrimps, isopods, barnacles, etc. 32.4%; insects: larvae of caddis flies (Trichoptera), water boatmen (Corixidae), nymphs of dragonflies and damselflies (Odonata), mayflies (Ephemerida), saltflies (*Ephydra*), beetles (Coleoptera), and miscellaneous 28%; mollusks (*Mytilus, Lymnea, Macoma, Nucula, Goniobasis, Nassarius, Littorina, Lacuna, Bittium, Mitrella*, etc.) 9.7%; fishes (Gasterosteidae, Cottidae, Cyprinidae, Poeciliidae, etc.) 3.2% (Cottam 1939).

Shells of *Lacuna vincta* and *Margarita* (*Margarites*) *helicina* found in stomachs of birds in Me. (Norton 1909). In the upper Chesapeake region: gastropods (*Aceteocina, Ilyanassa*), bivalves (*Volcella, Macoma, Brachidontes, Mulinia*), crustaceans (Gammaridae, Xanthidae), and insects (Trichoptera and Odonata larvae) (R. E. Stewart 1962). Preference shown for crayfishes in Ky., Ohio, and Mich. (Audubon 1838, Trautman 1940, Pirnie 1935). At Reelfoot L., insects 24.67%, snails 16.67%, fishes 14%, and crustaceans 7% (Rawls 1958).

Shells of *Mya arenaria* found in a stomach in Cal. (J. Grinnell et al. 1918). A nearly empty stomach from the Pribilof Is. contained remains of a molusk (*Modiolaria verrucosa*), barnacles, and sea urchins (Preble and McAtee 1923). Three other stomachs from the Pribilofs contained 68.3% animal matter, largely amphipods 55%, with fish remains 10%, and marine worms (Nereidae) 3.3%. In March in Alaska, fed on herring spawn (Willett 1921).

In Swiss waters, larvae of insects (Dytiscidae, Perlidae, Phryganeidae, Libellulidae), worms, small mollusks (*Pisidium, Limnaeus, Valvata*), occasionally small fish, especially sculpins (*Cottus gobio*) (Fatio 1904). On upper Rhine, chiefly the water flea (*Daphnia pulex*) (Heussler and Heussler 1896, Naumann 1905b).

In England, aquatic plants, crabs, fish, frogs, tadpoles, freshwater mussels and snails (*Physa fontinalis*), larvae of Neuroptera (Millais 1913a; Cordeaux, in A. G. Butler 1897). The food in estuarine and coastal marshes of Great Britain, principally crustaceans, particularly *Carcinus maenas*. Inland, largely insect larvae, especially of the caddis fly (*Hydropsyche angustipennis*). Mollusks unimportant but principally *Limnaea pereger* and *Hydrobia jenkinsi*. Very few fishes (Olney and Mills 1963). In salt water in Ireland, crustaceans, isopods (*Idothea*), mollusks (*Littorina, Lacuna, Rissoa, Montacuta*), and in fresh water, *Limneus, Ancylus, Neritina* (W. Thompson 1851). Leeches found in a fledgling in Montenegro (Reiser and Führer 1896). These annelids are considered a favorite food in Ireland.

Food in Denmark 98% animal, mainly mollusks and crustaceans. Bivalves (*Mytilus edulis, Cardium nodosum, Spisula subtruncata*) 21%, crustaceans (*Crangon vulgaris, Idothea* spp., *Gammarus locusta, G. dübeni, Carcinus maenas, Mysis flexuosa*) 41%, fish (*Gobius* spp., *Gasterosteus aculeatus*) 8%, and annelids 7% (Madsen 1954).

In the U.S.S.R. at Rybinsk Reservoir, caddis fly larvae formed 75% by volume of food in Sept.–Oct., while in April these larvae (mainly *Phryganea grandis*) formed only 46.5% and chironomid larvae 32%. In the Mologa R. valley, Odonata nymphs amounted to 45% in autumn, but in early spring 60% consisted of small fish and 20% of chironomid larvae (Dementiev and Gladkov 1952).

**Vegetable** Pondweeds (*Potamogeton* largely, *Zostera, Ruppia, Najas*, and *Zannichellia*) 8.6%, wild celery (*Vallisneria spiralis*) 3.4%, spatterdock (*Nymphaea*) 1.4%, cultivated grains (bait) 1.4%, bulrushes (*Scirpus*) 1.1%, and miscellaneous 10.2% (Cottam 1939). The food in the upper Chesapeake region was not essentially different (R. E. Stewart 1962).

398

Seeds of *Zostera* in Me., while another stomach contained a complete meal of *Scirpus subterminalis* (Norton 1909, Mendall and Gashwiler 1940). A bird in Mass. fed almost exclusively on seeds of pondweed, waterlily, bayberry, bur reed, buds and roots of wild celery (J. C. Phillips 1911). Two birds collected on the lower Hudson R. had eaten seeds of *Echinochloa*, *Najas*, and *Polygonum* (Foley and Taber 1951). The 32% of plant material in 15 stomachs from Reelfoot L. consisted of algae 6.67%, giant cutgrass (*Zizaniopsis miliacea*) 6%, coontail (*Ceratophyllum demersum*) 4.33%, and seeds of hackberry *(Celtis* spp.) 4% (Rawls 1958). In Ore., a bird made a complete meal of seeds of *Hippuris*, *Scirpus*, and *Myriophyllum* (Gabrielson and Jewett 1940). Three specimens from the Pribilofs had eaten seeds of *Potamogeton* which formed 32% of the diet (Preble and McAtee 1923). AWS

[The above summary is published about as submitted; it would be more meaningful if summarized for fresh and for salt water, and by season. The essential data are not always given in the original sources. Yet it is apparent, for example, that insects are important on fresh water, crustaceans on salt water. RSP]

## Barrow's Goldeneye

*Bucephala islandica* (Gmelin)

Moderate-sized diving duck; sexually dimorphic; mainly black and white (♂ Alt. Plumage) or grays and white with brownish head (other Plumages). Also shares with Common Goldeneye such characters as: nostrils nearer tip than base of bill; iris and legs and feet yellowish, after early life. Although the Alt.-Plumaged drake obviously is separable from Common Goldeneye by any of various characters (white crescent in front of eye, spotted scapulars, dark bar in white area of wing), distinctions sometimes claimed for other stages and both sexes cannot be depended on invariably; full details in A. Brooks (1920). However, the nail on bill of Barrow's tends to be elliptical (not tapering toward forehead, i.e., oval in outline). There are various indefinite and subtle differences, Barrow's having more tapering bill, rounder head, wider gray band on breast in some Plumages, perhaps fewer white secondaries in the Basic wing. Internally there is a difference in configuration of the frontal portion of the skull; it is most evident in mature individuals.

The tracheal apparatus of the drake has been described and/or illus. numerous times from 1827 on. Distally, the windpipe is enlarged gradually to about double its smallest diam., being of the larger diam. for about the middle ⅗ and with evenly arranged rings, then is gradually reduced to half the larger diam. just before it enters the body (*B. clangula* has a bulbous enlargement distally); the bony bulla at inner end is much the same in the 2 goldeneyes, except smaller in *islandica*. For figs. of the windpipe, see Gilpin (1878a) and especially P. A. Taverner (1919); for the entire tracheal apparatus of the 2 goldeneyes, drawn comparatively, see especially A. Brooks (1920).

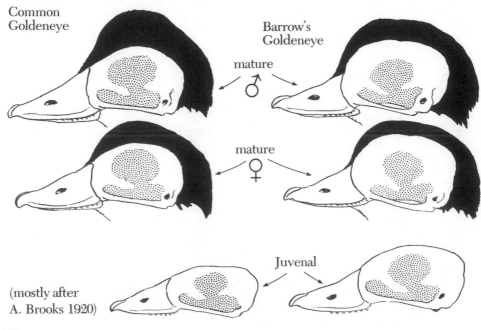

Common Goldeneye

Barrow's Goldeneye

mature ♂

mature ♀

Juvenal

(mostly after A. Brooks 1920)

400

DESCRIPTION    Two Plumages/cycle, sequence and timing as in Common Golden-eye, but apparently little individual variation in feathering. Terse treatment here; emphasis on known diagnostic characters.

▶    ♂ Def. Alt. Plumage (all feathering except tail and wing), worn from FALL into following SUMMER. **Bill** black, **iris** pale yellow. **Head** black, its sheen mostly ultramarine-violet, and a large white crescent between eye and side base of bill; **upperparts** mantle mostly black with some sheen as on head and black extends down the forward sides over end of folded wing; some shorter scapulars have white on inner webs, longer ones have an inner white area and black edges (terminal part of white breaks off, leaving black ends of the edges projecting beyond); the greater portion of the white scapular stripes is concealed, the exposed portions appearing as a row of roundish or oblong spots; neck and most of **underparts** white, the feathers on upper margins of sides and on the flanks have broad black border on outer web; feathers from vent to tail medium gray with light tips (latter wear off); legs and **feet** pale yellowish. Tail and wing are retained Basic feathering.

▶    ♂ Def. Basic Plumage (entire feathering), the head–body usually acquired beginning in JULY and succeeded by Alt. beginning in AUG., the wing and tail renewed toward end of Prebasic molt, well along in Aug. (duration of flightless period unknown). In general, like a dingy Alt. ♀, but has these distinguishing features: white areas in **wing** include many median wing coverts, some whitish feathers tend to remain in area where white crescent (of Alt. ♂) occurs on forward side of brownish **head** (of ♂ Def. Basic). **Tail** rounded, dark grayish. **Wing** differs from Juv. in having many coverts black (with sheen), the 2 outer primaries slightly tapered, and has a large interrupted white area: about half of secondaries plus tips of overlapping greater coverts, then a black bar (greater coverts except their ends), then median coverts and tips of some lesser coverts white; wing lining medium or darker grayish, axillars also.

▶    ♀ Def. Alt. Plumage (all feathering except tail and wing), acquired in FALL and worn into following SUMMER. **Bill** near orange-yellow with brown flecking in basal half (w. N. Am.), or varies with individual from essentially all to only distal third thus colored and remainder very dark (e. N. Am.), to (apparently without exception) only about the distal third orange-yellow (Iceland); this coloring is quite vivid from late winter through spring, in other seasons muted or bill all dark. **Iris** pale yellow. **Head** dark brownish, toward sepia (generally darker than Common Goldeneye), and some dark nape feathers. **Upperparts**, also ashy band on breast and along upper sides, av. darker than in the Common, so that any pale feather margins (which tend to wear off) appear more contrasty in new Plumage; most of neck, also lower **breast** to vent, white; vent to tail medium grayish. Legs and **feet** yellowish, webs dusky. Tail and wing are retained Basic feathering.

▶  ♀ Def. Basic Plumage (entire feathering), the head–body acquired beginning some time in SUMMER and retained into FALL, the tail and wing (after flightless period) acquired beginning some time in Aug. usually. Any yellowish in **bill** muted as compared to winter condition. Most obvious difference from ♀ Alt.: **neck** about as dark as breast and sides. **Tail** rounded, medium grayish. Much of **wing** blackish, but 5–6 middle secondaries white, the overlying greater coverts white and usually (but not invariably) with black ends (reverse of ♂), adjoining middle coverts have dark ends, and some lesser coverts are darkish with white margins (darkish patchy pattern where corresponding area in ♂ is white); wing lining and axillars as in ♂.

AT HATCHING   See comparison under Common Goldeneye, as the 2 may be indistinguishable on external characters. Early in the downy stage the head contour, in life, differs in the 2 goldeneyes; Barrow's appears somewhat larger headed and with "straight" forehead. Downy Barrow's have a proportionately much larger nail on the bill than downy Buffleheads; details in Linsdale (1933).

▶  ♂ Juv. Plumage (entire feathering), nearly grown at age about 8 weeks (when flight attained), then replaced by Basic I over a span of time in FALL, except wing retained into following summer. **Bill** dark, **iris** medium brownish. **Head** near fuscous, lower neck medium or lighter gray (not white); **upperparts** mostly various dark grays, the feathers with light grayish margins, scapulars fuscous (and short), rump toward brownish; **underparts** lower breast and belly off-white; upper breast, sides, flanks, and vent to tail darkish grays. **Tail** near dusky brownish, the feathers with notched ends. Legs and **feet** quite dark, but evidently become lighter in fall or soon after. **Wing** primaries and their coverts blackish brown, latter margined paler; secondaries 1–4 as primaries, 5 is broadly marked white at tip, 6–11 white except 11 has blackish brown patch on inner web, innermost secondaries as outermost; greater coverts dark with broad white tips, many of the smaller coverts have narrow white or light tips.

Distinguishable from ♀ Juv. only by greater av. size, as relative amount of white on wing coverts seems to vary independent of sex. Most Juv. Barrow's have less white on these coverts than do Juv. Commons. Shape of bill and its nail, perhaps also shape of head, may be useful in distinguishing the 2 goldeneyes in Juv. stage.

▶  ♀ Juv. Plumage (entire feathering), timing, etc., as ♂ and resembles ♂ except for smaller av. size.

▶  ♂ Basic I Plumage (all feathering except wing), the head–body begin to succeed the Juv. probably beginning about 9–10 weeks posthatching, in LATE SUMMER, and the new tail grows some time in fall; also during FALL, the Basic I head–body is succeeded by Alt. I (sometimes this is delayed until early winter). Drakes in Basic I have a much more clear-cut pattern than when in Juv. The **head** is darker (still without white crescent), the **neck** is white (for the first time), much of the **dorsum** is grayer, and the **belly**

402

is plain white. Thus it is very like Def. Basic, including the new tail, but the Juv. wing is retained.

▶   ♂ Alt. I Plumage (all feathering except tail and wing), generally begins to appear in OCT. or Nov. and all may be acquired by EARLY WINTER, but in some individuals molting is prolonged or interrupted, i.e., not completed until late winter. When fully acquired, resembles Def. Alt. in most respects, but possibly the facial crescent is smaller, the scapulars not as long. The Juv. wing and Basic I tail are retained. Then there is a molt of all feathering, beginning in SUMMER.

▶   ♀ Basic I and Alt. I (inclusive feathering of each as in ♂). Basic I is a FALL–WINTER Plumage, while Alt. I is acquired beginning in SPRING and continuing into early SUMMER; it is retained into SUMMER (usually July). The Juv. wing is retained throughout. Each of these Plumages has various characteristics of the corresponding definitive stage. Some time in fall or early winter the **iris** becomes pale yellowish; the **bill**, or part of it, lightens; the legs and **feet** become yellowish.

**Measurements** of birds from Alaska, B.C., Que., Me., and 1 Iceland, 12 ♂: BILL 32–36 mm., av. 34.3; WING 230–245, av. 239; TAIL 84–92, av. 88.2; TARSUS 40–43, av. 42;   12 ♀: BILL 30–33 mm., av. 31.7; WING 210–223, av. 218; TAIL 80–87, av. 84; TARSUS 37–40, av. 38 (ETS).

For series with WING meas. across chord, see J. C. Phillips (1925); for comparative meas. of nail on bill of Barrow's and Common Goldeneye, see A. Brooks (1920, or as quoted in Phillips).

Small series of "adults" from ne. N. Am.; 6 ♂: BILL 33–35 mm., av. 34; WING (across chord) 228–248, av. 234; TAIL 83–91, av. 87; TARSUS (of 5) 39.5–41.5, av. 40;   2 ♀: BILL 28–30; wing (across chord) 218; TAIL 79–81; TARSUS 34.5–37 (D. P. Olson).

**Weight** of 3 ♂ av. 2.4 lb. (1.09 kg.), max. 2.9 (1.3 kg.); 7 ♀ av. 1.6 lb. (0.73 kg.), max. 1.9 (0.86 kg.) (A. L. Nelson and Martin 1953). In ne. N. Am., "adults": 5 ♂ 38–42 oz., av. 41 (1.16 kg.), 2 ♀ 29 and 30 oz. (av. 0.84 kg.) (D. P. Olson).

When flightless in molt in ne. Alaska in Aug., there was a ¾-lb. difference between the sexes: 53 ♂ max. 2 lb. 8 oz., min. 1 lb. 8 oz., mean. 2 lb. 2 oz. (962 gm.); 14 ♀ max. 1 lb. 12 oz., min. 1 lb. 1 oz., mean 1 lb. 5 oz. (596 gm.) (Yocom 1970a). These birds were trapped Aug. 10 and held (without food?) for up to 5 days before weighing.

At Mývatn, Iceland, mean wt. of nesting ♀ ♀: 805 gm. (8 in 1968), 816 (6 in 1969), and 821 (6 in 1970) (Bengtson 1972c).

Wild **hybrids** are known with the Common Goldeneye, which see for details.

**Geographical variation** is most evident in pattern and color of bill of ♀; see above under ♀ Def. Alt. Plumage. In live drakes in Def. Alt., there are differences (hard to describe) in contour of head between birds of Iceland, e. N. Am., and w. N. Am. There may be other differences as yet not reported. RSP

FIELD IDENTIFICATION   See comparative remarks under Common Goldeneye. **RSP.**

VOICE   Much less is known of Barrow's than of the Common Goldeneye, since the latter (which see) has been studied at close range and in captivity.

The drake Barrow's usually is silent. During Kick display he has an *E–eng* call, quite

403

unlike any utterance of the Common. Both sexes are said to have a call during post-copulatory Rotations, but it is undescribed.

The duck utters a hoarse or grating croak. Young ♀ ♀ have a variant of it when "prospecting." Mature ♀ ♀ croak in various situations, as when going from nest to water to join the drake, when alarmed with young, and to contact her brood if separated from it. She is said sometimes to have a low clucking call, when in Prone posture.

Distress and social calls of downies are described below under "Reproduction."

A nonvocal "wing music" occurs in both goldeneyes, especially mature drakes. RSP

HABITAT    **Summer**    In w. N. Am., moderately alkaline lakes of small to medium size in parkland areas support the highest concentrations of Barrow's known except for a few localities in Iceland. Favored lakes are 5–15 ft. deep and have a dense growth of submerged aquatic vegetation, *Potamogeton pectinatus* and *Ruppia maritima* being the commonest species. Open water is essential, but lakes frequently are margined by dense stands of *Scirpus acutus*; less often they are bordered with forest or open range. In less alkaline lakes bordered with *Typha* or *Carex* the water is stained brown with finely suspended humic substances, which form a thick layer of bottom ooze. In spite of an abundance of invertebrate food, they are not heavily used by breeding goldeneyes. Females will go considerable distances from water to find nesting holes in dead or dying Douglas fir (*Pseudotsuga menziesii*), aspen (*Populus tremuloides*), cottonwood (*P. trichocarpa*), western yellow pine (*Pinus ponderosa*), or lodgepole pine (*P. contorta*). In some lakes with forested margins where the water level has been raised artificially, drowned trees form excellent nesting sites. In spring and early summer small sloughs of 2–3 acres as well as larger ponds and small lakes are used by territorial pairs, yearlings, and ♀ ♀ with broods, but molting postbreeders prefer larger water bodies. Very large, deep lakes with steep shorelines are not heavily used except on migration; food is not abundant in these lakes.

Breeders are more scattered at small subalpine and alpine lakes, beaver ponds, and streamside sloughs in the mountains throughout the breeding range in w. N. Am. The same applies to parts of Alaska. Such waters usually are surrounded by conifer forest and are clearer and have less aquatic vegetation than parkland sloughs. The sparseness is attributed chiefly to meager food supply, although scarcity of acceptable nesting sites also may be a factor.

In summary, in w. N. Am., breeding habitat of Barrow's Goldeneye and the Bufflehead are very similar, except the former is also on rivers, backwaters, and alpine lakes seldom used by the latter.

As yet, there is no really satisfactory information on breeding habitat in ne. N. Am., but the main area is presumed to be beyond the limits of sizable trees in interior Ungava; see Todd (1963). Presumably they nest in terrestrial cavities.

**During migrations** in spring and fall, ponds and lakes at lower elevations are utilized, being the first water areas to become free of ice in spring and the last to freeze over in fall. Many such ponds also are used for breeding. In Wash., spring migrants were observed in small numbers on deep, rockbound seepage lakes below dams, but not on scabland potholes (Johnsgard and Buss 1956).

**Molt migration**    In w. N. Am. the birds molt in groups on larger lakes within the overall breeding range, but possibly to some extent also away from it in Alaska; in e. N. Am., hundreds are known to occur in assemblies, at the season for molting, at localities on the perimeter of Ungava Bay, i.e., these birds have gone northward to molt.

In **winter** the bulk of the w. birds are found on coastal waters, in sheltered bays and inlets where rocky reefs and ledges in shallow water provide suitable feeding grounds. Barrow's on the w. coast appears to prefer waters of lower salinity than the Common Goldeneye, being found commonly on freshwater lakes and rivers of Vancouver I. and about the mouths of rivers on the mainland coast, but rarely on more saline waters of the e. side of Vancouver I. (J. Munro 1939). In Yellowstone Nat. Park they remain on waters kept open by hot springs and on rapid rivers that do not freeze. In ne. N. Am., on shallow marine waters and usually where it is rocky, some also on lower reaches of swift-flowing rivers that do not freeze.

In Iceland, where tree sites are lacking, Barrow's nests in natural cavities in rocks, also in cavities in structures such as sheep shelters built of rock; some nest under bushes; some in farm buildings and in nest boxes. Territorial pairs and females with broods occur on rivers and sheltered shallow bays of lakes. Drakes molt in flocks at Mývatn. In winter, both sexes are found in fjords and river mouths along the coast, while a few remain inland where hot springs prevent fresh waters from freezing. MFJ

DISTRIBUTION (See map.)   Barrow's Goldeneye apparently is of Nearctic origin. It has a discontinuous breeding distribution that corresponds roughly to the Nearctic–Icelandic portion of the range of the Harlequin. Center of abundance is in w. N. Am. and the writer suggests that Barrow's probably has bred in Iceland for a much longer time, or more continually, than in w. Greenland and on the Ungava Pen. The older records of distribution were presented fully by J. C. Phillips (1925) and part of these plus later ones for e. N. Am. were tabulated and mapped by Hasbrouck (1944c).

There have been problems and much confusion regarding various alleged records, hence occurrence, of Barrow's, a topic several authors have discussed. Stallcup (1952), for example, stated that all 6 specimens claimed for Kans. were found, on reexamination, to be *B. clangula*.

Because of fragmented distribution, the following summary is by regions, from w. to e., with seasonal status under each. There seems to be no information on exchange of individuals between regions; however, one might expect this to occur within continental N.Am. and possibly individuals from Iceland occasionally reach e. Greenland.

W. N. AM.   **Breeding**   The principal area is mainland B.C., spilling over into w. Alta., and extending northward into parts of s. Yukon Terr. and Alaska, and southward into conterminous w. U.S. where Barrow's is scattered and local.

The most northerly summer (not proven breeding) record is for a pair on June 30 in the upper Sheenjek valley, Alaska.

**Molt migration**   At least in Alaska and in the Ungava Pen., many Barrow's evidently go beyond nesting areas to molt. At Ohtig L., 40 mi. e. of Ft. Yukon in ne. Alaska, 2,697 molting birds were captured in 1960–61 and 359 in 1962 (King 1963). Turner (in Bent 1925) saw "great numbers" of these birds in late Sept. in Ungava Bay some 2 mi. from the mouth of the Koksoak R.

**Winter**   Recorded in the e. Aleutians at Unalaska; rare at Cold Bay (w. end of Alaska

Pen.). Usual range extends from the Kodiak I. area of Alaska southward on sheltered Pacific waters to cent., occasionally s., Cal.; also inland on some unfrozen waters, as at Yellowstone Nat. Park, Wyo. The bulk of the winterers evidently occur from somewhere in coastal B.C. down to include coastal Ore.

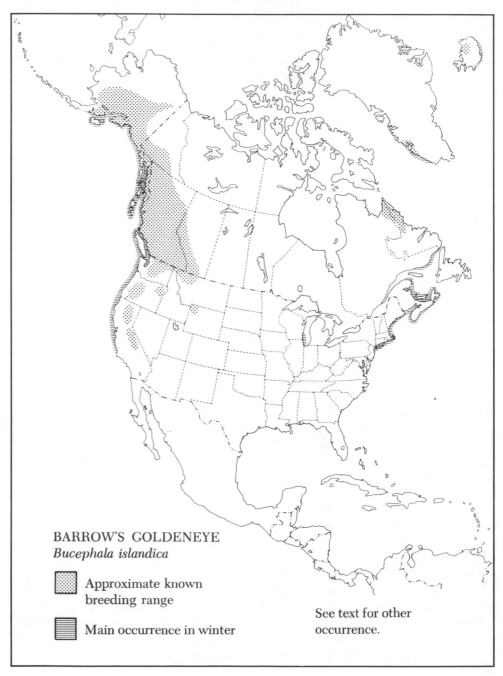

**BARROW'S GOLDENEYE**
*Bucephala islandica*

Approximate known
breeding range

Main occurrence in winter

See text for other
occurrence.

**Straggler** There are no reported occurrences on the Asiatic side of Bering Sea, but there are sightings of 2 drakes (1 accompanied by ♀ ♀, possibly of the same species) in May in the Pribilofs. There are 3 Aleutian records and, as mentioned above, it has been seen at outer end of the Alaska Pen. Barrow's has occurred (as a straggler?) inland away from known breeding range at several localities in Alta. and also in w. Mackenzie; for a listing, see Godfrey (1966).

To be certain whether southerly fall–winter records in the interior are of Pacific or Atlantic birds would, of course, be impossible without banding birds. W. of Texas, Barrow's has occurred in winter s. at least into Utah and Colo.

NOTE In the late 1870s, Carter (in Brewer 1879) found Barrow's plentiful and nesting in the Colo. mts., but there have been no nesting records in the state since 1886. Possibly there was an isolated breeding unit which became extinct and the region has not been repopulated. For historical data, see Bailey and Niedrach (1965).

**E. N. Am.** **Breeding** Based on various records of preflight broods (no nests have been located) and summer occurrence of mature birds, Barrow's definitely breeds near or along the upper half of the Labrador coast and probably it is a scattered nester inland in at least n. Ungava. Todd (1963) surmised that the Common nests in forested Ungava and Barrow's beyond in the unforested area. Hundreds of Barrow's and many more Commons molt in late summer to the north on the fringes of Ungava Bay.

In **migrations** on coastal salt water, also the Great Lakes–St. Lawrence drainage, but has straggled well away from usual places of occurrence.

In winter on salt, brackish, and to a very limited extent on unfrozen rapids and below dams on fresh water; from the Strait of Belle Isle southward regularly to Mass., occasionally to Long I. (N.Y.), and has occurred beyond as far down the coast as the Carolinas. Some remain inland, notably in s. L. Michigan and occasionally on open stretches of rivers in that general region.

**Straggler** to scattered inland localities s. to near Greenville in e. Texas, to Mo., Tenn., and w. N.C.

NOTES It is of interest that there are a very few Nfld. records—for March to May 19—in association with Common Goldeneyes.

According to Hantzsch (1908), Barrow's bred in considerable numbers e. of Ungava Bay in ne. Labrador prior to 1900, but he stated that Eskimos with guns virtually eliminated these birds by 1906.

In e. N. Am. there seem to be no gatherings in any season in numbers comparable to those seen on Pacific waters. For the inner St. Lawrence and Maritime waters, a large winter assembly might consist of 50–150 Barrow's; in Me., 10–40 in those winters when they arrive in greatest numbers.

GREENLAND Most records are for the Godthaab and Frederikshaab Districts; it has been recorded at least 3 times n. of the former, including once in Umanak Dist.; to the south it has been recorded occasionally in Julianehaab Dist. It was taken on the e. coast at Angmagssalik in summer of 1913. Barrow's has been seen or captured in all seasons, but usually in coastal waters from Nov. to April. Presumably it is resident, nesting not far from its winter quarters; no nests have been found (Salomonsen 1950, 1967a).

ICELAND Barrow's breeds mainly at Mývatn and along the R. Laxá; in the early 1970s, the number of mature birds may have approached 2,000 individuals. A few remain inland in winter, on fast stretches of rivers and at Mývatn where warm-water springs usually keep part of the lake open; others are on shallow waters along the s. coast.

**Straggler in the Palearctic** to Norway, Sweden, Finland, w. U.S.S.R. (a capture each for Lakes Ilmen and Onega), Poland (reportedly a small flock on March 31, 1957), Germany, Holland, Belgium, France, England, and Spain.

**No fossil record** (erroneously reported from the Pleistocene of Ore.). RSP

MIGRATION    Most of this section pertains to the largest regional population, that of w. N. Am., followed by brief mention of travels elsewhere.

Migration is characterized by lateness in fall, earliness in spring, relatively short distances covered, and a variety of routes. In w. N. Am. the birds are said to follow river systems such as the Fraser, Thompson, Okanagan, Columbia, Skeena, and others, which flow in an e.-w. or ne.-sw. direction, but cross overland readily, especially at night. Some of the birds at Yellowstone Nat. Park, Wyo., are only locally migratory; some breed at high mountain lakes, then winter on rivers and waters warmed by hot springs at lower elevations, but their numbers are augmented in spring by arrival of migrants that remain to breed (Skinner 1937).

Barrow's is locally migratory in Iceland and evidently even more so in sw. Greenland.

**Spring**    In B.C., adults leave coastal wintering areas in late Feb., March, or early April, in pairs or small groups; single males occasionally travel alone. The birds definitely travel at night, possibly also by day. Concentrations build up on lakes free of ice at lower elevations, especially in s. B.C. Then the birds disperse to breeding lakes as the ice melts on these in last half of April, early May, or later, depending on elevation and season. A few prebreeders (yearlings) accompany the older birds to interior B.C. in March and April, but others linger on coastal waters until late May. Most yearling ♀ ♀ arrive on breeding lakes during May. Many yearling ♂ ♂ do not go to nesting areas, i.e., they go from winter quarters to wherever they molt.

First arrival dates: L. Lenore, Wash., March 16 (Johnsgard 1955); pond  500 ft. above Okanagan L., B.C., March 9–22; Vaseaux L., B.C., Feb. 19 (J. Munro 1939); Redstone, Chilcotin Dist., B.C., March 31 (F. Shillaker); Atlin, in nw. B.C., April 23–29 (Swarth 1936). A few remain on the se. Alaska coast late into May (J. C. Phillips 1925).

On the Atlantic coast, most depart from Me. during the first 20 days of March (R. S. Palmer 1949); they are last seen in Mass. the last week in March or first week in April (Griscom 1945). They arrive on the Labrador coast by June 1 (Turner, in Bent 1925). They return to breeding areas in Iceland about the end of March (Millais 1913a).

**Summer and late summer**    Movements vary with age and sex. In interior B.C. 95% of adult drakes have a **molt migration** to unknown destinations in late May or early June, after clutches are complete and incubation has started. Postbreeding ♀ ♀ remain on breeding lakes or make only short local movements prior to molting and, afterward, have little tendency to wander prior to fall migration to wintering areas. Band recoveries indicate that young of the year have a considerable tendency to wander in late Aug., Sept., and Oct. in various directions apparently unrelated to direction of subsequent fall migration.

408

In ne. Alaska there is a notable concentration of molting birds of both sexes in Aug. at Ohtig L. 40 mi. e. of Ft. Yukon.

**Fall migration** In B.C., movement to coastal wintering areas occurs in late Oct.– early Nov. Prior to this, formation of ice on lakes at higher elevations, particularly in the north, results in concentrations of ♀ ♀ and young on open waters at lower elevations. They are first seen in the Vancouver region in the last week in Oct. After molting, postbreeding drakes evidently are scattered in interior B.C.; they arrive at coastal wintering areas in large flocks a few days ahead of ♀ ♀. Most ♀ ♀ and young of the year arrive during the next 2 weeks in smaller flocks. They leave the Okanagan Valley of B.C. the last week in Oct., just as Common Goldeneyes are arriving from the north (J. Munro 1918). They were last recorded at Atlin in nw. B.C. on Oct. 21, but probably remain later (Swarth 1936). They reappear on the se. Alaskan coast at end of Oct. (J. C. Phillips 1925).

In e. N. Am. they remain on the Labrador coast until early Nov. (Turner, in Bent 1925). They arrive in Me. chiefly in the latter half of Nov. (R. S. Palmer 1949). In Mass., they appear in late Nov. or early Dec.; the earliest recorded date for the state was Nov. 11 (Griscom 1945).

**Winter** There is some shifting about, since age and sex composition of local groups on the B.C. coast change as the season progresses, but the data are insufficient for analysis. MFJ

BANDING STATUS The total number banded in N. Am. was 12,784 through the year 1964 and there were 1,149 recoveries through 1961; main places of banding were B.C. and Alaska (data from Bird Banding Laboratory). Some Barrow's also have been banded in Iceland. RSP

REPRODUCTION Data mostly from B.C.; supplemented by available information from other areas. So far as known, both sexes **first breed** when approaching age 2 years (Bent 1925, J. C. Phillips 1925, J. Munro 1939). A captive-reared ♀ first bred at 2 years and annually thereafter (Wormald 1939). The birds are not in definitive feathering until well into their 2nd fall, when nearing age 1½ years. When younger, however, both sexes perform various pair formation displays and engage in nest hunting or "prospecting" activities (J. Munro 1939, present authors) and, in the Cariboo Dist. of B.C., a known-age (banded) yearling ♀ was trapped with a brood, which she may have adopted. No known yearling ♀ ♀ have been trapped on nests.

**Pair formation** activity of breeders occurs mostly on winter range, with 5–20 birds in displaying groups. A few individuals are paired as early as Dec., most before migrating in late March or April, and some may not be paired until after arrival in breeding areas. Birds behaving as pairs, and apart from displaying groups, are seen frequently from Jan. on, but the areas where they occur are neither consistently occupied nor defended. Each ♂, however, does defend his mate against other drakes in definitive feathering. Yet whether these winter-formed pairs have a durable bond remains unknown.

**Displays of the duck** include ROTARY PUMPING, both toward the ♂ (especially at beginning of a mutual Triumph ceremony) and in an indefinite form toward downies. JIVING is the same as in the Common Goldeneye. The NECK-DIP of the Common has not been seen in Barrow's. HEAD-UP is similar in the 2 species. The WATER-FLIP also is performed by the ♀.

**Displays of the drake**  Sawyer (1928) described and illustrated most of the pair formation displays, but the captions of his figs. were transposed. M. T. Myres has confirmed Sawyer's findings and has coined most of the display names used here.

HEAD-TURNING from side to side in a horizontal plane occurs in 2 situations: 1 during intervals between successive movements of the neck in Neck-withdrawing display and 2 during Postcopulatory steaming. In both, the action is similar to the corresponding movements of the Common Goldeneye. A clicking sound, evidently caused by the mandibles, is heard during Head-turning I. At intervals the neck is withdrawn quickly from this position into the shoulders, and shortened. It is then stretched upward again. Head-turning I resembles the Alarm posture. It is assumed most often when the drake is behind a duck, or between 2 of them; the ♂ appears to be in a mood of uncertainty as to the future actions of either the female(s) or himself.

HEAD-FLICK a tilting of the head once to right, then to left, is a regular finale of a number of displays, e.g., Kick, Rotary pumping, and during Threat. The bill points at a downward angle of about 35° as it passes in front of the bird. (It is also the finale of a number of displays of the Common Goldeneye.)

NECK-WITHDRAWING the drake stretches his neck vertically upward with beak held horizontally. The head is turned slightly from side to side while held in this position and the bill is opened and closed continually.

KICK is less elaborate in form than that of the Common Goldeneye. There are partial descriptions in A. Brooks (1920), J. C. Phillips (1925), Sawyer (1928), and J. Munro (1918, 1939). It is an obvious, striking display which appears to take 2 forms almost impossible to distinguish in the field. Film sequences indicate that the feet are kicked in both, which might indicate that they are homologous with the Slow and Fast forms of Headthrow-kick of the Common Goldeneye. If this is so, then Barrow's has no display comparable to the Headthrow of the other goldeneye. If, instead, the 2 forms of Kick are unevolved equivalents of Headthrow and Headthrow-kick respectively, then they have become hardly differentiated at all in Barrow's. It appears that the head does not touch the back in one form, while it does in the other. The body appears to sink more deeply into the water in the second form.

The first form was illus. in the Severn Wildfowl Trust *4th. An. Rept.* 1950–51 and in Sawyer's paper. The head is lifted and then swung backward until it is being held stiffly over the back at an angle of 45° and the beak is held almost vertically upward and is opened and a call uttered. This is a short, low, guttural note, which may be described as a thin *E-eng,* and it differs in tone from the calls in Headthrow and Headthrow-kick of the Common Goldeneye. The position is held only momentarily. A leg stroke appears to occur at the same moment as the call, for the breast sinks into the water. A Head-flick completes the display. The head is tilted over sideways when it is in the rearmost (raised) position. The display is rapid; there is no pause in it.

In the second form the head is thrown back into contact with the dorsum, the feet are thrust backward convulsively at the same time, and the whole body sinks into the water. A Head-flick completes the action.

These are differences from Common Goldeneye. 1 The head is tilted off center

410

plane. **2** The head is thrown back as if by the force of the jerk of the feet which is simultaneous. **3** The rear of the body is not elevated. The beak is opened and a call uttered as the propulsive movement is taking place. **4** The head and neck are not carried forward down to the water in front and then elevated, as in 2nd half of Headthrow-kick. The 2 forms of the Kick occur in (a) groups engaged in pair formation activities; (b) when a drake flies over a group on the water [the Red-breasted Merganser has a similar response when other birds, including gulls, fly over. (Curth 1954)]; (c) When a drake is alone, especially after alighting on the water; and (d) occasionally as a precopulatory activity. In displaying groups in breeding areas these movements are seen more from yearling than adult drakes. Some form of social stimulation occurs, since one performance generally is accompanied by the same display by another individual. In its various contexts it may have an appeasement function (which may be socially stimulated, in addition).

ROTARY PUMPING with TICKING    The head is lifted back and up (neck straight), then swung forward and finally brought back and down again so that the rotary movement in center plane may be repeated. Speed and amplitude of the movement range from weak jerks of the head to violent oscillations and the number of times it is repeated varies greatly. In forwardmost position the head is twice the distance from water that it is in Bowsprit-pumping of the Common Goldeneye and the neck axis forms an angle of 75° with the water line. In the rearmost position the neck is straight instead of curved. The beak tip follows a pear-shaped instead of elliptical path, owing mainly to the greater articulation of the head up-and-down.

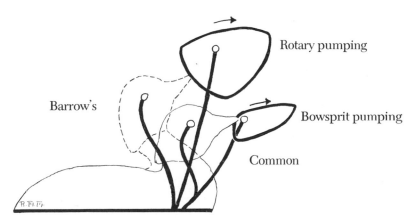

The above is seen when groups are displaying and it also is the main display of the drake toward his mate on territory. Generally it precedes Water-flips and Wing-and-leg-stretches of the precopulatory repertoire and may be reintroduced if that sequence is delayed or stopped. Rotary pumping is identical with the mutual "greeting" movement performed by adult ♀♀ and downy young.

At high intensities, and particularly when the movement is performed as a Triumph ceremony with the ♀ after a territorial border encounter with another drake, another display, TICKING, alternates with rotary pumping. The motivation appears to be aggressive, since the Threat posture is assumed. Ritualization has modified the signal

411

value of the display, for the beak is held wide open while a faint ticking or clicking noise occurs at the same time. The noise resembles that made by a pair of hand-operated hair clippers and occurs in bursts of 4–5 clicks. Evidently it is not produced in the same way as the sound heard in Head-turning. Generally 2 pumping movements alternate between each Ticking display, but the number of pumping movements is variable. Intergradations have been noticed, e.g., beak open while pumping. Sawyer (1928) and Stonor (1940) illustrated both the pumping and Ticking elements.

**Yearling drakes** have been seen to perform all ♂ displays listed above, but not with same proportionate frequency.

Pair bond form is single-clutch or **seasonal monogamy**; the bond is maintained until the ♀ is incubating, usually in late May or early June in B.C. Thereafter the ♀ ♀ are segregated from the ♂ ♂ until at least into early fall.

The birds **arrive** at nesting areas in B.C. in late March or in April, in pairs and small displaying groups, and congregate with other seasonally resident and migrant water-fowl on lakes or portions of them free of ice. As the ice melts, pairs move to breeding lakes and sloughs and establish or reestablish territories as soon as a sufficient area is free of ice. The ♀ ♀ return to the lakes where they were hatched, or to the nest sites they used in a previous year.

The defended (mated pair) **territory** is located on the water area closest to the nest site to which the ♀ has returned; it is used for copulating and feeding, although the pair not infrequently feeds elsewhere as well. (Brood territories are occupied by ♀ ♀ after their clutches hatch; these do not necessarily coincide with the territory used earlier by the pair, but may do so.) Size of territory depends on number of breeding pairs present, also on size and shape of water area where it is located. Ponds smaller than 2 acres usually are not occupied, but one of the 3 acres was occupied by 2 territorial pairs when the breeding population was high and only 1 when it was low. Territories are distributed around the periphery of larger lakes, either a long open shoreline or the outer boundary of a zone of emergent aquatic vegetation bordering the shore; that is, their number is limited by length of "shoreline" rather than size of water area. At a high breeding density (Cariboo Dist. of B.C. in 1952), on 2 lakes inhabited by a total of 38 pairs, each territory occupied 40–60 yds. of shoreline or margin; at lower densities the territories were larger and boundaries less well defined.

**Territorial defense** is undertaken most frequently by the drake against other *B. islandica* ♂ ♂ in Def. Alt. Plumage; yearling drakes are threatened less frequently. Females rarely defend territory, but occasionally threaten other ♀ ♀, especially when a ♀ returns to territory to find a yearling closely associated with her mate. Her display never is as intense as that of the drake, nor is the intruder chased to the territorial boundary, but merely away from the vicinity of the drake. Territorial drakes some-times attacked Common Goldeneye and Surf Scoter migrants, also seasonally resident Buffleheads, Redheads, Lesser Scaups, Ruddy Ducks, and young Coots (*Fulica americana*), at Westwick L., B.C. Conversely, a ♂ Bufflehead on territory attacked and drove off a ♀ Barrow's after her mate had departed and the goldeneye territory no longer was defended.

According to Erskine (1972a), the ♂ Barrow's attacks the ♂ Bufflehead; the ♀ Barrow's has attacked ♀ Buffleheads and possibly has killed the ducklings, as in an attack on Lesser Scaup reported by L. G. Sugden (1960); 2 ♀ Barrow's have been seen to kill their own young after the latter were color-marked, which suggests that Barrow's is unusually prone to attack ducks of any species. (Also see below.)

In summer on the River Laxá in Iceland, one knows when a drake Barrow's is approaching because the Harlequins become agitated and begin calling; they avoid Barrow's by taking flight, or swimming away, or even swimming to shore and walking away (R. S. Palmer).

**Threat and related displays** The weakest form of aggressive behavior is the CROUCH posture—the head lower and somewhat farther forward than in normal resting position. The "shoulders" are low, the tail depressed. This is assumed at times when no likely victims are in view. The bird often is restless, turning around and eyeing the environment.

Barrow's

Threat

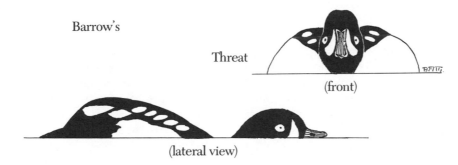

(front)

(lateral view)

The THREAT posture occurs at higher aggressive motivation than Crouch. The posture (but not pattern) is similar in both goldeneyes. The body is flattened and rather submerged. The bill may be pointed slightly upward so that the chin is raised above the surface, or may be lying along the water. Prominent features include the crescentic face patches, white "windows" on the sides of the back, and yellow irises (both eyes) against the dark of the head. It is very striking; the pattern visible to a potential victim is very different in the 2 goldeneyes. Front and side views sometimes may be visible to a victim, since the aggressor often swivels his body from side to side, possibly in order that he may view the opponent in monocular and binocular vision alternately, prior to diving.

An alarm posture (similar to that of the Common Goldeneye) seldom has been observed in border conflicts between equals on their territories. (An overt type of aggressive behavior is described under Common Goldeneye.)

Goldeneyes drive other ducks from their territories by underwater attack. Most diving attacks begin from about 20 down to 5 ft. from the intended victim, but sometimes an aggressor may travel as much as 300 yds. by a number of dives, surfacing in Threat posture between each. After the final dive the attacker may come up headfirst under its victim. Threat undoubtedly is derived from the posture indicating intention to dive, since there are all grades of posture from resting position through Crouched to full Threat followed by Diving. In an actual attack, the undersides of the victim are prodded or bitten.

On the breeding grounds various tactical situations may be distinguished. 1 Threat

413

may be assumed some distance from the territory boundary, or when no other individual is anywhere near the drake. **2** If each of 2 drakes is close to the boundary between their territories, they may dive continuously and parallel to each other without attacking and remain a constant distance apart. **3** Threat-posturing at the border may be followed by a fight, or there is an attack if the neighbor intrudes. **4** If an intruder flies into territory, assumption of Threat posture by the owner sometimes is sufficient to make it fly, or swim, away. Occasionally it escapes by diving.

If a potential victim manages to get into the air just before an attacking ♂ comes up beneath him and lands nearby, the aggressor may fly after him, land and dive in pursuit, the pursued having dived first. When struck from below, the victim seldom is capable of escaping by flight. Closer than 5 ft., the attacker rushes over the surface of the water at the victim. Generally the latter flaps wildly, with neck angled forward at 45° and wings beating rapidly against the water. When there is a displaying group, or the birds are on neutral ground, usually the aggressor desists, the victim lands, and both perform Upward-stretch, Wing-flap, Head-turning, and waggle their tails—a sure sign that the conflict is, for the time being, suspended. If the pursued is driven into his own territory, he turns and attacks, or dives toward, his opponent who flees in like fashion. When the chased bird turns to attack his tormentor, the birds may be seen fighting face to face, but only momentarily, necks lunging and wings beating. Fighting was described by A. Brooks (1920), Sawyer (1928), and J. Munro (1939). As indicated, however, fights in which 2 birds face each other breast to breast are a rare climax to aggressive behavior. Aggressive behavior by ♀♀ toward other ♀♀ is apparent mainly when a ♀ has young and occupies a brood territory close to a nest site of another individual.

**Mass display**  Occasionally a territorial boundary dispute between 2 drakes of adjacent pairs attracts several other territorial pairs and prebreeding drakes and develops into a mass display similar to that of groups during pair formation. All the drakes display toward a single ♀ and threaten each other; the other ♀♀ associate with the group, but take little part in display. After 15–20 min., display intensity decreases and the participants disperse.

**Common areas**, used but not defended, include open water in the centers of larger ponds and lakes and stretches of unoccupied shoreline. Such areas, if shallow, are used for feeding by territorial pairs and prebreeders; in deeper water, for resting and loafing, chiefly by prebreeders.

**Copulatory behavior** was discussed by Myres (1959b). The displays are described under the Common Goldeneye, since they are nearly identical in the 2 species. The PRONE posture was described and illus. by Sawyer (1928), who claimed that a low clucking call sometimes could be heard. The WATER-FLIP is indistinguishable from drinking—the head is dipped to water, then the beak raised rapidly to a 45° angle or more. This may be performed mutually on occasions other than during the precopulatory sequence. Sawyer described the WING-AND-LEG-STRETCH, which is similar in both goldeneyes. JABBING takes the form of a bout of dipping the beak to water, described accurately by Sawyer as "animated twitching of the water." It appears that Jabbing is homologous with the dipping of the beak which alternates with preening in the

414

Bufflehead and scoters. WING-PREEN is a momentary action. The precopulatory STEAMING posture is more upright and seemingly less stiff than in the Common Goldeneye. The head feathers are bristling. There is a WING-FLICK while the drake is mounted. Postcopulatory ROTATIONS and STEAMING are as in Common Goldeneye, but the neck is more curved and head not held quite as high in Steaming. Sawyer described and illus. both actions and stated that he heard a call, possibly from both members of the pair, during Rotations. He described Head-turning during post-copulatory Steaming ("proud swim") as a "regular ticktock movement." Other post-copulatory behavior: ritualized Bathing, Upward-stretch, and Wing-flap.

There is no information on when copulation occurs in relation to nesting in the wild. A captive ♀ was stated (Wormald 1939) to copulate daily when she came off her nest "during incubation."

**Comparison of *Bucephala* displays**   The only displays in which the 2 goldeneyes show almost no differences are the pre- and postcopulatory displays, Head-turning I, and Neck-withdrawing. The Water-flip, Wing-and-leg-stretch, Jabbing, Wing-preen, Upward-stretch, Wing-flap, and postcopulatory Bathing are derived quite clearly from comfort movements. This is made evident for Jabbing and Wing-preen displays by a comparison with the Bufflehead and scoters, in which these displays are less ritualized, and where they form the dominant displays of the precopulatory sequence (Myres 1959b).

The 2 goldeneyes have very different pair formation and maintenance displays that probably had common origins. The Headthrow-kick complex is more differentiated in the Common Goldeneye, where Headthrow also is the commonest display in display-ing groups (Rotary pumping is commonest in Barrow's). It may be assumed that Bowsprit and Rotary pumping are equivalent. The Common Goldeneye shows further specialization in having a Scoop display resembling the Bowsprit posture, but lacking Pumping, and it has a Masthead display. Neither are found in Barrow's.

Few pair formation displays of the Bufflehead can be homologized readily with goldeneye displays. The situations in which different types of tactics (e.g., Display-flights, "leading") are employed do, however, appear to be similar in many instances. Buffleheads, with fewer displays, seem to have a greater development of distinctive stereotyped "maneuvers" in their behavior. The greatest similarity between the Bufflehead and goldeneyes is in Rotations (Myres 1959b). Scoters lack these. The Bufflehead lacks the Water-flip, Wing-and-leg-stretch, and exaggerated steaming postures of the goldeneyes.

**Nest site**   Barrow's Goldeneye usually nests in dead stubs or in trees close to water where the territory is located. Most sites described have been either in trees standing in water or within 100 ft. of its edge, but 2 were found 400 and 500 yds. from it (A. Brooks 1903; MFJ). J. Munro (1939) observed a ♀ with newly hatched young appar-ently walking toward a lake 3 mi. distant. The nest site usually is the deserted cavity of a Pileated Woodpecker or Flicker, the latter enlarged by natural decay since otherwise it would be too small. Natural tree cavities also are used. Tree species commonly utilized in B.C. are quaking aspen (*Populus tremuloides*), Douglas fir (*Pseudotsuga menziesii*), and ponderosa pine (*Pinus ponderosa*), less commonly scrub pine (*Pinus contorta*).

415

Suitable holes usually are in dead or dying trees, or dead stubs. Unusual sites in B.C. include 4 old Crow nests (R. Y. Edwards 1953, L. G. Sugden 1963), hayloft of a deserted barn (J. Munro 1918), and a marmot burrow (J. Munro 1935). Near Atlin in n. B.C., young broods have been observed on alpine lakes in locations which preclude the possibility of tree nesting (Swarth 1926), i.e., presumably they nested in ground cavities.

In Ore. this goldeneye uses nest boxes (Griffee 1958). At L. Lenore in e. Wash., apparently they nest in holes in basalt cliffs (S. W. Harris et al. 1954). In McKinley Park, Alaska, they will utilize "rock crevices or similar situations" (A. Murie 1963); territorial drakes, alone or with mates, are seen there on ponds at a distance from any sizable trees. Presumably ground cavities are used to some extent on the Alaska Pen. This bird must be a ground nester in n. Ungava, certainly in Greenland. In Iceland it nests in cavities in stream banks, holes in lava rocks, under willow or birch on islets in rivers, among coarse grass or low scrub, or under large stones, and in artificial holes in turf walls of sheep shelters (Millais 1913a), also in dark corners of stables (J. C. Phillips 1925). The farmers provide various types of nesting quarters for these birds, some within buildings. At Mývatn in ne. Iceland, farmers have harvested duck eggs for 700 years; the law now requires that 4 eggs/clutch be left to hatch (Scott 1952).

The site is selected by the ♀, who returns to it each year as long as it remains usable. The nest trees and stubs frequently decay and fall; of 8 such sites observed in 1952–57 inclusive, 3 fell during the study period. If a previously used site no longer is suitable, another close by will be occupied. Competitors in B.C. for such sites include the Hooded Merganser, Wood Duck, Bufflehead, and American Kestrel. Rodents (Bushy-tailed Wood Rat, Flying Squirrel, Red Squirrel) sometimes nest in these cavities in summer, or fill them with sufficient debris in winter to render them unattractive to goldeneyes. Availability of usable sites may influence the number of breeders present, but J. Munro (1939) believed that food is more important in determining nesting density.

**No preparation** of the site is undertaken, except that the duck sometimes removes old egg shells and other detritus from the bottom of the cavity; more frequently, eggs are laid on top of matted nest down and shells of last season's nesting. In Iceland, nests under rocks contain a little grass and other vegetation (J. C. Phillips 1925). During the laying period a lining of **nest down** from the venter of the ♀ is added. This down is wholly white, or very pale gray (off-white), some with brownish tips; some intermingled feathers have the vane white with wide brown tip, others are wholly white. The amount of down in the nest varies, occasionally being insufficient for the duck to use in covering her clutch before departing. Individual ♀ ♀ differ as to time when the down is accumulated; in some nests a little is added with each egg laid, beginning with the first; in others, none is present until the clutch is nearly complete.

The **laying season** shows considerable variation in B.C. with latitude, season, and elevation, being chiefly dependent on when waters at breeding places become free of ice. In the Cariboo Dist., dates for first eggs in 22 nests varied from April 20 to May 26, av. May 6; dates for completion of these clutches varied May 2–June 10, av. May 21. J. Munro (1918) recorded downy young in the Okanagan Valley on May 22, indicating a completed clutch by April 20, and in the Creston region of s. B.C., young estimated a week old on May 11 (J. Munro 1950). Near Atlin in n. B.C., Swarth (1926) stated that downies were not seen until the first week in July, indicating that clutches were not completed there until early June.

Bent (1925) gave the following egg dates (some clutches undoubtedly longer incubated than others): B.C.—5 records May 12–May 31; Alta.—2 records May 28 and 30; Iceland—21 records May 19–June 30.

**Clutch size** 40 clutches in B.C. (28 examined by MFJ, others from the literature or museum data): 1 clutch (of 4), 10 (6), 5 (7), 3 (8), 5 (9), 7 (10), 3 (11), 3 (12), and 3 (13), av. 9.1/clutch. In Colo., 3 clutches—6, 7, and 10 (Brewer 1879). In a large series from Mývatn, Iceland, 1961–71 inclusive, mean clutch size and standard error varied from $10.15 \pm 0.32$ (20 clutches in 1964) to $10.73 \pm 0.38$ (11 clutches in 1969) (Bengtson 1971c). In a later paper on Mývatn, he gave mean clutch size as 10.9 in 101 "early" clutches and 10.0 in 78 "late" ones (Bengtson 1972c).

Clutches of 15 or more are presumed to be joint layings by at least 2 ♀♀. In 49 "dump nests" at Mývatn, the mean number of eggs was 17.4 (Bengtson 1972c).

One **egg** from each of 20 clutches (Iceland 15, w. Canada 3, conterminous U.S. 2) **size** length av. $62.02 \pm 1.58$ mm., breadth $44.06 \pm 1.31$, radii of curvature of ends $18.82 \pm 1.32$ and $12.50 \pm 0.99$, **shape** subelliptical, elongation $1.40 \pm 0.037$, bicone 0.00, asymmetry +0.203 (FWP). Seventeen eggs from B.C.: length 58.2–63.1 mm., av. 61.1, and breadth 42.0–44.9, av. 43.4 (MFJ). For other large series from unspecified localities, see J. C. Phillips (1925), Bent (1925), and Schönwetter (1961). They are smooth, with slight gloss when fresh. They are similar in **color** and shape to those of the Common Goldeneye, perhaps somewhat larger and harder shelled (Phillips).

The **rate of deposition** varies depending on individual, lateness of season, and number of eggs already laid, averaging about 1.5 days/egg. The interval between eggs, especially at start of laying, sometimes is as much as 3–4 days, frequently 2 days. In tardy seasons, or when clutches are nearing completion, eggs usually are laid on consecutive days. Yet there is considerable individual variation, some entire clutches being laid at rate of 1/day, others averaging one every 2 days. Most eggs are laid during the daylight hours, but some at night.

**Mixed clutches** The ♀ sometimes lays in the nests of other hole-nesting ducks, or 2 ♀ use the same cavity. A clutch from Enderby, B.C., contained 6 *B. islandica* eggs and 1 of *Aix sponsa;* another from the same area contained 11 *Mergus cucullatus* and 2 of *B. islandica.* In the Chilcotin Dist. of B.C., 15 *B. islandica* and 2 *B. albeola* eggs (Erskine 1959). In Iceland a *Mergus serrator* was incubating 4 *B. islandica* eggs (Brewer 1879). Very large clutches, presumably joint layings, of *B. islandica* include 18 in a cavity in B.C. (P. W. Martin) and 23 and 24 in Iceland (Millais 1913a). So-called "dump nests" in Iceland were mentioned earlier.

**Replacement clutches** in B.C., if any, are rare; also, the drakes depart from breeding areas fairly soon after incubation of initial clutches begins. Two eggs, laid June 11 and 12 near Williams L., were thought to comprise a replacement clutch, considering their number and date. More likely, however, the ♀ had lost part of her clutch and then had finished laying at another site. Of 31 B.C. clutches followed through laying and incubation, only 2 failed prior to hatching, both at the same site, an extremely exposed dead stub on open range. In 1952 the eggs were destroyed by an avian predator (probably Crow) during laying; in 1954 the incubating ♀ was attacked on the nest by an unknown predator and probably killed.

In 39 "renestings" at Mývatn, Iceland, mean clutch size was 7.5 eggs (Bengtson 1972c)—probably late and/or continued laying.

**Incubation** usually begins when the last egg is laid, occasionally 1–3 days earlier, sometimes 1–3 days after the last egg is laid. Its onset often is "premature" in late clutches and "delayed" in early ones, especially in cool weather. During the first 7–10 days the drake remains on territory while the duck is incubating; she joins him to feed and bathe and is accompanied by him on her return flight to the nest. At this time, ♀ prebreeders (yearlings) frequently form loose bonds with the drakes, associating with them on territory while the duck is incubating. As incubation proceeds, the pair bond is dissolved gradually; the drake tends to wander off territory more and more often, associating on neutral waters with other postbreeding drakes and prebreeders of both sexes. In late May or early June most of the mature drakes disappear, presumably migrating to molting lakes.

The **incubating rhythm** of the duck (data from recorders at 4 nests, some observations at 18 additional nests) varies with air temperature, stage in incubation, and the individual. Generally she is absent from the nest 1 to 4 times daily between sunrise and sunset, for periods varying from 30 min. to 5–6 hrs., usually totaling 2 to 4 hrs. or more daily. Most ♀ ♀ are absent once shortly before sunset, also earlier in the day, either 2–3 hrs. after sunrise, or at noon, or both times. On only 2 occasions was a ♀ absent after dark, both times on clear moonlit nights. Absences are less frequent but longer during the early part of incubation than later on. Absences tend to be less frequent and shorter on cold, rainy days than in hot, sunny weather. Nest temperatures during incubation varied 34°–39° C and showed positive correlation with external air temperatures, which varied 11°–30.5° C.

**"Prospecting"** While ♀ ♀ are incubating, groups of 2–20 adult and yearling ♀ ♀, occasionally joined by ♂ ♂, often fly rapidly in circles low over or through the forest, and back over the lake. One or more of the participants calls continuously while in flight, uttering an emphatic, monosyllabic, rather high-pitched, croaking note, rapidly and rhythmically repeated. The entire group sometimes splashes down noisily on the water, only to take off again and repeat the performance. Sometimes such a group will flutter persistently for up to an hour around an unoccupied nest hole, or even a dead stub or telephone pole in which there is no hole, the participants landing on the stub and taking off again in rapid succession. This behavior is seen only during the span when ♀ ♀ are incubating, usually in the morning or late evening, sometimes at night, especially if the moon is bright. Such activity by ♀ ♀ presumably is incipient nesting behavior of prebreeders and unmated older birds; it may serve to establish some degree of attachment to a particular place to which they will return the following year. Similar flights have been reported (many authors) for *B. clangula*, also for *B. albeola*.

**Incubation period** in the wild (10 clutches) 32–34 days, from laying of last egg to date when all hatched. J. C. Phillips (1925) gave the period as 31 days for eggs from Iceland hatched under a hen in England. When nesting in captivity, 30 days (Wormald 1939). Early reports of 21 days are erroneous.

418

**Hatching**  All young hatch within a few hrs. and remain in the nest an additional 24–36 hrs. During this period, and at intervals for several days before hatching, the duck frequently visits the part of the lake to which the brood is led and where they will remain for some weeks—**brood territory.** After the duck has surveyed the route, she returns to the nest for a short period, then flies to ground or water below the nest and repeatedly utters a series of *cuc* (MTM) or *kra* (Millais 1913a) notes, similar to those heard from "prospecting" ♀ ♀ and also to the alarm call of the ♀ when with very small young. The latter climb the inner nest wall, tumble out, and flutter to the ground or water below. (Presumably it is not necessary for the ♀ to "call" them; compare with Common Goldeneye.) They "literally pour out" (Millais) and the duck leads them off, walking overland or swimming to the brood territory. If the nest is close to shoreline, the ♀ may fly back and forth between it and the water as the young leave the nest and walk to the lake. Such behavior may have given rise to reports of goldeneyes carrying their young to water (J. Munro 1945). Most broods leave the nest during daylight; in one instance they were led off during darkness or early dawn, over an hr. before sunrise.

**Hatching success**  217 (91%) of 240 eggs in 39 nests hatched. Unhatched eggs resulted from infertility (9 eggs), death of embryo (8), breakage (1), and unknown causes (5). Clutch size in 27 nests in which all eggs hatched av. 8.1 eggs. In 12 nests in which one or more eggs failed to hatch, av. initial clutch size was 9.9; av. number of eggs hatching per nest was 8. Thus hatching success in larger clutches was generally lower than in smaller ones. A. Brooks (1903), however, saw 14 ducklings emerge from a nest.

Of 217 hatching in 39 nests, only 4 failed to leave the nest. Two of these died before the remainder of the brood had departed; the other 2 were left alive in the nest, probably because the remainder left early due to the observer's interference.

At Mývatn, Iceland, at high territorial density, 40% of clutches failed to hatch, chiefly from desertion, compared with 20% at lower densities; details in Bengtson (1972a, 1972c).

The **ducklings** develop extremely rapidly. They weigh 40–45 gm. at hatching and increase to about 200 gm. at about 3 weeks, when the first feathers appear in the scapular area. At 6 weeks ♂ ♂ weigh 750 gm., ♀ ♀ 550, or about ¾ adult wt. At about 8 weeks, ♂ ♂ 800–900 and ♀ ♀ 600–700 gm.

Captive young **drank** but did not feed during the first 24 hrs. after hatching. On the 2nd day they fed by skimming just below the surface of the water with their bills; a day or 2 later they began to up-end like Anatini when feeding, then to make short dives of 3–4 sec. duration. M. T. Myres observed young diving 1–5 sec. on first day after hatching. Feeding by skimming or up-ending rarely is seen after the young are 3 weeks old. Initial **preening** movements, seen in the nest before the ducklings are dry, are then uncoordinated; coordination develops in 48 hrs., but the oil gland probably is not functional until some time later. Upward-stretch with Wing-flap followed by tail wagging is seen in downies only a day or 2 old. Downies swim strongly from the first day; when alarmed they skitter over the surface of the water with head upstretched and wings extended. As noted earlier, "greeting" movements are performed by both the ♀ and her downies when individuals are reunited after being separated. Females do Rotary pumping, occasionally Jiving. In very young downies the "greeting" display is an up-and-down bobbing of the head; this is replaced by typical Rotary pumping by 3 weeks of age (Myres).

**Voice**    Downies have 2 distinct notes from day of hatching: 1 distress call—rather loud, rapidly repeated, disyllabic *pee-ap pee-ap pee-ap* (indefinite series) uttered when cold, hungry, or alarmed, and 2 social call—much quieter, more rapid, monosyllabic *pup-pup-pup-pup* (indefinite length). Both are most frequent in very young downies and are rarely heard after they are 3 weeks old.

**Brood territory**    Preferred locations are along shorelines where there is shallow water, 3—4 ft. deep, food is plentiful, there is ready access to deeper open water (for escape), and usually an exposed rock or log where the ♀ can brood the young when they are very small. This territory may be some distance from the nest tree and usually does not coincide with the mated-pair territory used earlier. Boundaries, and therefore size, are not rigidly defined. Females on brood territory threaten, attack, and drive off other ♀ ♀ with their broods; the invading ♀ is attacked first, then her young. Pre-breeders, nonbreeding, and probably failed-breeding adult ♀ ♀ may be tolerated; unattended young often are accepted into the brood, especially during the first 2 weeks after they hatch. The young rapidly learn the location of their own territory and will return to it independently if driven off and separated from the duck. Brood territory is occupied a variable length of time (see below); it may be abandoned and a new one established if the brood is severely disturbed.

In Iceland, Bengtson (1972c) "many times observed Barrow's Goldeneye females drown strange young or beat them badly." This reduced brood size of half-grown to large Barrow's to 3.0 when nesting density was high. As a result of aggressive behavior of ♀ ♀, the survival of ducklings of all species decreased with increasing goldeneye density (Bengtson 1972a).

In B.C., individual ♀ ♀ vary in **care of young**; some desert their broods within a day or 2 after hatching, but others are extremely attentive. Young in deserted broods frequently join other broods and are accepted by the ♀; composite broods of up to 25 young of varying ages led by one ♀ are not uncommon. Sometimes yearling ♀ ♀ attach themselves to ♀ ♀ with broods and possibly take over leadership of deserted young.

In Wyo., 2 downies not over a week old were captured from a brood of 10 and held over night; they were rejected by the ♀ when released, yet appeared to be doing satisfactorily on their own during the ensuing 10 days (Nickell 1966).

J. Munro (1958) reported ♀ ♀ (age-class?) attempting by force to acquire the broods of other ♀ ♀. He noted that such attempts often are successful, as indicated by ♀ ♀ escorting composite broods of up to 36 ducklings. In one instance a ♀ Mallard with 15 young was accompanied by a ♀ Barrow's. Even yearling ♀ Barrow's (prebreeders) are strongly influenced by presence of ducklings; he saw one "companioning" a successful breeder and her brood.

**Movements** of ♀ ♀ with young are infrequent except immediately after hatching, or when disturbed and driven off brood territory. In instances of the latter, movements of up to 3 mi. overland from one lake to another have been noted.

In cases where the **parental bond** is long maintained, it wanes gradually beginning about the 6th week, concurrent with waning of territorial behavior. Females with

420

broods on ponds and small lakes frequently leave their young to fly to larger lakes prior to wing molt about the beginning of Aug. Young from all broods on a lake frequently unite to form a loose-knit flock one or two weeks before they attain flight; either they keep to themselves or join with yearling and adult ♀ ♀. When alarmed, young not quite able to fly flap violently over the water surface, attempting to take wing. **Flight is attained** at about 8 weeks of age, by ♀ ♀ some earlier than ♂ ♂. MFJ MTM

SURVIVAL  Using the composite life table method of Hickey (1952), analysis of 277 recoveries from 1,996 "adult" ♀ ♀ banded by the B.C. Game Dept. in Cariboo and Kamloops Districts of B.C. from 1948 to 1952 indicated an av. annual mortality rate of 50%. Similar analysis of 400 recoveries from 2,799 first-fall birds of both sexes banded at same time and place gave a mortality rate of 78% for birds in their first calendar year. These calculated rates are too high to maintain the steady population level observed throughout the period (there was an annual productivity of 5.6 young/breeding pair surviving to Sept. 1). It is believed that mortality rates of 40%/year for "adults" and 60% for those in their first calendar year are more nearly representative of the true situation. Possibly there was high mortality at lakes accessible by road to both hunters and banding crews, which may be compensated for by an influx from inaccessible lakes.

In B.C., a ♀ banded as "adult" in 1950, was retrapped on her nest in 1952, 1953, 1954, and 1955, and shot in fall of 1955 at a minimum age of 7 years. Another, banded as a downy in 1948, was trapped on a nest in 1956, at 8 years of age. A third, banded as "adult" in Aug., 1949, was shot in Sept., 1957, at a minimum age of 10 years. There are no comparable data for drakes. MFJ

HABITS  Most of this section is based on fairly recent work in B.C., with occasional mention of the species as studied elsewhere.

**Prebreeders**  In B.C., yearlings of both sexes migrate later in spring than adults and do not appear in numbers at breeding lakes until the middle of May. Many yearling drakes do not reach the breeding grounds; most of those that do disappear with the postbreeding drakes in early June. Yearling ♀ ♀ form loose flocks on breeding grounds, or individuals associate rather closely with mated pairs or ♀ ♀ with broods. Some display is evident in yearlings of both sexes in May and June. Yearling ♀ ♀ show a marked tendency to return to natal lakes; of 75 ♀ ♀ banded as preflight young and recovered as molting yearlings, 80% were on natal lakes and 13% moved only from small sloughs to nearby larger lakes. Yearling ♀ ♀ molt on larger water bodies, in loose flocks with postbreeding ♀ ♀. The flightless period of yearlings commences before that of adults, in late July or early Aug. The limited evidence for yearling ♀ ♀ suggests that they do little wandering prior to migrating in late Oct. or early Nov.

**Postbreeding drakes** leave their mates early in the incubation period, gather in small flocks of 2–15 in late May or early June and, in B.C., soon disappear from breeding areas; only 5% of the mature drakes remain to molt on breeding grounds as scattered individuals with flocks of yearling ♀ ♀ and, later, with postbreeding ♀ ♀ and young of the year. The whereabouts of the greater part of the adult and yearling drake population is unknown from early June to late Oct.; then they appear on coastal wintering areas. J. Munro (1939) presumed that they went to salt water to molt, but no con-

421

centrations have been found there in molting season and no coastal band returns are reported before late Oct. Possibly they concentrate on a few molting lakes (as yet undiscovered) w. of main nesting areas but e. of the Cascades in B.C. Swarth (1926) observed flocks of drakes in June flying southward near Atlin L. in nw. B.C. In Yellowstone Nat. Park, drakes form part of the population present in summer (Skinner 1937). For some Alaskan data, see "Migration." In Iceland, postbreeding ♂ ♂ are segregated from ♀ ♀ ; they gather in flocks on Mývatn, not far from the bays and rivers where the ♀ ♀ raise broods (Millais 1913a). Data on wing molt of drakes in B.C. are meager, but flightless individuals in full or part of Basic head–body feathering have been trapped in interior B.C. between Aug. 7 and Sept. 3. Drakes apparently do not return to breeding localities after regaining flight, but presumably stay at molting lakes or elsewhere until late Oct. or early Nov., then migrate to coastal waters. Drakes that become flightless on breeding lakes remain there until they migrate to the coast with ♀ ♀ and young of the year.

**Postbreeding females**  In B.C., successful ♀ ♀ desert their broods prior to beginning the flightless stage of molting and congregate in loose flocks on lakes and larger sloughs within the breeding area. Many are flightless on breeding lakes, but those that nest near small sloughs move to larger water areas, usually within 5–10 mi. The longest recorded molt migration of a banded ♀ (Kamloops Dist. of B.C.) was 25 mi. The flightless period in B.C. commences Aug. 7 to 14 and terminates early in Sept. It may be delayed in a late nesting season. During molt the birds associate in loose flocks with young of the year, yearling ♀ ♀ , and a few yearling and adult drakes. Bonds between parent and offspring no longer are evident. Adult ♀ ♀ remain on molting lakes throughout Sept. and Oct., unless forced off by formation of ice or disturbance by hunters; they show no tendency to wander in fall as do young of the year.

**Young of the year** attain flight Aug. 14 to 31 in the Cariboo Dist. of B.C., occasionally earlier. At this time they associate in loose flocks with adult and yearling ♀ ♀ ; brood and parental ties are weak or absent. After sustained flight is achieved, they show a marked tendency to wander away from natal lakes in Sept. and Oct. The direction of this movement is governed by the location of suitable lakes and possibly by social bonds to other members of the species, but not by direction of migration undertaken later. They move in small flocks of 2–10 birds, chiefly during daylight. Some wander even as far as several hundred mi., well away from the center of breeding distribution; young banded near Williams L. in B.C. were recovered n. to Vanderhoof and Ft. Nelson, B.C., e. nearly to Edmonton, Atla., and s. to Flathead L., Mont. However, most remain within the chief breeding range in interior B.C. They usually associate with adult and yearling ♀ ♀ of their own species and migrate coastward with them in late Oct. or early Nov. Wandering probably is associated with learning recognition of visual landmarks within the general breeding area (Hochbaum 1955).

**Winter**  In coastal regions of B.C., Wash., and Ore., drakes arrive first, in large flocks of up to several hundred birds, then ♀ ♀ and young of the year together, several days later, in smaller flocks (3–20 birds). By mid-Nov. these units break up and isolated pairs or small flocks of mixed age and sex are encountered. In the Vancouver region, there are more ♂ ♂ than ♀ ♀ , and yearlings of either sexes are uncommon, but at Henderson L. on Vancouver I., in Nov. and Dec., J. Munro (1923b) found flocks of

5–50 birds, 90% young of the year, 8% adult ♀ ♀ , and 2% adult ♂ ♂ . Larger concentrations occur in favored feeding or resting areas, frequently in association with the Common Goldeneye, less often with scoters and Greater Scaup. Pairs and small flocks usually retain their identity within larger concentrations. Yearlings of both sexes become more abundant in the Vancouver region in late Feb. and March, associating with displaying parties of adults. As the adults move out toward the breeding grounds in March and April, small flocks of yearlings of both sexes are left on coastal wintering areas.

**Winter territorialism?**    Although pairs may occupy a specific area for short periods of time, there apparently is no establishment or defense of boundaries such as occurs on breeding territories. Band recoveries show that ♀ ♀ from local areas of breeding range are not isolated on local areas of winter range. Individuals from any one breeding area are scattered along the coasts of Ore., Wash., and B.C. This does not imply absence of tradition of homing to specific wintering areas, but merely that such tradition, if it exists, is a function of the individual.

**Daily routine**    On the s. B.C. coast the birds rest during the night on freshwater lakes and sheltered marine bays and coves, frequently in larger concentrations than are found during daylight. At daybreak they scatter to feeding grounds in pairs and small flocks, where they feed, display, and loaf alternately throughout the day. While activities in any one group are more or less synchronized, there is no regularly established rhythm. They return to sheltered areas before nightfall. Strong winds force flocks to seek sheltered resting areas (where food often is absent) during the day. Display is intensified in warm, sunny weather, even in Nov. and Dec.

**Flight** is similar to that of the Common Goldeneye. Barrow's rises laboriously from the water, in absence of wind, often "running" over the surface for some distance before becoming airborne. Once aloft, it is a strong flier; the wings produce a distinct whistling sound similar to that of the Common Goldeneye. On short flights the birds fly near the surface, often within 3–4 ft. of it, but on longer flights and over land they travel at greater heights. There is no information on flight speeds or wingbeats/sec. Barrow's **swims** readily in rapid streams and on quieter waters of lakes in Iceland (Millais 1913a), but not in turbulent sections that are the domain of the Harlequin. Skinner (1937) observed Barrow's coasting down swift rivers and over falls 3 ft. high in Yellowstone Nat. Park. The same may be seen in Iceland (R. S. Palmer). In **diving** the wings are not used under water, but are held tightly against the sides, and the tail is spread to the fullest extent, as in the Common Goldeneye (A. Brooks 1945). Duration of submergence varies with depth of water, usually being less than 1 min.

In w. N. Am., only minor **fluctuations in numbers** have been recorded in recent years. Barrow's was less seriously affected by loss of breeding habitat and overshooting in the 1930s than those species whose breeding range extends to the prairies. Although drought conditions at that time eliminated as breeding areas most sloughs and small lakes in cent. B.C. (T. Sorensen), larger or deeper lakes provided suitable breeding habitat for many birds. Recently, minor fluctuations in breeding density have been observed. In 1954 and 1955 in Cariboo Dist. of B.C., cold, wet weather delayed the breeding season 2 to 3 weeks and persisted throughout it, resulting in lowered survival of young birds. This was reflected in a decrease of about 40% in numbers of breeders in

1956 and 1957. Along the Atlantic coast, Griscom (1945) noted evidence of changes in small wintering assemblies: numbers reached a peak in the winter of 1935–36, then declined thereafter to 1941 and subsequently remained at a low level. (Loss of a local breeding unit in Colo. was mentioned earlier under "Distribution.")

**Factors affecting numbers** are varied. Females and young of the year are abundant in hunters' bags in interior B.C., but Barrow's rarely is taken on coastal waters. Adult drakes thus are subjected to very low hunting pressure, ♀ ♀ and young to considerably more. This may account, at least in part, for observed preponderance of drakes over ducks. Predation is not a major factor in controlling numbers. The main predator on breeding grounds is the Great Horned Owl and on wintering areas in coastal B.C. is the Bald Eagle (A. Brooks 1922); in Yellowstone Park, the Golden Eagle (W. M. Sharp 1951); in Iceland, the jaegers and Gyrfalcon to a slight extent. Many winter losses probably are of individuals first weakened by internal parasites or disease, then subjected to periods of cold, stormy weather that render feeding difficult. It is current logging practice in interior B.C. to remove many large Douglas firs, which provide nesting sites, but the effect of this on goldeneye numbers and local centers of abundance is not yet evident. Where adequate food supply and nesting sites are available, productivity of young is dependent chiefly on weather. They are very sensitive to cold wet weather immediately after hatching. In backward summers, both av. brood size and number of broods observed declines.

Barrow's is **less wary** of humans on interior B.C. breeding areas, even during the hunting season, than it is on coastal waters. In Iceland it is relatively tame during the breeding season, but shy in winter (Millais 1913a).

**Sex ratio** A few counts of mature birds in spring in B.C. show a preponderance of drakes; the samples, however, are too small to express a meaningful ratio.

**Feeding activities in winter** The birds concentrate in shallow water over rocky shelves and ridges, in contrast to Common Goldeneyes which frequently feed in somewhat deeper water. Favored localities vary with wind and tide. The birds feed by diving to bottom in 3–10 ft. of water. Larger items, such as mussels, are brought to the surface before being swallowed whole; smaller items are swallowed beneath the surface. At low tide, the birds sometimes feed in 3–6 in. of water, merely immersing their heads to reach toward bottom; they do not up-end as do surface-feeding ducks. There is no pronounced diurnal rhythm; feeding activities alternate frequently with displaying and loafing throughout the day. Marked local concentrations appear on freshwater lakes and streams where salmon spawn in fall and on herring grounds in spring. J. Munro (1923b) found Barrow's to be the commonest duck species feeding on salmon spawn at Henderson L. on Vancouver I. in Nov. and Dec. The birds went to salt water for the night and arrived at the lake 9 to 11 A.M.; there they fed by diving with 50–70 sec. submersion.

In **summer** breeding lakes abound with insect larvae and/or crustaceans, as well as pondweeds and other plant foods. J. Munro (1939) believed that adequate food supply is of greater importance than availability of nest sites in determining favored breeding lakes. The birds feed at any time of day, also on bright moonlit nights, but in incubating ♀ ♀, especially, feeding is intensified in midmorning and particularly just before sunset, except when the weather is stormy. Mated pairs frequently feed on territory, but

424

may fly to undefended areas also. Adults usually feed by diving to depths of 3–10 ft., rarely deeper. As in winter, small items are swallowed under the surface, but larger ones (as crayfish) are first brought to the surface. Duration of dive varies from 15–20 sec. in shallow water to 50–55 where it is deeper (J. Munro 1939). MFJ

FOOD   In general, diet is quite like that of the Common Goldeneye, but evidently more insects are consumed. Stomachs of 71 "adults" contained 78% animal matter, insects bulking larger than mollusks and crustaceans. Pondweeds and wild celery were of most importance in the 22% of vegetable matter. Five "juveniles" from B.C. had fed largely on insects, the total animal matter being 98.4% (Cottam 1939).

**Animal**   Insects: nymphs of damselflies and dragonflies (Odonata), larvae and cases of caddis flies (Trichoptera), water boatmen (Corixidae), back swimmers (*Notonecta*), larvae of midges (*Chironomus*), aquatic beetles and larvae (Dytiscidae), and miscellaneous totaled 30.4%; mollusks (*Mytilus edulis* mainly, *Littorina*, *Lacuna*) 19.2%; crustaceans: amphipods mainly, isopods, and crayfishes (*Astacus*) 17.7%; fishes, sculpins (Cottidae) mainly 1.1%; miscellaneous, water mites (Hydracarina), sea urchins, starfishes, earthworms, marine worms, hydroids, and freshwater sponges 3.3%.

**Vegetable**   Seeds of pondweeds (*Potamogeton, Ruppia, Zannichellia*) 8.2%; wild celery (*Vallisneria*) 1.6%, miscellaneous 12.6%.

**Some data by locality**   In B.C., crayfish, eggs and occasionally fry of sockeye salmon (J. Munro 1918, 1923b); in N.S., mollusks (*Littorina, Lacuna, Purpura*) (Gilpin 1878b); in ne. Labrador, mussels and snails (Hantzsch 1908); in Greenland, mollusks (*Margarita helicina, Modiolaria faba*) and small crustaceans (Salomonsen 1950). At Mývatn in ne. Iceland, Barrow's prefers to feed in the fast-flowing River Laxá; the adults eat chironomid larvae and *Lymnea*, also fish eggs in June–July; small ducklings feed chiefly on *Lymnea* and some larval and adult chironomids and, when full-grown, almost their entire diet is chironomids (Bengtson 1971b). At times, the chironomid larvae are so abundant in the river that adult Barrow's feed by scooping them up—a modified dabbling (R. S. Palmer). AWS

[As with the Common Goldeneye, the data on food of Barrow's are published about as submitted. A breakdown into fresh- and saltwater foods would be more meaningful, also data by season. It is apparent, however, that insects and their larvae are important on fresh water, and mollusks, crayfishes, etc., on salt water. RSP]

425

**Bufflehead**

*Bucephala albeola* (Linnaeus)

Very small duck; feathers on top and rear of head elongated (head has enlarged, rounded appearance); nostril about midway in bill (not nearer tip than base); iris dark in both sexes and all ages; feathering has essentially bicolored pattern—very dark plus very light or white (latter includes most or all of venter); sizable white patch extends back from behind eye, in ♂ Def. Alt. Plumage being continuous from side to side across rear of head. The drake's trachea is somewhat flattened, the bulla at inner end rather simple in form, flattened, and not markedly asymmetrical; for further details see J. C. Phillips (1925); no published illus. yet exists.

The sexes differ markedly in Alt. Plumage, but are much more alike (the darks not as dark and there is less white) in Juv. and Basic; all ♀ Plumages are fairly similar. Length ♂ to 15½ in., ♀ to 14½; wingspread ♂ to 24, ♀ to 23; usual wt. of ♂ about 1 lb., ♀ 12 oz. No subspecies.

DESCRIPTION Two Plumages/cycle in both sexes, with Basic II the earliest definitive Plumage; extent of feathering acquired in some predefinitive Plumages varies with individual; some individual variation in amount of white in wing in both sexes; total feathering often shows much fading. There is a summary of molting in Erskine (1972a).

▶ ♂ Def. Alt. Plumage (all of head–body), usually acquired mostly in SEPT., then retained through winter, and lost beginning in MAY and ending about MID-JULY. **Bill** medium bluish gray, **iris** dark brownish. **Head** and upper neck black with bluish, greenish, and violet iridescence; broad white area from behind eye to back of head (continuous there from side to side); lower neck white; **upperparts** back and rump black with some sheen; scapulars long, the middle ones black, others white with narrow black margins; upper tail coverts light gray. **Underparts** breast white, sides and flanks white with narrow black margins on dorsal webs of upper row of feathers; abdomen off-white, darkening somewhat posteriorly. Legs and **feet** pinkish. **Tail** and **wing** are retained Basic feathering, described below.

▶ ♂ Def. Basic Plumage (entire feathering); the head–body begin molting into Basic in EARLY MAY and have acquired it fully by about MID-JULY; then the tail and wing are molted (flightless period believed to be slightly longer than 3 weeks) and the head–body molt back into Alt., this completed usually in LATE SEPT. The Basic perhaps is best compared with ♀ Def. Alt., from which it differs as follows: **Head** darker, some feathers occasionally with some sheen; white patch on side of head larger; lower neck pale gray; **back** brownish gray; rump medium gray. **Underparts** upper breast, sides and flanks palish gray, remainder white or nearly white. **Tail** medium brownish gray and fades toward brownish, even yellowish. **Wing** flight feathers black, except 5–6 middle secondaries almost entirely white and some adjoining ones have white markings; coverts have rounded ends and are dusky to black, except wide white area that extends from white secondaries to leading edge of wing, also some inner lesser coverts have white edges; underwing mostly medium gray, but some white in smaller coverts; some axillars white, others all or predominantly medium gray.

426

BUFFLEHEAD

▶ ♀ Def. Alt. Plumage (head–body), acquired beginning in LATE AUG. or in SEPT., usually completed by OCT., and retained through winter, spring, and then succeeded by Basic in JULY–EARLY AUG. **Bill** blackish, **iris** dark brownish. **Head** and neck blackish brown, paling posteriorly and also on chin and ventral part of neck; broad white patch on side of head from below eye through auricular region. **Upperparts** upper back, mantle, and inner scapulars blackish brown, many feathers with indistinct grayish tips; lateral scapulars medium gray; rump black; upper tail coverts as rump. **Underparts** upper breast some variant of pale grayish, sides and flanks toward dusky, lower breast and belly white grading to dusky from vent to tail. Legs and **feet** brownish pink. **Tail** and **wing** are retained Basic, described below.

▶ ♀ Def. Basic Plumage (entire feathering), the head–body acquired beginning in JULY or AUG. (often before the duck leaves her brood) and ending usually about MID-AUG.; then the tail and wing are molted (av. flightless period about 3 weeks) and, as the new Basic ones grow, the head–body begin molting back into Alt. in LATE AUG.–SEPT. The molting into Basic is late in some ♀♀, perhaps being postponed if their nesting is late. The Basic tail and wing are retained nearly a year. No individuals in full Basic have been examined, but fall birds show 2 generations of feathers (during head–body molting from Basic to Alt.). Allowing for differential in fading, both generations apparently are much alike when new. **Tail** brownish gray (fades to washed-out brownish). **Wing** much as ♂ but browner, the white area usually limited to 4–5 secondaries (vs. 5–6 in the ♂) or also may include all or part of exposed area of several adjoining greater coverts; elongated innermost secondaries are slightly curved and have rounded ends; underwing as ♂.

AT HATCHING   See vol. 2, col. pl. facing p. 466. Distinguishable with certainty from downy young of the 2 goldeneyes, the bill and especially the feet being smaller in the Bufflehead. The legs and feet are neutral colored, while in both goldeneyes they show at least a hint of yellowish. Compared with downies of both goldeneye species, the nail on the bill of the Bufflehead is relatively, as well as actually, much smaller; further details in Linsdale (1933). Young Buffleheads become progressively more brownish and paler throughout the downy stage.

▶ ♂ Juv. Plumage (entire feathering), perfected approximately when flight is attained, at age about 50–55 days (LATE JULY to very EARLY SEPT.); then head—body and soon the tail molt into Basic I, commonly in SEPT.; the wing is long retained. **Bill** medium gray. **Head** and **upperparts** grayed brownish with indistinct white or whitish auricular area, whitish chin and throat; **underparts** lower breast and most of belly white or nearly white; legs and **feet** lead colored; **tail** fuscous, fading to pale brownish, the feathers with notched tips. **Wing** mostly very dark; about 5 middle secondaries largely white and some individuals have a white spot on 1 or more of the adjoining greater coverts (all of which are narrow). There is some geographical variation in color of the Juv. Plumage (see below).

▶ ♀ Juv. Plumage (entire feathering), timing apparently as ♂. General appearance as ♀, but perhaps usually identifiable in hand as ♂ by smaller size, including shorter wing. Browner overall than later ♀ Plumages (J. Munro 1942). As in the ♂, innermost secondaries short, straight, pointed, and soon become frayed. Also, as in the ♂, there is geographical variation in the Juv. Plumage.

NOTE   For a detailed description of growth and development of Buffleheads up to

427

flying age and an especially good photo of one in Juv. Plumage, see Erskine (1972a).

▶ ♂ Basic I Plumage (head–body plus tail), succeeds the corresponding parts of Juv. usually during SEPT. and, in turn, part of it may be succeeded by Alt. I in LATE OCT., but often much Basic I is retained until MARCH or even later. Thus Basic I is a "first winter" Plumage of many individuals. The pattern is clear-cut and contrasty and the sexes differ. **Head** blackish brown, the white area larger than in Juv.; **upperparts** back uniformly black or dark gray, some feathers tipped lighter; scapulars variable—in some, very dark, in others a frosted appearance; rump medium gray, contrasting with darker back and tail; **underparts** upper breast lighter (a pale gray) than in Juv., the feathers with white edging that wears off; flanks brownish gray; **tail** blackish brown, much darker than in succeeding Basics and shorter, the feathers with rounded ends. The **wing** is retained Juv. feathering. There probably is some geographical variation in coloring of Basic I in both sexes (Erskine 1972a).

▶ ♂ Alt. I Plumage (head–body); some drakes show some scattered incoming Alt. I feathers by LATE OCT., others not until the following SPRING, and some evidently acquire very little Alt. I, i.e., continue to retain variable amounts of Basic I head–body (plus Basic I tail and Juv. wing). Any Alt. I is retained until LATE JUNE–JULY. Feathering essentially as in later Alts. J. Munro (1942) stated that the long-retained Juv. flight feathers of the wing fade to drab and become so frayed as sometimes to hinder or even prevent flight. This does occur, in both sexes, also later with the Basic wing, and also in some other waterfowl. The molting out of Alt. I is earlier than the corresponding molting in succeeding cycles. However, some Juv. wing coverts often are retained into Aug.; as long as they are present they serve to identify yearlings from older drakes.

▶ ♀ Basic I Plumage—inclusive feathering and timing (acquired usually in SEPT.) as in ♂ Basic I, with individual variation in both factors. Differs thus from ♀ Def. Alt.: **head** and neck browner, many feathers of **upperparts** tipped fawn and gray, chest band more fawn than gray. As with the drake, the new **tail** (feathers have rounded ends) comes in early, usually by OCT. See comment on geographical variation under ♂ Basic I. Various Juv. feathers (always including the wing) are retained.

▶ ♀ Alt. I Plumage (head–body, but sometimes less feathering acquired); usually appears beginning in APRIL (before age 1 year) and retained into JULY. At least many ♀ ♀ in their first spring have mixed new (Alt. I) and old (Basic I) feathers, especially obvious on sides and flanks, both generations gray, the older feathers faded. Because of similarity of Plumages, rapid fading, and dearth of known-age specimens, not much is known about Alt. I. The Juv. wing and Basic I tail are retained.

▶ ♂ Basic II Plumage (entire feathering), the head–body acquired earlier than later Basics; while it is worn, the drake molts from Basic I tail and Juv. wing to Basic II tail and wing.

▶ ♂ Alt. II Plumage—definitive.

▶ ♀ Basic II Plumage (entire feathering), the head–body acquired beginning in summer (before age 1 year); the Basic I tail and Juv. wing are succeeded by Basic II later, apparently in late summer, then soon the head–body molt into Alt.

▶ ♀ Alt. II Plumage—definitive.

**Measurements** of birds from Alaska, Canada, and conterminous U.S.; 12 ♂: BILL 27–30 mm., av. 28.7; WING 169–175, av. 172.5; TAIL 70–78, av. 74.7; TARSUS 32–35, av. 33.7; 12 ♀: BILL 25–27 mm., av. 26; WING 152–161, av. 156; TAIL 59–70, av. 65.7; TARSUS 30–31, av. 30+ (ETS). For other series, WING meas. across chord, see J. C. Phillips (1925), and for WING meas. over the curve, Witherby (1939).

The Basic WING of drakes (chord, rather than flattened) av. about 2 mm. longer than the Juv. wing; the Basic I TAIL of drakes is about 8 mm. shorter than the Def. Basic tail (Erskine 1972a). There are no comparable data on ♀ ♀.

**Weight** averaged for the year: ♂ about 450 gm. (16 oz.) and ♀ 330 gm. (12 oz.). Both sexes are heaviest in autumn and lightest in winter; the ♀ ♀ are heavy when laying and very light during incubation. Some data, by month, for "fully grown" Buffleheads, were graphed for each sex by Erskine (1972a).

"Adults" in winter at Seneca L. in N.Y.: 21 ♂ (Jan. 8–April 16) 400–550 gm. (468 ± 11 gm.) and 20 ♀ (Jan. 6–March 26) 310–570 gm. (397 ± 19 gm.) (Ryan 1972). (The maxima for ♀ ♀ seem too high; possibly 1st-winter ♂ ♂ were included.)

Birds flightless during molting at Ohtig L. (40 mi. e. of Ft. Yukon), Alaska, in Aug.: 62 ♂ mean wt. 14.34 oz. (407 gm.), max. 22 oz. (624 gm.), min. 10 oz. (284 gm.), 10 ♀ mean 10.4 oz. (295 gm.), max. 12 oz. (340 gm.), min. 8 oz. (227 gm.) (Yocom 1970a). (These wts. are not representative of natural conditions, since the birds were confined and may not have fed for up to 5 days after capture before they were weighed.)

A newly hatched Bufflehead weighs 22–23 gm. (Erskine 1972a).

**Hybrids** are not known with absolute certainty in the wild. A wing, from near Thunder Bay, Ont., obtained in 1969 from a hunter, was too small for either species of goldeneye and too large for a Bufflehead; its upper surface was as in the Bufflehead, lower as in goldeneyes (A. J. Erskine). A drake Bufflehead that strayed to Japan formed a pair bond with a ♀ Common Goldeneye (Yamamoto 1963). In captivity, the Bufflehead reportedly has crossed with the Tufted Duck (*Aythya fuligula*).

**Geographical variation** In the Juv. Plumage the dorsum of birds from breeding areas in s. B.C. and n. Cal. is largely brownish, whereas in Alta., Yukon Terr., and probably Alaska, it is largely blackish gray. There are no useful data for areas e. of Alta. The same distinction "probably holds" for Basic I—most of the westerly ♀ ♀ and subadult ♂ ♂ are brownish, most of the easterly ones blackish—but this segregation is partly obscured by mixing of the birds during migration. Pale gray on scapulars seems to be restricted to the black drakes in Basic I. No geographical variation has been detected in drakes in definitive feathering.

There is some geographical variation in time of molting.

There is geographical variation in bleaching and fading; it is more pronounced in the arid sw. U.S. and in Mexico. (These data on variation are from Erskine 1972a.) RSP

FIELD IDENTIFICATION Buffleheads might be described as very active teal-sized goldeneyes. The white in the head (when visible) is behind the eye in the drake (extends to rear margin of head), but in the duck it appears as though under the eye (does not extend to rear of head). Compact body, puffy head, small stubby bill, and very short neck give a blocky appearance. Alt.-Plumaged drake on water appears to be mostly white (except head) and, in flight, shows broad white area completely crossing wing. Young drakes, also ♀ ♀ of any age, have more darkish and also have reduced white area behind eye (quite often not visible), but show white across wing in flight. A

♀ with young on water might be mistaken for goldeneyes, but the Bufflehead's small-ness, shape, and head pattern indicate its identity. Hardly to be confused with the long-crested and trim-bodied Hooded Merganser. Compare with the Smew, which is of about the same size but different in pattern. Buffleheads are lively and restless; they rise from the water with ease, unlike various bay ducks. Groups and singles often fly low, rapidly, with whirring wings. Usually singles, pairs, and small flocks, but also in assemblies in some localities and seasons. Usually by themselves. RSP

VOICE    Generally silent. Such sounds as are known seem like feeble imitations of goldeneyes. The drake has a somewhat squealing or growling call heard in late winter–spring; in April a paired drake growled, whereupon the ♀ flew to join him. In displays, when the duck is Following a drake, she has a sort of growl *grrrk* or *ik-ik-ik-ik* (in-definite series) call. She calls her brood with a low, somewhat buzzy *cuc-cuc-cuc-cuc* and sometimes gives a similar call when separated from them. (Based on Erskine 1972a.) RSP

HABITAT    As a breeder, the Bufflehead is a freshwater bird and a cavity nester. Nests primarily in mixed coniferous–deciduous woodland n. and w. of the Great Plains. Known areas of particular abundance are the Cariboo Parklands of B.C. and the Peace–Athabaska delta region in ne. Alta.

**Nesting** lakes and ponds typically are small, the water fresh or slightly alkaline, the margins shallow, bordered with semiopen stands of trees and standing dead trees in or near water. Larger lakes and ponds, especially at higher elevations, are not favored, nor are waters broadly margined with emergent or floating aquatic vegetation. Soper (1951) pointed out that, w. of L. Athabaska, the Bufflehead occurs in summer less in the delta itself than on more upland rivers and lakes. In n. B.C., lakes bordered with conifers (spruce, lodgepole pine, others) support a thin population, possibly an overflow from better habitat.

Nesting density probably is controlled locally by size and shape of ponds, nature of shorelines, availability of nest holes, and amount and nature of food present. Loafing sites—rocks, stranded logs, stumps, open shore—are used in breeding season more by ♀ ♀ than by ♂ ♂, but not much by either sex. All *Bucephala* species, in fact, spend much less time on solid ground than do dabbling ducks. Nesting density shows high correlation with presence of deciduous trees containing Flicker (*Colaptes*) holes, espe-cially aspen. The breeding range of the Bufflehead is within the combined ranges of several N. Am. forms of Flicker. Burned areas and parklike groves of aspen are espe-cially suitable for woodpeckers, hence also for Buffleheads. They seldom nest any great distance from water or in dense forest.

Breeding areas are shared mainly with scaups and /or goldeneyes. No conflicts with scaups are reported. Both goldeneye species attack Buffleheads and this is not re-stricted to territorial conflict between drakes. The ♀ Barrow's Goldeneye has been seen to attack the ♀ Bufflehead; the ♂ Bufflehead has attacked the ♀ Barrow's. (From Erskine 1972.)

In **migrations** occurs on shallow salt, brackish, and fresh water.

In **winter** Buffleheads occur on sheltered salt water, somewhat brackish water, and

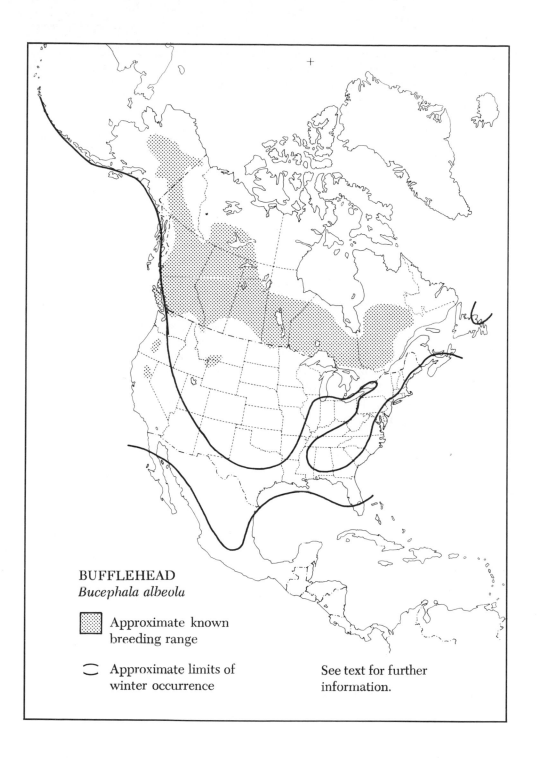

**BUFFLEHEAD**
*Bucephala albeola*

Approximate known
breeding range

Approximate limits of
winter occurrence

See text for further
information.

fresh water—the nonsaltwater winterers being concentrated on reservoirs and similar places in w. N. Am. just s. of the zone of general freezing of inland waters. They frequent small waters as well as large, even drainage ditches in s. B.C., which are shunned by Barrow's Goldeneye. Along both coasts they seem to prefer quite sheltered (though not necessarily small) harbors and bays, regularly spending much time quite distant from shore.

For much additional information, see various sections in Erskine (1972a). MTM

DISTRIBUTION    (See map.)    The reader also is referred to the several maps, which include some data on relative nesting density, and to the text in Erskine (1972a); the following is condensed from his text, with some additions. He devoted a chapter to the probable factors limiting distribution of this species.

**Breeding range** coincides quite closely with the combined continental breeding ranges of the 2 goldeneyes, while the Hooded Merganser is more southerly. Outside the principal area shown on the map, peripheral records, beginning with Mont. and going clockwise, are: nests in an area where the boundaries of Idaho, Mont., and Wyo. meet, and a questionable record for n.-cent. Mont.; ne. Cal.—has nested in an area there for at least 60 years; cent. Ore.—some records; B.C.—only 3 records w. of the mountains (1 on Vancouver I.); Alaska—a record for Kodiak I., may nest near head of John R. in Brooks Range; sw. corner of Keewatin—record for Kasba L.; Ont.—widely reported but very few definite records; e.-cent. Ungava—s. of L. Michikamau, present in summer; N.B. and Me.—quite likely nested in previous century; Mass.—near South Hanson, July 24, 1972, ten Bufflehead eggs incubated by a Wood Duck (1 egg was collected, 8 hatched, 1 embryo died) (D. Briggs); Vt.—Gale Meadows area in Windham Co., pair nested in 1971 (*Am. Birds* **25** 712, 1971); Iowa— possible record in 1880s, definitely in 1962 in Sac Co.; N.D.—records for 1873 and 1893, few recently; S.D.—brood in Marshall Co. in 1949.

The northernmost known regular nesting area of the Bufflehead is near the Alaska–Yukon Terr. boundary, just n. of the Arctic Circle. There seems to be no historical evidence of changes in breeding distribution, other than some contraction along the s. margin.

**Summer**    Buffleheads may be expected away from (including beyond) areas where they nest, at the time when they are molting and are flightless. This is known in Alaska and probably occurs in nw. Canada (Mackenzie drainage) and interior Ungava. Alaska: at Takslesluk L. (confluent with Baird Inlet), not distant from the Bering Sea coast, 204 "adults" were banded when flightless in 1963–65 inclusive.

**Winter** as mapped; essentially as detailed in J. C. Phillips (1925) and the 1957 A.O.U. *Check-list*. The bulk of westerly birds are in B.C., Wash., and Cal.; easterly ones in N.J., Md., Va., and N.C.

Limits of wintering: Aleutians and Alaska Pen.; down the Pacific coastal area into Baja Cal., Mexico; in the interior of the continent (including Great Lakes) at some unfrozen waters and thence down to include at least 6 states in Mexico (Chihuahua, Coahuila, Zacatecas, Jalisco, Guanajuato, State of Mexico); on the Gulf Coast from Texas eastward; in Atlantic waters in Nfld. regularly at a locality in Bonavista Bay, reportedly in the St. Lawrence estuary (but late fall occurrence is more probable), N.S.

432

and N.B. in small numbers, and thence down the coastal area into Fla. (to a line drawn from Tampa Bay to L. Okechobee to Palm Beach). The largest number of winterers on the Atlantic coast may be in N.C.

**Straggler** Most records are for fall–winter. BERING–PACIFIC Commander Is.—on Bering I., 2 ♂ and a ♀ (♂ shot), Jan. 19, 1883 (Stejneger 1885), also captured Jan. 13 and 19, 1911 (Hartert 1920c) [the statement, in Dementiev and Gladkov (1952), that it has been taken in winter in the Commanders on many occasions is an error]. Kamchatka—on e. coast at outlet of Vakhil R., ♂ shot Dec. 14, 1964, which had been banded Aug. 8 of the same year at Takslesluk L. in Alaska (see above under "summer"); estuary of the Khlamovitka R., Nov. 10, 1965, 2 seen (♂ shot) (Gerasimov 1968). Has straggled farther southward to the Kuril Is., also to Japan (several records, report of a flock). Hawaiian Is.—reported from Hawaii in 1959 and 1966, Maui in 1959 and 1965, Oahu in 9 years during 1929–70 inclusive, and Midway Atoll in 1965 (Berger 1972).

N. AND W. ATLANTIC W. Greenland— ♀ taken near Godhavn in Oct., 1827, and ♂ taken near Frederikshaab in 1891. Bermuda—in winter (not regular). Recorded from Cuba and Puerto Rico. Jamaica—near Kingston in 1961–63 (at least 3 seen). E. ATLANTIC–EUROPE England, Outer Hebrides, Scilly Isles—combined total of at least 5 records (1 summer), earliest about 1830, some details in Bruun (1971). Czechoslovakia— ♀ taken March 15, 1885.

The Bufflehead is recorded as **fossil** from the Pleistocene of Ore., Cal. (2 localities), Kans., Va., and Fla. (2 localities); also from the upper Pliocene of Nebr. (H. Howard, in Delacour 1964; Jehl 1966); and from **archaeological sites** in Alaska, Wash., Cal., Ill., and Fla.; for full references (aside from Nebr., just cited), see Brodkorb (1964a). RSP

MIGRATION This subject, including the relation of migratory movements to weather patterns, occupies 2 chapters with text figs. in Erskine (1972a); it is only outlined here.

Buffleheads travel comparatively late in spring and, mature birds especially, late in fall. Most overland movement is at night, the birds evidently in flocks by themselves.

**Routes** Birds from interior Alaska go to Kodiak I. and the Alaska Pen., also down the Pacific coast to the Alaska Panhandle and beyond even to Cal., and yet others more or less southeastward (destination unknown), but evidently most Alaskan birds winter in the Pacific area. Those from s. B.C. go sw. and s. to the coast from B.C. to n. Cal. (the majority to this portion of the coast), others s. in the interior, and still others se. across the Rockies. In Alta., some go sw. to the coast, some southward to s. Cal. and points e. to Texas, and still others se. to the Great Lakes and to the Atlantic coast. There is an area within Alta., that narrows rapidly northward, w. of which most birds go westward, e. of which eastward, and from within which a mixture (it includes most of those going southward). The mixing apparently extends e. into w. Sask., where Buffleheads are divided between southward and eastward migrants. Some of those of Man. go sse., down the Mississippi drainage; most go se. toward the Atlantic coast. There is not much known about other regional stocks; Buffleheads tend to move at night on a broad front across mts., coasts, etc., without regard for local topography.

Any crossing over to another route probably is done mainly by young birds. For example, one banded in B.C. was shot 2 years later in Me.

From banding, there is good evidence of homing by both sexes to particular breeding, molting, and wintering localities (Erskine 1961, 1972a).

**Spring**  Nearly all Buffleheads have left the Gulf and se. Atlantic coasts by the end of March. On the Pacific coast, the main movement is earlier (beginning around mid-March) than from along the Atlantic coast (beginning in early April). By April 20, many have reached breeding areas in s. B.C. and Alta. and, in 1962–64, the earliest birds had arrived near upper limits of breeding area in the Yellowknife section of N.W.T. around May 11. In 1962, first arrivals inland in Alaska were in early May.

There is a preponderance of mature drakes (i.e., many still unpaired) early in migration and a preponderance of prebreeders of both sexes late in migration. As the season advances and the ice melts, paired breeders move to smaller lakes and ponds, leaving behind the yearlings in flocks of about 15–20 individuals. These are not on every lake used in spring, but tend to gather on certain ones; then, at the time breeders are occupying or reoccupying their nesting places, the young drakes tend to disappear, evidently on molt migration.

On the Atlantic coast there is some evidence (from banding) that the birds are farthest s. during Dec. and, by Feb., already are moving up along the coast prior to beginning their overland migration northwestward. Many start overland from the mid-section, say Va. to N.J., of the coast. Departure from the New Eng. coast occurs from early April to around mid-May, in which period there are assemblies of birds on various marine bays. They form dense flocks; all birds dive nearly in unison, or rise to dash rapidly over the water. Soon they disappear, going overland at night, many headed for places as distant as wooded areas of the prairie provinces.

**Summer**  In June, postbreeding drakes have a **molt migration** to join flocks of molting yearlings. By the 2nd week in July, drakes of all age-classes are in molt and very wary. As the season progresses, flocks of molting yearling ♀ ♀ attract ♀ postbreeders (who leave their preflight young), also probably any failed-breeding ♀ ♀, and some drakes that have regained flight. Most molting areas are within the overall breeding range, i.e., the distance traveled to molt is not great. From recoveries of birds banded at some places in Alta. and Sask., "adults" show a different pattern from those of "immatures," the probable explanation being that the former have a molt migration after breeding.

Ohtig L., e. of Ft. Yukon, Alaska, is in the forest zone and also in the permafrost zone; a total of 1,245 molting Buffleheads were captured there in 1960–61 and 256 in 1962 (King 1963).

**Fall**  There is no evidence that the sexes or ages migrate independently; even the earliest flocks contain some mature drakes. The birds are in flocks and assemblies, on lakes where they molted or near which they nested, in Sept. prior to migration. Young of the year tend to scatter somewhat, few going very far. The major exodus of postbreeders occurs on approach of freeze-up. On the Pacific coast some older birds arrive at wintering areas in Oct., but the majority not until Nov. On the New Eng. coast, scattered birds occur after Aug. and scattered flocks beginning about mid-Oct., but the biggest movement apparently is in late Oct.–early Nov., when gatherings of 500–1,000 occur on some bays. As noted earlier, they reach their destinations in this month. There seems to be some segregation on winter range: mature drakes tend to winter farther n., but apparent changes during the season tend to mask this pattern. AJE  RSP

BANDING STATUS   The captions on certain figs. in Erskine (1972a) should have the following added, to show numbers banded through 1965: Alaska 5,258 and Sask. 289 (fig. 20); B.C. 2,116 and Man. 106 (fig. 21); Alta. 2,337 (fig. 22)); Ore. 190, Idaho 127, Texas 129, and Md. 390 (fig. 24); Utah 69, Okla. 29, N.Y. 834, N.C. 55, and all others 222 (fig. 25)—total 12,051. There were 630 recoveries through 1966. The banding data were utilized extensively by Erskine, on figs. showing places of banding and recovery, in text when estimating hunting kill and calculating rate of survival, in an appendix giving histories of 45 ♀ ♀ nest-trapped two or more times, and in other ways. RSP

REPRODUCTION   This section, for the most part, is a condensation of Erskine (1972a).

Buffleheads **first breed** at age approaching 2 years. Occasionally a yearling drake associates for a time with a particular ♀ known to be nesting, but probably after her mate has departed to molt. J. Munro (1942) believed that a yearling ♀ was nesting, but this was based on presumed Plumage and was not a known-age banded bird. Yearlings are largely in flocks when older birds begin nesting.

Breeders are paired before they establish a **territory**, which the drake defends against other Buffleheads and sometimes other waterfowl species. Females, on territory and elsewhere, after the pair bond is established, have been seen to reject the advances of strange drakes by threatening them. Both displays and copulation occur within the overall territory, but the birds also feed elsewhere at times. The territory includes an entire pond or as much as several hundred yds. of lake shore. At Watson L., B.C., nest trees were spaced rather closely, including 2 nests occupied simultaneously in the same tree. In late May–early June, ♂ ♂ are seen on water areas (part of territory) while ♀ ♀ are on their clutches and the drakes almost certainly know where their mates' nests are located (J. Munro 1942). After the drake leaves, the ♀ does not defend the nesting territory, but establishes a brood territory that usually does not coincide with the former and the dimensions of which may alter depending on circumstances.

Banding recoveries in B.C. indicate that ♀ ♀ return to the vicinity where they were hatched. All summer recoveries of banded ♀ ♀ at places more than 5 mi. from point of banding were on lakes where the birds go to molt.

Water areas unoccupied by territorial pairs are **common ground** where yearlings gather in flocks. These birds generally are not attacked by adults.

Pair bond form is **seasonal** (single-clutch) **monogamy** so far as known. Breeding drakes usually leave their mates after the midpoint of incubation and before the peak of hatching. It is exceptional to see a ♂ with a ♀ and brood, but not unusual to see drakes on a lake when early broods have appeared there. Many Buffleheads arrive on salt water in fall seemingly paired; the significance of this is unknown.

**Displays** may be seen as early as July, when drakes (having left their mates) associate with groups of yearlings that contain both sexes and possibly also contain ♀ failed breeders. Although display apparently does not occur during heavy molting, it is common when the birds return to salt water and continues throughout winter and spring, the latter being the season when most pairs are formed. On the New Eng. coast, about a third of the birds of breeding age are seen in pairs in April, before migra-

435

tion inland. In B.C., flocks of unpaired drakes have been observed in the same month; the unbalanced sex ratio (preponderance of ♂ ♂) on lakes there at that season is evidence that many drakes must have migrated that far prior to pair formation (Erskine 1961).

The relative importance or frequency of displays leading to pair formations is unknown. The actions of the ♂ always are directed toward a particular ♀, other ♀ ♀ present being ignored temporarily. At some stage, the ♀ shows an obvious positive response to a drake by Following him. Her Side-to-side and Sweep displays apparently are more frequent later.

Principal activities in displaying groups are 5 drake displays (Threat, Head-bobbing, Wing-lifting, Leading, Display-flight) and 2 ♀ displays (Head display, Side-to-side), which are among those described below. Precopulatory displays also are seen, but the entire copulatory sequence seldom is seen anywhere (but has been seen even in Cal. in Feb. and N.Y. in April). Yearling ♂ ♂ have all of the ♂ displays, including at least 2 from the precopulatory sequence, but their actions generally are of much lower intensity than in older age-classes, are less "complete" and, when displays are linked, the sequence is less predictable. Older birds seldom attack yearlings.

Threat often is linked with Head-bobbing. The ♂ may assume a crouched posture before another ♂ or ♀, then swing back and forth, presenting each of his sides in turn. He may do the same before a ♂ prior to attacking him. Concomitant with Threat and fleeing is overt attack. As 1 ♂ flees, the other dives and comes up under him, seizing him by the tail or bumping him ventrally. The attacked ♂ usually swims off rapidly, even using his wings as paddles, in which case the pursuer behaves similarly or flies low over the water; or the pursued drake may dive to escape; or fly away. Pursuit on the water generally is between ♂ ♂, while aerial pursuit flights generally include a ♀ and are more in the nature of pair formation activity. Surface pursuits often are followed by Wing-flapping and Head-bobbing.

**Pair formation and maintenance displays**   Although incomplete, important earlier studies were those of Pearse (1928) and J. Munro (1942). There is recent, probably complete, coverage in Myres (1959a) and as utilized in Erskine (1972a); some figs. in the latter show relative positions of displaying individuals.

**Displays of the duck**   HEAD-DISPLAY a threat posture as in ♂, but she holds her head farther forward and not drawn into her "shoulders." SIDE-TO-SIDE inconspicuous; the ♀ holds her head in a position intermediate between crouched and that assumed in Head-forward, and swims around the drake or back and forth beside him, keeping close to him, sometimes Leading, looking away, then toward him. SWEEP inconspicuous; when a ♀ and a closely accompanying ♂ meet another ♂, the ♀ may exaggerate lateral head-turning movements in Leading display and lower her bill and threaten the strange bird. This exaggeration grades into movements of alternating between "look at her own ♂" and "threaten the stranger." A ♀ may look toward "her own" ♂, dip her bill, then raise it out of water while pointed down at about 45° and go through what looks like a short, smooth Head-bobbing movement. This grades into a posture in which she looks along the water at the intruding ♂ with her bill lowered, similar to the Prone posture described below. FOLLOWING is the main positive response to the drake with whom she is paired or otherwise associated. The ♀ may follow the ♂ with

436

some energy when he swims away from her Leading. Since her position is at first farther away, then close behind the drake's tail, she is paddling about as fast as possible at the beginning. According to Myres, she ploughs forward, piling a wave at her bow. At first her neck is alternately stretched (fully upward) and shortened, later she Follows with it merely stretched. In the latter phase she utters a loud continuous grating call;

♀ Side-to-side Threat fleeing ♂

Wing-flapping

Display-flight

♀

braking after Display-flight

often linked in this sequence

Head-bobbing Wing-lifting

Leading often ends in Threat

Headshake forward Crest erection

♀ Head display ♀ Following Sweep

Water-twitch Preen-dorsally

437

the beak can be seen opening and closing. The drake is silent. Such Following is very similar to that of the Lesser Scaup. It occurs most often on breeding grounds, after a territorial encounter in which the ♂ is involved, but also is seen occasionally in winter. Sometimes positions are reversed, the ♀ going ahead of the ♂.

The **displays of the drake** are derived almost entirely from attack and escape behavior. THREAT differs from goldeneyes in that the neck is held lower and the body appears more buoyant. The head is lowered, back feathers raised slightly (humped appearance), tail not cocked. In full-front view the rounded back rises behind the threatening head; bird often paddles feet. Resembles prediving posture and, indeed, attack may take place by diving. Or wings may be flicked in and out of body feathers, or threat may lead to actual rush over water with flapping wings. After a diving attack, pursuer may come to the surface and be barely visible as he maintains Threat posture. HEAD-BOBBING is the most frequent action of displaying ♂ ♂. Starts with head lowered and rather crouched posture. Then head thrust violently up to fullest extent with neck axis some 70° forward; then it is lowered (nearly as rapidly) until tip of bill nearly touches water. No pause in extended position, but a clear pause in lowered stance. This jerking occurs in a sequence that includes Display flight, and at high intensity always is preceded by Wing-lifting. Crest-erection often follows a bout of bobbing, and Head-bobbing has been seen linked with Leading and Water-twitching. HEADSHAKE FORWARD is a slight amplification of a comfort movement which normally occurs at end of Upward-stretch plus Wing-flapping sequence. Consists of head thrust forward, all its feathers raised, and suddenly rolling the head violently on its side and back again. At the same time, the bill swings out to one side. [ED. NOTE Myres's description, above, and see fig. 94, perhaps is an action intermediate between Headshake forward and Water-twitch (see below), the head forward and bill swung sideways in the air. Erskine's definition of Headshake forward: the neck is bent forward and the head lowered and raised emphatically and suddenly; both after Wing-flapping and in the sequence leading to Head-bobbing, it is accompanied by an upward movement of the wings; in the former sequence the wings are raised off the back with the primaries horizontal, while the head is in lowered position; in the latter the primaries are raised, but the carpal joint often scarcely rises off the back, and this may occur as the head rises from the lowest position.] WING-LIFTING the wings are lifted upwards sharply, once, the tips well apart but scapular areas almost meet above the lowered neck. The bird appears to bob, or bow, forward in this movement. Wings then are snapped back into place as Head-bobbing (to which this display often is linked) commences. WING-FLAPPING is a comfort movement which appears often enough in display situations to earn recognition as a display. The bird rises on its tail, flaps 4–6 times, then settles down as wings flicked swiftly upward and closed just as swiftly, or primaries may be flicked once or twice as they are folded into place. (Rapid upward flick and sudden closure are very characteristic of Bufflehead and scoters, but not at all ritualized in goldeneyes.) The flick and closure occur also as part of termination of Display flight. It follows Splash-bathing in postcopulatory sequence, occurs after aggressive encounters between ♂ ♂, and at end of various sequences occurring in displaying groups. CREST-ERECTION a drake while swimming toward, beside, or behind a ♀, may slowly raise his head until the neck is fully extended, all of crest erected, cheek feathers sleeked. The

438

effect is to make the head appear almost circular in lateral view and its white area attains nearly twice normal size. The drake slowly turns his head, presenting a full side view to the ♀; he may swim past and turn to present the other side. This display thus is clearly directed at a particular ♀, seemingly when she has not responded to the ♂. LEADING the drake swims away from the duck, who is following close behind him. As he swims he turns his head from side to side as though mechanically, showing each side in turn about once/sec.; no sound has been reported. DISPLAY FLIGHT the drake starts in a position of alarm, then abruptly takes wing with a splashing run, his head forward and low. It is held rigidly in this lowered position during a short flight away from or toward a pair of Buffleheads. The flight is vibrant, with shallow wingbeats. As he starts to alight, the body is at a steep angle, the legs forward with the pink feet showing, braking his landing before the breast lowers to the horizontal on the water. The crest is erected. If the flight is away from a pair, the white areas of the wing as well as the pink feet are conspicuous. At the last moment he flicks the wings as they are clipped smartly into the sides.

This display may be preceded by Head-bobbing; usually it is followed by Headshake-forward, Wing-lifting, and Head-bobbing in that sequence. Myres noted that an unmated ♂ may start behind a pair, fly over them, land with quick wing closure, turn to face the pair, then do Wing-lift plus Head-bobbing for a few sec. He then drifts or swims, idly, toward or past the pair, before repeating the flying-over phase and remainder of sequence. C. W. Townsend (1916) stated that, on settling, the tail was jerked upward, but he probably referred to Wing-lifting.

The following, reported by earlier authors, have not been observed subsequently: (a) spreading and cocking the tail, the bill straight out forward and head feathers puffed, (b) occasional throwing back of the head in a sort of reverse bow—both from C. W. Townsend (1916); and (c) ♂ assumes erect posture on water and "struts about, as if supported by his feet and tail, with his bill drawn in upon his swelling bosom" (Bent 1925). The last could be an inaccurate description of terminal phase of Display-flight.

**Copulatory displays**, which have been described by Myres (1959a and 1959b) and Erskine (1972a), have been seen in complete sequence on breeding territory and rarely elsewhere. The precopulatory PRONE posture of the ♀ is as in goldeneyes flattened, stretched out in water, body almost submerged. In some instances the ♂ may mount almost before the ♀ is Prone, in others she may maintain it for some time beforehand, but never for 5 min. (the usual period in goldeneyes).

The drake has 2 pre- and 1 postcopulatory display, the last followed by ritualized comfort movements. WATER-TWITCH ♂ dips at least tip of bill in water, with slight sidewise movements of head water is sprayed to the side; almost indistinguishable from nearly similar comfort movement. Though repeated very frequently during the precopulatory phase, it does not become a series of seemingly frenzied Jabbings as in Goldeneyes. It is more frequent than the PREEN-DORSALLY, which often accompanies it in no fixed sequence. Drake's head is lifted and swung around to one side or the other; when the bill is brought over the back it is depressed and touched lightly to the feathers. The wing on the side to which the head has been swung usually is slightly lifted (or flicked) during this movement. ROTATING at termination of mounting, the drake slips off the back of the ♀, still holding her by her head feathers, and one bird or

439

the other is paddling. This causes 1 or 2 full-circle Rotations (in goldeneye manner; the Hooded Merganser also Rotates, but makes an incomplete circle), then drake releases hold on ♀ and, without moving very far from her, proceeds to bathe. Splash-bathing with Wing-flapping follows postcopulatory Rotations in both sexes. The deep plunge which the ♂ first performs on some occasions probably is an exaggeration of first dip of Splash-bathing.

**Comparison with goldeneyes** There are marked differences in displays. Head-bobbing, Crest-erection, and Wing-lifting seem to differ from goldeneye actions, whereas Threat, Water-twitch, Leading, Preen-dorsally, Rotating, and Splash-bathing seem to be similar (some have been designated by other names sometimes). Display flight of the Common Goldeneye is similar to that of the Bufflehead. A number of goldeneye displays are completely lacking in the Bufflehead. For detailed comparison of copulatory sequences, see Myres (1959b).

"**Prospecting**" is much less characteristic of Buffleheads than of the 2 goldeneyes. This appears to be an activity of prebreeding (yearling) ♀ ♀, sometimes accompanied by 1 or more ♂ ♂. The group makes circling flights and then the birds flutter around a tree or "inspect" a cavity. Such activity usually ends some time during the period when mature ♀ ♀ are incubating.

The **nest site** is a tree, generally near water, chosen by the ♀; some are used in consecutive years—2, 3, 4, even 6—by the same ♀, probably until rotted out or the tree falls. Some evidently suitable sites are not used in consecutive years, nor are all available sites used. There is rapid turnover, from deaths of ♀ breeders; also, Starlings, Bluebirds, and squirrels take over some cavities. If a ♀ returns, but not to last year's site, she does not go far (under 1 mi.) to another one. The sites most commonly used (based on 204 nests from Cal. to Alaska) were in quaking aspen (*Populus tremuloides*) 107, douglas fir (*Pseudotsuga menziesii*) 44, balsam poplar (*Populus tacmahaca*) and black cottonwood (*Populus trichocarpa*) 14, ponderosa pine (*Pinus ponderosa*) 12, poplar (*Populus* sp.) 11, and a few other coniferous and deciduous species. There is a decided preference for unaltered flicker (*Colaptes*) holes, but Pileated Woodpecker (*Dryocopus pileatus*) holes also are used. Holes enlarged by rotting are less characteristic as Bufflehead than as goldeneye sites.

**Exceptional sites** Raine (1892) reported 12 eggs in a "gopher" (*Spermophilus*) burrow in a brush-grown bank beside a lake in Sask.; some authors have questioned this, on the basis that he published erroneous information on other subjects. Broods have been found in areas remote from trees, as in S.D. and near Kindersley, Sask. Beyond the forest in the Brooks Range in Alaska, a ♀ was flushed from a dense mat of dwarf birch beside a pond, but no nest was found (J. M. Campbell 1969b).

**Interspecific competition** Relatively few Bufflehead nests are affected by the activities of other birds. Although most competition for cavities is from flicker species and from Starlings, Erskine mentioned 3 cavities that were deserted after the Bufflehead eggs were buried under material brought in by Mountain Bluebirds (*Sialia currucoides*) or Tree Swallows (*Iridoprocne bicolor*); there are 4 known instances of Buffleheads, attempting to use Barrow's Goldeneye nests, that were killed by the larger ducks. Joint clutches of Bufflehead–Barrow's and Bufflehead–Common Golden-

440

eye have been reported by 5 persons. More than 1 Bufflehead may lay in the same cavity in the same season.

In the Cariboo dist. of B.C., most Bufflehead nests are within 25 meters of water, exceptionally to 230 meters away, but in Alta. most are 25–75 meters away, exceptionally to 350 meters. There is no preference for trees standing in water, nor for a hole facing water, but it tends to face into the open. The nest entrance usually is 1–6.6 meters (3–20 ft.) above ground or water, but recorded heights range from 0.6 to about 27 meters. The Bufflehead's readiness (or lack of it) to use nest boxes varies in different localities. The Bufflehead and Hooded Merganser are nearly the same in girth, but the former can use cavities that will not accommodate the longer-bodied merganser. Nest-entrance dimensions, based on many data: 5.7–7.6 cm. wide by 5.7–12.7 cm. high, mostly about 6.3 × 6.3–7.6 cm. (2½ × 2½–3 in.); the internal diam. usually is about 15 cm. (6 in.), depth mainly 25–35 cm. (10–14 in.).

The ♀ may enter the cavity and remain for some time, during a period of up to several days before laying starts. Nothing is added to the cavity other than the nest **down** from the ♀ beginning after laying has started. The down is pale grayish with a brownish cast and with indistinct lighter centers; any intermingled feathers are small and white. The proximal portion of the shafts of breast feathers is dark (Broley 1950).

**Laying** Allowing for some variation, Buffleheads commonly lay on alternate days early in the clutch and successive days later on, i.e., the interval between egg depositions decreases from about 40–60 hrs. to 20–30 hrs. The most rapid sequence was 12 eggs in 14 days and 2 hrs.; at another nest there were only 5 eggs in 13 days. Most eggs are laid in the forenoon.

**Clutch size,** based on 263 clutches, commonly is 9 eggs, with 85% in the range 6–11, and little year-to-year overall variation. Yet there is very pronounced variation in clutch size from the same ♀ in successive years—for example, 7 and 13 eggs, 14 and 7 eggs. Most clutches of more than 12 presumably were produced by more than 1 ♀. Two "dump nests" each of 20 eggs, and not incubated, have been reported. There is no certain evidence that 2-year-olds lay smaller clutches than older ♀ ♀, yet there is no record of their laying more than 9 eggs. Late clutches av. smaller than early ones. There are 2 published records of "runt" eggs.

One **egg** from each of 20 clutches (13 Alta., 5 B.C., 2 Yukon Terr., 1 Mackenzie Dist.) size length 51.56 ± 1.64 mm., breadth 36.57 ± 0.72, radii of curvature of ends 13.97 ± 0.92 and 11.12 ± 1.31; **shape** between elliptical and subelliptical, elongation 1.40 ± 0.046, bicone −0.028 asymmetry +0.110 (FWP). One egg each from 62 clutches, meas. by Erskine: length 50.7 ± 1.7 mm., breadth 36.3 ± 1.1. Additional data, from Bent, Phillips, and other sources, were given in a table by Erskine (1972a). The shell is smooth, slightly glossy, and **color** varies from cream (like old ivory) to pale olive buff.

**Egg dates** Eggs have been found as early as April 29 in the Cariboo dist. of B.C. (A. J. Erskine) and May 8 on the upper Yukon R. and May 19 near Ft. Resolution (J. C. Phillips 1925). Clutches are completed over a period of 6 weeks or longer, beginning in early May (before May 11 each year 1958–61, based on hatching dates) in s. B.C. Based in part on hatching dates, there is a closer synchrony among breeding schedules farther

441

northward; most broods near Yellowknife, N.W.T., hatch within a 2-week period. Full clutches may be expected in interior Alaska beginning around June 10, but nesting presumably varies to some extent everywhere, being governed locally by time of thaw.

**Incubation**   The ♀ begins sitting after, or possibly sometimes shortly before, laying of the last egg, and she leaves the nest only to feed and preen. Generally speaking, Buffleheads are close sitters; some are tame, but others are shy and leave at the slightest noise. When undisturbed, they may leave and go to water at any hour during daylight (nests were not checked at night). **Incubation period** in 14 clutches 29–31 days (28–33 are normal extremes).

When the ducks are over half way through incubation, the drakes leave the territories, perhaps briefly at first, but soon completely. Thus most are gone in s. B.C. in early June. Evidently they gather in groups and then move to some location to molt. Since broods begin to appear early in June, drakes are seen near or in company of ♀ ♀ with broods occasionally.

**Hatching**   The time of peak hatching dates varies geographically and has been mapped by Erskine (1972a): roughly, mid-June in conterminous U.S., last third of June in w. Canadian provinces, early July in N.W.T., Yukon, and Alaska, and no data for e. N. Am. Usually all eggs hatch overnight and the ducklings remain in the nest, brooded by the ♀, for 24–36 hrs. Then they generally leave in the forenoon. The duck may "visit" the cavity repeatedly at the time the young are about ready to leave, but no vocalizing by her has been reported. After some "visiting," the ducklings climb to the entrance and drop to the ground or water and are led away by the duck. Few young fail to leave natural cavities, but in Cal. there was more failure from deep boxes orginally erected for Wood Ducks.

**Renesting** is "certainly uncommon or lacking in this species" (Erskine 1972a).

**Nesting success**   Probably at least some eggs hatch in 75%–80% of nests. In 88 successful nests (751 eggs), 700 (93%) hatched. Some eggs are infertile. In some others there are dead embryos. There is not much predation on nests. Many unsuccessful nests are deserted before incubation begins. Histories of some failed nests were given by Erskine (1972a).

The **brood** is led out to open water by the duck; seldom does a duck with young remain long on a pond under 2½ acres in size and the family will go overland to reach larger waters. At first the young are comparatively inactive, remain clustered about the duck, and probably get some food from the surface of the water and also are nourished by reserves of yolk for a few days. Then they become very active. They definitely are brooded during adverse weather and probably also on shore at night for some time. The brood rarely is unattended by the duck during the first month posthatching; usually by the 2nd week she has established a "brood territory" (or sooner if other broods are nearby and restrict movement). Once established on an area, a brood normally remains until age 5–6 weeks. Females vary in care of young. Some, especially on large lakes, readily abandon them; others stay until the young are well grown. As many as 18 young together have been seen (J. Munro 1942), and 19, 23, and 34 with a single ♀ (Erskine). It seems probable that small young that become separated from the rest of the brood may die unless they succeed in joining another brood. When older, they may join a flock of yearlings. Half-grown young often occur in unattended groups of up to

442

about 40 individuals. Also, yearling ♀ ♀ may join a ♀ with her brood, if not driven off by the parent ♀. When approached by a potential predator, the ♀ usually swims ahead of the young, her neck stretched fully upward, calling; the ducklings crowd close behind her or flap or skitter over the water to catch up with her. Brood cohesion lasts until the ♀ leaves to molt.

For much information on growth and development of young Buffleheads, based on known-age ducklings, see Erskine (1972a). They are almost fully feathered when approaching age 40 days; they have over 90% of "adult" dimensions (except WING) at that time, but only 80% of "adult" wt. Generally speaking, gains in wt. and growth level off at 55–60 days in both sexes. The primary feathers of the wing, however, continue to lengthen even after the young are flying.

**Age at first flight,** very closely estimated from observations of wild broods and from growth data on captured known-age young is about 50–55 days in s.-cent. B.C. Thus the Bufflehead attains flight later than teals of similar size, being more like the Ring-necked Duck (*Aythya collaris*).

Allowing 14 days for laying a 9-egg clutch, 30 days for incubation, and 55 for the preflight period, about 100 days are required if a ♀ starts laying as soon as she arrives in an area. Adding a week for prelaying and 2 weeks after first flight for the young to be readied for migrating would require an ice-free period of about 120 days. This available span extends northward and "closely parallels" tree line in n. Canada, "rather to the north" of the limit of nesting of the Bufflehead.

For instructions on rearing Buffleheads in captivity, see W. M. H. Williams (1971). AJE MTM

SURVIVAL   Probably about half of hatched young survive to flight age. It is not easy to check on birds after the breakdown of brood ties, since young of different broods may join forces. In 3 actual broods in B.C., survival to flight was attained by 12 young from 21 eggs (57%). There are too few "sexed immature" recoveries to give a first-year survival rate by sexes, but mortality of ♀ ♀ in their first year must exceed that of ♂ ♂, since "adult" ♂ ♂ outnumber "adult" ♀ ♀ in the population.

Erskine tried several methods of calculating estimated annual adult survival rates and concluded that, in B.C., it "seems likely" that breeders could not maintain their numbers unless survival rates of first-year birds or of mature ♀ ♀ or both were higher than he calculated from banding recoveries and recaptures. The figures from banding recoveries were, for adults only and of birds shot in their 2nd or later fall seasons, ♂ 52.8% ± 8.33 and ♀ 43.1 ± 614; first-fall birds (sexes combined) had a survival rate of only 27.8% ± 3.02. (Summarized from Erskine 1972a.) RSP

HABITS   According to Erskine (1972a)—the source of information in this section— "the general impression of Buffleheads at all seasons is one of activity, of whirring wings and splashing bodies."

**Flight**   Buffleheads take wing very easily, even from such places as large pools or ponds surrounded by thickets or trees. The wings beat rapidly, almost insectlike. Sometimes a bird or even a group takes wing, flies about, and then often alights near the point of takeoff. When going from one feeding area to another, the birds usually fly

443

within a few yds. of the water, rapidly, in rather ragged formation. Unlike goldeneyes, there is no audible whistle of wings. They fly higher when crossing overland locally and evidently much higher still when migrating. When alighting, they touch down at a good speed and quickly coast to a halt.

**Resting**   At least during daylight, Buffleheads rest on the water in a pseudosleeping posture, occasionally paddling with a foot (or both) to keep station in a group or with a companion. On a windy day the birds may avoid the crest of an oncoming wave by diving. They evidently do not attempt to feed in rough water. They preen a great deal when idling, rolling on a side and flashing their white underparts conspicuously. They sleep on the water. Seldom does a grown Bufflehead come ashore, except ♀ ♀ in breeding season, which may rest at the water's edge or on a log or stump.

**Feeding** occupies much time and is done very actively by diving in shallow water, often over tidal flats—more sheltered and shallower waters than typical of goldeneyes. The feathers are sleeked, the head drawn in, the tail usually on the surface, and the bird makes a forward plunge or leap, sometimes clear of the surface, and goes under. There it swims with feet only; the wings remain folded. Then the bird bobs buoyantly to the surface. Sometimes, in taking flight after a dive, a bird seems almost to fly out of the water. There is much synchrony in feeding activities; most of the birds are below the surface simultaneously. It is "frequently impossible" to count a flock without first mildly alarming the birds so that they stop diving. Usually they are submerged 15–25 sec. (in 6–10 ft. of water), with intervening pauses of 5–15 sec.; one was seen to make no less than 80 dives in 43 min. In very shallow water they make frequent, short, dives when gathering small organisms. Rarely do they feed by submerging only the head in merganser fashion.

**Flocking**   Singles, twos, and threes are more often seen than larger groups in all seasons. Yet gatherings of 40–200 molting birds are known and occasionally assemblies of hundreds of birds occur at stopping places in fall. In winter, flocks typically are small, about 5–10 birds. They show no inclination to associate with other waterfowl.

Little is known of parasites and not much about **predation,** but most of the natural predation evidently occurs during the preflight period. As a **gamebird,** the Bufflehead is "quite unimportant" at the present time. Evidently it was relatively more numerous until late in the previous century than during the few decades of unrestricted gunning that followed. The Bufflehead never became scarce in the west, although it certainly did in New Eng. and on the Great Lakes in 1910–30. At times these small waterfowl seem inquisitive, as well as unwary. They decoy readily and are easy to kill. At present the kill is, geographically, distributed quite unevenly, apparently depending on numbers of Buffleheads occurring and relative availability of more desirable targets. (See Erskine's monograph for a long discussion of hunting kill.)

An increase in Buffleheads in recent decades is more pronounced from N.J. northward than on the Great Lakes and in the southeast, while changes on the Pacific side of the continent have been relatively slight. There has been loss of nesting habitat along the n. margin of the prairies, notably in the parkland belt that stretches some 800 mi. from Minn. to Alta. Loss of this particularly favorable habitat must set the upper limit on possible recovery in numbers to a level well below that which most likely existed a hundred years ago.

444

Estimates of the **total number** of Buffleheads at the beginning of the 1970s vary, depending on method of arriving at a figure. The spring population, all ages included, probably is between ¼ and ¾ million individuals. RSP

FOOD  The nature of the many details—original data and from the literature—in Erskine (1972a) render his account difficult to condense; he discussed foods eaten on fresh and on salt water, by season.

The Bufflehead feeds primarily on **small animals:** aquatic insects, shrimps, snails, etc. (total 70%–90%), to a much lesser extent on seeds and other portions of **aquatic plants.** Downies feed almost exclusively on aquatic insects; food of young more than half grown does not differ appreciably from that of adults.

Main foods taken when on fresh water: in spring—insects; summer—insects; autumn—insects, gastropods, plant items; winter—mollusks (chiefly snails, but also others), a few insects, some plant items. On salt water (Oct.–early April): crustaceans, mollusks (chiefly in winter), with insects very minor. Thus the Bufflehead feeds chiefly on insects while on fresh water and crustaceans while on the sea, with mollusks consumed chiefly in winter. RSP

## Smew

*Mergus albellus* Linnaeus

Very small merganser (but larger than the Bufflehead); the short, relatively stoutish, serrated, dark bill has more ducklike proportions than bill of Hooded Merganser; secondaries dark with white tips in Juv. and Basic wing in both sexes; sexually dimorphic in color and to some extent in pattern; erectile nuchal crest (♂ Alt. Plumage); dark legs and feet. The tracheal apparatus has been described and figured repeatedly, beginning in 1798; see Beard (1951) for description and Schiøler (1926) and Heinroth and Heinroth (1928) for good illus.

The ♂ Smew measures 15–16 in. long, the ♀ to about 15. No subspecies.

♂ Def. Alt.     ♀ Def. Alt.

DESCRIPTION   Two Plumages/cycle in both sexes. The mature drake most of the year (Def. Alt. Plumage) is white, with sharply defined nearly black facial patch (bill to around eye), another in crest, and some in back, rump, wings, and 2 slim crescents down forward sides; more posteriorly, the sides appear gray (are vermiculated). The ♀, and ♂ in other than Alt.: lores, upperpart of head, and hindneck brownish, well delineated from white of lower sides of head and throat; upperparts including upper sides are various grays or toward brownish, grading to white belly. RSP

DISTRIBUTION   Breeds from n. Scandinavia e. across Eurasia into Yakutia, also in n. Kamchatka and in an area farther northward inland from Anadyr Gulf; from upper limits of forest or thereabouts s. into more temperate areas. Migratory. Rare spring and fall in Commander Is. Straggler to Novaya Zemlya and the Azores. For further details of range in all seasons, see Vaurie (1965). For Palearctic records from the Pleistocene, see Brodkorb (1964a).

**In our area**   Some of the following records listed as ♀ perhaps are of drakes in predefinitive feathering.

A ♀ was seen in the harbor at Buffalo, N.Y., at various times, Feb. 17–April 2, 1960; during this time it wandered to the Ont. side where the best photographs of it were taken on Feb. 21. Reports of this individual were summarized by Baillie (1964); also see Beardslee and Mitchell (1965, text and photos).

Either a ♀ or young ♂ was seen at Brantford in s. Ont. in late Dec. 1973.

Pribilofs—a young ♂ was taken on St. Paul I. on Nov. 20, 1961, and is specimen no. 476,206 in the Nat. Mus. of Nat. History.

446

In regard to the following Aleutian records (almost all from various issues of *Am. Birds*), here given from e. to w., it is of interest that Adak and Amchitka are centers of continued and very active field observation.

Adak I.—♀ seen Nov. 22–26, 1969, and probably the same bird on Feb. 4, 1970, when it was collected (Univ. of Alaska coll.); an adult ♀ seen on a pond on April 30, 1970, and last seen that year on Nov. 7; another ♀ seen June 5–6, 1971; 2 ♀ Oct. 17–23, 1972; 1 ♀ March 15–31, 1973; and 4 more Smew records for Adak in the interval thereafter to March 15, 1974.

Amchitka I.—a ♀ with Harlequins and Red-breasted Mergansers, Feb. 16, 1972.

Attu I. (outermost of the Aleutians)—2 ♂ "adults" on June 3, 1972, evidently the first Aleutian records of "adult" drakes.

Various older reports for N. Am., including the following, are unsatisfactory. Audubon (1838) claimed that he collected a ♀ at a lake "not far from New Orleans in the winter of 1819," which was the model for a plate in his *Elephant folio*. The specimen is not known to be in existence. A ♀ in the Brit. Mus. (Nat. Hist.), purchased from Hudson's Bay Co., is said to have come from Canada. RSP

OTHER TOPICS  Usually a silent bird, but the ♀ has a grating croak (as do other *Mergus*); the ♂ has a croak and a hissing whistle. For habitat, see comparison under Hooded Merganser. A hole nester, usually in trees not distant from water; also in nest boxes; in ne. Asia breeds even beyond the limit of trees, probably on the ground under creeping cedar (Portenko 1960). There are natural hybrids with *Bucephala clangula*— see Ball (1934) and J. M. Harrison (1943). The food of the Smew has been discussed at length by Madsen (1957). For further information, see Witherby (1939) for general account, Hollom (1937) and Lebret (1958b) for displays, and Delacour (1959) for brief text and col. pl. RSP

**Hooded Merganser**

*Mergus cucullatus* Linnaeus

Very small and trim merganser, distinguishable from all others by fan-shaped erectile crest in Def. Alt. Plumage (it is at least indicated, but is much reduced, in other Plumages). Serrations in the cylindrical bill are low, oblique, and not hooked. Sexes differ strikingly in Def. Alt., being much more alike in other Plumages. Trachea of ♂ has a smallish, lemon-shaped enlargement near inner end, close to the large bony bulla; the trachea of the ♀ is even in diam. and there is no bulla; for full descr. and illus., see Beard (1951).

The drake av. about 18 in. long, the ♀ about 17; wingspread ♂ to 26 in., ♀ to 24½; wt. of ♂ usually about 1½ lb., ♀ about 1¼. No subspecies.

DESCRIPTION   Two Plumages/cycle, the 2nd cycle earliest definitive. The innermost secondaries and some overlying coverts are renewed twice/cycle, the tail once/cycle. Because specimens in some younger stages and in Def. Basic are very scarce, treatment is somewhat sketchy here.

▶   ♂ Def. Alt. Plumage (head–body and some innermost feathers of wing), acquired in LATE SUMMER–EARLY FALL and retained through winter into following SUMMER. **Bill** black, **iris** yellow. Very large, black-bordered, white crest, remainder of **head** and the neck dark (latter has some greenish sheen); black of **mantle** continues as 2 bars down forward sides (anterior heaviest and sometimes continuous across breast); lower back blackish brown; upper tail coverts sepia with gray bloom when new and narrow buffy edging; **underparts** mostly white, this extending up sides of breast, including between the 2 black bars; rest of sides some variant of cinnamon-rufous or tawny, vermiculated black; under tail coverts white speckled dusky. Legs and **feet** vary with individual and/or season from yellow to light olive to light brownish, the webs dusky to black. In the **wing** the 4 innermost secondaries are elongated, curved distally, and have tapering ends; the proximal one is black with greenish sheen, the others are black with conspicuous and sharply defined median longitudinal white stripe; a few overlying coverts usually are black; remainder of wing, also the tail, are retained Basic feathering (described below).

▶   ♂ Def. Basic Plumage (entire feathering), the head–body is acquired in SUMMER, beginning probably in June or early July; then the wing and tail feathers are dropped and there is a flightless period (duration unknown, probably less than a month) during which the new wing and tail are growing; beginning in that span or some time afterward, the Basic head–body is succeeded by Alt. in EARLY FALL; the Basic tail and most of the wing are retained and worn with the Alt.

**Bill** toward dusky, paling to yellowish at base; **iris** light olive (1 individual). **Plumage** much resembles ♀ Def. Alt., but the very small crest, without white, is dusky (not warm brownish). **Tail** blackish brown, the feathers with some narrow pale brownish edging (may wear off). **Wing** most lesser and middle coverts are palish gray or buffy gray, forming a large light area not extending clear to leading edge; distal greater coverts black, the others with at least outer web white (forming short white bar) and

448

black ends (forming black bar); 4 outermost secondaries nearly black, then about 5 are white (forming white speculum), and the innermost ones (which are worn for some weeks beginning in summer) are short, some variant of sepia, with narrow darker border on exposed web; primaries and their coverts sepia, darker on outer web; wing lining and axillars white.

▶  ♀ Def. Alt. Plumage (head–body and some innermost feathers of wing), acquired during EARLY FALL, sometimes later, and retained through winter into following SUMMER. **Bill** upper mandible blackish green with orange edge, the lower muted orange or yellowish. **Iris** brownish buff or brownish olive. **Head** and neck various muted browns, sharply defined white chin and upper throat (both sometimes flecked brownish) and long cinnamon or rusty crest which is paler at its distal edge. **Upperparts** slaty brownish, the feathers with slightly paler (grayish or brownish) distal margins; rump and upper tail coverts darker. **Underparts** upper breast slaty and sides quite brownish since the feathers have warm brownish margins (a scalloped effect) that tend to fade or wear off; lower breast and belly white; under tail coverts grayish. In the **wing** the innermost secondaries are elongated, distally curved and tapering, and sepia with longitudinal white stripe in outer web; a few overlying coverts are dark and tapering; remainder of wing and the tail are retained Basic feathering (described below).

▶  ♀ Def. Basic Plumage (entire feathering), the head–body acquired in EARLY SUMMER, the tail and at least most of wing later (and after a flightless period). Differs from ♀ Def. Alt. in having almost no crest, and with plainer **head** and **upperparts** more brownish (less slaty). Tail as ♂, perhaps browner. **Wing** mostly brownish sepia, the middle covert area blackish brown (where the drake has a light area); some innermost greater coverts have white outer webs (form short white bar) and 6 inner secondaries have outer edge and terminal third of both webs white; the innermost secondaries (worn for a period beginning in summer) are not elongated and are sepia or darker. In LATE SUMMER or EARLY FALL, while the Basic wing and tail are growing, the head–body is losing Basic and acquiring Alt.; the Basic tail and almost all of wing are retained, and worn with Alt. head–body.

AT HATCHING  See vol. 2, col. pl. facing p. 466. Downies are plain around the eye and to base of bill, not patterned as are our 2 large mergansers. (Downy Smews are very different from all 3, being patterned and colored quite like young goldeneyes.) Internally, the tracheal bulla is present in ♂ Hoodeds at hatching.

▶  ♂ ♀ Juv. Plumage (entire feathering), estimated to be fully developed at age about 75–80 days, soon after flight attained, and the head–body soon begin to be succeeded by Basic I. The Juv. **head** has a hint of a crest—a sort of hairy fringe—and there is a poorly defined whitish area on chin; **upperparts**, breast, and sides brownish fuscous, various feathers margined paler; **abdomen** not plain white, being marked or mottled muted brownish; **tail** feathers taper, have notched ends, and match the dorsum in coloring. **Wing** has less white than the Basic wing; the coverts are narrower, browner, and paler with darkish tips; inner greater coverts have some white, also the inner secondaries, and the innermost secondaries are straight, comparatively short, brownish, and soon very frayed at the ends.

NOTE  Possibly the sexes differ, other than in av. size, in Juv. Plumage. It is said that ♀ ♀ have the innermost secondaries shorter and darker than do ♂ ♂, the one next

449

to the white-ended secondaries without indication of the frosting present in the ♂ (in Witherby 1939).

▶  ♂ Basic I Plumage (head–body, tail, and evidently the innermost feathers of wing), acquired probably beginning 80–90 days posthatching, in LATE SUMMER or EARLY FALL, and most of it retained only until LATE OCT. or NOV. Clear-cut overall pattern; earliest white-bellied ♂ Plumage. **Iris** yellow; **head** crest small and plain (darkish), chin white; **upperparts,** breast, and sides darkish, the feathers on sides broad ended and with wide pale margins (somewhat barred effect), those on flanks generally vermiculated gray; **tail** as ♂ Def. Basic. Most of the wing is retained Juv. feathering.

NOTE  Although this Plumage is well known to the few persons who have reared Hoodeds, good examples are very scarce in museum collections.

▶  ♂ Alt. I Plumage (head–body and innermost feathers of wing); in the last half of OCT. and in NOV. the young drake grows a fairly full dull brownish crest with a white patch in it; some black feathers may grow in the head, especially on crown and forepart of face; scattered black feathers grow on forward sides, indicating where the 2 dark bars will be in Def. Alt.; some brownish (chestnut) feathers, vermiculated black, are scattered on sides and especially on flanks; some birds get black feathers on chin and throat. Much of the other feathering—gray upper breast, white from lower breast to beyond vent, gray-brown in upper sides, and dorsal coloring—resembles ♀ Def. Alt. The tail is retained Basic I. Most of the wing is retained Juv.

Either acquisition of Alt. I sometimes is protracted or some birds begin late; some drakes are more "advanced" toward Def. Alt., having more black in head–neck, nearly full crest with much white, definite black stripes down forward sides, some black scapulars, some black-vermiculated tawny feathers in sides, and fairly long innermost secondaries having whitish or white internal longitudinal stripe.

▶  ♀ Basic I Plumage (head–body, tail, and evidently innermost feathers of wing), timing as ♂, i.e., a FALL Plumage; soon succeeded (except for tail) by Alt. I in late fall. Clear-cut pattern; earliest white-bellied ♀ Plumage. Judging from inadequate material, the head, upperparts, and sides somewhat darker and more uniformly colored than ♀ Def. Basic. The new tail feathers taper slightly, then have ends broadly rounded. Most of the Juv. wing, having narrower, browner coverts than Def. Basic, is retained.

▶  ♀ Alt. I Plumage (head–body and innermost feathers of wing), acquired beginning in LATE FALL (sometimes early winter) and retained into following SUMMER. Based on inadequate material, very like ♀ Def. Alt. Most of the wing, worn and frayed, is retained Juv. feathering.

**Measurements** 12 ♂: BILL 37–41 mm., av. 39.6; WING 191–207, av. 198.5; TAIL 86–96, av. 90.8; TARSUS 30–34, av. 32.4;   and 12 ♀: BILL 35–40 mm., av. 38.3; WING 180–191, av. 185.2; TAIL 81–93, av. 86.8; TARSUS 30–32, av. 31.3 (ETS).

For another series, WING meas. across chord, see J. C. Phillips (1926), and for WING meas. over the curve, Witherby (1939).

**Weight** 24 ♂ av. 1.5 lb. (0.68 kg.), max. 2 lb. (0.91 kg.); 20 ♀ av. 1.2 lb. (0.54 kg.), max. 1.5 lb. (0.68 kg.) (A. L. Nelson and Martin 1953); these agree closely with Kortright (1942).

On day of hatching one weighed 31.3 gm. (Smart 1965a).

**Hybrids** with the Common Goldeneye (*Bucephala clangula*) have occurred in the wild at least several times, the latest recorded specimen (Short 1969) being a young drake. An apparent cross between these species was seen in Feb., 1972, in s. Ont. (*Am. Birds* **26** 597. 1972). An apparent hybrid with the Red-breasted Merganser (*Mergus serrator*) was seen in April, 1951, near St. Paul, Minn. (Erickson 1952), and the same cross has occurred in captivity. It is said to have crossed in the wild with the Common Merganser (*M. merganser*) and a hybrid was raised in captivity. In captivity, a ♀ mated with a ♂ Wood Duck (*Aix sponsa*) and produced fertile eggs, but the young died in the shell just before hatching (Ripley 1956). The Hooded presumably has crossed with the Redhead (*Aythya americana*), presumably in captivity. See Gray (1958) for references to most of the relevant literature on hybrids.

**Geographical variation** apparently none. RSP

FIELD IDENTIFICATION    Small waterfowl, more streamlined than any duck of comparable size (Bufflehead, teals) or the Smew; rather stubby cylindrical bill; high forehead (rather rakish profile); fan-shaped erectile crest, varying in different Plumages from seemingly oversized to a mere hairy fringe. Drake most of the year (Def. Alt. Plumage) has black-bordered white crest, black upperparts, black bars down forward sides and rusty along sides, white belly and patchy wing pattern (white area at trailing edge). Young drakes have some white in the crest part of the year, but in some Plumages, and the ♀ always, have the crest plain, brown or tawny, the dorsum darkish gray or brown, the belly white or whitish, and patchy wing pattern with white wing lining. They are small, nervous-acting, darkish birds with stubby round bills. The Hooded stands quite erect, like a sea duck. Swims buoyantly, often jerking the head. May settle down in water (as other mergansers) rather than dive, and swim some distance before taking wing. Rises directly and easily from the water. Flies hard and straight; may change direction abruptly. Very trim in flight, the head somewhat low, bill directed forward (not angled downward), crest depressed, ♂ shows white streak at most. A rather quiet whistling of wings. May alight in the open, but usually swims to a sheltered place. Habitual preener, displaying its handsome feathering. Seldom vocal except during displays. Singles to small groups, occasionally a score or two, occasionally more at favored feeding places in early fall. Prefers company of its own kind. Not readily confused with Bufflehead or Smew. RSP

VOICE    The drake usually is silent except during display. Then he utters a guttural purring *crrroooooooo* during forward movement of Head-throw; it is somewhat reminiscent of the voice of the pickerel frog (*Rana palustris*) and is audible a half mile in calm air. A vernacular name of the Hooded in the Okefinokee Swamp in Ga. is "Frog Duck." The guttural purring is the most common call of the drake, heard in winter and spring. The first part occurs as a separate *car* syllable (Bagg and Eliot 1933), an explosive *kok* (Brewster 1924), or, after repeated Head-shake, drake lifts his head and utters a hollow *pop* (Johnsgard 1961d).

The usual call of the ♀ is a rough grunt *croo-croo-crook* quite like the call of various

451

sea ducks; it is feebler and less raucous than that of the Common Merganser; occasionally it is uttered in flight. A hoarse *gack* during Bobbing display (Johnsgard). After departure of drakes, sometimes 3–4 ♀ ♀ fly in company (see "Reproduction"), uttering *ca-ca-ca-ca-ca* (indefinite length), softer than that of ♀ Common Goldeneye; typically it occurs when incubation is advanced; later, the birds revert to the usual croaking (Brewster). A loud croaking to assemble the brood (Beard 1964).

A whistling of wings, not as loud or distinct as in goldeneyes, carries well in calm air. RSP

HABITAT   Very different from our large mergansers; a freshwater and forest-dependent hole nester. A bird of woodland waters (streams, rivers, swamps, ponds, and lake coves), often on fast streams having gravelly or cobbled bottoms. Ideal **nesting** habitat is flooded shoreline with standing drowned trees and with snags and stumps interspersed, but also nests in other locations where there are hollow trees (or nest boxes).

In **nonbreeding season,** also occurs in brackish estuaries and, along the Gulf Coast, in mangrove areas. Usually considered rare on salt water, but apparently does not avoid it along the nw. Pacific coast.

The Hooded of N. Am. is the closest ecological counterpart of the Smew of Eurasia; the latter seems to be less of a forest bird and it is decidedly more regular on salt water. RSP

DISTRIBUTION   (See map.) Apparently until after Audubon's time the Hooded Merganser occurred in numbers as a breeder in the U.S. from parts of the Mississippi drainage eastward and down into the Gulf states. Deforestation, with loss of nesting trees, and the era of unrestricted gunning were nearly as detrimental to this species as to the North American Wood Duck. For summary of older literature, see J. C. Phillips (1926), who chronicled the decline in numbers of this unwary little merganser.

An increase in the number of Hoodeds definitely became noticeable by the 1930s. Although there are large areas that probably never again will become suitable natural **breeding** habitat for Hoodeds, there now are scattered records of nesting s. into La., Miss., and Ala., although none for Fla. (where it bred in 1877). Some of the southerly records are for Hoodeds that have occupied nest boxes provided for Wood Ducks. At any rate, at present, and outside the main breeding areas in Canada and the U.S., there are vast areas where Hoodeds may nest occasionally. The first known nesting in Colo. occurred in 1971. Northwesterly, and on the Pacific slope, there has been an increase in Hoodeds lately; an expansion of breeding range apparently has occurred. There were several broods in the Chickamin R. area in se. Alaska in 1973.

In **summer** evidently a few non- or postbreeding individuals occur northward of breeding areas across interior Canada.

Mature drakes, especially, in mild **winters** occur about as far n. on the edges of the continent and in the interior as there is suitable open water. It winters in s. B.C. and locally nearly to the Canadian border elsewhere. As to southerly limits, there are small flocks down into the Gulf states and to s. Fla. The general increase, plus more observ-

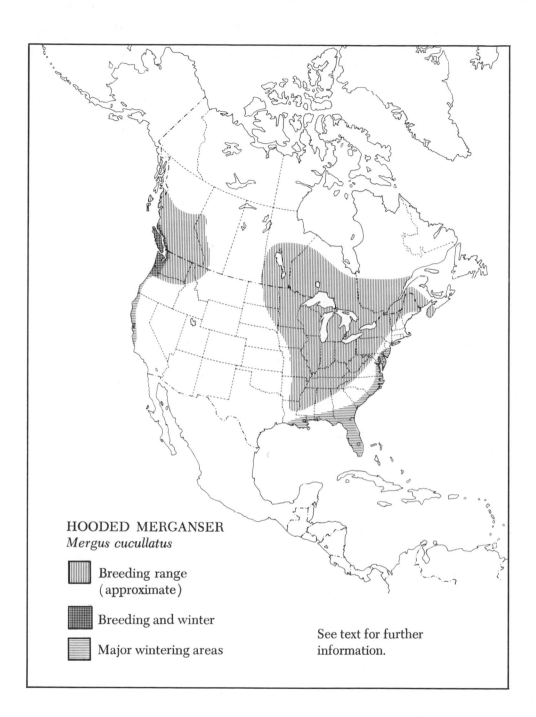

HOODED MERGANSER
*Mergus cucullatus*

Breeding range
(approximate)

Breeding and winter

Major wintering areas

See text for further
information.

ers and reporting, would account for reported recent occurrences, late fall into spring, on waters in the arid sw. U.S.

**Straggler** In Alaska the Hooded has occurred s. of the Alaska Pen. at Afognak I. (2 in Nov. 1956) and at the base of the Alaska Pen. at Katmai Nat. Monument (June 1968); in the interior it has occurred n. to near Fairbanks (Oct. 1970) and sw. from there on the Inoko R., lower Yukon drainage (♂, also 2 ♀ each with 5 young, midsummer 1927); and in the Bering Sea region it has occurred in the cent. Aleutians at Adak I. (Nov. 1970) and in the Pribilofs at St. Paul I. (Oct. 1961). There may be no reason to question a report (in E. W. Nelson 1887) that a flock was seen at St. Michael on Norton Sd. and a bird shot from it but not retrieved, Oct. 1865.

"Reported from Hawaii and Oahu" (Berger 1972).

On the Atlantic side it has straggled to Nfld. (several records), C. Breton I., Prince Edward I., Bermuda (winter, not regular), Cuba (several records), Puerto Rico, St. Croix in the Virgin Is., and Martinique in French W. Indies.

In Mexico, recorded s. into Baja Cal., also to Distrito Federal, Veracruz, and Tamaulipas.

There are 2 British and 3 Irish records, 4 in winter and 1 in July.

A drake was taken in what is presently W. Germany in 1906.

**Erroneously** recorded from Greenland.

**Fossil** in the Pleistocene on Kans., Okla., and 5 localities in Fla., and recorded from **archaeological sites** in Ill. (3 localities) and Fla. (4 localities); for references see Brodkorb (1964a). RSP

MIGRATION   Little useful information; J. C. Phillips (1926) discussed this topic tentatively, at a time when the Hooded was scarce. For an inland waterfowl, an early spring and late fall traveler. Goes in singles, twos, and small groups, usually flying quite high. Young in their first fall begin traveling earlier, and many go farther s., than the majority of older birds; mature drakes, especially, give an impression of keeping just ahead of freeze-up, thus the majority of them occur in colder parts of winter range. Judging from seasonal distribution (see map), there must be considerable more or less diagonal movement e. of the Rockies, from the n. interior (summer) toward the se. Atlantic and Gulf coasts (winter). Not many reach Mexico or Cuba.

**Spring** movement of easterly birds on winter range begins by mid-Feb., perhaps earlier (depending on season), all the way from the Gulf states n. at least to the Chesapeake area. Peak numbers are moving about a month later. There is much movement in the latitudes of about Mo.–Va. to Wis.–Me. from at least as early as mid-March into the last quarter of April. Migration does not end in n. half of breeding range e. of the Rockies until some time in May. West of the Rockies, return to breeding areas apparently occurs mostly from late March through April.

A dispersal or short **molt migration** occurs in summer. Drakes leave their mates early; Brewster (1924) found none at L. Umbagog on the Me.–N.H. border from the end of May until mid-Oct. (he discounted the idea that they molted into Basic Plumage and so remained without being recognized as ♂ ♂). They probably do not go far to molt; occasional birds do, however, occur (as in parts of Canada) some distance from the nearest places where ♀ ♀ would be likely to find nesting cavities. The ♀ ♀ leave their partly grown broods, but are presumed to molt nearby. Some movement of young birds occurs after they become experienced fliers, but most of this consists of seeking the nearest suitable feeding and resting areas.

**Fall** migration of easterly birds, s. into n. conterminous U.S., is negligible until well along in Sept. or (for postbreeders) some time in Oct. Peak numbers in e. U.S. down to about the Virginias occur in late Oct. or Nov. Some linger very far n. until late Nov., unless freeze-up comes early, and migration in southerly areas continues in diminishing amount into Dec. On the Pacific slope, movement is mainly in Nov., over shorter distances, to more northerly winter range. RSP

BANDING STATUS   A total of 347 had been banded through the year 1964 and there were 18 recoveries through 1961; main places of banding: Me., N.Y., Vt., La., and Mich. (data from Bird Banding Laboratory). Some papers cited in the next section were based, in part, on additional banding. RSP

REPRODUCTION   Age when **first breeds** in the wild is not known, but evidently 2 years; captive-reared birds first breed in their 2nd spring (Pilling, in T. E. Morse et al. 1969). Although pair formation is frequent in winter, the behavior of groups containing both sexes in late spring may indicate that some pairs are being formed even then. More than 1 drake displaying to a ♀ is frequent into spring.

Displays relating to **pair formation** and bond maintenance have been studied in captives by Johnsgard (1901d). The following is based on his paper.

**Displays of the duck**   BOBBING the head moves in jerky upward fashion, bill pointed downward, a hoarse *gack* uttered. It appears to be an intensive form of INCITING. PUMPING as in ♂.

♂ Crest-raising

**Displays of the drake**   CREST-RAISING is done independently or in combination with other displays; a "bump" on the foreneck. HEAD-SHAKE the crest is raised and there are several lateral shakes; it precedes Head-throw and, functionally, is homologous with Introductory shake of *Anas* (see Mallard). Sometimes, after several shakes, the ♂ does not perform Head-throw, but lifts head, opens bill, and utters a hollow *pop*. HEAD-THROW with TURNING-THE-BACK-OF-THE-THE-HEAD is directed toward a particular ♀ who may be stationed parallel to the drake; he utters a froglike call as the

455

head is thrown forward. PUMPING upward, then a forward and downward movement (in arc) of head and bill; the neck swollen; frequent and silent. Sometimes it is done simultaneously by both sexes. UPWARD-STRETCH upward, as HEAD-shake but without shake (as in other *Mergus* and *Bucephala*). Upward-stretch with WING-FLAP as preceding but with wings flapped several times (as other *Mergus* and *Bucephala*). DRINKING ritualized, with much-depressed crest; on upward movement the bill is raised to near vertical; used both in mate seeking and in precopulatory sequence. TAIL-COCKING ♂ usually swims ahead of ♀, the tailed cocked at 45° angle. CREST DEPRESSED directed toward ♀, the forehead feathers raised but crest strongly depressed; similar to Turning-the-back-of-the-head in ♂ *Anas*. TERTIAL-LIFTING repeated lifting of the tertials while performing the 2 preceding displays.

As with other mergansers, there is a certain amount of display even when the birds are ashore. Observations in the wild are too limited to indicate the relative frequency or order of occurrence of whatever displays are used during pair formation. The ♂ display most frequently noted is the Head-throw; sometimes it terminates with a forward dash for some yds. along the surface of the water.

**Copulation** The following is condensed from Johnsgard (1961d). The ♀ solicits copulation. The ♂ performs Drinking movements and swims near the ♀, who responds by DRINKING. After several such mutual displays, she assumes a PRONE position on the water. The ♂ immediately performs jerky forward and backward movements of the head, also occasionally does Upward-stretch. Suddenly he dips his bill and part of head rapidly and repeatedly in water while shaking his bill, the WATER-TWITCH. Then he abruptly stops, performs an Upward-stretch, with or without Wing-flap, then settles back on water and immediately Preens-behind-the-wing on side toward ♀. Then he swims with rapid, jerky, pointing movements toward the ♀, on a zigzag course TACKING-TOWARD-♀, so that he presents first one side and then the other of his crest to her full view. After mounting, he performs a single flick of the wings and, after successful treading, each bird ROTATES (incomplete circle) and then ♂ swims directly away with crest erect. Then ♀, or both, bathe. Thus the drake's sequence includes 6 displays, often more.

The **nest tree** usually is within a few rods of, or even standing in, water; frequently it is much weakened by decay. The cavity, at any height, may be a natural one or a rotted-out woodpecker hole; the only requirement is that it be big enough for bird and eggs. Exceptional sites: fallen hollow log, cavity in ground under a stump (Bent 1925). The duck, prior to departing, covers her early eggs with debris present in the cavity; beginning usually after most of the eggs are laid, the **nest down** is added over a period of time. Each down is pale gray with lighter center. Any intermingled breast feathers are narrow (they are narrow also in the Bufflehead, but wide in the Wood Duck) and the proximal portion of their shafts is light (it is dark in the Bufflehead) (Broley 1950). A site is used in successive years, probably often by the same bird. Nest boxes, preferably adjacent to water, are accepted readily (T. E. Morse et al. 1969).

Time of **onset of laying** varies geographically: early to late March (and 1 late Feb. record) at s. limits of nesting, and (T. E. Morse et al. 1969) in Benton Co., Ore., sometimes beginning in Feb., the majority in March, and no clutches begun after April; and in colder parts of its range laying must begin in April or even early May, judging from dates when clutches have been found. At Laurel, Md., the earliest clutch was begun March 14, 1961, the latest March 25, 1963 (McGilvrey 1966b). As in *Bucephala*, the interval between eggs is longer, commonly 2 days, early in laying; then some ♀ ♀ accelerate and lay several at the rate of 1/day; details in T. E. Morse et al. (1969).

Usual **clutch size** 8–12 eggs. From Morse et al.: in Ore., among ♀ ♀ that had nested in a previous year, clutch size decreased the later they began laying; ♀ ♀ laying for the first time also were late; when experienced and inexperienced birds were graphed, the result was a bimodal curve of clutch initiation. Ten ♀ ♀ that had nested at least 1 previous year laid an av. of 10.8 eggs/clutch, while 8 birds that presumably were nesting their first time av. 9.4.

Due to competition for nesting cavities, **combined layings** of ♀ Hoodeds, also **joint layings** with other hole nesters, especially Common Goldeneye and American Wood Duck, have been reported various times. Examples: 18 eggs of Hooded (Bent 1923); in a single year, 6 dump nests of 8 to 36 Hooded eggs, av. 18.2 (T. E. Morse et al. 1969); 30 Wood Duck eggs plus 5 Hooded (Peck 1896); several eggs of Common Goldeneye and about an equal number of Hooded on top of 2 addled eggs of the Barred Owl (Brewster 1924). In nw. N. Am. the Bufflehead and Barrow's Goldeneye were said (J. C. Phillips 1926) to "seek similar sites" to those of the Hooded, but actually they seldom compete (Erskine 1972a).

A **replacement clutch** is laid if the first is taken.

One **egg** each from 17 clutches (16 from conterminous U.S., 1 from N.B.) **size** length 54.34 ± 2.56 mm., breadth 43.73 ± 0.98, radii of curvature of ends 18.19 ± 1.38 and 13.39 ± 1.44; **shape** nearly elliptical, elongation 1.23 ± 0.058, bicone −0.099, and asymmetry +0.137 (FWP). The data on 116 eggs, in Bent (1923), are very similar. Their **color** is white, the shell glossy, thick, tough, and smooth except for widely separated coarse pits. Peck (1896) mentioned melanistic eggs.

Especially if disturbed, the ♀ is a restless sitter and often absent from the nest. In Ore., however, throughout **incubation** and until the ducklings left the nest boxes, ♀ ♀ routinely were absent in early morning, again at midday, and during late afternoon (T. E. Morse et al. 1969). That the **incubation period** is 31 days dates back to R. Owen (1866); the basis for this correct figure is unknown. Of 10 eggs laid by a captive ♀ and incubated under bantam hens, 9 hatched in 30½ days (Ripley 1956; Pilling, in Delacour 1959). At Laurel, Md., and assuming that eggs were laid 1/day (which is not true for many), 3 clutches in nest boxes hatched in 28, 36, and 37 days (McGilvrey 1966b). In Benton Co., Ore., in 32 nests, and assuming incubation began the day following laying of last egg in each, the mode was 33 days, the av. 32.6, and range was 29–37 (T. E. Morse et al. 1969). The period was given, without details, as 28 days by Johnstone (1970).

At intervals during laying, when mates are together, the ♀ is followed closely by the ♂ in flight. Then, approximately when incubation begins, the drake departs and presumably goes to an area where he will pass the flightless period of molting. After the drakes leave, 3–4 ♀ ♀ sometimes fly in company, perhaps circling a nest tree, uttering a continuous noisy croaking.

Recent data from N.Y.: in the literature there are at least 38 records, pertaining to about 44 nests and/or broods; other data, for the period 1949–73 (includes 145 records for the 1960s), brings the total to 229. Most clutches are found in boxes erected for Wood Ducks and joint layings are common. The 229 records are scattered in 26 counties (none for Long I.), but nesting is concentrated in areas s. of L. Ontario and in the Adirondacks. In 34 nests there was an av. of 9.9 eggs (range 1–20); most frequent was 10 and the range 9–12 includes nearly 60% of the sample. The av. size of 150 preflight broods was 5.4 ducklings, but perhaps not all young in some of them were seen. (Data from S. Browne.)

Fifty-five nests in Ore. contained 598 eggs; of these nests, 44 (containing 459 eggs) were successful, with 423 ducklings (av. 9.6/brood) **hatching** (T. E. Morse et al. 1969). After the fairly long process of hatching, the young usually remain a full day in the nest and then in the morning join the ♀ by climbing to the entrance and tumbling to the ground or water. They are tended by their very secretive mother, often on fairly rapid and secluded stretches of streams, and soon are expert divers. She abandons them during their preflight stage, however, perhaps at about 5 weeks of age (Mendall 1958, Beard 1964); brood members quite likely remain together thereafter until they can fly. Based on recapture and examination of marked individuals, **age at first flight** of 2 drakes was calculated as about 71 days, by McGilvrey (1966b).

For some information on rearing Hoodeds in captivity, see Ripley (1956), Pilling (in Delacour 1959), and W. M. H. Williams (1971). RSP

SURVIVAL   No useful information available.

HABITS   Seldom seen in gatherings of any size. An active daytime feeder. Most food is obtained by making short dives in shallow, and often rapidly flowing, water;

458

some also is gotten at the surface. It has been seen feeding with herons and a kingfisher in Fla. (Parks and Bressler 1963). Alleged use of wings in underwater swimming is not proved and was not seen in a captive in a tank. Morning and evening feeding flights to and from feeding areas, typical of many waterfowl, do not seem to be particularly evident in this little merganser, but Brewster (1924) saw evening flights from woodland streams and ponds to L. Umbagog in Me.; whether to feed or pass the night was not mentioned. It does not perch in trees, thus being like the goldeneyes and unlike the Wood Duck. It does, however, roost on snags, stranded logs, and rocks.

If alarmed, the Hooded becomes airborne more quickly than the large mergansers, trailing the feet or abdomen only a yard or so even in a flat calm. Molting, also injured, birds dive to escape and do not go ashore. It is a fast flier, its smallness increasing its apparent speed—"the pinions moving with a rapidity that almost creates a blur on each side of the body, the outline of the wing disappearing" (Elliot 1898). It has what might be termed the sea duck trait of following watercourses closely, rather than crossing areas by a more direct route, except when flying high in migration. It seems to appear from nowhere and pitches out in the open with a suddenness that surprises the observer, landing with a splash and forward spurt, and then, with jerky movements of the head, swims quickly to the shallows.

The destruction of forests in parts of its breeding range began early, but unrestricted gunning from the 1850s to about the turn of the century was the chief cause of its local extinction and general scarcity. Its fondness for small accessible bodies of water, its tameness, and its conspicuousness made it an easy target. Young Hoodeds, especially, are fair birds for the table. There seems to have been hardly more than an appreciable increase in the number of Hoodeds prior to the 1930s; increase has accelerated since but at a slower rate than that of the Wood Duck. Loss of habitat continues from forest cutting and drying of streams; the introduction of pike into various n. lakes is a hazard to the ducklings. The readiness with which the Hooded takes to nest boxes, however, suggests one measure for encouraging its increase. RSP

FOOD    The diet of the Hooded contains a much smaller proportion of fishes, about 44%, than that of our 2 large mergansers. The papers listed by Kitchen and Hunt (1969) indicate that small fishes and invertebrates (notably crayfishes and aquatic insects) comprise most of the diet and this is supported by additional information given in this section. Examination of 138 stomachs showed 96% animal and 4% vegetable matter, the latter probably taken incidentally (Cottam and Uhler 1937). Evidently some food is gotten from the surface, but most of it beneath the surface of very shallow water and from the bottom.

**Animal**    Fishes of little value for market and sport 24.5%; game, pan, and unidentified fishes 19.4%; crayfishes 22.3%; other crustaceans 10.3%; insects, mainly aquatic, 13.4% (Cottam and Uhler 1937). Eleven stomachs from Reelfoot L. contained only animal matter: fishes 81.36%, insects 12.64%, crustaceans 4.55%, and clams 0.45% (Rawls 1958). In the upper Chesapeake region, in estuarine and freshwater localities, the gullet and gizzard contents of 10 birds collected Nov.–March contained predominantly small fishes (*Anguilla rostrata*, Percidae, Centrarchidae, Ictaluridae, Cyprinidae, Cyprinodontidae); other items were mud crabs (Xanthidae), crayfishes

459

(*Cambarus* sp.), dragonfly nymphs (Libelluloidea), and caddis fly larvae (Trichoptera); see tabulation in R. E. Stewart (1962).

A drake taken July 23 in s. Keewatin contained remains of aquatic insects (Harper 1953). Two Me. birds had fed entirely on larvae of dragonflies (Mendall and Gashwiler 1940). At L. Umbagog fish not eaten; aside from a small amount of aquatic plants, stomach contents consisted of aquatic insects, especially Dytiscidae (Brewster 1924). Stomach of a Mass. bird contained only nymphs of caddis flies and dragonflies (J. C. Phillips 1911).

Crayfishes (*Cambarus virilis*, *C. propinquus*) taken extensively in Mich.; also yellow perch (*Perca flavescens*), bass and sunfish (Centrarchidae), muddler (*Cottus bairdii*), blunt-nosed minnow (*Hyborhynchus notatus*), rainbow darter (*Poecilichthys caeruleus*), aquatic insects, and frog (*Rana*) (Salyer and Lagler 1940, Pirnie 1935). Gizzard shad (*Dorosoma cepedianum*) and small mollusks at Buckeye L., Ohio (Trautman 1940). Two birds taken in Md. in Nov. had eaten respectively 12 and 20 tiny fish (Judd 1902).

**Vegetable**   Frogbit (*Limnobium*), water milfoil (*Myriophyllum*), water starwort (*Callitriche*), and bladderwort (*Utricularia*) are recorded (Yorke 1899). Seeds of tupelo gum (*Nyssa aquatica*) ingested in Ala. (A. H. Howell 1924). Fragment of buds of *Vallisneria* found in Mich. (Pirnie 1935). AWS

### Red-breasted Merganser

*Mergus serrator* Linnaeus

Fairly large merganser, or sawbill. The nostril is nearer the base of the bill than in *M. merganser*, being much closer to center of eye than to tip of bill; feathering at side base of upper mandible projects in rounded outline much farther forward than that on side base (and also ventrally on) lower mandible. In the wing the greater secondary coverts do not conceal the black bases of the secondaries; the ♂ Basic wing has 2 black bars (on white); the Juv. wing in both sexes and the ♀ Basic wing have one black bar toward leading edge of the white patch. After early life the eye is red in both sexes. There are many descriptions of the tracheal apparatus. Beard (1951), who described it for both sexes, stated that the ♂'s trachea has one enlargement just distal from the midpoint; this agrees with pl. 76 in Schiøler (1926), but pl. 248a in Heinroth and Heinroth (1928) shows a second, smaller, swelling about midway between the large one and the bulla. The huge tracheal bulla of the drake is best illus. in 2 views on pl. 76 in Schiøler.

Length ♂ to 26 in., ♀ to about 23; wingspread ♂ to 34 in., ♀ to 33; usual wt. of ♂ about 2½ lb., ♀ about 1¾. No subspecies are recognized here, although the w. Greenland birds are slightly differentiated.

DESCRIPTION   Two Plumages/cycle, Basic II is earliest definitive. Sequence, inclusive feathering (so far as known), and timing as in Common Merganser, except molting into Def. Basic in both sexes begins earlier. Perhaps in most molts, but certainly in Def. Prebasic and Prealt., it is usual for molting to be quite rapid at first and then to slow down and be prolonged. Interestingly, the ♀ in Def. Alt. usually acquires some black feathering typical of ♂ Def. Alt.

▶   ♂ Def. Alt. Plumage (head–body plus innermost feathers of wing), acquired within the span EARLY FALL into WINTER (usually complete by late Nov.) and succeeded by corresponding portions of Basic beginning in SPRING (often quite early) and continuing into SUMMER.

**Bill** near ruby with black dorsal stripe and nail; iris scarlet or ruby. **Head** and narrow stripe down nape black, former with greenish gloss; lower eyelid white; rest of neck white; the feathers on the occiput are much attenuated, forming an erectile 2-part crest. **Upperparts** mantle including inner scapulars black, other scapulars predomin-

461

antly white; black of mantle extends down on forward sides where there are at least several feathers with white centers and wide clear-cut black margins; middle of back to tail vermiculated dark on white (appears partly gray). **Underparts** breast cinnamon-rufous to quite brownish with variable amount of blackish markings that tend to be arranged in longitudinal rows; sides and flanks white, coarsely vermiculated black; belly to tail white, except some lateral under tail coverts may be vermiculated black. Legs and **feet** some variant of scarlet. In the **wing** the 2 secondaries adjoining the scapulars are black (as are their coverts) and 3 adjoining ones are white with sharply defined black stripe on at least the exposed margin and their overlying coverts are white with black or very dark bases. Remainder of wing and the tail are retained Basic feathering (described below).

▶ ♂ Def. Basic Plumage (entire feathering), the head–body acquired beginning in SPRING (sometimes as early as March, usually by early May, occasionally not until late June) and with molting continuing into SUMMER; then the Basic is succeeded by corresponding portions of Alt. beginning in FALL. The wing is molted rapidly, usually in July (duration of flightless period estimated as 4 weeks) and many drakes again are flying beginning some time in Aug. The Basic tail is acquired gradually, beginning some time in July or later. Most of the wing and the tail are retained about 11 mo.

In many respects quite ♀-like. Brown **head**, sometimes darker on crown, with sparse crest; brown of head and upper neck usually pales to white between eye and bill (with or without a darkish stripe from base of bill through eye) or same but continuous with white of chin–throat or even extending down center of foreneck; remainder of neck brownish; **upperparts** mantle feathers very dark with wide gray margins, lower back and rump variably gray; underparts feathers of lower neck, breast, sides, and flanks more or less gray or gray-brown with quite wide paler margins on sides and flanks; remainder of **venter** white except, at least sometimes, some dusky markings on lateral under tail coverts. **Tail** dark gray-brown, the feathers paler at edges.

In the **wing** the innermost secondaries are comparatively short and rounded, the 2 adjoining the scapulars very dark, then 3 are white with broad blackish border (wider than in Def. Alt.); these feathers are succeeded in fall by the longer Alt. ones. The small coverts at leading edge of wing and some nearest the body are darkish gray, most of the others white (large white area); most greater secondary coverts white with black bases which show (forming dark bar), and same for most secondaries (another dark bar or line), but a number of distal greater coverts and 2 or 3 distal secondaries are black; primaries and their upper coverts dusky to blackish; axillars and wing lining white except middle and greater primary coverts and some small coverts along leading edge are mostly dusky (some have white margins).

▶ ♀ Def. Alt. Plumage (head–body and innermost feathers of wing), acquired beginning in FALL (usually Sept.) and molting continues usually through Oct. and, to a limited extent, on some individuals into Nov. or even Dec.; then the Alt. is retained through WINTER and finally is replaced by Basic beginning (sometimes early) in SPRING.

**Bill** and **iris** as ♂, but usually less vivid coloring. **Head** crown and 2-part nuchal crest (lower part longest) usually more sepia than tawny, grading to pinkish cinnamon on sides of face and upper neck; white area on chin not sharply defined; lower eyelid

462

white, at least in some individuals; the amount of black on head–neck varies, from none (as just described), to patch around eye (mostly behind it), to much of forepart of face, around eye, more or less of chin, scattered feathers on throat, and even a black area near middle of foreneck. Color of neck (except where black) merges into that of body. **Upperparts** mantle gray-brown or even quite brownish (not the gray or blue-gray of Common Merganser), with paler rump, the feathers (especially scapulars) with grayish or somewhat buffy margins that are reduced by wear. **Underparts** upper breast, sides, and flanks essentially as mantle, with light feather margins prominent on sides and flanks; coloring of breast merges into unmarked white of remainder of venter. The ventral body down is quite dark—darker than in *M. merganser* in any season—but slightly paler than in ♀ Def. Basic. Legs and **feet** more or less scarlet-orange, webs somewhat muted in coloring. In the **wing** the 2 innermost secondaries are black or nearly black, then several adjoining ones are grayish margined blackish and the outermost of these may have white in outer web; overlying coverts are blackish; remainder of wing and the tail are retained Basic feathering (described below).

▶  ♀ Def. Basic Plumage (entire feathering), the head–body begin showing traces of Basic occasionally by very late Feb. or early March, commonly a few weeks later. Thus, in SPRING, there is new facial feathering, also at least foreneck, scattered feathers on dorsum and sides, and probably all of abdomen. The head–body are retained into FALL.

The **bill** becomes brownish pink along sides. **Head** face variably warm (to reddish) brown with no black areas, paling to nearly white at sides of and under bill (but no sizable white chin area in specimens seen); commonly a palish facial stripe extends from below and behind eye forward to side of bill, or there is a somewhat patchy pattern on forepart of face (palest at eye, also near bill); foreneck warm brownish, without black. Apparently the molting slows or ceases and is renewed beginning in the rearing period or after the young are abandoned. The head acquires a short, sparse, scraggly crest and **upperparts** are more or less buffy gray-brown; **underparts** lower neck to lower breast, sides and flanks, as dorsum with various feathers margined somewhat paler; a least a few lateral under tail coverts may have dusky markings. The ventral body down is medium gray-brown or darker. The **wing** is molted (onset of flightless period) in late summer or early fall and, while the new Basic wing is growing, the **tail** begins gradual renewal (Basic).

**Wing** lesser and middle coverts medium grayish; greater coverts black, except about 6 proximal ones have most of exposed area white with black edges; distal secondaries black, then about 6 middle ones white with black bases (form black bar); primaries and their coverts dusky; in summer some innermost secondaries are shorter, distally rounded, and ashy brown; they and their overlying dark coverts are succeeded in fall by Alt. feathers (see Alt., above); axillars and wing lining as ♂ Basic.

AT HATCHING  See vol. 2, col. pl. facing p. 466. Separable from Common Merganser by position of nostril, which is entirely within proximal third rather than nearer middle of mandible; the down extends farther forward at side of bill than on top. Lower mandible lighter reddish than upper. Bill slenderer than that of Common Merganser of same age. The facial pattern is variable, both in the Nearctic and Palearctic; some have a continuous white stripe or a line from under eye to side base of bill, others have the same more or less clouded or interrupted in midsection; some have white above eye, others lack it. Judging from photos of pl. 254 in Heinroth and Heinroth (1928) and in Curth (1954), the head pattern is variable even within a brood. Legs and feet variable, more or less reddish or lavender of flesh-color. A small white scapular spot shows on some individuals, but on others it is discernible only by parting the down. Internally, the tracheal bulla is partly developed in the ♂ and easily detected.

According to Strong (1912), on day of hatching the downies have a spiny or bristly appearance, the down filaments being held together by feather-germ material, but in a few days they become fluffy. This is not entirely correct. Waterfowl ducklings have delicate "waxy" sheaths on the down at hatching, which vanish within a few hrs.

▶ ♂ Juv. Plumage (entire feathering), head, body, and tail develop before the wings, which grow slowly; by the time flight is attained there already has begun some replacement of Juv. by incoming Basic I feathers. The facial striping soon becomes obscure or lost. The Juv. is characterized by **head** with dark malar stripe and light one above it, a mere fringe on nape (not an obvious crest); **upperparts** have a rather slaty (not brown) cast; **underparts** breast and sides nearly like mantle; the various feathers tipped or margined very pale; **tail** dark, the feathers with notched ends; **wing** quite like ♀ Def. Basic, but feathers (including all coverts) smaller and narrower; greater secondary coverts without dark edging; there is more or less gray on innermost secondaries (inward from edge of white speculum) which are darkest marginally and usually paler overall than in ♀ Juv.

▶ ♀ Juv. Plumage (entire feathering), as in ♂, replacement by Basic I begins early. **Feathering** as ♂ but innermost secondaries shorter and usually darker overall. Age for age, ♀♀ are smaller than ♂♂.

▶ ♂ Basic I Plumage (much, perhaps all, of head–body, also the tail and innermost feathers of wing), acquired during FALL (beginning before flight attained) and retained until later in FALL or even well into WINTER (individual variation in molting schedule).

Quite ♀-like. **Head** usually with dullish brown crown and a definite but rather sparse crest, the sides of head variably warm brownish (toward reddish brown) with rather diffuse buffy line from bill to or beyond eye and a diffuse darker one below it; chin whitish, which may end on upper throat or continue down midline of foreneck; **upperparts** gray-brown; **underparts** lower neck, upper breast, and sides variably gray-brown, the feathers (especially on sides) margined or tipped paler; lower breast to tail white. **Tail** feathers toward slaty, their ends rounded; they are acquired in Oct. or Nov. In the **wing** the innermost secondaries are very dark, with black edges, and their longer overlying coverts are very dark; remainder of wing is retained Juv. feathering.

▶ ♂ Alt. I Plumage (much, possibly all, of head–body, also the innermost feathers of wing), timing variable and feathering variable. In some individuals, much Alt. I is acquired in DEC., there being essentially continuous molting from Juv. to Basic I to Alt. I, but in many a midwinter pause after Basic I, then molting begins (or continues) from quite early in FEB. into (possibly through) SPRING. This feathering is succeeded by Basic II beginning in MAY or, sometimes, EARLY JUNE.

The **head** and upper neck variably reddish brown, the crown and 2-part nuchal crest same or nearer neutral colored and darker; occasionally an indication of facial patterning (indistinct stripes or patchy effect), the white of chin sometimes continuing down

464

foreneck. In "advanced" birds there is more or less black on sides of head and upper neck (especially foreneck). **Upperparts** mainly some variant of slaty gray, the feathers margined paler, some inner scapulars dark (black in "advanced" birds), the outer scapulars variable, usually more or less white or (in "advanced" birds) same with black vermiculations; center of back to tail grayish or (in "advanced" birds) more or less coarsely vermiculated black on white or pale gray. "Advanced" birds also have some feathers on forward sides white with broad dark or black margins. **Underparts** lower neck warm brownish, marked somewhat darker, and this continues so as to include much of breast; feathers of sides and flanks plain grayish or ("advanced" birds) white coarsely vermiculated black, or same mixed with gray feathers; whatever pattern occurs may continue onto lateral feathers beyond the vent; remainder of underparts unmarked white.

In the **wing** the innermost secondaries are very dark and some adjoining ones white margined very dark (to black) and the longer overlying coverts are very dark. Remainder of wing is retained Juv. feathering, the tail retained Basic I.

NOTE   As in the Common Merganser, the pattern and coloring vary depending on whether Alt. I is acquired early (meaning Basic I is worn rather briefly), in which case characteristics are more ♀-like, or acquired (or molting continues) after a winter pause, in which case various features resemble ♂ Def. Alt. But they are the same feather generation in both instances. It should be noted also that an occasional young drake acquires "advanced" (Def. Alt.) characteristics beginning early, sometimes even in Dec.

▶   ♀ Basic I Plumage (inclusive feathering as ♂ Basic I), timing evidently as ♂, i.e., acquired beginning early and individuals vary in how long they retain it (until very LATE FALL or well into WINTER).

The **head** tends to be 2 toned, crown and sparse crest darker and nearer neutral colored, remainder down to include upper neck a variant of reddish brown; some indication of a darkish stripe through eye; sometimes some whitish adjoining side of bill; a poorly defined white area restricted to chin or sometimes continues onto foreneck. The reddish brown coloring tends to end quite abruptly on the neck; the coloring below, on the nape, grades into that of mantle and, on foreneck, varies from nearly white to more or less brownish. **Upperparts** mantle variably slaty to somewhat brownish, the feathers margined somewhat paler. **Underparts** sides as mantle; upper breast to tail white. **Tail** more or less slaty, the feathers with rounded ends. **Wing** the 2 innermost secondaries very dark, some adjoining ones variably gray with very dark edges, and longer overlying coverts very dark; remainder of wing is retained Juv. feathering.

▶   ♀ Alt. I Plumage (inclusive feathering as ♂ Alt. I), time acquired equally variable, as in ♂; then the feathering retained into late spring or later. Thus it is a first WINTER Plumage.

**Head** (including 2-part nuchal crest), neck, and upper breast unicolor, variably reddish brown, with poorly defined white area on chin (not extending onto foreneck), and merging with gray-brown or **dorsum** and white of **venter**; no examples seen with any black in head; sides as mantle; in the wing the 2 innermost secondaries are very dark (sometimes black) and several adjoining ones variably gray margined black; their overlying coverts are very dark; remainder of wing is retained Juv. feathering, the tail retained Basic I.

465

▶ ♂ ♀ Basic II earliest definitive; the head–body portion is acquired before the Juv. wing (except innermost feathers) is lost.

**Measurements** of birds from continental N. Am., in various seasons; 12 ♂: BILL 57–60 mm., av. 59; WING 238–257, av. 248.5; TAIL 78–86, av. 82; TARSUS 45–48, av. 46.3; and 12 ♀: BILL 50–58 mm., av. 55; WING 213–239, av. 224; TAIL 69–78, av. 73.8; TARSUS 42–49, av. 44 (ETS).

In the w. Palearctic, part of the data in Schiøler (1926): flattened WING 19 ♂ Juv. 219–240 mm., av. 226, and 43 Basic 236–258, av. 244; ♀ 10 Juv. 210–223 mm., av. 215, and 23 Basic 204–235, av. 220.

For Palearctic birds, WING meas. over the curve, see Witherby (1939).

For comparative meas. (wing, bill, width of bill at base) of ♂ ♂ from N. Am., Greenland, and Sweden, see Vaurie (1965).

**Weight** few useful N. Am. data; ♂ 2 lb. 7 oz. to 2 lb. 14 oz., av. (of 15) 2 lb. 10 oz. (1,190 gm.); ♀ 1 lb. 7 oz. to 1 lb. 15 oz., av. (of 11) 1 lb. 13 oz. (825 gm.) (Kortright 1942).

Eighteen ♂ av. 2.5 lb., max. 2.9, and 17 ♀ av. 2.0, max. 2.8 (A. L. Nelson and Martin 1953).

At Anaktuvuk Pass in the Brooks Range in Alaska: 5 ♂ May 26–June 1 weighed 992–1,077 gm. and 3 ♀ May 30–June 24 weighed 808–975 gm. (Irving 1960).

Eleven on day of hatching weighed 38.6–50.7 gm., mean 44.5 (Smart 1965a).

Sources of Palearctic data: seasonal changes in wt. in the Black Sea region, see Ardamatskaya (1963); winter wt. in Denmark, Schiøler (1926); wt. at hatching, Koskimies and Lahti (1964). Mean wt. of nesting ♀ ♀ in Iceland: 1,026 gm. (10 in 1968), 955 (11 in 1969), and 1,018 (9 in 1970) (Bengtson 1972c).

**Hybrids** Among some Red-breasted Mergansers in Minn. in April a possible cross with the Hooded was seen (Erickson 1952). There is a very doubtful old report of the Red-breasted having crossed with the Mallard.

**Geographical variation** is slight, even though this species has the largest range of any merganser. Schiøler (1926) compared available material from the Palearctic, including Iceland, and from the Nearctic, but mostly Greenland specimens. He regarded the w. Greenland birds as a recognizable subspecies, which he had named in 1925. According to Vaurie (1965), in ♂ ♂ the wing does av. somewhat longer in Greenland and the bill somewhat narrower in N. Am. Although some individuals are identifiable as from w. Greenland, so great is individual variation in the species generally that it seems inadvisable to recognize any subspecies—B.O.U. subcommittee (*Ibis* 98 159. 1956), Rand (1947), Vaurie (1965), and present author. Schiøler stated that the young drake acquires less Alt. I Plumage in Greenland than in Denmark, a possible latitudinal variation in extent of molting, but there is great individual variation in the characteristics and timing of Alt. I in N. Am., as discussed earlier. RSP

FIELD IDENTIFICATION  In flight has the usual attenuated merganser outline—slim bill and the head, neck, and body are all in line—which makes the bird seem longer than it actually is. At a great distance it can, however, be confused even with the Mallard. It is not enough smaller than the Common Merganser for comparative size to be of much use as a field character in separating them. Both fly in long lines and chevrons. On the water the Red-breasted has a decided long-bodied appearance; the rather ragged 2-part crest (of both sexes) varies with age and season from slight to decidedly conspicuous.

The drake Red-breasted is separable at considerable distance from the Common by having a dark, rather than white, breast. The features usually mentioned as distinguishing the ♀ from the Common Merganser ♀, whether in flight or on water, are that the former has **1** white chin patch poorly defined and **2** mantle more toward brownish than blue-gray. These characters can be useful under favorable conditions. In practice, however, one usually reckons with differences in preferred habitat plus association of ♀♀ with indentifiable drakes, if such are present. The growing young are ♀-like in appearance. They are separable from young Commons with certainty by bill characters when in hand. From the time they are about half adult size, however, they have a more ruffled and dingy appearance than young Commons of corresponding age.

Older drakes in ♀-like Basic Plumage generally can be identified to species at least as late as early summer by retained remnants of Alt. Plumage, and to sex (unless the wing quills are molted) by the white patch extending nearly to leading edge of wing (♀ has white only from trailing edge part way inward).

When not nesting, generally in pairs and small groups, but occasionally in scattered bunches totaling thousands at places where food is plentiful and in some locations during migrations. A distinct whistling of wings is heard if they pass by at short range. RSP

VOICE   The drake usually is silent, except at times when feeding and during certain displays: in Salute a loud harsh purring approaching a double note *da-ah* or *yeoww*, uttered once (it is difficult to describe); in Curtsy a low purring or scraping variant, also uttered once. An exhalant quacking–rattling reported by Heinroth (1911) was never heard by Curth (1954). The calls of the ♀ are essentially as in Common Merganser. A single short *rock* or *wark* uttered by both sexes in flight (rarely on water) and much more frequently by the ♀, expresses alarm and also may be a contact call. Especially when alarmed with brood, the ♀ has a prolonged hoarse croaking, or series of croaking sounds, and a more quacking *kha-kha-* in indefinite series to assemble brood after danger has passed. A disturbed ♀ returning to her nest uttered ducklike quacks (Strong 1912). See Curth (1954) for a few more details. RSP

HABITAT   Much more marine than the Common Merganser. In **breeding season** inland waters (rivers, ponds, lakes) within and beyond the forest zone; also regular on coasts and marine is. Ideal breeding habitat is a small island or islet having low or prostrate woody growth or other low overhead shelter such as conifer limbs for the ground nest and, at nearby water, gravel bars, rocks that are nearly awash, or open strand, where the drake has his station early in the season and where, later, the brood may rest and preen. In **other seasons**, although some remain on interior waters such as large lakes and reservoirs, this bird is essentially a coastal migrant and a tidewater and inshore marine dweller. As such, it is not competitive with the Common Merganser. Often it is found on much less sheltered waters than preferred by the Common and it pursues a straighter coarse when fishing, i.e., it is more independent of depth of water. RSP

467

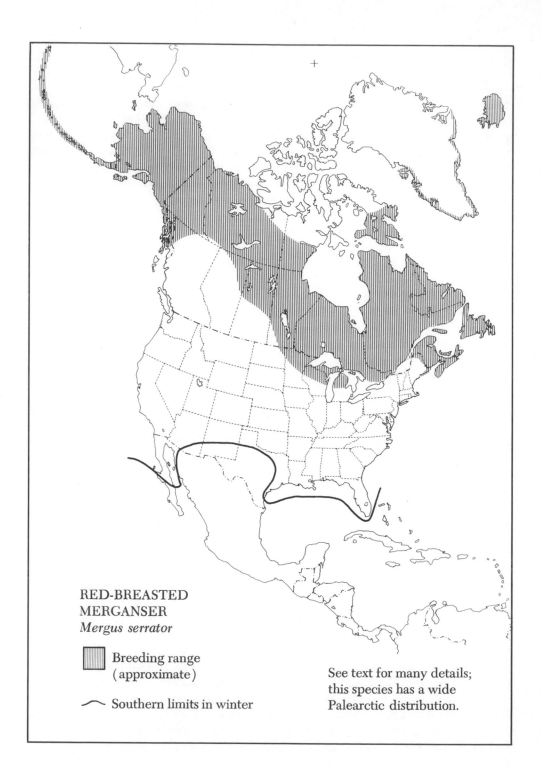

RED-BREASTED
MERGANSER
*Mergus serrator*

Breeding range
(approximate)

Southern limits in winter

See text for many details;
this species has a wide
Palearctic distribution.

DISTRIBUTION (See map.) Large Holarctic range. A boreal–subarctic species that has expanded into the arctic in postglacial time (Johansen 1956). The older distributional literature was summarized by J. C. Phillips (1926), whose accompanying map still is useful. He showed the w. Greenland birds as an extension from continental N. Am. via Baffin I. and those of the Faeroes and Iceland as an extension from the Palearctic mainland, assumptions which are reasonable.

In interior N. Am. there are various questionable nesting records, because of probable confusion with the Common Merganser, the most likely nester at southerly localities.

Prebreeding (yearling) Red-breasted Mergansers sometimes remain far s. of breeding range into, even throughout, summer; most such occurrences are on brackish and salt water.

NEARCTIC **breeding** Godfrey (1966) is followed for Canada and various sources are used for Alsaka, conterminous U.S., and Greenland. Peripheral records, clockwise, beginning in the w. Canadian arctic: Yukon Terr.—mainland opposite Herschel I.; se. Victoria I.—a scarce breeder in se. part; Baffin I.—scattered records in s. $2/5$; Greenland—breeds along w. side to Nugssuak Pen. and locally beyond into Upernavik Dist., and up the e. side locally to Scoresby Sd. and a record beyond (the only high-arctic record) for Sofia Sd.; Maritimes—regular offshore at Sable I., N.S.; Me.—coastal is. w. to include Penobscot Bay, occasionally (at least formerly) farther westward, and occasionally (formerly more numerous) at larger waters well inland; Mass.—bred at Ipswich in 1916 and, s. of C. Cod, has nested regularly on Monomoy I., occasionally also formerly on is. in Nantucket Sd.; N.Y.—a few records for Long I., also Gardiner's and Fisher's I., and at larger waters in n. interior; Mich. and Wis.—s. to cent. areas; nw. conterminous U.S.—only questionable records; B.C.—in n. part nests on both mainland and marine is.; Alaska—is. and mainland of se. Alaska and thence n. and w. to include the Alaska Pen. and nearby is. (Kodiak, others) throughout the Aleutians, and at least larger Bering Sea is. (Nunivak, St. Lawrence—evidently breeds but no nests yet found); no Pribilof breeding records; scattered throughout the Alaskan interior and more numerous peripherally, with records n. to the Barrow region and delta of the Colville.

In **winter** scattered on open waters inland, the major concentrations being along marine coasts. On the Pacific side: along the Aleutians and s. of the Alaska Pen. and continuing in coastal waters down to include n. Baja Cal. and coastal lagoons of adjacent Sonora in Mexico (but majority along coasts of conterminous U.S.); scarce in w. interior, but recorded down to s. Nev. and in New Mex. and to cent. Ariz.; from the Mississippi eastward it occurs regularly on open waters in the interior, the bulk of the birds southerly; in Atlantic waters: around at least most of Nfld. and thence southward to include all of Fla. (but most plentiful probably from Me. to N.J.); regular in Fla. Keys and occasional (possibly regular) in the Dry Tortugas; occurs in small numbers on larger waters throughout interior Fla.; most numerous in Fla. on the Gulf Coast (Hernando to Santa Rosa Cos.); in some numbers thence westward to include at least part of coastal Texas, and also in lesser numbers on open waters inland in Gulf Coast states.

Greenland—on open water along the sw. coast.

**Straggler** in Bering Sea to the Pribilofs; Pacific Ocean—Hawaiian Is. (Hawaii and

Oahu). In the Atlantic—to Bermuda (occasionally in winter), Bahamas (New Providence, sighting at Andros I.), Cuba, and Puerto Rico (♀, originally recorded as *M. merganser*).

**Erroneously recorded** (1957 A.O.U. *Check-list*) for St. Croix in the Virgin Is. (the bird was *M. cucullatus*).

Recorded in the Nearctic as **fossil** from the Pleistocene of Ore., Ill., and Fla. (abundant remains at Rock Spring); and from **archaeological sites** in Alaska (on 2 is.) and Fla.; references, except for Ore., in Brodkorb (1964a).

For the PALEARCTIC there are various published texts and maps; for text, Vaurie (1965) is useful.

On the Pacific side—in Commander Is. breeds sparingly and is present in winter; on the Chuckchee Pen. a scarce nester, absent from northerly and easterly portions. On the Atlantic side—in Iceland, present all year, most common in lowland areas, and a small portion of the birds migrates to Scotland; in the Faeroes it nests sparingly and occurs all year, but is more common in passage. The increase and spread of this merganser in Scotland was documented in detail by Mills (1962a). The Palearctic fossil and archaeological records were summarized by Brodkorb (1964a). RSP

MIGRATION   In N. Am. A late traveler in spring and prolonged through fall. There is meager evidence for determining the overall pattern, but the following is suggested as applicable to most of our area. Assuming those individuals that nest at or close to salt water remain fairly close by on salt water through the winter, then at least most birds of breeding age in such areas as the Aleutians, is. of se. Alaska and n. B.C., and Nfld., are relatively local all year; the young leave, migrating various distances. From within the continent, westerly birds go to Pacific waters, easterly ones to the Atlantic, and more or less of those in the middle move to southerly inland waters or (first-fall birds) reach the n. rim of the Gulf of Mexico. After older birds are on salt water, continuing movement is weather influenced and, for the most part, probably rather local. It is possible that mature ♀♀ travel farther than mature drakes, but the evidence is tenuous.

**Spring**   In much of conterminous U.S. there is migratory movement by early March; it gains momentum toward the end of the month, is sustained until late April, then dwindles in May. Spring flocks are much smaller than the assemblies of young birds in fall. Along the way, the birds are abundant at favored places, where they occur in many scattered groups and there is much display. Migration is earlier on the Pacific than on the Atlantic coast. Prebreeders, with breeders or separately, go to breeding localities. A few remain scattered down even to southerly winter range until well along in May, occasionally through summer. This merganser arrives at the big lakes in nw. Canada beginning about mid-May. It begins arriving in northerly and easterly interior Alaska in the last few days of May and very early June.

There is a considerable but variable lapse of time between arrival and nesting, which complicates any attempt to date back from dates for fresh clutches to estimate when migration occurred locally.

**Summer**   In most of the breeding range, beginning quite early in June, prebreeders move unknown and undoubtedly variable distances on **molt migration.** Presuma-

470

bly they do not go far. Mature drakes travel considerably later, in late June or early July. Little is known regarding summer activities of young birds or mature drakes, which some authors have described as being scattered and extremely secretive. There are a few reports of very small groups of flightless mature drakes. In summer there also are sizable assemblies, at least temporarily and at least sometimes, but details as to sex and age of the birds are lacking. Examples: 1,500–2,000 on July 7–8 at the Fox Is. in the Churchill area of s. Hudson Bay (Twomey, in Taverner and Sutton 1943); at L. Athabaska in nw. Sask., flock of about 50 (plus some Common Mergansers) fishing together on July 14, flock of about 250 far out on the lake on July 19, and "dense flock" of about 120 on a beach on July 24 (Nero 1963).

**Fall** First-fall birds begin traveling soon after they can fly, in Sept., and very large gatherings build up on some lakes and in coastal waters. Along several mi. of beach at Ipswich, Mass., in late Oct.–early Nov., the water was "covered" with these birds, at times perhaps 25,000 of them (C. H. Townsend, in Bent 1923). Peak numbers of "brown heads" occur in New Eng. coastal waters beginning in late Oct., in the Chesapeake region through Nov., and some still are moving on Atlantic coastal winter range until past mid-Dec. Timing on the Pacific coast is about as on the Atlantic; inland it is more variable. Older birds of both sexes are late everywhere, evidently not moving until freeze-up; most of their migratory movement occurs from the latter part of Oct. into Dec. and they do not go far. Some rather sizable northerly wintering flocks consist almost entirely of mature drakes.

Wayne (1010) stated that in S.C. "adult" ♂♂ are seldom if ever seen until the first week in Feb., but "towards the second week they make their appearance in large numbers." This sudden appearance is best explained (by J. C. Phillips 1926) as young ♂♂ then acquiring Alt. I Plumage rapidly. The same occurs in other areas where first-year birds are wintering.

**Greenland** Along the w. coast, migrants go northward in May–early June as the fjord ice breaks and inland lakes start to thaw; in Sept.–Nov. they return to sw. Greenland and are strictly marine in winter. Summering prebreeders are in scattered small groups in fjords and on other sheltered waters. Salomonsen (1950) thought that e. Greenland birds migrate to the Brit. Isles, but there still is no evidence.

A preflight young, banded at Mývatn in ne. Iceland on July 4, 1935, was shot at Tasiussarssuk, in Angmagssalik Dist. of e. Greenland, on Sept. 22, 1939 (M. T. Cooke 1945).

It is of interest that, in Iceland, many remain through winter on the s. and sw. coasts, but 8 of those banded in ne. Iceland have been captured as follows: 6 in Scotland, 1 Ireland, and 1 Holland. Those banded in Denmark are nearly sedentary (Boyd 1959b), but see Joensen (1973) for full discussion. RSP

BANDING STATUS The total number banded in N. Am. through 1964 was 187 and the number recovered through 1961 was 10; main places of banding were Alaska, Mich., and N.S. (data from Bird Banding Laboratory). In Greenland the total number banded 1946–65 inclusive was 65 (Salomonsen 1966) and there have been some recoveries.

In the Palearctic there has been banding in Iceland, Scandinavia (including Denmark), Germany, and elsewhere. Some interesting recoveries were mapped by Boyd (1959b). RSP

REPRODUCTION   In order to show the pattern more completely, the rather scant N. Am. data are supplemented by information from a number of studies done in the w. Palearctic.

Both sexes **first breed** when approaching age 2 years; authors are agreed on this, although there seems to bc no published evidence from banding. At least in captive-reared birds, the drake in 1st fall has some display (Heinroth and Heinroth 1928).

In Nov.–Dec., when many of the birds are on winter range, some of them already are behaving as mated pairs. **Pair formation** activity is common beginning in Feb. and continuing until at least well into spring. According to several European authors, some pairing occurs even after arrival at nesting areas; it is probable, however, that most of the display seen in the later stages of migration and afterward is related to bond maintenance and copulation, that as a rule they are paired before arrival. Many drakes already are molting out of Alt. Plumage by the time the birds arrive. The birds fly or swim to a gathering place where, in groups typically of several ♂ ♂ and a ♀, there are bouts of display that culminate in formation of a pair bond. The following summary of displays is based on both Nearctic and Palearctic sources.

**Displays of the duck**   As noted especially in spring, when the birds are in small parties, ♀ ♀ often respond aggressively to advances of ♂ ♂, making JABBING motions. The most conspicuous activity, however, is INCITING, in which the ♀ swimming (or even ashore) makes a short dash forward, her head high and forward with bill angled downward. A grating croak is uttered. NODDING may be related more to bond maintenance than to pair formation. UPWARDS-STRETCH and WING-FLAP, also BATHING, evidently are ritualized; they are interspersed among other activities and continue as long as the pair bond lasts. Also see below under "Copulation."

**Displays of the drake**   All motions are executed stiffly. CROUCHED threat posture, much as in *Bucephala*. SPRINT drakes make rushes on the water, near and among ♀ ♀, creating a conspicuous bow wave, a wake, and even a shower of spray thrown up behind the bird (somewhat as in Head-throw-kick of Common Goldeneye); the head is withdrawn slightly, crest depressed, neck curved (very snakelike profile), wings closed. Sometimes this is done in overt attack, but generally to take station near a ♀. Often it immediately precedes (is linked to) the next. SALUTE head suddenly brought forward so that neck, head, and bill are in a diagonal line; then, in a quick action, the head is jerked slightly downward as a nasal whining purr *yeow* is uttered. When the

Head-turning

Curtsy

drake's head is fully forward, the white of the neck and pattern on forward sides are shown to fullest advantage. CURTSY drake swims with head settled on mantle, crest erected, bill slightly up-tilted. Suddenly the crest is depressed; then the stretched-neck attitude (of Salute) is assumed and catlike call given. After a brief pause the neck and anterior body are submerged as if jerked downward under water from base of neck and the tail is tilted toward water simultaneously. In extreme form the rear of the bird rises until the feet are in air. The wings are lifted slightly so that the white area, contrasting with adjacent dark feathering, is conspicuous. In this display, neck and forward sides are out of sight, submerged, which is the opposite of the 2 preceding displays. The open bill is conspicuous. HEAD-TURNING, after Curtsy the drake resumes normal stance, his double crest spread fully, then his head is turned sideways and the bill opened to fullest extent and pointed toward a preferred ♀, or another ♂, and 2 faint catlike calls are uttered. In this and the previous display, the red lining of the mouth is conspicuous. The combination of Curtsy, Salute, and whatever follows, in all their variations, is the "Knicks" (bending) of the German literature, as in Curth (1954). Portions or variants of the sequence are seen among birds ashore at the edge of water. UPWARD-STRETCH, WING-FLAP, and BATHING are frequent and evidently ritualized.

If there is any related **aerial activity** other than chases, such as a mated pair with an interloping ♂ in pursuit, apparently it is not recorded. Such chases are common after many of the birds are mated.

**Copulation** In Devon, England, Dec.–March inclusive. Behavior always was the same before coition: the ♀ held the PRONE posture for several min. while the ♂ PREENED-DORSALLY and made DRINKING movements. Both birds are "repeatedly turning slowly" (which suggests Rotations). On dismounting, the ♂'s actions vary. He immediately "displays" (elements of Salute-Curtsy?) and the ♀ submerges her head repeatedly and also Wing-flaps. Once a ♀ SPRINTED, then the ♂ PLUNGED below the surface and she followed. On surfacing, she Preened and Wing-flapped. In another instance a ♂ Sprinted, then Plunged in violent manner; on surfacing, he swam toward the ♀, his head "between his shoulders," crest erected, and beak elevated (elements of Curtsy). (From Adams 1947.) In late June in the Hebrides: the ♂ Sprinted forward and mounted the Prone ♀; after he dismounted, the birds swam side by side very briefly; then the ♂ raised his head to near-vertical with bill partly open, silently. The ♀ responded by "writhing" the head–neck without opening her bill. After a minute or so the ♂ Plunged, then surfaced nearby in an almost vertical posture, Wing-flapped, and settled down and Preened. When the ♂ Plunged, the ♀ ceased "writhing" and began Preening. (From Sage 1962.) In spring in Sweden 10 copulations were observed by Nilsson (1965). The ♀ initiated the sequence by becoming Prone; there was no rapid swimming beforehand. The ♂ circled the ♀, his neck stretched forward (Salute position), then followed DRINKING-PREENING-DORSALLY and WATER-FLIP (a derivative of Drinking; compare with Barrow's Goldeneye). Union lasted 6–13 sec.; then the pair ROTATED, the ♂ performed more or less of the "Kicks" sequence, and both birds Bathed.

Some **aberrant situations** occur—♀♀ copulating with more than 1 drake, also a drake mated to 2 nesting ♀♀ (Ringleben 1936).

As noted in the w. Palearctic, the ♀ may search for or visit a **nest site** or its vicinity for 2–3 weeks prior to onset of laying. Such trips occur in the morning, only occasionally in the afternoon; the drake accompanies her on her travels, even when she is afoot sometimes, or sometimes remains behind at the water's edge. There are some Finnish banding data on ♀♀ returning to the same locality for more than 1 year.

Although the Red-breasted nests to some extent on river banks and lake shores, in most areas preferred sites are within about 10 meters of the water's edge on smaller is. in lakes, brackish waters, or the sea. Many thus are in the peripheral zone where flotsam is washed and blown ashore, providing secluded niches under stranded logs and tangles of debris. More or less overhead shelter is a requisite; open sites are exceptional. Favored places include: under conifers whose drooping lower branches are close to the ground, under fallen logs, between and under boulders, in shallow cavities or up against the bases of stumps, in tall grass, heather, bracken, patches of last year's reeds, and in nettles. In some instances the ♀ has a path, even a tunnel, through plant growth from nest to water. Sometimes there is more than a single path. If the nest is well away from shore, quite often it is at the edge of an opening, as under brush and facing a grassy area; it is unlikely that the ♀ can take wing from such a place, but probably she can do so from a steep slope.

Some Red-breasted Mergansers nest among Common Eiders, or near various other ducks, also in gulleries and terneries and react to the warning cries of their neighbors. Salomonsen (1950) mentioned 3 nests in Greenland that were 5 meters above the sea on coastal cliffs, in gulleries of Kittiwakes and the Iceland Gull. In some places the surface nests of the Red-breasted are near hole nests of Common Merganser.

J. C. Phillips (1926) pointed out that it is common to find 6–10 Red-breasted Merganser nests in close proximity; this reflects availability of preferred sites rather than social nesting.

In the Baltic, in the Finnish Archipelago, nesting boxes are provided for this merganser. A hole about 12.5 cm. square or a little smaller is sawed in the middle of the short side of relatively small, shallow boxes and these are placed near bushes or in vegetation, the hole facing the sea or a clearing (Grenquist 1958).

The Red-breasted lays later than the Common Merganser. In the Nearctic, **laying** begins in early May in most southerly areas; most of all first clutches in any area are initiated within a period of about a month and, even beyond lat. 55° N, nearly all clutches are begun by the end of June. In the sw. Baltic at Hiddensee, Curth (1954) gave the interval between deposition of eggs in clutches, for 265 eggs, as averaging about 1½ days (0.7 egg/24 hrs.) with the duck at the nest for 1–2 hrs. at laying.

The **nest down**, which is plentiful at least with first clutches, is deposited beginning after the laying of the 3rd to 5th egg and continues for some time, possibly into incubation; thus there is a liberal amount for surrounding a normal-sized clutch and for the duck to use in covering it before she departs. It is much darker than that of the Common Merganser; an individual down is relatively large, has a small whitish center, and the very tips are palish. In a mass it appears medium gray-brown, dotted light. Any intermingled feathers are rather small, have the vane white, and proximal portion of the shaft dark; see Broley (1950) for illus. Beginning with Audubon and his contemporaries, authors have stated or implied that the nest is lined with plant materials such as weeds, mosses, and the like. The probable explanation is that there is litter at the site and the sitting ♀ works more or less of it into the nest and its lining.

In N. Am., **first clutches** usually contain 7–10 eggs and presumably any number over 14 or 15 is the product of more than one individual. Compiled from scattered published sources, 40 presumed first clutches in N. Am.: 1 of 5 eggs, 4 (of 6), 5 (7), 6 (8), 8 (9), 12 (10), 1 (11), 1 (12), and 2 (13). In Iceland, 1961–70 inclusive, mean clutch size varied from 9.00 ± 0.41 (4 clutches in 1969) to 10.0 ± 0.43 (10 in 1966), the mean of the yearly means (total of 158 clutches in 10 years) being 9.50 ± 0.13 (Bengtson 1971c). In the Baltic at Hiddensee, 72 clutches in 1950 av. 9.9 eggs and 48 in 1951 av. 9.8 (Curth 1954). On Schleimunde, 22 ranged 6–15, av. 10.4 (Pflugbeil 1956). For details of a total of 765 clutches, or layings, of 5–21 eggs (but mostly 9–13), in the Black Sea Reserve, see Ardamatskaya (1963).

In sw. Finland, first clutches av. 9.6 eggs and 9 **replacement clutches** av. 6.2 (G. Bergman 1939). At Vejlerne in N. Jutland, Denmark, in 1966, clutches were progressively smaller the later they were started until mid-June, indicating that those started after that were replacement clutches; 15 first clutches av. 12.7 eggs and 10 presumed renestings av. 7.3 (Kortegaard 1968).

One **egg** each from 20 clutches (17 from scattered N. Am. localities, 1 Iceland, 2 Ireland) **size** length av. 64.36 ± 2.64 mm., breadth 43.96 ± 1.16, and radii of curvature of ends 15.98 ± 1.07 and 12.67 ± 0.77; **shape** between elliptical and subelliptical, elongation 1.46 ± 0.062, bicone – 0.040, and asymmetry + 0.111 (FWP).

Total of 280 eggs (Nearctic and Palearctic) length 57–70 mm., av. 64.9, and breadth 40.5–47.5, av. 45.1 (Schönwetter 1961) and 480 eggs in nw. Black Sea area length 57–71, av. 65.9, and breadth 39–48.8, av. 45.9 (Ardamatskaya 1963). The shell is smooth, **color** creamy or brownish buff when fresh, but Kortegaard (1968) stated that some become olive green while being incubated. In general, they are smaller and darker than those of the Common Merganser.

Possibly incubated **joint layings**, also "dump nests," are somewhat less frequent in this species than in waterfowl that nest in tree cavities where there is competition for available sites. However, practically all workers who have devoted any time to the Red-breasted have reported at least 16–20 eggs in occupied nests, presumedly joint layings. True "dump nests," without nest down and not incubated, contained 20 eggs in a number of instances. Curth's (1954) summary of Palearctic records included "30 and more," to 50, and he himself found 17, 22, and 56.

In N. Am. the Red-breasted has laid in the nests of several waterfowl; Pelzl (1971) listed Mallard, Gadwall, and Lesser Scaup as hosts in Wis., also Gadwall + Red-breasted Merganser clutch incubated by the latter. In the Palearctic the most frequent and widespread host is the Common Sheld-Duck, but the list includes Mallard, Gadwall, White-winged Scoter, and Common Gull (*Larus canus*). On the Black Sea Reserve is., where many Gadwalls nest in stands of reeds, 50 of 2,052 nests contained Sheld-Duck eggs, 24 contained Red-breasted Merganser eggs, and 10 contained both Sheld-Duck and merganser eggs (Ardamatskaya 1965). J. C. Phillips (1926) summarized some older reports: eggs of the Red-breasted in Barrow's Goldeneye nests (Iceland), in Common Sheld-Duck nests (Europe), and an egg of the Ancient Murrelet in a merganser's nest (Alaska).

During laying, the **drake** usually is not far away, on water or at a beach or other resting place, and the ♀ joins him when off duty from laying and incubation. **Incubation** usually begins on completion of the clutch, but sitting on the eggs sometimes occurs even before the last or next to last egg is laid; sometimes there is an interval after clutch completion before incubation begins; details in Curth (1954) and Pflugbeil (1956). At times during laying and into incubation there is some social grouping of off-duty ♀ ♀ and their mates, resting and preening ashore or afloat. Soon after incubation begins, however, the pair bond is terminated; small groups of drakes may remain in the vicinity for a while, then disappear.

In Russian Lapland, at 2 nests only a meter apart, the 2 ♀ ♀ alternated their periods of absence. Usually a sitter left twice a day, occasionally 1 or 4 times. A recorder was placed at one nest, where total daily absence av. 4 hr. and 5 min., with the pattern not varying either at beginning or end of incubation; the ♀ did, however, sit continuously for 20.5 hrs. during a drenching rain (Semenov-Tian-Shanskii 1960).

The **incubation period**, when part of the clutch was left with the ♀ and part placed under a domestic fowl, was 29 days minus a few hrs. in both situations (Strong 1912). In the Palearctic the period in 21 clutches in the wild was 29–35, av. 31.8 days (Curth 1954). Various other records are for 29–35, usually 32, days.

There is considerable evidence from the w. Palearctic that **fertility of eggs** is fairly high but that a considerable number are not hatched. In Pflugbeil's (1956) study at Schleimunde, slightly over half of the eggs hatched; in Kortegaard's (1968) study in cent. Sweden, over a quarter of the nests were abandoned, in successful nests an av. of just under 4 eggs (some with dead embryos, some infertile) did not hatch, and only 23% of clutches started produced any ducklings.

In the sw. Baltic the **young** remain in the nest 12–24 hrs. (Curth 1954) and then are led to water by the ♀ while she utters a croaking call. They travel close behind her, strung out slightly. At first they feed at the surface, but soon are making shallow dives. A duckling or two occasionally climbs onto the back of the ♀. In response to danger, the group skitters along the surface, like Common Mergansers, rather than diving as do goldeneyes. Mortality of preflight young apparently is low, but in N. Am. pike (*Esox* spp.) are a known predator and it is likely that the larger species of gulls also get some of the downies.

A ♀ may lose her brood to another ♀ with brood, or an untended group of young may be "adopted" by a tended or untended group. Tended crèches or "**flotillas**" of up to at least 64 young—not necessarily all the same age—are reported. Quite early in the preflight stage of the ducklings the adult ♀ ♀ depart to continue molting (become flightless) and the young, now on their own and capable of fending for themselves, may keep their groupings or combine and split in various numbers. Flocks of 20 or 30, even 40 or 50, individuals occur. Aggregations of hundreds were reported from Ireland (Treveleyan, cited in J. C. Phillips 1926). Not only are flotillas comprised of birds of assorted ages, but also some contain young Common Mergansers.

There are photos of captive-reared young at age 15 days in Heinroth and Heinroth (1928) and Strong (1912) described **growth** of a captive duckling, still downy at age 4 weeks. Based on captive-reared birds, age at first flight was estimated as 59 days by Heinroth and Heinroth (1928). In N. Am., late-hatched young in the wild still are flightless in Sept.

Moody (1944) had no difficulty in raising this merganser from eggs placed under domestic fowls. He noted that the young dive with remarkable swiftness for pieces of food tossed into the water. RSP

HABITS   The data here are mostly from N. Am., but they apply more widely.

Red-breasted Mergansers are busy birds, active almost constantly—swimming along in pairs or groups, preening when afloat or ashore, diving and feeding, splash bathing with great energy, displaying in late winter–spring, and they seem very alive even when quietly floating in pseudosleep with an eye open. They are wary. Small parties are the rule, but there are large gatherings, mostly of young birds, in fall, and the parties in spring congregate in large loose assemblies on sheltered coasts and on brackish waters. Goldeneyes, scoters, and other seafowl are intermingled at times.

To become airborne, the Red-breasted can rise directly even in calm air, but usually patters along the surface; it rises more easily than the Common and appears to be more buoyant and maneuverable in flight. It can pitch down with a certain suddenness and glide quickly to a halt. Flight is swift and seemingly purposeful, the birds usually in lines, or members of a pair close together, low over the water on local flights and usually higher than the Common Merganser on longer flights. Recorded flight speeds: av. of 29 observations in spring 72.4 km./hr (Ryden and Kallander 1964), also air speed of 80 mph (about 114 km./hr.) near an airplane for a short distance (M. C. Thompson 1961).

On the water the Red-breasted gives the appearance of riding lower than the Common, which may be an illusion. At times when swimming along they pump their heads back and forth, perhaps indicating mild alarm or flight intention. J. Munro (1923a) stated that they tend not to follow the shoreline when feeding, as does the Common Merganser, but move on a straight course, often on deeper water. They tend to be in a group when commencing to feed and can dive smoothly, one quickly after another so that the whole group may disappear, or the entire group makes a great commotion of splashing, plunging, surfacing, and jerking their heads as they rush about. In feeding, except in very shallow places, they generally are down for 10–30 sec., and the pauses between dives are brief. If they scatter while submerged, often they regroup on surfacing, in preparation for the next bout of diving. It is generally agreed that the legs are used for underwater propulsion, but several authors also have reported the wings used under exceptional circumstances. Sometimes they come to the surface with the wings out somewhat from the body. If they dive and swim to escape a pursuer, their submergence is longer than when feeding.

There are various reports of cooperative feeding, such as arranging themselves in an arc and driving fish fry into the shallows where, with a great thrashing and splashing, they capture and swallow their prey. Small items are swallowed beneath the surface; large ones are brought to or above it and the local gulls may be on the lookout for a chance to snatch a fish. Part of the commotion also consists of the mergansers trying to rob one another. For a good description of cooperative feeding by 7 individuals, see Des Lauriers and Brattstrom (1965), and for various herons benefitting from the fishing activity of this species, see Abdulali (1949), also Emlen and Ambrose (1970) and authors they cited.

Like the Common Merganser, the Red-breasted explores submerged terrain, pok-

477

ing its bill into holes, crevices, and between loose stones, to startle any fish that may be hiding. Such prey usually is caught crosswise, then manipulated into a head-first position for swallowing. Most of their prey is rather small, or at least slim, but there are known instances (as also in the Common Merganser) of individuals choking on large fish. For an interesting account of their catching eels in a brook in winter, and sometimes losing them to Herring Gulls, see Forbush (1925). They have the usual merganser habit of swimming along, dipping the head partly under the surface or even keeping it there while they move, seeking underwater prey. This also is a common method where the water is too shallow for effective diving.

Both of our large mergansers often rest on shore, close to the water's edge, an activity quite alien to the true diving ducks. The sides, breast, and belly are preened both when ashore and afloat, by elevating the forepart of the body; they also roll or "capsize" on the water, so that the belly is exposed for preening and a foot is in air.

A great local seasonal abundance of these mergansers is deceptive; they occur widely in N. Am., but total numbers are relatively small. They are not much hunted nowadays, but used to be shot in large numbers in spring; being sawbills or sheldrakes, they have coarse flesh and a literally unsavory reputation, but Turner (1886) stated that the Aleuts preferred them to any other duck. Their main claim to attention stems from the fact that they are voracious feeders—like the Goosander, "a notorious glutton" (J. C. Phillips 1926). There are hunters' tales of these birds having swallowed so much food that they had to disgorge it before they could take wing. They feed on whatever animal life of suitable size is available. Since they cannot stalk prey in murky water, they share with trout and young salmon a liking for clear water and can do local damage to the stocks of these fishes, as can any other fish-eating bird. Control measures against this merganser, however, are justifiable only when the birds are numerous in certain particular localities, as pointed out by J. Munro and Clemens (1937, 1939) and reaffirmed by other investigators. Consider, in their favor, the amount of trashy items they undoubtedly eat in the course of a year.

As reported from Conn. by Penner (1953), this merganser is the natural host of a fluke *Austrobilharzia variglandis*; the cercariae emerge from a snail and, in man, cause clam digger's itch. (Other bird species are hosts also.)

The reader who wishes to learn more of the activities and feeding methods of this merganser will find much of interest in papers cited in the following section. RSP

FOOD   The bulk consists of **fishes**, plus some crustaceans; minor items include insects, amphibians, and worms. Examination of 130 stomachs from N. Am. localities showed minnows, killifishes, and sticklebacks 34.2%; low-grade commercial fishes, principally carp and suckers, 3%; game and pan fishes 14.4%; unidentified fish fragments 25.1%; miscellaneous items, mainly crayfishes and shrimps, 23.3% (Cottam and Uhler 1937).

Adult birds in e. Canada had eaten fishes (*Salmo salar*, *Gasterosteus aculeatus*, *Apeltis quadracus*, *Fundulus diaphanus*, *Tautoglabrus adspersus*, *Notemigonus chrysoleucas*, and *Catostomus commersonii*) and ephemerid shrimps (mainly *Siphlonurus*). Young had eaten fishes (*Fundulus diaphanus* and *Pungitius pungitius*) and shrimp (*Crago septemspinosus*) (White 1937, 1957). Eels taken in Mass. (Forbush 1925) and elsewhere. A bird taken in S.C. in Jan. contained 295 top minnows (*Gambusia*) (Sprunt and Chamberlain 1949). Ten taken in Mich. had eaten fishes (*Perca flavescens*, *Lepomis macrochirus*, *Hyborhynchus notatus*, *Notropis cornutus*, *Nocomis biguttatus*, *Fundulus diaphanus*, *Poecilichthys exilis*), a frog (*Rana*), and small quantities of anisopteran and ephemerid nymphs (Salyer and Lagler 1940). Eleven at Buckeye L., Ohio, contained 1–9 gizzard shad each (Trautman 1940).

Rock bass and spotted shark recorded from Santa Cruz I., Cal. (Linton 1908). In fresh water in B.C., sculpins and eggs (*Cottus asper*) most important; also salmonoids, salmon eggs, sticklebacks (*Gasterosteus aculeatus*), shrimps (*Pandalus danae*), amphipods (*Gammarus limnaeus*), and larvae of crane flies and caddis flies. In salt and brackish waters, salmonoids, herring (*Clupea pallasii*), smooth sculpin (*Leptocottus armatus*), blennies (Blenniidae), rock fish (*Sebastodes*), shrimps (*Pandalus*, *Spirontocaris*), and crabs (*Lophopanopeus bellus*). Sculpins and herring of greatest importance (J. Munro 1930, J. Munro and Clemens 1931, 1939). Sticklebacks an abundant food in Alaska (E. W. Nelson 1887).

Insects are important to small young. Eleven young taken in N.S. had eaten ephemerid nymphs (*Siphlonurus* mainly, some *Baetis*), aquatic coleopterans and trichopterans, fishes (*Catostomus commersonii*, *Gasterosteus aculeatus*, *Pungitius pungitius*), and shrimps (*Crago septemspinosus*) (H. C. White 1937). Captive young were fed grasshoppers with questionable success (Strong 1912).

Some amphipods are taken in Greenland (Holbøll 1846). Two birds taken in Scoresby Sd. contained only polar cod (*Boreogadus saida*) (Salomonsen 1950). At Mývatn in ne. Iceland, both sexes feed predominantly on sticklebacks in shallow water near shores; young, for a time after hatching, ate sticklebacks, some adult insects, and some seeds (mainly *Carex*); 5 full-grown young had eaten sticklebacks, Cladocera, and traces of other items (Bengtson 1971b). Cod, stickleback, hake, pipefish, and crustaceans in Ireland. One was gorged on 24 sand eels (*Ammodytes*) (W. Thompson 1851). In 148 birds in Scotland: salmon (*Salmo salar*) in 113 stomachs and remains of salmonoids were most frequent, then *Petromyzon planeri*, *Phoxinus phoxinus*, *Gobius minutus*, and *Anguilla anguilla*, with 6 other fishes in lesser amounts; also some crustaceans and insects (Mills 1962b). Sixteen in Britain had eaten fishes (salmon, trout, roach, perch, eel, blenny, sand eel, dace, plaice, and stickleback) 75%, crustaceans 15%, insects 5% and annelids 5% (Collinge 1924–27). A drake taken in waters swarming with the fry of coalfish had eaten crabs only (H. W. Robinson 1909). Fishes formed 75%–80% of the food in Denmark. Most important, in order, were sticklebacks *Gasterosteus* spp.), gobies (*Gobius* spp.), blenny (*Zoarces viviparus*), and butterfish (*Pholis gunnellus*); the crustaceans were primarily shrimps (Cragonidae) and prawns (Palaemonidae) (Madsen 1957).

In U.S.S.R., 2 taken in May on Onega Bay, White Sea, had eaten smelts 6 cm. in length. On the Pechora R. the fish in 63% of stomachs were mainly *Phoxinus*, with some *Cottus* and *Thymallus*. One had eaten a frog. In 50% of stomachs were found larvae of caddis flies, and the water beetle *Dytiscus marginalis*. The stomachs of 3 birds taken in autumn at Rybinsk Reservoir were filled with *Phryganea grandis*. In winter at Lenkoran on the Caspian Sea the stomachs contained fish only, mainly carp 5–16 cm. in length, and *Alburnoides*. The esophagus of a bird taken on the Black Sea at Sukhumi in Dec. was filled with *Blennius*. (Summarized from Dementiev and Gladkov 1952.) AWS

## Common Merganser; Goosander

*Mergus merganser*

A large merganser, or sawbill. Nostrils nearer middle of bill than base, thus being about half way between center of eye and tip of bill. The bill is stouter than in the Red-breasted and its distal end tends to be somewhat bulbous and bent sharply downward, more prominently in Palearctic than in Nearctic birds. The feathering at side base of upper mandible projects forward in an acute angle, just above the tomium (serrated edge); the feathering on the underside of the bill (between the rami) projects as far as or farther forward than that on the side of the upper mandible. In the wing the median and lesser coverts are white in ♂ Basic; they are gray in ♂ Juv. and ♀ Juv. and Basic. The tracheal apparatus of both sexes has been described frequently; see, for example, Beard (1951). In the drake the trachea has a greatly flattened dilation in its distal third, a smaller one in middle third and, at its inner end, an enormous partly membranous and partly bony bulla (diam. over 5 cm.) with major protruberance on left side; the best illus. are on pl. 75 in Schiøler (1926).

The Am. subspecies: length ♂ to 27 in., ♀ to 25; wingspread ♂ to 36, ♀ to 34; usual wt. of ♂ about 3½ lb., ♀ about 2½. The 2 Palearctic subspecies are not very different from Nearctic birds in dimensions.

DESCRIPTION *Mergus merganser americanus.* Two Plumages/cycle, the 2nd cycle earliest definitive. Most standard works confuse Basic I with the Juv., because characters overlap and most of the former is worn briefly. After a pause, variable amounts of Alt. I are acquired, gradually, from early winter or (usually) from about Feb. through spring. The most useful paper on Am. birds is Erskine (1971), who was uncertain as to whether all of the venter is molted more than once/cycle (it is) and whose regional dates for molting need expansion in order to be more inclusive geographically. There are some additional data on molting in Anderson and Timken (1971). There are various conflicting statements in the literature, some here discarded and some others (but not all) reconciled through reinterpretation or from examining additional material.

▶ ♂ Def. Alt. Plumage (head–body and innermost feathers of wing), acquired within the span SEPT. into DEC. (sometimes even later); retained through winter–spring and succeeded by corresponding portions of Basic from about MID-JUNE to LATE AUG. (occasionally into Sept.)

**Bill** nearer scarlet than ruby, with dark area along top, dark nail, and scarlet-orange lining to mouth; **iris** dark brownish, sometimes with outer ring of yellow concealed in life by the eyelids. **Head** and upper neck almost black with greenish sheen, the feathers at rear of crown and on nape somewhat elongated (but smoothly contoured), exaggerating size of head; lower neck white or fugitive creamy; **upperparts** much of mantle glossy black, but center of back to tail medium gray, darkening toward tail; the inner scapulars are black, the lateral ones (nearest wing) white or creamy; **underparts** creamy white (except abdomen sometimes mottled gray) usually with pronounced salmon tinge that fades quickly after death (also in captives and does not recur after subsequent molting); flanks finely vermiculated gray; a palish area at side base of tail;

legs and **feet** some variant of scarlet; in the **wing** the elongated innermost secondary is black and the others (up to 6 feathers) are white with very narrow black margin on outer web. The remainder of the wing and the tail are retained Basic feathering (described below).

NOTE   The Alt. feathers of the dorsum are acquired gradually, while molting of head–neck begins later and proceeds quite rapidly (Erskine 1971). The abdomen is molted sufficiently gradually to mask any evident change from one feather generation to another.

▶   ♂ Def. Basic Plumage (entire feathering); head–body acquired within the span MID-JUNE to very EARLY AUG. and lost in the span SEPT.–EARLY DEC.; the tail and wing feathers are dropped in July or early Aug. (there follows a flightless period) and the Basic wing is fully grown between some time in Aug. and about mid-Sept. (then most of this feathering is retained approximately 10 mo.); the tail is renewed more gradually, often into early Nov., then retained until the following July or early Aug.

The drake in Basic is quite ♀-like, having a crested brown head, also has certain Juv.-like characteristics, but has the definitive ♂ wing. BILL muted scarlet with dusky brown ridge and nail; **head** and upper neck more or less cinnamon (crown often darker); the crest tends to be single and shorter and denser than in ♀ Def. Alt.; usually there is a light line from gape across lores and sometimes a white patch above it (or sometimes they coalesce); the white of chin varies from restricted in area (upper foreneck brown) to narrowly continuous down foreneck and center of breast; remainder of lower neck various grays; **upperparts,** including scapulars, toward sepia and medium grays—browner than ♀ Def. Alt.; **upperparts** white or faintly salmon, grading on sides and flanks to various grays and these feathers have paler margins; **tail** feathers very dark (sooty).

**Wing** boldly marked; distal upper surface black, inward to include the 3 outer secondaries; a wide white area crosses wing (to or almost to leading edge), into which, from the distal side, projects a black bar formed by black basal portions of some greater coverts; the inner coverts of the wing are dark; the middle coverts are unmarked white; the innermost Basic secondaries (which are not long retained) are shorter, with more rounded ends than in Alt., and have outer webs off-white with narrow dark border and inner webs quite dark gray; wing lining and axillars white, except under-primary coverts darkish gray.

NOTE   The Basic begins showing first on scapulars, sides and flanks; then the head–neck, remainder of back, and at least part of venter gradually. As to the wing, the flightless period (lasting perhaps nearly a month) begins about early Aug. at C. Breton I. in N.S., but Erskine (1971) also examined museum specimens from the Hudson Bay region that had become flightless 2–4 weeks earlier, i.e., in July. Many drakes in N. Am., which have departed from their mates in June, become flightless in July.

▶   ♀ Def. Alt. Plumage (head–body and innermost feathers of wing), usually worn from about OCT. into the following AUG. (details of molting are given below under Basic).

**Bill** quite vivid to slightly muted scarlet with dusky stripe along top and darkish nail, **iris** as ♂ or with an outer ring paler brown and outermost pale yellowish. **Head** and upper neck rich rusty or brownish red, with elongated filamentous crest (its lower por-

481

tion longest) of same color or some feathers may have blackish shafts, and sharply defined white patch on chin; **upperparts** from lower hindneck to tail medium bluish gray (lightest on rump), the feathers with quite dark shafts and most have pale edges (which become frayed or wear off); **underparts** mostly white, creamy white, or pale salmon (which, as in ♂, fades soon after death); sides of body as dorsum, the feathers with white margins; legs and **feet** muted scarlet, webs toward dusky; in the **wing** the innermost secondaries taper distally and are medium or darker gray, darkest at edges, and their overlying coverts are same color; remainder of wing and the tail are retained Basic feathering (described below).

▶ ♀ Def. Basic Plumage (entire feathering), most of head–body acquired beginning in MID- or LATE JULY and extending into EARLY FALL; part of the feathers of the dorsum and the venter molt gradually and continually, without clear separation from the succeeding (Prealt.) molt; in the 2nd half of Aug. or about then, the wing feathers drop (flightless period begins) and the tail and its coverts also begin molting; the new Basic wing is grown in about a month, but renewal of the tail often continues well into Nov. In late Sept. or early Oct. the body begins acquiring Alt. in place of Basic; the gradual molting of the head from Basic back into Alt. continues into or through Nov. In brief, the head–body show much Basic for a few weeks at most, in fall; most of the Basic wing and the tail are retained about 10 mo., i.e., are worn also with Alt. head–body.

The **bill** becomes muted in coloring, darker along top. The **head** is a muted brownish and at least usually there is a definite light (white or buffy) line extending from side base of bill back under eye; the brownish crest is rather short, scraggly, and seldom appears to have 2 parts; the white chin patch usually is well defined; upperparts toward gray-brown (less bluish than Alt.); **underparts** mostly whitish creamy, the belly often blotched darkish; sides of breast and body have darkish feathers, margined palish; under tail coverts have dark markings; **tail** ashy gray or darker.

**Wing** primaries and their coverts very dark; lesser and median coverts darkish gray; 4 outermost secondaries and their coverts black; then about 5–6 secondaries are white, with concealed black basal portion, and usually 6 overlying greater coverts are basally black (concealed), then white, then tips very dark (incomplete dark bar); the innermost Basic secondaries (worn rather briefly) are short, distally rounded, very dark, and are succeeded by the elongated, distally tapering, dark gray Alt. ones; axillars and wing lining white, except under primary coverts quite dark. In brief, the wing is dark with squarish white area proximally that extends from trailing edge inward and has a narrow and incomplete black bar within it.

AT HATCHING    See vol. 2, col. pl. facing p. 466. The nostril is within center third of mandible, i.e., nearer the tip than it is in the Red-breasted Merganser. The down extends at least a little farther forward on top midline of bill than on side. Head pattern variable in the species (and in the Red-breasted also); some Commons have a white stripe from below eye to base of bill (photo in Bent 1923) or the stripe may be clouded or more or less obscure (pl. 254 in Heinroth and Heinroth 1928); some have white above the eye, some only a trace, some none. The nature of this variation is not understood. For full description of downy pattern, see Erskine (1971). The feet usually are toward slaty. Internally, the tracheal bulla already is partly developed in the ♂, i.e., its presence is diagnostic of sex.

482

▶ ♂ Juv. Plumage (entire feathering), fully developed soon after flight is attained (at age 65–70 days) and soon much of the head–body is succeeded by Basic I. The Juv. contour feathers appear on the venter in the 4th week, the body is fully covered with feathers at 40 days, the tail fully grown at 50 days, the secondaries probably at about 65 days, and the primaries continue growing until about 85 days (Erskine 1971).

**Bill** somewhat yellowish, **iris** brownish yellow. **Head** and upper neck variably warm brownish with hint of a ragged crest; a pale buffy line or stripe extends from side base of bill back under eye, but (always?) is interrupted before eye; there is a small whitish spot above eye (always?); the white chin patch is well defined, at least anteriorly, but may be continued as whitish down foreneck and middle of breast; **upperparts** quite gray, the feathers soft, lax, with darkish shafts; **underparts** most of breast, the sides and flanks rather mottled gray and white; belly whitish (area not sharply defined); feathers from vent to tail whitish with indistinct drab blotches; legs and **feet** yellowish; **tail** feathers dark gray, the ends notched. In the **wing** the lesser and median coverts are pale gray (paler than in ♀ Juv.); the innermost secondaries and their overlying coverts are narrow, loosely structured, and soon become frayed.

▶ ♀ Juv. Plumage (entire feathering), timing as ♂; soft parts and feathering evidently as ♂ Juv. except the lesser and median **wing coverts** are quite gray, i.e., are darker.

▶ ♂ Basic I Plumage (all feathering except most of wing), very soon succeeds much of the Juv. in FALL, then molting is usually slower but continues; thereafter, more or less of Basic I is succeeded by Alt. I beginning in LATE WINTER (but sometimes as early as Dec.).

**Iris** brownish, grading to yellowish marginally. **Head** muted to rather warm brownish, including triangular crest; the pale stripe from bill to below eye of the Juv. generally persists late, then usually (but not invariably) an unbroken stripe reappears, white, in Basic I and sometimes there also is a white area above it (before eye); by the time all of Basic I is acquired, most of the head is unicolor, with white restricted to chin, i.e., not continuous down foreneck; **upperparts** variably slaty, the feathers with dark shaft streaks, and the bluish slaty extends onto underparts to include part of breast and upper sides of body; remainder of **underparts** unmarked white, except feathers from vent to tail have sharply defined dark markings. (At least much of the venter acquires Basic I early during the Prebasic molt.) Usually in Oct.–Nov. the **feet** become orange, then scarlet-orange. The notched Juv. tail feathers are succeeded by round-ended slaty Basic I feathers usually by some time in Oct., but in Nov. in some late-hatched young. In the **wing** the innermost secondaries are short, rounded, and mostly gray with dark edges; remainder of wing is retained Juv. feathering.

▶ ♂ Alt. I Plumage (at least much of head–body, also the innermost feathers of wing), succeeds corresponding portions of Basic I beginning at any time from at least as early as DEC. to as late as MARCH and molting in some instances continues gradually through spring; then, in LATE MAY or (usually) JUNE, the molting into Basic II begins.

**Bill** mostly scarlet-orange, but dark on top; **iris** mostly brownish. Some black appears in the **head,** usually most noticeable first in the white chin area, but also often around eye, and very dark feathers appear in upper neck, forming a dark ring adjoining the white of lower neck; scattered black feathers appear in the **dorsum,** including inner scapulars, and some white outer scapulars may grow; early during molting the **under-parts** become creamy white or even tinged salmon from lower neck to tail (no markings on feathers from vent to tail); the upper sides may become all white or have some feathers vermiculated gray; legs and **feet** orange or scarlet-orange; in the **wing** the new innermost secondaries have outer (sometimes both) webs pale grayish with very narrow black border; inner webs medium gray. The remainder of the wing is retained Juv. feathering, the tail retained Basic I.

NOTE    Alt. I is highly variable as to the nature of new feathering acquired and, to a considerable extent, in timing. Because many drakes in their first winter or spring begin showing some Def. Alt. characters (as described above), it does not follow that molting was limited to those portions of feathering. Drakes that have molted into Alt. I actually vary from quite ♀-like (essentially brown headed) to having scattered feathers like Def. Alt., to sometimes being even more "advanced"—much black in head and mantle, considerable white in outer scapulars, and vermiculation on upper sides. Regardless of such individual variation, the venter becomes unmarked clear to the tail. Some ♂♂ seem to be in overlapping molting—conclusion of Prebasic I concurrent with beginning of Prealt. I—in very late fall or early winter, but in others there is a spacing in between with Prealt. starting in late Feb. or March.

▶    ♀ Basic I Plumage (all feathering except most of wing), as in ♂, much of it succeeds the Juv. early, then molting continues more gradually in FALL; then more or less of Basic I is succeeded by Alt. I beginning at any time from about DEC. to MIDWINTER and continuing thereafter until or even through SPRING.

**Bill** mostly yellowish at first, but changes to orange or even scarlet-orange; **iris** brownish around pupil and remainder mostly yellowish. **Head** warm brownish, often the crown and short crest somewhat darker; since the head and upper neck usually are late in fully acquiring Basic I, the usually discontinuous pale stripe (as in Juv.) from bill to under eye persists until late, then usually is succeeded by a white stripe and a white area above it (but sometimes these are obscure); **upperparts** a variant of bluish slaty, the feathers with dark shaft streaks; underparts the dorsal coloring extends, in broken pattern, onto upper breast, sides, and flanks; remainder of **underparts** unmarked white or with creamy tinge, except feathers from vent to tail have sharply defined dark markings. (As in the ♂, the Basic I venter is acquired beginning early in Prebasic I molt.) Legs and **feet** yellowish, then become orange or even scarlet-orange. The Basic I **tail** feathers, with rounded ends, generally have succeeded the notched Juv. feathers by some time in Oct., but in some individuals in Nov. In the **wing** the innermost secondaries are rather short and dark; remainder of wing is retained Juv. feathering.

▶    ♀ Alt. I Plumage (evidently a variable amount acquired, but molting may be more extensive than is readily apparent), usually begins to appear before MIDWINTER and molting continues into or through SPRING; then Alt. I is succeeded by Basic II beginning in JUNE.

**Bill** usually scarlet-orange, dusky along top; **iris** mostly brownish. Any new feathering in **head** (including forepart of face, also the crest) and upper neck reddish brown; a sharply defined white area on chin; new feathers in **dorsum** are grayish blue; **underparts** more or less gray-blue feathers appear in upper breast and along upper sides of body; lower foreneck, midline of breast, and remainder of venter creamy (under-tail area unmarked); legs and feet variably orange or toward scarlet-orange; in the **wing** the new innermost secondaries approximate those of ♀ Def. Alt. and the remainder is retained Juv.; the tail is retained Basic I.

NOTE    Especially on the mantle, the antecedent Basic I feathers fade, so that the palish incoming Alt. I feathers are not very different in appearance. In "advanced" individuals, at least most of the head is rusty and the crest is well developed; as in the ♂ the venter is acquired early, often before there is appreciable change in the head.

▶    ♂ Basic II Plumage (entire feathering), definitive, differing from later Basics only in that it is acquired earlier—sometimes beginning in LATE MAY, generally by EARLY JUNE—and the Juv. wing still is retained while at least much of the Basic II head–body is growing.

▶    ♀ Basic II Plumage (entire feathering), definitive, apparently acquired beginning somewhat later than in the ♂, probably in JUNE.

NOTE    Some recent authors have emphasized an absence of molting during early winter. Mature birds usually finish by or during Dec., then seldom begin again until very late spring or early summer. Some first-winter birds, however, are molting through fall into early winter and may continue at a reduced rate for some time thereafter; a great many have a pause in early winter, then are actively molting from late winter on.

**Measurements** of birds from scattered N. Am. localities 12 ♂ : BILL 54–59 mm., av. 55.8; WING (flattened) 269–285, av. 278.1; TAIL 96–102, av. 100.4; TARSUS 48–52, av. 50.2;    and 12 ♀ : BILL 47–54 mm., av. 49.2, WING (flattened) 246–259, av. 253; TAIL 90–98, av. 93.3; TARSUS 45–51, av. 46.4 (ETS).

Birds from e. N.S., meas. by Erskine (1971), the WING flattened:

♂ "adult": BILL 49–60 mm., but was 52–56 in 40 (of 59) birds; WING 260–283, but was 266–277 in 41 (of 57) birds; TARSUS 47–60, but was 48–50 in 45 (of 60) birds.

♀ "adult": BILL 45–52 mm., but was 47–49 in 39 (of 56) birds; WING 230–259, but was 245–250 in 24 (of 55) birds; TARSUS 40–48, but was 44–46 in 43 (of 58) birds.

♂ "immature" (with Juv. wing): BILL 47–57 mm., but was 53–56 in 44 (of 73) birds; WING 239–277, but was 257–271 in 57 (of 75) birds; TARSUS 45–55, but was 48–50 in 57 (of 77) birds.

♀ "immature" (with Juv. wing): BILL 42–51 mm., but was 45–49 in 75 (of 94) birds; WING 230–259, but was 233–250 in 89 (of 99) birds, TARSUS 41–49, but was 44–46 in 82 (of 105) birds.

Based on a large sample of birds taken Nov.–March in S.D. and Okla., the flattened WING, both Juv. and Basic, was longer than 263 mm. in all ♂ ♂ ; there was overlap with ♀ ♀ in the range 263–269 mm., also 2 ♀ ♀ (of 41 birds) with Basic wing and 1 ♀ (of 34) with Juv. wing exceeded 263 mm., but all the others (98%) were shorter (Anderson and Timken 1971). As in waterfowl generally, in both sexes the Juv. wing is shorter than the Basic wing.

**Weight**    With adjustment for desiccation of specimens during storage and before weighing, and with contents of digestive tracts not removed, Erskine (1971) gave data on 301 specimens, subdivided by month and by sex and age. These are late fall data, when the birds are heaviest: "adult" ♂ (13 in Nov.) 1,528–2,054 gm., mean 1,709; and ♀ (11 in Oct.) 1,050–1,362 gm., mean 1,232; "immature" [first fall] ♂ (21 in Oct.)

1,348–1,617 gm., mean 1,491, and ♀ (14 in Oct.) 915–1,268, mean 1,122. See Erskine's paper for more figures and for graphs showing seasonal changes in wt.

Anderson and Timken (1972) reported on 319 fall–spring birds, from S.D., Minn., and Okla.; the food was removed from the esophagus and stomach and then the birds were weighed. Weight varied with sex, age, season, and locality; the mean for "adult" ♂ ♂ varied from a low of 1,600 gm. (Nov. 6–Dec. 13) in S.D. to a high of 1,900 (Jan. 4–Feb. 13); in Okla., figures for the same periods were higher: 1,725 and 1,950. In "adult" ♀ ♀ the means were much lower: in S.D. 1,175 (Nov. 6–Dec. 13) to 1,400 (Jan. 4–Feb. 13), and in Okla., 1,300 and 1,400. There was not much overlap between the sexes except when both were heaviest, in winter (Jan. 4–Feb. 13), and in birds from S.D.

The greatest increase in wt. occurred in ♀ ♀ in their first winter—34% greater than in fall; the increase was 25% in young ♂ ♂ , 23% in "adult" ♀ ♀ , and 22% in "adult" ♂ ♂ .

It was found that winter wt., in general, was about 10% greater in S.D. (where the climate is colder) than in Okla.

In N. Am. the upper limit of wt. of "adult" birds is about 2,100 gm. and ♀ ♀ to nearly 1,800; one would expect occasional heavier birds in the Palearctic, where they measure larger.

The mean wt. of 7 newly hatched young was 38.8 gm. (Smart 1965a).

**Hybrids** There are old reports of wild-taken crosses with Mallard (*Anas platyrhynchos*) and Common Goldeneye (*Bucephala clangula*), the latter more probable. This species has crossed in captivity with the Common Sheldrake (*Tadorna tadorna*), Common Goldeneye, and Hooded Merganser (*Mergus cucullatus*). The characteristics and behavior of Common Sheldrake × Common Merganser hybrids in captivity were described by Lind and Poulsen (1963).

**Geographical variation** is quite limited but obvious. In N. Am.: size av. smaller; bill less strongly hooked at tip; in the ♂ a black bar extends from distal edge into white area of wing; the ♂ in Alt. has a smoothly contoured head profile in life; in the ♀ and young the head and upperparts av. somewhat darker. Iceland and eastward across n. Eurasia: size av. larger; bill more strongly hooked; black bar in wing of ♂ usually concealed; the ♂ in Alt. has a "bumpy" forehead and, especially, nape. A montane population across cent. Asia differs from those that breed to the north in having shorter, slenderer bill, which is narrower at base, the wing is longer (which seems odd, since they are said to migrate only altitudinally); the ♀ has head and dorsum averaging somewhat paler.

Written descriptions and color illus. of downies of this species are not consistent, indicating at least individual variation. RSP

SUBSPECIES **in our area** *americanus* Cassin—described above; av. smaller than those listed below; migratory.

**Extralimital** *merganser* Linnaeus—breeds from Iceland (where present all year) eastward across n. Eurasia to Kamchatka and the n. Kuril Is.; mostly migratory, but some go very little distance; for many meas., including flattened WING, see Schiøler (1926); for a series with WING meas. over curve, see Witherby (1939); for BILL, its width at base, and flattened WING, of ♂ ♂ from Sweden, see Vaurie (1965).

*comatus* Salvadori—breeds on high plateaus across cent. Asia, limits not well known; said to migrate only to lower elevations; av. longer wing, but smaller bill, than the preceding; for meas. of 25 ♂ from Tibet and the high Himalayas, including flattened WING, see Vaurie (1965). RSP

FIELD IDENTIFICATION   (In N. Am.)   General appearance is that of an elongated duck, big enough so that a Mallard seems small in direct comparison.

In flight very often low over the water, the birds strung out, evenly spaced, in a line. Head, neck, and body are held in a straight line (as in other mergansers), which accentuates the length of the bird. The bill is long, slim, straight, and narrow. The drake's head appears black and the white (or pinkish) of the venter extends to include part of the dorsum, part of the remainder of the dorsum being black, and the very dark wing has a wide white portion extending clear across its inner portion. In dorsal view, not readily distinguished at a distance from ♂ Red-breasted Merganser. When passing overhead, shows more white than any of our other ducks (except the little Smew)— white venter and wing linings, and much white in inner wing. In summer the drake acquires a crested brown head and becomes otherwise considerably ♀-like prior to becoming flightless.

The ♀ has a crested brown head, blue-gray dorsum, and large white patch at inner trailing edge of wing with inner and outer blackish margins; most of the venter is very light. Differs from ♀ Red-breasted in having a sharply defined white chin patch rather than a poorly defined one, and the white of anterior underparts ends sharply instead of merging with brown of upper neck. The chin characteristics are useful only at close range, the differences in breast at somewhat greater distance. In general considerably larger and paler than the ♀ Red-breasted. The diagnostic characters become blurred as the ♀ molts into Basic in late summer.

On the water large and long-bodied, the bill held parallel to the water rather than angled downward. The drake's head appears black (shows no greenish) except in strong light at close range, the red bill is prominent, the mantle black and white, rump and tail gray, breast and sides white or a salmon tinge conspicuous in good light. The ♀ is largely blue-gray with crested brown head and with the clear-cut (rather than blurred) characters of chin and upper breast mentioned above.

At a distance Common Mergansers can be confused with Canvasbacks (J. C. Phillips 1926).

Downies of our 2 large mergansers are readily separable when in hand by location of nostril, which is nearer the tip in this species than in the Red-breasted, but not under usual field conditions. Growing young Commons lack most of the dingy and ruffled appearance that is especially characteristic of young Red-breasteds. Young of the 2 species intermingle.

Early predefinitive stages are more or less ♀-like; some ♂♂ in 1st winter, for example, have a crested brown head, but others have a mixture of ♂ and ♀ characters. RSP

VOICE   By no means silent in any season, but seldom heard in fall. Winter gatherings (include various ages and both sexes): low *qua-auks* "appeared to indicate feeding time," and there also was a low-toned alarm call (A. Roberts and Huntington 1959). The drake has distinctive calls, none with much carrying power, during these displays: Sprint—croaking, a hissing in close attack; Stretch-call—faint guttural call; Salute—high pitched, bell-like; and in postcopulatory sequence—a purring. When a tame young ♂ on a lake encountered a wild one, both hissed and fought briefly (H. C. White 1957).

Both sexes, when circling overhead in summer, utter an unmelodious squawk (Swarth 1911). Unpublished notes of A. A. Saunders indicate variability of spring calls of both sexes—shorter, higher pitched, and faster (syllables run together) to lower pitched and slower (syllables spaced apart).

The ♀'s alarm call is a repeated, coarse, harsh, guttural croaking *grrrk* or variant; when Inciting, a croak followed by a repeated *ack*-ing. When the young are going from nest to water, the ♀'s croaking is higher pitched, rapid, more or less continuous; it is much the same when she is alarmed while with brood on water later on. An incubating ♀ in a hole hissed when disturbed (Gilroy 1909). There is a hissing if the ♀ is cornered when with her brood. Young ♀♀, when "prospecting," quack like broody ♀♀ (H. C. White 1957).

A brood of large young, when the attending ♀ surfaced with a trout, begged with mouths open, throaty hisses, and flapping wings (A. Bailey 1927).

For some additional information, see Witherby (1939). RSP

HABITAT   (Mostly N. Am. data.)   Prefers shoal water, hence usually swims near shore.

Usually **nests** near the cool, clear waters of n. forests and w. mountains. Seldom lingers in any season where the water is muddy or full of weeds; needs good visibility when seeking prey. Usually nests in hollow trees, but some in cavities in cliffs or ground, typically well-protected sites. Accepts nest boxes. In B.C., restricted to lakes and rivers of main waterways; evidently absent from high, isolated lakes. The habitat of drakes in summer, after they leave their mates, is not well known; apparently it is northerly for interior birds, while those near coasts go to brackish tidal waters. Most ♀♀ and young spend the summer on lakes and rivers, gradually descending toward river mouths as the young grow older. In early fall in N.S., very few birds are seen on rivers in Sept., most being on bays and estuaries.

In **migrations** along coasts the birds keep near shore, where they can take advantage of any fresh or brackish water.

Most birds **winter** on fresh water, mature ♂♂ tending to be more northerly, at upper limits of unfrozen waters such as river rapids. Many on larger unfrozen waters in the interior, s. to include reservoirs in the arid southwest. Even those that winter along coasts actually stay as much as possible on fresh water ponds, lakes, and lagoons, and on brackish waters. Feeds in rapids as well as quiet waters. Comes out on rocks, sandbars, and ice to rest and preen.

In extralimital range, nesting habitat includes some areas that have no nesting trees, such as Iceland, parts of Scotland, and cent. Asian plateau. RSP

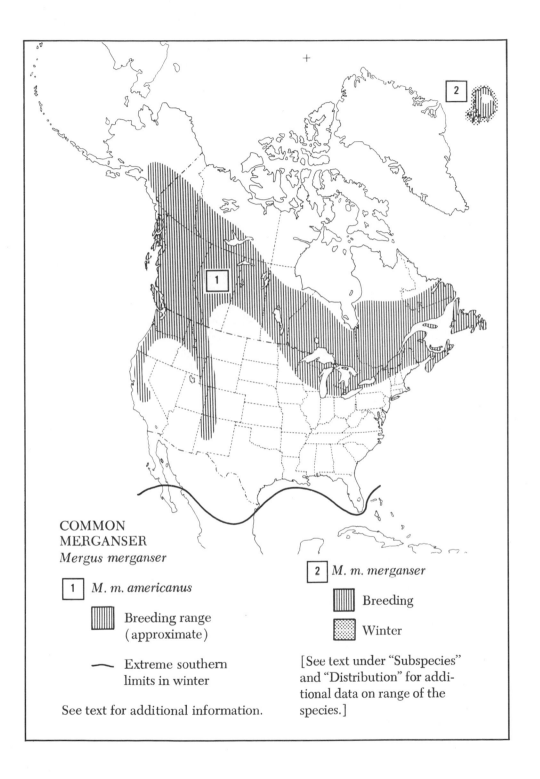

COMMON
MERGANSER
*Mergus merganser*

1 *M. m. americanus*

Breeding range
(approximate)

— Extreme southern
limits in winter

See text for additional information.

2 *M. m. merganser*

Breeding

Winter

[See text under "Subspecies"
and "Distribution" for additional data on range of the
species.]

DISTRIBUTION    (See map.)  *Mergus merganser americanus*—**breeding range** extends from part of southerly interior Alaska (and has bred on Kodiak I.) southward to include various is. of the Alaskan panhandle and of B.C. (including the Queen Charlotte Is. and Vancouver I.) and across a wide boreal area of the continent, then beyond on is. in Gulf of St. Lawrence and in part of Nfld. The most southerly breeding records are in the mountainous w. part of the continent, a parallel to the distribution of the species in the Palearctic. In N. Am. this large waterfowl has lost some of its southerly breeding range through man's activities, such as destruction of nest trees and disturbance of waters by power boats. The s. limits as mapped may reflect the fairly recent past more accurately than the present. The older distributional data, worldwide, were summarized fully by J. C. Phillips (1926).

This merganser nests, or has nested, well southward in Cal., Nev., Ariz., and a 1909 record for Chihuahua in Mexico; on the Atlantic side, s. of Mass. and cent. N.Y., there are records for Pa., Va., and 1 in N.C.

In **summer** in the interior some drakes occur away from (including north of) presumed limits of nesting, but the whereabouts of many is a mystery; others are on coastal waters.

In **migrations** occurs widely inland, especially along the larger waterways, also concentrated along coasts.

In **winter** occurs in small numbers w. to the cent. Aleutians (a ♂ from Adak is *M. m. americanus*) and sparingly beyond to Attu (presumably this subspecies); they are plentiful in se. Alaska and in B.C. in sheltered coastal waters and, to the south, numbers dwindle along the coast of Cal. In the interior they occur from the upper limits of unfrozen waters having available food throughout a broad zone to the south, within which there are changes through the season as waters freeze or thaw and probably if they deplete their food supply locally. There are many thousands on large reservoirs in the arid southwest. In the w. Atlantic coastal region, in numbers around part of Nfld. and in the Maritimes and down to se. New Eng., then scattered groups to the Chesapeake region, occasionally beyond.

**Straggler** to Kamchatka—young ♂ taken March 7, 1960 on lower Apuka R. in Koryak Highlands (Portenko 1963). Recorded from the Pribilofs, seasonally latest on Oct. 13. Recorded in Baja Cal. In interior Mexico s. into Jalisco, Guanajuato, Michoacan, and Distrito Federal (and note breeding record, above, for Chihuahua). Evidently now scarce on and near the Gulf Coast from Texas eastward, but occurred more commonly when winters were colder. Occasional in n. Fla. and there are sightings far beyond near Key West. Has occurred in Bermuda in winter. In Greenland a drake was taken March 10, 1906, near Sarfanquak, Holsteinborg Dist. (Schiøler 1926).

**Erroneously** recorded from Puerto Rico (J. Bond 1959).

In the Nearctic this species is recorded as **fossil** from the Pleistocene of Ore., Idaho, Ill., and 2 localities in Fla.; and from **archaeological sites** in Alaska on St. Lawrence I. and at Dutch Harbor, also in Cal; see Brodkorb (1964a) for references.

*Mergus m. merganser*—for details of **breeding** and of **winter** distribution see Dementiev and Gladkov (1960) and especially Vaurie (1965). Referring to the Palearctic, Slessers (1968) stated that, because of warming of the climate, this is one of the species that has extended its range northward during the past 50 years.

490

Those occurring in the Commander Is. presumably are of this subspecies. Nearly 90 years ago Stejneger called it an occasional breeder there, but Johansen (1961) saw it only in spring plus single individuals in winter. There are no records of the species from the Chuckchee Pen.

The Common Merganser is a widespread breeder in Iceland, where it is apparently only locally migratory; it occurs even on the n. coast in winter. Occasional winterer in the Faeroes. In Scotland it was first found breeding in 1871; it is now widespread, with rapid increase since about 1890; see Mills (1962a) for details. In Europe there is a disjunct breeding unit in the Alps.

In the Palearctic this species is recorded as **fossil** from the Pleistocene of Norway, Denmark (3 localities), Switzerland, Germany, Czechoslovakia, and Hungary (3 localities); references in Brodkorb (1964a). RSP

MIGRATION  (In N. Am.)  Unlike those waterfowl that travel in sizable flocks along traditional flight paths, this merganser goes in singles, pairs, and small groups, on a broad front. Short flights are low, along waterways; longer flights are high and direct. Along coasts, flights tend to be close to shore where the birds can use fresh- and brackish-water places for stopover. Some migration appears to be rather local, to nearest unfrozen fresh water or coastal waters. Young and ♀♀ are relatively widespread in winter; mature ♂♂ occur widely, but with concentrations near upper limits of range at that season.

**Spring**  The wintering of many on the Great Lakes, on river rapids in the Maritimes and New Eng., and other n. areas of open water, complicates dating. However, this is an early waterfowl, following the edge of the thaw northward and sometimes retreating in face of freezing storms. More southerly-wintering mature ♂♂ are first to start moving, in Feb.; there is much migration in March and continuing in April. At first, in n. parts of winter range, ♂♂ are preponderant; later, the sex ratio is nearer even and pair formation activity continues. Within the main breeding range, southerly nesters are present in April, perhaps earlier w. of the Rockies. The schedule for yearlings is about as for mature ♀♀.

**Summer**  After the ♀♀ are incubating, about mid-June in much of breeding range, both mature and yearling ♂♂ begin leaving the streams and few remain as late as mid-July. Most of them probably have a fairly short **molt migration** and wherever they go presumably they are more or less sequestered, in small groups, into fall. Many from near coasts go to tidewater. Harper (in J. C. Phillips 1926) saw a flock of about 21 ♂♂ far inland in V-formation, passing northward in the Athabaska delta region, about mid-June; during all the rest of the season not a single ♂ could be identified. Mature drakes, or prebreeders, or both categories occur in summer in places in nw. N. Am., and in the Palearctic even on the n. coast of the U.S.S.R. and beyond, well n. of breeding localities.

The postbreeding ♀♀ evidently have about the same pattern, varying with locality, but they move to a lesser extent and later. They leave before their young can fly and apparently are scattered. Yearling ♀♀ spend much of the summer–fall on the larger streams where the species nests.

**Fall**  A very late migrant. Young of the year and mature ♀♀ are traveling first, 2–4

weeks ahead of mature drakes (which move when forced by freeze-up); the former appear in coastal New Eng. waters in early Oct., with peak numbers in Nov. Peak numbers reach Md. by late Nov., and Fla. after mid-Dec.

Bandings in the Maritimes support the general picture, just outlined, of fall movements. All recoveries before Nov. were within 60 mi. of location where banded, and in Nov. the recoveries still were in the Maritimes; in Dec., in the Maritimes, but also 2 in Mass., 1 in R.I., and 1 in N.J.; in Jan., in the Maritimes plus 1 in Mass.; in Feb. there were 2 recoveries in N.S. and 1 in Nfld.—out of 71 recoveries (Erskine 1972c).

The pattern apparently is the same on the Pacific coast, but at higher latitudes.

For the w. Palearctic, some recoveries were mapped by Boyd (1959b). The Scandinavian birds tend to remain there except in hard winters, when some reach s. England. RSP

BANDING STATUS    The total number banded in N. Am. through 1964 was 1,718 and the total number of recoveries through 1961 was 142; main places of banding were N.Y., N.S., Okla., and N.B. (data from Bird Banding Laboratory). Some data from recoveries are given in the preceding section. RSP

REPRODUCTION    Both Nearctic and Palearctic data are cited. Both sexes **first breed** when approaching age 2 years. For details of gross examination of genital organs of both sexes, of birds in their first year and older, see Erskine (1971). Yearling drakes are not seen mated, but they have at least rudiments of display. As to ♀♀, 5 banded in N.B. as preflight young in 1952 were shot on the same rivers with broods in 1954, and 2 other young banded in the same area in 1953 were shot as "lone" (unmated) individuals in 1954 (A. J. Erskine).

The earlier literature on displays, as observed in the Nearctic, include Brewster (1911b) and C. W. Townsend (1916); the following paragraphs, however, are a condensation of Palearctic as well as Nearctic data. Activities leading to pair formation and subsequent bond maintanance are seen on warm days in winter but mostly in spring; pairing is most frequent in the latter season, since any local segregation of the sexes, such as occurs to a large extent in fall and limited extent in winter, is eliminated then by mixing of birds during migratory movement. In coastal Mass., there is a display in the first warm days of Feb., it occurs more constantly in March, and in April when more ♀♀ arrive and join the ♂♂.

**Displays of the duck**    INCITING is the main display—a quick sideways-pointing movement toward unfavored ♂♂, then a sudden forward spurt as though jumping, the neck forward and rigid, the crest spread, and guttural croakings uttered. Sometimes the feet throw up a considerable spray as the bird is propelled forward. A favored ♂ responds by swimming rapidly ahead of the Inciting bird, usually Turning-the-back-of-the-head toward her. Sometimes ♀♀ jump sideways, opening the bill and croaking. The aggressive behavior of ♀♀ toward intruding ♂♂ continues long after pair formation. UPWARD-STRETCH the ♀ rears up on water with her beak touching her breast. Stereotyped DRINKING is done by both sexes, as a greeting as well as a display (Christoleit 1927). WING-FLAP is frequent. The behavior of a displaying group, containing

492

both sexes, has a certain coordination of activities and Christoleit referred to this as "ceremonial swimming."

**Displays of the drake**  SPRINT consists of swimming so rapidly in an alert attitude that a conspicuous bow wave and wake are formed. Often a drake swims near or circles around a ♀. It seems to go on incessantly, at least in early spring. At high intensity, ♂ ♂ almost run on the surface, beating the water with their wings, or "race" toward one another, or even bump as they swerve or turn; they threaten, or a bird may strike another. A quickly repeated purring *dorr-dorr* or *krr-krr* is uttered, or series ending in an abrupt *cruk* or, instead, only the latter in series; in close attack a hissing sometimes. STRETCH-CALL frequent; an upstretching of the neck; erection of head feathers, and a faint *uig-a* twang uttered; the throat expands at each call. SALUTE from either an up-stretched or resting position, the head suddenly lifted and neck stretched to fullest extent; for a fraction of a second the bill points straight up and a faint high-pitched bell-like call is uttered; then the bird returns rapidly to starting position. It is reminiscent of Masthead display of the Common Goldeneye. Reports differ as to whether the bill is open or closed when pointed upward. At low intensity the bill is angled to about 45°, then returned to horizontal. TURNING-THE-BACK-OF-THE-HEAD to ♀ ♀, especially In-citing ones. TAIL-COCKING tail is tilted diagonally. UPWARD-STRETCH frequent; bird raises body upward so that only hindparts are in water, the head pulled back and bill (horizontal to water) rests on upper breast. The tinted underparts are prominent. WING-FLAP frequent; often linked to the preceding display. KICK drake's foot sends 3- to 4-ft. stream of water arching behind and he spurts forward from force of thrust; the foot not visible to human eye (unlike goldeneye homologue). DRINKING as ♀; see above.

Other ♂ activities include BOBBING the head; exaggerated DIVING (bird arches forward; nearly clear of water, and down; this exposes underparts and red feet); and stereotyped PREENING (various forms; in one the bird rolls on side, exposing a foot). It is possible that some form of display may occur under water.

Reported **aerial activity** is rather puzzling. A pair, or several of them, will perform aerial dives with neck extended and wings half-closed, producing a peculiar hollow sound (Christoleit 1927). In se. Alaska a "peculiar habit" made this merganser "quite conspicuous throughout the summer": individuals rose high in the air and circled for hours, uttering "at frequent and regular intervals a most unmelodious squawk". Both sexes were observed doing this and it continued to occur until about the end of Aug. (Swarth 1911). In late spring, after most pairs are formed, aerial chases are common.

**Copulation**  Either sex may initiate this by Drinking, which becomes a mutual ac-tivity; each time, the ♀ lifts her bill as she pumps her head forward, outward, then downward, with depressed crest. She then assumes a PRONE posture. According to Richmond (in Witherby 1939), the neck is stretched forward, crest splayed out and, finally the still-rigid neck is lowered, also the crest, as the bird sinks and becomes Prone. The ♂ sometimes circles (Sprints around) the ♀; he Drinks repeatedly (his crest depressed), interspersed with Preening (dorsally and/or behind-the-wing), also does Upward-stretch and sideways shaking of bill in water (suggests Water-twitch of Hooded Merganser and the goldeneyes). After copulation, he releases the ♀ and

193

swims away rapidly while Turning-the-back-of-the-head toward her, repeatedly uttering his purring call and with head feathers erected. The ♀ bathes and both Wing-flap.

So far as known, breeders **arrive** at nesting areas already paired, in twos and small groups. The ♀ presumably selects the **nest site;** her role thus is important in establishing the area that the ♂ will occupy for a time. The pair may utilize 2–3 mi. of river, this area overlapping that used by adjoining pairs. The latter rarely encroach on the most-used (defended) portion, which contains loafing and roosting rocks that are whitewashed with excreta and which probably are near the nest. The ♂ may threaten or rush other mature ♂ ♂, but ♀ -like birds (of either sex) are tolerated. Territory on lakes has not been described, but there are places where rocks are plentifully whitewashed and, presumably, even where a number of ♀ ♀ are nesting in relatively close proximity, each drake has his station.

Generally speaking, the Common Merganser nests in holes and dark recesses, while the Red-breasted nests on the ground under overhead shelter such as vegetation. Some Commons nest far from main waterways, up small tributaries, and bring their broods downstream. Many nests are in holes in trees and snags, the species of tree and height of cavity being unimportant, but the number of suitable tree cavities definitely is limited and must affect nesting distribution. In Switzerland there were 4 occupied cavities, containing a total of 21 eggs, in a single tree (Weber 1946). The usual site is near water, but H. C. White (1957) reported ♀ ♀ leading broods from as much as 200 yds. from a river and, in Sweden, Holmer (1955) reported a ♀ seen with brood in a forest almost a mile from water. Many Commons nest in dark places, such as beneath boulders and in tangles of roots where streams, when in flood, undercut their forested banks. Some nest in crevices in cliffs; see, for example, Nero (1963). There are various reports, from throughout breeding range, of ♀ ♀ going down chimneys or otherwise entering buildings. Dugan (1953) reported at least 12 ♀ ♀ trapped in cabins near Lake of the Woods, Ont.; it appeared that they had entered chimneys of unoccupied cabins at a time when high water had flooded all short stubs (their usual sites) thereabouts. Along the Indal R. in Sweden, people provide entrance holes into attics, with as many as 4 nests in an attic (Holmer 1955). Large nest boxes have been accepted in nw. N. Am., but many more are provided and used in the Baltic region.

In the Finnish Archipelago (Baltic), 63 of 100 nest boxes were occupied by Goosanders one year, with young hatching in 53. These boxes were made by cutting out the inner portions of sections of logs, then reassembling the outer portions to make a hollow log. The entrance should be $12 \times 12$ cm., with its lower edge 50–60 cm. from the bottom of the cavity and upper edge 20–35 cm. from the roof. A layer of soil is placed in the cavity. Such boxes, fastened to trees near shore, require some maintenance, and most were utilized when 2–14 years old. (Summarized from Grenquist 1953.) The writer has seen Finnish boxes made of rough-sawed lumber.

Nest sites are used repeatedly, probably by the same ♀; fragments of last year's egg shells are common in the debris under new clutches.

As to "**prospecting,**" during June and July, lone ♀ ♀ (presumably yearlings) fly among and alight in larger trees in stream valleys (H. C. White 1957), probably seeking a future nest site or at least establishing some attachment to a locality.

The Common begins **laying** earlier than the Red-breasted Merganser. Clutches are

494

started in early April in coastal B.C. and later in the interior there; laying schedules are more retarded in e. N. Am. than in the west. In the continental interior, clutches normally are initiated over 6 or 7 weeks, from about mid-April to early June in lat. 45°–48° in the east and 49°–52° in the west. This presumably includes replacement clutches. In Iceland, for some reason, these birds seem to be late in laying.

In Scotland in late April, an egg "appeared to be laid every other day" (Gilroy 1909), for a total of 8. Again Scotland: Ross (1938) stated "some birds lay every second day, some seem to have a longer interval"—of which an example was given—but also a 14-egg clutch laid at rate of 1/day.

The **nest down** is dark in the Red-breasted, but light in the Common Merganser. There is an interesting photograph on pl. 254b in Heinroth and Heinroth (1928), showing, side by side, the ventral surfaces of a ♀ of each of these species with half the contour feathers plucked; the difference between the downs is very striking. In nests, this is added usually beginning after several eggs in presumed first clutches have been laid. Various early authors, and down at least to Forbush (1925), stated that plant materials are added to the nest; such reports may indicate confusion of nests of the Red-breasted with this species, as suggested by C. W. Townsend and Allen (1907) for reports by A. P. Low.

The long **laying season** suggests that a replacement clutch is laid if the first is abandoned or destroyed. In w. Ont. a nest with 10 eggs in a chimney on June 11 and, 2 weeks later, "a second laying of eight eggs had been deposited" (Snyder 1953), but whether a replacement clutch by the original occupant is not evident. In N. Am., very late-hatched broods are common; there are young still flightless at the very end of Aug. and even in Sept.

**Clutch size** has not been reported on extensively in N. Am., but first clutches evidently av. at least 9 eggs, with 7–13 the usual spread. Stutz (1965b) gave an av. clutch size of 12.3 eggs, "as calculated from the literature." In Finland: clutch size 7–16 eggs in 63 occupied nest boxes (Grenquist 1953). Up to at least 19 eggs in a cavity indicate joint laying by at least 2 ♀ ♀. Raine (1904) reported half the eggs in a nest being different in shape and color from the others.

In the Palearctic a "dump nest" of 36 eggs (in Naumann 1905b). In Iceland, 2 Oldsquaw nests near one of a Common Merganser also contained eggs of the latter (Pearson and Pearson 1895).

One **egg** each from 20 clutches (19 from N. Am., 1 Lapland) **size** length av. 66.03 ± 2.40 mm., breadth 46.48 ± 0.97, radii of curvature of ends 17.31 ± 1.27 and 13.76 ± 1.26; **shape** subelliptical, elongation 1.41 ± 0.058, bicone −0.048, and asymmetry +0.108 (FWP). For comparison, averages for 93 N. Am. eggs (in Bent 1923) are 64.3 × 44.9 mm. and in the Palearctic 300 eggs (in Schönwetter 1961) av. 67.5 × 46.5. Egg **color** pale cream or buffy without luster; the shell is thick. They av. larger and generally are paler than those of the Red-breasted Merganser.

**Incubation**, by the ♀, probably begins on completion of the clutch or soon after. As with other waterfowl that have a nest down, including hole nesters, the ♀ covers her eggs before going to water. In the Lapland Reserve, U.S.S.R., using an automatic recorder, after a clutch was perhaps ⅔ incubated: the ♀ left the nest 2–3 times daily, for an av. daily total absence of 2 hrs. 32 min.; she incubated continuously at night, also uninterruptedly for a span of 18 ⅓ hrs. that included hatching and, on the following morning, the brood departed (Semenov-Tian-Shanskii 1960). Some authors have reported that the young remain longer, up to 2 days, before leaving the nest.

**Incubation period** probably about 32 days in the wild. Eggs from incomplete clutches in Man., hatched in an incubator in 28 days (Bent 1923). J. C. Phillips (1926) gave 28 days, citing Harper (1914), but the bird already was incubating when discovered and the young were on the water 28 days later. Icelandic eggs, incubated under domestic fowls, required 32–34½ days (Derscheid 1941). At the Berlin zoo, 32 days (Heinroth and Heinroth 1928), probably in an incubator or under domestic fowls. In Scotland in the wild, 34–35 days (Weber 1946). At the Wildfowl Trust in England, 30 days (Johnstone 1970).

The **young** climb to the entrance of tree cavities and tumble to ground or water. The duck is nearby, usually uttering a rather quiet but rapid croaking. The small downies are less awkward ashore than the young of most diving ducks and are nearly as fast afoot as dabbling ducks (although adults are awkward). They can make shallow dives from the time they reach water and are rapid swimmers. There are scattered reports of some occasionally riding on their mothers' backs where there is insufficient room for an entire brood. In se. Alaska, Swarth (1911), on several occasions, saw an adult "floating gently down a stream" with maybe a half dozen young surrounding her and 3 or 4 aboard.

The normal escape behavior of preflight young is "running" on the surface of the water. If they are startled at close range, however, small young may skulk under a bank or even in vegetation ashore, while the ♀ flaps away, along the surface, or dives. In one instance, in a narrow and shallow creek, a ♀ when chased led her brood ashore (Stutz 1965a). As they grow older, the young only skulk or dive if very hard pressed. Even when small, if orphaned they can survive by themselves; examples were given by H. C. White (1957).

There is a definite tendency to descend streams as the season progresses and, presumably, food fishes in the upper reaches become depleted; some go to lakes or estuaries, if accessible (H. C. White 1957). Such moving to larger waters seems to be the usual pattern.

While the young are entirely downy, broods tend to keep apart, seldom mixing with others of their own age or older; later, mixing of broods occurs frequently, partly from broods, when fleeing danger, entering the ranges of other broods, probably also partly from the aforementioned tendency of older young to descend toward river mouths through other occupied areas. Large groups of small young usually are accompanied by at least 1 ♀, sometimes more. Tended groups, also unescorted ones, and often groups containing individuals of different ages may contain both Common and Red-breasted Mergansers. The parent ♀ ♀ leave the partly grown young and evidently molt in seclusion. That is, they disappear.

H. C. White (1957) described the development of captive young from age about 3 weeks (captured July 2) on; 3 survived 344 days and then were released. Based on recaptured marked individuals in the wild, Erskine (1971) presented curves of growth—dimensions and wt.—by sex, for ages to 80 days posthatching; he also described the appearance of birds of various ages along his curves. In a long table, H. C. White (1957) gave the wt. of his 4 (later only 3) captives and wt. of fish they ate daily.

496

The ducklings av. 6 oz. in wt. on July 5 and ate an av. of 9.5 oz. of fish/day, to reach a maximum wt. or "full growth" as "immatures" in late Oct. Thereafter they ate an av. of 10.9 oz./day until mid-June, when they were liberated. It is of interest that they ate most heavily during March (15.5 oz./day) and were very active then.

According to Delacour (1959), this species was not bred in confinement until 1956 when 2 young were reared at the Wildfowl Trust in England.

Based on brood schedules plus data from recaptured marked young, flight is attained in 65–70 days and the primary feathers continue to grow until age about 85 days (Erskine 1971). The bond among broodmates, or in crèches, apparently endures quite often until some time after the young are flying. RSP

SURVIVAL  The only information at hand on the species is as follows. Boyd (in LeCren and Holdgate 1962) gave an estimated mean annual adult survival rate of $0.60 \pm 0.07$ for British-wintering individuals. RSP

HABITS  N. Am. data unless otherwise indicated. Except when nesting, Common Mergansers prefer to be in social groups of a few to about a score of individuals, which sometimes combine in assemblies of 50–75 birds. Under certain conditions there are very large winter assemblies; A. Roberts and Huntington (1959), for example, reported gatherings of 100 up to 1,500 on reservoirs in New Mex. Commons and Red-breasteds intermingle at times, apparently on good terms; on a reservoir in winter, however, Roberts and Huntington reported that 32 Red-breasteds were feeding by themselves and, when 200–250 Commons swam toward them, the former "registered their protest" and the Commons turned and continued on to the next cove. The latter sometimes associate quite closely with goldeneyes, occasionally with other diving ducks, while rarely if ever with dabbling ducks. Loons (*Gavia*) prevent mergansers (probably any species) from feeding in waters where the loons are rearing their young.

Common Mergansers—even the small young—are wary birds. If alarmed ashore, a merganser runs in an upright posture to water, to take wing or dive. Even when there is no wind, this merganser can become airborne without pattering along the surface, although ordinarily it does patter in more leisurely takeoff. In a moderate wind the drake rises at a fairly steep angle, the ♀ also and, being lighter than the ♂, can gain altitude faster. The ♀ can maneuver among tree branches, as when "prospecting," and enters and leaves tree cavities with ease. In the Palearctic this species is reported to perch on branches a few feet above the water sometimes, also well up in trees when "prospecting." In a winter enclosure $12 \times 4 \times 8$ ft., young ♂ ♂ could fly between platforms at either end; a ♀ would fly to the other end and turn back and return to the starting point (H. C. White 1957).

Once under way, the Common flies at a good speed. In local flights, generally the bird or group carefully follows every bend in a waterway, like other mergansers and the Harlequin. Known flight speeds include 45 mph (H. C. White 1957) and a ♀ maintained 45–50 when paced by auto for over a mile (A. J. Erskine). In s. Sweden in spring, a few were timed at about 70 km., or 50 mi., per hour (Ryden and Kallander 1964). Meinertzhagen (1955) reported 4.6 wingbeats/sec.

Except for nesting ♀ ♀, this merganser probably alights only on water; it swims or wades ashore and climbs out on ice regularly to rest, sometimes remaining for hours, and may preen as busily when ashore as when afloat. It spends the night ashore (A. Roberts and Huntington 1959) where not disturbed, otherwise on open water and moves shoreward to feed in daytime.

H. C. White (1957) took exception to statements, as in Bent (1923), of the larger mergansers swimming low in the water. It is true, of course, that birds when escaping from danger often dive again without fully surfacing from an earlier dive. White also disagreed that the birds leap clear of the water at start of a dive; they do go upward slightly but in a much less pronounced manner than, for example, the scaups. Underwater propulsion is by the feet only, except perhaps in unusual circumstances. From a study of captives in Sweden: legs stroke alternately at the surface, but in unison during diving; there is random searching, with bills, among and under submerged rocks and other objects under which fish might hide; small fishes are swallowed under water; and on ceasing diving a bird floats to the surface (Lindroth and Bergstrom 1959). When a tame bird saw a fish go into hiding it would probe beneath stones and often get the fish (H. C. White 1957). In se. Alaska in April there was a mixed group of Common and Red-breasted Mergansers; they swam back and forth slowly, necks outstretched and bills held just at the surface of the water, at a slight angle; their heads were submerged to the eyes and there was an audible gabbling noise; they were feeding in the manner of the Shoveler (Swarth 1911). For a general summary of feeding habits of this species, see Mills (1962a).

It is fairly common to see a line of these birds swimming along, more or less following the shoreline, and dipping their heads deep enough for underwater searching for prey. Various data on duration of submergence indicate (as do foods eaten) that this bird generally feeds close to the bottom in about a fathom of water. They regularly fish in rapids, shallow or deep. Exceptional recorded depths include: a bird taken on a troutline hook "in water 28 feet deep" (A. Roberts and Huntington 1959) and one in a gill net near bottom in 40 ft. of water (Harper 1953). In Okla., 96 birds were taken in gill nets measuring $6 \times 30$ ft. and set on bottom in 25–35 ft. of water (Heard and Curd 1959).

Roberts and Huntington reported that feeding began after daylight, they fed again in the afternoon, and were seen feeding at least once when it was becoming dark. Furthermore, as determined from contents of digestive tracts, they were not as successful at catching prey when wind velocity exceeded 20 knots. Usually they fed in groups of a few to a score of birds, loosely bunched, or strung out in a long line or, at times, more or less abreast. Assemblies of hundreds were spread out and divided into smaller units to feed, although sometimes they collectively formed a large crescent. There was a great commotion—a thrashing of water with feet and wings—as surfaced birds juggled fish into head-first position for swallowing; in calm air the noise from a flock in which birds thus were engaged could be heard farther than the mergansers could be seen with the unaided eye.

Sometimes one or more birds goes under, then most of the others in rapid succession in follow-the-leader pattern; then all emerge within seconds of when the first breaks the surface. Then again, in a small group, the individuals apparently dive quite independently of one another. Or there is a concerted rushing along the water, the birds apparently cooperating in driving fish into the shallows; if the birds dive and come up scattered, they re-form and continue on their course. At times they advance with much splashing made by their wings, evidently thus confusing and concentrating the fish. Flocks of up to 70 have been seen doing this in Ont. If fishes become scarce, those surviving take refuge beneath stones, where the mergansers search them out (H. C. White 1939).

The procedure in swallowing a large fish (head first) resembles that of a snake; the prey is taken in by a merganser with neck bent, then the neck is extended to work the mouth over the prey and re-flexed to swallow it, as described and illus. by H. C. White (1957). For details of upper limits of size of prey taken, see Latta and Sharkey (1966). On Vancouver I. a merganser in a creek captured a 12-inch trout, quickly threw it out on the ice, then followed it there and killed it with blows of the beak (J. L. Hart 1949). Alarmed birds have been seen to disgorge their food in order to become airborne; one was caught by hand as it tried unsuccessfully to rid itself of a carp weighing 1¼–1½ lb. (A. Roberts and Huntington 1959). That particular fish equaled in wt. the daily consumption of food of this merganser as estimated by Salyer and Lagler (1940). A bird shot and dying vomited a live pickerel and so Brewster (1924) thought that this merganser might transport fish into "waters untenanted by their kind." Bald Eagles have been seen stealing fish from this merganser (Grubb 1971); various gulls keep close watch on them and apparently get sufficient food to make the effort worthwhile.

Captive young Common Mergansers, if given more live fish than they could eat, killed and mauled the excess. They also played a sort of game of stealing fish from one another. They were supplied with green grass and watercress, which they ate in small quantities. (From H. C. White 1957.)

In former times, when spring shooting was allowed, the "salmonbelly" was shot commonly. It is not an easy bird to kill. And as food, the old birds seldom were admired but can be eaten "in a case of necessity" (J. C. Phillips 1926). Various persons have stated that the young in their first fall are palatable; one such claimant was William Brewster, whose tastes were more catholic than most people's.

The total number of Common Mergansers in N. Am. is small compared to many waterfowl, maybe several hundred thousand at very most. Owls, notably the Barred, are believed to capture many preflight young. Other predators in various seasons include man and the Bald Eagle. RSP

FOOD  Although names and percentages are given for foods eaten by the other mergansers included in this volume, in general, they all consume what is available to them in their particular habitats. For the Common Merganser in N. Am., there seems little point in giving the details for various samples of digestive tracts—74 (A. H. Howell 1932), 107 (Cottam and Uhler 1937), 67 (Timken and Anderson 1969), and so on. Studies done where trout or salmon occur include those of Elson (1962), Leonard and Shetter (1937), J. Munro and Clemens (1936, 1937), Salyer and Lagler (1940), and H. C. White (1936, 1957). In White's 1957 paper he reported on 887 stomachs. Differences among the findings of various workers reflect the fact that most birds taken by some authors were from salmon and trout waters, while birds taken by others were from a variety of circumstances. The Common Merganser in N. Am. has eaten at least 50 species of fish, also various fish eggs. Any indictment of the species as a serious predator on sport fish based on stomach analysis should be qualified by the circumstances under which the food samples were taken. It is clearly evident that the birds take what is available, roughly in proportion to its abundance and vulnerabliity.

Older summaries of data on food include those of J. C. Phillips (1926) and H. C. White (1957). Madsen's (1957) studies in Denmark are especially interesting, giving foods in freshwater and marine habitats; he also summarized the literature. The following consists of a scattering of observations in N. Am., to give some idea of the variety of items ingested.

In 6 ducklings, judged to be out of the nest only a few hours, each gizzard contained a wad of gauzy feathers (H. C. White 1957). Ducklings at first feed entirely on insects, catching most beneath the surface of the water, and soon they start to catch small fish (White). In a stream depleted of fish by these mergansers, a flock of 7 half-grown young reverted to the downy duckling habit of eating insects; there also was vegetation in their stomachs (White). White's captive young birds ate some green vegetation, as mentioned earlier under "Habits." [Interestingly, in Iceland, according to Hantzsch (1905), ♂ ♂ in the nesting season fed on water plants.]

Drakes are larger than ♀ ♀ , hence can eat larger items; suckers (*Catostomus*) over 11 in. long commonly are taken, the size of a sucker's head being the limiting factor; a brown trout 14½ in. long; eels up to 16 in. and a report of one 22 in. (H. C. White 1957, citing other authors). For other large items see Latta and Sharkey (1966).

These are some data for areas away from trout and salmon waters. Rough or forage fish in Okla. (Heard and Curd 1959) and Nev. (J. R. Alcorn 1953), and top minnows at Pyramid L., Nev. (E. R. Hall 1926); salamanders (*Ambystoma*) at L. Burford, New Mex., fish being absent (Wetmore 1920); elsewhere in New Mex. various mostly non-game fishes, including a very large number of gizzard shad (A. Roberts and Huntington 1959); 55 birds from Unakwik Inlet, Alaska, had eaten mainly sculpins, shrimp, and crested blenny (Fritsch and Buss 1958); and on the Me. coast in winter, mussels and other mollusks, shells and all being completely digested (Knight 1908).

The gizzard of a ♂ may contain a teaspoon of gravel and the harder bones of fishes may have the same function as grit (H. C. White 1957). RSP

## Ruddy Duck

*Oxyura jamaicensis*

The name Ruddy Duck includes subspecies having a combined distribution extending from northern N. Am. to southern S. Am.; another species, *O. vittata* of southern S. Am., may be called Lake Duck (Meyer de Schauensee 1966) rather than Argentine Ruddy Duck.

The Ruddy is a small stocky duck with the usual stifftail characters, including the shafts to the tail feathers and the very short tail coverts. Unlike the Masked Duck (*O. dominica*), it has no light area in the wing. The bill is broad, flat distally, with large nail angled back. Drake in Alt. Plumage (spring–summer): black crown, white cheeks, reddish chestnut neck and dorsum; in Basic ("winter"): white cheeks plus somber coloring elsewhere with some inconspicuous barring; the ♀ in all post-Juv. Plumages is quite like the drake in somber Basic, but the cheeks often are not quite white and this area contains a diffuse to distinct dark stripe; the Juv. ♂ ♀ also have a dark facial stripe, plus much barring on sides and dorsum.

No tracheal bulla. The skin of the neck is full and loose in both sexes, but only the drake has an inflatable tracheal air sac; it lies between the trachea and the esophagus, is pear-shaped (50–60 mm. long and 30–40 broad), and the drake habitually keeps it partly inflated even when diving; in addition, the larynx has within it a pad or flap that apparently is analogous in function to the mammalian epiglottis (Wetmore 1917b, 1918, 1926). The air sac was well illus. (photos: mature ♂ and large downy, the sac inflated) in figs. 90 and 91 in T. S. Roberts (1932).

In N.Am.: ♂ length 14½–16 in., wingspread to 24, wt. usually about 1¼ lb.; the ♀ av. smaller in size and wt., usually about 1 lb. (There are larger and heavier Ruddies in S. Am.) Four subspecies are recognized here, 2 in our area.

DESCRIPTION  *O. j. rubida* of continental N. Am. See col. pl. facing p. 504. Both sexes have a Basic ("dull") Plumage in winter and both molt into an Alt. ("display") Plumage in late winter–early spring. Ferrous staining is common on lighter feathers in all seasons. The first cycle in both sexes may be summarized thus: the Juv. is long retained; Basic I is acquired later in the year than subsequent Basics, is retained until later, and, as observed in captives, includes a new wing; Alt. I, being acquired late, is worn for less time than succeeding Alts. It is suspected that Prealt. molting begins progressively earlier through several cycles, finally being stabilized when beginning about mid-March.

The following important matters need further study. 1 Siegfried (1973a) presented good evidence that the wing is molted twice/cycle in both sexes of the Ruddy. The Prealt. wing molt occurs in late winter–early spring, the new feathers sometimes not fully grown until after spring migration. Although not described by Siegfried, the same molt includes head–body plus tail, i.e., all feathering is renewed twice/cycle. Evidently there is a flightless period, as yet unreported, before the birds leave winter quarters. 2 Based on museum material, it is unclear whether there is some sort of "offset" molting of some head feathers of 1 of 2 generations or whether certain follicles

501

are activated 3 times/cycle, i.e., there is a fleeting Suppl. Plumage (see below under ♂ Def. Alt. and ♂ Alt. I).

▶  ♂ Def. Alt. Plumage (all feathering), the head–body and tail usually fully acquired by some time in APRIL and retained into AUG. **Bill** turquoise-cobalt with brownish nail; **iris** reddish brown; **head** forehead, crown, and nape black; some feathers on side of crown erectile (a small "horn" on each side during display); cheeks white and this connects narrowly on chin. The neck appears especially stout in life when the tracheal air sac is inflated. **Upperparts** tawny to deep reddish chestnut (individual variation), fading in extreme cases to yellowish brown. **Underparts** sides and flanks as dorsum; most of remainder of venter silvery (the feather tips), but darker subterminal feather coloring shows more or less. Legs and **feet** bluish gray with dusky webs. **Tail** dusky brownish. **Wing** innermost secondaries elongated and quite sickle-shaped and their overlying coverts are rounded at their tips; most of the wing is very dark, its lining and axillars a mixture of white and grayed brownish.

NOTES   As the above feathering grows in spring, quite commonly there appear few to many black feathers (like crown) in white of cheeks and across the chin, occasionally so many as to form patches (cheeks nearly all black or patchy in specimens from as far n. as Kindersley, Sask.); evidently these feathers soon fall out (cheeks become all white).

Frith (1967) was the first to report double wing molt in *Oxyura*, in wild ♂ *O. australis* in Australia. In S. Africa, captive-reared *O. punctatus* of both sexes in the definitive cycle molted their wings as often as head–body, i.e., twice/cycle; neither period of molting began with wing molt or flightless period (Siegfried 1970).

In close confinement, drakes eventually molt from Alt. to Alt. (at least head–body), i.e., are "red" all year. Whether ♀ ♀ also molt from Alt. to Alt. is unknown.

The "blue" of the bill of the Ruddy is a physical phenomenon (not a pigment); some drakes have vivid blue bills in early March and most migrants have this appearance by the time they reach their breeding grounds; the bill appears black toward the end of July or in Aug. (Hays and Habermann 1969).

▶  ♂ Def. Basic Plumage (entire feathering); usually the wing is molted beginning in EARLY AUG. (flightless period probably lasts 3 weeks); the head–body and tail then are molting from Alt. into Basic and then the latter is retained until LATE WINTER or EARLY SPRING.

**Bill** blackish. **Head** forehead and crown very dark, usually somewhat browner and lighter on nape; cheeks white; much of neck smoke gray. **Upperparts** mantle and scapulars dark brownish with fine darker markings (also a buffy or chestnut tinge in some individuals); lower back dusky brown. **Underparts** upper breast gray tinged cinnamon, sides and flanks grayish mottled brownish (sometimes some chestnut mottling); belly to tail silvery white (patchy and darker when feather tips are frayed). Legs and **feet** grayed slaty. **Tail** nearly black, but fades and becomes much frayed. **Wing** innermost secondaries shorter, nearly straight, and broader ended than in Alt.; the upper surface of wing dark and unicolor except secondaries have pale tips, the wing lining and axillars variegated white and grayish brown.

NOTES   Apparently some yearlings become flightless earlier than older birds. Thus, most drakes that are flightless in July may be yearlings, those in Aug. mainly older cohorts.

The relation of head–body molt to wing molt varies; a flightless drake Aug. 20 had much of dorsum still in Alt.; another, flightless on Aug. 1, had head–body mostly in Basic.

Molting is late and prolonged in some drakes, with scattered Alt. (reddish) feathers sometimes retained as late as Jan.

▶ ♀ Def. Alt. Plumage (entire feathering), worn approximately from MARCH or EARLY APRIL into AUG., sometimes retained longer. **Bill** muted slaty, **iris** warm brownish. **Head** forehead, crown, and nape have black feathers with brownish tips; side of head and chin mostly white, with a clearly defined dark facial stripe from gape to ear coverts. **Upperparts** dark brownish, speckled and variously barred with light browns, often suffused chestnut; **underparts** sides as dorsum; upper breast brownish, the paler feather tips often tinged cinnamon; lower breast to tail silvery white; mottled on breast when darker parts of the feathers show from wear. Legs and **feet** grayed slaty. **Tail** dark dusky brownish, but webs may wear off the feathers entirely and leave only the faded and yellowish shafts. **Wing** innermost secondaries long, curved, and tapering distally, and their longer coverts also taper; remainder of wing essentially as described below for Basic.

NOTE   A mostly black (melanistic) ♀ was collected in Utah in early June.

▶ ♀ Def. Basic Plumage (entire feathering), about SEPT. into MARCH. No clear-cut facial stripe, but instead a diffuse and indistinct one. **Bill** very dark. Many feathers are shorter and have more broadly rounded ends than in Alt. Plumage; coloring quite like Alt., but **upperparts** more speckled and sometimes barred with buffs and grays. Legs and **feet** bluish gray. **Tail** dusky brownish. **Wing** variants of dusky brownish, the secondaries with paler ends and innermost ones are shorter and have broader ends than in Alt.

This Plumage evidently is acquired as follows: the ♀ leaves her preflight brood, then molts wings (onset of flightless period), and by then the entire new Basic feathering, or at least much of it, is growing.

AT HATCHING   See vol. 2, col. pl. facing p. 466. The downies appear oversized (they hatch from very large eggs) and with very large hind limbs placed far back (they cannot walk and must scoot on their bellies). The nail on the bill is large and angled somewhat backward. Overall appearance of downies might be described as inky looking, i.e., dark, with mostly blended pattern. Iris very dark; upper mandible dusky, lower more or less pinkish in life. Black forehead, crown, cheek stripe, dorsum (with pale spot on side of "shoulder"), and breast band merge with whitish of remainder. Legs and feet nearly black and very shiny. Downies cannot be sexed by presence of a tracheal bulla, since there is none in *Oxyura*; the tracheal air sac, however, is well developed in the newly hatched ♂ duckling.

NOTE   The dark facial stripe is present in both 1st and 2nd downs, plus the Juv. Plumage, in both sexes; also, either well- or poorly-defined, in all subsequent ♀ Plumages.

▶ ♂ ♀ Juv. Plumage (entire feathering), fully developed in 40–50 days, but the primaries continue growing for sometime thereafter. This Plumage is retained through most or all of FALL—longer than, for example, in most shoal-water ducks—then succeeded by incoming Basic I in NOV.–DEC. or even continuing into Jan. The Juv. is a

503

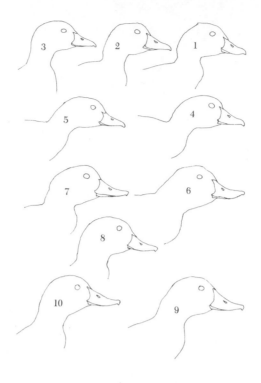

Masked Duck—figs. 1-5

*Oxyura dominica*

Two-striped facial pattern, except ♂ Alt. Plumages. On the dorsum, Alt. Plumages are longitudinally marked and Basic transversely marked. The head is rather similar in various Plumages. Following are some useful guidelines.

1   ♂ Def. Alt.—much of head black; much of remainder of feathering variably reddish; dark markings on dorsum longitudinal.

2   ♂ Def. Basic—striped face, the light areas variably buffy or tawny-buff; dark dorsum with light transverse markings.

3   ♂♀ Basic I—contrasty head pattern (not blended as in Juv.); stripe above eye white; venter palish buff (no rusty); dorsum transversely marked.

4   ♀ Def. Alt.—contrasty face; rusty or reddish in neck and similar edging on black feathers of dorsum; abdomen white.

5   ♀ Def. Basic—"washed out" coloring, except blacks; pale transverse dorsal markings on black background.

North American Ruddy Duck—figs. 6-10

*Oxyura jamaicensis rubida*

The drake has white cheeks (or same marked black) in Alt. and diffuse darkish stripe in Juv. and Basic I; the ♀ has a diffuse dark cheek stripe in Alt. and a more or less obscure one in other Plumages.

6   ♂ Def. Alt.
7   ♂ Def. Basic.
8   ♂ Basic I.
9   ♀ Def. Alt.
10  ♀ Def. Basic.
    (For a day-old downy in color, see vol. 2, plate facing p. 466.)

R. B. Bengel

very barred pattern. **Head** crown blackish brown; diffuse dark stripe across light cheeks. **Upperparts** back, especially scapulars, blackish brown with narrow buffy brownish crossbars spaced about 6 mm. apart. **Underparts** on breast and sides the darker areas are not as dark as the dorsum, the crossbars wider and browner. Belly white. **Tail** feathers narrow, tapering, dusky, and the antecedent down is large and firmly attached to the ends of the shafts, as described by Coues (1878). In the **wing** the innermost secondaries are short and straight; the upper coverts are narrow and somewhat angular ended rather than broad and smoothly rounded distally as in definitive feathering.

▶ ♂ Basic I Plumage (entire feathering), acquired in LATE FALL–EARLY WINTER and retained into LATE SPRING–EARLY SUMMER (May–early June). A soft blending throughout, with various (mostly fine) markings. **Head** crown not black, but a fine mixture of browns and black; cheeks whitish with very diffuse darkish area (not a stripe) or even largely white by some time in Dec. or early Jan.; throat gray; **upperparts** back toward dusky with peppered effect or narrow irregular barrings (individual variation), at least the barring coarser than in later Basics; **underparts** including sides more or less silvery with various dark markings. New Basic **tail** feathers are dusky and narrower than later Basics; some frayed and bleached Juv. tail feathers sometimes are retained all winter.

**Wing** At the Delta (Man.) Waterfowl Research Station, young Ruddies were captured and penned in the summer of 1971; all these birds molted the wing (including all flight feathers) between Dec. 18, 1971, and Jan. 18, 1972 (R. E. Jones). It should be emphasized that these birds, being confined, were prevented from migrating; also, their wing molt probably was "offset," i.e., followed the acquisition of at least most of Basic I head–body. There is a single flightless young Ruddy, taken on winter range (in Fla. in Jan.) in the collection of the Am. Mus. of Nat. Hist., which the writer has not examined and which is the only known wild-taken N. Am. Ruddy that was flightless in winter.

NOTE Tail molt in *Oxyura* differs from that of our other waterfowl, being very gradual; one finds full-length feathers of 2 generations present at the same time.

▶ ♂ Alt. I Plumage (head–body plus tail), acquired through MAY (occasionally beginning earlier) into JUNE and succeeded by Basic II in LATE SUMMER when age over 1 year. The earliest "red" Plumage; it is worn a much shorter time than later Alts. (which are acquired earlier in the calendar year). Acquired more gradually than subsequent Alts. Definitive pattern, but various feathers somewhat narrower and less firm in texture. The new **tail** is dark brownish. The **wing** evidently is retained Basic I; that is, the relatively briefly worn Alt. I is the only Plumage that does not have a new wing.

NOTE The drake, when Alt. I is incoming, quite commonly acquires scattered black feathers or patches of them on cheeks and chin; in some individuals, the light areas of the head become a smoky gray or brownish gray usually with black and white intermixed. Especially in these birds with darkish heads, some gray feathering appears on the neck and, scattered on back, sides, and flanks, are some brownish feathers that are speckled gray and tinged chestnut. All these fall out in a relatively short time. Then the cheeks are white. This phenomenon, which is present also in birds molting into later Alts., may relate somehow to the fact that Ruddies of the same species in S. Am.

vary from white- to speckled- to entirely black-cheeked throughout the time that they are in Alt. Plumage.

▶ ♀ Basic I Plumage (entire feathering, as described above for ♂ Basic I), timing evidently as ♂. Cheeks nearly white with a dark stripe. **Overall appearance** grayer than in the antecedent ♀ Juv. Throat and foreneck av. paler than in ♂ Basic I. **Upperparts** the back feathers have few to no fine barrings but sometimes fine vermiculations (individual variation). The new tail feathers are fairly narrow and have rounded ends; sometimes some of the very worn, frayed, and notched Juv. tail feathers are retained. In the few early-winter ♀ ♀ examined, the wing appeared to be at least mostly retained Juv. feathering.

NOTE In all ♀ Basics the dark cheek stripe is present, but typically (there is some individual variation) is a much less definite stripe than in Alt.

▶ ♀ Alt. I Plumage (head–body, tail, perhaps some inner feathers of wing); timing apparently as ♂, i.e., acquired during LATE SPRING–EARLY SUMMER and retained into VERY EARLY FALL—the ♀ Alt. worn the shortest time. Definitive pattern and coloring so far as known. As to the wing, the statement above at end of first paragraph under ♂ Alt. I applies here also.

**Measurements** of birds taken in various seasons in continental N. Am., 12 ♂ : BILL 36–44 mm., av. 41.6; WING 146–153, av. 150; TAIL 68–78, av. 72; TARSUS 32–35, av. 33.4; 12 ♀ : BILL 38–43 mm., av. 40.3; WING 139–150, av. 146; TAIL 63–74, av. 70; TARSUS 31–34, av. 33 (ETS).

According to Delacour (1959), without indication of whether W. Indian specimens were included: ♂ BILL 39–44 mm., WING (flattened?) 142–154, TAIL 74–78, TARSUS 31–36; ♀ BILL 37–42, WING (flattened?) 135–145.

Another series, which included "adult" and "subadult" individuals, the WING evidently meas. across chord, 31 ♂ : BILL 38.5–43.5 mm., av. 40.7; WING 135–148, av. 141.6; TARSUS 31.5–35.5, av. 33.3; 12 ♀ : BILL 36.5–42.5 mm., av. 39.6; WING 131–145, av. 137.1; TARSUS 30.5–34, av. 31.6 (H. G. Lumsden).

**Weight** of continental birds: 8 ♂ 1 lb. 3 oz. (539 gm.) to 1 lb. 12 oz. (794 gm.), av. 1 lb. 5½ oz. (610); 13 ♀ 11 oz. (312 gm.) to 1 lb. 7 oz. (652), av. 1 lb. 2 oz. (511) (G. B. Saunders et al. 1950); 12 ♂ av. 1.3 lb. (590 gm.), max. 1.8 (816), and 17 ♀ av. 1.1 (499), max. 1.4 (635) (A. L. Nelson and Martin 1953); "adults" in fall: 3 ♂ av. 1.35 lb. and 2 ♀ av. 1.21 (Bellrose and Hawkins 1947).

No **hybrids** are reliably reported, although it has been claimed that this species crossed in captivity with *Aythya marila*.

**Geographical variation in the species** The birds of continental N. Am. and the W. Indies are comparatively small, light-colored overall, and with narrow nail on bill. In Alt. Plumage the drake has white cheeks (quite commonly with some black or gray temporarily) and the duck has a conspicuous pale (to white) stripe above the dark cheek stripe. Southward through S. Am. the birds are increasingly larger. General coloring is increasingly darker southward, with decreasing (to no) white in cheeks of the drake in Alt. and the duck's head pattern becomes less contrasty. So far as known, the trend of increased darkness in general coloration is reflected even in the downy young.

NOTE Offhand, *Oxyura vittata* of the s. third of S. Am. might be likened to merely another population of rather small and very dark Ruddies, the drake having no white on the chin, but this species differs from the Ruddy in various respects. The drake's tracheal anatomy, as described by Wetmore (1926), is quite different. RSP

SUBSPECIES For northerly populations, 2 trinomials have been in use recently—*rubida* (Wilson) for continental birds, described in detail above and at least most of which are migratory; *jamaicensis* (Gmelin) for W. Indian birds, which are resident. This split was recognized in the 1957 A.O.U. *Check-list;* later, Delacour (1959) stated that continental Ruddies are "neither larger nor lighter in coloration" than those of the W. Indies. (Continental birds may migrate to at least the n. portion of the latter area, i.e., the Bahamas.) A small series of "adult" ♂ from W. Indian localities (not including the Bahamas), in the Am. Mus. Nat. Hist. and Nat. Mus. of Nat. Hist., were measured by H. Hays: BILL (of 10) 37.3–42.1 mm., av. 41.1; flattened WING (of 11) 135–145, av. 138.6; and a ♀ from Puerto Rico BILL 37.8, flattened WING 131. The bill thus matches that of continental birds but, sex for sex, the wing of W. Indian birds is decidedly shorter. On the basis of a difference in this single character, as measured in available specimens, a W. Indian subspecies is recognized here. This subject needs further study when more material is available.

Extralimital *andina* Lehmann V—size approximately as continental N. Am. birds, bill somewhat straighter, drake in Alt. Plumage has cheeks mixed black and white, lighter parts of ♀ rather dark, and downies are undescribed; inhabits montane waters of cent. and e. Colombia and probably has quite local seasonal movements. This subspecies was discussed in some detail, and various measurements given, by Borrero H. and Hernandez-Camacho (1958). At least some of the specimens they measured at Instituto de Ciencias Naturales in Bogota are included in a larger series which measures, 11 ♂ : BILL 39.2–42 mm., av. 40.7; flattened WING (of 10) 141–152, av. 146.5; TAIL 60–76, av. 70; TARSUS 31–34.7, av. 32.9; 11 ♀ : BILL 38–42.2 mm., av. 39.8; flattened WING 135–145, av. 140; TAIL 60–79.5, av. 67.3; TARSUS (of 9) 31–34.4, av. 32.5 (A. Olivares). In addition, 3 unusual TARSAL lengths were ♂ 39 mm., ♀ 39 and 50 mm. (!), as checked by both Olivares and H. Hays.

*ferruginea* (Eyton—largest, darkest overall (head of ♂ in Alt. Plumage has white only as a small patch on chin), downies dark and without white spots on rump; occurs from s. Colombia to Tierra del Fuego; seasonal movements probably local; see Delacour (1959) for meas. RSP

FIELD IDENTIFICATION In N. Am. Almost as small as the Bufflehead and even chunkier. Distinctive short thick neck and stout body. Upperparts are evenly dark. Drake has dark cap, white cheeks (or a little black intermixed), and upperparts are reddish brown (about April–Aug.) or brownish gray. The ♂ ♀ Juv. and ♀ in all seasons are more or less brownish gray with dark line through cheeks.

Patters over the water a long distance, taking flight with seeming difficulty; the short wings beat so rapidly as to be almost a blur—hence "bumblebee buzzer" and other vernaculars. Skims water at speed faster than any of our common ducks except Canvasback. Flies as though overloaded at stern (axis of body angled downward slightly). Migrants, in flocks of about 25–50, often rest on the water quite evenly spaced and in circular formation. On approach of danger they frequently dive rather than fly. For

507

example, an observer censusing ducks from a low-flying aircraft may first be aware of the presence of Ruddies by circles of ripples which, in turn, are arranged in a circular pattern and are made by a flock diving in unison. They also can submerge without a ripple. Ashore, the Ruddy stands or walks very upright, because the legs are far back.

Compare with the smaller Masked Duck, which sometimes occurs in same environment as the Ruddy. The Ruddy hardly can be confused with Cinnamon Teal or ♀ Bufflehead, but possibly might be mistaken at long distance for the much larger ♀ or young Common and Surf Scoters. FCB

VOICE   N. Am. Data. Apparently the **drake** is silent except for a call, which may be rendered as *raa-anh*, uttered during Bubble display. Displaying drakes have 2 non-vocal sounds: 1 a muffled flat sound which can be heard as the bill strikes the breast during the Bubble display; and 2 a short series of ascending and descending staccato sounds heard as drakes make short flying rushes across the water, usually toward ♀ ♀.

The **duck** has 2 vocal sounds: 1 a low, nasal *raanh* in threat, also to call her brood, and 2 a high-pitched, sharp *E* uttered when ready to form a pair bond.

Small **ducklings** have 1 a polysyllabic trill, perhaps a contact call, and 2 a sharp high note which reveals location of a strayed caller. Both are uttered from just before hatching until the young are about 7 weeks old.

Individuals of a brood that appeared to be about 6 weeks old uttered a high-pitched, nasal, mewing *kee-ow* (2nd syllable lower). It resembled the sound made by the drake Redhead during Head-throw display and was given at the end of Bubble display by the young Ruddies. Hatchery-reared birds, about 8 weeks old, uttered a low nasal *raanh* very similar to the ♀'s low note. This may be the same as the emphatic quack mentioned by van Rossem (1923).

The duck and ducklings hiss when threatened, but whether drakes hiss also is unknown. HH

HABITAT   In N. Am., **breeds** on freshwater marshes where the nests are built over shallow water in dense stands of emergent aquatics such as cattail (*Typha*), bulrush (*Scirpus*), whitetop (*Scholochloa festuca*), and reeds (*Pragmites communis*); the adjoining areas of open water are used for display, feeding, and resting. During **migrations,** Ruddies stop at sizable expanses of shallow fresh and brackish water, preferably where there is much aquatic plant growth and small mollusks are abundant. In **winter** on sheltered shallow brackish-and saltwater coastal areas, commonly also in ice-free inland waters.

In other parts of range of the species, primarily marsh-bordered lakes and ponds, often at considerable elevations, and extensive marshes having at least patches of open water. HH

DISTRIBUTION   (See map.) *O. j. rubida.* Older information was given in detail by J. C. Phillips (1926); there is a concise summary, containing later information, in the 1957 A.O.U. *Check-list;* Canadian breeding range was mapped and other seasonal occurrence was summarized in text by Godfrey (1966).

**Breeding** there is a tendency for single Ruddy pairs to nest, or small groups to form

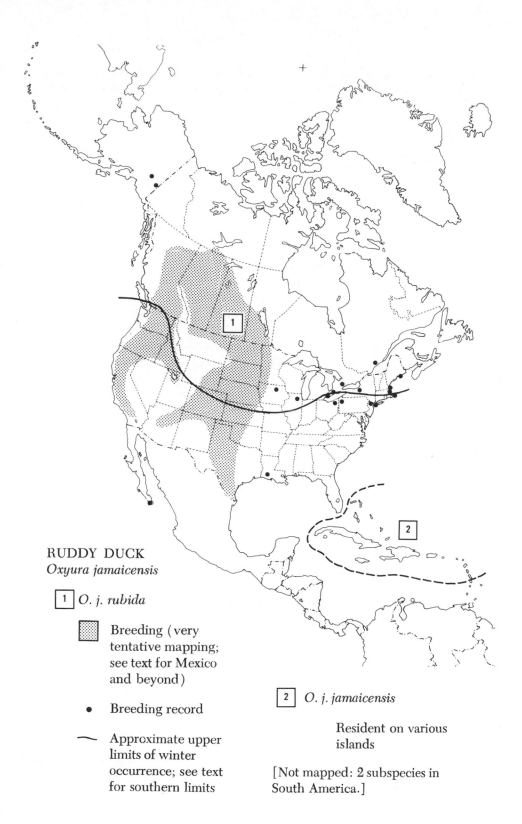

RUDDY DUCK
*Oxyura jamaicensis*

1 *O. j. rubida*

Breeding (very
tentative mapping;
see text for Mexico
and beyond)

• Breeding record

— Approximate upper
limits of winter
occurrence; see text
for southern limits

2 *O. j. jamaicensis*

Resident on various
islands

[Not mapped: 2 subspecies in
South America.]

breeding colonies, often short-lived, away from the usual breeding range. The scattered easterly Canadian records (from Godfrey), away from main breeding range, are shown on the map. Elsewhere in N. Am., acceptable records (from very old to recent) include at least the following: Alaska (Tetlin area in 1959 and 1961, Minto Lakes in 1963), Me. (Mt. Desert I. in 1953), Mass. (C. Cod in 1890, W. Newbury in 1931, Plum I. in 1968), N.Y. (Seneca R., Jamaica Bay Refuge in 1960s), N.J. (Hackensack Meadows, 1958 and later), Pa. (Pymatuning L.) Ohio, n. and sw. Ill., n. Iowa, and sw. La. (in the last in 1969). In Texas the Ruddy breeds locally s. to the Brownsville area. For Mexico there are old records for the s. tip of Baja Cal. and the Valley of Mexico. There are "colonies" of Ruddies on interior marshes of Mexico, but only a fraction of the former number of these because most of the suitable habitat has dried up (A. S. Leopold 1959). There is an old nesting record for Guatemala, at Duenas.

There are widespread **summer** and **early fall** occurrences at places in Alaska (Petersburg in 1916; Northway in 1957); at College, Harding L., and Minto Lakes in 1962 (also see above paragraph on breeding), data from Kessel and Springer (1966); ne. Man. (York Factory), e. Hudson Bay (Great Whale R.), and widely scattered to the south, including Va., also Fla. (near Tallahassee).

**Dispersal** and **migrations** The only valid record for Nfld. dates from Sept. 1, 1899. There are scattered records for the Maritimes, primarily in fall. At this season many are present some years in upper coastal New Eng. (Also see "Migration.")

Has **straggled** (presumably this subspecies) to the Hawaiian Is.—to Hawaii in 1952 and 1956 and Oahu in 1945—as listed by Berger (1972).

**Winter** Upper limits of normal occurrence are s. B.C., se. Ont. (Lakes Erie and Ontario), and Mass. (coastal waters and nearby ponds). The Ruddy occurs regularly and in some numbers in coastal N.Y. (Long I.). It winters up the lower Mississippi drainage, farther n. some years than others. It has occurred in winter on Bermuda. South of the U.S.–Mexican border only a small number of Ruddies (resident birds?) remain in the interior at this season; migrants are concentrated instead in coastal marshes, lagoons, and bays. A great many more are present on the Pacific than on the Atlantic side, with large numbers occurring (at least some winters) from s. Sinaloa into Guerero. An estimated 107,700 seen in 1952 at L. Coyuca, just w. of Acapulco in Guerero (A. S. Leopold 1959), may have been more than a third of the then existing N. Am. continental population.

In the Bahamas there are records assigned to *rubida* for New Providence, Watling, and Inagua; the species has been taken on Eleuthera, but whether resident *O. j. jamaicensis* or migratory *O. j. rubida* is unknown. It is a question whether *rubida* has occurred beyond the W. Indian area.

Southern limits of wintering of *rubida* apparently are in Mexico (Guerero); possibly the old Guatemalan breeding report, mentioned earlier, pertained to birds that were present all year.

*O. j. jamaicensis*—resident, or only a local traveler, in the Bahamas and Greater and Lesser Antilles; the various is. from which there are records were listed by J. Bond (1956).

Subspecies *andina* and *ferruginea*—their ranges in S. Am. were mentioned briefly earlier under "Subspecies."

510

**Feral birds**   The Ruddy has bred very successfully at the Wildfowl Trust in Slimbridge, Glos., England; either introduced birds or escapees now breed regularly in a feral state, mainly in the sw. part of England.

**Erroneous records**   Certain records of *rubida* that were included in the 1957 A.O.U. *Check-list* appear to be erroneous and are not included here.

The Ruddy is recorded as **fossil** from the Pleistocene of Ore., Cal., Va., and Fla., and from **archaeological sites** in Cal., Ill., and 2 Fla. localities; see Brodkorb (1964a) for details. RSP

MIGRATION   *O. j. rubida*. From interior breeding areas, apparently the majority of westerly birds trend toward the Pacific coast, many prairie birds go s. over the prairies and eventually reach w. Mexico, and easterly ones go toward the U.S.–Mexican Gulf Coast except perhaps 10,000–20,000 go to Atlantic coastal waters (Chesapeake Bay primarily). Many of the Atlantic coastal birds shift southward along the coast. Ruddies travel at night, generally in rather small flocks. It seems doubtful that any in the U.S. are permanent residents. In Cal., for example, they shift at least from breeding habitat to lower elevations, and in the other states bordering Mexico it seems likely that breeders move out and are replaced by transients and some winter residents. Possibly some Ruddies are permanently resident in some Mexican localities.

**Spring** migration probably begins in Feb. in Mexico. In conterminous U.S., migration extends from the very beginning of March well into May. In Chesapeake Bay there are peak numbers from about mid-March to mid-April. In N.Y. (Long I.) the sex ratio is quite even, or unbalanced in favor of ♀ ♀ , as the birds move from marine bays to freshwater ponds in March; in April the majority depart northward. At Delta, Man., Ruddies begin arriving toward the end of April (early flocks are comprised mainly of drakes) and others continue arriving until at least mid-May. In w. U.S., probably all breeders are on breeding areas by some time in April.

**Molt migration**   Usually well along in summer the drake, and later the duck, leave the nesting area and generally travel a rather short distance to an expanse of shallow water, where they molt their wings (and probably they never come ashore while flightless). There is much individual variation in timing; some drakes depart soon after their mates begin incubating, but some remain even into the rearing period. The duck usually takes leave of her brood well before the young have attained flight. It appears, however, that some Ruddies fly considerable distances before molting; for example, drakes (singles, also small groups) still in reddish feathering sometimes are found in Aug. at localities quite distant from nearest known breeding places.

**Fall**   First there is some dispersal of both old and young birds, primarily in Aug.–early Sept. Some mature birds, having moved away from breeding areas to molt, evidently may move again afterwards. In some years, hundreds of Ruddies occur in fall as far ne. as upper coastal New Eng.; quite a few are ♀ ♀ and young of the year which probably had a dispersal movement eastward prior to going southward.

Movement to **winter** range begins in early Sept. and extends into early Dec. in conterminous U.S., generally with a heavy flight toward coasts in early to late Oct. Ruddies arrive late in cent. Fla., with peak numbers present in Jan., and in some years many do not travel that far southward. Migration continues at least through Dec. in Mexico. RSP

*O. j. jamaicensis* is resident in the W. Indies. RSP

BANDING STATUS   The total number banded in N. Am. was 4,055 through the year 1964 and the total number of recoveries was 115 through 1961; main places of banding: Cal., Utah, Ore., and Alta. (data from Bird Banding Laboratory). RSP

REPRODUCTION   *O. j. rubida.* There is no definite information as to when Ruddies **first breed** in the wild. If some do not breed as yearlings, this might explain the presence of early summer gatherings of birds in Alt. Plumage that occur on waters in parts of the general breeding range. Another possibility would be that some birds in their first year nest comparatively late.

At first, more ♂ ♂ than ♀ ♀ arrive at breeding localities, but the sex ratio is nearer balanced later. From time of arrival until the parent(s) depart to molt, Ruddies tend to be quite sedentary, not shifting from one water area to another, and they are remarkably secretive once nesting has begun. Pair formation occurs after arrival, while the birds are in assemblies on open water. Ducks then are highly aggressive toward drakes, often gaping, with outstretched necks and ruffled scapulars.

So far as known, there is no defended area (territory); observed encounters between drakes occurred in the presence of ♀ ♀ or young.

Drakes that are evidently unpaired swim about near a ♀ who is diving. The drake's head is drawn into his scapulars and his crests are erect. At times he may swim to the spot where a ♀ has dived and dip his head under water. This seems to be the usual pattern of drakes when seeking prospective mates. In one instance the ♂ dipped his head down, caught the ♀, and copulation occurred before the ♀ surfaced.

**Displays of the duck** are primarily aggressive postures—swimming with head low and forward, gaping, and sometimes with dorsal feathering raised somewhat. They seem to have no stereotyped Inciting behavior. Occasionally they perform some variant of the drake's Bubble display.

**Displays of the drake**   BUBBLE the drake sits high on water, neck swollen (tracheal air sac inflated), head held as high as possible, tail angled forward so that its tip is near his nape. Then the head is drawn down 6–12 times in increasing tempo and, each time, the bill is slapped against the breast. Each jerk is shorter, until the head is merely bobbed against the breast, the bill striking the feathers near waterline (forces air from among feathers into water and bubbles form around breast; bill does not touch water), producing a hollow tapping sound. Then the neck is stretched forward as the tail is lowered, the bill angled upward, then opened, and a 2-syllabled *raa-anh* uttered. During this display the body feathering is raised slightly, also 2 crests, one on each side of crown, are prominent; the feathers at the back of the head (the rear margin of the "cap" is a conspicuous V in outline) remain depressed. RING-RUSH drake sits low in water, with fully spread tail held vertical. Then the tail is lowered as the body sinks so that water closes over the back. Suddenly the tail is snapped down and, with a shower of spray, the wings break the water surface and the ♂ completes a short rush to within a few ft. of the ♀. Both wings and feet propel the bird; the stiff tail (submerged) may

512

support the bird during rush (the feet, not the wings, produce the ringing sound). Scapulars and other body feathering are raised somewhat as the bird decelerates. Display ends abruptly as the drake settles back on water, or he immediately turns around and performs Bubble display. TAIL-FLASH duck and drake swim on close courses, but the latter leads (he maneuvers to keep ahead). He assumes a "dumpy" posture, the tail cocked a little forward (prominently displays the white under coverts), nape high, bill

Bubble display

Ring-rush

Hunch-rush          Head-flick          preflight)
                                        Cheecking

♂ Threat

♂ Threat (head-on view)

Appeasement:
Turning-the-back-
of-the-head

pseudosleeping

withdrawn toward breast. His body movements cause the tail to seesaw at right angles to the direction of his progress. When he displays thus (appeasement?), a duck may cease threatening and follow him. It is not directed toward other drakes. During this display the tracheal air sac is inflated and the feathers are held as they are during the Bubble display. BILL-HIDING ♂ turns bill away from an approaching ♂. Drake passing a pair will turn his head so that his bill is hidden and the black rear of his head is exposed toward them. Often a ♂ turns his head and buries bill in scapulars (pseudosleeping) and thus swims past another drake (this inhibits attack) and then he resumes "normal" posture. CHASE ♂ with scapulars raised, bill near water and open (threat posture), rushes toward another drake. HUNCH-RUSH ♂, after chase, rushes toward ♀; his tracheal sac is inflated, neck drawn back, bill on breast, and he swims "down at the stern" (rear submerged). The scapulars are raised, as though the ♂ still were aggressive. On nearing the ♀ he may Tail-flash or Bubble. Thus he returns without causing attack or escape in ♀♀, i.e., this posture of an aggressive ♂ has an appeasement function.

**Formation of pair bond** has been observed twice. A ♀, on being approached by a ♂, gives a sharp high cry and dives away from the ♂. He pursues, his scapulars raised. Other ♂♂ join the chase, diving after the ♀ as she continues calling, diving, and rushing across the water. Finally she surfaces and, instead of rushing away, "threatens" the nearest ♂. He turns and, swimming away from her, performs Tail-flash. She follows him, with repeated head-jerking movements and threatening. As they get farther from the other drakes, her display decreases in frequency, then ends. The 2 birds now feed, after which the ♀ moves into reeds and both birds appear to sleep.

**Copulation** evidently occurs on several days beginning just before the clutch is started. The drake gives a precopulatory HEAD-FLICK (much more exaggerated than when done as a maintenance activity)—he dips his bill repeatedly in the water, then flicks it up to near-vertical; there are accompanying lateral movements as the bill is raised (water flicked to both sides); from a distance, his bill appears to make a figure-8 movement. The duck assumes a PRONE postion, the drake mounts, and she is completely submerged as he treads. Afterwards, the drake gives his Bubble display and then usually preens vigorously.

In one instance (mentioned early in this section) copulation was seen on April 30, away from breeding range and between what appeared to be unpaired birds.

Pair bond form is **seasonal monogamy**. The bond lasts at least until the ♀ is incubating and some ♂♂ remain nearby after that (see below). However, if the drake approaches the duck while she is incubating, she threatens.

Beginning about the time the pair is formed—long before actual nest building occurs—both sexes (but the ♀ mainly) build platforms; their locations have no apparent relation to former or later nest sites. The **nest site** used is preferably in dense emergent vegetation such as *Typha* and usually no other Ruddy nest is nearby (though occasionally they are as close as 10 ft. apart; in captivity, ♀♀ have nested only inches apart). The duck first constructs an anchored floating platform of plant materials; on this she lays her eggs and, when the clutch is completed, she adds a rim and begins incubating. Sometimes she builds on an old coot nest or a muskrat house or feeding platform. Sites in dense cover are more successful because, if the water level rises, she has much additional vegetation at the site with which to build up the nest and so keep her eggs dry. The **nest down** is added, not in large quantity, during the first days of incubation; late nests have little down, or none. It is very light colored, small, and a specimen of it, when flattened, shows a dense white "center"; any breast feathers mingled in the down are brown, with white tips, and the darkened portion of the shafts are darker than the adjacent web (Broley 1950).

Complete **first clutches** may be expected in s. U.S., including part of Cal., by late April or early May (short-distance migrants?) and in the n. tier of states and n. Cal. from the very end of May to well into June (migrants). In all these areas, viable eggs are found thereafter for a very long span of time. In Man., a nest was begun as early as May 30 and latest hatching date at the same locality was Aug. 16, but hatchings also were seen in the first week in Sept. H. A. Hansen (1960) reported 5 downies on Aug. 25 somewhere not far from Tetlin, Alaska. For *O. j. jamaicensis*, Bent (1925) gave Dec. through March as Puerto Rican egg dates, while Bond (1961) stated Dec.–May, with height of season March, as the W. Indian season. In S. Am., broods of *O. j. andina* have been seen in Colombia in Dec., Feb., March, and May (J. I. Borrero).

"Dump nests" occur where the water level is unstable and the birds are flooded out or stranded from their own sites. Up to 80 eggs have been reported in a single such "nest," also Ruddy eggs in nests of other ducks, grebes, Am. Bittern, Am. Coot, and a gallinule.

In s. Man., **clutch size** in 44 first clutches: 1 (of 15 eggs), 1 (of 13), 5 (10), 7 (9), 6 (8), 9 (7), 12 (6), and 3 (5). In n. Cal., 8 nests in 1952 av. 8 eggs and 27 in 1957 av. 9.9 (Rienecker and Anderson 1960).

The eggs are remarkably large for the size of the duck; the clutch may weigh far more than the sitter. One **egg** from each of 20 clutches (localities from Pa. to Cal. and Ore., also Sask.) **size** length $62.30 \pm 1.70$ mm., breadth $46.12 \pm 1.13$, radii of curvature of ends $17.31 \pm 1.33$ and $13.58 \pm 1.72$; **shape** between elliptical and short subelliptical, elongation $1.34 \pm 0.042$, bicone $-0.095$, asymmetry $+0.109$ (FWP). For another series, of 80 eggs, see Bent (1925). The shell is thick and white, with a granular surface. Eggs are laid at rate of 1/day. When a clutch was lost after 3–4 days' incubation, a ♀ laid a **replacement clutch** of 10 eggs.

The duck begins sitting on the day the last egg is laid. **Incubation period** 23 days, as checked at 7 nests in Man. (it has been reported as 24 days in captive birds).

**Hatching success** in s. Man. in 1956, 28 (80%) of 35 nests hatched with 100% hatching success in these. In n. Cal., 45 of 64 eggs (70.4%) hatched in 8 successful nests in 1952, and 198 of 268 eggs (73.8%) in 27 nests in 1957, with 7 infertile eggs listed for the latter year; and 107 week-old broods av. 5.1 ducklings that year (Rienecker and Anderson 1960); and in 1963, 10 successful nests had 77 eggs and 55 hatched (83.3%) (W. Anderson 1965). The mean wt. of 5 incubator-hatched ducklings was 42.6 gm., the range being 38–45.5 (Smart 1965a). They are in a considerably more advanced stage of development than, for example, the young of *Aythya*. Weights of known-age Ruddy ducklings in s. Man.: 5 days (72.6 gm.), 11 (135.7 and 138), 16 (241), and 35 (446).

Ordinarily, the **ducklings** leave the nest when about 20 hrs. old (they imprint best at 12–14 hrs.) and dive well from the beginning. When first hatched, they push forward on their bellies, propelled by the feet stroking in unison. Four-day-old hatchery birds gave head-jerking movements very like the drake's Bubble display. A duck with downies was feeding when approached by several drakes. The latter seemed to rush and display toward the young as if they were mature ♀ ♀ and the downies threatened the drakes whenever they approached. A duckling only a few hrs. out of the nest threatened a coot. The duck usually stays with her brood for 3–4 weeks, then leaves to molt (there are no data on ♀ ♀ with late-hatched broods). In se. Idaho, Oring (1964) twice saw drakes accompanying ♀ ♀ with broods, a situation also reported in Bent (1925). The drake in such groups often distracted predators from the young. When the young are about half grown, both parents deserted the broods and molted together. He saw 3 other drakes leave their mates at start of incubation; such ♂ ♂ formed groups that were joined, in turn, by pairs that had remained together and subsequently deserted their broods, so that flocks containing a ratio of about 3 ♂ : 1 ♀ were seen commonly in late summer. Age at **first flight** about 6 weeks in wild birds; in hatchery-reared young, the primaries had ceased growing by age 8 weeks.

The Ruddy is single-brooded in the n. part of its breeding range, but there is some evidence that it is at least **occasionally double-brooded** elsewhere. This has occurred in captivity, both at the Wildfowl Trust (England) and in Salt Lake City (Utah). At the latter place, Calvin Wilson also has noted it twice in wild ♀ ♀ that were identified positively. The Ruddy may be double-brooded quite often in the sw. U.S. and perhaps in Mexico. As observed in Man., the drake still is nearby until after the duck and her young part company; if this ♂ behavior is a general characteristic, it could facilitate having 2 broods by the same drake. HH

SURVIVAL    No data.

HABITS    In continental N. Am. Outside the breeding season (also either tardy breeders or presumed prebreeders in summer), Ruddies generally occur in groups or flocks of up to a few dozen individuals, scattered about on sizable expanses of open water. Sometimes they dwell in weedy areas where there is almost no open water; there, if closely pursued, they dive and skulk away or take flight with seeming halfheartedness and drop back into the water to vanish from sight.

The Ruddy ordinarily does not associate with other ducks (nor decoys), but lone ones may join up briefly with company. The only regular associates are the Am. Coot (*Fulica americana*) and, in warmer parts of range, gallinules. A raft of Coots on winter range often contains patches of Ruddies, which scatter when feeding. Large wintering assemblies of Ruddies have few, if any, other ducks mingled with them.

Proportionate to body size, the Ruddy has very small pointed wings, the feathers slotted only minimally; the feet are very large and the hind limbs are far back on the body. Thus the Ruddy is quite grebelike. If disturbed, generally it dives instead of taking wing (migrants are somewhat more inclined to fly) and it can sink below the surface without a ripple. Ashore, it moves awkwardly; a nesting ♀ slips into the water, submerges, and surfaces only when some distance away. Her furtiveness then contrasts greatly with the unwary, almost confiding nature of Ruddies at other times that has inspired such vernacular names as "booby," "fool duck," "sleepy," and so on.

Flight intention is indicated by 2 different patterns of behavior which appear to have been derived from maintenance activities. These movements are seen when 2 or more birds fly together and apparently serve to coordinate the flight of a number of birds. CHEEKING the bird floats high in the water, neck upstretched in alarm posture. The neck then is lowered over the back and the cheek touched quickly to the back while moving lightly, once or twice, over the area just anterior to the preen gland. HEAD-SHAKING often, before flying, both ♂♂ and ♀♀ assume the alarm posture and very quickly shake their heads once or twice. The 2 patterns have not been observed linked together; also, when a drake took wing and no other Ruddies were nearby, neither pattern was performed.

The Ruddy patters along, becoming airborne gradually, but flies fast once it achieves full momentum. The short wings beat rapidly through a narrow arc. It travels by night and feeds by day. It does not roll on its side to preen, as many waterfowl do; often it rears up and treads water.

Usually the Ruddy dives and feeds on the bottom, judging from stomach contents such as seeds that had settled to the bottom. The dives usually are of short duration, 20 sec. or less. The Ruddy also feeds by dabbling occasionally. In some observed instances, presumably Ruddies were feeding on small invertebrates such as *Daphnia*, which were present in swarms. The Ruddies swam along the surface, their bills under water.

In most of the period of unrestricted gunning the Ruddy was not considered particularly edible, nor a worthy target, being an easy mark, though hard to kill. But eastern gunners, especially, beginning about the mid-1890s when some of the most desirable ducks began to decrease in numbers, discovered that the Ruddy was a fine table bird and shot them in numbers for the market. As a result, the Ruddy population declined greatly. With many restrictions subsequently on shooting, its numbers have not recovered. Because of continuing loss of breeding habitat, from drainage and drought, the Ruddy in N. Am. probably cannot again achieve more than a small fraction of its former numbers. The present N. Am. continental population is probably of the order of a very few hundred thousand individuals. RSP

FOOD  *O. j. rubida*. From examination of stomachs of 163 "adults": vegetable 72%, principally pondweeds and sedges, with some wild celery and algae; animal 28%, insects mainly with a few mollusks and crustaceans; and 14 "juveniles" had taken 63% animal and 37% vegetable food (Cottam 1939).

**Vegetable**  Pondweeds (*Potamogeton, Ruppia, Najas, Zannichellia, Zostera*) 30%, tubers and seeds of sedges (*Scirpus, Carex, Cyperus, Eleocharis*) 18.4%, algae (*Chara, Nitella*) 4.0%, wild celery (*Vallisneria*) 2.4%, smartweeds (*Polygonum*) 1.5%, coontail (*Ceratophyllum*) 1.4%, water milfoils (*Myriophyllum, Hippuris*) 1.2%, grasses (Gramineae) 1.1%, miscellaneous (*Brasenia, Myrcia, Sagittaria, Heliotropin, Lemna, Verbena*, etc.) 13.0% (Cottam 1939, R. E. Stewart 1962). The plant food of 65 birds from Reelfoot Lake, Tenn., amounted to 47.12%, the major item consisting of *Potamogeton* spp. (29.37%), and *Ceratophyllum demersum* (10.94%) (Rawls 1958).

A bird taken in Conn. had eaten 22,000 seeds of a pondweed (*Najas*) (Barrows 1912).

Cottam found in a single stomach from N.C. 200,000 of the minute oögonia of a muskgrass (*Chara*).

**Animal** Highest percentage in summer. Insects; mainly larvae of midges (Chironomidae), also larvae of caddis flies (Trichoptera), water boatmen (Corixidae), predaceous diving beetles, dragonfly and damselfly nymphs, etc. 22.0%; mollusks 2.8%; crustaceans, mainly amphipods, 2.5%; miscellaneous (marine worms, water mites, bryozoans, fishes, sponges, hydroids) 0.4% (Cottam 1939).

The animal food of 35 specimens from upper Chesapeake Bay consisted of Gastropoda (*Planorbis* sp., *Acetoecina canaliculata*, *Sayella chesapeakea*), Pelecypoda (*Macoma phenax*, *M. balthica*, *Mya arenaria*, *Mulinia lateralis*), Crustacea (*Cyathura* sp., *Chiridotea coeca*, Gammaridae, Xanthidae), and larvae of Chironomidae (R. E. Stewart 1962). Of the 52.89% of animal matter consumed at Reelfoot Lake, insects formed 45.47% (Rawls 1958).

Of 68 stomachs from Buckeye Lake, Ohio, Trautman (1940) found that 42 contained only gravel, and 16 a few mollusks (*Physa*, *Sphaerium*), aquatic insects, duckweed (Lemnaceae), hornwort (*Ceratophyllum*), and traces of gizzard shad. This shad is little consumed in spite of its abundance. Seen to eat small crayfish (*Cambarus*). The stomachs of 4 Mass. specimens contained 60% animal matter (Chironomid and Hydrophilid larvae) and 40% vegetable (seeds of bur reed, pondweed, bulrush, buds and seeds of *Najas*, and wild celery) (J. C. Phillips 1911).

Recently Siegfried (1973) studied Ruddies in sw. Man. in June–Aug. The basic diets of adults of both sexes and ducklings of all ages were similar—principally larvae and pupae of midges, especially *Chironomus*. At all ages, the birds foraged almost exclusively by diving and straining food organisms from soft mud on the bottoms of ponds.

For winter food of 44 birds from Currituck Sd., N.C., see Quay and Crichter (1965).

*O. j. jamaicensis*. In Cuba, seeds, tender plants, and small aquatic animals (Gundlach 1875). AWS RSP

**Masked Duck**

*Oxyura dominica* (Linnaeus)

A very small duck in the stiff-tailed group, hence quite like the Ruddy in various respects. It differs from other stifftails, including the Ruddy, as follows: smallest in size; bill comparatively narrow horizontally and thick vertically, with broader nail that is less angled back (retrorse); both sexes in all flying ages have a large white area well out on the wing; tail longer and more graduated (central feathers much the longest). The drake in Alt. Plumage has forward half of head black and remainder plus neck, dorsum, breast, and sides largely a rich reddish brown or rusty color; the drake in Juv. and Basic and the ♀ in all Plumages are more somber (toward a yellowish brown), with dark cap and 2 dark stripes on side of head (only 1 stripe in Juv.). The Juv. and all Basics have light transverse dorsal barring.

The drake's trachea has no bony bulla where it bifurcates; the trachea itself is enlarged in diam. for about an inch at its upper end (von Pelzeln 1870). On the ventral surface of the upper end of the trachea there is an elliptical aperture that opens into a sac, 10 mm. in diam. when inflated, also a somewhat larger extension that opens from another aperture on the dorsal surface (Wetmore 1965).

Length 13–15 in., wingspread to about 21, wt. to about 1 lb.; the ♀ av. slightly smaller than the ♂ in meas., but heaviest wts. recorded are for ♀ ♀. No subspecies.

DESCRIPTION   See col. pl. facing p. 504. Both sexes have 2 Plumages/cycle. As in other stifftails, the 2 head–body–tail molts of both sexes are spaced far apart temporally—probably about a half year in definitive cycles; that is, the ♂ Def. Basic is not a briefly worn "eclipse." Almost no specimens exist showing any molting of the wing, yet it is evident from the very different coloring of the margins of various feathers (coverts, some secondaries) of birds in Alt. vs. Basic head–body, that much, probably all of the wing is molted twice/cycle (but timing in relation to head–body molting is unknown). There is a dearth of information on predefinitive Plumages and on timing of all periods of molting.

▶   ♂ Def. Alt. Plumage (entire feathering) in Texas; reddish drakes have been seen

519

from EARLY SUMMER into LATE FALL. Blue bill, black "mask," and much reddish brown in dorsum.

**Bill** upper mandible quite vivid blue basally, paling to light greenish blue distally, the dorsal midline from nostrils to tip (including nail) and scattered spots elsewhere black; lower mandible grayed bluish grading to fleshy or pinkish distally, the intervening skin black; **iris** reddish brown; eyelids bluish. Much of **head** glossy black, abruptly changing to reddish brown approximately at the auricular region (the margin is irregular) and the latter color includes not only remainder of head but also neck, lighter portions of all feathering on **upperparts,** the breast, sides, and flanks. Some individuals have a white spot on the chin. The black internal areas of feathers of the dorsum and sides are elongated; the proportions of black to brown on particular feathers varies on different drakes. **Underparts** belly and rear of venter pale, to white. **Tail** black, the feathers somewhat less tapering than in Basic. Legs and **feet** mostly some variant of greenish olive.

**Wing** mostly blackish with large white patch which includes approximately the inner halves of 5 or 6 distal secondaries, also some other feathers; the innermost secondaries taper somewhat and there is more or less reddish brown (matches the dorsum) in their margins and in various (especially the larger) wing coverts; wing lining evenly dark, axillars white.

NOTES The writer has examined many drakes in both Def. Alt. and Basic, but not enough to establish fully their seasonal occurrence throughout the range of the species. Since there is no way to distinguish Alt. I from later Alts., birds in their first as well as later cycles may be included among these examples of reddish Alt.: Texas—summer, fall; Mexico—Sept.; Caribbean examples include Cuba—late. Jan. and in Feb. (molting Alt. to Basic), Jamaica—Feb. 2 (mostly into Alt.), Trinidad—Oct. 10; in Cent. Am., Costa Rica—July, Aug., Dec., and Panama—Dec., Jan.; in S. Am., Ecuador—Feb. 3, n. Peru—Sept. 22 (new Alt.), Sept. 24 (new Alt., also bird molting head Alt. to Basic), Brazil—Feb., Aug. 7 (molting Alt. to Basic), Paraguay—Jan. 12 to March 26 (5 ♂ in Alt.), also Sept.

In the Masked Duck (and other *Oxyura*), the tail is molted gradually, not (as in *Anas*) all at once. Beginning with the earliest (Prebasic I) tail molt in both sexes, specimens show long feathers of both the outgoing and incoming generations. In some individuals the central feathers tend to be replaced first, in others the order of replacement appears to be almost random.

▶ ♂ Def. Basic Plumage (entire feathering); few details on timing; at least some drakes in Texas acquire this Plumage in LATE FALL and retain it until LATE SPRING or EARLY SUMMER. A more or less tan Plumage, the head striped (not masked), the dorsum with broken or transverse barring (not longitudinal streaking).

**Bill** upper mandible mostly medium grayish, lower at least partly palish flesh. Eyelids apparently dark seasonally. **Head** facial pattern quite like ♀ Def. Alt., but differences include: lower facial stripe usually wider, chin generally has white- to buffy-ended blackish feathers (somewhat barred effect); **upperparts** most of the feathers are notched laterally with buffy brown or tan or have an internal light crossbar of same, i.e., lateral notches meet and coalesce; neck, upper breast, and lighter areas of dorsum have "washed out" coloring compared with ♂ Def. Alt.; **underparts** sides and flanks match dorsum in coloring, the feather shaving a dark internal area and light crossbar(s); lower breast to beyond vent white. Legs and **feet** more or less toward slaty. **Tail** very dark, but not black.

In the Basic **wing** the elongated innermost secondaries have quite broadly rounded ends and at least their exposed margins grade more or less from medium dark to buffy tan, or the latter may be concentrated in notches or as flecking along the edge; most upper wing coverts are terminally margined and laterally notched tan. Wing (including lining and the axillars) evidently otherwise as described earlier under Def. Alt.

▶ ♀ Def. Alt. and Def. Basic Plumages (each presumably includes all feathering); few details on timing; in Texas, at least some individuals acquire Alt. head–body in SPRING or later and molt back into Basic in LATE FALL or EARLY WINTER.

**Bill** upper mandible some variant of slaty; **iris** brownish. In both Alt. and Basic, the sides of the **head** have 2 dark stripes—a light superciliary line or stripe, a very dark transocular stripe, a broad light stripe next, then a dark stripe across cheek, then lower cheek and chin very pale; the pale areas of head are white or a variant of light buffy. When series of skins are compared, the crown appears uniformly colored nearly black in Alt., but not as dark and with brownish dots intermixed in Basic. **Dorsal feathers** tend to be longitudinally patterned dark with reddish brown margins in Alt. and they are very dark but crossbarred some variant of buff in Basic. Pattern and coloring of sides and flanks more or less corresponds with the dorsum of each Plumage. **Underparts** lower breast to beyond vent whitish in Alt. and toward tawny-buff or pale cinnamon in Basic (seldom as pale as ♀ Basic I). The basic venter becomes very ragged, exposing the darker portions of the feathers, after much wear. A Texas ♀ molting from Alt. to Basic on body had an apparently new tail on Jan. 2.

**Wing** general pattern as in the ♂, i.e., dark with a large and somewhat triangular white area. In Alt. the flight feathers are nearly black, the innermost secondaries somewhat tapering, and some proximal secondaries often have some reddish brown markings on their exposed margins. In the Basic wing the dark portions are more dusky (not blackish), innermost secondaries are quite broadly rounded at their ends, and sometimes the exposed margins of at least several secondaries are notched palish buff; the dark upper coverts also are marked palish buff (not reddish brown). The wing lining is dark, axillars white, in both Alt. and Basic.

NOTES The ♀ in definitive stages in superficially like the ♂ in Def. Basic; in the former, however, the chin–throat are white or nearly white and much more of the underparts is light-colored.

Dates for some museum specimens of ♀ Def. Basic: Cuba—Dec. to March 12, Colombia—late Jan. (one has unworn head–body on Jan. 29), n. Peru—Sept. 24.

The figures in color on pl. 27 in Delacour (1959) show the drake in Def. Alt., but the ♀ is in Basic.

AT HATCHING More or less black and yellow, while the downy Ruddy is black and white. The down is notably long and the bill has a less retrorse nail than in newly hatched Ruddies. The duckling is very dark dorsally with brownish breast and rest of venter buffy; sides of head, hindneck, a pair of small spots near top base of wing, and another pair on sides of rump, are yellowish buff. The one cheek stripe is prominent. This description is based on J. Bond (1961b), who included a photo of a dorsal view of a 4-day-old duckling; the tail prepennae were stated (and shown) to be "decidedly longer" than in young Ruddies.

▶ ♂ ♀ Juv. Plumage (entire feathering), the sexes similar, assuming the sex is recorded accurately on specimen labels.

**Head** face appears to have a single broad and very diffuse dark stripe across cheek; cap medium gray-brown; **upperparts** grayish brown, the feathers barred very pale (to white) and this barring is wider than in succeeding Plumages; rump marked or somewhat barred buffy or pale tan; **underparts** sides and flanks have dark feathers notched pale; remainder of underparts varies with individual—predominantly light, pale buffy, to a rich yellowish brown (resembles ferrous staining), in some with medium grayish barring. **Tail** nearly black, the feathers with protruding naked shafts. **Wing** innermost secondaries dark with whitish lateral notches and/or palish exposed edges; as in all flying ages, the dark wing has a white area near its midportion.

Trinidad—March 14 (specimen in Juv., another molting from Juv. into Basic I).

▶ Other early Plumages not fully described here for lack of adequate information. The above-described Juv. is retained for a considerable time, rather than (as in *Anas*) much of it being lost early. It shows much wear before it is succeeded by the very contrastingly patterned Basic I. An excellent photo on cover of *Aud. Field Notes* **22** no. 1 (Feb. 1968) shows 2 young birds with the contrasty 2-striped Basic I head pattern. The rump becomes heavily barred black and whitish, also sides and flanks. The belly is essentially white; the feathers on the venter, however, are darkish except terminally and so the area becomes blotchy when the light ends become ragged. This Plumage includes a new tail although, at least when first in Basic I head–body, the birds still have the full Juv. tail and occasionally even the long prepennae still attached to a few of the feathers. Presumably there is a new Basic I wing.

Specimens seen in Basic I include: Texas—Nov. 4 (photo), Panama—March 12, Argentina—Sept. 3.

▶ ♂♀ Alt. I Plumage—apparently indistinguishable from later Alts.

**Measurements** of birds from scattered parts of range of the species, 12 ♂: BILL 31–34 mm., av. 32.8; WING 142–148, av. 145; TAIL 81–85, av. 82; TARSUS 26–29, av. 27.6;   12 ♀: BILL 32–35 mm., av. 33.8; WING 136–148, av. 142.5; TAIL 74–86, av. 80; TARSUS 27–28, av. 27.4 (ETS).

For meas. of 5 ♂ and 5 ♀, the WING meas. across chord, see Wetmore (1965).

If the WING is renewed twice/cycle, it is possible that it does not measure the same both times.

**Weight** of birds without specified date or locality, mean and standard error: 4 ♂ 359 ± 36 gm. and 3 ♀ 368 ± 23.6 (F. A. Hartman 1961). In Cuba in mid-Sept., a ♂ "adult" 386 gm., "first year plumage" 275, and 2 corresponding ♀ 445 and 275 gm. (Ripley and Watson 1956).

**Hybrids** none reported.

**Geographical** variation none reported in morphological characters, but obviously it exists in timing of various events in the annual cycle that extends from one temperate zone to the other. RSP

FIELD IDENTIFICATION   The Masked Duck might be likened to an under-sized long-tailed Ruddy, with drake in Alt. Plumage having the black cap shifted so as to cover the front half of the head; and in other known post-Juv. Plumages of the drake and all Plumages of the duck, the face has 2 dark longitudinal stripes, 1 more than the Ruddy. The Juv. Masked Duck and the Ruddy in Juv. and Basic I, however, all have a single, diffuse, dark cheek stripe. Neck, dorsum, etc., of the Masked Duck vary from predominantly deep reddish brown (in drakes with black facial mask) to paler reddish browns to tan to grayish, depending on age and season, in birds with striped faces.

Singles are seen, also pairs and small groups, but flocks of over 20 seldom have been reported. Even more than in the Ruddy, the head of swimming Masked Ducks seems disproportionately large. When resting on the water or swimming in "normal" fashion, the tail may be on the surface of the water, or parallel and above it, or angled quite steeply upward, or sometimes vertical or even angled slightly forward. Or a bird may decrease its buoyancy until only the head and end of the vertical tail are visible, then vanish from sight altogether. This little duck tends to shun open expanses of water much of the time and stays close to or within stands of aquatic vegetation. The white patch within the wing is a diagnostic character when the Masked Duck is in flight. It seems unlikely that this species would be mistaken for a grebe, the Cinnamon Teal, or even the Ruddy Duck. For further information, see Slud (1964). RSP

VOICE   Generally silent. Its voice has not been adequately described.

Drake: very distinctive *kirri-kirroo kirri-kirroo kirroo kirroo kirroo* and will utter this in response to man-made noises (W. Percy, in Barbour 1923). An almost inaudible dull *oo-oo-oo* "low in the throat" (Slud 1964). Little puffing sounds when displaying (L. I. Davis) are nonvocal, as in the Ruddy's Bubble display.

Duck: short hissing noise, repeated several times (W. Percy, in Barbour 1923).

Sex not stated: a sound very like clucking of a hen to her chicks; another sound, reminiscent of a short note from a motor horn (English 1916).

"Immatures" utter high-pitched whistling peeping sounds (Johnsgard and Hagemeyer 1969). RSP

HABITAT   Pools, freshwater ponds, saltwater ponds with mangroves, lakes, lagoons, swamps, and quiet stretches of waterways; the ideal combination consists of at least some open water plus areas of emergent aquatic vegetation, such as gallinules inhabit. Also rice plantations in Cuba. See "Reproduction" for some information on location of nests. RSP

DISTRIBUTION   For the species throughout its range, older information was summarized by J. C. Phillips (1926). For the U.S., the recent paper by Johnsgard and Hagemeyer (1969), which cited numerous sources of information, is drawn on heavily here. In the U.S., the Masked Duck now **occurs all year,** and also **has bred,** in se. Texas; most or all occurrences elsewhere appear to be **storm-driven individuals,** probably from the Caribbean area.

**U.S. records prior to 1900,** in chronological order: Wis.—Nov. 1870, near New-ville, ♀ captured; Mass.—Aug. 27, 1889, near Malden, ♂ shot; Texas—1891, 5 mi. n.

of Brownsville, ♂ killed July 18 and, on July 22, a ♀ killed and several other Masked Ducks seen.

NOTE    Except for Forbush (1925), all compilers through 1969 consistently have listed as the first U.S. record the alleged capture of a drake in Vt., at Missisquoi Bay on L. Champlain, on Sept. 26, 1857. As first reported, it was claimed that this bird was flying when shot by a boy, also that it was acquired the same day by H. D. Morse. In Morse's name, the specimen was presented by Dr. Samuel Cabot, Jr., to the Boston Soc. of Nat. Hist. at a meeting on May 5, 1858. According to Howe (1902), "Mr. Samuel Henshaw has called my attention to the fact that the specimen . . . has its right wing clipped, and was thus probably not a wild straggler in Vermont, but an escaped tame bird."

**Present main range in U.S.** is in Texas. In addition to the 1891 occurrences just listed, the few records prior to 1941 were:  Eagle Nest L. (Brazoria Co.), Jan. 2, 1927, ♂ in flesh obtained from a hunter; Harlingen, Dec. 1936, one seen; near Brownsville, Sept. 1937, eight seen; Harlingen, "prior to 1941," singles seen on various occasions and breeding suspected.

In the 1940s it was recorded in Aransas Co.; in the 1950s in Hidalgo and in Cameron Co.; and in the period 1962–68 inclusive it was recorded in a total of 10 counties and scattered reports subsequently seem to indicate that it is now established at a few localities.

Seldom are more than several Masked Ducks seen together in Texas, rarely up to 9, plus a flock of 24 at the Aransas Nat. Wildl. Refuge in Dec. 1948.

The Masked Duck bred in Chambers Co. at the Anahuac Nat. Wildl. Refuge in 1967—4 small young on Oct. 2 and a young bird of another age on Nov. 16; and in Brooks Co. near Falfurrias, clutch of 6 eggs hatched successfully in fall of 1968.

**Other occurrences in U.S.** are listed here from s. to n. by locality:

Fla.—near Key West, April 13, 1955, bird found dead; L. Okechobee in 1956–57 hunting season, bird shot, and another in 1957; Loxahatchee Nat. Wildl. Refuge, Jan. 6, 1962, 3 seen, and in 1963 a bird seen Jan. 15, Feb. 11, and collected on March 5; near Lantana, Dec. 25–30, 1966, "immature" ♂ seen (2nd occurrence there in 4 winters); Loxahatchee Refuge, Feb. 13–March 2, 1971, ♂ seen. Thus records are mostly at or near the Loxahatchee Refuge, inland in se. Fla. s. of Palm Beach.

La.—a few mi. s. of L. Charles, Dec. 23, 1933, ♀ shot; n. of Holly Beach, ♂ seen in 1970 and ♀ shot Jan. 7, 1971.

Ga.—near Valdosta, April 11, 1961, bird seen and photographed.

Iowa—w. part of state, March 1965, ♂ seen.

Md.—Elkton, Sept. 8, 1905, ♂ shot.

N.J.—Brigantine Nat. Wildl. Refuge, Dec. 6 and 29, 1960, ♂ seen.

**Elsewhere**    Caribbean area—occurs virtually throughout the Antilles, including Grand Cayman and Swan I., but rare e. of Hispaniola (J. Bond 1961b). It was resident and breeding on Grand Cayman about 1916, but Johnston et al. (1971) reported "present status uncertain." Specimens were taken in Puerto Rico in 1943–46 (V. Biaggi, Jr.), but Westerman (1953) stated that this duck may have been extirpated there. This secretive duck seems able to hold its own in the Lesser Antilles, whereas the Ruddy has been virtually exterminated (J. Bond 1966).

Mexico—known distribution (probably resident in most places whence reported) is spotty; on Pacific side in Sinaloa, Nayarit, Jalisco, and Colima, and on Atlantic side in Tamaulipas and Veracruz.

S. Am.—has straggled away from usual range to near Concepción in Chile.

Reported as **fossil** in the Pleistocene of Brazil; see Brodkorb (1964a) for full citation. RSP

MIGRATION Evidently rather sedentary, with some shifting about to congregate for pair formation activities, also occasional wandering but more frequently driven by tropical cyclones of hurricane intensity. Probably a nocturnal traveler under normal conditions. RSP

REPRODUCTION Scant information. In Venezuela in May, groups of 5–15 individuals stayed on areas of open water (Conover, in Bent 1925); probably they display in such conspicuous gatherings. Almost nothing is known about **displays.** Near Harlingen, Texas, the only drake seen displayed during a period lasting several weeks. "When in display posture with tail spread and bill held down, it sometimes made little puffing sounds [compare with Bubble display of the Ruddy Duck]; it also made very fast bursts of speed, for short distances, with head held forward [compare with Ringrush of the Ruddy]" (L. I. Davis). The Bubble display of the Masked Duck, as seen in Venezuela, also was described by Ginés and Aveledo (1958). Nothing is known about spacing of **nests,** other than reports of a single pair on a pond or small water area. The nest bowl, made of reeds and the like, is concealed amidst growing vegetation. In w. Cuba the nests are on mattings of broken rice stems in among the growing rice (J. Bond 1958). There is an old report of a nest having very little "lining," evidently meaning nest down. Judging from fragments of data, going from s. to n., **full clutches** probably can be expected as follows: Sept.–Nov. in Argentina; Oct.–March in Panama; Nov.–Dec. in Martinique; June, Aug. (mainly?), and Nov. in Cuba; Nov.–Dec. in Yucatan; June–Aug. in w. Mexico; and at least Sept.–Oct. in Texas. Reports of **clutch size** vary from 4–6 eggs (Panama) to 8 clutches of 8–18 (Cuba), the 18 presumably joint laying by at least 2 ♀ ♀. Five **eggs** from Cuba: **size** length 53.7–55.6 mm. and breadth 40–41.6; they were subelliptical in **shape,** decidedly smaller and with smoother shell than Ruddy eggs, and **color** was pale buff to buffy white (J. Bond 1958). There is no information on incubation period, rearing stage, or age at first flight. Mature drakes are in Basic Plumage (have striped faces) at a time when the young still are growing.

NOTE Certain eggs, reported as of this species, from Jamaica, Trinidad, and Yucatan, are Ruddy Duck eggs; see J. Bond (1958) for details. RSP

HABITS Unwary, almost tame, where not molested. Feeds by day and probably travels mainly at night. It is a very expert diver. The Masked Duck usually is reported as occurring in pairs and small groups, seldom near other ducks except perhaps the Ruddy, in the same environment occupied by small grebes, coots, and gallinules. If disturbed, also sometimes when alighting, it pumps its head up and down. Escape behavior includes swimming away while submerging, like a leaking ship going down on an even keel (English 1916), or diving, and occasionally taking wing. It swims and crawls in the tangle of water plants; some museum specimens have the body feathering badly worn, the tail feathers reduced nearly to naked shafts. It rests on supporting vegetation, or floating objects, or at the water's edge, generally close to or in shelter of plant growth. It is said to be "quite agile" when on solid ground; also, adults readily climb up on marsh grasses in order to scan the surrounding area (Johnsgard and Hagemeyer 1969). It is known to flutter along the water surface while gaining momentum to become fully airborne (like the Ruddy), also to rise vertically (like a teal). It alights by skidding to a stop on open water, or by stalling in forward flight and then dropping vertically a few ft. Vertical takeoff and landing are necessary adaptations for getting out of and into plant growth or water strewn with flotsam. Although some authors claim that the Masked Duck seldom flies, Percy (in Barbour 1923) found that, in late summer and autumn in Cuba, they flew about a good deal, especially early and late in the day.

For additional information, see especially Bent (1925), J. C. Phillips (1926), Slud (1964), Wetmore (1965), and authors they cited. RSP

FOOD Apparently largely vegetable. Little precise information. Birds taken in Brazil and Jamaica had eaten seeds (von Pelzeln 1870, Gosse 1847). According to Gundlach (J. C. Phillips 1926), food consists of seeds of grasses, also roots, tubers, insects, and small crustaceans. Three birds collected in Cuba in Jan. had fed mainly on seeds of smartweed (*Polygonum hydropiperoides*) and a few seeds of a sedge (*Fimbristylis*), dodder (*Cuscuta*), sawgrass (*Cladium jamaicensis*), and waterlily (*Castalia*) (Phillips, Cottam 1939). AWS

## Literature Cited in Volumes 2 and 3

Book titles, when translated into English, are enclosed in brackets.

References listed below, and as cited in text, are to original publication or a stated edition, regardless of language; if an item also has been published in English translation, this information is added to the citation.

Initials usually are omitted, except when there is a need to distinguish among different authors having the same surname.

After an author's papers are listed, those of which he also is senior coauthor are listed chronologically rather than alphabetically by coauthor.

Abdulali 1949 *Journ. Bombay Nat. Hist. Soc.* **48** 585–86.    Aber and Vowinkel 1972 *Arctic* **25** 263–71.    Adams 1947 *Brit. Birds* **40** 186–87.    Addy 1953 U.S. Dept. Interior, Fish and Wildlife Serv., *Spec. Sci. Rept.—Wildlife* no. 19.    Ahlén and Andersson 1970 *Ornis Scandinavica* **1** 83–106.    Airey 1955 *Bird Study* **2** 143–50.    Alcorn, G. D. 1968 *Condor* **70** 185.    Alcorn, J. R. 1953 *Condor* **55** 151–52.    Aldrich 1946 *Wilson Bull.* **58** 94–103, Aldrich (ed.) 1949 U.S. Dept. Interior, Fish and Wildlife Serv., *Spec. Sci. Rept.—Wildlife* no. 1.    Aldrich and Baer 1970 *Wilson Bull.* **82** 63–73.    Alford 1920 *Brit. Birds* **14** 106–10.    Ali 1943 *Journ. Bombay Nat. Hist. Soc.* **44** 127–30, 1953 *The Birds of Travancore and Cochin* (Bombay).    Alison 1973 *Bird-Banding* **44** 61–62, 1974 *Auk* **91** 188.    Allen, A. A. 1951 *Nat. Geog. Mag.* **100** 514–39.    Allen, P. 1814 *Hist. of the Exped. under the Command of Captains Lewis and Clark* **2** (Philadelphia).    Alpheraky 1905 *The Geese of Europe and Asia* (London).    Am. Ornithol. Union 1957 *Check-list of North Am. Birds*, 5th ed. (Baltimore).    Anderson, B. W. et al. 1969 *Journ. Wildlife Mgt.* **33** 209–12.    Anderson, B. W., and Timken 1969 *Auk* **86** 556–57.    Anderson, B. W., and Werner 1969a *Bird-Banding* **40** 85–94, 1969b *Bird-Banding* **40** 198–207.    Anderson, D. R., and Henny 1972 U.S. Dept. Interior, Fish and Wildlife Serv., Bur. Sport Fisheries and Wildlife, *Resource Pub.* no. 105.    Anderson, D. W. 1970 *Condor* **72** 370–71.    Anderson, H. G. 1959 Ill. Nat. Hist. Surv. *Bull.* **27** 289–344.    Anderson, W. 1956 *Calif. Fish and Game* **42** 117–30, 1957 *Calif. Fish and Game* **43** 71–90, 1965 *Calif. Fish and Game* **51** 5–15.    Anderson, W., and Miller 1953 *Condor* **55** 152–53.    Ardamatskaya 1963 *Ornitologiya* no. 6: 293–302, 1965 *Ornitologiya* no. 7: 456–57.    Armstrong 1954 *Ibis* **96** 1–30, 1958 *The Folklore of Birds* (London).    Arnhem 1959 *Gerfaut* **49** 43–51.    Arnold 1963 *Condor* **65** 442.    Arthur 1920 *Auk* **37** 126–27.    Atkinson-Willes (ed.) 1963 *Wildfowl in Great Britain* (London), 1969 *Wildfowl* no. 20: 98–111.    Atlantic Waterfowl Council 1968 *The Black Duck . . . a Symposium* (Bolton, Mass.).    Atwater 1959 *Journ. Wildlife Mgt.* **23** 91–96.    Audubon 1835 *Ornithological Biography* 3, 1838 *Ornithological Biography* 4, 1843 *The Birds of America* 6 (New York and Philadelphia).    Austin, G. T. 1970 *Condor* **72** 474.    Austin, O. L., Jr., 1949 *Waterfowl of Japan* (Gen. Hq., Supreme Comdr. for Allied Powers, Nat. Resources Sect., Rept. no. 118. Tokyo).    Austin, O. L., Jr., and Kuroda 1953 *Bull. Mus. Comp. Zool. Harvard* **109** no. 4.    Aymar 1935 *Bird Flight* (Garden City, N.Y.).

Bagg and Eliot 1933 *Auk* **50** 430–31.    Bailey 1923 *Nat. Hist.* **23** 172–81, 1925 *Condor* **27** 197–207, 1927 *Auk* **44** 184–205, 1928 *Auk* **45** 271–82, 1930 *Condor* **32** 264–65, 1943 *Proc. Colo. Mus. Nat. Hist.* **18** no. 1, 1948 *Birds of Arctic Alaska* (Denver: Colo. Mus. Nat. Hist), 1956 *Auk* **73** 560.    Bailey et al. 1933 Chicago Acad. Sci. *Program of Activities* 4 no. 2.    Bailey and Niedrach 1965 *Birds of Colo.* 1 (Denver).    Baillie 1963 *Ont. Field Biol.* no. 17: 15–26, 1964 *Ont. Field Biol.* no. 18: 1–13, 1969 *Ont. Nat.* no. 1 (for 1969): 7, 28–30.    Baird, J. 1963 *Aud. Field Notes* **17** 4–8.    Baird, S. F. 1873 *Forest and Stream* **2** 5.    Baird, S. F. et al. 1884a *Water Birds of N. Am.* 1 (Boston), 1884b *Water Birds of N. Am.* 2.    Baker, E. C. S. 1929 *The Fauna of Brit. India . . . Birds*, 2nd ed. 6 (London).    Baker, E. J. 1954 *Bull. Me. Aud. Soc.* **10** 40–43, 1956 *Me. Field Nat.* **12** 77.    Baker, F. C. 1889 *Ornithol. and Ool.* **14** 139–40, 1890 *Proc. Acad. Nat. Sci. Phila.* for 1889 **41** 266–70.    Baker, J. R. 1938 *Proc. Zool. Soc. London* **108-A** 557–82.    Balát 1969 *Zool. Listy* **18** 247–52.    Balát and Folk 1968 *Zool. Listy* **17** 327–40.    Balham 1952 *Emu* **52** 163–91, 1954 *The Behavior of the Canada Goose . . . in Man.* (Univ. of Mo., Ph.D. thesis).    Balham and Miers 1959 N.Z. Dept. Internal Affairs, *Wildlife Pub.* no. 5.    Ball 1934 Peabody Mus. Nat. Hist. (Yale) *Bull.* no. 3.    Bangs 1918 *Proc. New Eng. Zool. Club* **6** 87–89.    Banko 1960 *N. Am. Fauna* no. 63.    Bannerman 1957 *The Birds of the Brit. Isles* 6 (Edinburgh), 1958 *The Birds of the Brit. Isles* 7.    Barbour 1923 *Mem. Nuttall Orn. Club* no. 6.    Barnes 1929 *Oologist* **46** 130.    Barnhart 1901 *Condor* **3** 67–68.    Barrows 1912 *Mich. Bird Life* (Lansing, Mich.).    Barry 1956 *Auk* **73** 193–202, 1962 *Journ. Wildlife Mgt.* **26** 19–26, 1968 *Can. Field-Nat.* **82** 140–44.    Barry and Eisenhart 1958 *Auk* **75** 89–90.    Bartlett, C. O. 1960 *Can. Field-Nat.* **74** 153–55.    Bartlett, L. M. 1955 *Auk* **72** 297.    Bartonek 1969 *Wilson Bull.* **81** 96–97, 1972 *Can. Field-Nat.* **86** 373–76.    Bartonek and Hickey 1969 *Condor* **71** 280–90.    Bartonek and Murdy 1970 *Arctic* **23** 35–44.    Bartonek et al. 1971 *Trans. 36th N. Am. Wildl. and Nat. Resources Conf.* 345–61.    Batty and Cave 1963 *Brit. Birds* **56** 190–91.    Bauer and Glutz von Blotzheim 1968 *Handb. d. Vögel Mitteleuropas* 2 (Frankfurt am Main), 1969 *Handb. d. Vögel Mitteleuropas* 3.    Baysinger 1971 *Auk* **88** 438.    Beals and Shenstone (eds.) 1968 *Science, History, and Hudson Bay* 1 (Ottawa: Dept. Energy, Mines, and Resources).    Beard 1951 *Wilson Bull.* **63** 296–301, 1964 *Journ. Wildlife Mgt.* **28** 492–521.    Beardslee and Mitchell 1965 *Bull. Buffalo Mus. Nat. Sciences* **22**.    Beckwith and Hosford 1957 *Am. Midland Nat.* **57** 461–73.    Beer 1968 *Bull. Brit. Orn. Club* **88** 4–15.    Beer and Boyd 1962 *Bird Study* **9** 91–99, 1963 Wildfowl Trust 14th *Rept.* 114–19.    Beetz 1916 *Auk* **33** 286–92.    Behle et al. 1963 *Wilson Bull.* **75** 450–56.    Bellrose 1943 *Auk* **60** 446–47, 1955 Ill. Nat. Hist. Surv. *Circ.* 45 (revised), 1957 Ill. Nat. Hist. Surv., *Biol. Notes* no. 36, 1958 *Wilson Bull.* **70** 20–40, 1968 Ill. Nat. Hist. Surv., *Biol. Notes* no. 61, 1972 U.S. Bur. Sport Fisheries and Wildl., *Wildl. Research Rept.* no. 2: 3–26.    Bellrose and Hawkins 1947 *Auk* **64** 422–30.    Bellrose and Chase 1950 Ill. Nat. Hist. Surv., *Biol. Notes* no. 22.    Bellrose and Sieh 1960 *Wilson Bull.* **72** 29–59.    Bellrose et al. 1961 Ill. Nat. Hist. Surv. *Bull.* **27**, art. 6, 1964 *Journ. Wildlife Mgt.* **28** 661–76.    Bellrose and Crompton 1970 Ill. Nat. Hist. Surv. *Bull.* **30** no. 3.    Belopolskii 1934 *Trudy Arkt. Inst.* **9** 23–44, 1957 [*Ecology of Colonial Seabirds of Barents Sea*] (Moscow and Leningrad) TRANSL. 1961 Israel Program for Sci. Transl. (Jerusalem).    Bëme et al. 1965 *Ornitologiya* no.

7: 20–28. Bendire 1875 *Proc. Boston Soc. Nat. Hist.* **18** 153–68. Bengtson 1966a Wildfowl Trust 17th *An. Rept.* 79–84, 1966b *Vär Fägelvarld* **25** 202–26, 1968 *Wildfowl* no. 19: 61–63, 1971a *Ornis Scandinavica* **2** 17–26, 1971b *Ornis Fenn.* **48** 77–82, 1971c *Ibis* **113** 523–26, 1972a Ecological Segregation . . . Duck Populations in Iceland (Univ. of Lund, Sweden, *Dissertation Summary* 12 pp.), 1972b *Ornis Scandinavica* **3** 25–43, 1972c *Oikos* **23** 35–58, 1972d *Bull. Brit. Orn. Club* **92** 100–01. Bengston and Ulfstrand 1971 *Oikos* **22** 235–39. Bennett 1937 *Auk* **54** 534, 1938 *The Blue-winged Teal; . . .* (Ames, Iowa). Benson 1966 *N.Y. State Conservationist* **21** no. 2: 14–15, 37. Benson and Foley 1962 *N.Y. Fish and Game Journ.* **9** 73–92. Benson and DeGraff 1968 *N.Y. Fish and Game Journ.* **15** 52–70. Benson and Browne 1969 *Trans. Northeast Sect. Wildlife Soc.* 1969: 91–110. Bent 1923 *U.S. Nat. Mus. Bull.* 126, 1925 *U.S. Nat. Mus. Bull.* 130, 1932 *U.S. Nat. Mus. Bull.* 162. Berger 1972 *Hawaiian Birdlife* (Honolulu). Berglund et al. 1963 *Acta Vertebratica* **2** no. 2. Bergman, G. 1939 *Acta Zool. Fennica* **23** no. 1, 1957 *Die Vogelwarte* **19** 15–25. Bergman, G., and Donner 1964 *Acta Zool. Fennica* **105** 1–59. Bergman, R. D. 1973 *Journ. Wildlife Mgt.* **37** 160–70. Bernhardt 1940 *Journ. f. Ornithol.* **88** 488–97. Berry 1951 *Proc. 10th Internat. Orn. Congr.* 339–40. Bertram and Lack 1933 *Ibis* **75** 283–301. Bertram et al. 1934 *Ibis* **76** 816–31. Beyer 1900 *Proc. La. Soc. Naturalists for 1897–1899:* 75–120. Beyer et al. 1907 *Auk* **24** 314–21. Bezzel 1960 *Journ. f. Ornithol.* **101** 276–81, 1968 *Vogelwelt* **89** 102–11, 1969 *Die Tafelente* (Wittenberg Lutherstadt: A. Ziemsen. Neue Brehm-Bücherei no. 405). Biaggi and Rolle 1961 *Auk* **78** 425. Bianki et al. 1967a *Problemy Severa* **11** 218–33 Transl. 1968 *Problems of the North* no. 11 269–74 (Ottawa: National Research Council), 1967b *Trans. Kandalaksh State Reserve* no. 5: 5–39. Billard and Humphrey 1972 *Journ. Wildlife Mgt.* **36** 765–74. Bird and Bird 1941 *Ibis* **83** 118–61. Bishop, L. B. 1895a *Auk* **12** 293–95, 1895b *Auk* **12** 295–97. Bishop, R. A., and Barratt 1970 *Journ. Wildlife Mgt.* **34** 734–38. Bjärvall 1968 *Wildfowl* no. 19: 70–80, 1969 *Wilson Bull.* **81** 94–96. Bjerke 1970 *Sterna* **9** 149–52. Blaauw 1903 *Ibis* 8th ser. **3** 245–47, 1905 *Ibis* 8th ser. **5** 137–38, 1909 *Ibis* **51** 188–89, 1916 *Ibis* **58** 252–54. Blaedel (ed.) 1961 *Nordens Fugle i. Farver* **5** (Copenhagen). Blair 1936 *Ibis* **78** 429–59 Blake 1948 *Condor* **50** 148–51. Blanchan [Mrs. Nelson Doubleday] 1898 *Birds that Hunt and are Hunted* (New York). Blurton Jones 1956 *Bird Study* **3** 153–70, 1960 Wildfowl Trust 11th *Rept.* 46–52. Boase 1959 *Brit. Birds* **52** 114–23. Boie 1822 *Tagebuch gehalten auf einer Reise durch Norwegen in Jahre 1817 . . .* (Schleswig). Bolam 1912 *The Birds of Northumberland and the Eastern Borders* (Alnwick, England). Bolen 1962 *Aud. Field Notes* **16** 482–85, 1964 *Texas Journ. Sci.* **16** 257–60, 1967 *Journ. Wildlife Mgt.* **31** 794–97, 1970 *Journ. Wildlife Mgt.* **34** 68–73, 1971a *Journ. Wildlife Mgt.* **35** 385–88, 1971b *Wilson Bull.* **83** 430–34. Bolen et al. 1964 *Southwestern Nat.* **9** 78–88. Bolen and Forsyth 1967 *Wilson Bull.* **79** 43–49. Bolen and Cain 1968 *Condor* **70** 389. Bolen and Beecham 1970 *Wilson Bull.* **82** 325–26. Bonaparte 1824 *Journ. Acad. Nat. Sci. Phila* ser. **1 3** 381–90. Bond, J. 1951 *Cassinia,* 1949–50: 33, 1956 *Check-list of Birds of the West Indies* (Philadelphia), 1958 *Third Suppl. to Checklist of Birds of the West Indies* (Philadelphia), 1959 *Fourth Suppl. . . . ,* 1960 *Cassinia* no. 43 (for 1958): 5, 1961a *Birds of the West Indies* (Boston),

1961b *Sixth Suppl. to check-list of Birds of the West Indies*, 1965 *Tenth Suppl.* . . ., 1966 *Eleventh Suppl.* . . ., 1967 *Twelfth Suppl.* . . ., 1973 *Eighteenth Suppl.* . . . Bond, R.M. 1934 *Auk* **51** 500–02, 1940 *Condor* **42** 246–50.    Borden and Hochbaum 1966 *Trans. 31st N. Am. Wildlife and Nat. Resources Conf.* 79–88. Borrero H. and Hernandez-Camacho 1958 *Caldasia* **8** 253–94.    Bossenmaier and Marshall 1958 *Wildlife Monogr.* no. 1.    Bowles 1917 *Auk* **42** 206–07.    Boyd 1953 *Behaviour* **5** 85–129, 1954 Wildfowl Trust 6th *Rept.* (1952–53): 73–79, 1956 *Journ. Animal Ecol.* **25** 253–73, 1957a *Bird Study* **4** 80–93, 1957b *Ibis* **99** 157–77, 1959a *Ibis* **101** 441–45, 1959b Wildfowl Trust 10th *Rept.* 59–70, 1961a Wildfowl Trust 12th *Rept.* 116–24, 1961b Wildfowl Trust 12th *Rept.* 153–56, 1963 Wildfowl Trust 14th *Rept.* 87–93, 1965 Wildfowl Trust 16th *Rept.* 34–40, 1968 *Wildfowl* no. 19: 96–107.    Boyd and Radford 1958 Wildfowl Trust 9th *Rept.* 42–46.    Boyd and Eltringham 1962 *Bird Study* **9** 217–41.    Boyd and Campbell 1967 Wildfowl Trust 18th *Rept.* 36–42.    Boyd and Ogilvie 1969 *Wildfowl* no. 20: 33–46.    Boyer 1959 *Can. Field-Nat.* **73** 1–5, 1966 Can. Wildlife Serv. *Occas. Pap.* no. 8.    Bradlee and Mowbray 1931 *Proc. Boston Soc. Nat. Hist.* **39** no. 8.    Bradley and Miller 1972 *Nature* 385–87.    Brakhage 1953 *Journ. Wildlife Mgt.* **17** 465–77, 1962 Mo. Fed. Aid in Wildlife Restoration Act, *Proj.* no. 13-R-16, 1965 *Journ. Wildlife Mgt.* **29** 751–71.    Brandt 1943 *Alaska Bird Trails* (Cleveland, Ohio).    Bray 1943 *Auk* **60** 504–36    Breckenridge 1956 *Journ. Wildlife Mgt.* **20** 16–21.    Bretherton 1896 *Oregon Nat.* **3** 45–49, 61–64, 77–79, 100–02.    Brewer 1879 *Bull. Nuttall Orn. Club* **4** 145–52.    Brewster 1900 *Auk* **17** 207–16, 1902 *Auk* **19** 183–88, 1911a *Condor* **13** 22–30, 1911b *Bird-Lore* **13** 125–27, 1924 *Bull. Mus. Comp. Zool. Harvard* **66** no. 1, 1925 *Bull. Mus. Comp. Zool. Harvard* **66** no. 2.    Brimley 1927 *Auk* **44** 427–28.    Brodkorb 1964a *Bull. Fla. State Mus.*, Biol. Sci. **8** no. 3, 1964b *Journ. Barbados us. and Hist. Soc.* **31** 3–10.    Broley 1950 *Journ. Wildlife Mgt.* **14** 452–56.    Brooks, A. 1903 *Auk* **20** 272–84, 1904 *Auk* **21** 289–91, 1920 *Auk* **37** 353–67, 1922 *Auk* **39** 556–59, 1926 *Condor* **28** 129, 1934 *Nat. Geog. Mag.* **66** 487–528, 1942 *Condor* **44** 33, 1945 *Auk* **62** 517–23.    Brooks, W. S. 1915 *Bull. Mus. Comp. Zool. Harvard* **59** no. 5.    Broun 1941 *Auk* **58** 266–68.    Brouwer and Tinbergen 1939 *Limosa* **12** 1–18.    Brown, B. W. 1973 *Proc. SE Conf. Fish and Game Commrs.* (1972) **27** 195–202.    Brown, D. E. 1924 *Murrelet* **5** (3): 11.    Bruemmer 1971 *The Beaver* outfit 302 (1) [summer issue] 4–13.    Bruggemann 1876 *Zool. Garten* (Berlin) **17** 366–68.    Bruijns and Tanis 1955 *Ardea* **43** 261–71.    Bruun 1971 *Brit. Birds* **64** 385–408.    Bryan and Greenway 1944 *Bull. Mus. Comp. Zool. Harvard* **94** no. 2.    Bryant, H. C. 1914 *Condor* **16** 217–39.    Bryant, W. E. 1893 *Zoe* **4** 54–58.    Bue et al. 1952 *Trans. 17th N. Am. Wildlife Conf.* 396–414.    Bull 1964 *Birds of the New York Area* (N.Y.: Harper and Row).    Burgess et al. 1965 *Journ. Wildlife Mgt.* **29** 89–95.    Burleigh 1958 *Georgia Birds* (Norman, Okla.).    Burnett and Snyder 1954 *Auk* **71** 315–16.    Burton 1961 Wildfowl Trust 12th *Rept.* 104–12.    Butler, A. G. 1897 *Brit. Birds with their Nests and Eggs* 4 (London).    Butler, A. W. 1898 *The Birds of Indiana* (Indianapolis).

Cabot 1963 Wildfowl Trust 14th *Rept.* 104–06.    Cade 1955 *Journ. Wildlife Mgt.* **19** 321–24.    Cadman 1953 *Brit. Birds* **46** 374–75, 1956 *Nature in Wales* **2** 348–

49.    Cadwallader et al. 1972 *Journ. Applied Ecol.* **9** 417–25.    Cahn 1947 *Condor* **49** 78–82.    Cain 1970 *Taius* (Texas A and I Univ. Studies) **3** 25–48, 1972 *Wilson Bull* **84** 483–85, 1973 *Wilson Bull.* **85** 308–17.    Campbell, J. M. 1969a *Condor* **71** 80–81, 1969b *Condor* **71** 80.    Campbell, J. W. 1936 *Brit. Birds* **30** 209–18, 1946 *Brit. Birds* **39** 226–32, 1947 *Ibis* **89** 429–32.    Carney 1964 U.S. Fish and Wildlife Serv., *Spec. Sci. Rept.–Wildlife* no. 82.    Carney and Geis 1960 *Journ. Wildlife Mgt.* **24** 372–81.    Carr 1969 *Game Breeders Gazette* **18** (4): 9–11.    Carroll 1932 *Auk* **49** 343–44.    Carter 1958 Can. Wildlife Serv. *Wildlife Mgt. Bull.* ser. 2 no. 9. Cartwright 1944 *Journ. Wildlife Mgt.* **8** 79–80.    Cartwright and Lloyd 1933 *Can. Field-Nat.* **47** 72–73.    Cartwright and Law 1952 *Waterfowl Banding* 1939–1950 (Winnipeg., Man.: Ducks Unlimited, 53 pp.).    Cawkell and Hamilton 1961 *Ibis* **103a** 1–27.    Cayouette 1955 *Les Carnets* **25** 113–17.    Chabreck 1966 *Auk* **83** 664.    Chamberlain 1925 *Auk* **42** 265–66, 1937 *Auk* **54** 383.    Chamberlain, Jr., 1960 Fla. Game and Fresh Water Fish Comm., *Tech, Bull,* no. 7.    Chapman, A. C. 1887 *Zoologist* ser. 3 **11** 3–21.    Chapman, F. M. 1934 *Handb. of Birds of E. N. Am.* (2nd rev. ed.) (New York City).    Chapman, H. H. 1942 *Auk* **59** 100–03.    Chapman, J. A. 1970 *Murrelet* **51** 34–37.    Chapman, J. A., et. al. 1969 *Wildlife Monogr.* no. 18.    Chattin et al. 1949 U.S. Fish and Wildlife Serv., *Spec. Sci. Rept.–Wildlife* no. 2: 115–27.    Childs 1969 *Biol. Papers Univ. of Alaska* no. 10.    Choate 1966 *Breeding Biol. of the Am. Eider* . . . (Univ. of Me., M.S. thesis), 1967 *Journ. Wildlife Mgt.* **31** 769–77.    Christensen et al. 1965 *Ibis* **107** 542–43.    Christmas 1960 *Auk* **77** 346–47.    Christoleit 1926 *Journ. f. Ornithol.* **74** 404–90, 1927 *Journ f. Ornithol.* **75** 385–404.    Chura 1961 *Trans. 26th. N. Am. Wildl. Conf.* 121–34, 1962 *Auk* **79** 484, 1963 *Wilson Bull.* **75** 90.    Clapp and Woodward 1968 U.S. Nat. Mus. *Proc.* **124** no. 3640.    Clark, A. H. 1910 U.S. Nat. Mus. *Proc.* **38** 25–74.    Clark, G. M. et al. 1958 *Journ. Wildlife Mgt.* **22** 204–05.    Clayton 1897 *Science,* n.s. **5** 585–86.    Cleaves 1947 *Field and Stream* **51** (10): 42–43.    Clegg 1971 *Brit. Birds* **64** 372–73.    Cleghorn 1942 *Auk* **59** 584–85.    Cockrum 1952 *Wilson Bull.* **64** 140–59.    Collett 1894 *Norges Fuglefauna* (Christiania, Norway).    Collias and Collias 1956 *Auk* **73** 378–400.    Collias and Jahn 1959 *Auk* **76** 478–509.    Collinge 1924–27 *The Food of Some Brit. Wild Birds* (York, England).    Conover 1926 *Auk* **43** 162–80.    Cooch 1952 *Can. Field-Nat.* **66** 111, 1955 *Wilson Bull.* **67** 171–74, 1961 *Auk* **78** 72–89, 1963 *Proc. 13th Internat. Orn. Congr.* 1182–94, 1964 *Auk.* **81** 380–93, 1965 Can. Wildlife Serv., *Wildlife Mgt. Bull.* ser. 2 no. 2.    Cooch and Beardmore 1959 *Nature* **183** 1833–34.    Cooch et al. 1960 *Auk* **77** 460–65.    Cook and Trainer 1966 *Journ. Wildlife Mgt.* **30** 1–8.    Cooke, F. 1969 *Ont. Nat.,* 1969 no. 4 (Dec.): 16–19.    Cooke, F., and Cooch 1968 *Evolution* **22** 289–300.    Cooke, F., and Ryder 1971 *Evolution* **25** 483–96.    Cooke, F., and Mirsky 1972 *Auk* **89** 863–71.    Cooke, M. T. 1933 *Auk* **50** 309–16, 1937 U.S. Dept. Agric. *Circular* no. 428, 1945 *Bird-Banding* **16** 123–29.    Cooke, M. T., and Knappen 1941 *Trans. 5th N. Am. Wildlife Conf.* 176–83.    Cooke, W. W. 1906 U.S. Dept. Agric., Biol. Surv., *Bull.* no. 26, 1913a *Nat. Geog. Mag.* **24** 361–80, 1913b *Wilson Bull.* **25** 1–7.    Cooper and Lysaght 1956 *Ibis* **98** 316–19.    Cooper, J. A., and Batt 1972 *Journ. Wildlife Mgt.* **36** 1267–70.    Cornwell 1969 *Fla. Wildlife* **22** (9): 26–28.    Cottam 1935 *Auk* **52** 432–41, 1936 *Journ. Wash. Acad. Sci.* **26** 165–77, 1939 U.S. Dept. Agric., *Tech.*

*Bull.* no. 643. Cottam and Uhler 1937 U.S. Dept. Agric., *BS Leaflet* no. 83. Cottam and Hanson 1938 Field Mus. Nat. Hist., *Zool. Ser.* **20** no. 34. Cottam and Knappen 1939 *Auk* **56** 138–69. Cottam et al. 1942 *Wilson Bull.* **54** 121–31, 1944 *Journ. Wildlife Mgt.* **8** 36–56. Cottam and Glazener 1959 *Trans. 24th N. Am. Wildlife Conf.* 382–95. Coues 1878 *Am. Nat.* **12** 123–24. Coulter 1954 *Bull. Me. Aud. Soc.* **10** 20–23, 1955 *Journ. Wildlife Mgt.* **19** 263–67, 1957 *Journ. Wildlife Mgt.* **21** 235–36. Coulter and Miller 1968 Vt. Fish and Game Dept. *Bull.* 68–2. Cowan 1974 *Auk* **91** 189–91. Cowardin et al. 1967 *Journ. Wildlife Mgt.* **31** 229–35. Craighead and Craighead 1949 *Journ. Wildlife Mgt.* **13** 51–64. Craighead and Stockstad 1958 *Journ. Wildlife Mgt.* **22** 206–07. 1964 *Journ. Wildlife Mgt.* **28** 57–64. Cringan 1971 *Trans. 36th N. Am. Wildlife and Nat. Resources Conf.* 296–312. Crissey (compiler) 1949 U.S. Fish and Wildlife Serv., *Spec. Sci. Rept.—Wildlife* no. 2. Cronan 1957 *Auk* **74** 459–63. Cruickshank 1936 *Auk* **53** 321–22. Curth 1954 *Der Mittelsäger* (Wittenberg Lutherstadt: A. Ziemsen. Neue Brehm-Bücherei no. 126). Cutler 1955 *Cassinia* no. 39: 33.

Daange 1950 *Behaviour* **3** 48–99. Dalgety 1933 *Bull. Brit. Oological Assoc.* (London) **3** no. 32: 79–91, 1936 *Ibis* **78** 580–91. Dalgety and Scott 1948 *Bull. Brit. Orn. Club* **68** 109–21. Dall and Bannister 1867 *Trans. Chicago Acad. Sci.* **1** 267–310. Dalquest and Lewis 1955 *Condor* **57** 243. Dane, B., et al. 1959 *Behaviour* **14** 265–81. Dane, B., and van der Kloot 1964 *Behaviour* **22** 282–328. Dane, C. W. 1965 *The Influence of Age on the Development . . . Blue-winged Teal* (Purdue Univ., Ph.D. thesis), 1966 *Auk* **83** 389–402, 1968 *Journ. Wildlife Mgt.* **32** 267–74. Danielson 1971 *Arctic* **24** 90–107. Davis, C.A. 1972 *Symposium on Rare and Endangered Wildlife in sw. U.S.* (Santa Fe: New Mex. Dept. Fish and Game) 46–50. Davis, N. L. 1895 *The Museum* **1** 114–16. Davison 1925 *Can. Field-Nat.* **39** 197–98. Dawson 1923 *The Birds of Calif.* **4** (San Diego, Los Angeles, and San Francisco). Dawson and Bowles 1909 *The Birds of Wash.* **2** (Seattle). Deane 1905 *Auk* **22** 321. Degerbøl and Möhl-Hansen 1935 *Meddel. om Grønland* **104** no. 18. DeGraff et. al. 1961 *N.Y. Fish and Game Journ.* **8** 69–87. Delacour 1951a *Ardea* **39** 135–42, 1951b *Am. Mus. Novitates* no. 1537, 1954 *Waterfowl of the World* **1**, 1956 *Waterfowl of the World* **2**, 1959 *Waterfowl of the World* **3**, 1964 *Waterfowl of the World* **4** (London), 1970 *Alauda* **38** 82–86. Delacour and Mayr 1945 *Wilson Bull.* **69** 3–55. Delacour and Zimmer 1952 *Auk* **69** 82–84. Dementiev (ed.) 1965 [*The Migrations of Birds and Mammals*] (Moscow: "Nauka" Pub. House). Dementiev and Gladkov (eds.) 1952 [*Birds of the Soviet Union*] **4** TRANSL. 1967 Israel Program for Sci. Transl. (Jerusalem). Dementiev and Gladkov 1960 *L'Oiseau* **30**, spec. no. Dennis 1964 Wildfowl Trust 15th *Rept.* 71–74. Denson and Murrell 1962 *Journ. Wildlife Mgt.* **26** 257–62. Derscheid 1938 *Brit. Birds* **32** 151–53, 1941 *Le Gerfaut* **31** 87–99. de Schauensee (*see* Meyer de Schauensee). Des Lauriers and Brattstrom 1965 *Auk* **82** 639. Dickey and van Rossem 1923 *Condor* **25** 38–50, 1928 Field Mus. Nat. Hist., *Zool. Ser.* **23**. Dickinson 1953 *Bull. Mus. Comp. Zool. Harvard* **109** no. 2. Dirschl 1969 *Journ. Wildlife Mgt.* **33** 77–87. Dixon 1924 *Condor* **26** 41–66. Dolgushin 1960 [*The Birds of Kazakhstan*] **1** (Alma-Ata). Donker 1959 *Ardea* **47** 1–27. Donovan 1971 *Me. Fish and Game* **13** (3): 2–4. Doty and Krus 1972 *Journ. Wildlife Mgt.* **36** 428–35. Dow, D. D. 1964 *Auk*

81 556–58.    Dow, J. S. 1943 *Calif. Fish and Game* **29** 3–18.    Dreis 1954 *Journ. Wildlife Mgt.* **18** 280–81.    Dresser 1877 *History of the Birds of Europe* **6** (London).    Drewien and Frederickson 1970 *Wilson Bull.* **82** 95–96.    Driver 1958 *Arctic* **11** 191–93, 1960 *Arctic* **13** 201–04.    Drury 1961 *Can. Field-Nat.* **75** 84–101.    Duben 1968 *Ornitologiya* no. 9: 347.    Duebbert 1966a *Wilson Bull.* **78** 12–25, 1966b *North Dakota Outdoors* **29** no. 2: 14.    Dugan 1953 *Wilson Bull.* **65** 279.    DuMont 1943 *Auk* **60** 109–10.    Dunbar 1969 *Arctic* **22** 438–41.    Dunthorn 1971 *Bird Study* **18** 107–12. Dwight 1914 *Auk* **31** 293–308.    Dzubin 1955 *Trans. 20th N. Am. Wildlife Conf.* 280–98, 1957 *Blue Jay* **15** 10–13, 1959 *Journ. Wildlife Mgt.* **23** 279–90, 1962 *Bird-Banding* **33** 152–53, 1964 *Blue Jay* **22** 106–08, 1965 *Condor* **67** 511–34, 1969 Can. Wildlife Serv. *Rept. Ser.* no. 6: 138–60.

Earl 1950 *Journ. Wildlife Mgt.* **14** 332–42.    Eaton 1910 *Birds of New York* **1** (N.Y. State Mus. *Mem.* **12** pt. 1).    Eckardt 1918 *Ornithol. Monatsschrift*, 1918: 70–80.    Eckert 1970 *Loon* **42** 34–35.    Edwards, E. P. 1943 *Auk* **60** 239–41.    Edwards, R. Y. 1951 *Avic. Mag.* **57** 185, 1953 *Wilson Bull.* **65** 197–98.    Einarsen 1965 *Black Brant* . . . (Seattle: Univ. Wash. Press).    Elder, W. H. 1946a *Journ. Wildlife Mgt.* **10** 93–111, 1946b *Trans. 11th N. Am. Wildlife Conf.* 441–46, 1955 Wildfowl Trust 7th *Rept.* 127–32.    Elder, W. H., and Elder, N. L. 1949 *Wilson Bull.* **61** 133–40.    Elder, W. H., and Weller 1954 *Journ. Wildlife Mgt.* **18** 495–502.    Elgas 1970 *Wilson Bull.* **82** 420–26.    Ellarson 1956 *A Study of the Old-squaw Duck on L. Michigan* (Univ. of Wis., Ph.D. thesis).    Elliot 1898 *The Wild Fowl of the U.S. and Brit. Possessions* (New York).    Ellis and Frye 1965 *Journ. Wildlife Mgt.* **29** 396–97.    Elson 1962 Fisheries Research Bd. Can., *Bull.* no. 133.    Eltringham 1963 *Bird Study* **10** 10–28.    Eltringham and Boyd 1963 *Brit. Birds* **56** 433–44.    Embody 1910 *Science* **31** 630–31.    Emlen and Ambrose 1970 *Auk* **87** 164–65.    English 1916 *Ibis* 10th ser. 4 17–35.    Erickson 1952 *Wilson Bull.* **64** 167.    Erskine 1959 *Can. Field- Nat.* **73** 131, 1961 *Auk* **78** 389–96, 1964 *Trans. Northeastern Wildlife Conf.*, 1964 unpaged (25 pp.), 1971 *Ibis* **113** 42–58, 1972a *Buffleheads* (Can. Wildlife Serv., Monogr. Ser. no. 4), 1972b *Auk* **89** 449–50, 1972c Can. Wildlife Serv., *Rept.* ser. no. 17.    Evans, A. H. 1899 *Birds* (Cambridge Nat. Hist. 9) (London).    Evans, C. D. 1951 *A Study of Movements of Waterfowl Broods in Man.* (Univ. of Minn., Ph.D. thesis).    Evans, C. D., et al. 1952 U.S. Fish and Wildlife Serv., *Spec. Sci. Rept.—Wildlife* no. 16.    Evans, W. 1909 *Brit. Birds* **3** 165–67.    Ewaschuk and Boag 1972 *Journ. Wildlife Mgt.* **36** 1097–106.    Evenden 1952 *Journ. Wildlife Mgt.* **16** 391–93.    qEvermann 1913 *Auk* **30** 15–18.    Eygenramm 1957 *Ardea* **45** 117–43.    Eyton 1838 *A Monogr. of the Anatidae, or Duck Tribe* (London).

F. L. B. 1891 *Forest and Stream* **36** 310.    Faber 1822 *Prodromus der isländischen Ornitologie, oder Geschichte der Vögel Islands* (Copenhagen), 1826 *Ueber das Leben der hochnordischen Vögel* (Leipzig).    Falla et al. 1966 *A Field Guide to the Birds of New Zealand* . . . (London: Collins).    Farley (compiler) 1955 U.S. Fish and Wildlife Serv., *Spec. Sci. Rept.—Wildlife* no. 27.    Farner 1955 Chap. 12 in *Recent Studies of Avian Biol.* ed. by Wolfson (Urbana: Univ. of Ill. Press).    Farner and King (eds.) 1972 *Avian Biology* **2** (New York: Academic Press).    Fatio 1904 *Faune* *des vertébrés de la Suisse. Hist. nat. des Oiseaux* pt. 2 (Geneva).    Fay 1961 Wildfowl Trust 12th *Rept.* 70–80.    Fay and Cade 1959 *Univ. Calif. Pub. Zool.* 63 no. 2.    Fedducia 1973 *Condor* 75 243–44.    Fencker 1950 *Dansk Orn. Foren. Tidsskr.* 44 61–65.    Ferry 1910 *Auk* 27 185–204.    Finn 1900 *Journ. Asiatic Soc. Bengal* (Calcutta) 69 147–49, 1904 *Avic. Mag.* n.s. 2 89–94, 1916 *Zoologist* ser. 4 20 78, 1919 *Bird Behaviour* (London).    Fish and Wildlife Serv. (compiler) 1952 U.S. Fish and Wildlife Serv., *Spec. Sci. Rept.—Wildlife* no 21.    Fisher, A. K. 1893 *N. Am. Fauna* no. 7.    Fisher, H. I. 1965 *Condor* 67 355–357, 1970 *Audubon* 72 62–63.    Fjeldså 1972 *Sterna* 11 145–63.    Flaherty 1918 *Geogr. Rev.* 5 433–58. Fleming 1912 *Auk* 37 445–48.    Flickinger et al. 1973 *Journ. Wildlife Mgt.* 37 171–75.    Flint 1954 *Zool. Zhurnal* (Moscow) 33 159–61, 1955 *Bull. Soc. Nat. Moscow Biol.* 60 58–63.    Flint et al. 1968 [*Birds of USSR* (field guide)] (Moscow: "Mysl" Pub. House).    Flock 1972 *Arctic* 25 83–98, 1973 *Wilson Bull.* 85 259–75.    Florence 1912 *Trans. Highland and Agric. Soc. Scotland* 5 180–219.    Foley and Taber 1951 N.Y. Cons. Dept. *Proj.* 47-R, 1953 N.Y. Cons. Dept. *Proj.* 52-R.    Foley et al. 1961 *N.Y. Fish and Game Journ.* 8 37–48.    Folk et al. 1966 *Zool. Listy* 15 249–60.    Folkestad and Moksnes 1970 *Sterna* 9 9–17.    Forbush 1912 *A Hist. of Game Birds, Wildfowl and Shore Birds* . . . (Boston), 1922 *Auk* 39 104–05, 1925 *Birds of Mass.* . . . 1 (Norwood, Mass.).    Franklin 1823 *Narrative of a Journey to the Polar Sea,* . . . (London).    Fraser 1957 *Can. Field-Nat.* 71 192–99.    Frederickson 1968 *Ornis Fennica* 45 127–30.    Freeman 1967 *Arctic* 20 154–75, 1970 *Can. Field-Nat.* 84 145–53.    Frère 1846 *Zoologist* 4 1249–50.    Freuchen and Salomonsen 1958 *The Arctic Year.* (New York City).    Friedmann 1934 *Journ. Wash. Acad. Sci.* 24 83–96, 1935 *Journ. Wash. Acad. Sci.* 25 44–51, 1941 *Journ. Wash. Acad. Sci.* 31 404–09, 1947 *Condor* 49 189–95, 1948 *Proc. Biol. Soc. Wash.* 61 157–58, 1949 *Condor* 51 43–44.    Friedmann et al. 1950 *Pac. Coast Avifauna* no. 29.    Friley 1960 *Journ. Wildlife Mgt.* 24 97-99.    Frings and Frings 1960 *Elepaio* (Hawaii Aud. Soc.) 20 46–48, 55–57.    Frith 1967 *Waterfowl in Australia* (Honolulu: East-West Center Press).    Fritsch and Buss 1958 *Condor* 60 410–11.    Fuller and Kevan (eds.) 1970 *Proc. Conf. on Production and Conservation of North Circumpolar Lands*, Edmonton, Alta., Oct. 15–17, 1969 (Morges, Switzerland: Internat. Union for Cons. of Natural and National Resources).

Gabrielson 1947 *Auk* 64 325.    Gabrielson and Jewett 1940 *Birds of Oregon* (Corvallis).    Gabrielson et al. 1956 *Auk* 73 119–23.    Gabrielson and Lincoln 1959 *Birds of Alaska* (Wash., D.C.: Wildlife Mgt. Inst.).    Gadamer 1855 *Naumannia* 3 89–92.    Gadow 1890 *Zool. Jahrb., Abth. fur Syst.* 5 629–46.    Gallagher 1960 *Ibis* 102 489–502.    Ganning and Wulff 1969 *Oikos* 20 274–86.    Gardarsson 1968 *Náttúrufraedingurinn* (Reykjavik) 37 76–92, 1969 *Náttúrufraedingurinn* 38 (for 1968) 165–75, 1972 *Ibis* 114 581.    Garden et al. 1964 *Bird Study* 11 280–87.    Gashwiler 1961 *Murrelet* 42 4–5.    Gates 1957 *Proc. Utah Acad. Sci.* 34 69–71, 1965 *Journ. Wildlife Mgt.* 29 515–23.    Gätke 1895 *Heligoland as an Ornithological Observatory* (Edinburgh).    Gavin 1940 *The Beaver* outfit 271 (Dec.): 6–9, 1947 *Wilson Bull.* 59 195–203.    Gavrin 1964 *Trudy Inst. Zool. Akad. Nauk, Kazakh SSR* 24 5–58.    Geis, A. D. 1959 *Journ. Wildlife Mgt.* 23 253–61, 1971 U.S. Bur. Sport

Fisheries and Wildlife, *Spec. Sci. Rept.—Wildlife* no. 144.    Geis, A. D., and Crissey 1969 *Journ. Wildlife Mgt.* **33** 861–66.    Geis, A. D., et al. 1971 U.S. Bur. Sport Fisheries and Wildlife, *Spec. Sci. Rept.—Wildlife* no. 139.    Geis, M. B. 1956 *Journ. Wildlife Mgt.* **20** 409–19.    Genelly 1955 *Condor* **57** 63.    Gerasimov 1968 *Ornitologiya* no 9: 345.    Gerasimova and Baranova 1960 *Trans. Kandalaksh State Reserve* no. 3: 8–90.    Gershman et al. 1964 *Journ. Wildlife Mgt.* **28** 587–89.    Geyr von Schweppenburg 1959 *Journ. fur Ornithol.* **100** 397–403, 1961 *Journ. fur Ornithol.* **102** 140–48.    Gibbs 1962 *Me. Field-Nat.* **18** 67–68.    Gigstead 1938 *Trans. 3rd N. Am. Wildlife Conf.* 603–09.    Gillham, E. H. 1957 *Brit. Birds* **50** 389–93, 1958 *Brit. Birds* **51** 413–26.    Gillam, E.H., et al. 1966 *Wildfowl Trust 17th Rept.* 49–65.    Gillham, M. E. 1956 *Bird Study* **3** 205–12.    Gilpin 1878a *Proc. and Trans. Nova Scotian Inst. Nat. Sci.* (1875–78) **4** 398–99, 1878b *Forest and Stream* **10** 75.    Gilroy 1909 *Brit. Birds* **2** 400–05.    Gines and Aveledo 1958 *Aves de caza de Venezuela* (*Monogr* 4, Soc. Cien. nat. La Salle).    Girard 1939 *Trans. 4th N. Am. Wildlife Conf.* 364–71, 1941 *Journ. Wildlife Mgt.* **5** 233–59.    Giroux 1953 *Les Carnets* **13** 115–19.    Gizenko 1955 [*Birds of the Sakhalin Region*] (Moscow: Acad. Sci. USSR).    Gjøsaeter et al. 1972 *Sterna* **11** 173–76.    Glasgow and Bardwell 1965 *Proc. 16th* [1962] *An. Conf. SE Game and Fish Commrs.* 175–84.    Glazener 1946 *Journ. Wildlife Mgt.* **10** 322–29.    Glegg 1951 *Ibis* **93** 305–06.    Glover 1956 *Journ. Wildlife Mgt.* **20** 28 –46.    Glover and Smith 1963 U.S. Fish and Wildlife Serv., *Spec. Sci. Rept. —Wildlife* no. 75.    Gochfeld 1968 *Condor* **70** 186–87.    Godfrey 1966 *The Birds of Canada* (Nat. Mus. Canada *Bull.* 203).    Gollop and Marshall 1954 *A Guide to Aging Duck Broods in the Field* (Mississippi Flyway Council, Tech. Sect., 14 pp., mimeo.).    Goodwin 1956 *Ont. Field Biol.* no. 10: 7–18.    Gordon et al. *Bird Study* **11** 280–87.    Gorman and Milne 1971 *Ibis* **113** 218–28, 1972 *Ornis Scandinavica* **3** 21–26.    Gosse 1847 *The Birds of Jamaica* (London).    Gottlieb 1963 *Journ. Compar. and Physiol. Psychol.* **56** 86–91.    Grandy 1972 *Auk* **89** 189–90.    Grant 1946 *Condor* **48** 143.    Grastveit 1971 *Sterna* **10** 31–33.    Gray 1958 *Bird Hybrids* (Farnham Royal, Bucks, England: Commonwealth Agric. Bureaux).    Greenway 1958 *Extinct and Vanishing Birds of the World* (Am. Committee for Internat. Wildlife Prot., *Spec. Pub.* no. 13).    Greij 1973 *Auk* **90** 533–51.    Grenquist 1953 *Suomen Riista* (Helsinki) **8** 49–59, 1958 *Suomen Riista* **12** 94–99, 1959 *Suomen Riista* **13** 73–92, 1962 *Suomen Riista* **15** 83–98, 1963 *Proc. 13th Internat. Orn. Congr.* 685–89, 1965 *Finnish Game Research* no. 27, 1968 *Sutmen Riista* **20** 112–17, 1970 *Suomen Riista* **22** 24–34.    Grice and Rogers 1966 *The Wood Duck in Mass.* (Mass. Div. Fisheries and Game).    Grieb 1970 *Wildlife Monogr.* no. 22.    Griffee 1958 *Murrelet* **39** 26.    Griffith 1946 *Auk* **63** 436–38.    Grimm 1952 *Birds of the Pymatuning Region* (Harrisburg: Pa. Game Comm.).    Grinnell, G. B. 1919 *Auk* **36** 561.    Grinnell, J. 1900 *Pac. Coast Avifauna* no. 1, 1909 *Univ. Calif. Pub. Zool.* **5** no. 2, 1910 *Univ. Calif. Pub. Zool.* **5** no. 12.    Grinnell, J., et al. 1918 *The Game Birds of Calif.* (Berkeley).    Grinnell, J., and Miller 1944 *Pac. Coast Avifauna* no. 27.    Griscom 1920 *Auk* **39** 517–30, 1945 *Auk* **62** 401–04.    Griscom and Snyder 1955 *The Birds of Mass.* (Salem, Mass.: Peabody Museum).    Gross 1937 *Auk* **54** 12–42, 1938 *Auk* **55** 387–400, 1944 *Wilson Bull.* **56** 15–26, 1945 *Auk* **62** 620–22, 1947 *Bull. Me. Aud. Soc.* **3** 50–51.    Grosz and Yocom 1972 *Journ. Wildlife Mgt.*

36 1279–82. Grubb 1971 *Auk* **88** 928–29. Gudmundsson 1932 *Beitr. z. Fortpflanzungsbiol. d. Vögel* **8** 85–93, 142–47, 1940 [*Eider Colonies and Down production in Iceland*] (Reykjavik: Ministry of Cultural Affairs 19 pp.), 1951 *Proc. 10th Internat. Orn. Congr.* 502–14, 1971 *Náttúrufraedingurinn* **41** 1–28, 64–98. Guignion 1968 *Nat. Canadienne* **95** 1145–52. Gullion et al. 1959 *Condor* **61** 278–97. Gundlach 1875 *Journ. f. Ornithol.* **23** 353–407, 1876 *Contribucion a la Ornitologia Cubana* (Havana). Gunn 1939 *Brit. Birds* **33** 48–50. Gusev 1962 *Ornitologiya* no. 5 149–60. Guthrie 1815 *A New Geogr., Hist., and Commercial Grammar*, 2nd Am. ed. **2** (Philadelphia).

Haapanen et al. 1973 *Suomen Riista* **33** 40–60. Hagar, C. 1945 *Auk* **62** 639–40. Hagar, J. A. 1954 *Northeastern Flyway* . . . (Mass. Div. Fisheries and Game 28 pp.). Hahn 1963 *Where is that Vanished Bird?* (Toronto: Roy. Ont. Museum). Halkett 1905 *Ottawa Nat.* **19** 104–109. Hall, E. R. 1926 *Condor* **28** 87–91. Hall, E. S., Jr., 1969 *Condor* **71** 76–77. Hall, F. A., and Harris 1968 *Condor* **70** 188. Hall, L. C., and McGilvrey 1971 *Journ. Wildlife Mgt.* **35** 835–36. Hall, M. S. 1969 *N.Y. Fish and Game Journ.* **16** 127. Halla 1966 *Proc. Northeast Sect. Wildlife Soc.* unnumbered pp. (15 pp.). Hambleton 1949 *Auk* **66** 198–99. Hamilton, R. D. 1950 *Auk* **6** 383. Hamilton, W. J., III 1953 *Wilson Bull.* **69** 279. Hammer 1970 *Wilson Bull.* **82** 324–25. Hammond and Mann 1956 *Journ. Wildlife Mgt.* **20** 345–52. Handley, C. O., Jr., 1950 *Wilson Bull.* **62** 128–32. Hanna 1917 *Auk* **34** 403–10, 1920 *Auk* **37** 248–54. Hansen, H. A. 1960 *Condor* **62** 136–37, 1961 *Journ. Wildlife Mgt.* **25** 242–48, 1962 *Trans. 27th N. Am. Wildlife Conf.* 301–20, (compiler) 1964 U.S. Bur. Sport Fisheries and Wildlife, *Spec. Sci. Rept.— Wildlife* no. 86. Hansen, H. A., and Oliver 1950 *Murrelet* **32** 3–7. Hansen, H. A., and Nelson 1957 *Trans. 22nd N. Am. Wildlife Conf.* 237–56. Hansen, H. A., and McKnight 1964 *Trans. 29th N. Am. Wildlife Conf.* 119–27. Hansen, H. A., and Hudgins (compilers) 1966 U.S. Bur. Sport Fisheries and Wildlife, *Spec. Sci. Rept.—Wildlife* no. 99. Hansen, H. A., et al. 1971 *Wildlife Monogr.* no. 26. Hanson, H. C. 1951a *Auk* **68** 164–73, 1951b *Journ. Wildlife Mgt.* **15** 68–72, 1954 *Auk* **71** 267–72, 1959 *Arctic* **12** 139–50, 1962a Arctic Inst. N. Am., *Tech. Paper* no. 12, 1962b Ill. Nat. Hist. Surv., *Biol. Notes* no. 49, 1965 *The Giant Canada Goose* (Carbondale, Ill.: S. Ill. Univ. Press). Hanson, H. C., and Smith 1950 Ill. Nat. Hist. Surv. *Bull.* **25** 67–210. Hanson, H. C., and Griffith 1952 *Bird-Banding* **23** 1–22. Hanson, H. C., et al. 1956 Arctic Inst. N. Am., *Spec. Pub.* no. 3. Hanson, H. C., and Currie 1957 *Arctic* **10** 211–29. Hanson, H. C., and Browning 1959 *Journ. Wildlife Mgt.* **23** 129–45. Hanson, H. C., and Eberhardt 1971 *Wildlife Monogr.* no. 28. Hantzsch 1905 *Beitrag zur Kenntnis der Vogelwelt Islands* (Berlin), 1908 *Journ. f. Ornithol.* **56** 177–202, 307–92 Transl. 1928 *Can. Field-Nat.* **42** 87–94, 123–25, 146–48, 172–77, 201–07, 221–27, 1929 *Can. Field-Nat.* **43** 11–18, 31–34, 52–59. Hardister et al. 1965 *Proc. 16th An. Conf.* [1962] *Southeastern Fish and Game Commrs.* 70–75. Hargrave 1939 *Condor* **41** 121–23. Harmon 1962 *Trans. 27th N. Am. Wildlife Conf.* 132–38. Harper 1914 *Bird-Lore* **16** 338–41, 1953 *Am. Midland Nat.* **49** 1–116. Harris, H. J. 1970 *Journ. Wildlife Mgt.* **34** 747–55. Harris, S. W. 1954 *Am. Midland Nat.* **52** 403–32. Harris, S. W. et al. 1954

*Murrelet* **35** 33–38.     Harris, S. W., and Shepherd 1965 *Journ. Wildlife Mgt.* **29** 643–45.     Harris, S. W., and Wheeler 1965 *Condor* **67** 539–40.     Harrison, C. J. O. 1962 *Bull. Brit. Orn. Club* **82** 90–91.     Harrison, J. G. 1949 *Brit. Birds* **42** 123–24, 1967 Wildfowl Trust, 18th *Rept.* 155– 56, 1969 *Bull. Brit. Orn. Club* **89** 72.     Harrison, J. M. 1943 *Ibis* **85** 253– 57, 1958 *Bull Brit. Orn. Club* **78** 105–07, 1968 *Bull Brit. Orn. Club* **88** 154–60.     Harrison, J. M., and Harrison 1959 *Bull. Brit. Orn. Club* **79** 135–42, 1963a *Bull Brit. Orn. Club* **83** 21– 25, 1963b *Bull. Brit. Orn. Club* **83** 101–08, 1965 *Bull. Brit. Orn. Club* **85** 107–11, 1968 *Brit. Birds* **61** 169–71, 1970 *Bull. Brit. Orn. Club* **90** 86–88, 1971 *Bull. Brit. Orn. Club* **91** 28–32.     Hart, H. C. 1880 *Zoologist* ser. 3 **4** 204–14.     Hart, J. L. 1949 *Can. Field-Nat.* **63** 213.     Hartert 1920a *Vogel Paalarktischen Fauna* (Berlin) pt. 10 (**2** no. 4), 1920b *Ibid.* pt. 11–12 (**2** no. 5–6), 1920c *Novitates Zoologicae* **27** 128–58.     Hartman, F. A. 1961 *Smithsonian Misc. Colls.* **143** no. 1.     Hartman, F. E. 1963 *Journ. Wildlife Mgt.* **27** 339–47.     Harvey 1971 *Can. Journ. Zool.* **49** 223–34.     Harvey et al. 1968 *Wilson Bull.* **80** 421–25.     Hasbrouck 1944a *Auk* **61** 93–104, 1944b *Auk* **61** 305–06, 1944c *Auk* **61** 544–54.     Hatter 1960 *Condor* **62** 480.     Haverschmidt 1947 *Wilson Bull.* **59** 209, 1970 *Vogelwarte* **25** 229–33.     Havlin 1964 *Folia Zoologica* **13** 178–80, 1966 *Bird Study* **13** 306–10, 1968 *Zool. Listy* **17** 341–50.     Hawkins and Bellrose 1940 *Trans. 5th N. Am. Wildlife Conf.* 392–95.     Haynes 1900 *Wilson Bull.* **12** 12–13.     Hays and Habermann 1969 *Auk* **86** 765–66.     Headley 1967 *Biology of Emperor Goose* (Univ. of Alaska, Coop. Wildlife Research Unit, unpub. MS 118 pp.).     Heard and Curd 1959 *Proc. Okla. Acad. Sci.* **39** 197–200.     Hebard 1941 Ga. Soc. Naturalists *Bull.* 3.     Hedgpeth 1954 *Condor* **56** 52.     Hein and Haugen 1966 *Journ. Wildlife Mgt.* **30** 657–68.     Heinroth 1906 *Orn. Monatsber.* **14** 111–15, 1910 *Journ. f. Ornithol.* **58** 101–56, 1911 *Proc. 5th Internat. Orn. Congress* 589–702, 1918 *Journ. f. Ornithol.* **66** 241–44.     Heinroth and Heinroth 1928 *Die Vögel Mitteleuropas* **3** (Berlin-Lichterfelde).     Hellmayr and Conover 1948 Field Mus. Nat. Hist., *Zool. Ser.* **13** pt. 1, no. 3.     Hemming 1966 *Condor* **68** 163–66.     Henny 1973 *Journ. Wildlife Mgt.* **37** 23–29.     Henry 1948 *Audubon Mag.* **40** 242–49.     Herman and Wehr 1954 *Journ. Wildlife Mgt.* **18** 509–13.     Hester 1965 *Proc. 16th An. Conf.* [1962] *Southeastern Assoc. Game and Fish Commrs.* 67–70.     Heusmann 1972 *Journ. Wildlife Mgt.* **36** 620–24.     Heussler and Heussler 1896 *Ornis* **8** 477–531.     Hewitt 1950 *Trans. 15th N. Am. Wildlife Conf.* 304–09.     Hewson 1964 *Brit. Birds* **57** 26 –31.     Heyland and Boyd 1970 *Dansk Orn. Foren. Tidsskr.* **64** 198–99.     Heyland et al. 1970 *Can. Field-Nat.* **84** 398–99.     Hickey 1952 U.S. Fish and Wildlife Serv., Spec. *Sci. Rept.—Wildlife* no. 15, 1956 *Wisc. Acad. Sci., Arts, and Letters* **45** 59–76.     Higgins 1969 *Journ. Wildlife Mgt.* **33** 1006–08.     Hildén 1964a *Suomen Riista* **17** 133–60, 1964b *Ann. Zool. Fenn.* **1** 153–279.     Hill 1965 *The Birds of Cape Cod, Mass.* (N.Y.: Wm. Morrow).     Hilprecht 1956 *Höckerschwan, Singschwan, Zwergschwan* (Wittenberg Lutherstadt: A. Ziemsen. Neue Brehm-Bücherei no. 177).     Hine and Schoenfeld (eds.) 1968 *Canada Goose Management* . . . (Madison, Wisc.: Dembar Educ. Research Services).     Hochbaum 1944 *The Canvasback on a Prairie Marsh* (Wash., D.C.: Am. Wildlife Inst.), 1946 *Wilson Bull.* **58** 62–65, 1955 *Travels and Traditions of Waterfowl* (Minneapolis: Univ. of Minn. Press), 1960 *Nat. History* **69** no. 6: 54–61.     Hocutt and Dimmick 1971 *Journ. Wildlife Mgt.* **35** 286–92.     Hoffman et al. 1959 Condor **61** 147–51.    Höhn 1947 *Proc. Zool. Soc. London* **117** 281–304, 1948 *Brit. Birds* **41** 233–35, 1957 *Auk* **74** 203–14, 1959 *Can. Field-Nat.* **73** 93– 114.    Holbøll 1846 *Ornithologischer Beitrag zur Fauna Grönlands* (Leip-zig).    Holgersen 1960 *Proc. 12th Internat. Orn. Congr.* 310–16.    Hollister 1919 *Auk* **36** 460–63.    Hollom 1937 *Brit. Birds* **31** 106–11.    Holman 1933 *Sheep and Bear Trails* (N.Y.: Frank Walters).    Holmer 1955 *Vår Fågelvarld* **14** 231– 35.    Hoogerheide 1950 *Ardea* **37** 139–61.    Hori 1962 Wildfowl Trust 13th *Rept.* 173 –74, 1963 Wildfowl Trust 14th *Rept.* 124–32, 1964 *Ibis* **106** 333–60.    Hørring 1937 *Rept. Fifth Thule Exped.*, 1921–24 **2** no. 6 (Copenhagen).    Hørring and Salomonsen 1941 *Medd. om Grønland* **131** no. 5.    Houston 1949 *Can. Field-Nat.* **63** 215– 41.    Hout 1967 U.S. Bur. Sport Fisheries and Wildlife, *Spec. Sci. Rept.—Wildlife* no. 103.    Howard, H. 1933 *Condor* **35** 235, 1971 *Condor* **73** 237– 40.    Howard, P. J. 1968 *Notornis* **15** 253.    Howard, W. J. 1934 *Auk* **51** 513– 14.    Howe 1902 *Auk* **19** 196.    Howell, A. H. 1924 *The Birds of Alabama* (Montgomery, Ala.), 1932 *Florida Bird Life* (Tallahassee).    Howell, T. R. 1959 *Condor* **61** 226–27.    Howley 1884 *Auk* **1** 309–13.    Hubbard 1971 *Auk* **88** 666– 67.    Huey, L. M. 1961 *Auk* **78** 260.    Huey, W. S. 1961 *Auk* **78** 428– 30.    Huey, W. S., and Travis 1961 *Auk* **78** 607–26.    Huggins 1941 *Ecology* **22** 148–57.    Hull 1914 *Wilson Bull.* **26** 116–23.    Humphrey 1957a *Condor* **59** 139–40, 1957b *Auk* **74** 392–94, 1958a *Condor* **60** 303–07, 1958b *Condor* **60** 129–35, 1958c *Condor* **60** 408–10.    Humphrey and Butsch 1958 *Smithsonian Misc. Colls.* **135** no. 7.    Humphrey and Clark 1961 *Condor* **63** 365–85.    Hundley 1970 *Maine Nature* (Brunswick, Me.) **1** no. 10: 2 (April).    Hunt, E. G., and Naylor 1955 *Calif. Fish and Game* **41** 295–314.    Hunt, E. G., and Anderson 1966 *Calif. Fish and Game* **52** 17– 27.    Hunt, G. S. 1963 *Wilson Bull.* **75** 198.    Hunt, R. A., and Jahn 1966 Wisc. Cons. Dept., *Tech. Bull.* no. 38.    Huntington, C. E. 1962 *Me. Field Nat.* **18** 69.    Huntington, D. W. 1903 *Our Feathered Game . . .* (N.Y.).    Huxley 1947 *Brit. Birds* **40** 130–34.    Hyde 1958 *Fla. Waterfowl Band Recoveries 1920–1957* (Fla. Game and Fresh Water Fish Comm. Proj. W-19-R).

Imber 1968 *Journ. Wildlife Mgt.* **32** 905–20, Imber and Williams 1968 *Journ. Wildlife Mgt.* **32** 256–67.    Imhof 1958 *Auk* **75** 354–57.    Ingolfsson 1969 *Bird Study* **16** 45– 52.    Irving 1960 U.S. Nat. Mus. *Bull.* 217.

Jackson, A. C. 1915 *Brit. Birds* **9** 34–42.    Jackson, M. F. 1959 *Auk* **76** 92– 93.    Jacoby and Jögi 1972 *Communications Baltic Commission for Study of Bird Migr.* **7** 118–39.    Jahn (chm.) 1963 *Wilson Bull.* **75** 295–325, (ed. bd. chm.) 1966 *Wood Duck Mgt. and Research: A Symposium* (Wash., D.C.: Wildlife Mgt. Inst.).    Jehl 1966 *Auk* **83** 669–70, 1967 *Condor* **69** 24–27.    Jenkins 1944 *Auk* **61** 31– 47.    Jennings and Singleton 1953 *Texas Game and Fish* **11** 10–11, 27.    Jensen, A. S., et al. 1934 *The Zool. of the Faroes* **3** pt. 2 (Copenhagen).    Jensen, G. H., and Nelson 1948 U.S. Fish and Wildlife Serv., *Spec. Sci. Rept.—Wildlife* no. 60.    Jewett 1931 *Condor* **33** 255, 1947 *Condor* **49** 126, Jewett et al. 1953 *Birds of Washington State* (Seattle: Univ. of Wash. Press).    Joensen 1964 *Dansk Orn. Foren. Tidsskr.* **58** 127– 36, 1968 *Danish Rev. Game Biol.* **5** no. 5, 1972 *Dansk Vildtforskning 1971–1972* 59–61, 1973 *Danish Rev. Game Biol.* **8** no. 4, Joensen and Preuss 1972 *Medd. om Grønland*

**191** no. 5.     Johansen 1934 [*Birds of the Commander Islands*] *Trudy Tomskogo Gos. Universitets* **86** 222–66, 1945 *Dansk Orn. Foren. Tidsskr.* **39** 106–27, 1956 *Acta Arctica* (Copenhagen) fasc. 8, 1959 *Journ. f. Ornithol.* **100** 314–36, 1961 *Auk* **78** 44–56.     Johns and Erickson 1970 *Condor* **72** 377–78.     Johnsen, P. 1953 *Medd. om Grønland* **128** no. 6.     Johnsen, S. 1938 *Bergens Museum Årbok 1937, Naturvidenskapelig rekke* nr. 3: 1–18.     Johnsgard 1955 *Condor* **57** 19–27, 1960 *Wilson Bull.* **72** 133–55, 1961a *Auk* **87** 3–43, 1961b *Am. Midland Nat.* **66** 477–84, 1961c Wildfowl Trust 12th *Rept.* 58–69, 1961d *Wilson Bull.* **73** 227–36, 1964a *Condor* **66** 113–29, 1964b Wildfowl Trust 15th *Rept.* 104–07, 1965 *Handbook of Waterfowl Behavior* (Ithaca, N.Y.: Cornell Univ. Press), 1967 *Am. Midland Nat.* **77** 51–63, 1968a *Waterfowl/Their Biol. and Nat. Hist.* (Lincoln, Nebr.: Univ. Nebr. Press), 1968b *Bull. Brit. Orn. Club* **88** 140–48, Johnsgard and Buss 1956 *Journ. Wildlife Mgt.* **20** 384–88, Johnsgard and Hagemeyer 1969 *Auk* **86** 691–95.     Johnson, A. R., and Barlow 1971 *Southwestern Nat.* **15** 394–95.     Johnson, C. S. 1947 *Journ. Wildlife Mgt.* **2** 21–24.     Johnson, N. F. 1971 *Journ. Wildlife Mgt.* **35** 793–97.     Johnson, O. W. 1961 *Condor* **63** 351–64, 1966 *Auk* **83** 233–39.     Johnson, R. A. 1942 *Aviculture* **12** 233–36 (Mar.–April).     Johnson, T. W. 1973 *Wilson Bull.* **85** 77–78.     Johnston et al. 1971 *Quart. Journ. Fla. Acad. Sci.* **34** no. 2.     Johnstone 1957a *Avicultural Mag.* **63** 23–25, 1957b Wildfowl Trust 8th *Rept.* 38–42, 1961 *Avicultural Mag.* **67** 196–97, 1970 *Avicultural Mag.* **76** 52–55.     Jones, H. L. 1966 *The Chat* **30** 4–7.     Jones, L. 1906 *Wilson Bull.* **18** 26.     Jones, R. D., Jr., 1963a Wildfowl Trust 14th *Rept.* 80–84, 1963b Wildfowl Trust 14th *Rept.* 175, 1965 Wildfowl Trust 16th *Rept.* 83–85, 1970 *Journ. Wildlife Mgt.* **34** 328–33, Jones, R. D., Jr., and Jones 1966 Wildfowl Trust 17th *Rept.* 75–78.     Jones, R. E., and Leopold 1967 *Journ. Wildlife Mgt.* **31** 221–28.     Jones, R. N., and Obbard 1970 *Auk* **87** 370–71.     Jones, T. 1951 *Avicultural Mag.* **57** 12.     Jordan 1953 *Journ. Wildlife Mgt.* **17** 304–11.     Jourdain 1922 *Auk* **39** 166–71.     Judd 1901 U. S. Dept. Agric. *Yearbook for 1900* 411–36, 1902 U.S. Dept. Agric., Biol. Surv. *Bull.* 17.     Jull 1930 *Nat. Geog. Mag.* **57** 326–71.     Junca et al. 1962 *Trans. 27th N. Am. Wildlife Conf.* 114–21.

Kaczynski and Geis 1961 U.S. Fish and Wildlife Serv., *Spec. Sci. Rept.—Wildlife* no. 59.     Kalmbach 1937 U.S. Dept. Agric., *Circular* no. 433, 1938 *Trans. 3rd N. Am. Wildlife Conf.* 610–23.     Kapitonov 1962 *Ornitologiya* no. 5: 35–48.     Kartaschev 1961 *Zool. Zhurnal* (Moscow) **40** 1395–410, 1962 *Journ. f. Ornithol.* **103** 297–98.     Kear 1961 *Brit. Birds* **54** 427–28, 1965 *Journ. Wildlife Mgt.* **29** 523–28, 1966 *Ibis* **108** 144–45, 1970 *Wildfowl* no. 21: 123–32, Kear and Burton 1971 *Ibis* **113** 483–93.     Keith 1961 *Wildlife Monogr.* no. 6, Keith and Stanislawski 1960 *Journ. Wildlife Mgt.* **24** 95–96.     Kennard 1919 *Auk* **36** 455–60, 1927 *Proc. New Eng. Zool. Club* **9** 85–93.     Kenyon 1961 *Auk* **78** 305–26, 1963 *Auk* **80** 539–41.     Kerbes et al. 1971 *Wildfowl* no. 22: 5–17.     Kessel and Cade 1958 Univ. of Alaska *Biol. Pap.* no. 2, Kessel and Springer 1966 *Condor* **68** 185–95.     Kilham 1954 *Auk* **71** 316.     King 1963 *Journ. Wildlife Mgt.* **27** 356–62, 1970 *Wildfowl* no. 21: 11–17.     Kinlen 1963 Wildfowl Trust 14th *Rept.* 107–14.     Kistschinskii 1968 [*Birds of the Kolyma Highlands*] (Moscow), 1971 *Wildfowl* no. 22: 29–34.     Kitchen and Hunt 1969 *Journ. Wildlife Mgt.* **33** 605–09.     Klein 1966 *Arctic* **19** 319–36.     Klopman 1958 *Wilson Bull.* **70** 168–83, 1962 *The Living Bird* 1st Annual 123–29.     Knight 1908 *Birds of Me.*

(Bangor, Me.).    Koenig 1911 *Avifauna Spitzbergensis* (Bonn).    Kokhanov 1967 *Trans. Kandalaksh State Reserve* no. 5: 40–48, 1974 Sixth All-Union Ornithol. Congr., Moscow, *Proc.* pt. 1: 207–08.    Kondla 1973 *Auk* **90** 890.    Korschgen 1955 Mo. Cons. Comm. *P–R Ser.* no. 14.    Kortegaard 1968 *Dansk Orn. Foren. Tidsskr.* **62** 37–67.    Kortright 1942 *The Ducks, Geese, and Swans of N. Am.* (Wash., D.C.: Am. Wildlife Inst.).    Koskimies 1957 *Ann. Zool. Soc. 'Vanamo'* **18** no. 9, 1958 *Suomen Riista* **12** 70–78, Koskimies and Routamo 1953 *Papers on Game Research* (Helsinki) no. 10, Koskimies and Lahti 1964 *Auk* **84** 281–307.    Kossack 1947 *Journ. Wildlife Mgt.* **11** 119–26, 1950 *Am. Midland Nat.* **43** 627–49.    Kozlik et al. 1959 *Calif. Fish and Game* **45** 69–82.    Krabbe 1926 *Vidensk. Medd. dansk Naturh. Foren. Kbh.* **80** 543–55, 1929 *Proc. 6th Internat. Orn. Congress* (1926) 173–80.    Krashkin 1962 *Ornitologiya* no. 4: 449–52.    Krechmar and Leonovich 1967 *Problemy Severa* no. 11: 229–34 TRANSL. 1968 *Problems of the North* no. 11: 283–89 (Ottawa: Nat. Research Council).    Krog 1953 *Condor* **55** 299–304.    Kubichek 1933 *Iowa State Coll. Journ. Sci.* **8** 107–26.    Kuhring (ed.) 1969 *Proc. World Conf. on Bird Hazards to Aircraft* (Ottawa: Nat. Research Council).    Kulachkova 1960 *Trans. Kandalaksh State Reserve* no. 3: 91–106.    Kumari (ed.) 1966 *Trans. Conf. for Study, Protection, and Propagation of the Common Eider* (Tartu, Estonia), 1968 *The Common Eider . . . in the U.S.S.R.* (Tallinn, Estonia: Proc. of a Conf., Estonia, May 1966), 1971 *Wildfowl* no. 22: 35–43.    Kumlien and Hollister 1903 *The Birds of Wisc.* (Milwaukee).    Kuroda 1929 *Condor* **31** 173–80, 1937 *Tori* **9** 273–99, 1952 *Tori* **13** 4–9, 1953 *Condor* **55** 100–01, 1959 *Dobutsugaku Zasshi* [Zool. Mag. Tokyo] **68** 330–34, 1960 *Dobutsugaku Zasshi* **69** 277–79, 1961a *Annotationes Zoologicae Japonenses* **34** 159–60, 1961b *Bull. Biogeogr. Soc. Japan* (1959) **21** 75–76, 1961c *Bull. Biogeogr. Soc. Japan.* (1959) **21** 77–78, 1968 *Tori* **18** 392–405, Kuroda and Kuroda 1960 *Annotationes Zoologicae Japonenses* **33** 61–65.    Kutz et al. 1948 N.Y. Cons. Dept. *Proj.* 20-R.    Kuyt 1962 *Can. Field-Nat.* **76** 224.

Lagler and Wienert 1948 *Wilson Bull.* **60** 118.    La Hart and Cornwell 1971 *Proc. 24th An. Conf.* [1970] *Southeastern Assn. Game and Fish Commrs.* 117–21.    Laidley 1939 *Avicultural Mag.* 5th ser. **4** 102–03.    Laing 1925 Canada, Dept. Mines *Mus. Bull.* no. 40.    Lampio 1961 *Suomen Riista* **14** 82–94.    Lanyon 1962 *Nat. History* **71** no. 7: 38–43.    Larionov 1956 *Zool. Zhurnal* (Moscow) **31** 89–95.    Larsen and Norderhaug 1964 *Sterna* **6** 153–68.    Latham 1790 *Index Ornithologicus* **2** (London), Latham and Romsey 1798 *Trans. Linn. Soc. London* ser. 1 **4** 90–128.    Latta and Sharkey 1966 *Journ. Wildlife Mgt.* **30** 17–23.    Lawrence 1846 *Ann. Lyceum Nat. Hist. N.Y.* **4** 171–72, 1874 Boston Soc. Nat. Hist. *Memoirs* **2** 265–319.    Lawson 1709 *A New Voyage to Carolina . . .* (London) (reissued 1714 *The Hist. of Carolina*).    Lebret 1947 *Ardea* **35** 79–131, 1951 *Brit. Birds* **44** 412–13, 1955 *Journ. f. Ornithol.* **96** 43–49, 1958a *Ardea* **46** 68–72, 1958b *Ardea* **46** 75–79.    Lech 1968 *Cassinia* no. 50: 9–11.    Le Cren and Holdgate (eds.) 1962 *The Exploitation of Natural Animal Populations* (Oxford, Eng.: Blackwell).    Lehmann V 1957 *Novedades Colombianas* no. 3: 101–56.    Leitch 1964 *Can. Field-Nat.* **78** 199.    Lemieux 1958 *Les Carnets* **18** 12–18, 1959a *Can. Field-Nat.* **73** 117–28, 1959b *Naturaliste Canadien* **86** 133–92.    Lemieux and Moisan 1959 *Trans. Northeastern Wildlife Conf.* (1958)

124–48.    Lensink 1968 *Journ. Wildlife Mgt.* **32** 418–20.    Leonard and Shetter 1937 *Trans. Am. Fisheries Soc.* **66** 335–37.    Leopold, A. 1921 *Condor* **23** 85–86.    Leopold, A. S. 1959 *Wildlife of Mexico* (Berkeley: Univ. Calif. Press). Leopold, F. 1951 *Condor* **53** 209–20.    Lévêque 1964 *Alauda* **32** 5–44, 81–96. Lévêque et al. 1966 *Condor* **68** 81–101.    Leverkühn 1890 *Journ. f. Ornithol.* **38** 168–232.    Levy 1964 *Audubon Field Notes* **18** 558–59.    Lewis, E. J. 1863 *The Am. Sportsman* (Philadelphia).    Lewis, H. F. 1931 *Can. Field-Nat.* **45** 57–62, 1933 *Bird-Banding* **4** 112–13, 1937 *Auk* **54** 73–95.    Lewis, L. B., and Domm 1948 *Physiol. Zool.* **21** 65–69.    Lewis, W. E. 1925 *Auk* **42** 441.    Ligon 1965 *Bull. Fla. State Mus., Biol. Sciences* **10** no. 4.    Lincoln 1926 *Condor* **28** 153–57, 1929 *Bull. Northeastern Bird-Banding Assoc.* **5** 92–94, 1935a U.S. Dept. Agric., *Circular* 363, 1935b *Trans. 21st N. Am. Game Conf.* 264–76, 1943 *Condor* **45** 232, 1950a U.S. Dept. Interior, Fish and Wildlife Service *Circular* no. 16, 1950b *Audubon Mag.* **52** 282–87.    Lind 1959 *Dansk Orn. Foren. Tidsskr.* **53** 177–219, Lind and Poulsen 1963 *Zeitschr. f. Tierpsychol.* **20** 558–69.    Lindroth and Bergstrom 1959 Inst. Freshwater Research, Drottingholm *Rept.* no. 40.    Lindsey 1946 *Auk* **63** 483–92.    Linduska (ed.) 1964 *Waterfowl Tomorrow* (U.S. Bur. Sport Fisheries and Wildlife, Fish and Wildlife Service).    Linsdale 1933 *Condor* **35** 38–39.    Linton 1908 *Condor* **10** 124–29.    Lippins 1937 *Gerfaut* **27** 122–23.    Lissaman and Shollenberger 1970 *Science* **168** 1003–5.    Littlejohn 1899 *Osprey* **3** 78–79.    Lokemoen 1966 *Journ. Wildlife Mgt.* **30** 668–81, 1967 Wilson Bull **79** 238–39.    Longacre and Cornwell 1964 *Journ. Wildlife Mgt.* **28** 527–31.    Longhurst 1955 *Condor* **57** 307–08.    Longstaff 1932 *Journ. Animal Ecol.* **1** 119–42.    Lönnberg 1926 *Fauna och Flora* **21** 193–208, 1927 *Fauna och Flora* **22** 1–3.    Løppenthin 1932 *Meddel. om Grønland* **91** no. 6.    Lord et al. 1962 *Science* **137** no. 3523: 39–40.    Lorenz 1941 *Journ. f. Ornithol.* **89** (Sonderheft): 194–293 TRANSL. 1951 *Avicult. Mag.* **57** 157–82, 1952 **58** 8–17, 61–72, 86–94, 172–84, 1953 **59** 24–34, 80–91, 1958 *Sci. American* **199** no. 6: 67–76, 78.    Lorenz and von de Wall 1960 *Journ. f. Ornithol.* **101** 50–60.    Loring 1890 *Ornithol. and Ool.* **15** 81–87.    Løvenskiold 1964 *Avifauna Svalbardensis* (Oslo: Norsk Polar-Institutt *Skryfter* **129**).    Low, A. P. 1906 *Rept. Dominion Gov't Exped. to Hudson Bay . . . on board D. G. S. Neptune 1903–1904.* (Ottawa).    Low, J. B. 1945 *Ecol. Monogr.* **15** 35–69.    Lowery 1931 La. Polytech. Inst. *Bull.* **29** no. 4, 1955 *Louisiana Birds* (Baton Rouge: La. State Univ. Press).    Lucas 1944 *Brit. Birds* **37** 199.    Lumsden 1959 *Trans. Northeast Wildlife Conf.* (1958) **1** 156–64.    Lynch 1939 *Auk* **56** 374–80, 1943 *Auk* **60** 100–02, Lynch et al. 1947 *Journ. Wildlife Mgt.* **11** 50–76.    Lysaght 1959 *Bull. Brit. Mus. (Nat. Hist.), Historical ser.* no. 6: 251–371.

Mabbott 1920 U.S. Dept. Agric. *Bull.* no. 862.    McAtee 1910 *Auk* **27** 337–39, 1911 U.S. Biol. Survey *Circular* no. 81, 1914 U.S. Dept. Agric. *Bull.* no. 58, 1915 U.S. Dept. Agric. *Bull.* no. 205, 1917 *Auk* **34** 415–21, 1918 U.S. Dept. Agric. *Bull.* no. 720, 1922 *Auk* **39** 380–86.    McCabe and McCabe 1935 *Condor* **37** 79–80.    McCartney 1963 *The Fulvous Tree Duck in La.* (New Orleans, La.: Wild Life and Fisheries Comm.).    McClanahan 1942 *Auk* **59** 589.    McCoy 1963 *Auk* **80** 335–51.    MacDonald 1954 Nat. Mus. Canada *Bull.* no. 132: 214–38.    McEwen 1958 *Can. Field-Nat.* **72** 122–27.    MacFarlane 1891 U.S. Nat. Mus. *Proceedings* **14** 413–

46.    MacGillivray 1852 *A List of Brit. Birds, indigenous and migratory* . . . **5** (London).    McGilvrey 1966a *Journ. Wildlife Mgt.* **30** 193–95, 1966b *Auk* **83** 477–79, 1966c *Journ. Wildlife Mgt.* **30** 577–80, (compiler) 1968 U.S. Bur. Sport Fisheries and Wildlife *Resource Pub.* no. 60, 1969 *Journ. Wildlife Mgt.* **33** 73–76.    McGilvrey and Uhler 1971 *Journ. Wildlife Mgt.* **35** 793–97.    McHenry 1968 *Wilson Bull.* **80** 229–30.    McIlhenny 1932 *Auk* **49** 279–306, 1943 *Auk* **60** 541–49.    MacInnes 1962 *Journ. Wildlife Mgt.* **26** 247–56, 1966 *Journ. Wildlife Mgt.* **30** 536–53.    MacInnes and Cook 1963 *Auk* **80** 77–79.    MacKay, G. H. 1890a *Auk* **7** 294–95, 1890b *Auk* **7** 315–19, 1891 *Auk* **8** 279–80, 1892 *Auk* **9** 330–37, 1894 *Auk* **11** 224.    Mackay, R. H. 1957 *Condor* **59** 339.    McKernan and Scheffer 1942 *Condor* **44** 264–66.    McKinney 1953 Severn Wildfowl Trust 5th *Rept.* 68–70, 1959 Wildfowl Trust 10th *Rept.* 133–40, 1961 *Behaviour* Suppl. 7: 124pp., 1965a Wildfowl Trust 16th *Rept.* 92–106, 1965b *Wilson Bull.* **77** 112–21, 1965c *Condor* **67** 273–90, 1967 Wildfowl Trust 18th *Rept.* 108–21, 1970 *Living Bird* 9th Annual: 29–64.    McKnight and Buss 1962 *Journ. Wildlife Mgt.* **26** 328–29.    McLaren and Bell 1972 Nova Scotia Mus. Sci. *Spec. Pub.* 50pp.    McLaughlin and Grice 1952 *Trans. 17th N. Am. Wildlife Conf.* 242–59.    McLean 1925 *Condor* **27** 116–17.    McMahan 1970 *Journ. Wildlife Mgt.* **34** 946–49.    McMahan and Fritz 1967 *Journ. Wildlife Mgt.* **31** 783–87.    Macpherson and McLaren 1959 *Can. Field-Nat.* **73** 63–81.    Macpherson and Manning 1959 Nat. Mus. Canada *Bull.* 161.    McRoy 1970 *On the Biol. of Eelgrass in Alaska* (Univ. of Alaska: Ph.D. thesis).    McRoy and Phillips 1968 U.S.Fish and Wildlife Service *Spec. Sci. Rept.—Wildlife* no. 114.    Madon 1935 *Alauda* ser. 3 **7** 546–68.    Madsen 1954 *Danish Rev. Game Biol.* **2** 157–266, 1957 *Danish Rev. Game Biol.* **3** 19–83.    Maher 1960 *Condor* **62** 138–39.    Maher and Nettleship 1968 *Auk* **85** 320–21.    Maillard 1902 *Condor* **4** 46.    Malone 1965 *Journ. Wildlife Mgt.* **29** 529–33, 1966 *Wilson Bull.* **78** 227–28.    Mann 1950 *Journ. Wildlife Mgt.* **14** 360–62.    Manniche 1910 *Meddel. om. Grønland* **45** no. 1.    Manning 1946 *Can. Field-Nat.* **60** 71–85, 1949 Appendix (pp. 155–224) to Manning, Mrs. Tom [Ella W.] *A Summer on Hudson Bay* (London: Hodder and Stoughton), 1952 Nat. Mus. Canada *Bull.* 125.    Manning and Coates 1952 *Can. Field-Nat.* **66** 1–35, 1961 *Trans. Roy. Can. Inst.* **33** pt. 2: 116–239.    Manning et al. 1956 Nat. Mus. Canada *Bull.* 143.    Marakov 1966 [ *Land Where Birds have no Fear; Animal Life of Commander Is.* ] (Moscow: "Nauka" Pub. House).    Marchant 1960 *Ibis* **102** 349–82.    Markgren 1963 *Acta Vertebratica* **2** 298–418.    Marquardt 1955 *Study of Waterfowl Productivity on an Unmanaged Sedge-Meadow Marsh in Me.* (Univ. of Me.: M.S. thesis).    Martin, A. C. et al. 1951 *Am. Wildlife and Plants* (N.Y.: McGraw-Hill).    Martin, F. W. 1964 *Behavior and Survival of Canada Geese in Utah* (Utah Dept. Fish and Game, *Information Bull.* no. 64.7).    Martinson and Hawkins 1968 *Auk* **85** 684–86.    Martz 1964 *Wilson Bull.* **76** 291–92.    Mathiasson 1963 *Acta Vertebratica* **2** 419–533, 1970 *Brit. Birds* **63** 414–24.    Matthews 1972 *Wildfowl* no. 22: 120–21.    Mauersberger 1958 *Beitr. z. Vögelkunde* **6** 122–36.    Mayaud 1962 *Alauda* **30** 148–50.    Mayhoff 1918 *Verhandl. der Ornithol. Gesellschaft in Bayern* **13** 351–59.    Meanley and Meanley 1958 *Auk* **75** 96, 1959 *Wilson Bull.* **71** 33–45.    Mednis 1968 *Ecol. of Waterfowl of Latvia/Ornithol. Study* no. 5:71–108 (Riga: Inst. of Biol., Acad. Sci).    Meinertzhagen 1955 *Ibis* **97** 81–117.    Meise *see*

542

Schönwetter.    Mendall 1949a *Trans. 14th N. Am. Wildlife Conf.* 58–64, 1949b
*Journ. Wildlife Mgt.* **13** 64–101, 1958 *The Ring-necked Duck in the Northeast* (Univ. of
Mc. *Bull.* **60** no. 16, *Univ. of Me. Studies* 2nd ser. no. 73).    Mendall and Gashwiler
1940 *Auk* **57** 245–46.    Merne 1972 *Ibis* **114** 584.    Mershon 1927 *Auk* **44** 95–96,
1928 *Auk* **45** 93.    Meyer de Schauensee 1966 *The Species of Birds of S. Am. with
their Distribution* (Narberth, Pa.: Livingston Pub. Co.).    Michael and Michael 1922
*Auk* **39** 14–23.    von Middendorff 1853 *Reise in den äussersten Norden und Osten
Sibiriens . . .* (St. Petersburg) 124–246.    Mihelsons and Viksne (eds.) 1968 *Ecol. of
Waterfowl of Latvia* (Riga: "Zinatne" Pub. House).    Mihelsons et al. 1968 *Ecol. of
Waterfowl of Latvia* 109–52.    Mikhel 1935 *Trudy Arkticheskogo Instituta* **31** 1–101.
Millais 1902a *Nat. Hist. Brit. Surface-feeding Ducks* (London and Bombay), 1902b
*Ibis* ser. 8 **2** 163–64, 1913a *Brit. Diving Ducks* **1** (London, N.Y., Bombay, Calcutta),
1913b *Brit. Diving Ducks* **2**, 1913c *Brit. Birds* **7** 69–80.    Miller, A. W., and Collins
1954 *Calif. Fish and Game* **40** 17–37.    Miller, H. W., and Dzubin 1965 *Bird-
Banding* **36** 184–91.    Miller, H. W., et al. 1968 *Trans. 33rd N. Am. Wildlife and Nat.
Resources Conf.* 101–19.    Miller, W. deW. 1925 *Auk* **42** 41–50, 1926 *Am. Mus. Novitates* no. 243.    Mills 1962a Wildfowl Trust 13th *Rept.* 79–92, 1962b *Freshwater Salmon Fish Research* (Edinburgh) no. 29: 3–10.    Milne 1963 *Ibis* **105** 428, 1965 *Bird
Study* **12** 170–80, 1969 *Ibis* **111** 278.    Milne and Robertson 1965 *Nature* **205** 367–
69.    Milne and Reed 1974 *Can. Field-Nat.* **88** 163–69.    Milonski 1958 *Trans. 23rd
N. Am. Wildlife Conf.* 215–28.    Miner 1940 *Pennsylvania Game News* **11** no. 6: 4–5,
28 (Sept.).    Minton 1968 *Wildfowl* no. 19: 41–60, 1971 *Wildfowl* no. 22: 71–
88.    Miskimen 1955 *Condor* **57** 179–84.    Moffitt 1931 *Calif. Fish and Game* **17**
20–26, 1932 *Calif. Fish and Game* **18** 298–310, 1937 *Condor* **39** 149–59, 1938 *Condor*
**40** 76–84, 1939 *Condor* **41** 93–97, 1940 *Condor* **42** 309.    Moffitt and Cottam 1941
U.S. Fish and Wildlife Service *Wildlife Leaflet* no. 204.    Moisan 1966 *Naturaliste
Canadienne* **93** 69–88.    Moisan et al. 1967 U.S. Bur. Sport Fisheries and Wildlife,
*Spec. Sci. Rept.—Wildlife* no. 100.    Monnie 1966 *Journ. Wildlife Mgt.* **30** 691–
96.    Monson, G., and Phillips 1964 *A Checklist of the Birds of Ariz.* (Tucson: Univ.
Ariz. Press).    Monson, M. A. 1956 *Condor* **58** 444–45.    Moody 1944 *Avicultural
Mag.* **9** no. 4: 86 (July–Aug.).    Moreau 1967 *Ibis* **109** 232–59.    Morris and Ogilvie
1962 Wildfowl Trust 13th *Rept.* 53–64.    Morse, J. 1950 *Kentucky Waterfowl Studies*
(Ky. Div. Fish and Game Proj. 11-R).    Morse, T. E., and Wight 1969 *Journ. Wildlife
Mgt.* **33** 284–93.    Morse, T. E., et al. 1969 *Journ. Wildlife Mgt.* **33** 596–
604.    Moynihan 1959 *Nat. Geog. Mag.* **116** 562–70.    Munro, D. A. 1960 *Proc. 12th
Internat. Orn. Congr.* 542–56, 1961 *Canadian Geogr. Journ.* **63** 58–63 Aug.    Munro,
D. (ed.) 1969 Can. Wildlife Service *Rept. Ser.* no. 6.    Munro, G. C. 1960 *Birds of
Hawaii* (Rutland, Vt.: C. E. Tuttle Co.).    Munro, J. A. 1918 *Condor* **20** 3–5, 1923a
*Can. Field-Nat.* **37** 70–74, 1923b *Can. Field-Nat.* **37** 107–16., 1930 *Condor* **32** 261,
1935 *Condor* **37** 82–83, 1936 *Wilson Bull.* **48** 137, 1938 *Wilson Bull.* **50** 288, 1939
*Trans. Royal Can. Inst.* **22** 259–318, 1941 *Can. Journ. Research* sect. D **19** 113–38,
1942 *Can. Journ. Research* **20** 133–60, 1944 *Can. Journ. Research* **22** 60–86, 1945 *Can.
Journ. Research* Sect. D **23** 17–103, 1949a *Can. Journ. Research Sect.* D **27** 289–307,
1949b *Am. Midland Nat.* **41** 1–38, 1949c *Can. Journ. Research Sect.* D **27** 149–78, 1950
B.C. Provincial Mus. *Occas. Pap.* no. 8, 1958 B.C. Provincial Mus. Nat. Hist. and

Anthropol. *Rept.* for 1957:1–18.     Munro, J. A., and Clemens 1931 Can. Biol. Board *Bull.* no. 17, 1936 *Can. Field-Nat.* **50** 34–36, 1937 Biol. Board Canada *Bull.* no. 55, 1939 *Journ. Wildlife Mgt.* **3** 46–53.     Munro, J. A., and Cowan 1947 *A Review of the Bird Fauna of Brit. Columbia* (B.C. Provincial Mus., Dept. of Educ.).     Munro, R. E., et al. 1968 *Auk* **85** 504–05.     Munsterhjelm 1922 *Meddel. fran Göteborgs Musei Zool. Avdelning* no. 13.     Murdoch 1885 *Rept. Internat. Polar Exped. to Point Barrow, Alaska,* . . . pt. IV Natural History, II Birds (Washington, D.C.: Gov't Printing Office). Murdy 1953 *Chronology of the 1951 Waterfowl Breeding Season* (S.D. Dept. Game, Fish, and Parks: Fed. Aid. Proj., Job Completion Rept. 44pp.). Murie, A. 1963 *Birds of Mt. McKinley Nat. Park, Alaska* (Mt. McKinley Nat. Hist. Assoc.).     Murie, J. 1867 *Proc. Zool. Soc. London,* 1867:8–13.     Murie, O. 1954 *A Field Guide to Animal Tracks* (Boston: Houghton Mifflin), 1959 *N. Am. Fauna* no. 61.     Murrell 1959 *Condor* **61** 374.     Murray 1931 *Auk* **48** 110–11.     Musacchia 1953 *Condor* **55** 305–12.     Myres 1959a *The Behaviour of the Sea-Ducks* . . . (Univ. of B.C.: Ph.D. thesis), 1959b *Wilson Bull.* **71** 159–68.

Naumann 1905a *Naturgeschichte der Vögel. Mitteleuropas,* Neuarbeitet von [Blasius et al.]. Edited by C. R. Hennicke. **9** (Gera-Untermhaus), 1905b *Naturgeschichte der Vögel* . . . **10.**     Naylor 1953 *Calif. Fish and Game* **39** 83–94, 1960 *Calif. Fish and Game* **46** 241–69.     Nechaev 1969 [*Birds of the southern Kuril Islands*] (Leningrad: "Nauka" Pub. House).     Neff 1948 *Condor* **50** 271.     Nellis et al. 1970 *Wilson Bull.* **82** 461–62.     Nelson, A. L. 1944 *Wilson Bull.* **56** 170.     Nelson, A. L., and Martin 1953 *Journ. Wildlife Mgt.* **17** 36–42.     Nelson, C. H. 1964 *Auk* **81** 219–21.     Nelson, E. W. 1887 *Rept. upon Nat. Hist. Colls. made in Alaska between the Years 1877 and 1881 (Washington, D.C.: Arctic Ser. Publ. in connection with Signal Serv., U.S. Army, no. 3).*     Nelson, H. K. 1952 *Auk* **69** 425–28, 1963 *Trans. 28th N. Am. Wildlife Conf.* 133–50. Nelson, U. C., and Hansen 1959 *Trans. 24th N. Am. Wildlife Conf.* 174–87.     Nero 1959 *Blue Jay* **17** 54, 1963 *Birds of L. Athabasca Region, Sask.* (Sask. Nat Hist. Soc., Spec. Pub. no. 5).     Newstead 1908 *Journ.* [Brit.] *Board Agric.* **15** no. 9 suppl.     Newton, A., and Newton 1859 *Ibis* ser. 1 **1** 365–79.     Newton I., and Campbell 1970 *Scottish Birds* **6** 5–18.     Nicholson 1930 *Ibis* **72** 395–428.     Nickell 1966 *Wilson Bull.* **78** 121–22. Nieman 1972 *Blue Jay* **30** 93–95.     Nilsson 1965 *Vår Fågelvärld* **24** 244–56, 1969 *Wildfowl* no. 20 112–18, 1971 *Vår Fågelvärld* **30** 180–83. Nisbet 1955 *Brit. Birds* **48** 533–37, 1959 *Brit. Birds* **52** 393–416.     Noll 1959 *Ornithol. Beobachter* **56** 128–30.     Nord and Bolund 1964 *Vår Fågelvärld* **23** 326.     Nordberg 1950 *Acta Zool. Fennica* **63** 1–62.     Norderhaug 1968 Norsk Polarinst. *Arbok* 1968:7–35, 1970 *Sterna* **8** 73–80.     Nordhoff 1902 *Auk* **19** 212–14.     Norton 1896 *Auk* **13** 229–34, 1897 *Auk* **14** 303–04, 1900 *Auk* **17** 16–18, 1909 *Auk* **26** 438–40.     Nowak and Monson 1965 *Condor* **67** 357.     Nuttall 1834 *A Manual of the Ornithol. of the U.S. and of Canada* **2** (Boston).

Oates et al. 1956 *Audubon Field Notes* **10** 347.     Ogilvie 1964 Wildfowl Trust 15th *Rept* 84–88, 1968a *Wildfowl* no. 19: 162–64, 1968b *Bird Study* **15** 2–15, 1969 *Wildfowl* no. 20: 79–85, Ogilvie and Matthews 1969 *Wildfowl* no 20: 119–25.     Ohlendorf and Patton 1971 *Wilson Bull.* **83** 97.     Oliver 1970 *Brit. Birds* **63** 388.     Olney 1963a

*Proc. Zool. Soc. London* **140** 169–210, 1963b *Ibis* **105** 55–62, 1965 *Ibis* **107** 527–32, 1969 *Biol. Conservation* **1** 71–76 (Sandy, Bedfordshire, Eng.: Roy. Soc. Prot. Birds). Olney and Mills 1963 *Ibis* **105** 293–300.    Olson 1965 *Trans. 30th N. Am. Wildlife and Nat. Resources Conf.* 121–35.    van Oordt 1921 *Ardea* **10** 129–70.    Oring 1964 *Journ. Wildlife Mgt.* **28** 223–33, 1966 *Breeding Biol. and Molts of the Gadwall . . .* (Univ. Okla. Ph.d. thesis), *1968 Auk* **85** 355–80, 1969 *Wilson Bull.* **81** 44–54.    Osburn 1921 *Science* **53** 451–53.    Ouweeneel 1971 *Limosa* **44** 84–101.    Owen, M. 1972 *Journ. Animal Ecol.* **41** 79–92.    Owen, M., and Kerbes 1971 *Wildfowl* no. 22: 114–19.    Owen, R. B., Jr., 1968 *Auk* **85** 617–32, 1970 *Condor* **72** 153–63.    Owen, R. 1866 *On the Anatomy of the Vertebrates* **2** (London).    Owre 1962 *Auk* **79** 270–71.

Palmer, R. S. 1949 *Maine Birds (Bull. Mus. Comp. Zool. Harvard* **102**), 1973 *Wildfowl* No. 24:154–157.    Palmer, W. 1899 "The Avifauna of the Pribilof Islands," in D. S. Jordan. The Fur Seals and Fur-Seal Is. of the N. Pacific Ocean. Pt. 3 (Washington, D.C.).    Paludan 1962 *Danske Vildtundersogelser* no. 10.    Parkes 1950 *Condor* **52** 91–93, 1953 *Condor* **55** 275–76, 1958 *Ann. Carnegie Mus.* **35** 117–25, 1960 *Can. Field-Nat.* **74** 162–63.    Parks and Bressler 1963 *Auk* **80** 198–99.    Parmelee and MacDonald 1960 Nat. Mus. Canada *Bull.* 169, Parmelee et al. 1967 Nat. Mus. Canada *Bull.* 222.    Parnell and Quay 1965 *Proc. 16th Conf.* [1962] *Southeastern Assoc. Fish and Game Commrs.* 53–67.    Patch 1922 *Can. Field-Nat.* **36** 101-05.    Paterson 1968 *Bull. Brit. Orn. Club* **88** 109–10.    Patterson and Ballou 1953 *Wyo. Wildlife* **17** 4–14, 36.    Paulson 1969 *Auk* **86** 759.    Pavlinen 1965 *Novosti Ornitologii* [=*Ornithol. News* (Moscow)] 281–83.    Payn 1941 *Ibis* **83** 456–59.    Paynter 1951 *Ecology* **32** 497–507, 1955 *Ornithogeogr. of Yucatan Pen.* (Yale Univ.: Peabody Mus. Nat. Hist. *Bull.* no. 9).    Pearse 1921 *Brit. Birds* **15** 70, 1928 *Condor* **30** 251–52, 1945 *Can. Field-Nat.* **59** 66–67, 1950 *Murrelet* **31** 14.    Pearson and Pearson 1895 *Ibis* ser. 7 **1** 237–49.    Peck 1896 *Oregon Nat.* **3** 84.    Pedersen 1942 *Meddel. om Gronland* **128** no. 2.    Pekulak and Littlefield 1969 *Wilson Bull.* **81** 464–65.    von Pelzeln 1870 *Zur Ornithologie Brasiliens* (Vienna).    Pelzl 1971 *Auk* **88** 184–85.    Pennant 1785 *Arctic Zoology* **2** (London).    Penner 1953 *Journ. Parasitol.* **39** (4, sect. 2):20.    Penny and Bailey 1970 *Journ. Wildlife Mgt.* **34** 105–14.    Perrins 1961 *Brit. Birds* **54** 49–54.    Perrins and Reynolds 1967 Wildfowl Trust 18th *Rept.* 74–84.    Persson, Borg, and Fält 1974 *Viltrevy* **9** no. 1. Peters 1931 *Check-List of Birds of the World* **1** (Harvard Univ. Press).    Pethon 1967 *Nytt Mag. Zool.* **15** 97–111.    Pettingill 1959a *Me. Field Nat.* **15** 58–71, 1959b *Wilson Bull.* **71** 205–07, 1962 *Wilson Bull.* **74** 100–01.    Petrovic and King 1972 *Auk* **89** 660. Pflugbeil 1956 *Die Vögelwelt* **77** 44–47.    Philippona 1972 *Die Blessgans* Wittenberg Lutherstadt: A. Ziemsen. Neue Brehm Bücherei no. 457),    Philippona and Mulder 1960 *Limosa* **33** 90–127. Phillips, A. R. 1959 *Journ. Ariz. Acad. Sci.* **1** 22–30.    Phillips, A. R., et al. 1964 *The Birds of Arizona* (Tucson: Univ. Ariz. Press).    Phillips, J. C. 1911 *Auk* **28** 188–200, 1912 *Auk* **29** 295–306, 1915 *Journ. Exper. Zool.* **18** 69–144, 1916 *Auk* **33** 22–27, 1923a *Nat. Hist. of the Ducks* **1** (Boston: Houghton Mifflin), 1923b *Nat. Hist. of the Ducks* **2**, 1925 *Nat. Hist. of the Ducks* **3**, 1926 *Nat. Hist. of the Ducks* **4**, 1928 U.S. Dept. Agric. *Tech. Bull.* no. 61, 1932 *Auk* **49** 445–53.    Phillips, R. C. 1964 U.S. Bur. Sport Fisheries and

Wildlife, *Spec. Sci. Rept.—Wildlife* no. 79. Picozzi 1958 *Brit. Birds* **51** 308. Pilcher and Kear 1966 *Brit. Birds* **59** 160–61. Pirnie 1935 *Mich. Waterfowl Management* (Lansing, Mich.), 1954 Mich. Agr. Exper. Sta. *Quarterly Bull.* **37** 95–104. Pitelka 1948 *Condor* **50** 113–23. Pitt 1944 *Bull. Brit. Ornithol. Club* **64** no. 45: 33–35 (March 9). Player 1971 *Wildfowl* no. 22: 100–106. Pleske 1928 Boston Soc. Nat. Hist. *Memoirs* **6** no. 3. Ploeger 1968 *Ardea* **56** 1–159. Poll 1911 *Proc. 5th Internat. Orn. Congr.* (1910) 399–468. Pollard and Walters-Davies 1968 *Wildfowl* no. 19: 108–16. Polunin and Eklund 1953 *Can. Field-Nat.* **67** 134–37. Pool 1962 Wildfowl Trust 13th *Rept.* 126–29. Poole 1940 *Auk* **57** 577–78. Porsild 1943 *Can. Field-Nat.* **57** 19–35, 1951 *Can. Field-Nat.* **65** 40–42. Portenko 1939 [*Fauna of the Anadyr Region. Birds*, pt. 2] *Trans. Inst. Polar Agric., Anim. Husbandry, . . .* ser.: *Hunting and Fishing Industry* **6** (Leningrad and Moscow), 1952 *Trudy Zool. Inst. A.N., USSR* **9** 1100–32, 1959 *Aquila* **66** 119–34, 1960 *Proc. 12th Internat. Orn. Congr.* **2** 615–20, 1963 *Proc. 13th Internat. Orn. Congr.* 1140–46, 1972 *The Birds of the Chukotsk Pen. and Wrangel I.* pt. 1 (Leningrad: "Nauka" Pub. House). Portmann 1945 *Archiv. suisses d'Ornithol.* **2** 181–84. Post 1968 *Kingbird* **19** 132–34. Potts 1961 *Dansk Orn. Foren. Tidsskr.* **55** 152–60. Potvin 1954 *Les Carnets* **14** 110–17. Poulsen 1949 *Dansk Orn. Foren. Tidsskr.* **42** 173–201. Preble 1908 *N. Am. Fauna* no. 27. Preble and McAtee 1923 *N. Am. Fauna* no. 46. Prevett et al. 1972 *Can. Field-Nat.* **86** 369–72. Prevett and MacInnes 1972 *Condor* **74** 431–38, 1973 *Condor* **75** 124–25. Prevett and Prevett 1973 *Auk* **90** 202–04. Price 1899 *Bull. Cooper Orn. Club* **1** no. 5: 89–93. Priklonskii et al. 1962 *Migrasti Zhivotnykh* no. 3 (Moscow): 145–59. Prince 1968 *Journ. Wildlife Mgt.* **32** 489–500. Prince et al. 1968 *Growth* **32** 225–33, 1969 *Auk* **86** 762–63, 1970 *Auk* **87** 342–52.

Quay and Crichter 1965 *Proc. 16th An. Conf.* [1962] *Southeastern Assoc. Game and Fish Commrs.* 200–09. Quorthrup and Holt 1940 *Journ. Am. Veterinary Med. Assoc.* **96** 543–44.

Radde 1863 *Reisen in Süden von Ost-Siberien in den Jahren 1855–1859 . . .* **2** *Die Festlands—Ornis des südöstlichen Siberiens* (St. Petersburg). Raine 1892 *Bird-Nesting in North-West Canada* (Toronto: Hunter, Rose and Co.), 1904 *Oologist* **21** 200–01. Raitasuo 1964 *Papers on Game Research* (Helsinski) no. 24. Rajala and Ormio 1970 *Papers on Game Research* (Helsinki) no. 31: 2–9. Ramsay 1956 *Wilson Bull.* **68** 275–81, 1961 *Anim. Behaviour* **9** 104–05. Rand 1946 Nat. Mus. Canada *Bull.* 105, 1947 *Auk* **64** 281–84, 1948a *Evolution* **2** 314–21, 1948b Nat. Mus. Canada *Bull.* 111. Ransom 1927 *Condor* **29** 170. Ranwell and Downing 1959 *Animal Behaviour* **7** 42–56. Rathbun 1934 *Murrelet* **15** 23–24. Raveling 1968 *Journ. Wildlife Mgt.* **32** 412–14, 1969a *Journ. Wildlife Mgt.* **33** 19–30, 1969b *Auk* **86** 671–81, 1970 *Behaviour* **37** 291–319. Raveling et al. 1972 *Wilson Bull.* **84** 278–95. Rawls 1958 *Reelfoot Lake Waterfowl Research* (Tenn. Game and Fish Comm., Proj. W-22-R). Ray, C. E., et al. 1968 *Smithsonian Misc. Colls.* **153** no. 3. Ray, John 1678 *The Ornithol. of Francis Willoughby . . . Translated into English* (London: Printed for A. C. by J. Martyn). Ray, M. S. 1912 *Condor* **14** 67–72. Reed

1964 *Trans. Northeast Wildlife Conf.* 20pp. (mimeo.), 1971 *Wildfowl* no. 22: 61– 62, 1972 *The Migr. and Mortality Rates of Breeding Eiders . . . St. Lawrence Estuary* (Ste.-Foy, Que., Can. Wildlife Serv.: 21pp., mimeo). Reed and Cousineau 1967 *Naturaliste Canadienne* **94** 327–34. Reif 1896 *Me. Field Nat.* **22** 112–14 (June). Reiser and Führer 1896 *Materiallen zu einer Ornis balcanica* 4 *Montenegro* (Vienna). Reynolds 1966 *Calif. Fish and Game* **52** 118. Riabov 1960 *Ornitologiya* no. 3: 384–95. Rich 1907 *Feathered Game of the Northeast . . .* (N.Y.: T. Y. Crowell). Richardson 1851 *Arctic Searching Exped.* (London). Rienecker 1965 *Calif. Fish and Game* **51** 132–46, 1968 *Calif. Fish and Game* **54** 17– 26. Rienecker and Anderson 1960 *Calif. Fish and Game* **46** 481–506. Ringleben 1936 *Ornithol. Monatsber.* **44** 178–79. Ripley 1951 *Minn. Naturalist* **2** 14–15 (Sept.), 1956 *Avicult. Mag.* **62** 181–82, 1961 *A Synopsis of the Birds of India and Pakistan* (Bombay Nat. Hist. Soc.), 1963 *Wilson Bull.* **75** 373–75. Ripley and Watson 1956 *Postilla* (Yale Peabody Mus.) no. 26. Roberts, A. A., and Huntington 1959 New Mex. Dept. Game and Fish *Bull.* no. 9. Roberts, B. 1934 *Ibis* **76** 239– 64. Roberts, E. L. 1966 Wildfowl Trust 17th *Rept.* 36–45. Roberts, T. S. 1932 *The Birds of Minn.* **1** (Minneapolis: Univ. of Minn. Press). Robertson, D. J. 1929 *Brit. Birds* **23** 26–30. Robertson, W. B., and Mason 1965 *Fla. Nat.* **38** 131– 38. Robinson, H. W. 1909 *Brit. Birds* **2** 311. Robinson, R. H. 1958 *Condor* **60** 256–57. Røen 1960 *Dansk Orn. Foren. Tidsskr.* **54** 128–35. Rogers 1964 *Journ. Wildlife Mgt.* **28** 213–22, 1967 *Wilson Bull.* **79** 339. Rogers and Korschgen 1966 *Journ. Wildlife Mgt.* **30** 258–64. Rogers and Hansen 1967 *Bird-Banding* **38** 234– 35. Rollin 1957 *Condor* **59** 263–65. Rolnik 1943 *Journ. Wildlife Mgt.* **7** 155– 62. Rollo and Bolen 1969 *Southwestern Nat.* **14** 171–88. Römer and Schaudinn 1900 *Fauna Arctica* **1** (Jena). Rosen and Bankowski 1960 *Calif. Fish and Game* **46** 81–90. Ross 1938 *Brit. Birds* **32** 153–54. van Rossem 1923 *Condor* **25** 31. Roth et al. 1902 *Deutsches Weidwerk unter der Mitternachtsonne* (Berlin). Rowan 1931 *The Riddle of Migration* (Baltimore: Williams and Wilkins Co.). Rowley 1877 *Ornithol. Miscellany* **2** pt. 6: 205–33 (London: Quaritch). Rudenko 1947 [*The ancient culture of the Bering Sea and the Eskimo problem*](Moscow-Leningrad: Pub. House Main Northern Sea Route) TRANSL. 1961 Arctic Inst. N. Am. *Anthropol. of the North, Transl. from Russian Sources* no. 1. Rutilevskii 1957 Arctic Scientific-Research Inst., Northern Sea Route Hq., Ministry of Sea Transport USSR *Trans.* **205** 33–62 (Leningrad: Marine Transport Pub. House), 1963 *Trans. Arctic and Antarctic Inst.* **224** 93–117. Ryan 1972 *Journ. Wildlife Mgt.* **36** 759–65. Ryden and Kallander 1964 *Vår Fågelvärld* **23** 151–56. Ryder, J. P. 1967 Can. Wildlife Serv., *Rept. Ser.* no. 3, 1969 *Auk* **86** 282–92, 1970 *Wilson Bull.* **82** 5–13, 1971a *Wildfowl* no. 22: 18–28, 1971b *Wilson Bull.* **83** 438–39, 1972 *Ardea* **60** 185–215, Ryder, J. P., and Cook 1973 *Auk* **90** 691–92. Ryder, R. A. 1955 *A Prelim. Analysis of Waterfowl Recoveries in Colo. . . .* (Colo. Cons. Comm., Fed. Aid Proj., Job Completion Rept.), 1959 *Auk* **76** 424–42, 1961 *Trans. 26th N. Am. Wildlife Conf.* 134–46. Rylander and Bolen 1970 *Auk* **87** 72–90.

Sage 1957 *Bull. Brit. Orn. Club* **77** 140, 1958 *Bull. Brit. Orn. Club* **78** 108–13, 1962 Wildfowl Trust 13th *Rept.* 171, 1963a *Brit. Birds* **56** 22–27, 1963b *Bull. Brit. Orn.*

*Club* **83** 75–77.    St. Quintin 1917 *Avicult. Mag.* ser. 3 **8** 248–51.    Salomonsen 1942 *Journ. f. Ornithol.* **89** 282–337, 1946 *Göteborgs Kungl. Vetenskaps-* . . . B **3** no. 10, 1948 *Dansk Orn. Foren. Tidsskr.* **42** 102–08, 1949 *Avicult. Mag.* **55** 59–62, 1950 *The Birds of Greenland* pt. 1 (Copenhagen: E. Munksgaard), 1957 *Dansk Orn. Foren. Tidsskr.* **51** 119–31, 1958 *Vidensk Meddel. Dansk Naturh. Foren.* **120** 43–80 (reissued 1958 Internat. Wildfowl Research Bureau pub. no. 4), 1959 *Dansk Orn. Foren. Tidsskr.* **53** 31–39, 1961 *Dansk Orn. Foren. Tidsskr.* **55** 197–208, 1965 *Dansk Orn. Foren. Tidsskr.* **59** 92—103, 1966 *Beretninger vedrørende Grønland 1966* no. 1: 46–51, 1967a *Fuglene på Grønland* (Copenhagen: Rhodos), 1967b *Dansk Orn. Foren. Tidsskr.* **61** 151–64, 1968 *Wildfowl* no. 19: 5–24, 1971 *Meddel. om Grønland* **191** no. 2, 1972 *Proc. 15th Internat. Orn. Congr.* 25–77.    Salt 1961 *Auk* **78** 427–28.    Salyer and Lagler 1940 *Journ. Wildlife Mgt.* **4** 186–219.    Samson 1971 *Bird-Banding* **42** 115–18.    Saunders, A. A. 1926 *Roosevelt Wild Life Bull.* **3** no. 3.    Saunders, G. B., et al. 1950 U.S. Fish and Wildlife Serv., *Spec. Sci. Rept.—Wildlife* no. 5.    Savage 1908 Buffalo Soc. Nat. Sci. *Bull.* **9** 23–28.    Savile 1951 *Can. Field-Nat.* **65** 145–57, Savile and Oliver 1964 *Can. Field-Nat.* **78** 1–7.    Sawyer 1928 *Wilson Bull.* **40** 5–17.    Saylor 1941 *Auk* **58** 92.    Schauensee (*see* Meyer de Schauensee).    Scheffer and Hotchkiss 1945 State of Wash., Dept. of Game, *Biol. Bull.* no. 7.    Scheider 1957 *Kingbird* **7** 14.    Schiøler 1908 *Dansk Orn. Foren. Tidsskr.* **2** 109–49, 1925 *Danmarks Fugle* **1** (Copenhagen: Nordisk Forlag), 1926 *Danmarks Fugle* **2**.    Sclater 1859 *Proc. Zool. Soc. London* **29** 205–06.    Schladweiler and Tester 1972 *Journ. Wildlife Mgt.* **36** 1118–27.    Schmidt-Nielsen and Kim 1964 *Auk* **81** 160–72.    Schneider 1965 *Growth and Plumage Dev. of Ducklings in Interior Alaska* (Univ. of Alaska, M.S. thesis).    Schönwetter (continued by W. Meise) 1960 *Handb. d. Oologie* Lieferung 2 (Berlin: Akademie-Verlag), 1961 *Ibid.* Lieferung 3.    Schorger 1947 *Wilson Bull.* **59** 151–59, 1964 *Wilson Bull.* **76** 331–38, 1968 *Wilson Bull.* **80** 228–29.    von Schweppenburg (*see* Geyr von Schweppenburg).    Sclater 1859 *Proc. Zool. Soc. London* **29** 205–06.    Scott 1951 *Wild Geese and Eskimos* (London: Country Life Ltd.), 1952 Severn Wildfowl Trust 5th *Rept.* 125–32, 1966 Wildfowl Trust 17th *Rept.* 20–26, 1970 *The Wild Swans at Slimbridge* (Slimbridge, Glos., England: Pub. by Wildfowl Trust, 12pp.).    Scott and Fisher 1953 *A Thousand Geese* (London: Collins).    Scott et al. 1953 Severn Wildfowl Trust 5th *Rept.* 79–115.    Scott and Boyd 1954 Wildfowl Trust 6th *Rept.* 79–81.    Scott "and the Wildfowl Trust" 1972 *The Swans* (London: Michael Joseph).    Sdobnikov 1959 *Trudy Inst. Biol. Yakut Affiliate Sibirsk. Otdel. Akad. Nauk USSR* no. 6: 119–43, 1959b [*Geese and Ducks of Western Taimyr*] Sci. Research Inst. Agric. Far North *Trans.* pt. 9 (Norilsk, USSR).    Sealy et al. 1971 *Condor* **73** 322–36.    Sedwitz 1958 Linn. Soc. N.Y. *Proc.* nos. 66–70: 61–70.    Seebohm 1880 *Siberia in Europe*; . . . (London: J. Murray), 1892 *Ibis* ser. 6 **4** 87–99.    Semenov-Tian-Shanskii 1960 *Trudy Problemnykh i Tematicheskikh Soveschanii, Zool. Inst. Akad. Nauk. USSR* no. 9: 279–86.    Semenov-Tian-Shanskii and Bragin 1969 *Byulleten Moskovskogo obshekestva isjytatelei prirody, Otdel. Biol.* **74** no. 5: 50–56.    Sennett 1878 *Bull. U.S. Geol. and Geogr. Surv. Terr.* **4** 1–66.    Serebrovsky 1941 *Doklady Akad. Nauk SSSR* **33** 471–73.    Shackleton 1956 *Brit. Birds* **49** 229–30.    Sharp, B. 1972 *Journ. Wildlife Mgt.* **36** 1273–77.    Sharp, W. M. 1951 *Journ. Wildlife Mgt.* **15**

224–26.    Sharpe and Johnsgard 1966 *Behaviour* **27** 259–72.    Sharpless 1832 *Am. Journ. Sci.* **22** (1st ser.): 83–90.    Shaw and Fredine 1956 U.S. Fish and Wildlife Serv. *Circular* no. 39.    Sheppard 1949 *Can. Field-Nat.* **63** 99–100, 1951 *Can. Field-Nat.* **65** 114.    Sherwood 1960 *Condor* **62** 370–77, 1967 *Trans. 32nd N. Am. Wildlife and Nat. Resources Conf.* 340–55.    Shevareva 1960 *Trudy Problemnykh i Tematicheskikh Soveschanii Zoologicheskii Institut Akad. Nauk USSR* no. 9: 146–50, 1965 *Ornitologiya* no. 7: 318–27, 1968 *Ornitologiya* no. 9: 249–69.    Shields 1899 *Bull. Cooper Orn. Club* **1** 9–11.

Shore-Bailey 1918 *Avicult. Mag.* ser. 3 **10** 15–16.    Short 1969 *Auk* **86** 84–105.    Shortt 1943 *Wilson Bull.* **55** 3–7, Shortt and Waller 1937 *Contr. Roy. Ont. Mus.* no. 10.    Sibley, C. G. 1957 *Condor* **59** 166–91,    Sibley, C. G., and Ahlquist 1972 Peabody Mus. Nat. Hist. (Yale Univ.) *Bull.* no. 39.    Sibley, C. L. 1938 *Proc. 9th Internat. Orn. Congr.* 327–35.    Siegfried 1965 *Ostrich* **36** 155–98, 1970 *Wildfowl* no. 21: 122, 1972 *Can. Field-Nat.* **86** 86, 1973 *Bull. Brit. Ornithol. Club.* **93** 98–99, 1973b *Can. Journ. Zool.* **51** 1293–97.    Siivonen 1941 *Ornis Fennica* **18** 39–45.    Simkin 1963 *Can. Field-Nat.* **77** 60.    Simms 1970 *Brit. Birds* **63** 302.    Singleton 1953 *Texas Coastal Waterfowl Survey* (Texas Game and Fish Comm., *FA Rept. Ser.* no. 11).    Siren 1957a *Suomen Riista* **11** 59–64, 1957b *Suomen Riista* **11** 130–33.    Skalinov 1960 *Trans. Kandalaksh State Reserve* no. 3: 191–94.    Skinner 1928 *Wilson Bull.* **40** 139–49, 1937 *Wilson Bull.* **49** 3–10.    Skryabin 1968 *Ornitologiya* no. 9: 277–81.    Sladen 1960 *Proc. Linn. Soc. London*, 171 Sess., 1958–59, pt. 1: 30–52, 1966 *Auk* **83** 130–35.    Slater 1901 *Manual of the Birds of Iceland* (Edinburgh).    Slessers 1968 *Arctic* **21** 201–03.    Slud 1964 *Birds of Costa Rica* (Am. Mus. Nat. Hist. *Bull.* **128**).    Smart 1965a *Auk* **82** 645–48, 1965b *Journ. Wildlife Mgt.* **29** 533–36.    Smith, I. D., and Blood 1972 *Can. Field-Nat.* **86** 213–16.    Smith, J. D. 1946 *Auk* **63** 73–81.    Smith, R. I. 1955 *The Breeding Territory and its Rel. to Waterfowl Productivity at Ogden Bay Bird Refuge* (Utah State Agric. College, M.S. thesis), 1968 *Auk* **85** 381–96, 1970 *Journ. Wildlife Mgt.* **34** 943–46.    Smith, R. I., and Jensen 1970 *Trans. 35th N. Am. Wildlife and Nat. Resources Conf.* 227–41.    Smith, T. G. 1973 *Can. Field-Nat.* **87** 35–42.    Smith, W. J. 1957 *Can. Field-Nat.* **71** 163–81.    Snow 1897 *Notes on the Kuril Islands* (London: J. Murray).    Snyder 1941a Roy. Ont. Mus. Zool. *Occas. Pap.* no. 6, 1941b *Contr. Roy. Ont. Mus. Zool.* no. 19: 25–92, 1953 *Trans. Roy. Can. Inst.* **33** 47–95, 1957 *Arctic Birds of Canada* (Univ. Toronto Press), 1963 *Can. Field-Nat.* **77** 128–29.    Snyder and Lumsden 1951 Roy. Ont. Mus. Zool. *Occas. Pap.* no. 10.    Sooter 1943 *Auk* **60** 96–97.    Soper 1942a Boston Soc. Nat. Hist. *Proc.* **42** no. 2, 1942 *Trans. Roy. Can. Inst.* **24** 19–97, 1946 *Auk* **63** 1–24, 1951 Can. Wildlife Serv. *Wildlife Mgt. Bull.* ser. 2 no. 2.    Southwick 1953a *Journ. Wildlife Mgt.* **17** 1–8, 1953b *Audubon Mag.* **54** no. 1: 44–47.    Soutiére et al. 1972 *Journ. Wildlife Mgt.* **36** 752–58.    Sowls 1948 *Journ. of Mammalogy* **29** 113–37, 1955 *Prairie Ducks* . . . (Washington, D.C.: Wildlife Mgt. Inst.).    Spangenberg 1960 *Byull. Mosk. Obshch. Isp. Prir. Biol.* n.s. **65** no. 2: 31–34.    Speirs 1945 *Auk* **62** 135–36.    Spencer, D. L., et al. 1951 *Trans. 16th N. Am. Wildlife Conf.* 290–95.    Spencer, H. E., Jr., 1953 *The Cinnamon Teal* . . . (Utah State Agric. College, M.S. thesis).    Spencer, R. 1969 *Brit. Birds* **62** 393–442, 1971 *Brit. Birds* **64** 137–

86.    Sprunt 1930 *Auk* **47** 244.    Sprunt and Chamberlain 1949 *South Carolina Bird Life* (Columbia, S.C.).    Stallcup 1952 *Wilson Bull.* **64** 43–44.    Steel et al. 1957 *Journ. Wildlife Mgt.* **21** 38–41.    Stejneger 1885 U.S. Nat. Mus. *Bull.* no. 29, 1887 U.S. Nat. Mus. *Proc.* **10** 117–45.    Stephenson and Smart 1972 *Auk* **89** 191–92.    Sterling and Dzubin 1967 *Trans. 32nd N. Am. Wildlife Conf.* 355–73.    Stewart, P. A. 1957 *The Wood Duck . . . and its Management* (Ohio State Univ., Ph.D. thesis), 1958a *Wilson Bull.* **70** 184–87, 1958b *Auk* **75** 157–68, 1959 *Audubon Mag.* **61** no. 2: 62–65, 1961 *Animal Kingdom* **64** 178–83, 1962 *Bird-Banding* **33** 85–89, 1968 *Bird-Banding* **29** 130, 1971a *Auk* **88** 425, 1971b *Wilson Bull.* **83** 97–99.    Stewart, R. E. 1958 U.S. Fish and Wildlife Serv. *Circular* no. 51, 1962 U.S. Fish and Wildlife Serv., *Spec. Sci. Rept.—Wildlife* no. 65.    Stewart, R. E., and Aldrich 1956 *Proc. Biol. Soc. Wash.* **69** 29–34.    Stewart, R. E., and Manning 1958 *Auk* **75** 203–12.    Stewart, R. E., et al. 1958 *Journ. Wildlife Mgt.* **22** 333–70.    Stieglitz 1972 *Journ. Wildlife Mgt.* **36** 422–28.    Stieglitz and Wilson 1968 *Journ. Wildlife Mgt.* **32** 921–934.    Stirrett 1954 *Trans. 19th N. Am. Wildlife Conf.* 211–21.    Stoddard 1922 *Wilson Bull.* **34** 67–79.    Stollberg 1950 *Journ. Wildlife Mgt.* **14** 214–17.    Stone, W. 1903 *Auk* **20** 209–10.    Stone, W. B., and Marsters 1970 *N.Y. Fish and Game Journ.* **17** 50–52.    Stonor 1940 *Courtship and Display Among Birds* (London: Country Life, Ltd.).    Stotts 1958a *Md. Conservationist* **35** no. 4: 11–15, 1958b *Proc. Southeastern Wildlife Conf.* (1958), 7 pp. (mimeo).    Stotts and Davis 1960 *Chesapeake Sci.* **1** 127–54.    Stoudt 1944 *Journ. Wildlife Mgt.* **8** 100–12.    Strange et al. 1971 *Journ. Wildlife Mgt.* **35** 786–93.    Streets 1876 *Bull. Nuttall Ornithol. Club* **1** 46–47.    Strong 1912 *Auk* **37** 479–88.    Stutz 1965a *Murrelet* **46** no. 3: 47, 1965b *Murrelet* **46** no. 3: 47–48.    Sugden, J. W. 1947 *Condor* **49** 93–96.    Sugden, L. G. 1960 *Can. Field-Nat.* **74** 163, 1963 *Condor* **65** 330, 1973 Can. Wild. Serv. *Rept. Ser.* no. 24.    Sugden, L. G., and Harris 1972 *Poultry Sci.* **51** 625–33.    Surrendi 1970 *Journ. Wildlife Mgt.* **34** 719–33.    Sutherland and McChesney 1965 *The Living Bird* 4th annual 99–106.    Sutton 1931 *Auk* **48** 335–64, 1932 Carnegie Mus. *Memoirs* **12** pt. 2, sect. 2, 1961 *Iceland Summer* (Norman: Univ. Okla. Press).    Swainson and Richardson 1831 *Fauna Boreali-Americana: Birds* (London: J. Murray).    Swanson and Bartonek 1970 *Journ. Wildlife Mgt.* **34** 739–46.    Swarth 1911 *Univ. Calif. Pub. Zool.* **7** no. 2, 1913 *Univ. Calif. Pub. Zool.* **12** no. 1, 1915 *Condor* **17** 115–18, 1924 *Univ. Calif. Pub. Zool.* **24** no. 3, 1926 *Univ. Calif. Pub. Zool.* **30** no. 4, 1934 Cooper Ornithol. Club, *Pacific Coast Avifauna* no. 22, 1936 *Proc. Calif. Acad. Sci.* **23** 35–38.    Swarth and Bryant 1917 *Univ. Calif. Pub. Zool.* **17** no. 11.    Sykes 1961 *Auk* **78** 441.

Tait 1949 *Can. Field-Nat.* **63** 43.    Talmadge 1947 *Condor* **49** 172–73.    Tamisier 1971 *Alauda* **39** 261–311.    Tate and Martin 1969 *Condor* **71** 81.    Taverner, J. H. 1963 *Brit. Birds* **56** 273–85, 1967 *Brit. Birds* **60** 509–15.    Taverner, P. A. 1919 *Can. Field-Nat.* **33** 57–58, 1926 *Birds of Western Canada* (Canada, Dept. Mines *Mus. Bull.* 41).    Taverner, P. A., and Sutton 1934 *Ann. Carnegie Mus.* **23** no. 1.    Taylor 1953 *Ibis* **95** 638–41.    Tennent 1948 *Brit. Birds* **41** 25.    Teplov 1957 *Trudy Pechoro-Iycheskogo Gosudaretvenn zapovednika* no. 6: 5–115.    Terres 1961 *Discovery: Great Moments in the Lives of Outstanding Naturalists* (Phila.: Lippincott).    Thayer and Bangs 1914 *Proc. New Eng. Zool. Club* **5** 1–48.    Thienmann 1903 *Journ. f. Ornithol.* **51** 161–231.    Thompson, D. Q., and Person 1963 *Journ.*

*Wildlife Mgt.* **27** 348–56. Thompson, D. Q., and Lyons 1964 *Wilson Bull.* **76** 282–85. Thompson, M. C. 1961 *Condor* **63** 265. Thompson, W. 1851 *The Nat. Hist. of Ireland* **3** (London). Thomson, A. L. 1964 *A New Dict. of Birds* (London: Nelson). Thorburn 1926 *British Birds* (new ed.) **3** (London: Longmans, Green). Ticehurst 1957 *The Mute Swan in England* (London: Cleaver-Hume Press). Tikhomirov 1959 [*Interrelations of the Animal World and the Plant Cover of the Tundra*] (Moscow and Leningrad: Bot. Inst. Acad. Sci. USSR). TRANSL. 1966 Israel Program Sci. Transl. (Jerusalem). Timken 1967 *Auk* **84** 588. Timken and Anderson 1969 *Journ. Wildlife Mgt.* **33** 87–91. Timmermann, A. 1962 *Limosa* **35** 199–218. Timmermann, G. 1949 *Die Vögel Islands* Erster Teil 2 Hälfte (Folge 2) und Zweiter Teil (*Visindafélag Islendinga* Societas Scientarum Islandica **28** 238–524). Tinbergen 1957 *Bird Study* **4** 14–27, 1958 *Curious Naturalists* (N.Y.: Basic Books, Inc.). Titman and Lowther 1971 *Can. Field-Nat.* **85** 323–24. Todd 1950 *Condor* **52** 63–68, 1963 *Birds of the Labrador Peninsula* (Toronto: Univ. Toronto Press). Tomlinson et al. 1973 *Condor* **75** 120–21. Tougarinov 1941 *Anseriformes* Fauna of USSR, Aves 1 no. 4 (Moscow and Leningrad: Acad. Sci. USSR). Townsend, C. W. (ed.) 1911 *Captain Cartwright and His Labrador Journal* (Boston: Dana Estes), 1916 *Auk* **33** 9–17. Townsend, C. W., and Allen 1907 Boston Soc. Nat. Hist. *Proc.* **33** 277–428. Townsend, G. H. 1966 *Can. Field-Nat.* **80** 74–88. Trainer and Hunt 1965 *Journ. Wildlife Mgt.* **29** 95–103. Trauger 1970 *34th Fed.-Prov. Wildlife Conf., Yellowknife, N.W.T., July 14–16 1970:* 29. Trauger et al. 1971 *Auk* **88** 856–75. Trautman 1940 *Birds of Buckeye Lake, Ohio* (Univ. Mich. Mus. Zool. *Misc. Pub.* no. 44), 1943 *Wilson Bull.* **55** 192, 1947 *Wilson Bull.* **59** 26–35. Truslow 1960 *Nat. Geog. Mag.* **118** 134–50. Tuck 1971 *Bird-Banding* **42** 184–209. Tuck and Lemieux 1959 *Dansk Orn. Foren. Tidsskr.* **53** 137–54. Tufts 1932 *Can. Field-Nat.* **46** 51–53, 1961 [= 1962] *The Birds of Nova Scotia* (Halifax: N. S. Museum). Turner 1885 U.S. Nat. Mus. *Proc.* **8** 233–54, 1886 *Contrib. to Nat. Hist. of Alaska* no. 2 (Washington, D.C.: Arctic Ser. Pub. issued in connection with Signal Service, U.S. Army). Twomey 1956 *Carnegie Mag.* **30** 41–45. Tyler 1916 *Condor* **18** 194–98.

Uspenskii, S. M. 1959 *Ornitologiya* no. 2: 7–15, 1960 Wildfowl Trust 11th *Rept.* 80–93, 1963a *Priroda* no. 9: 58–62, 1963b *Der Falke* **10** 13–15, 1965a *Die Wildgänse Nordeurasiens* (Wittenburg Lutherstadt: A. Ziemsen. Die Neue Brehm-Büchcri no. 352), 1965b Wildfowl Trust 16th *Rept.* 126–28, 1965c *Sbornik Trudov Zoologeskogo Muzeya MGU* **9** 63–97, 1967 *Problemy Severa* no. 11: 224–28 TRANSL. 1968 *Problems of the North* no. 11: 275–81 (Ottawa: Nat. Research Council), 1969 [*Life at High Latitudes*] (Moscow), 1972 *Die Eiderenten* (Wittenberg Lutherstadt, A. Ziemsen. Die Neue Brehm-Bücherei no. 452). Uspenskii, S. M., et al. 1962 *Ornitologiya* no. 5: 49–67, 1963 *Ornitologiya* no. 6: 58–67. Uspenskii, S. M., and Filin 1965 *Ornitologiya* no. 7: 494. Uspenskii, V. S. 1946 [*Eiders and Eider Management*] (SNK RSFSR Admin. of Reserves, Zooparks, and Zool. Gardens. Moscow, 36 pp.).

Vaught 1964 *Journ. Wildlife Mgt.* **28** 208–12, Vaught and Kirsch 1966 *Canada Geese of the Prairie Population* . . . (Mo. Dept. Cons. *Tech. Bull.* no. 3). Vaught et al. 1967 *Journ. Wildlife Mgt.* **31** 248–53. Vaurie 1965 *Birds of the Palearctic Fauna.*

*Non-Passeriformes* (London: Witherby).    Vermeer 1968 *Wilson Bull.* **80** 78–83, 1969 *Blue Jay* **27** 72–73, 1970 *Can. Journ. Zool.* **48** 235–40.    Vermeer et al. 1972 *Can. Field-Nat.* **86** 168.    Veselovsky 1953 *Sylvia* **14** 36–73.    Vibe 1967 *Meddel. om Gronland* **170** no. 5.    Vieillard 1970 *Alauda* **38** 87–125.    Vine 1950 *Brit. Birds* **43** 227.    Voous 1945 *Ardea* **33** 126–35, 1957 *The Birds of Aruba, Curaçao, and Bonaire* (Studies on Fauna of Curaçao and Other Caribbean Is. **7** The Hague), 1963 *Die Vogelwelt Europas und Ihre Verbreitung* [corrected ed.] (Hamburg and Berlin: Paul Parey).    Vorobev 1963 [*Birds of Yakutia*] (Moscow: Acad. Sci. USSR).    de Vos 1964 *Ardea* **52** 166–89.    de Vries 1944 *Limosa* **17** 89–94.

Waaramäki 1970 *Suomen Riista* **22** 89–96.    Walker 1970 *Wildfowl* no. 21: 99–104.    von de Wall 1963 *Journ. f. Ornithol.* **104** 1–15.    Walton 1937 *Journ. Exper. Biol.* **14** 440–47.    Ward and Middleton 1971 *Can. Journ. Zool.* **49** 11–14.    Washington 1972 *Avicult. Mag.* **78** 1–4.    Watson 1967 *Auk* **84** 424, 1970 *Auk* **87** 353–57.    Wayne 1910 *Birds of South Carolina* (Contr. Charleston Mus. no. 1).    Webbe 1958 *Dansk Orn. Foren. Tidsskr.* **52** 41–47.    Weber 1946 *Nos Oiseaux* (Paris) **18** 225–31.    Webster and Uhler 1964 U.S. Bur. Sport Fisheries and Wildlife *Leaflet* no. 458.    Weidmann 1956 *Zeitschr. Tierpsychol.* **13** 208–71.    Weidmann and Darley 1971 *Animal Behaviour* **19** 287–98.    Weller 1957 *Wilson Bull.* **69** 4–38, 1959 *Ecol. Monogr.* **29** 333–65, 1964 *Journ. Wildlife Mgt.* **28** 64–103, 1965 *Auk* **82** 227–35, 1967 *Auk* **84** 544–59, 1969 *Wildfowl* no. 20: 55–58, 1970 *Wilson Bull.* **82** 320–23, 1975 *Auk* **92** 280–97.    Weller and Ward 1959 *Journ. Wildlife Mgt.* **23** 427–33.    Weller et al. 1969 *Can. Field-Nat.* **83** 344–60.    Westermann 1953 *Nature Preservation in the Caribbean* (Utrecht: Pub. Foundation for Sci. Research in Surinam and Netherlands Antilles, no. 9).    Wetherbee and Wetherbee 1961 *Bird-Banding* **32** 141–59.    Wetmore 1916 U.S. Dept. Agric. *Bull.* no. 326, 1917a *Am. Nat.* **51** 753–55, 1917b U.S. Nat. Mus. *Proc.* **52** 479–82, 1918 *Condor* **20** 19–20, 1920 *Auk* **37** 221–47, –412, 1921 U.S. Dept. Agric. *Bull.* no. 936, 1926 U.S. Nat. Mus. *Bull.* 133, 1938 *Auk* **55** 51–55, 1943 U.S. Nat. Mus. *Proc.* **93** 215–340, 1944 *Auk* **61** 473, 1951 *Journ. Wash. Acad. Sci.* **41** 338–40, 1956 *Smithsonian Misc. Colls.* **131** no. 5, 1958 *Smithsonian Misc. Colls.* **135** no. 8, 1959 *Smithsonian Misc. Colls.* **138** no. 4, 1965 *Smithsonian Misc. Colls.* **150,** 1967 *Bull. Ga. Acad. Sci.* **25** 151–53, 1973 *Auk* **90** 910–11.    Wetmore and Peters 1922 *Proc. Biol. Soc. Wash.* **35** 41–46.    Wetmore and Swales 1931 U.S. Nat. Mus. *Bull.* 155.    Weydemeyer and Marsh 1936 *Condor* **38** 185–98.    Wheeler 1965 *Murrelet* **46** no. 3: 40–42.    Wheeler and Harris 1970 *Calif. Fish and Game* **56** 180–87.    White, E. F. G., and Lewis 1937 *Auk* **54** 440–44.    White, H. C. 1936 *Journ. Biol. Board Can.* **2** 299–309, 1937 *Journ. Biol. Board Can.* **3** 323–38, 1939 Fisheries Research Board Can. *Bull.* no. 58, 1957 Fisheries Research Board Can. *Bull.* no. 116.    Whitfield 1894 *Auk* **11** 323.    Widmann 1906 *Prelim. Cat. Birds of Mo.* (St. Louis, Mo.: *Trans. Acad. Sci.*).    Wilber and Yocom 1971 *Murrelet* **52** 16–19.    Wilke 1944 *Auk* **61** 655–56.    Willett 1919 *Condor* **21** 194–207, 1921 *Condor* **23** 156–59.    Willey 1968 *Trans. Northeastern Wildlife Conf. (1968)* 121–34. (mimeo.).    Williams, C. S. 1946 *Auk* **63** 438, 1956 *The Canada Goose, Its Habits, Requirements, and Management* (MS 399 pp.), 1967 *Honker* (Princeton, Toronto, London: D. Van Nostrand).    Williams, C. S., and Marshall

1938a *Journ. Wildlife Mgt.* **2** 17–19, 1938b *Journ. Wildlife Mgt.* **2** 29–48, 1938c *Trans. 3rd N. Am. Wildlife Conf.* 640–46.　　Williams, C. S., and Sooter 1941 *Trans. 5th N. Am. Wildlife Conf.* 383–87.　　Williams, C. S., and Kalmbach 1943 *Journ. Wildlife Mgt.* **7** 163–69.　　Williams, G. R. 1964 Wildfowl Trust 15th *Rept.* 140–46.　　Williams, L. 1946 *Condor* **48** 139.　　Williams, L. E., Jr., 1961 *Wilson Bull.* **73** 389, 1968 *Wilson Bull.* **80** 488–89.　　Williams, R. S. 1886 *Auk* **3** 274, 1888 *Auk* **5** 14–18.　　Williams, S. O. III 1975 *Auk* **92** 152–53.　　Williams, W. M. H. 1971 *Avicult. Mag.* **77** 58–65.　　Wilson, A. 1829 *Am. Ornithol.* **3** (Philadelphia).　　Wilson, A., and Bonaparte 1831 *Am. Ornithol.* **3** (London and Edinburgh).　　Wilson, G. 1929 *Wilson Bull.* **41** 177–85.　　Wilson, R. S. 1948 *Condor* **50** 124–29.　　Wingard 1952 *Journ. Wildlife Mgt.* **16** 228–30.　　Winge 1898 *Meddel. om Grønland* **21** no. 1, 1903 *Vidensk. Meddel. naturhist. Foren.* (Copenhagen) **55** (6th ser. 6) 61–109.　　Wingfield 1951 *A Waterfowl Productivity Study in Knudson Marsh, Salt Lake Valley, Utah* (Utah State Agric College, M.S. thesis). Wingfield and Low 1955 Utah Acad. Sci. *Proc.* **32** 45–49.　　Winterbottom and Middlemiss 1960 *Bull. Brit. Ornithol. Club* **80** 154–62.　　Witherby, H. F. (ed.) 1924 *Practical Handb. Brit. Birds* **2** pt. 1 (London: Witherby), 1939 *Handb. Brit. Birds* **3** (London: Witherby).　　Wolff, E. 1951 *Année Biol.* ser. 3 **27** 379–83.　　Wolff, W. J. 1966 *Ardea* **54** 230–70.　　Wolfson (ed.) 1955 *Recent Studies in Avian Biol.* (Urbana: Univ. Ill. Press).　　Wood 1964 *Journ. Wildlife Mgt.* **28** 197–208.　　Woolfenden 1957 *Wilson Bull.* **69** 181–82.　　Wormald 1939 *Avicult. Mag.* **5** 100–01.　　Worth 1940 *Auk* **57** 44–60.　　Wright, A. H. 1913 *Forest and Stream* **81** no. 4 110–11.　　Wright, B. S. 1954 *High Tide and an East Wind* (Harrisburgh, Pa.: Stackpole Co.).　　Wright, T. W. 1960 *Proc. 14th An. Conf. Southeastern Assoc. Game and Fish Commrs.* 14–17.　　Wrigley 1964 *The Field* **223** no. 5803: 627.　　Würdinger 1970 *Zeitschr. f. Tierpsychol.* **27** 257–302.　　Wüst 1960 *Proc. 12th Internat. Orn. Congr.* 795–800.　　Wynne-Edwards 1952 *Auk* **69** 353–91.

Yamamoto 1963 *Tori* **18** 12–14.　　Yamashina 1948 *Pac. Science* **2** 121–24.　　Yancey 1954 *La. Conservation* **6** no. 9: 10–11.　　Yarrell 1832 *Trans. Linn. Soc. London* **17** 1–4, 1845 *A Hist. of Brit. Birds* 2nd ed. **3** (London).　　Yeager 1970 *The Canada Geese of Southeastern Colo.* (Colo. Div. Game, Fish and Parks, *Tech. Pub.* no. 26).　　Yeates 1955 Wildfowl Trust 7th *Rept.* 146–52.　　Yelverton and Quay 1959 *Food Habits Canada Geese at L. Mattamuskeet, N.C.* (N.C. Wildlife Resources Comm.).　Yocom 1962 *Murrelet* **42** 13–20, 1963 *Murrelet* **44** 28–34, 1964 *Murrelet* **45** 30–36, 1970a *Murrelet* **51** 20–21, 1970b *Murrelet* **51** 26, 1970c *Auk* **87** 812–14, 1972 *Murrelet* **53** 33–34.　　Yocom and Harris 1965 *Journ. Wildlife Mgt.* **29** 874–77, 1966 *Murrelet* **47** 33–37.　　Yorke 1891 *Am. Field* **35** 641–43, 1899 *Our Ducks* (Chicago).　　Young 1970 *Ibis* **112** 330–35.　　Ytreberg 1960 *Sterna* **4** 11–26.

# INDEX TO VOLUMES 2 AND 3

Numbers in sans serif (2, 3) are volume numbers.

Numbers in **boldface** (**114**, **370**) refer to caption pages facing color plates.